Luxemburger Juristische Studien –
Luxembourg Legal Studies

edited by

Faculty of Law, Economics and Finance
University of Luxembourg

Volume 20

Kris Grimonprez

The European Union and Education for Democratic Citizenship

Legal foundations for EU learning at school

Nomos

The Deutsche Nationalbibliothek lists this publication in the Deutsche Nationalbibliografie; detailed bibliographic data are available on the Internet at http://dnb.d-nb.de

ISBN 978-3-8487-6074-9 (Print)
978-3-7489-0203-4 (ePDF)

British Library Cataloguing-in-Publication Data
A catalogue record for this book is available from the British Library.

ISBN 978-3-8487-6074-9 (Print)
978-3-7489-0203-4 (ePDF)

Library of Congress Cataloging-in-Publication Data
Grimonprez, Kris
The European Union and Education for Democratic Citizenship
Legal foundations for EU learning at school
Kris Grimonprez
807 pp.
Includes bibliographic references and index.

ISBN 978-3-8487-6074-9 (Print)
978-3-7489-0203-4 (ePDF)

Published by Nomos Verlagsgesellschaft, Baden-Baden, Germany 2020.
Printed and bound in Germany.

1st Edition 2020

To Linde, Sander, Niels, Elke, Lise, Thomas,
Zoë, Floor, Lotte and Wout
To all children in the EU
May they be educated in the spirit of the values of Article 2 TEU[1]

1 Article 2 Treaty on European Union: 'The Union is founded on the values of respect for human dignity, freedom, democracy, equality, the rule of law and respect for human rights, including the rights of persons belonging to minorities. These values are common to the Member States in a society in which pluralism, non-discrimination, tolerance, justice, solidarity and equality between women and men prevail.'.

Preface

The book that you have in your hands is the fruit of an exceptional path. Much more than a rigorous, careful and detailed revision of the PhD thesis that Kris Grimonprez defended brilliantly at the University of Luxembourg in December 2018, this book emerged from the author's commitment not only to legal academic research but also to social and political change. The unique combination at the genesis of this work, far from detracting from the intellectual value of the endeavour, has led the author to engage in an in-depth scientific analysis of a legal problem – the scattered dimensions of the right to education, of citizenship education and its relationship to EU citizenship – with a view to inform the normative development of the legal systems that shape and influence our collective life. The book has a dual audience. On the one hand, it is directed at the community of EU lawyers, in whose regard the author convincingly makes three main arguments. First, the absence of an EU dimension in education for democratic citizenship is the hidden face of the EU's democratic and civic deficit. Put in stronger terms, the author reminds us that without linking EU citizenship to citizenship education, attempts to remedy the widening gap between EU integration and citizens may easily continue to fail. Secondly, the general principles of law with which EU lawyers work and the status of EU citizenship have educational implications and there are enough legal normative grounds for establishing an EU dimension in education for democratic citizenship. Thirdly, the EU has competence to support education for democratic citizenship and its EU dimension. On the other hand, this book also addresses all professionals involved in citizenship education and educational policy. In their regard, Kris Grimonprez argues that law has a value for citizenship education and that EU law has necessary consequences for the content of citizenship education. Given the significance of the EU's impact on our societies and on citizens' rights, curricula of both primary and secondary education and teachers' training can no longer ignore the importance of EU learning, and, particularly, of the European dimension of education for democratic citizenship. While the reader is unlikely to be both an EU lawyer and an education scholar or practitioner, they should bear in mind the dual character of this work that makes the book unique. The critical reader should also be aware from the outset that the author does not shy away from the difficulties that her topic raises: that both citizenship education and EU citizenship are contentious matters is one of the reasons why this book should trigger a wider discussion on education for democratic citizenship in the European Union.

The book brings together a wealth of material on international law instruments and on EU law (as the impressive and lengthy list of primary sources can testify), analyzing both the interactions between them and their implications for EU law. Core issues of EU law are discussed in depth, always with the view to advance the argument on the legal foundations for EU learning at school. Thus, as the Council of Europe Charter on Education for Democratic Citizenship and Human Rights Education of 2010 and the right to education defined in international instruments (the 1966 International Covenant on Economic, Social and Cultural Rights and the 1989 Convention on the Rights of the Child) are two of the "anchor points" for citizenship education of EU citizens, the reader will find an accurate mapping of the different modes of reception of exogenic legal norms in the EU legal order. Similarly, because one of the aims of the book is to identify the substance of citizenship education of EU citizens, the reader is provided with an analysis of EU citizenship rights, of the democratic participation rights enshrined in the Title II of the Treaty on European Union and of other EU rights and obligations of both mobile and static citizens, all in light of the standards of education for democratic citizenship (identified by the author on the basis of the Charter of the Council of Europe). The book goes one step further: it identifies the learning content of citizenship education of EU citizens, showing how it can be included in mainstream education. For this purpose, the reader is presented with a possible teaching method, accompanied by a beautiful transformation of the case law of the Court of Justice of the European Union into stories that pupils could be taught in order to develop their critical thinking, to later exercise their rights and responsibilities as citizens, to value diversity and to play an active part in democratic life. Finally, because education is often treated as a matter of national policy and part of the states' duties and prerogatives, the whole work could stumble upon the competence of the European Union. The author therefore concludes her work with the analysis of the EU's supporting competence, as enshrined in Article 165 of the Treaty on the Functioning of the European Union, and of the principles of subsidiarity and proportionality, inquiring how, combined, this Treaty article and principles relate to the autonomy of the Member States in providing for the inclusion of an EU dimension in citizenship education.

The questions with which the book opens are many, complex and controversial. All are carefully intertwined in an analysis that only an author with a masterful domain of EU law and highly committed to citizenship education could successfully undertake. In times of deep challenges to the European Union, the arguments made in this book should be seriously considered by both critics and advocates of citizenship education; and, irrespective of where one stands in the debate, by those concerned with the democratic and civic deficits that spread deeper into the social and political structures of the state, while afflicting particularly the European Union.

Joana Mendes
Professor of Comparative Administrative Law
University of Luxembourg

Acknowledgements

My gratitude goes to all the people who have accompanied me on the journey to completion of the doctoral dissertation on which this study is based: 'The EU Dimension in Education for Democratic Citizenship—a Legal Analysis', defended at the University of Luxembourg on 20 December 2018. I would like to thank the members of the thesis supervision committee who have guided me from the very beginning: Professor Pascal Ancel, Professor Jörg Gerkrath, Professor Luc Heuschling, Professor Johan van der Walt, and, last but not least, Professor Herwig Hofmann. Conversations with him were precious in helping me to structure my wide-ranging ideas and lofty intentions on the basis of legal anchor points. My particular gratitude goes to Professor Joana Mendes, the dissertation supervisor, who mentored the final phase. I am indebted to the members of the defence committee, Professor Eleftheria Neframi (University of Luxembourg), Professor Christian Calliess (Freie Universität Berlin) and Professor Kurt Willems (KU Leuven). Their positive feedback has meant a lot to me and their pertinent comments were taken into account to improve the study. A special word of thank goes to ECtHR Judge Síofra O'Leary, who was a member of the defence committee but could not be present due to unexpected circumstances. She read the text in great detail and made many valuable suggestions. I benefited from her shared strong belief in the power of education.

I have had the privilege of discussing topics and ideas with many experts in the legal field and in multidisciplinary contexts. I would like to thank ECJ Judges Egils Levits, Sacha Prechal, and Christiaan Timmermans, and Professor Piet Van Nuffel. Exchanges with discussants at conferences deepened my insights (inter alia at FIDE (Fédération Internationale pour le Droit Européen), NECE (Networking European Citizenship Education), Lifelong learning platforms, European summit for critical thinking education, Politicologenetmaal).

I am grateful to the people who gave me a forum for testing learning methods for the EU dimension in citizenship education in practice, both in secondary schools and in Teacher Training at the KU Leuven (in particular Professor Ellen Claes).

My sincere gratitude also goes to Susan Pawlak, who skillfully improved my use of English. It was a pleasure working with her.

Numerous people have encouraged me warmly in the undertaking of this study. I thank my children for their loving support, and my grandchildren for their patience while watching their grandmother at her computer with curiosity.

Most of all, I want to thank my husband, Koen Lenaerts. During endless conversations—at the table, in the car, at the seaside, or in the forest—he listened, objected, nuanced, and increasingly shared my passion for the citizenship education of EU citizens.

My deepest motivation for this work comes from my belief in the values on which the EU is founded. As a proud Flemish, Belgian, and EU citizen, I am thankful to all those who have enhanced my awareness of these values in the past. I hope to be a solid link in the ongoing chain for the future. Democracy has to be born anew every generation, and education is its midwife (John Dewey). Wise efforts are more necessary than ever to educate citizens in our common values in order to ensure a peaceful and happy life in the European Union.

Kris Grimonprez
Luxembourg, 30 October 2019

Abbreviations

AFSJ	Area of Freedom, Security and Justice
AG	Advocate General
AT, BE, BG, CY, CZ, DE, DK, EE, EL, ES, FI, FR, HR, HU, IA, IT, LT, LU, LV, MT NL, PL, PT, RO, SE, SI, SK	EU Member States: Austria, Belgium, Bulgaria, Cyprus, Czech Republic, Germany, Denmark, Estonia, Greece, Spain, Finland, France, Croatia, Hungary, Ireland, Italy, Lithuania, Luxembourg, Latvia, Malta, Netherlands, Poland, Portugal, Romania, Sweden, Slovenia, Slovakia
Bull	Bulletin
BVerfG	Bundesverfassungsgericht (DE)
CADE	Convention Against Discrimination in Education
CFR	Charter of Fundamental Rights of the European Union
Charter on EDC/HRE	Council of Europe Charter on Education for Democratic Citizenship and Human Rights Education (CM/Rec(2010)7)
CM	Committee of Ministers (CoE)
CMLRev	Common Market Law Review
CoE	Council of Europe
Commission	European Commission (EU)
CoR	Committee of the Regions
Council	Council of the European Union
CRC	Convention on the Rights of the Child
CRELL	Centre for Research on Lifelong Learning
DG	Directorate-General of the European Commission
Dir	Directive
EAC	Education and Culture (DG)

EACEA	Education, Audiovisual and Culture Executive Agency
EC	European Community (Treaty establishing the European Community, 1992)
ECAS	European Citizen Action Service
ECHR	European Convention for the Protection of Human Rights and Fundamental Freedoms (Council of Europe)
ECI	European citizens' initiative
ECJ	Court of Justice of the European Union
ECRI	European Commission against Racism and Intolerance (CoE)
ECSC	European Coal and Steel Community
ECtHR	European Court of Human Rights
ed(s)	editor(s)
EDC	Education for Democratic Citizenship
edn(s)	edition(s)
EEC	European Economic Community (Treaty establishing the European Economic Community, 1957)
EERJ	European Educational Research Journal
EESC	European Economic and Social Committee
ELJ	European Law Journal
ELRev	European Law Review
EP	European Parliament
ESC	European Social Charter
ET	Education and Training
ET2020	Strategic Framework for European Cooperation on Education and Training ('ET 2020')
EU	European Union
fn(s)	footnote(s) external to the work
HRE	Human Rights Education
i.a.	Inter alia

ICCPR	International Covenant on Civil and Political Rights
ICCS	International Civic and Citizenship Education Study
ICESCR	International Covenant on Economic, Social and Cultural Rights
IEA	International Association for the Evaluation of Educational Achievement
INGOs	International Non Governmental Organisations
JCMS	Journal of Common Market Studies
JRC	Joint Research Centre (Commission)
JSSE	Journal of Social Science Education
MEP	Member of the European Parliament
MOU	Memorandum of Understanding between the EU and the Council of Europe
n/nn	footnote(s) internal to the work
OECD	Organisation for Economic Cooperation and Development
OHCHR	Office of the High Commissioner for Human Rights (UN)
OJ	Official Journal of the European Union
OSCE	Organisation for Security and Co-operation in Europe
PA	Parliamentary Assembly (CoE)
Parliament	European Parliament
Reg	Regulation
Res	Resolution
RFCDC	Reference Framework of Competences for Democratic Culture
Rn	Randnummer
TEU	Treaty on European Union (as amended by the Lisbon Treaty)
TFEU	Treaty on the Functioning of the European Union
UDHR	Universal Declaration of Human Rights

UN	United Nations
UN ComESCR	UN Committee on Economic, Social and Cultural Rights (ICESCR)
UN ComRC	UN Committee on the Rights of the Child (CRC)
UN HRCom (ICCPR)	UN Human Rights Committee (ICCPR)
UNESCO	United Nations Educational, Scientific and Cultural Organisation
UNGA	United Nations General Assembly
UNHRC	United Nations Human Rights Council
UNTS	United Nations Treaty Series

Abstract

Education for democratic citizenship equips learners with knowledge, skills and understanding and develops their attitudes and behaviour with the aim of empowering them to exercise and defend their democratic rights and responsibilities in society, to value diversity and to play an active part in democratic life (the consensual definition in the Charter on Education for Democratic Citizenship and Human Rights Education of the Council of Europe, 2010). What does this mean for EU citizens? The study reads this Charter in combination with EU law and argues that an EU dimension must be incorporated in national citizenship education. A method for objective, critical and pluralistic EU learning is proposed, a method based on the Treaties and on case teaching (stories for critical thinking).

Starting from EU law, suitable content for the EU dimension in mainstream education is then explored on the basis of four criteria: (i) additional content for national education for democratic citizenship, (ii) significant content, i.e. relating to foundational (EU primary law) values, objectives and principles, (iii) inviting critical thinking, (iv) affecting the large majority of EU citizens, including static citizens (who live at home in their own country). A broader view of EU citizenship is developed, beyond that resulting from classic citizenship rights.

Finally, it is argued that the EU has the legal competence to support the EU dimension in education. Member States are invited to take more action to ensure quality education, which must now include education for democratic citizenship and its EU dimension. Democracy in the EU needs an educational substratum.

Aide mémoire

Effects of a combined reading of EDC standards and EU law

Education for Democratic Citizenship (EDC) means:
- (a) education, training, awareness raising, information, practices and activities which aim
- (b) by equipping learners with knowledge, skills and understanding and developing their attitudes and behaviour
- (c) to empower the learners
  - (c-1) to exercise and defend their democratic rights and responsibilities in society
  - (c-2) to value diversity
  - (c-3) to play an active part in democratic life
- (d) with a view to the promotion and protection of democracy and the rule of law.[2]

Citizenship of the Union is hereby established. Every person holding the nationality of a Member State shall be a citizen of the Union. Citizenship of the Union shall be *additional* to and not replace national citizenship.[3]

Four criteria for determining relevant content for the **EU dimension of EDC in mainstream education** consistent with EU law:
- (i) *additional* content for national EDC
- (ii) significant content,
  i.e. relating to foundational (EU primary law) values, objectives and principles
- (iii) inviting critical thinking
- (iv) affecting the large majority of EU citizens, including 'static' citizens

2 Para 2 Council of Europe Charter on Education for Democratic Citizenship and Human Rights Education.

3 Art 20(1) Treaty on the Functioning of the European Union, Art 9 Treaty on European Union (emphasis added).

Table of Contents

Introduction

1 Why a study on this subject?

This study deals with the education of pupils as EU citizens in schools. 'Schools' are defined as institutions delivering primary and secondary education, by contrast with higher education institutions.[4]

The introduction first outlines two contrasting observations and the problem which gave rise to the idea for this study. It then points to the challenges inherent in formulating an adequate response and proposes three anchor points to that effect. Finally, it formulates the questions which this study aims to answer, explains the method used, and the general objectives pursued throughout.

Contrasting observations

2 High importance of the EU

The starting point is a puzzling contrast between two observations: the high importance of the EU in public life and the low importance of EU learning in many schools.

Europeanisation has multiple aspects and is difficult to quantify, yet its existence cannot be denied.[5] The paradigm of the 19th century nation state, perceived as being exclusively sovereign within its territory, has shifted.[6]

---

4 See Charter on EDC/HRE, para 2(c) on formal education; and text to n 1041 for a definition of formal learning (in schools). Definition of 'higher education institutions' in Regulation 1288/2013 of the European Parliament and of the Council of 11 December 2013 establishing 'Erasmus+': the Union programme for education, training, youth and sport and repealing Decisions 1719/2006, 1720/2006 and 1298/2008 [2013] OJ L347/50 (Erasmus+ Regulation 1288/2013), Art 2 (14); Commission Proposal for a Regulation of the European Parliament and of the Council establishing 'Erasmus': the Union programme for education, training, youth and sport and repealing Regulation (EU) No 1288/2013, COM(2018) 367 final, Art 2.

5 Formulated alternatively as 'The EU impinges directly on national policy-making': B Kohler-Koch and B Rittberger, 'The "Governance Turn" in EU studies' (2005) 44 JCMS 27, 35.

6 F Ost and M van de Kerchove, *De la pyramide au réseau? Pour une théorie dialectique du droit* (Facultés universitaires Saint-Louis 2002); HCH Hofmann, GC Rowe and AH Türk, *Administrative law and policy of the European Union* (Oxford University

Nations have gradually opened their borders. In the initial phase, they accepted the exercise of powers by the authorities of the European Coal and Steel Community (ECSC) and the European Economic Community (EEC, vertical opening of borders). In the second phase, they started recognising the decisions of other Member States (horizontal opening of borders). In the third phase, nation states have become integrated in networks.[7] As a result, EU measures now affect the everyday life of citizens in many respects. EU action is not limited to the internal market, but includes policy areas such as the environment, public health, or consumer protection. With the development of an area of freedom, security and justice, the EU reaches into ever more fields traditionally seen as a matter of national sovereignty, such as criminal law, immigration, asylum, security and defence policy.[8] In response to refugee crises, the EU adopts quotas,[9] and in the face of global financial crises, the EU asks for sacrifices, taking from some and giving to others. EU measures in the context of economic and monetary union (adopted in accordance with the ordinary legislative procedure) aim to enhance the coordination and surveillance of budgetary discipline and to reinforce economic governance of the Eurozone.[10] Newspapers report on a daily basis on the implications of EU membership ('EU

Press 2011) 5; K Nicolaïdis, 'European Demoicracy and Its Crisis' (2013) 51 JCMS 351, 366: European peoples have progressively left the shores of state sovereignty.

7 Hofmann, Rowe and Türk, *Administrative law and policy of the European Union* 5–11, with ECSC and EEC case law (first shift), Case 120/78 *Rewe-Zentral (Cassis de Dijon)* ECLI:EU:C:1979:42 and the subsequent line of case law (second), and integrated administration (third). See in general, legal pluralism, Ost and van de Kerchove, *De la pyramide au réseau? Pour une théorie dialectique du droit*; M Delmas-Marty, *Ordering Pluralism. A Conceptual Framework for Understanding the Transnational Legal World* (Hart 2009); M Avbelj and J Komárek, *Constitutional Pluralism in the European Union and Beyond* (Hart 2012).

8 Evolution in several fields, see P Craig and G de Búrca, *EU Law: Text, Cases, and Materials* (6th edn, Oxford University Press 2015); A Rosas and L Armati, *EU Constitutional Law: An Introduction* (Hart 2018) i.a. 12; K Lenaerts, 'L'apport de la Cour de justice à la construction européenne' (2017) 25 Journal de droit européen 134 (impact of EU law on several delicate issues during the last 30 years).

9 Council Decision (EU) 2015/1601 of 22 September 2015 establishing provisional measures in the area of international protection for the benefit of Italy and Greece [2015] OJ L248/80; Joined Cases C-643/15 and C-647/15 *Slovakia and Hungary v Council* ECLI:EU:C:2017:631.

10 Regulations in 'six pack' in 2011 (OJ [2011] L306); 'two pack' in 2013 (OJ [2011] L140). See i.a. Art 136 TFEU.

cautious with German dieselplan' or 'France gets three months to tweak budget') and speculate on the implications of Brexit.[11]

A substantive part of public power—legislative, executive as well as judicial—is exercised jointly by the EU and its Member States. Europeanisation of national law takes many different forms.[12]

By signing the Treaties, Member States agreed to limit their sovereign rights and created a common legal order which became an integral part of their domestic legal orders. The principle of the primacy of Union law, inherent in the specific nature of the EU[13] and a crucial corollary to the equality of Member States, is stated in a declaration annexed to the Lisbon Treaty.[14] The European Court of Justice (ECJ) has confirmed that 'it follows from well-established case-law that rules of national law, even of a constitutional order, cannot be allowed to undermine the unity and effectiveness of European Union law'.[15] National courts and administrations have an obligation to interpret national law in conformity with Union law and a duty to set aside conflicting national rules. In this context, national legislation voted within national parliaments—and even constitutional law—may become inapplicable. Every Member State body must ensure the full effectiveness in the national legal order of rights derived from Union law.[16] The unlawful consequences of a breach of Union law must be nullified, e.g. unlawful taxes must be refunded. National democracies adopting legislation on the basis of majority voting have to take into account, and

---

11 <www.euobserver.com/economic/126720>; <www.euobserver.com/environment/138681>; or 'L'Italie prépare l'affrontement avec l'Europe. La coalition populiste annoncera à la rentrée des mesures qui inquiètent déjà Bruxelles et les marchés' (<www.lemonde.fr/europe/article/2018/08/07/l-italie-prepare-l-affrontement-avec-l-europe_5340043_3214>).

12 See, i.a., F Snyder (ed) *The Europeanisation of Law: The Legal Effects of European Integration* (Hart 2000); N Jääskinen, 'Europeanisation of National Law: A Legal-theoretical Analysis' (2015) 40 ELRev 667. Further in Part three.

13 Case 6/64 *Costa v ENEL* ECLI:EU:C:1964:66; Case 11-70 *Internationale Handelsgesellschaft* ECLI:EU:C:1970:114.

14 Declaration No 17 concerning primacy [2010] OJ C83/344.

15 Case C-416/10 *Križan* ECLI:EU:C:2013:8, para 70 (the competent national authorities involved in the construction of a landfill site could not refuse public access to an urban planning document pursuant to European environmental provisions). See earlier: Case 106/77 *Simmenthal II* ECLI:EU:C:1978:49, paras 22–24; Case C-213/89 *Factortame I* ECLI:EU:C:1990:257, paras 14–15; Case C-409/06 *Winner Wetten* ECLI:EU:C:2010:503, para 61.

16 Art 4(3) TEU on sincere cooperation. See i.a. Case C-432/05 *Unibet* ECLI:EU:C:2007:163, para 38; Case C-404/13 *ClientEarth* ECLI:EU:C:2014:2382, para 52. Also Case C-282/10 *Dominguez* ECLI:EU:C:2012:33, paras 30–3.

give precedence to, rules adopted at the EU level on the basis of majority voting in accordance with the relevant Treaty procedures. A European directive adopted in accordance with the ordinary legislative procedure must be implemented by all Member States even if it would not have obtained the necessary majority in the national parliament.

Although estimating percentages is hard to do, national legislation often stems from EU law.[17] Moreover, beyond quantitative estimates, 'the law' in Member States has become a mixture of EU law and national law. EU law influences legal thinking and judicial interpretation of legislation in the Member States.[18]

Another aspect of the Europeanisation of law is that to a large extent the Member States take up the executive function for the EU.[19] EU law, including EU administrative law, has been described as an incoming tide, flowing into the estuaries and up the rivers, its waves relentless and impossible to hold back.[20]

Extensive legal review and remedies guarantee the correct application of this joint exercise of public power. Compliance by a Member State with

---

17 In 1988, Delors claimed that in 10 years, the EC would be the source of 80% of Member States' legislation (especially economic, may be even fiscal and social). Actual numbers, ranging from 1 to 80%, should be looked at with great care. See for the Netherlands, M Bovens and K Yesilkagit, 'The EU as lawmaker: the impact of EU directives on national regulation in the Netherlands' (2010) 88 Public Adminstration 57. For other Member States, see AE Töller, 'Concepts of Causality in Quantitative Approaches to Europeanization' in C Radaelli and T Exadactylos (eds), *Establishing Causality in Europeanization Research* (Palgrave Macmillan 2012): studies showed rather low shares of Europeanised national legislation (15% for the UK, 14 % for Denmark, 10% for Austria, 3 to 27% for France, 1 to 24% for Finland, yet 39% for Germany). The author concludes that these figures tell us little about the impact of EU-policy-making, i.a. because of differences in policy fields (the famous Delors 80% could be reality in agriculture, environment or financial market regulations). See also WC Muller and others, 'Legal Europeanization: comparative perspectives' (2010) 88 Public Administration 75.

18 Jääskinen, 'Europeanisation of National Law: A Legal-theoretical Analysis', distinguishing 'law' as legal order, legal system, jurisprudence or legal culture.

19 Hofmann, Rowe and Türk, *Administrative law and policy of the European Union*.

20 D Curtin, *Executive Power of the European Union. Law, Practices, and the Living Constitution* (Oxford University Press 2009) 278, referring to Lord Denning in *Bulmer v Bollinger* [1974] Ch 401 (418F): 'But when we come to matters with a European element, the Treaty is like an incoming tide. It flows into the estuaries and up the rivers. It cannot be held back. Parliament has decreed that the Treaty is henceforward to be part of our law. It is equal in force to any statute.'.

EU law is ensured through actions brought by the Commission,[21] by citizens[22] or by other Member States[23]. National courts have the task of implementing EU law in their capacity as the 'ordinary' courts within the EU legal order and have to ensure an effective remedy when rights and freedoms guaranteed by EU law are infringed (Article 47 Charter of Fundamental Rights of the European Union, hereafter CFR).[24] National judges have sent more than 10 000 references for preliminary rulings to the ECJ, asking for its help in the interpretation of EU law.[25] In *Wightman*, the ECJ noted that any withdrawal of a Member State from the EU 'is liable to have a considerable impact on the rights of all Union citizens'.[26]

This, then, is the first observation: the EU has become an important reality, a fact of life and law, with considerable impact on the society in which citizens live. This first observation is in stark contrast to the second observation, which follows now.

3 Low importance of EU learning in many schools

Have education systems adapted to the paradigm shift? Can national education systems embrace these developments flexibly and prepare young people for citizenship in the European system of multilevel governance? In her study of the field of education, Keating observes: 'Member States tend to reframe the notion of European citizenship to reflect the national model of citizenship and the histories, traditions, and socio-political priori-

---

21 Arts 258–260 TFEU, possibly leading to financial penalties being imposed on the defendant Member State. See Case C-304/02 *Commission v France* ECLI:EU:C:2005:444: France failing i.a. to carry out checks of fishing activities in accordance with Community provisions, was ordered to pay a lump sum of 20 million euros for past non-compliance and 57 million euros for each period of six months of future non-compliance; Case C-533/11 *Commission v Belgium* ECLI:EU:C:2013:659: Belgium failing i.a. to implement correctly Directive 91/271/EEC on urban waste-water treatment, was ordered to pay a lump sum of 10 million euros for past non-compliance and a penalty payment of 859 000 euros for each future six-month period of delay.

22 See §§ 242 243 . Citizens in national courts can rely on the direct effect of EU provisions when these are clear, precise and unconditional, or can claim damages against the defaulting Member State (private enforcement).

23 Art 259 TFEU and, e.g., Case C-591/17 *Austria v Germany* ECLI:EU:C:2019:504.

24 *Opinion 1/09* ECLI:EU:C:2011:123, para 80.

25 Court of Justice of the European Union, Annual Report 2017, Judicial activity, p 125 (10 149 new references for a preliminary ruling between 1952 and 2017).

26 Case C-621/18 *Wightman and Others* ECLI:EU:C:2018:999, para 64.

ties of the nation-state.'[27] Yet, the nation states as 'Masters of the Treaty' have chosen to transfer competences to the Union in respect of objectives which they consider they can achieve better together. It would be logical to explain this choice, the motives underpinning it, and its far-reaching consequences, to the young citizens at school. A significant percentage of national legislation may stem from EU directives. But what percentage of 18 years-olds has been taught what an EU directive is? Quite a degree of inertia characterises education systems operating within the old paradigm.

Based on successive surveys and analyses, it is fair to observe that learning about the EU in schools is fragmented.[28]

The 2013 *ICF GHK report 'Learning Europe at school'* concludes that Member States differ widely as to the aspects of the EU they expect to be taught in schools.[29] The European citizenship dimension, in particular, is rarely clearly defined. The EU curriculum is very fragmented in most countries, with little evidence of progressive building on basic facts towards complex understanding, and with little consistency and complementarity at different levels and in different subjects.[30] No clear picture is created of the EU as an entity. The functioning of EU institutions is neglected as a subject, compared to European history or geography. There is great disparity in teacher training about the EU, with limited evidence of EU study in initial teacher training programmes. Much depends on the teachers' motivation or personal convictions. In many school books, there is relatively little coverage of EU issues.

The results of the 2009 *International Civic and Citizenship Education Study*[31], which mainly tested 14 years-old pupils, are described by the Commission as follows:

---

27 A Keating, 'Educating Europe's citizens: moving from national to post-national models of educating for European citizenship' (2009) 13 Citizenship Studies 135, 147.

28 See further Part four (§ 311).

29 Commission, *Learning Europe at School* (DG for Education, Youth, Sport and Culture, ICF GHK, 2013).

30 'Curriculum' can be defined as 'a plan for learning in the form of the description of learning outcomes, of learning content and of learning processes for a specified period of study'. See CoE Reference Framework of Competences for Democratic Culture, Vol 3: Guidance for implementation (2018) 13.

31 The 2009 International Civic and Citizenship Education Study (ICCS) assessed lower-secondary students (8th grade) with regard to inter alia civic knowledge, identity, attitudes, engagement, participation. See D Kerr and others, *ICCS 2009 European Report: Civic knowledge, attitudes and engagement among lower-secondary*

> The European module data show that knowledge about the European Union is relatively good in EU countries ..., but there is still a clear need for improvement. In all participating EU countries more than 95% of pupils knew that their country was an EU Member State. Over 90% of pupils knew the flag of the European Union (...).[32]

Given the extensive impact of the exercise of EU public power on citizens' daily life, I wonder whether being able to recognise the flag of the EU should be deemed a sufficient learning outcome.[33] The 2016 International Civic and Citizenship Education Study, too, reports that the opportunities to learn about Europe vary substantially across Europe. Pupils mostly have the opportunity to learn about European history, but far less opportunity to study European political and economic integration or European political and social issues.[34]

Eurydice, a network consisting of 42 national units in 38 States—including all EU Member States—providing information and analyses of European education systems and policies,[35] concluded in 2012 that the European dimension is well represented in citizenship curricula.[36] Upon a closer look, however, significant disparities appeared in the quality and

---

students in 24 European countries (International Association for the Evaluation of Educational Achievement IEA, 2010).

32 Commission Staff working document 'Progress towards the common European objectives in education and training- Indicators and benchmarks 2010/2011', 105–109. 'European pupils score high in civic knowledge', titled the Commission in a 2010 press release, but continued: 'The study found large differences in pupils' levels of civic knowledge' <europa.eu/rapid/press-release_MEMO-10-599_en.htm>.

33 Former webpage <iccs.iea.nl/index.php?id=52> accessed 6 September 2017.

34 B Losito and others, *Young People's Perceptions of Europe in a Time of Change: IEA International Civic and Citizenship Education Study- 2016 European Report* (2017), 14–15 (reported learning opportunities about Europe at school, to a large or a moderate extent: on average 50% of the pupils).

35 Next to the EU Member States, also Albania, Bosnia and Herzegovina, the former Yugoslav Republic of Macedonia, Iceland, Liechtenstein, Montenegro, Norway, Serbia, Switzerland and Turkey. The coordinating unit in EACEA (Education, Audiovisual and Culture Executive Agency) supports the Commission in cooperative work the CoE and UNESCO.

36 Commission/EACEA/Eurydice, Citizenship Education in Europe (2012) 97. Earlier: Commission/EACEA/Eurydice, Citizenship Education at School in Europe (2005).

extent of the EU dimension of citizenship education in schools.[37] Eurydice reported in 2017 that '[a]s many as eight EU member states do not have an international dimension in the curriculum of secondary education' and that in most countries the citizenship education curriculum for vocational training does not mention the EU at all.[38]

Thus, while optional or extra-curricular activities may offer more opportunities for EU learning, surveys and authors report on patchy rules concerning the curricula of formal education.[39] They point, moreover, to a compliance gap, there being disparities between the intended curriculum and the implemented curriculum.[40] The inadequacies in EU learning may be the result of many factors: poorly-defined EU learning content, insufficient training of teachers on EU matters, non-mandatory EU learning, a lack of assessment, or tenacious convictions that the EU as a subject is too sensitive, too complex, or not essential in an overburdened curriculum. Education is often underpinned by an economic rationale, the need to prepare students for the job market, not for citizenship. Furthermore, sociological realities play a role: the autonomy of philosophical-ideological school platforms and of schools (private and public institutions), and the

---

37 Commission/EACEA/Eurydice, Citizenship Education in Europe (2012) 17 ff; for diversity in approaches and themes, see figure p 30; see also p 32 (in Germany, themes related to the European dimension were no longer included in the upper secondary level curriculum). Eurydice's concept of citizenship education in text to n 902.

38 Commission/EACEA/Eurydice, Citizenship Education at School in Europe (2017) 67 (based on questionnaires answered by national units, who used official recommendations, regulations as well as national strategies or action plans as primary information sources). See also ibid, pp 29, 58, 65; Commission/EACEA/Eurydice, Promoting citizenship and the common values of freedom, tolerance and non-discrimination through education: Overview of education policy developments in Europe following the Paris Declaration of 17 March 2015 (2016); European Parliament Resolution of 12 April 2016 on Learning EU at school [2018] OJ C58/57, recitals J-L. On problematic EU learning, further § 312 and text to n 1039 ff.

39 Many laudable initiatives organised *ad hoc* in or outside schools: Europe Days, 9 May actions, Spring Day in Europe, European Youth Parliament, Parlamentarium, EPAS, eTwinning, Your Europe Your Say, Back to School, guest speakers, special debates, conferences, competitions, exhibitions, chat sessions. See further text to n 1039 ff, § 152 . Concept of formal education in text to n 1040.

40 C Bîrzéa, 'EDC policies in Europe - a synthesis' in *All-European Study on Education for Democratic Citizenship Policies* (CoE 2005) 29. See also n 243.

freedom of teachers.[41] A worrying impression is that it is not only the teachers (trainers) themselves who may lack essential knowledge about the EU, but also the trainers of the trainers. Even scholars in the field of citizenship education sometimes fail to clearly distinguish between the EU and the Council of Europe[42], or between EU citizens and immigrants.[43]

In short, a huge number of pupils leave school at age 18 with impressive knowledge about science or literature, but in relative ignorance of the EU. The high importance of the EU contrasts with the low importance attached to EU learning in many schools.

These two observations are related to a wider problem.

---

41 Various factors described, i.a., in Kerr and others (n 31); H Walkenhorst, 'Problems of Political Education in a Multi-level Polity: explaining Non-teaching of European Union Issues in German Secondary Schooling' (2006) 14 Journal of Contemporary European Studies 353, 354: 'The European Union initiative "European Dimension in Education", designed to raise pupils' awareness and knowledge of European integration issues, is highly contested and has not always found its way into the school curricula of the Member States.' See further challenges documented in § 66 .

42 Unclear, e.g. E Féron, 'Citizenship Education in France' in VB Georgi (ed), *The Making of Citizens in Europe: New Perspectives on Citizenship Education* (Schriftenreihe Band 666, Bundeszentrale für politische Bildung 2008) 108, citing the ECHR as a founding text in courses on European citizenship and on European integration, with no mention of the EU Treaties. European citizenship is not founded on the ECHR (this convention is also valid for Turkish or Azerbaijan citizens). In the EU, the ECHR is at present an indirect source of general principles of law (Art 6(3) TEU, before accession to the ECHR).

43 Unclear questions asked to pupils in ICCS 2016 (how strongly do you agree: 'Immigrants should have the same rights that everyone else in the country has'): see Losito and others, *Young People's Perceptions of Europe in a Time of Change: IEA International Civic and Citizenship Education Study- 2016 European Report* 24, 27 (e.g. on the immigration of people from other EU Member States). See also D Sampermans and others, *ICCS 2016 Rapport Vlaanderen, Een onderzoek naar burgerschapseducatie in Vlaanderen. Eindrapport november 2017* (KU Leuven, Centrum voor Politicologie, 2017) 165 ('Politieke tolerantie is het geven van gelijke rechten aan alle groepen die deel uitmaken van de maatschappij, zodat iedereen op gelijke wijze zijn belangen kan verdedigden. Zonder deze gelijke rechten kan er van een volwaardige democratie geen sprake zijn').

The gap between the EU and its citizens

4 Problem of democratic and civic deficit

The legitimacy of the EU is questioned. The gap between the EU and its citizens is often referred to as the 'democratic deficit'.[44] The disconnect between the EU and its citizens can also be described by the concept of the 'civic deficit', highlighting other aspects than the 'democratic deficit'.[45] The EU civic deficit, the unacceptable distance between the EU and its citi-

44 Vast literature on democratic deficit and (social) legitimacy. See, i.a., AK Kiernan, 'Citizenship—the real democratic deficit of the European union? 1' (1997) 1 Citizenship Studies 323; C Blumann, 'Citoyenneté européenne et déficit démocratique' in C Philip and P Soldatos (eds), *La citoyenneté européenne* (Collection études européennes, Chaire Jean Monnet, 2000); C Philip and P Soldatos (eds), *La citoyenneté européenne* (Collection études européennes, Chaire Jean Monnet, 2000) (democracy, transparency and communication deficit); A Verhoeven, *The European Union in Search of a Democratic and Constitutional Theory* (European Monographs 38, Kluwer Law International 2002) 60; G Majone, *Dilemmas of European integration: the ambiguities and pitfalls of integration by stealth* (Oxford University Press 2005); S Smismans, *Law, Legitimacy, and European Governance: Functional Participation in Social Regulation* (Oxford Studies in European Law, Oxford University Press 2004); A Follesdal and S Hix, 'Why there is a democratic deficit in the EU: A response to Majone and Moravcsik' (2006) 44 JCMS 533; P Craig, 'Integration, Democracy and Legitimacy' in P Craig and G de Búrca (eds), *The evolution of EU law* (Oxford University Press 2011); Curtin, *Executive Power of the European Union. Law, Practices, and the Living Constitution*, 283 ff; P Norris, *Democratic Deficit: Critical Citizens Revisited* (Cambridge University Press 2011); J Habermas, 'The Crisis of the European Union in the Light of a Constitutionalization of International Law' (2012) 23 European Journal Of International Law 335, 345; JHH Weiler, 'In the Face of Crisis: Input Legitimacy, Output Legitimacy and the Political Messianism of European Integration' (2012) 34 Journal of European Integration 825.

45 Concepts of democratic and civic deficit overlap to some extent, e.g. with regard to 'distance' and 'transparency and complexity' issues as described by Craig, 'Integration, Democracy and Legitimacy' 13 and 30, but they emphasise different aspects. An extreme hypothesis to illustrate the difference: enlightened despotism, by definition suffering from a major democratic deficit, may only result in a minor civic deficit if a much-loved king or queen achieves popular outcomes and most people feel connected to the governing system and accept it. I make this point not to downplay the importance of democracy, but to clarify concepts. Recital F in European Parliament Resolution of 12 April 2016 on Learning EU at school [2018] OJ C58/57 refers to the democratic deficit.

zens,[46]has cognitive, affective and behavioural dimensions.[47] Fragmented learning about the EU in schools is relevant to the civic deficit (at least) in its cognitive dimension. Studies invariably reveal a lack of knowledge about the EU. A 2018 Eurobarometer survey found that 59 per cent of Europeans feel that they understand how the EU works (subjective knowledge), yet only 18 per cent answered questions on the EU correctly (objective knowledge).[48] Poor understanding easily turns into ambivalence, irritation about 'Brussels' or hostility. Negative referendum results and low turn-out rates at the European Parliament elections are significant.[49] A positive signal is that the increased turnout at the 2019 European Parliament elections was driven by greater participation by young people.[50] However, older people (over 55 years old) continued to constitute the main voter

---

46 The term 'civic deficit' was probably first used in a Report of the Australian Civics Expert Group, *Whereas the people: Civics and Citizenship Education* (Canberra 1994). See Dutch Ministry of Education Culture and Science, *Citizenship – made in Europe: living together starts at school* (2004) 11; V Pérez-Díaz, 'The European Civic Deficit' (2004) <www.essayandscience.com/article/24/the-european-civic-deficit/> ; L McNabb, 'Civic Outreach Programs: Common Models, Shared Challenges, and Strategic Recommendations' (2013) 90 Denver University Law Review 871, 872, 876 (on deficits in civic literacy and participation); M Chou and others, *Young people, citizenship and political participation: combatting civic deficit* (Rowman & Littlefield 2017). On the elite vs public divide, see T Raines, M Goodwin and D Cutts, *The Future of Europe: Comparing Public and Elite Attitudes* (Research Paper, Europe Programme, Chatham House, The Royal Institute of International Affairs, 2017).

47 On the affective crisis of European citizenship, see i.a. JHH Weiler, 'To be a European Citizen –Eros and Civilization' (1997) 4 Journal of European Public Policy 495. On dimensions of active citizenship: E Cresson, *Learning for active citizenship: a significant challenge in building a Europe of knowledge. Foreword* (1998); M Nussbaum, *Political Emotions: Why Love Matters for Justice* (Harvard University Press 2015).

48 Standard Eurobarometer 89, Public Opinion in the European Union (June 2018), 132: 18% of respondents were wrong with regard to 3 true/false statements (the euro area currently consists of 19 Member States; the Members of the EP are directly elected by the citizens of each Member State; Switzerland is a Member State of the EU). See Standard Eurobarometer 91, 'European citizenship' (August 2019): 57% of Europeans feel they know their rights as EU citizens, yet 68% would like to know more. See also n 1637.

49 Negative referenda outcomes (as in Denmark in 1992, France in 2005, Ireland in 2001 and 2008, the Netherlands in 2005) illustrate hesitation or opposition towards the EU on issues which are essentially a matter of national politics: J Habermas, *Zur Verfassung Europas. Ein Essay* (Suhrkamp 2011) 118.

50 Global turnout at EP elections: 42,61% (2014) and 50,62% (2019). Young voters' turnout: 27,8 % of 18–24 year-olds (2014), 42% in 2019.

population and some socio-demographic groups were poorly represented. About 49 per cent of the EU citizens did not vote.[51] The EU still has to strengthen its social legitimacy, i.e. the subjective acceptance by the public of the political system. Social legitimacy is based on deep common interests and feelings of loyalty.[52] Yet, a sense of alienation vis-à-vis the EU as a level of governance can be observed. The Brexit vote convincingly illustrates the structural consequences to which the gap with the citizens may lead, both for the Member State (UK) and for the whole of the EU. The causes of the Leave vote are complex and cannot simply be attributed to the failure to learn about the EU at school. However, it is thought-provoking that in the 2012 Eurydice study on 'citizenship education themes, as recommended in national curricula', some columns for the UK (though not for Scotland) were left empty, namely those relating to European identity and belonging, and European history, culture and literature.[53] In 2014, England made the study of 'Fundamental British Values' compulsory in schools.[54]

---

51 See Eurobarometer Survey 91.5 of the European Parliament, The 2019 post-electoral survey: Have European elections entered a new dimension? (September 2019), 22–23.

52 Concept and problem of social legitimacy in: S O'Leary, *The Evolving Concept of Community Citizenship: From the Free Movement of Persons to Union Citizenship* (European Monographs 13, Kluwer 1996) 312; Curtin, *Executive Power of the European Union. Law, Practices, and the Living Constitution* 284; Weiler, 'In the Face of Crisis: Input Legitimacy, Output Legitimacy and the Political Messianism of European Integration', 826; G Davies, 'Social Legitimacy and Purposive Power: The End, the Means and the Consent of the People' in D Kochenov, G de Búrca and A Williams (eds), *Europe's Justice Deficit?* (Hart 2015) 261.

53 Commission/EACEA/Eurydice, Citizenship Education in Europe (2012), 30 (not recommended in any level in national curricula). See also J Arthur and D Wright, *Teaching Citizenship in the Secondary School* (David Fulton 2001), only referring to some EU websites. Further B Hoskins, 'Brexit and its implications for Citizenship Education across Europe' 2 August 2016 <ec.europa.eu/epale/en/blog/brexit-and-its-implications-citizenship-education-across-europe>. For empirical studies on impact of citizenship education, see n 108. In the Brexit referendum 71 % of the 18–25 age group voted Remain, yet, apparently, only 30% of young people actually voted (YouGov opinion poll). See further J Curtice, 'Why Leave Won the UK's EU Referendum' (2017) 55 JCMS 19; L Gormley, 'Brexit - Never Mind the Whys and Wherefores? Fog in the Channel, Continent Cut Off!' (2017) 40 Fordham International Law Journal 1175; J Snell, 'European Union and National Referendums: Need for Change after the Brexit Vote?' (2017) 28 European Business Law Review 767.

54 See n 1180 and text.

One of the basic challenges to be resolved by the EU is how to bridge the gap with its citizens. This study will approach the problem of the democratic and civic deficit from the educational perspective by studying EU citizenship education.[55]

The term 'EU citizenship education' brings with it a two-fold challenge. The two subjects which this study aims to link—namely, EU citizenship and citizenship education—are to a certain extent each contentious in their own right.

The two-fold challenge for 'EU citizenship education'

5 *Which citizenship education?*

The first challenge is to find a neutral and commonly accepted concept of citizenship education. On the Beaufort scale, the winds in the field of citizenship education range from calm indifference, via light breeze, to strong gale, and storms causing structural damage. In the past, totalitarian regimes such as nazism or communism have demonstrated the potentially devastating effects of citizenship education. Today, 'citizenship education' is also provided by the Taliban (to boys only) and in Turkey (by loyal professors only). The fear of social engineering, of a religious or ideological nature, leads some to reject the need for citizenship education of any kind: neither states nor schools have to 'educate' citizens. Osler, an authoritative scholar on citizenship education, observes: 'Citizenship is a contested subject and it is therefore not surprising that education for citizenship in schools often tends to provoke heated debate and controversy'.[56] Talking about citizenship education is like opening Pandora's box.[57] A huge variety

55 Calls for research on this topic, in Walkenhorst, 'Problems of Political Education in a Multi-level Polity: explaining Non-teaching of European Union Issues in German Secondary Schooling' 354 (the democratic deficit is generally seen as an institutional-structural problem; '[a]stonishingly, few EU scholars have approached the issue of the democratic deficit from an educational perspective)'; see also Commission/EACEA/Eurydice, Citizenship Education at School in Europe (2005) 62; S Philippou, A Keating and D Hinderliter Ortloff, 'Citizenship education curricula: comparing the multiple meanings of supra-national citizenship in Europe and beyond' (2009) 42 Journal of curriculum studies 291, 296.

56 A Osler and H Starkey, 'Education for democratic citizenship: a review of research, policy and practice 1995–2005' (2006) 21 Research Papers in Education 433, 435, see also 455.

57 T Olgers, 'Escaping the Box of Pandora, in K O'Shea, EDC policies and regulatory frameworks' (Strasbourg, 6-7 December 2001).

of definitions, approaches, objectives, sceptical and even hostile reactions emerge. Sensitive questions often remain unspoken, e.g. how competent are teachers, or, do pupils think sufficiently critically? To avoid propaganda and the indoctrination of future voters, 'politics' is not considered to be an appropriate curriculum subject.[58] Although curriculum guidelines often include citizenship education, there is reticence about it in practice, as teachers want to avoid accusations of hidden agendas or the inappropriate influencing of young minds in schools. A recurring problem is that Member States fail to move beyond mere rhetoric on citizenship education. Citizenship education goals are set, but surveys and scholars point to an implementation gap.[59] Everyone is in favour of citizenship education (who would advocate having uneducated citizens?). How the abstract ideal is to be translated into reality, however, is open to discussion. In its 2017 report, Eurydice draws attention to the fluidity of citizenship education.[60]

Both 'citizenship' and 'education' are debatable concepts in themselves. Combining them in 'citizenship education' intensifies the debate. Brubaker is realistic: 'Citizenship and nationhood are intensely contested issues in European politics... They are likely to remain so for the foreseeable future'.[61] The same can be expected to hold true for citizenship education. Shaw describes citizenship as 'an open-textured concept', with a host of meanings, susceptible to interpretation and even ideological manipulation, with no consensus even as to the methods for approaching it.[62] Citizenship education can be accused of the same 'muddiness' as citizenship. It

58 Even the study of constitutional law at universities had to fight for acceptance. See L Heuschling, 'Wissenschaft vom Verfassungsrecht: Frankreich' in A von Bogdandy, P Cruz Villalón and PM Huber (eds), *Handbuch Ius Publicum Europaeum*, vol II Offene Staatlichkeit- Wissenschaft vom Verfassungsrecht (CF Müller Verlag 2007).

59 Bîrzéa, 'EDC policies in Europe - a synthesis' 29; Commission/EACEA/Eurydice, Citizenship Education at School in Europe (2017) 19–21.

60 Commission/EACEA/Eurydice, Citizenship Education at School in Europe (2017) 19–21; variations in organisation and content, i.a. p 43, 45. See also Commission/EACEA/Eurydice, Promoting citizenship and the common values of freedom, tolerance and non-discrimination through education: Overview of education policy developments in Europe following the Paris Declaration of 17 March 2015 (2016).

61 R Brubaker, *Citizenship and nationhood in France and Germany* (3rd edn, Harvard University Press 1996) 189.

62 J Shaw, 'The many pasts and futures of citizenship in the European Union' (1997) 22 ELRev 554, 558. See also B Hoskins and others, *Contextual Analysis Report: Participatory Citizenship in the European Union (Report 1)* (2012) 9- 12: countries have developed different citizenship models (liberal, communautarian, civic republi-

is not only citizenship which is a highly-charged concept: education in general is contentious, with all that implies for our children: 'What children should learn at school and how the learning process should be organized is the source of never-ending challenge and change.'[63] It is true that citizenship and education are the subject of rational reflection in political and social sciences, in philosophy or legal theory, yet, it must be recognised, both subjects reach into deeper layers of feelings, beliefs and values. Sir Bernard Crick, on whose recommendation citizenship was introduced into the English National Curriculum,[64] states that citizenship education is important, 'yet, it is also full of complications, conflicts and irrationalities'.[65] There are countless theories of education, and the diverging viewpoints of governments, parents, children, schools, and other stakeholders, have to be reconciled. In the case of citizenship education in particular, obstacles and inherent tensions are part of the game, and they are not infrequently accompanied by terms such as suspicion, perennial debate, painful, or malaise.[66]

How then can some common ground be found on the issue of citizenship education? In the Member States, citizenship education is defined and approached in many different ways because it is closely related to the historical, political and cultural traditions of the nation states concerned.[67] Even the terminology used to designate citizenship and citizenship educa-

---

can, critical) based on civic traditions, societal problems, or the political leaning of governing parties.

63 K Tomaševski, *Human rights obligations: making education available, accessible, acceptable and adaptable* (Right to education Primers No 3, 2001).

64 Advisory Group on Citizenship, *Education for citizenship and the teaching of democracy in schools: the Crick Report* (Qualifications and Curriculum Authority, 1998). See also n 594.

65 Foreword to D Heater, *Citizenship : the civic ideal in world history, politics and education* (3rd edn, Longman 2004) xi.

66 O Ichilov (ed), *Citizenship and Citizenship Education in a Changing World* (Woburn Press 1998); J Arthur, I Davies and C Hahn (eds), *The SAGE Handbook of Education for Citizenship and Democracy* (Sage 2008), Introduction by editors, see p 8; M Sundstrom and C Fernandez, 'Citizenship education and diversity in liberal societies: Theory and policy in a comparative perspective' (2013) 8 Education, Citizenship and Social Justice 103.

67 T Grammes, 'Different Cultures in Education for Democracy and Citizenship' (2012) 11 Journal of Social Science Education 3; J Ainley, W Schulz and T Friedman (eds), *ICCS 2009 Encyclopedia: Approaches to civic and citizenship education around the world* (International Association for the Evaluation of Educational Achievement IEA 2013) 20; Commission/EACEA/Eurydice, Promoting citizenship and the common values of freedom, tolerance and non-discrimination

tion varies.[68] Merely choosing one of the national models for citizenship education as a template for examining the situation of the EU citizen, would not be satisfactory. Scholarly writing on citizenship education does not offer a solution either. Definitions of the terms used in citizenship education are the subject of 'ongoing and vigorous academic dialogue'.[69]

6 *Which EU citizenship?*

The second challenge inherent in the concept of 'EU citizenship education' is the need to find a basic consensual view on the EU and EU citizenship before linking it with education.[70] The EU is not only complex, but it is, to say the least, the object of diverging visions and opinions. As it weathers the storms of financial and economic crises, migration, or Brexit, the EU finds itself contested in its fundamentals by some, in its nuances by others.[71] In its proposals for the EU27 by 2025, the Commission has set out five scenarios reflecting radically different visions of the EU.[72] The fragility

---

through education: Overview of education policy developments in Europe following the Paris Declaration of 17 March 2015 (2016), see annex with references to various national programs and websites.

68 Examples in n 480. Overview of terms in Bîrzéa, 'EDC policies in Europe - a synthesis', appendix I-II; as well as examples in Hoskins and others, *Contextual Analysis Report: Participatory Citizenship in the European Union (Report 1)* 18–21; and CoE, Government Replies to the Questionnaire, in 2016 Report on the State of citizenship and Human Rights Education in Europe. See also H Becker, 'Politische Bildung in Europa' Bundeszentrale für politische Bildung (2012) <www.bpb.de/apuz/148214/politische-bildung-in-europa?p=all> : 'Wer in der höchst diversen Szene politischer Jugend-, Erwachsenen- und Schulbildung schon in Deutschland heftig um Begriffe als Stellvertreter für Konzepte streitet, dem erscheinen die nationalen Ausprägungen und unterschiedlichen Begrifflichkeiten quer durch Europa erst recht unbezähmbar'.

69 W Schulz and others, *IEA International Civic and Citizenship Education Study 2016: Assessment Framework* (2016) 15.

70 Education in itself is a difficult topic in the EU context. See J Pertek, 'L'éducation et la Communauté: une relation mouvementée et incertaine' [2005] Law & European affairs 7.

71 Z Bańkowski and E Christodoulidis, 'The European Union as an Essentially Contested Project' (1998) 4 ELJ 341; L van Middelaar, *De passage naar Europa. Geschiedenis van een begin* (Historische uitgeverij 2009) 11–12: it is 'extremely tricky' to answer the question as to whether Europe exists as a political entity.

72 Commission White paper of 1 March 2017 on the future of Europe COM(2017) 2025 final; C Calliess, 'Bausteine einer erneuerten Europäischen Union- Auf der Suche nach dem europäischen Weg: Überlegungen im Lichte des Weißbuchs der Europäischen Kommission zur Zukunft Europas' (2018) 20 Neue Zeitschrift für Verwaltungsrecht 1.

of EU citizenship is apparent in civil and political society, where Eurosceptic views contrast with the ambitions of Eurofederalists for deeper integration.[73] In scholarly writing, conflicting ideas on the EU result from attempts to fit the EU as a political system into concepts traditionally used in political science. Demos or no demos, democracy or demoi-cracy, international, supra-national or trans-national organisation, ...: many opinions are canvassed.[74] Semantic debates appear to be about more than just semantics. Terms matter.[75] Choosing to label the EU as a constitutional order, a polity, a multilevel system of governance, an international organisation, intergovernmental cooperation by sovereign Member States, or an internal market, produces different answers to the question as to whether, in a given form, the EU should be linked with citizenship education. Citizenship education would appear to be the natural companion of a constitutional model but might seem superfluous in the context of intergovernmental cooperation or an internal market. In a pluralistic society the diversity of views about the EU is normal and healthy. However, what should schoolchildren be taught? Should the EU as a subject be excluded from the school curriculum because it is too controversial for citizenship education?[76] An author published by the German *Bundeszentrale für politsche Bildung* writes:

> Trotz der überragenden Bedeutung der EU für praktisch alle Politikbereiche lassen sich die einschlägigen Bücher an einer Hand abzählen. Ein akzeptiertes Konzept zur Beschäftigung mit Europa in der [Politische Bildung] ist bislang nicht in Sicht.[77]

---

73 See Eurobarometers, newspapers, think tanks, Bratislava meeting after Brexit.

74 See i.a. nn 1036 and 1702 and text.

75 L Azoulai and E Jaeger, 'Review: The Passage to Europe (van Middelaar)' (2014) 51 CMLRev 311, 311 (European integration, European project, European construction… terms carry important assumptions about the way we understand the EU).

76 JM Halstead and MA Pike, *Citizenship and Moral Education: Values in Action* (Routledge 2006) (controversial subjects in the classroom: death penalty, fox hunting, the EU, gay mariage). Cf AEC Struthers, 'Human Rights: A Topic Too Controversial for Mainstream Education?' (2016) 16 Human Rights Law Review 131.

77 R Müller, 'Politische Bildung (und Europa)' Bundeszentrale für politische Bildung (2016) <www.bpb.de/nachschlagen/lexika/177197/politische-bildung-und-europa> : 'In spite of the overriding importance of the EU in practically all areas of politics, relevant textbooks can be counted on the fingers of one hand. An accepted model for studying Europe in politics classes is not yet in sight.'.

Is it wise to wait until the waters calm and clear EU certainties appear? The answer this study advocates is: no, on the contrary. A society claiming to be democratic is supposed to make sure its citizens are on board.

With potentially high waves in the sea of citizenship education and strong winds forecast around EU citizenship, firm anchor points are needed.

Three anchor points

7 *First anchor point: Education for Democratic Citizenship (EDC) of the Council of Europe Charter on EDC/HRE*

The first anchor point is the concept of Education for Democratic Citizenship (EDC), with associated principles, as defined in the 2010 Charter on Education for Democratic Citizenship and Human Rights Education (hereafter Charter on EDC/HRE), recommended by the Council of Europe. It responds to the first challenge of finding a neutral and commonly accepted concept of citizenship education. Paragraph 2(b) contains the following definition:

> 'Education for democratic citizenship' means education, training, awareness raising, information, practices and activities which aim, by equipping learners with knowledge, skills and understanding and developing their attitudes and behaviour, to empower them to exercise and defend their democratic rights and responsibilities in society, to value diversity and to play an active part in democratic life, with a view to the promotion and protection of democracy and the rule of law.[78]

Hereafter, capital letters will be used for 'Education for Democratic Citizenship' (EDC) to refer specifically to this Council of Europe concept. Otherwise 'education for democratic citizenship' or 'citizenship education' will be the generic terms.[79]

---

78 CoE Recommendation CM/Rec(2010)7 of the Committee of Ministers to member states on the Council of Europe Charter on Education for Democratic Citizenship and Human Rights Education (11 May 2010). While the TFEU differentiates between 'education' (Art 165) and 'vocational training' (Art 166), in the EDC context, the concept of 'education' includes vocational training. 'Education' in the EDC concept is like the concept of 'lifelong learning' as defined in the Erasmus+ Regulation 1288/2013 (Art 2(1)).

79 For Eurydice's definition of citizenship education, see text to n 902; see also definition in text to n 99.

8 *Second anchor point: EU citizenship of the EU Treaties*

The second anchor point is the concept of EU citizenship and associated rights, as set out in the EU Treaties and the Charter of Fundamental Rights of the European Union (CFR), which constitute EU primary law.[80] Referring to the EU and EU citizenship as described in EU primary law is a response to the second challenge, that is, the need to start from a basic consensual view. The 1992 Maastricht Treaty established the legal concept of 'citizenship of the Union' (hereafter EU citizenship). EU citizenship is defined in Articles 9 TEU and 20(1) TFEU:

> Citizenship of the Union is hereby established. Every person holding the nationality of a Member State shall be a citizen of the Union. Citizenship of the Union shall be additional to and not replace national citizenship.

Since the adoption of the 1992 Maastricht Treaty and the 2009 Lisbon Treaty, the rights of EU citizens are set out in Title II 'Provisions on democratic principles' of the TEU (Articles 9–11 TEU) and in Part Two 'Non-discrimination and citizenship of the Union' of the TFEU (Articles 20–24 TFEU).

9 *Third anchor point: the right to education of the ICESCR and the Convention on the Rights of the Child (CRC)*

The third anchor point is the right to education as defined in the 1966 International Covenant on Economic, Social and Cultural rights (ICESCR) and the 1989 Convention on the Rights of the Child (CRC), which are binding international agreements ratified by all EU Member States. This will help to respond to the challenge of linking citizenship education and EU citizenship. Pursuant to Article 13(1) ICESCR:

> The States Parties to the present Covenant recognize the right of everyone to education. They agree that education shall be directed to the full development of the human personality and the sense of its dignity, and shall strengthen the respect for human rights and fundamental freedoms. They further agree that education shall enable all persons to participate effectively in a free society, promote understanding, toler-

---

80 Consolidated versions of the Treaty on European Union and the Treaty on the Functioning of the European Union [2016] OJ C202/1; Charter of Fundamental Rights of the European Union [2016] OJ C202/389 (proclaimed at Strasbourg on 12 December 2007 by the European Parliament, the Council and the Commission [2007] OJ C303/1).

> ance and friendship among all nations and all racial, ethnic or religious groups, and further the activities of the United Nations for the maintenance of peace.[81]

These educational aims are considered to be compulsory ('shall be directed to'). Article 13(1) ICESCR develops the aims for education set out in Article 26(2) of the Universal Declaration of Human Rights (UDHR) and is comparable to Article 29(1) CRC.[82]

Research questions, method and objectives

10 *Implications of a joint assessment of the anchor points for citizenship education of EU citizens*

Starting from the three anchor points (the Council of Europe Charter on EDC/HRE, the EU Treaties on EU citizenship, and the right to education in international agreements), the central question examined in the study is: What are the implications for citizenship education of EU citizens of a combined reading—as to form and substance—of the provisions on Education for Democratic Citizenship in the Council of Europe Charter on EDC/HRE, on EU citizenship in the EU Treaties, and on the right to education in the ICESCR and CRC? As to the substance, the three anchor points are directly relevant for citizenship education in the EU. As to the form, however, they are based on normative instruments of varying legal force: a Council of Europe recommendation, EU primary law and interna-

81 International Covenant on Economic, Social and Cultural Rights (adopted 16 December 1966 A/RES/2200 (XXI), entered into force 3 January 1976) 993 UNTS3 (emphasis added).

82 Art 29(1) CRC: 'States Parties agree that the education of the child shall be directed to: (a) The development of the child's personality, talents and mental and physical abilities to their fullest potential; (b) The development of respect for human rights and fundamental freedoms, and for the principles enshrined in the Charter of the United Nations; (c) The development of respect for the child's parents, his or her own cultural identity, language and values, for the national values of the country in which the child is living, the country from which he or she may originate, and for civilizations different from his or her own; (d) The preparation of the child for responsible life in a free society, in the spirit of understanding, peace, tolerance, equality of sexes, and friendship among all peoples, ethnic, national and religious groups and persons of indigenous origin; (e) The development of respect for the natural environment'.

tional agreements binding for Member States. This raises various questions.

What are the legal status and effects of these anchor points within the legal orders of the Member States and within the EU legal order, separately and taken together? How should the three anchor points be combined in a legal analysis as to *form* (sources of variable normativity) and as to *substance* (combining the components)? How do EDC and the right to education apply to nationals of Member States *in their capacity as EU citizens*? The EU, in which Member State nationals live, is a relatively young construction compared with nation states, whose structures enjoy deeply embedded authority. In the face of the above mentioned 'two-fold challenge' (diverging opinions on citizenship education and on EU citizenship), the aim is to use sources of law as a secure starting point. A central concern of this study is to identify suitable teaching content for the EU dimension in education. What are the implications of a combined reading of the Charter on EDC/HRE, EU law, and the right to education for what EU citizens should learn about the EU at school? Finally, the issue of competence to act in the field of citizenship education will be addressed. Does the EU have the legal competence to promote education for democratic citizenship for EU citizens? On a combined reading of the instruments mentioned above, to what extent do EU citizens have a right to EU citizenship education and do Member States have a corresponding obligation to provide it? How do human rights affect the exercise of competences by actors in the education field? The importance of these questions is clear if compared with the traditional view that education is the state's duty and prerogative. A member of the DARE network—Democracy and Human Rights Education in Europe—testifies: 'I do not know how often I have heard this killer phrase: "Your work is incredibly important, but education is subject to national policies"'.[83] How far does the discretion enjoyed by Member States with regard to the education of their citizens extend? Does citizenship education depend on the political views of the government which happens to be in power at any given time? Can Member States freely decide to include an EU dimension in the citizenship education which they provide for their nationals, or is their autonomy with regard to education policy con-

83 <dare-network.eu/>; Georg Pirker, *Arbeitskreis deutscher Bildungsstätten* in former webpage <dare-network.blogspot.com/2009/06/reflection-on-hearingexchange-of-views> accessed 16 October 2018. See also the recurring argument of Member State autonomy in education in debates before adoption of European Parliament Resolution of 12 April 2016 on Learning EU at school [2018] OJ C58/57.

strained by rights and obligations? Identifying rights and obligations could help to transform the rhetoric on citizenship education into actual implementation. Hence the need to examine the legal framework which Member States must take into account when designing their policies on citizenship education. Understanding the legal status and effects as to form and substance of the provisions on EDC, EU citizenship, and the right to education—especially when read together—will shed light on national educational autonomy.

11 *Global structure*

In order to answer the questions raised, the study is structured in four Parts, reflecting four consecutive steps.

Part one analyses the Charter on EDC/HRE as to form and substance within the Council of Europe legal order (first anchor point). It is argued that the recommendation of the Committee of Ministers on the EDC/HRE Charter has a high degree of normativity and produces legal effects for the EU Member States *as* member states of the Council of Europe. EDC standards reflect a European consensus, including with regard to the concept of EDC itself.

In *Part two*, EDC standards meet EU law. In an analysis as to *form*, I explain the normative reception of the EDC standards of the Council of Europe (fragmented, but convincing) in the EU legal order and demonstrate that the Charter on EDC/HRE should be taken into account in the interpretation of EU law on citizenship, democracy and education, while respecting EU autonomy.

Based on the foundations of Parts one and two, *Part three* provides an analysis as to *substance* focusing on EU citizenship (second anchor point). It is argued that national EDC in the Member States—in an adaptation perspective—should include an EU dimension consistent with EU law. The result of a combined reading of EU law and EDC standards is the recognition of an EU dimension to the various components of EDC relevant to mainstream education.

Part four examines the competence of the EU and of the Member States to bring this EU dimension into the national EDC curriculum and takes a human rights-based approach to education, considering inter alia the right to education (third anchor point) and its effects on the concept of quality education. It is posited that the EU can adopt incentive measures and recommendations to encourage EDC and its EU dimension.

12 *A legal analysis*

Analysis of legal sources will be the main method used to answer the research questions. Legal sources were consulted until 15 October 2019.[84]

Part one examines the normative framework on EDC in the Council of Europe legal order, including in relation to the ECHR and the case law of the European Court of Human Rights (ECtHR). The other Parts are based on an analysis of EU primary, secondary and case law, complemented by academic legal writing. The novel aspect of this study is that the three anchor points are not only read individually, but also in combination with one another. This enhances their significance.

Member State law occasionally supplements the analysis, but no exhaustive comparative study is made. Empirical material on the state of citizenship education in Member States is borrowed from reports on citizenship education, i.a. of actors in the Council of Europe (review cycles of the Charter on EDC/HRE), Eurydice, the International Civic and Citizenship Education Study, and by academic writers.

13 *The value of law for citizenship education*

This study will clarify the legal foundations for learning about the EU at school. An examination of the law helps to understand *why* it is important to learn about the EU at school, *what* pupils should be taught, *how* they should be taught, and *who* is legally competent to ensure that study of the EU is part of the curriculum.

Legal analysis contributes to the field of citizenship education in various ways. In conferences on citizenship education, I am frequently the only lawyer among the participants. Participants are government officials and policy makers, representatives of NGOs and youth organisations, educators and trainers of trainers, activists, and experts from multiple disciplines. The legal approach is often considered to be reductive.[85] Indeed, society is much richer than its written law alone. That said, the law has much to offer the field of citizenship education. While the law cannot impose 'truths' on pupils, it cannot, either, be neglected. As Ronald Dworkin and other legal theorists have argued, law is more than the technical rule in a given legal text. Law includes the objectives of the rule (*ratio legis*), the policies, and the underlying principles.[86] In a constant search for justice and

---

84 Links to websites were checked in July 2019.

85 See, e.g., RFCDC 2018, text to nn 303-304; also text to n 906.

86 R Dworkin, *Law's Empire* (Harvard University Press 1987); R Dworkin, *A matter of principle* (repr. edn, Clarendon 1992). Cp H Hart, *The Concept of Law* (2nd edn,

integrity, law cannot be separated from values and the underlying morality.[87] This is valid for EU law, with EU primary law embracing values, objectives and principles.[88] The application of the law often implies balancing those values, objectives and principles, and therefore requires critical thinking, which is especially pertinent to citizenship education. Admittedly, the analysis risks becoming 'embroiled in the conjunctions of law, morality and education'.[89] Yet working with the law is fertile ground for the field of citizenship education as it is a source simultaneously of objective support and challenge. It awakens the curiosity of all those concerned: the lawyer, the citizenship educator, and the pupil. For the lawyer, it may lead to the challenge of bridging the gap between, on the one hand, legal norms often considered to be self-evident because they are firmly established in primary law, and, on the other hand, legal culture or practice in contexts in which the norms in question are unfamiliar or even entirely unknown to the citizen. EU law is not an exception; it is even a very good example. The citizenship educator is challenged to go beyond communicating information about institutions and the pupil is invited to reflect and think critically, not just to absorb knowledge. EU law triggers several democratic citizenship competences (as defined further).[90]

The value of law for citizenship education is multifaceted. Law affects citizenship education from a number of different angles. It determines the legal competence of public authorities to set the school curriculum and sets limits to that competence, inter alia requiring respect for the constitution and for fundamental rights, such as freedom of education. In providing citizenship education, the right *to* education must be respected (compulsory aims of education) as well as rights *in* education (such as respect

---

Oxford University Press 1994); H Kelsen, *Pure Theory of Law* (Knight tr, 2nd edn, University of California Press 1967).

87 See also Jääskinen, 'Europeanisation of National Law: A Legal-theoretical Analysis', 669: 'legal order means a momentary and concrete order of legal norms, and combines the propositional and the concrete, whereas the legal system, that is, an order consisting of the conceptual and axiological elements of law, is both propositional and abstract'.

88 E.g. Arts 2- 6 TEU, Arts 18–19 TFEU.

89 M Minow, 'What the rule of law should mean in civics education: from the "Following Orders" defence to the classroom' (2006) 35 Journal of Moral Education 137.

90 CoE Reference Framework of Competences for Democratic Culture, Vol 1: Context, concepts and model (2018); Council Recommendation of 22 May 2018 on key competences for lifelong learning [2018] OJ C189/1.

for human dignity or freedom of expression).[91] Law governs the relationship between the actors in the field (schools, teachers, pupils, parents, churches, NGOs, ...). Citizenship education is also said to strengthen rights *through* education, because education unlocks the door to the exercise of rights (e.g. citizenship rights, various human rights).[92] Furthermore, law underpins the need for citizenship education in relation to basic legal principles, such as the rule of law, democracy and fundamental rights. Law provides substance for citizenship education.[93] A connection traditionally made is that between citizenship education and constitutions (learning about constitutional values, the political system of the state, the institutions).[94] The principle that education must be linked to the constitution has been confirmed by thinkers throughout history. Aristotle strongly encouraged the education of citizens in the spirit of their constitution: 'There is no profit in the best of laws ... if the citizens themselves have not been attuned, by the force of habit and the influence of teaching, to the right constitutional temper'.[95] Condorcet (a philosopher at the time of the French revolution who devoted much thought to how to educate the newly born 'citoyen') affirmed:

> une constitution vraiment libre, où toutes les classes de la société jouissent des mêmes droits, ne peut subsister si l'ignorance d'une partie des citoyens ne leur permet pas d'en connaître la nature et les limites, les oblige de prononcer sur ce qu'ils ne connaissent pas, de choisir quand ils ne peuvent juger; une telle constitution se détruirait d'elle-même après quelques orages, et dégénérerait en une de ces formes de gou-

---

91 See i.a. § 179 and n 592 (human rights education should underpin citizenship education).

92 See n 2167.

93 On the importance of law in general within citizenship education, H Oberreuter, 'Rechtserziehung' in W Sander (ed), *Handbuch politische Bildung* (Reihe Politik und Bildung 32, 3rd edn, Wochenschau 2005). The author considers the law to be more than the technical rule: 326 ('Recht erschöpft sich nicht in Rechtsnormen'); 329 ('Recht ist kein Instrument der Herrschenden'), 328 ('Politik ist dem Grundgesetz unterworfen'), 332 ('Rechtserziehung ist Wertevermittlung'). See further n 579, n 592, and n 1071.

94 On the link between citizenship education and constitutions, further i.a. § 89 (n 670), § 165 .

95 R Curren, 'A neo-Aristotelian account of education, justice, and the human good' (2013) 11 Theory and Research in Education 231.

vernement qui ne peuvent conserver la paix au milieu d'un peuple ignorant et corrompu.[96]

A constitution is incomplete without corresponding citizenship education.[97] Civics is defined by experts as 'the didactic transmission of factual information about constitutions and institutions'.[98] Yet, citizenship education is more than that definition of civics. Citizenship education refers to 'the knowledge, understanding, skills and dispositions that are connected with public life'.[99] Citizenship education potentially covers all aspects of society, from learning about traffic rules, to how to draw up a contract, but also–with some courage–discussing the Islamic headscarf or burqa. The

96 Condorcet, *Cinq mémoires sur l'instruction publique* (digital JM Tremblay edn, 1791), Premier Mémoire, IV : 'a constitution based on true freedom, where all social classes enjoy the same rights, cannot survive if the lack of education of some citizens does not enable them to understand its nature and limits, obliges them to express a view on things of which they are ignorant, to choose when they cannot judge; such a constitution would destroy itself after a few storms and degenerate into one of those forms of government which cannot preserve peace in the midst of an uneducated and corrupted people.' Concorcet was one of the most important educational philosophers of the French revolution, influential in the 19th and 20th century.

97 See also Talleyrand-Périgord, Rapport sur l'Instruction Publique, fait au nom du Comité de Constitution à l'Assemblée Nationale, les 10, 11 et 19 Septembre 1791 : 'Les pouvoirs publics sont organisés: la liberté, l'égalité existent sous la garde toute-puissante des Lois; la propriété a retrouvé ses véritables bases; et pourtant la Constitution pourroit sembler incomplette, si l'on n'y attachoit enfin, comme partie conservatrice et vivifiante, L'INSTRUCTION PUBLIQUE' (...) Enfin, et pour tout dire, la constitution existeroit-elle véritablement, si elle n'existoit que dans notre code; si de-là elle ne jettoit ses racines dans l'âme de tous les Citoyens; si elle n'y imprimoit à jamais de nouveaux sentimens, de nouvelles moeurs, de nouvelles habitudes?'; 'L'Instruction, considérée dans ses rapports avec l'avantage de la Société, exige, comme principe fondamental, qu'il soit enseigné à tous les hommes: 1º. A connoître la Constitution de cette Société; 2º. A la défendre; 3º. A la perfectionner; 4º. Et, avant tout, à se pénétrer des principes de la morale qui est antérieure à toute Constitution, et qui, plus qu'elle encore, est la sauve-garde et la caution du bonheur public.' See also: 'En attachant l'Instruction publique à la constitution, nous l'avons considérée dans sa source, dans son objet, dans ses rapports, dans son organisation, dans ses moyens'.

98 I Davies, 'Political Literacy' in J Arthur, I Davies and C Hahn (eds), *The SAGE Handbook of Education for Citizenship and Democracy* (Sage) 382.

99 J Arthur, I Davies and C Hahn, 'Introduction' in J Arthur, I Davies and C Hahn (eds), *The SAGE Handbook of Education for Citizenship and Democracy* (Sage 2008) 9; see also nn 902- 904.

law can give guidance in discussions and controversies.[100] Constitutions, and the law in general, may provide objective support for teachers and pupils in what are sometimes sensitive fields. Yet, caution is needed. The legal approach must remain dynamic and open. It should invite critical thinking, which is an essential component of citizenship education as well.

In short, law contributes to the rationale for citizenship education, to the means, the methods, the substance, and the limits.[101] The objective of this study is, therefore, not only to clarify the EU legal framework providing the basis for establishing effective measures for citizenship education for EU citizens. It will also consider the extent to which EU law provides the rationale, the method, the substance and the limits to citizenship education. To my knowledge, this has not been analysed before in a systematic way. The legal analysis will show that there is a normative basis (both formal and substantive) justifying the inclusion of an EU dimension in EDC. Considering citizenship education from the vantage point of EU law will be enriching in multiple ways.

14 Law in the context of various epistemological approaches

While law can make a valuable contribution to citizenship education, citizenship education cannot be studied in isolation by sole reference to the law. This study conjoins EU law with insights gained from other disciplines. I will sometimes refer to their contributions as *context* for the law, widening the field, giving depth to it, broadening the scope for critical reflection. Various other disciplines may shed light on the extent to which EU citizenship education can provide a solution to bridging the gap between the EU and its citizens.

The literature on citizenship education is substantial. In many Member States, citizenship education is a new field of academic study, yet in some Member States—such as France and Germany—it is founded on an established tradition.[102] Though individual country studies or comparative stud-

---

100 E.g. the proportionality principle as a tool in solving problems (text and n 1265). Law provides core content to be respected in citizenship education, see i.a. §§ 258 259 326 . Affective (irrational) dimensions of citizenship may need some legal constraints, see i.a. Nussbaum (nn 579-580).

101 Methods and substance of citizenship education cannot not always be distinguished, see S Reinhardt, *Teaching Civics: A Manual for Secondary Education Teachers* (Barbara Budrich 2015).

102 For France, see n 492 ff; for Germany n 497 ff. Arthur, Davies and Hahn, 'Introduction' (p 3–4: citizenship education has 'relative immaturity as an academic field' but insights from established disciplines such as political or social studies enhance understanding in the field).

ies are often cross-disciplinary,[103] differentiating epistemological approaches helps to master the wealth of literature. Studies in *history* examine the phenomenon of citizenship education throughout different historical periods, in peaceful and in disturbed times, and point to its effects, auspicious as well as devastating.[104] History provides evidence of the powerful role of citizenship education in the formation of nation states and the creation of national identities during the 19th century.[105] The teaching of history (or of the state's interpretation of history) is an important form of citizenship education.[106] The effects of citizenship education on society

---

103 D Kerr, S McCarthy and A Smith, 'Citizenship Education in England, Ireland and Northern Ireland' (2002) 37 European Journal of Education 179; K Haav, 'Civic Education in Estonia: Democratic or Authoritarian' (2008) 7 Journal of Social Science Education 121; J Krek and MK Sebart, 'Citizenship Education in Slovenia after the Formation of the Independent State' (2008) 9 Journal of Social Science Education 66; D Kavadias and B Dehertogh, *Scholen en Burgerschapseducatie : de totstandkoming van de vraag tot ondersteuning binnen scholen* (Koning Boudewijnstichting 2010); M Sandström Kjellin and others, 'Pupils' voices about citizenship education: comparative case studies in Finland, Sweden and England' (2010) 33 European Journal of Teacher Education 201; L Johnson and P Morris, 'Critical citizenship education in England and France: a comparative analysis' (2012) 48 Comparative Education 283; Sandström Kjellin and others, 'Pupils' voices about citizenship education: comparative case studies in Finland, Sweden and England'; M Jeliazkova and T Zimenkova, 'Beyond description: Civic and political education in Europe - dialogue and comparison' (2017) 16 Journal of Social Science Education 2.

104 Citizenship education was practiced in Ancient Greece and Rome; it was studied intensely in the Enlightenment (e.g. by Montesquieu and enlightened monarchs) and during the age of revolutions to form 'le citoyen' in the spirit of 'liberté, égalité, fraternité' (Condorcet, Talleyrand, Lepelletier); it was effective in nation-building during the 19th century, it was devastating in its use by totalitarian regimes and seen as one of the causes leading to World Wars. See D Heater, 'The history of citizenship education: a comparative outline' (2002) 55 Parliamentary Affairs (UK) 457; P Riesenberg, *A History of Citizenship: Sparta to Washington* (Anvil Series, Krieger 2002); D Heater, *A history of education for citizenship* (Routledge Falmer 2004); D Heater, *Citizenship: the Civic Ideal in World History, Politics and Education* (3rd edn, Manchester University Press 2004). Further on Montesquieu, Condorcet and Talleyrand, text to nn 96, 492, 1160, 1217-1220.

105 Brubaker, *Citizenship and nationhood in France and Germany*; BRO Anderson, *Imagined Communities: Reflections on the Origin and Spread of Nationalism* (revised edn, Verso 2006).

106 On the impact of history education in schools, K Tomaševski, *Human rights in education as prerequisite for human rights education* (Right to Education Primers

('socialisation') are researched in *sociology*.[107] *Empirical political science* analyses the effectiveness of citizenship education by the various actors in society and seeks to provide evidence of its concrete impact (to a greater or lesser degree).[108] *Normative political science, philosophy* (political and social),

---

No 4, Novum Grafiska 2001) 19; G Clemitshaw, 'Citizenship without history? Knowledge, skills and values in citizenship education' (2008) 3 Ethics and Education 135; K Korostelina, 'History Education and Social Identity' (2008) 8 Identity 25; A Osler, 'Patriotism, multiculturalism and belonging: political discourse and the teaching of history' (2009) 61 Educational Review 85; KV Korostelina and S Lässig (eds), *History education and post-conflict reconciliation: reconsidering joint textbook projects* (Routledge 2013); M Lücke and others (eds), *CHANGE – Handbook for History Learning and Human Rights Education* (Wochenschau Verlag 2016). See also n 278, n 2441.

107 Sociological approach, i.a., in DH Kamens, 'Education and Democracy: A Comparative Institutional Analysis' (1988) 61 Sociology of Education 114; J Brine, 'Educational and Vocational Policy and Construction of the European Union' (1995) 5 International Studies in Sociology of Education 145; RG Niemi and MA Hepburn, 'The Rebirth of Political Socialization' (1995) 24 Perspectives on Political Science 7; RG Sultana, 'A Uniting Europe, a Dividing Education? Euro-centrism and the Curriculum' (1995) 5 International Studies in Sociology of Education 115; G Delanty, 'Citizenship as a learning process: disciplinary citizenship versus cultural citizenship' (2003) 22 International Journal of Lifelong Education 597; MT Hallinan (ed) *Handbook of the sociology of education* (Springer 2006); A Keating, 'Developing a European dimension to the sociology of education' (2006) 27 British Journal of Sociology of Education 269; R Hedtke, T Zimenkova and T Hippe, 'A Trinity of Transformation, Europeanisation, and Democratisation? Current Research on Citizenship Education in Europe' (2007) 6 Journal of Social Science Education 5; S Philippou, 'Policy, curriculum and the struggle for change in Cyprus: the case of the European dimension in education' (2007) 17 International Studies in Sociology of Education 249; T Zimenkova and R Hedtke, 'The Talk-and-Action Approach to Citizenship Education. An Outline of a Methodology of Critical Studies in Citizenship Education' (2008) 7 Journal of Social Science Education 5; RM Brooks and JAK Holford, 'Citizenship, learning and education: themes and issues' (2009) 13 Citizenship Studies 85; K Dunn, 'Left-Right identification and education in Europe: A contingent relationship' (2011) 9 Comparative European Politics 292; F Borgonovi, 'The relationship between education and levels of trust and tolerance in Europe' (2012) 63 British Journal of Sociology 146; D Tröhler, 'La construction de la société et les conceptions sur l'éducation. Visions comparées en Allemagne, en France et aux États-Unis dans les années 1900' [2013] Education et sociétés 35; E Arbués, 'Civic Education in Europe: Pedagogic Challenge versus Social Reality' (2014) 4 Sociology Mind 226.

108 Empirical approach, i.a., in N Emler and E Frazer, 'Politics: the education effect' (1999) 25 Oxford Review Of Education 251; CL Hahn, 'Citizenship Education: an empirical study of policy, practices and outcomes' (1999) 25 Oxford Review Of Education 231; J Torney-Purta and others, *Citizenship and education in*

and *ethics* reflect on citizenship education in the light of its relationship to freedom, justice, equality, democracy, etc., and uncover its normative assumptions.[109] The need, aims and methods of citizenship education are studied further in *social sciences*, in *educational sciences* in particular. *Didacti-*

---

twenty-eight countries: Civic knowledge and engagement at age fourteen (IEA 2001); SE Finkel, 'Can democracy be taught?' (2003) 14 Journal of Democracy 137; RG Niemi and M Sanders, 'Assessing Student Performance in Civics: The NAEP 1998 Civics Assessment' (2004) 32 Theory & Research in Social Education 326; B Hoskins, B D'Hombres and J Campbell, 'Does Formal Education Have an Impact on Active Citizenship Behaviour?' (2008) 7 EERJ 386; E Quintelier, 'The effect of schools on political participation: A multilevel logistic analysis' (2008) 25 Research Papers in Education 137–154; E Claes, 'Schools and Citizenship Education. A Comparative Investigation of Socialization Effects of Citizenship Education on Adolescents' (PhD in Social Science KULeuven, Faculteit Sociale Wetenschappen 2010); M Hooghe and others, *Jongeren, politiek en burgerschap : politieke socialisatie bij Belgische jongeren* (Acco 2012); A Keating, T Benton and D Kerr, 'Evaluating the impact of citizenship education in schools: What Works and What are we Measuring?' in M Print and D Lange (eds), *Schools, Curriculum and Civic Education for Building Democratic Citizens* (Series Civic and Political Education 2, Sense 2012); J Lauglo, 'Do more knowledgeable adolescents have more rationally based civic attitudes? Analysis of 38 countries' (2013) 33 Educational Psychology 262; AM Martens and J Gainous, 'Civic Education and Democratic Capacity: How Do Teachers Teach and What Works?' (2013) 94 Social Science Quarterly 956; S Verhaegen, M Hooghe and C Meeusen, 'Opportunities to learn about Europe at school. A comparative analysis among European adolescents in 21 European member states' (2013) 45 Journal of Curriculum Studies 838; RL Claassen and JQ Monson, 'Does Civic Education Matter? The Power of Long-Term Observation and the Experimental Method' (2015) 11 Journal of Political Science Education 404; E Claes and M Hooghe, 'The Effect of Political Science Education on Political Trust and Interest: Results from a 5-year Panel Study' (2017) 13 Journal of Political Science Education 33; JF Ziemes, K Hahn-Laudenberg and HJ Abs, 'From Connectedness and Learning to European and National Identity: Results from Fourteen European Countries' (2019) 18 Journal of Social Science Education (3: European Citizenship Education: Business as Usual or Time for Change?) 5.

109 E Callan, *Creating Citizens: Political Education and Liberal Democracy* (Oxford University Press 1997); A Lockyer, B Crick and J Annette, *Education for Democratic Citizenship: Issues of Theory and Practice* (Ashgate 2003); E Callan, 'Citizenship and Education' (2004) 7 Annual Review of Political Science 71; C Lohrenscheit, 'Dialogue and Dignity - Linking Human Rights Education with Paulo Freire's "Education for Liberation"' (2006) 5 Journal of Social Science Education 126; T McCowan, 'Approaching the political in citizenship education: The perspectives of Paulo Freire and Bernard Crick' (2006) 6 Educate 57; A Scherb, Der Bürger in der Streitbaren Demokratie: Über die normativen Grundlagen Politischer Bildung (Springer Verlag 2008). See also nn 565-594.

cal sciences examine appropriate methods for the classroom, including ways to stimulate critical thinking.[110] Combining insights gained from other disciplines with EU law, I will propose an innovative learning method for EU citizenship education in schools in Chapter five.

15 Bridging EU law and citizenship education

Both EU law and the science of citizenship education are in flux. This study cannot comprehensively analyse all theories or issues in both fields, nor aim to give definitive answers. The objective is, rather, to link the fields and to raise awareness in each field of the other field of study. Too often, legal approaches to EU citizenship disregard the educational dimension and approaches to citizenship education lack the EU dimension. My ambition is to demonstrate, on the one hand, that in order to render EU citizenship more democratic, the development of an educational dimension is necessary, and that, on the other hand, in order to render citizenship education more adequate and acceptable in European society, an EU dimension needs to be interwoven into its component parts. In other words, it will be argued that the EU dimension must necessarily be part of the ongoing debates on citizenship education, and, conversely, that the educational dimension should be part of the thinking on EU citizenship.

I hope to convince EU law experts and constitutionalists in the Member States of the educational implications of the general principles they deal with on a daily basis. The principle of non-discrimination on grounds of nationality, for instance, is taught at universities all over the EU (and is a cornerstone of EU construction) but is not necessarily matched by culture and actual practice. While law has much to offer citizenship education, citizenship education also has something to offer law. Looking through the prism of EDC will enrich the legal approach to EU citizenship and shed light on it. Considering EU citizenship from the perspective of education for democratic citizenship and the right to education contributes to the originality of the study.

I also hope to convince citizenship education experts and curriculum designers of the EU implications of the educational principles *they* deal with on a daily basis. Educational aims in the EU Member States can only

---

110 W Sander (ed) *Handbuch politische Bildung* (Reihe Politik und Bildung 32, Bundeszentrale für politische Bildung 2005), see in particular W Sander on 'Politikdidaktik' as a science (21–35) and authors on 'Methoden und Medien politischer Bildung' (487–619); Reinhardt, *Teaching Civics: A Manual for Secondary Education Teachers*.

be achieved by including the EU dimension. The EU–driven by EU law–has evolved in a way which requires academic study of citizenship education to keep pace. Citizenship education should be systematically adapted to assure consistency with EU law (alignment). The empowerment of EU citizens fails when based on outdated content.

16 Education: The Necessary Utopia—empowering EU citizens

In 1996, Delors described education as 'the Necessary Utopia'.[111] That is even more true of citizenship education: it is necessary *and* utopian. At times, the 'two-fold challenge' of linking two uncertain subjects (citizenship education and EU citizenship) has given me a feeling of 'mission impossible'. However, the path forward must be waymarked. The normative assumption underlying this study is that if we are to take the values of democracy, the rule of law and respect for fundamental rights seriously, citizenship education becomes extremely important. Quality education is needed to strengthen values of human dignity, freedom, equality and solidarity, which belong to the core values underlying national constitutions, the EU Treaties, and the CFR. Two aphorisms come to mind: 'today's education is tomorrow's society'[112] and 'we are not born as a citizen, we are educated to be a citizen'[113]. Admittedly, citizenship education is closely connected to politics and power, and therefore a delicate enterprise.[114] Yet, the benefits of citizenship education largely outweigh the potential risks—

---

111 J Delors, 'Education: The Necessary Utopia' in *Learning: the Treasure Within, Report to Unesco of the International Commission on Education for the Twenty-first Century* (Unesco 1996). See also E Callan, 'A Note on Patriotism and Utopianism: Response to Schrag' (1999) 18 Studies in philosophy and education 197; H Starkey, 'Human rights, cosmopolitanism and utopias: implications for citizenship education' (2012) 42 Cambridge Journal of Education 21.

112 Cited by Mr Tibor Navracsics, EU Commissioner for Education, Culture, Youth and Sport, in CoE, *Learning to live together: Council of Europe Report on the state of citizenship and human rights education in Europe* (in accordance with the objectives and principles of the Council of Europe Charter on Education for Democratic Citizenship and Human Rights, 2017) 39.

113 Often repeated aphorism, see i.a. R Maxwell 'Citizens Are Made, Not Born: How Teachers Can Foster Democracy', in Citizens in the Making (2017 ASCD); Dutch Education minister A Slob, Citizenship to have key role in Dutch schools: 'children are not born democratic', in <www.dutchnews.nl/news/2018/06/citizenship-to-have-key-role-in-dutch-schools-children-are-not-born-democratic/>.

114 A Osler and YW Leung, 'Human rights education, politics and power' (2011) 6 Education, Citizenship and Social Justice 199.

risks which can, moreover, be contained.[115] The objective is to empower EU citizens, an empowerment advocated by many actors.[116] In the search for democracy in Europe, Calliess and Hartmann ask the central question: How does the public sphere develop in a transnational context?[117] This study will contribute part of the answer by highlighting the educational substratum of the public sphere. The EU dimension cannot be left out of citizenship education, because the EU exercises important parts of public authority. There is no other choice for EU Member States but to find ways of dealing with citizenship education to the best of their abilities and including an EU dimension in it. Given the 'two-fold challenge', criticism of this study is unavoidable and will be taken into account in all openness.[118]

I will use continuous numbering for the paragraphs and chapters.

---

115 See, i.a., human rights *in* education and multiple guidelines (§ 179).

116 Scholars, institutions, politicians, NGOs, ... see further Part one, i.a. n 562; also M Dougan, N Nic Shuibhne and E Spaventa (eds), *Empowerment and disempowerment of the European citizen* (Hart 2012); G Smith, 'The European Citizens' Initiative: A New Institution for Empowering Europe's Citizens?' in M Dougan, N Nic Shuibhne and E Spaventa (eds), *Empowerment and Disempowerment of the European Citizen* (Hart 2012); A Somek, 'The Individualisation of Liberty: Europe's Move from Emancipation to Empowerment' (2013) 4 Transnational Legal Theory 258; C Calliess and M Hartmann, *Zur Demokratie in Europa: Unionsbürgerschaft und europäische Öffentlichkeit* (Mohr Siebeck 2014); D Sarmiento and E Sharpston, 'European Citizenship and Its New Union: Time to Move on?' in D Kochenov (ed), *EU Citizenship and Federalism: The Role of Rights* (Cambridge University Press 2017) 226 ('only with the support of empowered citizens will the European Union have a real future'); and European Parliament Resolution of 18 May 2010 on 'An EU Strategy for Youth – Investing and Empowering' [2011] OJ C161E/21; Commission Citizenship Report 'Strengthening Citizens' Rights in a Union of Democratic Change, EU Citizenship Report 2017' COM(2017) 030 final/2; Commission Communication 'A Modern Budget for a Union that Protects, Empowers and Defends- The Multiannual Financial Framework for 2021-2027' COM(2018) 321 final.

117 Calliess and Hartmann, *Zur Demokratie in Europa: Unionsbürgerschaft und europäische Öffentlichkeit* 150: 'Wie entstehen Öffentlichkeiten in der transnationalen Konstellation?'.

118 Reactions to <www.kuleuven.be/wieiswie/en/person/00007631>.

PART I Education for Democratic Citizenship and the Council of Europe

Introduction: Relevance of Council of Europe norms on education for the EU and its Member States

17 Structure of Part one

Part one examines the Charter on EDC/HRE as an anchor point for a neutral and commonly accepted concept of citizenship education. That concept will be examined with regard to EU citizens in Parts two and three.

The Introduction to Part one provides an initial explanation as to why a Council of Europe instrument has been chosen as an anchor point and how it is relevant for the EU and its Member States.[119]

Chapter one is descriptive. The Charter on EDC/HRE is described as to its form (non-binding) and its substance (EDC concept and principles) in section A, and is then situated in its normative context in section B. The account of the genesis and the restatements of the Charter by Council of Europe bodies provides insight into the rationale and the consistency of Council of Europe action on EDC. Against this background, Chapter two assesses the effects of the Charter in the Council of Europe legal order through an analysis of case law of the ECtHR (sections A and B). The argument that EDC standards carry great weight is developed further in section C based on criteria borrowed from scholars. Strengths and weaknesses of the Charter are pointed out. The Charter on EDC/HRE has a high degree of normativity, reflecting the European consensus on the need for, the concept, and the principles of EDC and HRE. Finally, in section D, the Charter on EDC/HRE is examined in the context of some other epistemological approaches in order to establish its significance as an anchor point as to substance. Caveats about citizenship education in general should be acknowledged before addressing the question of citizenship education for the EU citizen. It will be concluded that the Charter on EDC/HRE and the EDC standards it contains, form a reliable anchor point for the analysis in the following parts of the study.

18 An unconvincing starting point?

One may wonder why a recommendation of the Council of Europe has been chosen as an 'anchor point' for this study. Recommendations are not

119 Further explained in Chapters two, three and four (see §§ 74 129 145).

binding and the Council of Europe has a relatively weak reputation.[120] Seen from the angle of EU law, where many binding norms have direct effect and primacy, causing national legislation to be set aside, this may appear to be a weak starting point. To motivate the reader for the subsequent analysis of Council of Europe instruments, I will first recall a number of provisions of the Council of Europe Statute, EU primary law, and the Memorandum of Understanding between the EU and the Council of Europe. The standards set by the Council of Europe are relevant both from the perspective of the EU Member States and from that of the EU.

19 Members of the Council of Europe, parties to the Statute

With regard to the EU Member States, it is recalled that all EU Member States (hereafter capitalised, as in the EU Treaties) are among the 47 member states of the Council of Europe (hereafter not capitalised, as in the Charter on EDC/HRE). They are parties to the Statute (Article 2), which is a binding international agreement.[121] The analysis of the legal status and effects of the Charter on EDC/HRE is relevant for them in their capacity as member states of the Council of Europe. In that capacity, EU Member States participate in the norm-setting of the Council of Europe and are called upon to give effect to the norms in their domestic legal orders. Each member state must accept the principles of the rule of law and of the enjoyment by all persons of human rights, and must collaborate sincerely and effectively to achieve the aims of the Council (Article 3 Statute, sanctioned by Article 8).

At the same time, EU Member States are actors in the EU. Their legislative, executive and judicial authorities are involved in the adoption, implementation and enforcement of EU decisions.[122] In that capacity, the three following arguments are also relevant for them.

---

120 G Sasse, 'The Council of Europe as a Norm Entrepreneur: The Political Strengths of a Weak International Institution' in N Walker, J Shaw and S Tierney (eds), *Europe's Constitutional Mosaic* (Hart 2011) 171. See also text to n 398.

121 Statute of the Council of Europe (signed in London, 5 May 1949; entry into force 3 August 1949), ETS No 001. See signatures and ratifications in <www.coe.int/en/web/conventions/full-list>. EU Member States who joined the CoE more recently are Hungary (1990); Poland (1991); Bulgaria (1992); Estonia, Lithuania, Slovenia, the Czech Republic, the Slovak Republic and Romania (1993); Latvia (1995); and Croatia (1996).

122 K Lenaerts and P Van Nuffel, *European Union Law* (R Bray and N Cambien, eds 3rd edn, Sweet & Maxwell 2011) 609 ff.

20 Sharing foundational values

From the perspective of the EU, three arguments stand out as a justification for an analysis of Council of Europe norms on EDC. Firstly, the Council of Europe and the EU share foundational values. Democracy, the rule of law and respect for human rights, which are at the core of the Council of Europe mission (Article 1 and 3 Statute), are also values on which the Union is founded (Article 2 TEU). Only European States which respect these values can become Member States of the Union (Article 49 TEU, and Article 7 TEU on a clear risk of a serious breach).

In the Council of Europe, as in the EU normative order, the rule of recognition is not neutral, but is value-charged.[123] In the preamble to the Statute, the governments of the member states of the Council of Europe reaffirm 'their devotion to the spiritual and moral values which are the common heritage of their peoples and the true source of individual freedom, political liberty and the rule of law, principles which form the basis of all genuine democracy'.[124] Promoting these values is its core mission[125] and the Council of Europe is '[f]irmly convinced that education and training play a central role in furthering this mission'.[126] Democracy, the rule of law and human rights are the values at the basis of the commitment of Council of Europe member states to the EDC project and of 'the standards they are setting themselves to achieve.'[127] Certainly, democracy and human rights are founded on law and institutions. Yet, as Mr. Thorbjørn Jagland, Secretary General of the Council of Europe observed:

---

123 For the CoE legal order, see Pinto de Albuquerque, Partly dissenting opinion in *Muršić v Croatia* no 7334/13 (ECtHR 20 Oct 2016), para 26.

124 Third recital.

125 Repeated over and over again in CoE instruments. All activities of the CoE must contribute to the fundamental objective of promoting human rights, democracy and the rule of law, see i.a. CoE Third Summit of Heads of State and Government, The Declaration and the Action Plan (Warsaw, 16-17 May 2005), para 1.

126 CoE Recommendation CM/Rec(2010)7 of the Committee of Ministers to member states on the Council of Europe Charter on Education for Democratic Citizenship and Human Rights Education (11 May 2010), second and third recital. See also CoE Recommendation Rec(2002)12 of the Committee of Ministers to member states on education for democratic citizenship (16 October 2002), para 1; and text to n 233.

127 Explanatory memorandum to CoE Recommendation CM/Rec(2010)7 of the Committee of Ministers to member states on the Council of Europe Charter on Education for Democratic Citizenship and Human Rights Education (11 May 2010), para 24.

> While democratic institutions are crucial, they will only work if they build on a democratic culture and a culture of human rights; and in building this culture, for each generation, we need our education systems to play a key role.[128]

The EU institutions, too, are convinced that education plays a central role in furthering a culture of democracy and human rights. The European Parliament, the Council and the Commission confirm the role of education in this respect.[129]

21 *Cooperation of the EU with the Council of Europe, in particular in education*

Secondly, the EU 'shall' cooperate with the Council of Europe in general (Article 220 TFEU) and on education in particular (Article 165(3) TFEU). Article 220 TFEU states that the Union *shall* establish all appropriate forms of cooperation with the organs of the Council of Europe. Article 165(3) TFEU provides a specific legal basis: the Union and the Member States *shall* foster cooperation with competent international organisations in the field of education, in particular the Council of Europe.[130]

While sharing values, the Council of Europe and the Union have different objectives, as appears from their constitutional documents.

For the EU, education is not a central preoccupation. Absent from the Treaty of Rome, for a long time education only appeared incidentally to Community action in the economic sphere. The first instance of Community action in the field of education dates from the 1970s (i.a. vocational training related to the single market).[131] The 1992 Treaty of Maastricht

---

128 CoE Proceedings of the Conference on 'Human Rights and Democracy in Action - Looking Ahead: The Impact of the Council of Europe Charter on Education for Democratic Citizenship and Human Rights Education' (Strasbourg, 29-30 November 2012), p 7. See also Thorbjørn Jagland's Foreword to CoE Reference Framework of Competences for Democratic Culture, Vol 1: Context, concepts and model (2018). Further CoE Third Summit of Heads of State and Government, The Declaration and the Action Plan (Warsaw, 16-17 May 2005); in the same way CoE Report of the Group of Eminent Persons of the Council of Europe, *Living together: combining diversity and freedom in 21st century Europe* (2011) 37.

129 See adopted instruments in i.a. §§ 118 120 124 127 .

130 Emphasis added. See also Art 167(3) TFEU (culture). Cp Art 166(3) TFEU on vocational training: no specific reference to the CoE.

131 For the key stages of Community action in education, see L Pépin, *The history of European cooperation in education and training. Europe in the making - an example* (European Commission 2006) 22–35.

conferred competences on the EU with regard to education, but only supporting competences.[132] The recent and limited nature of these competences explains why many legal instruments on education stem from outside the EU legal order.

For the Council of Europe, however, education has been part of its core mission since the very beginning. After the war, the Council of Europe was immediately seen as the appropriate forum for educational cooperation between states,[133] and it did pioneering work, for instance on adult education or language learning, fields in which the EU only later took an interest.[134] At present, education still constitutes a central focus of the standard-setting activities of the Council of Europe, a field in which it has developed significant expertise. Against this background of shared values but different objectives and competences, it is thus not so surprising that this study should start with Council of Europe standard-setting on EDC.

Examining the legal status and effects of Council of Europe recommendations on EDC will moreover make it possible to take a broader perspective. In the specific context of the EDC recommendations, the basic question becomes: are these recommendations appropriate as a reference framework for EU policy and how effective are they at a normative level?

22 Recognised benchmark and shared priority

Thirdly, the EU recognises that the Council of Europe sets the benchmark for human rights, the rule of law and democracy, and mentions EDC and HRE as a shared priority and focal area for cooperation in the Memorandum of Understanding (MOU).

The 2007 Memorandum of Understanding between the EU and the Council of Europe (MOU) was the response to a call by the Council of Europe Heads of State and Government at the 2005 Warsaw Summit 'to create a new framework for enhanced co-operation and interaction in areas of common concern, in particular human rights, democracy and the rule of law', as they were 'determined to ensure complementarity of the Council of Europe and the other organizations involved in building a demo-

132 Arts 126–127 Treaty on European Union, signed at Maastricht on 7 February 1992 [1992] OJ C191/1.

133 See i.a. CoE Standing Conference of European Ministers of Education, Resolution on the activities of international organisations in the fields of education and science (No 3) and Resolution on future meetings of the Ministers of Education (No 4) (The Hague, 12-13 November 1959).

134 Pépin, *The history of European cooperation in education and training. Europe in the making - an example* 51–52, 83, with other examples.

cratic and secure Europe'.[135] The Heads of State and Government of the member states stated among their principal tasks: 'We will make full use of the Council of Europe's standard-setting potential'.[136] Several provisions of the MOU are applicable to education for democratic citizenship and human rights.

Under its first heading, the Memorandum sets out 'Purposes and principles of co-operation', seeking 'to achieve greater unity between the states of Europe through respect for the shared values'.[137] In 'all areas of common interest', the relationship between the Council of Europe and the EU will be developed.[138] Paragraph 10 states that '[t]he *Council of Europe will remain the benchmark for human rights, the rule of law and democracy* in Europe.'[139] Cooperation 'will take due account of the comparative advantages, respective competences and expertise' (avoiding duplication and fostering synergy). It 'will search for added value and make better use of existing ressources'. It is understood that the Council of Europe and the EU 'will acknowledge each other's experience and standard-setting work, as

135 CoE Third Summit of Heads of State and Government, The Declaration and the Action Plan (Warsaw, 16-17 May 2005), para 10. Follow-up in J-C Juncker, *Council of Europe - European Union: 'A sole ambition for the European continent', Report to the attention of the Heads of State or Governments of the Member States of the Council of Europe* (2006). See earlier CoE Compendium of Texts governing the relations between the Council of Europe and the European Union (2001). On the cooperation, see F Benoît-Rohmer and H Klebes, *Council of Europe Law - Towards a pan-European legal area* (CoE 2005) 146 ff; T Joris and J Vandenberghe, 'The Council of Europe and the European Union: Natural Partners or Uneasy Bedfellows' (2008-2009) 15 Columbia Journal of European Law 1; E Cornu, 'The impact of Council of Europe Standards on the European Union' in RA Wessel and S Blockmans (eds), *Between Autonomy and Dependence: The EU Legal Order Under the Influence of International Organisations* (Asser Press 2013) 116–120.

136 CoE Third Summit of Heads of State and Government, The Declaration and the Action Plan (Warsaw, 16-17 May 2005), Action Plan, para 3, Guidelines, paras 1 and 3. See also CoE Second Summit of Heads of State and Government, Final Declaration and Action Plan (Strasbourg, 10-11 October 1997).

137 Memorandum of Understanding between the Council of Europe and the European Union (2007), paras 1 and 8.

138 Para 9, 'in particular the promotion and protection of pluralistic democracy, the respect for human rights and fundamental freedoms, the rule of law, ...'.

139 Emphasis added. Compared to previous documents, a new recognition, see M Kolb, *The European Union and the Council of Europe* (Palgrave Macmillan 2013) 153.

appropriate, in their respective activities.'[140] Undeniably, under these provisions of the first heading of the MOU, the Charter on EDC/HRE counts as an 'existing resource'. If it is a Council of Europe standard and to be seen as part of 'the benchmark for human rights, the rule of law and democracy in Europe', it is 'appropriate' that the EU 'acknowledges' the Council of Europe's experience and 'standard-setting work' in the field of EDC/HRE. It is thus relevant to examine the legal status and effects of norms on EDC and to see in what legal form the EU 'acknowledges' them.

Under a following heading, the Memorandum mentions EDC and HRE *expressis verbis* among the 'Shared priorities and focal areas for co-operation'.[141] In the area of common interest 'Human rights and fundamental freedoms', the Memorandum states that the EU 'regards the Council of Europe as the Europe-wide reference source for human rights', that 'the relevant Council of Europe norms will be cited as a reference in European Union documents' and that cooperation between the Council of Europe and the EU will include the promotion of human rights education.[142] Applying the provisions of this heading, the Charter on EDC/HRE undoubtedly qualifies as a 'relevant Council of Europe norm' to be cited as a reference in EU documents.[143] In the area of common interest 'Education, youth and the promotion of human contacts', it is stated that '[t]he Council of Europe and the European Union will co-operate in building a knowledge-based society and a democratic culture in Europe, in particular through promoting democratic citizenship and human rights education.'[144] In the youth field, cooperation will aim 'to empower young people to participate actively in the democratic process'.[145] The Council of Europe and the EU 'will draw on each other's expertise and activities to promote and strengthen democracy and good governance' as well as 'democratic stability'.[146] Applying these provisions, the relevance of an

140 Para 12. See also para 25: 'to the extent necessary the Council of Europe and the European Union will consult each other at an early stage in the process of elaborating standards'. A difficult provision in the negotiation, ibid, 153.

141 Para 14.

142 Paras 17 and 21.

143 Reception of the Charter on EDC/HRE in the EU legal order is analysed in Part two.

144 Para 36. See CoE Third Summit of Heads of State and Government, The Declaration and the Action Plan (Warsaw, 16-17 May 2005), Action plan, III, 3.

145 Para 37.

146 Paras 27 and 30.

analysis of the Charter on EDC/HRE from the perspective of EU law and EU citizenship speaks for itself.

Both the EU institutions and the Council of Europe continue to refer to the 2007 Memorandum of Understanding.[147] In the 2010 Stockholm Programme, the European Council defines strategic guidelines for the development of an area of freedom, security and justice. It considers that the 'work of the Council of Europe is of particular importance. It is the hub of the European values of democracy, human rights and the rule of law. The Union must continue to work together with the Council of Europe based on the Memorandum of Understanding'.[148] In line with the MOU, the Council of Europe and the EU do indeed cooperate on EDC/HRE 'within their respective policy frameworks' and in various forms.[149]

What is the legal value of the MOU? Admittedly, this question is the subject of discussion among academic writers.[150] It appears from the negotiating process that the EU did not want to create a legally binding instrument.[151] Moreover, the terminology used in the Memorandum is that of a non-binding instrument (e.g. constant use of 'will' instead of 'shall').[152] However, it cannot be denied that the MOU was signed by the EU, represented by the President of the Council and by the European Commis-

147 CoE Parliamentary Assembly Recommendation 2060(2015) 'The implementation of the Memorandum of Understanding between the Council of Europe and the European Union', para 6.

148 European Council, The Stockholm Programme — An open and secure Europe serving and protecting citizens [2010] OJ C115/1, 7(6). Further cooperation in line with the MOU: Commission Communication 'Strengthening the rule of law within the Union: A blueprint for action' COM(2019) 343 final; CoE Committee of Ministers Summary Report on co-operation between the Council of Europe and the European Union Helsinki (16–17 May 2019) CM(2019)67-final; CoE Parliamentary Assembly Recommendation 2151 (2019) 'Establishment of a European Union mechanism on democracy, the rule of law and fundamental rights'.

149 See § 124 ff.

150 See Kolb, *The European Union and the Council of Europe* 142–143, with references.

151 Ibid 152; see also 162: a main contentious issue of the MOU was its legal nature (the CoE preferred it binding, the EU was hesitant). The drafting of the text took over two years and was 'very difficult' (ibid, 146).

152 Ibid 143, 151 (only the preamble in the beginning of the document reminds of a treaty).

sion.[153] It is certainly an agreement expressing a political commitment.[154] It is thus relevant to examine how the Charter on EDC/HRE fits into the standard-setting work of the Council of Europe and in what way it is part of the benchmark for human rights, the rule of law, and democracy recognised by the EU. Although in EU law, most attention has been directed at the Council of Europe standards on human rights (EHCR), standards on democracy are just as important. Indeed, they belong to the shared priorities and focal areas for cooperation.

In the light of the provisions of EU primary law cited above, the Council of Europe Statute, and the MOU, it can be concluded that the analysis of the Charter on EDC/HRE which follows is relevant, both from the perspective of the Member States and that of the EU.

153 Signed in Strasbourg on 23 May 2007. Commissioner for External Relations, Benita Ferrero-Waldner, represented the European Commission. Germany had the presidency of the Council of the EU.

154 Kolb, *The European Union and the Council of Europe* 142.

CHAPTER 1 The Charter on Education for Democratic Citizenship and Human Rights Education (EDC/HRE)

A *Form and substance*

1. Legal status within the Council of Europe legal order

23 Terminology—endogenic and exogenic norms

The 'legal order' of the Council of Europe is the composite of valid legal norms based on the Statute of the Council of Europe–a treaty which functions as the founding text–and on statutory resolutions. [155] Some authors call it 'a common legal area', 'a pan-European legal area' ('un espace juridique paneuropéen'), or 'an autonomous legal order', and describe the Statute as 'constitutional'.[156] The expression 'legal instrument' is used in a wide sense, including conventions, recommendations, declarations, resolutions, guidelines, memoranda of understanding, etc.[157] Legal instruments contain 'norms', the term used to refer to the substance of the legal instrument. From the viewpoint of the EU, norms originating in normative systems other than that of the EU, are described as 'exogenic'; those norms originating in the EU legal order itself are 'endogenic'. The Charter on EDC/HRE is a norm exogenic to the EU, but a norm which the EU is committed to acknowledging (MOU). The first question here is: what are the legal status and effects of the Charter on EDC/HRE as a matter of Council

155 N 121.

156 I.a. Benoît-Rohmer and Klebes, *Council of Europe Law - Towards a pan-European legal area* ('constitutional charter'); B Haller, H Krüger and H Petzold (eds), *Law in Greater Europe: Towards a Common Legal Area* (Kluwer Law International 2000); HG Schermers and NM Blokker, *International Institutional Law: Unity within Diversity* (5th edn, Martinus Nijhoff 2011); Separate Opinion of Pinto de Albuquerque in *Baka v Hungary* no 20261/12 (ECtHR 23 June 2016), para 23 ('an autonomous legal order').

157 More on the *legal* quality of CoE instruments, text to n 402, n 409 ff. Also in the EU legal order, 'legal instrument' gets a wide definition; see European Convention, Working Group IX on Simplification (aimed at reducing the number of legal instruments available to the Union's Institutions, then 15 types); Legal acts (Art 288 TFEU).

of Europe law? The answer is directly relevant to the EU Member States in their capacity as Council of Europe member states. What is meant by 'a standard' and to what extent the Charter on EDC/HRE can be qualified as a standard will be examined step by step in this Part. In what legal form the EU then acknowledges the EDC standards, will be analysed in Part two (reception of exogenic norms).

24 A non-binding Charter

The term 'Charter' is ambiguous. International practice contains examples of binding Charters (such as the UN Charter or the EU CFR) as well as non-binding Charters (such as the European Charter on the Participation of Young People in Local and Regional Life[158]). However, there is no doubt that the Charter on EDC/HRE is a non-binding text, a document without treaty status. The Charter is set out in the appendix to Recommendation CM/Rec(2010)7. Recommendations are, by definition, non-binding legal instruments. It was the clear intention of the member states that the Charter should be 'non-binding as a matter of public international law'.[159] The explanatory memorandum records how in 2009, a binding and a non-binding draft text was presented to the members of the Steering Committee for Education at a plenary meeting. The first draft text was a convention, using the language of obligation ('shall'), and providing for a reporting mechanism by states and for external supervision. The second text used softer terms ('should') and relied on self-evaluation by states. An overwhelming majority chose the non-binding variant.[160] To seal the non-binding character, a subtitle 'Charter without the status of a Convention' was added. This subtitle was dropped later when it was decided to adopt the Charter 'in the framework of a recommendation' in accordance with the practice of the Council of Europe, as advised by the Legal Advice Department of the Council of Europe. Since the Charter was adopted in the form of an appendix to a recommendation, its non-binding character was not in doubt. At the same time, however, the authors of the Charter on EDC/HRE wanted to express their strong commitment by choosing the title and form of a 'charter', a more 'weighty' document than those previ-

---

158 CoE Congress of Local and Regional Authorities of Europe Recommendation 128(2003) on the revised European Charter on the Participation of Young People in Local and Regional Life (21 May 2003).

159 Explanatory memorandum para 32.

160 Explanatory memorandum paras 17–18. See text to n 518.

ously adopted.[161] The preamble of the Charter was reformulated as the preamble of the recommendation.[162]

25 Form: a recommendation of the Committee of Ministers addressed to member states

On 11 May 2010, under the terms of Article 15(b) of the Statute, the Committee of Ministers adopted 'Recommendation CM/Rec(2010)7 recommending the Council of Europe Charter on Education for Democratic Citizenship and Human Rights Education'.[163] Pursuant to Article 1(a) of the Statute, the Council of Europe aims 'to achieve a greater unity between its Members for the purpose of safeguarding and realizing the ideals and principles which are their common heritage and facilitating their economic and social progress'. To pursue this aim, the Committee of Ministers acts on behalf of the Council of Europe as the decision-making body (Article 13 Statute). It is important to note the representation of all EU Member States in this body, as the Committee of Ministers is composed of the Ministers for Foreign Affairs of each member state of the Council of Europe, or a representative, if possible, a member of Government (Article 14 Statute). The Committee of Ministers has meetings at ministerial level (generally once a year) and at deputies level (regularly), the latter taking decisions of the same legal value.[164] Under Article 15 of the Statute, norm-setting by the Committee of Ministers can take the form of conventions (paragraph a), which become binding for members who ratify them afterwards, or 'in appropriate cases' the form of recommendations to the governments of members (paragraph b), which are legally non-binding. By adopting norms in these two forms the Committee of Ministers contributes to the creation of a common European legal area.[165] Council of Europe standards

161 Explanatory memorandum para 32.

162 Explanatory memorandum paras 20–21, 23, 32. See text to n 466.

163 First preambular paragraph.

164 Meetings at deputies level are not provided for in the Statute. See Art 14 Rules of Procedure of the Committee of Ministers (each representative on the Committee of Ministers appoints a Deputy to act on its behalf when the Committee is not in session. They transact business and record decisions on behalf of the Committee of Ministers). More on the Committee of Ministers at Deputy level: CoE iGuide, Committee of Ministers: Procedures and working methods (24 September 2018).

165 Cornu, 'The impact of Council of Europe Standards on the European Union' 115. On the common legal space, more in G De Vel, *The Committee of Ministers of the Council of Europe* (CoE 1995); G De Vel and T Markert, 'Importance and Weaknesses of the Council of Europe Conventions and of the Recommenda-

(like UN standards) can thus be legally binding or non-binding. The fact that the member states have opted for a non-binding form, does not imply that they have not agreed on a common text containing 'a standard'.[166] The Council of Europe compendium of standards includes recommendations and guidelines adopted by the Committee of Ministers, the Parliamentary Assembly, the Congress of Local and Regional Authorities, the Commissioner for Human Rights, and the European Commission for Democracy through Law (hereafter the Venice Commission).[167]

Under the Statute, the strongest legal form for the Charter on EDC/HRE would thus have been a convention, ratified by all member states. In practice, however, the Committee of Ministers considers the field of education in general, and the sensitive field of education for democratic citizenship in particular, to be 'appropriate cases' (Article 15(b) Statute) for the use of recommendations. Scholars point to various advantages which make recommendations a politically interesting choice.[168] By contrast with conventions, which only become binding after a certain period of time

---

tions addressed by the Committee of Ministers to Member States' in B Haller, HC Krüger and H Petzold (eds), *Law in Greater Europe: Towards a Common Legal Area* (Kluwer Law International 2000) 353; Benoît-Rohmer and Klebes, *Council of Europe Law - Towards a pan-European legal area* 123; S Schmahl and M Breuer (eds), *The Council of Europe: Its Law and Policies* (Oxford University Press 2017). For the type of texts adopted by the Committee of Ministers, see <www.coe.int/en/web/cm/adopted-texts-information>.

166 Oxford dictionaries define a 'standard' as '[a] level of quality or attainment' or '[s]omething used as a measure, norm, or model in comparative evaluations'.

167 Compendium of standards, see e.g. CoE Secretary General, State of Democracy, Human Rights and the Rule of Law in Europe. Report 2014, 9; also n 414.

168 De Vel and Markert, 'Importance and Weaknesses of the Council of Europe Conventions and of the Recommendations addressed by the Committee of Ministers to Member States' 347, 351, 353; Benoît-Rohmer and Klebes, *Council of Europe Law - Towards a pan-European legal area* 123 (it is said in the CoE that to advance the rule of law, a good recommendation is preferrable to a bad convention). Bartsch explains a shift in 2000 from treaty obligations to recommendations, with more easily reached compromises: H-J Bartsch, 'The Acceptance of Recommendations and Conventions within the Council of Europe' in *Le rôle de la volonté dans les actes juridiques: Etudes à la mémoire du Professeur Alfred Rieg* (Bruylant 2000) 94. Sasse addresses four plausible explanations for the sustained norm production and credibility of the CoE, see Sasse, 'The Council of Europe as a Norm Entrepreneur: The Political Strengths of a Weak International Institution'. See also for international organisations in general, Schermers and Blokker § 1229: in some fields, as WHO, '[t]he speed and flexibility of recommendations are preferred to the cumbersome formality of legally binding regulations'.

and only on those who have ratified them, recommendations are immediately and universally applicable to all member states. While the process for the adoption of conventions tends to be lengthy and rigid because of the need for the consent of each state party, recommendations allow for a flexible and rapid response to changing circumstances. Moreover, the non-compulsory nature of recommendations ensures respect for member states' freedom, which is perceived as especially valuable in the education field, and even more so in the field of citizenship education, both areas which are traditionally closely associated with national sovereignty. What may be perceived as a legal weakness—namely, the non-binding form of the Charter on EDC/HRE—may actually be a political strength: the member states retain autonomy but commit to a common standard. It is therefore understandable that the Committee of Ministers has opted to use recommendations in many instances in the education field, inviting the governments of member states to act according to the norms set out in an appendix.[169] The Recommendation on the Charter on EDC/HRE is in keeping with this tradition. In accordance with the classic recommendation formula, the Committee of Ministers recommends that the governments of member states implement measures based on the provisions of the Charter on EDC/HRE set out in the appendix and ensure that the Charter is widely disseminated to the national authorities responsible for education and youth. The Secretary General of the Council of Europe is instructed to transmit the Charter on EDC/HRE to international organisations, such as the EU and the UN.

The Recommendation on the Charter on EDC/HRE entered into force upon adoption in 2010 and is addressed to 50 states: the 47 member states of the Council of Europe (all EU Member States, plus Azerbaijan, the Russian Federation, Turkey, Ukraine, etc.), as well as the parties to the European Cultural Convention who are not member states of the Council of Europe (Belarus, the Holy See, and Kazakhstan).[170] The Committee of Ministers thus contributed to a major objective of the European Cultural Convention added in 2004: '[c]reating conditions for full participation in democratic life'.[171]

---

169 E.g. nn (and text) 214, 223, 253, 273, 283, 339, 345, 355, 356.

170 European Cultural Convention (Paris, 19 December 1954) ETS No 18. See 50 ratifications in list (n 121).

171 Ministers responsible for culture, education, youth and sport from the States Parties to the European Cultural Convention, Wroclaw Declaration on 50 Years of Cultural Cooperation (9-10 December 2004) ETS No 18, i.a. section I: 'Less than 10 years after the end of World War II, the adoption of the European Cultural Convention within the framework of the Council of Europe reflected the

As to the form, it may be concluded that the legal status of the Charter on EDC/HRE is that of a recommendation of the Committee of Ministers under Article 15(b) of the Statute. It is non-binding in the Council of Europe legal order, but implies a weighty commitment, reflected in the use of the word 'Charter'. What is the substance of this Charter?

2. Concept and principles of Education for Democratic Citizenship (EDC)

26 *Substance*

The Charter on EDC/HRE has four sections: (I) General provisions, (II) Objectives and principles, (III) Policies, and (IV) Evaluation and cooperation. In documents of the Council of Europe, in academic writing and in practice, 'Education for Democratic Citizenship' or 'EDC' is widely used as an umbrella term, referring to principles and practices recommended in the Charter on EDC/HRE.[172] Essential elements covered by the overarching concept 'EDC' will be briefly described. For more precise information, and in response to the call for wide dissemination, I have attached the Charter in annex to this study.[173]

27 *Definitions of EDC/HRE and scope*

When compared with previous instruments on EDC, the Charter on EDC/HRE represents distinct progress. Firstly, it responds to a need for clear concepts in order to facilitate implementation. Earlier Council of Europe instruments tended to give lengthy descriptions of what EDC *included* rather than truly *defining* it.[174] Moreover, the Charter is the first to deal with education for democratic citizenship (EDC) and human rights education (HRE) in conjunction with one another and define their relationship. It was felt that this could no longer be postponed. Before 2010,

---

hope of future unity and a belief in the power of the humanistic spirit of education and culture to heal old and new divisions, prevent conflicts, and cement the democratic order'. See n 240.

172 Explanatory memorandum para 33 ('overarching concept'); M Hartley and T Huddleston, *School-community-university partnerships for a sustainable democracy: Education for Democratic Citizenship in Europe and the United States of America* (CoE 2010) 17.

173 Annex 1.

174 Explanatory memorandum para 34.

EDC and HRE were the subject of separate normative instruments.[175] Drawing on earlier documents of the Council of Europe[176] and of the UN[177], the Charter refines and extends the definitions of EDC and HRE in such a way that in both the words 'to empower' appear. Emphasis is placed on the outcome of education, which is not simply knowledge, but the empowerment of learners.[178] In accordance with the terms of paragraph 2(b) of the Charter,[179] the EDC concept can be studied in its various components. These components will be used as parameters to analyse the situation of EU citizens in Part three. For ease of reference in this study, I have numbered them (a) to (d).

EDC means:

(a) education, training, awareness raising, information, practices and activities which aim

(b) by equipping learners with knowledge, skills and understanding and developing their attitudes and behaviour

(c) to empower the learners
  (c-1) to exercise and defend their democratic rights and responsibilities in society
  (c-2) to value diversity
  (c-3) to play an active part in democratic life

(d) with a view to the promotion and protection of democracy and the rule of law.

The definition of HRE is structured similarly:

> 'Human rights education' means education, training, awareness raising, information, practices and activities which aim, by equipping learners with knowledge, skills and understanding and developing their attitudes and behaviour, to empower learners to contribute to the building and defence of a universal culture of human rights in society,

175 Explanatory memorandum paras 33, 37.

176 Further §§ 31 35 .

177 Reference to the right to education in the UDHR, ICESCR, and CRC, and to the World Conference on Human Rights, Vienna Declaration and Programme of Action (25 June 1993) A/CONF.157/23.

178 Explanatory memorandum para 35; and text to nn 201-202.

179 Definition cited in the Introduction § 7.

with a view to the promotion and protection of human rights and fundamental freedoms.[180]

EDC and HRE are 'closely inter-related and mutually supportive', as they 'differ in focus and scope rather than in goals and practices'. While EDC 'focuses primarily on democratic rights and responsibilities and active participation, in relation to the civic, political, social, economic, legal and cultural spheres of society', HRE looks at 'the broader spectrum of human rights and fundamental freedoms in every aspect of people's lives.'[181] EDC and HRE overlap, 'because the rights important to citizenship, for example, the rights to vote, to freedom of speech and to freedom of assembly, are classic human rights, which are as much the field of HRE as of EDC.'[182]

Given the interconnectedness of EDC and HRE, the use in this study of the term 'EDC' alone automatically implies HRE as well (only when EDC and HRE both need an explicit focus, will they be mentioned separately). In a legal analysis, human rights are part of the constitutional rights of democratic citizenship. If democracy and human rights are intrinsically related concepts[183], then EDC and HRE are intrinsically related too.[184] They are twin fields, with the same roots.[185]

The scope of the Charter does not cover areas related to EDC/HRE, such as intercultural education, equality education, education for sustainable development and peace education. Yet, 'where they overlap and interact' with EDC/HRE, the Charter principles apply.[186] The explanatory memorandum posits that all these areas have a specific focus (intercultural education addresses mutual understanding and respect in multicultural societies, education for sustainable development has an environmental focus, etc.),

180 Charter para 2(b), emphasis added.

181 Charter para 3.

182 Explanatory memorandum para 37.

183 As stated in CoE Conference of International Non-Governmental Organisations (INGOs), Declaration on genuine democracy (24 January 2013), V (a)-(c) ('Genuine democracy and human rights are intrinsically related concepts which cannot exist without each other. Political rights and freedoms form part of human rights, while respect for human rights is essential to the establishment and maintenance of a democratic system'). See Annex 2 to this study.

184 More on the relationship in text to n 515, § 294 and text to n 2205. See also A Osler, 'Human Rights Education: The Foundation of Education for Democratic Citizenship in our Global Age' in J Arthur, I Davies and C Hahn (eds), *The SAGE Handbook of Education for Citizenship and Democracy* (Sage 2008).

185 See also DARE network, Democracy and Human Rights Education in Europe.

186 Charter para 1.

but they are nevertheless covered to a large extent by the overarching concept of EDC/HRE.[187] The same is true for related areas which are not mentioned in the 2010 Charter but came to the fore later, such as education for global interdependence and solidarity[188], global citizenship education[189] and global development education.[190] Global education addresses the global dimensions of EDC, and encompasses 'Development Education, Human Rights Education, Education for Sustainability, Education for Peace and Conflict Prevention and Intercultural Education'.[191]

28 Objectives, principles and policies of EDC

In its second section, the Charter describes the 'Objectives and principles' which 'should guide member states in the framing of their policies, legislation and practice'.[192] The words 'should guide' were deliberately chosen, indicating neither a prescriptive blueprint nor a mere background consideration.[193] These objectives and principles are fleshed out in the third section 'Policies'. The aim of the Charter is that *every person* within the territory of the member states has the opportunity of EDC/HRE.[194] EDC/HRE are thus not only reserved to citizens in the legal sense of a state's own

---

187 Explanatory memorandum para 33, also para 7.

188 E.g. CoE Recommendation CM/Rec(2011)4 of the Committee of Ministers to member states on education for global interdependence and solidarity (5 May 2011). See n 2192.

189 E.g. UNESCO Global Citizenship Education: Preparing learners for the challenges of the 21st century (2014); UNESCO Global Citizenship Education: Topics and Learning Objectives (2015).

190 Global Development Education (GDE) in a cooperation CoE/EU, e.g. Intercultural Learning Exchange through Global Education, Networking and Dialogue (iLEGEND, project for school curricula helping 'to understand an increasingly interconnected world, and appreciate economic, political, environmental and cultural challenges that people from different countries face, from north to south'.

191 Definition of the CoE North-South Centre recalled in CoE Europe-wide Global Education Congress, European Strategy Framework For Improving and Increasing Global Education In Europe to the Year 2015 (Maastricht Global Education Declaration) (Maastricht, 15-17 November 2002), using the expression 'the global dimensions of Education for Citizenship'. See also Global Education Guidelines: a Handbook for Educators to Understand and Implement Global Education (Global Education Week Network, CoE, 2012); and United Nations Secretary-General's Global Education First Initiative, UN, NY, 2012.

192 Para 5.

193 Explanatory memorandum 40: the drafters did not choose the wording 'should base', nor the words 'should take into account'.

194 Charter para 5(a) (my emphasis).

nationals but apply to all residents in the member state. Strictly speaking, EDC should thus be differentiated from 'citizenship education' in the literal sense of the education of the state's own nationals. History has shown what a dangerous turn that concept may take.[195]

EDC/HRE is a lifelong learning process in which formal, non-formal and informal learning have a part to play.[196] EDC/HRE may be provided in schools in a structured way leading to certification (formal education). Member states should include EDC and HRE in the curricula at pre-primary, primary and secondary school level, as well as more generally in vocational education and training. They should also continue to support, review and update EDC and HRE in these curricula in order 'to ensure their relevance'.[197] In higher education, member states should promote the inclusion of EDC/HRE, with due respect for academic freedom.[198] EDC and HRE are also part of extra-curricular learning in planned education programmes outside schools to improve skills and competences (non-formal learning) and in daily life in the family and work environment, through media, etc. (informal learning).[199] Accordingly, the training of teachers and education professionals for EDC/HRE in schools, and the training of youth leaders, is vital and should be adequately planned and resourced by member states.[200]

Clarifying the objectives of EDC/HRE (already incorporated in their respective definitions), the Charter adds that, as preparation for living together in a democratic and multicultural society, EDC/HRE should develop the knowledge, understanding and skills for promoting social cohesion and handling differences and conflict,[201] and, crucially, should empower learners to participate in the democratic process:

> One of the fundamental goals of all education for democratic citizenship and human rights education is not just equipping learners with knowledge, understanding and skills, but also empowering them with

195 Citizenship education under totalitarian regimes, as nazism or USSR. See § 288 n 2137. Further Heater, 'The history of citizenship education: a comparative outline'. On a right to education *for all*, see § 241 and text to n 2008.

196 Charter para 5(b) and (c). See Annex 5 to this study.

197 Charter para 6.

198 Charter para 7.

199 Definitions in para 2 (c)-(e).

200 Charter paras 5(h), 7 and 9.

201 Charter paras 5(f) and 13.

the readiness to take action in society in the defence and promotion of human rights, democracy and the rule of law.[202]

To reach the objectives of EDC/HRE, schools themselves should be democratically governed, and provide learning activities in a way which reflects human rights and democratic values.[203] Effective EDC/HRE involves a wide range of stakeholders in society as a whole, including pupils and educational institutions and professionals, but also policy makers, non-governmental organisations, parents, youth organisations, media and the general public.[204] Member states should promote their role in EDC/HRE and encourage partnerships and collaboration at state, regional and local level.[205]

29 Respect for member states' responsibility: the paragraph-4 principle

An important EDC principle which underlies the whole Charter, is respect for member states.[206] The Committee of Ministers recommends EDC/HRE '[b]earing in mind that member states are responsible for the organization and content of their educational systems'.[207] An essential provision of the Charter is paragraph 4, which states that the objectives, principles and policies relating to EDC/HRE 'are to be applied with due respect for the constitutional structures of each member state, using means appropriate to those structures' and 'having regard to priorities and needs of each member state'. This paragraph-4 principle will arise from time to time throughout the study. The Charter thus leaves an important margin of appreciation to member states as to its application.[208] Furthermore, its implementation relies on a system of self-evaluation by member states and on the encouragement to cooperate. Member states should develop criteria themselves for the evaluation of the effectiveness of their EDC/HRE programmes,[209] should regularly evaluate their strategies and policies, and adapt them as appropriate. Member states should cooperate in follow-up activities, i.a. by pursuing topics of common interest and common priorities, by fostering the existing network of EDC/HRE coordinators, exchanging good practice, or supporting networks. Because of 'the international

202 Charter para 5(g).
203 Charter paras 5(e) and 8.
204 Charter paras 5(b) and (d).
205 Charter paras 10 and 5(i).
206 Explanatory memorandum para 29.
207 Preambular para 13.
208 To complement with text to n 394.
209 Charter paras 11 and 14; explanatory memorandum paras 41 and 53.

nature of human rights values and obligations and the common principles underpinning democracy and the rule of law', member states should cooperate internationally and regionally on EDC/HRE,[210] and share results achieved in the framework of the Council of Europe with other international organisations.[211]

Now that the form and substance of the Charter on EDC/HRE have been explained, I will examine how the elements of the Charter on EDC/HRE thus described—the definition of EDC (closely interlinked with HRE), its objectives and principles, including respect for member States' responsibilities, constitutional structures and priorities—form *standards* (hereafter EDC standards) and whether the Recommendation on the Charter on EDC/HRE has legal effects despite its non-binding character. To answer these questions, the Charter on EDC/HRE must first be situated in the context of the many normative instruments of the Council of Europe related to EDC. Its legal effects can then be appraised in Chapter two.

B Normative context

30 Ongoing process of standard-setting on EDC

The Charter on EDC/HRE was not drafted overnight by one or two well-intentioned authors. The Recommendation on the Charter on EDC/HRE is not some random recommendation of the Council of Europe. It is a milestone along a long path of persistent work and perseverence, involving numerous actors and spread over the course of several decades. The significance of the Charter on EDC/HRE cannot therefore be understood in isolation. The purpose of this section is to explain the Charter on EDC/HRE as a standard by putting it in the broader context of norm-setting on EDC and to provide insight into the rationale for so much joint action. This overview will provide the elements necessary to assess the legal effects of the Charter on EDC/HRE. The interpretation of a legal instrument depends not only on its wording, but equally on examining its provisions in their context and in the light of the objectives pursued.[212] Moreover, if the EU commits itself in the MOU to drawing on the expertise and activi-

---

210 Charter para 5(j).

211 Charter para 16.

212 Cf Art 31 Vienna Convention on the Law of Treaties. Explanatory reports do not provide authoritative interpretations, yet their interpretative value is recognised.

ties of the Council of Europe to promote democratic culture and to empower young people to participate actively in the democratic process, in particular through EDC and HRE, then it is important to gain an overview of the action the Council of Europe has taken in this field. Throughout this chronological account and in anticipation of possible effects in the EU legal order, it should be borne in mind that the EU Member States were always participants in the Council of Europe bodies adopting the EDC instruments in question.[213]

1. Genesis of the Charter on EDC/HRE (2010)

31 Early years: before 1997

As early as the seventies and eighties, the Council of Europe recommended essential principles of education for democratic citizenship, without actually naming it as such.[214] It was after the fall of the Berlin Wall (1989) that education for democratic citizenship became a central preoccupation. At their First Summit in 1993, the Heads of State and Government adopted the Vienna Declaration, welcoming former communist countries into the Council of Europe. With the aim of making Europe 'a vast area of democratic security', new member states were reminded that 'accession presupposes that the applicant country has brought its institutions and legal sys-

213 When in 1997 the work on EDC started, all the current EU Member States were members of the CoE (Croatia was the last to join the CoE, in 1996). See bibliography to this study for an overview of the various instruments per body of the Council of Europe. For organs and bodies, see Art 10 Statute and statutory resolutions.

214 CoE Recommendation R(83)13 of the Committee of Ministers to member states on the role of the secondary school in preparing young people for life (23 September 1983), appendix 'Principles for the guidance of those responsible for programmes concerned with preparing young people for life', see i.a. para 2. See also CoE Committee of Ministers Resolution (78)41 on the teaching of human rights (25 October 1978); CoE Recommendation R(83)13 of the Committee of Ministers to member states on the role of the secondary school in preparing young people for life (23 September 1983); CoE Recommendation R(85)7 of the Committee of Ministers to member states on teaching and learning about human rights in schools (14 May 1985); CoE Parlementary Assembly Recommendation 1111(1989) 'European dimension of education'; CoE Parliamentary Assembly Recommendation 1346(1997) 'Human rights education'; CoE Standing Conference of Ministers of Education, Resolution on 'the European dimension of education: teaming and curriculum content' (Vienna, 16-17 October 1991).

tem into line with the basic principles of democracy, the rule of law and respect for human rights'. Education was mentioned among the prime instruments for creating a cohesive yet diverse Europe.[215] In 1994, the European Ministers of Education (Standing Conference) emphasised 'the need for a coherent and sustained approach by schools to education for democratic citizenship', starting at an early age and making full use of possibilities in the formal curriculum and in extra-curricular activities.[216]

32 *Agenda setting: 1997*

At their Second Summit in 1997 (Strasbourg), the Heads of State and Government, taking account of the significant enlargement of the Council of Europe, underlined its essential standard-setting task. Conscious of the crucial role of education in achieving pluralist democracy and mutual understanding, they expressed the 'desire to develop education for democratic citizenship based on the rights and responsibilities of citizens, and the participation of young people in civil society'.[217] They outlined an Action Plan to strengthen democratic stability in the member states and launched the EDC project within one of the main areas for immediate action. A Steering Group for EDC/HRE was formed. In 1997, the European Ministers of Education adopted a work programme which comprised the EDC project.[218] The project unfolded in three phases.

33 *First phase: 1997–2000*

During this phase, EDC definitions were developed, and skills and competencies for effective democratic citizenship learning in schools were identified. Various sections of the Council of Europe cooperated, research was

---

215 CoE First Summit of Heads of State and Government, Vienna Declaration (Vienna, 9 October 1993).

216 CoE Standing Conference of European Ministers of Education, Resolution on education for democracy, human rights and tolerance (No 1) (Madrid, 23-24 March 1994), paras 4–6.

217 CoE Second Summit of Heads of State and Government, Final Declaration and Action Plan (Strasbourg, 10-11 October 1997) (enlargement of the CoE from 23 to 32 member states by 1995; most new members belonged to the former communist system).

218 Three projects: EDC, Learning and Teaching about the History of Europe in the 20th Century, and Language Policies for a Multicultural and Multilingual Europe. See CoE Standing Conference of European Ministers of Education, Resolution No 1 on trends and common issues in education in Europe, Resolution No 2 on fundamental values, aims and the future role of educational co-operation in the Council of Europe (Kristiansand, Norway, 22-24 June 1997).

done, and conferences held.[219] In a general 'Declaration and programme on education for democratic citizenship, based on the rights and responsibilities of citizens' (1999), the Committee of Ministers insisted on 'the urgency of strengthening individuals' awareness and understanding of their rights and responsibilities so that they develop a capacity to exercise these rights and respect the rights of others' and stressed 'the fundamental role of education in promoting the active participation of all individuals in democratic life at all levels: local, regional and national' (*the objective of this study is to add the EU level*). The Ministers called upon member states to make EDC 'an essential component of all educational, training, cultural and youth policies and practices', deeming it a high priority.[220] The Programme was added to the Declaration and underlined 'the evolving concept of democratic citizenship, in its political, legal, cultural and social dimensions'[221] (*I will argue that in this evolving concept, the EU dimension is increasingly important*).

During this phase, several instruments adopted by the Committee of Ministers and the Parliamentary Assembly highlighted *specific* aspects of EDC. The Committee of Ministers recommended EDC in secondary schools (reaffirming their 'decisive role')[222], at universities in European Studies (studies 'particularly well suited' to providing EDC)[223], and in social sciences ('strategic' for true democratic citizenship)[224]. The Parliamentary Assembly asked for the inclusion of duties and responsibilities in

219 The explanatory memorandum to the Recommendation on the Charter on EDC/HRE (paras 1–22) explains the 'background, origins and negotiating history'. Preambular paras 7–10 mention some important instruments in the genesis of the Charter.

220 CoE Committee of Ministers Declaration and programme on education for democratic citizenship, based on the rights and responsibilities of citizens (Budapest, 7 May 1999), paras 6–7, 14–15.

221 Heading 3(1) in Key issues.

222 CoE Recommendation R(99)2 of the Committee of Ministers to member states on secondary education (19 January 1999) .

223 CoE Recommendation Rec(2000)24 of the Committee of Ministers to member states on the Development of European Studies for Democratic Citizenship (20 December 2000), appendix para 2(d). EDC is seen as a general principle to be applied in European Studies (which are defined in para 1).

224 CoE Recommendation Rec(2000)12 of the Committee of Ministers to member states on the social sciences and the challenge of transition (13 July 2000), recalling 'that the process of transition from totalitarian regimes to democracy requires efficient and independent social sciences able to contribute to a true democratic citizenship' (social sciences cover 'disciplines aiming at improving the understanding and functioning of society, as well as its welfare: mainly soci-

EDC, not only rights.[225] The Assembly further recommended that EDC become a part of the fight against terrorism[226], against religious intolerance[227] and against extremism[228].

In 2000, the European Ministers of Education endorsed the results of the EDC project (welcoming their quality) and called for a recommendation from the Committee of Ministers on EDC drawing up common guidelines for all educational systems beyond national specificities.[229] During the first phase, experts developed Council of Europe materials and scholars reflected on EDC.[230]

34 Second phase: 2001–2005

EDC policies and networks continued to be developed with national EDC coordinators[231] and experts. The 2002 Recommendation of the Committee of Ministers to member states on education for democratic citizenship—

---

ology and anthropology, political science, contemporary history, psychology, educational science, economics *and law*' (emphasis added).

225 CoE Parliamentary Assembly Recommendation 1401(1999) 'Education in the responsibilities of the individual', see para 13.

226 CoE Parliamentary Assembly Recommendation 1426(1999) 'European Democracies facing up to terrorism'.

227 CoE Parliamentary Assembly Recommendation 1396(1999) 'Religion and democracy', paras 14(1), para 13(2)(a): 'teaching about religions as sets of values towards which young people must develop a discerning approach within the framework of education on ethics and democratic citizenship'.

228 CoE Parliamentary Assembly Recommendation 1438(2000) 'Threat posed to democracy by extremist parties and movements in Europe'.

229 CoE Standing Conference of European Ministers of Education, Resolution on results and conclusions of the completed projects on the 1997-2000 Medium-term programme: Educational policies for democratic citizenship and social cohesion: challenges and strategies for Europe (Cracow, 15-17 October 2000), see paras 9–10.

230 E.g. R Veldhuis, *Education for democratic citizenship: dimensions of citizenship, core competencies, variables and international activities* (CoE 1997); A Osler, 'European Citizenship and Study Abroad: student teachers' experiences and identities' (1998) 28 Cambridge Journal of Education 77; F Audigier, *Basic concepts and core competencies for education for democratic citizenship* (CoE 2000); C Bîrzéa, *Education for Democratic Citizenship: A LifeLong Learning Perspective* (CoE 2000); L Carey and K Forrester, *Sites of Citizenship: Empowerment, Participation and Partnerships* (CoE 2000); K Durr, V Spajic-Vrkaš and I Ferreira Martins, *Strategies of Learning Democratic Citizenship* (CoE 2000).

231 The Ministry of Education in each member state appointed a contact person within the EDC project, part of the network.

the forerunner of the 2010 Charter on EDC/HRE—was a landmark.[232] The Committee of Ministers affirmed that EDC was fundamental to the Council of Europe's primary task of promoting a free, tolerant and just society, and contributed 'to defending the values and principles of freedom, pluralism, human rights and the rule of law, which are the foundations of democracy'.[233] While respecting member state constitutional structures, national or local situations, and education systems, it recommended that national governments make EDC a priority objective of educational policy-making and reforms.[234] EDC should be 'seen as embracing any formal, non-formal or informal educational activity, including that of the family, enabling an individual to act throughout his or her life as an active and responsible citizen respectful of the rights of others'.[235] The Committee of Ministers set out general guidelines for EDC policies, outlined EDC objectives, content and methods as well as teacher training, and described the role of media and new information technologies. EDC could be a specific discipline but also be cross-curricular. Civic, political or human rights education could contribute to EDC without covering it completely. Multidisciplinary approaches were recommended, including history, philosophy, religion, languages, or social sciences. Priority was given to the acquisition of knowledge, attitudes and skills which reflected the fundamental values of human rights and the rule of law. The Committee of Ministers recognised that:

> education for democratic citizenship is a factor which promotes relations of trust and stability in Europe beyond the boundaries of the member states. The European dimension should consequently be a component as well as a source of inspiration when formulating the corresponding policies.[236]

Therefore, it was recommended that each state's contribution to the European and international debate on EDC should be reinforced by 'sites of cit-

232 CoE Recommendation Rec(2002)12 of the Committee of Ministers to member states on education for democratic citizenship (16 October 2002).

233 Para 1.

234 Para 3.

235 Para 2.

236 CoE Recommendation Rec(2002)12 of the Committee of Ministers to member states on education for democratic citizenship (16 October 2002), appendix, heading 1. Remark the same terminology 'European dimension' as in the 1992 Maastricht Treaty provision on education, now Art 165 TFEU.

izenship', European networks for practitioners and researchers, and fora for experimenting on and developing EDC.[237]

In 2004, the Parliamentary Assembly recommended that the Committee of Ministers should 'draft a European framework *convention* on education for democratic citizenship and human rights' [238] and the European Ministers asked for 'the setting of European standards by means of appropriate *conventional* mechanisms' to be considered, because 'the Council of Europe should strengthen its role as a center of excellence for policies to equip people with the knowledge, skills and attitudes for life in democratic societies'.[239] In their Wroclaw Declaration on 50 Years of Cultural Cooperation, one of the new objectives (added to the original objectives of the European Cultural Convention[240]) was to create the conditions for full participation in democratic life, with EDC being seen as central to educational *quality*.[241] European action on EDC matched with international action to achieve quality education linked with democratic citizenship.[242]

Responding to the implementation gap—the difference between words and deeds on EDC[243]—the 2005 European Year of Citizenship through Education disseminated good practice and directed different players to

---

237 Appendix heading 1–2.

238 CoE Parliamentary Assembly Recommendation 1682(2004) 'Education for Europe', para 8 (emphasis added).

239 Ministers responsible for culture, education, youth and sport from the States Parties to the European Cultural Convention, Wroclaw Declaration on 50 Years of Cultural Cooperation (9-10 December 2004) ETS No 18, heading III (emphasis added). See also CoE Conference of European Ministers responsible for Youth, Human dignity and social cohesion: youth policy responses to violence. Final Declaration (Budapest, 23-24 September 2005), calling for a framework policy document, and paras 4 and 11.

240 Text to n 171. The initial aim in 1954 was to contribute to the common cultural heritage of Europe (Article 1). Two other new objectives were 'A European dimension in standards, policy and practice' and 'Promoting cultural diversity and building up shared values'. See also 50 years of the European Cultural Convention (2004).

241 Heading I.

242 See 'Issues for discussion at meeting of OECD Ministers of Education' (18–19 March 2004): A meeting of Education Ministers from the Organisation for Economic Co-operation and Development (OECD) member states on the subject of 'Raising the Quality of Education for All': The issue for education is how to develop not only successful individuals with good workplace skills, but also 'democratic citizenship' — an outcome both linked to, and supportive of, social cohesion'.

243 JM Heydt, *Education for Democratic Citizenship: Words and Actions* (CoE 2001); K O'Shea, 'EDC policies and regulatory frameworks' (Strasbourg, 6-7 December

their responsibilities with regard to EDC (decision-makers in ministries, university vice-chancellors, school heads, teachers, trainers, NGOs, etc.).[244] Several states requested the assistance of the Council of Europe in developing their EDC policies and practice.[245] The 2005 Third Summit of Heads of State and Government was crucial. They reconfirmed the fundamental role of EDC/HRE and called for increased efforts. The action plan included 'Education: promoting democratic citizenship in Europe'.[246]

During the second phase too, EDC appeared in various *specific* Council of Europe instruments as an overarching concept, a platform for specific action within an integrated approach, a general principle informing, for example, history teaching[247], gender equality[248], e-learning[249], lifelong

---

2001), section 3(1): 'La question de l'écart entre la politique et la pratique demeure l'un des problèmes majeurs dans les Etats membres'. For a systematic description of EDC policies in different member states and the compliance gap, see All-European Study on Education for Democratic Citizenship Policies (CoE 2005).

244 CoE Recommendation CM/Rec(2010)7 of the Committee of Ministers to member states on the Council of Europe Charter on Education for Democratic Citizenship and Human Rights Education (11 May 2010), twelfth preambular para; explanatory memorandum para 4. See evaluation of the year during the third phase.

245 See CoE Committee of Ministers, Terms of reference of the Ad hoc Advisory Group on Education for Democratic Citizenship and Human Rights (ED-EDCHR) (5 February 2007) CM/Del/Dec(2007)985/7.2.

246 CoE Third Summit of Heads of State and Government, The Declaration and the Action Plan (Warsaw, 16-17 May 2005): 'We will make full use of the opportunity to raise public awareness of European standards and values provided by the "European Year of Citizenship through Education" (...) The Council of Europe will enhance all opportunities for the training of educators, in the fields of education for democratic citizenship, human rights, history and intercultural education.'.

247 CoE Recommendation Rec(2001)15 of the Committee of Ministers to member states on history teaching in twenty-first-century Europe (31 October 2001), for history teaching to strengthen 'trusting and tolerant relations within and between states', recommends that member states adopt an integrated approach, using in particular the EDC project.

248 CoE Recommendation Rec(2003)3 of the Committee of Ministers to member states on balanced participation of women and men in political and public decision making (12 March 2003), para 23.

249 CoE Recommendation Rec(2004)15 of the Committee of Ministers to member states on electronic governance ('e-governance') (15 December 2004), para 4.

learning[250] or promoting a Europe without divisions[251]. The Congress of Local and Regional Authorities of Europe adopted the Revised European Charter on the Participation of Young People in Local and Regional Life, which recognised that 'education about rights and duties of citizens in a democratic society must be made an integral part of any school curriculum to enable young people to contribute actively to democratic decision making'[252] and the Committee of Ministers recommended this Charter to member states.[253] To combat racism and intolerance, the European Commission against Racism and Intolerance (ECRI) adopted a general policy recommendation on school education referring to EDC and HRE.[254] During the second phase, new EDC materials were produced and scholars continued to reflect on the matter.[255]

---

250 CoE Recommendation Rec(2003)8 of the Committee of Ministers to member states on the promotion and recognition of non-formal education/learning of young people (30 April 2003), i.a. on role of lifelong learning 'in promoting active participation in democratic life'; CoE Recommendation Rec(2004)4 of the Committee of Ministers to member states on the European Convention on Human Rights in university education and professional training (12 May 2004).

251 CoE Parliamentary Assembly Recommendation 1682(2004) 'Education for Europe'.

252 CoE Congress of Local and Regional Authorities of Europe Recommendation 128(2003) on the revised European Charter on the Participation of Young People in Local and Regional Life (21 May 2003), para 13.

253 CoE Recommendation Rec(2004)13 of the Committee of Ministers to member states on the participation of young people in local and regional life (17 November 2004), with in appendix the Revised European Charter on the Participation of Young People in Local and Regional Life, i.a. para 15.

254 CoE ECRI General Policy Recommendation No 10 on combating racism and racial discrimination in and through school education (15 December 2006), having regard to CM Rec(2002)12; i.a. para II(2)(a) ensuring that HRE 'is an integral part of the school curriculum at all levels and across all disciplines, from nursery school onwards', (f) 'revising school textbooks to ensure that they reflect more adequately the diversity and plurality of the society'.

255 E.g. P Belanger, *Education for Democratic Citizenship: Methods, Practices and Strategies* (CoE 2001); O'Shea, 'EDC policies and regulatory frameworks'; C Naval, M Print and R Veldhuis, 'Education for Democratic Citizenship in the New Europe: context and reform' (2002) 37 European Journal of Education 107; K Forrester, 'Leaving the academic towers: the Council of Europe and the Education for Democratic Citizenship Project' (2003) 22 International Journal of Lifelong Education 221; Lockyer, Crick and Annette, *Education for Democratic Citizenship: Issues of Theory and Practice*; All-European Study on Education for Democratic Citizenship Policies (CoE 2005); D Kerr and B Losito, *Tool on Key Issues for EDC Policies* (CoE 2004); D Kerr, 'Western Europe Regional Synthesis' in *All-European Study on Education for Democratic Citizenship Policies* (CoE 2004);

35 Third phase: 2006–2009

The first two phases highlighted the need for EDC and HRE 'to become a permanent strategic goal for the Council of Europe and its member states'.[256] A multi-disciplinary Ad Hoc Advisory Committee on Education for Democratic Citizenship and Human Rights guided the third phase of the EDC project, during which sub-projects were initiated to develop standards for EDC and to link policy and practice.[257] In the light of the experience acquired in the 2005 European Year,[258] and in order to consolidate and fine-tune the work, the Parliamentary Assembly and other Council of Europe bodies called for a new, appropriate European framework policy document to set out basic EDC/HRE principles and to establish a follow-

---

C Bîrzea and others, *Tool for Quality Assurance of Education for Democratic Citizenship in Schools* (UNESCO, CoE, CEPS 2005); C Bîrzea, B Losito and R Veldhuis, 'Editorial' (2005) 4 Journal of Social Science Education; MH Salema, 'Teacher and Trainer Training in Education for Democratic Citizenship Competencies' (2005) 4 Journal of Social Science Education 39. One of the most popular manuals is 'Compass Manual on Human Rights Education with Young People', first published in 2002, now updated and translated in more than 30 languages <www.coe.int/en/web/compass>. See also Compasito, for children. National recommendatios for *Compass* in Denmark, Germany, Estonia and Austria (Commission/EACEA/Eurydice, Citizenship Education at School in Europe (2017) 82).

256 CoE Ad Hoc Committee of Experts for the European Year of Citizenship through Education (CAHCIT), Education for Democratic Citizenship and Human Rights: Programme of Activities (2006-2009), Learning and living democracy for all, DGIV/EDU/CAHCIT(2006)5.

257 CoE Committee of Ministers, Terms of reference of the Ad hoc Advisory Group on Education for Democratic Citizenship and Human Rights (ED-EDCHR) (5 February 2007) CM/Del/Dec(2007)985/7.2. Three lines of action for the 3rd phase in CoE Ad Hoc Committee of Experts for the European Year of Citizenship through Education (CAHCIT), Education for Democratic Citizenship and Human Rights: Programme of Activities (2006-2009), Learning and living democracy for all, DGIV/EDU/CAHCIT(2006)5 (ie education policy development and implementation for democratic citizenship and social inclusion; new roles and competences of teachers and other educational staff in EDC/HRE (defining competencies for teachers in EDC); and democratic governance of educational institutions). See also O Olafsdottir, 'Education for Democratic Citizenship and Human Rights: A Project by the Council of Europe' in VB Georgi (ed), *The Making of Citizens in Europe: New Perspectives on Citizenship Education* (Schriftenreihe Band 666, Bundeszentrale für politische Bildung 2008) 134.

258 CoE Evaluation Conference of the 2005 European Year of Citizenship through Education: Conclusions (Sinaia, 27-28 April 2006); D Kerr and J Lopes, *Implementation and outcomes of the 2005 European Year of Citizenship through Education: Learning and Living Democracy, Report DGIV/EDU/CAHCIT (2006)11* .

up mechanism.[259] In 2007, the European Ministers of Education recommended unanimously, with the exception of the Polish delegation, that the Steering Committee for Education should continue its work on EDC/HRE programmes and draw up a reference framework.[260] The culmination of the third phase was Recommendation CM/Rec(2010)7 of the Committee of Ministers to member states on *the Council of Europe Charter on Education for Democratic Citizenship and Human Rights Education*. The Steering Committee for Education had drafted the Charter on EDC/HRE in close collaboration with various Council of Europe bodies, member state EDC/HRE coordinators, experts and networks.[261] The Charter on EDC/HRE is effectively 'the outcome of international co-operation among the 47 member states of the Council of Europe—and in the education field, between all the States Parties to the European Cultural Convention',[262] illustrating that educational cooperation is one of the cornerstones of the Council of Europe.[263] By consensus, the member states of the Council of Europe adopted the Recommendation on the Charter on EDC/HRE, with its

259 CoE Parliamentary Assembly Recommendation 1791(2007) 'State of human rights and democracy in Europe', para 18(2), also para 2(3); CoE Parliamentary Assembly Recommendation 1849(2008) 'For the promotion of a culture of democracy and human rights through teacher education', paras 5–6. See also call in CoE Evaluation Conference of the 2005 European Year of Citizenship through Education: Conclusions (Sinaia, 27-28 April 2006) (n 258), paras 1, 3.

260 CoE Standing Conference of European Ministers of Education, Building a more humane and inclusive Europe: role of education policies, Resolution on the 2008-2010 programme of activities (Istanbul, 4-5 May 2007), paras 7–8 (also asking to reinforce work on indicators (with the European Commission) on quality assurance in the field of EDC/HRE). On front page: 'This resolution was adopted unanimously with the exception of the Polish Delegation'.

261 Details in explanatory memorandum to CoE Recommendation CM/Rec(2010)7 of the Committee of Ministers to member states on the Council of Europe Charter on Education for Democratic Citizenship and Human Rights Education (11 May 2010), paras 9–22. A study on the feasability of a reference framework for EDC/HRE had been submitted in 2007, drafted by an expert assisted by an informal group of experts. This was subsequently commented by numerous CoE consulted bodies, i.a. the Ad hoc Advisory Group on EDC and Human Rights, the Steering Committee on Human Rights, the Joint Council on Youth, the Steering Committee for Higher Education, the Bureau of the Steering Committee for Education, and in March 2008, the plenary Steering Committee for Education.

262 Explanatory memorandum para 40(j).

263 CoE Standing Conference of European Ministers of Education, Building a more humane and inclusive Europe: role of education policies, Resolution on the 2008-2010 programme of activities (Istanbul, 4-5 May 2007), para 14(1).

appendix, as was proposed by the Steering Committee for Education (CDED). Among them, as appears from the documents, were all the EU Member States, represented by their Ministers of Foreign Affairs or representatives thereof.[264] The EU representative to the Council of Europe was also present. No reservations were submitted.[265]

In addition to the general recommendation on EDC, *specific* instruments of Council of Europe bodies continued to refer to EDC, with EDC thus appearing as a general principle, a paradigm in which other issues were approached, or of which specific dimensions would be developed further. EDC was recommended in actions to promote the participation of young people in public life[266], new information and communications environment[267], gender equality[268], race equality[269], or the integration of migrants.[270] In 2008, the European Ministers for Foreign Affairs launched

---

264 Addendum 1 to the Minutes of the sitting held at the Palais de l'Europe, Strasbourg on 11 May 2010 (CM(2010)PV-Add 1. On voting procedures, text to n 423 ff.

265 See n 433 and text.

266 CoE Recommendation Rec(2006)14 of the Committee of Ministers to member states on citizenship and participation of young people in public life (25 October 2006), importance of youth associations (non-formal learning).

267 CoE Recommendation Rec(2006)12 of the Committee of Ministers to member states on empowering children in the new information and communications environment (27 September 2006); CoE Recommendation CM/Rec(2007)11 of the Committee of Ministers to member states on promoting freedom of expression and information in the new information and communications environment (26 September 2007); CoE Recommendation CM/Rec(2007)16 of the Committee of Ministers to member states on measures to promote the public service value of the Internet (7 November 2007): 'Member states should use the Internet and other ICTs in conjunction with other channels of communication to formulate and implement policies for education for democratic citizenship to enable individuals to be active and responsible citizens throughout their lives, to respect the rights of others and to contribute to the defence and development of democratic societies and cultures' (appendix, section I).

268 CoE Recommendation CM/Rec(2007)13 of the Committee of Ministers to member states on gender mainstreaming in education (10 October 2007), para 37.

269 CoE ECRI General Policy Recommendation No 10 on combating racism and racial discrimination in and through school education (15 December 2006) (fundamamental role of schools towards equality).

270 CoE Recommendation CM/Rec(2008)4 of the Committee of Ministers to member states on strengthening the integration of children of migrants and of immigrant background (20 February 2008), C(5) (ii): 'The school curricula should include education for democratic citizenship, human rights and intercultural competence.'.

the White Paper on Intercultural Dialogue, recognising that the competences necessary for intercultural dialogue are not automatically acquired but need to be learned, with EDC as one of the key areas of competence.[271] In the case of, for example, religious differences, teaching should be consistent with the aims of EDC and HRE, aiming at tolerance and critical thinking.[272] Public authorities should ensure that higher education institutions can fulfil their objectives, including 'preparation for life as active citizens in democratic societies'.[273] Categorising activities that foster the rule of law, the Committee of Ministers mentioned EDC and HRE as 'important activities that seek to promote the rule of law in indirect ways'.[274] One binding instrument is particularly noteworthy in this third phase: the 2005 Council of Europe Convention on the Prevention of Terrorism. It contains an *obligation* for member states to take appropriate measures in the field of education 'with a view to preventing terrorist offences and their negative effects'.[275] This instrument presaged the link between education and security, which was to become central in the next phase.

Throughout the third phase, materials were further developed to assist member states and practitioners with implementation (six manuals on EDC/HRE for school practice were included in an EDC Pack), scholarly reflections were published, and good practices shared.[276]

---

271 CoE Committee of Ministers, White Paper on Intercultural Dialogue: Living together as equals in dignity (2 May 2008), paras 76 and 93–94 ('Education for democratic citizenship is fundamental to a free, tolerant, just, open and inclusive society, to social cohesion, mutual understanding, intercultural and interreligious dialogue and solidarity, as well as equality between women and men'). Also explanatory memorandum to the Charter on EDC/HRE, para 7.

272 CoE Recommendation CM/Rec(2008)12 of the Committee of Ministers to member states on the dimension of religions and non-religious convictions within intercultural education (10 December 2008), appendix para 5.

273 CoE Recommendation CM/Rec(2007)6 of the Committee of Ministers to member states on the public responsibility for higher education and research (16 May 2007), preambular paras 17–18, and appendix para 5. See in the same line CM/Rec(2012)7 (n 281).

274 CoE Committee of Ministers, The Council of Europe and the Rule of Law, CM(2008)170, para 62 fn 19 (categorisation of activities that further the rule of law).

275 CoE Convention on the Prevention of Terrorism CETS No 196 (Warsaw, opened 16 May 2005, entered into force 1 June 2007), Art 3(1). The EU and all EU Member States signed the Convention, but some did not ratify (e.g. BE, EL, IE).

276 Osler and Starkey, 'Education for democratic citizenship: a review of research, policy and practice 1995–2005'; CD Dziuban and others, 'Developing the Euro-

2. EDC standards after 2010: authoritative value of Charter on EDC/HRE confirmed

36 *Fourth phase: the Charter on EDC/HRE as a frequently cited reference point*

In the ongoing normative work of the Council of Europe since 2010, the Charter on EDC/HRE has been a frequently cited reference point.[277] Various recommendations of the Committee of Ministers refer to it and go on to consider specific aspects or dimensions of EDC, for instance in relation to the teaching of history[278], in the context of disadvantaged neighbor-

pean Citizen: Investing in Europe's Democratic Future' (2007) 21 International Journal of Social Education 177; T Huddleston (ed) *Tool on Teacher Training for Education for Democratic Citizenship and Human rights Education* (revised, CoE 2007); Olafsdottir, 'Education for Democratic Citizenship and Human Rights: A Project by the Council of Europe'; Osler, 'Human Rights Education: The Foundation of Education for Democratic Citizenship in our Global Age'; HJ Abs (ed) *Introducing Quality Assurance of Education for Democratic Citizenship in Schools: A comparative Study on Ten Countries* (CoE 2009); P Brett, P Mompoint-Gaillard and MH Salema, *How all teachers can support citizenship and human rights education: a framework for the development of competences* (CoE 2009); B Guidetti, 'Intercultural education for citizenship in complex societies. Summary of the International Conference on Intercultural Education for citizenship' (2009) 4 Ricerche di Pedagogia e Didattica 1; A Keating, DH Ortloff and S Philippou, 'Citizenship Education Curricula: The Changes and Challenges Presented by Global and European Integration' (2009) 41 Journal of Curriculum Studies 145. For materials and good practices in this period, see R Gollob and P Krapf (eds), *Living in democracy: EDC/HRE lesson plans for lower secondary level* (EDC/HRE vol III, CoE 2008); R Gollob and P Krapf, *Exploring Children's Rights: Nine short projects for primary level* (EDC/HRE vol V, CoE 2007); R Gollob and P Krapf, *Teaching Democracy: A collection of models for democratic citizenship and human rights education* (EDC/HRE vol VI, CoE 2009); Human Rights Education in the School Systems of Europe, Central Asia and North America: A Compendium of Good Practice (CoE, OSCE/ODIHR, UNESCO, OHCHR, 2009) 187.

277 Almost in all instruments cited in this section B. See also Hartley and Huddleston, *School-community-university partnerships for a sustainable democracy: Education for Democratic Citizenship in Europe and the United States of America* 51.

278 CoE Recommendation CM/Rec(2011)6 of the Committee of Ministers to member states on intercultural dialogue and the image of the other in history teaching (6 July 2011) ('history teaching constitutes an integral part of education for democratic citizenship').

hoods[279], the participation of young people[280], the responsibilities of public authorities[281], or global interdependence and solidarity[282].

The 2012 Recommendation of the Committee of Ministers on ensuring quality education, which has (i.a.) regard to the Charter on EDC/HRE is particularly important. This Recommendation describes *quality education* not only by reference to employability, but also with an expectation that education will promote democracy, respect for human rights, and responsible citizenship.[283] In the 2013 Helsinki agenda for quality education, the European Ministers of Education share this view, recalling that one of the four main purposes of education is '[p]reparation for life as active citizens in democratic societies' (echoing Article 13(1) ICESCR, third anchor point).[284]

---

279 CoE Recommendation CM/Rec(2015)3 of the Committee of Ministers to member States on the access of young people from disadvantaged neighbourhoods to social rights (21 January 2015).

280 CoE Recommendation CM/Rec(2012)2 of the Committee of Ministers to member States on the participation of children and young people under the age of 18 (28 March 2012).

281 CoE Recommendation CM/Rec(2012)7 of the Committee of Ministers to member States on the responsibility of public authorities for academic freedom and institutional autonomy (20 June 2012) ('higher education fulfils the multiple purposes of preparation for the labour market, preparation for life as active citizens in democratic societies, personal development ...'); CoE Recommendation CM/Rec(2019)5 of the Committee of Ministers to member States on the system of the European Convention Human Rights in university education and professional training (16 October 2019).

282 CoE Recommendation CM/Rec(2011)4 of the Committee of Ministers to member states on education for global interdependence and solidarity (5 May 2011) (recommends a more prominent role for education for global interdependence and solidarity in the framework of the implementation of the Charter on EDC/HRE). See also CoE Parliamentary Assembly Recommendation 2157 (2019) 'Towards an ambitious Council of Europe agenda for gender equality'.

283 CoE Recommendation CM/Rec(2012)13 of the Committee of Ministers to member States on ensuring quality education (12 December 2012), preambular paras 25–26; appendix para 6 (d-f).

284 CoE Standing Conference of Ministers of Education, Governance and Quality Education (Helsinki, 26 -27 April 2013), see paras 6, 15, and 18 (1)-(2). See also CoE Standing Conference of European Ministers of Education, Final Declaration on 'Education for Sustainable Democratic Societies: the Role of Teachers' (Ljubljana, 4-5 June 2010), and especially CoE Standing Conference of Ministers of Education, Securing Democracy through Education: The development of a Reference Framework of Competences for Democratic Culture (Brussels, 11-12 April 2016), para 13.

In the 2012–2015 Strategy for the Rights of the Child, the Committee of Ministers builds on the achievements of the programme on EDC and HRE. In several policy cycles, the Charter on EDC/HRE appears among the *standards* protecting the child, and forms part of strategic objectives and priority areas.[285] Member states are supported in the effective implementation of the Charter on EDC/HRE, for instance through the pilot project scheme 'Human Rights and Democracy in Action' jointly funded by the EU and the Council of Europe.[286]

The importance of EDC continues to be confirmed by other Council of Europe bodies, such as the Conference of International Non-Governmental Organisations[287] and the Congress of Local and Regional Authorities, which uses the definition of EDC in the Charter and advocates 'draw[ing] up local policies, strategies and action plans for education for democratic citizenship'.[288] Unfortunately, the Venice Commission has not worked on EDC. This authoritative body sets standards on democracy with a focus on legal orders and the working of democratic institutions.[289]

37 *EDC as a security imperative*

Two interlinked developments mark the period after 2010. The first is that EDC gained momentum through its relationship with the issue of security

---

285 CoE Committee of Ministers, Council of Europe Strategy for the Rights of the Child (2012-2015) (15 February 2012) CM(2011)171final, third policy cycle, strategic objective 4 (p 8); CoE, *Council of Europe Strategy for the Rights of the Child (2012-2015): Implementation report* (2016), 8, 17, 24; CoE Committee of Ministers, Council of Europe Strategy for the Rights of the Child (2016-2021): Children's human rights (3 March 2016) CM(2015)175 final, para 10, priority areas 3 and 4 (paras 37, 40, 48, 60, on participation in and through school, violence, and digitial citizenship education).

286 CoE Committee of Ministers, Council of Europe Strategy for the Rights of the Child (2016-2021): Children's human rights (3 March 2016) CM(2015)175 final, para 40.

287 CoE Conference of International Non-Governmental Organisations (INGOs), Declaration on genuine democracy (24 January 2013), para 13 ('Recognising that education is the key means of developing democratic values in the young, and wishing to encourage them to exercise fully the rights and assume the responsibilities of citizenship').

288 CoE Congress of Local and Regional Authorities of the Council of Europe Resolution 332(2011) 'Education for democratic citizenship: tools for cities', paras 2, and 5–7, and explanatory memoranum paras 6–11.

289 CoE Committee of Ministers Resolution(2002)3, Revised Statute of the European Commission for Democracy through Law (Venice Commission) (21 February 2002). Especially Statute Art 1(2)(b) would allow work on EDC/HRE.

in Europe. EDC became a central preoccupation in the drive for 'democratic security' after the fall of the Berlin wall (1989), and renewed commitment to EDC has resulted from the challenges of radicalisation and terrorism. Acknowledging that these are complex phenomena, several Council of Europe and EU bodies have pointed to education for democratic citizenship and human rights as an important part of the response and a matter of urgency.[290] Most terrorist suspects are European citizens. EDC and HRE are also needed to address the problems resulting from the influx of migrants and refugees.

In the 2015 report on the 'State of democracy, human rights and the rule of law: A shared responsibility for democratic security in Europe', the Secretary General of the Council of Europe recalls the consensus among political scientists that 'democracies rarely go to war with each other.'[291] In order to assess the performance of each member state, five pillars of democratic security are distinguished (each broken down into parameters and detailed criteria). One of them is the 'Inclusive society and democratic citizenship' pillar, with EDC as a measurement criterion (to see whether specific action has been taken to increase the priority given to EDC/HRE in education policies). Curricula should be reviewed and updated in line with the Charter on EDC/HRE (country monitoring suggests that there are still large gaps).[292] EDC is one of the basic criteria for assessing the degree to which states promote inclusion and democratic citizenship. 'Building and reinforcing inclusiveness in our societies—and thereby empowering all citizens *to exercise and defend their rights, to value diversity and to play an active part in democratic life*—is an essential element of democratic security' (the three components of the definition of EDC in the Charter on EDC/HRE).[293] The successive reports on the state of democracy, human rights and the rule of law continue in the same vein, inter alia recommending

290 Discussed in various fora. See e.g. CoE Exchange on the religious dimension of intercultural dialogue: the role of education in the prevention of radicalisation leading to terrorism and violent extremism (Strasbourg, 9-10 November 2016); World Forum for Democracy 2016, Democracy & equality: does education matter? (Strasbourg, 7-9 November 2016); CoE Conference, Securing Democracy through Education (Nicosia, 22-23 March 2017). See also CoE Parliamentary Assembly Recommendation 2084(2016) 'Foreign fighters in Syria and Iraq'. See for EU reactions §§ 127 .

291 CoE Secretary General, State of democracy, human rights and the rule of law: A shared responsibility for democratic security in Europe. Report 2015, 6.

292 Ibid 13, 86–88. On practice, see text to n 523.

293 Ibid 75 (emphasis added); see also 86.

assessment of the need to make the Charter on EDC/HRE a binding legal instrument.[294] In 2016, the Charter on EDC/HRE was included in a Compendium of the most relevant Council of Europe texts in the area of democracy.[295]

38 The Reference Framework of Competences for Democratic Culture (RFCDC)

A further development was the work on a Reference Framework for Competences for Democratic Culture (RFCDC). In 2011, a 'Group of Eminent persons' was asked by the Secretary General of the Council of Europe, Thorbjørn Jagland, to analyse the threat of rising intolerance and discrimination and loss of democratic freedoms (i.a. through populism, xenophobic parties, and Islamic extremism). This Group regarded educators as the primary actors for change and urged them to develop 'intercultural competencies' as core elements in school curricula.[296] Intercultural and democratic competences were developed in the RFCDC at the insistence of the Committee of Ministers (Declaration and Action Plan), the European Ministers of Education, the Secretary General, and the Parliamentary Assembly.[297] The RFCDC was officially launched in April 2018 during the con-

---

294 CoE Secretary General, State of democracy, human rights and the rule of law—a security imperative for Europe. Report 2016, 81–101 (pillar on inclusive societies), 97 (criteria), 201 (binding); CoE Secretary General, State of democracy, human rights and the rule of law: Populism—How strong are Europe's checks and balances? Report 2017, 112 (narrowing implementation gaps); CoE Secretary General, State of democracy, human rights and the rule of law: Role of institutions—Threats to institutions Report 2018 (ch 5, education and culture for democracy).

295 CoE Secretariat, Compendium of the most relevant Council of Europe texts in the area of democracy CDDG(2016)Compendium, Chapter E. The Compendium has been drawn up by the SG, authorised for publication by the CM, reflecting 'the state of play as regards the texts adopted by Council of Europe bodies in areas that fall into the shared definition of democracy' and with 'no legal force nor authoritative status'.

296 CoE Report of the Group of Eminent Persons of the Council of Europe, *Living together: combining diversity and freedom in 21st century Europe*, p 37, 61, para 31. Joschka Fischer headed the Group; members were Emma Bonino (Italy), Timothy Garton Ash (UK), Martin Hirsch (France), Danuta Hübner (Poland), Ayşe Kadıoğlu (Turkey), Sonja Licht (Serbia), Vladimir Lukin (Russia) and Javier Solana (Spain).

297 CoE Committee of Ministers Declaration 'United around our principles against violent extremism and radicalisation leading to terrorism' (19 May 2015) CM(2015)74-final; CoE Committee of Ministers, The fight against violent extremism and radicalisation leading to terrorism - Action Plan (19 May 2015)

ference 'Democratic Culture—from words to action' (Copenhagen).[298] It aims to support member states in the implementation of the Charter on EDC/HRE and to increase effectiveness of EDC and HRE.[299]

The RFCDC has the Charter on EDC/HRE as a main source of inspiration and refers to the central conceptual foundations of EDC/HRE. The enormous value of having a single, consensual EDC concept in the Charter on EDC/HRE is underscored when it is compared with the *101* schemes on citizenship education audited to establish the model for the RFCDC.[300] The schemes examined—schemes drawn up by Council of Europe or EU bodies, UNESCO, OECD, member state governments, and academic

---

CM(2015)74 add final, especially heading 2(1)(1); CoE Standing Conference of Ministers of Education, Governance and Quality Education (Helsinki, 26 -27 April 2013), para 21(4); CoE Standing Conference of Ministers of Education, Securing Democracy through Education: The development of a Reference Framework of Competences for Democratic Culture (Brussels, 11-12 April 2016), see paras 12–14 (also on quality education), 20, 31, 37. See also CoE Committee of Ministers, Thematic debate: 'Living together implies having a level of common competences as regards intercultural and democratic dialogue, as well as a system of attitudes, behaviour and common values. Can these be taught?'—Follow-up (4 and 6 July 2012); CoE Committee of Ministers Action Plan on Building Inclusive Societies (2016-2019) (15-16 March 2016) CM(2016)25; CoE Secretary General, The fight against violent extremism and radicalisation leading to terrorism - Implementing the Action Plan. Report (18 May 2016); CoE Parliamentary Assembly Recommendation 2088(2016) 'Towards a framework of competences for democratic citizenship'. See also nn 291 and 294.

298 <www.coe.int/en/web/education/-/official-launch-of-the-reference-framework-of-competences-for-democratic-culture-rfcdc-and-of-the-implementation-network>.

299 More in text to n 300.

300 Competences for democratic culture: Living together as equals in culturally diverse democratic societies (CoE 2016) 3 (four phases). See CoE Committee of Ministers, The fight against violent extremism and radicalisation leading to terrorism - Action Plan (19 May 2015) CM(2015)74 add final, especially 2.1.1; CoE Standing Conference of Ministers of Education, Securing Democracy through Education: The development of a Reference Framework of Competences for Democratic Culture (Brussels, 11-12 April 2016), see paras 12–14 (also on the quality of education), 20, 31, 37. Also CoE Committee of Ministers, Thematic debate: 'Living together implies having a level of common competences as regards intercultural and democratic dialogue, as well as a system of attitudes, behaviour and common values. Can these be taught?'—Follow-up (4 and 6 July 2012); CoE Committee of Ministers Action Plan on Building Inclusive Societies (2016-2019) (15-16 March 2016) CM(2016)25; CoE Secretary General, The fight against violent extremism and radicalisation leading to terrorism - Implementing the Action Plan. Report (18 May 2016).

researchers—are evidence of the variety of approaches to citizenship education.[301] The proliferation of schemes, which moreover differ considerably, presents 'a dilemma to educational planners and policy makers who wish to find an authoritative model upon which to base their work'.[302] The Glossary to the RFCDC reiterates the definition of EDC (concept in para 2). It is interesting that the authors added this comment to the definition:

> As democratic citizenship is not limited to the citizen's legal status and to the voting right this status confers, education for democratic citizenship includes all aspects of life in a democratic society and is therefore related to a vast range of topics such as sustainable development, participation of people with disabilities in society, gender mainstreaming, prevention of terrorism and many others.[303]

EDC does indeed relate to *all* the rights and obligations which the law confers on citizens, including those concerning sustainable development, disability, gender, etc. Citizens' participation rights, moreover, relate to the prevention of terrorism and much more. All these subjects fall ipso facto under the definition of para 2 of the Charter on EDC/HRE. The legal status of citizens and component (c-1) cannot be construed narrowly.

The RFCDC proposes a model of 20 democratic competences needed for effective participation in a culture of democracy.[304] Democratic competence is defined as 'the ability to mobilise and deploy relevant psychological resources (namely values, attitudes, skills, knowledge and/or understanding) in order to respond appropriately and effectively to the demands, challenges and opportunities presented by democratic situations'.[305] The RDCDC sets out the values, attitudes, skills, and knowledge and critical understanding which an individual needs in order to be an

---

301 Appendix A. See also Grammes, 'Different Cultures in Education for Democracy and Citizenship'.

302 Competences for democratic culture: Living together as equals in culturally diverse democratic societies (CoE 2016), 27.

303 CoE Reference Framework of Competences for Democratic Culture, Vol 1: Context, concepts and model (2018), 72. See also definition of 'democratic culture', etc. in p 71 ff.

304 See Annex 3 to this study.

305 CoE Reference Framework of Competences for Democratic Culture, Vol 1: Context, concepts and model (2018), 32 (intercultural competences are defined likewise as a response to intercultural situations; for citizens who live within culturally diverse democratic societies, they are an integral aspect of democratic competence).

active participant in a 'democratic culture/society/group'[306]—there is, notably, no mention of the state.[307] It will be possible to apply these democratic competences in the EU context as they have been chosen to be multipurpose, flexible, open and dynamic.[308] An example is the competence specifying the expected knowledge and critical understanding of the world (including politics, law, human rights, etc.).[309] Moreover, 447 descriptors have been developed. Descriptors are 'statements referring to concrete observable behaviour of a person with a certain level of competence'.[310]

The RFCDC is 'not a prescribed or even recommended European curriculum'.[311] It is a reference document, a tool to enable European education systems to specify learning outcomes, and is destined for use in school curricula at different levels of formal education. The democratic competences in the RFCDC and their descriptors add precision to the EDC standards.

For the purposes of this study, the concept of EDC in the Charter on EDC/HRE is useful in itself, especially in its components (c-1–2–3), which set out the EDC and HRE objectives, i.e. empowering citizens to exercise and defend their democratic rights and responsibilities in society, to value diversity (in its behavioural aspects), and to play an active part in democratic life. These components will be used as parameters to apply EDC/HRE standards to the position of EU citizens under EU law. Furthermore, the EDC concept provides a common denominator from which to approach citizenship education, bridging the different political systems in the member states. It is possible to apply the EDC parameters and still

306 CoE Reference Framework of Competences for Democratic Culture, Vol 3: Guidance for implementation (2018), 12.

307 See § 150 statal thinking, i.a. text to n 1026.

308 Competences for democratic culture: Living together as equals in culturally diverse democratic societies (CoE 2016), 31.

309 See ibid 52–53 (also knowledge and critical understanding of culture, media, economies, environment, and sustainability...).

310 Including 135 key descriptors. See CoE Reference Framework of Competences for Democratic Culture, Vol 2: Descriptors of competences for democratic culture (2018), p 11; CoE Reference Framework of Competences for Democratic Culture, Vol 3: Guidance for implementation (2018), p 12: descriptors cover only those values, attitudes, skills, and knowledge and understanding which are learnable, teachable and assessable.

311 CoE Reference Framework of Competences for Democratic Culture, Vol 1: Context, concepts and model (2018), 20: 'The Framework is thus a tool for use in designing and developing curricula, pedagogies and assessments suitable for different contexts and education systems as determined by those responsible'. It provides a shared language.

respect national constitutional differences. Even within the EU, the political systems of the Member States differ widely (constitutional monarchies and republics; presidential, semi-presidential, and parliamentary systems; unitary states, federal systems, and states with devolved powers to certain regions; unicameral and bicameral parliaments, etc.). However, they are all representative democracies, their constitutions guaranteeing free elections and human rights. The concise common denominator of EDC is wide enough to embrace different national concepts and allow for diverse approaches in the member states. The democratic competences and their descriptors in the RFCDC provide additional detail.

39 Ongoing work on EDC

The follow-up activities since 2010 continue to involve a wide range of actors.[312] National public authorities, educational establishments, NGOs, youth organisations, partnerships, networks, and other stakeholders, put Council of Europe instruments into practice. Materials and tools for the implementation and assessment of EDC have been developed further and made available through Council of Europe publications.[313] Strategic support has been offered to policy makers.[314] EDC continues to be studied in social science.[315] At the 2016 Standing Conference, the Ministers of Educa-

---

312 See i.a. CoE Committee of Ministers, Terms of reference for the Steering Committee for education policy and practice (CDPPE), 1 January 2018 until 31 December 2019, CM(2017)131-addfinal (Education for Democracy).

313 R Gollob, P Krapf and W Weidinger (eds), *Taking Part in Democracy: Lesson plans for upper secondary level on democratic citizenship and human rights education* (EDC/HRE vol IV, CoE 2010); R Gollob, P Krapf and W Weidinger (eds), *Educating for democracy: Background materials on democratic citizenship and human rights education for teachers* (EDC/HRE vol I, CoE 2011). See also § 126 on the ACCI and the CCCI, in co-operation with the EU.

314 I.a. D Kerr and others, *Strategic support for decision makers: Policy tool for education for democratic citizenship and human rights* (CoE 2010); Curriculum Development and Review for Democratic Citizenship and Human Rights Education (prepared by Felisa Tibbits for UNESCO/CoE/Office for Democratic Institutions and Human Rights/Organization of American States, 2016).

315 E.g. Hartley and Huddleston, *School-community-university partnerships for a sustainable democracy: Education for Democratic Citizenship in Europe and the United States of America*; K Hüfner, 'The Human Rights Approach to Education in International Organisations' (2011) 46 European Journal of Education 117; D Kerr and A Keating, 'Intercultural, citizenship and human rights education: the challenges of implementation for policy, practice and research' (2011) 53 Educational Research 119; Becker, 'Politische Bildung in Europa'; Grammes, 'Different Cultures in Education for Democracy and Citizenship'; D Kerr, *Implementation of the Council of Europe Charter on Education for Democratic Citizenship and*

tion supported the development of a long-term strategy for a more coherent and comprehensive approach to EDC/HRE and requested the Council of Europe to consider ways of increasing the impact of the Charter.[316] Successive chairmanships of the Council of Europe mention education for democratic citizenship and human rights among their priorities.[317] Every five years, a Council of Europe report and a conference assess the impact of the Charter on EDC/HRE.[318]

Human Rights Education: Final Report (CoE Steering Committee for Educational Policy and Practice, 2012); J Menthe, 'Education for Democratic Citizenship: Values vs Process' in M Print and D Lange (eds), *Schools, Curriculum and Civic Education for Building Democratic Citizens* (Sense 2012); GH Helskog, *Democracy and diversity in education. Report of the International conference at Buskerud University College (Norway 12-13 March 2013)* ; Korostelina and Lässig, *History education and post-conflict reconciliation: reconsidering joint textbook projects*; M Print and D Lange (eds), *Civic Education and Competences for Engaging Citizens in Democracies* (Springer 2013); Arbués, 'Civic Education in Europe: Pedagogic Challenge versus Social Reality'; R Otte, 'The Council of Europe's work on "Education for Democratic Citizenship and Human Rights Education" and its links to the PIDOP project' in M Barrett and B Zani (eds), *Political and Civic Engagement: Multidisciplinary Perspectives* (Routledge 2014); Curriculum Development and Review for Democratic Citizenship and Human Rights Education (prepared by Felisa Tibbits for UNESCO/CoE/Office for Democratic Institutions and Human Rights/Organization of American States, 2016). See also A Osler, *General Rapporteur Conference report, in CoE Proceedings of the Conference on 'Human Rights and Democracy in Action - Looking Ahead: The Impact of the Council of Europe Charter on Education for Democratic Citizenship and Human Rights Education' (Strasbourg, 29-30 November 2012)* (2013).

316 CoE Standing Conference of Ministers of Education, Securing Democracy through Education: The development of a Reference Framework of Competences for Democratic Culture (Brussels, 11-12 April 2016), paras 22, 31.

317 E.g. Priorities of the Czech Chairmanship of the Committee of Ministers of the Council of Europe (May—November 2017) CM/Inf(2017)12, section 4; Priorities of the Finnish Presidency of the Committee of Ministers of the Council of Europe (21 November 2018–17 May 2019) CM/Inf(2018)30, point 3. See also Stocktaking of the Finnish Presidency CM/Inf(2019)16: 'The Expert Meeting of the Education Policy Advisers Network (EPAN) on Education for Democratic Citizenship and Human Rights was held on 16–17 April 2019 in Helsinki with a focus on implementing the Council of Europe's Reference Framework of Competencies for Democratic Culture (RFCDC)'.

318 First review cycle (2010–2012), see CoE Proceedings of the Conference on 'Human Rights and Democracy in Action - Looking Ahead: The Impact of the Council of Europe Charter on Education for Democratic Citizenship and Human Rights Education' (Strasbourg, 29-30 November 2012); see i.a. Kerr, *Implementation of the Council of Europe Charter on Education for Democratic Citizenship and Human Rights Education: Final Report*; and Osler, *General Rapporteur*

40 Conclusion

The genesis of the Charter on EDC/HRE and the period after its adoption have revealed its solid foundations, its authority and major political significance. The Charter is a cornerstone in the Council of Europe normative framework on EDC. A huge number of legal instruments containing EDC norms have been mentioned: about 30 recommendations of the Committee of Ministers, various declarations and action plans of the Committee of Ministers, about 10 recommendations of the Parliamentary Assembly, 3 declarations of Summits of Heads of State and Government, about 10 declarations of the Standing Conference of European ministers of Education, several Secretary General reports, and various instruments of the Conference of International Non-Governmental Organisations (INGOs), the Congress of Local and Regional Authorities of the Council of Europe, etc.[319] Together, these instruments demonstrate that EDC is a common objective, a paradigm in which all organs and bodies of the Council of Europe cooperate, a generally accepted principle. The *political* consensus is undeniable. EDC standards belong to the category of 'generally accepted rules, which would be politically embarrassing to neglect'.[320] The question is: what is their *legal* impact? Having clarified the normative context, I will now examine the legal effects.

Conference report, in CoE Proceedings of the Conference on 'Human Rights and Democracy in Action - Looking Ahead: The Impact of the Council of Europe Charter on Education for Democratic Citizenship and Human Rights Education' (Strasbourg, 29-30 November 2012). Second review cycle (2012–2017), see CoE Conference, Learning to Live Together: a Shared Commitment to Democracy: Conference on the Future of Citizenship and Human Rights Education in Europe (Strasbourg, 20-22 June 2017).

319 Overview in bibliography.

320 Applying Schermers and Blokker § 1226 (recommendations of international organisations reflecting the generally held view on a given matter).

CHAPTER 2 Effects of the Charter on EDC/HRE in the Council of Europe legal order

41 Perspectives for assessing the effects of the Charter on EDC/HRE

The effects of the Charter on EDC/HRE within the Council of Europe legal order are assessed, firstly, in the light of the case law of the ECtHR (sections A and B) and, secondly, according to criteria established by legal scholars, revealing strengths and weaknesses (section C). Section D draws on research and scholarship outside the legal field providing a context for further analysis.

A Relevance for the interpretation of ECHR provisions

42 The 2002 Recommendation cited in case law

The legal status of the Charter on EDC/HRE is that of a recommendation of the Committee of Ministers under Article 15(b) of the Statute (CM/Rec(2010)7). This recommendation is not mentioned in the case law of the ECtHR: it is not cited in any judgment, decision or opinion.[321] However, its predecessor is: the 2002 Recommendation of the Committee of Ministers on education for democratic citizenship (Rec(2002)12).[322] In *Seurot v France* (2004), a secondary school teacher was dismissed after he published an article with racist content inciting hatred in the school's newspaper ('unassimilable Muslim hordes'). In an application to the ECtHR, Seurot invoked the right to freedom of expression (Article 10 ECHR). The Court found that the dismissal did indeed interfere with his right to freedom of expression, but that that was necessary in a democratic society.[323] It pursued a legitimate aim of protection of the reputation and of the rights of others. The exercise of the right to freedom of expression 'carries with it duties and responsibilities' (Article 10(2) ECHR). These are of a special significance in the case of teachers, 'who are figures of authority to their

321 <hudoc.echr.coe.int> search in October 2019.

322 Rec(2002)12 of the Committee of Ministers to member states on education for democratic citizenship (text to n 232).

323 *Seurot v France* no 57383/00 (ECtHR Decision 18 May 2004).

pupils'.[324] In earlier case law, the concept of special duties and responsibilities had been applied to a certain extent to the teachers' activities outside the school and—continued the Court—the same must a fortiori apply to the activities of teachers *in* school. To support its reasoning, at this point, the Court cited the 2002 Recommendation noting that ('La Cour note d'ailleurs que') in the Recommendation Rec(2002)12 on education for democratic citizenship, the Committee of Ministers recalls that 'education for democratic citizenship is fundamental to the Council of Europe's primary task of promoting a free, tolerant and just society' throughout life and at each level of education (primary, secondary, ...). The Court held that such an education for democratic citizenship, which is essential ('indispensable') to combating racism and xenophobia, requires the mobilisation of responsible actors, in particular teachers. The Court explicitly referred to the provision on the teacher training necessary for education for democratic citizenship in the Appendix to the 2002 Recommendation.[325] The Court found the complaint to be manifestly ill-founded and unanimously declared the application inadmissible.[326]

The *Seurot* decision indicates that the ECtHR recognises the essential role of EDC. It gives some effect to the 2002 Recommendation in its interpretation and application of Article 10 ECHR, striking a fair balance between the fundamental right of the individual to freedom of expression and the legitimate interest of a democratic State.

Because the 2010 Recommendation builds on the 2002 Recommendation and contains similar provisions to those cited by the ECtHR,[327] it can be expected to produce the same effect.

In addition to this first argument militating in favour of the legal effects of the Charter on EDC/HRE, a more general argument will now be developed. Even though recommendations of the Committee of Ministers do not lead to obligations of compliance, judgments of the ECtHR show that such recommendations are not devoid of any legal effects. This second

---

324 Ibid; *Vogt v Germany* no 17851/91 (ECtHR 2 Sept 1996), para 60.

325 Rec(2002)12, para 4.

326 See also CoE Parliamentary Assembly, Motion for a resolution tabled by Mr Luca Volontè and other members of the Assembly, 'Respect for human rights in education for democratic citizenship in Spain' (3 June 2010): 305 parents and children lodged an application concerning compulsory 'Education for Citizenship' in Spain, in accordance with the 2002 Recommendation. Further Motos (n 462).

327 CM/Rec(2010)7 preamble ('Recalling the core mission... Firmly convinced'), appendix (Charter) paras 5, 6, 9.

argument will first be explained in general terms, then applied to the 2010 Recommendation on the Charter on EDC/HRE.

43 The ECtHR takes non-binding instruments into account to interpret the ECHR and to establish common European standards

The normative context in Chapter one has revealed a wide range of non-binding instruments on EDC adopted by various bodies of the Council of Europe. They all have potential legal relevance. Case law of the ECtHR demonstrates that non-binding instruments of the Council of Europe have been decisive in important cases.

In *Tănase v Moldova* (Grand Chamber),

> [t]he Court emphasises that it has consistently held that it must take into account relevant international instruments and reports, and in particular those of other Council of Europe organs, in order to interpret the guarantees of the Convention and to establish whether there is a common European standard in the field.[328]

In this case, the Court interpreted the right to free elections (Article 3 Protocol 1 ECHR) in the light of various non-binding instruments of bodies of the Council of Europe.[329] In *Mosley*, the ECtHR confirmed even more clearly that 'any standards set out in applicable international instruments and reports' are relevant to the interpretation of the ECHR and to the identification of 'any common European standard in the field'.[330] Indeed, throughout the case law of the ECtHR and in the context of many different ECHR rights, non-binding instruments of Council of Europe bodies

---

328 *Tănase v Moldova* no 7/08 (ECtHR 24 April 2010), paras 176–77. See earlier *Demir and Baykara v Turkey* no 34503/97 (ECtHR 12 November 2008), paras 74–76, 85–86; and later *Soltysyak v Russia* no 4663/05 (ECtHR 10 February 2011), para 51.

329 *Tănase*, paras 55–60 and 124: to assess proportionality, the ECtHR took account of conclusions and reports of the European Commission against Racism and Intolerance, the Code of Good Practice in Electoral Matters of the Venice Commission, and resolutions of the Parliamentary Assembly, i.a. PA Resolution 1619(2008) on the state of democracy in Europe (25 June 2008).

330 *Mosley v UK* no 48009/08 (ECtHR 10 May 2011), para 110; also *Çam v Turkey* no 51500/08 (ECtHR 23 February 2016), para 53; *Saadi v UK* no 13229/03 (ECtHR 29 January 2008), para 62. Concrete application in *Mosley*: see paras 56–60, 124, for interpretation of Art 8 ECHR taking PA resolutions into account (i.a. Resolution 1636(2008) on indicators for media in a democracy) as well as a Declaration and Programme of action adopted by the Cracow 2000 European Ministerial Conference (A media policy for tomorrow).

are relevant. The Court relies on them to determine the scope of provisions, interference or justification, often in unprecedented cases where it formulates new standards.[331] As early as the 1979 *Marckx* case, in order to interpret the word 'everyone' in Article 8 ECHR (everyone has the right to respect for his family life), the Court took note of the Committee of Ministers' Resolution on the social protection of unmarried mothers and their children (recommendations of the Committee of Ministers were initially called 'resolutions').[332] In *Telegraaf Media Nederland Landelijke Media*, the ECtHR used the definition of journalistic sources in the appendix of a recommendation of the Committee of Ministers in order to decide whether there was infringement of Articles 8 and 10 ECHR, and declared that '[p]rotection of journalistic sources is one of the basic conditions for press freedom, as is recognised and reflected in various international instruments including the [quoted] Committee of Ministers Recommendation'.[333] The ECtHR thus refers to Council of Europe recommendations to stress the importance of certain general principles.[334] In *Shtukaturov v Russia*, Article 8 ECHR was interpreted and applied by reference to a Committee of Ministers recommendation on principles concerning the legal protection of incapable adults: '[a]lthough these principles have no force of law for this Court, they may define a common European standard in this area'.[335] The Court held that Russian legislation contrary to these principles, constituted a disproportionate restriction on the right guaranteed by Article 8 ECHR. In the landmark *Demir* case, the Court recalled that it has

331 LR Glas, 'The European Court of Human Rights' use of non-binding and standard-setting Council of Europe documents' (2017) 17 Human Rights Law Review 97, 100, 102–103, 106–108, 119. In a sample of 795 judgments between 2012 and 2015, the ECtHR used CoE documents in a minority of cases (about 230), but these cases were relatively important and formulate new standards.

332 *Marckx v Belgium* no 6833/74 (ECtHR 13 June 1979), para 31 (CM Resolution (70)15 on the social protection of unmarried mothers and their children (15 May 1970) was an argument 'in addition'). See this and other examples in Pinto de Albuquerque (n 401). Text to n 402 on the role of soft law.

333 *Telegraaf Media Nederland Landelijke Media v the Netherlands* no 39315/06 (ECtHR 22 November 2012), paras 86 and 127 (quoting Recommendation No. R (2000) 7 of the Committee of Ministers to member states on the right of journalists not to disclose their sources of information).

334 Glas, 'The European Court of Human Rights' use of non-binding and standard-setting Council of Europe documents', 110, with examples.

335 *Shtukaturov v Russia* no 44009/05 (ECtHR 27 March 2008), para 95. Taking into account CoE Recommendation R(99)4 of the Committee of Ministers to member states on principles concerning the legal protection of incapable adults (23 February 1999).

never considered the provisions of the ECHR as the sole reference framework for interpreting the rights and freedoms therein. 'On the contrary, it must also take into account any relevant rules and principles of international law applicable in relations between the Contracting Parties'.[336] The Court 'has used, for the purpose of interpreting the Convention, intrinsically non-binding instruments of Council of Europe organs, in particular recommendations and resolutions of the Committee of Ministers and the Parliamentary Assembly'.[337] Here, the Court took account of a recommendation of the Committee of Ministers on the status of public officials in Europe to interpret the right to freedom of association (Article 11 ECHR).[338] In several cases, European Prison Rules, featuring as an appendix to recommendations of the Committee of Ministers just like the Charter on EDC/HRE, have played an important role in the interpretation of Article 3 (prohibition of torture or inhuman or degrading treatment or punishment) or of Article 8 ECHR (right to respect for private and family life).[339] In *S v Switzerland*, the ECtHR recognised the right of the accused to communicate with his lawyer out of hearing of third persons as a basic condition for a fair trial in a democratic society (Article 6(3)(c) ECHR). This right had been set forth in the Standard Minimum Rules for the Treatment of Prisoners (appendix to Resolution (73)5 of the Committee of Ministers). The Court held this to be a necessary right, considering that 'the Convention is intended to guarantee rights that are practical and effective'.[340] In *Salduz*, the ECtHR held that Article 6(1) ECHR included the suspect's right of access to a lawyer from the time of the first police

336 *Demir* (n 328), para 67.

337 *Demir* (n 328), paras 74–75. The Court has also supported its reasoning 'by reference to norms emanating from other CoE organs, 'even though those organs have no function of representing States Parties to the Convention, whether supervisory mechanisms or expert bodies'. See also para 85: When 'defining the meaning of terms and notions in the text of the Convention, [the Court] can and must take into account elements of international law other than the Convention, the interpretation of such elements by competent organs, and the practice of European States reflecting their common values'.

338 *Demir* (n 328), paras 46, 76, 104, using Recommendation No R(2000)6).

339 The European Prison Rules are the minimum standards to be applied in prisions. See CoE Recommendation Rec(2006)2 of the Committee of Ministers to member states on the European Prison Rules (1 January 2006), and earlier CoE Recommendation R(87)3 of the Committee of Ministers to member states on the European Prison Rules (12 February 1987). See also text to n 512.

340 *S v Switzerland* no 12629/87 (ECtHR 28 November 1991), para 48.

interrogation,[341] and also referred to several recommendations of the Committee of Ministers and of the European Committee for the Prevention of Torture and Inhuman or Degrading Treatment or Punishment.[342] In *Murray*, interpreting Article 3 ECHR, the ECtHR found support for its decision that prisoners should be given an opportunity to rehabilitate i.a. in recommendations of the Committee of Ministers confirming the rehabilitative aim of imprisonment—notwithstanding the fact that the ECHR does not guarantee such a right—and held that States have an obligation of means to provide this.[343] Finally, and without seeking to provide an exhaustive list of examples,[344] in *Baka,* the Court considered Hungary's alleged violation of Articles 6 and 10 ECHR in the light of 'international and Council of Europe standards on the independence of the judiciary and the procedural safeguards applicable in cases of removal of judges', including a Recommendation of the Committee of Ministers to member states on judges' independence, efficiency and responsibilities (with norms in the appendix also expressed in terms of 'should'), and in the light of other non-binding instruments of Council of Europe bodies, such as opinions of the Venice Commission.[345]

---

341 *Salduz v Turkey* no 36391/0227 (ECtHR November 2008), para 55, 'in order for the right to a fair trial to remain sufficiently "practical and effective"'.

342 Ibid, paras 37–38, 54–55 (i.a. CM Res(73)5, CM Rec(2006)2). See earlier *Perez v France* no 47287/99 (ECtHR 12 February 2004), para 72 ('the Court draws attention for information to the text of Recommendations Nos. R (83) 7, R (85) 11 and R (87) 21 of the Committee of Ministers ..., which clearly specify the rights which victims may assert in the context of -criminal law and procedure').

343 *Murray v the Netherlands* no 10511/10 (ECtHR 26 April 2016), paras 58, 60, 66, 70, 73, 76, 99, 103–04 (taking into account European Prison Rules, also CM recommendations Rec(2003)23, Rec(2003)22, R (98)7 and Resolution 76(2)). Various other international and European materials are referred to, i.a. country reports of the European Committee for the Prevention of Torture and Inhuman or Degrading Treatment or Punishment (paras 57, 62). Other case law on prison rules with role of non-binding CoE instruments, see i.a. *Enea v Italy* no 74912/01 (ECtHR 17 September 2009), para 101; *Vinter and Others v UK* no 66069/09 et al (ECtHR 9 July 2013), paras 114, 116, 119 (i.a. a report on Switzerland of the Committee for the Prevention of Torture).

344 Other examples in Pinto de Albuquerque (n 401), and Glas, 'The European Court of Human Rights' use of non-binding and standard-setting Council of Europe documents'.

345 *Baka v Hungary* no 20261/12 (ECtHR 23 June 2016), paras 77–79, 82–83, 114, 117, such as Opinion no. 1 (2001) of the Consultative Council of European Judges on standards concerning the independence of the judiciary and the irremovability of judge, CoE Recommendation CM/Rec(2010)12 of the Committee of Ministers of the Council of Europe on judges: independence, efficiency and

The interpretative value of Council of Europe recommendations, and recognition of their legal effect within the Council of Europe legal order, is comparable—mutatis mutandis—to the ECJ *Grimaldi* line of case law, acknowledging the legal effects of recommendations within the EU legal order. The ECJ stressed that recommendations cannot be regarded as having no legal effects:

> *national courts are bound to take recommendations into consideration in order to decide disputes submitted to them, in particular where they cast light on the interpretation of national measures adopted in order to implement them or where they are designed to supplement binding Community provisions.*[346]

To conclude, in its interpretation of the ECHR, the ECtHR is mainly guided by the rules of interpretation of the Vienna Convention on the Law of Treaties.[347] The ECHR 'cannot be interpreted in a vacuum but must be interpreted in harmony with the general principles of international law'.[348] When the ECtHR considers the object and purpose of ECHR provisions, it also takes account of the international law background to the legal question before it,[349] and relies on a wide range Council of Europe instruments: recommendations of the Committee of Ministers, resolutions or recommendations of the Parliamentary Assembly, declarations of European ministerial conferences, reports of Council of Europe bodies, etc. All

---

responsibilities (17 November 2010) (norms in appendix), opinions of the Venice Commission, or the European Charter on the Statute for Judges. See also Joint Concurring Opinion of Judges Pinto de Albuquerque and Devov, paras 6 and 17: 'The Court's direct recourse to international-law standards on judicial independence, including soft-law sources, as a source of law in order to address the applicant's situation is highly remarkable, and laudable.' Further *Murray v the Netherlands* no 10511/10 (ECtHR 26 April 2016), paras 57 ff, i.a. report of the European Committee for the Prevention of Torture and Inhuman or Degrading Treatment or Punishment (CPT) on its visit to Aruba and the Netherlands Antilles in 2007; and in *Vinter and Others v UK* no 66069/09 et al (ECtHR 9 July 2013), para 116, i.a. report on Switzerland of the CPT.

346 Case C-322/88 *Grimaldi* ECLI:EU:C:1989:646, para 18.

347 *Demir* (n 328), para 65, referring to Arts 31–33 Vienna Convention on the Law of Treaties.

348 *RMT v UK* no 31045/10 (ECtHR, 8 April 2014), para 76. The ECtHR consistently holds that the Convention cannot be interpreted in a vacuum; see i.a. *Al-Adsani v UK* no 35763/97 (ECtHR 21 November 2001), para 55; *Hassan v UK* no 29750/09 (ECtHR 16 September 2014), para 77.

349 *Demir and Baykara v Turkey* no 34503/97 (ECtHR 12 November 2008), para 76, also 67; *Saadi v UK* no 13229/03 (ECtHR 29 January 2008), para 63.

such instruments have featured in the normative context of the Charter on EDC/HRE and therefore have legal relevance.

44 *Taking account of the Charter on EDC/HRE and the establishment of common EDC standards*

In the light of the ECtHR case law set out above, the Charter on EDC/HRE can be seen as an instrument which is relevant for interpreting the ECHR and establishing common European EDC standards in the field of citizenship education. As stated in *Demir*:

> Being made up of a set of rules and principles that are accepted by the vast majority of States, the common international or domestic law standards of European States reflect a reality that the Court cannot disregard when it is called upon to clarify the scope of a Convention provision that more conventional means of interpretation have not enabled it to establish with a sufficient degree of certainty.[350]

By the same token, the EDC standards form 'a set of rules and principles that are accepted by the vast majority of States' and make up 'the common international or domestic law standards of European States'. They 'reflect a reality that the Court cannot disregard' in the interpretation of the Convention. In line with the *Demir*, *Tănase* and *Mosley* case law of the ECtHR, and taking into account all the relevant Council of Europe instruments on EDC which form its normative context, the Charter on EDC/HRE establishes a common European standard in the field of citizenship education.[351] In its definition of the EDC concept and principles, the Charter on EDC/HRE marks an important stage in a long-standing educational policy of the Council of Europe and is accepted throughout Europe as an important reference point.[352] Moreover, several bodies of the Council of Europe refer to the Charter on EDC/HRE as a 'standard'.[353] This common European standard on EDC/HRE is part of the Council of Europe *benchmark for*

350 *Demir* (n 328), para 76.

351 Text to n 328.

352 Explanatory memorandum para 1; Kerr, *Implementation of the Council of Europe Charter on Education for Democratic Citizenship and Human Rights Education: Final Report* 1; CoE, *Learning to live together: Council of Europe Report on the state of citizenship and human rights education in Europe*.

353 CoE Committee of Ministers, Council of Europe Strategy for the Rights of the Child (2012-2015) (15 February 2012) CM(2011)171final, p 3 and 8 (aims at an effective implementation of children's rights standards and works on the Charter on EDC/HRE in strategic objective 4); CoE, *Council of Europe Strategy for the Rights of the Child (2012-2015): Implementation report*, p 6 and 8; CoE Committee

human rights, the rule of law and democracy in Europe, which the EU has committed itself to respecting in the Memorandum of Understanding. Eurydice also states that the Council of Europe has set policy *standards* in the field of EDC and includes Council of Europe work in the basis for its reports.[354]

Case law on the Convention right to education (Article 2 Protocol 1 to ECHR) confirms a reading in the light of recommendations of the Committee of Ministers and of other non-binding Council of Europe instruments. At this point of the study, it is sufficient to draw attention to the use of non-binding instruments as a reference for understanding formal sources of law. The consequences of applying these instruments as to the substance will be considered in Parts three and four. In the area of education, the ECtHR regularly refers to non-binding instruments under the heading 'relevant Council of Europe documents' and incorporates them in the reasoning on the merits, for instance with regard to Roma children.[355] In *Horváth* the Court held that positive measures were to be taken to assist

---

of Ministers, Council of Europe Strategy for the Rights of the Child (2016-2021): Children's human rights (3 March 2016) CM(2015)175 final, para 40 and 62 (making the standards work, Charter in priority area 2(3)). See also CoE Secretary General, State of Democracy, Human Rights and the Rule of Law in Europe. Report 2014, p 9.

354 Commission/EACEA/Eurydice, Citizenship Education at School in Europe (2005), 7. In the 2012 report, Eurydice takes CoE studies on EDC as a basis for its work on citizenship education in national curricula, and updates and enriches it: see Commission/EACEA/Eurydice, Citizenship Education in Europe (2012), p 109 fn 95. Further Commission/EACEA/Eurydice, Citizenship Education at School in Europe (2017), 27.

355 Concerning Roma children, see *DH and Others v Czech Republic* no 57325/00 (ECtHR 13 November 2007), paras 54–61, 182, 216 (i.a. PA Recommendation No 1203(1993) on Gypsies in Europe; PA Recommendation No 1557(2002) on the legal situation of Roma in Europe; ECRI General Policy Recommendation No 3 and 7, with reference to definitions and explanatory memorandum); *Oršuš and Others v Croatia* no 15766/03 (ECtHR 16 March 2010), paras 65–76, 79–86, 147 (i.a. citing CoE Recommendation CM/Rec(2009)4 of the Committee of Ministers to member States on the education of Roma and Travellers in Europe (17 June 2009), with appendix; ECRI reports on Croatia; Opinions of Advisory Committee on the Framework Convention for the Protection of National Minorities; and reports of the Commissioner for Human Rights). Also in other education cases (not on Roma), non-binding CoE instruments form part of the reasoning: e.g. *Hasan and Eylem Zengin v Turkey* no 1448/04 (ECtHR 9 October 2007), paras 26–28, 52, 69, 74 (PA Recommendations 1396(1999) and 1720(2005) and ECRI General policy recommendation no 5); *Velyo Velev v Bulgaria* no 16032/07 (ECtHR 27 May 2014), paras 34–35, and para 41 (on CoE

Roma children who had difficulties following the school curriculum. The Court referred in this context to a recommendation of the Committee of Ministers according to which appropriate support structures should be put in place to enable Roma/Gypsy children to benefit from equal opportunities at school, in particular through positive action.[356] Like the EDC norms in the appendix to the Recommendation on the Charter on EDC/HRE, the relevant norms were set out in the appendix to the recommendation and framed in 'should' terms.

The fact that the ECtHR uses soft law instruments is often linked to the *living instrument* doctrine and the *effectiveness* ambitions of the Court. In *Leyla Şahin*, the Court notes that the substance of the right to education may vary from one time or place to another according to economic and social circumstances, and adds that

> it is of crucial importance that the Convention is interpreted and applied in a manner which renders its rights practical and effective, not theoretical and illusory. Moreover, the Convention is a living instrument which must be interpreted in the light of present-day conditions.[357]

The Court referred to recommendations of the Committee of Ministers and of the Parliamentary Assembly on access of minorities to higher education, in which 'the Council of Europe has stressed the key role and importance of higher education in the promotion of human rights and

---

Recommendation R(89)12 of the Committee of Ministers to member states on education in prison (13 October 1989)); *Altınay v Turkey* no 37222/04 (ECtHR 9 July 2013), paras 22, 43–44 (on CoE Recommendation R(98)3 of the Committee of Ministers to member states on access to higher education (17 March 1998), and appendix).

356 *Horváth and Kiss v Hungary* no 11146/11 (ECtHR 29 January 2013), para 104, see also paras 72–75, 114 (i.a. citing CoE Recommendation R(2000)4 of the Committee of Ministers to member States on the education of Roma/Gypsy children in Europe (3 February 2000), with relevant sections of the appendix; Opinion on Hungary of the Advisory Committee on the Framework Convention for the Protection of National Minorities, and Follow-up Report on Hungary (2002–2005) of the CoE Commissioner for Human Rights, and Report on Hungary of ECRI).

357 *Leyla Şahin v Turkey* no 44774/98 (ECtHR 10 November 2005), para 136; *Mihalache v Romania* no 54012/10 (ECtHR 8 July 2019), para 91.

fundamental freedoms and the strengthening of democracy'.[358] The Court reads Article 2 of Protocol 1 'in its context and having regard to the object and purpose of the Convention, a law-making treaty', stating that in a democratic society, the right to education is indispensable to the furtherance of human rights.[359]

Not only recommendations, but also the reports of various Council of Europe and international bodies have been used by the ECtHR to interpret and apply the right to education in specific cases.[360] It is not impossible that, in an appropriate and comparable way, the reports for the 2012 and 2017 review cycles of the implementation of the Charter on EDC/HRE, surveying national practices, may have legal relevance. They may point to standards in the same way as national reports in ECtHR case law have done in other fields.[361]

45 Caution: weight of standards is to be determined by the ECtHR

While recommendations of the Committee of Ministers may have important interpretative value and the ECtHR takes a wide array of non-binding sources of various Council of Europe bodies into account, the use of soft law instruments in the Council of Europe legal order is not straightforward. Doubts have been expressed as to whether it is appropriate that non-

---

358 *Şahin*, para 136, see also paras 66, 68–69 (on CoE Recommendation R(98)3 of the Committee of Ministers to member states on access to higher education (17 March 1998), with referral to preamble, and CoE Parliamentary Assembly Recommendation 1353(1998) on the access of minorities to higher education).

359 *Şahin*, para 137. See also para 141: 'This is not an extensive interpretation forcing new obligations on the Contracting States: it is based on the very terms of the first sentence of Article 2 of Protocol No 1 read in its context and having regard to the object and purpose of the Convention, a law-making treaty' (with reference to *Golder v UK* no 4451/70 (ECtHR 21 February 1975), para 36).

360 E.g. nn 355-356 (cases *DH*, *Oršuš*, and *Horvath*,); *Mansur Yalçin and Others v Turkey* no 21163/11 (ECtHR 16 September 2014), para 33.

361 See nn 330, 343 and 369 (and text); further Glas, 'The European Court of Human Rights' use of non-binding and standard-setting Council of Europe documents', 101, 104 (reports of independent experts, even of one person are taken into account). Reports on EDC: CoE, *Learning to live together: Council of Europe Report on the state of citizenship and human rights education in Europe*, see e.g. 51–52: the Analytical Summary of Replies to the Questionnaire for Governments, part of the 2016 Report on the State of citizenship and Human Rights in Europe, was drawn up in a collaboration of independent experts and academics. The ultimate goal of the report is to strengthen the Charter on EDC/HRE as 'an effective support instrument for the promotion of respect and dialogue through education'.

binding Council of Europe standards become binding indirectly via interpretation, as a result of their incorporation into ECtHR case law (judgments are binding on member states and precedents are created).[362] The answer to this question should start with the recognition that the incorporation of non-binding Council of Europe standards is far from automatic. The judges of the ECtHR do not adopt one single approach in this matter.[363] In ECtHR case law, the existence of recommendations of Council of Europe bodies (such as the Committee of Ministers or the Parliamentary Assembly) does not necessarily lead to corresponding interpretations. In *Velyo Velev*, the ECtHR held that '[w]hile the Court is aware of the recommendations of the Committee of Ministers to the effect that educational facilities should be made available to all prisoners ..., it reiterates that Article 2 of Protocol 1 does not place an obligation on Contracting States to organise educational facilities for prisoners where such facilities are not already in place'.[364] Ultimately it is the ECtHR which decides in the spe-

362 Glas, 'The European Court of Human Rights' use of non-binding and standard-setting Council of Europe documents' 98–99, 120.

363 Compare the open-minded attitude vàv soft law of Judges Pinto de Albuquerque and Tulkens with more reticent views: e.g. Concurring Opinion of Judge Wojtyczek in *National Union of Rail, Maritime and Transport Workers v UK* no 31045/10 (ECtHR 8 April 2014), para 4 (warning for judicial activism); Dissenting Opinion of Judge Keller, joined by Judge Popovic in *Ruiz Rivera v Switzerland* no 8300/06 (ECtHR 18 February 2014), para 17. Drawing judicial inspiration from exogenic soft law can be criticised as eroding the values of democracy and the rule of law. Further : F Tulkens, S Van Drooghenbroeck and F Krenc, 'Le soft law et la Cour européenne des droits de l'homme: questions de légitimité et de méthode' (2012) 23 Revue trimestrielle des droits de l'homme 433, 437, on the methodology of the use of soft law; and below n 401.

364 *Velyo Velev v Bulgaria* no 16032/07 (ECtHR 27 May 2014), para 34. Not following either: *Üner v the Netherlands* no 12629/87 (ECtHR 18 October 2006), paras 35–37, 55–56; *Muršić v Croatia* no 7334/13 (ECtHR 20 October 2016), with critical reaction of Pinto de Albuquerque, para 2 ('the majority assume that they are not bound by the standards set by the Committee of Ministers, the Committee for the Prevention of Torture (the CPT) and the Council for Penological Cooperation (PC-CP) of the European Committee on Crime Problems (CDPC) of the Council of Europe'). According to Glas, 'The European Court of Human Rights' use of non-binding and standard-setting Council of Europe documents', the Court usually follows standards of other CoE organs (p 113, with more examples of exceptions). The autonomy of the Court also appears in the interpretation of certain concepts vàv domestic legislators, see e.g. C Grabenwarter, *European Convention on Human Rights: Commentary* (Beck Hart Nomos 2014) 101, 108, 112.

cific case what weight is to be given to the various sources.[365] *The Court has attached 'considerable importance' or 'great weight' to various recommendations of the Committee of Ministers, while acknowledging that, in se, they have no binding force for the member states,*[366] *for* instance with regard to European prison standards.[367] Hence the question: what is the weight of the Charter on EDC/HRE? In the absence of case law on the Recommendation on the Charter on EDC/HRE, but in line with the ECtHR's reasoning in the cases cited above, situating the Charter in its normative context helps to appraise the weight of the EDC standards. The Charter on EDC/HRE is a standard which deserves to be given 'considerable importance' or 'great weight'. It is based on an impressive body of instruments on EDC emanating from all the Council of Europe bodies and has repeatedly been recalled as an authoritative instrument since its adoption. It is anchored in the core aims and values of the Council of Europe and is informed by a persistent rationale for democratic security. That soft law and hard law are profoundly interwoven,[368] should not only apply to prison standards or the protection of incapable adults (case law cited above) but should be relevant a fortiori for norms concerning the foundations of our society, namely democracy, the rule of law and human rights. In line with the *Leyla Şahin* case law[369] and on a reading based on the context and aims of the provisions, the ECtHR would probably consider the Recommendation on the Charter on EDC/HRE to be relevant to the interpretation of the right to education (Article 2 Protocol 1 to ECHR) and a standard of great weight contributing to rendering ECHR rights 'practical and effective, not theoretical and illusory'.[370] After all, EDC and HRE seek the empowerment of citizens, as appears from their definitions. Importantly, the Recommendation on the

365 *Tănase v Moldova* no 7/08 (ECtHR 24 April 2010), paras 176.

366 See also *Rivière v France* no 33834/03 (ECtHR 11 July 2006), para 72 ('la Recommandation du Comité des Ministres du Conseil de l'Europe relative aux aspects éthiques et organisationnels des soins de santé en milieu pénitentiaire, ... la Cour ... y attache un grand poids, même si elle admet qu'elle n'a pas en soi valeur contraignante à l'égard des Etats membres'); *Gülay Çetin v Turkey* no 44084/10 (ECtHR 5 March 2013), para 130.

367 See cases cited in Pinto de Albuquerque (n 401), para 35. While the ECtHR recognises the value of soft law instruments, it underlines at the same time the conceptually different role of the Court and the bodies drawing up soft law (preventive function, higher protection): see *Muršić v Croatia* no 7334/13 (ECtHR 20 October 2016), para 114.

368 Pinto de Albuquerque (n 401), para 18.

369 Text to nn 357-359.

370 *Şahin*, para 136.

Charter on EDC/HRE is fully in keeping with the Convention's aim of achieving 'effective political democracy' (preamble ECHR).[371] Former ECtHR Vice-President Françoise Tulkens underlines that the preamble's reference to effective political democracy is not rhetorical: 'In interpreting and applying the Convention, the European Court of Human Rights relies heavily on these principles not only as a source of inspiration but also as a basis for its action'.[372] The ECtHR frequently reiterates that democracy is a fundamental feature of the European *ordre public*,[373] and the only political model compatible with the ECHR.[374] While case law of the ECtHR on this aspect will be examined in Part four, the point may already be made that it seems highly unlikely that the Court would ignore EDC/HRE standards. EDC/HRE are basic pre-conditions for genuine democracy and respect of human rights, as recognised and reflected in the innumerable Council of Europe instruments on EDC, and in particular the Recommendation on the Charter on EDC/HRE. The Committee of Ministers, the highest decision-making body of the Council of Europe, and other bodies too, frequently repeat that the core mission of the Council of Europe is to promote human rights, democracy and the rule of law, and that they are firmly convinced that education and training play a central role in furthering this mission.

---

371 Preamble: 'Reaffirming their profound belief in those fundamental freedoms which are the foundation of justice and peace in the world and are best maintained on the one hand by an *effective political democracy* and on the other by a common understanding and observance of the human rights upon which they depend' (emphasis added).

372 F Tulkens, 'Freedom of Religion under the European Convention on Human Rights: A Precious Asset' [2014] Brigham Young University Law Review 509. See also S Marks, 'The European Convention on Human Rights and its Democratic Society' (1996) 66 The British Year Book of International Law 209; P van Dijk and others (eds), *Theory and practice of the European Convention on human rights* (4 edn, Intersentia 2006) 912.

373 *United Communist Party of Turkey and Others v Turkey* no 19392/92 (ECtHR 30 January 1998), para 45; *Karácsony and Others v Hungary* no 42461/13 et al (ECtHR 17 May 2016), para 141; *Selahattin Demirtaş v Turkey* no 14305/17 (ECtHR 20 November 2018), para 227.

374 *United Communist Party of Turkey and Others v Turkey* no 19392/92 (ECtHR 30 January 1998), para 45; *Hirst v UK* no 74025/01 (ECtHR 6 October 2005), para 58.

A possible reason why the ECtHR might not follow the recommendations adopted by Council of Europe bodies is that it disagrees with them.[375] This can hardly be imagined in the case of EDC/HRE, given the reference to the 2002 Recommendation in *Seurot v France* and the consensus in all Council of Europe bodies on the importance of recommending EDC. Another reason for refusing to follow a recommendation might be a disparity between required *minimum* human rights standards and recommended *desirable* standards.[376] Certainly, the desirable standards set out in recommendations do not automatically equate with the minimum standards protected by human rights. In the case of EDC standards, however, establishing a set of human rights in the ECHR as minimum standards (including participation rights, freedom of expression, etc.) but not at the same time providing for adequate education to empower citizens to exercise such rights, may deprive those rights of their essence and effectiveness.

EDC standards can be seen as belonging to internationally recognised general principles. Education for democracy and human rights are not only protected in Council of Europe instruments, but also vigorously defended in UN instruments.[377]

Applying criteria proposed by academic writers (section C) will provide additional arguments for appraising the weight of EDC standards.

Taking the Charter on EDC/HRE into account as a weighty standard when interpreting ECHR provisions, is not only relevant within the Council of Europe legal order. It will have knock-on effects in the national legal orders and in the EU legal order.

B Limitation of member states' margin of appreciation

46 A European consensus generally limits the margin of appreciation of member states

ECtHR case law shows that the existence of a European consensus, based on binding and/or non-binding standards, has consequences for the breadth of the margin of appreciation enjoyed by member states: 'where no consensus exists, the margin of appreciation afforded to States is gener-

375 Glas, 'The European Court of Human Rights' use of non-binding and standard-setting Council of Europe documents' 116 (example: disagreement among CoE bodies on the blanket ban on clothing designed to conceal one's face in public).

376 Ibid, 117.

377 Further text to n 442 ff and Part four § 294 .

ally a wide one'.[378] A contrario, finding a European consensus generally narrows the breadth of the margin of appreciation for member states.

47 A wide European consensus on EDC

The normative context of the Charter on EDC/HRE is evidence that the Charter on EDC/HRE is based on a wide European consensus, more particularly on the need for, the concept and the principles of EDC. The numerous legal instruments cited above adopted by the various Council of Europe actors demonstrate the political will of European leaders to bring about meaningful EDC. The main reason for the success of the EDC/HRE project is the acknowledgment by governments and other decision-makers of the crucial role of education in fostering the civic engagement of European citizens.[379] Over the course of 30 years work, there has been a consensus on the role of education as preparation for democracy, in other words, on the inseparable link between democratic citizenship and human rights on the one hand, and education on the other hand. EU Member States share this consensus on EDC standards. They have been continuous participants in the Council of Europe bodies which have adopted legal instruments on EDC.

The Committee of Ministers is 'the best intermediary of the European consensus': as the ECtHR has stated, it is 'through the Committee of Ministers' that 'the member states of the Council of Europe have agreed

378 *Mosley v UK* no 48009/08 (ECtHR 10 May 2011), para 110. See also *Fretté v France* no 36515/97 (ECtHR 26 February 2002), para 41; *Evans v UK* no 6339/05 (ECtHR 10 April 2004), paras 54, 59, 77; *Lautsi and Others v Italy* no 30814/06 (ECtHR 18 March 2011), para 70; *SH and Others v Austria* no 57813/00 (ECtHR 3 November 2011), para 94; *Siebenhaar v Germany* no 18136/02 (ECtHR 3 February 2011), para 39; *Sindicatul "Păstorul cel Bun" v Romania* no 2330/09 (ECtHR 9 July 2013), para 171. See also Joint Dissenting Opinion of Judges Tulkens, Hirvelä, Lazarova Trajkovska and Tsotsoria in *SH*, para 8: 'The differences in the Court's approach to the determinative value of the European consensus and a somewhat lax approach to the objective indicia used to determine consensus are pushed to their limit here, engendering great legal uncertainty.' Other examples and discussion in *Dialogue between Judges, European Court of Human Rights* (2008), 'The role of consensus in the system of the European Convention on Human Rights', concluding that consensus in the Convention sense is not unanimity, but 'more an expression of the common ground required for the collective approach underlying the Convention system and the interaction between the European and domestic systems'.

379 Olafsdottir, 'Education for Democratic Citizenship and Human Rights: A Project by the Council of Europe' 130; Arbués, 'Civic Education in Europe: Pedagogic Challenge versus Social Reality' 229.

that ...'.[380] The *intergovernmental* consensus, to which several scholars refer in order to argue the importance of Council of Europe recommendations in general,[381] is even more marked in the case of the Recommendation on the Charter on EDC/HRE, which was not only adopted by the Ministers of Foreign Affairs (Committee of Ministers), but corresponds to declarations of the Heads of State and Government (Summits) and of the Ministers of Education or Youth (Standing Conferences). Furthermore, the consensus reaches much deeper than an *intergovernmental* consensus. The Recommendation on the Charter on EDC/HRE is embedded in several recommendations and resolutions of the *Parliamentary Assembly*, thus involving representatives of national parliaments, and other bodies of the Council of Europe. Finally, the Council of Europe has recognised EDC as a complex and multifaceted undertaking for which rule-making should not be left to official institutions alone.[382] The Charter on EDC/HRE is the result of wide consultations with stakeholders and experts, civil society and grassroots organisations.[383] In keeping with its reputation as a norm entrepreneur,[384] the Council of Europe took into account the wealth of information resulting from its interaction with many actors. The Council of Europe works together with international NGOs (INGOs) and has civil-society programmes with national NGOs to increase the active participation of citizens in public life.[385] The consensus on EDC continues to be manifest in the period since the adoption of the Charter. A key conclusion after the second review cycle (2012–2017) of the Charter on EDC/HRE was that the implementation of EDC/HRE had gained importance in Europe, that education is increasingly recognised as an essential response to the challenges that our societies are facing, and that the Charter needs to be

380 *MC v Bulgaria* no 39272/98 (ECtHR 4 December 2003), para 162; Pinto de Albuquerque (n 401), para 40.

381 See § 55 , De Vel and Markert (n 168); Benoît-Rohmer and Klebes, *Council of Europe Law - Towards a pan-European legal area*.

382 Hartley and Huddleston, *School-community-university partnerships for a sustainable democracy: Education for Democratic Citizenship in Europe and the United States of America* 15. An open-ended list of stakeholders in Charter on EDC/HRE, paras 5(b)(d)(i), 10, 15 (b)(d)(e); explanatory memorandum para 40.

383 Conferences, working groups, text drafting sessions and revisions, see text to n 261. A commonly accepted standard, see also Durr, Spajic-Vrkaš and Ferreira Martins, *Strategies of Learning Democratic Citizenship*.

384 Sasse, 'The Council of Europe as a Norm Entrepreneur: The Political Strengths of a Weak International Institution' 175–176.

385 CoE Committee of Ministers Declaration on the Code of Good Practice for Civil Participation in the Decision-Making Process (21 October 2009).

further developed as a common framework for policy dialogue among and within countries.[386] Governments of 40 member states (Ministries of Education, in consultation with diverse partners) and almost 100 civil society organisations from 44 countries (NGOs and youth organisations) responded to the questionnaires on the implementation of the Charter on EDC/HRE.[387]

Admittedly, three EU Member States did not answer (DK, IT, and PL). Yet, sporadic dissonance does not destroy the European consensus, nor its relevance in ECtHR case law. The consensus does not require unanimity in order to carry weight. In *Demir*, the Court found it sufficient 'that the relevant international instruments denote a continuous evolution in the norms and principles applied in international law or in the domestic law of the majority of member [s]tates of the Council of Europe and show, in a precise area, that there is common ground in modern societies'.[388] The Court has referred in several cases to the 'great majority' of the member states.[389] Applied to EDC standards, the fact that some member states have reservations on a certain issue or at a particular time is not a contra-indication for a European consensus.[390] In the search for common ground among the norms on citizenship education in member states, the Charter on EDC/HRE is undoubtedly a widely accepted reference point, as confirmed in 2017: 'Although the charter is a non-binding legal instrument, it

386 CoE, *Learning to live together: Council of Europe Report on the state of citizenship and human rights education in Europe*, 7. See also CoE Proceedings of the Conference on 'Human Rights and Democracy in Action - Looking Ahead: The Impact of the Council of Europe Charter on Education for Democratic Citizenship and Human Rights Education' (Strasbourg, 29-30 November 2012), 12.

387 CoE, Government Replies to the Questionnaire, in 2016 Report on the State of citizenship and Human Rights Education in Europe.

388 See *Demir* (n 328), para 85–86, see also paras 77–78.

389 Pinto de Albuquerque (n 401), para 20: 'As a matter of constitutional principle guiding the Council of Europe, consensus is decoupled from unanimity', see e.g. 'great majority'of member states in *Tyrer* or *Marckx*. See also Discussion article 'The role of consensus in the system of the European Convention on Human Rights', in CoE, Dialogue between Judges, European Court of Human Rights (2008), concluding that consensus in the Convention sense is not unanimity, but 'more an expression of the common ground required for the collective approach underlying the Convention system and the interaction between the European and domestic systems.'.

390 A reservation of Poland has been noted in text to n 260.

provides a unique common European framework of reference and is a focus and catalyst for action in the member states'.[391]

48 Nuancing the 'killer phrase'

In the light of the previous considerations, the phrase 'Your work is incredibly important, but education is subject to national policies', which is perceived as a 'killer phrase' in European citizenship education networks,[392] requires nuancing. Situating the phrase in the wider legal context largely reduces its killer potential.[393] It is correct that education is subject to national policies (see, for instance, the paragraph-4 principle of the Charter on EDC/HRE, as well as Article 165(1) TFEU). However, this does not imply that member states have unlimited freedom in framing their national education policies and can educate their citizens as they wish. Common objectives like EDC and HRE are widely accepted limitations on member states' freedom. By adopting recommendations and numerous other legal instruments on EDC as actors in the Council of Europe, the member states have to a certain extent limited their wide discretion to regulate education. Even if EDC standards include due respect for state constitutional structures and national priorities and needs (the paragraph-4 principle), leaving a corresponding margin of discretion, member states have nevertheless accepted the principle that they should include EDC, as understood in the Charter, in the curricula for formal education at all school levels, that they should review and update EDC to ensure its relevance, and that they should provide adequate EDC for all (paragraphs 5 and 6). Not providing for EDC and HRE would be tantamount to disavowing the weighty European standard they themselves have established as actors in the Council of Europe legal order. Member states enjoy broad autonomy as to *how* they implement EDC standards in their country; yet, *that* they should provide for EDC and HRE is a matter of established consensus. Choosing not to provide for EDC is no longer an option. The margin of appreciation enjoyed by member states based on paragraph 4 of the Charter cannot be interpreted as giving them arbitrary powers to organise education curricula as they like.[394] It is the duty of national authorities in a

---

391 CoE, *Learning to live together: Council of Europe Report on the state of citizenship and human rights education in Europe*, 4.

392 Text to n 83.

393 Further nuances in Part three and four (obligations flowing from EU law and international agreements).

394 Supra text to n 208. See also *Fretté v France* no 36515/97 (ECtHR 26 February 2002), para 41.

democratic society to consider, within the limits of their jurisdiction, the interests of society as a whole.[395] The elementary EDC standards set out in the Charter on EDC/HRE reflect the interests of society as a whole and thus limit the margin of member state appreciation.

As appears from the explanatory memorandum, the intention of the authors of the Charter on EDC/HRE was to respect national differences. The authors acknowledge that education is an area where member states' systems differ widely, and that those differences—constitutional or organisational—must always be respected: '[a]ccordingly, all the policies and practices set out in the Charter are to be applied by individual states with due respect to those constitutional and structural systems'[396], no less, and no more. The authors' intention was not to allow member states to silently opt out of the European consensus on EDC. Even with regard to education, a field traditionally associated with national sovereignty, limits must be respected. Interdependence in Europe and the world is too great for just any type of national education to be acceptable. As an extreme example, national policy cannot be permitted to promote the style of education favoured by the Nazi regime in Germany. When formulating national policies, member states have to respect the ECHR, interpreted by taking the weighty EDC standards into account. They also have to respect the obligations flowing from international agreements at UN level and flowing from the EU Treaties and the Charter of Fundamental Rights, as will be examined further. In addition, they have to honour, in good faith, the commitments they have made based on norms which are not always hard law, but nevertheless have a certain normative intensity.[397] In order to understand this normative intensity, the strengths and weaknesses of the Charter on EDC/HRE will now be analysed.

C Strengths and weaknesses of the Recommendation on the Charter on EDC/HRE

49 Worthy but weak?

Given the challenges in the field of citizenship education, the purpose of Part one is to examine the Charter on EDC/HRE as the first anchor point. In order to deepen the analysis, I will now evaluate the Recommendation

395 Ibid, para 41.
396 Explanatory memorandum para 29.
397 Continuum, see text to n 402.

on the Charter on EDC/HRE as a legal instrument on the basis of criteria put forward by a number of legal scholars.

If one applies the criterion of enforceability in court, the Charter on EDC/HRE is of course weak. That, admittedly, is in keeping with the image of the Council of Europe as a 'worthy' but 'weak' organisation, as analysed by Sasse: a valuable creator of norms but lacking the means for enforcement. In its dual capacity as a developer and enforcer of norms, the Council of Europe succeeds in the first, but has wobbly credibility with regard to the second.[398] According to Lenaerts and Van Nuffel, the Council of Europe 'has not evolved any further than a forum of discussion, providing interesting ideas for European cooperation, but not affording any genuine prospects of realising them'.[399] So is the Charter on EDC/HRE nothing more than an interesting idea?

50 Factors strengthening recommendations

Schermers and Blokker recall that it is not only the existence of a legal obligation and the possibility of sanctions which justifies observance of a rule. In international law, sanctions often prove to be illusory. These authors mention eight factors which strengthen the recommendations of international organisations: constitutional provisions, structure of the organisation, method of enactment, formal acceptance, need for a rule, application by others, moral or legitimising effect, and restatement.[400] To what extent do these factors apply to the Recommendation on the Charter on EDC/HRE?

51 Factors hardening soft law

Pinto de Albuquerque, scholar and ECtHR judge, points to a *dégradé normatif*.[401] Without abandoning the formal theory of sources of law (still pre-

398 Sasse, 'The Council of Europe as a Norm Entrepreneur: The Political Strengths of a Weak International Institution' 172 (exploring the tension between 'weak' and 'worthy').

399 Lenaerts and Van Nuffel, *European Union Law* 6. Further text to n 533.

400 Schermers and Blokker § 1220–1240. The factor of formal acceptance does not apply and is left aside.

401 Pinto de Albuquerque, Partly dissenting opinion in *Muršić v Croatia* no 7334/13 (ECtHR 20 Oct 2016). See also Tulkens, Van Drooghenbroeck and Krenc, 'Le soft law et la Cour européenne des droits de l'homme: questions de légitimité et de méthode' i.a. 469: (tr) 'The *Tanase* ruling is not based on the binary logic of "all" or "nothing", but on a ternary form, a gradualist logic whereby a norm set out in a source which is intrinsically non-binding may nevertheless have some normative value, and whereby, moreover, that normative value—in the sense of

vailing), the influence of soft law has to be acknowledged: 'there is no water-tight, binary distinction between hard law and non-law, since European human rights law evolves by means of a rich panoply of sources that do not necessarily share the classic, formal features of hard international law'.[402] In the continuum from soft law to hard law, this author lists seven factors which may harden a text: prescriptive language or label; linguistic accuracy and content precision; the existence of *travaux préparatoires*,

---

being capable of influencing the interpretation and application of Convention guarantees—may vary in intensity. It is not a question of all or nothing, but of more or less, or, to employ the terms of the *Tanase* ruling itself, of differentiated "weight" within a set of external sources acknowledged to be "worth considering".'.

402 Pinto de Albuquerque (n 401), para 23, also para 2. There is no unique parameter to distinguish hard law from soft law. For deeper analysis of formal theory of sources of law and scholarly writing accepting or criticising soft law in the human rights field, see i.a. fns 2–4, and 40. The rich panoply includes non-ratified treaties; declarations of international organisations, e.g. UDHR; resolutions and recommendations of international organisations, e.g. of the CoE Committee of Ministers or Parliamentary Assembly; General Comments of international organisations, e.g. of UN treaties bodies; Codes of Conduct and Guidelines of international organisations, e.g. of the WHO, etc. (ibid, fn 43). Further para 24–26 on the rule of recognition of a democratic international community. See also Tulkens, Van Drooghenbroeck and Krenc, 'Le soft law et la Cour européenne des droits de l'homme: questions de légitimité et de méthode': that soft law is used by the ECtHR is clear, yet the question is the methodology for determining under which conditions and to what extent measures in the grey zone between law and non-law can be relied on. On soft law in EU law, see European Parliament Resolution of 4 September 2007 on institutional and legal implications of the use of 'soft law' instruments [2008] OJ C187E/75, recitals C and M; L Senden, *Soft Law in European Community Law* (Hart 2004); Hofmann, Rowe and Türk, *Administrative law and policy of the European Union* 566–67 (cp: 'one can distinguish three possible types of effects of a measure (including so-called soft law), direct, indirect and factual'). EU administrative law illustrates how the complexity of institutional practice transcends the dichotomy binding/non-binding. Unilateral administrative rule-making by the European Commission can take the form of recommendations and opinions, guidelines, rules as a form of regulation by information, interpretative communications, notes, notices, and memoranda, indicators, codes of practice, internal directions, and vademecums. They may have legal effects, depending on conditions specified in case law; see ibid, 544–566, and 566–579 for analysis of the legal character of these rules). The use of soft law as a source is debated in international law. See classic (critical of soft law) and other approaches (open to greater or lesser extents) mentioned in Tulkens, Van Drooghenbroeck and Krenc, 'Le soft law et la Cour européenne des droits de l'homme: questions de légitimité et de méthode', 448 ff.

explanatory reports and commentaries; the complexity of the deliberation procedure, including the voting pattern; wide publicity; follow-up mechanisms and an independent third body; and subsequent practice confirming or developing the standards.[403] Soft law not only enriches hard law by fulfilling an interpretative function, it can also be seen independently, containing standards in its own right: 'Where there is no hard law, ... soft law may exercise alone its normative claim, in accordance with the relevant hardening factors that it puts forward'.[404] The greater the number of attendant factors, the greater the normative intensity of the text.[405] At the end of the spectrum, 'hardened soft law is an imperative constraint, the flouting of which constitutes an internationally unlawful act'.[406] What is the place of the Charter on EDC/HRE in the continuum? In addition to its interpretative function, can the Charter on EDC/HRE stand alone as an independent source of normativity?

52 Testing the anchor point

The Charter on EDC/HRE will be tested as an anchor point by looking for the presence of the strengthening or hardening factors suggested as criteria by Schermers and Blokker, and by Pinto de Albuquerque. The criteria have been regrouped to draw attention to the strengths and weaknesses of the Charter on EDC/HRE as a legal instrument. This appraisal will deepen the understanding of this instrument in the Council of Europe legal order and provide additional arguments for considering the Recommendation on the Charter on EDC/HRE to be a European standard of 'great weight' or 'considerable importance'. At the same time, some of its weaknesses are acknowledged.

---

403 Pinto de Albuquerque (n 401), para 28 (the hardening factors relate either to the rule-making procedure or to the rule-application procedure). See also Tulkens, Van Drooghenbroeck and Krenc, 'Le soft law et la Cour européenne des droits de l'homme: questions de légitimité et de méthode': as parameters to distinguish which soft law to use and to what extent, Tulkens analyses 'legitimité' (consensus among the CoE member states) and 'effectivité' (accepted and practiced by member states).

404 Pinto de Albuquerque (ibid), para 33.

405 Para 24.

406 Para 27.

1. Strengths

53 Accordance with constitutional provisions

The first strengthening factor advanced by Schermers and Blokker relates to the constitutional provisions which underlie the powers of the body adopting the recommendation.[407] In this case, the Recommendation on the Charter on EDC/HRE fully conforms to the Statute of the Council of Europe. From a substantive point of view, the Recommendation directly relates to the core mission of the Council of Europe defined in Article 1 and the preamble.[408] From a formal point of view, the Recommendation is a *legal* act in the sense that it was issued by a competent body acting in accordance with its mandate and with respect for the procedural requirements of the Statute,[409] and thus correctly based on the internal rule of recognition.[410]

Bartsch and Jung highlight that recommendations of the Committee of Ministers are 'Council of Europe law', by contrast with European conventions. The latter are drafted within the ambit of the Council of Europe, but legally, they are international agreements signed by the member states as parties, not by the Council of Europe, and they have to be ratified to have a binding effect.[411] Recommendations of the Committee of Ministers, on the other hand, are decisions addressed to the governments of the member states which come into existence through the mere expression of the collective will of the Committee of Ministers *and* are adopted according to

407 Schermers and Blokker § 1221–1222.

408 Text to n 163 ff (Form and Substance).

409 Arts 14–21 Statute; CoE, Rules of Procedure of the Committee of Ministers (5th revised edn 2005); CoE Committee of Ministers, Rules of Procedure for the meetings of the Ministers' Deputies (4th revised edn 2005). See also CoE iGuide, Committee of Ministers: Procedures and working methods (24 September 2018).

410 M Desomer, *Reform of the Legal Instruments of the European Union* (Proefschrift, KUL 2008) 124.

411 Bartsch, 'The Acceptance of Recommendations and Conventions within the Council of Europe' 92–96.

predefined procedures.[412] Both are essential for determining the legal quality of Council of Europe recommendations.[413]

In this sense, the Charter on EDC/HRE thus has *legal* status in the Council of Europe normative system. Unfortunately, the legal status of non-binding standards of the Council of Europe gets lost in some Council of Europe documents which reflect the traditional concept of law, whereby the legal quality of a norm is essentially determined by its binding force. These documents categorise standards of the Council of Europe in terms of 'legal standards' (binding), and other standards (non-binding),[414] which may suggest to readers that they are of minor importance. If 'legal' is narrowly construed as only including what is binding and justiciable in court, the EDC Charter on EDC/HRE is certainly not a legal instrument. Yet, other Council of Europe documents consider both recommendations and conventions as 'legal standards' and cite the Charter on EDC/HRE among them.[415] The equation 'legal—binding' has also been

412 In the present Council of Europe structure, work on EDC falls in the mandate of the Directorate General of Democracy (DGII) '[t]o strengthen the democratic competencies of the citizens and their willingness to engage themselves in the democratic process'). Within this DGII, the 'Directorate of Democratic Citizenship and Participation' is composed of an Education Department and a Youth Department. The Education Department is concerned with the work of the Standing Conference of Ministers of Education, and includes a Steering Committee for Educational Policy and Practice (CDPPE). Art 17 Statute allows the CM to set up steering committees. See for practices and procedures, also Cornu, 'The impact of Council of Europe Standards on the European Union'.

413 Bartsch, 'The Acceptance of Recommendations and Conventions within the Council of Europe' 92. In the same sense: H Jung, 'Die Empfehlungen des Ministerskomitees des Europarates: zugleich ein Beitrag zur europäischen Rechtsquellenlehre' in JR Bröhmer and GR Gerhard (eds), *Internationale Gemeinschaft und Menschenrechte: Festschrift für Georg Ress* (Carl Heymanns Verlag 2005) 522, and Cornu, 'The impact of Council of Europe Standards on the European Union' 116.

414 In various documents or webpages, e.g. CoE Secretary General, State of Democracy, Human Rights and the Rule of Law in Europe. Report 2014, 9, or <www.coe.int/children> (legal standards only include conventions). The Venice Commission categorises standards in hard law and soft law, see CoE European Commission for Democracy through Law (Venice Commission), Rule of law checklist (11-12 March 2016), p 34.

415 E.g. CoE, *Council of Europe Strategy for the Rights of the Child (2012-2015): Implementation report*, 6 and 8.

abandoned by a number of scholars.[416] Variations in the legal effects of instruments (as seen in ECtHR case law above) transcend the black and white distinction between legal and binding versus non-legal and non-binding. Normative realities and governance in a globalised world are more complex than this binary categorisation suggests. In this context, there is no longer any justification for dismissing recommendations of the Council of Europe as insignificant because they are non-binding.[417] By the way, the MOU—in which the EU recognises the Council of Europe as a standard-setting authority—refers to 'standards' in general.[418]

It must be observed that in the EU legal order as well, recommendations are listed among the 'legal acts of the Union' (Article 288 TFEU). They are published in the L-series of the Official Journal and are included in the Directory of European Union legislation (EUR-Lex).[419] Von Bogdandy, Arndt and Bast state that '[a] non-binding operating mode cannot be equated with legal irrelevance'.[420] Indeed, 'non-binding instruments are an integral part of the legal order'.[421] Thus, Council of Europe recommendations are an integral part of the Council of Europe legal order. In a community based on the rule of law, they are of relevance.

---

416 Leaving Kelsen's equation *Recht-Zwang*. Also Jung, 'Die Empfehlungen des Ministerskomitees des Europarates: zugleich ein Beitrag zur europäischen Rechtsquellenlehre' 522–23 ('Kleine variation über das Thema "Geltung", "Authorität" und "Wirkung"'). This is not the place for an examination of legal theory. Further: A von Bogdandy, F Arndt and J Bast, 'Legal instruments in European Union law and their reform: A systematic approach on an empirical basis' (2004) 21 Yearbook of European Law 91, 111; Delmas-Marty, *Ordering Pluralism. A Conceptual Framework for Understanding the Transnational Legal World* 162–165 (on 'orderly cloud' models, i.a. pyramidal models with guaranteed consistency).

417 Jung, 'Die Empfehlungen des Ministerskomitees des Europarates: zugleich ein Beitrag zur europäischen Rechtsquellenlehre' 519, 523.

418 Paras 2, 16, 23, 25; exception in para 24 (standards in conventions, in the context of legal cooperation for their coherence).

419 C-series of Official Journal refers to information and notices. See overview 'Types of documents in EUR-Lex' (website): Sector 3 'Legislation' includes recommendations, opinions, resolutions, declarations, etc.

420 von Bogdandy, Arndt and Bast, 'Legal instruments in European Union law and their reform: A systematic approach on an empirical basis', 93: adopting a nominalist approach, all acts present in the L-series 'can be considered as a legal act and any adopting institution as a law-making institution'; see also 111.

421 Ibid, 112.

54 Structure of the organisation

A second factor strengthening recommendations relates to the structure of the organisation.[422] The adoption of the Recommendation on the Charter on EDC/HRE was not an isolated action by the Committee of Ministers. As is obvious from the normative context in Chapter one, several bodies within the institutional structure of the Council of Europe have been, and still are, actively engaged in the EDC project and in its implications in specific fields.

55 Method of enactment

The voting pattern leading to the adoption of recommendations increases their persuasive force and influences subsequent implementation. States which have supported a particular recommendation will be more inclined to give effect to it.[423] What was the voting pattern for the Recommendation on the Charter on EDC/HRE? Recommendations of the Committee of Ministers to governments of member states (Article 15(b) Statute) belong to the category of 'important matters' and fall under the rule of unanimity (Article 20(a)(i) Statute).[424] However, as an effect of the enlargement of the Council of Europe, the Ministers' Deputies decided in 1994 on the basis of a gentleman's agreement that no delegation would block the adoption of recommendations and accepted that the two-thirds majority rule would suffice.[425] In return, Ministers Deputies may issue reservations about the recommendations, approving the adoption of the text but reserving the right of their government to comply or not (Article 10(2)(c) Rules

422 Schermers and Blokker § 1223.

423 Ibid, § 1224–1230; also Pinto de Albuquerque (n 401), para 28.

424 They 'require the unanimous vote of the representatives casting a vote, and of a majority of the representatives entitled to sit on the Committee' ('Sont prises à l'unanimité des voix exprimées et à la majorité des représentants ayant le droit de siéger au Comité des Ministres les résolutions du Comité relatives aux questions importantes mentionnées ci après: i. les recommandations relevant de l'article 15.b').

425 CoE Ministers' Deputies, *Effects of enlargement of the Council of Europe, Report (4 November 1994) CM/Del/Dec(94)519bis/2.2* (1994); CoE Committee of Ministers Declaration on compliance with commitments accepted by member states of the Council of Europe (10 November 1994); CoE Committee of Ministers, Procedure for implementing the Declaration of 10 November 1994 on compliance with commitments accepted by member states of the Council of Europe (20 April 1995). Earlier CoE Committee of Ministers Statutory Resolution (93)27 on majorities required for decisions of the Committee of Ministers (14 May 1993).

of Procedure for the meetings of the Ministers' Deputies).[426] A quorum of two thirds of the representatives of the members is required.[427] In practice, the recommendations of the Committee of Ministers are adopted by consensus and 'usually cover all or nearly all member [s]tates'.[428] The Committee of Ministers takes care that all agree on the adoption of the recommendations and does not vote.[429] Thus, the adoption of recommendations constitutes 'a joint expression of European governmental opinion on a given subject, which obviously lends them considerable weight, even though they do not have the binding force of conventions.'[430] Admittedly, the opinion expressed is that of the government, without direct parliamentary support for the recommendations in the member states. This will be discussed in the next section.

Jung argues that the possibility of issuing reservations enhances the binding effect of Council of Europe recommendations.[431] Bartsch points out that

> by recording reservations in cases where they cannot fully apply a recommendation, member States implicitly recognize the quasi-legal authority of the instrument; they treat recommendations, although they are legally not bound by them, as if they contained treaty obligations; for strictly speaking, a reservation has no place in the acceptance of a non-binding instrument.[432]

---

426 CoE Committee of Ministers, Rules of Procedure for the meetings of the Ministers' Deputies (4th revised edn 2005).

427 Art 11 CoE, Rules of Procedure of the Committee of Ministers (5th revised edn 2005); Art 7 CoE Committee of Ministers, Rules of Procedure for the meetings of the Ministers' Deputies (4th revised edn 2005).

428 De Vel and Markert (n 168), 346.

429 Benoît-Rohmer and Klebes, *Council of Europe Law - Towards a pan-European legal area* 62–63.

430 De Vel, *The Committee of Ministers of the Council of Europe* 37.

431 Jung, 'Die Empfehlungen des Ministerskomitees des Europarates: zugleich ein Beitrag zur europäischen Rechtsquellenlehre' 524: 'ein Zugewinn an Bindungswirkung', agreeing with Bartsch. Jung gives another example on p 525, illustrating that member states feel as if recommendations are binding and therefore want to use the possibility of making reservations.

432 Bartsch, 'The Acceptance of Recommendations and Conventions within the Council of Europe' 94. See also Schermers and Blokker § 1225 ('By making an official declaration that it does not wish to be affected by a recommendation, a state places itself outside the scope of the recommendation. It thus considers the recommendation as a *res inter alios acta*, as an act between other parties, which is of no concern to it.').

At the adoption of the Recommendation on the Charter on EDC/HRE no reservations were expressed.[433] It follows that all EU Member State governments agreed.[434] As a matter of fact, Mrs. Androulla Vassiliou, the EU Commissioner responsible for Education, Culture, Multilingualism and Youth, wrote that '[i]n 2010, *all the Member States of the European Union adopted* the Council of Europe's Charter on Education for Democratic Citizenship and Human Rights Education'.[435]

56 Complexity of the deliberation procedure

The complexity of the deliberation procedure is a factor which hardens soft law. It helps to guarantee wide acceptance of the norms, which in turn tends to legitimise the normative claims of the text.[436]

Admittedly, recommendations of the Council of Europe can be criticised for lacking democratic legitimacy as they have not been approved by parliament or by the citizens of the member states (referendum), unlike conventions, which need to be ratified in order to be binding for any participating state.[437] Recommendations are decisions of the Committee of

---

433 No mention of reservations of Ministers' Deputies under Article 10(2)(c) of the Rules of Procedure (compare for instance reservations of Ireland in CoE Recommendation R(99)4 of the Committee of Ministers to member states on principles concerning the legal protection of incapable adults (23 February 1999)). Pro memorie, the reservation found for Poland concerned a resolution of the Standing Conference of European Ministers of Education (n 260). In the draft annotated agenda (Ministers' Deputies CM(2010)OJ1-final) for the 120th Session of the Committee of Ministers on 11 May 2010, in view of the important role of education for the promotion of knowledge on the ECHR and the fundamental rights enshrined therein, the Ministers were invited to adopt Recommendation CM/Rec(2010)7 'without debate' (item 2, para 5). However, 'Ministers will be able to speak on items on the agenda during the formal and the informal sessions. It is recalled that national position papers containing detailed statements may be distributed' (ibid, 'General comment'). All EU Member States were present, see text to n 264 (Genesis). The Charter was also adopted as a follow-up to CoE Committee of Ministers, Declaration and Action Plan, High Level Conference on the Future of the European Court of Human Rights (Interlaken, 19 February 2010), adopted unanimously.

434 See also CoE, *Learning to live together: Council of Europe Report on the state of citizenship and human rights education in Europe*, 23 : unanimous adoption.

435 Commission/EACEA/Eurydice, Citizenship Education in Europe (2012) 3, Foreword.

436 Pinto de Albuquerque (n 401), para 28.

437 Sasse, 'The Council of Europe as a Norm Entrepreneur: The Political Strengths of a Weak International Institution' 180, its 'institutional structure insulates the Council of Europe from direct public or democratic scrutiny'.

Ministers, thus adopted by ministers of member state governments and by their deputies, and are not directly based on a democratic parliamentary decision-making process. By way of comparison, recommendations in the EU legal order generally have greater democratic legitimacy, especially when adopted by ordinary legislative procedure, involving not only the Council (governments) but also the European Parliament and national parliaments (Title II TEU, Art 289 TFEU, Protocols Nos 1 and 2 annexed to the Treaties).

However, in particular with regard to the Recommendation on the Charter on EDC/HRE, there are several factors which increase its democratic legitimacy. As its genesis shows, this Recommendation was drafted on the basis of input from many state and non-state actors. The ministers conducting the EDC processes (Ministers of Foreign Affairs, of Education, etc.) are accountable vis-à-vis democratically elected national parliaments. The Parliamentary Assembly of the Council of Europe has at several stages recommended action on EDC and proposed guidelines, although only in consultative role (Article 22 Statute). Grassroots actors and stakeholders, NGOs, and numerous experts were involved in the drafting of the EDC standards during the three phases leading to the adoption of the Charter.[438] Governments continue to work with other stakeholders to implement the Charter on EDC/HRE and strong support comes from NGOs (88 per cent) and youth organisations (78 per cent).[439]

Compared to some European Commission recommendations or administrative rules in the EU legal order, the Recommendation on the Charter on EDC/HRE in the Council of Europe legal order withstands the test of normativity very well: it reflects a wide European consensus, is supported by wide-reaching consultation of stakeholders, and is based on a specific adoption procedure. Certain norms of the European Commission, which do have legal effects, are criticised for lacking a wide platform of support and for not being the result of standardised procedures.[440]

---

438 Text to n 261. Pinto de Albuquerque (n 401), para 25: 'The involvement of States and grass-roots non-State actors in the exercise of law-making powers ... reinforces the democratic nature of the process and the responsiveness of the international public policy-making system towards the European people'.

439 CoE, *Learning to live together: Council of Europe Report on the state of citizenship and human rights education in Europe*, 70.

440 See Hofmann, Rowe and Türk, *Administrative law and policy of the European Union* 544–45.

The Charter on EDC/HRE satisfies the Schermers and Blokker criterion of reflecting 'the generally held view on a given matter'[441], as shown by the normative context of the Charter on EDC/HRE.

57 Widespread acceptance

A particular strength of the Charter on EDC/HRE is its connection with the international right to education (third anchor point of the study) and its embeddedness in UN standards. This is clear from the preambular paragraphs to the Recommendation on the Charter on EDC/HRE.[442] The Charter on EDC/HRE is a regional instrument, congruent with UN action on education for democracy and human rights education, and in line with the compulsory educational aims in the ICESCR and CRC.[443] It is part of a contemporary interpretation of the international right to education, as will appear in Part four.[444] Starting from the right to education recognised in the UDHR and the post-World War rationale on non-totalitarian education, an international consensus developed on the importance of education for democracy and human rights.[445] The UN General Assembly adopted various resolutions on this.[446] Within the Council of Europe legal order, the ECtHR has held that UN General Assembly resolutions, although not legally binding, may provide an indication of the existence of an international consensus.[447] Education for democratic citizenship and human rights education, however they may be termed in national school curricula, have become universally accepted normative realities, goals to be

441 Schermers and Blokker § 1226–1230.

442 Fourth, fifth and eleventh preambular paragraphs; explanatory memorandum para 8.

443 Text to nn 81- 82. Convention Against Discrimination in Education (adopted 14 December 1960, entered into force 22 May 1962) (CADE); International Covenant on Economic, Social and Cultural Rights (adopted 16 December 1966 A/RES/2200 (XXI), entered into force 3 January 1976) 993 UNTS3; Convention on the Rights of the Child (adopted 20 November 1989 UNGA Res 44/25, entered into force 2 September 1990) 15777 UNTS 3. See Case C-540/03 *Parliament v Council* ECLI:EU:C:2006:429, para 37 (the CRC and ICESCR bind each of the Member States).

444 §§ 291 292 294 .

445 Also text to n 170; explanatory memorandum para 31. Further Part four, § 285 ff.

446 § 294 nn 2203-2204.

447 *V v UK* no 24888/94 (ECtHR 16 December 1999), para 73.

pursued, yet not always reached.[448] That the European consensus on EDC and HRE matches an international consensus is illustrated by the links between the Council of Europe and other international actors, and this, in turn, is one of the strengths of the Council of Europe as a norm-entrepreneur.[449] The EDC norms were adopted principally in partnership with the UN, the EU and the Organisation for Security and Co-operation in Europe (OSCE).[450] The Charter review processes are part of the contribution of the Council of Europe to the UN World Programme for Human Rights Education and the 2030 Education Agenda.[451] Council of Europe action on EDC is internationally recognised and supported. The 2016 World Forum on Democracy recommended Council of Europe member states to ensure full implementation of the Charter on EDC/HRE.[452]

---

448 Charter on EDC/HRE, para 5(j); S Bergan, T Gallagher and I Harkavy (eds), *Higher education for democratic innovation* (CoE Higher Education Series No 21, 2016). Comparable elements in concept of US Department of Education, Office of the Under Secretary and Office of Postsecondary Education, Advancing Civic Learning and Engagement in Democracy: A Road Map and Call to Action, Washington DC, 2012, 1: 'By "civic learning and democratic engagement" we mean educational experiences that intentionally prepare students for informed, engaged participation in civic and democratic life by providing opportunities to develop civic knowledge, skills, and dispositions through learning and practice. These include civics and government as subjects unto themselves but also service-learning and other approaches for integrating a civic and democratic dimension into other disciplines, such as science, technology, engineering, and math'. Compared to the European concept of EDC, in the US there is more emphasis on 'civic engagement', see Hartley and Huddleston, *School-community-university partnerships for a sustainable democracy: Education for Democratic Citizenship in Europe and the United States of America*. See also D Feith (ed) *Teaching America: the Case for Civic Education* (Rowman & Littlefield Education 2011).

449 Sasse, 'The Council of Europe as a Norm Entrepreneur: The Political Strengths of a Weak International Institution' 196.

450 Paras 5(j) and 16 Charter on EDC/HRE, para 56 explanatory memorandum; yearly Memoranda CoE-UN activities.

451 CoE, *Learning to live together: Council of Europe Report on the state of citizenship and human rights education in Europe*, 6 (Target 4.7 in Education Agenda).

452 World Forum for Democracy 2016, Democracy & equality: does education matter? (Strasbourg, 7-9 November 2016), 5; Human Rights Education in the School Systems of Europe, Central Asia and North America: A Compendium of Good Practice (CoE, OSCE/ODIHR, UNESCO, OHCHR, 2009): worldwide exemplary practices of human rights education, education for democratic citizenship and education for mutual respect and understanding, i.a. reference to longstanding tradition of CoE work on EDC.

58 Need for a rule

Schermers and Blokker point to the need for a rule as a powerful factor strengthening recommendations of international organisations. A non-binding yet genuinely necessary rule is stronger than a binding rule which is considered obsolete. What is determining is the opinion of the participating governments as to the need.[453] The need for a rule on EDC follows from the core values and aims of the Council of Europe expressed in the Statute (Article 1 and preamble). In the MOU, EDC is part of the shared priorities and focal areas for cooperation. Several Heads of State and Government have underlined the urgent need for common action on EDC to ensure democratic security, first because of the political changes in Europe since 1989 and, more recently, because of the challenges of terrorism and the refugee crisis. In their individual answers to the 2016 questionnaire on the implementation of the Charter on EDC/HRE, a large number of member states said they agreed 'to a great extent' that citizenship and human rights education are a means of addressing violent extremism and radicalisation leading to terrorism, the integration of migrants and refugees, and the deficit in the democratic participation of both vulnerable and non-vulnerable groups in society with the overall aim of building cohesive and equitable societies.[454] The usefulness of international cooperation and of EDC norms at Council of Europe level appears from surveys.[455] Many member states consider the review process of the Charter on EDC/HRE to be a support, e.g. as encouragement and motivation for more action and better quality, as an opportunity to promote good practice, a support tool for dialogue, and as a means of access to expertise from other countries and international institutions.[456] Council of Europe action on EDC is expected

---

453 Schermers and Blokker § 1233–1235, example: food standards of the *Codex Alimentarius* Commission. Pinto de Albuquerque (n 401), para 33: hard law should not be softened, only upgrading of soft law is possible (thus, the lack of a need cannot serve to downgrade hard law).

454 CoE, Government Replies to the Questionnaire, in 2016 Report on the State of citizenship and Human Rights Education in Europe, Q1, less importance to address the consequences of the economic crisis, austerity measures, or social exclusion.

455 CoE, *Learning to live together: Council of Europe Report on the state of citizenship and human rights education in Europe*, 22.

456 CoE, Government Replies to the Questionnaire, in 2016 Report on the State of citizenship and Human Rights Education in Europe, Q 24, many high ratings on various components. See also Foreword of Thorbjørn Jagland, Secretary General of the Council of Europe, to CoE, *Learning to live together: Council of Europe Report on the state of citizenship and human rights education in Europe*: 'edu-

to provide a shared reference framework and common standards, and member states are satisfied that this is the case.[457] A lesser expectation was authoritative encouragement to ensure compliance with commitments. Governments consistently marked a review of the Charter on EDC/HRE as being of high importance for formal education and more than two thirds of civil society organisations considered the Charter on EDC/HRE as useful or very useful (in non-formal educational activities).[458] Furthermore, the Charter on EDC/HRE is valued as the only international legal document which responds to the need to define education for democratic citizenship and human rights education in conjunction with one another.[459]

The fact that the 2010 Charter does not provide the last word on EDC/HRE is not a weakness. The need to respond to new challenges and to incorporate new ideas on effective implementation is inherent in the dynamic nature of citizenship education, a field 'constantly questioned, tested, reviewed and updated',[460] and is good for the health of a genuine democracy. In the meantime, the Charter remains a strong reference point.

59 Legitimising effect

In certain areas, norm-setting can be so complicated that member states prefer to use the standards of an international organisation rather than trying to formulate norms themselves and risking opposition from various parties. Recommendations of an international organisation increasingly tend to legitimise national action.[461] This is true of citizenship education,

---

cation is increasingly recognised as a tool for tackling radicalisation leading to terrorism, for successfully integrating migrants and refugees and for tackling disenchantment with democracy and the rise of populism'.

457 CoE, Government Replies to the Questionnaire, in 2016 Report on the State of citizenship and Human Rights Education in Europe, Q25: of 40 respondents, 30 marked 4 or 5 on a scale 1–5 (1 not useful, 5 very useful). Overview in CoE, *Learning to live together: Council of Europe Report on the state of citizenship and human rights education in Europe*, 75.

458 CoE, Government Replies to the Questionnaire, in 2016 Report on the State of citizenship and Human Rights Education in Europe, Q27; CoE, *Learning to live together: Council of Europe Report on the state of citizenship and human rights education in Europe*, 23, 87, 94.

459 CoE, *Learning to live together: Council of Europe Report on the state of citizenship and human rights education in Europe*, 25.

460 See perspectives in World Forum for Democracy 2016, Democracy & equality: does education matter? (Strasbourg, 7-9 November 2016); CoE, *Learning to live together: Council of Europe Report on the state of citizenship and human rights education in Europe*, 80.

461 Schermers and Blokker § 1236, 1238–39.

which can be quite a sensitive matter in certain domestic contexts. When confronted with critics or inertia in the education sector, some states will base their arguments in favour of changes in the curriculum on Council of Europe EDC recommendations. This happened in Spain, where domestic opposition was countered by referring to the implementation of the 2002 Council of Europe recommendation on EDC, the precursor of the 2010 Recommendation on the Charter on EDC/HRE.[462] In answer to the question about what would be needed to raise the priority of EDC and HRE, 82 per cent of the respondent governments in the 2016 survey identified 'some political pressure from regional and international institutions'.[463] Many civil society organisations use the Charter on EDC/HRE as an advocacy and lobbying tool vis-à-vis national and local authorities.[464]

60 Prescriptive language or label

Pinto de Albuquerque mentions 'the prescriptive language adopted in a text or the label attached to the instrument' as a factor hardening soft law. Admittedly, the provisions of the Recommendation on the Charter on EDC/HRE are framed in 'should' terms.[465]

However, some provisions take a more affirmative tone (paragraph 4 'are to be applied'; paragraph 5(c) 'have a part to play in'). In particular, the label 'Charter' indicates the high degree of normativity which the actors wished to attach to the text, differentiating it from the usual Council of Europe recommendations. The many preambular paragraphs (recalling the core mission of the Council of Europe, firmly convinced, having regard to, etc.) are reminiscent of a convention and reinforce the formal setting of norms in the Charter on EDC/HRE.[466]

---

462 CR Motos, 'The Controversy over Civic Education in Spain' (2010) 9 European Political Science 269, 270–71, on claims of the Catholic Church and other conservative actors that moral education was exclusively reserved for families, not for schools and government via EDC. Motos argues for a liberal democracy in which EDC stimulates critical thinking. In a political theory framework, he points to reasons justifying both content of EDC and competence of democratic government. See also n 2073.

463 CoE, *Learning to live together: Council of Europe Report on the state of citizenship and human rights education in Europe*, 98 (in addition to an improved awareness of relevance of EDC/HRE for meeting current challenges in society, 87%).

464 Ibid, 87, 94 (41%).

465 Text to n 193.

466 Text to n 162.

61 Travaux préparatoires, explanatory reports and commentaries

The normative intensity of a text is further increased by the existence of *travaux préparatoires*, explanatory reports and commentaries, and by giving wide publicity to the text.[467] These hardening factors all apply to the Recommendation on the Charter on EDC/HRE.[468]

The Committee of Ministers recommends wide dissemination of the Charter to the authorities responsible for education and youth, and says member states should cooperate in 'informing all stakeholders, including the public, about the aims and implementation of the Charter'.[469] Since the official languages of the Council of Europe are English and French (Article 12 Statute), the European Commission provided a translation into all the languages of the EU Member States of Recommendation Rec(2002)12 on education for democratic citizenship (precursor).[470] At present, almost all member states have translated the Charter on EDC/HRE into their languages and most states have published it on the website of their Ministries of Education or other relevant bodies.[471] However, the Charter on EDC/HRE only partially satisfies the criterion of wide publicity. It is, for instance, not available in Dutch and not published on the website of the Ministry of Education in the Netherlands.[472] Awareness of the Charter on EDC/HRE among young people, educationalists, and even governments, should be raised.[473] A key recommendation of the 2017

467 Pinto de Albuquerque (n 401), para 28.

468 Explanatory memorandum, and huge number of comments and materials published by the CoE (mentioned after each phase in the normative context, see Genesis).

469 Fifteenth preambular para; Charter para 15(d).

470 Hartley and Huddleston, *School-community-university partnerships for a sustainable democracy: Education for Democratic Citizenship in Europe and the United States of America* 51 (the EU has more financial means than the Council of Europe).

471 CoE, Government Replies to the Questionnaire, in 2016 Report on the State of citizenship and Human Rights Education in Europe, Q8. CoE, *Learning to live together: Council of Europe Report on the state of citizenship and human rights education in Europe*, 51–52, 64: 38 out of 40 made the Charter available in the official national language(s); 83% published it on the website of Ministries of Education or other relevant bodies; only 60% disseminated it by other means; see p 64 about minority languages).

472 See systematic 'No' answer on Q8. In Belgium, it does not exist 'in Flemish'.

473 CoE, *Learning to live together: Council of Europe Report on the state of citizenship and human rights education in Europe*, 23 ('according to the respondents from both governmental and civil society organisations, the charter is not well known in the countries).

Conference is to promote the Charter more widely among the stakeholders.[474]

62 Subsequent practice (positive)

This factor must be treated with caution. Schermers and Blokker note that in certain cases, 'the application by others' can strengthen recommendations.[475] Pinto de Albuquerque states that 'subsequent practice' confirming or developing the standards set out in the text, can reinforce the standard-setting function of the text. Of course, this does not mean that, in general, normativity depends on compliance, which would be putting the cart before the horse.[476]

To the extent that application by others and subsequent practice are strengthening factors, it must be acknowledged that in this respect the findings for the Charter on EDC/HRE are mixed. In 2015, the Secretary General of the Council of Europe stated that only 32 per cent of the member states provide for satisfactory EDC.[477] The 2017 Report on the state of citizenship and human rights education in Europe points to both achievements and gaps. It is positive that many member states provide for citizenship education in accordance with the EDC standards. All the member states (40) which replied to the 2016 questionnaire on the implementation of the Charter reported that concrete measures had been taken to promote citizenship and human rights education in accordance with the objectives and principles of the Charter (in 2012, only two thirds of respondents did). Substantial progress has been made and almost all governments foresee further action to promote it.[478] One of the main findings is that there is a shared working definition of EDC/HRE in 31 countries (78 per cent of the respondents).[479] This is an important strength of the Council of Europe

474 Ibid, 7, 25, 52 (also increased visibility in media, and advocacy by prominent personalities are asked for).

475 Schermers and Blokker § 1237. In the same sense Tulkens, Van Drooghenbroeck and Krenc, 'Le soft law et la Cour européenne des droits de l'homme: questions de légitimité et de méthode' 483–4: 'L'instrument de soft law pèsera d'autant plus sur l'interprétation conventionnelle si la norme qu'il véhicule a d'ores et déjà reçu dans le droit interne des Etats membres une certaine effectivité.'.

476 Pinto de Albuquerque (n 401), para 28, fn 55.

477 CoE Secretary General, State of democracy, human rights and the rule of law: A shared responsibility for democratic security in Europe. Report 2015, table p 87.

478 CoE, *Learning to live together: Council of Europe Report on the state of citizenship and human rights education in Europe*, 51–52, and conclusions p 77, 80.

479 Ibid, 52 (but only 17% of civil society respondents think the definition is shared).

norm on EDC/HRE, underscoring the legitimacy of using the EDC concept as an anchor point for this study.

It is impossible to give a comprehensive overview of the application of the Charter on EDC/HRE by the 47 member states of the Council of Europe, not even of that of the 27 EU Member States. The first difficulty is that the expression 'education for democratic citizenship' (EDC) is translated in many different ways and that its content is given many varied forms in the Member States. The diversity of terminology referring to 'citizenship education' is striking.[480] Citizenship education norms reach into many areas of the curriculum, for instance into history, geography, philosophy, or into topics like human rights, citizenship/civic education, democracy, intercultural education, and many—often optional—courses in social sciences. Most frequently, EDC and HRE are promoted through a cross-curricular approach and are therefore formulated in rather abstract norms.[481] Moreover, an overview would involve the examination of not 27 EU Member State educational systems, but in fact many more, as education policy is not centralised in every Member State. Because education is a regional competence in federal states, various regional versions of citizenship education exist (16 *Länder* in Germany, 3 communities in Belgium, etc.). Several States have also recognised devolved competences for autonomous regions, including for some aspects of education (e.g. Spain).

480 Civic education, social sciences, life skills, state and law, individuals and society, living together, principles of civil society, ... See overview of terminology in Bîrzéa, 'EDC policies in Europe - a synthesis', appendix II; CoE, Government Replies to the Questionnaire, in 2016 Report on the State of citizenship and Human Rights Education in Europe. Certain names are historically charged and therefore avoided (e.g. for some, 'citizenship education' recalls practice in the USSR). See also Becker, 'Politische Bildung in Europa', fns 8 and 11: there are differences even within the same language, e.g. in Austria usually 'politische Bildung', in Germany 'Demokratieerziehung', with translation of the Charter on EDC/HRE as 'Charta des Europarats zur Demokratie- und Menschenrechtsbildung', in Austria as 'Europarats-Charta zur Politischen Bildung und Menschenrechtsbildung'. But see also in Germany, the *Bundeszentrale für politische Bildung*. Political education is not necessarily the same as education for democracy (see, i.a., B Widmaier and B Overwien (eds), *Was heisst heute Kritische Politische Bildung?* (Non-Formale Politische Bildung, Band 2, Wochenschau Verlag 2013)).

481 CoE, *Learning to live together: Council of Europe Report on the state of citizenship and human rights education in Europe*, 67 : a crosscurricular approacht (88% of the respondents), obligatory (78%), whole school approach (73%), optional (45%). See Commission/EACEA/Eurydice, Citizenship Education at School in Europe (2017) and Commission/EACEA/Eurydice, Citizenship Education at School in Europe—Annexes: National Information and Websites (2017).

Further differentiation of citizenship education norms would be necessary to reflect different levels of education (primary or secondary education), different pupil age (grades) and different programmes and educational paths (general, technical, vocational, and numerous options). On top of this, ideological or religious schools may have their own curricula, and school freedom and the autonomy of educational institutions add to the complexity. It is not only the many actors and the autonomy they enjoy which make a comprehensive overview of norms on citizenship education a quite impossible task—it is also a never-ending task because of the frequent changes over time in the educational programmes. The political context plays a part in the formulation of citizenship education aims and changes in government may lead to changing curricula.

However, a few snapshots will provide a flavour of EDC in some EU Member States, with all due reservations.[482] Reports indicate that subsequent practice confirms the standards set out in the Recommendation on the Charter on EDC/HRE.

In several Member States, citizenship education is currently in the process of revision, aligning it with EDC standards.[483] The *Irish* Government reports that the revised Civic Social and Political Education 'incorporates all of the concepts expressed at [Council of Europe] level', an obligatory

482 For legislation supporting and promoting EDC/HRE mentioned by parliaments of five Member States (BE, EE, ES, FI, LT), see appendix II of CoE, Learning to live together: Council of Europe Report on the state of citizenship and human rights education in Europe, 82. See also Commission/EACEA/Eurydice, Citizenship Education at School in Europe (2017), Annex 3.

483 Commission/EACEA/Eurydice, Citizenship Education at School in Europe (2017), 10. See i.a. *Three Country Audit of the lower secondary citizenship and human rights education curriculum: Reflection of the principles of the Charter on Education for Democratic Citizenship and Human Rights Education in the curricula of France, Finland and Ireland* (2013). Also CoE, Government Replies to the Questionnaire, in 2016 Report on the State of citizenship and Human Rights Education in Europe, i.a. in *IE* (revisions to Civic Social and Political Education, which 'incorporates all of the concepts expressed at CoE level'), *NL* ('in 2015, the Dutch government launched an initiative to develop a new national curriculum for primary and secondary education, with EDC/HRE as one of the priorities'); *HU* (revisions mainly occur in lower secondary education); *BE* (n 485). See also Commission/EACEA/Eurydice, Promoting citizenship and the common values of freedom, tolerance and non-discrimination through education: Overview of education policy developments in Europe following the Paris Declaration of 17 March 2015 (2016), references to national measures.

subject at lower secondary level.[484] In *Belgium*, the Flemish Community hosted pilot projects for the Council of Europe RFCDC, in preparation for revision of the learning outcomes in the curricula ('eindtermen').[485] In various Member States, including *Bulgaria*, new curricula have been designed for more consistency with EDC standards.[486] The *Czech Republic* is working, for example, on participation in school governance.[487] In *Spain*, a new Strategic Plan for School Coexistence was drawn up by the Ministry of Education with the collaboration of autonomous communities.[488] The *Hungarian* Ministry of Human Capacities reports that the content of Moral Education is regulated by the National Core Curriculum and the Framework Curricula in line with the Act on Public Education, and that the New Moral and Religious Education subject is in line with EDC/HRE.[489]

In other Member States, the implementation of the Charter is an incentive to build further on EDC and HRE, a tool to deepen or complement certain aspects of existing citizenship education. *Austria* has done extensive

---

484 CoE, Government Replies to the Questionnaire, in 2016 Report on the State of citizenship and Human Rights Education in Europe.

485 *Vlaamse Gemeenschap*: <onderwijs.vlaanderen.be/nl/europees-kader-voor-burgerschap-en-democratische-waarden-in-het-onderwijs-van-reykjavik-tot-athene>; 'eindtermen' are under revision: Decreet 26 januari 2018 houdende wijziging van het decreet basisonderwijs van 25 februari 1997 en de Codex Secundair Onderwijs, wat de onderwijsdoelen betreft (opschrift gewijzigd door de commissie: ... tot wijziging van het decreet basisonderwijs van 25 februari 1997 en de Codex Secundair Onderwijs, wat onderwijsdoelen betreft, en tot wijziging van de decreten Rechtspositie onderwijspersoneel) BS 9 maart 2018, 2018030576; *Communauté française*: Décret relatif à l'organisation d'un cours et d'une éducation à la philosophie et à la citoyenneté (D 22-10-2015, MB 09-12-2015), inserting a number 11° in article 9 of 'décret du 24 juillet 1997 définissant les missions prioritaires de l'enseignement secondaire et organisant les structures propres à les atteindre'.

486 Reported by BG: 'The new curricula have been designed so as to target EDC/HRE to a greater extent'. See Law on Pre-School and School Education (2016); and new standard on civic, intercultural and environmental education to enact under the Educational Law (Q5).

487 CoE, *Learning to live together: Council of Europe Report on the state of citizenship and human rights education in Europe*, 46 (democratic administration of schools). See for PT, Decree-Law no. 139/2012, July 5, and a Reference Document 'Citizenship Education Guidelines'.

488 Ibid, 20, devised by the Ministry of Education, Culture and Sport, also with the Observatory for Racism and Xenophobia, the Institute for Women, and other tertiary-sector organisations.

489 See CoE, Government Replies to the Questionnaire, in 2016 Report on the State of citizenship and Human Rights Education in Europe, Q8 and 13.

work in the citizenship education field in accordance with the competence model.[490] The Workprogramme of the Federal government mentions the establishment of political education as a compulsory module, in order to prepare Austria for the future.[491]

In *France*, 'éducation à la citoyenneté' has roots in the French revolution (1789). The deep concern to educate and to form *le citoyen* according to the new constitution(s), led to the introduction of several education schemes at the end of the 18th century, i.a. by Condorcet and Talleyrand.[492] In the 19th century, education helped to turn 'peasants into Frenchmen'[493] and *l'amour pour la patrie* was (and still is) inculcated in schools.[494] Today, consistency with EDC standards can be seen in various legislative acts. Le *Code*

---

490 The concept of citizenship education is based on the competence model (Krammer, Kompetenz-Strukturmodell Politische Bildung, Wien, 2008). *Lehrpläne* in <www.politik-lernen.at/site/grundlagen/politischebildung>.

491 Work programme of the Austrian Federal Government 2013–2018, 27: Establish Political Education as a compulsory module from the 6th school grade as part of the subject History and Social Studies/Political Education.

492 Condorcet, *Cinq mémoires sur l'instruction publique;* Talleyrand-Périgord, Rapport sur l'Instruction Publique, fait au nom du Comité de Constitution à l'Assemblée Nationale, les 10, 11 et 19 Septembre 1791.

493 E Weber, *Peasants Into Frenchmen: The Modernization of Rural France, 1880–1914* (Stanford UP 1976).

494 About historic aspects of citizenship education in France, see e.g. M Lepelletier, *Plan d'Éducation Nationale, présenté à la Convention par Maximilien Robespierre au nom de la Commission d'Instruction publique, le 29 juillet 1793* (1793); F Buisson, *Dictionnaire de pédagogie et d'instruction primaire* (1911 edn, 1882-1887); G Compayré, *Histoire critique des doctrines de l'éducation en France depuis le seizième siècle* (4th edn, Hachette 1883); J Vaujany, *L'école primaire en France sous la Troisième République: les lois fondamentales, l'école nouvelle, l'évolution de l'école* (Perrin 1912); P Nora, 'Ernest Lavisse: son rôle dans la formation du sentiment national' (1962) 228 Revue Historique 73; A Prost, *Histoire de l'enseignement en France 1800-1967* (2nd edn, Colin 1970); M Gontard, *L'oeuvre scolaire de la Troisième République: l'enseignement primaire en France de 1876 à 1914* (2nd edn, CRDP 1976); J-F Chanet, *L'école républicaine et les petites patries* (Aubier 1996); R Grevet, 'La réforme des études en France au siècle des Lumières' (1997) 297 Revue Historique 85; B Baczko, *Une éducation pour la démocratie: textes et projets de l'époque révolutionnaire* (2nd edn, Droz 2000); R Grevet, *L'avènement de l'école contemporaine en France (1789-1835): laïcisation et confessionnalisation de la culture scolaire* (Presses universitaires du Septentrion 2001); F Audigier, 'L'éducation civique dans l'école française' (2002) 1 Journal of Social Science Education 1; JF Chanet, 'Instruction publique, éducation nationale et liberté d'enseignement en Europe occidentale au XIXe siècle' (2005) 41 Paedagogica Historica 9; A Ferrari, 'The problem of civic cohesion and the role of the state school in France and Italy: historical, religious and secular comparisons' (2006) 35 Journal of Moral

de l'Education states that '[a]u titre de sa mission d'éducation à la citoyenneté, le service public de l'éducation prépare les élèves à vivre en société et à devenir des citoyens responsables et libres, conscients des principes et des règles qui fondent la démocratie'.[495] More detailed programmes set out the curriculum to be followed and the objectives to be achieved.[496]

In Germany, at the prompting of the Allies after World War II, huge efforts were made to counter totalitarian tendencies through re-education. The *Bundeszentrale für politische Bildung* (Federal Agency for Civic Education) was established to educate German citizens about democratic principles.[497] The reunification of East and West Germany was also a spur for citizenship education.[498] 'Democracy calls for political education' was the

Education 533; L Heuschling and J Hummel, 'Le libéralisme du Vormärz : la figure du « professeur politique »' (2006) 24 Revue Française d'Histoire des Idées Politiques 227 (article revealing the context of the time, see also n 58).

495 Code de l'éducation, Art L121–4–1 (crée par la Loi d'orientation et de programmation pour la refondation de l'École de la République n 2013–595 du 8 juillet 2013).

496 Décret relatif au Socle commun de connaissances, de compétences et de culture: Bulletin Officiel n°17 du 23-4-2015; Circulaire n° 2016–092 du 20–6–2016 relative au parcours citoyen de l'élève; Circulaire relative aux orientations générales pour les comités d'éducation à la santé et à la citoyenneté; Arrêté fixant le programme d'enseignement moral et civique à l'école élémentaire et au collège (Arrêté du 12–6–2015, Journal officiel du 21–6–2015): Bulletin officiel spécial n° 6 du 25 juin 2015; Arrêté fixant les programmes d'enseignement moral et civique en classes de seconde générale et technologique, de première et terminale des séries générales (Arrêté du 12–6–2015, Journal officiel du 21–6–2015): Bulletin officiel n°6 du 25 juin 2015. See also overview of Féron, 'Citizenship Education in France'; and Johnson and Morris, 'Critical citizenship education in England and France: a comparative analysis'.

497 Established as Federal Agency for Homeland Services in 1952. See <www.bpb.de/die-bpb/147828/history-of-the-bpb>; <www.bpb.de/die-bpb/138853/our-mission-and-activities>: 'Considering Germany's experience with various forms of dictatorial rule down through its history, the Federal Republic of Germany bears a unique responsibility for firmly anchoring values such as democracy, pluralism and tolerance in people's minds'. Further § 319 .

498 W Sander, 'Theorie der politischen Bildung: Geschichte - didaktische Konzeptionen - aktuelle Tendenzen und Probleme' in W Sander (ed), *Handbuch politische Bildung* (Reihe Politik und Bildung 32, Bundeszentrale für politische Bildung 2005); S Reinhardt, 'The Case of (East-) Germany' (2008) 6 Journal of Social Science Education 67; J Bruen, 'From Dictatorship to Democracy? The Impact of the Collapse of the German Democratic Republic (GDR) on Political Education in its Schools' (2014) 10 Journal of Political Science Education 315.

title of the 1997 *Münchner Manifest*.[499] As a consequence, citizenship education in Germany builds on decades of remarkable work, based on various lines of academic research in social sciences.[500] German *Demokratiebildung* provides good examples of citizenship education norms for schools

---

499 Public statement of the heads of the *Bundeszentrale* and the *Landezentralen für politische Bildung* on 26 May 1997.

500 See, e.g., B Sutor, 'Politische Bildung im Streit um die "intellektuelle Gründung" der Bundesrepublik Deutschland. Die Kontroversen der siebziger und achtziger Jahre' (2002) 52 Aus Politik und Zeitgeschichte: APuZ 17; P Massing, 'Die Infrastruktur der politischen Bildung in der Bundesrepublik Deutschland - Fächer, Institutionen, Verbände, Träger' in W Sander (ed), *Handbuch politische Bildung* (Bundeszentrale für politische Bildung 2005); Sander, 'Theorie der politischen Bildung: Geschichte - didaktische Konzeptionen - aktuelle Tendenzen und Probleme', i.a. on 'Politikdidaktik'; G Weißeno, 'Standards für die politische Bildung' (2005) 55 Aus Politik und Zeitgeschichte: APuZ 32; Walkenhorst, 'Problems of Political Education in a Multi-level Polity: explaining Non-teaching of European Union Issues in German Secondary Schooling'; D Lange and G Himmelmann (eds), *Demokratiebewusstsein: Interdisziplinäre Annäherungen an ein zentrales Thema der Politischen Bildung* (VS Verlag für Sozialwissenschaften 2007); P Massing, 'Politische Bildung in der Grundschule: Uberblick, Kritik, Perspektiven' in D Richter (ed), *Politische Bildung von Anfang an: Demokratie-Lernen in der Grundschule* (Schriftenreihe Band 570, Bundeszentrale für politische Bildung 2007); D Richter (ed) *Politische Bildung von Anfang an. Demokratie-Lernen in der Grundschule* (Schriftenreihe Band 570, Bundeszentrale für politische Bildung 2007); D Lange, 'Citizenship Education in Germany' in VB Georgi (ed), *The Making of Citizens in Europe: New Perspectives on Citizenship Education* (Schriftenreihe Band 666, Bundeszentrale für politische Bildung 2008); G Weisseno (ed) *Politikkompetenz. Was Unterricht zu leisten hat* (Schriftenreihe Band 645, Bundeszentrale für politische Bildung 2008); M-B Vincent, '« La Constitution doit devenir un livre populaire »: Enseigner le patriotisme constitutionnel sous la République de Weimar' (2009) Histoire de l'éducation 71; A Eis, 'Concepts and Perceptions of Democracy and Governance beyond the Nation State: Qualitative Research in Education for European Citizenship' (2010) 9 Journal of Social Science Education 35, W Edelstein, 'Education for Democracy: reasons and strategies' (2011) 46 European Journal of Education 127; B Lösch and A Thimmel (eds), *Kritische politische Bildung: Ein Handbuch* (Reihe Politik und Bildung, Band 54, Wochenschau Verlag 2011); B Blessing, T Grammes and H Schluss, 'Civics Courses in the German Democratic Republic: A Case Study in the History of Curriculum and Educational Research' (2012) 11 Journal of Social Science Education 85; G Weisseno, 'Dimensionen der Politikkompetenz' in G Weiseno and H Buchstein (eds), *Politisch Handeln Modelle, Möglichkeite, Kompetenzen* (Schriftenreihe Band 1191, Bundeszentrale für politische Bildung 2012); K-P Hufer and D Richter (eds), *Politische Bildung als Profession: Verständnisse und Forschungen* (Schriftenreihe Band 1355, Bundeszentrale für politische Bildung 2013); Widmaier and Overwien, *Was heisst heute Kritische Politische Bildung?*; W Sander and P Steinbach

and higher education, best practices, and interaction with civil society (NGOs, networks, youth organisations, foundations[501]). Because education is in principle a *Länder* competence,[502] there are a variety of EDC/HRE policies in formal education in Germany. Yet, essential guidance is provided by resolutions of the German Standing Conference of the Ministers of Education and Cultural Affairs.[503] This Standing Conference recommends that education for democracy should be a central task in primary and secondary schools, and sets out content and objectives. The Education Ministers refer to the Council of Europe project on EDC/HRE, the RFCDC, and recommend the use of Council of Europe materials in schools.[504] The Standing Conference furthermore recommends that human rights educa-

---

(eds), *Politische Bildung in Deutschland* (Schriftenreihe Band 1449, Bundeszentrale für politische Bildung 2014); A Petrik (ed) *Formate fachdidaktischer Forschung in der politischen Bildung* (Gesellschaft für Politikdidaktik und politische Jugend- und Erwachsenenbildung, Band 14, Schwalbach/Ts 2015).

501 E.g. Society for Civic Education Didactics and Civic Youth and Adult Education (Gesellschaft für Politikdidaktik und politische Jugend- und Erwachsenenbildung), DARE (n 83), NECE (Networking Citizenship Education in Europe), or HREYN (Human Rights Education Youth Network).

502 Grundgesetz für die Bundesrepublik Deutschland Arts 7, 23(6), 72, 74, 91b; see HD Jarass and B Pieroth, *Grundgesetz für die Bundesrepublik Deutschland: Kommentar* (11th edn, Beck 2011). See also H-U Evers, *Die Befugnis des Staates zur Festlegung von Erziehungszielen in der pluralistischen Gesellschaft* (Duncker und Humblot 1979); I Hochbaum, 'The Federal Structure of Member States as a Limit to Common Educational Policy: The Case of Germany' in B De Witte (ed), *European Community Law of Education* (Nomos 1989); H-P Füssel, 'Cooperative Federalism in Education: About the Work of the Conference Education Ministers and the Joint Federal and Länder Commission on Education Planning and Research Promotion' in J De Groof and others (eds), *Power Sharing in Education: Dilemmas and Implications for Schools* (Acco 1998).

503 Commission/EACEA/Eurydice, Citizenship Education at School in Europe (2017), p 32, on the unique approach in Germany: 'Although subject curricula are defined at the level of each *Land*, several official documents dealing with human rights education, intercultural education, democracy education, media literacy, and historical and political education apply to all *Länder* and therefore make citizenship education a cross-curricular feature of the whole education system'. See also p 144.

504 Beschluss der Kultusministerkonferenz vom 06.03.2009, Stärkung der Demokratieerziehung (Strengthening of democracy education, KMK Resolution of 06.03.2009): 'Demokratie ist stets aufs Neue Gefahren ausgesetzt. Dies zeigt die deutsche Geschichte mit zwei Diktaturen im 20. Jahrhundert. (…) Erziehung für die Demokratie ist eine zentrale Aufgabe für Schule und Jugendbildung. Demokratie und demokratisches Handeln können und müssen gelernt werden' (in der Grundschule und Sekundarstufe, und Augabe aller Fächer).

tion should be one of the primary aims of education, a common task of all subjects and all teachers, and states that 'textbooks must take account of the content of this recommendation'.[505] The *Bundeszentrale für politische Bildung* also gives guidance by 'providing citizenship education and information on political issues to all people in Germany' in conformity with the German constitution, defining citizenship education in general as 'educating and encouraging citizens to actively participate in society and in the democratic process'.[506]

To conclude, the factor 'application by others' is relevant and strengthens the Recommendation on the Charter on EDC/HRE to a large extent.

63 Restatements

One last strength of the Charter on EDC/HRE is related to the factor 'restatement'. Schermers and Blokker explain how restatement of a recommendation of an international organisation in later recommendations strengthens the earlier one.[507] Pinto de Albuquerque notes that the further development of standards set out in a text hardens them.[508] The frequent recalling of the Charter on EDC/HRE in later instruments reinforces its authority.[509] One of the essential developments of the Charter on

---

Confirmed in Beschluss der Kultusministerkonferenz vom 06.03.2009 i. d. F. vom 11.10.2018, 'Demokratie als Ziel, Gegenstand und Praxis—historisch-politischer Bildung und Erziehung in der Schule',13, with reference to the CoE RFCDC.

505 'Schulbücher müssen dem Inhalt dieser Empfehlung Rechnung tragen. Dasselbe gilt für sonstige Lehr- und Lernmittel' para 4 in 'Beschluss der Kultusministerkonferenz vom 04.12.1980 i.d.F. vom 14.12.2000, Empfehlung der Kultusministerkonferenz zur Förderung der Menschenrechtserziehung in der Schule' (Resolution of the Standing Conference of the Ministers of Education and Cultural Affairs of 4 December 1980 in the version of 14 December 2000, Recommendation of the Standing Conference of the Ministers of Education and Cultural Affairs on the promotion of human rights in schools). Continued importance in Beschluss der Kultusministerkonferenz vom 04.12.1980 i.d.F. vom 11.10.2018, 'Menschenrechtsbildung in der Schule'.

506 <www.bpb.de/die-bpb/51236/the-federal-agency-for-civic-education>: 'Being an institution entrusted with providing *the kind of civic education specified in the German constitution …*' (emphasis added). Further § 319 .

507 Schermers and Blokker § 1240.

508 Pinto de Albuquerque (n 401), para 28. To that extent that the factor 'subsequent practice' of Pinto de Albuquerque means that organs of the international organisation confirm or develop the standards set out in the text, the Charter on EDC/HRE satisfies this criterion.

509 See § 36 - 39 .

EDC/HRE is the 2018 Reference Framework on Competences for Democratic Culture (RFCDC).

Thus, several factors strengthen the Recommendation on the Charter on EDC/HRE. However, its weaknesses must also be acknowledged.

2. Weaknesses

64 Linguistic accuracy and content precision

'The more accurate the terminology of a text and the more precise its content, the stronger is the normative claim', according to Pinto de Albuquerque.[510] This factor can probably be nuanced to the extent that some abstract norms have also proven to be powerful sources of law. Several human rights provisions are formulated as rather abstract principles and have little content precision, yet, since they are part of conventions or primary EU law, no one would call their binding, hard law character into question.[511] But it is true that the binding character of conventions usually goes hand in hand with the drafting of precise provisions, while the non-compulsory nature of recommendations allows for more generality.

On the one hand, it must be recognised that the Charter on EDC/HRE does not include precise provisions comparable to the European prison standards, which are considered by Pinto de Albuquerque as the prototype of hardened soft law. European prison standards can be crystal-clear, for instance, when they list the personal details to be recorded for each prisoner on admission.[512] By contrast, some provisions of the Charter on EDC/HRE are quite programmatic, such as paragraph 5, stating which 'objectives and principles should guide member states in the framing of their policies, legislation and practice'. The description of one of the fundamental goals of EDC and HRE as empowering learners with 'the readiness to take action in society in the defence and promotion of human

510 Second hardening factor, para 28. (Abstraction is here made of the 'should' terminology, it concerns another factor).

511 E.g. CFR Art 3(1) or 6(1); or Art 18 TFEU (many precise applications in case law; admittedly, it is easier for negatively formulated abstract rules to be hard law).

512 E.g. CoE Recommendation Rec(2006)2 of the Committee of Ministers to member states on the European Prison Rules (1 January 2006), para 15(1). See Pinto de Albuquerque (n 401), para 2 ('crystal-clear standards'); paras 34–35, citing cases where the ECtHR itself stated the 'considerable importance' or 'great weight' of prison standards.

rights, democracy and the rule of law' (paragraph 5(g)) does not excel as an example of precision.

On the other hand, while leaving an important degree of freedom to member states, EDC standards are, at the same time, sufficiently clear and precise to resolutely indicate to the member states the action they are to take. One clear aim is, for instance, to provide 'every person within their territory' with the opportunity of EDC and HRE (paragraph 5(a)). The content is sufficiently precise to make it clear that that there can be no exclusion or disregard of certain social groups of (young) citizens, such as Roma, or of some categories of school pupils, such as those taking vocational training classes. The various provisions of the Charter on EDC/HRE form one coherent and meaningful set of norms, frequently expanding the principles with more concrete elements (e.g. paras 9, 11, 12, 13). The Charter unambiguously states that member states should 'include [EDC and HRE] in the curricula for formal education at pre-primary, primary and secondary school level as well as in general and vocational education and training' and that member states 'should review and update' them 'in order to ensure their relevance' (paragraph 6). It must be remembered that one of the strengths of the Charter on EDC/HRE is that its drafters had the courage to put forward a well defined concept of EDC and HRE.[513] Admittedly, not all elements of the definition have sufficiently precise content—for instance, the reference to empowering learners 'to value diversity'. Yet, sometimes open-ended formulations are the price to pay for establishing any standards in the delicate area of citizenship education. They provide space for national traditions and expertise, which can render EDC standards more concrete.

From a legal point of view, components of the EDC concept could be criticised as overlapping. Component (c-1) is empowerment 'to exercise and defend democratic rights and responsibilities in society'. In a democratic society all rights are 'democratic rights', in the sense of rights created by democratic institutions and respecting procedures. Strictly speaking, democratic rights (c-1) therefore include the rights relating to valuing diversity (c-2) and participation rights (c-3). However, it seems that the authors of the Charter wanted to provide specific emphasis in a context of interdisciplinary cooperation. I will therefore retain the separate components, as they reflect a specific focus which is useful for the analysis. More-

513 Text to n 174.

over, it is crucial to respect the consensus which the Council of Europe was able to establish in the sensitive field of citizenship education.[514]

The relationship between EDC and HRE as defined in the Charter may also seem blurred. Rights of democratic citizenship arguably include human rights. This is true in most member states. However, in some self proclaimed 'democratic states', human rights are eclipsed by the governmental majority which come to power after elections. The risk is that the political majority of the day will limit freedom of expression and pluralism in society, and impose 'education for democratic citizenship' on its own terms (setting aside or neglecting the constitutional rights of minorities). In these cases, democratic citizenship rights do not include human rights, and EDC deviates from HRE. Both EDC and HRE should therefore be conceptually distinguished, yet necessarily belong together. I recall that in this study, the term EDC always implies HRE as well.[515]

The EDC concept and principles in the Charter on EDC/HRE are sufficiently clear to form the basis for unequivocal normative claims and guide progress towards preparing young citizens for responsible life in a free and democratic society—an ideal which will never be fully reached but must constantly be worked for. In the 2016 survey, civil society organisations state that the Charter on EDC/HRE has become 'the ready-to-use instrument' for fostering EDC and HRE.[516]

For the purposes of this study, the EDC concept and principles are sufficiently precise in terms of their content to serve as an anchor point for examining the citizenship education of EU citizens. Where needed in the analysis, elements from other sources will complement the EDC concept, such as the descriptors of the RFCDC.[517]

---

514 Jung, 'Die Empfehlungen des Ministerskomitees des Europarates: zugleich ein Beitrag zur europäischen Rechtsquellenlehre' 522: the frequent interdisciplinary genesis of recommendations has an impact on their terminology, but this genesis is usually beneficial for the quality of the content.

515 Text to n 184.

516 CoE, *Learning to live together: Council of Europe Report on the state of citizenship and human rights education in Europe*, 89. See CoE, Government Replies to the Questionnaire, in 2016 Report on the State of citizenship and Human Rights Education in Europe, answers to Q9: the Charter is most often considered moderately useful as a tool and resource (e.g. in AT, CZ, DE, EL, ES, FR, GR, HU, SE; while extensively useful in HR, and scarcely useful in BE, EE, IE, and LV). Publicity actions are now given more attention.

517 See CoE Reference Framework of Competences for Democratic Culture, Vol 2: Descriptors of competences for democratic culture (2018) (text to n 310).

65 Follow-up mechanisms and an independent third body

A hardening factor which the Charter on EDC/HRE is lacking is 'the delegation of authority for interpretation and conflict resolution to an independent third body'. An immediately apparent weakness is that the Charter relies on a system of self-evaluation (paragraph 14). During the adoption phase, a huge majority of member states rejected a draft text providing for external supervision.[518] However, the Statute allows the Committee of Ministers to request information from the governments of member states on the action undertaken with regard to recommendations under Article 15(b). This follow-up potential indicates that the Statute assumes that recommendations have legal effects. It is an incentive for implementation.[519] Paragraph 15 of the Charter recommends cooperation in follow-up activities. In order to follow up the Charter's implementation for the second review cycle (2012–2017), the Education Department of the Council of Europe organised a survey for governments and the Youth Department carried out a survey of civil society organisations.[520]

Pinto de Albuquerque mentions that for soft law to harden, non-compliance should not only have a reputational or political cost, but should lead to other negative consequences, such as an obligation of justification.[521] The Charter on EDC/HRE is weak in this respect. Non-compliance with the Charter leads to, at most, a reputational or political cost. As recommended after the first review cycle, government reports for the second review cycle have been made available for public scrutiny. The answers of

518 See text to n 160.

519 On follow-up mechanisms, see CoE Committee of Ministers Declaration on compliance with commitments accepted by member states of the Council of Europe (10 November 1994); CoE Committee of Ministers, Procedure for implementing the Declaration of 10 November 1994 on compliance with commitments accepted by member states of the Council of Europe (20 April 1995); Benoît-Rohmer and Klebes, *Council of Europe Law - Towards a pan-European legal area*.

520 On the procedure and actors, see CoE, *Learning to live together: Council of Europe Report on the state of citizenship and human rights education in Europe*, 57: the CoE Secretariat sent out a questionnaire to the representatives of the Steering Committee for Education Policy and Practice (CDPPE) with a copy to the EDC/HRE coordinators and Permanent Representations of the CoE member states, for completion by governments. The majority of the designated representatives worked in ministries, boards or national agencies dealing with education and youth. Many of them consulted key stakeholders in EDC/HRE.

521 Pinto de Albuquerque (n 401), para 28.

Ministries of Education are published on the Council of Europe website and were openly discussed at the 2017 conference.[522]

66 Subsequent practice (negative)

While it is positive that many member states provide for citizenship education in accordance with the EDC standards, challenges remain. The quality of EDC *de facto* provided in member states varies largely between and within the member states of the Council of Europe.[523] The majority of member states have not yet developed criteria for the evaluation of the effectiveness of EDC/HRE programmes (required in para 11 Charter on EDC/HRE).[524] Member states do not always explicitly refer to education for democratic citizenship and human rights in their education laws, policies, and strategic objectives (compare para 5 Charter on EDC/HRE). In their answers to a Council of Europe questionnaire, a significant number replied 'none' to 'scarcely' with regard to vocational education and training, and higher education.[525] A large majority of the respondent member states reported inconsistencies between policies (which include EDC/HRE

---

522 CoE Proceedings of the Conference on 'Human Rights and Democracy in Action - Looking Ahead: The Impact of the Council of Europe Charter on Education for Democratic Citizenship and Human Rights Education' (Strasbourg, 29-30 November 2012), 14; CoE Conference, Learning to Live Together: a Shared Commitment to Democracy: Conference on the Future of Citizenship and Human Rights Education in Europe (Strasbourg, 20-22 June 2017).

523 CoE Secretary General, State of democracy, human rights and the rule of law—a security imperative for Europe. Report 2016, 97; see also CoE Conference, Learning to Live Together: a Shared Commitment to Democracy: Conference on the Future of Citizenship and Human Rights Education in Europe (Strasbourg, 20-22 June 2017); and CoE, *Learning to live together: Council of Europe Report on the state of citizenship and human rights education in Europe*, 29, Greek Ombudsman for Children's Rights : 'Citizenship and human rights education is still a subject that is either taught theoretically and in fragment or is not included at all in the curriculum of many European schools'. See also Commission/EACEA/Eurydice, Citizenship Education at School in Europe (2017), i.a. p 45 (general guidelines, not specific), p 47 (challenges).

524 CoE, *Learning to live together: Council of Europe Report on the state of citizenship and human rights education in Europe*, 20, 53, 71.

525 CoE, Government Replies to the Questionnaire, in 2016 Report on the State of citizenship and Human Rights Education in Europe (n 520), Q11, also Q 31. CoE, *Learning to live together: Council of Europe Report on the state of citizenship and human rights education in Europe*, figure 7 on p 67, with a major concern that the trend is in decline; see also p 77, on a lack of feedback of national parliaments (about half of the countries), contrasting with the priority they say they accord to EDC/HRE policies.

in the curriculum) and practice (marginalised implementation in schools).[526] For Hungary, for instance, it is reported that there is not enough time for the development of the skills and attitudes needed for EDC/HRE, because the curriculum concentrates heavily on knowledge acquisition.[527] Governments pointed to a lack of support among education professionals, the media and the general public as the main obstacles, while civil society organisations indicated that EDC is not a priority among decision makers.[528] Some governments do not seem to be very aware of what goes on in schools and refer to the educational autonomy of educational institutions.[529] Curriculum overload is a key challenge in several member states, leading to significant inconsistencies between EDC/HRE curricula and teaching practices.[530] If democracy and human rights are to be taken seriously, as founding principles of our society, it is doubtful whether it is sufficient to treat EDC and HRE as residual categories, only entering into consideration if time and energy permit and after all other curricular subjects have been dealt with. Education for employability is a political priority, education for democratic citizenship is not. The 2017 Report concludes that, with a view to the long-term, EDC/HRE must be given greater political and pedagogical priority, potentially making the provision of EDC/HRE mandatory at least in formal education.[531] Admittedly, there is still a long way to go before EDC standards are actually met in every member state and in every school, yet the intention to achieve this is generally there.

Authors have described the Council of Europe as the place where good ideas can become ordinary ideas.[532] It is true that good ideas on EDC have over time become ordinary ideas, and this is an achievement in itself. Unfortunately, too often only lip service is paid to these ideas. Nevertheless, not putting the cart before the horse, as mentioned above, means that

526 Ibid, 16–17, 64: 66% of respondents, examples i.a. in BG, HR, EE, GR, LT, CY.

527 See CoE, Government Replies to the Questionnaire, in 2016 Report on the State of citizenship and Human Rights Education in Europe, Q8 and 13.

528 Ibid, 18, 98.

529 CoE, Government Replies to the Questionnaire, in 2016 Report on the State of citizenship and Human Rights Education in Europe, e.g. NL, SW on Q11.

530 See ibid, i.a. GR; CoE, *Learning to live together: Council of Europe Report on the state of citizenship and human rights education in Europe*, 52, 68. Text to n 41.

531 CoE, *Learning to live together: Council of Europe Report on the state of citizenship and human rights education in Europe*, 77.

532 Marcel Hicter, Belgian architect of cultural co-operation in Europe, cited in 50 years of the European Cultural Convention (2004), 7.

occasional disrespect for EDC standards should not detract from their legal status or degree of normativity. In this sense, EDC standards are more than mere 'interesting ideas' from 'a forum of discussion'.[533]

67 Conclusion: strong source

Having tested the Charter on EDC/HRE according to the criteria of Schermers and Blokker and Pinto de Albuquerque, I conclude that the Recommendation on the Charter on EDC/HRE is a strong source. The Recommendation satisfies at least six of the eight factors which, Schermers and Blokker have suggested, strengthen the recommendations of international organisations: constitutional provisions, structure of the organisation, method of enactment, need for a rule, moral or legitimising effect, and restatement. The assessment of 'application by others' produces a mixed result, because of the remaining challenges. In the continuum of the *dégradé normatif*, the Charter on EDC/HRE displays five of the seven hardening factors proposed by Pinto de Albuquerque: prescriptive language or label; existence of *travaux préparatoires*, explanatory reports and commentaries; the complexity of the deliberation procedure, including the voting pattern; wide publicity; and further development of the standards. It is weaker as to linguistic accuracy and content precision, follow-up mechanisms and monitoring by an independent third body. Challenges under the heading of subsequent practice must also be mentioned. On the basis of the five hardening factors, the Charter on EDC/HRE can, in addition to its interpretative function, stand alone as an independent source with a relatively high degree of normativity and 'exercise alone its normative claim'.[534] In spite of its weaknesses, the Charter on EDC/HRE is, as such, an important source for the EU Member States as member states of the Council of Europe, including in the light of the considerations in sections A and B.

Building on this conclusion, a final argument relates to the duty of good faith. Given that the Recommendation on the Charter on EDC/HRE is a Council of Europe standard of great weight and considerable importance, a strong source, it can be expected that member states acting in good faith will take EDC standards into account.

533 Lenaerts and Van Nuffel, *European Union Law*, text to n 399.
534 Applying Pinto de Albuquerque (n 401), para 33.

3. Implications for the duty to act in good faith

68 Good faith and recommendations in general

The duty of good faith has implications for Council of Europe recommendations in general. The principle of good faith is universally recognised.[535] The Statute and the ECHR, which are treaties binding upon the member states, must be performed and interpreted in good faith (Article 26 and 31 Vienna Convention).

De Vel and Markert develop a good faith argument linked to the Statute of the Council of Europe. Article 3 of the Statute states that '[e]very member state of the Council of Europe must accept the principles of the rule of law and of the enjoyment by all persons within its jurisdiction of human rights and fundamental freedoms, and collaborate sincerely and effectively in the realization of the aim of the Council'. As the Statute does not define 'the principles of the rule of law', De Vel and Markert argue that both conventions and recommendations are a privileged means of interpretation, and that even if the detail of recommendations is not binding on governments, their main principles are binding since member states have acceded to the Statute.[536] One might indeed question whether a member state which has approved the text of a recommendation but not adapted its domestic practice to the main principles thereof, is acting in good faith.[537] Even though they are not binding, recommendations do not discharge member states from the obligation of adopting a *bona fide* attitude and acting in line with the recommendation, collaborating sincerely and effectively for the aims of the Council of Europe. (A similar issue of good faith will arise in the EU legal order in the context of the principle of sincere cooperation of Article 4(3) TEU.[538])

With regard to the ECHR, member states' compliance with the duty to act in good faith has been examined in ECtHR case law in various contexts, for instance when determining whether member states' limitations on freedom of expression are 'necessary in a democratic society' (Article 10 ECHR). The ECtHR checks as a minimal requirement 'whether the respondent State exercised its discretion reasonably, carefully and in good

---

535 Vienna Convention on the Law of Treaties (adopted 23 May 1969, entered into force 27 January 1980) 1155 UNTS 331, preamble.

536 De Vel and Markert (n 168), 353.

537 De Vel and Markert (n 168), 351.

538 §§ 138 - 139 .

faith'.[539] Member states discretion is thus limited by the duty to act in good faith.

69 Good faith and provision of EDC

The duty of good faith has implications for the Recommendation on the Charter on EDC/HRE in particular. The normative history has shown the close involvement of the Council of Europe member states, including the EU Member States, in the genesis of the Charter on EDC/HRE. Not once, but consistently and at regular intervals, they adopted legal instruments on EDC (recommendations, declarations, resolutions, or plans of action). The normative context and the history of EDC standard-setting are testimony to the involvement of the member states, including all EU Member States, in the adoption of EDC standards. The *Committee of Ministers* took the decisions on EDC (Article 14 Statute). The EU is an observer without a right to vote in this Council of Europe body, but the Ministers of Foreign Affairs of all the EU Member States participated and had a vote (or their representatives did). The *Parliamentary Assembly*, the deliberative body of the Council of Europe with an advisory function, made many recommendations to the Committee of Ministers (Article 22 Statute) with regard to EDC. EU Member States have seats in this Assembly, where they are represented by nationals and members of their Parliaments whom they have elected or appointed (Article 25 Statute).[540] *Council of Europe Summits of Heads of State and Government* adopted declarations calling for action on EDC. The EU Heads of State and Government were among them. While the Council of the EU varies in its composition of ministers or state secretaries depending on the subject under discussion (10 configurations), in the Council of Europe the practice has developed of having standing conferences of specialised ministers. The *Standing Conference of the European Ministers of Education* regularly adopted declarations on EDC and asked the Committee of Ministers to adopt measures.[541] All EU Ministers of Educa-

539 Settled case law, see i.a. *Jersild v Denmark* no 15890/89 (ECtHR 23 September 1994), para 31; *Lindon and Others v France* no 21279/02 et al (ECtHR 22 October 2007), para 45; *Guja v Moldova* no 14277/04 (ECtHR 12 February 2008), para 69; *Navalnyy v Russia* no 29580/12 et al (ECtHR 15 November 2018), para 143. To note, supervision goes beyond that.

540 For number of seats at present, see fn 6 to Art 26 Statute.

541 The first was CoE Standing Conference of European Ministers of Education, Resolution on the activities of international organisations in the fields of education and science (No 3) and Resolution on future meetings of the Ministers of Education (No 4) (The Hague, 12-13 November 1959). Overview in <www.coe.int/en/web/education-minister-conference/previous-conferences>.

tion participated in these Conferences. EU Member States were involved in many other ways as well, for example in the *Congress of Local and Regional Authorities*, in the *Conference of International Non-Governmental Organisations (INGOs)* of the Council of Europe, or through the participation of national experts and practitioners in the wide consultations and common action on EDC.[542] This consistent involvement of member states throughout the process of Council of Europe standard-setting for EDC, including in the period after adoption of the Charter, shows an unmistakable commitment to EDC, i.e. to the education-democracy-citizenship-human rights link. This commitment is not only a political one but has legal implications. A combined reading of the Statute and the Recommendation on the Charter on EDC/HRE in the light of the principle of good faith leads to a legitimate expectation that member states will take EDC standards into account. The EDC standards of the Charter on EDC/HRE can in this way permeate domestic legal orders of Council of Europe member states via the principle of good faith. In the domestic legal orders, constitutional provisions on democracy and education cannot be interpreted and applied in good faith without taking EDC standards into account given that their Heads of State, Ministers or other members of government, parliamentary representatives, etc. have participated actively in EDC standard-setting in Council of Europe bodies for more than 30 years, advocating EDC and setting EDC norms in general and specific contexts.[543] Good faith is undermined if member states' national public authorities contest EDC standards, or pay lip service to EDC but neglect to provide it in practice. In a system based on the rule of law and honouring good faith, provisions in national constitutions on democracy, citizenship, human rights and education should be read in conjunction with the Council of Europe Statute and the Charter on EDC/HRE, because it is a European standard of great weight, based on a wide European consensus. In this sense, the margin of discretion of member states in the field of education is

542 Acting in their own capacity. See also members of ECRI, one per member state but independent from their government: Art 2(1) and (3) in CoE Committee of Ministers Resolution Res(2002)8 on the statute of the European Commission against Racism and Intolerance (13 June 2002).

543 In the context of the adoption of treaties, Heads of State or Government, Ministers for Foreign Affairs, heads of diplomatic missions, and representatives accredited by States to an international conference or to an international organisation or one of its organs, may all represent the State for the purpose of expressing the consent of the State (Art 7 Convention on the law of Treaties). For recommendations in the CoE, see i.a. Statute Arts 14, 15.

limited by their duty to act in good faith. This reasoning will be underscored by a reading in conjunction with international agreements such as the ICESCR and the CRC.[544] The human rights-based approach will highlight 'the international nature of human rights values and obligations and the common principles underpinning democracy and the rule of law'.[545]

D Law in context—some caveats

70 Complementary sources as to the substance of citizenship education

The effects of the EDC standards must be understood in the context of research and scholarly work in non-legal fields. Taking the Charter on EDC/HRE as an anchor point does not mean ignoring the contributions of academics, research associations, networks, or organisations operating best practices. These sources do not have the normative authority, legal status and effects of the Charter on EDC/HRE of the Council of Europe. Yet, they corroborate the concept of EDC in its essential components and add clarification and precision, possibly remedying certain weaknesses of the Charter itself. As law does not function in a vacuum, courts may take scientific knowledge into account. In order to evaluate the weight of Council of Europe standards, some ECtHR judges and judgments have placed them 'in the context of the knowledge gathered by social sciences'.[546] Moreover, beyond the possible legal value, the intention of this (too) short section is to honour multidisciplinary approaches to citizenship education and to draw attention to the rich perspectives they offer, informing the legal ones. These perspectives add depth to legal norms and to cardinal legal principles (such as democracy or equality). They may even identify critical pitfalls and stumbling blocks. Awareness of some of the ongoing debates in the citizenship education field in general is important, because —in my experience—the arguments used to contest a possible *EU dimension* in citizenship education, are often the same as those used to contest *citizenship education* itself. Such arguments and reservations are reflected in scholarly work on national citizenship education. The arguments used

544 § 285 ff.

545 Para 5(j) Charter on EDC/HRE. Further § 285 ff.

546 E.g. *Muršić v Croatia* no 7334/13 (ECtHR 20 October 2016), Joint partly dissenting opinion of Judges Sajó, López Guerra and Wojtyczek, para 5. Reference to social sciences in various judgments, i.a. *MC v Bulgaria* no 39272/98 (ECtHR 4 December 2003), para 146.

against the EU dimension in citizenship education may even reach into philosophical debate on *education* as such. Therefore, I will not only briefly discuss research on the assessment of citizenship education, but also some thought-provoking reflections and caveats advanced by non-legal scholars. The debates will not be resolved but are presented here in a nutshell in order to enhance understanding of *citizenship education in general* before tackling the subject of *EU citizenship education* in the following parts of the study.

71 *International Civic and Citizenship Education Study (ICCS)*

A widely recognised assessment of citizenship education is provided by the International Civic and Citizenship Education Study (hereafter ICCS). International research shows that in spite of national differences in the content and provision of citizenship education,[547] common patterns can be found. The International Association for the Evaluation of Educational Achievement (IEA) is an independent, international cooperative of national research institutions and governmental research agencies.[548] It regularly examines how young people are prepared for their roles as citizens. It operates worldwide, with 38 participating countries, including 14 EU Member States.[549] The conceptual underpinning of the 2016 International Civic and Citizenship Education Study (hereafter ICCS 2016) is

547 Ainley, Schulz and Friedman, *ICCS 2009 Encyclopedia: Approaches to civic and citizenship education around the world* 9 ('content and conduct of civic and citizenship education within and across countries varies considerably') and 20 (cross-curricular or as a separate subject, compulsory or not, at each educational level or not).

548 Schulz and others, *IEA International Civic and Citizenship Education Study 2016: Assessment Framework*. Much scholarly work has been done based on IEA or ICCS findings, i.a. Torney-Purta and others, *Citizenship and education in twenty-eight countries: Civic knowledge and engagement at age fourteen*; J Torney-Purta, 'The School's Role in Developing Civic Engagement: A Study of Adolescents in Twenty-Eight Countries' (2002) 6 Applied Developmental Science 203; J Torney-Purta and C Barber, 'Democratic School Engagement and Civic Participation among European Adolescents: Analysis of Data from the IEA Civic Education Study' (2005) 4 Journal of Social Science Education 13; Verhaegen, Hooghe and Meeusen, 'Opportunities to learn about Europe at school. A comparative analysis among European adolescents in 21 European member states'.

549 Participating Member States in the ICCS 2016 were BE-Flanders, BG, DE-North Rhine Westphalia, DK, EE, FI, HR, IT, LT, LV, MT, NL, SE, and SI (from 2 MS only one federal entity), plus Chili, Hong Kong, Mexico, the Russian Federation, etc.

based on broad expertise and scholarly work.[550] The civic and citizenship framework defines 'those aspects of cognitive and affective-behavioral content that should be considered important learning outcomes of civic and citizenship education'.[551] The field of civic and citizenship education includes 'cognitive aspects of learning as well as the development of attitudes towards aspects of civic life and dispositions to participate actively in the life of communities.'[552] One of the important contributions of the IEA was the emphasis on the role of cognitive skills:

> in order to participate effectively as citizens, young people need to possess a knowledge base and the capacity to reason about the institutions, events, actions and processes that exist in their civil and civic communities, as well as to develop and justify views and attitudes towards those things.[553]

To assess the cognitive domains, two categories are distinguished: 'knowing' (remembering or recalling information, and understanding) and 'reasoning and applying' (to new situations). To assess the affective-behavioural domains, 'attitudes' (including value beliefs) are differentiated from 'engagement'. Both the cognitive and affective-behavioural domains are applied to four content domains for 'civics and citizenship'. The first, 'civic society and systems', relates to citizens, including their roles, rights, responsibilities and opportunities for civic engagement, to State institutions and to civil institutions. The second content domain, 'civic principles', refers to the shared ethical foundations of civic societies (equity, freedom, sense of community and rule of law). The third content domain, 'civic participation', relates to decision-making, exercising influence and community participation (active citizenship). The fourth domain 'civic identities', concerns 'the personal sense an individual has of being an agent of civic action with connections to multiple communities', with civic self-image and civic connectedness as sub-domains.

Establishing an internationally accepted, overarching concept of citizenship and citizenship education for the ICCS was not an easy task. The identification of different domains (dimensions) and sub-domains testifies to

550 Schulz and others, *IEA International Civic and Citizenship Education Study 2016: Assessment Framework*, references to scholars from pages 67 to 82.

551 Ibid, 11. Cognitive and affective-behavioral 'domains' are also called 'dimensions'.

552 Ibid, 11.

553 Ibid, 11.

the richness of the concepts, but at the same time reveals their complexity. When comparing and weighing up the use of concepts in different national contexts, experts in the education field discuss and sometimes criticise distinctions with regard to their empirical relevance, validity and reliability.[554] I will not engage in these debates and am not qualified to do so. For the purpose of this study, it is sufficient to recognise the components of the ICCS concepts and note convergences with the Council of Europe concept. The EDC definition, for instance, inasmuch as it refers to 'knowledge, skills and understanding and developing their attitudes and behaviour', includes the cognitive and affective-behavioural domains pointed to in the ICCS concepts. I will use some of the specific ICCS elements mentioned to complement the EDC concept when examining the situation of the EU citizen in the following chapters.

72 *Scholars*

How do the reflections of academic writers relate to the EDC standards in the legal instruments of the Council of Europe? Much scholarly work is consistent with the consensus reflected in the Charter on EDC/HRE and confirms the essential components of the EDC concept. In the themes analysed by scholars, several elements of the EDC and HRE concepts and principles can be recognised, although they are sometimes worded or categorised differently.[555] Key themes include the foundations of citizenship education,[556] tensions between diversity and unity,[557]

---

554 S De Groof and others, *Burgerschap bij 14-jarigen. Vlaanderen in internationaal perspectief. Vlaams eindrapport van de International civic and citizenship education study* (Vlaams Ministerie van Onderwijs en Vorming, 2010) 23, 28.

555 See Commission/EACEA/Eurydice, Citizenship Education at School in Europe (2017), 23 (e.g. scholars about compositions of competences: knowledge, skills, attitudes, values, reflections), 24 (typology of approaches).

556 Discussed below.

557 A Osler and H Starkey, 'Citizenship Education and National Identities in France and England: Inclusive or exclusive?' (2001) 27 Oxford Review of Education 287; A Osler and H Starkey, 'Education for Citizenship: Mainstreaming the Fight against Racism?' (2002) 37 European Journal of Education 143; JA Banks and others, *Democracy and diversity: principles and concepts for educating citizens in a global age* (University of Washington 2005). There is an international consensus on key principles for citizenship education: 'students should learn about the complex relationships between unity and diversity in their local communities, the nation and the world'; 'they should study the ways in which people in their community, nation and region are increasingly interdependent with others around the world'; 'the teaching of human rights should underpin citizenship education in multicultural nation states' and 'students should be taught knowl-

democratic school culture,[558] teacher training,[559] and curriculum development.[560] Citizenship education topics for the classroom also feature,

---

edge about democracy and democratic institutions', thus related in Osler and Starkey, 'Education for democratic citizenship: a review of research, policy and practice 1995–2005', 442. Further: A Osler and H Starkey, *Changing citizenship : democracy and inclusion in education* (A Osler and H Starkey eds, Open University Press and McGraw-Hill Education 2005); JA Banks, 'Diversity, Group Identity, and Citizenship Education in a Global Age' (2008) 37 Educational Researcher 129; JA Banks, 'Educating citizens in diverse societies' (2011) 22 Intercultural Education 243 (challenging assimilationist conceptions of citizenship education, pleading for citizenship education that enables students 'to acquire the knowledge, skills, and commitments needed to become effective civic participants in their communities, nation-state, and the world.').

558 N 571.

559 Osler, 'European Citizenship and Study Abroad: student teachers' experiences and identities'; A Osler and H Starkey, *Teachers and Human Rights Education* (Trentham 2010); P Dusi, M Steinbach and G Messetti, 'Citizenship Education in Multicultural Society: Teachers' Practices' (2012) 69 Procedia - Social and Behavioral Sciences 1410; AJ Castro, 'What Makes a Citizen? Critical and Multicultural Citizenship and Preservice Teachers' Understanding of Citizenship Skills' (2013) 41 Theory & Research in Social Education 219; U Niens, U O'Connor and A Smith, 'Citizenship education in divided societies: teachers' perspectives in Northern Ireland' (2013) 17 Citizenship Studies 128; CL Hahn, 'Teachers' perceptions of education for democratic citizenship in schools with transnational youth: A comparative study in the UK and Denmark' (2015) 10 Research in Comparative and International Education 95.

560 E.g. WC Parker, A Ninomiya and J Cogan, 'Educating World Citizens: Toward Multinational Curriculum Development' (1999) 36 American Educational Research Journal 117; W Parker, 'Diversity, globalization and democratic education: Curriculum possibilities' in JA Banks (ed), *Diversity and citizenship education: Global perspectives* (2004); D Kerr and others, *Vision versus Pragmatism: Citizenship in the Secondary School Curriculum in England. Citizenship Education Longitudinal Study* (5th Annual Report, National Foundation for Educational Research, 2007); A Ross, 'Organizing a Curriculum for Active Citizenship Education' in J Arthur, I Davies and C Hahn (eds), *The SAGE Handbook of Education for Citizenship and Democracy* (Sage 2008); H Starkey, 'Diversity and citizenship in the curriculum' (2008) 6 London Review of Education 5; T McCowan, *Rethinking Citizenship Education: a Curriculum for Participatory Democracy* (Continuum 2009); M Print and D Lange (eds), *Schools, Curriculum and Civic Education for Building Democratic Citizens* (Series Civic and Political Education 2, Sense 2012); Curriculum Development and Review for Democratic Citizenship and Human Rights Education (prepared by Felisa Tibbits for UNESCO/CoE/Office for Democratic Institutions and Human Rights/Organization of American States, 2016).

such as peace, racism, extremism, feminism, sustainable development, or global citizenship.[561]

Many scholars emphasise the need for citizenship education, mirroring the Council of Europe EDC project. In his analysis of the aims of citizenship education throughout history, Wolfgang Sander, the educational scientist, finds three patterns: the aims of *Legitimation*, of *Mission* and of *Mündigkeit* (empowerment). He argues that in a democracy built on the premise of freedom for all citizens, *Mündigkeit* should be the central aim of education for democratic citizenship,[562] which echoes the empowerment of citizens, the central aim of the Charter on EDC/HRE.[563] James Arthur, Ian Davies and Carole Hahn (educationalists) conclude in a comparative perspective that international authors on citizenship education have this concept in common: citizenship education of young people aims to instil the knowledge, skills, attitudes, dispositions and values that will enable them to participate meaningfully in society, in the communities of which they are a part, locally, nationally, and globally (EDC components (b) and (c) appear).[564] Empowerment for participation is a recurring central aim of citizenship education discussed by scholars (EDC component c-3). In 1989, renowned political scientist Robert Dahl described 'enlightened understanding' by citizens as one of the five criteria for democracy. If civic education did not exist, he claimed, it would have to be invented in order to enlighten citizens.[565] Earlier, philosopher John Dewey had already argued for the crucial role of schools for democracy. He stated that the need for

---

561 M Nussbaum, 'Education for Citizenship in an Era of Global Connection' (2002) 21 Studies in Philosophy and Education 289; A Osler and H Starkey, 'Education for Cosmopolitan Citizenship' in VB Georgi (ed), *The Making of Citizens in Europe: New Perspectives on Citizenship Education* (Schriftenreihe Band 666, Bundeszentrale für politische Bildung 2008); N Hodgson, 'Educational research, governmentality and the construction of the cosmopolitan citizen' (2009) 4 Ethics and Education 177; W Sander and A Scheunpflug (eds), *Politische Bildung in der Weltgeschellschaft. Herausforderungen, Positionen, Kontroversen. Perspektiven politischer Bildung* (Schriftenreihe Band 1201, Bundeszentrale für politische Bildung 2011); A Keating, 'Are cosmopolitan dispositions learned at home, at school, or through contact with others? Evidence from young people in Europe' (2016) 19 Journal of Youth Studies 338. On specific themes, see also contributions in Richter, *Politische Bildung von Anfang an. Demokratie-Lernen in der Grundschule* 120–260.

562 Sander, *Handbuch politische Bildung* 13–17.

563 Central in the definitions of EDC and HRE.

564 Arthur, Davies and Hahn, 'Introduction' 5–6, 8–9.

565 RA Dahl, *Democracy and its critics* (Yale University Press 1989) 108–114; RA Dahl, *On democracy* (first edn 1998, Yale University 2000).

formal or intentional teaching and learning increases with the growing complexity of society's structures and resources (it might be observed that this is all the more true today in the EU). An often-cited quotation from John Dewey is 'Democracy has to be born anew every generation, and education is its midwife'.[566] In 1992, Czech writer and former dissident Václav Havel wrote:

> A moral and intellectual state cannot be established through a constitution, or through law, or through directives, but only through complex, long-term, and never-ending work involving education and self-education.[567]

He emphasised that schools 'must ... lead young people to become self-confident, participating citizens', people capable of thinking.[568] In the same vein, Chicago philosopher Martha Nussbaum writes that education is crucial to the health of democracy. Narrowly focusing on education in science and technology, or on internalising information, is dangerous for democracy's future. Rather than concentrating on utilitarian, profit-orientated training, education should focus on human development and should aim at three key abilities: critical thinking (critical examination of oneself and one's traditions), seeing oneself as a member of a heterogeneous nation and world, and 'narrative imagination' (empathy and understanding of others' stories).[569]

73 *Caveats for further reflection on EU citizenship education*

In addition to confirming EDC standards in general, scholarly work includes specific critical reflections which will complement the use of the Charter on EDC/HRE as a substantive source. Here I briefly draw attention to four caveats which must be borne in mind in the analysis which follows. They do not undermine the consensus on the EDC standards of the Charter on EDC/HRE, but they indicate that caution is needed.

---

566 J Dewey, *Democracy and education: an introduction to the philosophy of education* (Macmillan 1916), especially 9.

567 V Havel, *Summer Meditations* (P Wilson tr, Vintage Books 1992) 20.

568 Ibid, 117–118: 'The most basic sphere of concern is schooling. Every else depends on that.'.

569 M Nussbaum, 'Education for Profit, Education for Freedom' (2009) 95 Liberal Education 6; M Nussbaum, 'Education and Democratic Citizenship: Capabilities and Quality Education' (2006) 7 Journal of Human Development 385. For the three abilities applied in legal education, see M Nussbaum, 'Cultivating Humanity in Legal Education' (2003) 70 University of Chicago Law Review 265.

Scholars differ in the weight they attach to certain components of EDC/HRE and debate continues as to ways of proceeding. The Charter on EDC/HRE leaves the member states freedom and space to vary the emphasis.

The *first ongoing discussion* concerns the role of formal education (school education). Some scholars advocate citizenship education outside school in a non-formal or informal setting, for instance in the context of community involvement and volunteering.[570] One argument is that citizenship education should include the exercise of skills such as critical thinking, which can be problematic in an authoritative school climate.[571] The general question as to which institutions should provide citizenship education is a lasting source of conflict.[572] To what extent should the state, schools, civic society organisations, media, religious institutions, or the family, decide how to form the young citizen?[573] The Charter on EDC/HRE clearly expects schools to play a part, provided that they are democratically governed. At the same time, the Charter leaves room for all the other actors (paragraphs 5(i), 6, and 8).[574] This study will focus on schools (formal education), since the aim is to prepare *all* pupils for democratic participation, not only young people who engage in optional extra-curricular courses or occasional activities outside school.[575]

The *second caveat* concerns the role of citizenship education in forming identities. While acknowledging Council of Europe work on EDC/HRE, some scholars point to persisting ambivalence with regard to forms of citizenship education which instil national identities and (unconditional) loyalty to the nation.[576] History provides many examples. The 1965 German 'Gesetz über das einheitliche sozialistische Bildungswesen der DDR' stated:

---

570 Concepts of formal, non-formal and informal education, see n 1041. See also Annex 5 to this study.

571 S Macedo, 'Community, Diversity, and Civic Education: toward a Liberal Political Science of Group Life' [1996] Social Philosophy and Policy Foundation 240, argues for less citizenship education via the school curriculum. See other authors referred to in Osler and Starkey, 'Education for democratic citizenship: a review of research, policy and practice 1995–2005', 445–446.

572 E Callan, 'The Great Sphere: Education against Servility' (1997) 31 Journal of Philosophy of Education 221.

573 See i.a. debates in Spain (n 462): Motos, 'The Controversy over Civic Education in Spain' (role of church and family versus state).

574 N 196.

575 § 152 .

576 Osler, 'European Citizenship and Study Abroad: student teachers' experiences and identities'; J Sprogøe and T Winther-Jensen (eds), *Identity, education and citi-*

> Die Schüler, Lehrlinge und Studenten sind zur Liebe zur Deutschen Demokratischen Republik und zum Stolz auf die Errungenschaften des Sozialismus zu erziehen, um bereit zu sein, alle Kräfte der Gesellschaft zur Verfügung zu stellen, den sozialistischen Staat zu stärken und zu verteidigen.[577]

Today, instilling love for one's country is present in school education in many countries.[578] Martha Nussbaum pleads for patriotic education. She argues that patriotic political emotions are needed to give citizens a sense of duty vis-à-vis others and the common good even where that involves sacrificing self-interest. However, excesses must be prevented, given the unreliability of majority sentiment. Therefore, she continues, citizenship education should aim at critical thinking, and law and institutional structures are essential. One factor in obtaining 'the good out of patriotic education without the bad' is awareness of the constitutional rights of minorities.[579]

---

zenship - multiple interrelations (Comparative studies series 13 Peter Lang 2006); A Ross, 'Multiple Identities and Education for Active Citizenship' (2007) 55 British Journal of Educational Studies 286; S Freire and others, 'Identity Construction through Schooling: listening to students' voices' (2009) 8 EERJ 80; A Ross, *A European Education. Citizenship, identities and young people. European issues in Children's Identity and Citizenship* (Trentham Books, CiCe 2009); J Zajda, H Daun and L L. Saha (eds), *Nation-building, identity and citizenship education* (Springer 2009); A Osler, 'Teacher interpretations of citizenship education: national identity, cosmopolitan ideals, and political realities' (2011) 43 Journal of Curriculum Studies 1; A Ross, 'Controversies and Generational Differences: Young People's Identities in Some European States' (2012) 2 Education Sciences 91. See also work done in the 'Children's Identity and Citizenship in Europe Thematic Network' (CiCe).

577 In para 5(2). See Sander, 'Theorie der politischen Bildung: Geschichte - didaktische Konzeptionen - aktuelle Tendenzen und Probleme' 15. Other examples in 18th century French 'catéchismes', see AEX La Chabeaussière, *Catéchisme français, ou Principes de philosophie, de morale et de politique républicaine, à l'usage des écoles primaires* (L'An IV de la République, Chez Du Pont 1795). At present, softer forms, eg, preamble to Latvian Constitution: 'Loyalty to Latvia, the Latvian language as the only official language, freedom, equality, solidarity, justice, honesty, work ethic and family are the foundations of a cohesive society.'.

578 See i.a. research in Keating, Ortloff and Philippou, 'Citizenship Education Curricula: The Changes and Challenges Presented by Global and European Integration'. On identity and belonging, see i.a. text to n 1188.

579 M Nussbaum, 'Teaching patriotism: love and critical freedom' (2012) 79 University of Chicago Law Review 213, 227: 'So, we turn many things over to institutions and laws. Nonetheless, these institutions and laws will not sustain themselves in the absence of love directed at one's fellow citizens and the nation as a

This gives law additional importance within citizenship education, including in the EU dimension.[580]

The *third caveat* relates to the foundations and presuppositions of citizenship education. An important strand of literature highlights the significance of critical thinking in citizenship education, in line with normative instruments.[581] There is consensus on the necessary non-consensus within citizenship education. But how far does non-consensus go—or the personal autonomy and freedom of (young) citizens to think what they like? A liberal model for citizenship only allows 'thin' citizenship education. No

---

whole ..., it isn't sufficient to create good institutions and then run away and hide. We have to get our hands dirty by entering the feared emotional terrain'. However, '[l]aw and institutional structure are essential props to the good in patriotism'. See, further, M Nussbaum and J Cohen, *For love of country: debating the limits of patriotism* (Beacon 1996); M Nussbaum, 'Political Soul-Making and the Imminent Demise of Liberal Education' (2006) 37 Journal of Social Philosophy 301; M Nussbaum, 'Toward a globally sensitive patriotism' (2008) 137 Daedalus 78; Nussbaum, *Political Emotions: Why Love Matters for Justice*. On the affective dimension, also A Osler and H Starkey, 'Fundamental Issues in Teacher Education for Human Rights: a European perspective' (1994) 23 Journal of Moral Education 349; T Zimenkova, 'Citizenship Through Faith and Feelings: Defining Citizenship in Citizenship Education. An Exemplary Textbook Analysis' (2008) 7 Journal of Social Science Education 81. On the irrational in the crowd, G Le Bon, *The Crowd. A Study of the Popular Mind* (tr 'La psychologie des foules' 1895, Dover 2002).

580 See i.a. §§ 258 259 .

581 For normative instruments, see i.a. n 1064. Numerous scholars emphasise critical thinking: i.a. Dewey, *Democracy and education: an introduction to the philosophy of education*; PJM Costello, 'Education, citizenship and critical thinking' (1995) 107 Early Child Development and Care 105; H Mintrop, 'The Old and New Face of Civic Education: expert, teacher, and student views' (2003) 2 EERJ 446; G Ten Dam and M Volman, 'Critical thinking as a citizenship competence: Teaching strategies' (2004) 14 Learning and Instruction 359; T Grammes, 'Kontroversität' in W Sander (ed), *Handbuch politische Bildung* (Reihe Politik und Bildung 32, Bundeszentrale für politische Bildung 2005); SE Cuypers and I Haji, 'Education for Critical Thinking: Can it be non-indoctrinative?' (2006) 38 Educational Philosophy and Theory 723; SL Lamy, 'Challenging Hegemonic Paradigms and Practices: Critical Thinking and Active Learning Strategies for International Relations' (2007) 40 APSC Political Science Politics 112; DE Hess, *Controversy in the Classroom: The Democratic Power of Discussion* (Routledge 2009); Lösch and Thimmel, *Kritische politische Bildung: Ein Handbuch*; JW Mulnix, 'Thinking Critically about Critical Thinking' (2012) 44 Educational Philosophy and Theory 464; Widmaier and Overwien, *Was heisst heute Kritische Politische Bildung?*; G Biesta, *The Beautiful Risk of Education* (Paradigm 2014); M Davies and R Barnett (eds), *The Palgrave handbook of critical thinking in higher education* (Palgrave Macmillan 2015). Also authors in following notes.

prescriptive blueprint can be imposed by the state, no 'good citizen' mould for a predefined society. Scholars in the liberal tradition criticise the civic republican model, which aims to educate for the common good in the Aristotelian tradition.[582] Ute Frevert, the historian from Yale University, does not flinch from defining the Good European Citizen (GEC): a person of unblemished democratic convictions and attitudes, with both national and European sentiments, actively participating, informed, and with strong views on solidarity. The GEC model serves as a visionary goal and is founded on ethical assumptions.[583] Is Ute Frevert's GEC a reprehensible mould, limiting personal freedom? How can liberal and civic republican views be balanced? The consensus on EDC standards formulated in Council of Europe legal instruments leaves room for both the 'thin or 'thick' interpretations and implementations of citizenship education, in either a more liberal tradition or more civic republican tradition. Balancing the approaches, the following fundamental question for citizenship education emerges: how does one plan for citizenry with civic competences while respecting individual freedom?[584] This question relates to the more general educational paradox exposed by Immanuel Kant: there is a 'tension

582 E.g. P van der Ploeg and L Guérin, 'Questioning Participation and Solidarity as Goals of Citizenship Education' (2016) 28 Critical Review 248. On models of citizenship (liberal, communautarian, civic republican and critical) and implications for citizenship education, see Hoskins and others, *Contextual Analysis Report: Participatory Citizenship in the European Union (Report 1)* 9–17; and M Tarozzi, F Rapanà and L Ghirotto, 'Ambiguities of Citizenship. Reframing the Notion of Citizenship Education' (2013) 8 Ricerche di Pedagogia e Didattica - Journal of Theories and Research in Education 201.

583 U Frevert, 'How to become a Good European Citizen: Present Challenges and Past Experiences' in VB Georgi (ed), *The Making of Citizens in Europe: New Perspectives on Citizenship Education* (Schriftenreihe Band 666, Bundeszentrale für politische Bildung 2008) 41. See also F Galichet, 'La citoyenneté comme pédagogie: réflexions sur l'éducation à la citoyenneté' (2002) 28 Revue des sciences de l'éducation 105, i.a. 113 (liberal versus republican democracy, corresponding to human rights versus citizens' rights; a minimal level of citizenship education centres on education of human rights; the author proposes a higher level of citizenship, promoting mutual interest and mutual responsibility between citizens). Contextual reading: RD Putnam, 'Bowling Alone: America's Declining Social Capital' (1995) 6 Journal of Democracy 65; TH Sander and RD Putnam, 'Still Bowling Alone? The Post-9/11 Split' (2010) 21 Journal of Democracy 9.

584 Callan, 'Citizenship and Education' 81. See also, i.a., Macedo, 'Community, Diversity, and Civic Education: toward a Liberal Political Science of Group Life', 242; Nussbaum, 'Political Soul-Making and the Imminent Demise of Liberal Education'; M Papastephanou, 'Philosophical Presuppositions of Citizen-

between necessary educational influence and unacceptable restriction of the child's individual development and freedom of education in liberal democratic societies'.[585] On the one hand, liberalism demands respect for individual freedom and has thus to tolerate a diversity of views in order to preserve pluralism. In this context, it is easy to see citizenship education as 'despotism over the mind' (and quickly dismiss it as propaganda). Liberalism demands educational restraint. On the other hand, liberal democracy has to reproduce the civic virtues and skills necessary to sustain the liberal democratic society. This calls for citizenship education, planning for citizens with the necessary civic competences, with reasonable constraints on liberal ideas, for instance mitigating the personal views of (young) citizens who seek to propagate limits on democratic rights or on the freedom of minorities.[586] Despotism over the mind can also be prevented by applying the principles of the 'Beutelsbacher consensus'. As a result of debate in a party-political context and polarisation of views on citizenship education, German experts gathering in Beutelsbach (in the 1970s) reached a consensus on essential principles. The *Beutelsbacher Konsens* sets out three basic principles as the foundation of good political education: a prohibition on overwhelming the pupil (*Indoktrinationsverbot*), treating controversial subjects as controversial (*Gebot der Kontroversität*) and giving weight to the personal interests of pupils (*Prinzip der Schülerorientierung*).[587] An interesting framework for guaranteeing 'free citizenship education' is, further-

---

ship Education and Political Liberalism' in J Arthur, I Davies and C Hahn (eds), *The SAGE Handbook of Education for Citizenship and Democracy* (Sage 2008). Further reflections in § 325 .

585 See MH Redish and K Finnertyt, 'What did you Learn in School Today? Free Speech, Values Inculcation, and the Democratic Educational Paradox' (2002-2003) 88 Cornell Law Review 62; B Schaffar, 'Changing the Definition of Education. On Kant's Educational Paradox Between Freedom and Restraint' (2014) 33 Studies in Philosophy and Education 5.

586 E Callan, 'Beyond sentimental civic education' (1994) 102 American Journal of Education 190; E Callan, 'Liberal Legitimacy, Justice, and Civic Education' (2001) 111 Ethics: an international journal of social, political, and legal philosophy 141. See also n 1180 ('Actively promoting the values means challenging opinions or behaviours in school that are contrary to fundamental British values') and n 1257 (Popper).

587 H-G Wehling, 'Der Beutelsbacher Konsens: Entstehung und Wirkung' Landeszentrale für politische Bildung Baden-Württemberg (1977) <www.lpb-bw.de/wiebeutelbacherkonsensentstand.html>. See also Sander, 'Theorie der politischen Bildung: Geschichte - didaktische Konzeptionen - aktuelle Tendenzen und Probleme' 13, 18; Grammes, 'Kontroversität' 126, 128; S Reinhardt, 'The Beutelsbach Consensus' (2016) 15 Journal of Social Science Education 11 (at the

more, proposed by Bernard Crick, the English political theorist. He describes five presuppositions on which free citizenship education, as distinguished from education which indoctrinates, must be based: freedom, toleration, fairness, respect for truth, and respect for reasoning. Only when these five 'procedural values' are respected, can differences in substantive values be discussed and free critical thinking and (endless) debate be possible.[588] Belgian philosopher Patrick Loobuyck argues in the same vein for the need for citizenship education to respect, and aim to realise, the values of freedom, equality and solidarity. These values form an overlapping consensus.[589] It is philosopher John Rawls who describes the 'Overlapping Consensus' as one of the main ideas of political liberalism.[590] However, freedom as a value in itself leads to the fourth caveat. How free is the—democratic—majority of the day to decide on the content of citizenship education?

The *fourth caveat* concerns the dangers of the expression 'education for *democratic* citizenship'. Bernard Crick warns that unduly stressing 'democracy' in citizenship education 'can lead to definitional dogmatics about multiple meanings of the term'. Democracy is necessary, but not sufficient. Observing a risk of citizenship education which only accommodates the majorities, Audrey Osler and Hugh Starkey emphasise the essential role of human rights education.[591] They note within scholarly work 'a growing international consensus on human rights as the underpinning principles of EDC'.[592] As already explained, Martha Nussbaum also adjusts her idea of

---

40th anniversary of the consensus, it still has a big importance). Also citizenship education in Austria applies these Beutelsbacher consensus principles; see <www.politik-lernen.at/site/grundlagen/politischebildung/allgemeines>.

588 B Crick, 'The Presuppositions of Citizenship Education' (1999) 33 Journal of Philosophy of Education 337.

589 P Loobuyck, *Samenleven met gezond verstand* (Polis 2017). On citizenship education, see P Loobuyck, *Meer LEF in het onderwijs: levensbeschouwing, ethiek en filosofie voor iedereen* (Paul Verbraeken Lezing, VUBPress 2014).

590 J Rawls, *Political Liberalism* (2005 edn, Columbia University Press 1993), Part II (IV) on the Overlapping Consensus. Applied to the EU: an overlapping consensus on values in Art 2 TEU, see §§ 170 251 .

591 Osler, 'Human Rights Education: The Foundation of Education for Democratic Citizenship in our Global Age'; Osler and Leung, 'Human rights education, politics and power'; A Osler, 'Bringing Human Rights Back Home: Learning from "Superman" and Addressing Political Issues at School' (2013) 104 The Social Studies 67. Also Osler and Starkey, 'Fundamental Issues in Teacher Education for Human Rights: a European perspective'.

592 Osler and Starkey, 'Education for democratic citizenship: a review of research, policy and practice 1995–2005', 440. See text to nn 186 and 515.

patriotic citizenship education to include the constitutional rights of minorities. Bernard Crick aims at a form of democracy in which citizenship education concerns civic virtues and leads to participation (based on an underlying presupposition of civic republicanism).[593] Citizenship education should not aim to create a merely law abiding citizen, versed in the constitution and respectful of the rule of law, the law made by the majority. Citizenship education should seek to form the *active* citizen. When he introduced citizenship education in the English National Curriculum, he wrote in 1998 this (later frequently recited) paragraph:

> We aim at no less than a change in the political culture of this country both nationally and locally: for people to think of themselves as active citizens, willing, able and equipped to have an influence in public life and with the critical capacities to weigh evidence before speaking and acting; to build on and to extend radically to young people the best in existing traditions of community involvement and public service, and to make them individually confident in finding new forms of involvement and action among themselves.[594]

Bernard Crick emphasises that 'an education that creates a disposition to active citizenship is a necessary condition of free societies'. [595] Later UK governments took other approaches to citizenship education.

These caveats and critical reflections advanced by scholars with regard to citizenship education in general form the background for further reflection on citizenship education of citizens *as* EU citizens.[596]

Section D has shown that taking the Charter on EDC/HRE as an anchor point leaves room for clarifications and caveats from other sources, such as the ICCS and scholarly work.[597] These complementary sources on citizenship education display comparable elements to those of the Charter on

---

593 B Crick, 'Citizenship: the political and the democratic' (2007) 55 British Journal of Educational Studies 235, 243. See also text to n 1176.

594 Advisory Group on Citizenship, *Education for citizenship and the teaching of democracy in schools: the Crick Report*, para 1(5).

595 Crick, 'The Presuppositions of Citizenship Education', 343. See also B Crick, 'Education for Citizenship: the Citizenship Order' (2002) 55 Parliamentary Affairs 488; and G Biesta, *Learning Democracy in School and Society: Education, Lifelong Learning, and the Politics of Citizenship* (Sense 2011), on the promotion of democratic agency.

596 Especially when proposing a learning method (Chapter five).

597 Complementary EU sources, as the 2006 and 2018 Recommendation on key competences for lifelong learning and Eurydice 2017 are integrated in Parts two and three.

EDC/HRE, even if they do not always label, describe or categorise them in the same way. The Charter on EDC/HRE remains particularly attractive for my further analysis—as to the substance—because the consensual EDC standards include respect for the autonomy of member states, yet clearly and concisely set out the aims of citizenship education by isolating different components in the last part of the definition (c-1–2–3 in paragraph 2(a)). The Charter also defines the relationship between EDC and HRE.

Conclusion to Part one

74 The Charter on EDC/HRE is a reliable anchor point

The first challenge when analysing the issue of 'EU citizenship education' was to find a neutral and commonly accepted concept of citizenship education in general. The EDC concept and principles of the Charter on EDC/HRE have responded well to this challenge and proven to be a reliable and neutral anchor point. The legal status of the Charter on EDC/HRE is that of a recommendation of the Committee of Ministers of the Council of Europe. While not legally binding, it has potential legal effects for member states within the Council of Europe legal order. It can fulfil an interpretative function as a common European standard of great weight and is an indication of a wide European consensus which may limit the member states' margin of appreciation in line with ECtHR case law. While the weaknesses of the Charter on EDC/HRE as a formal source have been acknowledged, it also has many strengths. Several factors give it a high degree of normativity. It is legitimate to expect that member states acting in good faith will take EDC standards into account within their domestic legal order. As a substantive source, the Charter is attractive in various ways, and complementary sources have been designated as well.

In this study, 'EDC standards' refer to the elements of the Charter on EDC/HRE which have been described, i.e. the definition of EDC closely interlinked with HRE, its objectives and principles (including respect for member states' responsibilities, constitutions and priorities),[598] as further developed in other instruments of the Council of Europe normative framework.

598 See § 27 .

75 Proposal for recital

Based on the conclusion of Part one, the following phrase is suggested as a recital in the preamble of a hypothetical EU legislative act:

> *Whereas a European consensus exists on the need, the concept and principles of education for democratic citizenship and human rights, as expressed in the Council of Europe Charter on Education for Democratic Citizenship (EDC) and Human Rights Education (HRE).*

This is the first steppingstone in the reasoning of this study. The next step is to apply this common European standard to the situation of EU citizens in EU Member States.

76 For sceptical readers

Readers should not necessarily accept all the arguments I have advanced in Chapter two to develop the reasoning of this study (arguments on legal effects, evaluation of strengths, hardening of soft law, and good faith). As a premise for the analysis which follows, it is sufficient to take note of the legal realities described in the introduction and in Chapter one: provisions of the Treaties, the Statute, and the MOU; provisions of the Charter on EDC/HRE (form and substance), and the many Council of Europe instruments referred to in the normative context. Sceptical readers cannot deny their existence. The Recommendation on the Charter on EDC/HRE is part of the legal order of the Council of Europe, of which all EU Member States are members. The various Council of Europe instruments indicate there are commitments to EDC which it would, at least, be politically embarrassing to neglect.[599] This is certainly true for EU Member States, which claim to be established democracies (as appears from their constitutional provisions), and for the EU, which seeks to advance democracy and human rights in the wider world and aims to set an example in its external action (Articles 3(5) and 21 TEU). Even if one ignores the legal effects of the Charter on EDC/HRE as discussed in Chapter two and just starts from the text as a neutral standard which is widely accepted in Europe, one cannot avoid asking what this commitment to EDC implies for citizens living in Member States and, ipso facto, in the EU. At the very least, looking at the citizens in the EU through the glasses of another international organisation, namely the Council of Europe, is an interesting exercise. Applying the parameters of the EDC concept to the situation of the EU

599 Text to n 320.

citizen allows for an unprejudiced outsider's look. If the EU is eager to defend democracy and human rights worldwide, it should be ready for this confrontation.

PART II Education for Democratic Citizenship and the European Union

Introduction: The schema of modes of reception of exogenic norms

77 *EDC standards meet EU law*

Part two brings together the first and the second anchor point of this study (the concepts of EDC and EU citizenship) from the perspective of EU law. It contains an analysis *as to the form*: what are the legal status and effects of Council of Europe standards on EDC in the EU legal order? Whereas Part one concerned the Council of Europe legal order, Parts two, three and four address the question of citizenship education of EU citizens within the EU legal order.

EU citizenship and the associated rights are set out in the EU Treaties and the Charter of Fundamental Rights of the European Union (hereafter CFR). While the latter is a 'Charter' like the Charter on EDC/HRE, the difference between these legal sources is obvious: the CFR is EU primary law, a binding instrument in the EU legal order with the same legal value as the Treaties (highest-ranked norms); the Charter on EDC/HRE is a non-binding instrument in the Council of Europe legal order. The analysis of the legal status and effects of EU citizenship within the EU legal order is a story which has been told many times. The added value of the study will lie in a combined reading, as to form and substance, of EU law on EU citizenship, democracy and education with Council of Europe standards on EDC. Is this combined reading legitimate from a legal point of view? Part one examined the legal status and potential legal effects of the Charter on EDC/HRE for the EU Member States as member states of the Council of Europe. Part two answers the question of the normative value of Council of Europe standards for the Member States *as* EU Member States. Should the Recommendation on the Charter on EDC/HRE be taken into account in the EU legal order?

Readers with a particular interest in teaching content for EU learning at school could turn immediately to Part three. That Part will analyse the meaning of EDC for EU citizens *as to the substance*, starting with the Treaties which state that every national of an EU Member State is an EU citizen and that EU citizenship is additional to, and does not replace, national citizenship (Articles 9 TEU and 20(1) TFEU).

78 *Council of Europe standards on EDC are exogenic to the EU*
From the viewpoint of the EU, the Charter on EDC/HRE contains norms which are 'exogenic' to the EU since this instrument originates in another normative system.[600] Twins separated at birth, the EU and the Council of Europe have highly different legal orders.[601] None of the legal instruments adopted by the Council of Europe Committee of Ministers, the Parliamentary Assembly, the European Heads of State and Government, or the Ministers of Education, which form the normative context of the Charter on EDC/HRE in Part one, are part of the EU legal order. They do not belong to 'the law' of which the ECJ ensures observance (Article 19 TEU). In *Câmpean*, the referring court asked questions involving the interpretation of recommendations of the Committee of Ministers and resolutions of the Parliamentary Assembly of the Council of Europe. The ECJ declined jurisdiction.[602] This also applies to binding exogenic instruments. It is settled case law that 'the Court has no jurisdiction under Article 267 TFEU to rule on the interpretation of provisions of international law which bind Member States outside the framework of EU law', such as the European Social Charter.[603] The ECHR, a prime example, is not EU law. A fortiori, the Council of Europe Recommendation on the Charter on EDC/HRE does not have this status either, irrespective of its hardened soft law place in *le dégradé normatif* (as argued in Part one). The ECHR is binding for member states which have ratified it as a matter of public international law but is (as such) not binding on EU Member States as a matter of EU law. In *Kamberaj*, an Italian court asked whether it should directly disapply domestic law in the case of conflict with the ECHR, without first asking the Italian Constitutional Court. The ECJ held that the fundamental rights guaranteed by the ECHR constitute general principles of EU law (Article 6(3) TEU), but that 'Article 6(3) TEU does not govern the relationship between the ECHR and the legal orders of the Member States and nor does it lay down the consequences to be drawn by a national court in case of conflict

600 Exogenic norms defined in § 23 .
601 G Quinn, 'The European Union and the Council of Europe on the Issue of Human Rights: Twins Separated at Birth?' (2001) 46 McGill Law Journal 849.
602 Case C-200/14 *Câmpean* ECLI:EU:C:2016:494, para 34, i.a. on CoE Rec 2003(16) of the Committee of Ministers.
603 Case C-117/14 *Nisttahuz Poclava v Ariza Toledano* ECLI:EU:C:2015:60, para 43, concerning ILO Convention No 158 on the Termination of Employment (Geneva, 22 June 1982) and the ESC (Turin, 18 October 1961); Case C-457/09 *Chartry* ECLI:EU:C:2011:101, para 21: 'jurisdiction of the Court is confined to considering provisions of EU law only'.

between the rights guaranteed by that convention and a provision of national law.' Consequently, the national court was not required to directly apply the ECHR provisions, disapplying national law.[604] It is settled case law that the ECHR does not constitute a legal instrument formally incorporated into EU law until the EU has acceded to it.[605] This is not altered by the fact that two primary law provisions attach important effects to the ECHR in the EU legal order: fundamental rights recognised by the ECHR constitute general principles of EU law (Article 6(3) TEU) and the rights in the CFR which correspond to rights guaranteed by the ECHR are to have the same meaning and scope as those laid down by the ECHR (Article 52(3) CFR).[606] These primary law provisions do not convert the ECHR into EU law, but they give the Convention legal effects in the EU legal order. They function as a pathway from one legal order to the other, allowing the reception of exogenic ECHR norms in the EU legal order. This Part will search for similar pathways in EU law permitting the reception of EDC standards of the Council of Europe and giving them legal effects in the EU legal order.

There is no doubt about the starting point for this Part: the EDC standards adopted by the Council of Europe are not EU law. EU law consists of primary law (TEU, TFEU and CFR), international agreements concluded by the EU, secondary law, and ECJ case law. The legal acts of the Union take the form of regulations, directives, decisions, recommendations and opinions, adopted by EU institutions exercising Union competences. In addition to legislative acts (adopted by the legislative procedure), delegated and implementing acts may be adopted (Article 289–291 TFEU). A search for the Charter on EDC/HRE in legal acts in EUR-Lex produces the straightforward answer: 'no results found'.[607] However, that does not mean that EDC standards do not play any role in EU law.

---

604 Case C-571/10 *Kamberaj* ECLI:EU:C:2012:233, paras 59–63.

605 Case C-617/10 REC *Åkerberg Fransson* ECLI:EU:C:2013:280, para 44. See also Case C-523/12 *Dirextra Alta Formazione* ECLI:EU:C:2013:831, para 20; EU Accession to the ECHR *Opinion 2/13* ECLI:EU:C:2014:2454, para 179; Case C-398/13 P *Inuit Tapiriit Kanatami and Others v Commission* ECLI:EU:C:2015:535, para 45; Case C-601/15 PPU *N* ECLI:EU:C:2016:85, para 45.

606 As the ECJ formulates it in the cited paras 'whilst ...'.

607 Search for 'Charter on Education for Democratic Citizenship and Human Rights education' in legal acts on 15 October 2019. However, EUR-Lex found reference to the Charter in two other documents: the European Parliament Resolution of 13 December 2016 on the situation of fundamental rights in the European Union in 2015 (2018/C 238/01); Council Conclusions on the role of

79 *Effects of exogenic norms in the EU legal order: the schema of modes of reception*

The following analysis will explore the ways in which exogenic norms—mainly of the Council of Europe—produce effects in the EU legal order. Based on searches in EUR-Lex and ECJ case law, the reception of exogenic norms in the EU legal order can be categorised in various ways. Advocates General quite regularly mention Council of Europe instruments, parties sometimes invoke Council of Europe instruments in observations submitted to the Court, and national judges occasionally ask preliminary questions on them (overlooking the fact that they are not part of EU law). The Court, however, seems reticent about relying on Council of Europe instruments in the grounds and operative parts of judgments. The effects of recommendations of the Committee of Ministers in ECJ case law have to be searched for with a magnifying glass. Yet, they do exist. The schema of modes of reception of exogenic norms in EU law displays a variety of forms and intensity of legal effect. I will argue that acknowledgment by the EU of Council of Europe standards (a commitment in the Memorandum of Understanding[608]) can occur in six modes of reception: three stronger modes (Chapter three) and three weaker ones (Chapter four). At one end of the spectrum, the EU accedes to Council of Europe conventions (mode 1). At the other end, inspiration is shared, and the two legal orders are linked by *de facto* cooperation (mode 5). In between, EU law draws on exogenic norms to construct its own general principles (mode 2), refers to the title of Council of Europe instruments (mode 3) or incorporates the substance of Council of Europe norms (mode 4). Judicial interpretation complements these modes of reception to differing extents (mode 6). The ECJ takes Council of Europe norms into account on a contextual, historical, or teleological interpretation of EU law. Yet, in addition to a converging line of case law (consistent interpretation), there is a diverging line where the ECJ's interpretation differs from the exogenic norms in order to respect the specific objectives or characteristics of EU law.

Visualising the modes of reception in a legal landscape, the connections between the legal order of the Council of Europe and that of the EU can take the form of highways but also of mapped secondary roads, tracks, narrow paths and boreens, and even of hidden lanes and underground pas-

---

young people in building a secure, cohesive and harmonious society in Europe [2018] OJ C195/13 (see n 779 and 781). See for the ECtHR n 321.

608 Text to n 140.

sages. Through the landscape runs a red line which must not be crossed: the autonomy of the EU legal order. The EU has specific features and pursues specific objectives. What then are the implications for the reception of the Charter on EDC/HRE?

80 *Relevance of the schema*

The schema of modes of reception of exogenic norms in the EU legal order, introduced in Part two as a second step in the reasoning of the study, is important for several reasons.

Firstly, in the analysis as to the form, the schema will clarify the effects of the Council of Europe EDC standards in the EU legal order *de lege lata*. Each mode of reception will first be explained in general terms (with examples in various fields) and thereafter analysed as to its specific relevance for EDC standards. The place of the Recommendation on the Charter on EDC/HRE in the schema will be examined. Since in the Memorandum of Understanding (MOU), the EU recognises that the 'Council of Europe will remain the benchmark for human rights, the rule of law and democracy in Europe', the question is what form this recognition takes in the EU legal order. If the EU and the Council of Europe have committed to 'acknowledge each other's experience and standard-setting work, *as appropriate*, in their respective activities',[609] what does the EU consider *appropriate* with regard to EDC standards? It is important to understand what legal form the 'acknowledgment' of EDC standards by the EU currently takes. Moreover, effectiveness calls for a strong mode of reception of EDC standards, since they are named among the shared priorities and focal area for cooperation.[610] The reception of Council of Europe standards in other fields may provide precedents for EDC standards, uncover options for future EU action, and suggest which avenues can be taken *de lege ferenda*.

Secondly, the schema proposed applies equally to exogenic norms originating at UN level, norms which are highly relevant for EU citizenship education, such as the international agreements including the right to education (third anchor point) and UN standards on education for democracy, and which are used in Parts three and four.[611] The same normative reception mechanisms and effects in the interpretation apply to different types of exogenic norms.

609 MOU, para 12.
610 MOU, para 14.
611 Relevant for 'quality education' as a Treaty concept (§ 284).

Thirdly, the schema paves the way for the analysis of competences in Part four. Given the limited competence of the EU with regard to education and the respect for Member State autonomy, many educational norms stem from outside the EU and take the form of non-binding legal instruments. The Recommendation on the Charter on EDC/HRE is just one of many examples. EU legislative acts in the field of education frequently express a general intention to cooperate with the Council of Europe yet leave the legal effect of norms resulting from this cooperation unexplained. The proposed reception schema provides an overview of possible effects. Some modes are not mutually exclusive but overlap. Yet, distinguishing them sheds light on the relationship between the Council of Europe and the EU legal order and, importantly, shows the differing impact on Member State educational autonomy. The discretionary power of Member States to regulate education is not unlimited. According to settled case law, 'the fact that a matter falls within the competence of the Member States does not alter the fact that, in situations covered by European Union law, the national rules concerned must have due regard to the latter'.[612] This settled case law applies with regard to national rules on personal names, on direct taxation, or in the sphere of criminal legislation and procedure.[613] It is therefore legitimate to reason that it also applies to national rules on citizenship education. The schema of modes of reception will clarify which EU law Member States must have due regard to.

Finally, the EU legal order is not a closed system operating in a vacuum, but part of a network of interacting legal orders. The schema will indicate that what matters for Member States is not the binding or non-binding character of exogenic norms on EDC in their original legal order, but rather their effects in the EU legal order.

For these reasons, the schema of modes of reception of exogenic standards in the EU legal order remains relevant throughout the study. The schema may also be of interest as a general analysis of the way

---

612 Case C-135/08 *Rottmann* ECLI:EU:C:2010:104, para 41 (with cited case law in the sphere of criminal legislation and the rules of criminal procedure; law governing a person's name; national rules relating to direct taxation; national rules determining the persons entitled to vote and to stand as candidates in elections to the European Parliament; para 45 for the field of nationality). Further i.a. n 2408.

613 See § 323 , Case C-650/13 *Delvigne* ECLI:EU:C:2015:648 (§ 221); AG Poiares Maduro in Case C-135/08 *Rottmann* ECLI:EU:C:2010:104, para 20, with regard to nationality.

exogenic standards are received in the EU legal order, taking EDC standards as a case study.

CHAPTER 3 Stronger modes of reception of exogenic norms in the EU legal order

A Accession of the EU to conventions (mode 1)

1. General

81 After EU accession, conventions are an integral part of EU law

EU accession to conventions is the highway via which exogenic norms enter the EU legal order. International agreements which the EU concludes or to which the EU accedes, become binding upon the EU institutions and the Member States by virtue of Article 216(2) TFEU, and therefore are an integral part of EU law.[614] The ECJ can answer preliminary questions on interpretation and on validity.[615] In the hierarchy of norms, international agreements concluded by the EU rank below primary law and above secondary law. Pursuant to primary law, they must respect fundamental rights[616] and 'cannot affect the allocation of powers fixed by the Treaties or, consequently, the autonomy of the EU legal order, observance of which is ensured by the Court'.[617] Even on the highway (and especially there), the red line is thus protected. International agreements concluded by the EU prevail over secondary law and may affect the validity of acts of the institutions, subject to certain conditions. *As far as possible, consistent interpretation is sought. As is well-known, individuals can rely on the provisions*

---

614 EU Accession to the ECHR *Opinion 2/13* ECLI:EU:C:2014:2454, paras 179–180, with case law.

615 See Art 218 TFEU (procedure for the conclusion of international agreements by the Council); and Case 181-73 *Haegeman* ECLI:EU:C:1974:41, para 5; Case C-533/08 *TNT Express Nederland* ECLI:EU:C:2010:243, para 59.

616 Joined Cases C-584/10 P, C-593/10 P and C-595/10 P *Commission v Kadi* ECLI:EU:C:2013:518, para 22.

617 EU Accession to the ECHR *Opinion 2/13* ECLI:EU:C:2014:2454, para 201, see conditions in paras 160–162. Art 6(2) TEU ('Such accession shall not affect the Union's competences as defined in the Treaties'); Protocol (No 8) relating to Article 6(2) of the Treaty on European Union on the accession of the Union to the European Convention on the Protection of Human Rights and Fundamental Freedoms [2012] OJ C326/273, Art 1 and 2. See also Joined Cases C-402/05 P and C-415/05 P *Kadi* ECLI:EU:C:2008:461, para 282. Further AG Kokott on Opinion 2/13, para 201.

of an international agreement concluded by the EU if those provisions have direct effect (clear, precise, and unconditional) and if this is compatible with the spirit and general scheme of the agreement.[618]

82 *Few examples*

The highway is quite empty. To the disappointment of various authors, the EU has not been very active in pursuing accession to conventions drafted within the ambit of the Council of Europe.[619] Even where the Treaty provides that the EU 'shall accede' to the ECHR (Article 6(2) TEU), the process appears to be complex, with clear concerns not to cross the red line.[620]

Two cases illustrate the legal effects of exogenic standards resulting from conventions.

In 1978, the EEC acceded to 1976 European Convention on the Protection of Animals kept for Farming Purposes.[621] In *Compassion in World Farming*, the ECJ confirmed that this Convention had become an integral part of the Community legal order and tested the validity of an EU directive for consistency with its provisions.[622] It is interesting that in so doing the Court also took into account a recommendation adopted by a body

618 I.a. Joined Cases 21 to 24-72 *International Fruit Company* ECLI:EU:C:1972:115, para 20; Case 12/86 *Demirel* ECLI:EU:C:1987:400, para 14; Case C-280/93 *Germany v Council* ECLI:EU:C:1994:367, para 105; Case C-354/13 *FOA (Fag og Arbejde)* ECLI:EU:C:2014:2463, para 53. Lenaerts and Van Nuffel, *European Union Law*, 864; J Klabbers, 'Straddling the Fence: The EU and International Law' in D Chalmers and A Arnull (eds), *The Oxford Handbook of European Union Law* (Oxford University Press 2015).

619 Joris and Vandenberghe, 'The Council of Europe and the European Union: Natural Partners or Uneasy Bedfellows', 31–33 (out of 46 conventions allowing for accession, 11 were ratified by the EC in 2008); see also Cornu, 'The impact of Council of Europe Standards on the European Union'. On 15 October 2019, within the list of the 225 CoE treaties, 55 treaties allowed the EU to accede (source in n 121). Some were signed by the EU, i.a. the CoE Convention on preventing and combating violence against women and domestic violence (Istanbul); also treaties in the field of crime and terrorism, broadcasting by satellite, or animal protection (see <ec.europa.eu/world/agreements/default.home.do>).

620 EU Accession to the ECHR *Opinion 2/13* ECLI:EU:C:2014:2454, widely commented by scholars.

621 European Convention on the Protection of Animals kept for Farming Purposes (adopted on 10 March 1976 within the ambit of the CoE), approved by Council Decision 78/923/EEC of 19 June 1978 [1978] OJ L323/12. All Member States had become parties.

622 Case C-1/96 *Compassion in World Farming* ECLI:EU:C:1998:113, para 31 (about Directive 91/629). See also Case C-189/01 *Jippes* ECLI:EU:C:2001:420, on stan-

established under the Convention to ensure the implementation of the Convention principles.[623] In the mode of EU accession to international agreements, non-binding instruments, such as the recommendations of specific bodies set up under these agreements, acquire legal status in EU law.[624]

In 1994, the EU ratified the 1964 Convention on the Elaboration of a *European Pharmacopoeia*.[625] The *European Pharmacopoeia* is a reference work of pharmaceutical standards drawn up under the auspices of the Council of Europe. EU directives made the *European Pharmacopoeia* texts legally binding for the issuing of marketing authorisations, including in their regularly updated form ('dynamic reference', necessary for the quality control of medicines).[626] In *Novartis Pharmaceuticals*, the ECJ used these standards in a preliminary ruling to interpret concepts.[627]

---

dards of the International Office of Epizootics (IOE) and the International Animal Health Code (ninth edition, 2000).

623 Case C-1/96 *Compassion in World Farming* ECLI:EU:C:1998:113, paras 6, 35–36, on recommendations of the Standing Committee.

624 Case C-188/91 *Deutsche Shell* ECLI:EU:C:1993:24, para 17: 'Since measures emanating from bodies which have been established by an international agreement of that type, and which have been entrusted with responsibility for its implementation, are directly linked to the agreement which they implement, they form part of the Community legal order'; Opinion of AG Van Gerven, para 10: not the binding force of the act is decisive, but the direct connection between the act and the international agreement concluded by the Community. See also Opinion of AG Léger in Case C-1/96 *Compassion in World Farming* ECLI:EU:C:1998:113, para 128.

625 Convention on the Elaboration of a European Pharmacopoeia, ETS No 50 (22 July 1964) and Protocol ETS No 134; Council Decision of 16 June 1994 accepting, on behalf of the European Community, the Convention on the elaboration of a European Pharmacopoeia [1994] OJ L158/17.

626 9th edition in 2016.

627 Dir 2001/82–83/EC; Case C-106/01 *Novartis Pharmaceuticals* ECLI:EU:C:2004:245, paras 36–39. Before the EU in 1994 acceded to the 1964 Convention on the Elaboration of a European Pharmacopoeia, directives of the European Commission already referred to the *European Pharmacopoeia* by title (mode 3, below). The ECJ interpreted concepts in EU legislation accordingly.

2. Indirect relevance of accession to conventions for Education for Democratic Citizenship

83 UN conventions

The first mode of reception of exogenic norms into the EU legal order has limited direct relevance for EDC standards, which are—at present—not drawn up in conventions. However, some indirect effects may be deduced by analogy with convention effects.

At UN level, international agreements containing important norms on education have been signed and ratified by all the EU Member States, but not by the EU: the 1960 Convention Against Discrimination in Education (CADE), the 1966 International Covenant on Economic, Social and Cultural Rights (ICESCR), and the 1989 Convention on the Rights of the Child (CRC).[628] The European Parliament has called on the Commission to explore ways for the EU to accede to the CRC.[629]

It is worth noting the conclusion by the European Community of the 2006 UN Convention on the Rights of Persons with Disabilities.[630] In Article 24(1) of this Convention, States Parties recognise the right of persons with disabilities to education. With a view to realising this right without discrimination and based on equal opportunity, States 'shall' ensure an inclusive education system directed to ... '[e]nabling persons with disabilities to participate effectively in a free society' (Article 24(1)(c)). As a result of the conclusion of this convention, this provision has become an integral part of EU law. However restricted this provision may seem in terms of its scope, its meaning for education in general is important when seen in the broader context of international agreements binding on Member States. The wording of Article 24(1) of the Convention on the Rights of Persons

---

628 See n 443. The new Member States which acceded in 2004, 2007 and 2013 are also bound by these conventions. State parties at <indicators.ohchr.org/>. For for indirect legal effects, see *Intertanko*, § 100 .

629 European Parliament Resolution of 27 November 2014 on the 25th anniversary of the UN Convention on the Rights of the Child [2016] OJ C289/57, para 38.

630 Convention on the Rights of Persons with Disabilities (adopted 13 December 2006 A/RES/61/106, entry into force 3 May 2008); Council Decision of 26 November 2009 concerning the conclusion, by the European Community, of the United Nations Convention on the Rights of Persons with Disabilities [2010] OJ L23/35. To note, the EU has concluded some international agreements in the education field, but without specific consequences for citizenship education, e.g. Agreement between the European Community and the United States of America renewing a programme of cooperation in higher education and vocational education and training [2006] OJ L346/34.

with Disabilities on the right to education replicates the terms used with regard to the right to education in Article 13 of the 1966 ICESCR (Covenant ratified by all Member States, not by the EU). Both Article 24 of the Convention and Article 13 of the Covenant include an obligation for States Parties: they shall ensure an education system 'directed to' (i.a.) enabling 'to participate effectively in a free society'. Given the similarity in the wording, it can be indirectly inferred from the EU's conclusion of the Convention on the Rights of Persons with Disabilities that the EU adheres to the basic aims of education as expressed in the Article 13 of the ICESCR.[631] If it is part of EU law that the right to education includes the right for children with disabilities to an education directed to enabling effective participation in a free society, this must also be true for children without disabilities. This confirms the importance of the third anchor point of the study. Recognising a right to education directed to effective participation in a free society will have consequences when applied to the situation of the EU citizen.[632]

84 European conventions

At European level, several conventions laying down educational standards have not been acceded to by the EU.

The 2005 Council of Europe Convention on the Prevention of Terrorism is indirectly relevant, as it contains an obligation for Member States to take 'appropriate measures' in the field of education to prevent terrorist offences. If this provision is interpreted by taking account of other Council of Europe instruments, EDC and HRE are a necessary part of such measures.[633] However, while all EU Member States signed this Convention, not all ratified it. The EU signed the Convention, without ratifying it.[634] Thus it is not a part of EU law which Member States have to respect.

631 The 'programmatic' nature of provisions in the Convention on the Rights of Persons with Disabilities (Case C-363/12 *Z* ECLI:EU:C:2014:159, para 88) does not detract from this conclusion.

632 Parts three and four.

633 CoE Convention on the Prevention of Terrorism CETS No 196 (Warsaw, opened 16 May 2005, entered into force 1 June 2007), Art 3(1): 'Each Party shall take appropriate measures, particularly in the field of training of law enforcement authorities and other bodies, and in the fields of education, culture, information, media and public awareness raising, with a view to preventing terrorist offences and their negative effects while respecting human rights obligations'; explanatory memorandum paras 58. CoE action to take into account, see § 37 .

634 No ratification by BE, EL, IA, UK. Signature by the EU on 22 October 2015; Council Decision (EU) 2015/1913 of 18 September 2015 on the signing, on

The European Social Charter (ESC) is the convention on economic and social rights complementing the ECHR (which provides for civil and political rights). It is acknowledged to be the social constitution for Europe.[635] Neither the ESC (1961), nor the Revised ESC (1996) are open for signature by the EU. The Revised ESC was signed but not ratified by all Member States.[636]

The European Convention on the Exercise of Children's Rights was not signed or ratified by all Member States; it is open to the EU but has not been signed.[637] The 1997 Convention on the Recognition of Qualifications concerning Higher Education in the European Region, concluded in the ambit of the Council of Europe and jointly drafted with UNESCO, was signed and ratified by all EU Member States, except for Greece. Although it is open for signature by the EU, the EU has not become a party to it.[638]

It can be concluded that the first mode of reception of Council of Europe norms into the EU legal order is not directly relevant to the EDC issue. Yet, in the future this may change. The opinion has been voiced within the Council of Europe that the Recommendation on the Charter

---

behalf of the European Union, of the Council of Europe Convention on the Prevention of Terrorism (CETS No 196) [2015] OJ L280/22.

635 CoE Secretary General, State of democracy, human rights and the rule of law—a security imperative for Europe. Report 2016, 84.

636 European Social Charter ETS No 35 (Turin, opening 18 October 1961, entry into force 26 February 1965); European Social Charter (revised) ETS No 163 (Strasbourg, opening 3 May 1996, entry into force 1 July 1999), not ratified by CZ, DE, DK, ES, HR, LU, PL, and UK. See also Opinion of the Secretary General of the Council of Europe on the European Union initiative to establish a European Pillar of Social Rights (Strasbourg, 2 December 2016), 7: all EU Member States acceded to the treaty system of the CoE ESC, ratifying either the 1961 ESC or the 1996 revised ESC, yet with differing degrees of commitment. More in CoE European Committee of Social Rights, The relationship between European Union law and the European Social Charter (Working Document, 2014), appendix 1, for acceptance of specific provisions of the revised ESC by Member States ('à la carte' ratification system: States may choose the provisions they accept as binding international legal obligations).

637 European Convention on the Exercise of Children's Rights ETS No 160 (Strasbourg, opening 25 January 1996, entry into force 1 July 2000).

638 Convention on the Recognition of Qualifications concerning Higher Education in the European Region ETS No 165 (Lisbon, opening 11 April 1997, entry into force 1 February 1999), jointly drafted by the Coe and UNESCO, aiming replace six earlier conventions. Compare, e.g., European Agreement on the Instruction and Education of Nurses ETS No 59 (Strasbourg, opening 25 October 1967, entry into force 7 August 1969), not signed by all Member States, not open to the EU.

on EDC/HRE should become a convention. If this happens, the question which arises is whether the EU will be invited and willing to accede. However, it seems unlikely that any such steps will be taken soon, given the significance of education as an expression of Member State sovereignty.

B General principles of EU law (mode 2)

1. General

85 Genesis of general principles

Another strong mode of reception of exogenic norms are the general principles of EU law. They provide an attractive expressway in the legal landscape but are only recommended in the absence of other roads and for courageous drivers.

For a long time, the ECJ has fed the fundamental rights of the ECHR into the EU legal order as general principles of EU law, case law which is codified in Article 6(3) TEU.[639] Occasionally, the ECJ has also drawn on other exogenic human rights instruments to find (construct) general principles, such as the International Covenant on Economic, Social and Cultural Rights, the Convention on the Rights of the Child, the (Revised) ESC, or International Labour Organisation Conventions.[640] The question then arises as to what extent the ECJ is ready to draw inspiration from non-binding exogenic instruments, such as recommendations of the Council of Europe. Case law reveals two formulae: the ECJ draws inspiration from the guidelines supplied 'by international *treaties* for the protection of human rights'[641] (first formula) or 'by international *instruments* for the protection

---

639 Case 29-69 *Erich Stauder v City of Ulm - Sozialamt* ECLI:EU:C:1969:57, para 7; Case 11-70 *Internationale Handelsgesellschaft* ECLI:EU:C:1970:114, para 4; Case 4-73 *Nold* ECLI:EU:C:1974:51, para 13; Joined Cases C-402/05 P and C-415/05 P *Kadi* ECLI:EU:C:2008:461, para 283; EU Accession to the ECHR *Opinion 2/13* ECLI:EU:C:2014:2454, para 37.

640 E.g. Case 149/77 *Defrenne III* ECLI:EU:C:1978:130, paras 26–28; Case C-540/03 *Parliament v Council* ECLI:EU:C:2006:429, paras 37, 57. Indirectly, Case C-144/04 *Mangold* ECLI:EU:C:2005:709, paras 74–75 (refers to the preamble of Dir 2000/78 establishing a general framework for equal treatment in employment and occupation, which itself refers in recital 4 to, i.a., the UDHR and the ICESCR. See Craig and de Búrca, *EU Law: Text, Cases, and Materials* 386.

641 Case C-260/89 *ERT* ECLI:EU:C:1991:254, para 41; Case C-274/99 P *Connolly* ECLI:EU:C:2001:127, paras 37–38; Case C-94/00 *Roquette Frères* ECLI:EU:C:2002:603, para 23; Case C-112/00 *Schmidberger* ECLI:EU:C:2003:333, para 71;

of human rights on which the Member States have collaborated or to which they are signatories'[642] (second formula). The ECJ did, for example, rely on the CFR before it became binding on 1 December 2009.[643] The ECJ also draws inspiration from the constitutional traditions common to the Member States in order to establish general principles.

86 Significant legal effects

The legal effects of general principles of EU law are significant. In the hierarchy of norms, they are generally recognised as having constitutional status.[644] They are part of 'the law' of which the ECJ ensures observance (Article 19 TEU). EU law and national law falling within the scope of EU law are to be interpreted consistently with general principles. The infringement of general principles may result in the annulment or invalidity of EU measures. Within the substantive scope of EU law, Member State measures which fail to respect general principles must be set aside, as national courts must ensure the full effectiveness of EU law. Liability in damages may arise in some cases.[645]

Case C-36/02 *Omega Spielhallen* ECLI:EU:C:2004:614, para 33; EU Accession to the ECHR *Opinion 2/13* ECLI:EU:C:2014:2454, para 37.

642 Case C-540/03 *Parliament v Council* ECLI:EU:C:2006:429, paras 35–7 (the Court confirms that the ICESCR and the CRC are 'international instruments for the protection of human rights of which it takes account in applying the general principles of Community law'); Case C-244/06 *Dynamic Medien* ECLI:EU:C:2008:85, paras 39–40 (on CRC); Case C-305/05 *Ordre des barreaux francophones et germanophone et autres* ECLI:EU:C:2007:383, para 29 (on ECHR); Case C-229/05 P *PPK and KNK* ECLI:EU:C:2007:32, para 76 (on ECHR); Joined Cases C-402/05 P and C-415/05 P *Kadi* ECLI:EU:C:2008:461, para 283 (referring to UN Charter and Resolutions).

643 Case C-244/06 *Dynamic Medien* ECLI:EU:C:2008:85, para 41. Further HCH Hofmann and BC Mihaescu, 'The Relation between the Charter's Fundamental Rights and the Unwritten General Principles of EU Law: Good Administration as the Test Case' (2013) 9 European Constitutional Law Review 73.

644 T Tridimas, *The General Principles of EU Law* (Oxford University Press 2006), 6; Lenaerts and Van Nuffel, *European Union Law* 853 (on Treaty principles as sincere cooperation, conferral, subsidiarity, proportionality, or non-discrimination); Case C-282/10 *Dominguez* ECLI:EU:C:2012:33, Opinion of AG Trstenjak, para 95.

645 Arts 263 and 267 TFEU. For legal effects, see i.a. Case C-144/04 *Mangold* ECLI:EU:C:2005:709, paras 77–78; Case C-555/07 *Kücükdeveci* ECLI:EU:C:2010:21, paras 51–54, with cited case law. Further Tridimas, *The General Principles of EU Law* 29 ff; K Lenaerts and JA Gutiérrez-Fons, 'The constitutional allocation of powers and general principles of EU law' (2010) 47 CMLRev 1629, 1636 (consistent interpretation), 1650 (damages); Lenaerts and Van Nuffel, *European*

2. The bold proposition of a general principle on Education for Democratic Citizenship

Arguments in favour

87 *Common fundamental principles*

To consider EDC standards to be general principles of EU law is a bold proposition.[646] Several arguments militate in favour of this proposition and will first be explained (a). However, because there are strong counter-arguments, to be explained afterwards, the proposition will not be adopted (b).

EDC standards do not satisfy the definition of general principles as 'unwritten principles, recognised by the European Court of Justice, that have the status of higher law by the fact that they may be invoked as a standard for the review of Community acts'.[647] Neither 'education for democratic citizenship' nor 'citizenship education' appear in ECJ case law.[648] Yet, EDC standards could be labelled 'general principles' defined as 'the fundamental provisions of unwritten primary EU law which are inherent in the legal order of the European Union itself or are common to the legal orders of the Member States'.[649] EDC standards display several of the attributes which Tridimas describes as necessary for the elevation of a standard to the status of 'a general principle', inter alia 'to enjoy a degree of wide acceptance, i.e. represent "conventional morality"'.[650] The broad European consensus on EDC standards—standards moreover of great weight linked with the values of democracy, rule of law and human rights —is demonstrated in Part one. Throughout the four phases of the EDC project, instruments in the Council of Europe legal order show that EDC

Union Law 851; C Semmelmann, 'General Principles in EU Law between a Compensatory Role and an Intrinsic Value' (2013) 19 ELJ 457, 459: 'the well-known trouble with general principles as creatures *intra ius yet extra legem*'.

646 Cf Opinion of AG Mazák in Case C-411/05 *Palacios de la Villa* ECLI:EU:C:2007:604, para 89: considering the principle of non-discrimination on grounds of age as a general principle of EU law is 'a bold proposition'.

647 B de Witte, 'Institutional Principles: A Special Category of General Principles of EC Law' in U Bernitz and J Nergelius (eds), *General Principles of European Community Law* (Kluwer Law International 2000) 143.

648 Search on 15 October 2019.

649 M Schweitzer, W Hummer and W Obwexer, *Europarecht: das Recht der Europäischen Union* (Manz 2007) 65.

650 Tridimas, *The General Principles of EU Law* 26.

standards are accepted by member states as general principles with applications in diverse fields.[651]

88 *Guidelines supplied by international treaties and instruments for the protection of human rights*

Inspiration can be drawn from the guidelines supplied by international *treaties* for the protection of human rights (first formula in ECJ case law) and certainly from international *instruments* for the protection of human rights (second formula).[652]

As to the first formula, several treaties are relevant. Inspiration for a general principle of EDC can be found in the International Covenant on Economic, Social and Cultural Rights (ICESCR) and in the Convention on the Rights of the Child (CRC). Based on the UDHR (Article 26(2)), the provisions on the right to education in the ICESCR (Article 13(1)) and the CRC (Article 29(1)) stipulate that education 'shall be directed to' internationally agreed aims.[653] Education shall, i.a., enable all persons to participate effectively in a free society, develop respect for human rights and fundamental freedoms, and prepare for responsible life in a free society. EDC and HRE are direct responses to these compulsory educational aims. This is also evidenced by their expression and their development in UN instruments on education for democracy and human rights education.[654] EDC and HRE are crucial, in one form or another (in accordance with State priorities and constitutions), to the achievement of these educational aims. At the core of a general principle on EDC would be the need for EDC and HRE to reflect the compulsory educational aims of the International Covenant on Economic, Social and Cultural Rights and the Convention on the Rights of the Child, and the core components of EDC and HRE which, by consensus, develop these aims (such as in paragraph 2 of the Charter on EDC/HRE). It is to this core of EDC standards that I am referring when I use the expression 'a general principle of EDC'. As explained

---

651 Text to n 222 ff, 228 ff, 247 ff, 266 ff, 278 ff.

652 Formulas in text to nn 641-642.

653 See n 81-82. The 1996 Revised European Social Charter echoes some of them in Art 17: 'the right of children and young persons to grow up in an environment which encourages the full development of their personality and of their physical and mental capacities'; further Art 7 and 10. See also the aims in the UN Convention on the Rights of Persons with Disabilities, text to n 630.

654 §§ 285 294 .

above, the use in this study of the term 'EDC' automatically implies HRE as well.[655]

As to the second case law formula on general principles, inspiration can be drawn from 'the guidelines supplied by international *instruments* for the protection of human rights on which the Member States have collaborated or to which they are signatories', in this case the Recommendation on the Charter on EDC/HRE.[656] One of the requirements established in case law for general principles is their fundamental importance.[657] Against the backdrop of the dramatic consequences of education under totalitarian regimes and two World Wars, the authors of the provisions in international agreements on the right to education adopted compulsory educational aims which they considered pivotal for all human rights and society at large. Given their fundamental importance, the international (UN) and regional (Council of Europe) instruments which develop these aims further to include education for democracy and human rights education, arguably supply guidelines for a general principle of EDC/HRE in the EU legal order. In addition to the Charter on EDC/HRE—used as a reference instrument—the many other legal instruments described in the normative context in Part one provide further support.

89 Constitutional traditions common to the Member States

Alongside international guidelines, the common constitutional traditions of the Member States (Article 6(3) TEU) arguably also constitute a source for a general principle of EDC. An exhaustive analysis of constitutional law in all the Member States (including historical understanding, constitutional practice and case law) is impossible in the framework of this study. However, for the purposes of this study, sufficient indications can be drawn from the text of the constitutions.[658]

---

655 Text to n 181 ff.

656 See normative context (§ 85 ff) and participation in all organs (§ 162).

657 Case C-282/10 *Dominguez* ECLI:EU:C:2012:33, Opinion of AG Trstenjak, para 99.

658 More in P Häberle, *Verfassungslehre als Kulturwissenschaft* (2nd edn, Duncker und Humblot 1998); A Tschentscher, 'Comparing Constitutions and International Constitutional Law: A Primer' (10 February 2011) ; LFM Besselink and others (eds), *Constitutional Law of the EU Member States* (Kluwer 2014).

Provisions on democracy are to be found in all Member State constitutions, expressed in various terms.[659] They should be interlinked with standards on democracy, including the EDC standards to which all Member States are committed in the international context. A common constitu-

659 Some fragments of Member State constitutions (non-exhaustive; English translations as provided in database <www.refworld.org> or <www.unesco.org>): *Austria* Art 1 'Austria is a democratic republic. Its law emanates from the people'; *Czech Republic* Art. 1(1) 'The Czech Republic is a sovereign, unitary and democratic, law-abiding State, based on respect for the rights and freedoms of man and citizen'; Art 2(1) 'The people are the source of all power in the State; they exercise it through bodies of legislative, executive and judiciary powers.'; CZ Charter of Fundamental Rights and Basic Freedoms (part of the constitutional system, see Art 112 Constitution) Art 2(1) 'Democratic values constitute the foundation of the state, so that it may not be bound either to an exclusive ideology or to a particular religious faith'; *Finland* Section 2 Democracy and the rule of law: 'The powers of the State in Finland are vested in the people, who are represented by the Parliament. Democracy entails the right of the individual to participate in and influence the development of society and his or her living conditions'; *France* Art 1 'La France est une République indivisible, laïque, démocratique et sociale'; Art 2 'La devise de la République est « Liberté, Égalité, Fraternité ». Son principe est : gouvernement du peuple, par le peuple et pour le peuple'; Art 3 'La souveraineté nationale appartient au peuple qui l'exerce par ses représentants et par la voie du référendum'; *Germany* Art 20 '(1) The Federal Republic of Germany is a democratic and social federal state. (2) All state authority is derived from the people.); *Greece* Art 1 '2. Popular sovereignty is the foundation of government. 3. All powers derive from the People and exist for the People and the Nation'; Art 120(2) 'Respect towards the Constitution and the law concurrent thereto, and devotion to the Fatherland and to Democracy constitute a fundamental duty of all Greeks'; *Hungary* Article B (1) 'Hungary shall be an independent, democratic rule-of-law State'; (3) 'The source of public power shall be the people.' (4) 'The power shall be exercised by the people through elected representatives or, in exceptional cases, directly'; *Latvia* Art 1 'Latvia is an independent democratic republic'; Art 2 'The sovereign power of the State of Latvia is vested in the people of Latvia'; *Poland* Art 2 'The Republic of Poland shall be a democratic state ruled by law and implementing the principles of social justice'; *Romania* Art 1 (3) 'Romania is a democratic and social State governed by the rule of law, in which human dignity, the citizens' rights and freedoms, the free development of human personality, justice and political pluralism represent supreme values and shall be guaranteed'; Art 2(1) 'National sovereignty resides with the Romanian people, who shall exercise it through its representative bodies and by referendum'; *Sweden* Instrument of Government Art 1 'All public power in Sweden proceeds from the people. Swedish democracy is founded on the free formation of opinion and on universal and equal suffrage. It is realised through a representative and parliamentary form of government and through local self-government'.

tional tradition in respect of education can be deduced from a comparative analysis of provisions on the right to education in national constitutions, displaying 'a great uniformity'.[660] Several elements of the right to education in international agreements (ICESCR and CRC) recur, such as a right dimension and a freedom dimension; equal access for all, free of charge and compulsory up to a certain level; guarantees for the rights of parents; or some state supervision.[661] Importantly, several national constitutions encompass and develop the aims of education provided for in international agreements, and here *direct congruency* can be observed with EDC standards. The Portuguese Constitution adds with regard to the right to education that '[t]he state shall promote the democratisation of education ... to contribute to ... the development of the personality and the spirit of tolerance, mutual understanding, solidarity and responsibility, to social progress and to *democratic participation in collective life*.'[662] The Spanish Constitution specifies that '[e]ducation shall aim at the full development of human personality with due respect for the democratic principles of coexistence and for basic rights and freedoms'.[663] The Greek Constitution states that '[e]ducation constitutes a basic mission for the State and shall aim at ...their formation as free and responsible citizens'.[664] The Latvian Constitution provides in the chapter on 'fundamental human rights' that

---

660 G Gori, *Towards an EU Right to Education* (European Monographs 28, Kluwer Law International 2001) 321. See also G Gori, 'Article 14: Right to Education' in S Peers and others (eds), *The EU Charter of Fundamental Rights: a Commentary* (Hart 2014) 413.

661 See elements of the right to education i.a. in Constitution of Bulgaria Arts 23 and 53; Croatia Arts 64, 66–68; Cyprus Art 20; CZ Charter of Fundamental Rights and Basic Freedoms Art 33; Denmark § 76; Estonia § 37–38; Finland Section 16; Germany Art 7, also Art 5; Hungary Arts X-XI (i.a. X(3) 'Higher education institutions shall be autonomous in terms of the content and the methods of research and teaching'); Italy Art 33–34, Lithuania Arts 40–42; Luxembourg Art 23 (Constitution under revision); Malta Art 9–11; Poland Arts 33 and 70; Romania Art 32; Slovakia Art 42; Sweden Art 18. See also constitutions mentioned in other footnotes.

662 Art 73(2). See also Art 70 (1) and (2) on the aim 'to ensure the effective fulfilment of their economic, social and cultural rights' and 'effective integration into the active life, ... and a sense of community service', and Art 77(1) on democratic participation in education.

663 Art 27(2); see also (5) on partipation of all parties (as in Charter on EDC/HRE).

664 Art 16(2): 'Education constitutes a basic mission for the State and shall aim at the moral, intellectual, professional and physical training of Greeks, the development of national and religious consciousness and at their formation as free and responsible citizens.'.

'[e]veryone has the right to know about his or her rights'[665], which is like HRE and the concept of EDC in component (c-3). In the Austrian constitution '[d]emocracy, humanity, solidarity, peace and justice as well as openness and tolerance towards people are the elementary values of the school'. In addition to values, the aim is to develop independent judgement, social understanding, and attitudes of openness, as well as ensuring citizens are 'capable to participate in the cultural and economic life of Austria, Europe and the world and participate in the common tasks of mankind, in love for freedom and peace'[666], all of which is comparable to the EDC aim of empowering citizens to value diversity and to participate (parameters c-2–3). None of the constitutions which contain provisions directly related to citizenship education, deviate from EDC standards. The constitutional provisions on the promotion of the ideals of democracy[667],

665 Latvian Constitution Arts 112 and 90.

666 Constitution of Austria Art 14(5a) 'Democracy, humanity, solidarity, peace and justice as well as openness and tolerance towards people are the elementary values of the school (...) let them become healthy, self-confident, happy, performance-oriented, dutiful, talented and creative humans capable to take over responsibility for themselves, fellow human beings, environment and following generations, oriented in social, religious and moral values. Any juvenile shall in accordance with his development and educational course be led to independent judgement and social understanding, be open to political, religious and ideological thinking of others and become capable to participate in the cultural and economic life of Austria, Europe and the world and participate in the common tasks of mankind, in love for freedom and peace'; also Art 14(6). On values, see Belgium Art 24 (3–4) on moral education and equality; Romania, new Art 32 on access to culture (2) 'A person's freedom to develop his/her spirituality and to get access to the values of national and universal culture shall not be limited'; and Luxembourg proposal for new constitution (tr) Art 33 (1) Every person has the right to education, (3) Freedom of education shall be exercised respecting the values of democratic society founded on fundamental rights and public freedoms.

667 Sweden Instrument of Government Art 2 'the public institutions shall secure the right to employment, housing and education (...) The public institutions shall promote the ideals of democracy as guidelines in all sectors of society ... The public institutions shall promote the opportunity for all to attain participation and equality in society and for the rights of the child to be safeguarded'. See also France, preamble to the Constitution of 1946 (actual constitutional value), para 18: Faithful to its traditional mission, France desires to guide the peoples under its responsibility towards the freedom to administer themselves and to manage their own affairs democratically.

the common good[668], or quality education[669] are *indirectly congruent* with EDC standards.

In general, the implementation of EDC standards by Member States is closely linked to their constitutions, as constitutions provide for learning content (basic values, organisation of the State's institutions, fundamental rights, etc.)[670] and frame the way in which this learning is provided, for instance, the relationship between the right to education and State control, on the one hand, and the freedom of education and freedom of expression, on the other hand. According to the German and the Greek constitutions, freedom of education shall not release any person from the duty of allegiance to the constitution.[671] The requirement that freedom of education must respect constitutional provisions will have consequences with regard to EU primary law, interconnected with national constitutions.[672]

To sum up, common constitutional traditions exist with regard to education for democracy. Moreover, the trend for national practices implementing EDC is growing, as evidenced in the second review cycle of the Charter on EDC/HRE and in the 2017 Eurydice report on citizenship edu-

---

668 Constitution of Ireland Art 42(3- 2) 'The State shall, however, as guardian of the common good, require in view of actual conditions that the children receive a certain minimum education, moral, intellectual and social); see also Article 40 (6–1-i).

669 Cyprus Art 20(1); the Netherlands Art 23 ('eisen van deugdelijkheid'), Portugal Art 76(2); Slovakia Art 57 ('a proper education').

670 E.g. Beschluss der Kultusministerkonferenz vom 06.03.2009 'Stärkung der Demokratieerziehung', 4 ('erstärkte Vermittlung von Kenntnissen des Grundgesetzes und der Länderverfassungen' ('improving knowledge of the Basic Law and Land Constitutions'); Beschluss der Kultusministerkonferenz vom 06.03.2009 i. d. F. vom 11.10.2018, 'Demokratie als Ziel, Gegenstand und Praxis —historisch-politischer Bildung und Erziehung in der Schule' ('Das pädagogische Handeln in Schulen ist von demokratischen Werten und Haltungen getragen, die sich aus den Grundrechten des Grundgesetzes und aus den Menschenrechten ableiten lassen'). See for Austria <www.unsereverfassung.at/?lang=en>. Further § 165 .

671 Germany Art 5(3) Basic law '[t]he freedom of teaching shall not release any person from allegiance to the constitution'; see also Art 7(1) 'The entire school system shall be under the supervision of the state'; Greece Art 16(1) 'Academic freedom and freedom of teaching shall not exempt anyone from his duty of allegiance to the Constitution'; Cyprus Art 20(1) 'respect for the constitutional order'; see also Lithuania Art 28 (for all rights and freedoms).

672 See i.a. § 167. A constitutional core is to be respected, with room for balancing; see § 251 and text to n 2453.

cation.[673] In this respect constitutional traditions are converging. The greater the degree of convergence in national legal orders, the more inclined the ECJ will be to follow the national legal orders.[674] Besides, the ECJ rarely carries out a mathematical analysis to identify the lowest common denominator in national constitutional traditions, but adopts 'an evaluative approach', incorporating 'the solution provided for by the national legal orders that fits better or is in line with the objectives and structure of the Treaty'.[675] EDC standards fully fit in with this approach: they are in line with the objectives and structure of the Treaties (as will be argued below).[676] Responding to the absence of clear majority support in the national legal (and constitutional) systems for a principle of non-discrimination on grounds of age, Advocate General Kokott pointed to consistency with a specific task incumbent on the EU, to specific expression by the EU legislator, and to the mirroring of a more recent trend in the protection of fundamental rights.[677] A hypothetical general principle of EDC satisfies each of these terms. As abstract programmatic norms, EDC standards have been given specific expression by EU law (in modes 4 and 5, as will be analysed) and are thus codified to some extent.[678] Recognising a general principle of EDC would mirror a trend towards increased protection of democratic and human rights values in response to societal changes (radicalisation).

673 See n 478; CoE, *Learning to live together: Council of Europe Report on the state of citizenship and human rights education in Europe*; Commission/EACEA/Eurydice, Citizenship Education at School in Europe (2017), 10 (several Member States recently have put citizenship education in the spotlight).

674 K Lenaerts and JA Gutiérrez-Fons, 'The Role of General Principles of EU Law' in A Arnull and others (eds), *A Constitutional Order of States? Essays in EU Law in Honour of Alan Dashwood* (Hart 2011) 181.

675 Ibid, 183.

676 Analysis in text to n 934 ff.

677 Case C-550/07 P *Akzo Nobel Chemicals* ECLI:EU:C:2010:512, Opinion of AG Kokott, para 96. See also approach of AG Léger in Hautala (text to n 708); further Lenaerts and Gutiérrez-Fons, 'The Role of General Principles of EU Law', 183 (only the Finnish and the Portuguese constitutions); K Lenaerts and JA Gutiérrez-Fons, 'To Say What the Law of the EU Is: Methods of Interpretation and the European Court of Justice' (2014) 20 Columbia Journal of European Law 3, 51.

678 Just as Dir 2000/78 gave specific expression to the underlying general principle of non-discrimination on the grounds of nationality. See Case C-555/07 *Kücükdeveci* ECLI:EU:C:2010:21, para 21; Case C-144/04 *Mangold* ECLI:EU:C:2005:709, para 75; by analogy with Case 43/75 *Defrenne II* ECLI:EU:C:1976:56, para 54.

It is true that a general principle of EDC would put flesh on the bones of the Treaties and exercise a gap-filling function.[679]

Counterarguments

90 A precarious path

However, on a closer analysis, the arguments against considering EDC standards to be general principles of EU law in this study are strong.

Firstly, in general, giving effects to exogenic norms via general principles is a precarious path to take, prone to barriers and resistance. General principles are controversial, their genesis the subject of critical comment in legal literature, and so are, to an even greater degree, their wide-reaching legal effects.[680] Advocate General Mazák writes: 'it lies in the nature of general principles of law, which are to be sought rather in the Platonic heaven of law than in the law books, that both their existence and their substantive content are marked by uncertainty'.[681] The interface of general principles with provisions at constitutional and legislative level is the subject of debate.[682] Non-discrimination on grounds of age is an example of a general

679 On general principles putting flesh on the bones of the Treaties: Lenaerts and Gutiérrez-Fons, 'The constitutional allocation of powers and general principles of EU law', 1667; Case C-411/05 *Palacios de la Villa* ECLI:EU:C:2007:604, Opinion of AG Mazak, para 85. On the gap-filling function: Tridimas, *The General Principles of EU Law* 17.

680 Numerous comments on *Mangold*, i.a. D Martin, 'L'arrêt Mangold: Vers une hiérarchie inversée du droit à l'égalité en droit communautaire?' [2006] Journal des tribunaux du travail 941 ('motivation discutable'); J Mazák and M Moser, 'Adjudication by reference to general principles of EU law: a second look at the Mangold case law' in M Adams and others (eds), *Judging Europe's judges: The Legitimacy of the Case Law of the European Court of Justice* (Hart 2013); and Case C-411/05 *Palacios de la Villa* ECLI:EU:C:2007:604, Opinion of AG Mazák, paras 83, 88–89. For caution on general principles, see, i.a. M Herdegen, 'General Principles of EU Law: The Methodological Challenge' in U Bernitz and J Nergelius (eds), *General Principles of European Community Law* (European Monographs 25, Kluwer 2000); Lenaerts and Gutiérrez-Fons, 'The Role of General Principles of EU Law'; S Prechal, 'Competence creep and general principles of law' (2010) 3 Review of European administrative law 1.

681 Case C-411/05 *Palacios de la Villa* ECLI:EU:C:2007:604, Opinion of AG Mazák, para 86.

682 See three options in Semmelmann, 'General Principles in EU Law between a Compensatory Role and an Intrinsic Value', 464.

principle which has been criticised.[683] Recently, the ECJ has been reluctant to recognise or to use general principles. I think EDC standards are too important to jeopardise by taking a precarious path.

91 *Doubts about genesis*

Secondly, in particular with regard to a hypothetical general principle of EDC, the arguments relating to both the genesis and the legal effects are weak and problematic.

The doubts about the genesis of the principle concern the inspiration drawn from the ECHR (first formula in ECJ case law), from international instruments (second formula) and from common constitutional traditions.

92 *Doubts about the ECHR providing guidelines for EDC*

Can inspiration be drawn from the guidelines supplied by the ECHR, a treaty with 'special significance' to establish a general principle according to ECJ case law (first formula), treaty now mentioned as a direct source in Article 6(3) TEU? The answer is not straightforward. While the right to education in the ECHR does not militate against a potential EDC general principle, it does not, either, directly supply guidelines to conclude to the existence of a general principle of EDC. Article 2 of Protocol 1 to the ECHR essentially provides that '[n]o person shall be denied the right to education' (first and main sentence). Grafted onto this right to education are the rights of parents: in the exercise of the functions it assumes related to education and teaching, the State shall respect the rights of parents to education for their children in conformity with their religious and philosophical convictions (second sentence). If guidance is found, it is indirectly, based on settled case law in which the ECtHR interprets the right to education in a range of major principles.[684] Applying these interpretative principles to the EDC question provides some inspiration.

At first sight, the right to education does not give any indications as to EDC. The ECHR right to education primarily aims to guarantee a right of

---

683 *Mangold*, see text to n 680 ff.

684 I.a. *Kjeldsen, Busk Madsen and Pedersen v Denmark* no 5095/71 (ECtHR 7 December 1976), paras 50–54; *Campbell and Cosans v UK* no 7511/76 et al (ECtHR 23 March 1983), paras 36–37; *Valsamis v Greece* no 21787/93 (ECtHR 18 December 1996), paras 25–28; *Folgerø and Others v Norway* no 15472/02 (ECtHR 29 June 2007), para 84; *Hasan and Eylem Zengin v Turkey* no 1448/04 (ECtHR 9 October 2007), paras 47–55; *Lautsi and Others v Italy* no 30814/06 (ECtHR 18 March 2011), paras 59–62; *Catan and Others v Moldova and Russia* no 43370/04 et al (ECtHR 19 October 2012), paras 136–140; short referral in *Mansur Yalçin and Others v Turkey* no 21163/11 (ECtHR 16 September 2014), para 63.

equal access to the *existing* educational facilities.[685] It does not require States to establish any particular type or level of education at their own expense or to subsidise it.[686] The ECtHR repeatedly states that the setting and planning of the school curriculum in principle falls within the competence of the Contracting States and that it is not for the Court to rule on the questions of expediency, whose solution may legitimately vary according to the country and the era.[687] States enjoy a wide margin of appreciation with regard to the organisation and contents of their education systems. This is, by the way, consistent with Article 165 TFEU, which requires that the responsibility of Member States for the content of teaching be fully respected.

Upon a closer look, however, the ECHR right to education involves several aspects relevant to EDC. First, it includes more than a right of equal access.[688] A right to education would be illusory without a minimum degree of educational provision by the State. Positive obligations arise from ECtHR case law.[689]The right to education would, for instance, be meaningless if it did not imply the right to be educated in the national language or in one of the national languages.[690] The right to education 'by its

---

685 Emphasis added. See *Belgian Linguistic Cases* no 1474/62 et al (ECtHR 23 July 1968), para 4; *Kjeldsen, Busk Madsen and Pedersen v Denmark* no 5095/71 (ECtHR 7 December 1976), para 52; *Folgerø and Others v Norway* no 15472/02 (ECtHR 29 June 2007), para 84 (d); *Mehmet Reşit Arslan and Orhan Bingöl v Turkey* no 47121/06 et al (ECtHR 18 June 2019), para 51. See also L Veny, *Rechtsbescherming in het onderwijs* (Die Keure 1990) 30; B Vermeulen, 'The right to education (Article 2 of Protocol No. 1)' in P Van Dijk and others (eds), *Theory and practice of the European Convention on human rights* (4th edn, Intersentia 2006) 896; L Veny, *Onderwijsrecht 1: Dragende beginselen van het onderwijsbestel* (Die Keure 2010) § 191; LM Veny, 'The right to education according to the case-law of the European court of human rights' in EM Fodor (ed), *Education and law : interferences* (Pro Universitaria 2016).

686 *Belgian Linguistic Cases* no 1474/62 et al (ECtHR 23 July 1968), para 3; *Lautsi and Others v Italy* no 30814/06 (ECtHR 18 March 2011), para 61; Vermeulen, 'The right to education (Article 2 of Protocol No. 1)' 899.

687 *Valsamis v Greece* no 21787/93 (ECtHR 18 December 1996), para 28; *Folgerø and Others v Norway* no 15472/02 (ECtHR 29 June 2007), para 84 (g).

688 *Belgian Linguistic Cases* no 1474/62 et al (ECtHR 23 July 1968), para 4.

689 *Campbell and Cosans v UK* no 7511/76 et al (ECtHR 23 March 1983), para 37; *Valsamis v Greece* no 21787/93 (ECtHR 18 December 1996), para 27; *Mansur Yalçin and Others v Turkey* no 21163/11 (ECtHR 16 September 2014), para 72.

690 *Belgian Linguistic Cases* no 1474/62 et al (ECtHR 23 July 1968), para 3; *Catan and Others v Moldova and Russia* no 43370/04 et al (ECtHR 19 October 2012), para 137. On positive obligations, see Grabenwarter, *European Convention on Human*

very nature calls for regulation by the State'.[691] In *Campbell*, the ECtHR considered that 'the education of children is the whole process whereby, in any society, adults endeavour to transmit their beliefs, culture and other values to the young, whereas teaching or instruction refers in particular to the transmission of knowledge and to intellectual development.'[692] To that end, the State has the right to establish compulsory schooling and to verify and enforce educational standards. The State is responsible for the quality of education.[693] The ECtHR considers that in a democratic society, the right to education is indispensable to the furtherance of human rights and plays a fundamental role.[694]

A second inspirational element in case law is that the margin of discretion of States is limited by the obligation to respect parents' religious and philosophical convictions with the explicit aim of safeguarding the possibility of pluralism in education. This is essential for the preservation of the 'democratic society' as conceived by the Convention. This aim must primordially be achieved by means of State teaching.[695] An interpretative principle of crucial importance for EDC is that:

> the State, in fulfilling the functions assumed by it in regard to education and teaching, must take care that information or knowledge included in the curriculum is conveyed in an objective, critical and pluralistic manner. The State is forbidden to pursue an aim of indoctrination that might be considered as not respecting parents' religious and philosophical convictions.[696]

Rights: Commentary 394, especially in the knowledge-based society, 398; Vermeulen, 'The right to education (Article 2 of Protocol No. 1)' 901.

691 *Belgian Linguistic Cases* no 1474/62 et al (ECtHR 23 July 1968), para 5.

692 Para 33.

693 *Family H v UK* no 10233/83 (Commission, 6 march 1984) 37 DR 105; Vermeulen, 'The right to education (Article 2 of Protocol No. 1)' 901.

694 *Leyla Şahin v Turkey* no 44774/98 (ECtHR 10 November 2005), para 137 (also text to n 201); *Ponomaryovi v Bulgaria* no 5335/05 (ECtHR 21 June 2011), para 55; *Velyo Velev v Bulgaria* no 16032/07 (ECtHR 27 May 2014), para 33.

695 *Folgerø*, para 84(b); *Kjeldsen*, para 50.

696 *Folgerø and Others v Norway* no 15472/02 (ECtHR 29 June 2007) para 84 (h); emphasis added. Principle repeated in settled case law: see also *Kjeldsen, Busk Madsen and Pedersen v Denmark* no 5095/71 (ECtHR 7 December 1976), para 53; *Lautsi and Others v Italy* no 30814/06 (ECtHR 18 March 2011), para 62; *Osmanoglu and Kocabas v Switzerland* no 29086/12 (ECtHR 10 January 2017), para 91. On 'a certain margin of appreciation' and final decision resting with the ECtHR, see *Cölgeçen and Others v Turkey* no 50124/07 et al (ECtHR 12 Decem-

This constraint on the State must be understood in the historical context of the adoption of the ECHR: freedom of education is stressed throughout the preparatory works as a reaction to the education system enforced by the Nazi regime and with the aim of protecting the individual against State interference.[697]

Competing interests are at work: the State must guarantee a right to education for all and at the same time preserve freedom in education. A necessary balance is to be struck between the general interests of the community and individual rights and freedoms.[698] In *Valsamis*, parents brought a case on non-formal citizenship education in Greece before the ECtHR. Their daughter Victoria (in the first years of secondary school) had refused to take part in the school parade on the Greek National Day (28 October)[699] and had been punished with one day's suspension from school. Her parents, Jehovah's Witnesses, were opposed to extolling patriotic ideals in a school parade (with a military presence) and alleged a breach of their parental right to respect for their religious convictions. The ECtHR, without ruling on the State's school curriculum decisions, was 'surprised' about the compulsory attendance precincts on a holiday on pain of suspension from school. However, the Court discerned no offence to the parents' pacifist convictions: 'such commemoration of national events serve, in their way, both pacifist objectives and the public interest.' The parents were, moreover, not deprived of the right to enlighten their

---

ber 2017), para 48, *Leyla Şahin v Turkey* no 44774/98 (ECtHR 10 November 2005), para 154.

697 'We must not forget that Europe, at the time when the Convention was adopted, had just gone through years of suppression of the freedom of the peoples, where governments used all sorts of means and pressure to nazify the youth, especially through the schools and youth organisations. It was an important aim of the Convention that this should not be repeated and that the freedom of education should be protected', in partly dissenting opinion of Judge Terje Wold, in *Kjeldsen, Busk Madsen and Pedersen v Denmark* no 5095/71 (ECtHR 7 December 1976), arguing against positive claims against the State. See Preparatory work on Article 2 of the Protocol to the Convention (Strasbourg 9 May 1967), <www.echr.coe.int/LibraryDocs/Travaux/ECHRTravaux-P1-2-CDH%2867%292-BIL2292567.pdf>.

698 *Belgian Linguistic Cases* no 1474/62 et al (ECtHR 23 July 1968), para 13; *Folgerø*, paras 84(f), and 96; and *Valsamis*, para 27; *Lautsi and Others v Italy* no 30814/06 (ECtHR 18 March 2011), para 61; Vermeulen, 'The right to education (Article 2 of Protocol No. 1)' 897.

699 School and military parades in nearly all towns and villages commemorate the outbreak of war between Greece and Fascist Italy on 28 October1940.

children as educators and the imposed sanction was of limited duration.[700] The ECtHR concluded that there was no breach of Article 2 of Protocol 1.

The State is 'the ultimate guarantor of pluralism'.[701] The interpretative principles of the ECtHR on the right to education are consistent with the two sentences of Article 2 Protocol 1, with the Convention as a whole and 'with the general spirit of the Convention itself, an instrument designed to maintain and promote the ideals and values of a democratic society.'[702]

It can be concluded that the aims expressed in ECtHR case law with regard to the right to education match the EDC paradigm.[703] True, the Convention right to education does not directly imply an obligation to organise EDC, nor does the text contain indications as to content or aims of education, contrary to the International Covenant on Economic, Social and Cultural Rights and the Convention on the Rights of the Child. Yet, ECHR provisions must be interpreted in the light of these international agreements and international human rights standards, in line with Article 53 ECHR and case law. Even if Article 2 of Protocol 1 itself does not set out educational aims, when it is interpreted in the light of Article 13 of the ICESCR and Article 29 of the CRC, it does not countenance just any form of education. The ECtHR frequently restates that in interpreting and applying Article 2 of Protocol 1, 'account must also be taken of any relevant rules and principles of international law applicable in relations between the Contracting Parties and that the Convention should so far as possible be interpreted in harmony with other rules of international law of which it forms part'.[704] Moreover, as argued in Part one, the Charter on EDC/HRE must also be taken into account in the interpretation of Article 2 (in line with *Demir*, *Tănase, Mosley* and others) as a standard of great weight or considerable importance.[705] Furthermore, 'the Court emphasises that the object and purpose of the Convention, as an instrument for the

700 *Valsamis*, para 31.

701 *Mansur Yalçin and Others v Turkey* no 21163/11 (ECtHR 16 September 2014), para 70.

702 *Kjeldsen*, para 53. As a whole: *Folgerø*, para 84(a), *Lautsi,* para 54. I.a. in the light of Art 10 on the right to freedom of expression (including freedom to hold opinions and to receive and impart information and ideas without interference by public authority).

703 Also to value diversity, see *Folgerø,* para 84(f).

704 E.g. *Çam v Turkey* no 51500/08 (ECtHR 23 February 2016), para 53; *Catan and Others v Moldova and Russia* no 43370/04 et al (ECtHR 19 October 2012), para 136.

705 § 43.

protection of individual human beings, requires that its provisions be interpreted and applied so as to make its safeguards practical and effective'.[706]

The conclusion must thus be nuanced. Taking all aspects of the analysis together, the right to education in Article 2 of Protocol 1 to the ECHR supplies guidelines, to a certain extent, for acknowledgement of a general principle of EDC in EU law. Admittedly, it is not the text itself of Article 2 Protocol 1 ECHR on the right to education which supplies guidelines, but rather—as opponents might argue—a broad interpretation based on ECtHR case law. At the very least, the Convention right to education as interpreted by the ECtHR matches the EDC paradigm. To say that it inevitably leads to the recognition of EDC standards as general principles of EU law would be a bold step.

93 Doubts about international instruments

As to genesis based on international *instruments* for the protection of human rights, as in the second formula, the ECJ does not seem very interested in recommendations of the Committee of Ministers of the Council of Europe. In *Hautala*, advocating a general principle of access to documents and a right to information, Advocate General Léger drew attention to various recommendations of the Committee of Ministers.[707] They were part of the 'numerous unambiguous declarations' indicating the trend even before binding legislation was drafted. He found that '[i]t may suffice that Member States have a common approach to the right in question demonstrating the same desire to provide protection, even where the level of that protection and the procedure for affording it are provided for differently in the various Member States.'[708] The ECJ did not pursue this idea. In *Parliament v Council*, the European Parliament sought the annulment of provisions regarding third country nationals in a Directive on the right to family reunification.[709] The Parliament contended that the provisions did

706 *Leyla Şahin v Turkey* no 44774/98 (ECtHR 10 November 2005), para 136. Also text to n 357.

707 Case C-353/99 P *Hautala* ECLI:EU:C:2001:661, Opinion of AG Léger, para 59.

708 Ibid, para 62, reference i.a. to recommendations of the Committee of Ministers of the Council of Europe: No R (81) 19 on the access to information held by public authorities and No R (91) 10 on the communication to third parties of personal data held by public bodies.

709 Council Directive 2003/86/EC of 22 September 2003 on the right to family reunification [2003] OJ L251/12, recital 2: measures of family reunification should be adopted in conformity with the obligation to respect the family and

not respect the right to family life, referring to the ECHR, the International Covenant on Economic, Social and Cultural Rights, the Convention on the Rights of the Child, as well as to some recommendations of the Committee of Ministers.[710] The ECJ reasoned by reference to the ECHR and the Convention on the Rights of the Child, and considered that 'the remaining international instruments invoked by the Parliament do not in any event appear to contain provisions affording greater protection of rights of the child than those contained in the instruments already referred to'.[711] Case law on social rights also reveals the reticence of the ECJ. In *Dominguez*, Advocate General Trstenjak suggested to the Court that the entitlement of every worker to paid annual leave should be considered to be a general principle of EU law. This entitlement, she argued, has 'long numbered amongst internationally recognised social fundamental rights'. Citing many provisions of international public law, including various conventions, she found it 'unequivocally included among workers' fundamental rights'. [712] The ECJ was unmoved. The Court stated that the entitlement of every worker to paid annual leave must be regarded as 'a particularly important principle of European Union social law', without using the expression 'general principle of EU law'.[713] The ECJ has been criticised for failing, in its interpretation of CFR provisions, to recognise the persuasive authority of international human rights instruments other than the ECHR.[714] If even rights established in a panoply of conventions have not changed the mind of the Court, it can be presumed that EDC standards set out in recommendations will not be capable of doing so.

94 Doubts about common constitutional traditions

With regard to the genesis of a general principle on EDC based on the common constitutional traditions of the Member States,[715] a counterargument is that only a minority of constitutions contain explicit provisions on citizenship education which are directly congruent with EDC standards.

family life enshrined in many instruments of international law (in particular the ECHR and CFR).

710 Para 33.

711 Para 39.

712 Case C-282/10 *Dominguez* ECLI:EU:C:2012:33, Opinion of AG Trstenjak, paras 103–105, 114. Also Joined Cases C-569/16 and C-570/16 *Bauer* ECLI:EU:C:2018:871, para 38.

713 Case C-282/10 *Dominguez* ECLI:EU:C:2012:33, para 16.

714 Craig and de Búrca, *EU Law: Text, Cases, and Materials* 387.

715 Arguments in favour in § 89 .

Most constitutions provide for a right to education without reference to the content or educational aims.[716] EDC may then be seen as part of constitutional *practice.*

95 Doubts about legal effects

The legal effects of a hypothetical general principle of EDC are even more problematic. While it is conceivable that doubts as to genesis might be overcome—an issue which anyway has been selectively considered in ECJ case law—the main concern is that such a principle could have far-reaching legal effects, which would probably be hard to reconcile with respect for the constitutional allocation of powers in the Treaties, horizontally and vertically.[717] Construed as a general principle, EDC could become *un enfant terrible*, as described by Tridimas:

> the general principles of law are children of national law but, as brought up by the Court, they become enfants terribles: they are extended, narrowed, restated, transformed by a creative and eclectic judicial process.[718]

Horizontally, respect for the institutional balance and the separation of powers requires the ECJ not to encroach on the powers of the EU legislature. The establishment of general principles must respect legislative competence.[719] If more precision is needed than inherently implied in a general principle and legislative choices have to be made, the ECJ holds back. In *Audiolux*, the ECJ did not recognise a general principle of equal treatment of minority shareholders, because the general principle of equality could not determine the choice between various conceivable means of protection for minority shareholders. The protection of their interests required an element of detail in measures of secondary law.[720] A commonly accepted precondition for recognising a general principle is that it has 'a minimum ascertainable legally binding substance'.[721] Tridimas cites

716 E.g. Bulgaria, Croatia, Czech Republic, Denmark, Estonia, Finland, Hungary, Italy, Malta, the Netherlands, Poland, Romania, Slovakia (cp n 661).

717 Lenaerts and Gutiérrez-Fons, 'The constitutional allocation of powers and general principles of EU law'.

718 Tridimas, *The General Principles of EU Law* 6.

719 Lenaerts and Gutiérrez-Fons, 'The constitutional allocation of powers and general principles of EU law'; Prechal, 'Competence creep and general principles of law'.

720 Case C-101/08 *Audiolux* ECLI:EU:C:2009:626, paras 61–63.

721 Tridimas, *The General Principles of EU Law* 26. See also Case C-282/10 *Dominguez* ECLI:EU:C:2012:33, Opinion of AG Trstenjak, para 113.

the example of fairness, which is too vague to be a general principle. What is fair for one person, may appear unfair for the other. General principles must include an autonomous normative concept, an objective determination.[722] In this respect, a general principle of EDC falls short. What is perceived as an 'education for democratic citizenship' by some, will not qualify as such in the view of others. A hypothetical general principle of EDC leaves open a number of choices, to be made by the legislator. As observed in Part one, one of the weaknesses of the Charter on EDC/HRE is that it does not excel in content precision, which diminishes its normative claims. EDC is a quite abstract principle, akin to the principle of democracy, which the ECJ did not call a general principle of EU law either, but simply 'a principle'.[723] By contrast, the general principle of non-discrimination on grounds of age has autonomous content as a negative norm excluding provisions leading to unequal treatment based on the forbidden ground. In *Kücükdeveci*, this general principle was sufficient in itself to confer rights on individuals.[724] True, the components in the concept of EDC in paragraph 2 of the Charter on EDC/HRE contain quite precise elements, but the content of this paragraph is presumably more precise than that of a general principle of EDC. It is hard for a general principle of EDC to satisfy the criterion of self-sufficiency, for instance, for the ECJ to assess validity, or for national judges to give it full effectiveness as part of EU law.

Vertically, in construing a general principle of EU law, the ECJ must respect the principle of conferral. Recognition of a general principle of EU law on EDC, with the significant legal effects linked to the constitutional status, could be perceived as EU competence creep, encroaching on Member States powers in the field of education. Article 165(1) TFEU unambiguously states that the Union shall fully respect the responsibility of the Member States for the content of teaching.

96 *Interpretative function*

If, as Tridimas writes, judicial recourse to a general principle of EU law is essentially justified by its function in the EU legal order, making it possible to develop a notion of the rule of law appropriate for the EU polity while ensuring continuity with Member States' legal orders,[725] then there

722 Tridimas, *The General Principles of EU Law* 28, on the example of fairness.

723 Text to nn 954 ff.

724 About *Kücükdeveci*, see Case C-176/12 *Association de médiation sociale* ECLI:EU:C:2014:2, paras 46–49.

725 Tridimas, *The General Principles of EU Law* 20.

is probably no need to qualify EDC as a general principle. Semmelman considers:

> the soundest interpretation assigns general principles the role of an entry point for morality and values in legal determinations that reflect societal consensus, may change over time and substantiate more straightforwardly drafted provisions.[726]

For this role, an adequate and more direct entry point for EDC standards is to be found, inter alia, in Articles 2, 3, and Title II TEU, and their normative implications in terms of EDC standards. Rather than construing EDC as a general principle of EU law, EDC standards may operate as a tool for the interpretation of the relevant provisions of EU law, as will be argued in mode 6.

To conclude, weighing the arguments pro and contra, the second mode of reception is an unsafe path for the Charter on EDC/HRE. General principles of EU law are a complex option when other EU legal sources are silent.[727] In the case of EDC standards, the other EU legal sources are not silent.

C *Incorporation of the title of exogenic instruments in EU law (mode 3)*

1. General

97 *Reference to exogenic instruments*

In the legal landscape, a comfortable and safe secondary road bringing exogenic norms into the EU legal order is mentioning the title of an exogenic instrument in the corpus of EU law (not just in the preamble). This mode of direct entry can occur in both primary and secondary law and there are illustrations in many fields. The legal effects are not uniform but depend on the normative incorporation. The ECJ interprets EU law consistently with the incorporated exogenic norm but taking the autonomy of the EU legal order into account.

726 Semmelmann, 'General Principles in EU Law between a Compensatory Role and an Intrinsic Value', 487.
727 See, in general, ibid, 487.

Primary law incorporation of the title of an exogenic instrument

98 *The ECHR and indirect effects of Council of Europe recommendations*
The Treaties mention various exogenic instruments expressly, with different legal effects. Articles 6(3) TEU and 52(3) CFR refer to the ECHR. The fact that fundamental rights as guaranteed by the ECHR constitute general principles of EU law (Article 6(3) TEU) indirectly secures a way for Council of Europe recommendations to enter the EU legal order, i.e. to the extent that the ECtHR takes these recommendations into account to interpret provisions of the ECHR (*Tănase* and *Demir*[728]). This may actually happen with the EDC standards of the Charter on EDC/HRE as standards of great weight or considerable importance. The Recommendation on the Charter on EDC/HRE may thus have a cascading normative influence if taken into account by the ECtHR with a view to interpreting the ECHR and that ECHR interpretation is then incorporated into the general principles of EU law. Since the CFR has become EU primary law, the reception of ECtHR case law mainly occurs via the obligation of consistent interpretation in Article 52(3) CFR.[729] It is worth noting that the obligation of consistent interpretation 'shall not prevent Union law providing more extensive protection'.[730] Applying this last sentence of Article 52(3) CFR, the Recommendation on the Charter on EDC/HRE is therefore to be seen as a minimum, a starting point for a possibly further-reaching EU development.

Another example of an exogenic instrument to which EU primary law expressly refers by title is the *Geneva Convention relating to the status of refugees,* made binding in EU asylum policy by Article 78 TFEU. Secondary law regularly refers to the Geneva Convention, i.a. to determine who qualifies for refugee status and for the implications of that status.[731] The ECJ

---

728 See § 42 , i.a. *Tănase v Moldova* no 7/08 (ECtHR 24 April 2010), paras 176–77; *Demir and Baykara v Turkey* no 34503/97 (ECtHR 12 November 2008), paras 74–76, 85–86. For such an indirect reception through application of Article 52(3) CFR with regard to the right to vote, see however text to n 2294 ff.

729 The ECJ regularly refers to ECtHR case law, e.g. Case C-274/99 P *Connolly* ECLI:EU:C:2001:127, para 39 (same interpretation of freedom of expression as in *Handyside v UK* no 5493/72 (ECtHR 7 Dec 1976), para 33).

730 For cases going beyond or diverging from the ECHR, see Craig and de Búrca, *EU Law: Text, Cases, and Materials* 386.

731 Convention Relating to the Status of Refugees (Geneva, signed 28 July 1951, UNGA resolution 429 (V) of 14 December 1950, entered into force 22 April 1954) UNTS, Vol 189, p 150, No 2545 (1954); Protocol Relating to the Status of

interprets provisions of such secondary law 'in the light of its general scheme and purpose, while respecting the Geneva Convention'.[732] The *European Social Charter* does not enjoy this binding status in primary law, but has 'having in mind' status: Article 151 TFEU lists the objectives of the social policy of the EU and the Member States, having in mind fundamental social rights such as those set out in the ESC.[733] As to the *United Nations Charter,* several Treaty provisions require respect for its principles in the external action of the Union and in the common security and defence policy.[734]

Secondary law incorporation of the title of an exogenic instrument

99 *Exogenic standards incorporated into EU legislation in various fields*

In various fields the EU legislator chooses to incorporate standards originating outside the EU legal order. The intention is to avoid lagging behind and to adapt to evolving standards accepted in the international community. To this end, exogenic norms are often incorporated by a 'dynamic reference' to the title of the instrument, accepting future normative changes

---

Refugees (New York, 31 January 1967, entered into force 4 October 1967) (Geneva Convention). Secondary legislation, e.g. Council Directive 2003/86/EC of 22 September 2003 on the right to family reunification [2003] OJ L251/12, Art 2(b); Directive 2011/95/EU of the European Parliament and of the Council of 13 December 2011 on standards for the qualification of third-country nationals or stateless persons as beneficiaries of international protection, for a uniform status for refugees or for persons eligible for subsidiary protection, and for the content of the protection granted [2011] OJ L337/9; Regulation (EU) 2016/399 of the European Parliament and of the Council of 9 March 2016 on a Union Code on the rules governing the movement of persons across borders (Schengen Borders Code) [2016] OJ L77/1, see Art 4, requiring full compliance.

732 Joined Cases C-443/14 and C-444/14 *Alo and Osso* ECLI:EU:C:2016:127, paras 28–37, 44, 51; Joined Cases C-175/08, C-176/08, C-178/08 and C-179/08 *Salahadin Abdulla and Others* ECLI:EU:C:2010:105, para 53 (preliminary ruling on interpretation). Also preliminary rulings on the validity of secondary legislation in the light of the Geneva Convention, e.g. Case C-180/99 *Addou* ECLI:EU:C:2001:532.

733 See also preamble and Explanations to CFR.

734 Arts 3(5), 21(1), and 42 TEU; also Arts 208(2), 217(7) and 220 TFEU. See Case C-104/16 P *Council v Front populaire pour la libération de la saguia-el-hamra et du rio de oro (Front Polisario)* ECLI:EU:C:2016:973, paras 88, 90, 91, 93, referring to UN Charter and UN GA resolutions (concerning the Western Sahara).

in advance.[735] Some recommendations of the Committee of Ministers are also expressly mentioned in EU legal instruments. Case law amplifies the effect of normative reception by title. I will now briefly mention five examples. The purpose is to provide an insight into this mode of normative reception in order to assess to what extent the examples may serve as precedents for EDC standards (next section[736]). The first two examples, marine pollution and quality of wine, do not concern Council of Europe standards, yet they hint at the non-negligible effects of exogenic standards—binding or non-binding—in the EU legal order.[737] The last three examples highlight the effects of Council of Europe standards.

100 Standards for the discharge of polluting substances from ships

The International Convention for the Prevention of Pollution from Ships (Marpol 73/78) establishes standards to combat pollution of the marine environment.[738] These standards were received into the EU legal order by Directive 2005/35 of the European Parliament and of the Council, which refers to the Marpol Convention by title in Article 2.[739] In *Intertanko*, the ECJ held that the EU was not bound by the Marpol Convention and refused to assess the validity of the EU Directive in that light (even though the Directive had the objective of incorporating certain rules of the Marpol

---

735 Text to n 626.

736 Further §§ 105 106 .

737 Other example in Regulation (EC) No 1905/2006 of the European Parliament and of the Council of 18 December 2006 establishing a financing instrument for development cooperation [2006] OJ L378/41, e.g. Art 31: 'Tenderers who have been awarded contracts shall respect internationally agreed core labour standards, e.g. the ILO core labour standards'. See also the *Codex Alimentarius* (updated) published by the WHO and the FAO, containing standards for food safety in the form of -non-binding- recommendations. Legislation in many member states is based on it. For the EU, see i.a. Regulation (EC) No 183/2005 of the European Parliament and of the Council of 12 January 2005 laying down requirements for feed hygiene [2005] OJ L35/1, referring to the title of the *Codex Alimentarius*, taking it into account, but with sufficient flexibility (recital 15, Arts 21–22). Legal effects, e.g. Case C-236/01 *Monsanto Agricoltura Italia* ECLI:EU:C:2003:43, para 79 (defining a concept by referring to the *Codex Alimentarius*).

738 International Convention for the Prevention of Pollution from Ships (London, signed 2 November 1973); Protocol (17 February 1978) (Marpol 73/78).

739 Directive 2005/35/EC of the European Parliament and of the Council of 7 September 2005 on ship-source pollution and on the introduction of penalties for infringements [2005] OJ L255/11.

Convention into EU law).[740] But the fact that the Marpol Convention was binding on all Member States had consequences for the interpretation of provisions of secondary law which are within the scope of application of the Marpol Convention. The Court took account of the standards in the Marpol Convention in the interpretation of EU law 'in view of the customary principle of good faith, which forms part of general international law' and of the principle of sincere cooperation (now Article 4(3) TEU).[741] This *Intertanko* principle of 'taking account of' will be recalled in mode 6.[742] It is highly relevant for various exogenic instruments in the field of education, such as the International Covenant on Economic, Social and Cultural Rights and the Convention on the Rights of the Child. Like the Marpol Convention, these international agreements have been ratified by all the Member States, but not by the EU.[743]

101 Standards on quality of wine

A notable instance of effects in EU law are wine standards. An EU common agricultural policy Regulation refers in its corpus to recommendations of the International Organisation of Vine and Wine (OIV). In *Germany v Council*, the ECJ considered these recommendations to have been incorporated into EU law and attributed legal effects to them for the purpose of Article 218(9) TFEU.[744]

> In 2001, an Agreement to which many Member States are parties but not the EU, establishes the International Organisation of Vine and Wine (OIV), an intergovernmental organisation of a scientific and technical nature. To attain its objectives, the OIV draws up recommendations. In 2007, Council Regulation 1234/2007 refers in several specific provisions to OIV recommendations, e.g. stating that the methods of analysis concerning the composition of products in the wine sector and rules concerning authorised oenological practices 'shall be those recommended and published by the OIV'.[745] In an action for annul-

740 Case C-308/06 *Intertanko* ECLI:EU:C:2008:312, paras 49–52.

741 Para 52.

742 Text to n 981.

743 On the CRC, see further *Teixeira* Case C-480/08 ECLI:EU:C:2010:83.

744 *Germany v Council* Case C-399/12 ECLI:EU:C:2014:2258.

745 Art 120g of Council Reg 1234/2007 of 22 October 2007 establishing a common organisation of agricultural markets and on specific provisions for certain agricultural products (Single CMO Regulation) [2007] OJ 2007 L299/1 (as amended by Reg 1234/2010 of the European Parliament and of the Council of 15 December 2010 [2010] OJ 2010 L346/11). Several other references to OIV recommen-

ment of a Council Decision, the ECJ has to ascertain whether the OIV recommendations constitute 'acts having legal effects' as provided in Article 218(9) TFEU.[746] Germany claims that these acts only concern acts of international law binding on the EU.[747] Having regard to several specific provisions in the EU Regulation, the Court states that 'within the framework of the common organisation of the wine markets, the EU legislature *incorporates those recommendations into the legislation* adopted in that regard'.[748] The recommendations are 'capable of decisively influencing the content of the legislation adopted by the EU legislature in the area of the common organisation of the wine markets'.[749] The Court finds that the EU, while not a party to the OIV Agreement, was 'entitled to establish a position to be adopted on its behalf with regard to those recommendations, in view of their direct impact on the European Union's acquis in that area'.[750]

102 Council of Europe standards on data protection and standards on safety

An example of EU legislation incorporating a Council of Europe recommendation by title is the Regulation of the European Parliament and the Council on Europol. It provides that Europol 'shall take account of' and 'shall observe' the principles of the 1981 Council of Europe Convention for the Protection of Individuals with regard to Automatic Processing of Personal Data (not acceded to by the EU) and of Recommendation No R (87)15 of the Committee of Ministers to the member states on regulating the use of personal data in the police sector.[751] The preamble clarifies the aim that the data protection rules of Europol 'should be autonomous

dations, e.g. in Arts 120f(a), 120g and 158a(1)(2) of Reg 1234/2007 and Art 9 of Reg 606/2009 (para 36).

746 Para 56.

747 Paras 35–36.

748 Para 61 (emphasis added), with regard to the cited articles (Arts 120f(a), 120g and 158a(1)(2) of Reg 1234/2007 and Art 9 of Reg 606/2009).

749 Paras 62–63.

750 Para 64. The common position was not annulled. Germany, which had voted against the proposal of the Commission on a common position, had to accept the position on behalf of the EU.

751 Regulation (EU) 2016/794 of the European Parliament and of the Council of 11 May 2016 on the European Union Agency for Law Enforcement Cooperation (Europol) and replacing and repealing Council Decisions 2009/371/JHA, 2009/934/JHA, 2009/935/JHA, 2009/936/JHA and 2009/968/JHA [2016] OJ L135/53, Art 27. It concerns CoE Recommendation No R(87)15 of the Committee of Ministers to the member States 'on regulating the use of personal data in the police sector' (17 September 1987). See Convention for the Protection of

while at the same time consistent with other relevant data protection instruments applicable in the area of police cooperation in the Union', including the two Council of Europe instruments cited.[752]

Another EU instrument directly referring to the title of Council of Europe recommendations is the Council Resolution concerning police cooperation to prevent violence at football matches. To minimise risks, a Council of Europe checklist can be used. The list includes 11 Council of Europe recommendations.[753]

103 Council of Europe language education standards

The European reference standard for language education, the Common European Framework of Reference for Languages (CEFR), is a prominent example of a Council of Europe standard which has been received into the EU legal order in mode 3, i.e. by express reference to the title of the instrument. The Framework, use of which is recommended by the Committee of Ministers[754],'provides a common basis for the elaboration of language syl-

---

Individuals with regard to Automatic Processing of Personal Data ETS No 108 (Strasbourg, opened 28 January 1981, entered into force 1 October 1985), which has been ratified by all EU Member States, but is as such not open to the EU. For opening to the EU, see Additional Protocol to the Convention for the Protection of Individuals with regard to Automatic Processing of Personal Data, regarding supervisory authorities and transborder data flows No 181 (Strasbourg, opened 8 November 2001, entered into force 1 July 2004). This last instrument is not ratified by BE, EL, IT, MT, nor UK, not signed by SI, nor by the EU.

752 Recital 40.

753 Council Resolution of 3 June 2010 concerning an updated handbook with recommendations for international police cooperation and measures to prevent and control violence and disturbances in connection with football matches with an international dimension, in which at least one Member State is involved [2010] OJ C165/1. See section 2 in chapter nine, i.a. Rec (2001) 6 of the Committee of Ministers to member states on the prevention of racism, xenophobia and racial intolerance in sport. To note, the EU intends to accede to the CoE Convention on the Manipulation of Sports Competitions CETS No 215 (Magglingen, 18 September 2014) (signed by several Member States, not yet the EU), see COM/2015/086 final and COM/2017/0387 final.

754 CoE Recommendation CM/Rec(2008)7 of the Committee of Ministers to member states on the use of the Council of Europe's Common European Framework of Reference for Languages (CEFR) and the promotion of plurilingualism (2 July 2008): the Committee of Ministers recommends that governments of member states 'use every available means in accordance with their constitution, their national, regional or local circumstances and their education system to implement the measures set out in appendix 1 to this recommendation with respect

labuses, curriculum guidelines, examinations, textbooks, etc. across Europe.'[755] It serves as a reference tool for member states to develop and to implement consistent and transparent language education policies, inviting them to fully include language instruction in core educational aims.[756] Several EU secondary law instruments refer to the CEFR, e.g. in order to indicate required language levels.[757] Moreover, the European Commission has used the CEFR as a reference instrument for the European Qualifications Framework, Europass and the European Indicator of Language Competence.[758] Europass, the 'single Community framework for the transparency of qualifications and competences', has been set up, i.a. to include the European Language Portfolio, which the Council of Europe developed on the basis of the CEFR.[759] The European Indicator of Language Compe-

---

to the development of their language education policies'. The appendix details the 'Measures to be implemented concerning the use of the Council of Europe's Common European Framework of Reference for Languages (CEFR) and the promotion of plurilingualism'. See earlier CoE Recommendation R(98)6 of the Committee of Ministers to member states concerning modern languages (17 March 1998). Compare the less proactive action of the Committee of Ministers with regard to the RFCDC.

755 Council of Europe (2001) Common European framework of reference for languages: learning, teaching, assessment (CEFR), 1. Definition of six levels of foreign language proficiency: A1-A2, B1-B2, C1-C2, and three 'plus' levels, A2+, B1+, B2+.

756 Appendix 1, B(4).

757 E.g. Regulation (EU) No 1214/2011 of the European Parliament and of the Council of 16 November 2011 on the professional cross-border transport of euro cash by road between euro-area Member States [2011] OJ L316/1, Art 1(r) and Annex; Commission Directive (EU) 2016/882 of 1 June 2016 amending Directive 2007/59/EC of the European Parliament and of the Council as regards language requirements C/2016/3213 [2016] OJ L146/22, Annex; Council Recommendation of 22 May 2019 on a comprehensive approach to the teaching and learning of languages [2019] OJ C189/15, Art 4(g), Art 9(a).

758 CoE Recommendation CM/Rec(2008)7 of the Committee of Ministers to member states on the use of the Council of Europe's Common European Framework of Reference for Languages (CEFR) and the promotion of plurilingualism (2 July 2008), recital.

759 Decision 2241/2004 of the European Parliament and of the Council of 15 December 2004 on a single Community framework for the transparency of qualifications and competences (Europass) [2004] OJ L390/6, see recital 4, Art 8, and Annex V, with reference to the CoE ('The Europass-Language Portfolio (LP), developed by the Council of Europe, is a document in which language learners can record their language learning and cultural experiences and competences'). Europass includes also the Europass-CV.

tence was established in cooperation with the Council of Europe.[760] Various EU instruments recognise the CEFR and the European Language Portfolio as tools, i.a. to enhance the European dimension, or in the European strategy for multilingualism.[761] Further action has been undertaken to create a Europass framework, modernised and adapted to the EU context, providing a strategy for the coordination of services offered in Member States.[762]

It is promising that the RFCDC, developing EDC/HRE further, took the CEFR as a source of inspiration. By the same token, it is possible that RFCDC standards will enter the EU legal order just as the CEFR did, once they are the subject of a recommendation from the Committee of Ministers. At present, the RFCDC is only a reference document.[763]

104 Council of Europe standards on the rule of law

A crucial and thought-provoking example of exogenic norms received into the EU legal order in mode 3 are the rule of law standards of the Council of Europe. Initially, these standards were used as a foundation to fill a gap in the EU legal order, i.e. to address systemic threats to the rule of law without activating Article 7 TEU. Since December 2017, they constitute essential elements underpinning the grounds to activate Article 7 TEU for the first time in EU legal history—no mean legal effect for an exogenic

---

760 See, i.a., Commission Communication 'The European Indicator of Language Competence' COM(2005) 356 final; Commission staff working document, Language competences for employability, mobility and growth Accompanying the document Communication From the Commission Rethinking Education: Investing in skills for better socio-economic outcomes SWD(2010) 372 final.

761 I.a. Council Resolution of 19 December 2002 on the promotion of enhanced European cooperation in vocational education and training [2003] OJ C13/2; Council Resolution of 21 November 2008 on a European strategy for multilingualism [2008] OJ C320/1. On EU language policy: A Van Bossuyt, 'Is there an effective European legal framework for the protection of minority languages? The European Union and the Council of Europe screened' (2007) 32 ELRev 860; S van der Jeught, 'Conflicting Language Policies in the European Union and its Member States' (Proefschrift, Vrije Universiteit Brussel 2015). See also Commission/EACEA/Eurydice, The teaching of regional and minority languages in schools in Europe (2019).

762 Decision (EU) 2018/646 of the European Parliament and of the Council of 18 April 2018 on a common framework for the provision of better services for skills and qualifications (Europass) and repealing Decision No 2241/2004/EC [2018] OJ L112/42.

763 CoE Reference Framework of Competences for Democratic Culture, Vol 1: Context, concepts and model (2018), p 19. See on the RFCDC, § 106.

standard in the EU legal order. Confronted with Polish rules indicating undesirable political interference with regard to the Polish Constitutional Tribunal, the Commission adopted the Framework to strengthen the Rule of Law. The Framework refers to principles defining the core meaning of the rule of law as a common value of the EU in accordance with Article 2 TEU based inter alia on Council of Europe standards and building on the expertise of the European Commission for Democracy through Law (Venice Commission).[764] In two 2016 Recommendations (based on Article 292 TFEU), the Commission reiterated the reference to Council of Europe standards and recommended that the Polish authorities take the opinion of the Venice Commission fully into account.[765] In a third and a fourth Recommendation in 2017, the Commission relied even more heavily on Council of Europe standards on the rule of law, referring to well established European standards, inter alia the 2010 Recommendation of the Committee of Ministers of the Council of Europe on judges: independence, efficiency and responsibilities.[766] The Commission stated that the new Polish law conflicts with Council of Europe standards, in particular 'the principle of irremovability of judges as a key element of the independence of judges as enshrined in the 2010 Council of Europe Recommendation'.[767] The Polish authorities are recommended to 'ensure that any jus-

764 Commission Communication 'A new EU Framework to strengthen the Rule of Law' COM(2014) 0158 final, 3, 4, 6, 9.

765 Commission Recommendation (EU) 2016/1374 of 27 July 2016 regarding the rule of law in Poland [2016] OJ L217/53, recital 5 and para 74(c); Commission Recommendation (EU) 2017/146 of 21 December 2016 regarding the rule of law in Poland complementary to Recommendation (EU) 2016/1374 [2017] OJ L22/65, recital 4 and para 65(c).

766 Commission Recommendation (EU) 2017/1520 of 26 July 2017 regarding the rule of law in Poland complementary to Recommendations (EU) 2016/1374 and (EU) 2017/146 [2017] OJ L228/19, para 25, and fnn 15, 21, 23, referring to CoE Recommendation CM/Rec(2010)12 of the Committee of Ministers of the Council of Europe on judges: independence, efficiency and responsibilities (17 November 2010), also to the CoE Plan of Action on Strengthening Judicial Independence and Impartiality (13 April 2016) (CM(2016)36 final), and various opinions of the Venice Commission. The same line is continued in Commission Recommendation of 20 December 2017 regarding the rule of law in Poland complementary to Commission Recommendations (EU) 2016/1374, (EU) 2017/146 and (EU) 2017/1520 [2018] OJ L17/50, see i.a. para 6 ('independence of judges as enshrined in the case law of the Court of Justice and of the European Court of Human Rights, and in European standards', referring to the 2010 CM Recommandation), and fnn 20, 25, 30, 34, 35, 36, 77.

767 Ibid, fn 34, also fn 23.

tice reform upholds the rule of law and complies with EU law and the European standards on judicial independence'.[768] In December 2017, the Commission drafted a proposal for a 'Council Decision on the determination of a clear risk of a serious breach by the Republic of Poland of the rule of law' in accordance with Article 7(1) TEU.[769] The explanatory memorandum continued to rely on European standards and the Recommendation of the Committee of Ministers cited above.[770] Several non-EU actors were cited, not only the Council of Europe Committee of Ministers, but also the Parliamentary Assembly, the Venice Commission, the Commissioner for Human Rights, and of course, the ECtHR,[771] illustrating the impact of a wide European and international consensus at crucial moments of EU action to protect the rule of law.

Other EU institutions also refer to the Council of Europe standards on the rule of law. The European Parliament urged the Polish Parliament and Government 'to implement fully all recommendations of the Commission and the Venice Commission'.[772] In *Yanukovych*, the EU General Court interpreted and applied the value of the rule of law in Article 2 TEU by

---

768 Commission Recommendation (EU) 2017/1520 of 26 July 2017 regarding the rule of law in Poland complementary to Recommendations (EU) 2016/1374 and (EU) 2017/146 [2017] OJ L228/19, para 53(e); Commission Recommendation of 20 December 2017 regarding the rule of law in Poland complementary to Commission Recommendations (EU) 2016/1374, (EU) 2017/146 and (EU) 2017/1520 [2018] OJ L17/50, para 47(g). Infringement procedures have been started (Art 258 TFEU).

769 Commission Proposal for a Council Decision on the determination of a clear risk of a serious breach by the Republic of Poland of the rule of law COM(2017) 835 final (Reasoned proposal in accordance with Art 7(1) TEU). See recital 7, referring to CoE actors; and explanatory memorandum, referring to CoE instruments.

770 See e.g. paras 116 and 124, fn 54, 59, 64, 68, 69, 70, 111, 118, and 134. See also Commission Communication 'The 2019 EU Justice Scoreboard' COM(2019)198 final.

771 Proposal recital 7 and para 183. See CoE Parliamentary Assembly Resolution 2188(2017) 'New threats to the rule of law in Council of Europe member States: selected examples' (11 October 2017); Opinion 904/2017 CDL(2017)035 of the Venice Commission on the draft act amending the Act on the National Council of the Judiciary, on the draft act amending the Act on the Supreme Court proposed by the President of Poland, and on the Act on the Organisation of Ordinary Courts (CDL(2017)035), and Opinion 892/2017 CDL(2017)037 of the Venice Commission on the Act on the Public Prosecutor's Office as amended (CDL(2017)037).

772 European Parliament Resolution of 15 November 2017 on the situation of the rule of law and democracy in Poland (2017/2931(RSP)), para 7.

reference to the rule of law checklist adopted by the Venice Commission on 11–12 March 2016.[773] In *Commission v Poland* (2019), Advocate General Tanchev referred to various guidelines on judicial independence adopted by European and international bodies, inter alia the European Charter on the statute of judges. He noted that 'such guidelines are so-called "soft law" or non-binding norms, yet they embody a "normative consensus" of rules and principles shared by the Member States (and other jurisdictions) which provide a useful reference for the Court'.[774] In line with this finding, the ECJ referred in its judgment to an Opinion of the Venice Commission and gave effect to European and international standards on judicial independence and irremovability of judges. The Court held that Poland had failed to fulfil its obligations under the Article 19(1) TEU.[775]

In short, the title of exogenic Council of Europe standards on the rule of law—including the title of a recommendation of the Committee of Ministers—appears in several EU legal acts. Council of Europe standards, also referred to in ECJ case law, are essential elements for EU action protecting the rule of law in Member States. To what extent can the effects of the Council of Europe standards on the rule of law be seen as a precedent for Council of Europe standards on EDC?

2. Occasional reception of EDC standards by incorporation of the title

105 Reference to EDC standards

So far the Charter on EDC/HRE has not been mentioned by title in EU legislation (legal acts adopted by legislative procedure, Art 289(3) TFEU).[776] While EU legal acts in the education field repeatedly refer to

---

773 Case T-348/14 *Yanukovych* ECLI:EU:T:2016:508, para 99 (Case C-599/16P ECLI:EU:C:2017:785, appeal dismissed).

774 Case C-619/18 *Commission v Poland* ECLI:EU:C:2019:531, Opinion of AG Tanchev, para 72. See also W Hoffmann-Riem, 'The Venice Commission of the Council of Europe - Standards and Impact' (2014) 25 European Journal of International Law 579.

775 Case C-619/18 *Commission v Poland* ECLI:EU:C:2019:531, para 82. See Case C-64/16 *Juízes Portugueses* ECLI:EU:C:2018:117, paras 30–32 (for judicial independence in a Member State, no reference to the CoE, yet reference to Art 2 and Art 19 TEU). For a critical assessment, see S O'Leary, 'Europe and the Rule of Law' (Keynote speech, ESCB Annual Legal Conference, Frankfurt 6 September 2018). Further *Commission v Poland* Case C-192/18 pending.

776 No results in EUR-Lex (15 October 2019).

cooperation with the Council of Europe, they generally do not mention Council of Europe instruments or EDC standards in particular.[777] An exception is a 2018 Council recommendation on promoting common values, stating that Member States should 'make effective use of existing tools to promote citizenship education, such as the Council of Europe's Competences for Democratic Culture framework'[778] (which is intended to operationalise the Charter on EDC/HRE). Some policy documents and EU preparatory acts refer to the titles of Council of Europe instruments on EDC. In a resolution of 2016, the European Parliament calls on Member States to draw up national action plans for fundamental rights education and to implement the Council of Europe Charter on Education for Democratic Citizenship and Human Rights Education.[779] In the 2016 Council conclusions on developing media literacy and critical thinking through education and training, the Council expressly refers to the Council of Europe Framework of Competences of Democratic Culture. This can be categorised as a mode 3 reception of exogenic norms, albeit a watered-down version. The reference is not incorporated in a legislative act and the legal effects are minimal, as Member States are only invited to 'consider using' the Framework.[780] In 2018 the Council referred to the Charter on EDC/HRE in its conclusions on 'the role of young people in building a secure, cohesive and harmonious society in Europe' and invites the Member States and the Commission to

777 In youth policy, some recommendations of the Committee of Ministers have been recalled with regard to information, see Conclusions of the Council and the Ministers for Youth meeting within the Council of 30 November 1994 on the promotion of voluntary service periods for young people [1994] OJ C348/2, or Council Resolution of 31 March 1995 on cooperation in the field of youth information and studies concerning youth [1995] OJ C207/5. For mentioning of EDC standards in the preamble, see i.a. n 858.

778 Council Recommendation of 22 May 2018 on promoting common values, inclusive education, and the European dimension of teaching [2018] OJ C195/1, para 3.

779 European Parliament Resolution of 13 December 2016 on the situation of fundamental rights in the European Union in 2015 (2018/C 238/01). See also European Parliament resolution of 12 June 2018 on modernisation of education in the EU (2017/2224(INI)), recital.

780 Council Conclusions of 30 May 2016 on developing media literacy and critical thinking through education and training [2016] OJ C212/5, para 3 ('Invites the Member States'). See also Commission Communication supporting the prevention of radicalisation leading to violent extremism COM(2016) 379 final, 11.

> consider promoting and reinforcing, when and where relevant, the concept of 'Education for democratic citizenship and human rights education', which could be implemented in formal and non-formal learning environments and the peer-to-peer approach, respecting subsidiarity and freedom of education.[781]

Other instruments which expressly refer to the title of the Charter on EDC/HRE are joint programmes of the Council of Europe and the Commission. These programmes, though, only require that one EU Member State takes part besides other (non-EU) member states of the Council of Europe. They can thus hardly be seen as EU orientated.[782] It should be noted that the Committee of the Regions and the EESC also refer to EDC standards in their Opinions.[783]

While the reference to the Council of Europe instruments on EDC in the examples given may have only minor legal effects, they nevertheless show that EDC standards have been received into the EU legal order in mode 3 and are not considered alien to that legal order.

106 Attractive de lege ferenda

If in various fields EU legislation refers to standards originating outside the EU legal order by their title, the same pathway could be followed for EDC standards. If it was possible to use the third mode of reception for recommendations of the Committee of Ministers on data protection, safety, language education, and the rule of law, comparable normative value might be attributed to the Recommendation on the Charter on EDC/HRE in the EU legal order. From the perspective of legislative technique, there is no obstacle to referring to the title of this Recommendation, provided that there is a legal basis in the Treaties (examined in Chapter nine). Moreover, from the perspective of the Memorandum of Understanding, the EU

---

781 Council Conclusions on the role of young people in building a secure, cohesive and harmonious society in Europe [2018] OJ C195/13, para 35 (emphasis added), see also paras 16 and 34 and fn 3.

782 See map on <pjp-eu.coe.int/en/web/charter-edc-hre-pilot-projects/home>. Not involved in the Joint Programme 'Human Rights and Democracy in Action' (2013–2016) were, i.a., BE, DE, DK, IT, LU, NL, PT. See also text to n 898.

783 Opinion of the Committee of the Regions on the 'EU Citizenship Report 2010' [2011] OJ C166/3, para 12 (citing the 2002 Recommendation on EDC); Opinion of the European Economic and Social Committee on 'Education about the European Union' SOC/612 (21 March 2019), para 1.16 (referral to RFCDC). See also Commission/EACEA/Eurydice, Citizenship Education at School in Europe (2005), p 17. Text to n 35.

would be honouring its commitment that 'the relevant Council of Europe norms will be cited as a reference in European Union documents'.[784] In the field of education, the Charter on EDC/HRE certainly belongs to the category of 'relevant Council of Europe norms'. EDC is even considered to be a shared priority.

De lege ferenda EDC standards could conceivably be received into the EU legal order in a comparable way to standards on language learning. The Committee of Ministers sees the CEFR as a flexible tool which does not offer ready-made solutions, but which 'must always be adapted to the requirements of particular contexts'. This is true for EDC standards too. Moreover, language learning is not unrelated to citizenship objectives. The Committee of Ministers considers CEFR to be 'a tool for coherent, transparent and effective plurilingual education in such a way as to promote democratic citizenship, social cohesion and intercultural dialogue'.[785]

The precedent created by incorporating rule of law standards in EU legal acts on the basis of their title is appealing (though preferably without having to wait for dramatic non-compliance by a Member State). If institutions like the Commission, Parliament, and the ECJ (General Court) can enhance the capacity of the EU to ensure effective and fair protection of the *rule of law* in Member States by referring to the title of Council of Europe standards, including a recommendation of the Committee of Ministers, they could, equally, enhance the capacity of the EU to ensure effective democracy and respect for human rights, the other main values mentioned in Article 2 TEU, in Member States by referring to Council of Europe standards on EDC/HRE by title. Member States enjoy wide discretion in organising their judicial systems just as they do in relation to their educational systems. However, in exercising that discretion, they must respect the values of Article 2 TEU, in relation to which the European stan-

784 Para 17.

785 CoE Recommendation CM/Rec(2008)7 of the Committee of Ministers to member states on the use of the Council of Europe's Common European Framework of Reference for Languages (CEFR) and the promotion of plurilingualism (2 July 2008), appendix 1, A, 1. See also A Osler and H Starkey, *Citizenship and Language Learning: international perspectives* (Trentham Books 2005); and CoE Recommendation CM/Rec(2014)5 of the Committee of Ministers to member States on the importance of competences in the language(s) of schooling for equity and quality in education and for educational success (2 April 2014), appendix 6(d): 'all languages are conducive to the success of school learning processes as much as to individual fulfilment and preparation for active life and the exercise of citizenship'.

dards supported by a broad international consensus are relevant, as appears from the instruments of the EU institutions. The Commission underlines 'that where a constitutional justice system has been established, its effectiveness is a key component of the rule of law'.[786]

There is an understanding that the principles of the rule of law include:

> legality, which implies a transparent, accountable, democratic and pluralistic process for enacting laws ... Both the Court of Justice and the European Court of Human Rights confirmed that those principles are not purely formal and procedural requirements.[787]

Just like the rule of law, democracy is a value, expressed in terms of principles which 'are not purely formal and procedural requirements'. Substantive democracy needs EDC.[788] Compared to the quality of wine—important for the internal market—the quality of democracy and of respect for human rights is significantly more important, because it is the very foundation of life in society. Just as the EU cannot afford to lag behind internationally recognised standards on wine, it cannot—a fortiori—afford to fall behind internationally recognised standards on EDC/HRE, at least not in a Union which 'places the individual at the heart of its activities' (recital CFR), or a Union 'in which decisions are taken as openly as possible and as closely as possible to the citizen' (intention in Article 1 TEU).

786 Explanatory memorandum to Commission Proposal for a Council Decision on the determination of a clear risk of a serious breach by the Republic of Poland of the rule of law COM(2017) 835 final, para 91.

787 Commission Communication 'A new EU Framework to strengthen the Rule of Law' COM(2014) 0158 final, p 4.

788 Text to n 1684.

CHAPTER 4 Weaker modes of reception of exogenic norms in the EU legal order

A Incorporation of the substantive content of exogenic norms in EU law (mode 4)

1. General

107 Normative reception of substance

In the legal landscape, in addition to a few highways and a number of marked secondary roads leading through various fields, the Council of Europe and the EU legal order are connected by well-functioning tracks and smaller paths. The fourth mode of reception does not involve incorporation of the title, but of the substantive content of the exogenic instrument, to a lesser or greater extent. With a high degree of incorporation, exogenic norms are copy-pasted into the corpus of the EU legal instrument. With a lesser degree, similarities in the substance appear, even if the wording of the norms differs. In the spectrum of modes of reception in the EU legal order, more nuanced forms thus come to the fore. Principles or definitions from Council of Europe norms may be incorporated, but the rules are adapted to the specific needs of the EU and its Member States. This mode can work openly, with a reference to the exogenic instrument in the preamble, or tacitly, the content of an exogenic norm being absorbed without any explicit reference thereto.[789] In this mode, the legal source is not the copy-pasted exogenic norm, but the EU instrument, which may become the subject of preliminary rulings on validity or interpretation. In this latter process, interestingly, the exogenic norm often comes to life. Case law amplifies the fourth mode of normative reception by giving effect to the exogenic norms at the origin of EU law by interpret-

---

789 E.g. Directive 2003/88/EC of the European Parliament and of the Council of 4 November 2003 concerning certain aspects of the organisation of working time [2003] OJ L299/9. While the directive undoubtedly intends to comply with the rights enshrined in ESC, its preamble makes no reference to the ESC, as observed in CoE European Committee of Social Rights, The relationship between European Union law and the European Social Charter (Working Document, 2014), para 72.

ing EU law consistently with the exogenic norm, or taking it into account in a contextual, historic or teleological interpretation, or by giving *effet utile* to EU law provisions.[790]

The substantive content of Council of Europe conventions (a) as well as recommendations (b) has been incorporated—in whole or in part—in EU primary and secondary law. The following examples will raise a number of questions which fall to be answered in the following sections.

Incorporation of the substance of Council of Europe conventions

108 Transfrontier television: cases RTL and Commission v UK

The 1989 European Convention on Transfrontier Television is the object of both converging and diverging case law.[791] The EU was not party to this Convention, but adopted its own legal instrument in the same year, Council Directive 89/552, which constituted the legal framework for television broadcasting in the internal market. The Directive referred in its preamble to the Convention and had several quasi identical provisions.[792] In *RTL*, a preliminary question was referred about the interpretation of a Directive provision which had the same wording as a Convention provision. In order to interpret the term 'films made for television', having considered the wording, the Court adopted a historical and teleological interpretation.[793] To find the underlying aim, the Court referred to the explanatory report accompanying the European Convention.[794] This example of converging case law contrasts with the earlier case *Commission v UK*. The UK

790 The sixth mode of reception (interpretation) thus complements the fourth.

791 European Convention on Transfrontier Television (5 May 1989).

792 Council Directive 89/552/EEC of 3 October 1989 on the coordination of certain provisions laid down by law, regulation or administrative action in Member States concerning the pursuit of television broadcasting activities [1989] OJ L298/23, as amended by Directive 97/36/EC of the European Parliament and of the Council of 30 June 1997 [1997] OJ L202/60. Art 18(1) Dir is identical to Art 12(1) Convention; Arts 11(1), (3) and (4) Dir are quasi identical to Arts 14(1), (3) and (4) Convention. See also definition in Art 6(b).

793 Art 11(3) Dir and Art 14(3) Convention: 'The transmission of audiovisual works such as feature films and films made for television (excluding series, serials, light entertainment programmes and documentaries), provided their scheduled duration is more than 45 minutes, may be interrupted once for each period of 45 minutes...'.

794 Case C-245/01 *RTL Television* ECLI:EU:C:2003:580, paras 61- 63, see also para 97. RTL claimed that 'films made for television which provide, from their con-

had argued that Council Directive 89/552—which, according to the Commission, it had failed to implement correctly—was based on the European Convention on Transfrontier Television and that rules on intra-Community broadcasting could not differ radically from those of the Convention.[795] The ECJ did not accept this argument. In the light of a comparative analysis of the wording, scheme and aims of the Directive and of the Convention,[796] the Court underlined a substantive difference. The Directive was designed to establish the internal market in television services, while the Convention aimed to facilitate the transfrontier (re)transmission of television programme services.[797] Because of the difference in purpose, the Directive rules followed a different path.[798]

It can be deduced from this case law that exogenic norms can be received into the EU legal order through incorporation of elements of their substantive content into an act of EU law. That does not, however, necessarily lead to consistent interpretation of such an act with the exogenic norms at its origin. The specific aims of the EU must be respected. Does the EU have its own agenda for democracy and human rights which would legitimise a different approach and interpretation which diverges from EDC/HRE standards?

---

ception, for breaks for the insertion of advertising' do not come within the meaning of 'films made for television' in Article 11(3)'. The ECJ did not accept this view. RTL's claim did not fit with the purpose of Art 11, which was to establish 'a balanced protection of the financial interests of the television broadcasters and advertisers, on the one hand, and the interests of the rights holders, namely the writers and producers, and of consumers as television viewers, on the other'. See for earlier cases with a comparable converging reasoning: Joined Cases C 320/94, C 328/94, C-329/94, C-337/94, C-338/94 and C-339/94 *RTI and Others* ECLI:EU:C:1996:486, para 33, and Opinion of AG Jacobs, paras 6 and 31. Also Case C-11/95 *Commission v Belgium* ECLI:EU:C:1996:316, paras 24–25 (Convention used to determine the scope of the Directive).

795 Case C-222/94 *Commission v UK* ECLI:EU:C:1996:314, paras 43–44, concerning Council Directive 89/552/EEC of 3 October 1989 on the coordination of certain provisions laid down by law, regulation or administrative action in Member States concerning the pursuit of television broadcasting activities [1989] OJ L298/23, as amended by Directive 97/36/EC of the European Parliament and of the Council of 30 June 1997 [1997] OJ L202/60.

796 Para 45, i.a. comparing Art 2(1) Dir and Art 5(2) Convention.

797 Paras 49–50.

798 Paras 52–53. See also Case C-601/14 *Commission v Italy* ECLI:EU:C:2016:759.

109 Prisoners standards: case Ognyanov

Ognyanov illustrates the autonomy of an EU legislative act vis-à-vis a Council of Europe Convention: the ECJ did not refer to the Council of Europe Convention at the origin, but interpreted by referral to a specific EU objective, namely, the principle of mutual recognition.[799] The 1983 Council of Europe Convention on the Transfer of Sentenced persons, ratified by all Member States, aimed to further the social rehabilitation of foreign prisoners by allowing them to serve their sentence in their own country.[800] In 2011, the Council of the EU adopted Framework Decision 2008/909/JHA, replacing corresponding provisions of the European Convention in the relations between the Member States.[801] The Framework Decision copied Convention norms to a great extent (it contains some *verbatim* copy-pasted fragments and some adaptations in terminology[802]). The preamble of the Framework Decision referred to Council of Europe instruments and the need to further develop cooperation on the enforcement of criminal judgments. In addition to the aim of facilitating social rehabilitation, the EU had a further objective, considering that relations between the Member States are characterised by special mutual confidence in other Member States' legal orders and thus justify recognition by the executing State of decisions taken by the issuing State.[803] In the instant case a court in Den-

799 Case C-554/14 *Ognyanov* ECLI:EU:C:2016:835. See on mutual trust, essential characteristic of the EU: EU Accession to the ECHR *Opinion 2/13* ECLI:EU:C:2014:2454.

800 Convention on the Transfer of Sentenced Persons ETS No 112 (Strasbourg, opened 21 March 1983, entered into force 1 July 1985); Additional Protocol ETS 167 (Strasbourg, opened 18 December 1997, entered info force 1 June 2000), Art 3(1)(d) and Art 7.

801 Council Framework Decision 2008/909/JHA of 27 November 2008 on the application of the principle of mutual recognition to judgments in criminal matters imposing custodial sentences or measures involving deprivation of liberty for the purpose of their enforcement in the European Union [2008] OJ L327/27, as amended by Council Framework Decision 2009/299/JHA of 26 February 2009 [2009] OJ L81/24, Art 26.

802 E.g. 'issuing State' and 'executing State' instead of 'sentencing State' and 'administering State' in the Convention.

803 Recitals 4–5. Cp Art 6 Dec to Art 3 Convention. See, in that line, later amending legislation: Council Framework Decision 2009/299/JHA of 26 February 2009 amending Framework Decisions 2002/584/JHA, 2005/214/JHA, 2006/783/JHA, 2008/909/JHA and 2008/947/JHA, thereby enhancing the procedural rights of persons and fostering the application of the principle of mutual recognition to decisions rendered in the absence of the person concerned at the trial [2009] OJ L81/24.

mark (issuing State) had sentenced Mr Ognyanov to 15 years imprisonment. After spending some time in a Danish prison, Mr Ognyanov was transferred to Bulgaria (executing State). The Bulgarian judge had doubts as to whether the period during which Mr Ognyanov had worked in the Danish prison could be deducted from the length of the sentence still to be served in Bulgaria. While Bulgarian law provided for such a reduction, Danish law did not. The Framework Decision stated in Article 17 that 'the enforcement of a sentence shall be governed by the law of the executing State', but did not clarify whether enforcement began at the moment of delivery of the judgment or at the moment of transferral to the executing State.[804] The ECJ decided in favour of the latter option; a reduction in the sentence by reason of work carried out before the transfer may only be granted on the basis of the law of the issuing State. Contrary to the Advocate General Bot,[805] the Court did not refer to the original Council of Europe Convention, but interpreted Article 17 autonomously, on the basis of the place of that provision in the Framework Decision (internal context) and on the objective of respect for the principle of mutual recognition, which is the 'cornerstone' of judicial cooperation in criminal matters within the European Union.[806]

110 Education of nurses: case Commission v Germany

The autonomy of the EU legal order vis-à-vis the Council of Europe also appears from case law establishing that the requirement to implement EU law cannot be replaced merely by respecting Council of Europe norms. In *Commission v Germany*, the Commission claimed that Germany had failed to implement i.a. Directive 77/452. Germany argued that its administrative practice was in conformity with the 1967 European Agreement on the instruction and education of nurses, the provisions of which were almost identical to those of Directive 77/452.[807] The ECJ ruled that in the circumstances, the incorporation of the European Agreement into national law could not replace the proper implementation of the Directive.[808]

---

804 Para 32.

805 Case C-554/14 *Ognyanov* ECLI:EU:C:2016:835, Opinion of AG Bot, paras 96–98.

806 Para 34 and 46.

807 Case 29/84 *Commission v Germany* ECLI:EU:C:1985:229, para 34, concerning European Agreement on the Instruction and Education of Nurses ETS No 59 (Strasbourg, opening 25 October 1967, entry into force 7 August 1969).

808 Para 38. The ECJ concluded that Germany had failed to fulfil its obligations. See also Case C-601/14 *Commission v Italy* ECLI:EU:C:2016:759: Italy failed to adopt the necessary measures under the Council Directive 2004/80/EC of 29

111 Social standards

An example of converging case law in the field of social standards is *Khalil and Others.* The ECJ had to answer a preliminary question on whether a Regulation on social security schemes was valid in so far as it included stateless persons and refugees in its personal scope. In order to do so the ECJ situated the Regulation in its historical context, recalling i.a. the European convention on social security for migrant workers. The Court pointed to Regulation provisions which 'replicated content' or were 'substantively identical'. No factors were found affecting the validity of the Regulation.[809]

In general, the standards set by the Council of Europe and the EU on social rights largely converge: the 98 paragraphs of the Revised European Social Charter can be matched with binding provisions of EU primary or secondary law.[810] Many provisions of the CFR draw on articles of the European Social Charter, as appears from the CFR preamble and the Explanations.[811] However, it is important to recognise significant inconsistencies, which make the red line appear.[812] Due regard must be had to the

April 2004 relating to compensation to crime victims [2004] OJ L261/15. In the interpretation the Court took account 'not only of the wording of that provision, but also of the objectives pursued by that directive, and the system established by that directive of which it is part.' In the preamble, the Directive cited the European Convention of 24 November 1983 on the compensation of victims of violent crimes, but pursued its own objective of abolishing obstacle to free movement of persons and services.

809 Joined Cases C-95/99 to C-98/99 and C-180/99 *Khalil and others* ECLI:EU:C:2001:532, see paras 31, 42–43, 52–53, 58, concerning Council Regulation (EEC) No 1408/71 of 14 June 1971 on the application of social security schemes to employed persons, to self-employed persons and to members of their families moving within the Community, as amended and updated by Council Regulation (EEC) No 2001/83 of 2 June 1983 [1983] OJ L230/6, and specific context of (ia) European convention on social security for migrant workers (signed 9 December 1957). Question of compatibility with Art 51 EEC.

810 CoE European Committee of Social Rights, The relationship between European Union law and the European Social Charter (Working Document, 2014), para 19.

811 See CRF Explanations to Arts 14, 15, and 23, as well as Arts 25 till 35 CFR.

812 Opinion of the Secretary General of the Council of Europe on the European Union initiative to establish a European Pillar of Social Rights (Strasbourg, 2 December 2016), p 3, and appendix p 16, with table of provisions of the Revised ESC and corresponding guarantees in primary and secondary EU legislation where they exist. See also CoE European Committee of Social Rights, The relationship between European Union law and the European Social Charter (Working Document, 2014), para 27 ff, appendixes 2 and 3.

powers and tasks of the Union and to the principle of subsidiarity (preamble CFR). The ECJ interprets CFR provisions in keeping with the European Social Charter, but differences in the finetuning require a nuanced approach.[813] Mr Jagland, the Secretary General of the Council of Europe, asked the EU to formally incorporate provisions of the European Social Charter into the European Pillar of Social Rights, launched by the European Commission as a common benchmark.[814] Given the uncertainties and reticence as to the reception of the social standards of the Council of Europe—even though they are laid down in a (binding) convention, the European Social Charter[815]—there can be no expectation of automatic reception in EU law of EDC standards, which are only set out in (non-binding) recommendations. Can EDC standards be shared in principle, but with divergences in the finetuning, having due regard to the powers and tasks of the Union and to the principle of subsidiarity?

112 Converging and diverging lines of case law

In conclusion, European conventions whose substance is incorporated in EU law may have effects in a converging line of case law, where the ECJ interprets EU law consistently with the Council of Europe standards at its origin. However, this remains an autonomous interpretation of EU law in which the red line may emerge at any moment, as i.a. *Ognyanov* illustrated. Notwithstanding far-reaching reception of the substance of exogenic norms, EU law may pursue its own objectives or manifest specific features, and the interpretation of EU law provisions may consequently diverge from the original exogenic norms. This first reflection will provide food for thought in the section on the EDC standards. Do the Council of Europe recommendations on EDC fall under the converging or the diverging line of case law, or under both, depending on the particular subject-matter considered?[816]

---

813 See CoE European Committee of Social Rights, The relationship between European Union law and the European Social Charter (Working Document, 2014), appendix 2, column 4.

814 Opinion of the Secretary General of the Council of Europe on the European Union initiative to establish a European Pillar of Social Rights (Strasbourg, 2 December 2016), 4, 13. Compare Commission Communication 'Establishing a European Pillar of Social Rights' COM(2017) 250 final.

815 See n 636.

816 Further §§ 142 144 155 .

Incorporation of substance of Council of Europe recommendations

113 Blood standards: case Humanplasma

In addition to conventions, recommendations of the Committee of Ministers to the member states of the Council of Europe are received into the EU legal order by means of normative incorporation of their substance and judicial interpretation which takes them into account. A second reflection is that exogenic norms not only have effects in the interpretation of provisions incorporating their substance, but also in the broader context of EU law. Two cases will illustrate this.

In *Humanplasma*, the ECJ cited an article in the appendix to a recommendation of the Committee of Ministers (the Charter on EDC/HRE also features in the appendix of a recommendation) and used this article in the interpretation and application of the Treaty provisions on free movement of goods and the justification for restrictions on grounds of protection of health (Article 34 juncto 36 TFEU).[817] The Council of Europe standard provided additional support for the reasoning in the proportionality test.

> Austrian legislation only permits importation of blood or blood components from other Member States if blood donations have been made without any payment to the donors, even in terms of the coverage of costs. The ECJ holds this to be a measure of equivalent effect to a quantitative restriction on imports (Article 34 TFEU).[818] A restriction can be justified on grounds of the protection of human health, if it is appropriate and does not go beyond what is necessary to attain the objective (Article 36 TFEU).[819] The Court admits that the Member States have a discretion as to the level of protection of human health.[820] Yet, the fact that a number of other Member States reimburse blood donors' costs is relevant. Here, the Court refers to Council of Europe Recommendation (95)14 and an EU Directive in line with it (incorporating some substantive content).[821] Recommendation (95)14

---

817 Case C-421/09 *Humanplasma* ECLI:EU:C:2010:760, para 7: Art 2 of appendix to CoE Recommendation No R (95) 14 of the Committee of Ministers to the Member States of the Council of Europe on the protection of health of donors and recipients in the area of blood transfusion (12 October 1995) (Legal context, International rules). Then Art 28 EC juncto Art 30 EC.

818 Para 30.

819 Paras 31–36.

820 Paras 39–40.

821 Para 41.

of the Committee of Ministers to the member states of the Council of Europe 'on the protection of health of donors and recipients in the area of blood transfusion' stipulates in Article 2 of its appendix that 'voluntary, non-remunerated donation' of blood is compatible with small tokens, refreshments and reimbursements of direct travel costs.[822] Directive 2002/98 of the European Parliament and of the Council setting standards of quality and safety for the collection, testing, processing, storage and distribution of human blood and blood components refers in its preamble to 'relevant recommendations of the Council of Europe', considers that the efforts of the Council of Europe in the area of voluntary and unpaid donations should be supported, and that '[t]he definition of voluntary and unpaid donation of the Council of Europe should be taken into account'.[823] The Court recalls that both the Directive and Recommendation (95)14 aim to improve the health of donors or recipients of blood, but that they do not require that donations be completely unpaid.[824] Austrian legislation goes beyond what is necessary to attain the objective of ensuring the quality and safety of the blood and of the blood components.[825]

Health, like education, is an area where Member States have discretionary powers. Even so, the ECJ took a consensus in a Council of Europe recommendation into account in the interpretation of EU law.

114 Standards for the reception of applicants for international protection: case N

In case *N*, the ECJ referred to a recommendation of the Committee of Ministers of the Council of Europe in its interpretation and application of EU primary law provisions on the right to liberty and on limitations to this right (Articles 6 juncto 52(1) and (3) CFR). The validity of a provision of the 'Reception Directive' (Directive 2013/33/EU of the European Parliament and of the Council laying down standards for the reception of appli-

---

822 CoE Recommendation No R (95) 14 of the Committee of Ministers to the Member States of the Council of Europe on the protection of health of donors and recipients in the area of blood transfusion (12 October 1995); Directive 2002/98/EC of the European Parliament and of the Council of 27 January 2003 setting standards of quality and safety for the collection, testing, processing, storage and distribution of human blood and blood components and amending Directive 2001/83/EC [2003] OJ L33/30.

823 Directive 2002/98/EC, recitals 4, 23, 27.

824 Para 44.

825 Para 45.

cants for international protection) fell to be assessed in the light of the CFR Articles cited.[826] The provision in issue stated that an applicant may be detained 'when protection of national security or public order so requires'. As a limitation to the right to liberty protected by Article 6 CFR, it had to satisfy the criteria of Article 52(1) CFR, i.a. be 'necessary and genuinely meet objectives of general interest recognised by the European Union or the need to protect the right and freedom of others'.[827] Moreover, limitations to the right to liberty must be '*strictly* necessary', in view of its importance.[828] To assess strict necessity, the ECJ interpreted the Directive on the basis of its wording, context and legislative history.[829] It is at that point of the reasoning that the exogenic norm came in. Looking at the explanatory memorandum to the proposal for the Directive, the Court found that the grounds for detention were based on the 2003 Recommendation of the Committee of Ministers of the Council of Europe on measures of detention of asylum seekers and on detention standards in Guidelines of the UN High Commissioner for Refugees.[830] Noting in these exogenic instruments the strictly circumscribed conditions for detention, making it an exceptional measure of last resort, the Court found no factors affecting the validity of the provision at issue. It is interesting in this case that, notwithstanding the fact that they were not mentioned in the preamble of the Directive, Council of Europe exogenic norms nevertheless were given legal effect in the EU legal order. The effects of the UN guidelines cited should be noted as well, since they are relevant for Chapter nine.[831] In her View in the case *N*, Advocate General Sharpston also put the secondary law provisions in a historical context and pointed to similarities in the scope *ratione personae* of the Reception Directive and the Recommendation of the Committee of Ministers.[832] In the earlier case *El Dridi*, the Court had already based its ruling on a historic and teleological interpreta-

826 Case C-601/15 PPU *N* ECLI:EU:C:2016:85, concerning Directive 2013/33/EU of the European Parliament and of the Council of 26 June 2013 laying down standards for the reception of applicants for international protection [2013] OJ L180/96. The provision in litigation was Art 8(3)(e).

827 Para 50.

828 Para 56 (emphasis added).

829 Para 57.

830 Para 63. Repeated in Case C-18/16 *K* ECLI:EU:C:2017:680, para 46.

831 Text to n 2203.

832 Case C-601/15 PPU *N* ECLI:EU:C:2016:85, View of AG Sharpston, fn 48.

tion of Directive 2008/115, the predecessor of the Reception Directive, and had referred to guidelines of the Committee of Ministers.[833]

To sum up, the reception of exogenic norms in mode 4 unmistakably has effects in the interpretation and application of EU law. In *Humanplasma* and *N*, the exogenic norms—recommendations of the Committee of Ministers—were taken into account in the broader context of EU law in the interpretation and application of provisions relating to the internal market (Article 34 juncto 36 TFEU) and to the fundamental right to liberty (Article 6 juncto 52 CFR). Can recommendations of the Committee of Ministers containing EDC standards be taken into account in the interpretation and application of EU law provisions on citizenship and democracy in a comparable way?

The first question to be answered is: has the substantive content of EDC standards in Council of Europe instruments been received into the EU legal order?

2. Fragmented incorporation of the substantive content of EDC standards

115 *Endogenic norms related to citizenship education are drawn up in the EDC paradigm*

For EDC standards, the connecting routes between the Council of Europe and the EU legal order are predominantly situated in modes 4 and 5. This section will analyse the norms related to citizenship education originating within the EU legal order itself, thus endogenic (by contrast to the exogenic EDC norms of the Council of Europe). The substance of exogenic EDC standards can be identified to a significant degree within EU law. Admittedly, there is no extensive copy-pasting of the provisions of the Charter on EDC/HRE, nor any reference in the preambular provisions of EU legislation. Yet, similarities in substance and quasi identical expressions do appear. The fact that the EU embraces the Council of Europe EDC paradigm will be demonstrated in (1) EU primary law and (2) EU secondary law. To what extent this normative incorporation can be supplemented by an interpretation of EU law taking the exogenic standards into account, will be explored in mode 6.

833 Case C-61/11 PPU *El Dridi* ECLI:EU:C:2011:268, paras 43–44, and Directive 2008/115/EC of the European Parliament and of the Council of 16 December 2008 on common standards and procedures in Member States for returning illegally staying third-country nationals [2008] OJ L348/98, recital 3.

EU primary law: linking democracy and citizenship with education

116 A combined reading of Articles 10(3) TEU and 165(2) TFEU

In EU primary law, a clear link can be seen between citizenship and democracy on the one hand and education on the other hand. The similar wording of provisions inserted by the Lisbon Treaty in 2009 is striking. In the new Title II 'Provisions on democratic principles' in the TEU, Article 10(3) TEU provides that '[e]very citizen shall have the right to *participate in the democratic life of the Union*'. At the same time, the Lisbon Treaty added an extra sentence to Article 165(2) TFEU (which is the legal basis for EU education policy), stating that in education matters, Union action shall be aimed at 'encouraging the *participation of young people in democratic life in Europe*' (last part of fifth indent).[834] Admittedly, this extra sentence figures in an indent on youth policy, thus not on formal (school) education. Nevertheless, the comma preceding the phrase, added by the authors of the Lisbon Treaty, indicates its openness to education in general.[835] The provision is to be read in the light of Article 165 on education as a whole. On the basis of a textual interpretation, participation of young people in democratic life in Europe is undeniably an objective of EU education policy. On a contextual interpretation, reading Articles 10(3) TEU and 165(2) TFEU together, the congruence with the EDC objectives of the Council of Europe stands out. The EU norm seeking to encourage participation of young people in democratic life in Europe by education, is in substance the same as the Council of Europe concept of EDC, empowering them 'to play an active part in democratic life' (EDC component c-3).

---

834 My emphasis. Also similarities in other language versions. Cp Art 10(3) TEU 'Tout citoyen a le droit de participer à la vie démocratique de l'Union', 'Iedere burger heeft het recht aan het democratisch bestel van de Unie deel te nemen', 'Alle Bürgerinnen und Bürger haben das Recht, am demokratischen Leben der Union teilzunehmen', with Art 165(2) TFEU: 'encourager la participation des jeunes à la vie démocratique de l'Europe', 'deelneming van jongeren aan het democratisch leven van Europa aan te moedigen', 'verstärkte Beteiligung der Jugendlichen am demokratischen Leben in Europa'. See in context of Convention on the Future of Europe (2003) <european-convention.europa.eu/>, 'Document du Praesidium: project de titre VI du traité constitutionnel concernant la vie démocratique de l'Union (2 avril 2003)'.

835 No comma in the Treaty establishing a Constitution for Europe.

117 Council of Europe context of drafting

The drafting of Article 10(3) TEU and of the extra sentence in Article 165(2) TFEU dates from the 2004 Treaty establishing a Constitution for Europe.[836] The context in which it was drafted was one of intense action on EDC at Council of Europe level (first and second phase of the EDC project). Concurrent action by Member States in the Council of Europe and at EU level, and the cooperation of the EU and the Council of Europe, show their effects in parallel norm-setting. In addition to an identical objective—empowerment for participation—the wording is also very similar. In 1999, the Committee of Ministers had stressed 'the fundamental role of education in promoting *the active participation of all individuals in democratic life*'.[837] Similar terms are used in the 2002 Recommendation on EDC, the forerunner of the 2010 Recommendation on the Charter on EDC/HRE.[838] The Committee of Ministers recommended that the governments of member states make EDC a priority objective of educational policy-making and reforms.[839] The fact that the authors of the EU Treaty reform included the encouragement of participation in democratic life as one of the objectives of education by inserting the extra sentence in the fifth indent, is fully in keeping with the 2002 Recommendation.

EU secondary law: various aspects of EDC standards

118 EU legislative acts, variable terminology, same paradigm

In EU secondary law, much of the substantive of EDC standards is visible (mode 4) and certainly their inspiration (explained in mode 5). Even if the expressions 'education for democratic citizenship' or 'citizenship educa-

---

836 Treaty establishing a Constitution for Europe [2004] OJ C310/1. In Title VI ('The Democratic life of the Union') Art I-46 on 'The principle of representative democracy', para (3) has the same wording as Art 10(3) TEU. Art III-282 (1)(e) has the same wording as Art 165(2), but without a comma before 'encouraging'. Art 165 TFEU dates from the 1992 Maastricht Treaty (then Art 126 EC). The 1997 Amsterdam Treaty had no provision encouraging participation in democratic life.

837 CoE Committee of Ministers Declaration and programme on education for democratic citizenship, based on the rights and responsibilities of citizens (Budapest, 7 May 1999), para 7. See first and second phases.

838 CoE Recommendation Rec(2002)12 of the Committee of Ministers to member states on education for democratic citizenship (16 October 2002).

839 Para 3.

tion' are rarely used as such, components of the EDC concept, EDC objectives and underlying principles are present.[840] Obviously, norms on citizenship education appear more laterally and sporadically in EU legislative acts than in Council of Europe instruments. The Council of Europe tackles the subject systematically, comprehensively, and as part of its core mission. In the EU legal order, 'citizenship education' is not a directly conferred Treaty competence. Yet, with the widening of the scope of EU competences beyond those of a mere economic project, action has been taken which can be situated in the field of citizenship education.

Remarkably, where citizenship education is referred to in legal acts of the Union, the terms used are variable and often not defined, thus contrasting with the consistent use of 'education for democratic citizenship' in the normative framework of the Council of Europe, a well-defined concept embedded in standards developed over decades. In addition to 'civic competences' (used in the plural) and 'citizenship competence' (used in the singular),[841] EU legal instruments occasionally use the expression 'citizenship education'. Other expressions adopted are 'civic education and intercultural understanding', 'civic education courses', 'civic orientation programmes', 'promotion of civic competences', or 'human rights and citizenship education'.[842] However, regardless of the disparities in terminology, what matters is that the EU clearly embraces the EDC paradigm.[843] The following examples highlight the EDC aspects in the content of EU instruments.

840 See already early, Resolution of the Council and the Representatives of the Governments of the Member States, meeting within the Council of 29 May 1990 on the fight against racism and xenophobia [1990] OJ C157/1 (role of education in developing 'civic-mindedness and the values of pluralism and tolerance'); Resolution of the Council and the Representatives of Member States' Governments meeting within the Council of 23 October 1995 on the response of educational systems to the problems of racism and xenophobia [1995] OJ C312/1 ('European educational systems should continue as well as enhance their efforts at promoting education in values which encourage attitudes of solidarity and tolerance, as well as respect for democracy and human rights'). Also Case C-379/87 *Groener* ECLI:EU:C:1989:599, para 20: '[t]eachers have an essential role to play' in a policy of cultural and linguistic diversity.

841 Cp the 2006 and 2018 Recommendation on key competences for lifelong learning (below).

842 Instruments in next section. See also Commission Communication 'Improving and modernising education' COM(2016) 941 final (no citizenship education, but lateral mentioning of civic competences).

843 See § 40 (conclusion normative context).

119 Recommendations on key competences for lifelong learning

In the 2006 Recommendation on key competences for lifelong learning, the European Parliament and the Council developed a Reference Framework of key competences.[844]

On 22 May 2018 this Recommendation was replaced by a Council Recommendation on key competences for lifelong learning.[845] Because the 2006 Recommendation was, for a long time, the central text on key competences and was the basis for the 2018 Recommendation, the reception of exogenic EDC norms is here analysed on the basis of the 2006 instrument.[846]

The 2006 Recommendation did not refer to the title of Council of Europe instruments, nor did it duplicate any provisions thereof, but the development of the Framework occurred in cooperation with the Council of Europe, and similar substance and wording to the EDC standards were adopted.[847] During the preparatory work explicit reference was made to the EDC project (working group on active citizenship and social cohesion):

> The contribution of education and training to the development of active citizenship promoting inclusion and social cohesion is acknowledged by everyone. The Council of Europe's project on education for democratic citizenship is, moreover, actively supported by the Member States and the European Commission. [848]

---

844 Recommendation of the European Parliament and of the Council of 18 December 2006 on key competences for lifelong learning [2006] OJ L394/10 (Annex: Key Competencies for Lifelong Learning- A European Reference Framework).

845 Council Recommendation of 22 May 2018 on key competences for lifelong learning [2018] OJ C189/1.

846 The analysis as to the substance in Part three is based on the 2018 Recommendation.

847 Reference to cooperation with CoE in the work programme on the objectives of the education and training systems, see Commission Communication 'Education & Training 2010': The success of the Lisbon Strategy hinges on urgent reforms (Draft joint interim report on the implementation of the detailed work programme on the follow-up of the objectives of education and training systems in Europe) COM(2003) 0685 final, point 1.1.1.

848 Commission Report Implementation of the 'Education & Training 2010' programme - Supporting document for the draft joint interim report on the implementation of the detailed work programme on the follow-up of the objectives of education and training systems in Europe SEC(2003) 1250 final, heading 4 (Conclusion of the working groups), points 4.1.1 and 4.1.10 (Education and training for active citizenship).

Civic competences were identified as one of the eight key competences (together with, i.a., language, mathematical, or science and technology competences). They should be acquired before compulsory schooling ends and serve as the platform for any further learning. Competences were defined as 'a combination of knowledge, skills and attitudes appropriate to the context'. Key competences were 'those which all individuals need for personal fulfilment and development, active citizenship, social inclusion and employment'.[849] EDC components resonated in the description of social and civic competences:

> These include personal, interpersonal and intercultural competence and cover all forms of behaviour that equip individuals to participate in an effective and constructive way in social and working life, and particularly in increasingly diverse societies, and to resolve conflict where necessary. Civic competence equips individuals to fully participate in civic life, based on knowledge of social and political concepts and structures and a commitment to active and democratic participation.[850]

In a long paragraph the EU Recommendation describes the essential knowledge, skills and attitudes on which civic competences are based or which they include. 'Civic competence is based on knowledge of the concepts of democracy, justice, equality, citizenship, and civil rights (...).'[851] Skills include the ability to engage effectively with others in the public domain, to display solidarity and interest in solving problems, as well as critical and creative reflection and constructive participation in community activities and decision-making, in particular through voting.

---

849 Recommendation of the European Parliament and of the Council of 18 December 2006 on key competences for lifelong learning [2006] OJ L394/10 (Annex: Key Competencies for Lifelong Learning- A European Reference Framework).

850 Annex, heading 6.

851 Knowledge: 'Civic competence is based on knowledge of the concepts of democracy, justice, equality, citizenship, and civil rights, including how they are expressed in the Charter of Fundamental Rights of the European Union and international declarations and how they are applied by various institutions at the local, regional, national, European and international levels. It includes knowledge of contemporary events, as well as the main events and trends in national, European and world history. In addition, an awareness of the aims, values and policies of social and political movements should be developed. Knowledge of European integration and of the EU's structures, main objectives and values is also essential, as well as an awareness of diversity and cultural identities in Europe.'.

Attitudes include respect for human rights, including equality as a basis for democracy, understanding differences in value systems or religions, and demonstrating a sense of responsibility.[852]

The similarity of the Council of Europe concept of EDC and the EU concepts of civic and social competences is not surprising, given the recognition by the EU of the longstanding expertise of the Council of Europe in education and the involvement of all Member States in the genesis of the 2002 Council of Europe Recommendation on education for democratic citizenship adopted four years earlier.[853] The mutual influence of the Council of Europe and the EU can also be detected in later instruments. True, the authors of the 2010 Charter on EDC/HRE preferred not to adopt the term 'competences' (a cluster of skills, knowledge and attitudes focusing on outcomes) and continued to refer to the 'curriculum' (generally understood as focusing on learning objectives).[854] Yet the underlying principles remain the same. A comparison of the 2006 Recommendation with the 2010 Charter on EDC/HRE reveals the same central objective of the 'empowerment' of citizens and similar components. Component (c-2)—valuing diversity—appears *expressis verbis* as part of social competence in

852 Values, attitudes and participation: 'Full respect for human rights including equality as a basis for democracy, appreciation and understanding of differences between value systems of different religious or ethnic groups lay the foundations for a positive attitude.' Also 'a willingness to participate in democratic decision-making at all levels' and 'demonstrating a sense of responsibility, as well as showing understanding of and respect for the shared values that are necessary to ensure community cohesion, such as respect for democratic principles. Constructive participation also involves civic activities, support for social diversity and cohesion and sustainable development, and a readiness to respect the values and privacy of others'.

853 CoE Recommendation Rec(2002)12 of the Committee of Ministers to member states on education for democratic citizenship (16 October 2002), see, i.a., paras 2 and 3: some identical terms (knowledge, attitudes and skills) and certainly the same ideas (e.g. critical approach).

854 Explanatory memorandum para 43. See also CoE Reference Framework of Competences for Democratic Culture, Vol 3: Guidance for implementation (2018), 14: in Europe, the three main curriculum approaches are the knowledge-based curriculum (traditional), the objectives-based curriculum and the competence-based curriculum. Each approach determines which central element structures the curriculum, the remaining curriculum components follow from the central one; the competence-based curriculum is a further development of the objectives-based curriculum. Most curricula combine the three approaches. See also Commission Communication 'Empowering businesses and citizens in Europe's single market: An Action Plan for boosting Your Europe in cooperation with the Member States' COM(2013) 636 final.

the EU Recommendation on key competences.[855] Component (c-3)—playing an active part in democratic life—goes with equipping citizens 'to fully participate in civic life' and the 'commitment to active and democratic participation' in the EU Recommendation.

In the public consultations to review the 2006 Recommendation, a broad acceptance of the provisions on civic competences could be observed. Several contributors proposed better alignment with the EDC standards. One observer found that the definition of civic competence in the 2006 Recommendation lagged behind the better EDC/HRE standards of the Council of Europe.[856]

The 2018 Recommendation defines 'citizenship competence' as follows:

> Citizenship competence is the ability to act as responsible citizens and to fully participate in civic and social life, based on understanding of social, economic, legal and political concepts and structures, as well as global developments and sustainability.[857]

Components similar to those in the EDC standards continue to appear in the 2018 Council Recommendation on key competences for lifelong learning. Moreover, in the preamble the Council explicitly refers to the Council of Europe RFCDC (which further implements the Charter on EDC/HRE) and confirms that it took this into account when updating the Reference Framework on key competences.[858]

---

855 'Individuals … should value diversity and respect others, and be prepared both to overcome prejudices and to compromise.'.

856 Support of the stakeholder consultation in the context of the Key Competences Review: Report on the results of the stakeholder consultation EAC/2017/0150, pp 27, 51, 58, 59, 64, 72 (i.a. referring to Council of Europe model for Competences for Democratic Culture').

857 See Annex 4 to this study: EU Recommendation on key competences for lifelong learning (2018) for the description of essential knowledge, skills and attitudes related to the citizenship competence.

858 Council Recommendation of 22 May 2018 on key competences for lifelong learning, recital 15: 'the Council of Europe's Reference Framework of Competences for Democratic Culture presents a comprehensive set of values, skills and attitudes for an appropriate participation in democratic societies. All of these have been taken into due consideration when updating the Reference Framework.'.

120 Other EU instruments

There are other legal acts of the EU which are consistent with the EDC standards of the Council of Europe. While not necessarily referring to those standards, they encompass aspects of them.

In the 2012 *Decision on the European Year of Citizens (2013)*, Parliament and Council recognised the leading role of the Council of Europe and recalled that social and civic competences equip Union citizens to participate fully in civic life and 'empower them to exercise their rights' (words of the 2010 Council of Europe Charter on EDC/HRE). While the expressions 'citizenship education' and 'education for democratic citizenship' are absent, the three components (c-1–3) appear.[859]

In the *2013 Erasmus+ Regulation*, Parliament and Council state that cooperation with the Council of Europe in the field of education should be strengthened.[860] As to the substance (not the words), the definitions of formal, non-formal or informal education are similar to those in the Charter on EDC/HRE.[861] The Regulation does not use the expressions 'citizenship education' or 'education for democratic citizenship' either, but it recognises the role of education in promoting active citizenship, participation in democratic life, and European values (comparable objectives to the EDC standards).[862]

In the 2013 *Regulation establishing a Rights, Equality and Citizenship Programme for the period 2014 to 2020*, the Parliament and the Council seek to improve the exercise of citizens' rights and pursue this objective by 'enhancing awareness and knowledge of Union law and policies as well as

---

859 Decision 1093/2012/EU of the European Parliament and of the Council of 21 November 2012 on the European Year of Citizens (2013) [2012] OJ L325/1, recitals 14 and 19 ('equip them to fully participate in civic life and empower them to exercise their rights'), applying components (c-3) and (c-1) of the EDC concept, see also recital 19 ('Education policy plays an important role in informing citizens, particularly young people'); and Art 2 Objectives, i.a. Art 2(1) on rights and responsibilities and (2)(c) on valuing diversity.

860 Regulation 1288/2013 of the European Parliament and of the Council of 11 December 2013 establishing 'Erasmus+': the Union programme for education, training, youth and sport and repealing Decisions 1719/2006, 1720/2006 and 1298/2008 [2013] OJ L347/50, recital 20.

861 Compare Erasmus+ Regulation 1288/2013, Art 2 and Charter on EDC/HRE, para 2.

862 Arts 4, 11(1)(a), 14(1)(a), recitals 16,19 and 20. See also Strategic objective 3: Promoting equity, social cohesion and active citizenship, in Council Conclusions on the role of education and training in the implementation of the 'Europe 2020' strategy [2011] C70/1.

of the rights, values and principles underpinning the Union'. The types of actions envisaged include training and learning activities.[863] Exercising its budgetary powers, the Parliament labels these actions 'Ensuring the protection of rights and *empowering* citizens'.[864] Even if the Regulation does not mention the Council of Europe, or use the same wording, EDC standards underlie its provisions, in particular component (c-1) on citizens' rights.

The 2014 *Council Regulation establishing the 'Europe for citizens' programme for the period 2014–2020* is not directly targeted at education, but it includes awareness raising activities with similar objectives to EDC. Educational organisations do have access to the programme.[865] The aims are to enable and encourage citizens to participate in democratic life, to contribute to their understanding of the EU, and its values, politics, and history.[866] The expression 'citizenship education' is not used, nor was it in the previous instruments for the 'Europe for Citizens' programme.[867]

In the 2015 *Action Plan on Human Rights and Democracy* adopted by the Council in the external action field, 'human rights and civic education' are supported to invigorate civil society in third countries so as to strengthen the capacity to hold governments accountable.[868] In a 2012 Resolution on EU external action (human rights in the world), the European Parliament

863 Regulation 1381/2013 of the European Parliament and of the Council of 17 December 2013 establishing a Rights, Equality and Citizenship Programme for the period 2014 to 2020 [2013] OJ L354/62, Arts 4(2)a and Art 5(1)(b)(c).

864 Definitive adoption (EU, Euratom) 2017/292 of the European Union's general budget for the financial year 2017 [2017] OJ L51/1, Chapter 33 02 01 (my emphasis).

865 Listed in Art 6 among 'all stakeholders promoting European citizenship and integration'.

866 Council Regulation (EU) No 390/2014 of 14 April 2014 establishing the 'Europe for Citizens' programme for the period 2014-2020 [2014] OJ L115/3, Arts 1–3, recitals 1, 3, 4, and 19.

867 Citizenship education is not mentioned in Decision 1904/2006 of the European Parliament and of the Council of 12 December 2006 establishing for the period 2007 to 2013 the programme 'Europe for Citizens' to promote active European citizenship [2006] OJ L378/32, amended by Decision 1358/2008 [2008] L350/58, nor in Council Regulation (EU) No 390/2014 of 14 April 2014 establishing the 'Europe for Citizens' programme for the period 2014-2020 [2014] OJ L115/3.

868 Council Conclusions on the Action Plan on Human Rights and Democracy 2015-2019 (20 July 2015), 9, para 7(b). Other institutions are involved, see para 5 for the role of the High Representative, Commission and European Parliament. See also Council, EU Strategic Framework and Action Plan on Human Rights and Democracy (Luxembourg, 25 June 2012) 11855/12, 'Working with bilateral partners'. Furthermore, Joint Communication by the European Commission and the High Representative of the European Union for Foreign Affairs and

referred to the aim of 'building a real culture of human rights and democracy, particularly through *education for democratic citizenship and human rights*'[869] (an aim important in EU internal action as well[870]). This Resolution is one of the rare examples of an EU legal instrument using the expression 'education for democratic citizenship' *verbatim*.[871] Another example is a 2007 Resolution where the Parliament 'calls upon the Member States to develop policies of *education for democratic citizenship* based on citizens' rights and responsibilities' (c-1).[872]

A 2015 *Council resolution on encouraging political participation of young people in democratic life in Europe* refers to 'citizenship education' without defining it but reflects the same objectives and principles as EDC.[873]

In the 2016 *European Parliament resolution on Learning EU at school*, all the components of the EDC concept are present, some of them literally.[874] The Parliament does not refer to the Council of Europe. The expression 'education for democratic citizenship' does not appear, but 'citizenship education' does.[875]

The 2017 *European Pillar of Social Rights*, solemnly proclaimed by the European Parliament, the Council and the Commission, devotes its very first provision to education: 'Everyone has the *right to quality and inclusive*

Security Policy, Action Plan on Human Rights and Democracy (2015-2019) Keeping human rights at the heart of the EU agenda JOIN(2015) 16 final, para 41.

869 European Parliament Resolution of 18 April 2012 on the Annual Report on Human Rights in the World and the European Union's policy on the matter, including implications for the EU's strategic human rights policy [2013] OJ C258E/8, para 155 (emphasis added).

870 See also text to n 989.

871 See also reference in Opinion of the Committee of the Regions on the 'EU Citizenship Report 2010' [2011] OJ C166/3, para 12.

872 European Parliament Resolution of 13 December 2007 on combating the rise of extremism in Europe [2008] OJ C323E/494. Thus even before 2015, the Parliament was calling for citizenship education to combat extremism.

873 Council Resolution on encouraging political participation of young people in democratic life in Europe [2015] OJ C417/10, paras 18 and 34. Same underlying ideas in Council Resolution on the Structured Dialogue and the future development of the dialogue with young people in the context of policies for European cooperation in the youth field, post 2018 [2017] OJ C189/1 (education for active citizenship, values, and critical thinking).

874 European Parliament Resolution of 12 April 2016 on Learning EU at school [2018] OJ C58/57, para 15.

875 Para 10. See also European Parliament Resolution of 12 December 2017 on the EU Citizenship Report 2017: Strengthening Citizens' Rights in a Union of Democratic Change (2017/2069(INI)), para 32.

education, training and life-long learning in order to maintain and acquire skills that *enable* them *to participate fully in society* and manage successfully transitions in the labour market'.[876] Enabling full participation in society is consistent with the EDC-aim of empowerment for participation (c-3) and, moreover, echoes the aim of education in Article 13 of the International Covenant on Economic, Social and Cultural Rights ('education shall enable all persons to participate effectively in a free society').

In the 2018 *Recommendation on promoting common values, inclusive education, and the European dimension of teaching*, the Council states that Member States should make effective use of existing tools to promote citizenship education.[877]

It must be finally be noted that in various Opinions, the Committee of the Regions and the European Economic and Social Committee vigorously advocate citizenship education. The 'role of education in promoting active citizenship among young people' is emphasised.[878] Among 'the conditions for effectiveness of citizenship', the need for measures ensuring 'education and training in citizenship' is highlighted.[879] The Erasmus programme should support democratic citizenship and common European values.[880]

---

876 Commission Recommendation (EU) 2017/761 of 26 April 2017 on the European Pillar of Social Rights [2017] OJ L113/56, Chapter I 'Equal opportunities and access to the labour market', para 01 'Education, training and life-long learning'. See also Commission Communication 'Establishing a European Pillar of Social Rights' COM(2017) 250 final; Commission staff working document Report of the public consultation Accompanying the document Commission Communication Establishing a European Pillar of Social Rights SWD(2017) 206 final; Commission Staff working document Accompanying Commission Communication 'Establishing a European Pillar of Social Rights' SWD(2017) 201 final.

877 Council Recommendation of 22 May 2018 on promoting common values, inclusive education, and the European dimension of teaching [2018] OJ C195/1; see also recitals 10 and 13.

878 Opinion of the Committee of the Regions on 'Strengthening EU citizenship: promotion of EU citizens' electoral rights' [2013] OJ C62/26, paras 38–42. See also Opinion of the Committee of the Regions 'Strengthening European Identity through Education and Culture' [2018] OJ C 361/19, Policy recommendations point 3.

879 Opinion of the Committee of the Regions on the 'EU Citizenship Report 2010' [2011] OJ C166/3, para 37 (emphasis added).

880 Opinion of the EESC on 'Proposal for a regulation of the European Parliament and of the Council establishing "Erasmus": the Union programme for education, training, youth and sport and repealing Regulation (EU) No 1288/2013' [2019] OJ C 62/194, point 3.4.

B Inspiration and cooperation (mode 5)

1. General

121 *Mutual influence, a shared paradigm*

In addition to directly providing substance for EU norms, the exogenic norms of Council of Europe conventions and recommendations have—more generally—been a source of inspiration for the EU, as appears in primary and secondary law, in case law, in policies and in practice. Norm-setting does not occur in a vacuum. In the mode of reception based on inspiration, there is no incorporation of the title or of the actual substantive content of exogenic norms, but they can be recognised as a source of inspiration. Notwithstanding different wording and rules, similarities in the objectives and underlying principles is sometimes striking. Admittedly, the dividing line between modes 4 and 5 is not a sharp one, yet both modes have their place in the spectrum of mutual influence of normative systems. In particular, exogenic norms of high moral authority or expressing an international consensus may inspire the drafting of provisions in the home legal order. UN human rights instruments are at the origin of regional human rights instruments (compare the 1948 Universal Declaration of Human Rights and the 1950 ECHR). Member States' constitutions show similarities in style and substance. Cross-fertilisation of legal orders occurs in the process of norm-setting as well as in the interpretation of the norms.[881] The fact that EU law is also inspired by exogenic norms is thus perfectly natural. Moreover, the Treaties (Article 220 TFEU) and, quite regularly, secondary legislation emphasise the need for cooperation with international organisations.[882] The fifth mode of reception is a transition zone which includes the many *de facto* pathways between the Council of Europe and the EU legal order, resulting from dialogue at conferences, formal and informal meetings of politicians, judges, civil servants, or net-

---

881 Delmas-Marty, *Ordering Pluralism. A Conceptual Framework for Understanding the Transnational Legal World* 23. See also examples in S Breyer, *The Court and the World: American Law and the New Global Realities* (Vintage Books 2016).

882 See i.a. Council Decision of 28 February 2008 relating to the conclusion of an Agreement between the European Community and the Council of Europe on cooperation between the European Union Agency for Fundamental Rights and the Council of Europe [2008] OJ L186/6; Memorandum of Understanding between the Council of Europe and the European Union (2007), para 25: 'to the extent necessary the Council of Europe and the European Union will consult each other at an early stage in the process of elaborating standards'.

works of experts accredited by international organisations. A wide array of policy documents bear witness to this mutual inspiration. In mode 4, the EU legislator incorporates the substance of previously existing exogenic instruments; in mode 5, the same inspiration may lead to simultaneous and parallel norm-setting. Cooperation in the implementation of the norms thus shared fits into this mode. It is based on the same paradigm.

122 Cascades of norm-setting

In many fields, the Council of Europe did pioneer work before the EU acquired the competence to act. Norm-setting started at Council of Europe level and subsequently found its way into the EU legal order through the described modes of reception (accession, general principles, incorporation of title, of substance, or of inspiration). Smaller paths have become secondary roads, and sometimes highways. The cascading normative effects can take various courses. Often, Council of Europe recommendations prepare the ground, influence Council of Europe conventions, which influence interpretations in ECJ case law, which influence the drafting of new provisions in primary or secondary EU law.[883] Several provisions in the CFR (drafted in 2000) were inspired by earlier Council of Europe norms, such as the ECHR (1950) or the European Social Charter (1961, revised 1996). A good example is the right to data protection (Articles 8 CFR, 39 TEU and 16 TFEU), which was foreshadowed by recommendations of the Committee of Ministers (since 1970) and by the Convention for the Protection of Individuals with regard to Automatic Processing of Personal Data (1981).[884] The right to good administration (Article 41 CFR) is a codification (partly) of the general principle of good administration developed by the ECJ, which was preceded by Council of Europe norms dealing with

883 E.g. *European Pharmacopoeia,* see n 627. Other examples in Cornu, 'The impact of Council of Europe Standards on the European Union', i.a. p 126: 'negotiations within the Council of Europe have often facilitated the setting up of a common legal basis, including common values, on which the EU has then been able to elaborate more specific rules.' Analysis of the influence of the CoE on EU norms in various domains: Kolb, *The European Union and the Council of Europe*. See also Joris and Vandenberghe, 'The Council of Europe and the European Union: Natural Partners or Uneasy Bedfellows', 31: CoE conventions have been an important reference source for EU law in areas such as data protection, social policy and cooperation in justice and home affairs.

884 Convention for the Protection of Individuals with regard to Automatic Processing of Personal Data ETS No 108 (Strasbourg, opened 28 January 1981, entered into force 1 October 1985), ratified by all the Member States and referred to in the Explanations to the CFR.

underlying principles of good administration in a recommendation dating back to 1977.[885] In the field of cooperation in criminal matters and the fight against terrorism, various EU norms have their origin in Council of Europe standards and were then developed further, both in terms of substance and procedures.[886] In the area of freedom, security and justice, UN instruments setting out standards applying to detention (detention of refugees and asylum seekers) inspired Council of Europe recommendations of the Committee of Ministers, which in turn influenced EU directives, which partly copied the substantive content or used it as a source of inspiration.[887] The *N* and *El Didri* cases cited above illustrate the cascade effect from the UN to the Council of Europe to the EU legal order.[888] Where can EDC standards be situated in this ongoing cascade of norm-setting?

---

885 Hofmann, Rowe and Türk, *Administrative law and policy of the European Union* 191, referring to CoE Committee of Ministers Resolution 77 (31) On the Protection of the Individuals in Relation to the Acts of Administrative Authorities (28 September 1977) (this instrument does not use the term 'good administration' explicitly but laid down its fundamental principles, such as the right to be heard, access to information, etc.). See also Recommendation CM/Rec(2007)7 of the Committee of Ministers to member states on good administration (20 June 2007).

886 Cornu, 'The impact of Council of Europe Standards on the European Union' 126, with the example of Council Framework Decision 2008/919/JHA of 28 November 2008 amending Framework Decision 2002/475/JHA on combating terrorism [2008] OJ L330/21, which is closely linked to CoE Convention on the Prevention of Terrorism CETS No 196 (Warsaw, opened 16 May 2005, entered into force 1 June 2007) (see Decision recital 9, and compare its Art 3 with Arts 5, 6 and 7 of this Convention). See also examples in Delmas-Marty, *Ordering Pluralism. A Conceptual Framework for Understanding the Transnational Legal World* 21, and Kolb, *The European Union and the Council of Europe*, comparing CoE standards in the fight against terrorism and EU action.

887 See, i.a., Case C-601/15 PPU *N* ECLI:EU:C:2016:85, View of AG Sharpston, para 69.

888 Other examples of EU norms influenced by CoE norms: Art 3 CFR, of which the principles were already included in the CoE Convention on Human Rights and Biomedicine (ETS 164) and additional protocol (ETS 168), as the Explanations specify; or the Community Charter of the Fundamental Social Rights of Workers (adopted by eleven of the Heads of State and Government at the European Council of Strasbourg on 8 and 9 December 1989), inspired by the ESC (but only as poor reflection of it).

2. Shared inspiration and cooperation to implement EDC standards

123 Ongoing cooperation within education policy

Article 220 TFEU in general, and Article 165(3) TFEU in particular, require that the EU and the Member States 'shall' cooperate with the Council of Europe, which is referred to as the competent international organisation in the field of education. EU legal instruments repeatedly call for reinforced cooperation and the development of synergies.[889]

The cooperation of EU institutions with the Council of Europe in setting and implementing EDC standards in practice confirms the shared EDC paradigm.

889 I.a. Decision 1093/2012/EU of the European Parliament and of the Council of 21 November 2012 on the European Year of Citizens (2013) [2012] OJ L325/1, Art 6 and recital 24; EU Education Ministers and the Commissioner for Education, Culture, Youth and Sport, Paris Declaration on Promoting citizenship and the common values of freedom, tolerance and non-discrimination through education (17 March 2015), last para; Erasmus+ Regulation 1288/2013, recital 20; Council Regulation (EU) No 390/2014 of 14 April 2014 establishing the 'Europe for Citizens' programme for the period 2014-2020 [2014] OJ L115/3, Art 7 (joint contributions may be supported by the programme). *De facto* cooperation takes place in the International Contact Group on citizenship and human rights education (set up in 2011), including the UN High Commissioner for Human Rights (OHCHR), UNESCO, the Council of Europe, the European Commission, and the European Union Agency for Fundamental Rights (FRA). On the relationship EU-CoE, see Quinn, 'The European Union and the Council of Europe on the Issue of Human Rights: Twins Separated at Birth?'; O De Schutter, 'The two Europes of human rights: the emerging division of tasks between the Council of Europe and the European Union in promoting human rights in Europe' (2008) 14 Columbia Journal of European Law 509; Joris and Vandenberghe, 'The Council of Europe and the European Union: Natural Partners or Uneasy Bedfellows'; Kolb, *The European Union and the Council of Europe*; T Streinz, 'Fraternal twins: the European Union and the Council of Europe' in H de Waele and J-J Kuipers (eds), *The European Union's emerging international identity: Views from the Global Arena* (Martinus Nijhoff 2013); Schmahl and Breuer, *The Council of Europe: Its Law and Policies*; and in general, Joint Declaration on co-operation and partnership between the Council of Europe and the European Commission (2001), CoE Compendium of Texts governing the relations between the Council of Europe and the European Union (2001); CoE iGuide, Committee of Ministers: Procedures and working methods (24 September 2018), IX, 5–1.

124 EU support for the implementation of the Charter on EDC/HRE

In 2012, the EU Commissioner responsible for Education, Culture, Multilingualism and Youth, Mrs. Androulla Vassiliou, wrote to 'actively support the implementation of the Charter' on EDC/HRE.[890] That year, the Commission and the Council of Europe jointly organised a conference on the implementation of the Charter (first review cycle).[891] Senior officials of the European Commission underscored its significance: Director General for Education and Culture, Mr. Jan Truszczynski, underlined that '[t]he importance of the Charter, in the EU context as well, is that it provides a solid basis for designing and implementing policies aimed at educating citizens to know, respect, and practice democratic values we cherish'.[892] For the 2017 Conference (second review cycle), Mr. Tibor Navracsics, EU Commissioner for Education, Culture, Youth and Sport, stated in his key message that cooperation with the Council of Europe is stronger than ever:

> Our values are not a given. They must be learned, understood and owned by every citizen. Democracy is more than a process. Democracy is a mentality, an ethos, a reflex. … Considering that today's education is tomorrow's society, I firmly believe there is not a better place to pro-

---

890 Commission/EACEA/Eurydice, Citizenship Education in Europe (2012), 3 (Foreword). Earlier, Commission Report Implementation of the 'Education & Training 2010' programme - Supporting document for the draft joint interim report on the implementation of the detailed work programme on the follow-up of the objectives of education and training systems in Europe SEC(2003) 1250 final: 'The Council of Europe's project on education for democratic citizenship is, moreover, actively supported by the Member States and the European Commission'.

891 Commission/EACEA/Eurydice, Citizenship Education in Europe (2012), 8; CoE Proceedings of the Conference on 'Human Rights and Democracy in Action - Looking Ahead: The Impact of the Council of Europe Charter on Education for Democratic Citizenship and Human Rights Education' (Strasbourg, 29-30 November 2012).

892 Mr Jan Truszczynski, Director General for Education and Culture in the European Commission, in CoE Proceedings of the Conference on 'Human Rights and Democracy in Action - Looking Ahead: The Impact of the Council of Europe Charter on Education for Democratic Citizenship and Human Rights Education' (Strasbourg, 29-30 November 2012), 20. See also Mr Pierre Mairesse, Director for Lifelong Learning in the Directorate General for Education and Culture: education for employment and education for citizenship are complementary, and both are necessary (ibid, 21).

mote and pass on those values than families and schools—and no better vector than education to secure democracy.[893]

He cites as one of his responsibilities as Commissioner: '*Empowering* young people of all social and cultural backgrounds so that they can *participate fully in civic and democratic life*'.[894] In reports, evidence is given of the connectedness of the Council of Europe and the EU in the implementation of the Charter on EDC/HRE.[895]

Cooperating in order to implement is a form of reception of exogenic Council of Europe standards on EDC in the EU legal order, proving through action that the EU adheres to the EDC standards. The question is whether this cooperation is enough for the EU.[896]

---

893 CoE, *Learning to live together: Council of Europe Report on the state of citizenship and human rights education in Europe*, 39 (emphasis added); in the follow-up to the Paris Declaration there is Erasmus+ funding for more than 1200 projects, setting up of a network of role models, and extending e-Twinning as the largest teachers' platform in the world to third countries.

894 <ec.europa.eu/commission/commissioners/2014–2019/navracsics_en> (emphasis added).

895 For strong EU commitment and action, see CoE, *Learning to live together: Council of Europe Report on the state of citizenship and human rights education in Europe*, 39, declaration of Mr Navracsics, EU Commissioner for Education. In 2016, a huge number of member states reported to cooperate with the CoE (93%) and with the EU (90%) for the implementation of the Charter on EDC/HRE (in line with its Section IV). Reporting on joint projects, see ibid, p 73–74. Same trend earlier, Kerr, *Implementation of the Council of Europe Charter on Education for Democratic Citizenship and Human Rights Education: Final Report*, p 44. On EU-CoE cooperation on citizenship education in the eighties and nineties, see Naval, Print and Veldhuis, 'Education for Democratic Citizenship in the New Europe: context and reform' (also on the European dimension in education); B Hoskins and others, *Analytic Report: Participatory Citizenship in the European Union (Report 2)* (2012), p 20 (reference to the Charter on EDC/HRE), p 41 (the same experts are active in EU as in CoE context, the same materials used). In the EU, many good practices on education for democracy rely on Council of Europe projects, see J Krek and others, *Good Practices Report: Participatory Citizenship in the European Union (Report 3)* (2012).

896 E.g. CoE, *Learning to live together: Council of Europe Report on the state of citizenship and human rights education in Europe*, p 22, Recommendation 7 to Support and encourage international co-operation: 'Although co-operation among countries in the field of EDC/HRE has increased, opportunities for such cooperation are limited and do not meet the demand. Such co-operation ought to be further reinforced'. This is all the more true for the EU.

125 Joint programmes

Through several joint programmes of the Commission and the Council of Europe, EDC standards have become part of EU and Member States' practice. Since it has more means, the EU often contributes the larger part of the funding of the joint projects.[897] In the joint programme 'Human Rights and Democracy in Action', launched in 2013, the Charter on EDC/HRE provides a framework for this cooperation.[898] The programme supports citizenship and human rights education in participating countries and, since 2016, has also been helping to pilot the Council of Europe RFCDC, designed to implement the Charter on EDC/HRE.

126 Active citizenship: ACCI and CCCI indicators and Eurydice surveys

Questioned by an MEP on steps taken by the EU in the field of citizenship education, the Commission pointed to civic competences being a priority in the ET 2020 strategic framework, to relevant indicators and to Eurydice reports on citizenship education.[899]

The Active Citizenship Composite Indicator (ACCI) and the Civic Competences Composite Indicator (CCCI) were developed in cooperation between the EU and the Council of Europe in order to measure active citi-

---

897 Kolb, *The European Union and the Council of Europe* 43 (comparing budgets and persons working for the EU and CoE). See Memorandum of Understanding between the Council of Europe and the European Union (2007), paras 7–8 (enhanced cooperation), also Regulation (EU) No 235/2014 of the European Parliament and of the Council of 11 March 2014 establishing a financing instrument for democracy and human rights worldwide [2014] OJ L77/85.

898 CoE/EU Joint Programme- Human Rights and Democracy in Action- Pilot Projects Scheme; also CoE Committee of Ministers, Council of Europe Strategy for the Rights of the Child (2016-2021): Children's human rights (3 March 2016) CM(2015)175 final, para 40; CoE, *Council of Europe Strategy for the Rights of the Child (2012-2015): Implementation report*, p 17; CoE, *Learning to live together: Council of Europe Report on the state of citizenship and human rights education in Europe*, 73. Most joint programs aim at the promotion of democracy, rule of law and respect for human rights, see Joris and Vandenberghe, 'The Council of Europe and the European Union: Natural Partners or Uneasy Bedfellows', 23–25.

899 Written questions by Members of the European Parliament and their answers given by a European Union institution [2014] OJ C208/1. Referral also to the Jean Monnet action 'Learning EU at School', the joint programme on EDC and HRE, the campaign of the European Year of Citizens 2013, and the Youth in Action programme (non of these comprehensively define citizenship education).

zenship.[900] The composite indicators confirm the complexity of citizenship and citizenship education. They add precise information to components of the EDC concept in the Charter on EDC/HRE.

The concepts which Eurydice[901] uses to study citizenship education are inspired by the EDC project of the Council of Europe. The 2005 survey refers to the 2002 Recommendation on education for democratic citizenship and defines citizenship education as:

> school education for young people, which seeks to ensure that they become active and responsible citizens capable of contributing to the development and well-being of the society in which they live. While its aims and content may be highly diversified, three key themes are of particular interest. Citizenship education is normally meant to guide pupils towards (a) political literacy, (b) critical thinking and the development of certain attitudes and values and (c) active participation.[902]

---

900 See, i.a., CoE Committee of Ministers, Terms of reference of the Ad hoc Advisory Group on Education for Democratic Citizenship and Human Rights (ED-EDCHR) (5 February 2007) CM/Del/Dec(2007)985/7.2; B Hoskins and R Deakin Crick, *Learning to Learn and Civic Competences: different currencies or two sides of the same coin?* (European Commission, JRC, CRELL, 2008); B Hoskins and M Mascherini, 'Measuring Active Citizenship through the Development of a Composite Indicator' (2009) 90 Social Indicators Research 459; M Mascherini, AR Manca and B Hoskins, *The characterization of Active Citizenship in Europe* (European Commission, JRC, CRELL, 2009); Hartley and Huddleston, *School-community-university partnerships for a sustainable democracy: Education for Democratic Citizenship in Europe and the United States of America* 53; B Hoskins, M Saisana and C Harrison Villalba, *The 2011 Civic Competence Composite Indicator (CCCI-2): Measuring Young People's Civic Competence across Europe based on the IEA International Citizenship and Civic Education study* (Publications Office of the European Union, 2012). See also 4 reports of the Institute of Education, University of London, commissioned by the European Commission, Europe for Citizens Programme, 2012: Hoskins and others, *Contextual Analysis Report: Participatory Citizenship in the European Union (Report 1)*; Hoskins and others, *Analytic Report: Participatory Citizenship in the European Union (Report 2)*, pp 47, 56, 58, 60 (reference to education for democratic citizenship and suggestion of closer collaboration with the CoE to face challenges); Krek and others, *Good Practices Report: Participatory Citizenship in the European Union (Report 3)*; B Hoskins and D Kerr, *Final Study Summary and Policy Recommendations: Participatory Citizenship in the European Union (Report 4)* (2012).

901 Text to n 35.

902 Commission/EACEA/Eurydice, Citizenship Education at School in Europe (2005), p 10 (with description of attitudes and values). Several references to the CoE, i.a. p 9 (with reference to K O'Shea, 'A Glossary of terms for Education for Democratic Citizenship: Education for Democratic Citizenship 2001-2004,

The 2012 Eurydice report relies on the same conceptual framework.[903] Citizenship education encompasses the narrower concept of 'civic education', which is restricted to 'knowledge and understanding of formal institutions and processes of civic life (such as voting in elections)'.[904] Citizenship education 'is a broad concept, which encompasses not only teaching and learning in the classroom but also practical experiences gained through school life and activities in wider society.'[905] Interestingly, Eurydice observes that its 2012 report on citizenship education derives from an evolved concept of citizenship, 'acknowledging the fact that it goes far beyond the simple legal relationship between people and the state'.[906] The notion of 'active citizenship' is central, promoted at EU level by the Centre for Research on Education and Lifelong Learning.[907] Hoskins emphasises that active citizenship depends on explained citizenship: 'the evidence suggests that the main driver to enhance participatory forms of citizenship is learning'.[908] I would add, if citizenship is learned citizenship, then EU citizenship should be learned as well. Active citizenship is defined as 'partici-

---

Developing a Shared Understanding' CoE DGIV/EDU/CIT (2003)29; p 17 (referral to CoE Recommendation Rec(2002)12 of the Committee of Ministers to member states on education for democratic citizenship (16 October 2002)); p 69 (tables based on All-European Study on Education for Democratic Citizenship Policies (CoE 2005), 34–42).

903 Commission/EACEA/Eurydice, Citizenship Education in Europe (2012), p 8: 'citizenship education refers to the aspects of education at school level intended to prepare students to become active citizens, by ensuring that they have the necessary knowledge, skills and attitudes to contribute to the development and well-being of the society in which they live.'.

904 Ibid, 9, with reference to W Schulz and others, *ICCS 2009 International Report: Civic knowledge, attitudes, and engagement among lower-secondary school students in 38 countries* (International Association for the Evaluation of Educational Achievement IEA, 2010), p 22. This last concept is not used as such in the ICCS 2016 framework.

905 Ibid, 9. Further Commission/EACEA/Eurydice, Promoting citizenship and the common values of freedom, tolerance and non-discrimination through education: Overview of education policy developments in Europe following the Paris Declaration of 17 March 2015 (2016); Commission/EACEA/Eurydice, Citizenship Education at School in Europe (2017).

906 Ibid, 8.

907 Indicator-based evaluation and monitoring of education and training systems towards the Lisbon Agenda and the EU2020 objectives (<crell.jrc.ec.europa.eu/ >).

908 Hoskins and others, *Analytic Report: Participatory Citizenship in the European Union (Report 2)*, p 75. See also Hoskins and others, *Contextual Analysis Report: Participatory Citizenship in the European Union (Report 1)*; Hoskins and Kerr,

pation in civil society, community and/or political life, characterised by mutual respect and non-violence and in accordance with human rights and democracy'.[909] It is regrettable if these (indeed crucial) aspects of citizenship education were considered to fall outside any *legal* relationship. An in-depth, well understood and well grounded, legal approach to citizenship includes more aspects of active citizenship than experts in the education field sometimes presume.[910]

The 2017 Eurydice report on citizenship education continues to draw on the work of the Council of Europe and refers to EDC standards within its conceptual framework: the Charter on EDC/HRE and the RFCDC.[911]

127 *Citizenship education as a crisis measure*

The challenges of radicalisation leading to violent extremism have brought citizenship education to the fore. In the ensuing wave of intensified educational action by the EU, the similarities with the substance and objectives of EDC standards are even more striking than before. Several actors have adopted new instruments.

Final Study Summary and Policy Recommendations: Participatory Citizenship in the European Union (Report 4): citizenship is learnt citizenship. See comparable: Losito B and others, Young People's Perceptions of Europe in a Time of Change: IEA International Civic and Citizenship Education Study- 2016 European Report (2017).

909 B Hoskins and others, *Measuring active citizenship in Europe* (CRELL Research Paper 4, European Communities 2006), 10, developed by the research network on 'Active Citizenship for Democracy'. Confirmed in ICCS 2016 (n 550).

910 E.g. § 170 ff on foundational values and participation (Arts 2, 3, 9–11 TEU); § 176 ff. See also Introduction (a Dworkinian approach to law includes underlying principles and values).

911 Commission/EACEA/Eurydice, Citizenship Education at School in Europe (2017), 18, 23, 25, 48, 134. Citizenship education is understood 'as the subject area that is promoted in schools with the aim of fostering the harmonious co-existence and mutually beneficial development of individuals and of the communities they are part of. In democratic societies citizenship education supports students in becoming active, informed and responsible citizens, who are willing and able to take responsibility for themselves and for their communities at the local, regional, national and international level.' To reach these objectives, 'citizenship education needs to help students develop knowledge, skills, attitudes and values in four broad competence areas: 1) interacting effectively and constructively with others; 2) thinking critically; 3) acting in a socially responsible manner; and 4) acting democratically.' (p 9). See also Commission/EACEA/Eurydice, Promoting citizenship and the common values of freedom, tolerance and non-discrimination through education: Overview of education policy developments in Europe following the Paris Declaration of 17 March 2015 (2016).

In March 2015, in response to terrorist attacks, the *EU Ministers of Education and the Commissioner for Education* adopted the Paris Declaration on Promoting citizenship and the common values of freedom, tolerance and non-discrimination through education.[912] They pointed to synergies with ongoing work in the Council of Europe 'in the area of civic education and intercultural understanding'. Inclusive education should aim to promote citizenship and critical thinking. Action for citizenship education can be supported under the Erasmus+ programme.[913] In order to prevent radicalisation, the *Council and the Commission* added new priorities to the ET 2020 strategic framework, emphasising inclusive education, equality, equity, non-discrimination and the promotion of civic competences.[914] The *Council and the Representatives of the Governments* agreed that human rights and citizenship education represent powerful means of promoting common values and invited the Member States to promote citizenship education and to enhance social and civic competences.[915] In a 2016 Communication, the *Commission* stated that in the long run, 'high-quality education

---

912 EU Education Ministers and the Commissioner for Education, Culture, Youth and Sport, Paris Declaration on Promoting citizenship and the common values of freedom, tolerance and non-discrimination through education (17 March 2015).

913 Critical thinking as a skill is emphasised in the citizenship and civic competences mentioned in Resolution of the Council and of the Representatives of the Governments of the Member States, meeting within the Council, of 24 February 2016 on promoting socio-economic development and inclusiveness in the EU through education: the contribution of education and training to the European Semester 2016 [2016] OJ C105/1, and Council Conclusions of 30 May 2016 on developing media literacy and critical thinking through education and training [2016] OJ C212/5. See also Commission/EACEA/Eurydice, Promoting citizenship and the common values of freedom, tolerance and non-discrimination through education: Overview of education policy developments in Europe following the Paris Declaration of 17 March 2015 (2016).

914 Council Conclusions of 12 May 2009 on a strategic framework for European cooperation in education and training (ET 2020) [2009] OJ C119/2; Joint Report of the Council and the Commission on the implementation of the strategic framework for European cooperation in education and training (ET 2020) — New priorities for European cooperation in education and training [2015] OJ C 417/25 (see the Strategic Framework for European Cooperation on Education and Training ('ET 2020'), the renewed framework for European cooperation in the youth field (2010–2018), the EU Work Plan for Sport (2014–2017) and the Culture Work Plan (2015–2018).

915 Conclusions of the Council and of the Representatives of the Governments of the Member States, meeting within the Council, on the prevention of radicalisation leading to violent extremism [2016] OJ C467/3: Invitation to Member

from pre-school onward remains the best safety net against social exclusion, which can be for some a factor in radicalisation'.[916] Existing tools will be further implemented to support teachers, i.a. the RFCDC. The Commission proposed 'a Council Recommendation to enhance social inclusion and promote Europe's fundamental values through education and non-formal learning'.[917] The Commission asked for the possibility of establishing 'civic education courses in secondary schools' to be explored, in order to give third country nationals an understanding of the laws, culture and values of the receiving society. Member States are encouraged to '[o]rganise civic orientation programmes for all third country nationals as a way to foster integration into the host society and promote the understanding and respect of EU values'.[918] By a Decision of 2017, the Commission set up an Expert Group on radicalisation and referred to Council conclusions on

---

States to promote citizenship education. No definition, but call on Commission to work on a toolkit to develop democratic resilience, media literacy, tolerance, critical thinking, and conflict-resolution skills. Creation of a Working Group on Promoting citizenship and the common values of freedom, tolerance and non-discrimination through education (scope of Paris Declaration), including experts of the Council of Europe, and development of online compendium of good practices. Further Conclusions of the Council and of the Representatives of the Governments of the Member States, meeting within the Council, on Inclusion in Diversity to achieve a High Quality Education For All - Council Conclusions (17 February 2017).

916 Commission Communication supporting the prevention of radicalisation leading to violent extremism COM(2016) 379 final, p 9.

917 Ibid, p 11. See Council Recommendation of 22 May 2018 on promoting common values, inclusive education, and the European dimension of teaching [2018] OJ C195/1. Further on cooperation Conclusions of the Council and of the Representatives of the Governments of the Member States, meeting within the Council, on the prevention of radicalisation leading to violent extremism [2016] OJ C467/3; Commission Communication 'Eight progress report towards an effective and genuine Security Union' COM(2017) 0354 final: 'Education plays a key role in preventing radicalisation, and the Commission has taken a series of steps to implement the Paris Declaration'.

918 Commission Communication 'Action Plan on the integration of third country nationals' COM(2016) 377 final, point 4.1.5. Emphasis added. See already Commission Communication 'A Common Agenda for Integration - Framework for the Integration of Third-Country Nationals in the European Union' COM(2005) 389 final: 'civic orientation in introduction programmes and other activities for newly arrived third-country nationals with the view of ensuring that immigrants understand, respect and benefit from common European and national values'. See also Case C-579/13 *P and S* ECLI:EU:C:2015:369, paras 47–48 on the usefulness of a civic integration examination for third country nationals; the ECJ ruled that Dir 2003/109, which aims at the integration of third-

media literacy and critical thinking.[919] In these conclusions, the *Council* recalled Article 2 TEU and invited the Member States to '[e]ncourage sufficient attention to be paid to developing media literacy and critical thinking in education and training at all levels, including through citizenship and media education'.[920] Social and civic competences 'have a clear link to critical thinking, ensuring that people can *value diversity* and respect the views and values of others'.[921] Thus, essential components of EDC standards appear (such as c-2 and critical thinking).[922]

That crises favour increased focus on citizenship education is a matter of sociological observation.[923] Yet, this should not conceal the need to pursue citizenship education on a more permanent basis. Preparing citizens for life in a democratic society and in respect of fundamental rights should be a continuous and lasting objective.

---

country nationals who are settled on a long-term basis in the Member States, does not preclude Dutch legislation imposing the obligation to pass a civic integration examination, testing language proficiency and knowledge of the Netherlands society. It was not contrary to the principle of equal treatment (nationals were not required to pass such an examination, but the situations were not comparable). See also Opinion of AG Spunar, paras 93–94: The Council adopted Common Basic Principles for Immigrant Integration Policy in 2004 (confirmed by the Stockholm Programme), stating that 'basic knowledge of the host society's language, history and institutions is indispensable to integration and enabling immigrants to acquire this basic knowledge is essential to successful integration'. Mutatis mutandis applicable to the EU citizen in the EU society? More in E Bribosia and S Ganty, 'Arrêt Dogan: quelle légalité pour les tests d'intégration civique?" (2014) 22 Journal de droit européen 378.

919 Commission Decision of 27 July 2017 setting-up the High-Level Commission Expert Group on radicalisation [2017] OJ C252/3.

920 Council Conclusions of 30 May 2016 on developing media literacy and critical thinking through education and training [2016] OJ C212/5, paras 1 and 3. See alto text to n 780 (mode 3). Further Conclusions of the Council and of the Representatives of the Governments of the Member States, meeting within the Council, on the role of the youth sector in an integrated and cross-sectoral approach to preventing and combating violent radicalisation of young people [2016] OJ C213/1.

921 'Against this background, also notes that'. My emphasis.

922 See i.a. CoE Recommendation Rec(2002)12 of the Committee of Ministers to member states on education for democratic citizenship (16 October 2002), appendix para 2.

923 See also questions raised in France after the *Charlie Hebdo* attacks (e.g. <eduscol.education.fr/histoire-geographie/actualites/actualites/article/attentat-contre-icharlie-hebdoi-une-attaque-contre-la-liberte-la-democratie-et-la-republi>).

128 *Intermediate conclusion: partial normative incorporation of EDC standards*

The analysis of endogenic norms related to citizenship education has shown that normative reception of EDC standards occurs essentially in modes 4 and 5. There is a link in EU primary law between democracy, citizenship and education and EU secondary law contains provisions corresponding to the essential substance of EDC standards (mode 4) or—more generally—drawing inspiration from them (mode 5). Moreover, EU education policy occurs in close cooperation with the Council of Europe, including as regards the implementation of the Charter on EDC/HRE. Finally, EDC objectives are even more prominent in more recent EU legal instruments in response to the challenges of radicalisation. To sum up, the normative reception of EDC standards in EU law is fragmented, but convincing. Endogenic provisions relating to citizenship education partially incorporate the substance of the EDC standards of the Council of Europe and are drawn up on the basis of the EDC paradigm.

Before the sixth mode of reception—interpretation of EU law in the light of exogenic standards—is examined at close quarters, the reader may have a question which I will answer first.

129 *Why has no endogenic legal instrument on citizenship education been chosen as a prism through which to look at the position of EU citizens?*

If the EU has its own endogenic norms on citizenship education, such as the 2006 or 2018 Recommendation on key competences for lifelong learning, why have the EDC standards of the Council of Europe been chosen as a prism through which to look at the position of the EU citizen in this study? What value do they add?

Firstly, the Council of Europe was established in 1949 with the core mission to promote human rights, democracy and the rule of law. EDC is an integral and central part of this mission. The Council of Europe thus has a longstanding tradition in this field (as shown by the genesis of the Charter on EDC/HRE described above) and has developed an impressive set of EDC standards and materials. In contrast, the EU was established in 1957 with a very different mission as the European Economic Community. Competences in education were only inserted into the Treaties in 1992. They are lateral and limited. As a result, EU action on citizenship education is more recent, fragmented, and peripheral.[924] The EDC aspects highlighted in the EU legal instruments cited should not create the false

924 See Part four.

impression that EU law includes a comprehensive set of instruments on citizenship education.[925] In such an important field as democracy, the rule of law and human rights, it is wise for the EU to be guided by an organisation founded with those very goals in mind (in line with Articles 222 and 165(3) TFEU).

Secondly, as set out in Part one, the Charter on EDC/HRE reflects a European consensus carrying great weight. It limits the margin of appreciation of member states and has important strengths, including the link with UN standards and the right to education in international agreements.

Finally, the Council of Europe standards on EDC are neutral in the Eurosceptic/Europhile debate. A crucial argument in favour of using the Charter on EDC/HRE as a prism for academic analysis of EU citizenship is its objectivity as a Council of Europe standard.[926] Because it does not originate in the EU institutions, it cannot be distrusted on account of a 'pro EU' bias.[927] EU instruments do not focus on a neutral concept of citizenship education, but, as should be expected, tend to promote the EU aspects of it, such as closeness to the EU, or an EU identity.[928] When describing knowledge, skills and attitudes relating to civic competences, the 2006 Recommendation on key competences adds at a stroke in several provisions that they are applicable to local, regional, national, European and international levels.[929] The 2018 Recommendation, too, refers to 'constructive

925 The paragraph on citizenship competence in the Annex to the 2018 Recommendation on key competences for lifelong learning is at present one of the most relevant provisions.

926 See also the ECtHR principle in n 696.

927 EU institutions promoting EU learning: see i.a. European Parliament Resolution of 12 April 2016 on Learning EU at school [2018] OJ C58/57; earlier European Parliament Resolution of 26 September 2006 on initiatives to complement school curricula providing appropriate support measures to include the European dimension [2006] OJ C306E/100, para 1: 'Considers that all education systems should ensure that their pupils have by the end of their secondary education the knowledge and competences they need, as defined by their respective educational authorities, to prepare them for their roles as citizens and as members of the European Union'.

928 See i.a. Commission Communication on 'Strengthening European Identity through Education and Culture' COM(2017) 673 final; Commission Erasmus Proposal COM(2018) 367 final, Art 3(1): to the general objectives of the Erasmus Programme belongs the strengthening of European identity. Also Council Recommendation of 22 May 2018 on promoting common values, inclusive education, and the European dimension of teaching [2018] OJ C195/1.

929 Recommendation of the European Parliament and of the Council of 18 December 2006 on key competences for lifelong learning, Annex (6)(B).

participation in community activities, as well as in decision-making at all levels, from local and national to the European and international level'.[930] The placing of all these levels on an equal footing has been criticised for deflating the national level and inflating the European level.[931] Comparing the Council of Europe and the EU approach to citizenship education, scholars observe that the Council of Europe concentrates on education content, while the EU focuses on clarifying the benefits of European citizenship and supportive acceptance of EU institutions.[932] Because of its widespread international acceptance, the Council of Europe Charter on EDC/HRE constitutes an external and independent standard on citizenship education, which suits an academic analysis of the issue of citizenship education for the EU citizen.

The components of the Charter are without bias and based on universal values. They will be applied as neutral parameters in Part three, to explore their significance for citizens in the EU (as to the substance). But first, to complete the analysis of the effects of the Charter on EDC/HRE in the EU legal order (as to the form), I will explore to what extent the Charter on EDC/HRE should be taken into account in the interpretation of EU law.

C Interpretation of EU law taking account of exogenic norms (mode 6)

1. General

130 Interpretation methods

In the modes of reception described so far, case law illustrates that the ECJ gives effect to exogenic norms by using them in the interpretation and application of EU law. Interpretation of EU law thus operationalises the normative reception of exogenic norms in the EU legal order. This phe-

930 Council Recommendation of 22 May 2018 on key competences for lifelong learning, Annex (6), skills for citizenship competence.

931 Debate in workshop: K Grimonprez, 'Conflicting ideas of Europe: the role of values in citizenship education' (European Conference NECE, Networking European Citizenship Education, '1914-2014: Lessons from History? Citizenship Education and Conflict Management', Vienna, 16-18 October 2014).

932 P Schreiner (ed) *'Education for Democratic Citizenship' in the Context of Europe* (CSC/CEC 2013) 24; see also HJ Abs und S Werth in R Hedtke and T Zimenkova (eds), *Education for Civic and Political Participation: A Critical Approach* (Routledge 2013).

nomenon will be examined with special emphasis on its relevance for the effects of EDC standards within the EU legal order.

To ensure that 'the law' is observed (Article 19 TEU), the first step for the ECJ is a textual interpretation of EU law, including the endogenic norms incorporating the substance of, or drawing inspiration from, EDC standards. Next, where there is no clear and precise provision in all official languages, the ECJ may use contextual and teleological methods of interpretation (classic methods in line with the Vienna Convention on the Law of Treaties[933]).

The ECJ stated in *Cilfit:*

> every provision of Community law must be placed in its context and interpreted in the light of the provisions of Community law as a whole, regard being had to the objectives thereof and to its state of evolution at the date on which the provision in question is to be applied.[934]

On a historical interpretation, the *travaux préparatoires* are increasingly important.[935] They sometimes refer to exogenic norms.

Exogenic norms may furthermore play a role in ensuring interpretation in good faith and in the spirit of sincere cooperation. In general, a consistent interpretation with international law is aimed at, yet only as far as possible (red line): the autonomy of the EU legal order must be respected. In addition to converging lines of case law, diverging lines of case law are

---

933 Vienna Convention on the Law of Treaties (adopted 23 May 1969, entered into force 27 January 1980) 1155 UNTS 331, Arts 31–32. See text to n 790.

934 Case 283/81 *Cilfit* ECLI:EU:C:1982:335, para 20. See J Mertens de Wilmars, 'Réflexions sur les méthodes d'interprétation de la Cour de justice des Communautés européennes' (1986) 22 Cahiers de Droit européen 5, Lenaerts and Gutiérrez-Fons, 'To Say What the Law of the EU Is: Methods of Interpretation and the European Court of Justice'.

935 To the extent that the wording of EU law is unclear, the ECJ analyses the decision-making process leading to EU law. E.g. Case C-370/12 *Pringle* ECLI:EU:C:2012:756, paras 135–136, 138–141; Case C-583/11 P *Inuit Tapiriit Kanatami and Others v Parliament and Council* ECLI:EU:C:2013:625, paras 59, 66, 70. In line with the Vienna Convention on the Law of Treaties (adopted 23 May 1969, entered into force 27 January 1980) 1155 UNTS 331, Art 32. See Lenaerts and Gutiérrez-Fons, 'To Say What the Law of the EU Is: Methods of Interpretation and the European Court of Justice', 14, 16, 22, 24–31. Earlier: S Schenberg and K Frick, 'Finishing, Refining, Polishing: On the Use of Travaux Préparatoires as an Aid to the Interpretation of Community Legislation' (2003) 28 ELRev 149.

apparent, where interpretation differs from exogenic norms due to the specific objectives or features of EU law.[936]

What are the implications for EDC standards of these general reflections on the interpretation of EU law in the light of exogenic norms?

2. Taking account of the Charter on EDC/HRE in the interpretation of EU law

Textual, contextual and teleological interpretation

131 Interpretation in the light of Council of Europe EDC standards

Can the second anchor point of the study—'Every person holding the nationality of a Member State shall be a citizen of the Union. Citizenship of the Union shall be additional to and not replace national citizenship' (Article 20 TFEU)—be interpreted in the light of EDC standards, taking the Charter on EDC/HRE as a reference instrument? The partial normative incorporation of EDC standards into EU law could thus be reinforced by the interpretation-based mode. The two reflections expressed in the analysis of case law in mode 4 re-emerge.[937] To what extent do Council of Europe recommendations on EDC fall under the converging or the diverging line of case law? How can EDC standards have effects in the broader context of EU law?

Several Treaty provisions on citizenship, democracy, and education are broadly drafted and textual interpretation does not suffice to determine their content (*traité cadre*).[938] Applying the ECJ's statement of principle in *Cilfit* quoted above, placing EU law provisions on citizenship, democracy, and education in their *context* and interpreting them in the light of EU law as a whole, will amplify the effects of EDC standards incorporated in EU law. The *objectives* of EU law and its state of *evolution* also justify taking account of EDC standards in the interpretation of EU law. A closer look follows now at the first two elements of the *Cilfit* citation: context and objectives. The state of evolution has been considered in the previous sections: not only the growing impact of the EU in ever more policy fields

936 See conclusion to §111 .

937 §§ 112 113 .

938 Lenaerts and Gutiérrez-Fons, 'To Say What the Law of the EU Is: Methods of Interpretation and the European Court of Justice', 16 'traité cadre', 20 'a systematic interpretation enables the EU law provision in question to be in harmony with the context in which it is placed'.

and on the daily lives of citizens,[939] but also the recent challenges of radicalisation support an interpretation in the light of EDC standards.

132 Contextual interpretation

A contextual or systematic interpretation is premised on the idea of a rational legislator who has established a consistent legal order.[940] Each provision of EU law must be interpreted in harmony with the general scheme of the Treaties and with the context in which it is placed.

The general scheme of the Treaties includes the referential role for the Council of Europe (Article 220(1) TFEU). Article 165(3) TFEU requires that in the field of education cooperation is fostered in particular with the Council of Europe, the competent international organisation. With Article 165(3) TFEU in mind, various Council of Europe instruments cited in the normative context will be pertinent, i.a. for the interpretation of EU Treaty concepts such as 'quality education' or 'the European dimension in education' (Article 165(1) and (2) TFEU).

A contextual reading must also have regard to the general scheme of the Treaties embracing the EDC paradigm. This follows from a combined reading of Articles 10(3) TEU and 165(2) TFEU (linking democracy-citizenship-education). Other EU primary law provisions on democracy (Articles 9–12 TEU) and on citizenship (Articles 20–25 TFEU and 39–46 CFR) may be interpreted in the light of this paradigm.

Next, from Article 24(1)(c) of the UN Convention on the Rights of Persons with Disabilities (an integral part of EU law after accession), it can be inferred that the EU accepts that education shall be directed to effective participation in a free society, which is precisely the aim of EDC standards.[941]

There must also be consistent interpretation with the above-mentioned secondary law which partially incorporates EDC standards. The endogenic norms drawn up in the EDC paradigm in modes 4 and 5 are part of the EU legal order and together form the context for consistent interpretation of provisions on EU citizenship and democracy.

Furthermore, the interpretation of provisions on citizenship, democracy, and education in EU law in the light of EDC standards of the Coun-

939 Introduction and Part three.

940 Difference internal-external contextual interpretation, see Lenaerts and Gutiérrez-Fons, 'To Say What the Law of the EU Is: Methods of Interpretation and the European Court of Justice', 16. See for internal consistency, Art 7 TFEU. Structure of the Treaties, as in *Cilfit*.

941 Text to n 630.

cil of Europe is consistent with the EU's commitments in the Memorandum of Understanding recognising the Council of Europe as a benchmark for democracy. The Council of Europe and the EU will cooperate in building a democratic culture in Europe, in particular through promoting EDC and HRE.[942]

It is legitimate for the judge to take the Council of Europe origins of EU norms into account when analysing the decision-making process leading to the adoption of the norm.[943] As in other fields, the Court may interpret EU law with regard to citizenship education historically, on the basis of preparatory instruments, thus taking account of EDC standards.[944]

133 The value of democracy

The EU primary law context includes the provisions on foundational values (Articles 2 and 49 TEU), values shared with the Council of Europe.

The fact that 'democracy' is one of the founding values of the EU (Article 2 TEU) has normative implications which are reflected in EDC standards. Article 2 TEU states that the values to which it refers are 'common to the Member States'. Equally 'common to the Member States' is the association between democracy and education: democracy presupposes education for democracy. Democracy cannot be seen in isolation from the wide European consensus on EDC, as evidenced in the many Council of Europe instruments. The 2002 Recommendation on EDC affirmed that EDC is fundamental to defending the values of democracy, human rights, and the rule of law.[945] If democracy and human rights belong to the core nucleus of shared values[946], the EDC and HRE associated with them belong to the core nucleus as well.

Article 49 TEU provides that only a European State which 'respects' the values of Article 2 TEU and 'is committed to promoting them', can apply to be a member of the EU. This respect for, and commitment to promoting, the values of democracy and human rights must be interpreted in the

---

942 Paras 10 and 36; CoE Third Summit of Heads of State and Government, The Declaration and the Action Plan (Warsaw, 16-17 May 2005), Action plan, III, 3.

943 Lenaerts and Gutiérrez-Fons, 'To Say What the Law of the EU Is: Methods of Interpretation and the European Court of Justice', 16–17.

944 Text to n 848 and 957. See i.a. *RTL* (§ 108). To define for instance 'food safety', 'public health', 'handicap' or 'public interest', the ECJ wells in non-binding sources, i.a. text to n 737 (*Codex Alimentarius*).

945 CoE Recommendation Rec(2002)12 of the Committee of Ministers to member states on education for democratic citizenship (16 October 2002), para 1.

946 Lenaerts and Gutiérrez-Fons, 'The Role of General Principles of EU Law', 1663.

light of EDC/HRE standards. Promoting the value of democracy makes no sense without providing for EDC, based on international standards. What is expected of new Member States must, logically, be expected of existing Member States. Just as the value of the rule of law in Article 2 TEU has been interpreted by the European Parliament, the Commission and the ECJ (General Court)in the light of Council of Europe standards, including a Recommendation of the Committee of Ministers on judges' independence, efficiency and responsibilities, so too should the value of democracy in Article 2 be interpreted in the light of Council of Europe standards, including the Recommendation of the Committee of Ministers to member states on the Charter on EDC/HRE.[947] The substance of the norms of the Recommendation CM/Rec(2010)12 on judges' independence, efficiency and responsibilities is set out in the appendix, like those of the Charter on EDC/HRE. Admittedly, their content is in general more precise than that of the Charter on EDC/HRE. Nevertheless, there can be no doubt as to the essential principles, which are explained in a sufficiently clear way.[948]

The legal effects of the values in Article 2 TEU are increasingly important. Article 2 TEU was cited in an Order of the Court (Grand Chamber) imposing a periodic penalty payment on Poland in the context of interim measures in infringement proceedings concerning forest management (rule of law).[949] The Commission started the procedure under Article 7 TEU for determination of a clear risk of a serious breach by the Republic of Poland of the rule of law, as well as infringement procedures.[950] In *Wightman*, the ECJ underlined the importance of the values of liberty and democracy, part of the very foundations of the EU legal order. Not allowing a Member State (the UK) to reverse its decision to withdraw would be inconsistent with the aims and the values expressed in Article 1 and 2 TEU.[951]

134 Democratic principles pervading EU law

Title II of the TEU refers to 'democratic principles' in the plural ('Provi sions on democratic principles'). In the EU legal order, these democratic principles are not limited to the codification in Articles 9–12 TEU and can-

---

947 Text to n 765 ff.

948 See § 64 ('On the other hand').

949 Case C-441/17 R *Commission v Poland, Order of the Court* ECLI:EU:C:2017:877, para 102. See also the crucial role of Art 2 in Case C-64/16 *Juízes Portugueses* ECLI:EU:C:2018:117; and in Case C-216/18 PPU *LM* ECLI:EU:C:2018:586.

950 Text to n 769.

951 Case C-621/18 *Wightman and Others* ECLI:EU:C:2018:999, paras 61–63.

not be interpreted narrowly.[952] Democracy as a value is expressed in terms of democratic principles, which are further developed and codified in rules in secondary legislation. EDC standards are part of those democratic principles, giving substance to the value and contributing to its realisation. EDC standards contribute to making the democratic principles effective.[953]

The provisions of the Treaties and the CFR are to be interpreted in the light of their preambles. In the preamble to the TEU, the Member States confirm 'their attachment to the principles of liberty, democracy and respect for human rights and fundamental freedoms and of the rule of law'. In the preamble to the CFR, they proclaim that the Union 'is based on the principles of democracy and the rule of law' and that the Union 'places the individual at the heart of its activities'. It would be contrary to the general scheme of the Treaties to leave the individual—at the heart of the activities—without EDC.

ECJ case law repeatedly confirms the importance of the principle of democracy: 'participation reflects a fundamental democratic principle that the peoples should take part in the exercise of power through the intermediary of a representative assembly'.[954] In *Commission v Germany*, the ECJ stated that 'the principle of democracy forms part of European Community law', expressly enshrined in the Treaty as one of the foundations of the EU; '[a]s one of the principles common to the Member States, it must be taken into consideration when interpreting acts of secondary law'.[955] In other case law, the ECJ uses the principle of democracy as a ground of

---

952 On the concept of 'principles', see Semmelmann, 'General Principles in EU Law between a Compensatory Role and an Intrinsic Value', 460: 'A principle is a norm (understood in a broad sense) that shows a certain degree of inherent structural generality in the sense of an indeterminate, abstract, programmatic, non-conclusive or orientative character. Notwithstanding subsequent codification, principles are frequently unwritten'. See also Tridimas, *The General Principles of EU Law*, 1; A von Bogdandy, 'Founding Principles' in A von Bogdandy and J Bast (eds), *Principles of European Constitutional Law*, vol 8 (2nd edn, Hart Beck Nomos 2010).

953 Further Part three.

954 Case 138/79 *Roquette Frères* ECLI:EU:C:1980:249, para 33; Case 139/79 *Maizena v Council* ECLI:EU:C:1980:250, para 34; Case C 300/89 *Commission v Council (Titanium dioxide)* ECLI:EU:C:1991:244, para 20; Case C-155/07 *Parliament v Council* EU:C:2008:605, para 78. See also Joined Cases C-402/05 P and C-415/05 P *Kadi* ECLI:EU:C:2008:461, paras 303–304. Further K Lenaerts, 'The principle of democracy in the case law of the European Court of Justice' (2013) 62 International and Comparative Law Quarterly 271.

955 Case C-518/07 *Commission v Germany* ECLI:EU:C:2010:125, para 40, 51.

legality control of the acts of the institutions.[956] The principle of democracy pervades EU law. It should be interpreted in the light of EDC standards.

135 Teleological interpretation of EU legislation on education

EDC standards should be taken into account when interpreting EU law provisions on education teleologically, especially when they share objectives and the EU provisions were drafted in the period during which the Council of Europe was taking action in the same field, following the reasoning in *RTL*, *Humanplasma* and *N* in mode 4.

On the basis of a teleological and historical interpretation, the provisions on social and civic competences in the 2006 Recommendation on key competences for lifelong learning, should be interpreted in the light of the 2002 Recommendation on education for democratic citizenship, i.a. having regard to the preparatory works.[957] It must be admitted that uncertainty may arise as to how far the autonomy of the EU plays a role. Specific EU objectives deviating from Council of Europe objectives may lead to a divergent interpretation of—at first sight—comparable norms, as in *Commission v UK* on transfrontier television.[958] Together with the general objectives shared with Council of Europe instruments on EDC, the Recommendation on key competences has its own specific objectives. It recognises education in its dual role, social and economic, but the economic objectives seem predominant: the first aim mentioned in the preamble of the Recommendation on key competences is to respond to globalisation and the shift to knowledge-based economies (Lisbon European Council of March 2000).[959] Yet, I think that these economic objectives do not imply that the norms on civic and social competences should be interpreted as being at variance with EDC standards. On the contrary, durable economic prosperity can only be achieved in a society of mature citizens, aware of their rights and responsibilities, who value diversity and participate

---

956 See Case C-409/13 *Council v Commission* ECLI:EU:C:2015:217, paras 37, 96, 107: the ECJ dismissed the action for annulment of the Commission's withdrawal of a proposal; the Commission had not infringed 'the principle of democracy enshrined in Art 10(1) and (2) TEU' (principle of democracy as a ground for review of legality under Art 263 TFEU). Other case law on democracy in Part three.

957 Text to n 848.

958 N 795.

959 Presidency Conclusions of the Lisbon European Council of 23 and 24 March 2000.

actively in democratic life at various levels. An interpretation which converges with Council of Europe norms is therefore appropriate. The objectives of the 2018 Recommendation on key competences for lifelong learning require an interpretation in the light of the 2010 Recommendation on the Charter on EDC/HRE. Moreover, the preamble of the 2018 Recommendation refers to the RFCDC. Nevertheless, the issue of autonomy will be kept in mind when applying the Charter on EDC/HRE to the EU citizen.

EDC standards should also be taken into account when interpreting the Erasmus+ Regulation. Again, there may be doubts about a fully convergent interpretation because of the economic rationale. The general objective of the Erasmus+ Regulation is to contribute to the achievement of the Europe 2020 strategy for growth. The focus of the ET 2020 strategic objectives (European cooperation in education and training) is not citizenship education.[960] However, in the 2015 response to radicalisation, new priorities were added which did relate to citizenship education.[961] Mostly, the Erasmus+ Regulation shares the essential objectives of the Council of Europe's norms on EDC, i.e. promoting active citizenship, participation in democratic life, and European values.[962] Respect for the specific objectives of the EU should not therefore lead to a divergent interpretation, leaving EDC standards aside as some alien element.

136 EDC standards contribute to realising several EU objectives

EDC standards are fully consistent with several EU objectives. Accordingly, and in line with *Cilfit*, it is legitimate to take them into account

960 Art 4 (a) (b) and recital 5. Strategic objective 3 is not addressed to the population in general, but focuses on early school leavers, pre-primary education, migrants and learners with special needs. Strategic and specific objectives further developed in Part four.

961 Text to n 914.

962 Text to n 862. See also Strategic objective 3: Promoting equity, social cohesion and active citizenship, in Council Conclusions on the role of education and training in the implementation of the 'Europe 2020' strategy [2011] C70/ibid. Action in education combines an economic and social rationale, see, e.g., Council Conclusions on the role of youth work in supporting young people's development of essential life skills that facilitate their successful transition to adulthood, active citizenship and working life [2017] OJ C189/30; Commission Communication 'School development and excellent teaching for a great start in life' COM(2017) 248 final. Further Part three, and Commission Erasmus Proposal COM(2018) 367 final.

when interpreting EU law in a teleological way and giving *effet utile* to provisions.[963]

EDC standards are in harmony with the first aim of the EU, namely 'to promote peace, its values [such as democracy] and the well-being of its peoples' (Article 3 in conjunction with Article 2 TEU). They are congruent with Treaty objectives such as ensuring that the Union functions as a representative and participatory democracy (Articles 10–11 TEU), developing quality education (Article 165(1) TFEU), encouraging the participation of young people in democratic life in Europe through education (Article 165(2) TFEU), or protecting the rights of the child (Article 3(3) TEU). In its relations with the wider world, the EU aims to contribute to the protection of human rights, in particular the rights of the child (Article 3(5) TEU). Logically, it can be assumed that the EU accepts the standards on which there is a consensus in the international community, such as EDC standards.[964]

In its interconnection with human rights education, EDC is consistent with the objectives of the CFR.

EDC standards also help to advance objectives pursued in secondary law, contributing to the effectiveness of essential rules, i.a. on transparency and openness.[965]

---

963 See Lenaerts and Gutiérrez-Fons, 'To Say What the Law of the EU Is: Methods of Interpretation and the European Court of Justice', 16: 'The Treaties are imbued with a "purpose-driven functionalism"-their provisions provide the link between the objectives pursued by the EU and the means to attain them'; 32: 'teleological interpretation and systematic interpretation are often interlinked, since it is the latter that allows the ECJ to identify the objective pursued by the provision in question'; forms of teleological interpretation can be (1) functional, giving *effet utile*, (2) *sensu stricto*, interpreting an ambiguous provision in the light of its objectives, and (3) consequentialist, focusing on the consequences flowing from the interpretation advanced. See also M Ortino, 'A reading of the EU constitutional legal system through the meta-principle of effectiveness' [2016] Cahiers droit européen 91. On 'primacy, unity and effectiveness of EU law' see Case C-399/11 *Melloni* ECLI:EU:C:2013:107, para 60, and EU Accession to the ECHR *Opinion 2/13* ECLI:EU:C:2014:2454, para 188.

964 CoE Committee of Ministers, Council of Europe Strategy for the Rights of the Child (2012-2015) (15 February 2012) CM(2011)171final, p 8. EDC appears among the standards set to protect the child, part of strategic objectives. See n 285.

965 Further § 242 , examples in § 256 ff.

137 *Transparency and openness*

EDC standards can in the EU legal order be ranged under the umbrella principle of democracy, just like the principles of transparency and openness, with which they are closely interrelated.

The principles of transparency and openness follow from several primary law provisions (i.a. Articles 1, 10, 11, 16 TEU; 15 TFEU; and 42 CFR).[966] Secondary law and case law refer to them:

> Openness enables citizens to participate more closely in the decision-making process and guarantees that the administration enjoys greater legitimacy and is more effective and more accountable to the citizen in a democratic system. Openness contributes to strengthening the principles of democracy and respect for fundamental rights as laid down in Article 6 of the EU Treaty and in the Charter of Fundamental Rights of the European Union.[967]

In this citation, the word 'openness' could be replaced by 'EDC' inasmuch as it serves the same purposes. Like the right of public access to documents, EDC standards relate to the democratic nature of the institutions. Both public access and EDC must be assured as widely as possible.

EDC standards are in harmony with the EU objective of taking decisions 'as openly and as closely as possible to the citizen' (Article 10(3) TEU and preamble). Many EU law provisions corroborate the objective of informed citizenship. If the principles of transparency and openness point by their

---

966 Several components are codified, see i.a. Art 16(8) TEU on public meetings of the Council acting as a legislator; Art 42 CFR on the right of access to documents, Art 298(1) TFEU on an open European administration.

967 Recital 2 in the preamble to Regulation 1049/2001 of the European Parliament and of the Council of 30 May 2001 regarding public access to European Parliament, Council and Commission documents [2001] OJ L145/43 (see also Proposal COM(2008) 229 final). The 'right of public access to documents of the institutions is related to the democratic nature of those institutions'. See i.a. Case C-41/00 P *Interporc* ECLI:EU:C:2003:125, para 39; Joined Cases C-39/05 P and C-52/05 P *Sweden and Turco* ECLI:EU:C:2008:374, para 45; Case C-28/08 P *Commission v Bavarian Lager* ECLI:EU:C:2010:378, para 54; Joined Cases C-92/09 and C-93/09 *Schecke and Eifert* ECLI:EU:C:2010:662, para 68; Case C-506/08 P *Sweden v MyTravel and Commission* ECLI:EU:C:2011:496, para 72; Case C-280/11 P *Council v Access Info Europe* ECLI:EU:C:2013:671, paras 27–28; Case T-540/15 *De Capitani* ECLI:EU:T:2018:167. See also Commission Report on the application in 2018 of Regulation (EC) No 1049/2001 regarding public access to European Parliament, Council and Commission documents COM(2019) 356 final.

very nature to the 'opposite of opaqueness, complexity or even secretiveness'[968], the EDC standards do the same, only upstream, laying the foundations from the start for a basic understanding of the EU. The EDC standards are a corollary of the principles of openness and transparency (ontological assumptions). If democracy is a chain of legitimation from those governed to those governing,[969] EDC in schools is the essential first link of this chain. EDC standards are a crucial prerequisite if democratic systems are to work. Citizens must be empowered to take action and to hold public institutions accountable.

In *Sweden and Turco*, the ECJ held that the 'possibility for citizens to find out the considerations underpinning legislative action is a *precondition for the effective exercise of their democratic rights*'.[970] By the same token, EDC is a *precondition* for the effective exercise of democratic rights. With regard to the disclosure of an opinion of the legal service of the Council, the ECJ held that openness 'contributes to conferring greater legitimacy on the institutions in the eyes of European citizens and increasing their confi-

---

968 S Prechal and ME de Leeuw, 'Transparency: A General Principle of EU Law?' in U Bernitz, J Nergelius and C Cardner (eds), *General Principles of EC Law in a Process of Development* (Kluwer 2008). On transparency, see i.a. Commission Communication Follow-up to the Green Paper 'European Transparency Initiative' COM(2007) 127 final, and scholars: D Curtin and AJ Meijer, 'Does transparency strengthen legitimacy?' (2006) 11 Information Polity 109; P Kostadinova, 'Improving the Transparency and Accountability of EU Institutions: The Impact of the Office of the European Ombudsman' (2015) 53 JCMS 1077. On the difference between the principles of openness and transparency: A Alemanno, 'Unpacking the Principle of Openness in EU Law: Transparency, Participation and Democracy' (2014) 1 ELRev 72 (openness includes transparency and participation). On the question whether transparency and openness are general principles of EU law, see K Lenaerts, '"In the Union we trust": trust-enhancing principles of Community law' (2004) 41 CMLRev 317 (it can be hardly denied that the principle of transparency has evolved into a general principle of EU law); and Prechal and de Leeuw, 'Transparency: A General Principle of EU Law?' (authors scan manifold appearances of transparency in EU law, consider transparency too vague and uncertain to serve as an overarching a general principle, but find 'sub-principles'; the function of transparency as a guiding principle for interpretation is well-established).

969 Hofmann, Rowe and Türk, *Administrative law and policy of the European Union* 146. See also J Ziller, 'European models of government: Towards a patchwork with missing pieces' (2001) 54 Parliamentary Affairs 102.

970 Joined Cases C-39/05 P and C-52/05 P *Sweden and Turco* ECLI:EU:C:2008:374, para 46 (emphasis added). See also Case C-280/11 P *Council v Access Info Europe* ECLI:EU:C:2013:671, para 33; and Case C-57/16 P *ClientEarth* ECLI:EU:C:2018:660, para 84.

dence in them by allowing divergences between various points of view to be openly debated'.[971] Access to information in documents is 'intended to enable citizens to participate in public affairs'.[972] These considerations apply equally to EDC, which has the same objective of empowering citizens. What is the real value of transparency and openness without prior citizenship education? If, in the interests of transparency, the IT man repairing a computer opens the main cover to show the customer what is inside, the customer will see the complex components, wires and chips, but be none the wiser. Without pre-knowledge and some education, transparency and openness may prove to be quasi empty principles.

EDC standards coincide naturally with the aims of participation, legitimacy, and accountability. The academic writers referred to in Part one confirm this—for instance Sander, who considers that *Mission* (values), *Legitimation* and *Mündigkeit* are the essential aims of citizenship education.[973]

Lessig provocatively pleads against transparency.[974] Public availability of all information on the Internet can add to alienation and cynicism. A requirement, he argues, is that citizens are able to use the information; so, transparency must be accompanied by other measures. Information must be incorporated into 'complex chains of comprehension', such as political campaigns. I think that EDC should be part of the chain of comprehension. Naked transparency is clearly not sufficient in itself.

It can be concluded that a contextual and teleological interpretation of EU law provisions on citizenship, democracy and education should take account of EDC standards, as this interpretation corresponds to the structure of the Treaties and contributes to achieving the Treaties' objectives.[975]

---

971 Joined Cases C-39/05 P and C-52/05 P *Sweden and Turco* ECLI:EU:C:2008:374, para 59.

972 Joined Cases C-92/09 and C-93/09 *Schecke and Eifert* ECLI:EU:C:2010:662, para 31.

973 See text to n 562. In the same line other scholars, e.g. Crick, Dahl, Dewey (see § 71 ff).

974 L Lessig, 'Against transparency. The perils of openness in government' (2009) 240 The New Republic 37 (Harvard Law School).

975 Text to n 727. Some analogy with the principle of transparency: even if it is not clearly a general principle as such, it has an interpretative function: see Prechal and de Leeuw in n 968.

Interpretation in good faith and sincere cooperation

138 Good faith, universal principle

Th effects of the Charter on EDC/HRE in the EU legal order may also be felt through the principles of good faith and sincere cooperation.[976]

The universally recognised principle of good faith requires States to implement the international agreements they have concluded in good faith. Pursuant to Articles 26 and 31 of the Vienna Convention on the Law of Treaties, the EU Treaties must be performed and interpreted in good faith.[977] When interpreting and applying provisions of the EU Treaties on democracy and citizens' rights in good faith, Member States cannot deny the importance of EDC standards. Admittedly, good faith cannot function as a pathway for introducing non-binding norms into the EU legal order and conferring legally binding effect on them by means of interpretative incorporation. However, in the *dégradé normatif*, certain exogenic non-binding norms, such as recommendations, may be hardened according to the criteria set out by academic writers (who base their arguments on case law).[978] The consensus on which they rest may give them such a degree of legitimacy that good faith simply requires them to be taken into account. EDC standards are the reflection of an international consensus and have emerged as standards of great weight. The Charter on EDC/HRE represents the European *acquis* on EDC/HRE. The consistent nature of the commitments made over the course of 30 years work is too marked for Member States to be able to contest the relevance of EDC standards for EU citizens in any credible way. Member States cannot participate as members of the Council of Europe in the adoption of so many recommendations on EDC and then in good faith deny the implications of those standards for their citizens, who are—in addition to being national citizens—also EU citizens. A *bona fide* attitude means that the provisions on citizenship, democracy and education in EU law should be interpreted while taking account of Council of Europe commitments. Member States have a duty of good faith vis-à-vis one another and vis-à-vis their citizens, and citizens can legitimately expect Member States to adhere loyally to the rationale underlying EDC/HRE. If EDC standards inseparably link democracy, citizenship

976 §§ 160 and 162.
977 Vienna Convention on the Law of Treaties (adopted 23 May 1969, entered into force 27 January 1980) 1155 UNTS 331, see also preamble.
978 Schermers and Blokker, Pinto de Albuquerque, and Tulkens (Part one, §§ 50 51).

and education, that link does not cease to exist because another level of governance is concerned.[979] Democracy requires enlightened citizenship at any level of the exercise of public power. This must also apply in the EU context.

139 Sincere cooperation, duty to cooperate in good faith in EU law

Good faith acquires specific definition in EU law in the principle of sincere cooperation, also called the duty to cooperate in good faith (Article 4(3) TEU).[980] In *Intertanko*, the ECJ interpreted EU law by taking an international agreement into account 'in view of the customary principle of good faith, which forms part of general international law' and of the principle of sincere cooperation.[981] The *Intertanko* principle can be applied to EU law provisions on EU citizenship, democracy and education: in the light of the principles of good faith and sincere cooperation, these provisions must be interpreted taking into account international agreements, such as the ICESCR (Article 13) or the CRC (Article 29). Is the *Intertanko* principle only valid for (binding) international agreements? To what extent can the principle of sincere cooperation be an argument for interpreting EU law taking account of Council of Europe recommendations? One could argue that EU law should be interpreted by taking the Recommendation on the Charter on EDC/HRE into account 'in view of the customary principle of good faith, which forms part of general international law', and of the EU principle of sincere cooperation. The applicability of the principles of good faith and of sincere cooperation should not necessarily stand or fall on the basis of the black and white division binding/non-binding. In accordance with *le dégradé normatif*, EU law could be

979 Council of Europe, UN and EU instruments refer to various levels, e.g. CoE Committee of Ministers Declaration and programme on education for democratic citizenship, based on the rights and responsibilities of citizens (Budapest, 7 May 1999), para 7; UNGA Res 71/8 'Education for democracy' (17 November 2016) UN Doc A/RES/71/8, para 6 (see n 2210); EU Recommendations on key competences for lifelong learning, civic and citizenship competence (nn 929, 930).

980 Principle of 'federal good faith', see Lenaerts and Van Nuffel, *European Union Law* 147; W van Gerven, 'Gemeenschapstrouw: goede trouw in E.G.-verband' [1989-90] Rechtskundig Weekblad 1158, 1159. See also J Temple Lang, 'The Development by the Court of Justice of the Duties of Cooperation of National Authorities and Community Institutions under Article 10 EC' (2007-2008) 31 Fordham International Law Journal 1483.

981 Case C-308/06 *Intertanko* ECLI:EU:C:2008:312, para 52. Moreover, Dir 2005/35 expressly referred to the Marpol 73/78 Convention. Text to n 742.

interpreted as far as possible in a way consistent with commitments in international law, even if *sensu stricto* they are legally non-binding. The ECJ sees sincere cooperation as a general obligation the implications of which are to be determined in each individual case.[982] As explained in Part one, the Recommendation on the Charter on EDC/HRE has a high degree of normativity in itself.

When the EU selects *à la carte*, from the menu of Council of Europe norms, only whatever suits its own structure and purposes, can it afford to disregard the EDC standards—standards of considerable importance and possessing a high degree of normative intensity in the Council of Europe legal order, and relating to the common foundational values?

The duty of sincere cooperation has effects in both directions, from the EU to the Member States and from the Member States to the EU. The Member States gave commitments in the Council of Europe; the EU (institutions) should loyally cooperate with Member States to help them honour these commitments. The EU legal order cannot be out of kilter with Member State commitments in the Council of Europe legal order. Interpreting 'democracy' in EU law as embracing EDC standards (under the denominator of the democratic principles of Title II TEU) brings EU law into line with the commitments of EU Member States as member states of the Council of Europe. Conversely, the EU aims to uphold democracy and has—in the Memorandum of Understanding—committed itself to recognising the Council of Europe benchmark on democracy, including the EDC standards; logically, the Member States should loyally coöperate to achieve these aims. Interpreting EU law in the light of EDC standards is therefore a form of mutual sincere cooperation: 'Pursuant to the principle of sincere cooperation, the Union and the Member States shall, in full mutual respect, assist each other in carrying out tasks which flow from the Treaties' (Article 4(3) first subparagraph TEU). Respecting democratic principles is a task flowing from the Treaties (i.a. Articles 2, 3, 7, 49, Title II TEU, and other provisions read in the light of the preambles). The Union and the Member States must assist each other in the task of ensuring education for democracy. Interpreting provisions on citizenship, democracy

982 Case 78/70 *Deutsche Grammophon* ECLI:EU:C:1971:59, para 5. See also Case C-433/03 *Commission v Germany* ECLI:EU:C:2005:462, para 64. Further E Neframi, 'Principe de coopération loyale et principe d'attribution dans le cadre de la mise en oeuvre du droit de l'Union' (2016) 52 Cahiers droit européen 221. The human rights based approach in Part four will underscore the reasoning based on good faith and sincere cooperation by a reading in conjunction with with the ICESCR and the CRC.

and education in national and in EU law by taking EDC standards into account, is the first and most basic step. To refuse this combined reading could jeopardise the attainment of the Union's objectives, in breach of Article 4(3) third subparagraph TEU.

Article 4(3) second subparagraph TEU requires the Member States to take 'any appropriate measure, general or particular, to ensure fulfilment of the obligations arising out of the Treaties or resulting from the acts of the institutions of the Union'. Can providing for EDC be seen as an 'appropriate' measure to ensure fulfilment of Treaty obligations such as the requirement to uphold 'democratic' values (Articles 2, 7 and 49 TEU)? The ECJ has progressively widened the interpretation of obligations arising under the principle of sincere cooperation.[983] Member States are under 'a general duty of care'. They must use their own powers, e.g. to grant nationality, in a spirit of sincere cooperation, having due regard to EU law (if they grant nationality, the person becomes an EU citizen and enjoys the associated rights throughout the EU).[984] Equally, when exercising their competences in the field of education Member States must act in a spirit of sincere cooperation. They cannot just prepare their nationals for effective participation in the nation state. If they have a duty to adopt all the measures needed 'to guarantee the full scope and effect of Union law'[985], educating their nationals (who are also EU citizens) about the EU, and thus providing an EU dimension within EDC, must be part of that duty. Part three will analyse this on the basis of specific EU law provisions.

The Treaties reiterate the principle of sincere cooperation in the area of common foreign and security policy: 'The Member States shall support the Union's external and security policy actively and unreservedly in a spirit of loyalty and mutual solidarity and shall comply with the Union's action in this area' (Article 24(3) TEU). In response to the challenges of radicalisation, EDC and HRE have become part of security policy in the Council of Europe as well as in the EU.[986] To the extent that EDC and HRE concern the security of the Union, sincere cooperation is even more important.

---

983 Lenaerts and Van Nuffel, *European Union Law* 149.

984 Commission Report under Article 25 TFEU 'On progress towards effective EU citizenship 2013-2016' COM(2017) 32 final, p 4.

985 Lenaerts and Van Nuffel, *European Union Law* 150, 152; EU Accession to the ECHR *Opinion 2/13* ECLI:EU:C:2014:2454, para 173.

986 For the CoE see § 37 . For the EU see i.a. Commission Communication 'Eight progress report towards an effective and genuine Security Union' COM(2017) 0354 final, and text to n 917 ff.

Sincere cooperation is closely related to respect by the EU of international law.

Consistent interpretation with international law, as far as possible

140 Strict observance and development of international law

EDC standards may produce effects in the EU legal order seen from the perspective of EU respect for international law. The Union aims at 'the strict observance and the development of international law, including respect for the principles of the United Nations Charter' (Article 3(5) TEU). The commitment to respect international law flows from the general scheme of the Treaty and the CFR (see, i.a., Articles 3(5), 21(1), and 42 TEU, Article 208(2) TFEU, Article 52(3) CFR). As far as possible, the ECJ interprets EU law in the light of and consistently with international law.[987] The analysis of the substance of the specific rights of citizens in Part three will make it possible to develop this reasoning further.

The Recommendation on the Charter on EDC/HRE is part of international law, in a soft law form, yet displaying several hardening factors. The EDC standards of the Council of Europe can be seen as a further development and manifestation of rights and principles in the Universal Declaration of Human Rights, the International Covenant on Economic, Social and Cultural Rights and the Convention on the Rights of the Child.[988] Logically, EU law should be interpreted consistently with international law standards on education for democracy, to the extent possible. If the EU's ambition is to contribute to 'the development of international law' (Article 3(5) TEU), it should—at the very least—itself respect standards widely accepted in the international community, such as the EDC standards.

Since it aims to be an influential global player, the EU must take care to ensure consistency between its policies (Article 21(3) TEU).[989]

987 Lenaerts and Gutiérrez-Fons, 'To Say What the Law of the EU Is: Methods of Interpretation and the European Court of Justice', 60. Klabbers, 'Straddling the Fence: The EU and International Law', 67. See, e.g., Case C-340/08 *M and Others* ECLI:EU:C:2010:232, paras 8, 11, 45, 49 ('for the purpose of interpreting Regulation No 881/2002, account must also be taken of the wording and purpose of Resolution 1390 (2002) which that regulation, according to the fourth recital in the preamble thereto, is designed to implement'). This is also an example of mode 3: incorporation of substance and preamble reference.

988 See i.a. § 57 , § 292 .

989 Craig and de Búrca, *EU Law: Text, Cases, and Materials* 378–9.

In development cooperation, the Union and the Member States 'shall comply with the commitments and take account of the objectives they have approved in the context of the United Nations and other competent international organisations' (Article 208(2) TFEU). Citizenship and human rights education are part of the commitments and objectives (to invigorate civil society in third countries, to strengthen governments' accountability[990]). If these commitments and objectives are an obligation ('shall comply with') in (external) development cooperation, they are a fortiori valid in the (internal) policies of the EU and the Member States. The principle of consistent interpretation may thus indirectly give effect to EDC standards. However, the red line means caution is necessary.

141 Ambivalence—limits to consistent interpretation

Even in the light of the 'strict observance of international law' to which the Union 'shall contribute' (Article 3(5) TEU), the principle of consistent interpretation has limits. The ECJ has to accommodate this principle with the constitutional autonomy of EU law and the 'characteristic features' of the EU.[991] The relationship between EU law and international law is ambivalent.[992] In the early landmark cases *Van Gend & Loos* and *Costa v Enel*, the ECJ established its position with regard to the relative autonomy of EU law vis-à-vis international law, and further developed this in cases such as *Kadi* and especially in *Opinion 2/13*.[993] Vis-à-vis the Council of Europe, too, the EU demonstrates dependency and autonomy.[994] The reluctance of the ECJ to cite Council of Europe recommendations or, occa-

990 Text to nn 868 and 868.

991 Case 283/81 *Cilfit* ECLI:EU:C:1982:335, para 17. Lenaerts and Gutiérrez-Fons, 'To Say What the Law of the EU Is: Methods of Interpretation and the European Court of Justice', 7–8, 37 ff.

992 Klabbers, 'Straddling the Fence: The EU and International Law', 55, 61 (relationship 'characterised by a high degree of complexity and ambivalence'; the approach of the ECJ can 'hardly be qualified as völkerrechtsfreundlich'). See also P Eeckhout, 'Human Rights and the Autonomy of EU Law: Pluralism or Integration?' (2013) 66 Current Legal Problems 169.

993 Case 26-62 *Van Gend & Loos* ECLI:EU:C:1963:1; Case 6/64 *Costa v ENEL* ECLI:EU:C:1964:66; Joined Cases C-402/05 P and C-415/05 P *Kadi* ECLI:EU:C:2008:461; EU Accession to the ECHR *Opinion 2/13* ECLI:EU:C:2014:2454.

994 RA Wessel and S Blockmans, *Between Autonomy and Dependence: The EU Legal Order Under the Influence of International Organisations* (Asser Press 2013), 47. See also R McCrea, 'Singing from the Same Hymn Sheet? What the Differences between the Strasbourg and Luxembourg Courts Tell Us about Religious Freedom, Non-Discrimination, and the Secular State' (2016) 5 Oxford Journal of Law and Religion 183.

sionally, other international instruments has been acknowledged.[995] EU law is protected, adjusted or finetuned in its interpretation in order to respect the autonomy of the EU legal order. This is true where EU law incorporates the substance of binding exogenic norms (*Commission v UK* and *Commission v Germany*), and a fortiori of non-binding exogenic norms. Applying the Recommendation on the Charter on EDC/HRE to the situation of EU citizens in the next part will require constant prudence and care to respect the specificity of the EU legal order.

Respect for the autonomy of the EU and its specific characteristics

142 A closer look at the red line

The ECJ operates in the five modes of normative reception and brings exogenic norms to life in case law. At the same time, however, the ECJ points to limits. In principle, unless there is a specific reason not to do so, EU law on citizenship, democracy and education should be interpreted in a way which takes account of EDC standards in general and of the Charter on EDC/HRE in particular. Yet, specific EU characteristics or objectives may lead to exceptions to the principle. What does the red line mean for the normative reception of EDC standards in the EU legal order and interpretation of EU law in their light?

143 Opinion 2/13

In *Opinion 2/13*, in the context of the intended accession of the EU to the ECHR, the ECJ explained the autonomy of the EU. The High Contracting Parties had agreed in Protocol No 8 (which has the same legal value as the Treaties) that the agreement on EU accession to the ECHR 'shall make provision for preserving the *specific characteristics of the Union and Union law*' and must not affect the competences of the Union, the powers of its institutions, or the situation of the Member States in relation to the ECHR.[996] A Declaration had clarified that the '*specific features of EU law*' were to be preserved.[997] Referring to these conditions, the ECJ briefly

995 I.a. nn 707, 773.

996 Protocol (No 8) relating to Article 6(2) of the Treaty on European Union on the accession of the Union to the European Convention on the Protection of Human Rights and Fundamental Freedoms [2012] OJ C326/273, Arts 1 and 2; in line with Art 6(2) TEU. Emphasis added.

997 Declaration on Article 6(2) TEU by the Intergovernmental Conference (emphasis added); EU Accession to the ECHR *Opinion 2/13* ECLI:EU:C:2014:2454, para 162. See para 159 for 'compliance with various conditions'.

described what was meant by these specific characteristics[998] and held that the ECHR accession agreement was 'liable adversely to affect the specific characteristics of EU law and its autonomy'.[999] The specific characteristics relate to the constitutional structure of the EU, i.e. the principle of conferral of powers (Arts 4(1) and 5(1)(2) TEU) and to the institutional framework (Articles 13–19 TEU). Moreover, specific characteristics arise from the very nature of EU law, stemming from the Treaties as an independent source of law, with primacy over the law of the Member States and many of its provisions having direct effect.[1000] The legal structure of the EU is based on the fundamental premise of a shared set of common values (Article 2 TEU), recognised by the Member States, and justifying the mutual trust between the Member States.[1001] At the heart of the legal structure are fundamental rights (CFR). The pursuit of the EU's objectives (Article 3 TEU) is entrusted to a series of fundamental provisions, such as those on free movement of goods, services, capital and persons, EU citizenship, or the area of freedom, security and justice. They contribute to the process of integration that is the *raison d'être* of the EU itself.[1002]

144 Respect for constitutional principles when applying EDC standards

Like the ECHR, the Recommendation on the Charter on EDC/HRE is directed to States and, as is well known, the EU is not a State.[1003] Therefore, appropriate considerations are to be taken into account if these exogenic norms are nevertheless to enjoy a form of reception in the EU legal order (reception occurring in different modes and for different reasons). Applying the considerations in *Opinion 2/13 mutatis mutandis* to the reception and interpretation of EU law in the light of EDC standards, it must be ensured that the specific characteristics of EU law are preserved. Reception and interpretation require conformity with the 'basic constitutional charter, the Treaties'.[1004] The 'constitutional principles' of the Treaties cannot

998 See paras 165–176, 179 ff (about the 'The specific characteristics and the autonomy of EU law'). See also Joined Cases C-402/05 P and C-415/05 P *Kadi* ECLI:EU:C:2008:461, para 285.

999 In several respects, see paras 200, 258 (not compatible with Art 6(2) TEU and Protocol No 8).

1000 Paras 165–166.

1001 Paras 168, 172, 191.

1002 Paras 170, 172.

1003 EU Accession to the ECHR *Opinion 2/13* ECLI:EU:C:2014:2454, paras 156–158, 193.

1004 Para 163.

be prejudiced.[1005] When applying EDC standards as to their substance to the situation of the EU citizen in the next Part, this constitutional red line will be constantly borne in mind. The same obviously applies in relation to Member State constitutions. Moreover, not undermining constitutional principles is part of the EDC standards themselves, in line with the paragraph-4 principle of the Charter on EDC/HRE. This paragraph requires EDC/HRE objectives, principles and policies to be applied 'with due respect for the constitutional structures of each member state, using means appropriate to those structures' and 'having regard to the priorities and needs of each member state'. If the Charter on EDC/HRE is applied to the EU citizen, the EU as structure must also benefit from the privilege of the paragraph-4 principle. Consequently, based on EU primary law, ECJ case law, as well as the EDC standards themselves, the analysis which follows will display caution with respect to the autonomy of the EU, the constitutional allocation of powers, both horizontally and vertically, and to Member States' constitutions. As long as EU primary law and Member State constitutions are respected, there is no reason to deviate from the wide European consensus on EDC standards or classify the EDC standards in the diverging line of case law.[1006]

Conclusion to Part two

145 Place of EDC standards in the schema of modes of reception

To recapitulate, in the framework of the Council of Europe and the European Cultural Convention, 50 states adopted the 2010 Recommendation on the Charter on EDC/HRE, a reference instrument setting out EDC standards. Among the 50 states are all EU Member States. For them, the Charter on EDC/HRE acquires specific meaning seen from the perspective of EU law. The question addressed in Part two was: what are the legal status and effects of the Charter on EDC/HRE in the EU legal order? The answer is that the Charter on EDC/HRE is an exogenic norm, not part of EU law, but EU law gives it effects to a certain degree. To analyse the effects, this Part has formulated a schema of modes of reception of exogenic norms in the EU legal order, comprising three stronger modes of

1005 Joined Cases C-402/05 P and C-415/05 P *Kadi* ECLI:EU:C:2008:461, para 285 ('the constitutional principles of the EC Treaty, which include the principle that all Community acts must respect fundamental rights').

1006 Criterion (ii) is meant to ensure this respect, see §§ 155 169 173 .

reception and three weaker ones. The spectrum ranged from—the most significant mode in terms of legal effects—EU accession to conventions (mode 1), to reception via general principles of EU law (mode 2), reference to the title of exogenic instruments (mode 3), incorporation of the substance of exogenic norms (mode 4), to—least consequential mode of reception—sharing inspiration and *de facto* cooperation (mode 5). Judicial interpretation complements these modes of normative reception (mode 6). At all times, reception has to respect the autonomy of the EU legal order (the red line).

Situating Council of Europe standards in the schema, the EU can thus 'acknowledge' them (Memorandum of Understanding) on the basis of six possible modes of reception, with varying legal effects. The reception of EDC standards mostly occurs in mode 4 via partial incorporation of the substance of the norms and in mode 5 on the basis of inspiration and cooperation in the field (working in the same paradigm). Occasionally, some references to the title of EDC instruments are to be found (mode 3). Overall, the normative reception of EDC standards in the EU legal order is fragmented but convincing. As a complement to their normative reception, EDC standards produce effects when taken into account in the interpretation of EU law (mode 6; contextual and teleological interpretation, interpretation in good faith and in sincere cooperation, and consistently with international law). EDC standards fit perfectly into the landscape of EU law, since they are inextricably linked to the EU's values of democracy, respect for fundamental rights, and the rule of law, anchored in the Treaties. However, there is a red line which must not be crossed, as appears from ECJ case law: respect for the EU's autonomy, the specific objectives and characteristics of the EU stemming from the Treaties, and constitutional principles. In a way, this reservation is inherent in the EDC standards themselves, pursuant to the paragraph-4 principle of the Charter on EDC/HRE. It can be concluded that a combined reading of EU law provisions on citizenship, democracy and education with EDC standards is legitimate.

In Part three, the significance of EDC standards for democracy beyond the nation state will be explored. Again (just as at the end of Part one), for the sceptical reader it is not necessary to agree with all aspects of the preceding analysis. Independently of the effects which EU law assigns to EDC standards (as to form), the academic exercise of applying these widely accepted standards (as to substance) to the EU citizen, remains interesting *per se*.

Admittedly, the fact that ECJ case law shows both a converging and a diverging line of interpretation leaves the Council of Europe instruments on EDC in an uncomfortable position with regard to their effects in the EU legal order. This contrasts with the overriding importance of democracy and human rights as foundational values, and with the status of EDC as a shared priority and focal area for cooperation in the Memorandum of Understanding. In order to be effective, EDC requires a strong mode of reception.[1007] 'Acknowledging' Council of Europe standards, the EU concluded a convention on animal protection (mode 1), developed a general principle on access to documents (mode 2), incorporated the title of language standards (mode 3), directly copy-pasted substantive rules on transfrontier television with a reference in the preamble (mode 4). There is no shortage of precedents, including on less important topics than EDC. EDC deserves to benefit from at least comparable efforts. Some joint programmes exist on EDC, which are valuable, but none the less very limited compared to the 500 million inhabitants of the EU.[1008] Given the close interdependence of EU Member States on each others' democracies, the fragmented normative reception of EDC standards and their interpretative value in the EU legal order (uncertain, given the red line) are not sufficient. EDC standards may enjoy 'great weight' or 'considerable importance' in the Council of Europe legal order, but their acceptance in the EU legal order is indirect and complicated. It has taken two chapters and many pages to explain the effects of EDC standards. EU action could remedy this within its sphere of competence.

EDC standards should follow the course of other Council of Europe standards in a cascade of norm-setting.[1009] In the area of EDC/HRE, the chain of ongoing normative interaction at present probably only reaches halfway. UN instruments containing educational standards, including on education for democracy[1010], have influenced Council of Europe recommendations, such as the 2002 and 2010 Recommendations on EDC, which in turn have seen their substance and inspiration influence EU instruments on education, citizenship and democracy. Given the precedents, the further course of the cascade might imply ECJ interpretations taking the Charter on EDC/HRE into account and the adoption of specific EU instru-

1007 MOU, para 14.
1008 Text to n 898.
1009 Text to n 883 ff.
1010 UNGA resolutions on education for democracy, see n 2203.

ments incorporating EDC substance while adapting EDC standards to the specific EU context (which, I will argue, is needed and possible, based on Article 165 TFEU). If democracy and human rights are to be taken seriously, one must expect the chain to be continued.

Part two provides several arguments for the adoption of a comprehensive (non-fragmented) EU legislative act on EDC for the EU citizen, i.e. EDC adapted to the EU and its Member States.[1011] Firstly, as to the form, it would provide a direct source on EDC in EU law. It would meet the concerns of the hesitant reader who prefers legal certainty in legal texts, rather than contextual, teleological, *effet utile*, or *bona fide* interpretations taking exogenic EDC standards into account. Secondly, as to the substance, an EU legislative act on EDC would be an opportunity to develop and adapt the Council of Europe norms specifically to the EU context, as has happened in many other fields.[1012] An EU instrument could explain how specific features of the EU impact on EDC/HRE (further analysed in Part three). Thirdly, an EU instrument could remedy the weaknesses of the Recommendation on the Charter on EDC/HRE with regard to effectiveness, encouraging Member States to seek higher quality education (Article 165(1) TFEU). The latest review cycle of the Charter on EDC/HRE shows the persisting challenges to its implementation.[1013] The adoption of an EU instrument would not prevent further cooperation with the Council of Europe.

147 Proposal for recital

Based on Part two, the following phrase could be added as a recital in the preamble of a hypothetical EU legislative act:

> *Whereas EDC standards of the Council of Europe are not EU law and–as to their form–only have indirect effects in the EU legal order via partial normative reception and via an interpretation of EU law taking EDC standards into account while respecting the autonomy of the EU.*

1011 Adaptation perspective in § 151 .The 'civic competence' described in the Recommendation on key competences for lifelong learning could be developed in an EU legal act, with adequate accompanying materials and evaluation as in the Council of Europe, respecting Member States competences (Part four).

1012 Examples in *RTL* and *Ognyanov*.

1013 CoE, *Learning to live together: Council of Europe Report on the state of citizenship and human rights education in Europe*, p 53.

PART III Content for the EU dimension in Education for Democratic Citizenship

Introduction: Criteria for determing content for the EU dimension

148 Effects of a combined reading of EDC standards and EU law

The central question for Part three is: what are the effects of a combined reading of EDC standards and EU law, as to the substance, for citizenship education of EU citizens? What are the implications for the content of EU learning at school? Provisions on EU citizenship, democracy, and education will be interpreted by taking account of EDC standards.

An additional question is to be kept in mind, in preparation for Part four on legal competence to provide for quality education. When setting norms for national education curricula, Member States must respect the minimum standards included in the international right to education. EDC standards, as analysed in Part one, are the development of compulsory educational aims laid down in international agreements, binding for all Member States. The International Covenant on Economic, Social and Cultural Rights and the Convention on the Rights of the Child list the aims to which education 'shall be directed'. The aims include the preparation of the child for responsible life and effective participation in a free society, respect for human rights and fundamental freedoms, and promoting understanding, tolerance and friendship among all nations.[1014] The corollary of the international right to education and to quality education, is the obligation for States to provide for available, accessible, acceptable and adaptable education (the 4 A scheme, explained in Part four).[1015] What are the consequences of EU membership? To what extent does acceptable and adaptable education in EU Member States need an EU dimension? What is the impact of EU citizenship on the compulsory educational aims, the hallmark of quality education? Quality education is 'adapted to the requirements of modern, complex societies' and ensures that pupils' 'full potential

1014 Arts 13 ICESCR and 29 CRC. Core to all education is the full development of the human personality and the sense of its dignity. See n 81-82.

1015 See Part four text to nn 2149- 2150.

as citizens' is developed'.[1016] Part three will provide elements for the analysis in Part four of the EU's competence to support quality education.

How should learning content for 'EU citizenship education' be defined? The adjectives used by scholars in their reflections on EU citizenship paint a discouraging picture: thin, pale, uncertain, fragile, frail, Cinderella, pseudo, small c, unstable, muddy, debated, immature, contentious, loose, ...[1017] These adjectives do not seem to support the need for genuine EU citizenship education; rather, they suggest that a thin, pale, uncertain, ... version of citizenship education will do. However, the full picture should be drawn, using EDC standards as a prism through which to look at EU law as a whole. What happens—as to the substance—when EDC standards meet EU law?

1016 CoE Recommendation CM/Rec(2012)13 of the Committee of Ministers to member States on ensuring quality education (12 December 2012), appendix paras 2 and 23. Definition of quality education in para 6.

1017 See i.a. S O'Leary, 'The relationship between Community citizenship and the protection of fundamental rights in Community law' (1995) 32 CMLRev 519 (p 537: 'As it stands, citizenship could be regarded as a cosmetic exercise'); W Maas, 'Unrespected, unequal, hollow? Contingent Citizenship and Reversible Rights in the European Union' (2008-2009) 15 Columbia Journal of European Law 265 (the rights derived from EU citizenship are pale compared to national citizenship; author sketches three challenges: EU citizenship rights can be disrespected, contested, and fragile in their enforcement, 'rights remain reversible, and citizenship remains contingent'); D Kochenov, 'Ius tractum of many faces: European citizenship and the difficult relationship between status and rights' (2009) 15 Columbia Journal of European Law 169 (p 234 'reform of European citizenship is needed to make sure that is it "not merely a hollow or symbolic concept"'); N Nic Shuibhne, 'The Resilience of EU Market Citizenship' (2010) 47 CMLRev 1597 (small c, pseudo); J Shaw, 'Citizenship: Contrasting Dynamics at the Interface of Integration and Constitutionalism' in P Craig and G de Búrca (eds), *The evolution of EU law* (Oxford University Press 2011) (text to fnn 41, 128, 152: a rather thin transnational concept); citizenship of the Union has—for most people—a Cinderella status (p 605); citizenship still has an uncertain 'constitutional' role in the EuropeanUnion); D Kochenov and R Plender, 'EU Citizenship: From an Incipient Form to an Incipient Substance? The Discovery of the Treaty Text' (2012) 37 ELRev 369 (quasi, thin, incipient); D Kochenov, 'The Right to Have What Rights? EU Citizenship in Need of Clarification' (2013) 19 ELJ 502; Craig and de Búrca, *EU Law: Text, Cases, and Materials*, 890 (reference to criticism of thinness); K Lenaerts, 'EU citizenship and the European Court of Justice's "stone-by-stone" approach' (2015) 1 International Comparative Jurisprudence 1.

149 Search for balanced 'EU citizenship education'

In general, 'citizenship education' is meant to educate individuals to be informed, responsible and active citizens. Since the 1992 Maastricht Treaty introduced EU citizenship into the Treaties, it seems natural to extend the expression 'citizenship education' by adding the word 'EU', and to consider 'EU citizenship education' to be the education of individuals as informed, responsible and active EU citizens, thus taking citizenship of the Union and the rights attached to this status since the Maastricht Treaty as the substance. However, this approach is unsatisfactory seen from two sides. It is both reductive, seen from the EU perspective, and excessive, seen from the Member State perspective. This approach does not go far enough, inasmuch as the EU citizen is more than 'citizenship of the Union' and the rights usually attached to that status imply (Articles 20–24 TFEU).[1018] At the same time, this approach goes too far, inasmuch as it may suggest that EU citizenship is a new citizenship to be forged by EU citizenship education in order to replace national citizenship. The aim of EU citizenship education should not be to create new citizens faithful to an EU super state in a huge social engineering exercise, neglecting national allegiances. Using the term 'citizenship education' in relation to the EU may create just such a false impression. For some, 'EU citizenship education' awakens high expectations of cultivating a sense of EU identity and feelings of belonging. For others, it leads to suspicion and fear that it will only further undermine national sovereignty and the nation state.[1019] Citizenship education is traditionally associated with states (a statal concept) and as such cannot be transposed to the EU. It needs a translation adequate (acceptable and adaptable) for the EU.[1020]

EU citizenship education needs to find a balanced position. On the one hand, the sphere of the Member States must be safeguarded, national iden-

1018 See i. a. § 240.

1019 About fear of centralised 'superstate', see i.a. European Parliament Committee on Constitutional Affairs, Report on the Treaty of Lisbon (29 January 2008), Explanatory Statement to European Parliament resolution of 20 February 2008 on the Treaty of Lisbon, 1.4.

1020 See in general, N Walker, 'Postnational constitutionalism and the problem of translation' in JHH Weiler and M Wind (eds), *European Constitutionalism Beyond the State* (Cambridge University Press 2003); N Walker, 'European Constitutionalism in the State Constitutional Tradition' (2006) 59 Current Legal Problems 51, 51, on the question of 'translatability' of constitutionalism from the state tradition to the EU. See also GW Anderson, 'Beyond "Constitutionalism Beyond the State"' (2012) 39 Journal of Law and Society 359.

tities and the division of competences between the EU and the Member States must be respected (Articles 4 and 5 TEU). Ambitions with regard to EU citizenship and the realities of the nation state must be reconciled.[1021] The Convention on the Rights of the Child includes among compulsory educational aims 'development of respect for the own cultural identity, language and values, for the national values of the country in which the child is living, the country from which he or she may originate' (Article 29(1)(c)). On the other hand, Member States must respect EU law. As 'Masters of the Treaty', they have chosen to transfer competences to the EU in the Treaties and the EU exercises public power together with them. This inevitably has consequences for citizenship education. It requires learning about the EU.

'EU citizenship education' should therefore not be under-stated, nor over-stated (nor over-Stated, modelled on the State). It must find a path along the edge of both abysses, a nuanced approach. The constitutions of the Member States and the EU Treaties and CFR offer trustworthy and objective guidance, a basis for developing a balanced form of 'EU citizenship education'.

150 Statal thinking

Are EDC standards applicable to the EU as a polity?[1022] Is postnational citizenship education possible? The classification of the EU within traditional concepts of political theory lead to contrasting views on EU citizenship

1021 P Kirchhof, 'The European Union of States' in A von Bogdandy and J Bast (eds), *Principles of European Constitutional Law*, vol 8 (2nd edn, Hart Beck Nomos 2010) 738; E Spaventa, 'Article 45: Freedom of Movement and of Residence' in S Peers and others (eds), *The EU Charter of Fundamental Rights: a Commentary* (Hart 2014) 1169.

1022 Cf Shaw, 'The many pasts and futures of citizenship in the European Union', 563: 'One insight to emerge from a discussion of citizenship as a background to the specific Union context has been that many of the concepts of nationality, national identity and nation which underlie the more "statist" approaches to the notion of citizenship are plastic in character'. See on the influence of globalisation on citizenship education in the nation state: Keating, 'Educating Europe's citizens: moving from national to post-national models of educating for European citizenship'; Philippou, Keating and Hinderliter Ortloff, 'Citizenship education curricula: comparing the multiple meanings of supranational citizenship in Europe and beyond'; KJ Kennedy, 'Global Trends in Civic and Citizenship Education: What are the Lessons for Nation States?' (2012) 2 Education Sciences 121, 125 ('If the idea of citizenship is changing, it follows that ideas about civic and citizenship education should also be changing. Yet such changes are by no means simple. Civic and citizenship education

education. If qualified as an international (intergovernmental) organisation, the EU does not need 'citizenship' education.[1023] Qualified as an emerging federal State, it does. Pure statal thinking causes much discomfort. In the context of statal thinking oriented towards the nation state, citizenship education aims at confirming the national identity and will perceive every form of EU citizenship education as a threat. In the context of statal thinking oriented towards the EU, EU citizenship education aims at creating the EU super state, nation-building for the United States of Europe. Neither forms of pure statal thinking can be reconciled with the Treaties: Member States have transferred competences to the EU level, on the one hand, but, on the other hand, the EU has no 'Kompetenz-Kompetenz' and must respect the national identity of the Member States.[1024] Binary thinking must be left behind. Balanced EDC does not glorify the nation state, nor does it serve as a federalising device enlarging the sphere of influence of the EU, 'humiliating the state'.[1025]

It is worth noting that the concept of EDC in the Charter on EDC/HRE is not defined by reference to a state. EDC is about empowering learners 'to exercise and defend their democratic rights and responsibilities *in society*, to value diversity and to play an active part *in democratic life*, with a view to the promotion and protection of democracy and the rule of law' (para 2). EDC 'focuses primarily on democratic rights and responsibilities and active participation, in relation to the civic, political, social, economic, legal and cultural *spheres of society*'.[1026] Instruments at UN level and scholars confirm that the perspective starts from the individual in society, not the State. Weiler writes: 'Democracy is not about States. Democracy is about the exercise of public power—and the Union exercises a huge amount of public power'.[1027]

---

has been embedded in traditional theoretical frameworks that assume it is linked to the needs of individual nations.').

1023 Text to n 74.

1024 Text to n 1029.

1025 Cp G Davies, 'The humiliation of the state as a constitutional tactic' in F Amtenbrink and PAJ van den Berg (eds), *The Constitutional Integrity of the European Union* (Asser Press 2010); K Lenaerts and JA Gutiérrez-Fons, 'Epilogue on EU Citizenship: Hopes and Fears' in D Kochenov (ed), *EU Citizenship and Federalism: The Role of Rights* (Cambridge University Press 2017).

1026 In the same sense, UN instruments, see i.a. n 979 and accompanying text. See also n 307, and text to n 2208 ff.

1027 JHH Weiler, 'United in Fear: The Loss of Heimat and the Crises of Europe' in L Papadopoulou, I Pernice and JHH Weiler (eds), *Legitimacy issues of the Euro-*

151 The adaptation perspective: adding an EU dimension to national EDC

The issue of 'EU citizenship education' can be approached in four meta-theoretical ways (by analogy to Walker's four meta-theoretical perspectives on the relationship between State, constitution, and EU).[1028] From the *miscategorisation* perspective, 'EU citizenship education' is impossible: citizenship education is part of the State tradition and does not apply to the EU, because the EU is not a State and not intended to become one.[1029] From the *continuity* perspective, 'EU citizenship education' is a prolongation of national citizenship education, because the EU can be considered a form of federal State, or, at least, has sufficient state-like features.[1030] Both the miscategorisation and the continuity perspective remain 'under the shadow of the state'.[1031] The *nominalist* perspective perceives the issue as a matter of 'only semantics'.[1032] Here 'EU citizenship education' is freestand-

---

pean Union in the face of crisis: Dimitris Tsatsos in memoriam (Nomos 2017) 366. Further text to nn 2208 ff.

1028 Walker, 'European Constitutionalism in the State Constitutional Tradition'. The question of 'EU citizenship education' and the label 'constitution' for EU primary law have this point in common: the discomfort caused by the state paradigm.

1029 Art 4(2) TEU; EU Accession to the ECHR *Opinion 2/13* ECLI:EU:C:2014:2454, i.a. paras 156 and 193. See also analysis in Kirchhof, 'The European Union of States', 754 ('the EU lacks the essential characeristics of a modern state'); C Calliess, 'EU-Vertrag (Lissabon) Art 1' in C Calliess and M Ruffert (eds), *EUV/AEUV: das Verfassungsrecht der Europäischen Union mit Europäischer Grundrechtecharta : Kommentar* (5th edn, Beck 2016), Rn 27 ff, Rechtsnatur der EU.

1030 GF Mancini, 'Europe: The Case for Statehood' (1998) 4 ELJ 29; GF Mancini, 'The making of a constitution for Europe' (1989) 26 CMLRev 595. On federalism and the EU: K Lenaerts, 'Constitutionalism and the Many Faces of Federalism' (1990) 38 The American Journal of Comparative Law 205; C Schönberger, 'European Citizenship as Federal Citizenship: Some Citizenship Lessons of Comparative Federalism' (2007) 19 European Review of Public Law 63; K Lenaerts, 'EU Federalism in 3-D' in E Cloots, G De Baere and S Sottiaux (eds), *Federalism in the European Union* (Hart 2012); Calliess, 'EU-Vertrag (Lissabon) Art 1', Rn 27 ff; D Kochenov (ed) *EU Citizenship and Federalism: The Role of Rights* (Cambridge University Press 2017); D Kochenov, 'On Tiles and Pillars: EU Citizenship as a Federal Denominator' in D Kochenov (ed), *EU Citizenship and Federalism: The Role of Rights* (Cambridge University Press 2017), i.a. p 17 fn 74.

1031 Walker, 'European Constitutionalism in the State Constitutional Tradition', 54.

1032 Ibid, 53 ('constitutionalism can mean whatever we want it to mean within the very broad framework of whatever may be considered desirable by way of the regulation of political authority').

ing, independent of the state tradition, and based on its own definition according to what is desirable, *sui generis*.[1033] If the EU is a *sui generis* supranational organisation, *sui generis* citizenship education may be appropriate. I will not defend such a position, as Member States' traditions are deeply rooted and are the basis for the current way of framing citizenship education. Statal thinking is in our genes and it forms the starting point. The preamble of many constitutions of Member States bear witness to the past suffering of the nation and affirm the sovereignty and independence of the State.[1034] Respect for Member States' histories, opinions and feelings of belonging, and for constitutional structures, however, does not exclude the incorporation of an EU *dimension* in national citizenship education. From the *adaptation* perspective, state citizenship education remains the key contemporary frame, but is flexible and open, acceptable and adaptable to the EU and EU citizenship through the addition of an EU dimension. It is 'taking the state tradition seriously without being paralysed by its legacy'.[1035]

Acknowledging the many debates on the nature of EU citizenship and the EU (and on their contours for the future),[1036] it is from the adaptation perspective that the following analysis will explore how to add an EU dimension to EDC which respects EU law and national constitutions. This

---

1033 For arguments against the *sui generis* qualification, see R Schütze, 'On "federal" Ground: The European Union as an (Inter)national Phenomenon' (2009) 46 CMLRev 1069, 1091–2.

1034 See i.a. preamble to the constitution of the Czech Republic, Croatia, Ireland, Italy, Lithuania, Poland, Slovenia. National identities are to a certain extent constructed, i.a. by recalling (or selectively remembering) common historic experiences. See E Hobsbawm and T Ranger (eds), *The Invention of Tradition* (first published 1983, Cambridge University Press 1992); Anderson, *Imagined Communities: Reflections on the Origin and Spread of Nationalism*.

1035 Walker, 'European Constitutionalism in the State Constitutional Tradition', 55 (see p 56 ff).

1036 For further reflections on the nature and possible qualifications of the EU, see nn 1030, 1702 and text. Further i.a. K Lenaerts, 'Interlocking Legal Orders in the European Union and Comparative Law' (2003) 52 International and Comparative Law Quarterly 873; Schermers and Blokker, *International Institutional Law: Unity within Diversity*; C Timmermans, 'How to Define the European Union?' in F Goudappel and E Hirsch Ballin (eds), *Democracy and Rule of Law in the European Union: Essays in Honour of Jaap W de Zwaan* (Springer 2014); Klabbers, 'Straddling the Fence: The EU and International Law'; N Walker, 'The Philosophy of European Union Law' in D Chalmers and A Arnull (eds), *The Oxford Handbook of European Union Law* (Oxford Handbooks Online 2015); Rosas and Armati, *EU Constitutional Law: An Introduction* 7 (an elephant that cannot be defined).

will adjust traditional citizenship education to the EU supranational system, a multilevel system of governance. The German Constitutional Court, for instance, has emphasised that the EU is not a State and that it should not be compared to one for its democratic legitimation. Participation of Germany in the EU does not mean that a federal State is coming into being, but is about 'an *extension* of the constitutional federal model by a supranational cooperative *dimension*'.[1037] Applying this reasoning to EDC, the national EDC model needs *extending* by a supranational *dimension*. At present, citizens experience the EU predominantly through the lens of their own Member State.[1038] Education has to connect to this (statal) reality. In an adaptation perspective, I will explore how to extend existing national EDC with a view to including an EU dimension consistent with EU law.

152 EDC in mainstream education

How can relevant content for an EU dimension of EDC adapted to *mainstream education* be defined? Inside and outside school, there may be valuable EU learning projects, often provided ad hoc, or by enthusiastic teachers doing more than is required by the curriculum.[1039] While they deserve due credit for this, the concern is that this EU learning only ever reaches small numbers of young EU citizens. EDC standards aim to educate *all* learners for democracy, not a group of voluntary learners, not a select group. Article 10(3) TEU provides that *every citizen* shall have the right to participate in the democratic life of the Union. The Charter on EDC/HRE states that member states should be guided by the 'aim of providing *every person* within their territory with the opportunity of education for democratic citizenship and human rights education'.[1040] In view of this aim, this analysis will explore what is relevant content for an EU dimension of EDC in mainstream education in schools. 'Mainstream education' refers to the

---

1037 *BVerfG, 2 BvE 2/08 (Lissabon)* 30 June 2009, Absatz-Nr (1-421), para 277 ('Nicht nur aus der Sicht des Grundgesetzes handelt es sich bei der Beteiligung Deutschlands an der Europäischen Union indes nicht um die Übertragung eines Bundesstaatsmodells auf die europäische Ebene, sondern um die Erweiterung des verfassungsrechtlichen Föderalmodells um eine überstaatlich kooperative Dimension').

1038 See C Schönberger, 'Foreword. European citizenship as federal citizenship: studying EU citizenship through the federal lens' in D Kochenov (ed), *EU Citizenship and Federalism: The Role of Rights* (Cambridge University Press 2017) xxviii.

1039 See n 39. Also first caveat, text to n 570 ff.

1040 Charter on EDC/HRE, para 5 (a). See also § 241 .

compulsory levels of 'formal education', defined as 'the structured education and training system that runs from pre-primary and primary through secondary school and onto university'.[1041] Formal education is normally provided by general or vocational educational institutions. Schools are institutions providing formal education at primary and secondary level.[1042] Formal learning is the foundation for lifelong learning and is important in qualitative and quantitative terms. Delors observes that it is very tempting to focus on the educational potential of the modern media, yet he warns that people will not be able to make good use of potential resources outside schools unless they have received a sound basic education, fostering intellectual curiosity:

> nothing can replace the formal education system, where each individual is introduced to the many forms of knowledge. There is no substitute for the teacher—pupil relationship, which is underpinned by authority and developed through dialogue. This has been argued time and time again by the great classical thinkers who have studied the question of education.[1043]

Moreover, at present, learning through and from the media has been undermined because of fake news or disinformation. More than half of the respondents in a 2018 European Barometer tend not to trust media.[1044] The quantitative importance of formal learning is illustrated by the huge

---

1041 Charter on EDC/HRE, para 2 (leading to certification), also para 6. See further definitions in Art 2 Erasmus+ Regulation 1288/2013. See also para 5(c): all means of education have to play a part, also non-formal and informal. Overview in figure in Annex 5 to this study.

1042 Text to n 4.

1043 Delors, 'Education: The Necessary Utopia', 19. Additionally important: Resolution of the Council and of the Representatives of the Governments of the Member States, meeting within the Council, on the recognition of the value of non-formal and informal learning within the European youth field [2006] OJ C168/1. In several contexts, I will argue that information and awareness-raising do not suffice, education is needed (see i.a. text to n 1587).

1044 Standard Eurobarometer 89, Public Opinion in the European Union (June 2018): on average 56% of respondents in the EU tend not to trust the media (e.g. FI 23%, DK 36%, LU 42%, DE 47%, HU 60%, FR 66%, EL 77%), while 40% tend to do so. See also Flash Eurobarometer 464, Fake News and Disinformation Online (March 2018): traditional sources are more trusted, such as radio (70%), television (66%) and printed media (63%); online sources are trusted less, such as online newspapers and magazines (47%), video hosting websites and podcasts (27%) and online social networks and messaging apps (26%).

number of hours which pupils spend in classrooms. On average, 15 years of life are spent in schools. Instruction in classroom settings absorbs a large proportion of public investment, which is crucial to effective schooling.[1045] Given its aim of not only preparing young people for employability, but also for life as responsible citizens in a democratic society, formal learning should reach as many young EU citizens as possible in a systematic way. To that effect, I propose that EU learning should be included in compulsory levels of mainstream education, in general curricula in primary and secondary schools, adapted for different levels of difficulty. The last years of secondary education are a particularly valuable time for exercising critical thinking with regard to the EU. Accordingly, higher education programmes for future teachers, multipliers of EU knowledge, need to be adapted (an EU dimension in the training of trainers).[1046]

A 2017 Eurobarometer reports:

> A large majority (89%) agree national governments should strengthen school education about rights and responsibilities as EU citizens. More than eight in ten also agree that learning about European matters, such as the functioning of the EU and its institutions, EU history or European culture, should be part of compulsory school education (83%).[1047]

In principle, mainstream education includes all curricula, not only specialised curricula with a special focus on the EU, such as economics, and not only curricula targeted at the more gifted pupils before they attend university. It also includes vocational training curricula. Given an observed 'middle-class bias' (higher representation of members of the middle class

---

1045 See overview in Commission/EACEA/Eurydice, Compulsory Education in Europe 2019/20—Facts and Figures, 6. Profiles in OECD, *Education at a Glance 2017: OECD Indicators* (OECD 2017), 61. ISCED levels in Commission/EACEA/Eurydice, Citizenship Education in Europe (2012), 106 (ISCED 2: Lower secondary education; ISCED 3: Upper secondary education).

1046 See on teacher training, Charter on EDC/HRE, paras 7 and 9; CoE, *Learning to live together: Council of Europe Report on the state of citizenship and human rights education in Europe*, i.a. 53, 61, 69–70, 87 (EDC/HRE provision in teacher training is considered as insufficient).

1047 Flash Eurobarometer 455, European Youth (January 2018); interviewed respondents were aged 15–30 (survey conducted by TNS political & social at the request of the European Commission, DG Directorate-General for Education, Youth, Sport and Culture). See also Flash Eurobarometer 319b, Youth on the Move: Education and training, mobility, employment and entrepreneurship (May 2011), 9.

in participation forums),[1048] the EU dimension should be inserted into technical and professional education programmes. Future doctors and future electricians, future white- and blue-collar workers are all future EU citizens whom the EU seeks to put at the centre of its project and who must be empowered to participate in the democracy aspired to. They all deserve an EU dimension in the various forms and levels of education they receive.[1049] Therefore, by analogy with the mainstreaming of gender equality in education,[1050] it is submitted that an EU dimension too should be mainstreamed in education, in application of EDC standards.

153 Four criteria for determining relevant content for the EU dimension of EDC

Possible content for the EU dimension in mainstream education will be explored. The EU is active in many policy fields influencing citizens' lives. Manuals to introduce students in higher education to the EU and textbooks on EU law cover hundreds (thousands) of pages. What should be selected for pupils in schools? Obviously, not all pupils need to know about the right to deduct value added tax and the conditions for doing so pursuant to Directive 2006/112, nor about the obligation to respect milk quotas in the common agricultural policy. Schools can emphasise different aspects of the EU dimension of EDC in general or vocational training, depending on curriculum specialisations.[1051] The purpose of this Part is to explore those aspects of EU law which may have particular relevance for an

---

1048 Opinion of the European Economic and Social Committee on 'The transition towards a more sustainable European future— a strategy for 2050' [2018] OJ C81/44, paras 3.4.6 and 5.2.4.

1049 Facts in *Education at a Glance 2017: OECD Indicators.* See also Special Eurobarometer 471, Fairness, inequality and inter-generational mobility (December 2017): 41% of the respondents had completed secondary education, 16% had completed primary education. Working respondents are manual workers (41%), white collar workers (23%), managers (21%), 15% self-employed.

1050 CoE Recommendation CM/Rec(2007)13 of the Committee of Ministers to member states on gender mainstreaming in education (10 October 2007), para 37; Explanatory memorandum to the Charter on EDC/HRE, para 6. See also recital 5 in Decision 1093/2012/EU of the European Parliament and of the Council of 21 November 2012 on the European Year of Citizens (2013) [2012] OJ L325/1; and Struthers, 'Human Rights: A Topic Too Controversial for Mainstream Education?'.

1051 Certain EU policies have more relevance depending on specific curricula (e.g. chemistry, finance, commerce, economy, culture, agriculture, joinery, electricity, or technology and environment). Examples in section on EU rights (i.a. text to n 2061).

EU dimension of EDC in mainstream education on the basis of four criteria. The criteria (i-iv) are based on a combined reading of EU primary law and EDC standards as explained in Part one. All four criteria (i-iv) are applied to the concept of EDC as defined in Chapter One, including its three empowerment aims (c-1 to c-3). This confirms the importance of having identified a commonly accepted concept of citizenship education in Part one and having analysed its effects in the EU legal order in Part two.[1052]

154 (i) Additional content

In national EDC, pupils (supposedly) learn about the concepts of democracy, citizenship rights, values such as equality, justice, etc., based on Member State law and structures.[1053] They exercise skills, such as critical thinking, and develop attitudes based on respect and tolerance. They are introduced to human rights, which are universal. What does the EU level of governance have to add to this? A combined reading of EU primary law defining EU citizenship (Articles 9 TEU and 20 TFEU) and the Charter on EDC/HRE (paragraph 2) leads to the first criterion for the EU dimension: does it provide *additional* content for national EDC?

The 1992 Maastricht Treaty established the legal concept of 'citizenship of the Union'. The 1997 Amsterdam Treaty added that Union citizenship 'shall complement and not replace national citizenship'. The 2009 Lisbon Treaty replaced the word 'complement' by 'additional', reinforcing the idea that, in principle, EU citizenship does not detract from national citizenship rights, but adds further rights.[1054] Reiterating article 9 TEU, Article 20(1) TFEU states that:

1052 § 129 .

1053 Council Recommendation of 22 May 2018 on key competences for lifelong learning, Annex: A European Reference Framework, 6: Citizenship competence ('knowledge of basic concepts'). See concepts mentioned in Recommendation of the European Parliament and of the Council of 18 December 2006 on key competences for lifelong learning, Annex, Civic competences.

1054 Cp ex Art 8 of Treaty on European Union, signed at Maastricht on 7 February 1992 [1992] OJ C191/1; ex Art 17 of the Treaty on European Union; and Art 20(1) TFEU. See Treaty of Lisbon amending the Treaty on European Union and the Treaty establishing the European Community, signed at Lisbon on 13 December 2007 [2007] OJ C306, Art 2(34) amending Art 17 of the Treaty establising the European Community. Already in 1992, Closa wrote: 'The distinctive element of the concept of citizenship of the Union is the enjoyment of rights and the subjection to the obligations granted by the Treaty (Article 8.2). This determines the first characteristic of citizenship: additionality': C Closa,

> Every person holding the nationality of a Member State shall be a citizen of the Union. Citizenship of the Union shall be *additional* to and not replace national citizenship.[1055]

The relationship between national citizenship and EU citizenship is not 'either/or' but 'both/and'.[1056] EU citizenship is not self-standing; nor is EU citizenship education. The legal status of EU citizenship is derived from national citizenship inasmuch as Member States define who are their nationals and these nationals automatically become EU citizens by virtue of the definition in the Treaties. This legal automatism is (unfortunately) not an educational automatism: education as an EU citizen does not automatically follow from education as a national citizen. Extra efforts are needed to transform national citizens, additionally, into empowered EU citizens.

Because EU citizenship is additional to national citizenship, 'EU citizenship education' can be defined as national citizenship education with an additional EU dimension; in other words, as national EDC which incorporates an EU dimension. The expression 'the EU dimension of EDC' is to be preferred to 'EU citizenship education', as the latter may raise suspicions of an intention to replace national citizenship with EU citizenship, and national identities with an EU identity, which would be in breach of the Treaties.

'The concept of citizenship in the Treaty on European Union' (1992) 29 CMLRev 1137, 1160. See also Shaw, 'Citizenship: Contrasting Dynamics at the Interface of Integration and Constitutionalism', text to fn 109 ff.

1055 My emphasis. Cp 'La citoyenneté de l'Union s'ajoute à la citoyenneté nationale et ne la remplace pas'; 'Die Unionsbürgerschaft tritt zur nationalen Staatsbürgerschaft hinzu, ersetzt diese aber nicht'; 'Het burgerschap van de Unie komt naast het nationale burgerschap doch komt niet in de plaats daarvan'. See also Art 9 TEU.

1056 EDH Olsen, 'European Citizenship: Mixing Nation State and Federal Features with a Cosmopolitan Twist' (2013) 14 Perspectives on European Politics and Society 1, 4. See also European Parliament Resolution of 26 September 2006 on initiatives to complement school curricula providing appropriate support measures to include the European dimension [2006] OJ C306E/100, para 13 ('Stresses that the European dimension complements national content, but neither replaces nor supplants it); M van den Brink, 'The Court and the Legislators: who should define the scope of free movement in the EU?' in F De Witte, R Bauböck and J Shaw (eds), *Freedom of movement under attack: Is it worth defending as the core of EU citizenship?* (EUI Working Papers RSCAS 2016/69, 2016), 25 ('EU citizenship is not about the centralisation of rights and about replacing the democratically legitimated substance of national laws by uniform European ones').

Part three aims to analyse the additional EU dimension of EDC *based on EU law*. EDC aims to empower citizens 'to exercise and defend their democratic rights and responsibilities in society' (c-1), 'to value diversity' (c-2), and 'to play an active part in democratic life' (c-3), with a view to the promotion and protection of democracy and the rule of law.[1057] To achieve this empowerment, EDC equips learners with 'knowledge, skills and understanding' and develops 'their attitudes and behaviour' (b). In the context of Council of Europe standard- setting, the components of EDC standards have been chosen to be multi-purpose, flexible, and dynamic, in order 'to allow member states to adapt them to suit their own needs and the distinct cultural contours of their own societies'.[1058] They can thus be adapted to suit the needs of EU Member States. The intention in adopting an EDC common denominator was to allow for diversity of approach.

In order to apply EDC standards to democracy beyond the State, and without going into theoretical reflections on democracy and postnational citizenship, I will—pragmatically—formulate content for the components of the EDC concept of the Charter on EDC/HRE on the basis of EU law, in interaction with national law.[1059] This empirical approach, based on legal realities, ensures a stable (safe) start for EDC. It cannot be contested

1057 Definition of EDC in Charter on EDC/HRE, para 2. Components numbered in § 27 .

1058 See i.a. Thorbjørn Jagland, CoE Secretary General, Preface in Competences for democratic culture: Living together as equals in culturally diverse democratic societies (CoE 2016), 8, also 31.

1059 Literature on democracy and the EU is immense. See, i.a., E Stein, 'International integration and democracy: no love at first sight' (2001) 95 American Journal of International Law 489; Verhoeven, *The European Union in Search of a Democratic and Constitutional Theory*; W Durner, 'Streitbare Demokratie' (2003) 128 Archiv des oeffentlichen Rechts 340; A Peters, 'European democracy after the 2003 Convention' (2004) 41 CMLRev 37; D Halberstam, 'The bride of Messina: constitutionalism and democracy in Europe' (2005) 30 ELRev 775; JP McCormick, 'Habermas, Supranational Democracy and the European Constitution' (2006) 2 European Constitutional Law Review 398; G de Búrca, 'Developing Democracy beyond the State' (2007-2008) 46 Columbia Journal of Transnational Law 221; Habermas, *Zur Verfassung Europas. Ein Essay*; F de Witte, 'Union Citizenship and Constrained Democracy' in M De Visser and AP van der Mei (eds), *The Treaty on European Union 1993-2013: Reflections from Maastricht* (Intersentia 2013); J Habermas, 'Democracy, Solidarity and the European Crisis' (KU Leuven, 26 April 2013); Lenaerts, 'The principle of democracy in the case law of the European Court of Justice'; Nicolaïdis, 'European Demoicracy and Its Crisis'; S Rummens and S Sottiaux, 'Democratic Legitimacy in the Bund or 'Federation of States': the Cases of Belgium and the EU' (2014) 20 ELJ 568; L Van Middelaar and P Van Parijs (eds), *After*

that national EDC needs to be consistent with EU law.[1060] EU law contributes to the content of the EU dimension of EDC since it inevitably impacts on the components of the EDC concept. Starting from the EDC concept as defined in the Charter on EDC/HRE, my purpose is to explore the effects of EU law on the component parts of EDC. To what extent does EU law, in interaction with Member State law, produce *additional* democratic rights and responsibilities for EU citizens in society (c-1), *additional* elements to value diversity (c-2) and *additional* elements enabling them to play an active part in democratic life (c-3)? To empower EU citizens, which *additional* knowledge, skills, attitudes and behaviour (b) are needed, adapting national EDC? As for HRE, what is the additional EU dimension needed (interconnected with EDC) in order to contribute to the building and defence of a universal culture of human rights in European society?

155 *(ii) Significant content, i.e. relating to foundational values, objectives and principles laid down in EU primary law*

Some of the *additional* content for EDC components, satisfying criterion (i), may be of marginal significance for the average pupil, e.g. rights or obligations relating to fisheries. Therefore, a second criterion for main-

---

the Storm: How to Save Democracy in Europe (Lannoo 2015); J Hoeksma, *From Common Market to Common Democracy: A Theory of Democratic Integration* (Wolf Legal Publishers 2016). See further mentioned scholars on constitutionalism and on citizenship. Also EF Isin and BS Turner, *Handbook of Citizenship Studies* (Sage 2002); D Kostakopoulou, 'Ideas, Norms and European Citizenship: Explaining Institutional Change' (2005) 68 The Modern Law Review 233; S Besson and A Utzinger, 'Introduction: Future Challenges of European Citizenship - Facing a Wide-Open Pandora's Box' (2007) 13 ELJ 573; D Kostakopoulou, 'European Union Citizenship: Writing the Future' (2007) 13 ELJ 623; M Aziz, 'Implementation as the Test Case of European Citizenship' (2009) 15 Columbia Journal of European Law 281; G Davies, 'The entirely conventional supremacy of Union citizenship and rights' in J Shaw (ed), *Has the European Court of Justice Challenged the Member State Sovereignty in Nationality Law?* (EUI Robert Schuman Centre for Advanced Studies Paper 62, 2011); A Iliopoulou-Penot, 'The Transnational Character of Union Citizenship' in M Dougan, NN Shuibhne and E Spaventa (eds), *Empowerment and Disempowerment of the European Citizen* (Hart 2012); EF Isin, 'Citizens without Nations' 30 Environment and Planning D: Society and Space 450; A Iliopoulou-Penot, 'Citoyenneté de l'Union, mobilité et intégration dans l'espace européen' (2014) 134 Revue de l'OFCE 29; D Kostakopoulou, 'Scala Civium: Citizenship Templates Post-Brexit and the European Union's Duty to Protect EU Citizens' (2018) 56 JCMS 1.

1060 On the solidity of EU primary law as a basis for EDC, see text to nn 1141-1086, and following section.

stream education is proposed: is the additional content *significant* in the sense of relating to foundational values, objectives and principles laid down in EU primary law? This second criterion guarantees, moreover, that EDC is connected to the specific characteristics of the EU. It responds to the need to guard the constitutional red line.[1061] As is clear from Part two, applying the EDC standards of the Council of Europe in the EU legal order must at all times respect the specific characteristics of the EU. EU primary law and its foundational values, objectives and principles will constitute an essential pillar in the learning method proposed in Chapter five. The second criterion is also in line with EU secondary law on civic and citizenship competences, by reference to the foundational values, objectives or principles.[1062]

156 (iii) Inviting critical thinking

A third criterion for examining the relevance of content for the EU dimension of EDC in mainstream education is: does it invite critical thinking? In order to empower the learner, EDC needs to do more than merely convey additional and significant knowledge.[1063] EDC standards aim to educate learners for active and responsible citizenship. The purpose is not to imbue pupils with common EU orthodoxies without reflection, but to encourage

1061 See §§ 142 – 144 .

1062 See, i.a., Council Recommendation of 22 May 2018 on key competences for lifelong learning, para 2.7, Annex: A European Reference Framework, 6: Citizenship competence. Before: Recommendation of the European Parliament and of the Council of 18 December 2006 on key competences for lifelong learning. Within the description of civic competences, an EU dimension is present: reference to the CFR and application of the concepts mentioned by institutions at EU level; moreover, '[k]nowledge of European integration and of the EU's structures, main objectives and values is also essential, as well as an awareness of diversity and cultural identities in Europe.' See further Regulation 1381/2013 of the European Parliament and of the Council of 17 December 2013 establishing a Rights, Equality and Citizenship Programme for the period 2014 to 2020 [2013] OJ L354/62, Art 4(2)(a) (aim at better exercise of the rights of citizens and pursue this objective by 'enhancing awareness and knowledge of Union law and policies as well as of the rights, values and principles underpinning the Union'); Erasmus+ Regulation 288/2013, Art 4f (the promotion of European values in accordance with Art 2 TEU); Council Regulation (EU) No 390/2014 of 14 April 2014 establishing the 'Europe for Citizens' programme for the period 2014-2020 [2014] OJ L115/3, Art 2.

1063 Charter on EDC/HRE, para 5(g), explanatory memorandum para 35 ('In both [EDR and HRE] there is an emphasis on the outcome of such education being not simply knowledge but empowerment, leading to appropriate action').

them to think critically, which is an essential part of competences in a democratic culture. The importance of critical thinking is clear from Parts one and two and has been continuously stressed by all actors.[1064] In line with the controversy principle in citizenship education,[1065] uncertainties

1064 Critical thinking is part of EDC standards in the CoE and in the EU context. While not mentioned as such in the Charter on EDC/HRE, it is an essential in the Competences for democratic culture: Living together as equals in culturally diverse democratic societies (CoE 2016), p 10–11 (3 bodies of knowledge and critical understanding), p 13 ('Analytical and critical thinking skills are the skills required to analyse, evaluate and make judgments about materials of any kind (e.g. texts, arguments, interpretations, issues, events, experiences, etc.) in a systematic and logical manner; see also p 44–46); also CoE Reference Framework of Competences for Democratic Culture, Vol 1: Context, concepts and model (2018), Glossary: critical understanding involves active reflection on and critical evaluation of that which is being understood and interpreted (as opposed to automatic, habitual and unreflective interpretation); ibid, p 15: aims of education: 'The corresponding pedagogy is not only instrumental but also educational. It reflects a long education tradition, based on humanistic ideas and reflected in the concept of *Bildung*: the lifelong process enabling people to make independent choices for their own lives, to recognise others as equals and to interact with them in meaningful ways'. See CoE Reference Framework of Competences for Democratic Culture, Vol 2: Descriptors of competences for democratic culture (2018), i.a. key descriptors i.a. 120, 122, 124, 125, 127, 131, 134, also descriptors 2047- 2049. See earlier CoE Recommendation CM/Rec(2008)12 of the Committee of Ministers to member states on the dimension of religions and non-religious convictions within intercultural education (10 December 2008), appendix para 5. In the EU: Council Recommendation of 22 May 2018 on key competences for lifelong learning [2018] OJ C189/1, recitals 7 and 17, Annex 'Key competences' and 'Citizenship competence' ('This involves critical thinking and integrated problem solving skills, as well as skills to develop arguments and constructive participation in community activities, as well as in decision-making at all levels, from local and national to the European and international level'); see also critical thinking as skill in literacy, digital, and entrepreneurship competence. Before: Recommendation of the European Parliament and of the Council of 18 December 2006 on key competences for lifelong learning (critical thinking present throughout the Reference Framework). See also Commission/EACEA/Eurydice, Citizenship Education in Europe (2012), 8. See in general the need for critical thinking in the caveats raised by scholars with regard to EDC or citizenship education, i.a. in text to n 581, with significant academic work. For Germany, see the controversy principle of the Beutelsbacher consensus. Further, the increased attention to critical thinking to prevent radicalisation in Part two (§§ 127 128), including the Paris declaration; and Council Conclusions of 30 May 2016 on developing media literacy and critical thinking through education and training [2016] OJ C212/5. See also n 1221.

1065 Text to nn 587 and 1243.

and the controversial aspects of the EU and EU citizenship must be acknowledged in the classroom. Because of its importance, the criterion of critical thinking is given special attention in the section on case teaching (second pillar of the learning method proposed in Chapter five).

157 (iv) Affecting the large majority of EU citizens, including 'static' citizens

Finally, some of the additional (i) and significant (ii) content of the EU dimension of EDC may seem irrelevant to mainstream education because it relates to limited categories of citizens or to very specific situations. This leads to a fourth criterion (leaving what is probably the most problematic question to the end): does the EU dimension content 'affect' the large majority of citizens, who are mainly 'static'? Static citizens are citizens who live at home in the Member State of which they are a national and are EU citizens as a consequence of that State being an EU Member State (Article 9 TEU).[1066] The word 'affect' is used here in a broad sense, not necessarily requiring a legal relationship of rights and duties, but in a social sense: is the content of the EU dimension relevant to more than a small fraction of the population? Should all pupils be given the opportunity of learning about it, in keeping with EDC standards? The EU is sometimes perceived as a market, of importance only for economic actors, or as a norm-setter for crossborder situations, important only for mobile citizens. The Commission defines 'mobile citizens' as EU citizens residing in another EU Member State.[1067] Making this definition somewhat more specific, I propose to adopt the following working definition (commonly used for statistics): the mobile citizen is the citizen who lives for at least one year in another Member State.[1068] Less than 4 per cent of EU citizens are mobile,

---

1066 Cp Special Eurobarometer 346, New Europeans (April 2011), 5.

1067 Commission, Press release 'European Commission upholds free movement of people' (2014); the Commission relates that 'at the end of 2012, 14.1 million citizens were living in a Member State other than their own for one year or more'. The OECD Economic Survey of the EU 2012 reports that 0.29% of the EU citizens are mobile (annual cross-border mobility rate in the EU compared to the USA and Australia).

1068 J Salamońska and E Recchi, *Europe between mobility and sedentarism: Patterns of cross-border practices and their consequences for European identification* (EUI Working Paper RSCAS 2016/50, 2016), 2; Eurostat Glossary; see also Regulation (EC) No 862/2007 of the European Parliament and of the Council of 11 July 2007 on Community statistics on migration and international protection and repealing Council Regulation (EEC) No 311/76 on the compilation of statistics on foreign workers [2007] OJ L199/23, Art 2(1)(b). Working definition reconsidered in text to nn 1457 ff.

more than 96 per cent are static.[1069] To what extent is an EU dimension of EDC relevant for the static citizen? In 2011, Shaw reflected: 'Whether and how additionality might play out as Union citizenship gradually becomes more significant within rather than solely across the boundaries of the Member States is as yet unclear'.[1070] I will explore the relevance of EU law for those who stay within the boundaries of their Member State and examine what it adds to the components of EDC.

158 Simplicity is not a criterion

To determine relevant content for the EU dimension of EDC in mainstream education, all four criteria should preferably be satisfied. Ideally, seen from the perspective of the learner, the additional content of the EU dimension should also be easy to understand. However, simplicity has not been chosen as a criterion for EDC content. Living together as 27 Member States in one space is not simple. Balancing various interests often requires complex rules. Awareness of complexity and learning how to handle it, is part of education for democracy and respect for pluralism. The complexity of the EU is sometimes used as a counterargument: the EU is too complex for learning at school. However, its complexity is precisely why EU learning is necessary. The essential elements of the EU must be explained and reflected on in schools to empower EU citizens. Adult citizens rarely use their leisure time to discover what an EU directive is. Education teaches us how to address complex issues. The Latin texts of Cicero and mathematical problems are not simple either. Teachers and pupils should not be underestimated. Challenges are an inherent part of all learning. Citizenship education and the EU are no exception. Democracy and the rule of law are not only required in simple situations, on the contrary.

This does not mean that the (sometimes complex) rights and arguments in the following analysis are intended to serve as didactic material for schools. Rather, the analysis should function as legal fieldwork, a foundation for schools and for educational authorities who intend to add an EU dimension to EDC in mainstream education. These actors must develop adequate materials, simplifying EU law while keeping the fundamentals

---

1069 See <ec.europa.eu/eurostat/statistics-explained/index.php/Migration_and_migrant_population_statistics>: on 1 January 2017, 16.9 million persons lived in one EU Member State with the citizenship of another EU Member State (Romanian, Polish, Italian, Portuguese and German citizens were the five biggest groups of EU-citizens living in other EU Member States in 2017).

1070 Shaw, 'Citizenship: Contrasting Dynamics at the Interface of Integration and Constitutionalism', sub-heading D 1.

intact. This is a challenging but unavoidable task in a society based on democracy, fundamental rights and the rule of law.[1071]

159 Outlining the content for the EU dimension

Applying the four relevance criteria, I will now use a combined reading of EU law and EDC standards as a basis for specific EU learning content. The aim is to analyse how EU law impacts on the components of EDC and to determine what additional content is needed to empower the citizens living in the EU: what is the EU dimension of the exercise of rights and responsibilities (c-1), the EU dimension of valuing diversity (c-2), and the EU dimension of playing an active part in democratic life (c-3), with a view to the promotion and protection of democracy and the rule of law?[1072] Juxtaposing EU law and the empowerment aims of EDC standards automatically produces content for the EU dimension, as the simplified outline below shows.

Content for the EU dimension in Education for Democratic Citizenship

EDC standards	**+ EU law**	**➔ EU dimension in EDC**
Education for Democratic Citizenship empowers citizens to - exercise their rights and responsibilities in society - value diversity - play an active part in democratic life	- Classic EU citizenship rights (Arts 20–24 TFEU) - Participation rights (Title II TEU) - All other EU rights and obligations (EU law in general) ⇧⇧⇧ EU values, objectives, principles (e.g. Arts 2–5 TEU, Arts 18–19, 28, 45 TFEU, CFR)	Relevance criteria ✓ Additional content ✓ Significant content ✓ Critical thinking ✓ Affects the large majority of EU citizens

1071 See in general on a hard core relevant for political education, different from positivist law: Oberreuter, 'Rechtserziehung'.

1072 Charter on EDC/HRE, para 2; components numbered in § 27 .

To answer the question of content for the EU dimension, I will first look at the 'classic' citizenship rights, i.e. the rights listed in Articles 20–24 TFEU and usually associated with EU citizenship by EU lawyers (Chapter six). Their relevance for mainstream education is explored on the basis of the four criteria set out above[1073]: do they provide additional (i) and significant (ii) content for national EDC, invite critical thinking (iii) and affect the large majority of citizens, who are static (iv)? At first glance, classic citizenship rights at once provide the obvious content for the EU dimension of EDC components (c-1) and (c-3): they consist of rights and responsibilities and relate to playing an active part in democratic life. However, the exercise of formulating content for the EU dimension does not stop there. Secondly, in Chapter seven, the participation rights in Title II TEU are addressed. I will explain how EU citizenship rights—i.e. rights conferred by virtue of the status of citizen of the Union—extend beyond the classic list of citizenship rights. The (often forgotten) citizenship right to participate in the democratic life of the Union, laid down in Article 10(3) TEU, deserves particular attention. The various expressions of this right will be examined as to their relevance for the EU dimension. Thirdly, in Chapter eight, a still broader look on the legal position of EU citizens is taken. The many other rights which citizens derive from EU law, simply known as 'EU rights' and corresponding obligations, constitute an even more persuasive basis for the EU dimension of EDC according to the four criteria. These three categories of rights supply content for the core of an EU dimension of EDC, as they impact on the three empowerment aims of EDC (c-1–2–3), to greater and lesser extents.

160 More than just narrow legal content

The approach which explains rights and obligations is not only valuable per se, but it is the starting point for widening perspectives and for reflection. At first sight, the three following chapters may seem to limit the content for the EU dimension of EDC to rights and obligations. Yet, the narrow legal view must be transcended. The value of law for the field of citizenship education has already been explained.[1074] In the following analysis of rights and obligations, 'law' is more than the technical rule in legal instruments. It includes the deeper layers of values, objectives and principles which EU law embraces, or aims to embrace, and thus opens the door for debate, essential in citizenship education. In each chapter, rights and

1073 §§152-157 .
1074 § 13 .

obligations are supported by the foundational values, objectives and principles of the EU and will provide significant content (ii). They pervade the society in which EU citizens live and are directly relevant for education in various key competences. In order to attain the deeper layers and to widen perspectives, Chapter five proposes an adapted learning method to bring this content in classrooms.

161 *Aide mémoire*

This schema restates the focus of this study in order to guide the reader through the further analysis. Letters will be used to refer to EDC components and to criteria for relevance for mainstream education.

Effects of a combined reading of EDC standards and EU law

> **Education for Democratic Citizenship** (**EDC**) means:
> (a) education, training, awareness raising, information, practices and activities
> which aim
> (**b**) by equipping learners with knowledge, skills and understanding and developing their attitudes and behaviour
> (c) to empower the learners
> (**c-1**) to exercise and defend their democratic rights and responsibilities in society
> (**c-2**) to value diversity
> (**c-3**) to play an active part in democratic life
> (d) with a view to the promotion and protection of democracy and the rule of law.[1075]

> **Citizenship of the Union** is hereby established. Every person holding the nationality of a Member State shall be a citizen of the Union. Citizenship of the Union shall be *additional* to and not replace national citizenship.[1076]

> Four criteria for determining relevant content for the **EU dimension of EDC in mainstream education** consistent with EU law:
> (i) *additional* content for national EDC
> (ii) significant content,
> i.e. relating to foundational (EU primary law) values, objectives and principles
> (iii) inviting critical thinking
> (iv) affecting the large majority of EU citizens, including 'static' citizens

1075 Para 2 Council of Europe Charter on Education for Democratic Citizenship and Human Rights Education.

1076 Art 20(1) Treaty on the Functioning of the European Union, Art 9 Treaty on European Union (emphasis added).

CHAPTER 5 Objective, critical and pluralistic EU learning

162 Innovative learning method

Analysing the effects of a combined reading of EDC standards and EU law as to the substance, I essentially want to demonstrate *that* an EU dimension should be included in EDC and give indications as to its content in mainstream education according to the four criteria (i-iv). In itself, this leaves open the question as to *how* to include this EU dimension in the classroom. Teachers enjoy educational freedom as to methods. They are academically trained, skilled in didactics, and experienced. Yet, the substance and methods of imparting citizenship education are closely interrelated.[1077] Many interlocutors responded to my thesis that EDC standards require an EU dimension to national EDC, with the question: 'yes, ... but how?'. Therefore, to prepare for the analysis of the content of EDC in the following Chapters, I will set out a personal proposal bearing on the 'how' question. The proposed learning method follows from the adaptation perspective and the criteria explained in the Introduction to Part three and will be illustrated in the analysis of the rights of EU citizens in Chapters six, seven and eight. Obviously, the method proposed is not the only possible one.[1078] 'Best practices' for EDC exist in various formats and an EU dimension can be incorporated in all of them. However, this is a contribution for an innovative practice from a legal perspective.[1079]

1077 Reinhardt, *Teaching Civics: A Manual for Secondary Education Teachers*.

1078 Other methods for EU learning, see i.a. <beucitizen.eu/teaching-packages/>; <europa.eu/teachers-corner/>; <www.schooleducationgateway.eu/en/pub/teacher_academy/teaching_materials/united-in-diversity>; <www.europaindeklas.be/>; <www.bpb.de/internationales/europa/europaeische-union/>.

1079 Without making any scientific claims, the proposed method is based on limited but positive experiences in classrooms. I was able to test the method with pupils in secondary education (17–18 years old, Heilig Hartinstituut Heverlee Belgium, and European School Luxembourg), as well as in university Teacher Training and workshops with students of various faculties (KU Leuven). The response was in general enthusiastic. In a simplified version, the method was also used in primary education (11 years old, European School Luxembourg). Method discussed in workshop: Grimonprez, 'Conflicting ideas of Europe: the role of values in citizenship education'. See call for innovative practice in Council Recommendation of 22 May 2018 on key competences for lifelong

163 *Providing the EU dimension in an objective, critical and pluralistic manner, with no aim of indoctrination*

As a balanced method for providing an EU dimension at school, the following package is proposed: on the one hand, a stable platform based on EU primary law, offering pupils an understanding of EU foundational values, objectives and principles, and on the other hand, room for dialogue and critical thinking, based on case teaching. This responds to EDC standards, as well as to the ECtHR requirement that the State, in fulfilling its educational functions, must take care to convey the information or knowledge included in the curriculum 'in an *objective, critical and pluralistic* manner', with no aim of indoctrination.[1080] Teaching must occur in an 'unbiased and objective way, respectful of the freedoms of opinion, conscience and expression'.[1081] Teachers should not take advantage of their position to indoctrinate or exert improper influence in another way on pupils during lessons.[1082]

Objectivity is enhanced by an EU dimension in EDC based on EU primary law in conjunction with national constitutions (rather than based on the subjective views of educators). Educating in accordance with the tenets of EU primary law ensures respect for several interests and values, including Member State and EU interests. Law reflects the fundamental values and choices of society in an objective and neutral way. Law makes it possible to take emotion out of the debate.[1083] At the same time, discussing case law leaves room for *critical thinking and pluralism*, in accordance with the right to freedom of expression (Article 10 ECHR, Article 11 CFR), and empowers citizens to exercise this right.[1084]

---

learning, Annex: A European Reference Framework, 'Supporting the development of key competence, b(c); also Recommendation para 3: Member States should 'facilitate the acquisition of key competences by making use of good practices to support the development of the key competences'.

1080 My emphasis. Settled case law: see n 696 and text to n 2449.

1081 CESCR General Comment No. 13, cited above, para 28.

1082 *Vogt v Germany* no 17851/91 (ECtHR 2 Sept 1996), para 60. Also n 696 and text to n 2449.

1083 See i.a. § 258 ; Nussbaum (nn 579-580).

1084 Education as an empowerment right (n 2167).

A EU primary law: objectivity

1. A European constitutional space

164 *EU primary law constitutes an objective, consensus-based foundation for the EU dimension of EDC*

The incorporation of an EU dimension into EDC should be based on the Treaties and the CFR, which are interconnected with Member State constitutions. The fact that the Treaties and CFR have been agreed to by all Member States in accordance with their constitutional requirements, confirms their soundness as a pillar for EDC. The requirement of objectivity in education postulated by the ECtHR is satisfied. This approach also ensures respect for the principles of the Beutelsbacher consensus on citizenship education: using the texts of the Treaties and the CFR in classrooms cannot be seen as overwhelming pupils, nor as presenting controversial viewpoints.[1085] Contesting the validity of the Treaties and the CFR as an objective and stable basis for an EU dimension of EDC would be tantamount to denying the very essence of EU membership.

Now and again, civic educators and curriculum designers invoke uncertainties about the EU and EU citizenship as an argument for not including much EU learning. Scholars outside the legal field sometimes too easily dismiss the Treaties and the CFR (my experience at citizenship education conferences, the Treaties sometimes being considered to be 'just a document'). For readers who are less familiar with EU law, the following brief summary serves to recall how the Treaties came into being, demonstrating the fundamental consensus on which they are based. The procedures for adoption, amendment, accession, and withdrawal, all reflect the same basic principle and reality: the agreement on the Treaties is anchored in each Member State's own constitution.[1086]

The Treaties were *adopted* in accordance with the Vienna Convention on the Law of Treaties.[1087] Each Member State voluntarily agreed to the text. To underscore the authoritative value of the Lisbon Treaty, it is recalled

1085 § 164 . The primary law texts as such are consensus-based, yet their application and balance may be controversial (see next section, case teaching).

1086 The formula 'in accordance with their respective constitutional requirements' appears all over the Treaties: Arts 42, 48, 49, 54 TEU (see also Art 50); Arts 25, 218, 223, 262, 311, 357 TFEU.

1087 Vienna Convention on the Law of Treaties (adopted 23 May 1969, entered into force 27 January 1980) 1155 UNTS 331, Art 2, Art 9, Arts 11–15, Art 52.

that, firstly, the representatives of the governments of the Member States adopted the Lisbon Treaty by common accord in an Intergovernmental Conference;[1088] secondly, the Heads of State or Government of all the Member States signed it (Lisbon, 13 December 2007),[1089] and thirdly, and crucial for democratic legitimacy, all the Member States ratified the Lisbon Treaty in accordance with their respective constitutional requirements (as stipulated in the amended EU and EC Treaties, and in the Lisbon Treaty[1090]). Most national constitutions required the approval of the national parliament, in some cases a referendum was necessary.[1091] The Member States' agreement to the Treaties is a matter of fact. The instruments of ratification by the High Contracting Parties are deposited with the Government of the Italian Republic in all official languages of the EU.[1092] Several Member States adapted their constitutions to reflect EU membership and its implications.[1093] The Lisbon Treaty was challenged before some national constitutional courts, but none decided that the

---

1088 Final Act (2007/C306/02), Conference of the Representatives of the governments of the Member States [2007] OJ C306/231.

1089 Treaty of Lisbon amending the Treaty on European Union and the Treaty establishing the European Community, signed at Lisbon on 13 December 2007 [2007] OJ C306. The list of plenipotentiaries is not reproduced in the Consolidated versions of the Treaty on European Union and the Treaty on the Functioning of the European Union [2016] OJ C202/1, but see—for evidence of the consensus—ten pages of signatures of the 2007 Final act (preceding note), p 239–248. See also preamble TEU: 'His Majesty the King of the Belgians, her Majesty the Queen of Denmark, the President of the Federal Republic of Germany, the President of Ireland' etc. (and new members since then). Comparable in TFEU.

1090 Art 6 Treaty of Lisbon; Art 54 TEU and Art 357 TFEU.

1091 After a first negative referendum in Ireland on 12 June 2008, a second referendum on 2 October 2009 was positive (after guarantees on some Irish concerns).

1092 Art 54 TEU and Art 357 TFEU (deposit), Art 55 TEU (languages).

1093 E.g. the Croatian constitution develops in Title VIII, 'European Union', the legal grounds for membership and transfer of constitutional powers (Art 143), participation in EU institutions (Art 144), EU law and the rights of EU citizens (Art 145–6). Exercise of EU rights equated with the exercise of rights under Croatian law, Croatian courts must protect subjective rights based on the EU *acquis communautaire*, and governmental agencies, bodies of local and regional self-government and legal persons vested with public authority must apply European Union law directly. Text to n 1319. See further on changes in national constitutional law resulting from EU accession: C Grabenwarter, 'National Constitutional Law Relating to the European Union' in A von Bogdandy and J Bast (eds), *Principles of European Constitutional Law* (2nd edn, Hart Beck Nomos 2010).

Treaty was incompatible with the national constitutional order.[1094] The Lisbon Treaty entered into force on 1 December 2009,[1095] creating a new legal order. The three foundational documents resulting from the Lisbon Treaty are the TEU, the TFEU and the CFR.[1096] As is well known, the TEU sets out the fundamental principles governing the EU, while the TFEU organises the functioning of the Union and determines its competences (areas, delimitation and arrangements for exercise).[1097] The CFR is not incorporated into the Treaties, but the TEU explicitly provides that the Union recognises the rights, freedoms and principles therein, and states that the CFR shall have the same legal value as the Treaties.[1098]

The adoption of Treaty *amendments*, just like the adoption of the Treaties themselves, requires the approval of each Member State (pursuant to both the ordinary and simplified revision procedure). The unanimity rule is striking (kept by the Treaty of Lisbon), as is also the anchoring of any revision in national constitutional requirements (Article 48 TEU).[1099]

1094 Czech Constitutional Court, 26 November 2008 (PL ÚS 19/08) and 3 November 2009 (Pl. ÚS 29/09); *BVerfG, 2 BvE 2/08 (Lissabon)* 30 June 2009, Absatz-Nr (1-421). For cases in Austria, Hungary and Poland, see D Edward and R Lane, *Edward and Lane on European Union Law* (Edward Elgar 2013) 26–28.

1095 Art 6(2) Treaty of Lisbon. More on the drafting history in Lenaerts and Van Nuffel, *European Union Law* 59–67.

1096 The Treaty on European Union, the Treaty on the Functioning of the European Union, the Charter of Fundamental Rights of the European Union; see Art 1(3) TEU, Art 1(2) TFEU, Art 6(1) TEU. The Protocols and Annexes form an integral part of the Treaties (Art 51 TEU). For Protocols and Declarations added to the Lisbon Treaty, see Consolidated versions of the Treaty on European Union and the Treaty on the Functioning of the European Union [2016] OJ C202/1.

1097 Art 1(1) TFEU.

1098 Art 6(1) TEU. The Charter of Fundamental Rights of the European Union of 7 December 2000 was drafted by the Praesidium of the Convention. On 12 December 2007, the European Parliament, the Council and the Commission solemnly proclaimed an adapted text, replacing it from 1 December 2009 onwards (entry into force of the Treaty of Lisbon). See G de Búrca, 'The Drafting of the EU Charter of Fundamental Rights' (2001) 26 ELRev 126.

1099 See on the unanimity rule, F-X Priollaud and D Siritzky, *Le traité de Lisbonne: Commentaire, article par article, des nouveaux traités européens (TUE et TFUE)* (La documentation française 2008). For case law on amendment procedures, see Lenaerts and Van Nuffel, *European Union Law* 83.

Accession of new Member States to the Union requires 'ratification by all the contracting States in accordance with their respective constitutional requirements'.[1100]

Finally, Member States have the right to *withdraw* from the EU in accordance with their own constitutional requirements (Article 50 TEU).[1101] Belonging to the Union is an ongoing deliberate and individual choice by each Member State (as Brexit illustrates).[1102] Member States which have not withdrawn are presumed to agree to and are bound by EU primary law.

It can be concluded that the TEU, TFEU and CFR provide a solid basis as a starting point for formulating content for the EU dimension of EDC. Negotiated, adopted, signed, and ratified by all Member States in accordance with their own constitutional requirements, EU primary law sources

---

1100 Art 49 TEU; Art 2(1) Treaty of Accession of the Republic of Bulgaria and Romania [2005] OJ L157; Art 3 Treaty of Accession of Croatia [2012] OJ L112. Consensus of all appears in full name, e.g. 'Treaty between the Kingdom of Belgium, the Republic of Bulgaria, the Czech Republic, the Kingdom of Denmark, the Federal Republic of Germany, the Republic of Estonia, Ireland, the Hellenic Republic, the Kingdom of Spain, the French Republic, the Italian Republic, the Republic of Cyprus, the Republic of Latvia, the Republic of Lithuania, the Grand Duchy of Luxembourg, the Republic of Hungary, the Republic of Malta, the Kingdom of the Netherlands, the Republic of Austria, the Republic of Poland, the Portuguese Republic, Romania, the Republic of Slovenia, the Slovak Republic, the Republic of Finland, the Kingdom of Sweden, the United Kingdom of Great Britain and Northern Ireland (Member States of the European Union) and the Republic of Croatia concerning the accession of the Republic of Croatia to the European Union', signed 9 December 2011, signatures pp 15–20. In accordance with Art 142 of the Croatian constitution, a referendum was held on 22 January 2012 (66% in favour of accession). The instruments of ratification were deposited with the Government of the Italian Republic by 30 June 2013. Croatia significantly adapted its constitution for EU membership (n 1093).

1101 Art 53 TEU, Art 356 TFEU (unlimited period). See J-V Louis, 'Le droit de retrait de l'Union européene' (2006) 42 Cahiers de Droit européen 293; Lenaerts and Van Nuffel, *European Union Law*, 69.

1102 See Case C-621/18 *Wightman and Others* ECLI:EU:C:2018:999 (a Member State can revoke unilaterally the notification of its intention to witdraw from the EU); European Council Decision (EU) 2019/584 taken in agreement with the United Kingdom of 11 April 2019 extending the period under Article 50(3) TEU [2019] OJ L 101/1. See also P Eeckhout and E Frantziou, 'Brexit and Article 50: a constitutionalist reading' (2017) 54 CMLRev 695 (reading of Art 50 informed by key constitutional features of the EU legal order); Gormley, 'Brexit - Never Mind the Whys and Wherefores? Fog in the Channel, Continent Cut Off!'.

were created by the Member States and their peoples.[1103] Political philosopher Van Middelaar speaks of 'the pact' at the innermost sphere of the EU, legally defined, offering stability and order.[1104]

The first argument in favour of considering EU primary law as a pillar of the proposed learning method for the EU dimension of EDC is that EU primary law satisfies the criterion of objectivity, as it consists of texts on which there is a fundamental consensus. An important additional argument is based on the constitutional functions of EU primary law. The significance of constitutions for citizenship education in general is explained first. Then an analysis of the constitutional characteristics of the EU Treaties and CFR underscores their relevance for the EU dimension of EDC.

165 Significance of constitutions for EDC/HRE

The Member State constitutions are significant for citizenship education and the application of EDC standards in several respects.[1105] Member States' practices link citizenship education with their constitutions, aiming at constitutional literacy.[1106] As the foundational texts on which public life and the organisation in a given society are based, constitutions clearly provide essential content for the components of EDC (c-1–2–3), i.e. exercising and defending democratic rights and responsibilities, valuing diversity and

1103 Further text to nn 1119, 1125.

1104 L van Middelaar, *The passage to Europe: How a Continent became a Union* (L Waters tr, Yale University Press 2013) 12–24. Confronted with conceptual unclarities and the 'extremely tricky' question as to whether Europe exists as a political entity, the author proposes a new paradigm. He explains Europe as a set of three spheres, concentric globes, each sphere with its own principles of dynamism and order. The outermost sphere of Europe is that of the sovereign states on the continent, driven by the pursuit of their own national interests, ordered by balance of power and territorial borders, delineated in geography and history. The innermost sphere is that of the EU as created by the founding Treaty, 'a pact' signed by States, offering stability and order in an expanding action area of participating Member States, inspired by the idea of the 'European project' and legally defined. ('[t]he inner sphere derives its order and footing from the pact'; 'the treaty offers solid ground'). The intermediate sphere refers to Member States functioning sometimes in the inner and sometimes in the outer sphere, driven by national interests and by a growing consciousness of common interests.

1105 See also §§ 13 29 89 ; the para 4- principle of the Charter on EDC/HRE.

1106 See i.a. § 89 .

playing an active part in democratic life.[1107] Constitutions define human rights, the subject of HRE. It is not only constitutional literacy in the cognitive sense which is the aim of EDC. Constitutions reflect ethical choices, the vision of the common good, and the blueprint for the society on which the constituents have agreed.[1108] They are the highest legal expression of the value system.[1109] As constitutions thus lay down the basic choices for society, it is not only legitimate, but also necessary to educate citizens in the spirit of their constitutions, as Aristotle proclaimed in Ancient Greece.[1110] At present, some Member States' constitutions even explicitly limit freedom of education by requiring allegiance to the constitution.[1111] Yet, learning in respect for the constitution does not mean that citizens must be trained in uncritical obedience. Ensuring that the substance of EDC and HRE is in keeping with the constitution of the Member State does not exclude critical thinking.[1112] Constitutions are living documents and may evolve in accordance with the evolution of civil society; preferably constituted by educated citizens prepared for responsible action. A basic understanding of constitutional norms enables informed participation by citizens at moments of constitutional change. The relationship

---

1107 See e.g. 'Unsere Verfassung!' in AT: <www.politik-lernen.at/site/grundlagen/politischebildung> and <www.unsereverfassung.at/?lang=en>.

1108 Prescriptive or constructivist function of constitutions (also n 96). See i.a. MA Wilkinson, 'Political Constitutionalism and the European Union' (2013) 76 The Modern Law Review 191 (teleological aspect inherent in any constitutional discourse; '[t]he right question is not therefore "what sort of polity is the European Union?" but rather, "what sort of polity is it *becoming*?"').

1109 B de Witte, 'Community Law and National Constitutional Values' (1991) 18 Legal Issues of Economic Integration 1. On the crystallization of common ends and values in constitutions and amplifying effects, Walker, 'European Constitutionalism in the State Constitutional Tradition', 65. Further VC Jackson, 'Paradigms of public law: transnational constitutional values and democratic challenges' (2011) 8 International journal of constitutional law 517; and Calliess in nn 1185 ff.

1110 Curren, 'A neo-Aristotelian account of education, justice, and the human good': 'There is no profit in the best of laws ... if the citizens themselves have not been attuned, by the force of habit and the influence of teaching, to the right constitutional temper'. Text to n 95.

1111 Germany Art 5(3) Basic law, Greece Art 16(1), Cyprus Art 20(1). See n 672 and text.

1112 Cf JW Müller, 'A general theory of constitutional patriotism' (2007) 6 International Journal of Constitutional Law 72: 'The object of patriotic attachment is a specific constitutional culture that mediates between the universal and the particular, while the mode of attachment is one of critical judgment.'.

between constitutions and education is dynamic and dialectical: the constitution influences education, and, in the long term, education may influence the constitution.[1113] Beaumont writes that 'the complex intersections between education and the Constitution have helped define the contours of American governance, citizenship, civil liberties, and civil society in every era'.[1114]

166 *Constitutional features of EU primary law*

Are the EU Treaties and CFR the constitution of the EU? The significance of being called a constitution[1115] reaches into the field of citizenship education. As citizenship education and constitutions are concepts traditionally associated with states, transposing them to the level of the EU raises questions pertinent for both. Recognising the constitutional nature of the Treaties and CFR may affect opinions on the need for citizenship education of EU citizens.

While many scholars recognise the constitutional character of the EU Treaties and CFR, the persistence of debate must be acknowledged.[1116] The EU treaties and CFR display constitutional features to a certain extent. To the extent that they fulfil a constitutional role, they are an essential basis for all EDC of citizens. Yet, lacking the full constitutional weight of a state constitution, their suitability as pillar for an EU dimension of EDC may be criticised.

1113 Cf evolutionary, deliberative constitutionalism, see i.a. M Vargova, 'Democratic Deficits of a Dualist Deliberative Constitutionalism: Bruce Ackerman and Jürgen Habermas' (2005) 18 Ratio Juris 365, on Habermas' discursive constitution, open to new social and historical circumstances.

1114 E Beaumont, 'Education and the Constitution: Defining the Contours of Governance, Rights, and Citizenship' in M Tushnet, MA Graber and S Levinson (eds), *The Oxford Handbook of the US Constitution* (2015) 968. See also E Reilly, 'Education and the Constitution: Shaping Each Other & the Next Century' (2000-2001) 34 Akron Law Review 1; J Haubenreich, 'Education and the Constitution' (2012) 87 Peabody Journal of Education 436; FH Pina, 'Constitution, Education and Research' (2013) 12 EERJ 34. Cp Crick, 'The Presuppositions of Citizenship Education', 346 (sceptical as to constitution learning, because of focus on active citizenship); also Commission/EACEA/Eurydice, Citizenship Education at School in Europe (2017).

1115 Cf M Poiares Maduro, 'The importance of being called a constitution: Constitutional authority and the authority of constitutionalism' (2005) 3 International Journal of Constitutional Law 332 (on functions of constitutionalism as a normative theory of power in the EU).

1116 See overview of the debate in Calliess, 'EU-Vertrag (Lissabon) Art 1', Rn 51 ff.

The founding Treaties and CFR can be considered from two angles: the angle of the *instrumentum*—a treaty—and the angle of the *negotium*—the substance (this distinction appears clearly in the '*Treaty* establishing a *Constitution* for Europe'). There are no doubts about the *instrumentum* insofar as the Treaties have been ratified and *pacta sunt servanda*. This is the minimalist view. Some scholars plead in favour of viewing the founding Treaties and CFR as a contractual constitution as far as genesis is concerned (taking the form of treaties) and as a functional constitution as far as substance is concerned.[1117] Calliess speaks of a 'Verfassungsvertrag'.[1118] The EU Treaties and CFR do not satisfy some of the traditional conditions for constitutionalism. The EU missed its 'constitutional moment' and has an uncertain 'demos'. Whereas the constitutional moment is significant for a constitution's integrative and identity-building force, as emphasised by Ackerman,[1119] the Treaty establishing a Constitution for Europe was rejected. After this failure, the Intergovernmental Conference omitted several too state-like provisions, dropping the terminology 'constitution', as well as 'European law', 'European framework law', or 'Union Minister for Foreign Affairs', and deleting references to the symbols of the Union (flag, anthem and Europe day).[1120] As Kirchhof wrote, the Member States rejected the 'constitutionalisation' of EU law to the extent that the term 'constitution' suggests the emergence of statehood.[1121] Pernice saw no need for an EU constitution if this implied the constitution of a European

1117 Functions in text to n 1127.

1118 Calliess, 'EU-Vertrag (Lissabon) Art 1', Rn 65.

1119 B Ackerman, 'Revolution on a Human Scale (Moments of Change: Transformation in American Constitutionalism)' (1999) 108 Yale Law Journal 2279, 2341. See further BA Ackerman, *We the People*, vol 2: Transformations (Harvard University Press 1998); N Walker, 'The Legacy of Europe's Constitutional Moment' (2004) 11 Constellations 368; D Grimm, 'Integration by constitution' (2005) 3 International Journal of Constitutional Law 193, 200–201; N Walker, 'Europe's constitutional momentum and the search for polity legitimacy' (2005) 3 International Journal of Constitutional Law 211.

1120 Presidency Conclusions of the Brussels European Council of 21-22 June 2007, Annex I: IGC Mandate: the European Council asked to amend the existing EU and EC treaties, instead of adopting one single Treaty text, and to drop the constitutional character. The amendments provide instead for 'legislative acts' (legislative procedure, now Art 289(3) TFEU) and a 'High Representative of the Union for Foreign Affairs and Security Policy' (now Art 18 TEU).

1121 Kirchhof, 'The European Union of States' 737.

federal State.[1122] Weiler emphasises that the *content* of a constitution and a treaty may be identical (a functional constitution), but suggests that the *form* of a 'true' constitution depends on two hallmarks: amendment by a (privileged) majority and approval by a (growing) demos.[1123] A recurrent argument against a constitutional label for the EU Treaties is that there is not a 'people' of Europe sufficiently homogenous to form a democratic will.[1124] The EU has no constitutional authority in the sense of a *pouvoir constituant*, the power of a polity to define its own destiny.[1125]

Several scholars see the rejection of the Constitution of Europe as the rejection of formal constitutionalism. The substantive constitution remains, a 'functional constitution'.[1126] The Treaties and CFR fulfil the *constitutive* function of constitutions, establishing the institutions of a

---

1122 I Pernice, 'Does Europe need a Constitution?' in *Arnull A and others (eds), A Constitutional Order of States: Essays in EU Law in Honour of Alan Dashwood* (Hart 2011) 77 (however, in another sense a constitution may be necessary).

1123 JHH Weiler, 'A Constitution for Europe? Some hard choices' (2002) 40 JCMS 563, 565–569: contrary to a constitutional treaty, a 'true' constitution (first) does not require unanimity for amendments (unanimity is typical for internationalism, majority is sign of a polity) and (second) is approved by the peoples of Europe not in their status as national communities, but as such (demos). Further JHH Weiler, *The constitution of Europe: do the new clothes have an emperor? and other essays on European integration* (reprint edn, Cambridge University Press 2004).

1124 D Grimm, 'Does Europe Need a Constitution?' (1995) 1 ELJ 282; P Craig, 'Constitutions, Constitutionalism, and the European Union' (2001) 7 ELJ 125, 136–139 (the *no-demos* thesis); Grimm, 'Integration by constitution', 208. Cp Calliess, 'EU-Vertrag (Lissabon) Art 1', Rn 43, considering the establishment of EU citizenship in the Maastricht Treaty as an important step (also seen Arts 22, 23 TFEU).

1125 Much commented, see i.a. Poiares Maduro, 'The importance of being called a constitution: Constitutional authority and the authority of constitutionalism', 356; Vargova, 'Democratic Deficits of a Dualist Deliberative Constitutionalism: Bruce Ackerman and Jürgen Habermas'; C Möllers, 'Pouvoir Constituant-Constitution-Constitutionalisation' in A von Bogdandy and J Bast (eds), *Principles of European Constitutional Law*, vol 8 (2 edn, Hart Beck Nomos 2010); Calliess, 'EU-Vertrag (Lissabon) Art 1', Rn 56–57. See also D Grimm, 'The Democratic Costs of Constitutionalisation: The European Case' (2015) 21 ELJ 460 (lack of public sphere, lack of legitimacy, overconstitutionalisation of the EU).

1126 Weiler, 'A Constitution for Europe? Some hard choices' (p 569: 'Europe, of course, has a Constitution—in the same way that, say, the United Kingdom has one'); K Lenaerts, 'A Community Based on a "Constitutional Charter": Community Law as a Complete and Coherent Constitutional System' in MP Maduro and L Azoulai (eds), *The Past and Future of EU Law: The Classics of EU Law Revisited on the 50th Anniversary of the Rome Treaty* (Hart 2010) 298 (the

political society; the *attributive* function, empowering these institutions; and the *regulative* function, regulating and limiting the exercise of public

---

Treaty has 'the classical functions of a constitution, in terms of the horizontal division of powers between the European institutions, the vertical division of powers between the Community and the Member States and the protection of fundamental rights'); Pernice, 'Does Europe need a Constitution?', 75–76, 92; Calliess, 'EU-Vertrag (Lissabon) Art 1', 64. See also C Reh, 'The Lisbon Treaty: De-Constitutionalizing the European Union?' (2009) 47 JCMS 625, 629. On EU constitutionalism or constitutional characteristics, see further: J Gerkrath, *L'émergence d'un droit constitutionnel pour l'Europe* (Ed de l'Université de Bruxelles 1997); P Eleftheriadis, 'Begging the Constitutional Question' (1998) 36 JCMS 255; Craig, 'Constitutions, Constitutionalism, and the European Union'; J Habermas, 'Why Europe needs a constitution' (2001) New Left Review 5; Poiares Maduro, 'The importance of being called a constitution: Constitutional authority and the authority of constitutionalism'; R Bellamy, 'The European Constitution is Dead, Long Live European Constitutionalism' (2006) 13 Constellations 181; K Lenaerts, 'La constitutionnalisation de l'ordre juridique de l'Union européenne' in *Mélanges en l'honneur du Professeur Francis Delpérée: Itinéraires d'un constitutionnaliste* (Bruylant 2007); J Shaw, 'One or Many Constitutions: The Constitutional Future of the European Union in the 2000s from a Legal Perspective' (2007) 52 Scandinavian Studies in Law 393; F Amtenbrink, 'The multidimensional constitutional legal order of the European Union - A successful case of cosmopolitan constitution building?' (2008) 39 Netherlands Yearbook of International Law 3; KH Ladeur, '"We, the European People..."- Relâche?' (2008) 14 ELJ 147; N Walker, 'Not the European Constitution' (2008) 15 Maastricht journal of European and comparative law 135; T Christiansen and C Reh, *Constitutionalizing the European Union* (Palgrave MacMillan 2009); J Wouters, L Verhey and P Kiiver (eds), *European Constitutionalism beyond Lisbon* (Intersentia 2009); A Arnull and others (eds), *A Constitutional Order of States: Essays in EU Law in Honour of Alan Dashwood* (Hart 2011); Habermas, *Zur Verfassung Europas. Ein Essay*; TV Olsen, 'The political constitution of the EU citizen rights regime' (2011) 18 Journal of European Public Policy 35; P Cardonnel, A Rosas and N Wahl, *Constitutionalising the EU judicial systems: essays in honour of Pernilla Lindh* (Hart 2012); Habermas, 'The Crisis of the European Union in the Light of a Constitutionalization of International Law'; P Berthelet, 'Les fondements théoriques du droit européen à l'épreuve de la constitutionnalisation de l'ordre juridique de l'Union: Entre permanence et changement' [2015] Revue du droit de l'Union européenne 529; P Craig, 'The Financial Crisis, the European Union Institutional Order, and Constitutional Responsibility' (2015) 22 Indiana Journal of Global Legal Studies 243; K Lenaerts, 'Demoicracy, Constitutional Pluralism and the Court of Justice of the European Union' in L Van Middelaar and P Van Parijs (eds), *After the Storm: How to Save Democracy in Europe* (Lannoo 2015); D Grimm, *The Constitution of European Democracy* (Oxford University Press 2017) (the Treaties function as a constitution; the EU is even over-constitutionalised).

power.[1127] The Treaties constitute the EU: Article 1 TEU states that '[b]y this Treaty, the High Contracting Parties establish among themselves a European Union...'. The constituent acts of the International Labour Organisation and the World Health Organisation are also named 'constitutions'. The Treaties attribute public powers to the EU and, together with the CFR, they limit the use of this public power (vertically and horizontally). Like many constitutions, the Treaties and CFR define rights-based limitations on governmental power.[1128] Such rights will provide the content of component (c-1) in EDC, i.e. exercising and defending democratic rights and responsibilities in society. Functioning as the *Grundnorm* in the EU legal order and protecting fundamental rights, the Treaties and CFR operate as a constitution. The ECJ repeatedly qualifies the Treaties as 'the basic constitutional charter'.[1129] All measures adopted by the EU institutions and by the Member States when implementing EU law, must be in conformity with the Treaties and the CFR. Review of legality by the ECJ is a constitutional principle. The adjective 'constitutional' appears frequently in ECJ case law, e.g. constitutional charter,—principles,—significance,—

1127 LFM Besselink, 'The notion and nature of the European constitution after the Lisbon Treaty' in J Wouters, L Verhey and P Kiiver (eds), *European Constitutionalism beyond Lisbon* (Intersentia 2009) 264. See also functions described in Calliess, 'EU-Vertrag (Lissabon) Art 1', Rn 64. Further European Parliament Committee on Constitutional Affairs, Report on the Treaty of Lisbon (29 January 2008), Explanatory Statement to European Parliament resolution of 20 February 2008 on the Treaty of Lisbon, paras 1.2—4, and 2.2 (a constitution can be defined as 'a fundamental act governing the exercise of power in a political entity'); and European Parliament Resolution of 20 February 2008 on the Treaty of Lisbon [2009] OJ C184E/25.

1128 Craig, 'Constitutions, Constitutionalism, and the European Union', 141; essential constitutional feature, see Raz in n 1133.

1129 I.a. Case 294/83 *Parti écologiste 'Les Verts' v Parliament* ECLI:EU:C:1986:166, para 23; Case C-15/00 *Commission v European Investment Bank* ECLI:EU:C:2003:396, para 75; Joined Cases C-402/05 P and C-415/05 P *Kadi* ECLI:EU:C:2008:461, para 281 ('the Community is based on the rule of law, inasmuch as neither its Member States nor its institutions can avoid review of the conformity of their acts with the basic constitutional charter, the EC Treaty, which established a complete system of legal remedies and procedures designed to enable the Court of Justice to review the legality of acts of the institutions'); EU Accession to the ECHR *Opinion 2/13* ECLI:EU:C:2014:2454, para 163.

status,—guarantee,—structure.[1130] EU primary law expresses the 'constitutional consensus'.[1131]

Constitution and constitutionalism have divergent meanings. Depending on the definition, the Treaties and CFR have some of the features of a constitution. Walker distinguishes 'constitutional' in juridical frame terms, in institutional terms, in authoritative terms, and in social terms.[1132] The Treaties and CFR are, at least, a 'thin' constitution as defined by Raz, i.e. the law establishing and regulating 'the main organs of government'.[1133] According to some scholars, such as Pernice,[1134] the Treaties and CFR also possess several features of Raz' constitution in a 'thick' sense: in addition to being constitutive, defining the main organs of government and their powers,[1135] the Treaties and CFR are intended to be stable, normally enshrined in written documents; they are superior law and justiciable;[1136] they are entrenched, needing special amendment procedures, thus withdrawn from normal politics and ordinary legislation;[1137] and they express a common ideology. Here, reference is made to norms on democracy, rule of law, and fundamental rights, which 'express the common beliefs of the population

1130 *Opinion 2/94* ECLI:EU:C:1996:140, para 35 ('*constitutional significance*'); Joined Cases C-402/05 P and C-415/05 P *Kadi* ECLI:EU:C:2008:461, para 285 ('the *constitutional principles* of the EC Treaty, which include the principle that all Community acts must respect fundamental rights'), para 316 ('a *constitutional guarantee*'); EU Accession to the ECHR *Opinion 2/13* ECLI:EU:C:2014:2454, paras 158 and 177 ('*constitutional framework*'), para 163 ('*basic constitutional charter*') para 165 ('the *constitutional structure* of the EU, which is seen in the principle of conferral of powers referred to in Articles 4(1) TEU and 5(1) and (2) TEU, and in the institutional framework established in Articles 13 TEU to 19 TEU') (emphasis added).

1131 K Lenaerts and JA Gutiérrez-Fons, 'The Place of the Charter in the EU Constitutional Edifice' in S Peers and others (eds), *The EU Charter of Fundamental Rights: a Commentary* (Hart 2014), 142 (by contrast to the legislative consensus).

1132 N Walker, 'Opening or Closure? The Constitutional Intimations of the ECJ' in MP Maduro and L Azoulai (eds), *The Past and Future of EU Law: The Classics of EU Law Revisited on the 50th Anniversary of the Rome Treaty* (Hart 2010) 335.

1133 J Raz, 'On the Authority and Interpretations of Constitutions: Some Preliminaries' in L Alexander (ed), *Constitutionalism* (Cambridge University Press 2001) 152–153.

1134 Pernice, 'Does Europe need a Constitution?' 88; see also Craig, 'Constitutions, Constitutionalism, and the European Union', 126–129.

1135 E.g. Arts 13–19 TEU, 223–309 TFEU.

1136 E.g. Arts 19 TEU; Arts 258, 260, 263, 265 TFEU; Case C-50/00 P *Unión de Pequeños Agricultores v Council* ECLI:EU:C:2002:462, paras 38–40.

1137 Art 48 TEU.

about the way their society should be governed'.[1138] It is worth noting the use of the word 'society', not 'state'.[1139]

Whether the Treaties and CFR form a 'thin' or a 'thick' constitution is not decisive for the purposes of EDC. What matters is, firstly, that an undeniable consensus exists on the adopted texts (objectivity, as discussed in §164) and, secondly, that the texts adopted fulfil certain of the functions of a constitution. In an approach giving the Treaties a low degree of constitutional intensity, the Treaties nevertheless retain their status as agreements binding on the Member States, consent anchored in the national constitutions, and they establish and regulate some of the main organs of government at EU level. The *instrumentum* provides a stable pillar for an EU dimension of EDC, impacting on the content of EDC components (c-1–3), e.g. on the rights and obligations of citizens and on participation in democratic life. In an approach recognising a high degree of constitutionality as to the substance of the Treaties (*negotium*), the Treaties are an even more important basis for incorporating an EU dimension into EDC. Calliess describes the Treaties as a substantive constitution, with the essential functions and content of a constitution, supplementing Member State constitutions.[1140] The function of the Treaties and CFR as *Grundnorm*, their status as EU *primary* law, at the top of the hierarchy of norms in the EU legal order, is relevant for citizens. EU primary law gives numerous EU rights and principles entrenched status.[1141] If the EU primary law sources are the basis on which the legal order of the EU is constructed, shaping the society in which EU citizens live, a fortiori they must be sufficiently strong to have educational consequences for EU citizens. Functioning as the constitutional charter for the EU (ECJ), the Treaties and CFR provide guidance for the *EU dimension* of EDC, as national constitutions do for *national EDC*, in a comparable dialectical relationship between constitution and education.[1142]

That the Treaties and the CFR function as a constitution is underscored by their interconnectedness with Member State constitutions.

1138 Craig, 'Constitutions, Constitutionalism, and the European Union', 127. Craig adds that the EU Treaties and CFR 'contain rights of a kind that would be found in many national constitutions', such as provisions on citizenship rights (Arts 20–24 TFEU) and on prohibition of discrimination (Arts 18–19 TFEU).

1139 Further text to n 2208.

1140 Calliess, 'EU-Vertrag (Lissabon) Art 1', Rn 64–66.

1141 Entrenched, in the sense of not changeable through normal legislative processes.

1142 See nn 1113, 1114.

167 Interconnection of EU primary law and Member State constitutions

EU primary law and Member State constitutions are interconnected in various ways and cannot be adequately understood in isolation.[1143] The Treaties and CFR refer to Member State constitutions at several points,[1144] and most Member State constitutions contain provisions related to the EU Treaties. They refer to EU membership in diverse ways, to greater or lesser extents, for instance in structural guarantee clauses,[1145] procedural conditions for the transfer of public authority,[1146] norms on informing the national parliament on EU matters,[1147] provisions on European Parliament elections,[1148] or on rights of EU citizens (nationals of other Member States)[1149]. Some constitutions state that the EU Treaties and provisions of EU law form part of the internal legal order and are directly applicable; some refer to the supremacy of EU law over national law.[1150] Other

---

1143 On the interdependency and reciprocal linking of constitutions, Grabenwarter, 'National Constitutional Law Relating to the European Union', 127; Calliess, 'EU-Vertrag (Lissabon) Art 1', i.a. Rn 46. See also H Bauer and C Calliess (eds), *Constitutional principles in Europe* (Bruylant 2008).

1144 Art 42 TEU (common Union defence policy), Arts 48, 49, 50, 54 TEU (amendment, accession, withdrawal, ratification of the TEU); Art 55 TEU (Treaty languages); Art 4 (2) TEU (national identities), Art 6 TEU and Art 52(4) CFR (fundamental rights and common constitutional traditions); Art 53 (level of protection); Art 25 TFEU (adding new citizenship rights to the list in Art 20(2) TFEU); Art 218(8) TFEU (accession to the ECHR), Art 223 (EP elections), Art 262 (ECJ jurisdiction and European intellectual property rights), Art 311 (categories of EU resources), Art 357 (ratification of the TFEU).

1145 E.g. Art 23(1) German Basic Law (tr 'Germany shall participate in the development of the European Union that is committed to democratic, social and federal principles, to the rule of law, and to the principle of subsidiarity, and that guarantees a level of protection of basic rights essentially comparable to that afforded by this Basic Law'); Art 7(5)-(6) Portuguese constitution; Art 143 Croatian constitution. Further Kirchhof, 'The European Union of States', 742–743.

1146 E.g. constitution of Belgium Art 168; and Sweden Ch 10 Art 6.

1147 E.g. constitution of Bulgaria, Art 105(3)-(4); Finland Section 97; France Art 88(4); Greece Art 70(8); Hungary Art 19; Sweden Ch 10 Art 10.

1148 E.g. constitution of Austria Art 23(a)(b); Belgium Art 168 bis; Sweden, Ch 8 Art 2.

1149 See nn 1318-1319.

1150 Constitutional Act on membership of the Republic of Lithuania of the EU, para 2 ('The norms of the European Union law shall be a constituent part of the legal system of the Republic of Lithuania. Where it concerns the founding Treaties of the European Union, the norms of the European Union law shall be applied directly, while in the event of collision of legal norms, they shall have supremacy over the laws and other legal acts of the Republic of Lithua-

national constitutions do not specifically refer to EU membership, but provide for compliance with international obligations[1151], precedence over national law[1152], or have concordant constitutional practices, which confirm the minimalist approach mentioned above.

The interconnectedness of the EU Treaties and CFR with Member State constitutions is reflected in the concept of 'a European constitutional area' formed by the Member States' constitutions and the partial or complementary constitution in EU law.[1153] In a common area of constitutionalism, national and international constitutional guarantees interact to uphold common European constitutional values.[1154] Scholars (Pernice, Besselink) refer to the European constitutional space as a composite constitutional area, a *Verfassungsverbund*, a true compound of the EU 'constitution', the Member States' constitutions, and the ECHR.[1155] Calliess qualifies the EU

---

nia'); constitution of Portugal Art 8(3) and (4) ('The provisions of the treaties that govern the European Union and the norms issued by its institutions in the exercise of their respective competences are applicable in Portuguese internal law in accordance with Union law and with respect for the fundamental principles of a democratic state based on the rule of law.') For importance, see text to n 1828 (section).

1151 E.g. constitution of Slovenia Art 8; of Spain Art 96. Member States which do not mention EU membership in their constitution may have constitutional practices consistent with the Treaties (e.g. by means of judicial interpretation in Estonia).

1152 E.g. Art 25 German Basic Act.

1153 von Bogdandy, 'Founding Principles' 24.

1154 See in this context, A von Bogdandy and P Sonnevend (eds), *Constitutional Crisis in the European Constitutional Area: Theory, Law and Politics in Hungary and Romania* (Hart Beck 2015).

1155 I Pernice, 'Bestandssicherung der Verfassungen: Verfassungsrechtliche Mechanismen zur Wahrung der Verfassungsordnung' in R Bieber and P Widmer (eds), *Der europäische Vefassungsraum* (Schulthess Juristische Medien 1995) 261; Besselink, 'The notion and nature of the European constitution after the Lisbon Treaty' 262, 279. See also LFM Besselink, *A Composite European Constitution* (Europa Law 2007); A Voßkuhle, 'Multilevel cooperation of the European Constitutional Courts: Der Europäische Verfassungsgerichtsverbund' (2010) 6 European Constitutional Law Review 175, von Bogdandy, 'Founding Principles' 38; N Walker, J Shaw and S Tierney, *Europe's Constitutional Mosaic* (Hart 2011) (on the 'constitutional mosaic' methaphor, and the increasingly dense networks of constitutional authority within the European space); Lenaerts and Gutiérrez-Fons, 'The Place of the Charter in the EU Constitutional Edifice'; A Voßkuhle, 'European Integration Through Law: The Contribution of the Federal Constitutional Court' (2017) 58 European Journal of Sociology 145. On the theme of constitutional pluralism, see i.a. N Walker, 'The Idea of Constitu-

as a 'Staaten- und Verfassungsverbund'.[1156] In this 'Verbund', citizens act in a dual capacity as national citizens and as EU citizens, subjects conferring legitimacy on the political system.[1157]

The fact that Member State constitutions and EU Treaties are inextricably interwoven, should be reflected in EDC. Education of citizens aiming at national constitutional literacy and national constitutional values should be interwoven with education for literacy with regard to the EU Treaties and the values they enshrine. In other words, national EDC needs an EU dimension. Calliess describes a paradigm shift which requires more transparency and more interest from EU citizens in EU objectives. He defines the EU as 'a federal type of multi-level constitutionalism, in which state sovereignty is reduced and the constitutional orders of the EU and its Member States are mutually interlocked'.[1158] Therefore, if in the Aristotelian tradition citizens are to be educated in the spirit of their constitution ('to the right constitutional temper'[1159]) then that should apply with regard to Member State constitutions, the Treaties and the CFR. The 'spirit of law' (*L'esprit des lois*) is also central for Montesquieu, who argued that education must relate to the principle of government.[1160] In a play on

---

tional Pluralism' (2002) 65 Modern Law Review 317; R Barents, 'The Precedence of EU Law from the Perspective of Constitutional Pluralism' (2009) 5 European Constitutional Law Review 421; Avbelj and Komárek, *Constitutional Pluralism in the European Union and Beyond*; K Lenaerts, 'EU Values and Constitutional Pluralism: The EU System of Fundamental Rights Protection' (2014) XXXIV Polish Yearbook of International Law 135; Lenaerts, 'Demoicracy, Constitutional Pluralism and the Court of Justice of the European Union'.

1156 Calliess, 'EU-Vertrag (Lissabon) Art 1', Rn 44: Pernice's 'Verfassungsverbund' is problematic to the extent that it unifies EU and Member State levels. Member States first allow the 'Verfassungsverbund' as 'offene Verfassungsstaaten'. The 'Staaten- und Verfassungsverbund' is characterised by 'das inhaltliche Zusammenwirken, das Aufeinander-Angewiesensein und die gegenseitige Verzahnung der Ebenen'. (The alliance of States and constitutions is characterised by cooperation as to substance, consideration for one another and interlocking of levels).

1157 Calliess and Hartmann, *Zur Demokratie in Europa: Unionsbürgerschaft und europäische Öffentlichkeit* 80, 149 ('die geteilten Bürger').

1158 C Calliess, 'Europe as Transnational Law: The Transnationalization of Values by European Law' (2009) 10 German Law Journal 1367, 1375.

1159 N 95.

1160 Montesquieu, *De l'esprit des lois* (digital JM Tremblay 2002 edn, Barillot 1748), Livre quatrième- Que les lois de l'éducation doivent être relatives aux principes du gouvernement. I Des lois de l'éducation (…) 'Les lois de l'éducation seront

words, the EU has been said not to be a state, but a state of mind.[1161] Articles 1–6 TEU define the mind, the spirit.[1162] They give substance to the attitudes of Member States and EU citizens and, as far as the latter are concerned, relate to affective-behavioural aspects of citizenship education.[1163]

2. Foundational values, objectives and principles of the EU

168 The ground rules of play: constitutional norms as EDC content

Citizens should understand the ground rules of play of the system in which they live. EU primary law, interconnected with Member State constitutions, provides the EU dimension in the ground rules of play in the European constitutional space. If the society in which EU citizens live is based on a composite constitution, then EDC seeking to ensure constitutional literacy should correspond to the interconnected constitutional sources.[1164] National citizenship education linked solely with national con-

---

donc différentes dans chaque espèce de gouvernement. Dans les monarchies, elles auront pour objet *l'honneur*; dans les républiques, la *vertu*; dans le despotisme, la *crainte*.' (The laws on education must relate to the principles of government. The laws of education therefore will differ for each kind of government: in monarchies they will be concerned with honour, in republics with virtue, where there is despotism, they will aim at creating fear.) Haller refers to Montesquieu in his classic 'Spirit of Laws 1748': 'it is not enough to devise ideal models of constitutions but one must also take into consideration the social conditions which make a constitution really "work"'; see M Haller, *European Integration as an Elite Project: the Failure of a Dream?* (Routledge 2008) Preface xxiv.

1161 See i.a. K Lenaerts and M Desomer, 'Bricks for a Constitutional Treaty of the European Union: Values, Objectives and Means' (2002) 27 ELRev 377; J Subotic, 'Europe is a State of Mind: Identity and Europeanization in the Balkans' (2011) 55 International Studies Quarterly 309.

1162 See also Schuman (Strasbourg, 16 May 1949), text to n 1890. Further n 1890. Cf the spirit of the Treaty, used in the interpretation in settled case law of the ECJ, e.g. Case 294/83 *Parti écologiste 'Les Verts' v Parliament* ECLI:EU:C:1986:166, para 25.

1163 See in general CoE Recommendation CM/Rec(2010)7 of the Committee of Ministers to member states on the Council of Europe Charter on Education for Democratic Citizenship and Human Rights Education (11 May 2010), para 5(f). On belonging and identity formation, see i.a. text to nn 1187-1191, n 1191.

1164 The fourth meaning of constitutionalism as described by Craig is particularly appropriate in the context of linking constitutionalism with citizenship education: '[Constitutionalism] is used to connote not whether a legal system has

stitutions, lacking an EU dimension, will increasingly prove to be insufficient and inadequate for preparing citizens for life in a society where public power is dispersed across several levels. If constitutionalism has become multilevel,[1165] EDC should correspond, highlighting the interaction between constitutions at various levels. This is consistent with the paragraph-4 principle of the Charter on EDC/HRE (objectives, principles and policies on EDC/HRE are to be applied with due respect for the constitutional structures of each member state), as well as with the constitutional red line affecting the reception of exogenic standards in the EU.[1166] Not educating citizens in the spirit of the composite constitutional system may backfire: in just a day a popular vote could wipe away the carefully constructed architecture of interlocking constitutional rules meticulously developed over decades.

169 The DNA of the EU

To understand the system governing the society in which they live, EU citizens need some understanding of the norms on which that system is based, especially those of Articles 1–6 TEU. These provisions set out the foundational values, objectives and principles of the EU. They are the DNA of the EU and should be central to all EU learning. EDC should—to the extent possible—relate to the 'intrinsic nature of the EU',[1167] not to superficial

---

the features of a constitution, but also the extent to which it satisfies desirable precepts of good governance which go beyond those normally expressed within the constitution itself', with issues as accountability, good administration and mainstreaming of human rights. See Craig, 'Constitutions, Constitutionalism, and the European Union', 127–128.

1165 Callies n 1158; I Pernice, 'Multilevel constitutionalism in the European Union' (2002) 27 ELRev 511. On multilevel governance, see further C Harlow and R Rawlings, 'Promoting Accountability in Multilevel Governance: A Network Approach' (2007) 13 ELJ 542; A Lansbergen and J Shaw, 'National membership models in a multilevel Europe. Symposium: The Evolving Concept of Citizenship in Constitutional Law' (2010) 8 International Journal of Constitutional Law 50; N Bolleyer and C Reh, 'EU legitimacy revisited: the normative foundations of a multilevel polity' (2012) 19 Journal of European Public Policy 472; R Bauböck, 'The three levels of citizenship within the European Union' (2014) 15 German Law Journal 751.

1166 Text to nn 1205 ff.

1167 On the 'intrinsic nature', see EU Accession to the ECHR *Opinion 2/13* ECLI: EU:C:2014:2454, para 193. On the 'DNA' of the EU, also JHH Weiler, 'Deciphering the Political and Legal DNA of European Integration' in X Dickson and P Eleftheriadis (eds), *Philosophical Foundations of European Union Law* (Oxford University Press 2012).

information, such as the number of Members of the European Parliament or the date of accession of Bulgaria, to be learnt by heart and then forgotten. To empower EU citizens to exercise their rights and responsibilities, to value diversity, and to participate in the democratic life of the Union, they need to understand the *raison d'être* of the EU and how their Member State participates in it. The self-perception of Member States, and of their nationals, is incomplete if it lacks an EU dimension.

For the purposes of EDC, the terminology 'values', 'objectives' or 'principles' as used in EU primary law suffices.[1168] The adjective 'foundational' indicates that they are drawn from EU primary law. Admittedly, to the extent that the Treaties and CFR constitute a functional or material constitution, the values, objectives and principles they lay down may very well be labelled EU 'constitutional' values, objectives and principles. Calliess argues that using the label 'constitutional' is not only legitimate but also necessary for transparency reasons and closeness to EU citizens as a matter of honest politics.[1169] However, to ensure a safe start for an EU dimension

---

1168 Scholars consider values to be like ethical convictions, more indeterminate, while legal principles have a more defined structure, capable of producing legal effects. For legal theory, see i.a. R Alexy, 'On the Structure of Legal Principles' (2000) 13 Ratio Juris 294; von Bogdandy, 'Founding Principles' (p 14: 'The relationship between the principles discourse in legal philosophy and that in legal doctrine is as blurred as it is complicated'). C Hilson, 'Rights and principles in EU law: a distinction without foundation?' (2008) 15 Maastricht journal of European and comparative law 193; S Besson and P Pichonnaz (eds), *Les principes en droit européen/ Principles in European Law* (Schultess 2011). Formerly the Treaties referred to principles instead of 'values' (Art 6(1) TEU 'The Union is founded on the principles of liberty, democracy, respect for human rights and fundamental freedoms, and the rule of law, principles which are common to the Member States'). See also L Pech, 'A Union Founded on the Rule of Law': Meaning and Reality of the Rule of Law as a Constitutional Principle of EU Law' (2010) 6 European Constitutional Law Review 359, 366–367 (in the Lisbon Treaty '[a] distinction between the Union's fundamental moral values (human dignity, freedom, etc.) on which the Union is founded, and the structural constitutional principles (democracy, the rule of law, etc.) on the basis of which the Union must function, would have been more appropriate'). On rights and principles in the CFR, see S Peers and S Prechal, 'Article 52: Scope and Interpretation of Rights and Principles' in S Peers and others (eds), *The EU Charter of Fundamental Rights: a Commentary* (Hart 2014); also M Van Roosmalen and others, *Fundamental rights and principles: liber amicorum Pieter van Dijk* (Intersentia 2012). See Rosas and Armati, *EU Constitutional Law: An Introduction*, for an introduction to the essential values, principles and objectives of EU integration.

1169 Calliess, 'EU-Vertrag (Lissabon) Art 1', Rn 63.

in EDC at school, I consider that it is at present more appropriate to use the expression 'foundational' values, objectives and principles of the EU, in order not to encroach on political sensitivities in multidisciplinary contexts, and acknowledging the debate on the constitutional nature of the EU. Outside the legal field, the word 'constitutional' is less frequently used with regard to the EU and it could lead to reticence on the part of national curriculum designers and citizenship educators.[1170] Citizenship educationalists tend to be highly sensitive to any hint of an intention to create an EU super state. The word 'constitutional' could—unfairly—suggest such an intention and is better avoided. The word 'foundational' is in line with expressions in the Treaties and ECJ case law. The TEU and TFEU are the Treaties on which the EU is 'founded' (Article 1 TEU, third sentence).[1171] ECJ case law regularly refers to 'the very foundations' of the Union.[1172] Alternative expressions to 'foundational' may be 'founding', 'systemic' or 'core' values, objectives and principles.[1173] At a later stage, when citizens

1170 Searching in databases for 'constitutional & EU' mostly leads to law journals, legal conferences and books in the field of law.

1171 See Arts 1, 2, 10 TEU (the EU is 'founded' on the Treaties, on values, on representative democracy). See also earlier EEC Treaty, Part II 'Foundations of the Community'; and ECJ case law related to it (n 1172).

1172 Joined Cases C-402/05 P and C-415/05 P *Kadi* ECLI:EU:C:2008:461, paras 282, 290, 304 ('the principles that form part of the very foundations of the Community legal order, one of which is the protection of fundamental rights'). Earlier settled case law repeats that 'form part of the (very) foundations of the Community': the common market, the principle of free movement of goods, free movement of workers, free movement of persons, or equal pay. See i.a. Joined Cases C-482/01 and C-493/01 *Orfanopoulos and Oliveri* ECLI:EU:C:2004:262, para 62; Case C-215/03 *Oulane* ECLI:EU:C:2005:95, para 16; Case 43/75 *Defrenne II* ECLI:EU:C:1976:56, para 12.

1173 See e.g. choice of terms in A von Bogdandy, 'Founding Principles of EU Law: A Theoretical and Doctrinal Sketch' (2010) 16 ELJ 95 (p 7: founding principles defined as 'those norms of primary law which, in view of the need to legitimise the exercise of public authority, determine the general legitimatory foundations of the Union'); A von Bogdandy, 'The European Union as a Human Rights Organisation? Human Rights and the Core of the European Union' (2000) 37 CMLRev 1307; Decision 1093/2012/EU of the European Parliament and of the Council of 21 November 2012 on the European Year of Citizens (2013) [2012] OJ L325/1 Art 2(2)(c) ('the core values of the Union, as enshrined in the TEU and the TFEU and in the Charter of Fundamental Rights of the European Union'); Pech, 'A Union Founded on the Rule of Law': Meaning and Reality of the Rule of Law as a Constitutional Principle of EU Law', 362 ('The rule of law as a foundational principle'). Further Case

are more confident about the system, the label constitutional can be introduced and discussed.

170 Foundational values

There is a huge amount of literature on values and education.[1174] From a legal perspective, it is legitimate to focus on the values expressed in EU primary law, in particular Article 2 TEU:

C-419/16 *Simma Federspiel* ECLI:EU:C:2017:997, Opinion of AG Wahl, para 57 ('foundational principles of EU law, including, but not limited to, direct effect and State liability'; 'principes fondamentaux du droit de l'Union'). The Oxford dictionaries define foundational as '[d]enoting an underlying basis or principle; fundamental'. The adjective 'foundational' is seldom used in EU law.

1174 See i.a. RM Gordon, 'Freedom of expression and values inculcation in the public school curriculum' (1984) 13 The Journal of Law and Education 523; TM Lorenz, 'Value Training: Education or Indoctrination? A Constitutional Analysis' (1992) 34 Arizona Law Review 593; H Starkey, 'Back to Basic Values: Education for Justice and Peace in the World' (1992) 21 Journal of Moral Education 185; RC Salomone, 'Common Schools, Uncommon Values: Listening to the Voices of Dissent' (1996) 14 Yale Law & Policy Review 169; T Winther-Jensen (ed) *Challenges to European Education: Cultural Values, National identities, and Global Responsibilities* (Comparative Studies Series 6, Peter Lang 1996); D Evans, H Grassler and J Pouwels (eds), *Human Rights and Values Education in Europe: Research in educational law, curricula and textbooks* (Fillibach Verlag 1997); D Rowe, 'Value pluralism, democracy and education for citizenship' in *Values, Culture & Education* (1999); Redish and Finnertyt, 'What did you Learn in School Today? Free Speech, Values Inculcation, and the Democratic Educational Paradox'; S Macedo, 'School Choice, Civic Values and Problems of Policy Comparison,' in P Wolf and S Macedo (eds), *Educating Citizens: International Perspectives on Civic Values and School Choice* (Brookings Institution Press 2004); PJ Wolf and S Macedo (eds), *Educating Citizens: International Perspectives on Civic Values and School Choice* (Brookings Institution Press 2004); Halstead and Pike, *Citizenship and Moral Education: Values in Action*; K Sebart and J Krek, 'Citizenship education in educational research: description of knowledge, skills and values and their explanation in school evaluation' in B Kovzuh and others (eds), *New paradigms and methods in educational and social research* (University of California 2007); Clemitshaw, 'Citizenship without history? Knowledge, skills and values in citizenship education'; K Orlenius, 'Tolerance of intolerance: values and virtues at stake in education' (2008) 37 Journal of Moral Education 467; JS Hendricks and DM Howerton, 'Teaching values, teaching stereotypes: sex education and indoctrination in public schools' (2011) 13 University of Pennsylvania Journal of Constitutional Law 587; CJ Russo and WE Thro, 'Reflections on the Law and Curricular Values in American Schools' (2012) 87 Peabody Journal of Education 402; J Sayer and L Erler (eds), *Schools for the Future Europe: Values and Change beyond Lisbon* (Continuum 2012); J Arthur and T Lovat, *The Routledge international handbook of edu-*

The Union is founded on the values of respect for human dignity, freedom, democracy, equality, the rule of law and respect for human rights, including the rights of persons belonging to minorities. These values are common to the Member States in a society in which pluralism, non-discrimination, tolerance, justice, solidarity and equality between women and men prevail.[1175]

---

cation, religion and values (Routledge 2013); L Blum, 'Three educational values for a multicultural society: Difference recognition, national cohesion and equality' (2014) 43 Journal of Moral Education 332. See also Grimonprez, 'Conflicting ideas of Europe: the role of values in citizenship education'.

1175 See also CFR preamble: 'Conscious of its spiritual and moral heritage, the Union is founded on the indivisible, universal values of human dignity, freedom, equality and solidarity; it is based on the principles of democracy and the rule of law'. Fairness is another value appearing in EU primary law: it is given expression in various forms, as a horizontal aim, i.a. in CFR Arts 8, 17, 31, 41, or 47; TEU Art 3; TFEU Arts 39, 67, 79, 101, or 165. See categories of European values in C Calliess, 'Europa als Wertegemeinschaft — Integration und Identität durch europäisches Verfassungsrecht?' (2004) 59 JuristenZeitung 1033, 1369. Within the extensive literature on values in the EU, see further Lenaerts and Desomer, 'Bricks for a Constitutional Treaty of the European Union: Values, Objectives and Means'; F Benoît-Rohmer, 'Valeurs et droits fondamentaux dans la Constitution' [2005] Revue trimestrielle de droit européen 261; B de Witte, 'Non-market values in Internal Market Legislation' in N Nic Schuibhne (ed), *Regulating the Internal Market* (Edward Elgar 2006); S Besson, F Cheneval and N Levrat, *Des valeurs pour l'Europe? Values for Europe?* (Bruylant Academia 2008); M Kuisma, 'Rights or privileges? The challenge of globalization to the values of citizenship' (2008) 12 Citizenship Studies 613; Calliess, 'Europe as Transnational Law: The Transnationalization of Values by European Law'; P Leino and R Petrov, 'Between "Common Values" and Competing Universals —The Promotion of the EU's Common Values through the European Neighbourhood Policy' (2009) 15 ELJ 654; AT Williams, 'Taking Values Seriously: Towards a Philosophy of EU Law' (2009) 29 Oxford Journal of Legal Studies 549; A Freyberg-Inan, 'Equity as the missing link: the values of the European Union' (2010) 10 Romanian Journal of European Affairs 5; AT Williams, *The Ethos of Europe: Values, Law and Justice in the EU* (Cambridge University Press 2010); Lenaerts, 'EU Values and Constitutional Pluralism: The EU System of Fundamental Rights Protection'; L Potvin-Solis (ed) *Les valeurs communes dans l'Union européenne* (Bruylant 2014); Editorial Comments, 'Safeguarding EU values in the Member States—Is something finally happening?' (2015) 52 CMLRev 619; P Ferreira da Cunha, *Political Ethics and European Constitution* (Springer 2015); D Kochenov, G de Búrca and A Williams (eds), *Europe's Justice Deficit?* (Hart 2015); L Azoulai, 'Transfiguring European Citizenship: From Member State Territory to Union Territory' in D Kochenov (ed), *EU Citizenship and Federalism: The Role of Rights* (Cambridge University Press 2017) (see 193 ff); Kochenov, 'On Tiles and Pillars: EU Citizenship as a Federal Denomi-

These values, also expressed in the CFR, are not the natural qualities of individuals or of nation states. If they are to reflect more than the pathos of a Treaty text, they presuppose education as well as the persistent diligence of enlightened citizens. Active citizenship is not an objective *per se* but must be value-based.[1176] The EU and the Member States share a strong belief in the role of education to promote values.[1177] The Charter on EDC/HRE recalls that EDC overlaps with value education.[1178]

---

nator', 40. Also, among the many reflections on values in the context of citizenship rights and EU rights in the further analysis, see on equality i.a. §§ 258 259 , on solidarity questions i.a. text and n 1959.

1176 Values are an essential basis for participation of citizens: see Mascherini, Manca and Hoskins, *The characterization of Active Citizenship in Europe* (p 10: 'action alone is not considered active citizenship, the examples of Nazi Germany or Communist Europe can show mass participation without necessarily democratic or beneficial consequences'); and Hoskins concept of (value based) active citizenship in text to n 909. See underlying presuppositions of civic republicanism (n 593).

1177 See i.a. Erasmus+ Regulation 1288/2013, Art 4(f); EU Education Ministers and the Commissioner for Education, Culture, Youth and Sport, Paris Declaration on Promoting citizenship and the common values of freedom, tolerance and non-discrimination through education (17 March 2015); European Parliament Resolution on Follow-up of the strategic framework for European cooperation in education and training (ET2020) [2018] OJ C91/6; European Parliament Resolution of 12 April 2016 on Learning EU at school [2018] OJ C58/57, paras 2, 3, 6, 9, 13, 14, 21, 41. See also Commission Staff working document on the Application of the EU Charter of Fundamental Rights in 2016 Accompanying the document Communication from the Commission on 2016 Report on the Application of the EU Charter of Fundamental Rights SWD(2017) 162 final, 41 'Education policies are instrumental in addressing inequalities, fostering inclusion and tolerance, and promoting the common values of democracy, fundamental rights and the rule of law'; Commission Citizenship Report 'Strengthening Citizens' Rights in a Union of Democratic Change EU Citizenship Report 2017' COM(2017) 030 final/2, p 12: 'EU citizens expect more to be done to promote EU common values. They suggested that this should be done in particular through education, mobility of young people and cultural activities'); and earlier Commission Communication on Article 7 of the Treaty on European Union: Respect for and promotion of values on which the Union is based COM(2003) 606 final, 7. Further Commission/EACEA/Eurydice, Promoting citizenship and the common values of freedom, tolerance and non-discrimination through education: Overview of education policy developments in Europe following the Paris Declaration of 17 March 2015 (2016); JHH Weiler, 'The European Union belongs to its citizens: three immodest proposals' 22 ELRev 150, XIV, highlighting the need for education in the necessary *virtues*, which are a personal disposition to act to achieve *values*, the moral or ethical propositions; also JHH Weiler, 'On the Distinction between Values and

Applying the criterion of additionality for the EU dimension of EDC, the question arises as to whether the values in Article 2 TEU add content to national EDC. Admittedly, these so called 'EU values' have a universal vocation and national EDC already introduces pupils to them.[1179] The UK Department of Education, for instance, gave all schools a duty to actively promote 'Fundamental British Values'. These 'British' values included democracy, the rule of law, individual liberty, and mutual respect and tolerance.[1180] However, even if national values are the same as the 'EU values' in Article 2 TEU, there are additional challenges in striving to ensure

---

Virtues in the Process of European Integration' (IILJ International Legal Theory Colloqium, The Turn to Governance: The Exercise of Power in the International Public Space, New York Law School, 3 March 2010, unpublished).

1178 CoE Recommendation CM/Rec(2010)7 of the Committee of Ministers to member states on the Council of Europe Charter on Education for Democratic Citizenship and Human Rights Education (11 May 2010), paras 5(e)(f)(j), also para 2(e) and explanatory memorandum. See also CoE Recommendation CM/Rec(2019)9 of the Committee of Ministers to member States on fostering a culture of ethics in the teaching profession (16 October 2019).

1179 Member State constitutions express values, often in preambles. See, e.g., for the Czech Republik, preamble mostly written by Václav Havel: 'resolute to build, protect and develop the Czech Republic in the spirit of the inalienable values of human dignity and freedom as the home of free citizens who are aware of their obligations towards others and of their responsibility to the community, as a free and democratic State founded on respect for human rights and on *principles of civil society*, as a member of the family of European and World democracies'- emphasis added); or for Latvia: 'Loyalty to Latvia, the Latvian language as the only official language, freedom, equality, solidarity, justice, honesty, work ethic and family are the foundations of a cohesive society. Each individual takes care of oneself, one's relatives and the common good of society by acting responsibly toward other people, future generations, the environment and nature.' See also Germany in Government replies to questionnaire 2016 (n 386—387), Q14: 'Educating the individual to respect human dignity and to communicate the basic values, as stipulated in the Basic Constitutional Law, represents a key task of higher education institutions in the Federal Republic of Germany. The aim is, in addition to communicating knowledge and information, to form an understanding of the free democratic basic order of the Federal Republic and to impart consideration, tolerance and respect for other cultures, as well as a fundamental responsibility towards society'. See also n 666, and text to n 670.

1180 The Education (Independent School Standards) (England) Regulations 2010 contain a standard for the spiritual, moral, social and cultural development of pupils (in Part 2, Schedule 1). This standard was amended in 2014 (Education (Independent School Standards) (England) (Amendment) Regulations 2014 (come into force on 29th September 2014)): all schools, both independent and state-maintained schools, 'have a duty to "actively promote" the fundamental

respect for these values in a single area without internal frontiers with 500 million citizens. In one space encompassing 27 Member States, 24 official languages, with great diversity of regions, cultures, traditions, religions, etc., additional EU content is needed to clarify and to understand the concrete significance of these values for EU citizens, and—importantly—to reflect on the balancing of values (value hierarchy) and objectives.[1181] Moreover, some values (or principles) are specifically EU related, such as equality between Member States, or mutual trust and mutual respect.[1182] Mutual trust between the Member States 'is based on the fundamental premiss that Member States share a set of common values on which the European Union is founded, as stated in Article 2 TEU'.[1183] In *Wightman*, the ECJ recalled that 'the European Union is composed of States which have freely and voluntarily committed themselves to those values'.[1184] Calliess

---

British values of democracy, the rule of law, individual liberty, and mutual respect and tolerance of those with different faiths and beliefs'. This was designed to strengthen the barriers to extremism. See UK Department of Education, Promoting fundamental British values as part of SMSC [spiritual, moral, social and cultural development] in schools: Departmental advice for maintained schools (November 2014); UK, Department of Education, Improving the spiritual, moral, social and cultural (SMSC) development of pupils: supplementary information: Departmental advice for independent schools, academies and free schools (November 2014). No mention of 'Europe' or 'European'. See, e.g., para 5(b)(ii) 'enable pupils to distinguish right from wrong and to respect the civil and criminal law of England'; (b)(iv) 'enable pupils to acquire a broad general knowledge of and respect for public institutions and services in England'. Critical reactions followed. Members of the National Union of Teachers voted to include 'international rights' ('fundamental British values' set a tone of 'inherent cultural supremacism'); see also H Starkey, 'Fundamental British Values and citizenship education: tensions between national and global perspectives' (2018) 100 Geografiska Annaler: Series B, Human Geography 1: 'the obligation on schools in England since 2014 to promote FBVs [Fundamental British Values] can be read as an attempt to reinstate the national'). Cp education in France for 'les valeurs de la République'.

1181 Perceptions of Europeans on values in Special Eurobarometer 451, Future of Europe (December 2016): 45% say the EU best embodies peace and freedom of opinion, 43% social equality and solidarity, 41% tolerance and openness to others.

1182 Equality can be seen as a value and as a principle (see § 85 ff). The same can be argued for mutual trust; the ECJ formulates it as a principle. See text to nn 1203, 1207, 1208.

1183 Case C-64/16 *Juízes Portugueses* ECLI:EU:C:2018:117, para 30; also EU Accession to the ECHR *Opinion 2/13* ECLI:EU:C:2014:2454, para 168.

1184 Case C-621/18 *Wightman and Others* ECLI:EU:C:2018:999, para 63.

argues that even if EU values are common to the Member States, they have independent content. This content needs elaboration and concretisation. Value interaction leads to a 'Union of values' ('Werteverbund'), the basis for the EU as a 'Union of European States and constitutionalism' ('europäischer Staaten- und Verfassungsverbund').[1185] The establishment of common values in EU primary law is only the first step along the path to achieving a Union based on common values. For these values to have the power to effect integration, Calliess writes, the EU requires convincing institutions and effective procedures (functional and formal integration).[1186] It should be added that the education of citizens is also required, in keeping with EDC standards. Education is one of the shared values recognised by the Member States since the Enlightenment as being of central importance.

With shared values, a sense of a common EU identity may grow.[1187] However, creating a feeling of belonging is not a central objective of EDC/HRE standards, and this theme has therefore not been developed in this study.[1188] Words such as belonging, identity, feeling, or affective

---

1185 C Calliess, 'EU-Vertrag (Lissabon) Art 2' in C Calliess, M Ruffert and H-J Blanke (eds), *EUV/AEUV: das Verfassungsrecht der Europäischen Union mit Europäischer Grundrechtecharta : Kommentar* (Beck 2016), Rn 10, 14 ('Europäische Werte haben einen selbständigen Gehalt, der im europäischen Verfassungsverbund jedoch eng mit den nationalen Werteinhalten der Mitgliedstaaten verknüpft ist').

1186 Calliess, 'Europe as Transnational Law: The Transnationalization of Values by European Law', 1381.

1187 Calliess, 'Europa als Wertegemeinschaft — Integration und Identität durch europäisches Verfassungsrecht?', 1039; Peters, 'European democracy after the 2003 Convention', 77; Calliess, 'Europe as Transnational Law: The Transnationalization of Values by European Law', 1370: identity development through differentiation, not through discrimination of a common enemy.

1188 On belonging and EU identity, see furthermore S Dufeu, *Valeurs et constitutions européennes. Une identité politique entre deux mythes: universalité et frontière* (Questions contemporaines, L'Harmattan 2005); Ross, 'Multiple Identities and Education for Active Citizenship'; Verhaegen, Hooghe and Meeusen, 'Opportunities to learn about Europe at school. A comparative analysis among European adolescents in 21 European member states'; Calliess, 'EU-Vertrag (Lissabon) Art 2', Rn 4; A Somek, 'Europe: Political, Not Cosmopolitan' (2014) 20 ELJ 142; A Ross, *Finding Political Identities: Young People in a Changing Europe* (Springer 2018); JF Ziemes, K Hahn-Laudenberg and HJ Abs, 'From Connectedness and Learning to European and National Identity: Results from Fourteen European Countries' (2019) 18 Journal of Social Science Education (3: European Citizenship Education: Business as Usual or Time for Change?) 5 (teachers should foster identity complexity).

dimension, do not feature in any central way in the Charter on EDC/HRE. In the 2006 Recommendation on key competences for lifelong learning, they are present, yet the broadly worded aspirations remain prudent: civic competences include 'displaying both a sense of belonging to one's locality, country, the EU and Europe in general and to the world'. Still, social competences essentially include '[u]nderstanding the multi-cultural and socio-economic dimensions of European societies and how national cultural identity interacts with the European identity'.[1189] The 2018 Council Recommendation on key competences for lifelong learning explicitly refers to a 'vision towards a European Education Area that would be able "to harness the full potential of education and culture as drivers for jobs, social fairness, active citizenship as well as means to experience European identity in all its diversity"'.[1190] This connects to component (c-2) of the EDC concept, i.e. valuing diversity (c-2).[1191]

171 Foundational objectives

The Member States established a European Union on which they conferred competences to attain objectives they have in common (Article 1 TEU). The Union shall act only within the limits of the competences conferred upon it by the Member States in the Treaties 'to attain the objectives set out therein', objectives which they cannot sufficiently achieve alone (Article 5(2) and (3) TEU). The narrative in the Treaties is almost utopian. Among the foundational objectives are promoting peace and the well-being of the peoples, offering an area of freedom, security and justice without internal frontiers, ensuring free movement of persons, establishing an internal market, working for sustainable development, economic growth, full employment and social progress, protecting the environment, combating social exclusion and discrimination, promoting solidarity among Member States, and respecting cultural and linguistic diversity (Article 3 TEU). Together with Article 2 on Union values and the CFR, Article 3

1189 Recommendation of the European Parliament and of the Council of 18 December 2006 on key competences for lifelong learning.

1190 Council Recommendation of 22 May 2018 on key competences for lifelong learning, recital 1. See also Annex: A European Reference Framework, 6: Citizenship competence: 'Knowledge of European integration as well as an awareness of diversity and cultural identities in Europe and the world is essential. This includes an understanding of the multi-cultural and socioeconomic dimensions of European societies, and how national cultural identity contributes to the European identity'.

1191 Charter on EDC/HRE, paras 2, 5(f), and 13. See also text to n 1878.

paints the vision of a society where it is good to live. If democracy and EU citizenship are to be taken seriously, the foundational EU objectives should be part of compulsory learning outcomes in mainstream education. Quality education cannot stop at describing the EU as a peace project. Every achievement starts with a dream. There is wisdom in this metaphor: if you want people to build a ship, don't give orders, don't explain which tools to use, but tell them about the wide sea.[1192] The EU is not a goal in itself,[1193] but a way of attaining common objectives, reaching added value, the wide sea. In history classes, pupils may read the Schuman Declaration of 9 May 1950. It is time to put Articles 1–6 TEU next to this Declaration. As part of school curricula, the content of Articles 2 and 3 TEU should be discussed in classrooms, as a kick off for participation in an EU civil society, enhancing the growth of a European public space.[1194] Only if they are made aware of the European 'project', can individuals guide the 'process' and the 'product' through democratic processes as responsible and active EU citizens. The EU is an objective driven polity and should be understood as such and monitored by Europeans.[1195] Moreover, a shared sense of

---

1192 'If you want to build a ship, don't drum up the men to gather wood, divide the work and give orders. Instead, teach them to yearn for the vast and endless sea': quote attributed to Antoine de Saint-Exupéry, Citadelle (1948).

1193 K Lenaerts, 'De Europese Unie: doel of middel?' (1998) 21 Rechtskundig Weekblad 689.

1194 On the process towards creating a European public space, see Calliess and Hartmann, *Zur Demokratie in Europa: Unionsbürgerschaft und europäische Öffentlichkeit.*

1195 Lenaerts and Desomer, 'Bricks for a Constitutional Treaty of the European Union: Values, Objectives and Means'. Authors conclude that the real question does not concern the kind of 'constitution' we want, but what kind of Union, in terms of shared values, common objectives and means; clarifying these elements is essential to ensuring acceptance by EU citizens as a body politic. Further F Reimer, 'Ziele und Zuständigkeiten: Die Funktionen der Unionszielbestimmungen' (2003) 38 Europarecht 992; G Palombella, 'Whose Europe? After the constitution: A goal-based citizenship' (2005) 3 International Journal of Constitutional Law 357; J Schwarze, 'Die Abwägung von Zielen der europäischen Integration und mitgliedstaatlichen Interessen in der Rechtsprechung des EuGH' (2013) 48 Europarecht 253; J Larik, 'From specialty to a constitutional sense of purpose: on the changing role of the objectives of the European Union' (2014) 63 International and Comparative Law Quarterly 935 (a more far-reaching role than that related to the principle of conferral; 'the EU stands for certain values and has been endowed with powers, the exercise of which is guided by promoting these various aspects of the "common good"'); Davies, 'Social Legitimacy and Purposive Power: The End, the Means and the Consent

purpose is needed to respond to multiple crises in the EU.[1196] Education about the foundational values and objectives (the deep common interests) will enhance the social legitimacy of the EU.[1197]

172 Foundational principles

The Treaties define various systemic principles (TEU Title I Common provisions TEU) which are the backbone of the EU construction. They are essential to understanding the EU as a system, and the place of one's own Member State in it, and are thus essential to empowering EU citizens.[1198] A central axis in the EU constitutional construction is the principle of conferral: the EU can only act within the limits of the competences conferred upon it by the Member States in the Treaties to attain the objectives set out; competences not conferred upon the EU remain with the Member States (Article 4(1) TEU, 5(2) TEU).[1199]

Citizens are unaware of this principle.[1200] The high expectations of citizens with regard to EU citizenship and the EU (and of legal writers commenting on ECJ case law) cannot always be reconciled with the principle of conferral.[1201] When expecting the EU to 'humanise' or remedy certain

---

of the People'. See also Weiler, 'Deciphering the Political and Legal DNA of European Integration': 'political messianism' constitutes the political and legal (cultural) DNA of European integration.

1196 The response to the multiple crises of the EU 'should be built on a common perspective, and on the shared conviction that by coming together, each of us will be better off', see Commission White paper of 1 March 2017 on the future of Europe COM(2017) 2025 final. See also F Amtenbrink, 'Europe in Times of Economic Crisis: Bringing Europe's Citizens Closer to One Another?' in M Dougan, N Nic Schuibhne and E Spaventa (eds), *Empowerment and Disempowerment of the European Citizen* (Hart 2012) 187.

1197 Cf Curtin, *Executive Power of the European Union. Law, Practices, and the Living Constitution* 284.

1198 On the concept of 'principles', i.a. text to n 952, n 1168. Further Bauer and Calliess, *Constitutional principles in Europe*; constitutional principles also in Calliess, 'EU-Vertrag (Lissabon) Art 1', Rn 29 (integration); Rn 78 (closeness to citizens; transparency); Rn 90 (other, such as coherence and solidarity).

1199 I.a. Case C-589/15 P *Anagnostakis* ECLI:EU:C:2017:663, Opinion of AG Mengozzi, para 62. See E Neframi, *Objectifs et compétences dans l'Union européenne* (Droit de l'Union européenne Colloques, Bruylant 2013).

1200 See i.a. text to nn 1517, 1533 (e.g. citizens' initiative proposals not infrequently concern matters outside the EU competence sphere).

1201 Perceptions in civil society: the EU should act in the Spain/Catalonia crisis, should grant social rights, etc. See Commission Report under Article 25 TFEU 'On progress towards effective EU citizenship 2013-2016' COM(2017) 32 final. See also academic writers in debates on wholly internal situations, reverse dis-

situations,[1202] citizens should keep the limits to EU action in mind. If citizens consider these limits as too constraining, they should be empowered to instigate change through democratic participation, even to 'the pact'. The constitutional allocation of powers in the EU has either to be respected or to be adapted. If the EU is an autonomous legal order, the reverse side is that it is a limited field. Both aspects should be understood by citizens. This foundational principle should be explained in schools as a matter of elementary knowledge and is not so complicated in itself. It could reduce distrust and avoid misunderstandings and disappointment in civil society.

Other systemic principles to explain in EDC are, inter alia, subsidiarity and proportionality (Article 5(3) and (4) TEU), respect for national (constitutional) identities (Article 4(2) TEU), loyal (or sincere) cooperation (Article 4(3) TEU), and respect for fundamental rights (Article 6 TEU, CFR). Foundational principles include democratic principles (Articles 9–12 TEU), the principle of non-discrimination on grounds of nationality (Article 18 TFEU), non-discrimination based on sex, race, religion, etc. (Article 19 TFEU), free movement of citizens (Article 21 TFEU), and fundamental freedoms in the internal market (Articles 28, 45, 49, 56, 63 TFEU). The ECJ refers to principles, such as primacy, unity and effectiveness, and—of fundamental importance—the principles of mutual trust and mutual recognition.[1203]

Educating about EU foundational values, objectives and principles is relevant for mainstream education, as it satisfies the four criteria. It provides

---

crimination, citizenship linked to the material scope of EU law, or on fundamental rights protection, i.a. Kochenov, 'On Tiles and Pillars: EU Citizenship as a Federal Denominator', 4: 'How to unlock the potential of EU citizenship to make it work fo the benefit of all Europeans, while strictly adhering to the principle of conferral, is the core question behind this volume.'.

1202 E.g. Kochenov, 'On Tiles and Pillars: EU Citizenship as a Federal Denominator', 51: 'EU citizenship is bound to assume a structural role, should the ideals of dignity, equality, democracy and the Rule of Law prevail'.

1203 EU Accession to the ECHR *Opinion 2/13* ECLI:EU:C:2014:2454, paras 188–189 (primacy, unity and effectiveness), para 191 (mutual trust). Further K Lenaerts, 'La vie après l'avis: Exploring the principle of mutual (yet not blind) trust' (2017) 54 CMLRev 805; also Lenaerts, '"In the Union we trust": trust-enhancing principles of Community law', on general principles and the role of principles such as transparency, equality of arms, the precautionary principle, or sound administration. Mutual recognition in legislation, e.g. Regulation (EU) 2019/515 of the European Parliament and of the Council of 19 March 2019 on the mutual recognition of goods lawfully marketed in another Member State and repealing Regulation (EC) No 764/2008 [2019] OJ L 91/1.

additional (i) and significant (ii) content to EDC (knowledge, understanding, and attitudes), and provides ample food for thought (iii), preparing citizens for active participation. Foundational values, objectives and principles furthermore concern all EU citizens, mobile and static, 'founding' the society in which they live (iv). This will be illustrated when the EU dimension of EDC components is given more concrete form on the basis of EU primary law. Educating about EU foundational values, objectives and principles is consistent with EDC standards, with EU endogenic norms on citizenship competences, and with scholarly writing on citizenship education.[1204] Moreover, it respects the autonomy of the EU.

173 Applying EDC standards respects, even upholds, the specific characteristics of the EU

A limit to the reception of exogenic norms in the EU legal order—red line not to be crossed—was prejudice to the constitutional principles of the Treaties.[1205] This is not a problem when in application of EDC standards, an EU dimension is incorporated into EDC, on the contrary. Full respect for the specific characteristics of the EU is more likely when citizens are educated about them. Adding an EU dimension to EDC based on EU primary law upholds those specific characteristics since it enlightens citizens about the specificity of the EU and empowers them to exercise their rights and responsibilities, to value diversity and to participate in this system, which is not a state, yet exercises public power in conformity with the Treaties and the CFR. The following analysis will provide various examples.[1206]

1204 Values of democracy, human rights and the rule of law were the essential motivating factors in the genesis of the Charter on EDC/HRE (Part one). See the EU Council Recommendation of 22 May 2018 on key competences for lifelong learning, Annex: A European Reference Framework, 6: Citizenship competence ('involves an understanding of the European common values, as expressed in Article 2 of the Treaty on European Union and the Charter of Fundamental Rights of the European Union'). Before: Recommendation of the European Parliament and of the Council of 18 December 2006 on key competences for lifelong learning, Annex 6 B. See also Sander (*Mission*), text to n 562.

1205 EU Accession to the ECHR *Opinion 2/13* ECLI:EU:C:2014:2454, i.a. paras 164–177.

1206 E.g. learning about the principle of conferral and the right to a ECI (§ 209); about the right to vote for the EP and its specificity in the EU (§ 222); about respect for the rule of law and fundamental rights, internal market implications, concept of directives, etc. (§ 265).

An EU dimension to EDC will also reinforce mutual trust. The ECJ has ruled that the principle of mutual trust between the Member States is 'of fundamental importance in EU law, given that it allows an area without internal borders to be created and maintained'. [1207] The shared set of common values justifies mutual trust.[1208] Mutual trust presupposes measures in each Member State to create a citizenship culture consistent with the fundamental values of the EU, including respect for the rule of law and fundamental rights. Mutual trust has to be deserved by public authorities and citizens.[1209] Recognising the autonomy of the EU and its constitutional principles requires more EDC rather than less. The Council of Europe norms on EDC and HRE are a minimum. Specific EU features and the complexity of the EU—which nevertheless aims at democracy—call for even greater attention to be paid to EDC standards and more extensive circumspection than in a traditional nation state with a long-standing history.

Making EU primary law a pillar of the EU dimension of EDC guarantees that the additional EU dimension respects the basic constitutional charter, the Treaties, and the CFR.

174 The Union 'acquis' culture

Before accession, candidate States have to accept the Union *acquis*. The *acquis*, referred to in the Treaties, Acts of Accession, and in some national constitutions, is the body of rights and obligations inherent in the system of the Union and its institutional framework. Future Member States are required to accept the provisions of the Treaties, the decisions taken by the

---

1207 *Opinion 2/13*, paras 191–192 ('the principle of mutual trust requires, particularly with regard to the area of freedom, security and justice, each of those States, save in exceptional circumstances, to consider all the other Member States to be complying with EU law and particularly with the fundamental rights recognised by EU law'; 'Thus, when implementing EU law, the Member States may, under EU law, be required to presume that fundamental rights have been observed by the other Member States, so that not only may they not demand a higher level of national protection of fundamental rights from another Member State than that provided by EU law, but, save in exceptional cases, *they may not check whether that other Member State has actually, in a specific case, observed the fundamental rights guaranteed by the EU*' (emphasis added).

1208 Ibid, para 168: 'This legal structure is based on the fundamental premiss that each Member State shares with all the other Member States, and recognises that they share with it, a set of common values on which the EU is founded, as stated in Article 2 TEU. That premiss implies and justifies the existence of mutual trust between the Member States that those values will be recognised and, therefore, that the law of the EU that implements them will be respected'.

1209 Further in § 247 .

institutions pursuant to the Treaties, and ECJ case law, and must adopt the measures necessary to satisfy these conditions.[1210] It would conflict with good faith and acceptance of the Union *acquis* to reject an EU dimension of EDC based on the Treaties, or to consider such a dimension to be indoctrination.[1211] It is not sufficient to incorporate the *acquis* into national legislation, it must also be fashioned into a Union '*acquis* culture', to be fostered and, ideally, to be incorporated into all levels of education. Consistency between national EDC and the Union *acquis* can be expected of newly acceding States, and, hopefully leading by example, of the existing Member States. Certainly, the *acquis* goes far beyond what is relevant for mainstream education, but the notion shows that EU law has a hard core which must be accepted by its Member States. Citizens should be educated in a spirit corresponding to the Union *acquis*.

175 Counterargument: EU primary law is too complex for schools

True, the Treaties and the CFR are not written for the neophyte who wants an easy learning tool about the EU. Ideally, a simplified version the Treaties and CFR would be made available for the EU dimension of EDC, just as some Member State constitutions are presented in simplified form for national citizenship education.[1212] Admittedly, nothing is more complicated than simplifying; however, there is no escape: all education starts with elementary steps, a route to more complexity later on. For teaching purposes, Homer, Shakespeare, and Balzac have been simplified, re-cast in readable booklets for pupils. The UN Convention on the Rights of the

---

1210 Art 20 TEU; Presidency Conclusions of the Copenhagen European Council of 21-22 June 1993, Bull EC 6-1993 (Copenhagen criteria); Commission, Europe and the challenge of enlargement (24 June 1992) Bull EC Suppl 3-92, 11: 'Membership implies the acceptance of the rights and the obligations, actual and potential, of the community system and its institutional framework—the Community's acquis, as it is known'. Referral to the *acquis*, e.g., in Arts 9, 133, 145, 146, 152 Croatian constitution. See generally D Chalmers, A Arnull and C Hillion, *Accession and Withdrawal in the Law of the European Union* (Oxford University Press 2015); also Lenaerts and Van Nuffel, *European Union Law* 93.

1211 See n 1080.

1212 See, i.a., simplified version of the constitution in Germany: D Hesselberger, *Das Grundgesetz: Kommentar für die politische Bildung* (13 edn, Bundeszentrale für politische Bildung 2003); or brochure *Das Grundgesetz Uber den Staat* (einfach Politik, 2016, Bundeszentrale für politische Bildung); in Denmark *My Constitutional Act, with explanations* (Folketinget, 2014, 12th edn, Text Susannah Pedersen, Journalist; Adviser on legal aspects: Jens Peter Christensen, Supreme Court Judge, Professor, LLB); in Austria explanations per theme in <www.unsereverfassung.at>.

Child has been 'translated' into a child-friendly version for children and the ECHR exists in a simplified version for educational purposes.[1213] At the very least, the founding tenets of the EU as agreed in the Treaties could be formulated in understandable versions for teachers (non-lawyers) and pupils. Could the European Parliament draft—or at least support—a school-friendly version of the essential provisions of EU primary law? Foundational values, objectives and principles must be placed in the spotlight. The counterargument that foundational values, objectives and principles are too complex for EDC in schools, must be rebutted. Teachers manage to explain numerous complex subjects in formats adapted to their students. In Member States with a federal system, national EDC has to tackle complex situations anyway. Democracy requires enlightened citizenship.[1214] Democracy in the EU requires enlightened EU citizenship. Logically this must start at school.

B Case teaching: critical thinking and pluralism

176 Case teaching supports a pluralist EU dimension

The learning method proposed for an EU dimension of EDC in the classroom is founded on two pillars: texts and stories. In addition to EU primary law (texts), which enhances objectivity, case teaching (stories) invites independent, pluralist and critical thinking. EU primary law is a stable basis for EDC, yet it must not lead to uncritical acceptance of any norm. Education should not mould EU citizens to obey the general will as understood by Rousseau. Rousseau considered law to be the expression of the general will. He advocated patriotism as the most effective method of ensuring conformity with it.[1215] In his view, the purpose of education (from a very early age) was to shape souls in patriotism, civic virtue, over-

---

1213 See <www.unicef.org/rightsite/files/uncrcchilldfriendlylanguage.pdf>; <ork.lu/index.php/en/rights-of-the-child/the-convention-of-1989/simplified-version-of-the-crc>; <www.coe.int/en/web/compass/european-convention-on-human-rights> (simplified version of selected articles, prepared by the Directorate of Communication of the CoE).

1214 Dahl, *On democracy* (text to n 565).

1215 See in general J-J Rousseau, *Emile ou de l'éducation* (1762, Flammarion ed 2009), and in particular, for Rousseau's ideas on the need and ends of citizenship education, *Discours sur l'économie politique* (1755) and *Considérations sur le gouvernement de Pologne (1771)*.

coming self-interest, and thus compliance with the general will.[1216] In contrast to Rousseau, Condorcet argued that the end of instruction was not to instill pre-established opinions, but to submit all opinions to reason (Enlightenment).[1217] Reason alone should guide citizens, not beliefs (moral principles should also be based on reason) or blind feelings of love for the fatherland.[1218] According to Condorcet, we must embrace the law but also be capable of judging it ('Il faut qu'en aimant les lois, on sache les juger').[1219] The purpose of instruction is to give citizens the means of achieving a more perfect constitution, better law, and more complete freedom.[1220]

Today, in the light of the experience of patriotic but totalitarian education and its disastrous consequences in two world wars, independent and critical thinking has become an essential component of EDC standards, a recurrent aim in normative instruments on education.[1221] It is one of the compulsory aims of education, part of the development of the human per-

---

1216 To the Polish government, Rousseau gave the advice: 'It is education that you must count on to shape the souls of the citizens in a national pattern and so to direct their opinions, their likes and dislikes that they shall be patriotic by inclination, passionately, of necessity' (J-J Rousseau, *The government of Poland* (W Kendall tr, Bobbs-Merrill 1972) 19): see KW Clausen, 'Alternative education versus the common will' (2010) 45 Journal of Thought 95, 108 (fn 5). For influence of Rousseau's ideas on education, see D Heater, *A Brief History of Citizenship* (New York University Press 2004) 67–72; Heater, *Citizenship: the Civic Ideal in World History, Politics and Education*, 40–41 (Robespierre attempted to apply his ideas during the French revolution).

1217 Condorcet, *Cinq mémoires sur l'instruction publique* , 36–37.

1218 Condorcet thus disagrees with philosophers who want citizens to become attached to the existing constitution and law of their fatherland through 'a blind feeling' and passion. See ibid, 44.

1219 (tr) For citizens to love the law without losing their freedom, for them to retain the power of independent thought without which the fervour for liberty is mere passion and not a virtue, they must be taught the principles of natural justice, these essential rights of man: in Condorcet, *Rapport et project de décret relatifs à l'organisation générale de l'instruction publique, Présentation à l'Assemblée législative (20 et 21 avril 1792)* (1792).

1220 'lui préparez, par une instruction générale, les moyens de parvenir à une constitution plus parfaite, de se donner de meilleures lois, et d'atteindre à une liberté plus entière': ibid.

1221 In chronological order: CoE Recommendation Rec(2002)12 of the Committee of Ministers to member states on education for democratic citizenship (16 October 2002), appendix para 2: key competencies include the ability to 'develop a critical approach to information, thought patterns and philosophical, religious, social, political and cultural concepts, at the same time remain-

sonality in all its aspects.[1222] As explained above, in accordance with ECtHR case law, the State is prohibited from pursuing an aim of indoctri-

---

ing committed to fundamental values and principles of the Council of Europe'; Recommendation of the European Parliament and of the Council of 18 December 2006 on key competences for lifelong learning: critical thinking is part of the fifth key competence, i.e. learning to learn, and is a theme applied throughout the Reference Framework (p 394/14); CoE Recommendation CM/Rec(2010)7 of the Committee of Ministers to member states on the Council of Europe Charter on Education for Democratic Citizenship and Human Rights Education (11 May 2010) (no explicit mentioning of critical thinking, yet, it is present in the skills and attitudes, which are part of the definition of EDC; as illustrated in other instruments); CoE Recommendation CM/Rec(2012)13 of the Committee of Ministers to member States on ensuring quality education (12 December 2012), appendix para 6: quality education is education which (e) 'enables pupils and students to develop appropriate competences, self-confidence and critical thinking to help them become responsible citizens and improve their employability'; EU Education Ministers and the Commissioner for Education, Culture, Youth and Sport, Paris Declaration on Promoting citizenship and the common values of freedom, tolerance and non-discrimination through education (17 March 2015); European Parliament Resolution of 12 April 2016 on Learning EU at school [2018] OJ C58/57, paras 6, 15; Council Conclusions of 30 May 2016 on developing media literacy and critical thinking through education and training [2016] OJ C212/5, paras 1 and 3; Competences for democratic culture: Living together as equals in culturally diverse democratic societies (CoE 2016), scheme p 11 (analytical and critical thinking skills, knowledge and critical understanding); Conclusions of the Council and of the Representatives of the Governments of the Member States, meeting within the Council, on Inclusion in Diversity to achieve a High Quality Education For All - Council Conclusions (17 February 2017), p 5 para 2; Commission Staff working document on the Application of the EU Charter of Fundamental Rights in 2016 Accompanying the document Communication from the Commission on 2016 Report on the Application of the EU Charter of Fundamental Rights SWD(2017) 162 final, p 38 (action on media literacy and dissemination of critical thinking tools); Commission/EACEA/Eurydice, Citizenship Education at School in Europe (2017), 9 ('citizenship education needs to help students develop knowledge, skills, attitudes and values in four broad competence areas: 1) interacting effectively and constructively with others; 2) thinking critically; 3) acting in a socially responsible manner; and 4) acting democratically'), also 10, 11, 48, 52, 55, 61, 62; CoE, Learning to live together: Council of Europe Report on the state of citizenship and human rights education in Europe, 29, 30, 33, 34, 40; Council Recommendation of 22 May 2018 on key competences for lifelong learning (see n 1064).

1222 Aims in UHDR, ICESCR, CRC (see nn 81-82, § 288). See also UNESCO Recommendation concerning Education for International Understanding, Co-operation and Peace and Education relating to Human Rights and Fundamental Freedoms (adopted 19 November 1974), paras 13–14; UN ComRC 'General

nation and must take care that information or knowledge included in the curriculum is conveyed 'in an objective, *critical and pluralistic* manner' (interpreting Article 2 second sentence Protocol 1).[1223] The ECtHR has ruled that 'one of the principal characteristics of democracy is the possibility it offers of resolving a country's problems through dialogue, without recourse to violence, even when they are irksome. Democracy thrives on freedom of expression.'[1224] During the European Convention, the Working Group on Simplification found that the 'ability to criticise is a key factor for democracy, citizens must be able to understand the system so that they can identify problems, criticise it, and ultimately control it'.[1225] Almost all Member States include critical thinking in their curricula to develop social and citizenship competence[1226] and numerous scholars, as well as (young) citizens point to its importance.[1227] Revelations of the hijacking of social media in order to influence voters point in an even

---

Comment No 1 (2001)- Article 29(1): The Aims of Education' Doc CRC/GC/2001/1, paras 4 and 9; UNESCO-UNICEF, A Human Rights-Based Approach to Education for All: A framework for the realization of children's right to education and rights within education (2007), p 68–69.

1223 See n 1080. My emphasis.

1224 *Socialist Party and Others v Turkey* no 20/1997/804/1007 (ECtHR 25 May 1998), para 45. See also ECJ case law on freedom of expression.

1225 European Convention, Final report of Working Group IX on Simplification (29 November 2002) CONV 424/02 , 1.

1226 Commission/EACEA/Eurydice, Citizenship Education at School in Europe (2017), i.a. 11, 62 (see 'Thinking critically' and 'Exercising judgment' in figure 1.15).

1227 For academic writers, see Part one, i.a. third caveat (§ 73). See also É Dacheux, 'La communication publique de l'Union européenne ne rapproche pas l'Europe des citoyens' (2017) 77 Hermès, La Revue 45: author contrasts persuasive communication (marketing) versus deliberative communication ('faire émerger une culture commune'); this is what the EU needs: involving citizens in the discussions on the intended solutions. For young citizens, see i.a. Flash Eurobarometer 455, European Youth (January 2018) (Q4): One of the three ideas for the future of Europe that young people most agree with is the promotion of critical thinking and the ability to search for information in order to combat fake news and extremism (49% agree); also Commission, 12 Ideas for The Future of Europe: New narrative for Europe Communications campaign (2017), 7. For citizens, see Flash Eurobarometer 466, The European Education Area (May 2018), (Q7.5): Seven in ten respondents think increasing the teaching of creativity or of critical thinking in European schools or universities is useful for young people in the EU; Flash Eurobarometer 464, Fake News and Disinformation Online (March 2018): 85% think that the existence of fake news is a problem in their country, at least to some extent; 83% see this as a problem for democracy in general.

more compelling way to the importance of learning how to exercise critical and independent thinking in schools. The response to fake news must be EDC/HRE with all its components, including the EU dimension, being fully developed.[1228]

If one applies the principle that EDC is more than teaching top down about constitutional structures, then the EU dimension must be more than an additional layer of theoretical knowledge about EU primary law. EU primary law is consensus-based, yet (like most constitutions) its application leaves room for discussion, as witnessed by ECJ case law and academic writing. Many provisions are programmatic (certainly in the CFR). The rights of EU citizens enshrined in EU law may, moreover, collide with each other. Foundational values, objectives, and principles may compete and require balancing.[1229]

Case teaching is used in various fields of study all over the world (economics, medicine, ethics, psychology, law, public policy, international relations, etc.), widely commented on as to its advantages and limits.[1230]

1228 L Jackson, '"The Best Education Ever": Trumpism, Brexit, and new social learning' (2018) 50 Educational Philosophy and Theory 441; see also J Oelkers, 'The European Crisis and Education for Democracy' (2017) 22 The European Legacy 832.

1229 See on balancing, R Alexy, 'The Construction of Constitutional Rights' (2010) 4 Law and Ethics of Human Rights 21 (constitutional rights imply a debate on proportionality analysis; author argues that balancing of principles is not irrational; he develops a rational legal argument, the 'Weight Formula').

1230 On case teaching in the context of citizenship education, see i.a. Naylor, 'Educating for citizenship with law-related education' (1981) 20 Theory into Practice 194; R Coles, *The Call of Stories: Teaching and the Moral Imagination* (1990); VL Golich, 'The ABCs of Case Teaching' (2000) 1 International Studies Perspectives 11; C Menkel-Meadow, 'Telling Stories in School: Using Case Studies and Stories to Teach Legal Ethics' (2000-2001) 69 Fordham Law Review 787; S Kenney, 'Using the master's tools to dismantle the master's house: can we harness the virtues of case teaching?' (2001) 20 Journal of policy analysis and management 346; Nussbaum, 'Cultivating Humanity in Legal Education'; JS Lantis, 'Ethics and Foreign Policy: Structured Debates for the International Studies Classroom' (2004) 5 International Studies Perspectives 17; RJ Hardy, C Rackaway and LE Sonnier, 'In the Supreme Court Justices Shoes: Critical Thinking Through the Use of Hypothetical Case Law Analyses and Interactive Simulations' (2005) 38 Political Science and Politics 411; Massing, 'Institutionenkundliches Lernen'; Oberreuter, 'Rechtserziehung'; Halstead and Pike, *Citizenship and Moral Education: Values in Action*; G Biesta and R Lawy, 'From teaching citizenship to learning democracy: Overcoming individualism in research, policy and practice' (2006) 36 Cambridge Journal of Education 63;

Ample empirical and other evidence underscores its effectiveness.[1231] Cases are stories which, as precisely as possible, recount real events or problems, so that learners experience the ambiguities and uncertainties which the

---

McCowan, 'Approaching the political in citizenship education: The perspectives of Paulo Freire and Bernard Crick'; Nussbaum, 'Education and Democratic Citizenship: Capabilities and Quality Education'; D Eichner, 'Fallanalysen im Sachunterricht als Möglichkeit des Demokratie-Lernens' in D Richter (ed), *Politische Bildung von Anfang an: Demokratie-Lernen in der Grundschule* (Schriftenreihe Band 570, Bundeszentrale für politische Bildung 2007); Lamy, 'Challenging Hegemonic Paradigms and Practices: Critical Thinking and Active Learning Strategies for International Relations'; Zimenkova and Hedtke, 'The Talk-and-Action Approach to Citizenship Education. An Outline of a Methodology of Critical Studies in Citizenship Education'; D Hess and PG Avery, 'Discussion of Controversial Issues as a Form and Goal of Democratic Education' in J Arthur, I Davies and C Hahn (eds), *The SAGE Handbook of Education for Citizenship and Democracy* (Sage 2008); Hess, *Controversy in the Classroom: The Democratic Power of Discussion*; Z Beutler and D Lange (eds), *Schlüsselkompetenzen für aktive BürgerInnenschaft. Handbuch für die Sekundarstufe* (Voice Agora Politische Bildung 2010); Gollob, Krapf and Weidinger, *Educating for democracy: Background materials on democratic citizenship and human rights education for teachers*; A Osler and J Zhu, 'Narratives in teaching and research for justice and human rights' (2011) 6 Education, Citizenship and Social Justice 223; DAJ Telman, 'Langdellian limericks (case teaching method)' (2011) 61 Journal of Legal Education 110; J Vandenabeele, E Vanassche and D Wildemeersch, 'Stories of/on citizenship education: a case of participatory planning' (2011) 30 International Journal of Lifelong Education 171; GE Fischman and E Haas, 'Beyond Idealized Citizenship Education: Embodied Cognition, Metaphors, and Democracy' (2012) 36 Review Of Research In Education 169; J Murdoch, *Protecting the right to freedom of thought, conscience and religion under the European Convention on Human Rights* (Council of Europe Human Rights Handbooks, 2012); G Weisseno and H Buchstein (eds), *Politisch Handeln. Modelle, Möglichkeiten, Kompetenzen* (Schriftenreihe Band 1191, Bundeszentrale für politische Bildung 2012); I Davies and others, 'Young People's Community Engagement: What Does Research-Based and Other Literature Tell us About Young People's Perspectives and the Impact of Schools' Contributions?' (2013) 61 British Journal of Educational Studies 1; Osler, 'Bringing Human Rights Back Home: Learning from "Superman" and Addressing Political Issues at School'; HPD Maurer and C Neuhold, 'Problem-Based Learning in European Studies' in S Baroncelli and others (eds), *Teaching and Learning the European Union: Traditional and Innovative Methods* (Springer 2014); DE Hess, *Courting Democracy: Teaching about Constitutions, Cases, and Courts* (Routledge 2016); D Duda, 'Case Teaching in der politikwissenschaftlichen Lehre' (2017) 27 Journal of Political Science 259. See in general also CR Christensen and AJ Hansen, *Teaching and the Case Method* (Harvard Business School 1987).

1231 Golich, 'The ABCs of Case Teaching', 11–12, 14 (long lists of references).

original participants had to face.[1232] Cases can be based on newspaper articles, films, literature, etc.[1233] For active EU learning, I propose to base case teaching on well-chosen examples of ECJ case law, as the basis for telling an 'it really happened story' appealing to pupils, awakening their interest in the EU dimension in concrete situations. Depending on the educational level of pupils, the stories (Eurostories) can be told in accurate detail or in a simplified version to highlight the problem and the underlying (competing) principles.

Introduced by Langdell as the core of legal education[1234], the case method based on court cases is used by numerous law schools. At European universities and abroad, learning EU law is largely based on ECJ case law. At secondary school level, case-law-based teaching is less widespread, yet several models exist: it is used in several best practices in citizenship education in Member States[1235], in human rights education with cases of the ECtHR (for learning about the ECHR)[1236] and in US secondary schools with Supreme Court cases (for learning about the US constitu-

1232 Ibid, 12.

1233 For the importance and examples of stories based on literature, see Coles, *The Call of Stories: Teaching and the Moral Imagination*.

1234 Telman, 'Langdellian limericks (case teaching method)', 110–1.

1235 Human Rights Education in the School Systems of Europe, Central Asia and North America: A Compendium of Good Practice (CoE, OSCE/ODIHR, UNESCO, OHCHR, 2009), i.a. 54–5, 106–8, 119, 127, 133, 143. See also Oberreuter, 'Rechtserziehung' 333; Massing, 'Institutionenkundliches Lernen' 317–323 (learning about institutions should not be limited to formal and abstract rules; the author describes four didactical principles and applies them to learning about the German *Bundesverfassungsgericht* and its case law: *Erfahrungsorienterung, Problemorienterung, Binnenorienterung* (including play-acting) and *Handlungsorienterung;* in dimensions of polity (institution), politics (processes) and policy (contents)); Naylor, 'Educating for citizenship with law-related education'.

1236 Attractive model in *Freedom(s) - Learning activities for secondary schools on the case law of the European Court of Human Rights* (edited by P Kirschschlaeger, G Peter, B Dumont and D Hayward, Council of Europe 2015), with Preface of Thorbjørn Jagland (these learning materials for HRE in schools were developed on the basis of cooperation between educational science and law (Glasgow Prof Jim Murdoch). See S Krüger, 'Learning Human Rights through Landmark Decisions of the European Court of Human Rights' (CoE Education Department, 2010). Also *Compass*, one of the most popular EDC/HRE materials provided by the CoE, working with stories, concrete experience, and taking inspiration in ECtHR cases: Compass - Manual on human rights education with young people (CoE, 2012). Further examples in new communication tool: <www.coe.int/en/web/impact-convention-human-rights/about>.

tion)[1237]. These models confirm that case teaching can be adapted to the needs of secondary schools, stimulating discussion, providing differing arguments, as well as tools for reasoning.[1238] A comparable method should be developed for EU learning.[1239]

177 The importance of controversy in the classroom for exercising democracy

Cases provide material for interesting debates in the classroom and developing competences for participation in democratic life. Learners are 'moved to question, prepared to reason, and called to act'.[1240] Diane Hess, an authoritative US scholar in the field of civic education, underlines the need to include controversy in the classroom to prepare pupils for democracy.[1241] Her reasoning is applicable to citizens in the EU. Like US

1237 JB Raskin, *We the Students: Supreme Court Cases for and about Students* (4th edn, Sage 2015); JB Raskin, M Ahranjani and AG Ferguson, *Youth Justice in America* (2 edn, Sage 2015). Prof Jamin Raskin founded the 'Marshall-Brennan Constitutional Literacy Project', 'designed to mobilize talented upper-level law students to teach courses on constitutional law and juvenile justice in public high schools'; headquartered in Washington College of Law (Washington, DC) and with chapters in some 20 law schools (<www.wcl.american.edu/impact/initiatives-programs/marshallbrennan/>). Can a comparable project be launched in the EU (an 'EU constitutional literacy project' or, more cautiously, an 'EU Treaties literacy project')? Similar practice of Prof Emily Buss in Chicago Law School; see further Supreme Court cases in <www.icivics.org/>; Hardy, Rackaway and Sonnier, 'In the Supreme Court Justices Shoes: Critical Thinking Through the Use of Hypothetical Case Law Analyses and Interactive Simulations' (teachers simulate Supreme Court decision making; this equips them for later case teaching in classrooms); Hess, *Controversy in the Classroom: The Democratic Power of Discussion* (with examples).

1238 N 1265.

1239 The 'Fonds Lenaerts-Grimonprez, voor een sterkere EU dimensie op school' founded at KU Leuven (Belgium) works with this aim, in cooperation with the University's Teachers training programmes <www.allea.org/allea-prize-used-set-fund-lenaerts-grimonprez-stronger-eu-dimension-school/>.

1240 Expression repeatedly cited at the Harvard Law School Bicentennial (October 2017).

1241 Hess, *Controversy in the Classroom: The Democratic Power of Discussion*: 'purposeful inclusion of controversial issues in the school curriculum, when done wisely and well, can communicate by example the essence of what makes communities democratic while simultaneously building the skills and dispositions that young people will need to live in and improve such communities'; controversial political issues are issues of public policy that spark significant disagreement among a group of people. See also Hess, *Courting Democracy: Teaching about Constitutions, Cases, and Courts*: 'Courting Democracy encourages social

Supreme Court cases, ECJ cases, too, have the potential to 'communicate by example the essence of what makes communities democratic while simultaneously building the skills and dispositions that young people will need to live in and improve such communities'.[1242] ECJ cases can be used to identify EU rights or principles about which there are varying degrees of debate or controversy, and to transparently examine them. They thus comply with the requirement of critical and pluralistic education established by the ECtHR, as well as the controversy principle of 'the Beutelsbacher consensus' (that which is a matter of controversy in science and politics must also be presented as controversial to students).[1243] Case study is a means of delving into deeper layers of the EU legal order, reaching into principles and values. Dworkin analyses 'hard cases' and points to the principles and background morality underlying the—often complex and technical—rules.[1244]

Stories based on ECJ case law are tools giving pupils a good grasp of EU fundamentals (*what do the foundational texts say?*) as well as space to reflect (*what do you think?*).[1245] Examples in ECJ case law which invite critical thinking are not hard to find. Law can be conceived as a constant set of

---

studies educators to teach civic and democratic education by harnessing the pedagogical possibilities of the controversy that permeates the legal sphere'.

1242 Preceding note.

1243 See n 587. Cf Müller, 'Politische Bildung (und Europa)', about a trend to criticise 'Educating for Europe' ('Erziehung zu Europa') because incompatible with (1) The prohibition on overwhelming students with ideas (a pupil must not be pressurised to adopt a desired opinion and prevented from making his own independent judgement) and (2) The controversy principle (that which is a matter of controversy must be presented as controversial): 'Education for Europe' conflicts with both principles. Further Schulz and others, *IEA International Civic and Citizenship Education Study 2016: Assessment Framework* (case teaching relates to elements in various content domains, see i.a. p 21 negotiation/resolution, i.e. the concept that peaceful resolution of differences is essential to community well-being and that negotiation is the best way to attempt to reach resolutions; engagement, i.e. the 'concept that citizens need to concern themselves with issues and information in their communities in order to participate effectively'; see p 27 empathy).

1244 R Dworkin, 'Hard Cases' (1975) 88 Harvard Law Review 1057 (author criticises positivist adjudication; resolution of hard cases should be based on arguments of principle, not of policy). See also Alexy, nn 1168 and 1229.

1245 In Raskin's case book on citizenship education *We, the Students* (n 1237), a recurring section under each case (or sets of cases) is: 'What do you **Think**?' See also Youth project 'Empowering through Storytelling'; and J Schuitema and others, 'Guiding classroom discussions for democratic citizenship education' (2017) 44 Educational Studies 377.

questions.[1246] Case teaching is constructed around questions, inciting pupils to think, to react, to analyse, to understand, to feel, to compare, to propose, to compromise, to evaluate.[1247] By way of example, in the following analysis of EU rights, some questions for discussion will be raised. Questions should preferably be such as to bring EU foundational values, objectives and principles to the fore. EU primary law does not have all the answers but provides the rules of play which must be known by those who are playing *and* those who are watching the game (active and less active citizens).

> Should playing at killing be allowed in Germany because it is allowed in the UK (*Omega Spielhallen*)? Can Mr Schmidberger rely on the motorway to Italy being open or should a pro-environment demonstration be allowed to take place? Should Ms Jippes have the right to vaccinate her beloved sheep and goats, and what about EU rules on common agricultural policy and the internal market? Can a boat sail freely up and down between Helsinki and Tallin, just under another flag and with workers being paid less (*Viking*)? Should solidarity work to the advantage of Swedish workers or Latvian workers (*Laval*)? What do freedom, equality, or justice mean in the specific situation? Must Belgian universities accept all French students who are rejected under the numerus clausus in France (*Bressol*)?[1248]

1246 See i.a. Minow, 'What the rule of law should mean in civics education: from the "Following Orders" defence to the classroom': 'The dilemma posed for the soldier who must learn both to obey orders and to resist illegal orders [leading to atrocities] offers a rich focal point for students in middle and high school settings.' Law must be questioned. Civic instruction should deepen students' abilities 'to bring their conscience to bear in many settings where obedience and conformity jeopardize adherence to law and morality'. See also B de Witte, 'Democratic Adjudication in Europe: How Can the European Court of Justice Be Responsive to the Citizens?' in M Dougan, NN Shuibhne and E Spaventa (eds), *Empowerment and Disempowerment of the European Citizen* (Hart 2012). It is interesting for the ECJ to hear the opinion of citizens if the Court is to serve their interests (Art 13(1) TEU), not only to read opinions of academic writers.

1247 For the types of questions to guide the course of discussion, see Golich, 'The ABCs of Case Teaching', 19–20.

1248 Case C-36/02 *Omega Spielhallen* ECLI:EU:C:2004:614; Case C-112/00 *Schmidberger* ECLI:EU:C:2003:333; Case C-189/01 *Jippes* ECLI:EU:C:2001:420; Case C-438/05 *Viking* ECLI:EU:C:2007:772; Case C-341/05 *Laval* ECLI:EU:C:2007:809; Case C-73/08 *Bressol, Chaverot and Others* ECLI:EU:C:2010:181. Some stories discussed further in Chapter eight.

In my experience, such (provocative) questions awaken the class and guarantee dialogue and debate.[1249] Stories and issues arising in them create an EU public sphere in the classroom and lay the foundations for deliberative democracy (just counting votes does not give true legitimacy to democratic decisions). They are the start of active EU citizenship.[1250] Case teaching is in keeping with the EU's constitutional culture, which 'is about taming raw sovereignty, and establishing a politics of compromise, civilised confrontation and mutual learning.'[1251]

178 *Multiperspectivity and coping with complexity*

The main strength of case teaching based on ECJ case law is its inherent multiperspectivity. A single story can be used to encourage pupils to look at the same problem from various angles: the opposing standpoints of the different parties, the submissions of Member States or EU institutions to the Court; the judgment of the ECJ. It is an application of structured academic controversy.[1252] This multiperspectivity inspires open-mindedness. Case teaching strengthens attitudes such as tolerance and respect, equality, appreciation of diversity, a sense of justice, mutual trust, responsibility, empathy and solidarity.[1253] Case teaching encourages a thoughtful

---

1249 Using green and red cards, e. g., pupils can indicate which party in court they would support, or which arguments they find compelling.

1250 In line with, i.a., Commission recommendations to engage with citizens on European issues and to encourage participation of citizens in EU policymaking. See Commission Recommendation (EU) 2018/234 of 14 February 2018 on enhancing the European nature and efficient conduct of the 2019 elections to the European Parliament [2018] OJ L45/40, recital 7; earlier Commission Communication 'The Commission's contribution to the period of reflection and beyond - Plan-D for Democracy, Dialogue and Debate' COM(2005) 494. On deliberative democracy, see i.a. Verhoeven, *The European Union in Search of a Democratic and Constitutional Theory*; L Huyse, *De democratie voorbij* (Van Halewijck 2014). On the concept of public sphere, see n 1743.

1251 JW Müller, 'A European Constitutional Patriotism? The Case Restated' (2008) 14 ELJ 542, 552.

1252 Structured Academic Controversy (SAC): learning in small groups by considering a controversial subject from several perspectives. See i.a. Hess, *Controversy in the Classroom: The Democratic Power of Discussion*, 86.

1253 Menkel-Meadow, 'Telling Stories in School: Using Case Studies and Stories to Teach Legal Ethics', 815: 'Stories and role enactments allow multiple levels of analysis to be explored at the same time and with the different points of view of those in role (the acting "lawyers" or "clients") and those outside of role who watch, analyze, criticize and contribute to the ethical dialogue which follows'; Grammes, 'Exemplarisches Lernen' 99. Historic cases also require multiperspectivity, see CoE Education for democracy, *Tackling today's challenges*

response to the tensions inherent in daily life, in politics, within the Member State, the EU and a globalised world. ECJ case study increases pupils' awareness of complexities in real life and teaches them ways of coping with complexity. Pupils realise that situations are not one-dimensional and that problems seldom have simple solutions. They learn to consider the positive and negative aspects of the options available and to balance rights, objectives and principles. In this way case teaching can deter and shield against populism expressed in one-liners.[1254] Moreover, studying cases helps to understand the rationale behind EU legal frameworks. Case teaching permits a differentiated approach, learning in flexible pathways, learner centred. This is in keeping with the conclusions of the Council and the Representatives of the Governments of the Member States, who emphasised that 'education systems must move away from the traditional "one -size -fits all" mentality'.[1255]

Case teaching thus assumes an important place in the pedagogical toolkit of EDC, a powerful teaching tool complementing other forms of teaching such as lecturing.[1256] What is essential is to trigger interest and debate, not necessarily to achieve a consensus in the classroom. Even though trying to reach a consensus is an interesting exercise in taking on the role of the legislator, diverse opinions must be respected.[1257] The flexibility of case teaching makes it possible to inform pupils step by step about the relevant norms (EU primary law), after having initially described the facts and the issues in the story and given pupils the opportunity of brainstorming ways of solving the problem. After class debate, the decision of the ECJ can be explained, at least in its essential lines (such as the rights or

---

together: Biased history teaching. See in this context the historic background for Case C-364/10 *Hungary v Slovakia* EU:C:2012:630.

1254 Golich, 'The ABCs of Case Teaching', 12, 14 ('Cases offer dramatic proof that realworld problems do not have simple, easily prescribed solutions. Working through cases gives students vital practice in confronting "messy" problems and formulating tools for analysis and resolution').

1255 Conclusions of the Council and of the Representatives of the Governments of the Member States, meeting within the Council, on Inclusion in Diversity to achieve a High Quality Education For All - Council Conclusions (17 February 2017) ('Equal opportunities for all are crucial, but not sufficient: there is a need to pursue "equity" in the aims, content, teaching methods and forms of learning being provided for by education and training systems to achieve a high quality education for all').

1256 Eichner, 'Fallanalysen im Sachunterricht als Möglichkeit des Demokratie-Lernens' 343–4.

1257 How far does freedom of expression extend? See also § 326 .

responsibilities and foundational EU values, objectives or principles at stake). Pupils are free to discuss the ECJ's ruling.[1258] Finally, they can reflect on what they have learned from the case, draw possible conclusions for their own lives, and thus reinforce experiential learning.[1259]

179 Guidelines for case teaching

There are many resources on case teaching as a general method.[1260] They may be useful tools for developing teaching based on ECJ case law. Case teaching must be provided in a climate of respect for fundamental rights *in* education, such as respect for freedom of expression, freedom of thought, equality and non-discrimination, the participation rights of the child, privacy rights, best interests of the child, human dignity. Rights in the learning environment also include respect for identity, integrity, and the evolving capacities of the child.[1261] Fundamental rights *in* education are often distinguished from the fundamental right *to* education and fundamental rights *through* education. Case teaching as a tool also reinforces the EU dimension of fundamental rights *through* education (HRE).[1262]

1258 In cases where pupils can grasp the decisive points of the judgment, they are free to disagree. In some cases, however, reservations must be expressed if the ECJ judgment cannot be explained in accurate legal terms in secondary schools. Pupils understand this. In my experience, they realise that cases are mostly an occasion to discuss and to experience the EU dimension at work.

1259 Last phase described by Kolb (renowned American educational theorist) in the process of experiential learning (concrete experience; reflection on that experience; formation of abstract concepts based on the reflection; application of the new abstract concepts): DA Kolb, *Experiential Learning: Experience as the Source of Learning and Development* (Prentice-Hall 1984). For didactic work methods, such as discussions (small groups or classroom), role playing, simulations, written work, or creative problem solving, see Telman, 'Langdellian limericks (case teaching method)', 112, 125; also broad palette of forms in Compass (n 255).

1260 I.a. Kolb (n 1259); Golich, 'The ABCs of Case Teaching'; 'procedural values' of Crick (n 588); T Huddleston, *Teaching about controversial issues: guidance for schools* (Citizenship Foundation 2003); BP Shapiro, *Hints for case teaching* (Harvard Business 2014).

1261 Rights relevant within education: UDHR Arts 1, 2; ICCPR Arts 18, 19, 27; CRC Arts 2, 3, 5, 12–16, 19, 28, 29. See UN ComRC 'General Comment No 1 (2001)- Article 29(1): The Aims of Education' Doc CRC/GC/2001/1, paras 6 and 8; UNESCO-UNICEF, A Human Rights-Based Approach to Education for All: A framework for the realization of children's right to education and rights within education (2007), vii, 35.

1262 Para 2 Charter on EDC/HRE.

The Council of Europe recommends 'safe spaces' for handling controversial subjects in the classroom.[1263] Using EU primary law as a basis, it is possible to develop safe spaces for an EU dimension of EDC while respecting rights in education. When political issues arise, teachers should not promote partisan political views.[1264] Safe spaces can be created by linking the issues being debated to the foundational EU texts. Generally accepted reasoning techniques or schemes, such as the rule of reason or the principle of proportionality, can be suggested as tools to frame discussions and to balance principles or values.[1265] But the open space must be protected.

1263 See T Huddleston and D Kerr, *Managing controversy: developing a strategy for handling controversy and teaching controversial issues in schools* (CoE 2017), 57 (a safe space is 'an environment in which practitioners and participants can have rich and meaningful discussions about controversial issues, and in which young people feel safe discussing those issues'; all views can be expressed, no questions are 'silly' or 'wrong'). See earlier CoE, Pilot project, Teaching controversial issues: developing effective training for teachers and school leaders (2014); and proposed action in CoE Secretary General, State of democracy, human rights and the rule of law—a security imperative for Europe. Report 2016, 104 (develop a 'safe spaces' project drawing up guidelines that allow teachers and pupils 'to address difficult and controversial issues relating to faith, culture and foreign affairs, while respecting each other's rights and upholding freedom of expression'). Such a project is applicable to EU matters to the extent that some EU matters are controversial (e.g. 'benefit tourism', refugee quotas, austerity measures) or are still considered to fall under 'foreign affairs'. Guidance for lively yet respectful discussions, see DE Hess, 'Discussions that drive democracy' (2011) 69 Educational Leadership 69, 70; also Hess, *Controversy in the Classroom: The Democratic Power of Discussion*; Hess and Avery, 'Discussion of Controversial Issues as a Form and Goal of Democratic Education'; A Heijltjes, T van Gog and F Paas, 'Improving students' critical thinking: Empirical support for explicit instructions combined with practice' (2014) 28 Applied Cognitive Psychology 518. Further Reinhardt, *Teaching Civics: A Manual for Secondary Education Teachers*; *Compass* with guideline for educators (n 1236): 'The young people you are working with must feel free to explore and discover, and to interact and share with each other. Be genuine, friendly, encouraging and humorous'. Also Manifesto on critical thinking education (KU Leuven, CRITINKEDU, 2019: to model, to induce, to declare and to surveil).

1264 Cf guidance on the teaching of controversial issues in many states, see i.a. Standard in UK (Education (Independent School Standards) (England) (Amendment) Regulations 2014 (come into force on 29th September 2014), above n 1180), para 5(c).

1265 Many free movement cases which offer occasions for 'balancing' in the classroom, are in fact based on the same reasoning scheme, highly accessible for teachers. Simply put: which right is the case about? which measure has limited this right? was there a good reason for this limiting mesure (a legitimate objec-

180 *Learning outcomes of case teaching*

The learning outcomes of the proposed case teaching method relate to the EU dimension of component (b) of EDC: equipping learners with knowledge, skills and understanding and developing their attitudes and behaviour.[1266] Critical thinking is connected with knowledge, skills and attitudes.[1267] Discussion paths towards the learning objectives can be proposed while still respecting educational freedom. Triggered by a telling example in a story, chosen to advance the (EU) essentials, learning develops in an inductive way from the concrete to the abstract.[1268] Teachers help pupils to identify foundational EU values, objectives and principles in concrete situations. Knowledge and understanding grow—bottom up—about what it means to be an EU citizen. Stories based on case law lead to representative 'islands' of EU knowledge, 'rooted' understanding.[1269] Evidence shows that case teaching leads to knowledge 'sticking' more effectively than information given top down about rules or institutions. In addition to explicit knowledge, tacit understanding is gained from the experience of the stories and is more likely to be applied in later life.[1270] From real cases, pupils learn to recognise the EU dimension in situations

---

tive)? was this measure a good way of achieving that objective (appropriate)? did it not do more than was necessary and was it not excessive (necessary and proportional)? The principle of proportionality can be understood on the basis of clear steps, e.g. in *Schecke* (§ 263). For case law on this principle, see Case C-413/99 *Baumbast* ECLI:EU:C:2002:493, paras 85–86, 91; Case C-200/02 *Zhu and Chen* ECLI:EU:C:2004:639, para 32; Joined Cases C-92/09 and C-93/09 *Schecke and Eifert* ECLI:EU:C:2010:662, para 74; Case C-165/14 *Rendón Marín* ECLI:EU:C:2016:675, para 45. See also Y Borgmann-Prebil, 'The Rule of Reason in European Citizenship' (2008) 14 ELJ 328.

1266 Charter on EDC/HRE, para 2; skills as explained in Competences for democratic culture: Living together as equals in culturally diverse democratic societies (CoE 2016), 13–14. See Council Recommendation of 22 May 2018 on key competences for lifelong learning, Annex: A European Reference Framework, i.a. concepts competence, key competence and learning to learn competence.

1267 Davies and Barnett, *The Palgrave handbook of critical thinking in higher education.*

1268 Preparation for case teaching means matching learning objectives with case facts and norms, see Golich, 'The ABCs of Case Teaching', 16; Grammes, 'Exemplarisches Lernen' 96, on 'Elementaria und Fundamentalia', key concepts, key problems, and learning to learn.

1269 Grammes, 95 ('Inselbildung', 'Einwurzelung des Wissens').

1270 Golich, 'The ABCs of Case Teaching', 15. See also D Gentner and LA Smith, 'Analogical Learning and Reasoning' in D Reisberg (ed), *The Oxford Handbook of Cognitive Psychology* (Oxford Handbooks Online, Oxford University Press 2013).

where they would never expect to find it: they learn which EU rights are involved, which limitations apply, and why. They learn on types of EU rules (what is a directive, a regulation) and have a greater awareness of the EU rights of others (responsibilities). They see EU institutions at work in practice and experience the interaction of EU and Member State levels of governance in concrete situations.

Case teaching sharpens several skills which empower pupils as future citizens: analysing complex problems; creative, nuanced and critical thinking; forming an independent opinion; communicating effectively; speaking clearly and persuasively; listening carefully to other arguments; interpreting; working collectively to solve problems; negotiating; evaluating solutions; summarising; compromising; building consensus and a sense of community.[1271] Case teaching based on ECJ case law combines EU learning with problem solving, an essential component of EDC standards.[1272] It corresponds to the Charter on EDC/HRE which states that member states should promote educational approaches and teaching methods which enable 'learners to acquire the knowledge and skills to promote social cohesion, value diversity and equality, appreciate differences ... and *settle disagreements and conflicts in a non-violent manner with respect for each other's rights*, as well as to combat all forms of discrimination and violence'.[1273] Problem-based learning and conflict resolution are a form of peace education.

Case teaching furthermore is in keeping with the 2018 Council Recommendation on key competences for lifelong learning, which states that:

> Skills for citizenship competence relate to the ability to engage effectively with others in common or public interest, including the sustain-

---

1271 Frequently mentioned skills. See in the same vein, i.a. CoE Recommendation Rec(2002)12 of the Committee of Ministers to member states on education for democratic citizenship (16 October 2002), appendix, 2; Council Recommendation of 22 May 2018 on key competences for lifelong learning, Annex: A European Reference Framework, 6: Citizenship competence. Also RFCDC, ICCS, and scholars in §§ 38 71 73 .

1272 On the need to exercise problem solving skills see i.a. UN ComRC 'General Comment No 1 (2001)- Article 29(1): The Aims of Education' Doc CRC/GC/2001/1, (9) 'Basic skills include not only literacy and numeracy but also life skills such as the ability to make well-balanced decisions; to resolve conflicts in a non-violent manner'; Charter on EDC/HRE, para 13 ('settle disagreements and conflicts in a non-violent manner with respect for each others' rights').

1273 Para 13 (emphasis added). For differences between faith and ethnic groups in particular, see e.g. text to n 1946.

> able development of society. This involves critical thinking and integrated problem solving skills, as well as skills to develop arguments and constructive participation in community activities, as well as in decision-making at all levels, from local and national to the European and international level.[1274]

Case teaching on the EU dimension of EDC can be seen as good practice consistent with a competence-oriented approach. It allows for cross-discipline learning and underlines the connectivity between different subjects. It develops knowledge, skills and positive attitudes in several key competences.[1275]

Beyond and interlinked with the cognitive dimension, case teaching reaches the affective and behavioural dimensions of citizenship and citizenship education.[1276] Stories trigger feelings, which are an essential part of citizenship.[1277] As Shaw wrote on social citizenship, 'the affective dimension of the European project is critical to the Union'.[1278]

1274 Council Recommendation of 22 May 2018 on key competences for lifelong learning, Annex: A European Reference Framework, 6: Citizenship competence.

1275 Council Recommendation of 22 May 2018 on key competences for lifelong learning [2018] OJ C189/1, Annex: A European Reference Framework, 'Supporting the development of key competences', a.(a). See below Stories for case teaching, strengthening digital, social and citizenship key competences through cases on EU equality rights, privacy rights, rights in the digital single market, etc.

1276 See i.a. text to n 551 ff. See also in Germany the Resolution of the Standing Conference of the Ministers of Education and Cultural Affairs of 4 December 1980 in the version of 14 December 2000, Recommendation of the Standing Conference of the Ministers of Education and Cultural Affairs on the promotion of human rights in schools: human rights education cannot be limited to the transmission of knowledge; it must include emotional and behavioural components.

1277 See i.a. n 1215, 1216, Nussbaum (n 579).

1278 Shaw, 'The many pasts and futures of citizenship in the European Union', 555, 557 (on 'social citizenship'). On the interaction of cognition and emotion, see text to n 1450.

181 Experiential learning about values and EU citizenship

Cases lead to imaginative experiencing of the EU within the classroom.[1279] Cases and stories give contextual knowledge.[1280] The extra-legal conditions for a functioning democracy include the cognitive and ethical capacities of citizens.[1281] Democracy cannot be learned in books but has to be experienced in society. Cases bring society into the classroom. Pupils will sympathise with one party but must be encouraged to consider the opponent's situation (e.g. through role playing or simulations). Many citizenship educators agree that the 'most powerful way of learning is through participation and experience'.[1282] Case teaching is a bridge between formal education in schools and the experience of informal learning.[1283] Stories based on ECJ case law are a form of experiential learning, providing a path from the theory of EU primary law to practice, turning EU citizenship into 'a tangible reality'.[1284] Pupils recognise the relevance of the EU for their daily life. EU foundational values, objectives and principles do not remain vague, abstract academic truths, but acquire real significance and are often decisive in conflict resolution.

182 Active learning prepares for active citizenship

An important advantage of the case method is active learning. Cases make it possible to switch from a knowledge-based approach to a competence-based approach, and encourage teachers and pupils to take action.[1285] The stories of individuals who have stood up for their rights create a disposi-

---

1279 'Tell me, and I will forget. Show me, and I may remember. Involve me, and I will understand.' (Confucius); 'A child is not a vase to be filled, but a fire to be lit.' (Francois Rabelais, quoted in <changingthepresent.org>).

1280 Menkel-Meadow, 'Telling Stories in School: Using Case Studies and Stories to Teach Legal Ethics', 793: perhaps the strongest argument for the use of stories and real cases is the value placed on contextual knowledge and decision-making, preferably in 'thick descriptions'. Who did what, how, why, and what can be done?

1281 Peters, 'European democracy after the 2003 Convention', 77.

1282 CoE, *Learning to live together: Council of Europe Report on the state of citizenship and human rights education in Europe*, 29 (yet, a lot remains to be done).

1283 Applying the model used by Kolb (n 1259).

1284 Cf the priority set by European Council, The Stockholm Programme — An open and secure Europe serving and protecting citizens [2010] OJ C115/1: 'European citizenship must become a tangible reality.'.

1285 World Forum for Democracy 2016, Democracy & equality: does education matter? (Strasbourg, 7-9 November 2016), 4, Conclusions and recommendations.

tion for active citizenship.[1286] As a result of debate, simulation, or role playing, pupils feel more able to approach the relevant authorities in their later civic life. Beyond personal interest and the empowerment to exercise one's own rights, cases also provide an understanding of the societal choices which must be made in accordance with the Treaties and CFR and national constitutions. Learning based on cases prepares for participation in democratic processes. To be fully effective, case teaching based on ECJ case law requires teachers to explain that the case is more than a story about two parties (a precedent, with incorporation of judicial interpretation in the meaning and scope of the rule[1287]). Starting from apparently insignificant stories, case teaching may thus demonstrate the power of the active citizen and amplify the political interest of pupils and teachers.[1288] The (educated) citizen has the last word. As Lenaerts formulates it: *cogito ergo civis europaeus sum.*[1289] Independent and critical thinking are an essential part of being an EU citizen.

183 Choice of cases

There is no shortage of books on ECJ case law.[1290] Yet, appropriate cases for study in secondary schools will not necessarily be the classics of EU law

---

1286 See n 594, 595 (Crick report 'We aim at no less than...').

1287 Joined Cases C-581/10 and C-629/10 *Nelson and TUI Travel* ECLI:EU:C:2012:657, para 88.

1288 As asked by Co-creating European Union Citizenship: A Policy review (European Commission, 2013), 46: 'Professionals in the education sector should focus on amplifying the political interest of young people. Educational programmes in civic/citizenship education should be aimed primarily at enabling young people to acquire an interest in political and civic affairs; fostering their knowledge and understanding of political and civic matters; and supporting the development of the skills which they require to participate effectively in the political and civic life of their community and country.'.

1289 K Lenaerts, 'Cogito ergo civis europaeus sum: Discours à l'occasion de l'attribution du titre de docteur honoris causa de l'Université de Poitiers' (10 October 2016). For reflection with pupils.

1290 I.a. J Boulouis and R-M Chevallier, *Grands arrêts de la Cour de justice des Communautés européennes* (6 edn, Dalloz 1994); *Het recht van de Europese Unie in 50 klassieke arresten* (Juridische Uitgevers 2010); D Chalmers, G Davies and G Monti, *European Union Law: cases and materials* (2 edn, Cambridge University Press 2011); Craig and de Búrca, *EU Law: Text, Cases, and Materials*; J Meeusen, *Recht van de Europese Unie: basisjurisprudentie* (3 edn, Intersentia 2015); MQM Karpenschif and CQC Nourissat, *Les grands arrêts de la jurisprudence de l'Union européenne* (PUF 2016); F Nicola and B Davies (eds), *EU Law Stories: Contextual and Critical Histories of European Jurisprudence* (Cambridge University Press 2017).

(*Van Gend en Loos*, *Costa v Enel*, and similar cases[1291]). To achieve the aims of EDC, cases should be chosen on a different basis.

Firstly, in the concern for objectivity, the selection of cases should be guided by EU primary law. In the general debate on case teaching in classrooms, academic writers point to the risks of non-neutral selection of cases.[1292] Admittedly, the choice of particular ECJ cases can influence pupils' opinions. Yet, the same concern exists when choosing literature for schools (and literature is not excluded from the curriculum just for that reason). Cases for the EU dimension of education based on the Treaties and CFR have to illustrate foundational values, objectives and principles, and provide content to EDC components (c-1–3), e.g. entrenched EU rights.[1293]

Next, cases should preferably satisfy all the criteria for relevance to the EU dimension of EDC (additional content to that of national EDC, significant, inviting critical thinking and affecting the large majority of citizens).[1294]

Furthermore, because subjective involvement is an important factor for successful EDC,[1295] it is best if cases relate to real life situations of pupils or to their field of interest. European dilemmas in concrete conflicts between

1291 M Poiares Maduro and L Azoulai (eds), *The Past and Future of EU Law: The Classics of EU Law Revisited on the 50th Anniversary of the Rome Treaty* (Hart 2010).

1292 Menkel-Meadow, 'Telling Stories in School: Using Case Studies and Stories to Teach Legal Ethics', 794, 796 ('the on-going debate about the validation of stories, with the question of who decides whether a story is true/accurate/representative? Is the story valid on its own terms for teaching or some other reason?... Who decides which stories we teach from?'); Reinhardt, *Teaching Civics: A Manual for Secondary Education Teachers* 119.

1293 Condorcet entrusted enlightened learned societies, formed freely and independently of the State, to exercise final authority on citizenship education: see Condorcet, *Rapport et project de décret relatifs à l'organisation générale de l'instruction publique, Présentation à l'Assemblée législative (20 et 21 avril 1792)* ('sociétés savantes librement formées').

1294 Criteria i-iv in text to nn 1053 ff.

1295 Beutelsbacher consensus, third principle: giving weight the personal interests of pupils (text to n 587); CoE, *Learning to live together: Council of Europe Report on the state of citizenship and human rights education in Europe*, 18 ('it is essential to demonstrate the relevance of democracy and human rights for everyday life').

citizens trigger interest, but conflicts between Member States, institutions, or even continents (EU versus US) also provoke lively debates.[1296]

Beyond their personal interest, young citizens also need to be made aware of the common good.[1297] Confronted with societal issues, pupils are quick to react: 'this is not fair'. These natural reactions can be used as a basis for further critical thinking, including on the EU dimension.

Finally, the chosen cases should be amenable to simplification while keeping the essentials intact.

The cases in the following analysis will not be analysed comprehensively, yet they serve to illustrate EU rights, foundational values, objectives and principles, often in challenging constellations. They are not intended for direct use in schools. I will explore to what extent they are appropriate for EDC. If appropriate, the legal analysis can be used to underpin stories in case teaching and provide a basis for developing didactic material for pupils and for teacher training.

Rather than using the names of the parties, cases can be given more appealing titles: the story about playing at killing, the student versus Facebook, the angry farmers, the so-called princess, the lady with four sheep and two goats, the Hungarian President and the statute, the five lorries stranded on the Brenner motorway, the tourist in Paris, the Spanish businessman versus Google, the Swedish catechist on the internet, Liselotte and her vineyard, Dieter and his diploma, and (of course) the story of the stewardess. They are good (and fun) examples for incorporating the EU dimension into EDC.[1298]

1296 E.g. their interest in EU/US confrontations in cases such as Case C-366/10 *Air Transport Association of America and Others* ECLI:EU:C:2011:864, or Case C-362/14 *Schrems* ECLI:EU:C:2015:650 (§ 265); EU/UN in Joined Cases C-402/05 P and C-415/05 P *Kadi* ECLI:EU:C:2008:461; or EU/major economic actors such as Microsoft in Case T-167/08 *Microsoft* ECLI:EU:T:2012:323 (abuse of a dominant position, refusal of the dominant undertaking to supply and authorise the use of interoperability information, and a periodic penalty payment of EUR 860 million).

1297 Reinhardt, 'The Beutelsbach Consensus', 12 (the third principle of the Beutelsbacher consensus, focus on students' interests, was an appropriate choice 40 years ago, seeking to avoid subordination, yet it should not lead to ruthless defence of own interests; it should be mitigated by consideration of the interests of others and notions of the common good). This certainly applies to the EU dimension of EDC.

1298 Corresponding to ECJ cases Case C-36/02 *Omega Spielhallen* ECLI:EU:C:2004:614; Case C-362/14 *Schrems* ECLI:EU:C:2015:650; Joined Cases C-92/09 and C-93/09 *Schecke and Eifert* ECLI:EU:C:2010:662; Case C-208/09 *Sayn-Wittgenstein* ECLI:EU:C:2010:806; Case C-189/01 *Jippes* ECLI:EU:C:2001:420; Case

SOLVIT cases, containing simpler problems than those in ECJ judgments, are also an interesting source of material.[1299] In addition to real cases, hypothetical cases (inspired by real cases) or fictional stories can be developed.[1300] In its EU citizenship reports, the Commission inserts small stories as examples of citizenship rights (e.g. 'Frederico, a young cook from Portugal decided to go to Sweden to look for a new job...'[1301]).

184 Challenges

Awareness of the limits of the case teaching method is important.[1302] In addition to the risk of tendentious choice of cases (answered above), there may be reticence because of the time and work involved. Compared to traditional lecturing, it demands greater intellectual and emotional energy from both pupils, who have to abandon their passive role, and teachers, who have to master the subject and direct class discussion on the basis of questions.[1303] Some authors raise the risk of too much teacher direction.[1304]

C-364/10 *Hungary v Slovakia* ECLI:EU:C:2012:630; Case C-112/00 *Schmidberger* ECLI:EU:C:2003:333; Case 186/87 *Cowan* ECLI:EU:C:1989:47; Joined Cases C-154/15 and C-307/15 *Gutiérrez Naranjo and Others* ECLI:EU:C:2016:980; Case C-101/01 *Lindqvist* ECLI:EU:C:2003:596; Case 44/79 *Liselotte Hauer* ECLI:EU:C:1979:290; Case C-19/92 *Dieter Kraus* ECLI:EU:C:1993:125; Case 43/75 *Defrenne II* ECLI:EU:C:1976:56 (some examples are developed below).

1299 Commission Recommendation of 17 September 2013 on the principles governing SOLVIT [2013] OJ L249/10; Commission Communication 'Compliance Package- Action plan on the Reinforcement of SOLVIT: Bringing the benefits of the Single Market to citizens and businesses' COM(2017) 255 final. See 'Problems solved' in <ec.europa.eu/solvit>. SOLVIT is 'a service provided by national administrations throughout the EU and the EEA. National SOLVIT centres take on board citizens' complaints and cooperate via an online database to help citizens solve their problems out of court and free of charge.' See also text to n 1904.

1300 As practised for HRE, see Compass - Manual on human rights education with young people (CoE, 2012). On the power of fictional stories, e.g. to educate for values, see Menkel-Meadow, 'Telling Stories in School: Using Case Studies and Stories to Teach Legal Ethics'; Cole (n 1233).

1301 Commission EU Citizenship Report 2013: EU citizens: your rights, your future COM(2013) 269, 7.

1302 See n 1230.

1303 Golich, 'The ABCs of Case Teaching' 13–14 (role of the teacher as an orchestra conductor).

1304 Pleading for more freedom in education, fewer pre-established learning outcomes and results, accepting uncertainty and unpredictability, see Biesta, *The Beautiful Risk of Education*. Further Hess, *Controversy in the Classroom: The*

Case teaching based on ECJ case law, in particular, is a challenging exercise. Teachers usually have no law degree, let alone a knowledge of EU law. Therefore, source materials should be developed to make their work possible (based on existing models in other fields, such as HRE[1305]). During their higher education and in continuing education, teachers should be taught about the fundamentals of the EU.[1306] Best practices can be developed, for instance allowing university students to assist teachers in case teaching in secondary schools and to write academic papers on these training sessions.[1307] The purpose, after all, is not to educate pupils as EU lawyers but as EU citizens. Osler and Zhu argue with regard to narratives in HRE that the advantages outweigh the challenges: they have a valuable part to play in teaching human rights and justice.[1308] This applies, by analogy, to narratives for teaching EU rights and justice. The challenges are considerable, but the reward is even greater. Given concerns about the gap between the EU and the citizen (and the warning of the Brexit vote), case teaching can help to move into a higher gear and prepare EU citizens for the EU dimension of a society based on democracy, fundamental rights and the rule of law—based, of course, on an understanding of foundational EU values, objectives and principles.

185 Conclusion

The proposed learning method for an EU dimension of EDC at school is based on two pillars: EU primary law (objectivity) and case teaching (critical thinking and pluralism). Using EU texts and stories corresponds to EDC standards and to the ECtHR requirement to convey education in an objective, critical and pluralistic manner, with no aim of indoctrination. It respects the Treaties and the CFR, as well as Member State constitutions. It contributes to achieving the compulsory educational aims defined in the International Covenant on Economic, Social and Cultural Rights, the

---

Democratic Power of Discussion, p 53 ff (discussion of the extent of free speech by students, also with case law of the US Supreme Court).

1305 See i.a. n 1236.

1306 As they are also prepared for courses on chemistry, mathematics or literature. Training with regard to some ECJ cases can be included.

1307 E.g. experience discussed with Prof Emily Buss in October 2017 at the University of Chicago Law School (winwin situation for all parties, credits for students). See also J Murdoch, 'Using self- and peer assessment at honours level: bridging the gap between law school and the workplace' (2015) 49 The Law Teacher 73.

1308 Osler and Zhu, 'Narratives in teaching and research for justice and human rights', 233.

Convention on the Rights of the Child, in particular the aim of preparing EU citizens for responsible life and effective participation in a free society. Cases give pupils the opportunity to observe, imitate and practice critical agency in classrooms.[1309] They are the beginnings of a European public sphere. Classrooms are an obvious first forum in which EU citizens can make their voices heard and discuss issues together.[1310] If 'the source of legitimacy is not the predetermined will of individuals, but rather the process of its formation, that is deliberation itself',[1311] then such deliberation should be practised in education. It will enhance the social legitimacy of the Union.

1309 Ten Dam and Volman, 'Critical thinking as a citizenship competence: Teaching strategies', 375 ('If education is to further the critical competence of students it must provide them with the opportunity at the level of the classroom and the school to "observe, imitate and practice" critical agency').

1310 Response to Smith, who points to the inadequate development of a 'European public sphere' and a lack of an obvious forum for discussion, see Smith, 'The European Citizens' Initiative: A New Institution for Empowering Europe's Citizens?', 278. See also Commission White Paper of 1 February 2006 on a European Communication Policy COM(2006) 35.

1311 Smith, 'The European Citizens' Initiative: A New Institution for Empowering Europe's Citizens?', 287. On deliberative democracy, also n 1250.

CHAPTER 6 The EU dimension based on classic EU citizenship rights

186 EU citizens as holders of citizenship rights attached to their status by Articles 20–24 TFEU

Given the stated aim of objective, critical and pluralistic EU learning, content for the EU dimension of EDC can first be found in the citizenship rights traditionally associated with EU citizenship, read together with EDC standards. In EU primary law, 'citizenship of the Union' refers both to the legal status of all nationals of Member States (Articles 9 TEU, 20 TFEU) and to 'the rights conferred by virtue of their status as citizens of the Union' ('rights attaching to the status of EU citizen').[1312]

Since the entry into force of the 1992 Maastricht Treaty, 'citizens of the Union shall enjoy the rights and be subject to the duties provided for in the Treaties'.[1313] The rights of citizens of the Union are listed in sub-paragraphs (a) to (d) of (now) Article 20(2) TFEU and further elucidated in Articles 21 to 24 TFEU (hereafter: the classic citizenship provisions). The provisions are drafted in the following style: every citizen of the Union shall have the right to... The bundle of rights attached to the status of citizenship of the Union consists of the right to move and reside freely within the territory of the Member States; the right to vote and to stand as a candidate in European Parliament and municipal elections in the Member State of residence on the same conditions as nationals; the right to enjoy, in the territory of a third country in which one's own Member State is not represented, diplomatic and consular protection by authorities of any Member State on the same conditions as its nationals; the right to petition the European Parliament, to apply to the European Ombudsman, and to communicate with EU institutions in a Treaty language. Strengthening the protection of the rights and interests of the nationals of the Member States

---

1312 Case C-34/09 *Ruiz Zambrano* ECLI:EU:C:2011:124, para 42. Before Case C-135/08 *Rottmann* ECLI:EU:C:2010:104, para 42.

1313 Art 20(1) TFEU. See also Art 9 TEU: 'In all its activities, the Union shall observe the principle of the equality of its citizens, who shall receive equal attention from its institutions, bodies, offices and agencies. Every national of a Member State shall be a citizen of the Union. Citizenship of the Union shall be additional to and not replace national citizenship.' Also text to n 1054.

was a fundamental objective of the introduction of citizenship of the Union by the Maastricht Treaty.[1314]

After the 1997 Amsterdam Treaty and the 2001 Nice Treaty confirmed the citizenship provisions, the 2007 Lisbon Treaty introduced the right to a citizens' initiative in Article 11(4) TEU, which has since then been generally listed among the classic citizenship rights. The CFR (possessing the same legal value as the Treaties) restates citizens' rights in Title V (Articles 39–46). The European Council sought to make the overriding importance of fundamental rights more visible to the Union's citizens through the CFR and wanted to include the fundamental rights that pertain only to EU citizens.[1315]

The result is that citizens' rights are truly entrenched in EU primary law ('constitutional' rights[1316]), set out in three different EU primary law sources (TEU, TFEU, and CFR), sometimes with slight differences in the text. The CFR does not alter the system of rights conferred by the Treaties: the CFR rights for which provision is made in the Treaties shall be exercised under the conditions and within the limits defined by those Treaties (Article 52(2) CFR).[1317]

1314 See i.a. preamble of Council Directive 93/109/EC of 6 December 1993 laying down detailed arrangements for the exercise of the right to vote and stand as a candidate in elections to the European Parliament for citizens of the Union residing in a Member State of which they are not nationals [1993] OJ L329/34, amended by Council Directive 2013/1/EU of 20 December 2012; and of Council Directive 94/80/EC of 19 December 1994 laying down detailed arrangements for the exercise of the right to vote and to stand as a candidate in municipal elections by citizens of the Union residing in a Member State of which they are not nationals [1994] OJ L368/38, amended by Council Directive 96/30/EC of 13 May 1996.

1315 Presidency Conclusions of the Cologne European Council of 3-4 June 1999, 150/99 REV 1, Annex IV, 43.

1316 See i.a. M Dougan, 'The Constitutional Dimension to the Case Law on Union Citizenship' (2006) 31 ELRev 613; E Spaventa, 'Seeing the wood despite the trees? On the scope of union citizenship and its constitutional effects' (2008) 45 CMLRev 13; J Shaw, 'The constitutional development of citizenship in the EU context: with or without the Treaty of Lisbon' in I Pernice, Tanchev, E (ed), *Ceci n'est pas une Constitution - Constitutionalisation without a Constitution?* (Nomos 2009); L Azoulai, 'Constitution économique et citoyenneté de l'Union européenne' (2011) 25 Revue internationale de droit économique 543; Olsen, 'The political constitution of the EU citizen rights regime'; H van Eijken, *European Citizenship and the Constitutionalisation of the European Union* (Europa Law 2015).

1317 See also Art 51(1) CFR and Explanations. The CFR is thus not a freestanding source of law for EU citizens.

The EU citizenship rights provide additional content for EDC components. Some Member State constitutions explicitly refer to the citizenship rights of EU citizens.[1318] The Croatian constitution, for instance, states that '[c]itizens of the Republic of Croatia shall be European Union citizens and shall enjoy the rights guaranteed by the European Union acquis communautaire', and reproduces all rights set out in Article 20 TFEU.[1319] Several constitutions specify how the right to vote in European Parliament elections is to be regulated in the Member State.[1320] Even if their national constitution adopt these EU citizenship rights, young citizens have to understand that the rights originate at EU level. When national law restates EU citizenship rights, these rights must be interpreted in conformity with EU law (criterion i).

Because the right to free movement is commonly seen as the central right of EU citizenship,[1321] its relevance for EDC will be analysed in some detail.

A *The right to move and to reside freely*

187 Cluster of sub-rights

Article 21(1) TFEU grants every citizen of the Union the right to move and reside freely within the territory of the Member States (Articles 20(2)(a), Article 45 CFR).[1322] This primary and individual right stands for a cluster of sub-rights which have become increasingly important since 1992. Article 21 TFEU entitles mobile citizens (i.e. citizens exercising their right to free movement) to oppose to restrictive Member State measures.[1323]

1318 E.g. on rights in municipal or European Parliament elections: constitution of Finland Section 14; France Art 88–3; Hungary Art XXIII; Latvia Art 101; Portugal Art 15(4).

1319 Croatian constitution Art 146.

1320 See i.a. Belgian constitutional provisions referring to the European Parliament: Arts 39ter, 46, 65, 117, 118, 168bis, 195.

1321 Central: see i.a. Commission Third Report on Citizenship of the Union COM(2001) 506, 13; F de Witte, R Bauböck and J Shaw (eds), *Freedom of movement under attack: Is it worth defending as the core of EU citizenship?* (EUI Working Paper RSCAS 2016/69, 2016). See also n 1614 and text.

1322 For the individual, the CFR provision does not add much to Articles 20/21 TFEU: see Spaventa, 'Article 45: Freedom of Movement and of Residence', 1176.

1323 Further Craig and de Búrca, *EU Law: Text, Cases, and Materials* 884 ff, with case law.

Throughout the various illustrations in the following analysis, it will be shown that the various sub-rights into which the free movement right can be divided supply additional (i) and significant (ii) content to national EDC. Some of them invite critical thinking (iii). Their relevance for the large majority of citizens, who are static (iv), will be argued in a separate section at the end.

The fact that Article 21(1) TFEU contains additional rights for citizens, providing specific EU content for EDC component (c-1), is underscored by its direct effect. In *Baumbast* and *Zhu and Chen*, the ECJ confirmed that the right to move and to reside in the territory of the Member States is granted directly to every citizen of the Union by a clear and precise provision of the Treaty.[1324] Independently of national law, EU citizens enjoy the right to free movement and can oppose to obstacles to this freedom created by the home or the host Member State. As nationals of a Member State, citizens can rely on Article 21 TFEU: the right to free movement is attached to their EU citizenship status. The person concerned is not required to be engaged in an economic activity. Since the Maastricht Treaty, the template is no longer the market citizen but the EU citizen (pre-Maastricht free movement rights concerned workers, self-employed persons, and service providers).[1325] Mr Baumbast and baby Zhu were both economically inactive EU citizens. EU citizenship results in a *Grundfreiheit ohne Markt* (a fundamental freedom unrelated to the market).[1326]

188 No discrimination on grounds of nationality

EU law protects the EU citizen against the actions of public authorities who restrict free movement rights linked to equal treatment rights (Arti-

1324 Case C-413/99 *Baumbast* ECLI:EU:C:2002:493, para 84; Case C-200/02 *Zhu and Chen* ECLI:EU:C:2004:639, para 26. See also Directive 2004/38 of the European Parliament and of the Council of 29 April 2004 on the right of citizens of the Union and their family members to move and reside freely within the territory of the Member States [2004] OJ L158/77, recital 11.

1325 Ex Arts 39 EC, 43 EC and 49 EC. After Maastricht: Case C-413/99 *Baumbast* ECLI:EU:C:2002:493, paras 81, 83.

1326 D Kochenov, 'The essence of EU citizenship emerging from the last ten years of academic debate: beyond the cherry blossoms and the moon?' (2013) 62 International and Comparative Law Quarterly 97, 108 (with references to scholars). See also F Wollenschläger, 'A New Fundamental Freedom beyond Market Integration: Union Citizenship and its Dynamics for Shifting the Economic Paradigm of European Integration' (2011) 17 ELJ 1; Kochenov, 'On Tiles and Pillars: EU Citizenship as a Federal Denominator' 35 ('"market citizenship" can only be a logical aberration').

cles 21 and 18 TFEU). Recognising the importance primary law attaches to the status of citizen of the Union, the ECJ has reiterated in settled case law, starting with *Grzelczyk* in 2001, the famous mantra that

> *the status of citizen of the Union is destined to be the fundamental status of nationals of the Member States*, enabling those among such nationals who find themselves in the same situation to receive, as regards the material scope of the [TFEU] Treaty, the same treatment in law irrespective of their nationality, subject to such exceptions as are provided for in that regard.[1327]

Article 18 TFEU provides that '[w]ithin the scope of application of the Treaties, and without prejudice to any special provisions contained therein, any discrimination on grounds of nationality shall be prohibited.' The reasoning of the ECJ is that the situation of EU citizens who exercise their right to free movement, conferred by Article 21 TFEU, falls within the material scope of application of the Treaties for the purposes of Article 18,[1328] and thus, as a matter of principle, they enjoy the right to equal treatment. In other words, 'Article 21 TFEU contains not only the right to move and reside freely in the territory of the Member States but also ... a prohibition of any discrimination on grounds of nationality'.[1329] The Treaty of Lisbon confirmed the jurisprudential link between EU citizenship and the right to equal treatment, as it brought Articles 18 and 19 together with Articles 20 and 21 in Part Two TFEU, entitled 'Non-discrim-

1327 Case C-184/99 *Grzelczyk* ECLI:EU:C:2001:458, para 31 (emphasis added); Case C-224/98 *D'Hoop* ECLI:EU:C:2002:432, para 28; Case C-413/99 *Baumbast* ECLI:EU:C:2002:493, para 82; Case C-148/02 *Garcia Avello* ECLI:EU:C:2003:539 para 22; Case C-200/02 *Zhu and Chen* ECLI:EU:C:2004:639, para 25; Case C-147/03 *Commission v Austria* ECLI:EU:C:2005:427, para 45; Case C-135/08 *Rottmann* ECLI:EU:C:2010:104, para 43; Case C-391/09 *Runevič-Vardyn and Wardyn* ECLI:EU:C:2011:291, para 60; Case C-34/09 *Ruiz Zambrano* ECLI:EU:C:2011:124, para 41; Case C-75/11 *Commission v Austria* ECLI:EU:C:2012:605, para 38; Joined Cases C-523/11 and C-585/11 *Prinz* ECLI:EU:C:2013:524, para 24; Case C-359/13 *Martens* ECLI:EU:C:2015:118, para 21; Case C-165/14 *Rendón Marín* ECLI:EU:C:2016:675, para 69; Case C-115/15 *NA* ECLI:EU:C:2016:487, para 75; Case C-621/18 *Wightman and Others* ECLI:EU:C:2018:999, para 64. See also recital 3 Directive 2004/38.

1328 Case C-224/98 *D'Hoop* ECLI:EU:C:2002:432, para 29; Case C-148/02 *Garcia Avello* ECLI:EU:C:2003:539, para 24; Case C-209/03 *Bidar* ECLI:EU:C:2005:169, para 33.

1329 Case C-391/09 *Runevič-Vardyn and Wardyn* ECLI:EU:C:2011:291, paras 60–62, 65.

ination and citizenship of the Union'.[1330] The effects of the link are considerable. Mobile citizens have the right not to be discriminated against on grounds of nationality, either directly or indirectly, in the host or in their home Member State.[1331]

189 No hinderance to free movement

EU law, moreover, protects the EU citizen against national measures which constitute a restriction on free movement whether they are discriminatory or not (Article 21 TFEU). It is settled case law that national legislation cannot place nationals at a disadvantage simply because they have exercised their freedom to move and to reside in another Member State.[1332] An EU citizen who has moved to another Member State and returns home cannot receive less favourable treatment than that which he would enjoy if he had not availed himself of the opportunities offered by the Treaty in relation to free movement.[1333] Neither the home nor the host Member State can place limitations on the free movement of EU citizens. The ECJ protects the citizenship right to free movement by checking whether restrictive national measures comply with EU law, including the general principle of proportionality.[1334] Settled case law says that limitations to the right to move and to reside freely, for instance for reasons of public policy, public security and public health, must be interpreted strictly, because they constitute a derogation from the fundamental principle of freedom of movement for persons (pointing to significant content for EDC (ii)). Their scope cannot be determined unilaterally by the Mem-

---

1330 J Shaw, 'The Treaty of Lisbon and Citizenship' [2008] The Federal Trust for education & research (June): the Lisbon Treaty could have incorporated the 'fundamental status' mantra of the ECJ, adding gravitas and weight to EU citizenship, but it did not. It did, however, confirm and strengthen citizenship rights.

1331 Case C-103/08 *Gottwald* ECLI:EU:C:2009:597, para 27 (indirect discrimination: all covert forms of discrimination which, by the application of other distinguishing criteria, lead to the same result, e.g. residence).

1332 Case C-353/06 *Grunkin and Paul* EU:C:2008:559, paras 21–28; Case C-208/09 *Sayn-Wittgenstein* ECLI:EU:C:2010:806, para 53; Case C-391/09 *Runevič-Vardyn and Wardyn* ECLI:EU:C:2011:291, para 68; Case C-359/13 *Martens* ECLI:EU:C:2015:118, para 25; Case C-300/15 *Kohll and Kohll-Schlesser* ECLI:EU:C:2016:361, paras 42–44. See also Case C-22/18 *TopFit and Biffi* ECLI:EU:C:2019:497, para 47 (amateur sport less attractive for mobile EU citizens).

1333 Case C-224/98 *D'Hoop* ECLI:EU:C:2002:432, para 30.

1334 Case C-413/99 *Baumbast* ECLI:EU:C:2002:493, paras 85–86, 91; Case C-200/02 *Zhu and Chen* ECLI:EU:C:2004:639, para 32; Case C-165/14 *Rendón Marín* ECLI:EU:C:2016:675, para 45.

ber States.[1335] Since the Lisbon Treaty included citizens' rights in the CFR, the limits and conditions which Member States place on these rights must comply with Article 52(1) CFR: they must be provided for by law, respect the essence of the right, be proportional, necessary and genuinely meet objectives of general interest recognised by the Union, or the need to protect the rights and freedoms of others. International law may also justify limitations to the right of free movement, as was accepted by the ECJ in the case of an EU citizen who was the President of Hungary. Slovakia had refused his entry into its territory.[1336] This case certainly does not affect the large majority of EU citizens (iv), but the story is an interesting way of explaining to pupils the basic right of EU citizens to move freely throughout the Union. It is, moreover, a case of conflict between two Member States, Hungary and Slovakia. It reinforces awareness that historic tensions are still felt today but are now embedded in EU cooperation.

Article 21 TFEU grants EU citizens *additional* rights (i) based on EU law with direct effect, allowing them to invoke these rights vis-à-vis the host or the home Member State. The free movement rights which EU citizenship adds to national citizenship provide content for the EU dimension of EDC. While the centrality of national citizenship remains,[1337] the cluster of sub-rights with regard to mobility, complement what national citizenship can offer. The law of Member State A cannot oblige Member State B to allow nationals of Member State A to enter the territory of Member State B, reside there freely and enjoy equal rights. EU citizenship rights on mobility are genuinely additional to national citizenship rights.

The citizenship right of EU citizens to unrestricted mobility and to equal treatment, protected by the ECJ and national courts, has found application in many—unexpected—fields of daily life, for instance relating to taxes, social benefits, surnames, languages, or education.[1338] Some of them would be of interest to pupils and are now being described further.

1335 Case C-50/06 *Commission v the Netherlands* EU:C:2007:325, para 42; Case C-165/14 *Rendón Marín* ECLI:EU:C:2016:675, para 58.

1336 Case C-364/10 *Hungary v Slovakia* EU:C:2012:630, para 51.

1337 Craig and de Búrca, *EU Law: Text, Cases, and Materials* 854. Cp Bauböck, 'The three levels of citizenship within the European Union', emphasising the multi-level perspective: EU citizenship is not a mere appendix with a few additional rights.

1338 Case law on strengthened rights of non-discrimination in Craig and de Búrca, *EU Law: Text, Cases, and Materials* 884, i.a. on social and tax benefits. For implications for workers, see i.a. Case C-138/02 *Collins* ECLI:EU:C:2004:172, para 63; Case C-258/04 *Ioannidis* ECLI:EU:C:2005:559, para 22.

On multiple occasions, Member States have had to adapt practices, interpret national legislation consistently with EU law, or adopt new legislation. This confirms that EU law on the right to free movement of citizens provides additional content for national EDC (i).

190 Surnames

The rules governing a person's surname are a matter falling within the competence of the Member States. However, the Member States must exercise that competence in compliance with EU law.[1339] Two cases illustrate how the mobility rights of EU citizens provide additional content to national citizenship.

An early case on surnames was *Konstantinides.*

> Konstantinidis is a Greek national residing and working in Germany as a self-employed person. He asks the *German authorities to* change the spelling of his name in Roman characters from 'Kons*tadi*nidis' to 'Kons*tanti*nidis', *which is closer to the correct Greek pronunciation. They refuse. In* December 1992 (even before the Maastricht Treaty entered into force), Advocate General Jacobs, in his Opinion, made the famous statement *'civis europaeus sum'*:
> 'a Community national who goes to another Member State as a worker or self-employed person ... is entitled not just to pursue his trade or profession and to enjoy the same living and working conditions as nationals of the host State; he is in addition entitled to assume that, wherever he goes to earn his living in the European Community, he will be treated in accordance with a common code of fundamental values, in particular those laid down in the European Convention on Human Rights. In other words, he is entitled to say "civis europeus sum" and to invoke that status in order to oppose any violation *of his fundamental rights'.*[1340]
> *The ECJ holds that the refusal of German authorities to change his name interferes with the freedom to exercise the right of establishment, as clients might confuse him with some other person.*[1341]

1339 Case C-148/02 *Garcia Avello* ECLI:EU:C:2003:539, para 25; Case C-353/06 *Grunkin and Paul* EU:C:2008:559, para 16; Case C-208/09 *Sayn-Wittgenstein* ECLI:EU:C:2010:806; Case C-391/09 *Runevič-Vardyn and Wardyn* ECLI:EU:C:2011:291, para 63. Further § 323 .

1340 Case C-168/91 *Konstantinidis* ECLI:EU:C:1993:115, Opinion of AG Jacobs, para 46.

1341 Ibid, paras 16–7.

While in Konstantinidis, an internal market freedom is applied (not citizenship rules), the quote in the Opinion remains popular, still cited by Advocates General and scholars.[1342]

After the Maastricht Treaty introduced citizenship rules, EU citizens have successfully opposed to national rules on surnames when these restrict their rights of free movement and equal treatment.

Mr Garcia Avello, a Spanish national residing in Belgium, is married to Ms Weber, a Belgian national. Their two children are born in Belgium and have dual Spanish and Belgian nationality. Under Belgian law, their surname is registered as 'Garcia Avello', the name of the father. The Spanish Embassy, however, registers the surname 'Garcia Weber', the name of the father and the mother, in accordance with Spanish law and tradition. As a result, the children have different names in Belgian and Spanish law. The parents request the Belgian administrative authorities to change the surname 'Garcia Avello' to 'Garcia Weber' (adopting the Spanish rule), which is refused. In a Belgian court, the children invoke Articles 18 and 21 TFEU as EU citizens. In a preliminary ruling, the ECJ finds that the Belgian refusal is an unjustified restriction of the principles of equal treatment and free movement of citizens. The discrepancy in surnames is liable to cause the children serious inconvenience, both professionally and privately. Difficulties may, for instance, arise if they seek to benefit in one Member State from the legal effects of diplomas or documents drawn up in the surname recognised in the other Member State of which they are also nationals.[1343] The parents should be able to choose Garcia Weber as the name of the children.

1342 '*civis europaeus sum*' (sometimes spelled '*civis europeus sum*') referred to, i.a., in Case C-380/05 *Centro Europa* 7 ECLI:EU:C:2008:59, 16; Case C-228/07 *Petersen* ECLI:EU:C:2008:494, Opinion of AG Ruiz-Jarabo Colomer, para 16; Case C-34/09 *Ruiz Zambrano* ECLI:EU:C:2011:124, Opinion of AG Sharpston, para 83; Case C-270/13 *Haralambidis* ECLI:EU:C:2014:2185, Opinion of AG Wahl, para 51. See also K Lenaerts, '"Civis Europaeus Sum": From the Cross-border Link to the Status of Citizen of the Union' in P Cardonnel, A Rosas and N Wahl (eds), *Constitutionalising The EU Judicial System—Essays in Honour of Pernilla Lindh* (Hart 2012); Lenaerts, 'Cogito ergo civis europaeus sum: Discours à l'occasion de l'attribution du titre de docteur honoris causa de l'Université de Poitiers'; V Trstenjak, 'Civis Europeus Sum: Union Citizenship and the Influence of the Court of Justice of the European Union' (2015) 23 European Review 71.

1343 Case C-148/02 *Garcia Avello* ECLI:EU:C:2003:539, para 36. Other cases on surnames of EU citizens: Case C-353/06 *Grunkin and Paul* EU:C:2008:559 (Ger-

Garcia Avello shows how the citizenship right to free movement supplies additional content to several EDC components (i). Crossing borders provides a nexus with EU law which is stronger than nationality as a connecting factor. The EU citizen can rely on citizenship rights in EU law to oppose to the Member State. EU citizenship limits the application of national rules on surnames and gives parents in crossborder situations the freedom to choose which national law should apply to the name of their child.[1344]

Through discussion about a true story like *Garcia Avello*, pupils will sense the importance of the underlying principles of free movement and equal treatment more effectively than when teachers instruct them in the rules top-down.[1345] The rights of EU citizens with regard to surnames, which are sub-rights of the overarching category of the right to move and reside freely, reflect the foundational values, objectives and principles of EU law (ii). The deeper rationale for these sub-rights is the objective of free

---

man law did allow the double-barrelled Danish surname); Case C-208/09 *Sayn-Wittgenstein* ECLI:EU:C:2010:806 (Austrian law did not permit the use of titles in surnames; justified restriction on grounds of public policy); Case C-391/09 *Runevič-Vardyn and Wardyn* ECLI:EU:C:2011:291 (Lithuanian legislation required names to comply with the spelling rules of the official national language); Case C-438/14 *Bogendorff von Wolffersdorff* ECLI:EU:C:2016:401 (Germany did not recognise the surname containing a nobility title acquired in the UK by a citizen with double German-British nationality; proportionality of public policy justification). See also overview in K Lenaerts, 'In the Name of EU Citizenship' in A Verbeke and others (eds), *Confronting the Frontiers of Family and Succession Law - Liber Amicorum Walter Pintens* (Intersentia 2012).

1344 Lenaerts, 'In the Name of EU Citizenship', 837. Belgium adapted its Civil Code in 2014 (making it possible to give a child the name of its father, mother, or both) in response to observations of the Commission (see Commission Report under Article 25 TFEU 'On progress towards effective EU citizenship 2013-2016' COM(2017) 32 final, 9).

1345 They should, of course, not be expected to understand ECJ rulings in overloaded sentences such as that in Case C-438/14 *Bogendorff von Wolffersdorff* ECLI:EU:C:2016:401, para 84 ('that Article 21 TFEU must be interpreted as meaning that the authorities of a Member State are not bound to recognise the name of a citizen of that Member State when he also holds the nationality of another Member State in which he has acquired that name which he has chosen freely and which contains a number of tokens of nobility, which are not accepted by the law of the first Member State, provided that it is established, which it is for the referring court to ascertain, that a refusal of recognition is, in that context, justified on public policy grounds, in that it is appropriate and necessary to ensure compliance with the principle that all citizens of that Member State are equal before the law.').

movement in an open area, implying that EU citizens should be able to move throughout the EU with the same surname. For EU citizens with dual nationality, a discrepancy in surnames which is liable to cause 'serious inconvenience', constitutes an obstacle to free movement. Justifications for restrictions to free movement are possible, but must be based on objective considerations and proportionate to the legitimate aim pursued, as illustrated by several surname cases.[1346] The objective of free movement is to be balanced with respect for Member States' constitutional identities and cultures.[1347] Here, in addition to the rights of citizens (EDC component c-1), the importance of valuing diversity comes to the fore (EDC component c-2).[1348] In *Sayn-Wittgenstein* the ECJ allowed Austria to prohibit the use of a title of nobility in the surname registered in Germany (Fürstin von Sayn-Wittgenstein) out of respect for the national constitutional identity of Austria (Article 4(2) TEU). An Austrian law with constitutional status had abolished nobility.[1349]

Admittedly, rights relating to the surnames of mobile citizens do not affect the large majority of EU citizens (iv). Yet, the cases on surnames are occasions for critical thinking about the system itself (iii).[1350]

191 Languages

Another example of the way the right to free movement provides specific additional content to national citizenship (c-1) concerns the use of languages in court.

> Ms Rüffer, a German national, has a skiing accident in Italy, which, she says, is caused by Ms Pokorná, a Czech national. She brings a claim for damages in an Italian court in Bolzano, using German. However, Italian law only grants the right to use the German language in civil

1346 Case C-148/02 *Garcia Avello* ECLI:EU:C:2003:539, para 36; Case C-353/06 *Grunkin and Paul* EU:C:2008:559, paras 23–9, Case C-208/09 *Sayn-Wittgenstein* ECLI:EU:C:2010:806, paras 67, 69, 70, 81; Case C-391/09 *Runevič-Vardyn and Wardyn* ECLI:EU:C:2011:291, paras 68, 76, 83.

1347 Case C-391/09 *Runevič-Vardyn and Wardyn* ECLI:EU:C:2011:291, paras 84–7. Earlier Case C-379/87 *Groener* ECLI:EU:C:1989:599, para 19.

1348 Further text to n 1880, about core values of the Union and respect for national identities. Also Lenaerts, 'In the Name of EU Citizenship', 841.

1349 Case C-208/09 *Sayn-Wittgenstein* ECLI:EU:C:2010:806. A fun story for pupils, yet not relevant to their daily life.

1350 Academic writers comment and question, see i.a. LFM Besselink, 'Case C-208/09 Ilonka Sayn-Wittgenstein v Landeshauptmann von Wien: respecting constitutional identity in the EU' (2012) 49 CMLRev 671; Kochenov, 'On Tiles and Pillars: EU Citizenship as a Federal Denominator', 40.

proceedings to Italian citizens domiciled in Bolzano. The ECJ rules that Articles 18 and 21 TFEU must be interpreted as precluding such a national rule.[1351]

In criminal as well as in civil proceedings, an EU citizen who is a national of another Member State is entitled to rely on language rules on the same basis as nationals of the host State (additional content for component c-1).[1352] It is an expression of valuing diversity (component c-2). Again, this citizenship right may not appear crucial to the large majority of citizens, who neither ski, nor are likely to be involved in this type of court case (iv) However, it is important for all citizens to know that whenever they travel in the EU, for work or leisure, they have, in principle, the same rights as those enjoyed by the nationals of the host Member State (i, ii).

192 The Citizens' Rights Directive

Citizens' right to move and to reside is subject to the limitations and conditions laid down in the Treaties and by the measures adopted to give them effect (Articles 21(1) TFEU, Article 52(2) CFR). To give them effect, the European Parliament and the Council adopted Directive 2004/38 (hereafter the Citizens' Rights Directive).[1353] Because 'Union citizenship should be the fundamental status of nationals of the Member States when they exercise their right of free movement and residence', the Directive brought together the rights previously existing under separate instruments.[1354] The Directive applies to EU citizens who move to a host Member State and lawfully reside there on the basis of the Directive, and to

1351 Case C-322/13 *Rüffer v Pokorná* ECLI:EU:C:2014:189. On language rights as EU citizens, also Art 24 TFEU (§ 206).

1352 Case C-274/96 *Bickel and Franz* ECLI:EU:C:1998:563, illustrating the same link Art 21–18 TFEU.

1353 Directive 2004/38 of the European Parliament and of the Council of 29 April 2004 on the right of citizens of the Union and their family members to move and reside freely within the territory of the Member States [2004] OJ L158/77; E Guild and S Peers, *The EU Citizenship Directive: A Commentary* (Oxford University Press 2014).

1354 Recitals 3 and 4: repealing Council Dir 68/360/EEC of 15 October 1968 on the abolition of restrictions on movement and residence within the Community for workers of Member States and their families, Council Dir 73/148/EEC of 21 May 1973 on the abolition of restrictions on movement and residence within the Community for nationals of Member States with regard to establishment and the provision of services, Council Dir 90/364/EEC of 28 June 1990 on the right of residence, Council Dir 90/365/EEC of 28 June 1990 on the right of residence for employees and self-employed persons who have ceased

their family members.[1355] The Directive grants residence rights to mobile citizens subject to varying time limits.

Ideally, pupils should hear about this central secondary law instrument in mainstream education, at least in advanced levels of EDC (possibly starting with a story). It allows them to learn about the concepts of EU citizenship, citizenship rights, EU legislation, directives, and, essentially, the principle of conferral.[1356] A basic understanding of the Directive prepares pupils for nuanced thinking and informed participation in the democratic life of the Union, as will be illustrated in the sensitive fields of social benefits and rules applying to third country nationals. The Directive is an interesting example for pupils of the way EU law aims to strike a proper balance between EU and Member State interests. The purpose of the Directive is to reinforce the right of free movement and residence of all EU citizens, while allowing Member States to impose certain conditions and limits.[1357] EU citizens' rights to move and reside freely should not become an unreasonable burden on the host Member States.[1358] Therefore, the right of residence extending for more than three months is subject to conditions, such as having sufficient resources and comprehensive sickness insurance cover.[1359] For a period of less than three months, citizens can move freely and reside merely on the basis of holding a valid identity card or passport.[1360] EU citizens who have resided legally for a continuous period of five years in the host Member State have an unconditional right of permanent residence.[1361] As stated in the preamble of the Directive, the European Parliament and the Council aim to strengthen the feeling of EU citizenship and to promote social cohesion as a fundamental EU objective.[1362] Member States can impose limitations on the right of residence of EU citi-

their occupational activity and Council Dir 93/96/EEC of 29 October 1993 on the right of residence for students.

1355 Art 3 on beneficiaries.

1356 Directive 2004/38 is a legislative act, adopted in accordance with the ordinary legislative procedure (majority in the European Parliament and qualified majority in the Council), on the legal bases of ex Arts 12, 18, 40, 44 and 52 TEC (now Arts 18, 21, 46, 50, 59 TFEU).

1357 Recitals 4, 10, 30. See also Case C-434/09 *McCarthy* ECLI:EU:C:2011:277, para 28; Case C-127/08 *Metock* ECLI:EU:C:2008:449, paras 59, 82.

1358 See recitals 10, 16 and 'burden' appearing in Arts 7(1)(b)(c), Art 12(2), Art 13(2) and Art 14(1) of Directive 2004/38.

1359 Art 7(1)(b)(c). No such condition for workers or self-employed persons (a).

1360 Art 5 (right of entry), Art 6 (right of residence for up to three months).

1361 Art 16 Directive 2004/38, without the conditions of chapter III of the Dir.

1362 Recitals 17–8.

zens on grounds of public policy, public security or public health, but not for economic reasons.[1363]

Citizenship rights based on the Directive provide additional (i) and significant (ii) content to the EDC components. They empower citizens to exercise rights and responsibilities in society (c-1). A counterargument could be that national law anyway incorporates the essential EU norms of the Directive, since directives are binding as to the results to be achieved (Article 288 TFEU). This counterargument can be used against introducing an EU dimension based on the content of any directive. True, the boundaries between citizenship rights based on national law and those conferred by EU law are blurred when Member States implement EU directives and EU norms become national law. The Citizens' Rights Directive was indeed addressed to the Member States, obliging them to transpose it into national law within a period of two years.[1364] Through implementation, the rights which EU law confers on EU citizens (Article 21 TFEU and the Citizens' Rights Directive read together)—partially—take the form of national rights.[1365] However, this does not mean that the Directive is irrelevant to national EDC. EU primary and secondary law constitute an autonomous legal order. Accordingly, an autonomous EU dimension must be added to national EDC. EU law on free movement of citizens—Treaty law and the Directive—supplies additional and significant content of which empowered EU citizens need to be aware, and this is for several reasons.

Firstly, the EU origin of national legislation should be made clear because of the principle of consistent interpretation. National law implementing EU law must be interpreted in the light of the EU legislation from which it stems.[1366] National law interpreted in the light of a directive can thus produce additional rights relevant for EDC.[1367] Secondly, if directives are not correctly implemented, their provisions may apply directly,

---

1363 Art 27(1) Directive 2004/38. See on strict interpretation of derogations and no unilateral determination by Member States, i.a. Case C-165/14 *Rendón Marín* ECLI:EU:C:2016:675, paras 57–8, 67.

1364 Art 40 Directive 2004/38.

1365 The Member States communicated to the Commission the text of national provisions according to the provisions of the Directive. Implementation was partially imperfect. See n 1371.

1366 N 1823; Lenaerts and Gutiérrez-Fons, 'To Say What the Law of the EU Is: Methods of Interpretation and the European Court of Justice'.

1367 See i.a. n 1823; also *Folk* (§ 272).

under certain conditions.[1368] Informed citizens can be important protagonists in such situations.[1369] Of course, it would be stretching the point to suggest that this is therefore material for school education. Yet, the message of the autonomy of EU law, conferring rights and responsibilities on citizens independently of national law, must somehow be transmitted to pupils in component (c-1) of EDC in mainstream education. A third reason why pupils should be made aware of the Directive is that citizens need a basic understanding of its objectives and nuances in order to participate in an informed way in public debate (no, we do not have to pay for the subsistence and sickness insurance of all foreigners[1370]). In an EU based on the rule of law and democracy, the fundamental objectives of EU secondary law should not remain unknown to EU citizens, diluted or lost in 27 versions of national law implementing the Directive to a lesser or greater degree.[1371] The centralised legal framework supporting EU citizenship diverges from decentralised national practices.[1372] As participants in democratic processes relating to citizenship rights, both at national and EU level, citizens must be informed about their rights, the underlying rationale and the balancing of interests. Awareness of common objectives is crucial to the EU as a purpose driven polity (Article 1 and 3 TEU).

In a combined reading of EDC standards, EU primary law and the Citizens' Rights Directive, some specific citizenship rights falling within the cluster of sub-rights of free movement will now be examined more closely: students' rights, because of their special interest for pupils (potential future mobile students), rights to social benefits, and rights for third country

1368 N 1823.

1369 See below Stories for case teaching.

1370 Analysis in text to nn 1414, 1438 ff.

1371 Numerous infringement procedures of the Commission after expiry of the deadline: Craig and de Búrca, *EU Law: Text, Cases, and Materials* 859. On problematic implementation, see also Commission Report under Article 25 TFEU 'On progress towards effective EU Citizenship 2011-2013' COM(2013) 270 final, 4–5; U Neergaard, C Jacqueson and N Holst-Christensen (eds), *Union Citizenship: Development, Impact and Challenges - The XXVI FIDE Congress in Copenhagen, 2014 Congress Publications Vol 2* (DJØF 2014), i.a. 172, 196. Ongoing problems in implementation, see Commission Report under Article 25 TFEU 'On progress towards effective EU citizenship 2013-2016' COM(2017) 32 final, 8–9 (main issues concern third country nationals who are family members, and the expulsion of EU citizens).

1372 N Nic Shuibhne, 'The Developing Legal Dimensions of Union Citizenship' in D Chalmers and A Arnull (eds), *The Oxford Handbook of European Union Law* (Oxford University Press 2015) 484–485. See citizenship reports under Art 25 TFEU (n 1614), i.a. complaints of citizens.

nationals, because they relate to sensitive areas (themes in elections, c-2–3) and to the responsibilities of EU citizens (c-1). Their relevance for EDC will be argued.

193 Students

Discussing the rights which mobile students derive from EU citizenship is an appropriate topic for an EU dimension of EDC. It is an exercise in nuanced thinking, as not all these rights are simple and straightforward, and it certainly invites critical thinking (iii) (many cases even lead to heated debate). Moreover, this topic complies with the EDC guideline on subjectively involving pupils: students' rights affect their daily lives.

Students enjoy rights pursuant to several Treaty provisions: as workers or children of workers (Article 45 TFEU), as recipients of services (Article 56 TFEU), or just in their capacity as EU citizens (Article 21 TFEU), or they can profit from the principle of non-discrimination on grounds of nationality (Article 18 TFEU). Here I will focus on the last two categories. Students who are EU citizens have 'the right, enshrined in Articles 18 and 21 TFEU, to move and reside freely within the territory of a Member State, ... without being subject to direct or indirect discrimination on grounds of their nationality'.[1373] The right of students to be treated equally to the nationals of the host Member State has been applied in various contexts and needs a balanced approach. Equal access to higher education, equal enrolment fees, equal qualification requirements, and equal financial support, are the subject of extensive case law based on EU primary and secondary law (the Citizens' Rights Directive).

Firstly, students have—in principle—the right of equal access to higher education, based on the principle of non-discrimination on grounds of nationality in Article 18 TFEU.[1374] This first right enjoyed by mobile students—equal access—satisfies criteria (i), (ii) and (iii) of relevance for mainstream education, and criterion (iv) to a lesser extent, as it concerns mobile citizens.

Originally, the ECJ ruled that the situation of students comes within the scope of Article 18 TFEU by invoking Union competence with regard to

1373 Case C-73/08 *Bressol, Chaverot and Others* ECLI:EU:C:2010:181, para 33; Case C-75/11 *Commission v Austria* ECLI:EU:C:2012:605, para 41; Case C-233/14 *Commission v the Netherlands* ECLI:EU:C:2016:50, para 78.

1374 Exceptionally, restrictions can be justified (n 1385).

vocational training (*Gravier*).[1375] Today, the situation of mobile students is brought within the scope of the Treaty for the purposes of Article 18 via Article 21 TFEU (*Bressol*).[1376] Whether triggered by the application of the Treaty provisions on Union competence in education or on EU citizenship, once the situation of a student falls within the scope of the Treaties, the application of the Treaty principle of non-discrimination on grounds of nationality leads to the same outcome. An appealing story for case-teaching is *Gravier*.

> Ms Françoise Gravier is a French national who wants to study strip cartoon art at the *Académie royale des Beaux-Arts* in Liège. The *Académie* requires her to pay an enrolment fee (a minerval) which it does not require from Belgian students. Françoise claims that she is being discriminated on grounds of nationality. In a preliminary ruling, the ECJ qualifies the courses in strip cartoon art as vocational training, defined broadly, which brings the situation within the scope of the Treaties (as the Union has competence with regard to vocational training).[1377] The ECJ considers that the charging of the fee constitutes discrimination on grounds of nationality. Belgium cannot impose, as a condition of access, an entrance fee which it does not require from its own nationals.[1378]

The *Gravier* case of 1985 has been cited ever since.[1379] The action of one student, an active citizen defending her rights in court, had wide-ranging consequences: Member States adapted their policies, universities changed

1375 See reference to ex Art 128 EEC, ex Art 149–150 EC (now Arts 165–6 TFEU) in Case 293/83 *Gravier* ECLI:EU:C:1985:69, para 30 (broad interpretation of vocational training), see also para 23, Case C-65/03 *Commission v Belgium* ECLI:EU:C:2004:402, para 25; Case C-147/03 *Commission v Austria* ECLI:EU:C:2005:427, paras 32–4. In *Bressol*, the ECJ only makes this link in second instance (para 32).

1376 Case C-73/08 *Bressol, Chaverot and Others* ECLI:EU:C:2010:181, paras 30–32; also Case C-224/98 *D'Hoop* ECLI:EU:C:2002:432, para 29.

1377 Case 293/83 *Gravier* ECLI:EU:C:1985:69, paras 25, 30–1, ex Art 128 EEC. See previously Case 152/82 *Forcheri* ECLI:EU:C:1983:205: in certain circumstances, making access to vocational training for nationals of other Member States subject to payment of a registration fee which is not required of home students, may fall within the scope of the Treaty.

1378 Paras 14, 15, 26.

1379 See with regard to competences, Part four, text to n 2087.

their practices, and at EU level, work on student mobility programmes was pursued with conviction (such as the *Erasmus* programme).[1380]

Since *Gravier*, students have a right to equal treatment with regard to the conditions of access to vocational training. Mobile students have the right to the same enrolment fees as those paid by nationals of the host Member State,[1381] and can only be required to meet the same qualification requirements for access. In *Commission v Belgium* and *Commission v Austria,* the ECJ held that Member States cannot impose additional conditions of access for nationals of other Member States.

> Belgium and Austria adopt a liberal higher education system, giving students an easy access. They are confronted with a large influx of respectively French and German students who are trying to escape the restrictions on access to higher education in their home Member State (the advantage for these students is that their mother tongue is the same as that of the home and host MS). To limit the flood, Belgium and Austria impose additional qualification requirements for access on non-nationals. The Commission brings the matter before the ECJ. In both cases, *Commission v Belgium* and *Commission v Austria*, the Court makes a finding of indirect discrimination: the extra requirements place the nationals of other Member States at a disadvantage.[1382] The ECJ considers that the very essence of 'the principle of freedom of movement for students guaranteed by the Treaty' is the possibility for EU students who have obtained their secondary education diploma in one Member State to have access to higher or university education in

1380 HM Gilliams, 'Van "Gravier" tot "Erasmus": over de bijdrage van het Hof van Justitie tot de uitbouw van een Europees onderwijsbeleid' [1989-90] Rechtskundig weekblad 494; J Shaw, 'Education and the Law in the European Community' (1992) 21 Journal of Law & Education 415, 431; J Shaw, 'From the Margins to the Centre: Education and Training Law and Policy' in P Craig and G de Búrca (eds), *The evolution of EU law* (Oxford University Press 1999), 564; A Corbett, *Universities and the Europe of Knowledge: Ideas, Institutions and Policy Entrepreneurship in European Union Higher Education Policy* (Palgrave Macmillan 2005).

1381 Case 293/83 *Gravier* ECLI:EU:C:1985:69, para 25 (about a minerval); Case 24/86 *Blaizot* ECLI:EU:C:1988:43, paras 15–21 (about supplementary enrolment fees at universities); Case 263/86 *Humbel* ECLI:EU:C:1988:451, paras 8–20 (about access fees for secondary education); Case 42/87 *Commission v Belgium* ECLI:EU:C:1988:454, para 7 (about State finance for students at higher education establishments not of university level).

1382 Case C-147/03 *Commission v Austria* ECLI:EU:C:2005:427, paras 42–47; Case C-65/03 *Commission v Belgium* ECLI:EU:C:2004:402, para 29.

> another Member State under the same conditions as holders of diplomas awarded in that Member State.[1383]

These cases, which like *Gravier* have been criticised for going too far, lead to interesting debates with pupils. *Can a Member State with a liberal higher education system limit the influx of mobile students who have not been accepted in their own Member State (not selected because of a numerus clausus)? What about the argument that neither mobile students nor their parents have paid taxes to finance the education system in the host Member State?* Academic writers argue that selective application of the principle of free movement would put the EU at risk. Member States must accept both the positive and the negative implications of free movement. *Must Member States take 'the bitter with the sweet' in free movement law?*[1384]

In *Bressol*, continuing the education saga, the ECJ holds that the right to equal access to higher education cannot be restricted by a numerus clausus applying only to non-resident students, unless justified on the basis of specific evidence.[1385]

> Because of the continuing influx of French students, a decree of the French Community in Belgium establishes a *numerus clausus* to limit the access to nine medical and paramedical university programmes by non-resident students.[1386] Nicolas Bressol, Céline Chaverot, and other French students, bring an action for the annulment of the decree in the Belgian Constitutional Court, which sends preliminary questions to the ECJ. The ECJ acknowledges that Member States have the power

---

1383 Case C-147/03 *Commission v Austria* ECLI:EU:C:2005:427, para 70 (it therefore is not abuse of right); repeated in Case C-73/08 *Bressol, Chaverot and Others* ECLI:EU:C:2010:181, para 79.

1384 K Lenaerts, 'Federalism and the Rule of Law: Perspectives from the European Court of Justice' (2011) 33 Fordham International Law Journal 1338, 1343, 1349.

1385 Case C-73/08 *Bressol, Chaverot and Others* ECLI:EU:C:2010:181. See on the saga, S Garben, 'Case C-73/08, Nicolas Bressol and Others, Céline Chaverot and Others v. Gouvernement de la Communaute française, Judgment of the Court (Grand Chamber) of 13 April 2010' (2010) 47 CMLRev 1493; AP van der Mei, 'Movement of Students and the Protection of National Educational Interests: Reflections on Bressol and Chaverot' (2011) 13 European Journal of Migration and Law 123.

1386 For non-resident students, new enrolments were restricted to a maximum of 30% of enrolments in the preceding academic year (for each university institution and for each course). Beyond this percentage lots were drawn (see para 43).

to organise their education systems (Articles 165(1) and 166(1) TFEU), but the fact remains that, when exercising that power, Member States must comply with EU law, in particular the provisions on the freedom to move and reside within Member State territory.[1387] As the students are EU citizens exercising their freedom to move and reside, they fall within the scope of the Treaties and thus of the principle of non-discrimination on grounds of nationality (Article 18 TFEU). The decree, providing for unrestricted access for resident students and for limited access for non-resident students, constitutes indirect discrimination. The residence requirement is more easily satisfied by Belgian nationals. As to the justification, the difference in treatment can be accepted if it pursues a legitimate objective, is appropriate and proportionate, i.e. does not go beyond what is necessary to attain the objective.[1388] The Belgian Government, supported by the Austrian Government, alleges as a justification the excessive burdens on the financing of higher education, which the ECJ rejects.[1389] However, the ECJ accepts the objective of achieving a high level of protection of health in the Member State as a possible justification.[1390] The Member State may take protective measures in anticipation of a shortage of health professionals (French students tend to leave Belgium after obtaining their diploma). The restrictive measure is only appropriate and proportionate if it is based on specific evidence, with solid and consistent data for each of the nine courses covered by the decree. The referring court must assess this.[1391]

1387 Para 28, with cited case law.

1388 Paras 47–48. For justifications applied in the educational context, see i.a. Case C-209/03 *Bidar* ECLI:EU:C:2005:169, para 54; Case C-147/03 *Commission v Austria* ECLI:EU:C:2005:427, paras 60–6; Case C-524/06 *Huber* ECLI:EU:C:2008:724, para 75; Case C-158/07 *Förster* ECLI:EU:C:2008:630 paras 48–55; Case C-73/08 *Bressol, Chaverot and Others* ECLI:EU:C:2010:181, paras 77–81.

1389 Paras 49–51.

1390 AG Sharpston dealt with the justification based on quality education separately (Case C-73/08 *Bressol, Chaverot and Others* ECLI:EU:C:2010:181, Opinion of AG Sharpston, paras 100–113): the objective of maintaining high quality education was a legitimate concern, but the material available to the Court fell short of what would be required to justify this discriminatory treatment ('patchy information' on some aspects of student enrolment on some courses, not the basis for a prudent legislator). Also, less discriminatory measures could resolve the problem.

1391 Paras 64–5, 71–2, 82.

Secondly, mobile students have—to a certain extent—the right to equal financial support. Before the 2004 Citizens' Rights Directive was adopted, generous ECJ case law gave students—in their capacity as EU citizens exercising the right to free movement—an entitlement to various social benefits on the same footing as nationals: non-contributory minimex, tideover allowances, or maintenance grants, if they were legally resident and could show a certain degree of integration in the society of the host Member State. In *Grzelczyk*, *D'Hoop* and *Bidar*, all these benefits fell within the scope of Article 18 TFEU.[1392]

> Ms Nathalie D'Hoop is a Belgian national who has obtained her secondary education diploma in France. She is seeking her first job in Belgium. The Belgian State refuses a tideover allowance (allowance bridging the gap between the end of education and payment of the first salary) because Belgian legislation requires the secondary education diploma to have been obtained at a Belgian educational establishment. The ECJ holds that Nathalie can rely on the EU law provision on EU citizenship, as she holds the nationality of a Member State and EU citizenship is destined to be her fundamental status (as stated in *Grzelczyk*).[1393] A citizen cannot receive less favourable treatment from her home Member State when she has made use of the opportunities afforded by the Treaty on freedom of movement. These opportunities would not be fully effective if a national of a Member State could be deterred from availing herself of them by obstacles raised on return to the home Member State. Refusing to grant the tideover allowance penalises Nathalie for having used her right to free movement, places her at a disadvantage, and is 'contrary to the principles which underpin the status of citizen of the Union, that is, the guarantee of the same treatment in law in the exercise of the citizen's freedom to move.'[1394] The ECJ finds this particularly important in the field of education, considering that the Union objectives in the Treaty include a contribution to quality education and, inter alia, aim at encouraging mobility in education.[1395]

1392 Case C-184/99 *Grzelczyk* ECLI:EU:C:2001:458; Case C-224/98 *D'Hoop* ECLI:EU:C:2002:432; Case C-209/03 *Bidar* ECLI:EU:C:2005:169. See summary of previous case law in Case C-75/11 *Commission v Austria* ECLI:EU:C:2012:605, para 42.

1393 Case C-224/98 *D'Hoop* ECLI:EU:C:2002:432, paras 27–8.

1394 Paras 34–5.

1395 Para 32.

In 2004, the Citizens' Rights Directive introduced several limitations, and accordingly, more restrictive ECJ case law followed.[1396] The Directive, in principle, recognises equal treatment rights for EU citizens residing in a host Member State (Article 24(1), the specific expression of Article 18 TFEU[1397]), but immediately sets limits on social assistance and maintenance grants for studies (derogation in Article 24(2)). Students who are not economically active have no equal rights to 'student grants or student loans'. ECJ case law applies the right to equal treatment to anything outside this category, e.g. to reduced transport costs as illustrated in *Commission v Austria*.

> Some *Länder* in Austria grant the right to reduced fares on public transport only to students whose parents are in receipt of family allowances in Austria. The Commission brings proceedings against Austria in the ECJ for failure to fulfil its obligations under the Treaties (Article 258 TFEU). The ECJ considers that a scheme for reduced transport fares for students comes within the scope of the TFEU in so far as it enables them, directly or indirectly, to cover their maintenance costs.[1398] The ECJ rules that there is indirect discrimination of non-national students studying in Austria, since the requirement that parents must be receiving family allowances in Austria is more easily fulfilled by Austrian students (their parents do as a rule receive those allowances).[1399] The derogation from equal treatment concerning 'student grants or student loans' in Article 24(2) of the Citizens' Rights Directive is not applicable, because it has to be interpreted narrowly (as an exception to Article 18 TFEU). The finding that only maintenance aid in the form of student grants or student loans comes within the derogation is based on a literal interpretation (wording) and a structural interpretation ('the Court's obligation to interpret that derogation in accordance with the provisions of the Treaty, including those

1396 I.a. Case C-158/07 *Förster* ECLI:EU:C:2008:630 (the requirement of five years prior residence for entitlement to a maintenance grant was justified, proportional to the objective of guaranteeing a certain degree of integration into society of the host Member State). See also M Dougan, 'Fees, grants, loans and dole cheques: Who covers the costs of migrant education within the EU?' (2005) 42 CMLRev 943; M Dougan, 'Cross-border educational mobility and the exportation of student financial assistance' (2008) 33 ELRev 1.

1397 Case C-333/13 *Dano* ECLI:EU:C:2014:2358, para 61 (specific expression).

1398 Case C-75/11 *Commission v Austria* ECLI:EU:C:2012:605, para 43.

1399 Para 50.

relating to Union citizenship').[1400] The ECJ finds no objective considerations to justify the unequal treatment and the restriction on free movement of citizens. The enrolment in an educational establishment, accredited or financed by the host Member State, attests to a genuine link with the host Member State.[1401] The condition of receipt of Austrian family allowances is not justified.[1402] By granting reduced fares on public transport in principle only to students whose parents are in receipt of Austrian family allowances, Austria has failed to fulfil its obligations under the combined provisions of Article 18–21 TFEU and Article 24 of the Citizens' Rights Directive.

In contrast to *Gravier* and *Bressol*, where students took action to defend their rights to equal treatment, in the transport fares case, it was the Commission (guardian of the Treaties) who brought proceedings against the Member State to protect the rights of citizens and oblige it to respect EU law.[1403]

Thirdly, students (EU citizens) have *the right not to be hindered* in the exercise of free movement (prohibition of non-discriminatory obstacles based on Article 21 TFEU). Again, EU law provides for additional content to national rights (i). Several cases follow a comparable line of reasoning.[1404]

Ms Martens, a Netherlands national, opposes to her home Member State because she has been refused funding for higher education in Curaçao (portable study finance). The reason for the refusal by the Netherlands is that she has not satisfied the 'three out of six years rule' (a condition for funding is to have resided lawfully in the Netherlands for at least three out of the last six years prior to enrolment). Ms Martens lived in Belgium (where her father worked) before her enrol-

---

1400 Paras 54–6.

1401 Paras 57–61 (EU law allows for a certain degree of solidarity, yet without it becoming an unreasonable burden for the social assistance system of the host Member State (recital 10 Directive 2004/38); proving a genuine link with the host Member State can reflect a legitimate objective justifying restrictions).

1402 Para 65. Cp Case C-233/14 *Commission v the Netherlands* ECLI:EU:C:2016:50: financial support for travel costs as framed in the Netherlands' legislation is regarded as student grants or loans.

1403 See also n 1382.

1404 Joined Cases C-11/06 and C-12/06 *Morgan and Bucher* ECLI:EU:C:2007:626; Joined Cases C-523/11 and C-585/11 *Prinz* ECLI:EU:C:2013:524; Case C-275/12 *Elrick* ECLI:EU:C:2013:684; Case C-220/12 *Meneses* ECLI:EU:C:2013:683; Case C-359/13 *Martens* ECLI:EU:C:2015:118.

ment in Curaçao. In an earlier case *Commission v the Netherlands* (2012), the ECJ ruled that the three out of six years rule constituted indirect discrimination, infringing the right to free movement of workers.[1405] Here, the ECJ appraises this rule on the basis of the citizenship right to free movement.[1406] The ECJ recalls that Member States retain their competence in the field of education (Article 165(1) TFEU) and adds that EU law does not impose any obligation to provide for a system of funding. However, if Member States provide a system of funding for higher education, the rules for the award of that funding cannot create an unjustified restriction of the right to move and reside within the territory of the Member States.[1407] The ECJ recalls settled case-law: national legislation placing certain nationals at a disadvantage simply because they have exercised their freedom to move and to reside in another Member State constitutes a restriction on the freedoms conferred by Article 21(1) TFEU on every citizen of the Union.[1408] As in *D'Hoop*, the Court reasons on the basis of effectiveness:

'the opportunities offered by the Treaty in relation to freedom of movement for citizens of the Union cannot be fully effective if a national of a Member State could be dissuaded from using them by obstacles resulting from his stay in another Member State because of legislation of his State of origin penalising the mere fact that he has used those opportunities'.[1409]

1405 Case C-542/09 *Commission v the Netherlands* ECLI:EU:C:2012:346 (indirect discrimination, contrary to Art 45 TFEU and Art 7(2) Reg 1612/68).

1406 As Ms Martens' father was a former frontier worker in the Netherlands, a preliminary question was whether the '3 out of 6' this rule was precluded by the freedom of movement of workers (her father) or that of citizens (the status of Miss Martens). AG Sharpston opined that the provision on workers applied (para 99).

1407 Paras 23–4.

1408 Para 25.

1409 See paras 26–7: 'That consideration is particularly important in the field of education in view of the aims pursued by Article 6(e) TFEU and the second indent of Article 165(2) TFEU, namely, inter alia, encouraging mobility of students and teachers'. See also Joined Cases C-11/06 and C-12/06 *Morgan and Bucher* ECLI:EU:C:2007:626, para 26; Joined Cases C-523/11 and C-585/11 *Prinz* ECLI:EU:C:2013:524, para 28; Case C-275/12 *Elrick* ECLI:EU:C:2013:684, para 24; Case C-220/12 *Meneses* ECLI:EU:C:2013:683, para 23. Earlier effectiveness reasoning in Case C-224/98 *D'Hoop* ECLI:EU:C:2002:432, para 31; Case C-224/02 *Pusa* ECLI:EU:C:2004:273, para 19.

> The three-out-of-six rule, even though it applies without distinction to Netherlands nationals and other EU citizens, restricts the right to freedom of movement and residence.[1410] The Court does not accept a justification based on the objective of integration, because the national rule is not considered proportionate.[1411]

Finally, mobile students have residence rights. Based on the Citizens' Rights Directive, students have a right of residence in the host Member State for more than 3 months if they satisfy three conditions: enrolment in an establishment for the purposes of study, comprehensive sickness insurance, and sufficient resources (Art 7(1)(c)).[1412]

To conclude, students' rights are highly relevant to EDC. Various cases illustrate how the rights of mobile students, EU citizens, provide additional content to national EDC (i). EU law creates advantages which students would not enjoy under national law. The content is significant (ii), relating to foundational values (such as equality and freedom), objectives and principles (free movement, proportionality), and certainly invites critical thinking (iii). To a certain extent, these rights indirectly affect static citizens (iv), who have the advantages of studying with students from other Member States but also have to bear the consequences of that. Adapted conditions for access to higher education or for scholarships, for instance, apply to all citizens.

194 Social benefits

With rights come responsibilities. The following two topics—rights of economically inactive citizens to social benefits and rights of third country nationals—are of particular interest for EDC because they involve all aspects of citizenship education (as defined in the ICCS[1413]): cognitive domains (knowing, understanding the rules), affective (attitudes, different feelings, such as empathy, solidarity, irritation, hostility), and behavioural domains (influencing civic participation, such as voting for Eurosceptic

---

1410 Para 33.

1411 Para 43.

1412 Also Art 12(3): after the departure of an EU citizen from the host Member State or after his death, children and the parent who retains custody, keep their residence rights in order to complete their studies. Further Case C-337/07 *Ibrahim* ECLI:EU:C:2008:744; Case C-480/08 *Teixeira* ECLI:EU:C:2010:83; P Starup and MJ Elsmore, 'Taking a logical step forward? Comment on Ibrahim and Teixeira' (2010) 35 ELRev 571. Directive 2004/38 repealed Council Dir 93/96/EEC of 29 October 1993 on the right of residence for students.

1413 § 71 .

parties or voting 'Leave', or—other civic behaviour—volunteering in associations).

Pursuant to the controversy principle in EDC,[1414] uncertainties and controversial aspects of social entitlements of EU citizens must be discussed openly in the classroom. There are many questions which can trigger dialogue. *If EU citizens have the right to move and to reside freely within the territory of Member States, does this mean 'as long as they are healthy and well'? What are the responsibilities corresponding to the rights? One of the values mentioned in the second part of Article 2 TEU is 'solidarity'. How far should solidarity and the right to equal treatment stretch with regard to social benefits? What do you think of 'benefit tourism' as denounced by some media and some politicians?* Economically inactive citizens are suspected of deliberately moving to the Member States with the highest social benefits, to reside there, and then to ask for equal treatment.[1415] Gradually, teachers can bring in more information during the discussions. At advanced levels of EDC, the rules of the Citizens' Rights Directive provide essential knowledge. The Directive distinguishes three periods and several categories of citizens (workers or self-employed persons, jobseekers, economically inactive persons, students, family members) and links them with different levels of financial solidarity.[1416] In the period between three months and five years, economi-

1414 Text to n 1243.

1415 See N Nic Shuibhne and J Shaw, 'General report' in U Neergaard, C Jacqueson and N Holst-Christensen (eds), *Union Citizenship, FIDE Congress 2014* (DJØF 2014), on 'welfare tourism', i.a. p 216; European Parliament Resolution of 16 January 2014 on respect for the fundamental right of free movement in the EU [2016] OJ C482/114, para 7.

1416 The EU citizen has a right of exit and a right of entry into the territory of Member States with a valid identity card or passport (Arts 2 and 5). During the first three months, EU citizens have an unconditional right of residence in the host Member State provided they have a valid identity card or passport (Art 6). In the period between three months and five years, they have a right of residence only if they satisfy one of the conditions of Art 7: they must (a) be a worker or self-employed person in the host Member State; (b) have sufficient resources for themselves and their family members not to become a burden on the social assistance system of the host Member State as well as a comprehensive sickness insurance cover; (c) be an enrolled student with equally sufficient resources and comprehensive sickness insurance; (d) be a family member of the former categories. After a continuous period of five years legal residence in the host Member State (in compliance with the conditions of the Directive), EU citizens enjoy an unconditional right of permanent residence (Art 16). For case law for several categories of citizens: see Craig and de Búrca, *EU Law: Text, Cases, and Materials* 872 ff.

cally inactive persons only have a right of residence if they have sufficient resources for themselves and their family members not to become a burden on the social assistance system of the host Member State as well as a comprehensive sickness insurance cover (Article 7(b)). The right to equal treatment is limited by Article 24(2).[1417] The Directive also allows Member States to refuse to recognise rights in cases of abuse of rights or fraud.[1418] Member States have social responsibility for tackling misuse of their social welfare system, but without discriminating on grounds of nationality and subject to the conditions of the Directive.[1419] The fact that case law and academics continue to search for the exact delimitation of the sub-rights in the cluster of free movement rights under Article 21 TFEU should not be hidden from pupils.[1420] Some scholars criticise EU law for constructing EU citizenship piecemeal, in a 'patchwork of personhoods rather than a uni-

---

1417 I.a. no obligation of equal treatment for 'maintenance aid for studies, including vocational training, consisting in student grants or student loans'; see case mentioned in n 1398.

1418 Art 35, recital 28.

1419 European Parliament Resolution of 16 January 2014 on respect for the fundamental right of free movement in the EU [2016] OJ C482/114, para N (10). See also Case C-333/13 *Dano* ECLI:EU:C:2014:2358 (n 1426).

1420 See, also on social citizenship and solidarity questions, i.a. M Dougan and E Spaventa, '"Wish you weren't here..." New Models of Social Solidarity in the European Union' in M Dougan and E Spaventa (eds), *Social welfare and EU law* (Hart 2005); N Ach, 'La citoyenneté européenne au service d'une Europe sociale' [2006] Journal des Tribunaux- Droit européen 129; S Maillard, *L'émergence de la citoyenneté sociale européenne* (Presses Universitaires d'Aix-Marseille 2008); O'Brien, 'Real links, abstract rights and false alarms: the relationship between the ECJ's "real link" case law and national solidarity' (2008) 33 ELRev 643; A Somek, 'Solidarity decomposed: being and time in European citizenship' (2007) 32 ELRev 787; M Wind, 'Post-national citizenship in Europe: the EU as a "welfare rights generator"?' (2009) 15 Columbia Journal of European Law 239; J Menéndez, 'European Citizenship after Martínez Sala and Baumbast: Has European Law Become More Human but Less Social' in M Maduro and L Azoulai (eds), *The Past and Future of EU Law; The Classics of EU Law Revisited on the 50th Anniversary of the Rome Treaty* (Hart 2010); K Lenaerts, 'EU Citizenship and the Social Solidarity Link' in M-C Foblets, M Hildebrandt and J Steenbergen (eds), *Liber Amicorum René Foqué* (Larcier 2012); TO Dalessio, *Socializing Europe—Solidifying EU Citizenship* (Wolf Legal Publishers 2013); F de Witte, *Justice in the EU: The Emergence of Transnational Solidarity* (Oxford Studies in European Law, 2015); K Hailbronner, 'Union Citizenship and Access to Social Benefits' (2015) 42 CMLRev 1245; D Thym, 'The Elusive Limits of Solidarity: Residence Rights of and Social Benefits for Economically Inactive Union Citizens' (2015) 52 CMLRev 17; S Reynolds, 'Union citizenship: Placing limitations on a human-centred approach?' in N Ferreira

tary status', where equal welfare entitlements depend on circumstances, and there is no coherent vision of the 'fundamental status' of EU citizens.[1421] The cluster of sub-rights under the heading of the right to move and reside freely pursuant to Article 21 TFEU does not grant mobility rights to EU citizens equally.[1422] Mobile workers have stronger 'citizenship rights' under the Citizens' Rights Directive than economically non-active citizens. *Is 'the Good European Citizen' a hard working 'market citizen', preferably crossing borders?*[1423] In reliance on the Treaty rights of free movement and non-discrimination, the ECJ initially produced quite liberal case law, such as *Trojani* and *Bidar* (criticised by some for going too far).[1424] After 2006 and giving effect to the Citizens' Rights Directive, ECJ case law took a more moderate approach (criticised for not reaching far enough, or for inconsistency with previous case law). The *Dano* case law was welcomed by

---

and D Kostakopoulou (eds), *The Human Face of the European Union: Are EU Law and Policy Humane Enough?* (Cambridge University Press 2016); van den Brink, 'The Court and the Legislators: who should define the scope of free movement in the EU?'.

1421 See i.a. C O'Brien, 'I trade, therefore I am: legal personhood in the European Union' (2013) 50 CMLRev 1643; Nic Shuibhne, 'The Developing Legal Dimensions of Union Citizenship', III. See also Proposal for the future of D Kochenov, 'The Citizenship Paradigm' (2013) 15 Cambridge Yearbook of European Legal Studies 197 ('The citizenship paradigm of European integration consists of deploying European citizenship as an integration tool which would function alongside the internal market').

1422 I.a. O'Leary, *The Evolving Concept of Community Citizenship: From the Free Movement of Persons to Union Citizenship* 278: the logic of Union citizenship should be all about equality and the abolition of frontiers; Kochenov, 'Ius tractum of many faces: European citizenship and the difficult relationship between status and rights', 194–196; D Kochenov, 'Citizenship without Respect: The EU's Troubled Equality Ideal' (2010) 8 Jean Monnet Working Paper No 08/10; Kochenov, 'The essence of EU citizenship emerging from the last ten years of academic debate: beyond the cherry blossoms and the moon?', 123; PJ Neuvonen, *Equal Citizenship and its Limits in EU Law: We the Burden?* (Hart 2016). See, generally, also Kuisma, 'Rights or privileges? The challenge of globalization to the values of citizenship'.

1423 For discussion in classrooms. Cf the question raised by Frevert (n 583 ff). See also Azoulai, 'Transfiguring European Citizenship: From Member State Territory to Union Territory' (p 193 ff, analysis of the 'Good citizen' in ECJ case law); Kochenov, 'On Tiles and Pillars: EU Citizenship as a Federal Denominator', 40 (totalitarian idea of the 'Good [Europen] citizen').

1424 Case C-456/02 *Trojani* ECLI:EU:C:2004:488; Case C-209/03 *Bidar* ECLI:EU:C:2005:169. See earlier Case C-85/96 *Martínez Sala* ECLI:EU:C:1998:217. Critical: C Calliess, 'Der Unionsbürger: Status, Dogmatik und Dynamik' (2007) 42 EuropaRecht 7.

some as 'more cautious and more conciliatory with regard to Member State concerns than the earlier cases'.[1425]

Ms Elisabeta Dano (22 years old) and her son Florin are Romanian nationals residing in Germany and economically inactive. Since their arrival in Leipzig, they have been living in Ms Dano's sister's apartment. Ms Dano has limited German language skills, has not been trained in a profession, and has not worked in Germany or Romania. There is no indication that she is looking for a job, although her ability to work is not in dispute. Applying German law, German public authorities refuse to grant social assistance. The ECJ points to the fact that Ms Dano and her son did not have a right of residence under the Citizens' Rights Directive, as they did not have sufficient resources for themselves (Article 7(1)(b)). To grant persons who do not have a right of residence under the Directive a right of access to social benefits equal to that of nationals, would run counter to an objective of the Directive, namely preventing Union citizens who are nationals of other Member States from becoming an unreasonable burden on the social assistance system of the host Member State.[1426] Economically inactive Union citizens cannot use the host Member State's welfare system to fund their means of subsistence (aim of Article 7(1)(b)).[1427] The ECJ rules that a Member State must therefore have the possibility (based on Article 7) to refuse social benefits 'to economically inactive Union citizens who exercise their right to freedom of movement solely in order to obtain another Member State's social assistance although they do not have sufficient resources to claim a right of residence.'[1428] Germany can refuse the social benefit to Ms Dano and her son.[1429]

1425 See Craig and de Búrca, *EU Law: Text, Cases, and Materials* 874; van den Brink, 'The Court and the Legislators: who should define the scope of free movement in the EU?', 23 (cp critical comments of F de Witte, in the Kick off contribution).

1426 Case C-333/13 *Dano* ECLI:EU:C:2014:2358, para 74 (on the concept of social assistance, see para 63).

1427 Para 76.

1428 Para 78.

1429 Para 84.

It is, in principle, for the legislation of each Member State to lay down conditions establishing the right to social assistance.[1430] Yet, in exercising their competences, Member States have to respect EU law, including the principle of equal treatment and the conditions and limitations of the Citizens' Rights Directive.[1431] For access to social benefits, an EU citizen can claim equal treatment with nationals of the host Member State only if his residence in the territory of the host Member State complies with the conditions of the Citizens' Rights Directive. The rule set out in *Dano* was confirmed in later case law.[1432] In order to assess the right to equal treatment of economically inactive citizens, the circumstances of each case must be considered carefully, including in the light of the principle of proportionality.[1433]

The topic of social benefits rights of EU citizens satisfies the criteria for relevance for mainstream education. The additional content (i) has a bearing on component (c-1) of the EDC concept, i.e. 'rights and responsibilities' (citizens are responsible for taking care of one another, citizens exercising the right to free movement are responsible for not abusing the system). The topic provides significant content, relating to foundational values, objectives and principles laid down in EU primary law (ii) and invites critical thinking (iii). It affects many citizens (iv) to the extent that it regularly features in the media and static citizens are involved in the public debate. Instances of abuse should be addressed, and the feasibility of a social Europe reflected on. It requires some courage to speak to young EU citizens at school about social realities and EU challenges. Nevertheless, the principle of democracy means that pupils must be informed, enabled to exercise critical thinking in the classroom, and prepared for participation in society. *Should solidarity be national or European?* (the 'correct' answer should not be pre-established). States traditionally harness solidar-

---

1430 Case C-333/13 *Dano* ECLI:EU:C:2014:2358, para 89; Case C-308/14 *Commission v UK* ECLI:EU:C:2016:436, para 65. See also European Parliament Resolution of 16 January 2014 on respect for the fundamental right of free movement in the EU [2016] OJ C482/114, para H.

1431 See also Regulation (EC) No 883/2004 of the European Parliament and of the Council of 29 April 2004 on the coordination of social security systems [2004] OJ L166/1, as amended.

1432 Case C-67/14 *Alimanovic* ECLI:EU:C:2015:597; Case C-308/14 *Commission v UK* ECLI:EU:C:2016:436.

1433 Craig and de Búrca, *EU Law: Text, Cases, and Materials* 876: despite the retreat of the ECJ in *Dano*, key elements of the earlier more liberal rulings continue to play out (as in *Trojani*, *Baumbast* or *Grzelczyk*).

ity at national level.[1434] During discussions, teachers can refer to foundational values and objectives, and to principles such as freedom of movement, non-discrimination on grounds of nationality, abuse of law, burden on the social assistance system of the host Member State, and a genuine link with the host Member State.[1435] The fight against populism includes promoting class room discussions on these sensitive issues.[1436]

195 Third-country nationals, family members

Another sensitive area which relates to cognitive, affective and behavioural domains in citizenship education, are the rights of third-country nationals. Third-country nationals who are family members of a mobile EU citizen have derived rights (deriving from the rights of the mobile EU citizen). Pupils should understand the basic distinction between EU citizens and third country nationals (largely unknown, even among civic educators and scholars in the field[1437]). EU primary law confers the right to free movement on EU citizens (thus on nationals of Member States), not on third-country nationals. Free movement is a 'citizenship right', attaching to the status of EU citizenship. The difference clearly appears in Article 45 CFR: while '[e]very citizen of the Union has the *right* to move and reside freely within the territory of the Member States', for third country nationals '[f]reedom of movement and residence *may* be granted' when they legally reside in the territory of a Member State.[1438] Mobile EU citizens are not 'immigrants' (often confused in the media and in public opinion[1439], even

---

1434 See thinkers pleading for patriotism, as this orients citizens towards the common good: Nussbaum in § 73 and Rousseau in n 1216.

1435 'Principles' in a wide sense (not only in EU primary law, but in EU law in general, e.g. in Directive 2004/38).

1436 Concern about populism expressed i.a. in CoE Secretary General, State of democracy, human rights and the rule of law: Populism—How strong are Europe's checks and balances? Report 2017, Council Recommendation of 22 May 2018 on promoting common values, inclusive education, and the European dimension of teaching [2018] OJ C195/1, recital 3.

1437 E.g. unclarities in Losito and others, *Young People's Perceptions of Europe in a Time of Change: IEA International Civic and Citizenship Education Study- 2016 European Report*, p 24.

1438 Emphasis added. See also Art 8 TEU.

1439 Nic Shuibhne and Shaw, 'General report', 216 (the distinction EU citizen/third country national has not been assimilated in public discourse; inaccurate terminology). See on media and EU citizenship more generally, ibid, 198 ff: reporting is often 'inaccurate, sensationalist, and riddled with loaded terminology', 'almost always correlated with a generallly Euro-sceptic outlook or bias' (p 209); exceptionnally, media educates about EU citizenship, but in general a

by national public authorities[1440]). Third country nationals are immigrants, subject to immigration policy, which must be based on fairness. The Treaties state that in the area of freedom, security and justice, a common policy shall be framed, based on solidarity between Member States and 'fair towards third-country nationals'.[1441] Whereas EU citizenship is 'constructed around the paradigm of individual *rights*' based on EU primary law, immigration policy for third country nationals is traditionally grounded in an ethos of *permission.*[1442] Obviously, the human rights of third country nationals must be respected.[1443]

The Citizens' Rights Directive grants derived rights to third-country nationals who are family members of mobile EU citizens: residence rights and a right to equal treatment under certain conditions.[1444] The reason is that EU citizens should be able to exercise the right to free movement 'under objective conditions of freedom and dignity'.[1445] If 'the very essence

---

fragmented picture is given (p 210); in the majority of Member States, issues of benefit tourism, social dumping and poverty migration prevail (p 211), also criminality of foreigners, including EU citizens (p 213); as a result, public opinion is often biased. See for public opinion, Special Eurobarometer 469, Integration of immigrants in the European Union (April 2018), i.a. summary p 2 (immigrants are defined as people born outside the EU who have moved away from their country of birth and are at the moment staying legally in an EU Member State; during the interviews, it was repeated that 'we are not talking about EU citizens').

1440 Nic Shuibhne and Shaw, 'General report', 216 (a tendency among national actors—administrative, legislative, and judicial—not to apply the distinction appropriately).

1441 Art 67. The EU can take action on a legal basis with regard to policies on border checks, asylum and immigration. See Arts 77, 78 and 79 TFEU. Explanations to CFR.

1442 See Nic Shuibhne and Shaw, 'General report', 193, 195.

1443 On the motivations underlying the distinction between EU citizens and third country nationals, see D Thym, 'Citizens' and 'Foreigners' in EU Law: Migration Law and its Cosmopolitan Outlook' (2016) 22 ELJ 296; the author argues that there is no move to create 'fortress Europe' ('EU migration law can be construed as an endeavour to replace traditional notions of alienage with constitutional rules with a cosmopolitan outlook'). See also n 1454. For reflection, A Hoogenboom, 'In Search of a Rationale for the EU Citizenship Jurisprudence' (2015) 35 Oxford Journal of Legal Studies 301.

1444 Art 7(2) Directive 2004/38; Arts 12–13 (Retention of the right of residence by family members in the event of death or departure of the Union citizen, or divorce, annulment of marriage or termination of registered partnership); Art 16(2); Art 24(1) second sentence Directive 2004/38.

1445 Directive 2004/38, recitals 5, 15. Considerations in line with Article 7 CFR.

of EU citizenship is to ensure that *EU citizens feel at home wherever they are in the EU*',[1446] it is natural to allow them to be accompanied by their family members, irrespective of the nationality of those family members. In addition to respect for family life, the effectiveness of citizens' free movement rights is relevant here. The impossibility for EU citizens of being accompanied or joined by their family would interfere with their freedom of movement by discouraging them from exercising their right of entry into and residence in the host Member State. This is the purpose and justification for derived rights for third country nationals in ECJ case law.[1447]

While the *ratio legis* of the rules is easy to understand, their implementation is complex and sensitive. Abuses and cases of 'legal engineering' cause mistrust in civil society: artificial strategies have been used to obtain the eagerly desired rights of residence, such as arranging a marriage of convenience with an EU citizen, or having a child born in the territory of a Member State which will grant the child its nationality (so it becomes an EU citizen and the parent acquires derived rights).[1448] Member States are reluctant to grant rights to third-country nationals.[1449]

The rights of third country nationals have a relatively high degree of relevance for the EU dimension of EDC. They are additional to national citi-

---

1446 M Meduna, 'Institutional report' in U Neergaard, C Jacqueson and N Holst-Christensen (eds), *Union Citizenship: Development, Impact and Challenges - The XXVI FIDE Congress in Copenhagen, 2014 Congress Publications Vol 2* (DJØF 2014) 293 (emphasis in the original). See also Lenaerts and Gutiérrez-Fons, 'Epilogue on EU Citizenship: Hopes and Fears', 763.

1447 Case C-40/11 *Iida* ECLI:EU:C:2012:691, paras 63, 68; see also Case C-127/08 *Metock* ECLI:EU:C:2008:449, para 63; Case C-87/12 *Ymeraga* EU:C:2013:291, para 35; Case C-165/14 *Rendón Marín* ECLI:EU:C:2016:675, para 73. On same sex marriage and derived right of residence in application of Art 21 TFEU, see Case C-673/16 *Coman* ECLI:EU:C:2018:385.

1448 See facts and arguments in Case C-200/02 *Zhu und Chen* ECLI:EU:C:2004:639; Case C-34/09 *Ruiz Zambrano* ECLI:EU:C:2011:124. Recital 28 Directive 2004/38.

1449 European Parliament Resolution of 2 April 2009 on the application of Directive 2004/38/EC on the right of citizens of the Union and their family members to move and reside freely within the territory of the Member States [2010] OJ C137E/6, para S, examples in fn 15; Nic Shuibhne and Shaw, 'General report' 222 ff. (PL 'Several letters of complaint and petitions addressed to EU Institutions highlight the fact that some Member States are reluctant to fully recognise their rights to third countries family members'). See also S Adam and P Van Elsuwege, 'EU Citizenship and the European Federal Challenge through the Prism of Family Reunification' in D Kochenov (ed), *EU Citizenship and Federalism: The Role of Rights* (Cambridge University Press 2017).

zenship (i), concern foundational values, objectives and principles (ii), and certainly invite critical thinking (iii). It is true that the derived citizenship rights of third-country nationals lack direct relevance for the large majority of EU citizens (iv), who are static or, if they do move within the Union, usually have no third-country nationals as family members. Statistically, these rights concern a minority of the population. However, as with the rights to social benefits of non-economically active citizens, a lack of knowledge of the rules, leads to incomprehension and serious tensions in civil society, especially among static citizens. Cognition and emotion are interlinked.[1450] The public debate is not always an informed debate.[1451] Citizens should know about the choices made by Member States at EU level in both EU primary law and secondary law, and about the rationale for these choices. This allows informed participation in democratic processes leading to possible change in the law and policies. Many 'Leave' voters in the Brexit referendum wanted fewer 'immigrants', equating EU citizens with third country nationals.[1452] Hostility towards free movement in the EU is partly due to its assimilation in public discourse with immigration in general.[1453] Clarification of free movement rules in EDC is therefore desirable in order to get the (legal) facts straight. To the extent that

1450 See cognitive theories asserting that cognition (thoughts) frequently precedes emotions (also cognitive psychology). See i.a. Aaron Beck's cognitive model, GB Moskowitz, *Social cognition: understanding self and others* (Guilford 2005). Also 'cognitive reconstruction' in D Goleman, *Emotional intelligence* (Bantam Books 1997) 117 ff. Further J Storbeck and GL Clore, 'On the interdependence of cognition and emotion' (2007) 21 Cognition & Emotion 1212; P Luiz, 'On the relationship between emotion and cognition' (2008) 9 Nature Reviews Neuroscience 148; Gentner and Smith, 'Analogical Learning and Reasoning'; JR Huntsinger and S Schnall, 'Emotion–Cognition Interactions' in D Reisberg (ed), *The Oxford Handbook of Cognitive Psychology* (Oxford Handbooks Online, Oxford University Press 2013). See also emphasis of ICCS on the role of the cognitive skills, text to n 553. For reflection, Epictetus in the Enchiridion: 'Men are disturbed not by things, but by the views which they take of them'.

1451 N 1440. See also Special Eurobarometer 469, Integration of immigrants in the European Union (April 2018), Divided public perceptions (summary); less than four in ten Europeans feel well-informed about immigration and integration related matters (p 28); a clear majority sees an important role for the EU (p 28); 17% totally disagree that the integration of immigrants would be supported by ensuring the same rights as nationals in access to education, healthcare and social protection (p 21).

1452 Brexit surveys, i.a. <lordashcroftpolls.com/2016/06/how-the-united-kingdom-voted-and-why>.

1453 Nic Shuibhne and Shaw, 'General report', 198.

cognition precedes emotion, understanding rights, their rationale, and the conditions attaching to them can lead to more tolerant attitudes. What is called 'EU immigration' should be recognised as the 'free movement of EU citizens' and 'EU immigrants' as 'mobile EU citizens'. Mobile EU citizens have certain citizenship rights (if they satisfy certain conditions). Immigrants have—at least—human rights. An informed debate can then follow.

Questions as a basis for reflection (some deliberately provocative or probing) are: *What do you think of the distinction between 'us' and 'them', EU citizens and third country nationals?*[1454] *What explains this distinction in EU primary law? Can EU citizens availing of the right to free movement bring their non-EU spouse and all their children with them? How can we ensure respect for human dignity and family life, while fighting rights abuse? What do you think of 'Fortress Europe'?*

A lot of ECJ case law on third country nationals is available as food for thought and discussion. A substantive part of ECJ case law on 'citizenship of the Union' in fact concerns third-country nationals. In *Rendón Marín*, the ECJ specified that in principle third-country nationals have a derived right of residence 'only when it is necessary in order to ensure that a Union citizen can exercise effectively his rights to move and reside freely in the European Union'.[1455] The case reaffirms that, in principle, purely internal situations do not fall within the scope of Articles 20–21 TFEU on citizenship rights. It is only in very particular situations that derived rights are granted to third-country nationals to prevent static EU citizens from being deprived of the genuine enjoyment of the substance of their right to move and reside freely in the territories of the Member States (because, if their

1454 In simple terms, explaining third country nationals to pupils: the 'first' country is your own, this is the country of which you are a national; 'second' countries are countries who are also members of 'your club' or 'your family', that is the EU, thus the 27 EU Member States; 'third' countries are countries which are not EU Member States, the rest of the world. The fact that nationals of members of 'the club' or 'the family' have more rights is comparable to real life where ties with family or club members are closer (have a lot in common, are invited home, etc.) This does not mean that neighbours or other people should not be respected. Everyone has fundamental rights, different from citizenship rights.

1455 Case C-165/14 *Rendón Marín* ECLI:EU:C:2016:675, para 36. National legislation cannot automatically limit the derived right of residence on the sole grounds that the parent has a criminal record.

family member, a third country national, had to leave, they would be compelled to go with him and leave the EU completely).[1456]

1456 Para 78. In *Rottmann* (para 42) the ECJ had considered that '[it] is clear that the situation of a citizen of the Union who, like the applicant in the main proceedings, is faced with a decision withdrawing his naturalisation, adopted by the authorities of one Member State, and placing him, after he has lost the nationality of another Member State that he originally possessed, in a position capable of causing him to lose the status conferred by Article 17 EC and the rights attaching thereto *falls, by reason of its nature and its consequences, within the ambit of European Union law*' (emphasis added). In *Ruiz Zambrano*, the ECJ found that 'Article 20 TFEU precludes national measures which have the *effect of depriving citizens of the Union of the genuine enjoyment of the substance of the rights conferred by virtue of their status as citizens of the Union*'. See also Opinion of AG Sharpston in *Zambrano*. The cases *Rottmann* and *Ruiz Zambrano* raised hope and were extensively commented: i.a. Davies, 'The entirely conventional supremacy of Union citizenship and rights'; K Hailbronner and D Thym, 'Gerardo Ruiz Zambrano v. Office national de l'emploi (Onem)' (2011) 48 CMLRev 1253; D Kochenov, 'A Real European Citizenship: A New Jurisdiction Test; A Novel Chapter in the Development of the Union in Europe' (2011) 18 Columbia Journal of European Law 56 ('We are witnessing the creation of a real European citizenship by the Court'); D Kochenov, 'Two Sovereign States vs. a Human Being: CJEU as a Guardian of Arbitrariness in Citizenship Matters' in J Shaw (ed), *Has the European Court of Justice Challenged the Member State Sovereignty in Nationality Law?* (EUI Robert Schuman Centre for Advanced Studies Paper 62, 2011); H van Eijken and SA de Vries, 'A New Route into the Promised Land? Being a European Citizen after Ruiz Zambrano' (2011) 36 ELRev 704. However, in later case law, it became clear that the 'genuine enjoyment' criterion is only applicable in very specific situations: see i.a. Case C-434/09 *McCarthy* ECLI:EU:C:2011:277; Case C-256/11 *Dereci* ECLI:EU:C:2011:734, Case C-40/11 *Iida* ECLI:EU:C:2012:691; Joined Cases C-356 and 357/11 *O, S & L* ECLI:EU:C:2012:776; Case C-87/12 *Ymeraga* ECLI:EU:C:2013:291; Case C-86/12 *Alokpa* ECLI:EU:C:2013:645; Case C-115/15 *NA* ECLI:EU:C:2016:487; Case C-304/14 *CS* ECLI:EU:C:2016:674. Further S Adam and P Van Elsuwege, 'Citizenship rights and the federal balance between the European Union and its member states: comment on Dereci' (2012) 37 ELRev 176; Kochenov and Plender, 'EU Citizenship: From an Incipient Form to an Incipient Substance? The Discovery of the Treaty Text'; Lenaerts, 'EU Federalism in 3-D'; K Lenaerts, 'The concept of EU citizenship in the case law of the European Court of Justice' (2013) 13 ERA Forum 569; Lenaerts, 'EU citizenship and the European Court of Justice's "stone-by-stone" approach'; Nic Shuibhne, 'The Developing Legal Dimensions of Union Citizenship' (Section III, 1(a)); Azoulai, 'Transfiguring European Citizenship: From Member State Territory to Union Territory'; Kochenov, *EU Citizenship and Federalism: The Role of Rights* (see references at 10, fn 40).

196 Static citizens
Obviously, criterion (iv) for determining relevance for EDC needs particular attention: does the right to free movement affect the large majority of citizens, who are static? Sceptics with doubts as to the need for an EU dimension of EDC point out this fact: more than 96 per cent of the population is static, living in one Member State. Does EDC in mainstream education really need to be adapted to include learning about the mobility rights when they are only relevant for less than 4 per cent of citizens?[1457]

There are many facets to the answer.

Firstly, all EU citizens have a right to free movement. They all come within the personal scope of Article 21 TFEU just by virtue of being a national of a Member State (for the sake of clarity, nationals of Member States which are not part of the Schengen zone enjoy this right too; this is sometimes misunderstood).[1458] The right to free movement is an expression of the foundational value of freedom within the EU (Article 2 TEU) (ii). All citizens have the freedom to move and live wherever they want in the territories of the EU, a freedom which enhances their capacity for self-awareness and self-realisation.[1459] The right to free movement is seen as a public good.[1460] Freedom of movement guarantees equality of opportunity.[1461] In

---

1457 See text to n 1069.

1458 European Parliament Resolution of 16 January 2014 on respect for the fundamental right of free movement in the EU [2016] OJ C482/114, para C.

1459 Contributions in de Witte, Bauböck and Shaw, *Freedom of movement under attack: Is it worth defending as the core of EU citizenship?*: Floris De Witte (Kick off contribution) argues that EU citizenship should be primarily about free movement; 'the central thing that EU citizenship should be about: it is what makes EU citizenship distinctive from, and genuinely supplementary to, national citizenship'); see also contributions of Saara Koikkalainen (Free movement and EU citizenship from the perspective of intra-European mobility, at 17); and Kieran Oberman (What to Say to Those Who Stay? Free Movement is a Human Right of Universal Value, at 30: citizens who do not move, make use of the freedom of movement by choosing to stay). Further Kochenov, 'The essence of EU citizenship emerging from the last ten years of academic debate: beyond the cherry blossoms and the moon?', 134 ('EU citizenship directly affects all the holders of this status, as it offers Europeans a radically broadened horizon of opportunities and in this sense seriously contributes to liberty in the Union through empowering individuals').

1460 Ibid: see Floris De Witte (EU Citizenship, Free Movement and Emancipation: a rejoinder, at 44).

1461 See F Vandenbroucke, 'EU citizenship should speak to both the mobile and the non-mobile European' in M Ferrera and R Bauböck (eds), *Should EU citizenship be duty-free?* (EUI Working Papers RSCAS 2017/60, 2017), 9–10, for the

Eurobarometers, the right to free movement consistently ranks highly, as the right most cherished by EU citizens.[1462] Citizens consider free movement to be the essence of EU citizenship. The fact that only a fraction of EU citizens *exercises* the right to free movement, does not reduce the value of the right. Even if not exercised, the right to free movement, just like the right to vote, to freedom of expression or to freedom of association, is important,[1463] and should therefore be part of EDC. How empowered are EU citizens if they are not even aware of their free movement rights (their 'fundamental status')? As explained in examples above, Article 21 TFEU grants the EU citizen additional rights based on EU law, allowing him or her to oppose to the host or the home Member State. The extra rights which EU citizenship adds to national citizenship are content for the EU dimension of EDC.

Next, mobility rights can be exercised in various forms and levels of intensity. Scholars (and statistics) often categorise the population as either 'mobile citizens' or 'static citizens'.[1464] This *summa divisio* is inadequate for understanding the relevance of Article 21 TFEU for the large majority of EU citizens. Mobility rights do not only concern mobile citizens defined as those residing in another Member State for more than one year (the 4 per cent

---

deeper rationale of free movement (also in the internal market, not only a matter of efficient allocation of factors of production).

1462 Standard Eurobarometer 89, Public Opinion in the European Union (June 2018): 58% of the respondents found free movement of people, goods and services within the EU to be the most positive outcome of the EU, 54% pointed to peace among the Member States; 53% said they benefited from no or fewer border controls when traveling abroad; 37% from improved consumer rights when buying products or services in another EU country.

1463 De Witte, 'EU Citizenship, Free Movement and Emancipation: a rejoinder' in de Witte, Bauböck and Shaw, *Freedom of movement under attack: Is it worth defending as the core of EU citizenship?*, 43.

1464 Apart from the legal relevance of a cross border element, mobility also appears to be a relevant (or determining) factor for economic success in life, for pro European integration attitudes, or feelings of belonging. See, i.a., De Witte, Kick off contribution, in ibid, 1; Bauböck, Rainer, The New Cleavage Between Mobile and Immobile Europeans, in ibid, 19, 20 ('The new European cleavage is different because of divergent political spaces and time horizons. Mobile citizens regard Europe as their emerging space of opportunity and increasingly also of identity, whereas the immobile ones look back to the time when closed nation-states provided comprehensive social protection.'). See also E Recchi, 'Pathways to European identity formation: a tale of two models' (2014) 27 Innovation: The European Journal of Social Science Research 119.

figure).[1465] The Citizens' Rights Directive already distinguishes three periods (from less than three months, between three months and five years, and more than five years). In reality, EU citizens trigger free movement rights as soon as they cross a border, even if they are just going to a concert in a neighbouring Member State, or a Christmas market, a football match, a wine-tasting, a day out shopping, a weekend city trip, a holiday, or a visit to a child who is an Erasmus student.[1466] Only purely internal situations do not fall within the scope of Article 21 TFEU or Article 18 TFEU, that is to say situations 'which have no factor linking them with any of the situations governed by European Union law and which are confined in all relevant respects within a single Member State'.[1467] For the large majority of citizens living in a single area without internal frontiers, many situations in daily life are not purely internal, e.g. situations in which they actually or potentially move as tourists, workers, students, pensioners, businessmen, artists, patients, volunteers, consumers, ... The 'static' citizens (in the statistical sense) may in reality be extremely mobile. Hundreds of millions of 'static' citizens (living at home in their Member States) travel across Europe for family, tourism, or business reasons every year and 1.7 million 'static' Europeans commute to another Member State every day.[1468] Every morning, some 177 000 frontier workers cross the borders of France, Belgium or Germany to work in Luxembourg.[1469] In fact, being 'mobile' is a characteristic of a moment, not of a citizen. Citizens *are* seldom mobile *or* static. Sociological empirical research gives a diversified picture of mobility. Salamońska and Recchi reveal a palette of cross-border practices and

1465 Working definition of mobile citizens, text to n 1068.

1466 E.g. skiiing holiday, in Case C-322/13 *Rüffer v Pokorná* ECLI:EU:C:2014:189 (n 1351). See also Commission Report under Article 25 TFEU 'On progress towards effective EU citizenship 2013-2016' COM(2017) 32 final, 5.

1467 Settled case law, see i.a. Case C-434/09 *McCarthy* ECLI:EU:C:2011:277, para 45. See further S O'Leary, 'The Past, Present and Future of the Purely Internal Rule in EU Law' in M Dougan, N Nic Schuibhne and E Spaventa (eds), *Empowerment and Disempowerment of the European Citizen* (Hart 2012); also text to nn 1455-1456, nn 1617- 1618.

1468 Commission White paper of 1 March 2017 on the future of Europe COM(2017) 2025 final: 'For the 1.7 million Europeans who commute to another Member State every day, and for the hundreds of millions who travel across Europe for family, tourism or business reasons every year, borders are a thing of the past.' However, borders have been reintroduced because of security concerns.

1469 Published on 30 December 2016 <luxtimes.lu/archives/3731-close-to-180-000-cross-border-workers-in-luxembourg> (in the third quarter of 2016, close to 90,000 come from France, 43 000 from Belgium, and 43 000 from Germany).

demonstrate how 'mobilities, in their plural and multidimensional manifestations, shape the everyday lives of Europeans on a much larger scale than has been recognised so far.'[1470] Some 30 per cent of the respondents are 'locals': they rarely cross national borders, either physically or virtually. Most respondents show diverse patterns of cross-border mobility.[1471] The right to free movement is part and parcel of the broader mobility mix of transnational practices, e.g. with 52 per cent of the respondents having visited other Member States in the last 24 months. From this diversified picture of the exercise of mobility, it can be inferred that the dichotomy mobile citizens/static citizens does not correspond to reality and that free movement rights are relevant for large numbers of EU citizens. The working definition of the 'mobile citizen' as the citizen who lives for at least one year in another Member State,[1472] should be replaced by the concept of the mobile citizen who crosses a border, even for a very short time, in other words, the citizen in a crossborder situation.

Furthermore, all citizens—including the 'locals'—live in an area without internal frontiers. All citizens are affected by free movement rights inasmuch as free movement of persons pervades society, altering the sociological landscape. On a daily basis the 'locals' meet mobile citizens on the work floor, in local pubs and shops, in cultural and sports activities, on the train, the bus or the road. Static citizens feel the effects of changes made to

---

1470 Salamońska and Recchi, *Europe between mobility and sedentarism: Patterns of cross-border practices and their consequences for European identification*, 11 (based on data collection in DE, DK, ES, IT, RO, UK). See also E Recchi and others, 'Cross-border mobilities in the European Union: An evidence-based typology' in *EUCROSS, Final report, 'The Europeanisation of Everyday Life: Cross-Border Practices and Transnational Identifications Among EU and Third-Country Citizens'* (2014), 8–28; E Recchi and A Favell (eds), *Pioneers of European Integration. Citizenship and Mobility in the EU* (Edward Elgar 2009).

1471 Authors build a typology of European cross-border practices, distinguishing five groups, i.e. transnationals, visitors, tourists, networked, and locals. Physical mobility is ranged in a continuum from high to low permanence, including staying abroad for more than 3 years, holidaying, and short trips abroad. Virtual mobility (without crossing a border physically) includes having a foreign spouse or family member, having family members or friends in a foreign country, foreign neighbours, business partners, clients, or colleagues; planning relocation in a foreign country; sending children abroad; adhering to international associations; interacting with foreigners through social networks; making foreign investments; and buying foreign products online. See Salamońska and Recchi, *Europe between mobility and sedentarism: Patterns of cross-border practices and their consequences for European identification*, 2, 8–9, i.a. table 3.

1472 N 1068.

national legislation in order to adapt it to EU rules on free movement and non-discrimination. In a society governed by the rule of law, the rights of mobile citizens must be respected.[1473] For all citizens, free movement has an impact on responsibilities (EDC component c-1), on valuing diversity (c-2) and on participation in democratic life (c-3). All citizens have a right to participate democratically in future decisions on mobility or the closing of borders. This presupposes a basic understanding of free movement rules. There are, preferably, more options than just 'leave' or 'remain'.[1474] The EU is not a product, *à prendre ou à laisser*. The EU is a project and a process, shaped by the decisions of many actors. The ECJ has been an important actor in the development of EU citizenship and mobility rights.[1475] If EU citizens, too, are to be actors, EDC standards require that they be educated about the rights, responsibilities and challenges of free movement.[1476] For a critical understanding of society pervaded by free movement, citizenship competence needs to include an EU dimension.

Lastly, mutual trust—a specific EU characteristic—requires that all EU citizens understand the basic mobility rules. Free movement is part of the DNA of the system in which all EU citizens live (ii). Free movement presupposes mutual trust in what will happen when a border is crossed. While the con-

1473 Under conditions, free movement rights have a horizontal direct effect (text to n 1840ff).

1474 De Witte (n 1460), 44: 'Brexit reveals a more structural problem for the EU ...the EU cannot institutionalize contestation appropriately (...) The only possible way to contest the normative orientation of the European market is to leave the EU'. Further J Shaw, 'The quintessentially democratic act? Democracy, political community and citizenship in and after the UK's EU referendum of June 2016' (2017) 39 Journal of European Integration 559.

1475 I.a. Edward and Lane, *Edward and Lane on European Union Law* 433: case law has interpreted Article 21 TFEU so 'as to augment substantially, maybe fundamentally, the rights of citizens'.

1476 Recital 5 of Decision 1093/2012/EU of the European Parliament and of the Council of 21 November 2012 on the European Year of Citizens (2013) [2012] OJ L325/1 ('The message should be conveyed that Union citizens themselves also have a critical role to play in strengthening those rights through their participation in civil society and democratic life'); Dahl, *On democracy* on enlightening citizens (n 565). See also L Damay and H Mercenier, 'Free movement and EU citizenship: a virtuous circle?' (2016) 23 Journal of European Public Policy 1139, critical on tunnel vision limiting EU citizenship to free movement and suggesting opening up a space for controversy and debate, including the 'stayers', who are also European citizens; and S Huyghe, 'Construire une citoyenneté européenne' in P Boniface (ed), *Quelles valeurs pour l'Union européenne?* (Puf 2004).

troversy principle in citizenship education demands that the controversial is presented as controversial,[1477] conversely, what is based on consensus must be highlighted as such, in keeping with the spirit of the shared constitutional values. Free movement belongs to the core values, objectives and principles, established in the founding Treaties and CFR, and agreed to by all Member States in accordance with their constitutional requirements. Defining the precise limits to citizenship rights occurs through the dynamic interaction of secondary law and case law but is always based on EU primary law. Limitations and conditions must respect the essence of the right (Article 52(1) CFR). Leaders of the EU institutions and Member States repeatedly confirmed during the Brexit talks that the essence of the right to free movement is non-negotiable.[1478] In *Opinion 2/13,* the ECJ included the provisions on EU citizenship and free movement among the 'fundamental provisions' of the EU, part of the process of integration and the *raison d'être* of the EU itself.[1479]

1477 Text to n 587. On mutual trust, see n 1183.

1478 On 26 June 2016, 'Jean-Claude Juncker and Donald Tusk were uncompromising in their stance after meeting with the 27 EU leaders'. In the Brexit talks the 'French and German leaders also made clear that the freedom of movement of EU citizens was non-negotiable. ...European Council President Donald Tusk said the UK could not pick and choose' (<www.bbc.com/news/world-europe-36659900>). Junker addressing the European Parliament: 'Freedom of movement is a basic principle of the European Union since the very beginning and I'm not prepared to change this' (<www.irishtimes.com/news/world/europe/eu-free-movement-not-negotiable-says-juncker-1.1973337>) Angela Merkel, in the context of talks with the UK before Brexit: 'But it also goes without saying that there are things that are non-negotiable. That there are achievements of European integration that cannot be haggled over, for example the principle of free movement and the principle of non-discrimination' (<www.telegraph.co.uk/news/worldnews/europe/germany/angela-merkel/11932797/EU-freedom-of-movement-non-negotiable-says-Angela-Merkel>). Ministers in Finland, Norway, and Sweden wrote in a letter sent in 2014 to the Financial Times that '[f]ree movement of persons is the essence of European citizenship'; see Nic Shuibhne, 'The Developing Legal Dimensions of Union Citizenship', IV Conclusion ('EU migrants who work and contribute financially to building our societies should not be made scapegoats for loopholes in national benefit schemes'). See in 2014, European Parliament Resolution of 16 January 2014 on respect for the fundamental right of free movement in the EU [2016] OJ C482/114, i.a. having regard to Articles 21, 45, 47, and 151 of the TFEU, on free movement of citizens, of workers, and social policy.

1479 EU Accession to the ECHR *Opinion 2/13* ECLI:EU:C:2014:2454, paras 168, 170, 172, 191. Text to n 1207.

The conclusion which can be drawn from the foregoing considerations is that the right to move and reside freely in Article 21 TFEU is relevant content for EDC for the large majority of citizens.

197 Concluding remarks

The right to move and reside freely—established in Article 21 TFEU and commonly seen as the central EU citizenship right—encompasses a cluster of sub-rights which have an important impact in the EU and the Member States. A combined reading of EU law and EDC standards leads to the conclusion that the right to move and to reside freely should be part of the EU dimension of EDC. The four criteria for relevance in mainstream education are largely satisfied.

Firstly, the various sub-rights which make up the right to free movement contribute *additional* content to the EDC components of empowerment (c-1) exercising rights and responsibilities, (c-2) valuing diversity and (c-3) taking active part in democratic life, as has been illustrated (criterion i). They also add to EDC component (b), knowledge, skills and understanding, and to attitudes such as openness, tolerance, and mutual respect.

Secondly, free movement rights provide *significant* content (criterion ii), relating to foundational values, such as freedom, equality, and solidarity (Article 2 TEU), foundational objectives, such as offering citizens an area of freedom, security and justice without internal frontiers, ensuring free movement of persons (Article 3 TEU), and foundational principles, such as non-discrimination on grounds of nationality, or proportionality (Article 5(4) TEU, Article 18 TFEU). Free movement is part of the DNA of the EU and cannot be ignored in schools.[1480] At advanced levels of EDC, the rationale, advantages, and challenges of free movement of EU citizens must be explained and reflected on.

Thirdly, while the core of free movement and equal treatment is based on consensus (EU primary law), the outer limits are amenable to *critical thinking*, which, precisely, is a goal of EDC (criterion iii). Free movement rights constitute an exemplary field in which to exercise skills valued in EDC. One should not wait until doubts about EU citizenship have been dispelled and the rights clearly delineated (if ever) before educating EU citizens about them. EDC standards do not require consensus before a subject is introduced to pupils. Besides, the compulsory school curriculum includes 'art' and 'literature', even though there is no consensus about these concepts and their outer limits. One of the fundamental goals of all

1480 Or just mentioned superficially. See reports on EU learning at school.

EDC and HRE is 'empowering [learners] with the readiness to take action in society in the defence and promotion of human rights, democracy and the rule of law'.[1481] In an area without internal frontiers, this fundamental goal cannot be reached without learning about free movement. Admittedly, this right is complex, inter alia due to the conditions laid down in the Citizens' Directive. Yet, as has been observed, simplicity is not a required criterion for relevance for EDC. Balancing the interests of 27 Member States cannot be managed in simple, easy rules. EU citizens must learn to live with diversity, in respect for one another, and on the basis of political compromises reflected in nuanced legislation, not in one-liners. The provisions on the right to free movement of citizens in EU primary law and their development in the Citizens' Rights Directive provide safe spaces, ensuring objectivity in education. At the same time, ECJ case law and SOLVIT[1482] offer a multitude of cases on free movement, and potential for stories, stimulating critical and pluralistic thinking in the classroom.

Finally, mobility rights affect the *large majority* of citizens, in various ways (criterion iv). Adding the mobility rights of EU citizens to the EU dimension of EDC ultimately produces a win-win situation for all participants. The (future) mobile citizens see their horizons broaden and opportunities increase. Static citizens gain a better understanding of the rationale of the system and develop a view about the conditions and limits to the rights of mobile citizens, which leads to peaceful coexistence and better conflict resolution. All citizens gain from greater awareness of the EU's foundational values, objectives and principles through informed debate and more adequate preparation for democratic participation. Member States gain from having their nationals move with ease in the European space, an internal market and open area without internal frontiers, contributing to the economic substratum of the State and to social cohesion,

1481 Charter on EDC/HRE para 5g.

1482 For a simple illustration, see Commission Communication 'Compliance Package- Action plan on the Reinforcement of SOLVIT: Bringing the benefits of the Single Market to citizens and businesses' COM(2017) 255 final, 3: 'An Austrian artist wanted to register as a resident in Luxembourg. He handed in all the necessary papers to the local authorities but they refused to register him unless he presented a statement of support from a resident in Luxembourg. SOLVIT pointed out that this additional requirement was not in line with EU law. The local authority revised its position and issued the registration certificate. Thanks to SOLVIT's intervention, the case was solved within one week.' More challenging cases for discussion in ECJ case law.

supporting the EU dimension of personal, social, citizenship, and entrepreneurship competences (competences referred to in the 2018 Council Recommendation on key competences for lifelong learning).[1483] The EU benefits for the same reasons, and, additionally, from progress towards the realisation of foundational values and objectives. Indeed, as Delors wrote, education is the Necessary Utopia.[1484]

B Other EU citizenship rights

198 Overview

In addition to the right to free movement, Articles 20–24 TFEU list other citizenship rights, i.e. rights attaching to the status of EU citizen. Some of them add significant content to the EDC components, especially to exercising rights and responsibilities (c-1) and playing an active part in democratic participation (c-3). Their relevance for EDC based on the four criteria will be explored. The citizenship rights in Articles 21 to 23 TFEU are directed at citizens crossing borders (within the EU or outside the EU). A new category of citizenship rights appears in Article 24 TFEU, directly relevant for *all* EU citizens, including the static ones (iv). Citizens have the right to petition the European Parliament, to apply to the European Ombudsman, to communicate with EU institutions and advisory bodies in a Treaty language, and to participate in a citizens' initiative. At first sight, none of this appears so spectacular as to require instant adaptation of national EDC. However, upon a closer look, the political rights which Article 24 TFEU adds to national citizenship are significant (i, ii). By their very nature they call for critical thinking (iii). The right to petition and to apply to the European Ombudsman constitute powerful instruments for democratic control by EU citizens of EU governance (EU institutions and Member States implementing EU law). Together with the citizens' initiative, these rights constitute a means of direct communication with the EU, tools for participatory democracy.[1485] However, it is under Title II TEU that the most important participation rights for EU citizens will arise (Chapter seven).

1483 Council Recommendation of 22 May 2018 on key competences for lifelong learning, competences in Annex: A European Reference Framework.

1484 § 16 .

1485 See on concept and forms of participatory democracy, text to n 1659 ff.

1. The right to equal treatment in European Parliament and municipal elections

199 A right of mobile citizens in the host Member State

Article 22 TFEU grants the mobile EU citizen a right to equal treatment with regard to the right to vote and to stand as a candidate at European Parliament and municipal elections in the host Member State. As the ECJ states in *Spain v UK* and *Eman & Sevinger*, Article 22 TFEU is 'confined to applying the principle of non-discrimination on grounds of nationality to the right to vote and stand for election'.[1486] Conditions which Member States attach to the electoral rights of their nationals, e.g. period and proof of residence, must be identical for residing nationals of other Member States.[1487] The mobile citizen has the freedom to exercise these electoral rights in the home or the host Member State.[1488] The possible loss of electoral rights at European Parliament or municipal level as a result of moving to live in another Member State cannot be allowed to become a discriminatory obstacle to free movement.

Not many EU citizens make use of the political rights associated with their free movement rights.[1489] Strictly speaking, Article 22 TFEU is irrelevant for the large majority of citizens (iv). Yet, static citizens must accept that non-national EU citizens residing in their country are equals and entitled to have an input in democratic life.[1490]

1486 Case C-145/04 *Spain v UK* ECLI:EU:C:2006:543, para 66; Case C-300/04 *Eman and Sevinger* ECLI:EU:C:2006:545, para 53; Case C-650/13 *Delvigne* ECLI:EU:C:2015:648, para 42. See also L Khadar and J Shaw, 'Article 39: Right to Vote and to Stand as a Candidate at Elections to the European Parliament' in S Peers and others (eds), *The EU Charter of Fundamental Rights: a Commentary* (Hart 2014) 1037: Dir 93/109 'does not affect the rights of nationals of a Member States for EP elections in their own countries'.

1487 Art 3(b) in both Directive 93/109 (on European Parliament elections) and Directive 94/80 (on municipal elections).

1488 Ibid, Art 4(1).

1489 Nic Shuibhne and Shaw, 'General report', 170; Commission Report under Article 25 TFEU 'On progress towards effective EU citizenship 2013-2016' COM(2017) 32 final, 11–13; Eurobarometers.

1490 For discussion (with 'Is it fair?' questions), see A Balthasar and A Prosser, '"Every citizen shall have the right to participate in the democratic life of the union": serious commitment or vain promise in an "ever closer union"?' (International Conference on electronic governance and open society, St Petersburg, 22 November 2016).

200 *Additional and significant right*

The right in Article 22 TFEU adds significant content to national EDC (i, ii). It relates to the foundational objective of free movement: the authors of the Treaty aimed at better integration of EU citizens in the host Member State and therefore considered this right to be a corollary of the right to move and reside freely.[1491] However, this rationale has not been fully followed through, as the right does not concern national elections.[1492] Member States protect their sovereignty in a careful balancing exercise. In the preamble to the Directives on the implementation of equal electoral rights, the Council specifies that they do 'not presuppose complete harmonisation of Member States' electoral systems'.[1493] EU law must not go beyond what is necessary to achieve its objective, which is essentially to abolish the nationality requirement for European Parliament and municipal elections in the host Member State (principle of proportionality).[1494]

1491 Directives in n 1487, preamble: 'Whereas citizenship of the Union is intended to enable citizens of the Union to integrate better in their host country'.

1492 For criticism and proposals, see i.a. J Shaw, *The Transformation of Citizenship in the European Union: Electoral Rights and the Restructuring of Political Space* (Cambridge University Press 2007); D Kochenov, 'Free movement and participation in the parliamentary elections in the member state of nationality: an ignored link?' (2009) 16 Maastricht Journal of European and Comparative Law 197; Kochenov, 'Ius tractum of many faces: European citizenship and the difficult relationship between status and rights'; Lansbergen and Shaw, 'National membership models in a multilevel Europe. Symposium: The Evolving Concept of Citizenship in Constitutional Law'. Further the ECI 'Let me vote' in n 1593; and Opinion of AG Tizzano in Spain v UK and Eman and Sevinger (n 1668), paras 67–69. Also Commission Report under Article 25 TFEU 'On progress towards effective EU citizenship 2013-2016' COM(2017) 32 final, p 12–13 (response to complaints, questions, petitions, i.a. on the problem of disenfranchisement: mobile citizens cannot vote in national elections in the host Member State, but cannot either in their home Member State when this State deprives its citizens of the right to vote once they have resided abroad). Earlier: Commission Recommendation of 29 January 2014 addressing the consequences of disenfranchisement of Union citizens exercising their rights to free movement [2014] OJ L32/34.

1493 Directives in n 1487.

1494 Derogations to the equal treatment rule inasfar as they are 'warranted by problems specific to a Member State' (as in Luxembourg and Belgium): if in the host State the proportion of residing EU citizens of voting age who are nonnationals exceeds 20% of the total number of residing EU citizens of voting age, then the host State may restrict the right to vote by requiring a minimal period of residence for the nationals of other Member States. See Art 14 Directive 93/109 (on European Parliament elections); Art 12 Directive 94/80 (on

Some Member States have not been eager to let non-nationals exercise these political rights. In particular, participation in municipal elections is sensitive, encroaching on what always has been part of national sovereignty (in contrast to the European Parliament elections).[1495] In many Member States, the constitutional requirement of nationality as a condition for exercising voting rights was an obstacle to implementing the TFEU provisions and the Directives based on them. Several constitutional courts of Member States have handed down judgments on this matter. In the face of non- or problematic implementation of the Directives, the Commission started a number of infringement proceedings before the ECJ.[1496] Overall, in formal terms, Member States' implementation of electoral rights is satisfactory.[1497] National electoral law has been adapted where needed; Member States have amended their constitutions to allow non-national EU citizens to vote.[1498] In practical terms, however, the situation may still be complicated.[1499]

---

municipal elections). See also Meduna, 'Institutional report', 294 (because the derogations seem at odds with the objectives of EU citizenship and the gradual deepening of European integration, Meduna considers that these derogations are likely to be eroded in the future). The ECJ takes a cautious approach with respect to electoral rights, respecting Member State competence to determine who can vote on their territory, while guaranteeing EU rights for Union citizens, including the equal treatment right of Article 22 TFEU, as further implemented by secondary law, and the principles of proportionality: see e.g. Case C-535/08 *Pignataro* ECLI:EU:C:2009:20 (with regard to a condition of residence for eligibility in regional elections in Sicily, the Court found it had no jurisdiction). See cases in n 1486.

1495 About differences between the rules and objectives of EP and municipal elections, see i.a. van Eijken, *European Citizenship and the Constitutionalisation of the European Union*, and Nic Shuibhne and Shaw, 'General report', 162–163.

1496 Case C-323/97 *Belgium v Commission* ECLI:EU:C:1998:347: Belgium failed to bring into force within the prescribed period the laws, regulations and administrative provisions necessary to comply with Council Dir 94/80/EC. See also Commission Report under Article 25 TFEU 'On progress towards effective EU citizenship 2013-2016' COM(2017) 32 final, p 13 (proceedings against Czech Republic, Latvia, Lithuania and Poland for not allowing non-national EU citizens to found or become members of political parties in the host Member State).

1497 Nic Shuibhne and Shaw, 'General report', 171.

1498 Preamble to Directive 93/109 (on European Parliament elections): 'seeks to abolish the nationality requirement which currently has to be satisfied in most Member States in order to exercise those rights'. For decisions of constitutional courts, as well as adaptations of national constitutions (in Spain, Germany, Belgium, France, Austria, Poland, Greece, ...), see i.a. Shaw, *The Transformation*

Despite limits as to scope, the political rights set out in Article 22 TFEU are significant for the construction of democracy in the EU. Equal electoral rights in the host Member State are the first rights which the CFR mentions in the Title on Citizens' rights (Articles 39 and 40), even before the right to free movement. Some scholars see Article 22 TFEU as a promising step towards a growing EU demos.[1500] These political rights can foster feelings of belonging at both the transnational and subnational level in a Member State of which the citizen is not a national.[1501] The EU constitutes the political nexus between non-national EU citizens and the Member State of residence.[1502] Article 22 TFEU illustrates the interconnectedness between levels of governance in the EU, a composite polity where political

---

of Citizenship in the European Union: Electoral Rights and the Restructuring of Political Space; Craig and de Búrca, *EU Law: Text, Cases, and Materials* 888 fn 188 (Greece); van Eijken, *European Citizenship and the Constitutionalisation of the European Union* 161.

1499 Nic Shuibhne and Shaw, 'General report', 161 ('Member States continue to lag behind the vision spelled out in the Treaties and by the EU legislature'), 192 ('a damp squib' in practice). For the implementation of political rights in Member States, see national reports in Neergaard, Jacqueson and Holst-Christensen, *Union Citizenship: Development, Impact and Challenges - The XXVI FIDE Congress in Copenhagen, 2014 Congress Publications Vol 2.*

1500 I.a. Calliess, 'EU-Vertrag (Lissabon) Art 1', Rn 43.

1501 S Besson and A Utzinger, 'Towards European Citizenship' (2008) 39 Journal of Social Philosophy 196, 195 ('If nationals and nonnationals are, to an increasing degree, treated equally, people's loyalty and their feelings of belonging are expected to be less exclusively directed toward the national state').

1502 Several scholars point to the significance of the citizenship rights in Article 22 TFEU. See, i.a., Shaw, *The Transformation of Citizenship in the European Union: Electoral Rights and the Restructuring of Political Space*, 48 (and the transformation, Chapter 4); J Shaw, 'E.U. Citizenship and Political Rights in an Evolving European Union' (2007) 75 Fordham Law Review 2549; J Shaw, 'Political Rights and Multilevel Citizenship in Europe' in S Carrera and E Guild (eds), *Illiberal Liberal States: Immigration, Citizenship and Integration in the EU* (Ashgate 2009); J Shaw, 'Citizenship and Political Participation: The Role of Electoral Rights Under European Union Law' in B Fanning and R Munck (eds), *Immigration and the Irish Experience of European and Global Social Transformation* (Ashgate 2010/11); Lenaerts and Van Nuffel, *European Union Law* 190 fn 61 (the fact that any member of the European Parliament can be elected by nationals of several Member States, powerfully reflects the direct relationship between the EU and its citizens); Meduna, 'Institutional report', 293 (the political rights conferred on nationals of the Member States 'contribute to the very construction of democracy upon which the EU is founded' and are part of the process contributing to the creation of the ever closer Union).

rights are part of a complex balance.[1503] The analysis of the participation rights of EU citizens based on Title II TEU will confirm this interconnectedness.

2. The right to equal diplomatic or consular protection

201 Expressing a bond

Admittedly, the right enshrined in Articles 23 TFEU and 46 CFR does not affect the large majority of citizens (iv): in a third country where their Member State is not represented, EU citizens have a right to protection by the diplomatic or consular authorities of another (represented) Member State under the same conditions as the nationals of that State. Nevertheless, it is an additional right (i) and it has a significance (ii), as an expression of European solidarity.[1504] It indicates a bond between Member States and EU citizens, a feeling of belonging to one protective family. This citizenship right is the least well known of the rights listed.[1505]

3. The right to petition the European Parliament

202 Important tool in participatory democracy

Every citizen of the Union (iv) has the right to petition the European Parliament, individually or in association with others, on matters which come within the EU's fields of activity and which directly affect him or her (Article 24 in conjunction with Article 227 TFEU, Article 44 CFR).[1506] The

1503 See, i.a., van Eijken, *European Citizenship and the Constitutionalisation of the European Union* 163. On the question of multiple political allegiances and transformative Europeanisation of national citizenship, see Besson and Utzinger, 'Towards European Citizenship'.

1504 See Council Directive (EU) 2015/637 of 20 April 2015 on the coordination and cooperation measures to facilitate consular protection for unrepresented citizens of the Union in third countries and repealing Decision 95/553/EC [2015] OJ L106/1, i.a. recital 3.

1505 Flash Eurobarometer 430, European Union citizenship (March 2016).

1506 Rules of Procedure of the European Parliament: 8th parliamentary term (January 2017), Rule 215 Right of petition; European Parliament Resolution of 15 December 2016 on the activities of the Committee on Petitions 2015 [2018] OJ C238/132.

scope of this right is broad.[1507] Citizens can speak out against EU institutions and bodies as well as against Member States implementing EU law. They may complain of disrespect for their rights under EU law, draw attention to unacceptable implementation of EU law, or call for EU legislative action. The right to petition invites critical thinking on EU matters (iii). It is a key instrument of participatory democracy in the EU, effectively protecting the right of every citizen to play a direct part in the democratic life of the Union (significant, ii).[1508] Given the limited standing of individuals before the ECJ (Article 263 TFEU), the right of petition is a tool for bridging the gap between citizens and EU institutions, especially important in times of Euroscepticism and on matters where the citizens distrust the EU.[1509] It is a means of ensuring dialogue between EU citizens and their representatives, a direct EU level contact point in cases where citizens feel that they have not been heard by national administrations or judges.[1510] It adds content to national citizenship (i). Besides judicial action in the national courts, which can submit preliminary questions to the ECJ, 'petitions provide an alternative and independent avenue of inquiry and checks on compliance with EU legislation'.[1511] This right is thus not only important for the citizens themselves, but also for the EU institutions and Member States, as petitions are a source of first-hand information from citizens about problematic implementation of EU law at national level. They are a barometer for monitoring and identifying loopholes. As a follow-up, infringement proceedings may be started or legislative processes adapted.[1512] Furthermore, petitions make it possible to assess the impact of EU law on the daily life of citizens. They relate to a wide range of fields, such as the environment, consumer rights, fundamental rights, free movement rights, discrimination, children's rights, labour law, or access to information.[1513]

In *Schönberger*, the ECJ held that the decision of the European Parliament that a petition does not meet the necessary conditions (Article 227

1507 More in M Lindfelt, 'Article 44: Right to Petition' in S Peers and others (eds), *The EU Charter of Fundamental Rights: a Commentary* (Hart 2014) 1157.

1508 European Parliament Resolution of 15 December 2016 on the activities of the Committee on Petitions 2015 [2018] OJ C238/132, recital I.

1509 Lindfelt, 'Article 44: Right to Petition', 1160.

1510 Case C-261/13 P *Schönberger* ECLI:EU:C:2014:2423, para 17.

1511 European Parliament Resolution of 15 December 2016 on the activities of the Committee on Petitions 2015 [2018] OJ C238/132, para AG.

1512 Ibid, paras 5,13, 15.

1513 Ibid, paras U-W, AA, 25.

TFEU) or the refusal to consider it, is amenable to judicial review. Once the Parliament accepts the petition as meeting the conditions, it has a broad discretion—of a political nature—as to how to deal with it.[1514]

203 Insufficiently known

Unfortunately, the right of petition is not exercised to any great extent. The European Parliament's Committee on Petitions received 1400 petitions in 2015.[1515] Out of a population of more than 500 million citizens, this is almost negligible (0.00028 per cent). Is it sufficient to create a web portal to publicise the right to petition,[1516] when citizens are not educated about their rights and about the basic functioning of the EU? Another worrying aspect is that a large number of petitions are inadmissible because of confusion about the EU's competences and fields of activity. While the European Parliament and academics conclude that this suggests the EU still has much to do in terms of information and communication, [1517] I deduce that the right of petition should be included in the EU dimension of EDC in schools, and explained as a tool for democratic control, empowering active EU citizens. Adequate citizenship education means explaining which instruments of democratic participation are available, in keeping with the compulsory educational aim of enabling effective participation in a free society.[1518] Discussing the right to petition is an opportunity for explaining the foundational principle of conferral (ii) and reflecting with pupils on competences necessary to achieve foundational objectives (iii).

1514 Case C-261/13 P *Schönberger* ECLI:EU:C:2014:2423, paras 22, 24.

1515 Commission Report under Article 25 TFEU 'On progress towards effective EU citizenship 2013-2016' COM(2017) 32 final, 14. See also European Parliament Resolution of 15 December 2016 on the activities of the Committee on Petitions 2015 [2018] OJ C238/132, paras B-C.

1516 The Petitions Web Portal informs citizens how to start a petition. <petiport.secure.europarl.europa.eu/petitions/en/home>.

1517 European Parliament Resolution of 15 December 2016 on the activities of the Committee on Petitions 2015 [2018] OJ C238/132, para D ('there is still widespread confusion about the EU's fields of activity as is shown by the high number of inadmissible petitions received', 33.8% in 2015;); Lindfelt, 'Article 44: Right to Petition', 1158–1160.

1518 Art 13 ICESCR, Art 29 CRC.

4. The right to apply to the European Ombudsman

204 Complaints about maladministration

Every citizen of the Union (iv) has the right to apply to the European Ombudsman, a right firmly anchored in EU law (Article 24 in conjunction with Article 228 TFEU, Article 43 CFR). While Article 24 TFEU reads 'may apply', Article 43 CFR clearly states, 'has the right to'. It is thus a real right, even a fundamental right (ii). The European Ombudsman receives complaints about maladministration in the activities of EU institutions, bodies, offices or agencies (except concerning the ECJ in its judicial role), examines them and reports on them.[1519] This right is thus narrower in scope than the right to petition, which also includes action against Member States' implementation of EU law. Instances of integrated administration are grey areas where EU and Member State levels of governance are hard to distinguish from one another.[1520] The first purpose of the right to refer to the Ombudsman is to provide the ordinary citizen with an extra possibility of redress against maladministration (informal, cost-free and fast), as an alternative to judicial remedies (formal, implying costs and delays) and to petitioning the European Parliament. The second purpose is to contribute to higher quality administration at EU level and to enhance accountability.[1521] The complainant does not necessarily need to be personally affected by the maladministration, nor does he or she need to

1519 'Statute' of the European Ombudsman: Decision of the European Parliament on the Regulations and General Conditions governing the performance of the Ombudsman's duties [1994] OJ L113/15, amended by Decisions of 14 March 2002 and 18 June 2008; Decision of the European Ombudsman adopting Implementing Provisions [2016] OJ C321/1; Emily O'Reilly, Network in Focus 2017. For reports, see <www.ombudsman.europa.eu/en/activities/annualreports.faces>.

1520 Hofmann, Rowe and Türk, *Administrative law and policy of the European Union* 784–785, with examples of agencies. See also I Harden, 'Article 43: European Ombudsman' in S Peers and others (eds), *The EU Charter of Fundamental Rights: a Commentary* (Hart 2014) 1150, suggesting deeper cooperation in the European Network of Ombudsmen.

1521 A Peters, 'The European Ombudsman and the European constitution' (2005) 42 CMLRev 697, 711; Hofmann, Rowe and Türk, *Administrative law and policy of the European Union* 780. See also PN Diamandouros (ed) *The European Ombudsman: Origins, Establishment, Evolution* (Office for Official Publications of the European Communities 2005).

demonstrate specific interest. An 'actio popularis' is possible.[1522] Apart from answering the individual complaint, the European Ombudsman can formulate general recommendations. His *European Code of Good Administrative Behaviour* contains the general principles applicable to all relations between the institutions and their administrations and the public.[1523] The principles reach beyond the law; public bodies must also be service-minded, putting the EU citizen at the centre. Neither the decisions of the Ombudsman nor the European Code are legally binding. Yet, there is an overlap with the fundamental right to good administration, set out in Article 41 CFR, which is a binding provision. In addition to improving good administration, the Ombudsman's ultimate goal is to help to increase accountability and transparency at EU level, and to improve the quality of democracy in the EU.[1524] By triggering action of the European Ombudsman at a systemic level, the ordinary citizen thus takes part in the democratic life of the Union (ii). The EU dimension of EDC should therefore empower citizens to exercise this right. Citizens may for instance use referrals to the Ombudsman or petitions to the European Parliament to put pressure on the Commission to start infringement proceedings against Member States for non-compliance with EU law, or at least to explain its reasons for not starting them. The Commission's discretion with regard to infringement proceedings has limits. Individual EU citizens thus have 'a forum of accountability' where they can express dissatisfaction and receive answers.[1525]

The importance of the action of the European Ombudsman for citizens is reflected in ECJ case *European Ombudsman v Lamberts*, where the full

---

1522 I Harden, 'When Europeans Complain: The Work of the European Ombudsman' (2000) 3 Cambridge Yearbook of European Legal Studies 199, 214, with examples at 233.

1523 In 2013 the Ombudsman published a new version of the original Code of 2001 (own initiative inquiry, approved by the European Parliament). See Art 3.

1524 European Parliament Resolution of 15 January 2015 on the annual report on the activities of the European Ombudsman 2013 [2016] OJ C300/14, paras 3 and 9 ('transparency is a cornerstone of an advanced democracy, making it possible to scrutinise the activities of public authorities, evaluate their performance and call them to account'). See also (improving quality of democracy in the EU), i.a. Decision of the European Ombudsman closing her own-initiative inquiry OI/9/2013/TN concerning the European Commission (4 March 2015).

1525 Harden, 'Article 43: European Ombudsman', 1146–47, with examples of successful complaints. See also Peters, 'The European Ombudsman and the European constitution', 720; van Eijken, *European Citizenship and the Constitutionalisation of the European Union* 169.

Court accepted the principle of the non-contractual liability of the EU for mishandling of a complaint by the Ombudsman.[1526] The ECJ specified however that this depended on 'very exceptional circumstances' in which a citizen could demonstrate 'that the Ombudsman has committed a sufficiently serious breach of [Union] law in the performance of his duties likely to cause damage to the citizen concerned'.[1527] The Ombudsman is merely under an obligation to use his best endeavours and he enjoys wide discretion. A breach of EU law is sufficiently serious when an EU institution or body manifestly and gravely disregards the limits on its discretion.[1528] In *European Ombudsman v Staelen*, the ECJ applied these principles and confirmed the order of the General Court for the European Ombudsman to pay Ms Claire Staelen EUR 7000 as compensation for non-material damage.[1529] The Courts had found a sufficiently serious breach by the Ombudsman of his duty to act diligently, thus gravely disregarding the limits on his (wide) discretion when analysing the complaint of Ms Staelen on maladministration by the Parliament in its management of the list of suitable candidates in an open competition.

205 Often incorrectly applied

Both the right of petition and the right to apply to the European Ombudsman are empowering mechanisms for democratic participation by the EU citizen.[1530] Like petitions, the complaints to the Ombudsman concern a variety of matters, frequently related to consumer protection, taxation, social security, healthcare, or issues related to banks.[1531] Transparency is a

---

1526 Case C-234/02 P *European Ombudsman v Lamberts* ECLI:EU:C:2004:174, para 49 (applying the three conditions of settled case law: 'the rule of law infringed must be intended to confer rights on individuals; the breach must be sufficiently serious; and there must be a direct causal link between the breach of the obligation resting on the author of the act and the damage sustained by the injured parties').

1527 Para 52.

1528 Paras 49- 50; 82. Mr Lamberts had failed the oral test in an internal competition in the Commission for members of the temporary staff. He attributed this to medication causing fatigue and reducing concentration, and complained that he had not been able to ask for a postponement of this test.

1529 Case C-337/15 P *European Ombudsman v Staelen* ECLI:EU:C:2017:256, i.a. paras 109, 126, 131.

1530 Harden, 'Article 43: European Ombudsman', 143.

1531 Ombudsman Emily O'Reilly, Annual report 2016 (16 May 2017), p 31–34; Ombudsman Emily O'Reilly, Annual report 2018 (14 May 2019), p 3- 12. See also figures in Commission Report under Article 25 TFEU 'On progress towards effective EU citizenship 2013-2016' COM(2017) 32 final, p 14.

primary concern.[1532] Regrettably, as in the case of petitions, there is a clear lack of public knowledge. Many complaints to the Ombudsman do not satisfy the conditions required. They often fall outside the scope of the Ombudsman's mandate, for instance, because they relate to issues outside the work of the EU institutions and bodies, concern purely political issues (such as legislation) or the judicial activity of the Court.[1533] Even if citizens know about the right to apply to the Ombudsman, many do not know how to submit a correct application.[1534] As with petitions, better communication by the EU about this right has been recommended. Yet, as Hofmann, Rowe and Türk suspect, it is doubtful whether the EU administration may realistically be expected to enthusiastically promote the right to complain about its own maladministration.[1535] Therefore, the right to apply to the Ombudsman should be incorporated in the EU dimension of EDC. One of the objectives in inserting the right to apply to the European Ombudsman into the Maastricht Treaty was to reduce the alienation and scepticism of the public regarding the 'Brussels' administration.[1536] This rationale is still topical and makes the right relevant for mainstream education today. The right to address the European Ombudsman ensures necessary and meaningful protection of EU citizens as a corollary to the use of

1532 European Parliament Resolution of 16 November 2017 on the annual report on the activities of the European Ombudsman in 2016 (2017/2126(INI)), para 12. Data analysis in Kostadinova, 'Improving the Transparency and Accountability of EU Institutions: The Impact of the Office of the European Ombudsman' (author concludes that concerns about transparency and accountability dominate citizens' complaints, and that the majority of EU institutions follow the European Ombudsman's recommendation to increase transparency or accountability). See Commission Staff working document on the Application of the EU Charter of Fundamental Rights in 2016 Accompanying the document Communication from the Commission on 2016 Report on the Application of the EU Charter of Fundamental Rights SWD(2017) 162 final, 101: in 2016 the Ombudsman helped 15 756 citizens.

1533 Annual report 2016 (n 1531), p 34 (see also p 31: in 2016, 1880 complaints were handled, 235 inquiries were opened on the basis of complaints, 58% concerned the European Commission, 29% transparency (access to information), 28% personnel issues, 25% services (citizen friendliness, language...), 18% discretion, 4% respect for fundamental rights).

1534 Hofmann, Rowe and Türk, *Administrative law and policy of the European Union* 790: 'If there is any profound weakness in the system as it stands it may not lie in ... but rather in the relatively slow awareness among the European citizenry of the potential advantages of the institution.'.

1535 Ibid, 790.

1536 Peters, 'The European Ombudsman and the European constitution', 699.

public power at EU level. Related to the foundational value of the rule of law (Article 2 TEU), it is a significant building block for an EU governed by law, not by power,[1537] and thus a significant right to add to national EDC (i, ii).

To conclude, the rights to petition the European Parliament and to address the European Ombudsman satisfy the four criteria of relevance for mainstream education. Their significance is considerable inasmuch as these rights contribute to the safeguarding and implementation of the foundational values, objectives and principles underlying EU citizenship (ii): the rule of law, protection of fundamental rights, democracy, transparency, and good administration, and thus improve the accountability and legitimacy of EU governance, reducing the gap with the citizen.[1538] They are the corollary of the exercise of public power by the EU. The very existence of these rights shows the average citizen that governance at EU level directly impacts on his or her daily life. Even if the rights have a limited material scope, the underlying principles are important for the functioning of a healthy democracy. They stimulate critical thinking on EU matters (iii) and are rights granted to all EU citizens (iv). Reading Article 24 TFEU jointly with EDC standards, these rights should be inserted into the EU dimension of EDC to empower EU citizens to exercise them to their full potential.

5. The right to communicate in a Treaty language

206 Closeness to citizens

Every citizen of the Union (iv) has the right to address institutions and advisory bodies of the EU in one of the languages of the Treaties and to obtain a reply in the same language (Articles 24 TFEU fourth sentence, 41(4) CFR). This is an aspect of the right to good administration. The right to communicate in a Treaty language is crucial for a Union which 'places the individual at the heart of its activities, by establishing the citizenship of

1537 Ibid, 723.

1538 Ibid, 723–741; A Tsadiras, 'The European Ombudsman's remedial powers: an empirical analysis in context' (2013) 38 ELRev 52; A Tsadiras, 'Maladministration and life beyond legality: The European Ombudsman's paradigm' (2015) 3 International Review of Law 11.

the Union'.[1539] The right to use one's own language is an additional and significant citizenship right (i, ii), relevant to mainstream education to the extent that it underlines the aim of closeness to citizens and participatory democracy. The consequences of this right may be a topic for critical reflection (iii). The right to communicate or be communicated with in one of the EU official languages means that many translators and interpreters have to be recruited as civil servants (24 Treaty languages). Pupils can discuss whether they would prefer a smaller EU 'bureaucracy' and the possibility of contacting EU institutions only, for instance, in English, French, or German.[1540]

6. The right to a European citizens' initiative

207 Relevance in general for the EU dimension

Every citizen of the Union (iv) has the right to participate in the democratic life of the Union through the mechanism of the European Citizens' Initiative (hereafter ECI). This right is not included in the CFR, nor in the list of citizenship rights in Article 20 TFEU, yet it is set out in Article 11(4) TEU and benefits from the legal basis for secondary law in Article 24 TFEU. The fact that the legal basis is included amid citizenship rights sug-

1539 Preamble CFR. See also Art. 55(1) TEU and Art 342 TFEU; and Case C-377/16 *Spain v Parliament* ECLI:EU:C:2019:249. On EU language policy, see i.a. Commission Directive (EU) 2016/882 of 1 June 2016 amending Directive 2007/59/EC of the European Parliament and of the Council as regards language requirements C/2016/3213 [2016] OJ L146/22; Decision 1934/2000 of the European Parliament and of the Council of 17 July 2000 on the European Year of Languages 2001 [2000] OJ L232/1; Council Conclusions of 20 May 2014 on multilingualism and the development of language competences [2014] OJ C183/26; European Parliament Resolution of 24 March 2009 on Multilingualism: an asset for Europe and a shared commitment [2010] OJ C117E/59 , 59; Council Recommendation of 22 May 2019 on a comprehensive approach to the teaching and learning of languages [2019] OJ C189/15. See also Van Bossuyt, 'Is there an effective European legal framework for the protection of minority languages? The European Union and the Council of Europe screened'; G Guliyeva, 'Education, Languages and Linguistic Minorities in the EU: Challenges and Perspectives' (2013) 19 ELJ 219; van der Jeught, 'Conflicting Language Policies in the European Union and its Member States'.

1540 See N Vogiatzis, 'The linguistic policy of the EU institutions and political participation post-Lisbon' (2016) 41 ELRev 176 (analysis in the light of democratic participation rights, 'united in diversity', and considerations of resources and efficiency).

gests that the Treaty drafters considered the ECI to be a citizenship right, although they did not adapt the list of rights in Article 20(2) TFEU. Since EU lawyers, too, usually discuss it in the category of citizenship rights attaching to the EU citizen status,[1541] I have included this right in the chapter on classic citizenship rights. The ECI is enshrined in EU primary law and the 2011 ECI Regulation sets out the procedures and conditions for exercise of the right.[1542] From 1 January 2020 onwards, Regulation 2019/788 will apply.[1543]

On a combined reading of EU law and EDC standards, the citizens' initiative should have a prominent place in the EU dimension of national EDC, partly because of its potential for democracy, partly as a hook on which to hang other EU learning. It provides additional (i) and significant (ii) content, invites critical thinking in several ways (iii) and affects all EU citizens (iv). Learners should be equipped with knowledge, skills and understanding (EDC component b) of this right and of the DNA of the EU in general in order to effectively exercise this right (c-1) and—to the extent possible—to play an active part in democratic life of the Union (c-3). If education aims to enable citizens to participate effectively in a free society (Article 13 ICESCR), knowledge of the citizens' initiative should be part of the compulsory curriculum as an occasion for presenting the EU's ground rules of play, in particular the foundational principle of conferral.

1541 Case T-561/14 *One of Us and Others* ECLI:EU:T:2018:210, para 99. See also text to n 1652. Commonly seen as a citizenship right, e.g. in citizenship reports under Art 25 TFEU, i.a. Commission Report under Article 25 TFEU 'On progress towards effective EU citizenship 2013-2016' COM(2017) 32 final, 15.

1542 Regulation (EU) No 211/2011 of the European Parliament and of the Council of 16 February 2011 on the citizens' initiative [2011] OJ L 65/1 (legal basis of Art 24(1) TFEU). Further, i.a., Commission Implementing Reg (EU) No 1179/2011 of 17 November 2011 laying down technical specifications for online collection systems pursuant to Regulation (EU) No 211/2011 of the European Parliament and of the Council on the citizens' initiative [2018] OJ L301/3; Commission Delegated Regulation (EU) No 887/2013 of 11 July 2013 replacing Annexes II and III to Regulation (EU) No 211/2011 of the European Parliament and of the Council on the citizens' initiative [2013] OJ L247/11; Commission Delegated Regulation (EU) 2015/1070 of 31 March 2015 amending Annexes III, V and VII of Regulation (EC) No 211/2011 of the European Parliament and of the Council on the citizens' initiative [2015] OJ L178/1; Commission Report on the application of Regulation (EU) No 211/2011 on the citizens' initiative COM(2015) 145 final.

1543 Regulation (EU) 2019/788 of the European Parliament and of the Council of 17 April 2019 on the European citizens' initiative [2019] OJ L130/55 (hereafter the 2019 ECI Regulation).

At the same time, the question of the impact of the ECI on the democratic life of the Union cannot be avoided and calls for reflection. These elements will now be explained.

208 *Participation right*

All EU citizens can launch an ECI, inviting the Commission within the framework of its powers to submit any appropriate proposal on matters where they consider that a legal act of the Union is required for the purpose of implementing the Treaties. It requires the support of at least one million eligible signatories.[1544] This right is an additional right directly granted by EU law (i) to all EU citizens who are entitled to vote in elections to the European Parliament (iv).[1545] The right provides for two forms of democratic participation: organising or signing an ECI. Organisers form a citizens' committee to prepare the initiative and to submit it. Signatories complete a statement of support after the ECI has been registered by the Commission. The right is significant, in the sense of relating to foundational values, objectives, and principles, especially to the principle of democracy (ii). Whereas the functioning of the EU is in general founded on representative democracy (Article 10(1) TEU), the ECI is an expression of participatory democracy. The tone is ambitious: the ECI is an 'important and innovative tool in the European decision-making process, in the spirit of true European citizenship'; 'Europeans are at the heart of the European venture and this mechanism could help overcome the democratic deficit'.[1546] The ECI is intended to involve EU citizens actively in the EU decision-making process by offering them an indirect form of the right to initiate legislation. Like the Parliament and the Council, EU citizens, too, may request the Commission to submit an appropriate proposal.[1547] It provides an element of direct democracy.

Admittedly, this 'direct' participation is indirect in the sense that citizens can only propose to propose. A successful ECI does not oblige the Commission to make a proposal. The democratic input of citizens is limited to making suggestions for agenda-setting. After a huge effort by citizens to collect one million signatures, the Commission still has a free

---

1544 2011 ECI Regulation Art 2; 2019 ECI Regulation Art 3. See Art 11(4) TEU.

1545 2011 ECI Regulation Art 3(1) and (4); cp 2019 ECI Regulation Art 2.

1546 Preamble 2011 ECI Regulation; Opinion of the European Economic and Social Committee on The European Citizens' Initiative (review) [2016] OJ C389/35, paras 1.1 and 3.11.

1547 Arts 225 TFEU (Parliament); 241 TFEU (Council), 11(4) TEU citizens.

hand.[1548] The ECI does not affect the Commission's near-monopoly of legislative initiative (Articles 17(2) TEU, 289 TFEU). The Commission must communicate its legal and political conclusions on the ECI, the action it intends to take—'if any'—and the reasons for this.[1549] It is in order to promote the general interest of the EU that the Commission takes appropriate initiatives and determines the subject-matter, objective and content of its proposals for legislation.[1550]

Though indirect and limited, the ECI is an established participation right and a step towards a transnational democracy, as it necessarily involves citizens of several Member States. Article 11(4) TEU requires the signatures of one million citizens who are nationals of 'a significant number of Member States'. The 2011 ECI Regulation requires the organisers to form a citizens' committee of at least seven persons who are residents of at least seven different Member States, and the signatories of an ECI must come from at least one quarter of the Member States.[1551] That the ECI promotes the development of an EU public sphere, crucial for democracy in the EU, can be seen from the debates on various initiatives. The ECI topics and standpoints attract attention and provoke transnational discussion, whether on diversity in Europe, wage differences, refugees, or plastic in the sea. Four ECIs have reached the one million signatures threshold: 'Right2Water', 'One of us' (to stop the financing of research which implies destruction of human embryos), 'Stop vivisection' (to abolish testing on

---

1548 Case T-561/14 *One of Us and Others* ECLI:EU:T:2018:210, para 119, the applicants expect an influence proportional to the huge effort invested.

1549 2011 ECI Regulation Art 10(1)(c); 2019 ECI Regulation Art 15(2). In *One of us* (ibid), the General Court considered a communication of the Commission as an act which can be challenged under Art 263 TFEU (paras 66 ff). On the near-monopoly, see Case C-409/13 *Council v Commission* ECLI:EU:C:2015:217, Opinion of AG Jääskinen, para 43; Case T-561/14 *One of Us and Others* ECLI:EU:T:2018:210, paras 109–12 (dismisses the action on the ECI). Further Case C-418/18 P *Puppinck and Others v Commission* pending, and Opinion of AG Bobek. For criticism of the Commission's near-monopoly on the right of legislative initiative, see i.a. Opinion of the European Economic and Social Committee on 'The transition towards a more sustainable European future— a strategy for 2050' [2018] OJ C81/44, para 5.2.2.

1550 Case C-409/13 *Council v Commission* ECLI:EU:C:2015:217, para 70. See also n 1553.

1551 2011 ECI Regulation Arts 3 and 7; 2019 ECI Regulation Arts 2, 3 and 5. The minimum number of signatories per Member State is specificied in the Annex to the Regulations. See also Smith, 'The European Citizens' Initiative: A New Institution for Empowering Europe's Citizens?', 280, on explicit transnational ambition of the ECI.

animals), and 'Ban glyphosate and protect people and the environment from toxic pesticides'.[1552] The Commission formulated proposals responding to some of them.[1553] It is incontestable that the ECI invites citizens to think critically (iii), a crucial component of EDC and an intrinsic element of the ECI. It stimulates reflection on the state of play in the Union and on suggestions for new legal acts. Moreover, the right itself is a topic for critical reflection.

Looking through the prism of EDC standards, the most important aspect which requires attention is the requirement that a proposed ECI does not manifestly fall outside the Commission's powers. This requirement will now be analysed in order to draw conclusions with regard to EDC.

209 The need to include the principle of conferral in the EU dimension

The EU dimension of EDC may help to empower citizens to overcome the 'not-manifestly-outside-the-powers' obstacle of the ECI.

The text of Article 11(4) TEU is clear: the Commission may be invited 'within the framework of its powers' to submit a proposal on matters where citizens consider that 'a legal act' is required 'for the purpose of implementing the Treaties'. The ECI 2011 and 2019 Regulations lay down as a condition for registration that the proposed ECI does not manifestly fall outside the framework of the Commission's powers to submit a proposal for a legal act of the Union for the purpose of implementing the Treaties.[1554] The ECI cannot either be manifestly contrary to the values of the Union as set out in Article 2 TEU.[1555] Citizens are thus assumed to understand the foundational principles related to competences (conferral and legal bases) and the foundational values (ii). The main hurdle is the first. It underlines the relevance of an EU dimension of EDC and the need to provide basic knowledge about EU primary law (first pillar), about the

---

1552 <ec.europa.eu/citizens-initiative/public/initiatives/successful>. Full name of the ECI 'Right2Water' is 'Water and sanitation are a human right! Water is a public good, not a commodity!'.

1553 For action in follow-up of concrete ECIs, Commission Report under Article 25 TFEU 'On progress towards effective EU citizenship 2013-2016' COM(2017) 32 final, 15. E.g., the ECI 'One of us' did not lead to corresponding action of the Commission; as a follow-up to the ECI 'Ban glyphosate and protect people and the environment from toxic pesticides', the Commission adopted a proposal to revise the General Food Law Regulation.

1554 2011 ECI Regulation Art 4(2)(b); 2019 ECI Regulation Art 6(3)(c) 'none of the parts', but (4) allows partial registration.

1555 2011 ECI Regulation Art 4(2)(d); 2019 ECI Regulation Art 6(3)(e).

principle that the EU may only act within the limits of the competences conferred on it to achieve certain objectives (objective driven polity) and about the role of EU institutions in the legislative process. The condition that the ECI may not fall manifestly outside the Commission's powers has led the Commission to refuse the registration of many ECIs.[1556]

As a *first example* for (advanced) case teaching, the story of Mr Anagnostakis invites critical thinking about the EU and its policies, as well as about the ECI itself.[1557]

> Mr Alexios Anagnostakis is a Greek citizen living in Athens. He submits an ECI entitled 'One million signatures for a Europe of solidarity'. The objective is to enshrine in EU law the principle of 'the state of necessity': when the financial and political existence of a Member State is threatened by the servicing of abhorrent debt, then the refusal to repay that debt is necessary and justifiable. He proposes Articles 119 to 144 TFEU as legal basis, i.e. the economic and monetary policy of the Union. The Commission decides to refuse registration of this ECI because it manifestly falls outside the scope of its powers. The Commission rejects the Treaty Articles cited as a legal basis and can find no other possible legal bases. Mr Anagnostakis brings an action for annulment of the decision of the Commission. The General Court dismisses this action, because the ECI does indeed manifestly fall outside the scope of the Commission's powers and the decision of the Commission is moreover sufficiently reasoned. On appeal, the ECJ recalls that the right to initiate an ECI constitutes (like the right to petition the Parliament) an instrument relating to the right of citizens to partici-

1556 Opinion of the European Economic and Social Committee on The European Citizens' Initiative (review) [2016] OJ C389/35, para 3.10.2: around 40% of the ECIs were declared inadmissible at the registration phase. See Commission Report on the application of Regulation (EU) No 211/2011 on the citizens' initiative COM(2018) 157 final: in 2018, the Commission registered 48 initiatives and refused registration of 22. For the registered ('open-closed') and rejected ECIs, see <www.citizens-initiative.eu/eci/>. See Case C-589/15 P *Anagnostakis* ECLI:EU:C:2017:663, Opinion of AG Mengozzi, para 6: the condition of Article 4(2)(b) 'should not be interpreted too broadly, in my view, as the European right of initiative, the importance of which I have already stressed, would become devoid of substance'. See also Case C-420/16 P *Izsák and Dabis v Commission* ECLI:EU:C:2019:177, para 64. Further A Karatzia, 'The European Citizens' Initiative in Practice: Legal Admissibility Concerns' (2015) 40 ELRev 509.

1557 Case C-589/15 P *Anagnostakis* ECLI:EU:C:2017:663. The case is probably of particular interest for secondary school curricula focusing on economics and finance.

pate in the democratic life of the Union (Article 10(3) TEU).[1558] Having regard to the very nature of an ECI and the possible impact of a decision to refuse to register a proposed ECI, the Commission must state the reasons justifying the refusal in a clear way (in casu, why the ECI manifestly falls outside the scope of the powers). Mr Anagnostakis had only very briefly referred to the economic and monetary policy of the Union, mentioning the Treaty Articles. The ECJ considers that in these circumstances the Commission's reasons are sufficient (without there being any need to explain the Treaty Articles cited one by one, nor any other Treaty Article).[1559] The ECJ finds that the proposed initiative is manifestly not a measure of financial assistance which the Council can adopt based on Article 122(2) TFEU. Neither does the proposed principle of necessity fall within the terms of Article 136(1) TFEU, which concerns strengthening the coordination and surveillance of Member States' budgetary discipline. Furthermore, the mere existence of a principle of the state of necessity in international law does not suffice for EU action: 'it is only if competence is conferred in the Treaties to this effect that the Commission may propose the adoption of a legal act of the Union'. The Court refers to the principle of conferral (Article 5 TEU): the Union shall act only within the limits of the competences conferred upon it by the Member States *in the Treaties* to attain the objectives set out *therein*. The EU institutions must act within the limit of the powers conferred on them *in the Treaties* (Article 13(2) TEU).[1560] The ECJ dismisses the appeal.

The *Anagnostakis* case illustrates—in the context of the ECI—the importance of the principle of conferral and of the Treaties as foundational texts of the EU. This case moreover invites pupils to reflect critically on EU policies in the context of the financial crisis, on austerity measures, or on the level of democracy in the economic governance of the EU. Economic governance is based on EU regulations but also on intergovernmental agreements (e.g. establishing the European Stability Mechanism).[1561] *Anagnos-*

1558 Para 24.

1559 Para 38.

1560 Emphasis not in the ECJ judgment, but taken from the Opinion of AG Mengozzi, para 61. AG Mengozzi advises Mr Anagnostakis, if necessary, to submit a new ECI which might be registered if better reasoned, more detailed and precise.

1561 Treaty establishing the European Stability Mechanism (ESM) (Brussels, 2 February 2012). See, i.a., Case C-370/12 *Pringle* ECLI:EU:C:2012:756.

takis indicates that action based on EU law guarantees more democratic input than action through intergovernmental agreements.[1562] If a legal basis is provided in the Treaties, a citizens' initiative can be registered. By contrast, as observed by scholars, intergovernmental agreements are largely based on the bargaining power of parties (governments), negotiated behind closed doors. The democratic input is likely to be limited to the ratification by parliaments of the finished product. *Do we understand European integration as the product of intergovernmental bargaining or as something more?* Pupils are invited to reflect. *To what extent can EU legitimacy be based on negotiations between Member States' governments?*[1563] If the EU is purely seen as an intergovernmental bargain between Member State governments, the degree of democratic legitimacy would be satisfactory 'as long as the Council and the Member State executive bureaucrats retain formal control over the decision-making process'.[1564] Democratic legitimacy is then understood as formal accountability. If democracy is seen as the existence of multiple overlapping spheres of decision-making with input from citizens, giving access to multiple forums for debate,[1565] then the EU dimension to EDC is relevant.

A second example for case teaching in this respect is *Efler*, concerning the ECI 'STOP TTIP'.[1566] The case reveals the tensions and the transnational debate about the democratic input of citizens when the EU concludes international agreements. *Efler* highlights the importance attached to the ECI as a tool for democratic participation. By upholding the right to an ECI, the General Court safeguards EU citizens' rights of democratic participation when the EU concludes international agreements. If more free trade agreements are to be concluded, EU citizens should know about this tool for participation.

1562 For EU conclusion of international agreements, see Arts 216–9 TFEU.

1563 See, i.a., Halberstam, 'The bride of Messina: constitutionalism and democracy in Europe'; S Garben, *EU Higher education law. The Bologna Process and harmonization by stealth* (European Monographs 76, Kluwer Law 2011) 213 (deals are largely removed from parliamentary scrutiny', 231 ('the EU for all its democratic defects is still more democratic than the intergovernmental *smoke-filled rooms* of the Sorbonne and Bologna Declarations'); van Middelaar, *The passage to Europe: How a Continent became a Union*, 12 (intermediate sphere; bargaining in the sense of: you do something for my people in your country and I will do something for your people in my country).

1564 Halberstam ibid, 797.

1565 Ibid, 775.

1566 Case T-754/14 *Efler* ECLI:EU:T:2017:323.

The ECI 'STOP TTIP' seeks to prevent the conclusion by the EU of an international agreement with Canada (CETA) and with the US (TTIP). It asks the Commission to propose that the Council cancels the negotiation mandate for TTIP and does not conclude CETA.[1567] The citizens' committee argues that these agreements have provisions threatening democracy and the rule of law. The ECI i.a. wants to avoid 'opaque negotiations leading to a weakening of the rules on employment protection, social protection, environmental protection, protection of private life and of consumers'.[1568] The Commission refuses registration, claiming that this initiative does not propose a 'legal act' in the sense of Article 11(4) TEU, but only relates to a preparatory act allowing the Council to open negotiations and to conclude an international agreement. The Commission argues that citizens should not interfere in these processes and that, together with the Council, it has sufficient indirect democratic legitimacy to act until a definitive agreement is concluded (a legal act producing legal effects vis-à-vis third parties). Michael Efler and other members of the citizens' committee ask the General Court to annul the decision of the Commission refusing to register the ECI. The General Court recalls the importance of the principle of democracy and the objective of the ECI of improving the democratic functioning of the EU by granting every citizen a general right to participate in democratic life. This requires 'an interpretation of the concept of legal act which covers legal acts such as a decision to open negotiations with a view to concluding an international agreement, which manifestly seeks to modify the legal order of the European Union'.[1569] Because TTIP and CETA seek to modify the EU legal order, and because the object of the ECI is to prevent the conclusion of TTIP and CETA, the proposed legal act contributes to the implementation of the Treaties.[1570] Nothing justifies excluding from democratic debate legal acts seeking the withdrawal of a decision authorising the opening of negotiations for an international agree-

1567 CETA stands for the 'Comprehensive Economic and Trade Agreement' of the EU with Canada; TTIP for the 'Transatlantic Trade and Investment Partnership' of the EU with the US. See, i.a., J Mendes, *Participation in a New Regulatory Paradigm: Collaboration and Constraint in TTIP's Regulatory Cooperation* (IILJ Working Paper 2016/5 2016).

1568 Other critical issues concern i.a. dispute resolution between investors and States. The proposed legal bases are Arts 207 and 218 TFEU.

1569 Case T-754/14 *Efler* ECLI:EU:T:2017:323, para 37. See also para 36.

1570 Para 41.

ment as well as acts seeking to prevent the signing and conclusion of an international agreement.[1571] The Court considers that 'far from amounting to an interference in an ongoing legislative procedure, ECI proposals constitute an expression of the effective participation of citizens of the European Union in the democratic life thereof, without undermining the institutional balance intended by the Treaties'.[1572] The General Court annuls the Commission Decision which refused the registration.[1573]

The *Anagnostakis* and *Efler* examples demonstrate the importance of the ECI as a tool for participation in the democratic life of the Union, as well as its limits, given the requirement that the initiative may not manifestly fall outside the powers of the Commission.[1574] While the Commission has refused many ECIs on this ground, it recently adopted a more flexible approach by partially registering ECIs, i.e. to the extent that they do not manifestly fall outside the Commission's powers.[1575] To ensure that as

---

1571 Para 43.

1572 Para 47.

1573 After the judgment, the ECI was registered but collected 0 signatures. In 2015 the 'self-organised' (non-registered) ECI had collected more than 3 million signatures (<www.citizens-initiative.eu/eci/>).

1574 On the obligation for the Commission to give reasons when refusing to register an ECI, see Art 4(3) 2011 ECI Regulation, Art 6(4) 2019 ECI Regulation. Sufficient reasons were found in Case T-44/14 *Costantini and Others* ECLI:EU:T:2016:223 (on ECI 'Right to Lifelong Care'); insufficient reasons in Case T-646/13 *Bürgerausschuss für die Bürgerinitiative Minority SafePack — one million signatures for diversity in Europe* ECLI:EU:T:2017:59, leading to annulment of the Commission's decision refusing to register. See also Case C-589/15 P *Anagnostakis* ECLI:EU:C:2017:663, Opinion of AG Mengozzi, para 24 (refusals need 'a very explanatory approach, given that not all authors of such proposed initiatives are necessarily experienced specialists in EU law').

1575 Cp the 2015 and 2018 reports: Commission Report on the application of Regulation (EU) No 211/2011 on the citizens' initiative COM(2015) 145 final and Commission Report on the application of Regulation (EU) No 211/2011 on the citizens' initiative COM(2018) 157 final, table: Overview of initiatives (2 refused between 4/2015 and 3/2018, 17 registered). Registered, e.g. Commission Decision (EU) 2019/1564 of 4 September 2019 on the proposed citizens' initiative entitled 'Stop corruption in Europe at its root, by cutting off funds to countries with inefficient judiciary after deadline' [2019] OJ L 241/6; Refused, e.g. Commission Decision (EU) 2019/1182 of 3 July 2019 on the proposed citizens' initiative entitled 'EU law, minority rights and democratisation of Spanish institutions' [2019] OJ L 185/46.

many initiatives as possible are registered, the 2019 ECI Regulation now expressly provides for registering partly.[1576]

The ECI does not meet the high expectations it engendered. The tool is intended to be 'clear, simple and user-friendly'.[1577] Despite the assistance provided to organisers[1578], flaws have been pointed out by citizens, civil society organisations, scholars, and some EU institutions and bodies.[1579]

1576 Art 6(4)(b), recital 19.

1577 2011 ECI Regulation, recital 2 ('so as to encourage participation by citizens and to make the Union more accessible').

1578 For the duty of the Commission to provide assistance and advice to the organisers, see Art 4(1) and recital 4 of 2011 ECI Regulation. Support, i.a., by initiatives such as the European Citizens' Initiative Day, websites, or publications, e.g. European Economic and Social Committee, European Passport to Active Citizenship (2015).

1579 See, i.a., Decision of the European Ombudsman closing her own-initiative inquiry OI/9/2013/TN concerning the European Commission (4 March 2015); European Parliament Resolution of 28 October 2015 on the European Citizens' Initiative [2017] OJ C355/17; Opinion of the European Economic and Social Committee on The European Citizens' Initiative (review) [2016] OJ C389/35, para 3.3, see also paras 1.3, 1.4.5, 3.9.2, 5.2, and 6.1.5 (excess of powers of the Commission with regard to the ECI; suggestion of a separation of the roles of institutional mentor and judge to respond to the conflict of interests); Opinion of the European Economic and Social Committee on 'The transition towards a more sustainable European future— a strategy for 2050' [2018] OJ C81/44, para 5.2.2. See also analyses of J Pilcher and B Kaufmann (eds), *The European Citizens Initiative: Into New Democratic Territory* (Intersentia 2010); M Dougan, 'What are we to make of the citizens' initiative?' (2011) 48 CMLRev 1807; P Ponzano, 'L'initiative citoyenne européenne: la démocratie participative à l'épreuve' [2012] Revue du droit de l'Union européenne 615; Smith, 'The European Citizens' Initiative: A New Institution for Empowering Europe's Citizens?'; F Dehousse, *The European Citizens' Initiative: Next Big Thing of New False Good Idea?* (Egmont Paper 59, Academia Press 2013); J Organ, 'Decommissioning Direct Democracy? A Critical Analysis of Commission Decision-Making on the Legal Admissibility of European Citizens Initiative Proposals' (2014) 10 European Constitutional Law Review 422; Karatzia, 'The European Citizens' Initiative in Practice: Legal Admissibility Concerns'; M Conrad, 'The ECI's Contribution to the Emergence of a European Public Sphere' in M Conrad, A Knaut and K Böttger (eds), *Bridging the Gap? Opportunities and Constraints of the European Citizens' Initiative* (Nomos 2016); E Van Rijckevorsel, 'Initiative citoyenne et "dérapages démocratiques" dans l'Union européenne' (2016) 24 Journal de droit européen 52; A Karatzia, 'The European Citizens' Initiative and the EU institutional balance: On realism and the possibilities of affecting EU lawmaking' (2017) 54 CMLRev 177 (i.a. on current mismatch between EU citizens' expectations and the ECI's capacity to lead to legislative output).

The mythical EU citizen who launches an initiative, collects one million signatures for his or her idea, and persuades the Commission to adopt a proposal for EU legislation is an illusion. The high threshold means that the support of major civil society organisations with shared interests is necessary, and is costly.[1580] The 2019 ECI Regulation aims to make the ECI more accessible, less burdensome and easier to use in order to achieve its full potential.[1581] To achieve the full potential of the ECI for citizens, I suggest that Member States incorporate the ECI within the EU dimension of national EDC and that the EU—as an additional measure—promotes this EU dimension in education.[1582] One of the main challenges which institutions and stakeholders repeatedly point out, is the lack of knowledge and awareness of the ECI tool. Realising the full potential of the ECI is therefore not only a matter of resolving technical, organisational or bureaucratic difficulties. It requires, in addition, that citizens are aware that 'the EU legal order is governed by the principle of conferral of powers and [that] participatory democracy, which Article 11(4) TEU seeks to bring to life, can thus be exercised only within these limits'.[1583] Even if the new ECI Regulation introduces clearer, simpler, and user-friendlier procedures and conditions, 'proportionate to the nature of the ECI so as to encourage participation by citizens and to make the Union more accessible',[1584] even if organisers of an ECI receive enhanced support and assistance upon request,[1585] the effectiveness of the ECI requires elementary pre-knowledge and understanding of the EU. Including the ECI in the EU dimension of components (c-1) and (c-3) of EDC in the classroom is a good way to bring these essentials aspects of the EU to the fore. Academic writers look at the ECI from the vantage point of the non-specialised EU citizen and highlight

---

1580 Smith, 'The European Citizens' Initiative: A New Institution for Empowering Europe's Citizens?', 286 ('mythical citizen'); Opinion of the European Economic and Social Committee on The European Citizens' Initiative (review) [2016] OJ C389/35, para 3.10.5. See, e.g., experience of students organising ECI 'Teach for Youth—Upgrade to Erasmus 2.0', which collected 421 signatures, <teachforyouth.wixsite.com/teachforyouth>.

1581 Recital 5. See also Commission Staff working document Accompanying the document Proposal for a Regulation of the European Parliament and of the Council on the European citizens' initiative SWD(2017) 294 final.

1582 Proposed legal basis: Arts 165–6 TFEU together with Art 11(4) TEU and Art 24 para 1 TFEU. See competences in Part four.

1583 Case C-589/15 P *Anagnostakis* ECLI:EU:C:2017:663, Opinion of AG Mengozzi, para 2.

1584 2011 ECI Regulation, recital 2.

1585 2019 ECI Regulation Art 4(1), recital 13.

the fact that the ECI requires substantial knowledge of EU legislative competences and the EU institutional framework.[1586] EDC can meet these concerns to some extent on the basis of general EDC standards. Of course, one cannot expect the EU dimension to introduce pupils to all the legal bases in the Treaties (even EU experts discuss their limits). Yet, the average citizen should learn about the DNA of the EU, to which Articles 5(2) and 13(2) TEU belong. Citizens would then be more motivated to sign an ECI and better able to understand the assistance of the Commission when organising it.

Certainly, the proposed extra information and communication strategies are essential to remedy the unsatisfactory use of the ECI.[1587] However, taking democracy and participation rights seriously, more fundamental steps are needed. *Educating* citizens is more effective than *informing* citizens. In line with international standards, the underlying citizenship competence must be addressed.[1588] A combined reading of Article 24 TFEU and EDC standards requires the inclusion of this democratic participation tool in the EU dimension of EDC in mainstream education. An effective use of the ECI by all citizens not only presupposes awareness of the right, but also an understanding of the multilevel system of governance, including the principle of conferral. While the *existence* of direct participation tools increases the perception of empowerment of EU citizens,[1589] *using* them may lead to frustration and disillusionment if not preceded by appropriate citizenship education. Negative experiences with the ECI are likely to further alienate

---

1586 Smith, 'The European Citizens' Initiative: A New Institution for Empowering Europe's Citizens?', 283; Karatzia, 'The European Citizens' Initiative in Practice: Legal Admissibility Concerns', 528–9; M Conrad and F Steingrímsdóttir, 'A Tool for European Citizens? A Typology of ECI Organizers 2012–2015' in M Conrad, A Knaut and K Böttger (eds), *Bridging the Gap?: Opportunities and Constraints of the European Citizens' Initiative* (Nomos 2016).

1587 2019 ECI Regulation Art 4; Opinion of the European Economic and Social Committee on The European Citizens' Initiative (review) [2016] OJ C389/35, paras 1.6.1, 6.3.1, 3.9.1; Commission Staff working document Accompanying the document Proposal for a Regulation of the European Parliament and of the Council on the European citizens' initiative SWD(2017) 294 final, i.a. stakeholders p 58; Commission Report on the application of Regulation (EU) No 211/2011 on the citizens' initiative COM(2018) 157 final.

1588 Core consensus on EDC (Part one); see further at UN level, i.a. § 294 .

1589 Smith, 'The European Citizens' Initiative: A New Institution for Empowering Europe's Citizens?', 284 (with reference to research), 289 ('the ECI embodies the idea of an empowered European or transnational citizenship, but in practice this will not be realised to the extent that the rhetoric of supporters suggests').

citizens from 'Brussels'. To avoid disappointment, the EU dimension of EDC should draw attention to the limits of the ECI as a tool for democratic participation and situate it—for proper understanding—in the context of other forms of participation in democratic life. The support of one million citizens for the single issue in an ECI must be understood in the general context of European society. Whereas an ECI typically concerns a single issue and reflects the specific interests of certain groups of citizens, the legislator has to strive for the common good of 500 million citizens and must take account of many other (competing) interests. The ECI as an instrument of participatory democracy is complementary to representative democracy. The action of the European Parliament and national parliaments remains crucial for the common good. A nuanced approach is thus necessary.

210 Engaging young citizens

A supplementary argument for including the ECI in the EU dimension of EDC is that under the 2019 ECI Regulation the Member States may set the minimum age entitling to support an initiative at 16 years, and are encouraged to do so.[1590] Setting the minimum age at 16 is indeed a useful way of engaging young people in democratic processes and raising their awareness about the EU and its functioning.[1591] Preparing pupils for this participation tool in secondary schools is an obvious additional step, empowering them for involvement in EU debates. The ECI is also food for reflection about the right itself, for instance about its limited material scope. The ECI is not designed for the re-writing of Treaty provisions, but only for implementing them. This confirms the importance of the Treaties, the first pillar in the proposed EDC learning method. However, the fact that citizens are required to respect the limits of the Treaty can be criticised. The ECI does not allow EU citizens to think out of the box. *Can Treaty content be excluded from democratic debate?* Some scholars have argued for a 'de-

---

1590 2019 ECI Regulation Art 2, recital 7. Cp 2011 ECI Regulation, Art 3(1) and (4).

1591 Commission Staff working document Accompanying the document Proposal for a Regulation of the European Parliament and of the Council on the European citizens' initiative SWD(2017) 294 final, 4.2.1. Lowering the age was recommended by several stakeholders, see ibid, para 4.2.2 (i.a. Parliament, CoR, EESC, and ECI Campaign); e.g. in Luxembourg, citizens of at least 15 years of age can support public petitions. See also Opinion of the European Economic and Social Committee on The European Citizens' Initiative (review) [2016] OJ C389/35, para 6.1.4.

constitutionalisation' of some Treaty content to facilitate legislative initiatives.[1592] The emerging European public sphere should not be limited to EU secondary law.[1593] In this sense, even ECIs refused registration may serve a purpose and have an impact, just like unsuccessful ECIs (registered, but closed without reaching the threshold of one million signatures) or ECIs which were successful but not acted upon by the Commission. They all, at least, draw some attention to the live issues in civil society.[1594]

211 *An unsuccessful ECI on citizenship education*

Unfortunately, one last example must be noted in the context of the live issues in civil society, or more precisely, the not-so-live issues. The ECI entitled 'More than education—Shaping active and responsible citizens' was unsuccessful. It aimed at incentive measures coordinating citizenship education among the Member States 'so that global and European concepts and values are taught to citizens and the citizens are equipped with the competences to actively, responsibly participate in our democratic society'. The proposed action included setting up a long-term agenda, creating and evaluating benchmarks, providing support and exchanging practices in civic education.[1595] The ECI was registered by the Commis-

---

1592 See, eg, Grimm, *The Constitution of European Democracy*. Also D Grimm, 'The Power of Restraint in the European Union' in L Van Middelaar and P Van Parijs (eds), *After the Storm: How to Save Democracy in Europe* (Lannoo 2015), i.a. 116 ('Treaties without democracy'; consequences of negative integration on labour legislation and welfare state); FW Scharpf, 'After the Crash: A Multilevel European Democracy' in L van Middelaar and P Van Parijs (eds), *After the Storm: How to Save Democracy in Europe* (Lannoo 2015), i.a. 147 ('the stranglehold of overextended Treaty law'); P Van Parijs, 'Justifying Europe' in L van Middelaar and P Van Parijs (eds), *After the Storm: How to Save Democracy in Europe* (Lannoo 2015), i.a. 253 (agrees with former authors: de-constitutionalisation to facilitate legislation at EU level towards more justice).

1593 As an exception to the quite rigid application by the Commission of the condition that ECIs must stay within the Treaty limits, scholars point to the registration of the ECI 'Let me vote', which aimed under Article 20(2) TFEU to give citizens living abroad an equal right to vote in all political elections in their country of residence, also the national elections. For analysis: Karatzia, 'The European Citizens' Initiative in Practice: Legal Admissibility Concerns' (closer examination of Art 25 TFEU indicates that a Treaty amendment is not necessary to achieve the objectives). See also text to n 1492.

1594 For Swiss experiences and the impact of unsuccessful initiatives in direct democracy, see Smith, 'The European Citizens' Initiative: A New Institution for Empowering Europe's Citizens?', 284.

1595 See <morethaneducation.eu>. NGO behind the initiative was AEGEE ('Association des États Généraux des Étudiants de l'Europe'), European Students'

sion, but it only collected 1314 signatures.[1596] Although the initiative clearly reflected EDC standards, the interest in it was low. Apparently, citizenship education does not rank among the subjects which mobilise citizens. The good news, however, is that the Commission registered the ECI, accepting Articles 165–166 TFEU as a legal basis. It thus considers that incentive measures for EDC do not manifestly fall outside its powers to propose legislation. I will return to this finding in Chapter nine.[1597]

C *The ambiguities of EU citizenship do not preclude the relevance of EU citizenship rights for EDC*

212 *Ambiguities of EU citizenship*

The analysis of the EU citizenship rights granted by Articles 20–24 TFEU has revealed that these rights in general satisfy the criteria of relevance for mainstream education. They provide additional content (i) to national EDC and are significant (some more than others) (ii). In particular, the rights in Article 24 TFEU by their very nature invite critical thinking (iii) and are relevant for all EU citizens, static and mobile ones (iv).

However, it must be admitted that EU citizenship suffers from ambiguities and paradoxes. Awareness of the questions they raise is appropriate when applying EDC standards. Issues of (in)equality have already been discussed.[1598] Ambiguities also exist as to the attachment of rights to the status of EU citizenship. Scholars have expressed criticism.[1599] On the one

---

Forum ('one of Europe's biggest interdisciplinary student organisations, striving for a democratic, diverse and borderless Europe').

1596 Closed on 6 October 2017.

1597 Other registered yet unsuccessful ECIs in the field of education: High Quality European Education for All; Teach for Youth—Upgrade to Erasmus 2.0; Do not count education spending as part of the deficit! Education is an investment! See registered and ongoing ECI: Commission Decision (EU) 2019/434 of 27 February 2019 on the proposed citizens' initiative entitled 'Europe CARES — Inclusive Quality Education for Children with Disabilities' [2019] OJ L 75/103 (legal basis 19, 165–166 TFEU).

1598 See i.a. free movement rights and equality (lack of): text to nn 1421 ff. In general, text to n 1017.

1599 See i.a. Calliess, 'Der Unionsbürger: Status, Dogmatik und Dynamik'; U Liebert, 'The European Citizenship Paradox: Renegotiating Equality and Diversity in the New Europe' (2007) 10 Critical Review of International Social and Political Philosophy 417; N Nic Shuibhne, 'Three paradoxes of EU citizenship (Editorial)' (2010) ELRev 129; Nic Shuibhne, 'The Resilience of EU Mar-

hand, rights are conferred on EU citizens 'by virtue of their status as citizens of the Union',[1600] in contrast to the limited rights of third country nationals, and independently of economic activities.[1601] On the other hand, the category of EU citizens, i.e. nationals of Member States, cannot simply be equated with the category of holders of citizenship rights under Articles 20–24 TFEU.[1602] Entitlement to citizenship rights is not unambiguous. As Davis writes: '[t]he legal definition of a Union citizen is incompatible with the scope of most Union citizens' rights'.[1603] Paradoxically, so-called citizenship rights are (1) attributed to a larger group than EU citizens and (2) of benefit to a much smaller group than EU citizens. The 'citizenship rights' are not necessarily enjoyed by *only* EU citizens, nor by *all* of them. Sometimes, the personal scope is broadened to include *every person*, while, conversely, at other times, the scope of the right is narrowed down by certain conditions, so that not all citizens of the Union derive benefits from these rights.

(1) Citizenship rights are not exclusively for EU citizens. The rights attaching to the status of EU citizenship do not create an exclusive relationship

---

ket Citizenship'; Shaw, 'Citizenship: Contrasting Dynamics at the Interface of Integration and Constitutionalism'; D Kostakopoulou, 'When EU Citizens become Foreigners' (2014) 20 ELJ 447; J Menéndez, 'Which Citizenship? Whose Europe? - The Many Paradoxes of European Citizenship' (2014) 15 German Law Journal 928; Kochenov, 'On Tiles and Pillars: EU Citizenship as a Federal Denominator'; Sarmiento and Sharpston, 'European Citizenship and Its New Union: Time to Move on?'.

1600 Case C-34/09 *Ruiz Zambrano* ECLI:EU:C:2011:124, para 42. See also questions in text to n 1691.

1601 Text to n 1442.

1602 RW Davis, 'Citizenship of the Union...rights for all?' (2002) 27 ELRev 121; Kochenov, 'Ius tractum of many faces: European citizenship and the difficult relationship between status and rights', on the complicated relationship between the status of EU citizenship and the rights attached to it, see i.a. 214 ff, 222 ff; N Cambien, 'Citizenship of the Union as a cornerstone of European integration: a study of its impact on policies and competences of the Member States' (KU Leuven 2011), the personal scope of EU citizenship, see i.a. 401 (the bottom-line is that it hinges on the delicate balance between conflicting interests); D Thym, 'Ambiguities of Personhood, Citizenship, Migration and Fundamental Rights' in L Azoulai, S Barbou des Places and E Pataut (eds), *Constructing the Person in EU Law: Rights, Roles, Identities* (Hart 2016); Lenaerts and Gutiérrez-Fons, 'Epilogue on EU Citizenship: Hopes and Fears', 765. Earlier: O'Leary, 'The relationship between Community citizenship and the protection of fundamental rights in Community law'.

1603 Davis, 'Citizenship of the Union...rights for all?', 136.

between nationals of Member States and the EU.[1604] The rights to apply to the European Ombudsman and to petition the European Parliament are conferred on EU citizens by Article 24 TFEU, but are recognised for every residing person by the CFR (but in the Title on Citizens' rights).[1605] The right to good administration and language rights also appear in the Title Citizens' rights, yet are granted to 'any person'.[1606] Davis wrote in 2002 that EU citizens only enjoy two exclusive rights, i.e. the right to vote in European Parliament and municipal elections in any Member State, and the right to diplomatic and consular protection, which gave him 'little cause for excitement'.[1607] However, in 2006 the ECJ held in *Spain v UK* that:

> while citizenship of the Union is destined to be the fundamental status of nationals of the Member States, enabling those who find themselves in the same situation to receive the same treatment in law irrespective of their nationality ..., that statement does not necessarily mean that the rights recognised by the Treaty are limited to citizens of the Union.[1608]

In Gibraltar, non-EU citizens could vote in European Parliament elections under UK law.[1609] The personal scope of citizenship rights is also widened

---

1604 Ibid, 121, 136; Kochenov, 'Ius tractum of many faces: European citizenship and the difficult relationship between status and rights', 175 ('the absolute majority of citizenship rights can be enjoyed by those not possessing such status'), 222–234. See also O'Leary, 'The relationship between Community citizenship and the protection of fundamental rights in Community law' 525.

1605 Arts 43 and 44 CFR.

1606 Art 41, Art 42 adds 'residing'. The other CFR rights are not linked with citizenship, but are in general granted to 'everyone'.

1607 Davis, 'Citizenship of the Union...rights for all?', 137. See text to n 1625. Examples of the *exclusionary* as well as *privileged* character of citizenship as laid down in the CFR are Arts 15(2), 39, 40, 45, 46: see Nic Shuibhne, 'The Developing Legal Dimensions of Union Citizenship'.

1608 Case C-145/04 *Spain v UK* ECLI:EU:C:2006:543, para 74; see also para 73 (the Treaty recognises rights which are linked neither to citizenship of the Union nor even to nationality of a Member State, such as the right to petition or to make a complaint to the European Ombudsman).

1609 See paras 95–96; *Spain v UK* did not directly concern the equal electoral rights of EU citizens under Art 22 TFEU, but rather the personal scope of a right to vote for the EP. While a Member State can widen the scope of the the right to vote (*Spain v UK*), opposite, a Member State can also withhold electoral rights from certain nationals as long as citizens in the same situation are not treated differently (Case C-300/04 *Eman and Sevinger* ECLI:EU:C:2006:545).

in the case of derived rights of third-country nationals who are family members of mobile EU citizens. Moreover, any legally residing third-country national, even without such family ties, may be granted freedom of movement and residence under Article 45(2) CFR.[1610]

That 'citizenship rights' are attached to the status of EU citizenship and that third country nationals may have 'similar rights' is shown by the reaction of the Commission to the ECI 'EU Citizenship for Europeans: United in Diversity in Spite of jus soli and jus sanguinis', submitted after the Brexit referendum. The Commission clarified that there is no legal basis in the Treaties for adopting a legal act for the purpose of implementing the Treaties in order to grant citizenship of the Union to persons who do not hold the nationality of a Member State. Having the nationality of a Member State is a prerequisite for being an EU citizen.[1611] Yet, the Commission registered the ECI (partly), having understood that it sought to propose a legal act to ensure that the citizens of a country which has withdrawn from the Union 'can continue to benefit from *similar rights* to those which they enjoyed whilst that country was a Member State'. To the extent that it aims to 'implement the Treaties in the field of rights of *third country nationals* residing legally in a Member State, including the conditions governing freedom of movement and residence', it did not fall manifestly outside the Commission's powers to submit a proposal.[1612]

(2) Not all EU citizens fall within the scope of provisions on citizenship rights. While so-called citizenship rights are not necessarily limited to EU citizens, conversely, they are not necessarily enjoyed by all EU citizens inasmuch as their exercise must occur in accordance with the conditions and limits defined by the Treaties and by the measures adopted under the Treaties

---

1610 Case C-40/11 *Iida* ECLI:EU:C:2012:691, para 36 (on Dir 2003/109 and national law determing conditions for legal residence of third country nationals). International agreements can grant rights to third country nationals (e.g. to Norwegians (EEA), or Turcs (association agreements); or extend the right to diplomatic and consular protection).

1611 Commission Decision (EU) 2017/599 of 22 March 2017 on the proposed citizens' initiative entitled 'EU Citizenship for Europeans: United in Diversity in Spite of jus soli and jus sanguinis' [2017] OJ L81/18, (2) and (3), also (7). See also Commission Decision 18 July 2018 on the proposed citizens' initiative entitled 'Permanent European Union Citizenship' [2018] OJ C264/4, recital 5 ('rights similar to rights of citizens of the Union').

1612 Commission Decision (EU) 2017/599 of 22 March 2017 on the proposed citizens' initiative entitled 'EU Citizenship for Europeans: United in Diversity in Spite of jus soli and jus sanguinis' [2017] OJ L81/18, Art 1, recital (8). Emphasis added.

(Article 20(2) TFEU last sentence). EU citizenship is not a monolithic concept leading to equal enjoyment of rights.[1613] In order to fall within the scope *ratione materiae* of the central citizenship rights in Articles 20–24 TFEU in the first place, borders must be crossed. In this sense, EU citizenship seems essentially relevant for the mobile citizen.[1614] Paradoxically, those citizenship rights which are relevant for static citizens, i.e. the right to petition the European Parliament, to apply to the European Ombudsman, and the language rights in communications with the EU institutions, have been granted to everyone. The fact that EU citizenship is essentially relevant for the mobile citizen, has led scholars to qualify it as a 'thin' citizenship.[1615] The 'dormant' EU citizen awakens when he crosses borders.[1616] Crossing borders is the nexus required to activate rights, such as

---

1613 Kochenov, 'Ius tractum of many faces: European citizenship and the difficult relationship between status and rights', 173.

1614 See, i.a., Directive 2004/38; preambles of Directive 94/80 (on municipal elections) and Directive 93/109 (on European Parliament elections): 'Whereas citizenship of the Union is intended to enable citizens of the Union to integrate better in their host country' (in the context of Art 22 TFEU). In Commission reports based on Article 25 TFEU, the effects for static citizens are limited: see Commission Report under Article 25 TFEU 'Progress towards effective EU Citizenship 2007-2010' COM(2010) 602 final; Commission EU Citizenship Report 2010 'Dismantling the obstacles to EU citizens' rights COM(2010) 603 final; Commission Report under Article 25 TFEU 'On progress towards effective EU Citizenship 2011-2013' COM(2013) 270 final; Commission Report under Article 25 TFEU 'On progress towards effective EU citizenship 2013-2016' COM(2017) 32 final. Also in earlier reports: Commission Report on the Citizenship of the Union COM(93) 702 final; Commission Second Report on Citizenship of the Union COM(97) 230 final; Commission Third Report on Citizenship of the Union COM(2001) 506; Commission Fourth Report on Citizenship of the Union (1 May 2001—30 April 2004) COM(2004) 695 final; Commission Fifth Report on citizenship of the Union (1 May 2004 —30 June 2007) COM(2008) 85 final.

1615 Text to n 1017. 'Potential' versus 'full' EU citizens, see Kochenov, 'Ius tractum of many faces: European citizenship and the difficult relationship between status and rights', 175. See also Shaw, 'The many pasts and futures of citizenship in the European Union', 557 ('in both the Treaty provisions and the associated case law, it is the (economic) rights associated with free movement (especially free movement of persons) which represent the central pillar of Union citizenship, rather than either fundamental rights which construct a universalistic vision of individual status, or political participation rights which construct the citizen as the "sovereign" figure in the Union polity'); Nic Shuibhne, 'Three paradoxes of EU citizenship (Editorial)' ('the "big" consequences of EU citizenship are still felt mostly in the relatively "small" sphere of crossborder mobility. This means that EU citizenship does not yet evoke anything tangible for

the right to non-discrimination on grounds of nationality (linking Articles 21 and 18 TFEU).[1617] Problems of reverse discrimination arise.[1618] The Citizens' Rights Directive further imposes a number of conditions, rendering EU 'citizenship' rights in reality quite unequal.[1619] The different weighting of votes in European Parliament elections adds to the perceived inequalities of EU citizens (differences established to the advantage of smaller Member States).[1620] These inequalities contrast with the traditional (statal) concept of citizenship, where '[c]itizenship denotes an intrinsic status and a set of rights that adhere inherently and equally to all citizens.'[1621] EU citizenship may arouse hopes and fears: hopes that it will lead to a more equal, united and politically integrated supranational society, fears that a broad interpretation of EU citizenship unduly affects the vertical

---

most EU citizens. We continue to lack a more rounded application of citizenship within the European Union and we definitely still lack a shared feeling of that citizenship'); Shaw, 'Citizenship: Contrasting Dynamics at the Interface of Integration and Constitutionalism', text to fn 54 ('the "static" European citizen, in contrast to the mobile transnational one, does not seem to derive many benefits from the institution of citizenship as a fundamental building block of the European Union'); de Witte, Bauböck and Shaw, *Freedom of movement under attack: Is it worth defending as the core of EU citizenship?*. On the scope ratione personae and materiae, see Spaventa, 'Seeing the wood despite the trees? On the scope of union citizenship and its constitutional effects', 14. On ECJ case law widening rights with *Rottmann* and *Ruiz Zambrano*, and circumscribing them later, see i.a. text to n 1456.

1616 In this sense, N Cambien, 'When does someone become a citizen? Dormant and active citizenship in recent case law of the European Court of Justice' (Politicologenetmaal, Maastricht, 12-13 June 2014) ('in accordance with well-established case law, an EU citizen, in principle, only "activates" his EU citizenship after exercising his right to free movement, by residing in another Member State. This leaves the large majority of Member State nationals with a "dormant" EU citizen status, which they cannot invoke as long as they continue to reside in their home Member State.').

1617 No nexus in purely internal situations, see text to n 1467.

1618 On reverse discrimination, see n 1467, text to nn 1804 and 1938. Further O'Leary, 'The Past, Present and Future of the Purely Internal Rule in EU Law'.

1619 See § 220 ff and n 1416 ff. By the way, Member State law also lays down conditions and limitations on the exercise of citizenship rights of nationals.

1620 Kochenov, 'Ius tractum of many faces: European citizenship and the difficult relationship between status and rights', 203 (the weight of the citizen's vote is dependent on the place where the vote is cast). See also *BVerfG, 2 BvE 2/08 (Lissabon)* 30 June 2009, Absatz-Nr (1-421), para 279 aa. Further text to n 1689.

1621 W Maas, 'The Origins, Evolution, and Political Objectives of EU Citizenship' (2014) 15 German Law Journal 797, 812. See also n 1422.

allocation of powers in the Treaties.[1622] The fundamental status is more an aspiration than a realisation.[1623]

213 Yet, relevance for the EU dimension of EDC

The implementation of EDC standards should not depend on the resolution of the ambiguities and paradoxes of EU citizenship. It cannot be denied that the EU citizenship rights listed in Articles 20–24 TFEU are distinct rights which the EU legal order autonomously grants to EU citizens in addition to the entitlements conferred by national law (i). They are genuine, real and concrete rights.[1624] From the adaptation perspective, building further on national citizenship education, EU citizenship rights add content to the EU dimension of EDC components (c-1), to empower EU citizens to exercise their rights and responsibilities, (c-2), to value diversity, and (c-3), to play an active part in democratic life. It is true, to some extent, that the citizenship rights in Articles 20–24 TFEU may give 'little cause for excitement', because of their limited scope (Davis).[1625] Yet, reality shows that for large groups of citizens, both mobile and static (iv), citizenship rights are great cause for excitement, as the Brexit vote and ongoing debates on citizenship rights in and outside the UK illustrate.[1626] Moreover, they are significant (ii). As Craig and de Búrca argue, citizenship

---

1622 See Lenaerts and Gutiérrez-Fons, 'Epilogue on EU Citizenship: Hopes and Fears', 751. Cp Kochenov, 'On Tiles and Pillars: EU Citizenship as a Federal Denominator'; see also other contributions in this work.

1623 Shaw, 'Citizenship: Contrasting Dynamics at the Interface of Integration and Constitutionalism' (text to fn 5); R de Lange, 'Paradoxes of European Citizenship' in P Fitzpatrick (ed), *Nationalism, racism and the rule of law* (Aldershot 1995) 111: 'the suggestion that citizenship is a homogeneous, non-contested concept is in fact part of an EC rule-of-law ideology: as long as we talk about citizenship, we won't have to talk about democracy.'.

1624 Already in Commission Fourth Report on Citizenship of the Union (1 May 2001—30 April 2004) COM(2004) 695 final, 4 ('The importance of Union citizenship lies in the fact that the Union citizens have genuine rights under Community law'), 10 ('Citizenship of the Union has developed over twelve years of existence into a source of real and concrete rights'). See also Maas, 'Unrespected, unequal, hollow? Contingent Citizenship and Reversible Rights in the European Union', 267.

1625 Text to n 1689. O'Leary, 'The relationship between Community citizenship and the protection of fundamental rights in Community law', 527.

1626 See also considerable interest in 'citizenship rights' after the Brexit referendum, in Commission Staff working document on the Application of the EU Charter of Fundamental Rights in 2016 Accompanying the document Communication from the Commission on 2016 Report on the Application of the EU Charter of Fundamental Rights SWD(2017) 162 final, 98. See Case

rights may be limited in scope, but they lay the groundwork and indicate a direction for the future.[1627] Citizenship of the Union has proven to be more than symbolically important, contrary to expectations when it was introduced in the 1992 Maastricht Treaty ('a pie in the sky').[1628] EU citizenship is not an empty normative shell, as concrete cases have shown and as is witnessed by the unrest of thousands of mobile UK citizens in the EU and EU citizens in the UK.[1629] The tools which EU law gives to its citizens may be criticised for their limited impact, but EU citizens should at least be empowered to use them. This would be EU citizenship 'with respect'.[1630]

EDC standards do not require congruence with statal conceptions of citizenship and rights before citizens are enabled to exercise their rights. Citizens are supposed to be active and aware of their rights, whatever the level of governance in which the rights originate. Rights which do not fit into pre-established statal categories[1631] are equally worthy of protection under the rule of law. Notwithstanding ambiguities in personhood in EU law

---

C-221/17 *Tjebbes and Others* ECLI:EU:C:2019:189, on the consequences of the loss of the nationality of the Member State and thus of EU citizenship.

1627 Craig and de Búrca, *EU Law: Text, Cases, and Materials* 891, where authors conclude: 'A successful future for the EU urgently requires greater political and democratic participation, and the provisions on EU citizenship attempt to lay the groundwork for this'. See for the future: E Sharpston, 'Citizenship and Fundamental Rights—Pandora's Box or a Natural Step Towards Maturity?' in P Cardonnel, A Rosas and N Wahl (eds), *Constitutionalising the EU Judicial System: Essays in Honour of Pernilla Lindh* (Hart 2012); Kochenov, 'On Tiles and Pillars: EU Citizenship as a Federal Denominator'.

1628 HU Jessurun d'Oliveira, 'Union Citizenship: Pie in the Sky?' in A Rosas and E Antola (eds), *A citizens' Europe? In search of a new order* (Sage 1995).

1629 Cp Thym, 'Citizens' and 'Foreigners' in EU Law: Migration Law and its Cosmopolitan Outlook', section II C (text to fn 49), on discrepancy with social realities: 'Union citizenship pretends to be more than it is. It may even be presented as a misnomer or an empty normative shell. (...) Legally, EU citizenship moves towards federal structures irrespective of whether the social substratum follows suit. In the EU Treaties, citizenship is a virtual, a legal reality'. See on impact of EU citizenship, also A Wiener, 'Going Home? "European" Citizenship Practice Twenty Years After' in D Kochenov (ed), *EU Citizenship and Federalism: The Role of Rights* (Cambridge University Press 2017).

1630 Also the failing EU dimension in education suggests the lack of respect for EU citizenship. Cp Kochenov, 'Citizenship without Respect: The EU's Troubled Equality Ideal'.

1631 TH Marshall, *Citizenship and Social Class* (Cambridge University Press 1950) (evolution of rights: civil rights (18th century), political (19th) and social rights (20th century). This pattern of evolution in England does not fit the EU, as

and 'the conceptual puzzle at the heart of the European project'[1632], citizenship education cannot wait until new Treaties, new EU legislation, case law, or doctrine produce perfect clarity. On the contrary, democratic processes demand input from citizens, and thus EDC. Citizens should know what the legal *status quo* is and understand the constitutional tenets of the system. They should be informed and prepared for democratic participation by a system of education which includes the opportunity for critical thinking. EU citizenship has undergone a process of dynamic evolution through changes in primary law (1992, 2009), secondary law (before and after the Citizens' Rights Directive) and case law. Doubts and uncertainties are inherent in a process of navigating uncharted—supranational—waters. EDC empowers citizens to be actors in the process of societal change, not merely passive recipients of rights and duties, not merely citizens to whom information is 'communicated'.

214 Appeal to scholars

Another ambiguity must be pointed out in this context. EU citizenship is frequently the centre of attention in EU law, ECJ case law, and in legal scholarship. However, in spite of this, the large majority of EU citizens are, paradoxically, neglected. They are static and live at home in their Member State. The ECJ and scholars are preoccupied by 'the genuine enjoyment of the substance of the rights' of EU citizens. Yet, this concern is articulated in cases based on peculiar sets of facts which are irrelevant to most citizens. It is easy to associate EU citizenship with cases like *Rottmann, Zu and Chen, Ruiz Zambrano* or *McCarthy*. The paradox is that the so-called 'citizenship' cases which attract attention are far removed from the real-life situations of the average EU citizen, who is not stateless, has no criminal record in another Member State, no Chinese, Columbian or Jamaican family mem-

---

analysed by scholars: see references in Kochenov, 'Ius tractum of many faces: European citizenship and the difficult relationship between status and rights', 197 fn 178. See also categories of rights in O'Leary, *The Evolving Concept of Community Citizenship: From the Free Movement of Persons to Union Citizenship*, 14–16; F Goudappel, *The Effects of EU Citizenship* (TMC Asser Press 2010); SL Greer and T Sokol, 'Rules for Rights: European Law, Health Care and Social Citizenship' (2014) 20 ELJ 66; van Eijken, *European Citizenship and the Constitutionalisation of the European Union* 98, 123, 143 (civil, social, political).

1632 Thym, 'Ambiguities of Personhood, Citizenship, Migration and Fundamental Rights', 125.

bers claiming residence rights.[1633] The average EU citizen is, most often, not even mobile. Associating EU citizenship with such peculiar cases carries the risk of losing sight of the real EU citizen. The false impression is given that EU citizenship is quite problematic, and that complex reasoning is required to guarantee citizenship rights. In scholarly writing, interest in the situation of ordinary EU citizens is often missing, i.e. the citizens who live in their Member State, occasionally cross borders, but have no knowledge about their EU citizenship rights. This general lack of knowledge far more frequently stands in the way of genuine enjoyment of the substance of citizenship rights than the peculiar situations in the cases mentioned. In the absence of an EU dimension to EDC, citizens may miss out on the genuine enjoyment of the substance of their rights. To preserve EU citizenship —scholars explain—it is important for them to analyse its conceptual foundations, explore the limits to citizenship rights, comment on curious cases, and propose theories for encapsulating EU citizenship (statal, post-national, demoi-cratic, federalist, etc.[1634]). This leads to an impressive body of diverging (atomist) scholarly opinions on 'EU citizenship'. Yet—and this is an appeal to scholars—in order to preserve EU citizenship, it is equally important to underscore the consensual core of EU citizenship and the rights pertaining to it, which are firmly anchored in EU primary law. This may motivate curriculum designers and civic educators to include an EU dimension in EDC, so that this core can become part of legal culture and the culture of society. At present, curriculum designers and civic educators tend to hide behind the picture of uncertainty and complexity. The EU dimension does not get adequate attention in curricula. Yet, it is a necessary prerequisite for guaranteeing the future of EU citizenship. The genuine enjoyment of the substance of citizenship rights should be guaranteed

---

1633 Case C-135/08 *Rottmann* ECLI:EU:C:2010:104; Case C-200/02 *Zhu and Chen* ECLI:EU:C:2004:639; Case C-34/09 *Ruiz Zambrano* ECLI:EU:C:2011:124 (Ruiz Zambrano was criticised for 'legal engineering' in a decision of the Belgian 'Office des Etrangers', see para 31); Case C-434/09 *McCarthy* ECLI:EU:C:2011:277; etc.

1634 Constitutional... 'and who cares what it "really" is?' (Kochenov, 'On Tiles and Pillars: EU Citizenship as a Federal Denominator', 20). While the majority of scholars concentrate on specific situations of mobile citizens, there are exceptions, see i.a. L Azoulai, S Barbou des Places and E Pataut, 'Being a Person in the European Union' in L Azoulai, S Barbou des Places and E Pataut (eds), *Constructing the Person in EU Law: Rights, Roles, Identities* (Hart 2016); S Iglesias Sánchez, 'A Citizenship Right to Stay? The Right Not to Move in a Union Based on Free Movement' in D Kochenov (ed), *EU Citizenship and Federalism: The Role of Rights* (Cambridge University Press 2017).

for the large majority of EU citizens, not only the EU children of non-EU parents who are at risk of expulsion from EU territory.[1635]

215 All rights are important under the rule of law

Democracy cannot be reduced to black and white categories. The EU is growing in democratic intensity and legitimacy. It must be acknowledged that the democratic participation rights of EU citizens in Articles 20–24 TFEU are of limited scope and do not meet the initial ambition that they should be instruments for the participation of EU citizens 'at the heart of the European project'. However, the rights are part of the available armory and EU citizens should be empowered to use them.

To conclude, even if the EU citizenship rights listed in Articles 20–24 TFEU are (partly) ambiguous, imperfect, fragmented, unequal, unstable, limited, or non-exclusive, they are relevant to the EU dimension of EDC. In a system based on the rule of law, citizens are supposed to know the rights which the EU legal order confers upon them (whatever the ongoing reflections in legal or political theory as to the nature of these rights and regardless of the continuing search for their limits in case law). These rights supply content for components (c-1), (c-2), and (c-3) of EDC. Adding citizenship rights to the EU dimension of EDC is even more important in the light of the insufficient levels of knowledge indicated by reports and Eurobarometer. Even if many citizens say they are familiar with the term 'citizen of the Union' and about half of them say they 'feel informed' about their rights,[1636] there are many obstacles along the path to

---

1635 E.g. Case C-165/14 *Rendón Marín* ECLI:EU:C:2016:675 line of case law.

1636 In Flash Eurobarometer 430, European Union citizenship (March 2016), 87% of respondents said they were familiar with the term 'citizens of the European Union'; 42% said they felt informed about their rights as citizens of the Union. Progress is measured in Standard Eurobarometer 91, 'European citizenship' (August 2019): 73% feel they are an EU citizen, 57% feel they know their rights as an EU citizen, yet 68% would like to know more about their rights as EU citizens. In Commission Citizenship Report 'Strengthening Citizens' Rights in a Union of Democratic Change EU Citizenship Report 2017' COM(2017) 030 final/2, 11, the Commission wrote that 'Europeans are more than ever aware of their status as citizens of the Union and the majority of them now consider they know their rights as EU citizens. They also feel better informed about these rights, though not necessarily all of them, for example awareness of the right to consular protection remains low'. Yet, for a proper understanding of the figures, the procedure used should to be taken into account: the question was 'In your opinion, which of the following rights does an EU citizen have?' and the rights were first read out to respondents. This does not necessarily mean that citizens have active knowledge and are well informed about citizen-

full realisation of citizenship rights, inter alia because of a lack of knowledge.[1637] An increasing proportion of citizens want to know more about their rights.[1638] Research shows that EU citizenship is still a fragile construction, insufficiently interwoven with civil society and the Member States' culture of rights.[1639] The citizen is 'entitled to be aware of his citizenship rights' (as the Commission states).[1640] Reading Articles 20–24 TFEU in the light of EDC standards, it is clear that there is much work still to be done to empower EU citizens to exercise their citizenship rights.

The work ahead is even more challenging. The significance of EU citizenship for the purposes of EDC does not stop at the rights listed in Articles 20–24 TFEU.

---

ship rights. Other instruments point to exactly the opposite: a lack of knowledge (following note). See also lack of knowledge of the essential distinction between EU citizens and third country nationals (in Nic Shuibhne and Shaw, 'General report', n).

1637 On hurdles, persistent obstacles, and actions in response, see i.a. Commission Report under Article 25 TFEU 'Progress towards effective EU Citizenship 2007-2010' COM(2010) 602 final, 3; Commission Report under Article 25 TFEU 'On progress towards effective EU Citizenship 2011-2013' COM(2013) 270 final, 3–4; Commission EU Citizenship Report 2013: EU citizens: your rights, your future COM(2013) 269 (Actions 21–25, i.a. Raising citizens' awareness about EU citizenship and the rights attached to this status), and follow up in Commission Report under Article 25 TFEU 'On progress towards effective EU citizenship 2013-2016' COM(2017) 32 final; Commission Citizenship Report 'Strengthening Citizens' Rights in a Union of Democratic Change EU Citizenship Report 2017' COM(2017) 030 final/2.

1638 Commission Citizenship Report 'Strengthening Citizens' Rights in a Union of Democratic Change EU Citizenship Report 2017' COM(2017) 030 final/2, 11 (the Your Europe portal receives more than 1.4 million visits per month).

1639 Nic Shuibhne and Shaw, 'General report', 226 ('a worrying note of frailty').

1640 Commission Fourth Report on Citizenship of the Union (1 May 2001—30 April 2004) COM(2004) 695 final, 4.

CHAPTER 7 The EU dimension based on democratic participation rights in Title II TEU

216 Broadening the list of EU citizens' rights

The concept of 'citizenship rights' is unclear. Are they limited to those enumerated in Article 20(2) TFEU and listed in Articles 20–24 TFEU (the classic citizenship provisions), or do they extend beyond the list? Article 25 TFEU sets out a cumbersome procedure for strengthening or adding to the rights listed, requiring unanimous action by the Council, the consent of the European Parliament, and approval by the Member States in accordance with their constitutional requirements. This suggests that the list of EU citizenship rights is limited. However, the enumeration in Article 20(2) is preceded by the words 'inter alia', which could support the opposite interpretation.[1641]

The Treaties should be read in an evolving context. The words 'inter alia' were added by the Lisbon Treaty.[1642] EU citizens enjoy other rights than those listed in Articles 20–24 TFEU.[1643] An obvious example is the right to participate in the democratic life of the Union granted to every cit-

1641 O'Leary, *The Evolving Concept of Community Citizenship: From the Free Movement of Persons to Union Citizenship*, 105 ('inter alia'); A Tryfonidou, *The impact of Union citizenship on the EU's market freedoms* (Hart 2016), 26; W Kluth, 'AEUV Art 20' in C Calliess and M Ruffert (eds), *EUV/AEUV: das Verfassungsrecht der Europäischen Union mit Europäischer Grundrechtecharta : Kommentar* (5th edn, Beck 2016), Rn 11; Kochenov, 'On Tiles and Pillars: EU Citizenship as a Federal Denominator' 27. Cp Lenaerts and Gutiérrez-Fons, 'Epilogue on EU Citizenship: Hopes and Fears', 752: a limited list ('Otherwise, the constitutional allocation of powers sought by the authors of the Treaties would be disturbed').

1642 2007 Lisbon Treaty, Art 2(34)(b), amending Art 17 of the Treaty establishing the European Community.

1643 Art 25 TFEU reflects an expectation that rights will evolve. See also Closa, 'The concept of citizenship in the Treaty on European Union', 1167: 'Therefore, the character of the union citizenship is determined by the progressive acquisition of rights stemming from the dynamic development of the Union. That is, the gradual acquisition by the European citizen of specific rights in new policy-areas transferred to the Union. This evolutive character, which is in itself the most characteristic feature of the citizenship of the Union, was developed by the contributions to the conference as a channel for incorporating controversial socioeconomic rights.'.

izen by Article 10(3) TEU in Title II 'Provisions on Democratic Principles' (explained hereafter). In addition to democratic participation rights, citizens' rights include the right to good administration and the right of access to documents (Articles 41–42 CFR in Title V 'Citizens' rights').[1644] Moreover, the CFR recognises for every citizen of the Union the freedom to seek employment, to work, to exercise the right of establishment, and to provide services in any Member State (in Title II 'Freedoms').[1645] Some apparent inconsistencies (or seemingly sloppy drafting) in citizenship rights can be explained by the historical context. The rights in Articles 20–24 TFEU originate in the 1992 Maastricht Treaty and were influenced by the Adonnino Committee which sought to bring Europe closer to the citizen. They are—in the context of the time—more closely linked with mobility. The participation rights in Title II TEU originate in the work done in the Convention on the Future of Europe and the Treaty establishing a Constitution for Europe, which was partially incorporated into the Lisbon Treaty.[1646] These rights aim to strengthen democracy in the EU and increase the participation of EU citizens in EU governance.

It is safe to state that EU citizens have more rights than those listed in Articles 20–24 TFEU, independently of the question whether they are labelled 'citizenship rights' from the perspective of EU law. For the purposes of EDC, this label is not essential. All EU citizens' rights provide relevant content for EDC component (c-1) 'to exercise and defend their democratic rights in society'.

1644 Settled case law had developed general principles of good administration. The CFR codified them (partly). Further BC Mihaescu Evans, *The right to good administration at the crossroads of the various sources of fundamental rights in the EU integrated administrative system* (Luxembourg Legal Studies 7, Nomos 2015). Also Hofmann, Rowe and Türk, *Administrative law and policy of the European Union*, 190–204.

1645 Art 15(2) CFR; Art 56 TFEU. Thym, 'Ambiguities of Personhood, Citizenship, Migration and Fundamental Rights', 124: 'it seems that supranational rules on citizenship, migration and human rights are excellent examples to illustrate the inherent ambiguity of conceptions of personhood in EU law'; 'EU law deconstructs old conception of nation-state membership or alineage and, yet, it is unclear how to explain the new setting positively'.

1646 Convention on the Future of Europe (2003) <european-convention.europa.eu/>; Treaty establishing a Constitution for Europe [2004] OJ C310 (signed in Rome on 29 October 2004, ratified by 15 of 25 Member States, no entry into force).

217 Linking EU citizenship and democracy (Title II TEU)

That the Treaties see EU citizens as political actors has become clear from the democratic participation rights in Articles 20–24 TFEU (Chapter six). Yet, the core political rights of EU citizens are not established in these citizenship provisions. EU primary law recognises the role of EU citizens as political actors in many other ways. Title II TEU, which connects the provisions on democratic principles with EU citizenship, is the hard core for the EU dimension of EDC.[1647] Firstly, Title II obliges the Union to observe the principle of equality of EU citizens (Article 9 TEU). Next, Title II sets the scene with a mixture of systemic principles, institutional obligations, individual rights as well as opportunities for EU citizens, individually or collectively. It is a matter of debate among scholars as to the extent to which justiciable individual rights are established by democratic principles, institutional provisions, or obligations on institutions and Member States when implementing EU law. For the purposes of EDC, this is not a decisive factor. To the extent that EU primary law grants democratic participation *rights*, it adds content to EDC component (c-1) 'to exercise rights'. To the extent that EU primary law grants democratic participation *opportunities*, it adds content to EDC component (c-3) 'to play an active part in democratic life'. Both share the objective of 'the promotion and protection of democracy and the rule of law' (component d).[1648]

Title II TEU must be interpreted in the context of many other provisions of the Treaties. EU secondary law, too, gives concrete expression to democratic principles. The principle of democracy pervades EU law, giving citizens a context of participation, yet with specific EU features.[1649] In legal terms, nationals of a Member State are 'citizens *of* the Union' (Treaty expression, e.g. in Article 9 TEU). In reality, they are human beings, living

1647 Commission Recommendation of 12 March 2013 on enhancing the democratic and efficient conduct of the elections to the European Parliament [2013] OJ L79/29, recital 3 ('The Treaty of Lisbon enhances the role of citizens of the Union as political actors, establishing a solid link between citizens, the exercise of their political rights and the democratic life of the Union'). See analysis by Shaw, 'Citizenship: Contrasting Dynamics at the Interface of Integration and Constitutionalism', 4.2—3; Lenaerts and Gutiérrez-Fons, 'Epilogue on EU Citizenship: Hopes and Fears' 752, 756.

1648 Definition of EDC in Charter on EDC/HRE, para 2.

1649 Transparency rights, rights of freedom of expression, freedom of assembly and association i.a. in political matters, provisions on political parties, etc. See Lenaerts and Gutiérrez-Fons, 'Epilogue on EU Citizenship: Hopes and Fears' 752.

in a country which is an EU Member State: they are simply citizens *in* the Union.[1650] Do they understand the system in which they live? This system claims to be democratic. What are the implications when applying EDC standards?

A The right to participate in the democratic life of the Union

218 A citizenship right fundamental to the EU dimension of EDC

Article 10(3) TEU states that '[e]very citizen shall have the right to participate in the democratic life of the Union' and that '[d]ecisions shall be taken as openly and as closely as possible to the citizen'. Based on a textual and contextual interpretation, the right granted by Article 10(3) TEU is an authentic citizenship right, defined as a right conferred by virtue of the status of citizen of the Union (a right attaching to the status of EU citizen): purely by being a Member State national, the EU citizen has the right to participate in the democratic life of the Union.[1651] It is noteworthy that the right of Article 10(3) is drafted in the same style as the citizenship rights listed in Article 20–24 TFEU ('Every citizen ... shall have the right to ...'). The link between Title II TEU and the citizenship rights in Articles 20–24 TFEU is guaranteed, moreover, by the ECI, inserted into Article 11(4) TEU by the Lisbon Treaty, but with a legal basis in Article 24 TFEU.[1652]

Article 10(3) TEU satisfies the four criteria of relevance for mainstream EDC. The right to participate in the democratic life of the Union provides additional content for national EDC (i) in both components (c-1) and (c-3), and indirectly in (c-2). Since it is not included in the list of Articles

---

1650 Distinction between citizens *of* and *in* the Union in Shaw, 'Citizenship: Contrasting Dynamics at the Interface of Integration and Constitutionalism', i.a. text to fn 152 ('the challenge of constructing an effective political citizenship both *of and in* the Union). Shaw emphasises for citizens *in* the Union the political dimension and their role in the Union as a polity evolving beyond the State. In my approach, which is slightly different, citizenship *of* the Union includes the 'citizenship right' of Art 10(3) TEU, including the role in the polity evolving beyond the State. See also the distinction between EU citizenship and European citizenship in Besson and Utzinger, 'Towards European Citizenship' ('the benefit of EU citizenship ensues from its dynamic interplay with existing national citizenships. Hence, the idea of *European citizenship*, that best reflects the transformative Europeanization of national citizenship in Europe').

1651 See also text to n 1691.

1652 Text to n 1541.

20–24 TFEU, the right is often neglected as a citizenship right by scholars and in reports.[1653] It deserves much more attention. It is unnecessary to mention that the right relates to foundational values, objectives and principles, i.e. democracy (ii). True, the content of this citizenship right is quite abstract. Arguably, the right as such does not create rights which are justiciable (the provision on the right 'to participate in the democratic life of the Union' can hardly be deemed clear, precise and unconditional). Yet, given its place in the TEU (the Treaty which contains the essential provisions and principles of the EU, further developed in the TFEU), it is at least as important as the classic citizenship rights listed in the TFEU and mostly exercised by mobile citizens. EU institutions repeatedly confirm its importance, e.g. 'the most fundamental area of citizenship, namely the right to participate in the democratic process'.[1654] The right invites critical thinking (iii) about the EU and input in democratic processes, as well as about the right itself. *How exactly can citizens participate in 'the democratic life of the Union'? Does participating in a Union of 500 million citizens matter?*[1655] Finally, this right is granted to all citizens. Not dependent on mobility, it is a crucial right for static EU citizens (iv), therefore relevant for mainstream education.

The relevance of the right to participate in the democratic life of the Union for EDC is supported in EU primary law when Article 10(3) TEU is read in conjunction with Article 165(2), first and fifth indent, TFEU.[1656] Under the general objective of quality education, the EU can adopt incentive measures aimed at 'developing the European dimension in education' and 'encouraging the participation of young people in democratic life in Europe' (Article 165 TFEU).[1657]

1653 Not mentioned as such: i.a. Nic Shuibhne and Shaw, 'General report', 161 ff, Craig and de Búrca, *EU Law: Text, Cases, and Materials* 854, 888; K Lenaerts and P Van Nuffel, *Europees Recht* (6 edn, Intersentia 2017) 115–127.

1654 European Parliament Resolution of 11 November 2015 on the reform of the electoral law of the European Union [2017] OJ C366/7, recital AC ('whereas harmonisation of the voting age, and of the minimum age for candidates, would be highly desirable as a means of providing Union citizens with real voting equality, and would enable discrimination to be avoided in the most fundamental area of citizenship, namely the right to participate in the democratic process').

1655 See text to nn 1866 ff.

1656 See Part two, §§ 116 132 .

1657 Further Part four, § 305 ff.

219 A general right relating to representative and participatory democracy
The abstract wording of Article 10(3) TEU can be given concrete substance in various ways. Does it imply representative or participatory democracy?

On a narrow view, it only covers forms of participatory democracy. The verb 'to participate in' in Article 10(3) TEU connects with the adjective 'participatory'. On a broader view, it is also associated with representative democracy, as voting in elections is the means *par excellence* of participating in the democratic life of the Union; the other means of participation are complementary. Interpretation based on the *travaux préparatoires* does not produce any definitive answers.[1658] What pleads in favour of representative democracy, on the one hand, is that in the Treaty establishing a Constitution for Europe, this right was set out in Article I-46, entitled 'The principle of representative democracy' (just after the provisions which now form Article 10(1) and (2) TEU). Participation in democratic life is traditionally associated with voting to determine the composition of the parliamentary bodies representing citizens. What pleads in favour of participatory democracy, on the other hand, is that in the proposal of the Praesidium on the democratic life of the Union (Title VI), the right was included in Article 34 'The principle of participatory democracy'. [1659]

Given the arguments on both sides, the right in Article 10(3) TEU can be interpreted as an overarching right, relating to both representative and participatory democracy. Institutions and scholars use it in both con-

---

1658 See also B Kohler-Koch, 'Does participatory governance hold its promises?' in B Kohler-Koch and F Larat (eds), *Efficient and democratic governance in the European Union* (CONNEX Report Series No 9, Mannheim 2008) 266: not much deliberation on the provision; 'the Constitutional Convention was not a body that engages in theoretical reasoning'.

1659 Praesidium European Convention, The democratic life of the Union (2 April 2003) CONV 650/03, Art 34(1) 'Every citizen shall have the right to participate in the democratic life of the Union'; 'Draft Article 34 sets out the main elements of participatory democracy, and is intended to provide a framework and content for the dialogue which is largely already in place between the institutions and civil society' (p 2, also p 8). Further Convention on the Future of Europe (2003) <european-convention.europa.eu/>; Peters, 'European democracy after the 2003 Convention', 44; S Smismans, 'The constitutional labelling of "the democratic life of the EU": "representative" and "participatory" democracy' in A Follesdal and L Dobson (eds), *Political Theory and the European Constitution* (Routledge 2004); L Burgorgue-Larsen, A Levade and F Picod (eds), *Traité établissant une Constitution pour l'Europe, Partie II La Charte des droits fondamentaux de l'Union: Commentaire article par article* (Bruylant 2005); J Mendes, *Participation in EU Rule-Making: A Rights-Based Approach* (Oxford University Press 2011) 27, 140.

texts.[1660] The right to a citizens' initiative, to petition the European Parliament, or to refer to the Ombudsman are expressions of the general right in Article 10(3) TEU.[1661] The general right underpins the specific political rights of EU citizens.[1662] Article 10(3) TEU acquires further substance when read in conjunction with EU law provisions on the institutions.

The relevance of specific political rights to the EU dimension of EDC will now be examined, in respect of representative democracy in sections B and C, in respect of participatory democracy in section D.

B The right to vote for the European Parliament

220 The European Parliament in EU primary law

Voting in elections for the European Parliament is central to the image of active EU citizenship. It constitutes obvious learning content for the EU dimension of EDC in mainstream education. The topic provides additional (i) and significant (ii) content to national EDC, invites critical thinking about the state of play in the EU (iii), and it affects all EU citizens (iv).

The Treaties do not state that every citizen of the Union shall have the right to vote in elections to the European Parliament. While the 1989 'Declaration of fundamental rights and freedoms' of the European Parliament

---

1660 See i.a. European Parliament Resolution of 11 November 2015 on the reform of the electoral law of the European Union [2017] OJ C366/7, recital U ('a common European voting day would better reflect common participation by citizens across the Union, reinforce participatory democracy ...'); S Smismans, 'New governance: the solution for active European citizenship, or the end of citizenship?' (2007) 13 Columbia Journal of European Law 595, 599, 606; Lenaerts and Van Nuffel, *European Union Law* 737; Khadar and Shaw, 'Article 39: Right to Vote and to Stand as a Candidate at Elections to the European Parliament' 1039; S Smismans, 'Regulating interest group participation in the European Union: changing paradigms between transparency and representation' (2014) 39 ELRev 470, 604; M Ruffert, 'EU-Vertrag (Lissabon) Art 10' in C Calliess and M Ruffert (eds), *EUV/AEUV: das Verfassungsrecht der Europäischen Union mit Europäischer Grundrechtecharta : Kommentar* (5th edn, Beck 2016), Rn 11–12 ('ein demokratisches Grundrecht', both for representative and participatory democracy); Lenaerts and Gutiérrez-Fons, 'Epilogue on EU Citizenship: Hopes and Fears' 775 (Art 10(3): participation is primarily carried out by means of electing the members of Parliament). See also concept of 'participation' in Mendes (n 1738).

1661 Case C-589/15 P *Anagnostakis* ECLI:EU:C:2017:663, para 24.

1662 For the link between Art 10(3) TEU and access to documents, see Case C-57/16 P *ClientEarth* ECLI:EU:C:2018:660, para 84.

explicitly formulated that right,[1663] the authors of the Treaty were not so explicit. The right of EU citizens to vote in elections for the European Parliament can be deduced from a contextual reading of democratic principles together with the provisions on the institutions (Titles II and III TEU). Article 10 TEU states that '[t]he functioning of the Union shall be founded on representative democracy' and that '[c]itizens are directly represented at Union level in the European Parliament' (paras 1 and 2). It is noteworthy that before the 2009 Treaty of Lisbon, the members of the European Parliament were called 'representatives of the peoples of the States'.[1664] Since 2009, the European Parliament is composed of 'representatives of the Union's citizens' (Article 14 para 1 TEU). The obligation formulated in Article 39(2) CFR corresponds to that of Article 14(3) TEU: 'Members of the European Parliament shall be elected by direct universal suffrage in a free and secret ballot'.[1665] It was to this obligation that the ECJ linked the right to vote in the landmark decision *Delvigne*.[1666] The second paragraph of Article 39 CFR, corresponding to Article 14(3) TEU, thus constitutes an essential provision for the EU dimension of EDC.

221 Delvigne: the right to vote in elections for the European Parliament

In settled case law, the ECJ recalls that 'participation reflects a fundamental democratic principle that the peoples should take part in the exercise of power through the intermediary of a representative assembly'.[1667] While the right to vote had arguably already been implicitly recognised in *Eman v Sevinger* and in *Spain v UK* (pre-Lisbon),[1668] the explicit recognition by the

1663 European Parliament Resolution of 12 April 1989 adopting the Declaration of fundamental rights and freedoms [1989] OJ C120/51, Art 17 (3).

1664 Art 189(1) TEC.

1665 Correspondance confirmed by the Explanations to the CFR.

1666 Case C-650/13 *Delvigne* ECLI:EU:C:2015:648.

1667 Case 138/79 *Roquette Frères* ECLI:EU:C:1980:249, para 33; Case C 300/89 *Commission v Council (Titanium dioxide)* ECLI:EU:C:1991:244, para 20; Case 139/79 *Maizena v Council* ECLI:EU:C:1980:250, para 34.

1668 Case C-300/04 *Eman and Sevinger* ECLI:EU:C:2006:545; Case C-145/04 *Spain v UK* ECLI:EU:C:2006:543. The ECJ was not as explicit as AG Tizzano, who had argued in his Opinion (para 69) that all EU citizens enjoy the right to vote in European elections, primarily by virtue of the principles of democracy on which the EU is based, and in particular of the basic principle of universal suffrage. Implicit recognition argued in Shaw, 'Citizenship: Contrasting Dynamics at the Interface of Integration and Constitutionalism', text to fn 118 ff; analysis in Khadar and Shaw, 'Article 39: Right to Vote and to Stand as a Candidate at Elections to the European Parliament' 1037–9, 1042–3; in the same sense, Lenaerts and Gutiérrez-Fons, 'Epilogue on EU Citizenship: Hopes and

ECJ in *Delvigne* (post-Lisbon) of the right of EU citizens to vote for the European Parliament was a significant development.[1669] The case concerned the right to vote of an EU citizen in the Member State of which he is a national, thus the situation of a static citizen vis-à-vis his own Member State.

Thierry Delvigne, a French national, is sentenced in France to 12 years imprisonment for murder and, under French law, he is deprived of his right to vote in elections. An administrative commission decides to remove him from the electoral roll of the municipality where he resides (Lesparre-Médoc). Mr Delvigne challenges this decision alleging unequal treatment. A French Court (Bordeaux) asks the ECJ whether the deprivation of the right to vote is compatible with Article 39 CFR on elections to the European Parliament. The French, Spanish and UK Governments claim that the ECJ has no jurisdiction: the provisions of the CFR are addressed 'to the Member States only when they are implementing Union law' (Article 51(1) CFR),[1670] which, they say, is not the case here. The ECJ recalls that, indeed, the fundamental rights guaranteed in the EU legal order are only applicable in situations governed by EU law, but finds that, in this case, the situation is governed by EU law. It is true that the definition of the persons entitled to exercise the right to vote falls within the competence of each Member State, as the Electoral Act of 1976 does not define them and states that the electoral procedure shall be governed in each Member State by its national provisions.[1671] However, when exercising that competence, the Member States must comply with EU law. They are

---

Fears', fn 118. The UK Supreme Court (*Chester and McGeoch*) disputed that EU law contained an individual right to vote in European Parliament elections. Comparison with *Delvigne*: H van Eijken and JW van Rossem, 'Prisoner disenfranchisement and the right to vote in elections to the European Parliament: Universal suffrage key to unlocking political citizenship?' (2016) 12 European Constitutional Law Review 114, 118–9; S Coutts, 'Delvigne: A Multi-Levelled Political Citizenship' (2017) 42 ELRev 867, 872–4.

1669 Case C-650/13 *Delvigne* ECLI:EU:C:2015:648.

1670 Para 25. On this condition, see i.a. Case C-617/10 *Åkerberg Fransson* ECLI:EU:C:2013:280, paras 17, 19, 22.

1671 Para 31 (no express and precise definition of who is entitled to the right in Arts 1(3) and 8 Electoral Act). See Act concerning the election of the representatives of the Assembly by direct universal suffrage [1976] OJ L278/5 (Electoral Act), as amended, Art 7; Council Decision of 25 June 2002 and 23 September 2002 amending the Act concerning the election of the representatives of the European Parliament by direct universal suffrage, annexed to Decision 76/787/

bound by the EU law obligation to ensure that the election of Members of the European Parliament occurs by direct universal suffrage, free and secret, as set out in Article 14(3) TEU and in Article 1(3) of the Electoral Act. When they exclude an EU citizen from the elections, they are implementing EU law. The action thus falls within the scope of EU law.

As to the substance, the ECJ applies the distinction between the two paragraphs of Article 39 CFR in accordance with the Explanations to the CFR. The first paragraph of Article 39 CFR is not applicable as it only concerns mobile citizens and Mr Delvigne's situation is that of a static citizen. The second paragraph of Article 39, which corresponds to Article 14(3) TEU, is applicable. The ECJ states that Article 39(2) CFR 'constitutes the expression in the Charter of *the right of Union citizens to vote in elections to the European Parliament* in accordance with Article 14(3) TEU and Article 1(3) of the 1976 Electoral Act'.[1672] It is this right which has been limited by the decision of the French administrative commission depriving Mr Delvigne of his voting rights. Yet, the limitation is justified under Article 52(1) CFR: it is provided by law, respects the essence of the right as well as the principle of proportionality (excluding a person convicted of a serious crime).

As explained by Lenaerts and Gutiérrez-Fons, what is important in *Delvigne* is that it links EU citizenship and EU representative democracy:

> It has helped to make explicit the link between EU citizenship and democratic governance of the EU. It shows that the political dimension of EU citizenship is not limited to Articles 20–25 TFEU, but also involves other provisions of EU law, notably Article 14(3) TEU and Article 1(3) of the 1976 Act.[1673]

ECSC, EEC, Euratom [2002] OJ L283/1. See also European Parliament Resolution of 11 November 2015 on the reform of the electoral law of the European Union [2017] OJ C366/7.

1672 Para 44.

1673 Lenaerts and Gutiérrez-Fons, 'Epilogue on EU Citizenship: Hopes and Fears', 779; earlier K Lenaerts, 'Linking EU Citizenship to Democracy' (2015) 11 Croatian Yearbook of European Law and Policy VII, ix. Further J Gundel, 'Der Verlust der bürgerlichen Ehrenrechte als Eingriff in die Grundrechtecharta—Neues zur Reichweite des EU-Grundrechtsschutzes gegenüber den Mitgliedstaaten und zur lex-mitior-Garantie' (2016) 51 Europarecht 176; also significance in van Eijken and van Rossem, 'Prisoner disenfranchisement and the right to vote in elections to the European Parliament: Universal suffrage key to

Van Eijken and van Rossem consider that the 'most spectacular finding of the Court in *Delvigne* is that Union citizens have the right, *qualitate qua*, to vote in elections to the European Parliament'.[1674] This fundamental right, based on a combined reading of the TEU, the CFR and the Electoral Act, strengthens the political dimension of EU citizenship. Coutts finds the recognition of a free-standing right to vote for European Parliament elections more radical than one might suppose: it affirms a political right directly applicable even in the home Member State in wholly internal situations, associated with the status of EU citizenship, unrelated to free movement or non-discrimination. Whereas the Treaties link EU citizenship and direct democracy in the ECI, here the ECJ extends the link to representative democracy.[1675] In *Delvigne*, EU citizenship shifts beyond an economic and transnational citizenship towards a political and supranational citizenship.[1676] At the same time, EU citizenship remains derived multi-level citizenship. Member States can limit the right, and in the case in question, the ECJ even accepted the limit quite easily.[1677]

Importantly, in *Delvigne* the ECJ connected the right to vote for the European Parliament with paragraph 2 of Article 39 CFR, not with paragraph 1 (which corresponds to Article 22 TFEU and is limited to conferring a right of equal treatment on mobile citizens in the host Member State[1678]). This political fundamental right of EU citizens falls within the scope of the Treaties, including with regard to citizens who do not cross borders. Admittedly, the order of the provisions in Article 39 CFR is curious, first setting out the equal treatment right for mobile citizens and

---

unlocking political citizenship?', 130–2; Coutts, 'Delvigne: A Multi-Levelled Political Citizenship'.

1674 van Eijken and van Rossem, 'Prisoner disenfranchisement and the right to vote in elections to the European Parliament: Universal suffrage key to unlocking political citizenship?', 123 (emphasis added).

1675 Coutts, 'Delvigne: A Multi-Levelled Political Citizenship', 875.

1676 Ibid, 881 (political rights in Art 22 TFEU are in fact transnational rights; see Dir 93/100 and 94/80).

1677 Ibid, 881 (remarkable discretion). See also comparison with ECtHR case law in van Eijken and van Rossem, 'Prisoner disenfranchisement and the right to vote in elections to the European Parliament: Universal suffrage key to unlocking political citizenship?'; and Gundel, 'Der Verlust der bürgerlichen Ehrenrechte als Eingriff in die Grundrechtecharta—Neues zur Reichweite des EU-Grundrechtsschutzes gegenüber den Mitgliedstaaten und zur lex-mitior-Garantie'.

1678 *Delvigne* para 42; text to n 1486.

thereafter the right of universal suffrage. It should probably be seen in the historic drafting context.[1679]

Delvigne furthermore shows that fundamental rights may not be incorporated into the substantive rights attaching to the status of EU citizens by means of judicial interpretation.[1680] The rights in the CFR are not self-standing. It is the scope of the Treaty provision corresponding to a CFR right which determines the scope of the CFR right, here Article 14(3) TEU determining the scope of Article 39(2) CFR.[1681] The ECJ recognised the right to vote without linking it to the citizenship rights listed in Articles 20–24 TFEU. As Lenaerts and Gutiérrez-Fons emphasise, the Court left the scope ratione personae of Article 20(2)(b) TFEU and Article 22 TFEU untouched. It is in 'implementing' the obligations imposed by Article 14(3) TEU and the Electoral Act that the Member States must respect the CFR (in application of Article 51(1) CFR), also in regard to EU citizens who are nationals.[1682]

The recognition of the right of EU citizens to vote and the political dimension of EU citizenship in Title II TEU are a significant development for EU citizenship and for the application of EDC standards.

222 *Relevance of the right to vote for the European Parliament for mainstream education*

On a reading of EU primary law provisions on the European Parliament, in particular Articles 10(1)(2), 14(3) TEU, and 39(2) CFR, jointly with

1679 Khadar and Shaw, 'Article 39: Right to Vote and to Stand as a Candidate at Elections to the European Parliament', 1053.

1680 Lenaerts and Gutiérrez-Fons, 'Epilogue on EU Citizenship: Hopes and Fears' 779; Lenaerts, 'Linking EU Citizenship to Democracy', ix (against the incorporation doctrine 'à l'Européenne').

1681 Lenaerts, 'Linking EU Citizenship to Democracy', xvi.

1682 Lenaerts and Gutiérrez-Fons, 'Epilogue on EU Citizenship: Hopes and Fears' 779. For comments on *Delvigne*, see i.a. van Eijken and van Rossem, 'Prisoner disenfranchisement and the right to vote in elections to the European Parliament: Universal suffrage key to unlocking political citizenship?', 122 (quite foggy, circular, remarkably broad interpretation, 'a set of general principles is deemed sufficient to activate the scope of EU law'); Gundel, 'Der Verlust der bürgerlichen Ehrenrechte als Eingriff in die Grundrechtecharta—Neues zur Reichweite des EU-Grundrechtsschutzes gegenüber den Mitgliedstaaten und zur lex-mitior-Garantie', 187 (on the link with EU law: 'zwar dünn... aber unbestreitbar vorhanden'—admittedly tenuous... but indisputably there). On the scope of application of the CFR, see i.a. Case C-390/12 *Pfleger* ECLI:EU:C:2014:281: para 36 (derogation from free movement rules must comply with the CFR).

EDC standards, the right to vote in European Parliament elections adds significant content to national EDC (i, ii), in both components (c-1) and (c-3).

Sceptics doubt whether electoral rights in respect of the European Parliament really provide additional content for national EDC (i). Asked about EU citizenship and the EU dimension of citizenship education in schools, the head of one of the main school networks responsible for specifying the curriculum in a Member State, answered that it suffices for pupils to have learned about the national parliament; learning about another parliament (the European Parliament) does not add much to their civic knowledge.[1683] Admittedly, the act of voting is the same in parliamentary elections at regional, national, or EU level. Citizens do not need much additional empowerment to go to a polling station and tick a box on an electoral list for the European Parliament. From the perspective of *formal* or *procedural* democracy, additional educational preparation is superfluous. However, from the perspective of *substantive* democracy[1684], EU citizens need to be empowered to participate meaningfully in elections at EU level. For a non-negligible group of nationals, paradoxically, the *EU* dimension of voting in European Parliament elections needs to be explained. European Parliament elections should be more than popularity tests of national politicians or parties.[1685]

The increasingly important role of the European Parliament in the institutional framework of the EU provides additional content for national EDC (i). The European Parliament exercises legislative and budgetary functions jointly with the Council, functions of political control and consultation, and elects the President of the Commission (Art 14 (1) TEU).

1683 Studiedag KU Leuven, ICCS Vlaanderen, 'Burgerschap op school: hoe ga je ermee aan de slag?' (Brussels, 8 February 2018).

1684 Rosas and Armati, *EU Constitutional Law: An Introduction* 140: 'substantive principles and rules with constitutional status may contribute to democratic legitimacy, provided that they are based on values which are generally accepted and are articulated in an open deliberative process in which political institutions, judges and civil society can take part. This is what we mean by substantive democracy'. This conception of democracy presupposes 'agreeing up-front what the Union is based on and what the integration process is for'. See also D Van Reybrouck, 'Democratie is meer dan een bolletje kleuren' *De Standaard* (19 November 2016) <www.standaard.be/cnt/dmf20161118_02579747> .

1685 See also European Parliament Resolution of 11 November 2015 on the reform of the electoral law of the European Union [2017] OJ C366/7, para L (electoral campaigning remains national).

The Commission is as a body responsible to the European Parliament (Article 17(8) TEU). In many policy fields, the European Parliament is co-legislator together with the Council. Numerous legislative acts create EU rights or obligations for citizens and have an impact on their daily lives.[1686] It therefore is not sufficient to have learned about the national parliament. If the will of EU citizens is to be represented, these citizens need to be aware of the role of the European Parliament in their lives.[1687]

The electoral rights at EU level invite critical thinking about the EU and its policies, as well as about the European Parliament itself (iii). The European Parliament does not have the typical features of a parliament in the statal context. EU citizens' votes do not have equal weight.[1688] Article 14(2) TEU defines the criteria for the composition of the European Parliament, the minimum and maximum numbers of seats, and a system of degressive proportionality.[1689] Pupils should have some idea about the specific fea-

1686 EU rights, next chapter. See also Commission Recommendation (EU) 2018/234 of 14 February 2018 on enhancing the European nature and efficient conduct of the 2019 elections to the European Parliament [2018] OJ L45/40, recital 7.

1687 Commission Recommendation of 12 March 2013 on enhancing the democratic and efficient conduct of the elections to the European Parliament [2013] OJ L79/29, recitals 4 and 9; Case C-650/13 *Delvigne* ECLI:EU:C:2015:648, Opinion of AG Cruz Villalón, para 99. Flash Eurobarometer 431, Electoral Rights (March 2016): 84% of respondents think that turnout at European elections would be higher if more information was provided on the impact of the EU on their daily lives.

1688 See i.a. *BVerfG, 2 BvE 2/08 (Lissabon)* 30 June 2009, Absatz-Nr (1-421), para 279: 'The democratic basic rule of equal opportunities of success ("one man, one vote") only applies within a people, not within a supranational representative body, which remains a representation of the peoples linked to each other by the treaties albeit now with special emphasis on citizenship of the Union'; para 284: 'As a result the weight of the vote of a citizen from a Member State with a small population may be about twelve times the weight of the vote of a citizen from a Member State with a large population'.

1689 European Council Decision (EU) 2018/937 of 28 June 2018 establishing the composition of the European Parliament [2018] OJ L165I/1 (legal basis Art 14(2) TEU) sets the seats for the 2019–2024 parliamentary term after Brexit (i.a. BE 21, DE 96, FR 79, LU 6, RO 33), defining degressive proportionality: 'the ratio between the population and the number of seats of each Member State before rounding to whole numbers is to vary in relation to their respective populations in such a way that each Member of the European Parliament from a more populous Member State represents more citizens than each Member of the European Parliament from a less populous Member State and, conversely, that the larger the population of a Member State, the greater its entitlement to a large number of seats in the European Parliament'.

tures of representative democracy in the EU, which has to balance the principles of equality of its citizens and equality of Member States. If the minimal voting age for the European Parliament is harmonised at 16 years,[1690] EU learning at school becomes even more relevant.

Finally, the right to vote for the European Parliament is granted to every EU citizen. It affects static citizens too (iv), as illustrated by *Delvigne*.

In short, electoral rights for the European Parliament are relevant for mainstream education. They satisfy all criteria. The explicit recognition by the ECJ of the right to vote in the European Parliament underscores its relevance for mainstream education.

While the right to vote for the European Parliament is as such relevant to the EU dimension of EDC, labelling it a 'political right attaching to the status of EU citizen' would provide an even stronger argument in favour of an EU dimension to EDC. Yet, caution is needed for a proper understanding of this label.

223 A political right attaching to the status of EU citizen?

Lenaerts and Gutiérrez-Fons state that 'the political dimension of EU citizenship is not fully captured by the political rights attaching to the status of EU citizen' and 'the rights attaching to that status do not fully capture the link between EU citizenship and the democratic governance of the EU'.[1691]

True, as Lenaerts writes, the political dimension 'is not only about rights, but also about ensuring that representative democracy at EU level is

---

1690 Recommendation to enhance electoral equality and bring the EU closer to young citizens: European Parliament Resolution of 11 November 2015 on the reform of the electoral law of the European Union [2017] OJ C366/7, paras AC and 15.

1691 Lenaerts and Gutiérrez-Fons, 'Epilogue on EU Citizenship: Hopes and Fears': 'the new Treaty provisions on democratic principles reveal that EU citizenship has a political dimension that is not only about the political rights attaching to the status of EU citizen, but also about ensuring that representative democracy at the EU level is effective, and, most importantly, legitimate [fn: see Art 14 TEU, Arts 223–234 TFEU]. This means that the rights attaching to that status do not fully capture the link between EU citizenship and the democratic governance of the EU' (at 752); see also 780. Respect for the principle of representative democracy may require the EU institutions and the Member States to fulfil obligations not only flowing from Articles 20(2), 22(2) and 24 TFEU. See also Lenaerts, 'Linking EU Citizenship to Democracy', viii-ix. Cp critical comments of Kochenov, 'On Tiles and Pillars: EU Citizenship as a Federal Denominator' 27.

effective, and most importantly, legitimate'.[1692] Institutions and Member States must indeed fulfil obligations not only based on Articles 20(2), 22(2) and 24 TFEU, but also based on the other provisions of EU law which concretely express democratic principles. Importantly, here EDC standards come into play.

However, doubts may arise where Lenaerts and Gutiérrez-Fons seem to limit the category of 'political rights attaching to the status of EU citizen' to the rights listed in Articles 20(2), 22(2) and 24 TFEU.

In my view, the right to vote for the European Parliament is also a political right attaching to the status of EU citizen. As explained, the category of citizenship rights is not so clear: EU law grants EU citizens more rights than those listed in Articles 20–24 TFEU.[1693] In *Ruiz Zambrano* and *Rottman*, the ECJ used the expression 'rights attaching to the status of EU citizen' or 'rights conferred by virtue of their status as citizens of the Union', and referred in this context to 'the rights and duties laid down by the Treaty'.[1694] If the concept of 'rights attaching to the status of EU citizen' is defined as (tautologically, who will object?) rights which are granted purely because an individual has the EU citizen status, thus granted ipso facto because he or she is a national of a Member State, then the right to vote for the European Parliament is a political right 'attaching to the status of EU citizen'. Individuals have the right to vote in elections for the European Parliament just because they have the status of EU citi-

---

1692 Lenaerts, 'Linking EU Citizenship to Democracy', xviii.

1693 See text to n 594.

1694 Case C-34/09 *Ruiz Zambrano* ECLI:EU:C:2011:124, para 42 ('Article 20 TFEU precludes national measures which have the effect of depriving citizens of the Union of the genuine enjoyment of the substance of the *rights conferred by virtue of their status as citizens of the Union*'), para 45 ('Article 20 TFEU is to be interpreted as meaning that it precludes a Member State from refusing a third country national upon whom his minor children, who are European Union citizens, are dependent, a right of residence in the Member State of residence and nationality of those children, and from refusing to grant a work permit to that third country national, in so far as such decisions deprive those children of the genuine enjoyment of the substance of *the rights attaching to the status of European Union citizen*'). See Case C-135/08 *Rottmann* ECLI:EU:C:2010:104, para 44 ('Article 17(2) EC attaches to that status *the rights and duties laid down by the Treaty, including* the right to rely on Article 12 EC in all situations falling within the scope ratione materiae of Union law'), para 46 ('the conditions in which a citizen of the Union may, because he loses his nationality, lose his status of citizen of the Union and thereby be deprived of *the rights attaching to that status*'). Emphasis added. See i.a. text to n 1456.

zen, 'qualitate qua'.[1695] Article 39(2) is, moreover, a provision in the Title 'Citizens' rights' of the CFR. The right to vote is an expression of the right in Article 10(3) TEU, which is a citizenship right as well, i.e. attaching to citizen status.[1696] Recognising the right to vote for the European Parliament as a citizenship right is not inconsistent with Article 25 TFEU, which lays down a cumbersome procedure for adding new citizenship rights. Article 25 TFEU starts with '*on this basis*, and without prejudice to the *other provisions of the Treaties*'. The 'this basis' relates to the previous provision on Commission reports 'which shall take account of the development of the Union'. The right to vote for the European Parliament must be seen in the light of the development of the Union as reflected in the Lisbon Treaty and its new provisions on the European Parliament ('representatives of the Union's citizens', no longer of 'the peoples') and inclusion of democratic principles in the TEU. The 'other provisions of the Treaties' include Title II and Article 14 (3) TEU. Recognising the right to vote for the European Parliament as 'a political right attaching to the status of EU citizenship' is not pushing at the boundaries of the vertical delimitation of powers between the EU and the Member States but is respectful of the constitutional framework of the Treaties. It is the corollary of EU primary law obligations on Member States to organise free elections to the European Parliament and is confirmed by a contextual interpretation. It does not open the door to jurisprudential recognition of any further right of interest for EU citizens. The right concerns the very foundations of the Union, democracy.

In any case, irrespective of its label 'political right attaching to the status of EU citizen', the right to vote for the European Parliament is relevant for the EU dimension in mainstream education.

224 A right limiting the margin of appreciation of Member States

The fact that the right of EU citizens to vote in elections to the European Parliament is expressed in a provision of the CFR (Article 39(2)) has legal consequences for the relationship of static citizens with their own Member State.[1697] As appears from *Delvigne*, it affects the determination by the Member State of the members of the electorate, even though this determination is a matter of national competence. Limitations of CFR rights must

1695 See also Van Eijken and van Rossem in text to n 1695 ('qualitate qua').

1696 See § 218 .

1697 *Delvigne*, para 44: Article 39(2) CFR 'constitutes the expression in the Charter of the right of Union citizens to vote in elections to the European Parliament in accordance with Article 14(3) TEU and Article 1(3) of the 1976 Electoral Act'.

respect the conditions in Article 52(1) CFR. Other general rules of the CFR must also be respected (interpretation and level of protection of the CFR right, as determined in Articles 52–53 CFR). The margin of appreciation of Member States, even when they are exercising national competences, is thus limited by EU law.

What conclusions can be drawn from this finding with regard to the relationship between static citizens and their own Member State in the field of education? Can the CFR right to vote in European Parliament elections also affect the norm-setting by Member States with regard to EDC and limit their margin of appreciation, even if education falls within national competence? This will be analysed in Part four.[1698]

C The right to vote for the national parliament and its EU dimension

225 Specific features of democracy in the EU: dual democratic legitimacy

The right to vote for the national parliament is based on national law and voting primarily means taking part in the democratic life of the *Member State*. However, voting in national elections is at the same time indirect participation in the democratic life of the *Union*, because Member State parliaments and governments are important actors at EU level and Member States' democracies are interdependent.[1699] The Commission puts it succinctly: 'Full participation of EU citizens in *the democratic life of the EU at all levels* is the very essence of Union citizenship'.[1700] Representative democracy in the EU follows two tracks: citizens choose their representatives in the national parliament as well as in the European Parliament. Article 10(2) TEU is the basis for what is commonly referred to as the dual structure of democratic legitimacy of the Union: citizens are directly represented at Union level in the European Parliament (to which the Commission is accountable) and Member States are represented in the European Council by their Heads of State or Government and in the Council by

---

1698 The exercise of competences has to comply with fundamental rights. See in particular §§ 323 and 325 .

1699 See also I Pernice, 'Editorial: Nationale Wahlen sind Europäische Wahlen' [2017] Europäische Zeitschrift für Wirtschaftsrecht 441.

1700 Commission EU Citizenship Report 2013: EU citizens: your rights, your future COM(2013) 269 p. 5; note also the commas at p 20: 'Bolstering EU citizens' full participation in the democratic life of the EU, *at all levels,* is the very essence of EU citizenship'; they indicate that democratic life *includes* all levels. Levels are local, national or EU.

their governments, who in turn are themselves democratically accountable to their national parliaments or to their citizens.[1701] In this sense, the EU can be seen as a Union of citizens and States.[1702] Undeniably, these specific features of democracy in the EU system need to be explained and discussed with pupils. They provide additional (i) and significant (ii) content for EDC. In order to participate meaningfully in both tracks of representative democracy, some insight is needed into the delicate vertical and horizontal balance of powers in the system: the delimitation of powers between the EU and the Member States, with the pivotal principle of conferral,[1703] and the separation of powers between the institutions.[1704] Here EU primary law texts provide solid content for EDC. Even so they leave ample room for exercising critical agency (iii), as evidenced by a huge body of scholarly

1701 Lenaerts and Van Nuffel, *European Union Law*, 743; A von Bogdandy, 'The European lesson for international democracy: the significance of Articles 9 to 12 EU Treaty for International Organizations' (2012) 23 European Journal of International Law 315, 325; Calliess and Hartmann, *Zur Demokratie in Europa: Unionsbürgerschaft und europäische Öffentlichkeit*, 80, 152; Lenaerts and Gutiérrez-Fons, 'Epilogue on EU Citizenship: Hopes and Fears' 755–6; Commission Recommendation (EU) 2018/234 of 14 February 2018 on enhancing the European nature and efficient conduct of the 2019 elections to the European Parliament [2018] OJ L45/40 ('the Union's ... democratic legitimacy, which rests on the dual pillars of direct representation of citizens in the European Parliament and their indirect representation by governments of the Member States in the European Council and the Council'); Case C-411/06 *Commission v Parliament and Council* ECLI:EU:C:2009:518, Opinion of AG Poiares Maduro, para 6 fn 5. See also *BVerfG, 2 BvE 2/08 (Lissabon)* 30 June 2009, Absatz-Nr (1-421), para 36.

1702 See analysis by Timmermans, 'How to Define the European Union?' (other qualifications of the EU at 82). See also n 1036; further R Schütze, *European constitutional law* (2 edn, Cambridge University Press 2016) 75 (the EU is a Federation of States); Hoeksma, *From Common Market to Common Democracy: A Theory of Democratic Integration*. Before the Lisbon Treaty: W van Gerven, *The European Union: A Polity of States and Peoples* (Hart 2005).

1703 *BVerfG, 2 BvE 2/08 (Lissabon)* 30 June 2009, Absatz-Nr (1-421), para 265 ('To safeguard democratic principles, it may be necessary to clearly emphasise the principle of conferral in the treaties and in their application and interpretation, in order to maintain the balance of political forces of Europe between the Member States and the level of the Union as the precondition for the allocation of sovereign powers in the association').

1704 See, i.a., Case C-411/06 *Commission v Parliament and Council* ECLI:EU:C:2009:518, Opinion of AG Poiares Maduro, para 6; on vertical and horizontal division of powers: Lenaerts and Van Nuffel, *European Union Law* 298; also Schütze, *European constitutional law*.

writing (e.g. on EU 'demoi-cracy').[1705] At EU level, neither the European Parliament nor the national parliaments play the traditional role of a parliament in a State.[1706] Pupils can discuss many questions. *Is EU membership eroding national democracy? Why have Member States opted for membership? How can national parliaments play a more prominent role in EU matters?* Finally, the last criterion for relevance for mainstream education is also satisfied, since the specific features of EU democracy affect all EU citizens (iv).

226 National parliaments as actors in the EU

The EU dimension of EDC enables citizens to make informed choices when voting for the European Parliament as well as for national parliaments. The role of national parliaments in the EU provides additional and significant content to national EDC (i, ii). This role (again) underscores the EU dimension of the relationship of static citizens with their own Member State. National parliaments 'contribute actively to the good functioning of the EU' in the six ways described in Article 12 TEU and in

---

1705 K Nicolaïdis, 'The New Constitution as European "Demoi-cracy"?' (2004) 7 Critical Review of International Social and Political Philosophy 76; R Bellamy, '"An Ever Closer Union Among the Peoples of Europe": Republican Intergovernmentalism and Demoicratic Representation within the EU' (2013) 35 Journal of European Integration 499; R Bellamy and D Castiglione, 'Three models of democracy, political community and representation in the EU' (2013) 20 Journal of European Public Policy 206; F Cheneval and F Schimmelfennig, 'The Case for Demoicracy in the European Union' (2013) 51 JCMS 334; Nicolaïdis, 'European Demoicracy and Its Crisis'; F Cheneval, S Lavenex and F Schimmelfennig, 'Demoi-cracy in the European Union: principles, institutions, policies' (2015) 22 Journal of European Public Policy 1; Lenaerts, 'Demoicracy, Constitutional Pluralism and the Court of Justice of the European Union'; T Hüller, 'Out of time? The democratic limits of EU demoicracy' (2015) 22 Journal of European Public Policy 1; A Schlenker, 'Supranational, Intergovernmental or Demoicratic Legitimacy? Citizens' Evaluations of the EU' (2015) 16 European Politics and Society 581; Lenaerts and Gutiérrez-Fons, 'Epilogue on EU Citizenship: Hopes and Fears' 779 ('the idea of demoicracy suggests that both types of citizenship should coexist in a mutually reinforcing system of multilevel governance').

1706 C Sprungk, 'A New Type of Representative Democracy? Reconsidering the Role of National Parliaments in the European Union' (2013) 35 Journal of European Integration 547, 548: national parliaments play the role of gatekeepers (preventing rather than shaping legislation), of networkers (cooperating with other parliaments and supranational institutions), and of unitary scrutinisers (a uniform mode of control of government across all party groups); analysis of how France, Germany and Poland perform these roles.

accordance with Protocols No 1 and 2.[1707] Article 12 TEU illustrates how EU democracy depends on Member State democracy. National parliaments are actors in the EU at 'constitutional' moments, such as Treaty ratification or revision.[1708] They have responsibilities in the genesis of EU secondary law. Protocol 1 encourages greater involvement of national parliaments in the EU. Seeking to take decisions 'as closely as possible to the citizens of the Union', Protocol 2 establishes a system for monitoring the principles of subsidiarity and proportionality (Article 5 TEU, Article 69 TFEU). Commission consultation documents and draft legislative acts are forwarded to national parliaments, who can send reasoned opinions on non-compliance with the principle of subsidiarity (Early Warning System). Draft legislative acts may have to be reviewed, subject to conditions.[1709] Furthermore, national parliaments act in legislative implementation at national level, e.g. transposing directives. Last but not least, national parliaments play an essential role in guaranteeing ministerial accountability.[1710] National governments are accountable to the national parlia-

1707 Protocol (No 1) On the role of the National Parliaments in the European Union [2012] OJ C326/1; Protocol (No 2) On the application of the principles of subsidiarity and proportionality [2012] OJ C326/1.

1708 Arts 12(d) and 48 TEU. Withdrawal takes place in accordance with national constitutional requirements (Art 50 TEU).

1709 Protocol (No 1) On the role of the National Parliaments in the European Union [2012] OJ C326/1, Arts 1–3; Art 9 (interparliamentary cooperation); Protocol (No 2) On the application of the principles of subsidiarity and proportionality [2012] OJ C326/1, Arts 4–6, Art 7 (obligation to review the draft legislative act for non-compliance with the principle of subsidiarity). See P Kiiver, 'Analysis and reflections: The early-warning system for the principle of subsidiarity: The national parliament as a Conseil d'Etat for Europe' (2011) 36 ELRev 98; E Miklin, 'Beyond subsidiarity: the indirect effect of the Early Warning System on national parliamentary scrutiny in European Union affairs' (2016) 23 Journal of European Public Policy 1 (national parliaments are under normative pressure to engage in the Early Warning System). Example of the effect of a yellow card from national parliaments: Commission Decision to withdraw the Proposal for a Council Regulation on the exercise of the right to take collective action within the context of the freedom of establishment and the freedom to provide services COM(2012) 130.

1710 Protocol (No 1) On the role of the National Parliaments in the European Union [2012] OJ C326/1: 'the way in which national Parliaments scrutinise their governements is a matter for constitutional organisation and practice of each Member State' (preamble). See P Kiiver, 'European Treaty reform and the national parliaments: towards a new assessment of Parliament-friendly Treaty provisions' in J Wouters, L Verhey and P Kiiver (eds), *European Constitutionalism beyond Lisbon* (Intersentia 2009) 133; Lenaerts and Van Nuffel, *European*

ments for their actions at EU level, e.g. negotiations in the European Council or Council, the nomination of Commissioners, actions in committees, etc.[1711] The interface between national parliaments and the EU thus has multiple facets.

The effective exercise by national parliaments of this multifaceted role in the EU depends on the awareness of their members of EU policies and of the importance they attach to them. Members of national parliaments are sometimes criticised for being passive recipients of EU law.[1712] National citizens can influence the involvement of their representatives in EU matters by their votes and through the national public sphere. If closely observed (even mistrusted[1713]) by informed citizens, representatives will be more inclined to use the available tools. Through letters to newspapers, blogs, likes or dislikes in social media, citizens can prompt members of national parliaments to act in EU matters, or to intensify scrutiny of accountability or respect for subsidiarity. Therefore, citizens (and, of course, members of national parliaments) need an understanding of the EU. If national parliaments are empowered to act in the democratic life of the Union, citizens must be empowered to choose representatives fit for these processes. Ideally, taking democracy seriously, journalists and at least a substantive part of the public should be informed about the mechanisms for involving national parliaments in the work of the EU.

Admittedly, the potential role of national parliaments in the EU can be criticised as unsatisfactory.[1714] Yet, the possibilities for action in the cur-

---

Union Law 741–5; Sprungk, 'A New Type of Representative Democracy? Reconsidering the Role of National Parliaments in the European Union', 553; Grimm, *The Constitution of European Democracy*, ch 9.

1711 Kiiver, 'European Treaty reform and the national parliaments: towards a new assessment of Parliament-friendly Treaty provisions' 133: the principle of ministerial accountability can be seen as a cornerstone of national parliamentary involvement in EU affairs.

1712 Ibid 134.

1713 I Krastev, 'Democracy of Rejection' in L Van Middelaar and P Van Parijs (eds), *After the Storm: How to Save Democracy in Europe* (Lannoo 2015), 149, 161: for the success of democracy, it is vital to organise mistrust; it 'keeps elected representatives on their toes'; new democratic age gives profound primacy to the individual.

1714 T van den Brink, 'National Parliaments and EU Economic Governance. In Search of New ways to Enhance Democratic Legitimacy' in F Goudappel and E Hirsch Ballin (eds), *Democracy and Rule of Law in the European Union: Essays in Honour of Jaap W de Zwaan* (Springer 2015), 15, 19, 22 (the author raises questions about a more substantial role in the field of economics and fiscal sovereignty).

rent state of EU law are not always used to the full. If a more democratic EU is to be achieved, the ball is to a large extent in the court of the Member States (who are, moreover, responsible for education[1715]) and their parliaments.[1716] National EDC must be given an EU dimension which reflects the EU dimension of the role of national parliaments.

227 The EU dimension of democratic life within the Member State

The EU dimension of national democracies cannot be denied. Domestic votes have important crossborder repercussions. The whole of Europe attentively follows (and sometimes holds its breath) when national elections take place in Germany, France, Italy, Poland, Greece, Spain, or Hungary, just to cite some examples. Elections for national parliaments and national presidential elections have a crucial EU dimension.[1717] They determine whether more Eurosceptic or Europhile political parties will come to power and who will be the actors in the European Council and the Council. Whether Merkel, Macron, Kaczyński, Tsipras, Orban, or others, are the protagonists on the national political stage is highly relevant for the EU. National voters exert strong influence on the future of the EU by giving support to ideas born of 'illiberal democracy', to inward looking parties, and to exclusionary attitudes, or to the opposite. The ultimate example of the EU's dependence on national voters is the Brexit referendum. The national citizen has the last word. Given the interdependence of national democracies in the EU, the quality of national democracy is decisive for the quality of EU democracy.[1718] In other words, if there is a democratic deficit in the EU, it is related to a democratic deficit in the Member States. How 'democracy' (condition for EU membership) is assured in the Member States depends on the votes of their nationals in national elections. Needless to say, nationals are mostly static EU citizens (iv). Accordingly, applying EDC standards is not only a national matter. Incorporating an

1715 Part four.

1716 Kiiver, 'European Treaty reform and the national parliaments: towards a new assessment of Parliament-friendly Treaty provisions' 132.

1717 See, e.g., after parliamentary elections in Italy: 'Italian crisis felt in Spain and wider EU', <euobserver.com/economic/141934>.

1718 R Bauböck, 'Still United in Diversity? The State of the Union Address' (Florence, 5 May 2017): '... in a Union of states, the primary level of citizenship is that of the member states. The value of EU citizenship depends on the quality of democracy in the member states'.

EU dimension into EDC in mainstream education for the large majority of (static) citizens is crucial for the future of the EU.

228 Dual democratic legitimacy calls for an EU dimension to EDC on both tracks of legitimacy

Dual democratic legitimacy[1719] demands acceptable and adaptable EDC on both tracks of EU legitimacy. Adding an EU dimension to EDC is relevant to both national and European Parliament elections. Given the doubts about the European Parliament as an equivalent track of legitimacy (its characteristics not matching up to those of a national parliament), it is sometimes argued that the legitimacy of the EU is in essence based on that of the Member States.[1720] If this is so, this legitimacy can be questioned to the extent that the citizen's vote in national elections is not based on adequate enlightenment about EU matters. The legitimacy which Member States claim, cannot be based on uninformed citizenship.

Looking at it simplistically, *national* EDC prepares young citizens for democracy at *Member State* level, focusing on elections for the national parliament, and the *EU dimension* of EDC prepares them for democracy at *EU* level, focusing on elections for the European Parliament. In the EU's integrated multilevel system of governance, however, realities are more complex. So far in this study, it has been argued that an EU dimension must be added to national EDC to strengthen *EU* democracy. Paradoxically, adding an EU dimension to EDC is also needed to guarantee *national* democracy.

National parliaments are supposed to represent the will of the citizens. What is the credibility of representatives in national parliaments acting (or failing to act) at EU level if they have been chosen by citizens lacking understanding of EU matters? How legitimate is the mandate given directly by citizens to their parliaments, and indirectly to their governments, to act at EU level, if these citizens have no understanding of the *what*, *why* and *how* questions of the EU system or of the EU issues on which the national actors must adopt a position? Democratic elections of national parliaments presuppose at least minimal insight on the part of nationals as to the involvement of their country in EU matters and EU

1719 Text to n 1701.

1720 See i.a. Weiler, 'In the Face of Crisis: Input Legitimacy, Output Legitimacy and the Political Messianism of European Integration' ('Any solution to the crisis of Europe will have to draw upon the deep legitimacy resources of the national communities, the member states'); *BVerfG, 2 BvE 2/08 (Lissabon)* 30 June 2009, Absatz-Nr (1-421), i.a. paras 262, 276 ff, 289, 293.

foundational values, objectives and principles. As *economic* actors in the market, citizens can only conclude a contract if they are informed about its constitutive elements and conditions. The consumer has a right to be informed. Before the consumer can be bound by a contract, the trader has an obligation to provide clear and comprehensible information.[1721] As *political* actors, citizens do not enjoy such protection. No prior adequate information seems to be required for the social contract[1722]. Even votes based on fake news and false promises lead to valid votes. Therefore, at least, all reasonable efforts must be made to provide quality EDC in schools, including the EU dimension, to equip nationals with a basic preliminary understanding of the system in which they live and to develop their critical agency. The task of democracy is to educate citizens who will think critically throughout a political campaign and take responsibility for their votes.[1723] Because the Member States are actors in the EU composite legal order through the institutional framework (European Council, Council, national parliaments) and through the many mechanisms for cooperation and administrative entwinement, the national public sphere and national political life should include an informed EU dimension.[1724] On a reading of EU and national law in the light of EDC standards, this requires the incorporation of an EU dimension into EDC, strengthening both tracks of democratic legitimacy.

229 Conclusion for representative democracy

As recognised, citizens do not need an EU dimension to EDC in order to tick a box in an electoral list and cast a valid vote. However, it is assumed that democracy is more than procedural or institutional democracy. To

1721 See i.a. Art 5(1) Directive 2011/83/EU of the European Parliament and of the Council of 25 October 2011 on consumer rights, amending Council Directive 93/13/EEC and Directive 1999/44/EC of the European Parliament and of the Council and repealing Council Directive 85/577/EEC and Directive 97/7/EC of the European Parliament and of the Council [2011] OJ L304/64.

1722 It would be interesting to explore the political philosophical question on the need for information or for education in the context of 'le contrat social' as understood by Hugo Grotius, Thomas Hobbes, and John Locke.

1723 Oelkers, 'The European Crisis and Education for Democracy'. See also Jackson, '"The Best Education Ever": Trumpism, Brexit, and new social learning'.

1724 See VA Schmidt, *Democracy in Europe: the EU and national polities* (Oxford University Press 2006): the democratic deficit of the EU is mainly due to the sustained failure of political communication at Member State level; national politicians do not explain the supranational level of governance and the new realities.

increase the democratic legitimacy of the EU, it is not sufficient to organise procedurally correct elections or reinforce the institutional role of the European Parliament and the national parliaments in EU decision-making.[1725] To increase democratic legitimacy, these elections must, moreover, be held in conditions of genuine representativeness, that is: based on the votes of informed citizens, who are aware of the EU dimension of their votes. The EU dimension of EDC makes it possible to attain the compulsory educational aim of preparing citizens for effective participation and responsible life in a free society,[1726] in this instance participating by means of voting in elections for the European Parliament and for national parliaments. To the extent that Member States are actors in the EU political processes, the quality of democracy at *EU* level is contingent on the quality of democracy at *national* level, which is in turn contingent on EDC and its EU dimension.

To conclude, the right to vote for the European Parliament and for a national parliament constitutes core content for the EU dimension of EDC, satisfying all the criteria for relevance for mainstream education.

D Rights and opportunities in participatory democracy

230 Complementarity of EDC for representative and for participatory democracy

The role of active citizens in the democratic life of the Union is not limited to periodically casting a vote in elections for the European Parliament and for national parliaments. In between elections, EU citizens can observe, blog, twitter, protest, spread their views via the internet.[1727] Besides the participation rights of Article 24 TFEU (ECI, petition, Ombudsman), they can use the additional tools for participation provided by Article 11 TEU as a means of participatory democracy. If representative and participatory democracy are complementary, so is preparing for them in the classroom through EDC. I will explain how the EU dimension of EDC lays the foundations for participatory democracy in a different way than for representative democracy. Participatory democracy starts from a perspective differing

1725 Neither for the rule of law, nor for democracy do purely formal and procedural requirements suffice; see Commission Communication 'A new EU Framework to strengthen the Rule of Law' COM(2014) 0158 final, para 2.

1726 Aims in Art 13 ICESCR and Art 29 CRC.

1727 Krastev, 'Democracy of Rejection' 149.

from that of representative democracy. While a vote in an election usually expresses general views on society and on the common good (advocated by political parties), participatory democracy is more oriented towards single issues and protection of one's interests, directly and, most often, indirectly via interest groups and civil society organisations.[1728] Representative democracy puts the European Parliament and national parliaments centre-stage; participatory democracy provides EU citizens with opportunities for contact with other institutions, in particular the Commission (Article 11(3) TEU). The question is to what extent the content of Article 11 TEU is relevant for mainstream EDC. The fourth criterion for relevance, in particular, may cause hesitation: does this opportunity to participate affect the large majority of EU citizens (iv)? Is it not, in reality, intended for EU lobbyists in Brussels?

231 *(i) Additional content for EDC*

The first criterion for relevance for mainstream education is satisfied: Article 11 TEU provides additional content for EDC, especially in component (c-3), to play an active part in democratic life. The participatory tools of Article 11 are framed as obligations for the EU institutions: they shall 'by appropriate means, give *citizens and representative associations* the opportunity to make known and publicly exchange their views *in all areas of Union action*' (para 1), 'shall maintain an open, transparent and regular dialogue with *representative associations and civil society* (para 2), and the Commission 'shall carry out broad consultations with *parties concerned* in order to ensure that the Union's actions are coherent and transparent (para 3).[1729] These provisions do not formulate rights for EU citizens (EDC component (c-1), to exercise and defend their democratic rights). Only the ECI, another expression of participatory democracy (para 4), is generally seen as a citizenship right.[1730] Introduced in the Lisbon Treaty, Article 11 TEU has institutionalised existing practices of civil dialogue and consultation of

1728 Kohler-Koch, 'Does participatory governance hold its promises?' 268–9, 271. See also Mendes, *Participation in EU Rule-Making: A Rights-Based Approach* 33–5 (participation of citizens can relate to two realities: defending collective interests which may coincide with public interests (*uti cives*), and defending their own private rights and interests where public powers interfere in their legal sphere (*uti singuli*). Mendes also sees the latter as a form of participatory democracy; the distinction is a matter of degree, not clear-cut). Further on complementarity, text to n 1779. See also *BVerfG, 2 BvE 2/08 (Lissabon)* 30 June 2009, Absatz-Nr (1-421), paras 272–4.

1729 Emphasis added for criterion (iv), see n 1756.

1730 Text to n 1541.

stakeholders in EU governance.[1731] The existing practices were oriented towards higher *output legitimacy*, better policy-making through the external expertise of stakeholders, evidence based, and reducing costs. Governance assigned civil society organisations an instrumental role. Concerned by the interests of stakeholders, these organisations have contributed to efficient problem solving, higher quality and greater compliance.[1732] The inclusion of Article 11 in Title II TEU on democratic principles underscores the additional rationale of *input legitimacy*. Instruments of participatory democracy thus aim to increase both output and input legitimacy. It must be observed that practices of interest representation, consultation and civil dialogue are not situated in the legal field.[1733] The legal aspect of participation is limited to the right to be heard before an individual measure which would affect him or her adversely is taken (Article 41(2)(a) CFR; included in the right to good administration). The right to be heard is not applicable to the public at large seeking to reinforce democratic principles.[1734] The Lisbon Treaty has been criticised for not making participation

1731 Commission White Paper of 25 July 2001 on European Governance COM(2001) 428 final; Commission Communication 'The Commission's contribution to the period of reflection and beyond - Plan-D for Democracy, Dialogue and Debate' COM(2005) 494; Kohler-Koch, 'Does participatory governance hold its promises?' 266 (Art 11 builds further on existing practice); L Bouza García, 'How Could the New Article 11 TEU Contribute to Reduce the EU's Democratic Malaise?' in M Dougan, N Nic Shuibhne and E Spaventa (eds), *Empowerment and Disempowerment of the European Citizen* (Hart 2012), 255 (civil society organisations lobbied for participatory democracy). See for a historical overview and assessment of forms of participation in EU governance: Mendes, *Participation in EU Rule-Making: A Rights-Based Approach* 78 ff (participatory governance in the sense of 'policy-making underpinned by participation').

1732 Kohler-Koch and Rittberger, 'The "Governance Turn" in EU studies' 270; Bouza García, 'How Could the New Article 11 TEU Contribute to Reduce the EU's Democratic Malaise?' 256. See rationale in recitals 2 and 3 to Commission Proposal for a Interinstitutional Agreement on a mandatory Transparency Register COM(2016) 0627 final.

1733 Difference between concepts of interest representation, consultation and civil dialogue (oriented to different 'publics') in D Curtin and J Mendes, 'Transparence et participation: des principes démocratiques pour l'administration de l'Union Européenne' (2011) 137 Revue Française d'Administration Publique 101, 112–3. Consultation is the most flexible concept.

1734 Ibid, 111. See Mendes, *Participation in EU Rule-Making: A Rights-Based Approach* 161 ff, on the right to be heard and formal boundaries of participation rights. General rule in Case 17/74 *Transocean Marine Paint Association* ECLI:EU:C:1974:106, para 15: 'a person whose interests are perceptibly affected by a deci-

in civil dialogue a citizens' right.[1735] The participatory democracy instruments described above remain in the vague domain of non-rights and seem still mostly oriented to output efficiency.[1736] To the extent that paras (1) to (3) of Article 11 TEU concern participation *practices* and *opportunities* rather than participation *rights*, it is not in component (c-1) of EDC that Article 11 TEU provides additional content to national EDC (to exercise and defend democratic rights), but in component (c-3) of EDC, i.e. empowering citizens to play an active part in democratic life.

232 *(ii) Significant content*

The place of Article 11 in Title II TEU, 'Provisions on democratic principles', proves its significance. It is a supplementary expression of democracy, which is a foundational value, objective and principle. A textual, contextual and teleological interpretation makes a reading in the light of EDC standards a logical next step.

A contextual interpretation based on the place of Article 11 in Title II TEU has normative implications. As Mendes argues:

> For the first time at Treaty level participation in decision-making beyond political representation is explicitly linked to democracy. The democracy of the Union now rests, by force of Article 11 TEU, also on the links it establishes directly with its citizens. Participation is therefore one of the foundations of democracy in the EU. As such, it can no longer be approached merely as an aspect of process efficiency and policy outputs, detached from democratic values such as equality and transparency. (....) Article 11 TEU postulates a transition from the instrumental usages of participation typical of participatory gover-

---

sion taken by a public authority must be given the opportunity to make his point of view known.'.

1735 A contrario Commission Proposal for a Interinstitutional Agreement on a mandatory Transparency Register COM(2016) 0627 final Art 3 (non-applicability with regard to fundamental or procedural rights, such as the right to be heard, the fundamental right of a client to a fair trial, including the right of defence in administrative proceedings). Before 2009: Smismans, 'New governance: the solution for active European citizenship, or the end of citizenship?', 608, 611: 'new governance provides hardly any legally enforceable participation rights', it contributes to participation practice rather than ensuring equal participation rights.

1736 Smismans, 'New governance: the solution for active European citizenship, or the end of citizenship?', 604–5.

nance to participation conceived as a basis of participatory democracy.[1737]

Mendes concludes that the fundamental link between participation and democracy has normative implications and argues for law to have a larger role: the scope of participation rights in EU administrative law should be extended, i.a. in executive rule-making procedures in the EU.[1738] In the same paradigm, I conclude that this fundamental link has normative implications for the field of education and argue that, when reading Article 11 TEU jointly with EDC standards, public and educational authorities have a responsibility to extend the scope of national EDC to include an EU dimension so as to prepare EU citizens for their role in participatory democracy.[1739] The challenge is to turn the participatory governance practices oriented towards an instrumental rationale (output legitimacy) into genuine democratic participation tools for citizens (additional source of input legitimacy).[1740] As Mendes argues, the way participation in the EU

1737 J Mendes, 'Participation and the role of law after Lisbon: a legal view on Article 11 TEU' (2011) 48 CMLRev 1849, 1850.

1738 See Mendes, *Participation in EU Rule-Making: A Rights-Based Approach*. In this work, participation refers to 'the procedural intervention of natural and legal persons whose substantive rights and interests are potentially affected by EU regulatory measures, irrespective of the form in which the latter are adopted' (p 25, also p 76). This contrasts with a vague concept of 'participation at large', i.e. 'the possibility of taking part in decision-making processes', which can take various forms and degrees (p 27). The author defends two layers of participation rights: 'those of holders of subjective rights and those of holders of legally protected interests' (p 24; no clear cut distinction, see p 42). Participation rights can, from a procedural perspective, be broadly defined as advantageous positions that allow their holders to influence the exercise of decisional power (p 77). The extension of participation rights in EU administrative law is 'required by legal values that underpin the EU legal order, it is coherent with principles and rules of EU law, and it is consonant with the fact that participation is constitutionally relevant feature of the EU legal and political system' (p 469). These arguments are mutatis mutandis valid for the extension of EDC by an EU dimension. See also Mendes, 'Participation and the role of law after Lisbon: a legal view on Article 11 TEU' ('the normative shift which Article 11 TEU postulates, limits the discretion of the institutions in shaping participation practices').

1739 On Member States' competence, obligations, and limitation of the margin of appreciation, see Part four.

1740 Bouza García, 'How Could the New Article 11 TEU Contribute to Reduce the EU's Democratic Malaise?' 274.

is perceived needs to be transformed, to reflect the fact that participation is now a founding legal principle in EU democratic life.[1741]

Normative consequences moreover follow from a teleological interpretation of Article 11 TEU. EDC standards are inextricably linked to any form of democracy. They aim to achieve representative as well as participatory democracy objectives. Article 11 must also be linked to compulsory educational aims in binding international agreements ('to participate effectively').[1742]

233 (iii) Inviting critical thinking

Article 11 TEU invites critical reflection on EU policies, e.g. environment policy, or on how the EU handles specific single issues. Public debate, starting in the classroom, contributes to a growing European public sphere, as transnational alliances on single issues transcend borders.[1743] It is also possible to think critically about the tools of participatory democracy themselves. The democratic effects of participatory instruments are questioned.[1744] Problematic aspects include short periods of consultation in complex matters, limited feedback after consultations, and the selection

---

1741 Mendes, 'Participation and the role of law after Lisbon: a legal view on Article 11 TEU', 1850, 1857: 'the relationships between the citizens and representative associations, on the one hand, and the EU decision-makers, on the other, need to be reconsidered with respect to their value for the individual, so as to ensure voice independently of problem-solving needs as well as equal treatment of participants.' See also Smismans, 'Regulating interest group participation in the European Union: changing paradigms between transparency and representation' (paradigms in participation, evolution).

1742 Art 13 ICESCR.

1743 European Parliament Resolution of 7 September 2010 on journalism and new media - creating a public sphere in Europe [2011] OJ C308E/55 (recital G: 'whereas a public sphere can be understood as a space in which public policies may be better understood by, and discussed with, all EU citizens and all sections of the population, in all its diversity, with a view to meeting their expectations more effectively, and whereas it must be a venue both for the provision of information and for wide-ranging consultations transcending national borders and fostering the development of a sense of shared public interest throughout the EU'; see also para 13 on EU learning); Further, Bouza García, 'How Could the New Article 11 TEU Contribute to Reduce the EU's Democratic Malaise?'; S Smismans, 'Should participatory democracy become the normative model for EU governance?' [2012] Re-Public.

1744 See analysis of Kohler-Koch, 'Does participatory governance hold its promises?'; Mendes, *Participation in EU Rule-Making: A Rights-Based Approach* i.a. 14, 128 ff; Bouza García, 'How Could the New Article 11 TEU Contribute to Reduce the EU's Democratic Malaise?' 258.

of participants (some and not others).[1745] Unequal access to participation instruments is at odds with equality of citizens, which is essential to democracy, and is hardly reconcilable with the aim of increased democratic legitimacy.[1746] If characterised by elitist representation and professional lobbying on the Brussels circuit, participatory governance is not the same thing as participatory democracy.[1747] Several questions can be discussed in the classroom. *Is filling out an online questionnaire without deliberation 'effective participation'?*[1748] *What form can effective participation take in a Union of 500 million citizens? How can more citizens be involved on an equal basis? Are citizens interested at all in these participation tools (or, provocatively, do they prefer to watch television)?*[1749] Citizens may have doubts about the impact of their participation. Institutions have no obligation to meet the demands of civil society. Notwithstanding its enhanced legal status since the Lisbon Treaty—because it is included in Title II TEU—civil dialogue merely results in an invitation to the Commission to act in a certain direc-

1745 Frequently criticised. See i.a. Bouza García, 'How Could the New Article 11 TEU Contribute to Reduce the EU's Democratic Malaise?' 266 (Art 11(3) TEU refers to parties concerned, not 'the' parties concerned). Broad discretion of the Commission, see i.a. Smismans, 'New governance: the solution for active European citizenship, or the end of citizenship?', 604. Assessment of democratic potential, see Kohler-Koch and Rittberger, 'The "Governance Turn" in EU studies'; B Kohler-Koch and B Finke, 'The Institutional Shaping of EU–Society Relations: A Contribution to Democracy via Participation?' (2007) 3 Journal of Civil Society 205; Curtin and Mendes, 'Transparence et participation: des principes démocratiques pour l'administration de l'Union Européenne' (analysis as to what extent rules and practices of EU administration encourage realisation of the democratic principles of the TEU); Mendes, *Participation in EU Rule-Making: A Rights-Based Approach*.

1746 Kohler-Koch, 'Does participatory governance hold its promises?' 280; Curtin and Mendes, 'Transparence et participation: des principes démocratiques pour l'administration de l'Union Européenne', 118. See earlier: P Magnette, 'European Governance and Civic Participation: Beyond Elitist Citizenship?' (2003) 51 Political Studies 144 (practices underpinned by an élitist and functionalist philosophy).

1747 Kohler-Koch, 'Does participatory governance hold its promises?' 286 ('Such an elitist system is equal to representation for the people, but not by the people').

1748 Ibid, 280.

1749 Civil dialogues are not always attended by many citizens. See also JW Van Deth, 'In Search of the "Good European Citizen": WYSIWYG?' in B Kohler-Koch and F Larat (eds), *Efficient and democratic governance in the European Union* (CONNEX Report Series No 9, 2008) (What You See Is What You Get): the Good European Citizen seems to be a national citizen who is not interested in participation and EU matters (EDC should awaken him).

tion (like the ECI). The Commission has a wide discretion and is not obliged to give reasons for not taking account of opinions expressed in dialogue or consultations.[1750] Are the tools of 'democratic' governance disguised attempts to 'sell Europe', a form of window dressing?[1751] Participation may be reduced to 'public-making', letting the public know.[1752] Creating a European public space or a European civil society through participatory governance is still work in progress.[1753]

Scepticism also exists about the strengthening of EU legitimacy where interest representation is—not infrequently—based on professional relationships between clients and intermediaries. True, the institutions are quite open about the representative organisations and groups with which they interact. Only after registration in a mandatory Transparency Register can interest representatives engage in activities with the institutions (to promote certain interests 'with the objective of influencing the formulation or implementation of policy or legislation, or the decision-making process within these institutions', e.g. participation in public consultations).[1754] However, if mainly representative organisations, stakeholders, experts, or professional actors are involved, the question, critical for EDC in mainstream education, is to what extent the participatory instruments are intended for the ordinary citizen. This leads to the last criterion.

234 *(iv) Affecting the large majority of EU citizens*

The question as to what extent the ordinary citizen is involved in participatory democracy and governance is a matter of debate.[1755]

1750 Bouza García, 'How Could the New Article 11 TEU Contribute to Reduce the EU's Democratic Malaise?' 258.

1751 Kohler-Koch, 'Does participatory governance hold its promises?' 272.

1752 Mendes, *Participation in EU Rule-Making: A Rights-Based Approach* 118, with reference to Neil Walker.

1753 Ibid, 136–8, about participation rationales and results: in fact, under the new legitimacy garment participation remains, as before, essentially output-oriented; 'pragmatic governance'.

1754 Commission Proposal for a Interinstitutional Agreement on a mandatory Transparency Register COM(2016) 0627 final, i.a. Arts 2, 3(1), 5. See also European Parliament Decision of 15 April 2014 on the modification of the interinstitutional agreement on the Transparency Register [2017] OJ C443/228; Commission Communication 'Completing the Better Regulation Agenda: Better solutions for better results' COM(2017) 651 final. Recital 11: This does not affect the rights under Art 11(4) TEU (ECI) and Art 227 TFEU (petition the European Parliament).

1755 See i.a. O De Schutter, 'Europe in Search of its Civil Society' (2002) 8 ELJ 198; Smismans, *Law, Legitimacy, and European Governance: Functional Participation*

Article 11 TEU is poorly drafted and gives the impression of a shopping list (see italics above).[1756] Opportunities for the exchange of views shall be given 'by appropriate means'. Article 11 TEU, secondary legislation, and policy documents refer to a variety of actors, such as citizens, representative associations, civil society, parties concerned, organisations, stakeholders, experts, the public.[1757] While the forms of participation are not always clearly defined (such as interest representation, consultation and civil dialogue), it is nevertheless clear that Article 11 offers participation *opportunities* to many EU citizens, directly or indirectly.

---

in Social Regulation; Kohler-Koch and Rittberger, 'The "Governance Turn" in EU studies'; S Borrás and T Conzelmann, 'Democracy, Legitimacy and Soft Modes of Governance in the EU: The Empirical Turn' (2007) 29 Journal of European Integration 531; S Smismans, 'New Modes of Governance and the Participatory Myth' (2008) 31 West European Politics 874; A Wimmel, 'Theorizing the Democratic Legitimacy of European Governance: a Labyrinth with No Exit?' (2009) 31 Journal of European Integration 181; D Curtin, P Mair and Y Papadopoulos (eds), *Accountability and European Governance* (West European politics Series, Routledge 2010); S Bredt, 'Prospects and Limits of Democratic Governance in the EU' (2011) 17 ELJ 35; Mendes, 'Participation and the role of law after Lisbon: a legal view on Article 11 TEU' ('despite the rhetoric of connecting the EU to its citizens and to civil society, participation kept on serving very much the same purposes as before and maintained fairly the same traits it had acquired in the decades that preceded the White Paper'); Mendes, *Participation in EU Rule-Making: A Rights-Based Approach* 128–130; C Shore, '"European Governance" or Governmentality? The European Commission and the Future of Democratic Government' (2011) 17 ELJ 287 ('far from laying the grounds for a more inclusive, participatory and democratic political order, the Commission's model to governance represents a form of neoliberal governmentality that is actually undermining democratic government and promoting a politics of exclusion').

1756 Italics in text to n 1729. See Mendes, 'Participation and the role of law after Lisbon: a legal view on Article 11 TEU', 1851, 1854 (shopping list). See also Curtin and Mendes, 'Transparence et participation: des principes démocratiques pour l'administration de l'Union Européenne', 112–3 (on the difference between the concepts of interest representation, consultation and civil dialogue; oriented to different 'publics', consultation is the most flexible concept).

1757 See also Interinstitutional Agreement between the European Parliament, the Council of the European Union and the European Commission on Better Law-Making [2016] OJ L123/1, i.a. paras 19 and 28 (public and stakeholder consultation; experts and public consultations).

Directly, citizens can participate in instruments such as online consultations or citizens' dialogues, frequently organised by the Commission.[1758] Interaction of individual citizens with the European Parliament, the Council or the Commission does not require prior registration in the transparency register.[1759]

Indirectly, citizens can participate via their interest representatives. Whereas the original concept of participatory democracy implies the direct participation of citizens, it has evolved to mean participation of citizens through functional representatives. Functional representation allows all citizens to participate indirectly in the complex EU multilevel governance.[1760] It should be noted that here direct democracy has evolved into another form of 'representative' democracy.[1761] Functional interest representation and thus indirect participation of citizens in EU governance also occurs by means of organic participation through the European Economic

---

1758 Commission Recommendation (EU) 2018/234 of 14 February 2018 on enhancing the European nature and efficient conduct of the 2019 elections to the European Parliament [2018] OJ L45/40, recital 7: since 2015, 478 Citizens' Dialogues have been held, also in cooperation with institutional partners, and before 9 May 2019, around 500 more will take place. In its priority for 'a Union of Democratic Change', the Commission aims at better law making and refers i.a. to public consultations, including internet based. See Commission Communication 'Commission Work Programme 2017: Delivering a Europe that protects, empowers and defends' COM(2016) 710 final, Section 10; Commission Communication 'Commission Work Programme 2018 An Agenda for a more united, stronger and more democratic Europe' COM(2017) 650 final/2; Section II 'A Union of Democratic Change'; Commission Recommendation (EU) 2018/234 of 14 February 2018 on enhancing the European nature and efficient conduct of the 2019 elections to the European Parliament [2018] OJ L45/40.

1759 Commission Proposal for a Interinstitutional Agreement on a mandatory Transparency Register COM(2016) 0627 final, Art 3(2)(e): does not cover communication of citizens acting solely in their personal capacity. At present: European Parliament Decision of 15 April 2014 on the modification of the interinstitutional agreement on the Transparency Register [2017] OJ C443/228.

1760 See evolution in Smismans, 'Should participatory democracy become the normative model for EU governance?'.

1761 By way of parenthesis, the labels 'representative' and 'participatory' democracy may mislead. Voting in elections (representative democracy) is a form of participation in democratic life and could thus literatim be ranked under 'participatory' democracy. Conversely, participatory practices (participatory democracy) mostly occur via representative organisations and could textually be ranked under 'representative' democracy. However, the usual meaning is to connect representative democracy with official representation in parliaments.

and Social Committee and the Committee of the Regions, representing the economic, social, and regional interests of citizens,[1762] as well as through dialogue with social partners (Article 152 TFEU). In *UEAPME*, the General Court considered that:

> the principle of democracy on which the Union is founded requires — in the absence of the participation of the European Parliament in the legislative process — that the participation of the people be otherwise assured, in this instance through the parties representative of management and labour.[1763]

For functional representation, the essential point is a sound connection between the basis and its representatives, and here EDC standards come in. Scholars criticise the level of grass roots input in civil society organisations.[1764] Bouza García points to the distance of participatory tools from ordinary citizens: 'the civil dialogue scheme does not seem capable of fostering debate beyond the organisations already well established and interested in European policy-making.'[1765] Nor do online consultations easily reach the public. To give Article 11 TEU *effet utile* and reading this provision in the light of EDC standards, an EU dimension must be incorporated in EDC in mainstream education. An EU dimension to EDC prepares citizens for informed participation, direct and indirect, with reliable interaction between the grassroots and the top of civil society organisations, as well as between the top of those organisations and the institutions. Only when they understand what is at stake, can citizens responsibly choose representatives to protect their interests and receive nuanced feedback.[1766]

1762 Compulsary consultation on various policies (e.g. Art 46, 50, 100, 114 TFEU). See also Lenaerts and Van Nuffel, *European Union Law* 745; Mendes, *Participation in EU Rule-Making: A Rights-Based Approach* 31.

1763 Case T-135/96 *UEAPME v Council* ECLI:EU:T:1998:128, para 89.

1764 Bouza García, 'How Could the New Article 11 TEU Contribute to Reduce the EU's Democratic Malaise?' 270–2.

1765 Conclusion after empirical research, see ibid, 272 (support and control from grassroots citizens is lacking), also 261–2 ('as legitimate as civil society organisations consultation may be, the involvement of civil society organisations in policy-making is not a form of citizens' direct participation unless members of the organisations are effectively consulted and involved in the process'). See also Kohler-Koch, 'Does participatory governance hold its promises?'.

1766 On the distance from grassroots levels in general, see Kohler-Koch, 'Does participatory governance hold its promises?' 272, 284 ('When civil society representatives want to reach down to grassroots activists, arguing across the many

To conclude, paragraphs 1 to 3 of Article 11 TEU affect the large majority of citizens (iv) by giving them an opportunity to participate directly, and mostly indirectly, through representative organisations. To the dual tracks of democratic legitimacy, participatory democracy adds the functional representation of citizens, stakeholders and interests.[1767] The claim that functional representation gives citizens at grassroots level a voice in interaction with the institutions is undermined if the distance between grassroots and the top is widened by a lack of understanding of EU matters.

The affirmation that EU citizens participate in the democratic life of the Union (Article 10(3) TEU) through opportunities based on Article 11 TEU and that the democratic legitimacy of the EU is thus enhanced, sounds hollow if the participating citizens lack the most elementary understanding of the EU's DNA. How meaningful are discussions of citizens with EU officials, when these citizens identify the EU with the Commission (a common perception, even among civic educators) and are unfamiliar with the principle of conferral?

To grow beyond the activities of specialised actors and to increase input legitimacy, participation opportunities require a preparatory EU dimension in EDC.

That the EU dimension implies a different approach to that oriented to representative democracy will now be explained.

235 Effective interest protection

Participatory democracy gives citizens a voice. The EU dimension of EDC gives them an informed and more influential voice. Productive interaction with officials of EU institutions (be it through interest representation, consultations, dialogues, or other participatory opportunities) require prior EU knowledge and understanding. Firstly, the EU dimension of EDC should raise citizens' awareness of the existence of participatory instruments and encourage their use.[1768] Secondly, active and passive members of interest groups need some insight into the EU dimension of their specific interest field. Thirdly, single issue campaigners are handicapped if

---

layers of the multi-level system is time and resources consuming. Basic messages travel more easily').

1767 Ibid, 288 (the author defines participatory democracy by two core components: (1) NGOs, which constitute organised civil society and (2) civil dialogue, which enables them to participate in public policy making, at 274).

1768 Citizens lack motivation, see Van Deth, 'In Search of the "Good European Citizen": WYSIWYG?' (n 1749).

they cannot situate their single issue in the whole EU picture. To defend their cause persuasively, they need an understanding of related cross-cutting issues in other areas of EU policy and of the institutional balance of powers.[1769] A farmer who understands the principles of the common agricultural policy will have more influence than the farmer who only sees the issues affecting his land. The consumer who understands free movement rules in the internal market and knows about the existing consumer rights in EU law, their scope and limits, will have better arguments than the consumer who merely sets out the terms of his complaint. The social activist who understands the principle of conferral and has a view on EU competences in employment and social policy, will be better equipped to argue with the officials of EU institutions than someone who is limited to describing unjust and unfair situations in his own region. The same is true for issues relating to the environment, gender equality, minority protection, etc. In order to counter vested interests, to increase the visibility of particular interests, and to confidently play a role in the EU's participatory governance, citizens and their representatives need to be empowered. They will participate more effectively if the EDC they received at school was not limited to the nation state, but has introduced them to the foundational values, objectives and principles of the EU. Adequate interest representation requires a view on *what* happens at EU level, *why* it happens and *how*. Prior EDC with an EU dimension makes stakeholders and civil society organisations valuable partners for EU institutions in dialogues and consultations. Otherwise, the 'dialogues' or 'consultations' are camouflaged institutional 'communication' and 'information' sessions, with a top down bias.[1770] Certainly, *through* participation in dialogues or consultations, citizens' knowledge and ownership of the EU will increase. Participation has a learning effect.[1771] Yet, EU learning *before* participation will make this participation more effective. Knowledge of EU rights and obligations in relevant fields of interest contributes to the well-founded defence of interests at EU level (or in mixed bodies or agencies).[1772]

1769 On the so-called 'value and rights based' associations with a narrow focus, yet related to cross-cutting issues, see Kohler-Koch, 'Does participatory governance hold its promises?', 285–7.

1770 Bouza García, 'How Could the New Article 11 TEU Contribute to Reduce the EU's Democratic Malaise?' 272.

1771 Ibid 257, 262.

1772 Concept and examples of *EU rights*, Chapter eight.

Not only the EU dimension of *EDC*, but also the EU dimension of *HRE* (human rights education)[1773] is relevant for interest groups. The representatives and the citizens they represent should know about the rights and principles of the CFR which concern them and about the applicability of those rights and principles to EU institutions and Member States when implementing EU law. Examples are: the right to form and to join trade unions; the freedom to conduct a business; non-discrimination rights; the EU obligation to respect cultural, religious and linguistic diversity; the rights of the elderly and of persons with disabilities; workers' right to information and consultation within the undertaking; the right of collective bargaining and action; the right to working conditions which respect health, safety and dignity; rights with regard to social security and social assistance, health care, environmental protection, or consumer protection.[1774] Effective interest representation is a further reason why vocational training, too, should have an EU dimension. In order to defend the interests of their sector, future electricians, carpenters, car mechanics, decorators, cooks, hotel managers, ICT technicians, etc., need to understand the EU dimension of their professional activities. As part of quality education, the EU dimension will give them competitive advantages for work in the internal market, crossborder but also at home (area without internal frontiers). Respect for EU norms on safety, privacy, consumer or environment protection, are examples of horizontal themes relevant to many professions. The EU dimension will moreover empower them to play a role in participatory democracy, i.a. as active or passive members of professional organisations. The ordinary citizen who wants to participate in the democratic life of the Union may be intimidated when surrounded by professional consultancies, law firms, self-employed consultants, trade and business associations, trade unions, professional associations, think tanks, etc.[1775] Equipped with citizenship competence (a combination of knowledge, skills and attitudes[1776]), introduced to the rules of the game, he or she will be better armed to take up the challenges at EU level and to resist

---

1773 Defined in para 2(b) of the Charter on EDC/HRE (Part one).

1774 Resp CFR Arts 12, 16, 21, 22, 23, 25, 26, 27, 28, 31, 35, 37, 38. See also below Chapter eight.

1775 See categories of interest representatives signing up to the Transparency Register: Commission Proposal for a Interinstitutional Agreement on a mandatory Transparency Register COM(2016) 0627 final, Annex I.

1776 Council Recommendation of 22 May 2018 on key competences for lifelong learning, Annex: A European Reference Framework, 'Key competences', 6: Citizenship competence.

the temptation to withdraw to the perspective of the individual and the nation state, which only allows a limited response to the issues of globalisation.

236 Effective participation

The Member States have agreed in binding international agreements that 'education shall enable all persons to *participate effectively* in a free society' and 'shall strengthen the respect for human rights and fundamental freedoms'.[1777] Applying the compulsory educational aims in EU society—consistently with EU law—the opportunities for participatory democracy, including those related to fundamental rights, are relevant to the EU dimension of EDC. The EU dimension of EDC should enable citizens to use the *participation* tools of Article 11 TEU, and even to use them *effectively*. Read in the light of EDC standards, Article 11 TEU and its *effet utile* require an EU dimension to EDC in mainstream education.

In conclusion, an EU dimension of EDC at school is needed if citizens are to use participatory instruments effectively to defend their economic and non-economic interests (in professional and civic life). A general precondition for effective participation is transparency, where that implies intelligibility.[1778] EDC is a necessary step for attaining this. Preparing for participatory democracy thus implies a different and complementary perspective to preparing for representative democracy.[1779] Participatory instruments call for other qualities than are needed to vote in elections. They require more 'active citizenship' qualities than merely ticking a box in an electoral list. Acquiring a voice in participatory democracy is more difficult to achieve, influence must be fought for and deserved. To the extent that EU institutions have discretionary powers when organising participatory processes, or choosing and listening to parties[1780], it is preferable that these partners are well-informed. Adding an EU dimension to EDC to empower citizens for participatory opportunities is therefore at least as important as empowering them to exercise the (automatic) rights of representative democracy. Effective participatory democracy should not be reserved for the happy few, i.e. those who know how the system works, or those who don't, but can afford to pay intermediaries to represent their professional interests.

1777 Art 13 ICESCR; see also Art 29 CFR.
1778 Van Parijs, 'Justifying Europe' 258.
1779 Text to n 1728.
1780 N 1745.

237 Conclusion on the democratic participation rights in Title II TEU

In EU primary law, Title II TEU occupies a central position to which EDC standards must be linked. All EU citizens have the right to participate in the democratic life of the Union (Article 10(3) TEU). This general right is expressed in several specific democratic participation rights. With regard to representative democracy, EU law directly grants all EU citizens a right to vote in elections for the European Parliament (Articles 10(1)(2) and 14(3) TEU and 39(2) CFR). This has repercussions for the relationship of static citizens with their own Member State (*Delvigne*). Furthermore, EU law adds an important EU dimension to the right of citizens to vote for their national parliament (Article 12 TEU). With regard to participatory democracy, Article 11 TEU creates rights and various opportunities for participation by EU citizens.

Reading Title II TEU in conjunction with EDC standards, the democratic participation rights and opportunities described above provide additional (i) and significant (ii) content for national EDC in components (c-1) to exercise and defend democratic rights and responsibilities in society and (c-3) to play an active part in democratic life. They invite critical thinking (iii) and are relevant for the large majority of EU citizens, including static citizens (iv). They thus satisfy the criteria of relevance for mainstream education, moreover in complementary ways. In short, the EU dimension of EDC aims to empower EU citizens to exercise the participation rights based on Title II TEU and thereby to participate in the democratic life of the Union. Including an EU dimension in EDC enhances the quality of democracy at EU level and at national level, broadens the dual track of democratic legitimacy and strengthens social legitimacy.

Title II TEU, which was included in the 2009 Lisbon Treaty, provides the hard core for the EU dimension of EDC as it connects provisions on democratic principles with EU citizenship.[1781] Ten years later, in an evolving process towards more democratic legitimacy, the next step is to connect democratic principles and EU citizenship with EDC standards. Accordingly, young citizens should be systematically informed in main-

---

1781 Commission Recommendation of 12 March 2013 on enhancing the democratic and efficient conduct of the elections to the European Parliament [2013] OJ L79/29, recital 3 ('The Treaty of Lisbon enhances the role of citizens of the Union as political actors, establishing a solid link between citizens, the exercise of their political rights and the democratic life of the Union'). See analysis by Shaw, 'Citizenship: Contrasting Dynamics at the Interface of Integration and Constitutionalism', 4.2, 4.3; Lenaerts and Gutiérrez-Fons, 'Epilogue on EU Citizenship: Hopes and Fears' 752, 756.

stream education about the participation rights and opportunities in the EU and invited to reflect on the way forward.

CHAPTER 8 The EU dimension based on other EU rights and obligations

A Relevance of EU rights and obligations for Education for Democratic Citizenship

238 Two widening movements

The question of Part three was: how does EU law impact on the components of EDC to empower citizens living in the EU? What content is relevant for the EU dimension in mainstream EDC in application of the four criteria? To recapitulate: firstly, the EU dimension of the components of EDC was set out based on the classic EU citizenship rights listed in Articles 20–24 TFEU (Chapter six). Secondly, this list was broadened to include the participation rights based on Title II TEU (Chapter seven). Thirdly, in this Chapter eight, also other rights derived from EU law will be considered. In application of EDC standards, *all the democratic rights and responsibilities* enjoyed by citizens must be taken into account (EDC component c-1) and, moreover, the perspective should be opened up to include *all persons*, not only citizens. These two widening movements, to include all rights and all persons, add further substance to the EU dimension of EDC. As recognised, the status of the individual in EU law is ambiguous. Personhood in the EU is not uniform. EU primary law mentions several categories of rights holders, using expressions such as 'nationals of a Member State', 'citizen of the Union', 'nationals of their countries', 'workers', 'any natural or legal person', etc. In secondary law, legal instruments have varying personal scope and the categories of rights holders change over time.[1782] For the purposes of EDC—which starts from the learner's perspective—*all* rights guaranteed by EU law are relevant to the EU dimension: rights linked to the status of EU citizenship, EU rights of citizens, and EU rights

---

1782 See Thym, 'Ambiguities of Personhood, Citizenship, Migration and Fundamental Rights', 121–4 ('citizenship-foreigner-cleavage'; changes over time); Thym, 'Citizens' and 'Foreigners' in EU Law: Migration Law and its Cosmopolitan Outlook'. See also D Thym, 'Frontiers of EU Citizenship: Three Trajectories and Their Methodological Limitations' in D Kochenov (ed), *EU Citizenship and Federalism: The Role of Rights* (Cambridge University Press 2017).

of every person, including third country nationals, with corresponding responsibilities. In short, the EU dimension of EDC relates to all aspects of the individual's life which come within the ambit of EU law.

239 EU citizens as holders of all rights deriving from EU law (EU rights)

The commonly used name for Directive 2004/38, the 'Citizens' Rights Directive', may (wrongly) suggest that the rights of EU citizens are essentially those of the mobile citizen based on Article 21 TFEU.[1783] EU citizenship is much more than this admittedly quite 'thin' citizenship, which is much discussed in legal literature.[1784] In EU law, it is usual to associate EU citizenship with entitlement to the rights set out in Articles 20–24 TFEU. However, EU citizenship cannot be reduced to entitlement to the rights based on the classic citizenship provisions in the TFEU, even when those are broadened to include the rights based on Title II TEU. How far the legal category of citizenship of the Union stretches to engender rights 'attaching to the status' (apart from other legal categories) is a matter of debate,[1785] but for the purposes of EDC, this legal discussion is not so relevant. In the context of EDC standards, the focus shifts from EU citizenship rights (in a narrow sense, i.e. deriving from the status of citizenship of the Union) to 'EU rights', defined as all rights deriving from EU law, irrespective of the legal category on which these rights are based (they could be called citizenship rights in a broad sense).[1786]

The expression 'EU rights' appears in legislation and in various documents adopted by the institutions, yet the terminology used and the categorisation of rights of citizens is at times inconsistent.[1787] In Commission reports under Article 25 TFEU, entitled 'On progress towards effective EU

1783 The full name is Directive 2004/38 'on the right of citizens of the Union and their family members to move and reside freely within the territory of the Member States' (n 1353).

1784 Text to n 1017.

1785 The legal effect of citizenship of the Union beyond Arts 20–25 TFEU is 'a vital question that has not been properly resolved', see Nic Shuibhne, 'The Resilience of EU Market Citizenship', 1616–7. See thesis of Kochenov, *EU Citizenship and Federalism: The Role of Rights* 27 ff; Kochenov, 'Ius tractum of many faces: European citizenship and the difficult relationship between status and rights'. Also text to n 1691.

1786 Further text to n 1793.

1787 Regulation 1381/2013 of the European Parliament and of the Council of 17 December 2013 establishing a Rights, Equality and Citizenship Programme for the period 2014 to 2020 [2013] OJ L354/62, Arts 2 and 4, see also recitals 1, 13, 14, distinguishing *rights deriving from citizenship of the Union* and *rights deriving*

citizenship', the Commission explains developments with regard to equality rights in legislation based on Article 19 TFEU (combating discrimination based on sex, racial or ethnic origin, religion or belief, disability, age or sexual orientation).[1788] In the 2017 report, under the heading of Article 22 TFEU, the development in *Delvigne* is reported as well as action for the efficient conduct of European Parliament elections (even though this does not concern citizenship rights under Articles 20–24 TFEU). The opening up of the perspective beyond the rights of mobile citizens and the narrow list in Articles 20–24 TFEU appears even more pronounced in the accompanying EU citizenship report.[1789] The European Commissioner for Justice, Consumers and Gender Equality, and the European Commissioner for Migration, Home Affairs and Citizenship have set out priorities for further 'strengthening *citizenship rights*'. A wide range of rights are mentioned, whereby the expression 'EU rights' is used, including transparency

---

from Union law, i.a. but not only, for individuals in their capacity as consumers or entrepreneurs in the internal market. See also Decision 1093/2012/EU of the European Parliament and of the Council of 21 November 2012 on the European Year of Citizens (2013) [2012] OJ L325/1; Commission Recommendation of 17 September 2013 on the principles governing SOLVIT [2013] OJ L249/10, I(A): 'SOLVIT aims to deliver fast, effective and informal solutions to problems individuals and businesses encounter when their *EU rights in the internal market* are being denied by public authorities' (emphasis added); Directive (EU) 2015/2302 of the European Parliament and of the Council of 25 November 2015 on package travel and linked travel arrangements, amending Regulation (EC) No 2006/2004 and Directive 2011/83/EU of the European Parliament and of the Council and repealing Council Directive 90/314/EEC [2015] OJ L326/1, Annex I, concerning EU rights applying to package travel contracts. Case C-206/13 *Cruciano Siragusa* ECLI:EU:C:2014:126, para 26 ('fundamental EU rights'; context of the CFR); Joined Cases C-411/10 and C-493/10 *NS* ECLI:EU:C:2011:865, Opinion of AG Trstenjak, para 173; Case C-282/10 *Dominguez* ECLI:EU:C:2012:33, Opinion of AG Trstenjak, para 98 ('fundamental EU rights'); Case C-61/14 *Orizzonte Salute* ECLI:EU:C:2015:655, Opinion of AG Jääskinen, paras 35, 37.

1788 Commission Report under Article 25 TFEU 'Progress towards effective EU Citizenship 2007-2010' COM(2010) 602 final; Commission Report under Article 25 TFEU 'On progress towards effective EU Citizenship 2011-2013' COM(2013) 270 final; Commission Report under Article 25 TFEU 'On progress towards effective EU citizenship 2013-2016' COM(2017) 32 final. Citizenship reports under Art 25 TFEU (regarding the application of Part Two TFEU, Non-discrimination and citizenship of the Union).

1789 Commission Citizenship Report 'Strengthening Citizens' Rights in a Union of Democratic Change EU Citizenship Report 2017' COM(2017) 030 final/2, i.a. 11, 12, 36, 46.

rights, consumer rights, rights of victims and procedural rights in the area of freedom, security and justice. For information on 'EU rights', the Commission refers to the Your Europe web portal, which also relates to many sectors of the daily life of static citizens and encompasses many different rights.[1790] The Commission has published a handbook 'Did you know? 10 *EU rights* at a glance', with the aim of presenting 'in a clear, concise and readable way, the *rights attached to EU citizenship*', designed for use in schools, particularly in citizenship education programmes.[1791] The 10 *EU rights* in the handbook (a small brochure of 23 pages) are entitled: 'European and local elections, making your voice heard, free movement, health, consumer rights, travel, telecoms, cross-border divorces and separations, crime victims' rights and a fair trial, and information and guidance'.[1792]

240 Empowering for the exercise of all EU rights (not only citizenship rights)

Reading EU law in conjunction with EDC standards, I adopt the wider view of rights of EU citizens (first widening movement). To ensure consistency in terminology, they will not be called EU citizenship rights, but EU rights. EU citizens have more points of contact with the EU than just their status as nationals of a Member State. There are other connecting factors than just nationality which bring their situation within the scope of application of EU law and trigger EU rights and responsibilities in addition to those listed in Articles 20–24 TFEU and in Title II TEU.[1793] EU rights

1790 Ibid, 11. See <europa.eu/youreurope> (Travel, Work & Retirement, Vehicles, residence formalities, Education & Youth, Health, Family, Consumers).

1791 Commission EU Citizenship Report 2013: EU citizens: your rights, your future COM(2013) 269, 20. See Did you know? 10 EU rights at a glance (European Commission Publications Office 2014) (some of them are for static citizens, especially buying/selling products, consumer protection). Commission Citizenship Report 'Strengthening Citizens' Rights in a Union of Democratic Change EU Citizenship Report 2017' COM(2017) 030 final/2, 25, 46: 'Action 12', 'promoting EU citizens' awareness of their *EU citizenship rights*, and in particular their electoral rights, by launching on Europe Day in May 2014 a handbook presenting those *EU rights* in clear and simple language' (emphasis added).

1792 The so-called update of the handbook is more oriented towards the internal market: 'Your Europe, your rights: A practical guide for citizens and businesses on their rights and opportunities in the EU's single market (European Commission, 2015).

1793 Shaw, 'The many pasts and futures of citizenship in the European Union', 557: The 'formal legal existence of Union citizenship' includes 'a set of rights within the Treaties located not only in Part Two of the E.C. Treaty (Article 8 et seq. E.C.), but also in the free movement provisions and the institutional sec-

include the EU citizenship rights, rights attaching to the status of EU citizenship.

Pursuant to paragraph 2 of the Charter on EDC/HRE, EDC aims to empower learners 'to exercise and defend their democratic rights and responsibilities in society' (c-1). On a combined reading with Article 20 TFEU, which states that citizens of the Union shall enjoy 'the rights and be subject to the duties provided for in the Treaties', the EU dimension of EDC should empower the citizen to exercise and defend the rights and to take up the duties provided for in the Treaties. That includes not only those rights listed in Articles 20–24 TFEU, but encompasses *all* rights under the TEU, TFEU and CFR. The *ratio legis* of the EDC standards, as set out in Part one, is not to empower citizens in respect of a limited legal category of rights. Nor would such a restricted aim match the compulsory aims of education laid down in international agreements (such as enabling effective participation in a free society). A contextual interpretation of EU citizenship as that term is used in the Treaties and CFR confirms that EU citizenship is more than entitlement to the rights attaching to the status of EU citizenship. Article 1 TEU states that the aim is to create a Union 'in which decisions are taken as openly as possible and as closely as possible to the citizen'.[1794] The CFR 'places the individual at the heart of [the EU's] activities, by establishing the citizenship of the Union and by creating an area of freedom, security and justice' (preamble). These provisions are clearly not only addressed to the mobile citizen or the citizen as a political actor. EDC standards aim to empower citizens to exercise rights and responsibilities irrespective of the legal sources from which they stem. In a society based on the rule of law, seen from the perspective of its citizens, it is irrelevant at which level of governance rights and obligations originate. Citizens must be empowered to exercise and respect them all. The EU citi-

tions of the Treaty, and elsewhere within the Treaty framework including Article F(2) TEU which guarantees fundamental rights protection within the Union'; at 564: Rights can also be drawn from diverse 'hard' and 'soft' law instruments in the various fields of Union policy. Citizenship of the Union can only be fully understood by reference to a broader theory of citizenship and the dynamic, open-ended nature of that process. It leads to 'a recognition of citizenship as an integral part of the Union polity understood as a dynamic governance structure'. Further S Seubert and others (eds), *Moving Beyond Barriers: Prospects for EU Citizenship* (Edward Elgar 2018).

1794 See i.a. Presidency Conclusions of the Birmingham European Council of 16 October 1992, Birmingham Declaration 'A Community close to its citizens', Bull EC 10-1992.

zen lives in a legal space where several public authorities exercise public power together in a multilevel system of governance. He or she is a citizen *of* the Union and a citizen *in* the Union.[1795] Citizens' rights do not originate solely in national law anymore. The various (integrated) levels of governance produce rights and imply responsibilities. It is this interconnected set of rights and responsibilities based on Member State law interlinked with EU law, which must form the basis for EDC content. Acceptable and adaptable education ensures that EU citizens learn about this interconnected set of rights, and thus prepares them to live responsibly and participate effectively in a free society.[1796] The EU dimension of EDC will highlight those rights and responsibilities originating at EU level.

By way of parenthesis, this wider approach of looking at EU rights as citizenship rights in the broad sense helps to surmount an impasse pointed out by some scholars. Viewing the right in Article 21 TFEU as the core right of EU citizenship and the EU citizen as essentially mobile, leads to a cleavage between the mobile and the stayers. Academic writers reflect on ways of resolving this.[1797] I propose to look at EU law as a whole, beyond the provisions of Articles 20–24 TFEU, in order to bridge the cleavage. On a holistic approach, citizens derive far more rights from EU law than those narrowly attached to their status by the 1992 Maastricht Treaty. EU law does not only matter for the mobile, as many examples in the next section will illustrate.[1798]

To conclude, looking through the lens of EDC standards, the EU citizen is the holder of all rights and the bearer of all responsibilities which flow from EU law.

241 Empowering every person (not only EU citizens)

Non-citizens are not asked to leave the classroom when 'citizenship' education starts. EDC standards are intended to apply to every person, not only to citizens in the legal sense of own nationals (second widening movement). The Council of Europe Charter on EDC/HRE stipulates that member states should have the 'aim of providing *every person* within their territory with the opportunity of education for democratic citizenship and human rights education'.[1799] In the Reference Framework of Competences

---

1795 N 1650.

1796 Text to n 1015.

1797 See i.a. GLOBALCIT forum debate: M Ferrera and R Bauböck (eds), *Should EU Citizenship Be Duty-Free?* (EUI Working Paper RSCAS 2017/60, 2017).

1798 Text to nn 1917 ff.

1799 Para 5(a), emphasis added.

for Democratic Culture, the term 'citizens' does not only refer to 'those who hold legal citizenship and the passport of a particular state', but denotes 'all individuals who are affected by democratic decision-making and who can engage with democratic processes and institutions'.[1800] International agreements and other normative instruments consistently grant the right to education to every person.[1801] The rights of the child, to which EDC has been linked,[1802] do not depend on the citizenship or nationality of the child.

In practice, EDC learners are residents of Member States. All learners need to be prepared for the EU dimension in society. Social cohesion in society presupposes education for all, not only for EU citizens, and not only about the rights and responsibilities of EU citizens. The EU legal order also impacts on third country nationals. They derive rights and responsibilities from EU law, e.g. in the area of freedom, security and justice, or with regard to equality, food safety, etc.[1803] Learners—ideally—should understand the whole catalogue of rights and the corresponding

---

1800 Conceptual model in Competences for democratic culture: Living together as equals in culturally diverse democratic societies (CoE 2016), 15. See also Commission/EACEA/Eurydice, Citizenship Education at School in Europe (2017), 19 ('Normally, students are subject to citizenship education regardless of whether they are formal citizens of the country they live in').

1801 Art 26 UDHR; Art 13 ICESCR; Art 28 CRC ('the child', defined in Art 1 as every human being below the age of 18); Art 2 Protocol No 1 ECHR; Art 14 CFR. Further: UNESCO World Declaration on Education For All (Jomtien, Thailand, 1990); World Conference on Human Rights, Vienna Declaration and Programme of Action (25 June 1993) A/CONF.157/23; UNESCO The Dakar Framework for Action (Education for All) - Education for All: Meeting our Collective Commitments, adopted at the World Education Forum (Dakar, 26-28 April 2000); UNESCO World Education Forum 2015, Incheon Declaration - Education 2030: Towards inclusive and equitable quality education and lifelong learning for all. For applications, see K Willems and J Vernimmen, 'The fundamental human right to education for refugees: Some legal remarks' (2017) 17 EERJ 219, 224 (right to education for all, also refugee children). Other example: the German Federal Agency for Civic Education gives guidance by 'providing citizenship education and information on political issues to *all people in Germany*' (emphasis added).

1802 Part one, i.a. CoE Committee of Ministers, Council of Europe Strategy for the Rights of the Child (2016-2021): Children's human rights (3 March 2016) CM(2015)175 final.

1803 E.g. third-country nationals with an employment contract in a Member State have rights and obligations under the directives based on Art 19 TFEU. See i.a. Thym, 'Ambiguities of Personhood, Citizenship, Migration and Fundamental Rights'; Thym, 'Citizens' and 'Foreigners' in EU Law: Migration Law and its

responsibilities flowing from EU law. Inclusive 'citizenship education' means education about rights in all their diversity, of varying personal and material scope, citizenship rights and human rights. Inequalities between EU citizens and third country nationals, and inequalities between EU citizens in crossborder or in wholly internal situations (reverse discrimination) should not be hidden.[1804] Pupils have interesting viewpoints. All learners, EU citizens and non-EU citizens, should be empowered to exercise their rights and responsibilities (c-1), to value diversity (c-2), and to use the existing channels of democratic participation (c-3), preparing for responsible life in European society and striving to uphold the values of Article 2 TEU.[1805] Statistically, the group of learners will largely consist of EU citizens, which is of relevance for the political participation rights in Title II TEU. Only a small minority will be third country nationals.[1806]

Having widened the perspective, this section will explore the relevance of EU rights in general as content for the EU dimension of EDC in mainstream education, on the basis of the four criteria (i-iv). In section B, some examples (stories) will illustrate relevant content as well as the method proposed in Chapter five for EU learning at school. When referring to EDC, the word citizen may sometimes be used in a non-technical sense, applying to every person.[1807]

Cosmopolitan Outlook'. For critical thinking with pupils, see MA Becker, 'Managing diversity in the European Union: inclusive European citizenship and third-country nationals' (2004) 7 Yale Human Rights and Development Law Journal 132 (proposal that third country nationals should also be able to acquire EU citizenship status).

1804 Text to n 1938.

1805 See i.a. reflections of D Thym, 'The Failure of Union citizenship beyond the Single Market' in B De Witte, R Bauböck and J Shaw (eds), *Freedom of movement under attack: Is it worth defending as the core of EU citizenship?* (EUI Working Paper RSCAS 2016/69, 2016) 5.

1806 <ec.europa.eu/eurostat/statistics-explained/index.php/Migration_and_migrant_population_statistics>.

1807 In the same sense: Commission EU Citizenship Report 2013: EU citizens: your rights, your future COM(2013) 269, 2 ('in this report, the term citizens can also refer to any person who resides within the EU in accordance with EU primary and seondary law').

1. Additional content

242 *The EU dimension of EDC based on direct effect and primacy of EU law*

The following citation taken from settled ECJ case law is a crucial argument for incorporating EU rights into the EU dimension of EDC:

> EU law is characterised by the fact that it stems from an independent source of law, the Treaties, by its primacy over the laws of the Member States ... and by the direct effect of a whole series of provisions which are applicable to their nationals and to the Member States themselves.[1808]

The principles of direct effect and primacy of EU law—essential features of the EU legal order—underscore in general how EU law provides binding additional content for national citizenship, satisfying the first relevance criterion for EDC (i). Combined with the principle of effective judicial protection, direct effect and primacy require EU rights to be included in component (c-1) for EDC to be adequate and consistent with EU law. Acceptable and adaptable education should take the EU dimension into account, based on the EU's autonomous legal order. Citizens should know the whole story, not only the national part. In political science, the perception persists that EU citizenship is almost entirely 'isopolitical', i.e. relating to the equal treatment of citizens who move to another Member State.[1809] Yet, EU citizenship gives rise to many more rights, including 'sympolitical' rights, i.e. relating to the binding decisions of a common authority for all members of the participating communities.[1810]

Firstly, many EU law provisions directly grant rights to citizens, independently of Member State law *(direct effect)*. On a superficial reading, the Treaties are addressed to Member States. Many provisions contain obliga-

---

1808 EU Accession to the ECHR *Opinion 2/13* ECLI:EU:C:2014:2454, para 166. Settled case law, i.a. Case 26-62 *Van Gend & Loos* ECLI:EU:C:1963:1; Case 6/64 *Costa v ENEL* ECLI:EU:C:1964:66; *Opinion 1/09* ECLI:EU:C:2011:123, para 65; Case 11-70 *Internationale Handelsgesellschaft* ECLI:EU:C:1970:114, para 3; Case C-399/11 *Melloni* ECLI:EU:C:2013:107, para 59; Case C-573/17 *Popławski II* ECLI:EU:C:2019:530, para 52.

1809 See Kick off contribution of M Ferrera in Ferrera and Bauböck, *Should EU Citizenship Be Duty-Free?*, p 3; cp A rejoinder, p 72; also contribution of P Van Parijs, p 61.

1810 For the distinction between isopolitical and sympolitical rights, see P Magnette, 'How can one be European? Reflections on the Pillars of European Civic Identity' (2007) 13 ELJ 664, 669, 674 (isopolitical rights are horizontal; sympolitical rights are vertical).

tions or prohibitions for Member States.[1811] Yet, it is firmly established in EU law that provisions containing obligations or prohibitions for Member States directly confer rights on citizens when certain conditions are satisfied (if the provisions are clear, precise, and unconditional).[1812]

The fact that EU rights are directly relevant to the EU dimension of EDC is shown by this statement by the ECJ in *Van Gend & Loos* (1963):

> the [European Union] constitutes a new legal order of international law for the benefit of which the States have limited their sovereign rights, albeit within limited fields, and the subjects of which comprise not only Member States but also their nationals. Independently of the legislation of Member States, [EU] law therefore not only imposes obligations on individuals but is also intended to confer upon them rights which become part of their legal heritage.[1813]

From the Treaty prohibition preventing Member States from introducing new custom duties or increasing them (standstill obligation in Article 12 EEC) the ECJ derived rights for citizens (citizens in the broad sense, Van Gend & Loos was an importer).[1814] Article 12 EEC had direct effect and created individual rights which national courts must protect. The impact of the judgment was considerable: 'by heralding the doctrine of direct effect, the *Van Gend en Loos* ruling demonstrated that the EU is a rights-based legal order'.[1815] EU law imposes obligations and creates rights which become part of the legal position of individuals: 'Those rights arise not only where they are expressly granted by the Treaty but also by virtue of obligations which the Treaty imposes in a clearly defined manner both on individuals and on the Member States and the [Union] institutions'.[1816] Since the 1963 judgment, Member States have limited their sovereign

---

1811 I.a. Arts 18, 28, 30, 34–37, 45 TFEU.

1812 On direct effect, direct applicability, and conditions, see Lenaerts and Van Nuffel, *European Union Law* 810–12; B de Witte, 'Direct Effect, Supremacy, and the Nature of the Legal Order' in G De Búrca and P Craig (eds), *The Evolution of EU Law* (Oxford University Press 2011).

1813 Case 26-62 *Van Gend & Loos* ECLI:EU:C:1963:1.

1814 For the customs union, see now Art 28 TFEU.

1815 K Lenaerts, 'Some thoughts on the State of the European Union as a rights-based legal order' [2015] Il Diritto dell'Unione Europea 5, with further considerations on limits to rights, balancing, and the role of the ECJ.

1816 Joined Cases C-6/90 and C-9/90 *Francovich and Bonifaci* ECLI:EU:C:1991:428, para 31.

rights in ever wider fields, and the ECJ continues to uphold the same principle.[1817]

The conferral of rights on individuals through directly effective provisions of EU law adds significant content to EDC. It creates a personal sphere of self-determination free from State interference.[1818] In many areas of EU law, EU rights can be invoked by individuals vis-à-vis public authorities (vertical direct effect) and sometimes vis-à-vis other individuals (horizontal direct effect).[1819] In this way, the EU pervades the daily life of citizens, whether they move or not (iv). In addition to several Treaty provisions recognised by the ECJ as having direct effect,[1820] regulations are directly applicable in all Member States, binding in their entirety, and lead to the setting aside of conflicting national legislation (Article 288 TFEU).[1821] Directives, too, can directly create rights: 'individuals are entitled, as against public bodies, to rely on the provisions of a directive which are unconditional and sufficiently precise'.[1822] When a Member State fails to correctly implement a directive, the *nemo auditur propriam turpitudinem allegans* principle leads to vertical—not horizontal— direct effect. While EU law with direct effect is a direct source of EU rights and obligations, it becomes an indirect source of EU rights and obligations when directives are implemented in national law and national norms are interpreted consistently with EU law.[1823]

Secondly, the *primacy* of EU law over the laws of the Member States indicates even more strongly that EU rights add content to the EDC compo-

1817 See i.a. B de Witte, 'The Continuous Significance of *Van Gend en Loos*' in M Poiares Maduro and L Azoulai (eds), *The Past and Future of EU Law: The Classics of EU Law Revisited on the 50th Anniversary of the Rome Treaty* (Hart 2010) 11.

1818 E.g. the right to move; Lenaerts, 'Some thoughts on the State of the European Union as a rights-based legal order', 7.

1819 Edward and Lane, *Edward and Lane on European Union Law* 296 ff. Example: Case 43/75 *Defrenne II* ECLI:EU:C:1976:56.

1820 de Witte, 'The Continuous Significance of *Van Gend en Loos*', 10: the contribution of *Van Gend en Loos* is that the ECJ decides on the direct effect of specific Treaty provisions. For enumeration of articles granted direct effect, Lenaerts and Van Nuffel, *European Union Law* 811 fn 293.

1821 For direct effect of decisions, see e.g. Case 9/70 *Grad (Leberpfennig)* ECLI:EU:C:1970:7); Lenaerts and Van Nuffel, *European Union Law* 917.

1822 Case 41/74 *van Duyn* ECLI:EU:C:1974:133; Case C 578/08 *Chakroun* ECLI:EU:C:2010:117, paras 41–43, 52; Case C-404/13 *ClientEarth* ECLI:EU:C:2014:2382, paras 54–5. See also case in text to n 2033.

1823 I.a. Case C-282/10 *Dominguez* ECLI:EU:C:2012:33, paras 30–3; see also cases *CHEZ* (n 1945); *Lindqvist* (n 1964); *Folk* (n 2048).

nent (c-1)—rights and responsibilities—independently of national legislation. Primacy is a cornerstone principle of EU law, proclaimed by the ECJ in *Costa v ENEL* and confirmed since then.[1824] Because of its special and original nature, stemming from the Treaties as an independent source of law, EU law cannot be overridden by domestic legal provisions, however framed, without being deprived of its character as EU law: 'The transfer by the States from their domestic legal system to the [Union] legal system of the rights and obligations arising under the Treaty carries with it a permanent limitation of their sovereign rights'.[1825] A later act which is unilaterally adopted and incompatible with the concept of the EU, cannot prevail. The principle of primacy is a corollary of the general principle of equality of Member States (Article 4(2) TEU). In accordance with the principle of primacy, provisions of the Treaties and directly applicable measures adopted by EU institutions automatically render conflicting provisions of national law inapplicable and preclude the adoption of new conflicting national legislation.[1826] The ECJ added in *Popławski II* that 'in order to ensure the effectiveness of *all* provisions of EU law, the primacy principle requires, inter alia, national courts to interpret, to the greatest extent possible, their national law in conformity with EU law and to afford individuals the possibility of obtaining redress where their rights have been impaired by a breach of EU law attributable to a Member State'.[1827] Some constitutions expressly refer to the direct effect and primacy of EU law.[1828]

If indeed, as Lenaerts writes, the EU is a rights-based legal order and 'the very essence of EU law is the principle that the individual rights it creates are directly enforceable before national courts and prevail over conflicting national norms',[1829] the consequence is that acceptable and adaptable education needs an additional EU dimension to EDC to empower the individual to exercise these EU rights (c-1). Understanding EU rights and obliga-

---

1824 Case 6/64 *Costa v ENEL* ECLI:EU:C:1964:66; Case C-399/11 *Melloni* ECLI:EU:C:2013:107, para 59. See Declarations concerning provisions of the Treaties: Declaration 17 concerning primacy (the Conference recalls settled ECJ case law and attaches the Opinion of the Council Legal Service of 22 June 2007). Some EU law provisions have direct effect, all EU law has primacy: de Witte, 'The Continuous Significance of *Van Gend en Loos*'.

1825 Case 6/64 *Costa v ENEL* ECLI:EU:C:1964:66.

1826 Case 106/77 *Simmenthal II* ECLI:EU:C:1978:49, para 17; Case C-573/17 *Popławski II* ECLI:EU:C:2019:530, paras 53, 64–68.

1827 *Popławski II*, para 57 (emphasis added).

1828 Text to n 1150 ff.

1829 Lenaerts, 'Some thoughts on the State of the European Union as a rights-based legal order', 7.

tions is, moreover, relevant to valuing diversity (c-2) and prepares citizens for active participation in democratic life (c-3).[1830]

243 The EU right to effective judicial protection

Because EDC aims to empower individuals to exercise their rights, the right to effective judicial protection is pivotal. Article 19(1) TEU obliges Member States to provide remedies sufficient to ensure effective legal protection in the fields covered by EU law and requires the ECJ to 'ensure that in the interpretation and application of the Treaties the law is observed'.[1831] The Treaties have established a complete system of legal remedies.[1832] The linchpin of the EU as a rights-based legal order is Article 47 CFR, protecting the individual's right to an effective remedy and to a fair trial. The EU standard of effective judicial protection under Article 47 of the CFR is composite, coherent, and autonomous.[1833]

The ECJ has ruled that 'the guardians of [the EU] legal order and the judicial system of the European Union are the Court of Justice and the courts and tribunals of the Member States'.[1834] For the courts to be able to fulfil their role as guardian, citizens must be empowered to bring cases before them. This presupposes that an EU dimension of EDC will provide knowledge about EU rights and a basic understanding of the interlocking system in which national judges assume the role of EU judge. The fact that the Member States ensure judicial protection of an individual's rights

---

1830 Illustrations in section B, stories.

1831 Ibid: 'For every EU right, there must also be a judicial remedy. It is on this constitutional axiom that the entire EU system of judicial protection is based'. See Case C-362/14 *Schrems* ECLI:EU:C:2015:650, para 95: 'The very existence of effective judicial review designed to ensure compliance with provisions of EU law is inherent in the existence of the rule of law'. Also Case C-64/16 *Juízes Portugueses* ECLI:EU:C:2018:117; and n 1863.

1832 Joined Cases C-402/05 P and C-415/05 P *Kadi* ECLI:EU:C:2008:461, para 281; Case C-583/11 P *Inuit Tapiriit Kanatami and Others v Parliament and Council* ECLI:EU:C:2013:625, paras 90–2; Case C-456/13 P *T & L Sugars* ECLI:EU:C:2015:284, para 45.

1833 M Safjan and D Düsterhaus, 'A Union of Effective Judicial Protection: Addressing a Multi-level Challenge through the Lens of Article 47 CFREU' (2014) 33 Yearbook of European Law 3 (composite, as the different levels of EU law adjudication complement each other through the protection they respectively grant; autonomous definition of what exactly constitutes effective legal protection in a shared legal order based on loyal cooperation and mutual trust).

1834 *Opinion 1/09* ECLI:EU:C:2011:123, para 66. See also Case C-64/16 *Juízes Portugueses* ECLI:EU:C:2018:117, paras 32–4.

under EU law is an expression of the principle of sincere cooperation.[1835] How many citizens know that national judges enforce the rights they derive from EU law? Case teaching in particular can illustrate how citizens can take action in court to protect their EU rights. Examples of proactive citizens who win their cases, may motivate others to take an interest in EU norms and monitor the use of public power.

244 Obligations of EU citizens

EDC does not only aim to empower learners to defend their rights, but also to assume their responsibilities in society (c-1).[1836] Which additional responsibilities are linked to EU citizenship? In contrast with statal traditions, EU citizens have no duty to serve an EU army or pay direct EU taxes on their income. EU primary law contains many obligations which are addressed to the institutions and Member States. Article 20(2) TFEU states in general terms that citizens of the Union shall enjoy the rights and be subject to 'the duties provided for in the Treaties'. However, in the list which follows ('inter alia'), no duties appear. Nor does Title II TEU mention the duties of citizens. Some EU citizens have an obligation to vote for the European Parliament, but this is based on national electoral law (e.g. Belgium). Academic writers continue to debate whether the absence of legal duties (obligations) is a weakness of EU citizenship and they formulate proposals for the future.[1837]

In my view, EU citizens already do have duties under EU law. As explained, the perspective must be widened from EU citizenship rights and obligations attaching to citizenship status, to include EU rights and obliga-

---

1835 Case C 432/05 *Unibet* EU:C:2007:163, para 38; Case C-404/13 *ClientEarth* ECLI:EU:C:2014:2382, para 52.

1836 On the importance of including duties in EDC, see n 225; also CoE Reference Framework of Competences for Democratic Culture, Vol 2: Descriptors of competences for democratic culture (2018), key descriptors 37, 39–43, 118, descriptors 701–710, and possible EU dimension to define.

1837 Shaw, 'Citizenship: Contrasting Dynamics at the Interface of Integration and Constitutionalism' (text to fn 11); J Shaw (ed) *Has the European Court of Justice Challenged the Member State Sovereignty in Nationality Law?* (EUI Robert Schuman Centre for Advanced Studies Paper 62, 2011); Weiler, 'In the Face of Crisis: Input Legitimacy, Output Legitimacy and the Political Messianism of European Integration'; D Kochenov, 'EU Citizenship without Duties' (2014) 20 ELJ 482; R Bellamy, 'A Duty-Free Europe? What's Wrong with Kochenov's Account of EU Citizenship Rights' (2015) 21 ELJ 558; Ferrera and Bauböck, *Should EU Citizenship Be Duty-Free?* : see proposals in Kick off contribution of M Ferrera, 'to add stuff to the container' of EU citizenship, and following discussions (food for critical thinking with pupils).

tions deriving from EU law in general. The values of the rule of law and of respect for fundamental rights on which the EU is based (Article 2 TEU and CFR) imply the duty to respect EU law, including EU fundamental rights.[1838] EU law provisions set out a number of obligations for persons within their scope, in addition to the obligations resulting from national citizenship. Citizens are under the obligation to respect EU law vis-à-vis public authorities, and—sometimes—also have duties vis-à-vis other citizens. Such obligations may be based on the horizontal direct effect of EU primary law and of secondary law. Regulations with direct effect contain obligations which individuals must respect, including horizontally.[1839] EU rules on free movement of persons (workers), on freedom to provide services, and on non-discrimination on grounds of nationality (Articles 18, 45 and 56 TFEU) create EU rights for citizens, rights which must be respected by the State (defined broadly) and by non-public organisations laying down collective rules.[1840] When given horizontal direct effect, they imply obligations between individuals. In *Angonese*, the ECJ found that Article 48 EC was designed to ensure the absence of discrimination on the labour market and that the prohibition of discrimination therefore applies to private persons.[1841] However, to deduce generalised EU obligations between individuals from these provisions would be premature. It is still unclear whether the non-discrimination provisions in the Treaties lead to generalised horizontal EU obligations which can be relied upon between private persons.[1842] Some concrete examples of legal EU obligations follow in section B.[1843]

1838 See i.a. text to n 1887.

1839 Lenaerts and Van Nuffel, *European Union Law* 812.

1840 E.g. Case 36/74 *Walrave and Koch* ECLI:EU:C:1974:140, para 21–2 (prohibition of discrimination applying to the rules of a sporting federation); also Case C-415/93 *Bosman* ECLI:EU:C:1995:463, para 84. For trade unions, see Case C-438/05 *Viking* ECLI:EU:C:2007:772, para 61 (a private undertaking can rely on Art 43 EC against a trade union or association of trad unions); also Case C-341/05 *Laval* ECLI:EU:C:2007:809.

1841 Case C-281/98 *Angonese* ECLI:EU:C:2000:296, paras 33–6 (between Mr Angonese and a private bank, now Art 45 TFEU). See in relation to Art 119 EEC, *Defrenne* (n 1940).

1842 Lenaerts and Van Nuffel, *European Union Law* 230; Craig and de Búrca, *EU Law: Text, Cases, and Materials* 799. See i.a. Joined Cases C-569/16 and C-570/16 *Bauer* ECLI:EU:C:2018:871.

1843 See i.a. in section B Stories: obligations corresponding to equality rights, social rights, privacy rights, and consumer rights (i.a. text to n 2043). See also responsibilities above in § 194 (rights of economically inactive EU citizens to social benefits).

Responsibilities may, furthermore, flow from a contextual or teleological interpretation of provisions of EU law. Employers and posted workers, for instance, have responsibilities regarding social rights. In *Altun*, the ECJ allowed a national court to disregard certificates obtained fraudulently in another Member State.[1844] It is the basic civic duty of citizens in the EU not to abuse EU rights. The Commission observes that EU citizens are not always aware that 'benefiting from the rights stemming from EU citizenship also entails some responsibilities', e.g. EU citizens must report the loss and theft of their identity and travel documents promptly to reduce the risks of fraud.[1845] Other illustrations of responsibilities are to be found in the Area of Freedom, Security and Justice (AFSJ). Individuals committing acts punishable under the law of one Member State cannot escape their responsibilities by fleeing to another Member State. They must answer for their deeds in the Member State where they committed the act in question.[1846] In the case of serious crime, or suspicion of serious crime, a European arrest warrant (EAW) may be issued anywhere in the EU: a person can be arrested in one Member State and surrendered to another Member State for the purposes of criminal prosecution or the enforcement of a custodial sentence or detention order there.[1847] Mutual recognition of judicial decisions in civil and criminal matters is a cornerstone of the AFSJ.[1848] Here EU law replaces classic international law (under which States can refuse to surrender their own nationals to another State). Free movement cannot lead to impunity.

1844 Case C-337/07 *Altun* ECLI:EU:C:2018:63. Further Dir 2018 of the EP and the Council amending Dir 96/71/EC concerning the posting of workers in the framework of the provision of services, i.a. recitals 22, 25, 28. See also Directive 2004/38, Art 35 on abuse of rights, or Art 34 on information concerning the rights and obligations of Union citizens on subjects covered by the Dir.

1845 Commission Citizenship Report 'Strengthening Citizens' Rights in a Union of Democratic Change EU Citizenship Report 2017' COM(2017) 030 final/2, 11.

1846 See i.a. Case C-66/08 *Kozłowski* ECLI:EU:C:2008:437 and Opinion of AG Bot.

1847 Council Framework Decision of 13 June 2002 on the European arrest warrant and the surrender procedures between Member States - Statements made by certain Member States on the adoption of the Framework Decision 2002/584/JHA [2002] OJ L190/1 (Art 1: EAW is a judicial decision issued by a Member State). Facts for pupils: persons surrendered under the EAW system include 'a failed London bomber caught in Italy; a German serial killer tracked down in Spain; a suspected drug smuggler from Malta extradited from the UK; a gang of armed robbers sought by Italy whose members were then arrested in six different EU countries'. See <ec.europa.eu/justice/criminal/recognition-decision/european-arrest-warrant/index_en.htm>.

1848 Arts 67, 81(1) and 82(1) TFEU.

Finally, beyond legal duties (obligations), there are social responsibilities which flow from membership of a community, the EU.[1849] Admittedly, EU citizenship is not like 'romantic citizenship', implying allegiance and loyalty, dying for one's country, and military duties,[1850] in contrast to national citizenship and national identity, which evolved in the 19th century.[1851] However, EU citizenship is not only about claiming one's EU rights, either. As academic writers suggest, it should be associated with moral duties too, such as striving for justice, equality and solidarity within the EU.[1852] The EU is not a 'take the money and run' project, an opportunity to extract advantages for one's own Member State and leave problems to other Member States (e.g. immigrant flows at their external borders). Article 2 TEU sets out the ethical foundations of the Union. Using EU primary law as a pillar for the EU dimension of EDC at school should be accompanied by reflection about the responsibilities inherent in those foundational values, for instance through case teaching.[1853]

245 An EU 'dimension', not an 'ad hoc' supplement

The word 'additional' as used in criterion (i) (relevant content should be 'additional content' for national EDC) corresponds to Article 9 TEU which states that EU citizenship is 'additional' to national citizenship and does

---

1849 See i.a. Schuman (n 1890); Peters, 'European democracy after the 2003 Convention', 77 (on European identity: 'it must be admitted that such a collective identity is not in itself a pre-requisite of democratic culture, but consists in the virtues which ostensibly flow from it, namely *responsibility*, solidarity, a willingness to compromise, trust, and tolerance. (...) The formation and growth of these virtues however, require citizens to have minimum ethical and cognitive capacities'). Emphasis added.

1850 See A Sangiovanni in Ferrera and Bauböck, *Should EU Citizenship Be Duty-Free?*, 18 (and exclusion of foreigners, the others).

1851 See authors on construction of nation states, i.a. Anderson, Hobsbawm (n 1034); also Brubaker, *Citizenship and nationhood in France and Germany*.

1852 I.a. A Sangiovanni in Ferrera and Bauböck, *Should EU Citizenship Be Duty-Free?*. Cp Kochenov, 'EU Citizenship without Duties', pleading that EU citizenship is based on rights, with no room for duties. See Bellamy, 'A Duty-Free Europe? What's Wrong with Kochenov's Account of EU Citizenship Rights', arguing that a 'thicker' kind of EU citizenship entails developing civic duties towards the EU; at 565: 'to the degree that the EU has become already and develops in the future as a juridical order distinct from the Member States, then so one can expect the duties of EU citziens to support and control it to grow'. See, e.g., academic writers on equality (n 368), on solidarity (n 1959); also, the issue of citizenship rights of economically inactive citizens.

1853 Cases such as *Dano*, *Chez*, *Omega Spielhallen*, etc.

not replace it. The use of this word should not create the false impression that the EU dimension is additional in the sense of an extra layer added on at the end, like a topping added to a cake. In reality, the EU *dimension* is not *on* the cake but *in* the cake, in the kneading of the dough.

The word 'dimension' must be given its full weight. The complications of Brexit and the undoing of integration in the EU illustrate this only too well. There is no neat separation between EU rights and national rights. Citizens derive rights from national legislation implementing EU directives and these 'national rights' have to be interpreted in the light of EU directives, making them simultaneously 'EU rights', originating at EU level.[1854] National and EU law are intertwined and EDC should reflect this throughout the school curriculum. In order to effectively educate citizens for democracy, the EU dimension should ideally pervade the curriculum across the board, in a wide range of subjects (history, geography, economics, languages, sciences, information and communication technology, media, climate, environment, values, moral education, etc.). The EU dimension can be part of developing the eight key competences for lifelong learning.[1855] Member States are in the EU, but, more significantly, the EU is in the Member States, part of their very fabric. Authentic EU learning cannot be ticked off with an odd chapter added ad hoc to the last pages of a school textbook.[1856]

2. Significant content

246 EU fundamental rights

EU rights and obligations provide significant content for the EU dimension in EDC in different ways, satisfying the second criterion for relevance for mainstream education (ii). The fundamental rights protected by EU

1854 E.g. Case C-149/15 *Wathelet* ECLI:EU:C:2016:840, text to n 2024.

1855 Council Recommendation of 22 May 2018 on key competences for lifelong learning; Commission/EACEA/Eurydice, Developing Key Competences at School in Europe: Challenges and Opportunities for Policy (2012). See also Editorial Comments, 'EU law as a way of life' (2017) 64 CMLRev 357; and on a holistic approach: Opinion of the European Economic and Social Committee on 'Education about the European Union' SOC/612 (21 March 2019), para 1.2.

1856 In history textbooks, the EU often appears as an isolated chapter added after the chapter on WWII; in geography textbooks, a chapter on the EU will figure next to chapters on China or the Middle East (as if they were comparable subjects).

law are paramount examples. Consistency with EU law requires the inclusion of an EU dimension in both EDC and HRE.[1857] The Charter on EDC/HRE describes HRE as 'concerned with the broader spectrum of human rights and fundamental freedoms in every aspect of people's lives'.[1858] In various areas of life, the fundamental rights based on the CFR or on general principles of EU law (Article 6(3) TEU) add an EU dimension to national fundamental rights (i). Within the scope of application of the Treaties, the CFR applies.[1859] The examples in the next section will highlight the significance of fundamental rights, and their relationship with foundational values, objectives and principles (ii), and illustrate that the EU dimension of fundamental rights affects the daily life of many people (iv).[1860] Education about EU fundamental rights will enhance the social legitimacy of the EU. Fundamental rights protection is an essential part of the social contract of the citizens with the EU.[1861]

The significance of the EU dimension of HRE for mainstream education is, furthermore, underscored by a specific feature of the EU: mutual trust.

247 Mutual trust presupposes an EU dimension in mainstream EDC and HRE

Mutual trust is based on the fundamental premiss that Member States share a set of common values on which the EU is founded, as stated in

---

1857 Because of the interconnectedness of EDC and HRE, the term 'EDC' used alone in the study has automatically implied HRE as well. Here, a specific focus is needed on HRE. See text to n 183. See Council Recommendation of 22 May 2018 on key competences for lifelong learning, Annex: A European Reference Framework, 6: Citizenship competence: 'Respect for human rights as a basis for democracy lays the foundations for a responsible and constructive attitude.'.

1858 Para 3.

1859 Art 51(1) CFR. See i.a. Case C-399/11 *Melloni* ECLI:EU:C:2013:107; Case C-617/10 *Åkerberg Fransson* ECLI:EU:C:2013:280. On the the link between citizenship and fundamental rights in the CFR, see already Commission Fourth Report on Citizenship of the Union (1 May 2001—30 April 2004) COM(2004) 695 final, 9; Commission EU Citizenship Report 2010 'Dismantling the obstacles to EU citizens' rights COM(2010) 603 final, 2. See also Commission 2017 Annual Report on the Application of the EU Charter of Fundamental Rights COM(2018) 396 final ('It has never been more important to highlight that respect for the Charter of Fundamental Rights is not an option but an obligation for EU institutions and the Member States when implementing EU law').

1860 E.g. cases on human dignity, equality, privacy (section Stories).

1861 O'Leary, *The Evolving Concept of Community Citizenship: From the Free Movement of Persons to Union Citizenship* 314: protection of the individual is 'the central element of the Community's social contract with Member States and their nationals'.

Article 2 TEU.[1862] The principle of mutual trust, a specific characteristic of the EU, includes the presumption that other Member States comply with EU law and particularly with the fundamental rights recognised by EU law. Member States 'may not check whether that other Member State has actually, in a specific case, observed the fundamental rights guaranteed by the EU' (save in exceptional cases).[1863] This specific feature of EU law has far-reaching implications. Mutual trust should not just be proclaimed, a legal fiction, leaving realities as they are, hoping for the best. For mutual trust to be deserved, a substratum must be built by educating citizens in the Member States according to the same (minimum) standards. If mutual trust is a specific feature of the EU, it should be prepared for and worked at. Mutual trust requires more than informing national civil servants about fundamental rights. It requires EDC and HRE for the entire population, leading to a human rights culture, including in its EU dimension.[1864] To be credible and effective, mutual trust presupposes a minimal level of education of EU citizens about EU fundamental right standards, based on the composite constitutional structure.[1865] Respect for EU (fundamental)

1862 See n 1183.

1863 EU Accession to the ECHR *Opinion 2/13* ECLI:EU:C:2014:2454, paras 191–2. See also Case C-64/16 *Juízes Portugueses* ECLI:EU:C:2018:117, para 30; Case C-216/18 PPU *LM* ECLI:EU:C:2018:586, paras 35–37. Further Joined Cases C-404/15 and C-659/15 PPU *Aranyosi and Căldăraru* ECLI:EU:C:2016:198: When a judicial authority is asked to surrender an individual, it must assess whether the fundamental right guaranteed by Art 4 CFR will be respected, seek information, and not surrender if the conditions for detention of the individual in the issuing Member State expose him to a real risk of inhuman or degrading treatment. In exceptional circumstances, this limits the principles of mutual trust and mutual recognition, EU characteristics which the ECJ put centre stage in Opinion 2/13. See paras 78, 85, 88, 93 ff (evidence of the existence of such deficiencies that is objective, reliable, specific and properly updated; existence of a real risk that the individual concerned will be subject to inhuman and degrading treatment in the issuing Member State). Also Editorial [JS], 'Is Opinion 2/13 Obsolescent?' (2017) 42 ELRev 449; Lenaerts, 'La vie après l'avis: Exploring the principle of mutual (yet not blind) trust'; H van Eijken and TP Marguery, 'The Federal Entrenchment of Citizens in the European Union Member States' Criminal Laws: Or How EU Citizenship Is Shaping Criminal Law' in D Kochenov (ed), *EU Citizenship and Federalism: The Role of Rights* (Cambridge University Press 2017); and text to n 1207.

1864 Some analogy with the argument in Minow, 'What the rule of law should mean in civics education: from the "Following Orders" defence to the classroom' (n 1246).

1865 § 167 and text to n 1155.

rights and the need to strengthen the substratum for mutual trust directly touch the foundations of the EU (ii).

248 Counterargument: the EU mammoth

A frequent objection levelled against the EU dimension of EDC and the alleged significance of its content, is that it is illusory to assume that the individual citizen can influence the EU.[1866] The participation of the individual citizen seems meaningless in a mammoth polity with some 500 million citizens. In popular language: 'Everything is decided at the top by the large Member States and by the Commission bureaucracy. Adding an EU dimension to EDC is wasted energy. It is better for education policies to focus on the nation state.'

Robert Dahl (Yale) underlined the dilemma in these terms:

> Although enlarging the boundaries of a political system may make it more effective in dealing with problems of importance to citizens—defence, environmental issues, and trade, for example—the larger political system will also be more remote from citizens, less accessible, and less participatory.[1867]

In the face of this challenge, every reasonable measure must be taken. One of them is to enlighten citizens through citizenship education, as emphasised by Dahl,[1868] and in the EU this implies the incorporation of an EU dimension in EDC. Responding to the 'mammoth' objection, it should be noted here that—in addition to their input via democratic participation as developed in previous sections—individuals have in the past significantly contributed to shaping the face of the EU through court actions. Casebooks on EU law bear witness to the importance of judicial action taken by the ordinary citizen for the construction of the EU legal order. Preliminary rulings of the ECJ which have started with steps taken by an individual have an impact *erga omnes*: the EU norm as interpreted by the ECJ is

1866 Cf Standard Eurobarometer 89, Public Opinion in the European Union (June 2018) (D72.1): In response to the statement 'My voice counts in the EU', on average 45% of respondents agree (13% agree, 32% tend to agree) and 49% of respondents disagree (e.g. agree in DK 66%, in SE and DE 65%; disagree in EL 73%, EE 70%, CZ 67%). Positive evolution: Eurobarometer Survey 91.5 of the European Parliament, The 2019 post-electoral survey: Have European elections entered a new dimension? (September 2019), 89: 56% of Europeans agree that their voice counts in the EU.

1867 RA Dahl, 'Justifying democracy' (1998) 35 Society 386, 392. See also Aristotle on democracy in the polis: size matters (n 95).

1868 Part one, text to n 565.

binding throughout the EU.[1869] Adding EU rights to national EDC is therefore significant.

249 David and Goliath: the power of the individual defending EU rights

The names of hundreds of individuals have become shortcuts for denoting EU norms clarified in case law, often milestones in EU law and part of EU 'mythology'.[1870] Compliance with EU law is enforced not only by the infringement actions brought by the Commission against Member States (Article 258 TFEU), but also from below through the action of individuals.[1871] As long ago as *Van Gend en Loos* (1963) the ECJ acknowledged that the vigilance of individuals in protecting their rights amounted to effective supervision supplementing supervision by the Commission and the Mem-

---

1869 Craig and de Búrca, *EU Law: Text, Cases, and Materials* 464 ff; Lenaerts, 'Cogito ergo civis europaeus sum: Discours à l'occasion de l'attribution du titre de docteur honoris causa de l'Université de Poitiers' (The cardinal principles of the EU legal order were established in cases referred to the Court of Justice by national courts in proceedings between individual citizens and national authorities).

1870 Some individuals who impacted on the EU legal order: Hans Åkerberg Fransson; Nazifa Alimanovic; Roman Angonese; Ms Baumbast; Horst Otto Bickel and Ulrich Franz; Dany Bidar; Nabiel Peter Bogendorff von Wolffersdorff; Jean-Marc Bosman; Céline Bressol and Nicolas Chaverot; Calfa Donatella; HC Chavez-Vilchez; Mario Costeja González; Flaminio Costa; Nathalie D'Hoop; Elisabeta and Florin Dano; Gabrielle Defrenne; Erich Stauder; Paola Faccini Dori; Gert Folk; Andrea Francovich and Danila Bonifaci; Carlos Garcia Avello; Arthur Gottwald; Françoise Gravier; Anita Groener; Stefan Grunkin and Dorothee Regina Paul; Rudy Grzelczyk; Liselotte Hauer; Nimco Hassan Ibrahim and Maria Texeira; Ms H Jippes; Yassin Abdullah Kadi; Servet Kamberaj; Karl Robert Kranemann; Dieter Kraus; Seda Kücükdeveci; Deborah Lawrie-Blum; Bodil Lindqvist; Werner Mangold; María Martínez Sala; Shirley McCarthy; Ms CPM Meeusen; Stefano Melloni; Aleksei Petruhhin; Thomas Pringle; Alfredo Rendón Marín; Janko Rottman; Malgožata Runevič-Vardyn and Łukasz Paweł Wardyn; Ilonka Sayn Wittgenstein; Volker and Markus Schecke and Hartmut Eifert; Maximillian Schrems; Roland Schumacker; Michael Schwarz; Christopher, Gabriel and Alana Sturgeon; Michel Trojani; Kari Uecker and Vera Jacquet; Yvonne Van Duyn; Yvonne Watts; Gerardo Ruiz Zambrano; Kunqian Catherine Zhu and Man Lavette Chen; and many more. Some of them were truly active EU citizens.

1871 E.g. Shaw, 'Education and the Law in the European Community', 422 (about *Gravier*): 'This is a classic example of the enforcement and promotion of Community law from below so as to foster the interest of integration against the interests of nationalism, acting, in a sense, as the primary law-making power at supra-national level.'.

ber States.[1872] These forms of enforcement prove that EU law is a source of additional content to national EDC, protecting rights different from those in national law (i). In a system based on the rule of law (ii), judicial participation is a crucial form of participation. Empowering EU citizens to exercise their rights and responsibilities is beneficial for citizens, for Member States and for the EU. Various policy areas in EU law rely on private enforcement.[1873]

Several cases have taken the form of a 'David versus Goliath' battle. An air hostess, a student, a father, a business man, and many more vigilant citizens (a farmer, a teacher, a footballer, ...) have proactively defended their EU rights in court (assisted by lawyers, certainly), obtained satisfaction in terms of their personal interests, and achieved large scale beneficial effects for others (in civic republican terms, effects for the common good).[1874]

Individuals have caused EU institutions and Member States to adapt legislation, to recognise judicial interpretations, and to change their practices. When courts are the agents of social change, the process is quite often initiated by citizens. In this way, citizens have an impact on EU and Member State policies, even on the norms in force on other continents.[1875] Defrenne, Schrems, Gutiérrez Naranjo, and Costeja González were—by the way—all static citizens.

It can be concluded that individuals are important actors, key to the EU system.[1876] The EU can only function adequately under the control of the citizen. If individuals are to ensure accountability and respect for EU law

1872 Calliess and Hartmann, *Zur Demokratie in Europa: Unionsbürgerschaft und europäische Öffentlichkeit* 148, citizens mobilised to enforce EU law.

1873 Examples in administrative law, Hofmann, Rowe and Türk, *Administrative law and policy of the European Union* 702–03.

1874 *Defrenne, Schrems, Gutiérrez Naranjo, Costeja González (Google Spain), Schecke, Groener, Bosman,* ... Also Joined Cases C-402/07 and C-432/07 *Sturgeon* ECLI:EU:C:2009:716; Case T-540/15 *De Capitani* ECLI:EU:T:2018:167 (Emilio De Capitani wins against the European Parliament, which was supported by the Commission and the Council; as a result, the institutions have to change their practices and increase access to documents).

1875 E.g. effects of Case C-362/14 *Schrems* ECLI:EU:C:2015:650 (text to n 963); Case C-131/12 *Google Spain* ECLI:EU:C:2014:317 (text to n 1969).

1876 On the role of citizens, see further Shaw, 'The many pasts and futures of citizenship in the European Union', 559; Maas, 'Unrespected, unequal, hollow? Contingent Citizenship and Reversible Rights in the European Union', 274; Thym, 'Ambiguities of Personhood, Citizenship, Migration and Fundamental Rights', 118–9.

by the institutions and public authorities in the Member States via judicial action, they need to be empowered. It is about rights, and at the same time, about much more. EU rights are linked to the DNA of the EU. They reflect the foundational values, objectives and principles. Beyond the atomist defense of their own rights and interests, individuals point out the challenges facing European society, e.g. regarding the values of equality, freedom, or solidarity. In short, in addition to democratic participation mechanisms (as argued above), citizens' action in courts is significant. As Lenaerts observes:

> À mon sens, l'un des principaux ennemis du progrès, que ce soit au niveau régional, national ou européen, réside dans l'apathie citoyenne. Si les citoyens ne sont pas prêts à défendre leurs propres droits, la flamme de la démocratie, de la solidarité et de la justice risque de s'éteindre lentement mais sûrement.[1877]

From that perspective, EU rights can provide significant content to add to national EDC in component (c-1), of relevance for mainstream education. Including an EU dimension engages and empowers citizens, even in the face of 'the mammoth'.

EU rights also add significant content to EDC component (c-2), learning to value diversity.

3. Inviting critical thinking

250 Valuing diversity in the EU

Many EU rights and obligations invite critical thinking in the classroom. Satisfying the third criterion (iii), they provide relevant content for the EU dimension in EDC in mainstream education. Diversity is an appropriate theme for exercising critical agency in the classroom. EDC standards aim

1877 K Lenaerts, 'Au droit citoyen: Discours à l'occasion de l'attribution du titre de docteur honoris causa de l'Université de Namur' (50 ans de la Faculté de Droit de Namur, 13 October 2017) : tr 'In my view, one of the principal enemies of progress—be it at regional, national, or European level—is apathy on the part of citizens. If citizens are not prepared to defend their own rights, the flame of democracy, solidarity and justice is likely to be extinguished slowly but surely.' See also on active citizenship: Lenaerts and Gutiérrez-Fons, 'Epilogue on EU Citizenship: Hopes and Fears' 753, 781.

to empower learners to value diversity (c-2).[1878] Both diversity and unity are EU objectives, reflected in the European motto 'United in diversity'. Because the EU is a Union of 27 Member States, the EU dimension intrinsically includes diversity. Pupils readily engage in discussions, e.g. about national sensitivities or traditions.

Respect for diversity is a foundational principle, expressed in various ways in the Treaties and CFR, and further developed in secondary law. As a result, many EU rights and obligations relate to EDC component (c-2). Article 2 TEU mentions among the values on which the EU is founded 'respect for human rights, including the rights of persons belonging to minorities' and refers to 'a society in which pluralism, non-discrimination, tolerance, justice, solidarity and equality between women and men prevail'. Among the foundational objectives of the EU, Article 3(3) TEU provides that the Union shall combat social exclusion and discrimination, promote social justice and protection, equality between women and men, and solidarity between generations. It 'shall respect its rich cultural and linguistic diversity, and shall ensure that Europe's cultural heritage is safeguarded and enhanced'. One of the foundational principles is respect for the equality of the Member States as well as their national identities, inherent in

1878 Charter on EDC/HRE paras 2, 5(f), and 13, explanatory memorandum para 40. See also Art 13 ICESCR; Art 29 CRC; UNESCO World Education Forum 2015, Incheon Declaration - Education 2030: Towards inclusive and equitable quality education and lifelong learning for all, UN Sustainable Development Goal (SDG) 4. The EU also sets out objectives with regard to valuing diversity in education: see i.a. Joint Report of the Council and the Commission on the implementation of the strategic framework for European cooperation in education and training (ET 2020) — New priorities for European cooperation in education and training [2015] OJ C 417/25; EU Education Ministers and the Commissioner for Education, Culture, Youth and Sport, Paris Declaration on Promoting citizenship and the common values of freedom, tolerance and non-discrimination through education (17 March 2015); Conclusions of the Council and of the Representatives of the Governments of the Member States, meeting within the Council, on Inclusion in Diversity to achieve a High Quality Education For All - Council Conclusions (17 February 2017); Council Recommendation of 22 May 2018 on key competences for lifelong learning, Annex: A European Reference Framework, 6: Citizenship competence. See also academic writers, e.g. Osler and Starkey, 'Citizenship Education and National Identities in France and England: Inclusive or exclusive?'; Banks and others, *Democracy and diversity: principles and concepts for educating citizens in a global age*; Osler and Starkey, 'Education for democratic citizenship: a review of research, policy and practice 1995–2005'; Osler, 'Teacher interpretations of citizenship education: national identity, cosmopolitan ideals, and political realities'; Nussbaum, 'Teaching patriotism: love and critical freedom'.

their fundamental political and constitutional structures (Article 4(2) TEU). In all its activities, the Union must observe the principle of the equality of its citizens (Article 9 TEU). Discrimination on grounds of nationality and based on sex, racial or ethnic origin, religion or belief, disability, age or sexual orientation is prohibited (Articles 18–19 TFEU, Article 21 CFR). Respect for diversity is also mentioned in several areas of Union policy: cultural and linguistic diversity in education policy (Article 165 TFEU), national and regional diversity and promoting cultural diversity in cultural policy (Article 167 TFEU), taking account of the diversity of situations in the various regions of the Union in environment policy (Article 191 TFEU).[1879] The CFR confirms that the EU must respect cultural, religious and linguistic diversity (Article 22). The many 'Freedoms' in Title II CFR lead to respect for diversity through, inter alia, freedom of thought, conscience and religion, freedom of expression, freedom and pluralism of the media, and freedom of assembly and association.

All these expressions of 'valuing diversity' are illustrated in the case law of the ECJ.[1880] Case teaching provides opportunities for highlighting the

1879 See also taking diversity into account in Art 152 (role of social partners) and 207(4)(a) TFEU (common commercial policy).

1880 E.g. Case C-36/02 *Omega Spielhallen* ECLI:EU:C:2004:614 (text to n 1921 ff); Case C-110/05 *Commission v Italy* ECLI:EU:C:2009:66 (safe motocycling in Italy); Case C-208/09 *Sayn-Wittgenstein* ECLI:EU:C:2010:806; and Case C-438/14 *Bogendorff von Wolffersdorff* ECLI:EU:C:2016:401 (surnames, see also text to nn 1347-1349); Case C-81/12 *Accept* ECLI:EU:C:2013:275 and Case C-673/16 *Coman* ECLI:EU:C:2018:385 (same sex marriage); Case C-379/87 *Groener* ECLI:EU:C:1989:599; and Case C-202/11 *Las* ECLI:EU:C:2013:239 (languages). On languages, see Van Bossuyt, 'Is there an effective European legal framework for the protection of minority languages? The European Union and the Council of Europe screened'; van der Jeught, 'Conflicting Language Policies in the European Union and its Member States'. Further Craig and de Búrca, *EU Law: Text, Cases, and Materials*, 760–761; A Levade, 'Citoyenneté de l'Union européenne et identité constitutionnelle' [2011] 1 Law & European affairs 97; G van der Schyff, 'The constitutional relationship between the European Union and its Member States: the role of national identity in article 4(2) TEU' (2012) 37 ELRev 563; E Cloots, *National Identity in EU Law* (Oxford University Press 2015). Debate is possible about the ECI 'Minority SafePack— one million signatures for diversity in Europe', asking the EU 'to improve the protection of persons belonging to national and linguistic minorities and strengthen cultural and linguistic diversity in the Union'. The Commission refused registration. See Case T-646/13 *Bürgerausschuss für die Bürgerinitiative Minority SafePack — one million signatures for diversity in Europe* ECLI:EU:T:2017:59, and Case T-391/17 *Romania v Commission* ECLI:EU:T:2019:672.

core principles and, at the same time, invites critical thinking in the classroom (iii). Valuing diversity in specific situations sometimes makes it necessary to strike a difficult balance between different rights. Should the freedom to conduct a business prevail, or the freedom and pluralism of the media and the freedom of EU citizens to receive information?[1881] Should the right to free movement of goods prevail, or the right to freedom of expression when disagreement takes the form of protests which disrupt the normal functioning of society?[1882] Case law also respects diversity by leaving a margin of discretion to Member States in certain fields or by making assessments on a case-by-case basis.

Consequently, EU law adds significant content (i, ii) to EDC components (c-1) and (c-2), preparing citizens living in a single area without internal frontiers—including static citizens (iv)—to value diversity and to reflect on it (iii). If an essential element of all EDC is 'the promotion of social cohesion and intercultural dialogue and the valuing of diversity and equality' (as paragraph 5(f) of the Charter on EDC/HRE provides), then the EU dimension has a natural place in this. The importance of valuing diversity in citizenship education is also underlined in other normative instruments. The 2006 Recommendation on key competences for lifelong learning includes in its description of civic competence the awareness of diversity and cultural identities in Europe, as well as full respect for equality, as a basis for democracy. Social competence includes intercultural communication, respect, and being prepared to overcome prejudices.[1883] While democracy is based on the opinions of the majority, minorities must also be protected. Here again, EDC is necessarily interlinked with HRE.[1884]

251 Valuing unity in the EU

Upholding the motto 'United in diversity' is quite challenging in an open area without internal frontiers. A multilevel system of governance is characterised by tensions between unity and diversity.[1885] Choices must be

1881 Case C-283/11 *Sky Österreich GmbH v Österreichischer Rundfunk* ECLI:EU:C:2013:28, para 59.

1882 Case C-112/00 *Schmidberger* ECLI:EU:C:2003:333.

1883 Further Council Recommendation of 22 May 2018 on key competences for lifelong learning: diversity is a recurring theme in several competences. Also Commission, Preparing teachers for diversity: the role of initial teacher education, Publications Office of the European Union (2017).

1884 See § 27 .

1885 Maas, 'The Origins, Evolution, and Political Objectives of EU Citizenship', 818.

made on the basis of democratic processes with the input of enlightened citizens. Where society is fractured by the presence of opposing forces, social cohesion is a constant aim.[1886] The Venice Commission states that the rule of law can only flourish when inhabitants 'feel collectively responsible for the implementation of the concept, making it an integral part of their own legal, political and social culture'.[1887] In order to build a supportive legal culture in European society, aiming at the peaceful coexistence of 27 different Member States, 500 million inhabitants, numerous regions, languages, religions, traditions, and—accordingly—different expectations, elementary legal literacy must be included as part of EDC.[1888] There needs to be, at least, an 'agreement that the law must be obeyed, plus a shared understanding of what the law is and how it can be changed'.[1889] An EU dimension should introduce pupils to basic EU rights and obligations.

Schuman stated that reconciling nations in a supranational association would 'safeguard the diversities and aspirations of each nation while coordinating them'. He saw the European spirit as a unifying force: '[t]he European spirit signifies being conscious of belonging to a cultural family and

---

1886 See Council Recommendation of 22 May 2018 on key competences for lifelong learning, Annex: A European Reference Framework, combining unity and diversity in the description of citizenship competence: 'Knowledge of European integration as well as an awareness of diversity and cultural identities in Europe and the world is essential. This includes an understanding of the multi-cultural and socioeconomic dimensions of European societies, and how national cultural identity contributes to the European identity'. See also E-W Böckenförde, *Staat, Verfassung, Demokratie: Studien zur Verfassungstheorie und zum Verfassungsrecht* (Suhrkamp 1991); M Kunkler and T Stein (eds), *Ernst-Wolfgang Böckenförde. Constitutional and political theory: selected writings* (Oxford University Press 2017), on the need for a unifying ethos, a sense of community; the state plays a major regulatory role in creating relative homogeneity.

1887 CoE European Commission for Democracy through Law (Venice Commission), Rule of law checklist (11-12 March 2016), paras 42–3.

1888 Civic competences include legal literacy (see also public consultations before the adoption of the 2018 Recommendation on key competences for lifelong learning, i.a. p 63). Further Oberreuter, 'Rechtserziehung'; Reinhardt, *Teaching Civics: A Manual for Secondary Education Teachers* i.a. 46.

1889 CoE Report of the Group of Eminent Persons of the Council of Europe, *Living together: combining diversity and freedom in 21st century Europe*, 33, para 1. See for reflection also Bauböck, 'Still United in Diversity? The State of the Union Address'; and *Lautsi and Others v Italy* no 30814/06 (ECtHR 18 March 2011), paras 68–69: Europe is characterised by great diversity, but invoking a tradition cannot relieve States of their obligation to respect the ECHR.

to have a willingness to serve that community in the spirit of total mutuality, without any hidden motives of hegemony or the selfish exploitation of others'.[1890] The EU dimension of EDC, while valuing diversity, seeks to educate citizens in the core values of the EU formulated in the Treaties and CFR. The EU is a Union of transnational values, where the common value basis leads to homogeneity. Article 2 TEU sets out a constitutional core, a 'Verfassungskern' for the EU.[1891] Common values have a legitimising effect.[1892] In the EU, Rawls' overlapping consensus is expressed in the values of Article 2 TEU. However, the third caveat with regard to citizenship education (Part one) should not be forgotten: to what extent can citizenship education educate for the common good without becoming a despotism over the mind?[1893] The aim in including an EU dimension in EDC is not to define and delineate the core values of the EU (who can?) but to increase pupils' awareness of them and encourage reflection.[1894]

In addition to the 'constitutional' consensus on the core values in EU primary law and the legislative consensus in secondary law, judicial interpretation strikes a balance between values in concrete cases. The balance sought also concerns 'European commonality' versus 'national particularism', the twin objectives of European unity and diversity. Moderate 'constitutional pluralism' implies that the ECJ ensures uniformity with regard to the 'core nucleus of key shared values vital to the Union's integrity',[1895] but that beyond this core, the Court exercises a degree of judicial deference with regard to national constitutional traditions and their cultural, histori-

---

1890 Strasbourg, 16 May 1949: 'The 19th century saw feudal ideas being opposed and, with the rise of a national spirit, nationalities asserting themselves. Our century, that has witnessed the catastrophes resulting in the unending clash of nationalities and nationalisms, must attempt and succeed in reconciling nations in a supranational association. This would safeguard the diversities and aspirations of each nation while coordinating them in the same manner as the regions are coordinated within the unity of the nation.'.

1891 Calliess, 'EU-Vertrag (Lissabon) Art 2', Rn 7, 10–11. It can be connected to the search for the essence of fundamental rights in ECJ case law.

1892 Calliess, 'Europe as Transnational Law: The Transnationalization of Values by European Law', 1368, 1371.

1893 §73 n 590.

1894 Commission Citizenship Report 'Strengthening Citizens' Rights in a Union of Democratic Change EU Citizenship Report 2017' COM(2017) 030 final/2, 12: 'Union citizenship also means benefiting from equal treatment and sharing in a system of common values which the Union upholds, including respect for human dignity, equality and human rights, and inclusion, tolerance and respect for diversity'.

1895 Lenaerts and Gutiérrez-Fons, 'The Role of General Principles of EU Law', 197.

cal and social heritage.[1896] The *Omega Spielhallen* case (a story for case teaching in the next section) will illustrate this respect for diversity.[1897] In several areas, significant moral, religious and cultural differences between the Member States are accepted. Another example of diversity is gambling. In the absence of harmonisation, each Member State can determine what is required to protect the interests at stake in accordance with its own scale of values.[1898] Yet, national diversity must be compatible with the foundational values and principles of the Treaties and the CFR, upheld by the ECJ. The ECJ did not accept the German diversity regarding (so it was argued) 'consumer protection' and 'health' in the *Cassis de Dijon* case. The German rule fixing a minimum alcohol content in alcoholic beverages (higher than the alcohol percentage required in France and thereby excluding imports of Cassis de Dijon) was incompatible with the Treaty provisions on free movement of goods, a fundamental freedom in the internal market.[1899]

In the balancing of values, it is the legislator who has the last word, not the courts. The European Parliament and the Council decide where the balance between unity and diversity is to be struck, on the basis of democratic processes.

> Striking the right balance between European unity and national diversity has largely been achieved through the judicial protection of the individual rights contained in EU law, but is ultimately a task for the political process, with the representative democracy as a touchstone.[1900]

1896 Lenaerts, 'Some thoughts on the State of the European Union as a rights-based legal order', 23. See also Lenaerts, 'EU Values and Constitutional Pluralism: The EU System of Fundamental Rights Protection'.

1897 See text to n 1921. On legal effects of values and how to resolve conflicts, see Calliess, 'Europe as Transnational Law: The Transnationalization of Values by European Law', 1379 (value conflicts may turn into competence conflicts).

1898 Case C-42/07 *Liga Portuguesa de Futebol Profissional* ECLI:EU:C:2009:519, para 57.

1899 Case 120/78 *Rewe-Zentral (Cassis de Dijon)* ECLI:EU:C:1979:42.

1900 Lenaerts, 'Some thoughts on the State of the European Union as a rights-based legal order', at 6 (the three EDC elements can, by the way, be recognised in the three parts of this article: rights, valuing diversity, participation). Norms clarified in ECJ case law have been incorporated in several legislative instruments, e.g. Dir 2004/18, see also text to n 1977. Further reflection: de Witte, 'Democratic Adjudication in Europe: How Can the European Court of Justice Be Responsive to the Citizens?'.

In order to participate in these democratic processes, EU citizens need to be enlightened about EU rights and responsibilities, EU values and objectives, and the challenges in achieving them. The EU dimension in EDC components (c-1), (c-2) and (c-3) is interlinked. When fundamental choices about rights and responsibilities (c-1) and diversity (c-2) have to be made, citizens must be involved through democratic participation (c-3). In short, the ultimate balancing of values in the EU must be the result of a democratic process, which presupposes the involvement of enlightened citizens, which—in turn—presupposes the incorporation of an EU dimension in EDC.

4. Affecting the large majority of citizens

252 EU rights and obligations in many EU policy fields

EU law generates rights and obligations in various policy areas. The examples are practically endless. Many of them are relevant for static citizens, and thus satisfy the fourth relevance criterion for content for the EU dimension of EDC in mainstream education (iv).

EU rights and obligations include all rights and obligations deriving from EU law irrespective of the legal category. They may be based on status as a citizen of the Union, but also on a person's capacity as a buyer or seller of goods in the internal market, a provider or receiver of services, a worker, a tourist, a pensioner, a third country national, a refugee, etc. They may be EU fundamental rights, potentially affecting all individuals. Ideally, the EU dimension of EDC will empower individuals to exercise all their rights and responsibilities flowing from EU law, whenever their situation comes within the personal and substantive scope of EU law.

The Charter on EDC/HRE describes EDC as focusing 'primarily on democratic rights and responsibilities and active participation, in relation to the civic, political, social, economic, legal and cultural spheres of society'.[1901] The EU has an impact in all these spheres of society because of the competences which the Member States conferred on it in the Treaties (exclusive, shared or supporting, Articles 3–6 TFEU). The EU's policies and internal actions are set out in the 25 Titles of the TFEU. The enumeration of these policy fields in EU primary law in itself proves that the EU is not just a market but exercises public power in many fields affecting many EU

1901 Para 3.

citizens. The 25 Titles include the internal market; free movement of goods; agriculture and fisheries; free movement of persons, services and capital; the area of freedom, security and justice; transport; competition; taxation and harmonisation; economic and monetary policy; employment; social policy; education, vocational training, youth and sport; culture; public health; consumer protection; trans-European networks; industry; economic, social and territorial cohesion; research and technological development; environment; energy; tourism; civil protection; and administrative cooperation.

253 EU crossborder rights

Crossing borders (even briefly) as a citizen or as an actor in the internal market triggers a range of EU rights (Articles 20, 21, 45, 49, 56 TFEU). Freedom of establishment, for instance, includes the right to take up and pursue activities as a self-employed person and to set up and manage an undertaking.[1902] All EU citizens live in the internal market, 'an area without internal frontiers in which the free movement of goods, persons, services and capital is ensured' (Article 26(2) TFEU). Pupils should understand the EU rights related to the internal market and the foundational objectives and principles necessary to make this single area function, such as the principle of mutual recognition or the need for harmonisation, and be aware of the challenges in balancing market and other objectives.[1903]

Linked to the four freedoms of the internal market are the EU policies protecting additional EU rights. Mobile citizens have, for instance, social security rights (e.g. patients' rights to cross-border healthcare); rights to the recognition of educational, academic and professional qualifications; passenger rights (for travel by air, rail, ship, bus, or coach); consumer rights (e.g. package holidays); rights when registering a vehicle or exchanging a driving licence; rights related to the end of roaming charges; etc.[1904]

1902 Art 49 TFEU.

1903 Story for the classroom: Case 120/78 *Rewe-Zentral (Cassis de Dijon)* ECLI:EU:C:1979:42. See also Regulation (EU) 2019/515 of the European Parliament and of the Council of 19 March 2019 on the mutual recognition of goods lawfully marketed in another Member State and repealing Regulation (EC) No 764/2008 [2019] OJ L 91/1.

1904 SOLVIT deals with crossborder problems in various legal areas: Commission Communication 'Compliance Package- Action plan on the Reinforcement of SOLVIT: Bringing the benefits of the Single Market to citizens and businesses' COM(2017) 255 final, p 5, in diminishing order of intervention: social security, free movement of persons and right to reside, recognition of professional qualifications, taxation and customs, vehicles and driving licences, free move-

Even when they do not cross borders, citizens enjoy EU rights.

254 EU rights at home

Static citizens enjoy EU rights relevant for mainstream education. The EU dimension of life at home is often unnoticed. True, EU law on free movement rights does not apply in wholly internal situations: a crossborder element is needed to ensure a nexus with EU law. Yet, the crossborder element does not necessarily have to involve a mobile citizen; it is sufficient if goods or services cross the border. Citizens at home buy products originating in other Member States on a daily basis and often take advantage of crossborder services. Here the 'market citizen' can be linked with the 'genuine EU citizen', in the sense of any national of a Member State.[1905] EU rights related to free movement of goods and services (and capital) have implications for all residents. The setting-up of an area without internal frontiers includes many measures which affect citizens at home, contributing to the EU dimension of life *within* the Member State. EU rights to gender equality or working time rights, for example, affect all citizens. As early as 1995, O'Leary observed:

> The effect of Community Law is thus mostly felt by Member State nationals internally in their own Member State, or when resident in another Member State, via directives and national implementing legislation, and Community law therefore affects the relationship which the individual traditionally enjoys with his or her own Member State of origin or residence and does not generally give rise to a direct relationship between Member State nationals and the Community or Union.[1906]

---

ment for goods, services, workers, access to education. SOLVIT publishes examples of individual cases on its website (text to n 1299). EU rights follow from e.g. Directive 2011/24/EU of the European Parliament and of the Council of 9 March 2011 on the application of patients' rights in cross-border healthcare [2011] OJ L88/45 (Patients' Mobility Directive); or Commission Implementing Regulation (EU) 2016/2286 of 15 December 2016 laying down detailed rules on the application of fair use policy and on the methodology for assessing the sustainability of the abolition of retail roaming surcharges and on the application to be submitted by a roaming provider for the purposes of that assessment [2016] L344/46.

1905 Shaw, 'Citizenship: Contrasting Dynamics at the Interface of Integration and Constitutionalism' 297. See Maduro, i.a. Case C-72/03 *Carbonati Apuani* ECLI:EU:C:2004:506, Opinion of AG Maduro, para 58.

1906 O'Leary, 'The relationship between Community citizenship and the protection of fundamental rights in Community law' 530.

Citizens at home are also affected by EU action in the AFSJ. A foundational objective of the Union is to 'offer its citizens an area of freedom, security and justice without internal frontiers, in which the free movement of persons is ensured in conjunction with appropriate measures with respect to external border controls, asylum, immigration and the prevention and combating of crime' (Article 3(2) TEU). Crime and terrorism are matters of concern to all citizens. Victims, including victims of terrorism, have EU rights (e.g. the right to receive information, the right to interpretation and translation, the right to be heard, to legal aid).[1907]

255 Harmonisation affects the lives of all citizens

Of particular relevance for all EU citizens, including those at home, are EU harmonisation measures. The EU has the competence to harmonise national law, to eliminate disparities between the Member States when they form obstacles to free movement in the internal market, or to achieve certain objectives. In order to guarantee fair competition in the internal market, EU measures aim at creating a level playing field. Measures concerning health, safety, environmental protection, and consumer protection are based on a high level of protection. In addition to the general legal bases for harmonisation (Articles 114 and 352 TFEU), specific legal bases give the EU the competence to formulate its own policies, e.g. in agriculture, transport, economic policy, or social policy.[1908]

Where there has been EU harmonisation, the primacy of EU law requires non-application of conflicting Member State law.[1909] EU rights are, to that extent, not just additional to national rights (i), but even

1907 Directive 2012/29/EU of the European Parliament and of the Council of 25 October 2012 establishing minimum standards on the rights, support and protection of victims of crime, and replacing Council Framework Decision 2001/220/JHA [2012] L315/57 (Victims' Rights Directive). See also Directive 2011/36/EU of the European Parliament and of the Council of 5 April 2011 on preventing and combating trafficking in human beings and protecting its victims, and replacing Council Framework Decision 2002/629/JHA [2011] OJ L101/1 (Anti-Trafficking Directive); Commission Citizenship Report 'Strengthening Citizens' Rights in a Union of Democratic Change EU Citizenship Report 2017' COM(2017) 030 final/2, Action 7 p 43. For reflection, see i.a. E Herlin-Karnell, 'Is the Citizen Driving the EU's Criminal Law Agenda?' in M Dougan, NN Shuibhne and E Spaventa (eds), *Empowerment and Disempowerment of the European Citizen* (Hart 2012).

1908 Arts 40–41, 91, 121, 153 TFEU.

1909 As to levels of harmonisation, see, e.g., text to n 2041; Lenaerts and Van Nuffel, *European Union Law* 296; Craig and de Búrca, *EU Law: Text, Cases, and Materials* 625.

replace national rights, a fortiori of relevance for EDC. Living in one area, all residents feel the effects of EU rules on food safety and market surveillance, product safety, or on standards for passports and travel documents.[1910] It is worthwhile discussing with pupils how far EU uniformity or standardisation (and protection) should go, for instance in the context of the safety of toys.[1911]

From the general overview in section A, the conclusion can be drawn that many EU rights and obligations satisfy the four criteria (i-iv) and provide relevant content for the EU dimension of EDC. These rights and obligations reach into the deeper layers of values, objectives and principles of the EU and widen the perspective beyond law, as the following examples will illustrate.

B Stories for case teaching

256 Islands of knowledge; reflection on values

In the analysis of relevant content for the EU dimension of EDC in mainstream education, it is impossible to comprehensively list all the rights and responsibilities which EU citizens derive from EU law (c-1), to cover all aspects of valuing diversity (c-2), just as it was impossible to comprehensively analyse the various ways EU citizens can participate in democratic life (c-3). However, examples can provide 'islands of knowledge' for the EU dimension and foster values within the 'citizenship competence' as recommended by the 2018 Council Recommendation on key competences

1910 Council Regulation (EC) No 2252/2004 of 13 December 2004 on standards for security features and biometrics in passports and travel documents issued by Member States [2004] OJ L385/1; for continued action in the context of terrorism and security, see Commission Communication 'Action plan to strengthen the European response to travel document fraud' COM(2016) 790 final, 31; Regulation (EU) 2019/1157 of the European Parliament and of the Council of 20 June 2019 on strengthening the security of identity cards of Union citizens and of residence documents issued to Union citizens and their family members exercising their right of free movement [2019] OJ L 188/67.

1911 Directive 2009/48/EC of the European Parliament and of the Council of 18 June 2009 on the safety of toys [2009] OJ L170/1. Applying the New Approach principles (Council Resolution of 7 May 1985 on a new approach to technical harmonisation and standards), it sets out only the essential safety requirements for toys. See also n 1909.

for lifelong learning.[1912] The intention is to trigger pupils' interest in the EU dimension of citizenship. Examples show that the EU dimension can provide useful knowledge enabling citizens to enforce their EU rights. At the same time, beyond the personal benefits, the examples aim to provide some insight into the role and purpose of the EU as a whole. Questions arise as to the significance of EU rights and obligations for the common good. What type of society do pupils (want to) live in? What is the concrete meaning of the values in Article 2 TEU and the CFR? Paradoxically, the concrete reveals the abstract: the study of actual cases may be necessary to disclose the underlying values and principles. A specific story and the parties' viewpoints are a medium for understanding EU rights and lead to reflection about the DNA of the EU, its foundational values, objectives and principles. Pupils can discuss the rationale and added value of EU norms for the individual, for the Member State, and for the EU. Understanding EU rights and obligations and reflection on Treaty values prepares them for effective participation and responsible life in a free society, which are compulsory aims of education.[1913]

ECJ case law is extensive and includes many captivating stories. Some cases have already been described in the previous chapters, e.g. the stories of Françoise Gravier, Nathalie D'Hoop, or Elisabeta Dano.[1914] The following examples have been chosen in the light of the guidelines set out above for case teaching.[1915] Furthermore, they illustrate that—contrary to common perceptions—the citizen whose rights are protected in EU law, is not necessarily a market citizen nor a mobile citizen.[1916] Most citizens in the examples are static.[1917]

1912 Council Recommendation of 22 May 2018 on key competences for lifelong learning, para 2.7, and Annex: A European Reference Framework, 6: Citizenship competence.

1913 Arts13 ICESCR and 29 CRC.

1914 Text to nn 1420, 1426; 1375; 1385.

1915 Text to n 1291 ff.

1916 Cp Kochenov, 'On Tiles and Pillars: EU Citizenship as a Federal Denominator'.

1917 Other interesting cases for stories are Case C-189/01 *Jippes* ECLI:EU:C:2001:420; Case C-388/01 *Commission v Italy* ECLI:EU:C:2003:30 (equal admission rates in museums); Case C-109/04 *Kranemann* ECLI:EU:C:2005:187; Case C-42/07 *Liga Portuguesa de Futebol Profissional* ECLI:EU:C:2009:519; Case C-103/08 *Gottwald* ECLI:EU:C:2009:597; Case C-555/07 *Kücükdeveci* ECLI:EU:C:2010:21; Case C-236/09 *Test-Achats* ECLI:EU:C:2011:100; Case C-673/16 *Coman* ECLI:EU:C:2018:385.

In order to provide the EU dimension in an objective, critical and pluralistic manner, with no aim of indoctrination, the cases will be linked to EU primary law (the first and second pillar of the proposed learning method).[1918] They provide the 'educational substance'[1919], the legal material which educators can turn into stories adapted to the curriculum, interest, and educational level of the pupils.

1. Free movement rights and fundamental rights

257 *Free movement of services balanced against the right to human dignity: Omega Spielhallen*

The story of playing at killing

The right to human dignity is the basis of all fundamental rights: 'Human dignity is inviolable. It must be respected and protected' (Article 1 CFR).[1920] That this universal human right has an interesting EU dimension in its application in the Union, is illustrated in *Omega Spielhallen*, an excellent example for case teaching in secondary schools.[1921] Building respect for human dignity is an essential part of EDC standards.[1922]

Omega is a German company setting up a laserdrome in Bonn (Germany). To practice laser sport, 'guns' are used (gun-type laser targeting

1918 Text to n 1080 ff.

1919 Reinhardt, *Teaching Civics: A Manual for Secondary Education Teachers* 120.

1920 See also Case C-377/98 *The Netherlands v Parliament and Council* ECLI:EU:C:2001:523, para 70 (on 'the fundamental right to human dignity and integrity', general principle of Community law); C Dupré, 'Article 1: Human Dignity' in S Peers and others (eds), *The EU Charter of Fundamental Rights: a Commentary* (Hart 2014); C Dupré, 'Re-Thinking European Constitutionalism: Dignity, Humanism, Democracy' in *The Age of Dignity: Human Rights and Constitutionalism in Europe* (Hart 2015). Human dignity is a central value in international human rights sources (e.g. Art 1 UDHR, Art 10 ICCPR, Art 13 ICESCR, Art 28, 37 CRC, Art 3 ECHR; and in many national constitutions.

1921 Case C-36/02 *Omega Spielhallen* ECLI:EU:C:2004:614.

1922 CoE Recommendation CM/Rec(2010)7 of the Committee of Ministers to member states on the Council of Europe Charter on Education for Democratic Citizenship and Human Rights Education (11 May 2010), para 5(f). See also EU Education Ministers and the Commissioner for Education, Culture, Youth and Sport, Paris Declaration on Promoting citizenship and the common values of freedom, tolerance and non-discrimination through education (17 March 2015), and an increased focus on citizenship education to prevent radicalisation, see § 127 .

devices) to hit sensory tags fixed in the firing corridors or on the jackets of players. Omega obtains this equipment from the British company Pulsar. Even before the opening of the laserdrome, part of the population of Bonn manifest their opposition to the project. The Bonn police authority examines the situation and warns Omega that it will prohibit the game if sensory tags are fixed to the players' jackets, because this would result in 'playing at killing'. Omega does not comply with this condition. The Bonn police authority issues an order prohibiting the game, on pain of DEM 10 000 for each game played by firing a laser beam at human targets. The Bonn police considers this game to be a danger to public order: the simulation of homicide and the trivialisation of violence are contrary to fundamental values prevailing in public opinion. In court, Omega invokes its EU right of freedom to provide services (now Article 56 TFEU), since the laserdrome uses equipment from the British company Pulsar. In reply to a preliminary question from the Federal Administrative Court, the ECJ rules that the order prohibiting Omega from operating the game is indeed a restriction on the freedom to provide services. Such a restriction can be justified for reasons of public policy (Article 62 TFEU). What constitutes public policy cannot be unilaterally determined by each Member State without EU control. It requires 'a genuine and sufficiently serious threat to a fundamental interest of society'. Yet, the ECJ acknowledges that the competent authorities have a margin of discretion. The justification on grounds of public policy is acceptable because according to a prevailing conception (public opinion and national courts) the commercial exploitation of games involving the simulated killing of human beings infringes a fundamental value enshrined in the national constitution, namely human dignity (Article 1 in the German Basic Law). The restriction is not disproportionate simply because one Member State chooses a system of protection different from that of another Member State (in the UK, the game is allowed). The ECJ concludes that EU law allows a Member State to prohibit the commercial exploitation of a game simulating acts of homicide on grounds of public policy because it is contrary to human dignity.

Based on the Reinhardt manual for teaching civics,[1923] questions can be used to guide the case analysis through four steps: the outside perspective (*what is the issue? who is involved? what is the EU dimension of the situation of citizens living in Bonn? which EU rights and fundamental principles are concerned? why is the EU right limited? what are the aims?*), the inside perspective (*what would you do in the role of …? how do the actors feel? do you think the measure is excessive, or is it proportional to the aim?*), a political judgment (*what is the broader significance of this problem? should legislation be adapted? by whom?*), and generalisation (*do the parties represent groups in society? what is the significance of this story for the Member States, for the EU? what do we mean by human dignity?*).[1924] Human dignity is protected differently in Germany (mindful of its role in two World Wars) and in the UK, where the game is not deemed to be contrary to public policy. While the core fundamental right of human dignity is universal, Member States have a margin of discretion to determine its limits in specific applications. A specific EU dimension appears in EDC component (c-1) exercising rights and responsibilities and in component (c-2) valuing diversity (in considering the justification of restrictions in the internal market). This case illustrates the value attributed to diversity in the EU, even in the context of a fundamental Treaty freedom, namely the freedom to provide services (a market freedom). No uniform concept of public policy is imposed on the Member States. The ECJ recognises that justification on grounds of public policy 'may vary from one country to another and from one era to another'.[1925] The economic objectives of the EU are balanced against national constitutional traditions and perceptions among the population.[1926]

1923 Reinhardt, *Teaching Civics: A Manual for Secondary Education Teachers* 122, 130. Compare steps for case study (at 125). Sibylle Reinhardt is Prof em of Social Science Studies Education at the Institute of Political Sciences, Martin-Luther-University, Halle, Germany. Her book is regarded as a seminal text in the German speaking world and translated into English. The steps for case analysis are applicable to all the following illustrations, but I have not systematically worked through them (they may be developed by teachers or in teaching materials for the EU dimension).

1924 See also recurrent reasoning scheme in n 1265.

1925 Para 31; Case 41/74 *van Duyn* ECLI:EU:C:1974:133, para 18. See also gambling (n 1898).

1926 Lenaerts, 'Some thoughts on the State of the European Union as a rights-based legal order'. On disagreements on the level of protection of fundamental rights in Member States, see N de Boer, 'Addressing rights divergences under the Charter: Melloni' (2013) 50 CMLRev 1083.

Cases such as *Omega Spielhallen* help to answer the question raised in Part one: how do we balance liberal and civic republican views on citizenship education?[1927] The essence of human dignity has to be respected. The hard core of this fundamental right is not in question, but critical discussion is allowed at the margins.[1928] Article 52(1) CFR provides guidance in the debate.

Another excellent example for balancing freedoms in the internal market with fundamental rights is the *Schmidberger* case. Balancing free movement of goods against freedom of expression provides food for lively debate in the classroom.[1929]

2. Equality rights and obligations

258 Prohibition of discrimination on any ground

Education to promote equality is an essential element of EDC standards.[1930] The Charter on EDC/HRE states that equality education and EDC overlap and interact.[1931] For people living in the Member States,

1927 Third caveat, § 73 (i.a. on the GEC of Ute Frevert).

1928 See Callan on a sphere of respectable contention (n 1257).

1929 Case C-112/00 *Schmidberger* ECLI:EU:C:2003:333; J Morijn, 'Balancing Fundamental Rights and Common Market Freedoms in Union Law: Schmidberger and Omega in the Light of the European Constitution' (2006) 12 ELJ 15. Other cases related to the internal market could be 'la guerre des fraises', or concern 'the Polish plumber' (i.a. Directive 2006/123 of the European Parliament and of the Council of 12 December 2006 on services in the internal market [2006] OJ L376/36: provisions for the 'exercise of the freedom of establishment for service providers and the free movement of services, while maintaining a high quality of services' (Art 1)). Balancing interests, furthermore, in Case C-438/05 *Viking* ECLI:EU:C:2007:772; Case C-341/05 *Laval* ECLI:EU:C:2007:809. Further: S de Vries, 'Grondrechten binnen de Europese interne markt: een tragikomisch conflict tussen waarden in de "Domus Europaea"' (2016) 64 SEW - Tijdschrift voor Europees en economisch Recht 99 (highlighting the legal foundations of EU construction, legitimacy, and the importance of clear reasoning by the ECJ in balancing interests). Also LW Gormley, 'Keeping EU Citizens out is wrong' (2013) 21 Journal de droit européen 316.

1930 On the essential role of equality in citizenship education, see i.a. EU Education Ministers and the Commissioner for Education, Culture, Youth and Sport, Paris Declaration on Promoting citizenship and the common values of freedom, tolerance and non-discrimination through education (17 March 2015). Also G Liu, 'Education, Equality, and National Citizenship' (2006) 116 The Yale Law Journal 330 (duty of US Congress to ensure educational adequacy for equal citizenship). See also Nussbaum in caveat 3, text to n 579 (one factor in

equality has an important EU dimension, providing relevant content for mainstream education and satisfying the four criteria. 'Equality' is expressed in various ways in the foundational values, objectives and principles of the EU (i.a. Articles 2, 3(3) and 9 TEU, 18–19 TFEU). Article 19 TFEU allows the Council to 'take appropriate action to combat discrimination based on sex, racial or ethnic origin, religion or belief, disability, age or sexual orientation'. The CFR prohibits '[a]ny discrimination based on any ground such as sex, race, colour, ethnic or social origin, genetic features, language, religion or belief, political or any other opinion, membership of a national minority, property, birth, disability, age or sexual orientation' (Article 21) and states that equality between women and men must be ensured in all areas, including employment, work and pay (Article 23). Various instruments in secondary legislation implement the principle of non-discrimination and set out equality rights, justiciable in court.[1932] As

getting 'the good out of patriotic education without the bad', is awareness of the constitutional rights of minorities).

1931 Charter on EDC/HRE, para 1.

1932 I.a. Council Directive 2000/43/EC of 29 June 2000 implementing the principle of equal treatment between persons irrespective of racial or ethnic origin [2000] OJ L180/22 (Racial Equality Directive); Council Directive 2000/78/EC of 27 November 2000 establishing a general framework for equal treatment in employment and occupation [2000] OJ L303/16 (the Employment Equality Directive, prohibiting discrimination in employment and occupation on the grounds of religion or belief, disability, age and sexual orientation); Council Directive 2004/113/EC of 13 December 2004 implementing the principle of equal treatment between men and women in the access to and supply of goods and services [2004] OJ L373/37 (Directive on Gender Equality); Directive 2006/54/EC of the European Parliament and of the Council of 5 July 2006 on the implementation of the principle of equal opportunities and equal treatment of men and women in matters of employment and occupation [2006] OJ L204/23 (legal basis ex Art 141(3) TEC, now Art 157 TFEU, equal pay for equal work); Directive 2010/41/EU of the European Parliament and of the Council of 7 July 2010 on the application of the principle of equal treatment between men and women engaged in an activity in a self-employed capacity and repealing Council Directive 86/613/EEC [2010] OJ L 180/1; Commission Recommendation of 7 March 2014 on strengthening the principle of equal pay between men and women through transparency [2014] OJ L 69/112. See also Commission Joint Report on the application of Council Directive 2000/43/EC of 29 June 2000 implementing the principle of equal treatment between persons irrespective of racial or ethnic origin (Racial Equality Directive) and of Council Directive 2000/78/EC of 27 November 2000 establishing a general framework for equal treatment in employment and occupation (Employment Equality Directive) COM(2014) 2 final. For promotion of equality in programmes and European Year, see i.a. Regulation 1381/2013 of the European

reiterated in settled case law, the general principle of equality requires that similar situations are not treated differently, unless differentiation is objectively justified.[1933] For EU norms on equality to apply, situations must fall within the scope of the Treaties or secondary law. The Commission reports on the transposition of the Racial Equality Directive, the Employment Equality Directive, and the Directive on Gender Equality[1934] by the Member States, but warns that the main challenge is to raise awareness of the rights and protection in practice.[1935] This echoes Condorcet: 'Les lois

---

Parliament and of the Council of 17 December 2013 establishing a Rights, Equality and Citizenship Programme for the period 2014 to 2020 [2013] OJ L354/62 (legal basis Arts 19(2), 21(2), 114, 168, 169 and 197 TFEU): 'an area where equality and the rights of persons as enshrined in the TEU, in the TFEU, in the Charter and in the international human rights conventions to which the Union has acceded, are promoted'; earlier Decision 771/2006/EC of the European Parliament and of the Council of 17 May 2006 establishing the European Year of Equal Opportunities for All (2007)—towards a just society [2006] OJ L146/1 (legal basis ex Art 13(2) TEC, now Art 19 TFEU). Further E Ellis and P Watson, *EU Anti-Discrimination Law* (2 edn, Oxford University Press 2012); Craig and de Búrca, *EU Law: Text, Cases, and Materials*, 892–963; LS Rossi and F Casolari, *The Principle of Equality in EU Law* (Springer International 2017); E Muir, *EU Equality Law: The First Fundamental Rights Policy of the EU* (Oxford Studies in European Law, OUP 2018). Also G Davies, *Nationality discrimination in the European internal market* (European Monographs 44, Kluwer Law International 2003); J Shaw, 'Mainstreaming Equality and Diversity in the European Union' (2005) 58 Current Legal Problems 255; V Guiraudon, 'Equality in the making: implementing European non-discrimination law' (2009) 13 Citizenship Studies 527; L Potvin-Solis, 'La liaison entre le principe de non-discrimination et les libertés et droits fondamentaux des personnes dans les jurisprudences européennes' (2009) 20 Revue trimestrielle des droits de l'homme 967; Kochenov, 'Citizenship without Respect: The EU's Troubled Equality Ideal'.

1933 Joined Cases 117/76 and 16/77 *Ruckdeschel* ECLI:EU:C:1977:160, para 7.

1934 N 1932. See also Commission Proposal for a Council Directive on implementing the principle of equal treatment between persons irrespective of religion or belief, disability, age or sexual orientation COM(2008) 426 final (Horizontal Anti-Discrimination Directive); Commission Citizenship Report 'Strengthening Citizens' Rights in a Union of Democratic Change EU Citizenship Report 2017' COM(2017) 030 final/2, 34: to ensure a level playing field in terms of equality throughout the Union, it is vital to conclude the negotiations on the proposed Horizontal Anti-Discrimination Directive.

1935 Commission Report under Article 25 TFEU 'On progress towards effective EU citizenship 2013-2016' COM(2017) 32 final, 2–3. Websites provide information (see i.a. <ec.europa.eu/info/policies/justice-and-fundamental-rights/combating-discrimination_en>, including on members of the LGBTI community (Lesbian, Gay, Bisexual, Transgender, Intersex).

prononcent l'égalité dans les droits, les institutions pour l'instruction publique peuvent seules rendre cette égalité réelle.'[1936] Case teaching is an appropriate tool for promoting equality, inclusion, and tolerance, which are common values of EU citizens.

Non-discrimination on grounds of *nationality* (mentioned in the context of citizenship rights) has interesting applications when linked with internal market freedoms.[1937] In purely internal situations, outside the scope of the fundamental freedoms, problems of reverse discrimination may arise, which may be suitable material for reflection at advanced levels of EDC.[1938] Pupils will also be able to debate the issue of financial solidarity and the economic cost of upholding the principle of non-discrimination on grounds of nationality.[1939]

Non-discrimination on grounds of *gender* has been an objective of the EU since the very beginning (EEC) to ensure a level playing field in the common market. Many cases illustrate the principle of gender equality, i.a. the landmark case *Defrenne* on equal pay for equal work (the story of the stewardess).[1940] The Council of Europe recommends gender mainstreaming in education. This essential part of EDC standards undeniably has an

---

1936 Condorcet, *Cinq mémoires sur l'instruction publique* , 29, see also 52 (Laws may enshrine the principle of equality, but only the institutions responsible for public instruction can turn it into reality). Condorcet's humanistic ideal saw the transmission of basic knowledge as a unifying force for all citizens, religious or secular, noblemen or workers, in city or rural localities. Above all, Condorcet aimed at progress through reason and enlightenment towards a better mankind. Real equality and real freedom, and effective rights are central objectives of Condorcet's system of citizenship education.

1937 For interesting stories related to the internal market (recognising tourists as recipients of services brings situations within the scope of Art 18 TFEU), see i.a. Case 186/87 *Cowan* ECLI:EU:C:1989:47 (the story of a tourist in Paris); Case C-111/91 *Commission v Luxembourg* ECLI:EU:C:1993:92 (preferential rates for nationals for admission to museums, monuments, galleries, archaeological digs, parks and gardens classified as public monuments, discriminating against non-nationals). For non-discrimination as a citizenship right, see i.a. § 188 .

1938 On reverse discrimination, text to n 1467.

1939 *Grzelczyk* Case C-184/99 ECLI:EU:C:2001:458 (para 44); *Dano* (text to n 1426).

1940 EU primary law provisions on equality may have horizontal direct effect, e.g. Article 157 TFEU (ex Article 119 EC), which requires that male and female workers receive equal pay for equal work or for work of equal value. Case 43/75 *Defrenne II* ECLI:EU:C:1976:56, para 39. Also Case 149/77 *Defrenne III* ECLI:EU:C:1978:130; S Prechal, 'Defrenne: de Europese gelijkebeloningsaga met verstrekkende gevolgen' in Schutgens and others (eds), *Canon van het recht* (Ars Aequi Libri 2010); Lenaerts and Van Nuffel, *European Union Law* 811.

important EU dimension.[1941] The EU dimension of the principle of gender equality adds content to national citizenship (Ms Defrenne's case is evidence of this), is significant, invites critical thinking, and affects all citizens (i-iv). The huge impact of the principle of gender equality on society and daily life of EU citizens demonstrates that EU citizenship encompasses far more than the list of classic citizenship rights suggests. This broader view on the scope of EU citizenship implies taking account of all rights enjoyed by virtue of EU law by both static and mobile citizens.

Furthermore, EU law establishes the right to non-discrimination on grounds of *age, religion, sexual orientation, and disability*.[1942] These are topics which readily engage pupils' interest and cause them to reflect on the EU dimension. Different angles of the same case can be discussed, e.g. on the question whether the employer can prohibit employees from wearing any visible signs of their political, philosophical or religious beliefs in the workplace. In *Egenberger* and *Cresco*, the Court of Justice confirmed: 'The prohibition of all discrimination on grounds of religion or belief is mandatory as a general principle of EU law. That prohibition, which is laid down in Article 21(1) of the Charter, is sufficient in itself to confer on individuals a right which they may rely on as such in disputes between them in a field covered by EU law'.[1943]

There are many stories which are suitable for case teaching on equality and a number were mentioned in Chapter six.[1944] The following case illustrates the prohibition of discrimination on grounds of *ethnic origin*.

1941 Gender equality in EDC standards, see CoE Recommendation CM/Rec(2010)7 of the Committee of Ministers to member states on the Council of Europe Charter on Education for Democratic Citizenship and Human Rights Education (11 May 2010), para 5(f); CoE Recommendation Rec(2002)12 of the Committee of Ministers to member states on education for democratic citizenship (16 October 2002), para 2. See also CoE Recommendation CM/Rec(2007)13 of the Committee of Ministers to member states on gender mainstreaming in education (10 October 2007).

1942 Art 19 TFEU.

1943 Case C-193/17 *Cresco* ECLI:EU:C:2019:43, para 76; Case C-414/16 *Egenberger* ECLI:EU:C:2018:257, para 76.

1944 Above in §§ 190 to 194 (non-discrimination on the basis of *nationality*). Examples of non-discrimination on the basis of *gender*: Case C-236/09 *Test-Achats* ECLI:EU:C:2011:100. For age: Case C-555/07 *Kücükdeveci* ECLI:EU:C:2010:21, paras 50–6 (EU law precludes national legislation which provides that periods of employment completed by an employee before reaching the age of 25 are not taken into account in calculating the notice period for dismissal; the national court, hearing proceedings between individuals, must ensure compliance with the principle of non-discrimination on grounds of age, as given

259 The right to equal treatment irrespective of racial or ethnic origin: CHEZ

The story of Roma and the electricity meters on pylons

The *CHEZ* case illustrates (once more) the EU dimension of the daily life of citizens at home in their own Member State, in this case Bulgaria. EU norms on non-discrimination can apply in internal situations in the Member States (only involving nationals and lacking crossborder elements), yet falling within the scope of EU legislation.[1945] The case concerns the Racial Equality Directive, which implements the principle of equal treatment between persons irrespective of racial or ethnic origin.[1946]

> Ms Nikolova runs a grocer's shop in a Bulgarian town. Most inhabitants of the particular town district are of Roma origin. She complains that she cannot check the correctness of her electricity bills because CHEZ, the electricity distributor, has installed the electricity meters on pylons at a height of six or seven meters to avoid fraudulent tampering by Roma. In other districts, the meters are placed at a height of less than 2 meters. The Bulgarian Commission for Protection against Discrimination orders CHEZ to end this discriminatory practice. The Administrative Court of Sofia refers preliminary questions to the ECJ concerning the Racial Equality Directive. CHEZ argues that the EU has not laid down any rule about the height of electricity meters. The ECJ recalls that the Directive is an expression of the general principle of equality in EU law and that its scope cannot therefore be defined restrictively. The Directive forbids direct and indirect discrimination

---

expression in Dir 2000/78, if necessary by disapplying any contrary provision of national legislation; the ECJ grants horizontal direct effect to this general principle of EU law (see also Art 21 CFR)). Further Lenaerts and Van Nuffel, *European Union Law* 811. See also Case C-144/04 *Mangold* ECLI:EU:C:2005:709 ('general principle of European Union law prohibiting all discrimination on grounds of age, as given expression in Directive 2000/78'). For non-discrimination on the basis of *religion*, see Cases C-157/15 and C-188/15 188 *Achbita and Bougnaoui* ECLI:EU:C:2017:203 (related to Dir 2000/78); on the basis of *sexual orientation*, Case C-81/12 *Accept* ECLI:EU:C:2013:275 (a patron of a football club excludes hiring a homosexual); Case C-673/16 *Coman* ECLI:EU:C:2018:385; on the basis of *disability*, Case C-354/13 *FOA (Kaltoft)* ECLI:EU:C:2014:2463 (dismissal on grounds of obesity; static citizen in Denmark); non-discrimination of a *transgender*, Case C-451/16 *MB* ECLI:EU:C:2018:492.

1945 Case C-83/14 *CHEZ (Nikolova)* ECLI:EU:C:2015:480.

1946 Council Directive 2000/43/EC of 29 June 2000 implementing the principle of equal treatment between persons irrespective of racial or ethnic origin [2000] OJ L180/22 (Racial Equality Directive) (legal basis ex Art 13 TEC, now Art 19 TFEU) (n 1932). See also Case C-54/07 *Feryn* ECLI:EU:C:2008:397.

based on racial or ethnic origin, i.a. in relation to 'access to and supply of goods and services which are available to the public'. As this covers the supply of electricity, the situation falls within the scope of the Directive.[1947] The ECJ holds that the concept of 'discrimination on grounds of ethnic origin' applies in the circumstances of the case: while Ms Nikolova is not of Roma origin herself, the fact remains that it is the Roma origin of most of the other inhabitants of the district which has given rise to her complaint. The Court indicates elements which the Bulgarian Court must consider when assessing the existence of discrimination, direct or indirect, based on the Directive. The practice of installing high meters in the district is compulsory, widespread and lasting, irrespective of whether individual meters have been tampered with or have given rise to unlawful connections, and is still applied 25 years after it was first introduced. This practice is of an offensive and stigmatising nature, suggesting that the inhabitants of the district are considered as a whole to be potential perpetrators of unlawful conduct. The practice constitutes direct discrimination if such less favourable treatment in comparable situations is related to the ethnic origin common to most of the inhabitants of the district. If the practice is indirect discrimination (an apparently neutral practice putting persons of an ethnic origin at a particular disadvantage), it may be objectively justified by a legitimate aim.[1948] CHEZ contends that the practice was necessary to prevent fraud and abuse, because in that district, electricity meters had been frequently damaged, tampered with, and unlawfully connected. The ECJ accepts that these aims are legitimate, yet the risks must be proven and cannot be based on 'common knowledge'. The Administrative Court in Sofia must assess whether the practice is appropriate, necessary to achieve the legitimate aims, and is not disproportionate. Other electricity distribution companies have restored all meters to a normal height and used other techniques to achieve the same aims.

A case such as *CHEZ* is a colourful story for teaching the EU dimension of EDC. It provides additional content (i) to EDC component (c-1) exercising rights and responsibilities (national law is to be interpreted in the light of

1947 Para 42; Racial Equality Dir Art 3(1)(h); applicable (i.a.) in relation to conditions for access to employment, social protection, education, or the supply of public goods and services in the Member State. See also Case C-391/09 *Runevič-Vardyn and Wardyn* ECLI:EU:C:2011:291.

1948 Paras 84, 86, 87, 91; Racial Equality Dir Art 2 (a) and (b).

directives) as well as (c-2) valuing diversity. The content is significant (ii), because it relates to foundational values, objectives and principles of the EU Treaties and CFR. The case shows how EU objectives and legislation seeking to realise these objectives have effects for the large majority of citizens, including static citizens (iv). In a climate of increased intolerance and racism,[1949] the case invites critical thinking (iii), with application of the principle of proportionality.[1950] The four criteria for relevance for mainstream education are satisfied.

3. Social rights and obligations

260 *Rights regarding working time: Günther Fuss*

The story of the fireman

EU competences in the field of social policy are defined in Title X TFEU.[1951] EU legislation creates social rights in the working place. The Working Time Directive lays down minimum safety and health requirements for the organisation of working time. The content affects the large majority of citizens (iv), as the Directive is applicable to all sectors of activity, public and private. The Directive determines EU rights regarding daily rest, breaks, weekly rest periods, maximum weekly working time, annual leave, night work, etc., which must be guaranteed by the Member States through the transposition of the Directive in national law. Every worker is entitled to a minimum daily rest period of 11 consecutive hours per 24-hour period. Where the working day is longer than six hours, every worker is entitled to a rest break. Per seven-day period, every worker is entitled to a minimum uninterrupted rest period of 24 hours plus the 11 hours' daily rest. The average working time for each seven-day period, including over-

---

1949 Communication Report on the Application of the EU Charter of Fundamental Rights COM(2017) 239 final, 6; see action concerning Roma at 7. See Special Eurobarometer 493, 'Discrimination in the EU (including LGBTI)' (October 2019).

1950 Further Council Recommendation of 9 December 2013 on effective Roma integration measures in the Member States [2013] OJ C378/1. On action concerning Roma, see Commission Report under Article 25 TFEU 'On progress towards effective EU citizenship 2013-2016' COM(2017) 32 final, 3.

1951 See Arts 151–161 TFEU.

time, cannot not exceed 48 hours. Every worker is entitled to paid annual leave of at least four weeks.[1952]

> Mr Günther Fuss is a fire fighter employed by the City of Halle (Germany). As a Station Fire Officer in an operational service, he has to work more than 48 hours per week. He requests the City of Halle to ensure that his weekly working time no longer exceeds the maximum average limit of 48 hours laid down in the Working Time Directive. As a result, the City of Halle (his employer) transfers him to a non-operational service, where the working time limit is respected. Mr Fuss contests this compulsory transfer: he prefers to continue to work in the operational service, yet subject to the working time limit. The ECJ interprets the Directive and holds that the Directive precludes such a compulsory transfer.[1953]

Mr Fuss' EU rights were additional to those enjoyed under German law.[1954]

Why can the EU lay down rules about working time? The interests of the various parties and diverging viewpoints should be considered.[1955]

Social rights and solidarity (an Article 2 TEU value) are fertile subjects for discussions about the EU dimension of citizenship. The rights listed in the European Pillar of Social Rights[1956] are the subject of a shared commitment by the EU, the Member States and the social partners, to be imple-

---

1952 Directive 2003/88/EC of the European Parliament and of the Council of 4 November 2003 concerning certain aspects of the organisation of working time [2003] OJ L299/9, Arts 3–7.

1953 Case C-243/09 *Fuß* ECLI:EU:C:2010:609.

1954 See also Commission Report on the implementation by Member States of Directive 2003/88/EC concerning certain aspects of the organisation of working time COM(2017) 254 final.

1955 Another suitable case for discussion, illustrating the great relevance of EU law to static citizens is *CCOO v Deutsche Bank Case* C-55/18 ECLI:EU:C:2019:402 (on employers' obligation to set up a system to measure the duration of time worked each day by each worker). Also Joined Cases C-569/16 and C-570/16 *Bauer* ECLI:EU:C:2018:871 (on the right to paid annual leave and horizontal effects).

1956 Commission Recommendation (EU) 2017/761 of 26 April 2017 on the European Pillar of Social Rights [2017] OJ L113/56, i.a. paras 2, 3, 6, 7, 16, 20: Everyone has the right to equal treatment and opportunities—regardless of gender, racial or ethnic origin, religion or belief, disability, age or sexual orientation—regarding employment, social protection, education, and access to goods and services available to the public. Other social rights and principles concern access to the labour market, fair working conditions, and social pro-

mented within their respective spheres of competence. Some of the rights are already part of the Union *acquis*, but much still remains to be done.[1957] They provide material for reflection, e.g. through cases such as *Viking, Laval,* or *Altun,* which highlight rights as well as obligations.[1958] Citizenship cases discussed in Chapter six, such as *Dano*, *Gravier* or *Bressol*, also fit into this context.[1959]

---

tection and inclusion, e.g. workers have the right to fair wages that provide for a decent standard of living and the right to be informed in writing at the start of employment about their rights and obligations, including during a probationary period; everyone has the right to timely access to affordable, preventive and curative health care of good quality; and a right of access to essential services of good quality, including water, sanitation, energy, transport, financial services and digital communications.

1957 See i.a. Directive (EU) 2019/1152 of the European Parliament and of the Council of 20 June 2019 on transparent and predictable working conditions in the European Union [2019] OJ L 186/105; and Directive (EU) 2019/1158 of the European Parliament and of the Council of 20 June 2019 on work-life balance for parents and carers and repealing Council Directive 2010/18/EU [2019] OJ L 188/79.

1958 Case C-438/05 *Viking* ECLI:EU:C:2007:772; Case C-341/05 *Laval* ECLI:EU:C:2007:809; Case C-337/07 *Altun* ECLI:EU:C:2018:63. See in EU law i.a. Arts 151, 152, 157, 168 TFEU; and case law relating to Council Directive 2001/23/EC of 12 March 2001 on the approximation of the laws of the Member States relating to the safeguarding of employees' rights in the event of transfers of undertakings, businesses or parts of undertakings or businesses [2001] OJ L82/16 ; Directive 2003/88/EC of the European Parliament and of the Council of 4 November 2003 concerning certain aspects of the organisation of working time [2003] OJ L299/9; Council Directive 2010/18/EU of 8 March 2010 implementing the revised Framework Agreement on parental leave concluded by BUSINESSEUROPE, UEAPME, CEEP and ETUC and repealing Directive 96/34/EC [2010] OJ L68/13.

1959 Text to nn 1420, 1426; 1375; 1385. For further reflection on solidarity and social policy, see i.a. Art 222 TFEU (solidarity clause in case of terrorist attack or disasters); example of concrete action: Regulation (EU) 2018/1475 of the European Parliament and of the Council of 2 October 2018 laying down the legal framework of the European Solidarity Corps and amending Regulation (EU) No 1288/2013, Regulation (EU) No 1293/2013 and Decision No 1313/2013/EU [2018] OJ L 250/1. Further C Barnard, 'EU "Social" Policy: from Employment Law to Labour Market Reform' in P Craig and G de Búrca (eds), *The evolution of EU law* (Oxford University Press 2011); M Ross, 'The Struggle for EU Citizenship: Why Solidarity Matters' in A Arnull and others (eds), *A Constitutional Order of States: Essays in EU Law in Honour of Alan Dashwood* (Hart 2011); I Domurath, 'The Three Dimensions of Solidarity in the EU Legal Order: Limits of the Judicial and Legal Approach' (2012) 35 Journal of European Integration 459; Lenaerts, 'EU Citizenship and the Social Solidarity

4. Privacy rights and obligations

261 EU fundamental rights to privacy

The EU fundamental rights to privacy are entrenched in EU primary law: 'Everyone has the right to respect for his or her private and family life, home and communications' (Article 7 CFR) and 'Everyone has the right to the protection of personal data concerning him or her' (Articles 8(1) CFR, 16 TFEU). These rights are not absolute, but must be considered in relation to their function in society.[1960] Because a balancing of interests is involved, case teaching related to EU privacy rights encourages pupils to think critically (iii) and at the same time reveals some of the essentials of the EU (ii). Protection of privacy has to be balanced against economic objectives, security objectives (terrorism), or transparency objectives (public administration and use of tax money).[1961] Privacy is a concern affecting the personal lives of pupils; the possibility that 'big brother is watching

---

Link'; S O'Leary, 'The Charter and the Future Contours of EU Social and Employment Law' in P Cardonnel, A Rosas and N Wahl (eds), *Constitutionalising the EU judicial systems: essays in honour of Pernilla Lindh* (Hart 2012); Habermas, 'Democracy, Solidarity and the European Crisis'; I Pernice, 'Solidarität in Europa: Eine Ortsbestimmung im Verhältnis zwischen Bürger, Staat und Europäischer Union' in C Calliess (ed), *Uberlegungen im Kontext der Krise im Euroraum* (Mohr Siebeck 2013); A Sangiovanni, 'Solidarity in the European Union' (2013) 33 Oxford Journal of Legal Studies 1; C Barnard, 'EU employment law and the European social model: the past, the present, and the future' (2014) 67 Current Legal Problems 199; P Eleftheriadis, 'The Content of European Citizenship' (2014) 15 German Law Journal 777 (EU citizenship 'is best understood as a form of transnational solidarity which gives effect to the moral responsibilities of Member States and their peoples under a principle of fairness'). Also text to n 1416. Further Special Eurobarometer 471, Fairness, inequality and inter-generational mobility (December 2017). Early, Marshall, *Citizenship and Social Class*.

1960 Joined Cases C-92/09 and C-93/09 *Schecke and Eifert* ECLI:EU:C:2010:662, para 48; Case C-291/12 *Schwarz* ECLI:EU:C:2013:670, para 33.

1961 *Schecke* (n 1967). On balancing privacy/security, see i.a. Joined Cases C-203/15 and C-698/15 *Tele2 Sverige and Watson and others* ECLI:EU:C:2016:970; L Colonna, 'Schrems vs. Commissioner: A Precedent for the CJEU to Intervene in the National Intelligence Surveillance Activities of Member States?' (2016) 2 Europarättslig tidskrift 208. On balancing privacy/freedom of expression, see Case C-345/17 *Buivids* ECLI:EU:C:2019:122. See also CoE Recommendation CM/Rec(2018)7 of the Committee of Ministers to member States on Guidelines to respect, protect and fulfil the rights of the child in the digital environment (4 July 2018), i.a. the need for appropriate education (para 13), and link with the right to education (para 40).

you' is an easily understood peril. The criterion of subjective involvement is respected (or the Beutelsbacher consensus requirement of giving weight to the personal interests of pupils).[1962] Most EU citizens—including those at home—are 'digital citizens', users of the internet.[1963] Case teaching contributes to empowering them to exercise their rights and responsibilities in the additional EU dimension (i). The following stories all concern static citizens (iv): a Swedish lady living in Sweden, German farmers in Germany, a Spanish businessman in Spain, an Austrian student in Austria. Faced with concrete problems at home, their EU rights and obligations made the difference (i).

262 *EU obligations: Lindqvist*

The story of the catechist in Sweden

The fact that privacy rights deriving from EU law also imply responsibilities for citizens was something Ms Lindqvist experienced for herself.[1964]

> As a catechist in a parish in Sweden, Ms Lindqvist sets up internet pages to inform parishioners about preparation for confirmation. On the webpages, which are linked to the Swedish Church website, she includes (probably with the best of intentions) information about 18 colleagues in the parish: their names or first names, jobs, hobbies, family circumstances, phone numbers, and information about the foot injury of one colleague, who is therefore working halftime on medical grounds. Ms Lindqvist has to pay a large fine, because she has infringed Swedish law on personal data, i.a. for processing personal data without prior written notification and sensitive (medical) personal data without authorisation. This Swedish law implements the

---

1962 Wehling, 'Der Beutelsbacher Konsens: Entstehung und Wirkung' ('Pupils must be put in a position to analyse a political situation and to assess how their own personal interests are affected as well as to seek means and ways to influence the political situation they have identified according to their personal interests').

1963 Figures in Salamońska and Recchi, *Europe between mobility and sedentarism: Patterns of cross-border practices and their consequences for European identification*; a third of Europeans share their profiles and their ideas on general social media. Also Flash Eurobarometer 443, e-Privacy (July 2016). A lot of literature on privacy in the EU, i.a. B Petovka, 'Data Privacy Rights and Citizenship: Notes on Federalism All the Way Up' in D Kochenov (ed), *EU Citizenship and Federalism: The Role of Rights* (Cambridge University Press 2017). See also <ec.europa.eu/info/strategy/justice-and-fundamental-rights/data-protection_en>.

1964 Case C-101/01 *Lindqvist* ECLI:EU:C:2003:596.

Data Protection Directive.[1965] Ms Lindqvist argues that she is not guilty of any infringement, that she was not carrying out an economic activity, and that EU law was not applicable. As Swedish law must be interpreted consistently with the Directive, the Swedish Court asks a preliminary question. The ECJ answers that the essential objective of the Directive is to eliminate obstacles to the functioning of the internal market deriving from disparities between different national legislation. It would therefore not be appropriate to require that, in each individual case, it is determined whether free movement is concerned. The charitable or religious activities of Ms Lindqvist do not fall under any exception in the Directive. The ECJ recalls that the Directive aims at balancing, on the one hand, the establishment and functioning of the internal market which leads to the increase of cross-border flows of personal data, and, on the other hand, protection of that data. Ms Lindqvist's freedom of expression on the internet pages must be weighed against the protection of the private life of the colleagues about whom she has placed data on the website. Sanctions must be proportionate. On the basis of these guidelines, the ECJ invites the national court to ensure a fair balance in the concrete circumstances of the case.

Studying a case like *Lindqvist* in EDC draws the attention of pupils to their responsibilities. Living in a system based on the rule of law means that citizens must also respect obligations flowing from EU law. Responsible use of interactive media requires awareness of underlying legal and ethical principles. This fits in with learning to develop digital competence, increasingly important for empowering citizens in society.[1966] Digital competence has an essential EU dimension. The case may also trigger reflection

1965 Directive 95/46/EC of the European Parliament and of the Council of 24 October 1995 on the protection of individuals with regard to the processing of personal data and on the free movement of such data [1995] OJ L281/31 (as amended). Legal basis ex TEC Art 100a (ex Art 95 EC, now Art 114 TFEU). Dir repealed by the GDPR (n 1999).

1966 Council Recommendation of 22 May 2018 on key competences for lifelong learning, Annex: A European Reference Framework, 4: Digital competence ('Digital competence involves the confident, critical and responsible use of, and engagement with, digital technologies for learning, at work, and for participation in society'). See in the same vein earlier: Recommendation of the European Parliament and of the Council of 18 December 2006 on key competences for lifelong learning. See further Commission Communication on the Digital Education Action Plan COM(2018) 22 final.

on the foundational principle of conferral (*why does privacy have an EU dimension?*)

263 *Balancing the right to protection of personal data with transparency: Schecke*

The story of the angry farmers

The problem in *Schecke* provoked commotion and indignation among static (local) citizens. Case analysis makes it possible to distinguish clear steps in the reasoning.[1967]

> Volker und Markus Schecke have an agricultural firm in the *Land* of Hesse in Germany. Together with the farmer, Mr Eiffert, they receive funds under the EU common agricultural policy. Their problem is that their names and the precise amounts they receive are published on the website of a German Federal Agency and the information is available to everybody (a global website with a search function). They ask the *Land* Hesse to withdraw the personal data, but Hesse refuses, referring to an obligation in an EU Regulation to publish the information. In the first step of its reasoning, the ECJ decides that publication of the data without consent is a limitation of the rights enshrined in Articles 7 and 8 CFR (respect for private and family life and protection of personal data). In the second step of its reasoning, the Court examines whether this limitation can be justified. The conditions of Article 52(1) CFR must be fulfilled. Here, the interference is provided for by law (Regulation) and meets an objective of general interest recognised by the EU, i.e. increasing the transparency of the use of EU funds in the common agricultural policy (reinforcing public control of the use of the money and thus accountability in a democratic system). Publication is an appropriate means of attaining the objective, yet the measure goes beyond what is necessary to achieve the objective with regard to natural persons (proportionality test). A proper balance is to be struck between the privacy rights guaranteed by Articles 7 and 8 CFR and the transparency objective: limitations on the right to protection of personal data can only apply in so far as they are strictly necessary.[1968] The ECJ declares the Regulation partly invalid, i.e. to the extent that its

---

1967 Joined Cases C-92/09 and C-93/09 *Schecke and Eifert* ECLI:EU:C:2010:662. Text to n 1265.

1968 *Schecke*, paras 77, 86; Case C-73/07 *Satakunnan Markkinapörssi Oy and Satamedia* ECLI:EU:C:2008:727, para 56. See also Case C-291/12 *Schwarz* ECLI:EU:C:2013:670, paras 34 and 46 (Art 52 CFR).

> provisions impose an obligation to publish personal data of natural persons without distinction as to periods, frequency, nature or amount. In the case of legal persons, the publication obligation does not go beyond what is necessary to achieve the objective.

The facts provide a basis for critical discussion as to how the right balance should be struck: *should citizens know how public money is used (EU principle of transparency) or should the EU right to privacy prevail?* The principle of proportionality can be a guide for such a discussion.

264 *The right to be forgotten: Google Spain*

The story of the Spanish businessman and Google

Another interesting case encouraging pupils to think independently is *Google Spain*.[1969] Opposing interests are weighed against one another in the light of foundational values.

> Mario Costeja González is a Spanish citizen who resides in Spain. When his name is entered into the Google search engine a link appears to an article published ten years earlier in a widely circulated Spanish newspaper (*La Vanguardia*). The article mentions his social security debts and the public sale of his property (real-estate auction) necessary to pay off the debts. Mr Costeja González asks the newspaper to remove the e-article, arguing that the debt proceedings have in the meantime been resolved and have become irrelevant for the reader. The newspaper refuses. He then requests Google Spain to remove the links. Google Spain forwards the request to Google Inc. in the US. Mr Costeja González takes his complaint to the Spanish Data Protection Agency, who requires Google Spain and Google Inc. to withdraw the data. Google Spain and Google Inc. bring actions in the Spanish National High Court. Uncertain about the interpretation of the Data Protection Directive, the High Court refers preliminary questions to the ECJ. One of them is: can the data subject (Mr Costeja González) require the operator of a search engine to remove from the list of results certain information which he wishes to be 'forgotten' after a certain time? Google Spain, Google Inc., the Greek, Austrian and Polish Governments, and the Commission contend that there should not be any such right to be forgotten. Mr Costeja González, the Spanish and the Italian Governments, on the other hand, argue that the fundamental rights to the protection of personal data and to privacy encom-

1969 Case C-131/12 *Google Spain* ECLI:EU:C:2014:317.

pass the right to be forgotten.[1970] Interpreting the Data Protection Directive, the ECJ upholds a right to be forgotten (without calling it that), in particular where the Directive states that Member States shall guarantee every data subject the right to obtain from the controller the rectification, erasure or blocking of incomplete or inaccurate data, and the right to object to the processing of his data on compelling legitimate grounds.[1971] Even if the information causes no prejudice, the data subject has the right, after a certain time, to request that certain personal information is erased from the list of search results linked to his name, because in the course of time, data may become inadequate, irrelevant, or excessive in relation to the purposes of the processing (here, 16 years later, the debts have been paid and the public sale of property for that end is no longer relevant to the general public).[1972] The Court balances several interests: the economic interest of the operator of the search engine, the fundamental rights of the data subject under Articles 7 and 8 CFR, and the interest of internet users in having access to information. The fundamental rights in Article 7 and 8 CFR 'override, as a rule, not only the economic interest of the operator of the search engine but also the interest of the general public in having access to that information upon a search relating to the data subject's name'. In specific cases, the ECJ adds, the balance may be different, e.g. where the data subject plays a role in public life.[1973] The ECJ holds that even if the newspaper has not withdrawn the information from its webpages, the operator of the search engine can be obliged to remove the links to these webpages of the newspaper in certain circumstances.

Case teaching based on *Google Spain* is attractive for several reasons.

The story of a conflict between a citizen and Google easily captures the interest of pupils. It triggers animated debate in the classroom on the question of which right should prevail: the right to be forgotten and privacy rights, or the right to freedom of expression and freedom of information. The case shows how EU fundamental rights reflect foundational values on which all seem to agree, but which may lead to disagreement when

1970 Para 90.

1971 See conditions in Art 12(b), 'as appropriate'; and Art 14.

1972 Paras 92–94, 99.

1973 See paras 81, 91, 99. See also Art 7(f), requiring balancing of interests (the legitimate interests of the controller, third parties, or parties to whom the data are disclosed, can be overridden by interests or fundamental rights of the data subject).

applied in practice. *Do people searching Google have the right to* all *the information about somebody, or should some degree of privacy be respected?* Public debate starts in the classroom. Reasonable people may have different viewpoints. In his Opinion in the case Advocate General Jääskinen defended the opposite view to that taken by the ECJ. He was not prepared to limit the pivotal rights to freedom of expression and information when balancing them against the right to protection of private life. Acknowledging a right to be forgotten on a case by case basis, he argued, would moreover lead to an unmanageable number of requests.[1974] The issues in *Google Spain* provide an opportunity for exercising skills throughout different phases of problem based learning: defining the problem and its causes, understanding which interests are affected, understanding the viewpoints of the parties in the case, creatively finding a solution, formulating one's own opinion and listening with respect to other opinions, and foreseeing the consequences of proposed solutions.[1975] In the 'judgment' phase (or 'generalisation' of the case analysis), *Google Spain* demonstrates how an individual can defend his rights in court and thus have an impact on the evolution of the EU legal order. Triggered by the action taken by Mr Costeja González, a static and active EU citizen, the *Google Spain* ruling provoked increased awareness worldwide of privacy rights in social media.[1976] The case shows how, in the end, fundamental choices fall to be made through the political process. In 2016, the EU legislator, i.e. the European Parliament and the Council, on a proposal from the Commission, decided how to balance the fundamental rights in question.[1977] They codified the right to be forgotten in Article 17 of the new General Data Protection Regulation: the right to erasure.[1978]

1974 Opinion of Advocate General Jääskinen in Case C-131/12 *Google Spain* ECLI:EU:C:2014:317, paras 128, 133, 137. Among the innumerable comments on the judgment in legal literature, i.a., D Stute, 'Privacy Almighty? The CJEU's Judgment in Google Spain SL v AEPD' [2015] Michigan Journal of International Law 649.

1975 Reinhardt, *Teaching Civics: A Manual for Secondary Education Teachers* 96–102.

1976 Rules in various legal instruments worldwide have been adapted to include the right to be forgotten (see comments in wikipedia on Google Spain).

1977 Lenaerts, 'Some thoughts on the State of the European Union as a rights-based legal order', on legislative consensus. See a comparable question in another field, van den Brink, 'The Court and the Legislators: who should define the scope of free movement in the EU?'.

1978 Regulation (EU) 2016/679 of the European Parliament and of the Council of 27 April 2016 on the protection of natural persons with regard to the processing of personal data and on the free movement of such data, and repealing

The case provides an occasion for explaining concepts of EU legislation. A regulation is directly applicable, confers rights and obligations which are directly effective in daily life, and has primacy over national rules. The case shows the EU institutions in action,[1979] highlighting their role in the adoption of EU legislation and the interaction between judges and the legislator. The case demonstrates that citizens are actors in both judicial processes (defending their case in court) and legislative processes (i.a. as participants in—European and national parliament—elections or in public debate). For both processes, citizens need knowledge of their rights and awareness of problems in society. An EU dimension to EDC empowers them to exercise their rights (c-1) and to play an active part in democratic life (c-3).

In general, *Google Spain* illustrates that on a combined reading of EDC standards and EU law, it is not sufficient for pupils to learn about the history of the European Communities or the geography of Europe. The EU dimension of EDC is a source of many other fascinating subjects, of fresh and stimulating content for young EU citizens.

265 *Fundamental rights to respect for private life, protection of personal data, and to an effective remedy: Schrems*

The story of the student and Facebook

The *Schrems* case is a thought-provoking and quite spectacular case, appropriate for advanced levels of EDC.[1980] Since pupils use social media on a daily basis, they will have no difficulty engaging with the facts (subjective involvement). The relevant EU primary law provisions are Articles 7, 8 and 47 CFR and Article 16 TFEU.

Directive 95/46/EC [2016] OJ L119/1 (General Data Protection Regulation), Art 17: 'The data subject shall have the right to obtain from the controller the erasure of personal data concerning him or her without undue delay and the controller shall have the obligation to erase personal data without undue delay where one of the following grounds applies: (a) the personal data are no longer necessary in relation to the purposes for which they were collected or otherwise processed ...', see also recitals 65–66.

1979 Reinhardt, *Teaching Civics: A Manual for Secondary Education Teachers* 119: 'The innovation of case teaching is that we no longer have to oppose teaching by cases to teaching about institutions: students can learn about institutions by studying current cases. Specific cases show institutions in action, thereby helping learners grasp their structure and function by way of example and in context'. The case here is content and not simply a hook.

1980 Case C-362/14 *Schrems* ECLI:EU:C:2015:650. For details on the procedural steps, see Max Schrems' website <europe-v-facebook.org/EN/en.html>.

Maximillian Schrems is a student at the University of Vienna. He is an Austrian national and lives in Austria. When he created his Facebook account in 2008, he ticked the box to agree with the general conditions for use and thus concluded—like all Facebook subscribers in the EU—a contract with Facebook Ireland (a subsidiary of the parent company Facebook US). The data of European subscribers are transferred to servers in the US and kept there. In 2013, Maximillian learns of the revelations of Edward Snowden: the National Security Agency (NSA) has unrestricted access to European mass data stored on the servers (via PRISM, a US intelligence service programme). A month later, Maximillian lodges a complaint with the Irish Data Protection Commissioner, claiming that the law and practices of the US do not offer real protection of his data stored in the US. The Commissioner refuses to examine the complaint, because of a lack of evidence that the NSA accesses Mr Schrems' data, and because of the 2000 Safe Harbour Decision of the European Commission.[1981]

In the *Safe Harbour Decision*, the European Commission established that the US ensured an adequate level of protection of transferred personal data. Under this Decision, more than 3000 US companies self-certified that they adhered to the Safe Harbour Privacy Principles issued by the US Department of Commerce. Among them were Google, Facebook, Microsoft, Apple, and Yahoo, who transferred the personal data of hundreds of millions of users in Europe to the US. Yet, a significant number of the self-certifying companies did not comply in practice. US law also allowed large-scale collection and processing of personal data beyond what was strictly necessary and proportionate for national security.[1982] This seemed to contrast with the EU *Data Protection Directive*, on which the Safe Harbour Decision was based. The *Data Protection Directive* protects the fundamental right to privacy with respect to the processing of personal data.[1983] Processing of personal data includes collection, storage, consultation, or disclo-

---

1981 Commission Decision 2000/520/EC of 26 July 2000 pursuant to Directive 95/46 on the adequacy of the protection provided by the safe harbour privacy principles and related frequently asked questions issued by the US Department of Commerce [2000] OJ 2000 L215/7.

1982 *Schrems*, paras 21–25, with reference to Communication COM(2013) 847 final.

1983 Directive 95/46/EC of the European Parliament and of the Council of 24 October 1995 on the protection of individuals with regard to the processing of personal data and on the free movement of such data [1995] OJ L281/31 (as amended) (see n 1965).

sure of personal data.[1984] The principle is that Member States shall provide that the transfer to a third country of personal data intended for processing after transfer, may only take place if the third country ensures an *adequate level of protection* (Article 25). The Commission may conclude that the third country ensures this by reason of its domestic law or of international commitments (Article 25(6)). Moreover, each Member State shall establish a supervisory authority, a public authority responsible for monitoring the application of the Directive within its territory and acting with complete independence.[1985]

Maximillian contests the refusal of the Irish Data Protection Commissioner to examine his complaint in the High Court of Ireland. The High Court considers that surveillance and interception of personal data serves legitimate counter-terrorism objectives, but that the mass and undifferentiated accessing of personal data by the NSA interferes disproportionally with the right to privacy guaranteed by the Irish constitution. Based on Irish law, the Commissioner could not have refused to examine Mr Schrems' complaint. However, the High Court concludes that it cannot decide the case based on Irish law, as it concerns the implementation of EU law (Article 51 CFR), and refers a preliminary question to the ECJ.

The ECJ reads Article 25(6) of the Directive in the light of the fundamental right to respect for private life (Article 7 CFR), to protection of personal data (Article 8 CFR) and to effective judicial protection (Article 47 CFR).

First, the Court rules on the powers of the supervisory authority. The establishment of an independent supervisory authority is an essential component of the protection of individuals with regard to the processing of personal data (as Article 16(2) TFEU requires). This authority must ensure a fair balance between the right to privacy and economic interests. Member States cannot adopt measures contrary to the Safe Harbour Decision of the Commission (a decision is a legal act of the Union and is binding on all the Member States to which it is

1984 Arts 1 and 2 Dir: personal data is defined as 'any information relating to an identified or identifiable natural person'; processing is 'any operation or set of operations which is performed upon personal data, whether or not by automatic means, such as collection, recording, organisation, storage, adaptation or alteration, retrieval, consultation, use, disclosure by transmission, dissemination or otherwise making available, alignment or combination, blocking, erasure or destruction'.

1985 Art 28 Dir.

addressed).[1986] However, this does not prevent the national supervisory authority from examining the claim of a person who contends that there is not an adequate level of protection in the processing of his personal data. Otherwise, that person would be denied his fundamental rights. It is, moreover, settled case-law that the EU is 'a union based on the rule of law in which all acts of its institutions are subject to review of their compatibility with, in particular the Treaties, general principles of law and fundamental rights'.[1987] The Commission cannot escape such review of the validity of its Safe Harbour Decision.

Then, the ECJ examines whether that Decision is valid. An adequate level of protection in a third country must essentially be equivalent to the level of protection in the EU legal order.[1988] In the EU, restrictions on the rights in Articles 7 and 8 CFR must be laid down in clear and precise rules and only apply in so far as is strictly necessary (proportionality principle).[1989] The Court considers that legislation permitting public authorities to have access on a generalised basis to the content of electronic communications compromises the essence of the fundamental right to respect for private life (Article 7 CFR).[1990] Moreover, legislation not providing for any possibility for an individual to pursue legal remedies in order to have access to his personal data, or to obtain their rectification or erasure, does not respect the essence of the fundamental right to effective judicial protection (Article 47 CFR).[1991] The Court declares the Safe Harbour Decision invalid.

While—admittedly—the full story is not suitable for younger students in secondary education, the advantages of case teaching based on *Schrems* at more advanced levels are multiple.[1992]

1986 Para 52; Art 288 TFEU.

1987 Para 60 (settled case law). Also text to n 1831 ff.

1988 Para 73.

1989 Para 92.

1990 Para 94. Also Joined Cases C-293/12 and C-594/12 *Digital Rights Ireland* ECLI: EU:C:2014:238, para 39.

1991 Para 95: 'The very existence of effective judicial review designed to ensure compliance with provisions of EU law is inherent in the existence of the rule of law' (settled case law).

1992 The case can be schematised into its essential principles (also visually in slides), adapted to the level of students (see for instance, a version for a not necessarily legally trained audience: Lenaerts, 'Cogito ergo civis europaeus sum: Discours à l'occasion de l'attribution du titre de docteur honoris causa de l'Université de Poitiers'). The notion of adequacy (an adequate level of protection) is abstract, but pupils of 17- 18 can grasp it.

Firstly, the case can motivate pupils to engage in active citizenship, as it demonstrates the potentially high impact of the action of a simple citizen. Maximillian Schrems, a student (like Françoise Gravier[1993]) has, by taking legal action, shaken established systems in society, mobilising many important actors in the EU and even worldwide. While his immediate adversary in Court was the Irish Data Protection Commissioner (joined by Digital Rights Ireland), observations were also submitted by Ireland, the governments of Belgium, the Czech Republic, Italy, Austria, Poland, Slovenia, and the UK, plus the European Parliament, the European Commission, and the European Data Protection Supervisor. The Court's judgment had consequences for EU-US trade and even beyond. The end of Safe Harbour provoked reactions in the press, among politicians and scholars.[1994] Various EU and US industry associations and companies expressed their concern in an open letter to Commission President Juncker. Because data transfers are an integral part of commercial exchanges between the EU and the US, the Commission immediately devised an alternative system to ensure the continuity of transatlantic trade.[1995] Data transfers from the EU to other third countries were questioned, as they were based on comparable conditions to those declared invalid. Intensive talks with the US Government were needed to ensure that a new system would provide an equivalent level of protection.[1996] In 2016, a new framework was established, the *EU-US Privacy Shield*, as a response to the conditions set out by the ECJ in *Schrems*,[1997] to ensure an adequate level of protection.[1998] The Data Protection Directive was repealed and replaced by the *General Data Protection*

1993 Text to n 1377.

1994 See numerous notes in Eurlex.

1995 Commission Communication on the Transfer of Personal Data from the EU to the United States of America under Directive 95/46/EC following the Judgment by the Court of Justice in Case C-362/14 (Schrems) COM(2015) 566 final, 1.

1996 Ibid, 3, 14.

1997 Commission Implementing Decision (EU) 2016/1250 of 12 July 2016 pursuant to Directive 95/46/EC of the European Parliament and of the Council on the adequacy of the protection provided by the EU-U.S. Privacy Shield [2016] OJ L 207/1.

1998 See also European Parliament Resolution of 6 April 2017 on the adequacy of the protection afforded by the EU-US Privacy Shield ; Commission Report on the first annual review of the functioning of the EU–US Privacy Shield COM(2017) 611 final; Commission Communication 'Exchanging and Protecting Personal Data in a Globalised World' COM(2017) 07 final: 'The protection of personal data is part of Europe's common constitutional fabric and is enshrined in Article 8 of the EU Charter of Fundamental Rights.'.

Regulation (GDPR, based on Article 16 TFEU).[1999] This Regulation aims to strengthen citizens' fundamental rights and lays down rules for companies in the digital single market. It directly grants EU rights to data subjects (persons), such as the right of access, to rectification, etc.[2000] The GDPR refers to several elements of the *Schrems* judgment.[2001] Maximillian Schrems' legal action is ongoing.[2002]

Furthermore, case teaching based on *Schrems* provides an opportunity for reinforcing the EU dimension of (inter alia) digital, social and citizenship competence.[2003] Cognitive structures are deepened (concepts such as directives, decisions, third country, precedent; role of institutions such as the Commission; interaction between national and EU law, national and EU courts). The skills of nuanced and critical thinking are exercised (learning to balance conflicting objectives). The case illustrates how EU rights provide additional (i) and significant (ii) content to national EDC. The Irish High Court solves the case, not just on the basis of the Irish constitution, but also in the light of EU law. *Schrems* shows how the abstract foundational values, objectives and principles of the EU have concrete outcomes in practice. Through a story, pupils in the classroom experience what being a Union 'based on the rule of law' and 'respecting fundamental

---

1999 Regulation (EU) 2016/679 of the European Parliament and of the Council of 27 April 2016 on the protection of natural persons with regard to the processing of personal data and on the free movement of such data, and repealing Directive 95/46/EC [2016] OJ L119/1 (General Data Protection Regulation), adopted by the ordinary legislative procedure. See also legal basis in Art 39 TEU. More in P Valcke, 'General Report' in JL da Cruz Vilaça and others (eds), *The internal market and the digital economy*, vol 1 (XXVIII FIDE Congress Lisbon/Estoril (23-26 May 2018), Almedina 2018)143 ff and national reports. Simplified information (pupils), see <ec.europa.eu/info/law/law-topic/data-protection/reform/rights-citizens/my-rights/what-are-my-rights_en>. See on impact beyond the EU, 'New EU privacy rules to benefit Facebook users globally' <euobserver.com/digital/141520>: 'The GDPR is unique in the world, but has the possibility of setting a global standard because it will apply to any internet company that targets European consumers. Facebook's boss implied that non-Europeans will also benefit from the new rules. "We intend to make all the same controls and settings available everywhere, not just in Europe," he said.'.

2000 I.a. Arts 15 ff, including the right to be forgotten, to restriction of processing, to data portability, to object, etc.

2001 See e.g. recital 104 and 117. See also Regulation (EU) 2018/1725.

2002 Case C-311/18 *Facebook Ireland and Schrems* pending. See also Case C-498/16 *Schrems* ECLI:EU:C:2018:37 (concept of consumer, and class action).

2003 Council Recommendation of 22 May 2018 on key competences for lifelong learning (n 1966).

rights' actually means. The fundamental rights of individuals (the right to private life and data protection, the right to an effective remedy) are grounds for the ECJ to declare a decision of the Commission invalid.[2004]

Finally, questions for the 'political judgment' and 'generalisation' phase of the case analysis can be discussed: *Why can the EU act in this field? What is the added value of EU action? Can privacy and personal data be sufficiently protected by a Member State acting alone? Schrems* is an opportunity for explaining the foundational principles of conferral, subsidiarity and proportionality. Without EU cooperation, a Member State's privacy rights do not carry any weight against US law and practices. *Schrems* encourages reflection on the added value of EU action in a globalised world (speaking with one voice, the EU can require the US to offer equivalent protection to EU privacy rules) and, at the same time, invites critical thinking. Pupils become aware of the risks of inadequate EU legislation and policies. (This may motivate them to take part in the democratic life of the Union, in addition to attentively monitoring respect for their own individual EU rights.) The internet, free movement in the internal market (e.g. of services) and the expansion of international trade inevitably lead to a cross-border flow of personal data, including that of the static citizen. The foundational objectives of the EU have to be reconciled in the light of the principle of proportionality: an economic union with a free flow of data, on the one hand, and a right to privacy and data protection, on the other hand. The judicial balancing of interests in *Schrems* has been continued in legislative action: the GDPR aims to contribute to an area of freedom, security and justice *and* to an economic union, to economic *and* social progress, to economies in the internal market *and* to the well-being of persons.[2005] In a Union based on mutual trust it is necessary to develop a culture of human rights; discussing cases such as *Schrems* at school can contribute to such a culture.

266 EU obligations: Schwarz

The story of the fingerprints

As a final note, to counterbalance the success story of *Schrems*, the case of Mr Schwarz may add a touch of realism. It shows pupils that invoking EU rights is not a *deus ex machina* automatically leading to system changes.

2004 Also Joined Cases C-293/12 and C-594/12 *Digital Rights Ireland* ECLI:EU:C:2014:238.

2005 Recital 2 GDPR.

> When Michael Schwarz applies to the Stadt Bochum for a passport, he refuses to have his fingerprints taken. He argues that this infringes his EU right to privacy and personal data protection (Articles 7 and 8 CFR) and disputes the validity of the EU Regulation setting out the obligation to take the fingerprints of persons applying for passports. The ECJ rules that this indeed is a limitation of privacy rights but recalls that privacy rights are not absolute. They must be considered in relation to their function in society. Taking fingerprints is justified by the legitimate aim of preventing fraudulent use of passports, and is proportional, as it does not go beyond what is necessary to achieve this objective.[2006]

In conclusion, privacy is an appropriate topic to include in the EU dimension of EDC, relevant for mainstream education (satisfying criteria i-iv). Five stories have illustrated how (static) active citizens enforced their EU rights (*Schecke*, *Google Spain*, and *Schrems*) or were obliged to respect their EU obligations (*Lindqvist, Schwarz*).

5. Consumer rights and obligations

267 Relevance for EDC

Consumer rights and obligations based on EU law are relevant to mainstream education. They provide additional content to national EDC (i) and are significant (ii), relating to foundational values, objectives and principles. Competence has been conferred on the EU to promote consumers' interests and ensure a high level of consumer protection. To achieve these objectives, the EU 'shall contribute to protecting the health, safety and economic interests of consumers, as well as to promoting their right to information, education and to organise themselves in order to safeguard their interests' (Article 169(1) TFEU). The EU can adopt harmonisation measures in the internal market (Article 114 TFEU) or use its supporting competence (Article 169(2)(3) TFEU). When defining and implementing other Union policies and activities, consumer protection requirements must be taken into account (Art 12 TFEU). The CFR confirms in the Title 'Solidar-

2006 Case C-291/12 *Schwarz* ECLI:EU:C:2013:670; Council Regulation (EC) No 2252/2004 of 13 December 2004 on standards for security features and biometrics in passports and travel documents issued by Member States [2004] OJ L385/1, as amended by Regulation (EC) No 444/2009 of the European Parliament and of the Council of 6 May 2009 [2009] OJ L142/1.

ity' that 'Union policies shall ensure a high level of consumer protection' (Article 38).[2007]

Case teaching in the field of consumer protection connects with the sense of fairness felt by teachers and pupils (subjective involvement) and leads to critical thinking (iii). *How is it possible to achieve the foundational EU objective of combating social exclusion and discrimination, and promoting social justice (Article 3 TEU)?* Finally, consumer protection reveals an EU dimension to everyday situations which is relevant to all citizens (iv). Static citizens have EU consumer rights; local sellers of goods or suppliers of services must also respect EU obligations. Rights and obligations deriving from EU law on consumer protection concern (logically) all consumers, irrespective of nationality, residents in Member States' territories or abroad (export).

Case teaching about EU consumer rights can be based on a wide range of cases. Shopping online, product safety, telecoms, transport, energy, financial services, etc. often include crossborder elements. Citizens also enjoy important EU rights in so-called wholly internal situations (situations where all relevant elements are confined within a single Member State), as will appear in the following examples. Consumer interests are protected by an extensive body of EU secondary law.[2008]

2007 To be implemented by EU institutions and Member States within the scope of EU law (Art 52(5) CFR).

2008 See Art 3(1) of Regulation (EU) 2017/2394 of the European Parliament and of the Council of 12 December 2017 on cooperation between national authorities responsible for the enforcement of consumer protection laws and repealing Regulation (EC) No 2006/2004 [2017] OJ L 345/1: 'Union laws that protect consumers' interests' means the Regulations and the Directives, as transposed in the internal legal order of the Member States, which are listed in the Annex. The Annex contains 26 regulations and directives. See i.a. Regulation (EC) No 1333/2008 of the European Parliament and of the Council of 16 December 2008 on food additives [2008] OJ L354/16; Directive 2009/48/EC of the European Parliament and of the Council of 18 June 2009 on the safety of toys [2009] OJ L170/1; Regulation (EU) No 181/2011 of the European Parliament and of the Council of 16 February 2011 concerning the rights of passengers in bus and coach transport and amending Regulation (EC) No 2006/2004 [2011] OJ L55/1; Regulation (EU) 2017/826 of the European Parliament and of the Council of 17 May 2017 on establishing a Union programme to support specific activities enhancing the involvement of consumers and other financial services end-users in Union policy-making in the area of financial services for the period of 2017-2020 [2017] OJ L129/17. On the EU right to compensation from the air carrier for a delayed flight: Regulation (EC) No 261/2004 of the European Parliament and of the Council of 11 February 2004 establishing

268 *Rights protecting against unfair terms in consumer contracts: Gutiérrez Naranjo*

The story of unfair interest rates

Consumers derive EU rights from the Directive on unfair terms in consumer contracts. This Directive, adopted in 1993, illustrates that the internal market cannot function without the harmonisation of certain issues. The Directive aims to protect consumers and to avoid the distortion of competition resulting from disparities in national legislation on consumer protection.[2009] The large majority of citizens sign pre-formulated standard contracts (including general conditions often printed in lower case letters).[2010] A contractual term which has not been individually negotiated is unfair 'if, contrary to the requirement of good faith, it causes a significant imbalance in the parties' rights and obligations arising under the contract, to the detriment of the consumer'.[2011] The story of Mr Gutiérrez Naranjo illustrates once more the power of the individual citizen who takes legal action. By exercising his EU rights, he obtained satisfaction of his own claims and, at the same time, created added value for large groups of citizens all over the EU.

> Like numerous other Spanish citizens, Mr Francisco Gutiérrez Naranjo concludes a mortgage loan with his bank containing a 'floor clause' in the general conditions. 'Floor clauses' in loan agreements fix a minimum rate below which the variable rate of interest cannot fall. When market interest rates rise, consumers must pay higher rates (variable), but when the rates go down (even significantly), they cannot benefit from the lower rates as they must pay the contractual minimum rate, which is to the advantage of the banks. Mr Francisco

---

common rules on compensation and assistance to passengers in the event of denied boarding and of cancellation or long delay of flights, and repealing Regulation (EEC) No 295/91 [2004] OJ L46/1; Joined Cases C-402/07 and C-432/07 *Sturgeon* ECLI:EU:C:2009:716; Joined Cases C-581/10 and C-629/10 *Nelson and TUI Travel* ECLI:EU:C:2012:657; Case C-315/15 *Pešková and Peška* ECLI:EU:C:2017:342. Examples in Did you know? 10 EU rights at a glance (European Commission Publications Office 2014). Consumer (pupils) friendly information on <europa.eu/youreurope/citizens/consumers/index_en.htm>.

2009 Council Directive 93/13/EEC of 5 April 1993 on unfair terms in consumer contracts [1993] OJ L95/29 (before the EU was given the competence to protect consumers; legal basis in Art 100a EEC: approximation of provisions for the establishing and functioning of the internal market).

2010 Ibid (still in force).

2011 Art 3.

Gutiérrez Naranjo and three other citizens take legal action to protest.[2012] The Spanish Supreme Court applies the Directive on unfair terms in consumer contracts and decides that the 'floor clauses' are fair in the formal sense, i.e. grammatically intelligible for consumers, but not in the substantive sense because they are not transparent 'due to insufficient information for the borrowers as to the material consequences of their application in practice'.[2013] The Supreme Court declares the unfair 'floor clauses' void, but only with effect for the future, invoking reasons of legal certainty and the risk of serious economic repercussions. As a result, hundreds of thousands of Spanish consumers cannot claim reimbursement of the amounts of money overpaid to the banks. Several national lower courts refer preliminary questions to the ECJ on this temporal limitation of the effects of the judgement. Spanish newspapers follow the Luxembourg case closely (which indicates the relevance of this additional EU dimension for national citizens). The ECJ rules that the temporal limitation does not comply with EU law to the extent that it affects the substance of the right enjoyed by the consumer under the Directive, that is, the right not to be bound by unfair clauses. The objective of the Directive is to achieve more effective protection of consumers through the adoption of uniform rules of law on unfair terms, rules applicable to all contracts concluded between sellers or suppliers and consumers.[2014] A finding that a term is unfair 'must allow the restoration of the legal and factual situation that the consumer would have been in if that unfair term had not existed, by inter alia, creating a right to restitution of advantages wrongly obtained, to the consumer's detriment, by the seller or supplier on the basis of that unfair term'.[2015] Not granting reimbursement for the period before the judgment amounts to incomplete and insufficient protection and does not prevent the continued

2012 Joined Cases C-154/15 and C-307/15 *Gutiérrez Naranjo and Others* ECLI:EU:C:2016:980. The three joined cases concerned floor clauses in a mortgage loan of (1) Mr Francisco Gutiérrez Naranjo with Cajasur Banco SAU, (2) Ms Ana María Palacios Martínez with Banco Bilbao Vizcaya Argentaria SA, and (3) Mr Emilio Irles López and Ms Teresa Torres Andreu concluded with Banco Español SA.

2013 Para 21. For assessment of fairness, see Art 4(2) Dir 93/13 (terms must be in 'plain intelligible language').

2014 Recital 10 Dir 93/13.

2015 Para 66.

use of those types of terms.[2016] The ECJ interprets the Directive in such a way that when a national court makes a finding of unfairness, it cannot limit the restitutory effects to amounts overpaid *after* that finding.[2017]

Active citizenship was rewarding. The action taken by Mr Francisco Gutiérrez Naranjo and three other citizens leading to the ruling that unfair 'floor clauses' are also retroactively invalid, had wide repercussions. The Spanish national judiciary had to adapt their case-law and financial institutions all over the EU were obliged to adapt contracts and change their practices.

Other stories involving consumer rights are probably more directly related to the daily lives of pupils than mortgage loans, e.g. **renting an apartment.**

Dirk and Katarina (Asbeek Brusse and de Man Garabito) are private persons living in the Netherlands. They rent a residential property from a commercial company for EUR 875 per month. The tenancy agreement is based on the standard terms of a professional real-estate association and includes a penalty clause: if they fail to pay in time, 1% interest is due per month and 25 EUR per day. The couple do not pay the rent agreed and after some months receive a bill of EUR 13 897 from the commercial company. Dirk and Katarina consider this excessive and contest the bill in court. The ECJ (preliminary ruling) holds that the national court must examine of its own motion whether a contractual term is unfair, without being asked to do so by the consumer. This compensates for the imbalance between the consumer and the seller or supplier.[2018] The ECJ (on the basis of a teleological interpretation) draws attention to the objective of the Directive, i.e. to raise the standard of living and the quality of life throughout the EU.[2019] The rules are similar to national rules of public policy. If the national court finds that a penalty clause in a tenancy agreement is unfair, it may not merely reduce the amount of the penalty but must exclude the application of that clause in its entirety (as a deterrent).[2020]

2016 Art 7(1) Dir 93/13.

2017 Para 75. See contrary Opinion of AG Mengozzi.

2018 Case C-488/11 *Asbeek Brusse and de Man Garabito* ECLI:EU:C:2013:341, paras 38- 40.

2019 Paras 43–4.

2020 Paras 59–60. See Art 6(1) Dir (the contract continues to bind the parties if this is possible without the unfair term).

Pupils may reflect on the question: *why is there an EU dimension in this wholly internal situation?*[2021]

269 Rights of buyers and obligations of sellers: Sabrina Wathelet

The story of the second-hand car

Problems related to buying a car may appeal to pupils. The following example concerns Directive 1999/44 on certain aspects of the sale of consumer goods and associated guarantees.[2022] Sellers have an EU obligation to deliver goods in conformity with the contract of sale.[2023]

> In Belgium, Ms Sabrina Wathelet purchases a second-hand car at a local garage and pays EUR 4000 to the garage. The car breaks down. She refuses to pay EUR 2000 for the repair. It appears then that, in fact, the garage had acted as an intermediary and sold the car on behalf of a private owner, without saying so. The Belgian court applies provisions of Belgian law (Civil Code), which are intended to implement the Directive and must therefore be interpreted in the light of the Directive. Doubting whether the garage is a 'seller' in the sense of the Directive, the Belgian court asks a preliminary question.[2024] The ECJ recalls that the need for the uniform application of EU law requires that the concept of 'seller' is given an independent and uniform interpretation throughout the EU ('seller' is an autonomous concept of EU law). Taking account of the context and the objective of the EU law provision[2025] the Court then concludes that the concept of 'seller' cov-

2021 Link to the principle of conferral. See preamble; also nn 2009 and 2039 (functioning of the internal market and consumer protection).

2022 Directive 1999/44/EC of the European Parliament and of the Council of 25 May 1999 on certain aspects of the sale of consumer goods and associated guarantees [1999] OJ L171/12. See now Directive (EU) 2019/771 of the European Parliament and of the Council of 20 May 2019 on certain aspects concerning contracts for the sale of goods, amending Regulation (EU) 2017/2394 and Directive 2009/22/EC, and repealing Directive 1999/44/EC [2019] OJ L 136/28.

2023 Art 2(1). In the case of lack of conformity, the consumer has the right to a free of charge repair or replacement (unless this is impossible or disproportionate), to an appropriate price reduction, or rescission of the contract (unless the lack of conformity is minor). See Art 3.

2024 Case C-149/15 *Wathelet* ECLI:EU:C:2016:840. Dir 1999/44 defines the seller as 'any natural or legal person who, under a contract, sells consumer goods in the course of his trade, business or profession' (Art 1(2)(c)). In Belgian law, seller is 'any natural or legal person who sells consumer goods in the course of his trade, business or profession' (implementation of Dir).

2025 Paras 28–9.

> ers a trader who acts as an intermediary on behalf of a private owner, even if he has not duly informed the consumer of that fact.[2026]

The *Wathelet* case deepens knowledge (directive, conferral) and provides an opportunity to discuss the implications of the internal market, including for those at home. Many other stories can be selected from case law according to the interests of pupils and teachers.[2027]

270 The right of withdrawal in distance contracts: Faccini Dori

The story of the lady who made an impulsive purchase at a railway station

Consumers have an EU right of withdrawal when concluding distance or off-premises contracts.[2028] An early case was *Faccini Dori*.[2029]

> Ms Paola Faccini Dori is waiting for her train at Milan Central Railway Station and is approached by someone selling English language correspondence courses. She agrees on the spot to conclude a contract. Some days later, she regrets her action and writes a letter to cancel her order. The company refuses and claims payment. She initiates proceedings before an Italian court, relying on the right of cancellation for a period of at least seven days, a right provided for by the Directive.[2030] The Italian court doubts whether the Directive can be relied on directly, given that Italy has failed to transpose it in time in national law, and asks a preliminary question. The ECJ rules that Ms Paola Faccini Dori cannot rely on a right of cancellation provided for by the

---

2026 Para 45 (irrespective of the question as to whether the intermediary is remunerated for this service or not).

2027 E.g. the story of Ms Duarte Hueros who purchases a car with a sliding roof (Spain), but finds rain water leaking in through the roof, which is impossible to repair (Case C-32/12 *Duarte Hueros v Autociba SA and Automóviles Citroën España SA* ECLI:EU:C:2013:637); the story of Mr Wittmer in Germany who buys tiles for the roof of his house, but when two thirds of the tiles have been laid, he notices shading on the tiles (Joined Cases C-65/09 and C-87/09 *Weber and Others* ECLI:EU:C:2011:396). In the field of copyright, the appealing story of 'Suske en Wiske' (Spike and Suzy) illustrates another autonomous concept in EU law, i.e. 'parody' (Case C-201/13 *Deckmyn and Vrijheidsfonds v Vandersteen and Others* ECLI:EU:C:2014:2132).

2028 Directive 2011/83 on consumer rights, Art 9 (period of 14 days to withdraw from a distance or off-premises contract, without giving any reason).

2029 Case C-91/92 *Faccini Dori* ECLI:EU:C:1994:292.

2030 The (then applicable) Council Directive 85/577/EEC of 20 December 1985 to protect the consumer in respect of contracts negotiated away from business premises [1985] OJ L372/31.

> Directive vis-à-vis the trader with whom she concluded the contract. A directive cannot directly impose obligations on an individual. However, the national court must interpret national law as far as possible in the light of the wording and purpose of the Directive.[2031] If this is impossible, Ms Faccini Dori can ask the Italian State to make good the loss she suffered. If Member States fail to transpose a directive, EU law requires them to make good the damage caused to individuals, in accordance with the conditions for State liability.[2032]

The facts of the case are easy for pupils to relate to. The relevance of EU law for the static citizen is demonstrated once more (iv). The story provides an opportunity for explaining that directives contain obligations for Member States (Article 288 TFEU). If a Member State does not transpose a directive in time, individuals can rely on their rights under the directive in their relationship with the Member State (vertical direct effect), because the State cannot take advantage of its own failure to comply with EU law. However, directives do not impose obligations on individuals (no horizontal direct effect).[2033] This is, admittedly, content which is only suitable for advanced levels of EDC. Still, it illustrates specific features of the EU legal order and shows how EU law functions as a multilevel system, thus providing additional content to national citizenship (i).

271 Rights in the Digital Single Market: Content Services

The story of so-called 'free' software

The Digital Single Market is another interesting theme for pupils. When shopping online, the static citizen is protected by EU consumer rights (iv).[2034] The *Content Services* case illustrates the challenges, the need to

---

2031 Para 30.

2032 Para 27. Conditions in Joined Cases C-6/90 and C-9/90 *Francovich and Bonifaci* ECLI:EU:C:1991:428, paras 39–41.

2033 Case 152/84 *Marshall* ECLI:EU:C:1986:84, para 48; Case C-555/07 *Kücükdeveci* ECLI:EU:C:2010:21, para 46; Case C-176/12 *Association de médiation sociale* ECLI:EU:C:2014:2, para 36. See text to n 1822. Condition of clear, precise and unconditional provisions.

2034 I.a. Commission EU Citizenship Report 2013: EU citizens: your rights, your future COM(2013) 269, 5; see n 2008; also JL da Cruz Vilaça and others (eds), *The internal market and the digital economy*, vol 1 (XXVIII FIDE Congress Lisbon/Estoril (23-26 May 2018), Almedina 2018). 'The Digital Single Market ensures free movement of persons, services and capital and allows individuals and businesses to access seamlessly and to exercise online activities under conditions of fair competition, high level of consumer and personal data protec-

enhance consumer trust, and the response in the form of EU norms.[2035] Pupils and teachers will recognise this situation: when downloading 'free' software from the internet, they fill in a registration form, tick a box to accept the general conditions, and then receive a message of welcome to the community of subscribers... with the contractual obligation to pay.

> 'Free' downloading is possible on the website of Content Services, a company operating in Germany and accessible in Austria (in German). The problem is that by accepting the general conditions, the internet users—unknowingly—waive their right of withdrawal. They receive an email with their username and password to access the website, followed by an invoice of EUR 96 for 12 months. The invoice states that there is no option of cancelling the contract as the user has waived the right of withdrawal. An Austrian body protecting the rights of consumers challenges this practice in court in Vienna. Austria has implemented EU Directive 97/7 on the protection of consumers in respect of distance contracts, which requires information on the right of withdrawal to be provided to the consumer.[2036] On the Content Services website this information is only accessible by clicking on a hyperlink on the sign-up page or in the email. The ECJ recalls that the purpose of the Directive is to afford consumers extensive protection by giving them a number of rights in relation to distance contracts, i.a. to avoid a reduction of the information provided to the consumer.[2037] The ECJ interprets the Directive to the effect that a business practice making the required information accessible only via a hyperlink on a website is not sufficient, since that information is neither 'given' by that under-

---

tion, irrespective of nationality or place of residence', in <ec.europa.eu/commission/priorities/digital-single-market_en>.

2035 Commission Communication 'A Digital Single Market Strategy for Europe' COM(2015) 0192 final; European Parliament Resolution of 26 May 2016 on the Single Market Strategy [2018] OJ C76/112; Commission Communication on the Mid-Term Review on the implementation of the Digital Single Market Strategy: A Connected Digital Single Market for All COM(2017) 228 final. See also Regulation (EU) 2017/2394 of the European Parliament and of the Council of 12 December 2017 on cooperation between national authorities responsible for the enforcement of consumer protection laws and repealing Regulation (EC) No 2006/2004 [2017] OJ L 345/1.

2036 Directive 97/7/EC of the European Parliament and of the Council of 20 May 1997 on the protection of consumers in respect of distance contracts [1997] OJ L144/19, Art 5(1).

2037 Dir 97/7, recital 11; Case C-49/11 *Content Services Ltd* ECLI:EU:C:2012:419, para 36.

taking nor 'received' by the consumer and a website is not a 'durable medium' as required by the Directive.[2038]

Consumer rights, including those related to distance contracts, are currently to be found in the Consumer Rights Directive (2011).[2039] The Directive is imperative in nature: contractual terms which waive or restrict the rights resulting from the Directive cannot be binding on the consumer.[2040] The Member States cannot provide for a different level of consumer protection, neither more nor less (i).[2041] An evaluation report by the Commission points to the lack of awareness among consumers and traders of the Directive's provisions (one of the factors limiting its effectiveness).[2042] In addition to pilot projects to raise awareness of EU consumer rights and trader responsibilities,[2043] I propose to incorporate EU consumer rights in the EU dimension of EDC in mainstream education. This is in keeping with EDC standards (c-1). Empowered consumers are, moreover, a significant driver of growth.[2044] The EU's supporting competence can be used via

---

2038 Para 51.

2039 Directive 2011/83 on consumer rights, Art 1 (legal basis Art 114 TFEU); 'through the achievement of a high level of consumer protection, to contribute to the proper functioning of the internal market by approximating certain aspects of the laws, regulations and administrative provisions of the Member States concerning contracts concluded between consumers and traders'.

2040 Consumer Rights Dir, Art 25. On the right of withdrawal, Art 9 (and Ch III). Other possible case for EDC: Case C-112/11 *ebookers.com Deutschland* ECLI:EU:C:2012:487.

2041 Consumer Rights Dir, Art 4 (level of harmonisation).

2042 Commission Report on the application of Directive 2011/83/EU of the European Parliament and of the Council of 25 October 2011 on consumer rights COM(2017) 259 final, i.a. point 5; Commission Staff working document Evaluation of the Consumer Rights Directive Accompanying the document Report from the Commission to the European Parliament and the Council on the application of Directive 2011/83/EU of the European Parliament and of the Council of 25 October 2011 on consumer rights SWD(2017) 169 final, i.a. points 4.3 and 6.1.1 (low and uneven enforcement is linked to consumers' and traders' low level of awareness about their rights and duties).

2043 Commission Report on the application of Directive 2011/83/EU of the European Parliament and of the Council of 25 October 2011 on consumer rights COM(2017) 259 final, point 6, conclusion.

2044 Commission Staff working paper 'Consumer Empowerment in the EU' SEC(2011) 469 final: empowered consumers intensify competition and innovation; 'Consumer empowerment depends not only on good cognitive skills, but also on knowledge of consumer rights and information, well-known and effective non-governmental organisations and public authorities, an active media and simple and accessible means of redress.'.

a contextual interpretation of the legal bases in Articles 165 juncto 169 TFEU.[2045]

6. Environmental rights and obligations

272 The right to clean water: Folk

The story of the Austrian fisherman

Cases such as *Folk* and *ClientEarth* illustrate the influence of static citizens proactive with regard to the environment (iv). Whether they act alone (*Folk*) or in an environmental organisation (*ClientEarth*), citizens play an essential role in making their own governments comply with EU directives protecting the environment.

> Gert Folk likes fishing in his part of the river Mürz in Austria. He has fishing rights on a stretch of the river about 12 km long. To his regret, a hydroelectric powerplant situated upstream causes significant variations in the water level. Some areas normally submerged under water dry up rapidly, small and young fish are trapped and cannot follow the downstream flow of the river, and die. He submits a complaint about environmental damage resulting in the increased mortality of fish to the Austrian authorities. The authorities reject the claim of environmental damage, because the Governor of the Land (Styria) has issued an authorisation for the operation of the hydroelectric plant in accordance with Austrian law. On appeal, Mr Folk claims that Austrian law is incompatible with the Environmental Liability Directive. This Directive is based on the 'polluter-pays' principle in order to prevent and remedy environmental damage.[2046] Mr Folk argues that the existence of damage to water cannot be denied on the grounds that it is covered by an authorisation under national law, but that water damage must be defined in accordance with the Directive, i.e. any damage which has a significant adverse effect on the ecological, chemical or

---

2045 See § 282 .

2046 Directive of the European Parliament and of the Council of 21 April 2004 on environmental liability with regard to the prevention and remedying of environmental damage [2004] OJ L143/56, as amended (The Environmental Liability Directive), Art 1, recital 2 ('an operator whose activity has caused the environmental damage or the imminent threat of such damage is to be held financially liable').

quantitative status or ecological potential of the water.[2047] In answer to a preliminary question on the interpretation of the Directive, the ECJ rules that the definition of water damage in the Directive precludes national law which excludes, generally and automatically, water damage from being categorised as environmental damage just because it is covered by an authorisation.[2048] Moreover, the Directive grants individuals a right to a review procedure. Persons affected by environmental damage have the right to submit observations about that damage (or an imminent threat of such damage) and to request the competent authority to take action.[2049] The ECJ rules that national law cannot deny the right to initiate a review procedure—following environmental damage—to persons holding fishing rights.[2050]

This case clearly illustrates how EU law provides additional content to the rights which Gert Folk derives from national law (i). This content is of actual relevance to all citizens, including those who do not cross borders, like the man fishing in his local river (iv). It concerns several foundational objectives and principles of the EU (ii). The Union shall work for the sustainable development of Europe, aiming at a high level of protection and improvement of the quality of the environment (Article 3 TEU, developed in Article 191(1) TFEU).[2051] These aims must be integrated into the policies of the EU (Article 37 CFR). The foundational principles on which environmental policy is based are the precautionary principle and the principles that preventive action should be taken, that environmental damage should as a priority be rectified at source, and that the polluter should pay (Article 191(2) TFEU). *Folk* illustrates the principle of conferral (the legal basis for the Environmental Liability Directive is Article 192 TFEU).[2052] Environmental rights invite critical thinking (iv). *Can an individual person*

2047 Art 2(1)(b).
2048 Case C-529/15 *Folk* ECLI:EU:C:2017:419, para 34.
2049 Environmental Liability Dir, Art 12.
2050 Para 49.
2051 See also Art 3(5), Art 21(2)(d-f) TEU (external action); and Art 114 TFEU (harmonisation).
2052 Then Art 175 TEC. See on that legal basis also: Decision No 1386/2013/EU of the European Parliament and of the Council of 20 November 2013 on a General Union Environment Action Programme to 2020 'Living well, within the limits of our planet' [2013] OJ L354/171 (the 7th Environment Action programme); Regulation (EU) No 1293/2013 of the European Parliament and of the Council of 11 December 2013 on the establishment of a Programme for the Environment and Climate Action (LIFE) and repealing Regulation (EC)

complain about environmental damage by a company, even when the company has been given a national authorisation? If a Member State allows a company to act within its territory, can the EU impose more stringent EU standards?

Furthermore, *Folk* illustrates how individuals, like a simple fisherman, can successfully defend their rights, even against powerful opponents (Member States and a hydroelectric powerplant) and thus contribute to the achievement of foundational EU objectives.[2053]

273 *The right to clean air: ClientEarth*

The story of air quality plans

By the deadline set by the Air Quality Directive,[2054] the pollutants in the ambient air in the UK have exceeded limit values. The UK omits to fulfil its obligation to apply for postponement of the deadline by submitting an air quality plan, setting out appropriate measures to keep the exceedance period as short as possible. ClientEarth, a non-governmental organisation for the protection of the environment, asks the Secretary of State for revised air quality plans to see how conformity with the nitrogen dioxide limit values will be achieved, but the claim is dismissed in court. In response to a preliminary question from the UK Supreme Court, the ECJ rules that natural or legal persons who are directly concerned by the exceeded limit values, must be in a position to require the competent authorities to establish an air quality plan complying with the Directive, if necessary by bringing an action in court. Individuals can rely on unconditional and sufficiently precise provisions of a directive against public bodies (vertical direct effect). This applies particularly in respect of a directive whose objective is to reduce atmospheric pollution and to protect public health.[2055] Pursuant to the principle of sincere cooperation, Member States must ensure judicial protection of an individual's rights based on EU law.[2056]

No 614/2007 [2013] OJ L347/185 ; Directive 2011/92/EU of the European Parliament and of the Council of 13 December 2011 on the assessment of the effects of certain public and private projects on the environment [2012] OJ L26/1 (amended by Directive 2014/52/EU).

2053 See also Case C-723/17 *Craeynest and Others* ECLI:EU:C:2019:533.

2054 Directive 2008/50/EC of the European Parliament and of the Council of 21 May 2008 on ambient air quality and cleaner air for Europe [2008] OJ L152/1, especially Art 23(1). Dir based on Art 175 TEC, in force.

2055 Case C-404/13 *ClientEarth* ECLI:EU:C:2014:2382, paras 54–5.

2056 Arts 4(3) and 19(1) TEU; Case C 432/05 *Unibet* EU:C:2007:163, para 38.

The battle for clean air continues.[2057] Empowered citizens, taking action to exercise their EU rights—even procedural rights—have an impact on environmental protection. In *Schmidberger*, the right to freedom of expression and freedom of association of an environmental association in the Tirol was able—proportionally to the objective—to limit an internal market freedom.[2058] Alongside citizens, the Commission, too, enforces Member States' obligation to respect environmental directives.[2059] Member States cannot evade EU obligations by issuing national authorisations. The EU acts as a neutral observer to monitor environmental protection in the regions of Europe and guards the application of elementary Treaty-based principles, such as 'the polluter pays'.

Climate change and the added value of EU action can also be discussed in the classroom on the basis of cases such as *Air Transport Association of America* (involving major US airlines in Europe) and the Kyoto Protocol.[2060] The Directive establishing the scheme for greenhouse gas emission allowance trading was adopted to comply with commitments made by the EU and the Member States under the Kyoto Protocol.[2061] While an individual Member State alone may be quite powerless against a global actor

---

2057 I.a. Commission Decision (EU) 2019/1565 of 4 September 2019 on the proposed citizens' initiative entitled 'Actions on Climate Emergency' [2019] OJ L 241/8. National case law and media, e.g. <euobserver.com/environment/140764>.

2058 Text to n 1929.

2059 I.a. Case C-441/17 *Commission v Poland* ECLI:EU:C:2018:255: the Commission claims that Poland has failed to fulfil its obligations under the Habitats Directive and Birds Directive (Dir 92/43/EEC and Dir 2009/147/EC) in its forest management plan for the Białowieża Forest District.

2060 Case C-366/10 *Air Transport Association of America and Others* ECLI:EU:C:2011:864, involving also American Airlines Inc., Continental Airlines Inc. and United Airlines Inc.

2061 Directive 2003/87/EC of the European Parliament and of the Council of 13 October 2003 establishing a scheme for greenhouse gas emission allowance trading within the Community and amending Council Directive 96/61/EC [2003] OJ L275/32. The EU approved the Kyoto Protocol (its provisions thus are an integral part of the EU legal order). In *ATAA*, the ECJ finds no factor affecting the validity of Directive 2008/101/EC of the European Parliament and of the Council of 19 November 2008 amending Directive 2003/87/EC so as to include aviation activities in the scheme for greenhouse gas emission allowance trading within the Community [2009] OJ L8/3. See, as an example for the classroom in the field of technology, Regulation (EU) 2019/631 of the European Parliament and of the Council of 17 April 2019 setting CO2 emission performance standards for new passenger cars and for new light commercial vehicles, and repealing Regulations (EC) No 443/2009 and (EU) No

like the US, objectives may be more easily achieved through cooperation in the EU context. The EU is better placed to uphold the foundational values, objectives and principles in a globalised world, and its added value is clear—but so are the ongoing challenges it faces.[2062]

274 The EU dimension of education for sustainable development

The State Parties to the Convention on the Rights of the Child agree that education shall be directed to the 'development of respect for the natural environment' (Article 29(e)).[2063] In EU Member States, this compulsory educational aim cannot be achieved without an EU dimension. Clear water and clean air do not stop at national borders. EU citizens should be empowered to act to protect the natural environment and have some notion of the EU's competences in this field (conferral). Citizens who want to have a say about a wind turbine project (EU funded) in their local area, struggle to identify the authority responsible.[2064] In a complex governance structure, accountability problems arise. All reasonable steps are must be taken to increase transparency, including adding a basic EU dimension to EDC. The environment is an important concern of young

---

510/2011 [2019] OJ L 111/1 (both civic competences and competences in science and technology have an EU dimension, in that regard overlapping competences); see n 1051.

2062 See also Regulation (EU) 2018/1999 of the European Parliament and of the Council of 11 December 2018 on the Governance of the Energy Union and Climate Action, amending Regulations (EC) No 663/2009 and (EC) No 715/2009 of the European Parliament and of the Council, Directives 94/22/EC, 98/70/EC, 2009/31/EC, 2009/73/EC, 2010/31/EU, 2012/27/EU and 2013/30/EU of the European Parliament and of the Council, Council Directives 2009/119/EC and (EU) 2015/652 and repealing Regulation (EU) No 525/2013 of the European Parliament and of the Council [2018] L 328/1. Further J Scott, 'Can the EU Deliver on Citizen Expectations in the Fight against Climate Change?' in M Dougan, NN Shuibhne and E Spaventa (eds), *Empowerment and Disempowerment of the European Citizen* (Hart 2012).

2063 UN ComRC 'General Comment No 1 (2001)- Article 29(1): The Aims of Education' Doc CRC/GC/2001/1, para 13. See further UNGA Res 70/1 'Transforming our world: The 2030 Agenda for Sustainable Development' (25 September 2015) A/RES/70/1; and SDG 4. See for operationalisation, CoE Reference Framework of Competences for Democratic Culture, Vol 2: Descriptors of competences for democratic culture (2018), key descriptor 122, also 2043.

2064 Commission White paper of 1 March 2017 on the future of Europe COM(2017) 2025 final, scenario 5.

citizens.[2065] Education for sustainable development overlaps and interacts with EDC and, to that extent, comes within the scope of the Charter on EDC/HRE and of EDC standards in general.[2066] An adequate EU dimension empowers citizens to exercise their rights and responsibilities regarding the environment (c-1) and to participate in democratic life with those aims in mind (c-3).

275 Many other examples

The foundational principles such as conferral, subsidiarity, proportionality, or sincere cooperation, and the role of the European Parliament, the Council, or the Commission as constitutional actors, can be illustrated in cases such as *Council v Commission*, *Tobacco Advertising*, or *Commission v Austria*.[2067] Case law also illustrates the role of the EU in resolving tensions between Member States (in accordance with the foundational objective of peace, Article 3(1) TEU).[2068] Disagreement with regard to refugee quotas, for instance, were the object of *Slovakia and Hungary v Council*.[2069]

2065 See Flash Eurobarometer 455, European Youth (January 2018) (50% of respondents finds that protection of the environment and the fight against climate change should be a priority for the EU); confirmed by consistent action of the European Youth Climate Movement. See also Lindfelt, 'Article 44: Right to Petition', 1158 (environment is the most important concern in their exercise of the right to petition; 'This is hardly surpising as the division of labour between the EU and the Member States as to competences is by no means clear to the citizen').

2066 Charter on EDC/HRE, explanatory memorandum para 33. See also H Lödén, MS McCallion and P Wall, 'Teaching Citizenship: What if the EU Is Part of the Solution and Not the Problem?' (2014) 10 Journal of Political Science Education 386, choosing environmental issues to show how EU education can be part of citizenship education.

2067 Case C-409/13 *Council v Commission* ECLI:EU:C:2015:217 (withdrawal of legislative proposal); Case C-376/98 *Germany v Parliament and Council ('Tobacco Advertising')* ECLI:EU:C:2000:544; *Commission v Austria* (n 1382). Other: Case C-295/90 *European Parliament v Council* ECLI:EU:C:1992:294; Case C-65/93 *Parliament v Council* ECLI:EU:C:1995:91; Case C-411/06 *Commission v Parliament and Council* ECLI:EU:C:2009:518; Case C-540/03 *Parliament v Council* ECLI:EU:C:2006:429; Case C-128/17 *Poland v Parliament and Council* ECLI:EU:C:2019:194. See also the role of the institutions in *Schrems* and its follow-up.

2068 E.g. Case C-145/04 *Spain v UK* ECLI:EU:C:2006:543; Case C-364/10 *Hungary v Slovak Republic* ECLI:EU:C:2012:630; Case C-457/18 *Slovenia v Croatia* pending; Case C-591/17 *Austria v Germany* ECLI:EU:C:2019:504.

2069 Joined Cases C-643/15 and C-647/15 *Slovakia and Hungary v Council* ECLI:EU:C:2017:631.

It should be emphasised that—in all the examples cited—the aim is not to technically 'explain' the cases to pupils, but to give context so that pupils engage with the issues at stake. Diverging viewpoints, complexities, criticism of EU action, and uncertainties as to how to uphold the foundational values of Article 2 TEU should be addressed.[2070] The aim is to empower EU citizens by developing citizenship competences in the fullest sense (knowledge, skills, attitudes) and increasing awareness of the common values of Article 2 TEU.

Conclusion to Part three

276 A combined reading of EDC standards and EU law leads to substantial content for the EU dimension of EDC in mainstream education

In the search for balanced 'EU citizenship education', the discomfort caused by statal thinking has been resolved by using the consensual concept of EDC of the Council of Europe Charter on EDC/HRE and by pragmatically determining relevant content for its components based on EU law in interaction with Member State law. To respect EU primary law and Member State constitutions, existing national EDC should be extended by a genuine 'EU dimension', adapting it to the multilevel system of governance in which citizens in the EU live (adaptation perspective).[2071] Four criteria have been identified for determining relevant content for the EU dimension of EDC in mainstream education: (i) additional content for national EDC, (ii) significant content, i.e. relating to foundational (EU primary law) values, objectives and principles, (iii) inviting critical thinking and (iv) affecting the large majority of EU citizens, including static citizens (those at home).

The effects of a combined reading of EDC standards and EU law are considerable. EU law impacts so definitively and specifically on the EDC components that EDC of EU citizens is no longer adequate if it lacks an

2070 See e.g. the story of *Dano* (text to n 1426), *Gravier* and *Bressol* (text to n 1381). Various cases have led to conflicting observations of Member States and of commentators—which is healthy in a democracy (e.g. *Viking*, *Laval*, *Deutsche Bank*, etc). In particular, austerity cases can illustrate complexity, e.g. *Anagnostakis* (n 1557); Joined Cases C-8/15 P to C-10/15 P *Ledra* ECLI:EU:C:2016:701. See C Kilpatrick, 'On the Rule of Law and Economic Emergency: The Degradation of Basic Legal Values in Europe's Bailouts" (2015) 35 Oxford Journal of Legal Studies 325' (2015) 35 Oxford Journal of Legal Studies 325.

2071 § 151 .

EU dimension. The analysis in Part three has indicated that acceptable and adaptable education in EU Member States must include an EU dimension to ensure that pupils realise their full potential as citizens.[2072] Learning content for the EU dimension is based, firstly, on the classic EU citizenship rights listed in Articles 20–24 TFEU, secondly, on the participation rights based on Title II TEU, and thirdly, on all the rights derived from EU law and corresponding obligations. In application of the four relevance criteria, they provide relevant content for the EU dimension in respect of several EDC components, such as (b) knowledge, skills and understanding, attitudes and behaviour, especially where the aim is to empower learners to (c-1) exercise rights and responsibilities, (c-2) value diversity, and (c-3) play an active part in democratic life. The EU dimension in education is not, of course, limited to rights and obligations. However, their impact on the three empowerment aims is undeniable. Alignment of EDC with EU law therefore requires adaptation of the substance of national EDC. The incorporation of an EU dimension in mainstream education ensures consistency of (citizenship) education with EU law. Moreover, exploring rights and obligations may be a bridge to other areas of EU learning, e.g. in historical, cultural or economic aspects, and may reach into deeper consideration of the foundational values, objectives and principles on which the EU is based. Learning about and reflecting on the DNA of the EU may give pupils a greater sense of their own European identity.

The content and method for EU learning must be seen in context. In order to enhance objective, critical and pluralistic EU learning in school, with no aim of indoctrination, two pillars are proposed: EU primary law and case teaching. Thus, Part three consists of legal fieldwork which may help actors in the education field to translate the EU dimension of EDC into learning outcomes. It provides a basis for teachers and their trainers to develop teaching packages adapted for general or vocational training. There is no point waiting for consensus on the democratic legitimacy of the EU before educating citizens for democracy. Certainly, there are unsatisfactory aspects to some EU rights—especially citizenship rights—and ambiguities must be acknowledged. Yet, *notwithstanding* the non-statal features of the political rights of EU citizens and the specific characteristics of democracy in the EU, and even *because* of them, EDC standards require additional content in education, respecting the autonomy of the EU and vertical and horizontal balances of power. If EU citizenship is additional to national citizenship (Article 9 TEU), a corresponding additional EU

2072 Text to n 1016.

dimension of EDC is necessary. In a society based on the rule of law, EDC standards should be commensurate with the legal position of EU citizens and empower them to exercise their rights and meet their obligations whatever the legal source (EU or Member State level) and however complex the struggle for academic categorisation from the statal perspective.

While the schema of modes of reception of exogenic norms in the EU legal order has clarified how EDC standards of the Council of Europe produce effects in the EU legal order, the red line has to be respected, reflecting the specific characteristics of the EU. Therefore, using mainly Council of Europe standards is not the optimal route for educating EU citizens, as they leave areas of uncertainty. The consequences of EU membership are substantial. EU norms should be adopted setting out a framework for an adequate and adapted dimension of EDC for EU citizens. The EU dimension of EDC is an indispensable element in the progressive realisation of a more democratic Union.

277 *Proposal for recitals*

Based on the analysis in Part three, these recitals for the preamble of a hypothetical EU legislative act are proposed:

> *Whereas EU law provides relevant content for the EU dimension to be incorporated into national EDC in mainstream education (hereafter 'the EU dimension of EDC').*
> *Whereas the content of the EU dimension of EDC is additional to existing national EDC; is significant, i.e. relating to foundational values, objectives and principles of the EU (based on EU primary law); invites critical thinking; and affects the large majority of EU citizens, including 'static' citizens.*
> *Whereas the EU dimension of EDC empowers EU citizens to exercise and respect the rights and obligations provided for under the Treaties and the Charter of Fundamental Rights of the EU, empowers to value diversity and to play an active part in democratic life at EU and at Member State level.*

The time has come to analyse the competences for this hypothetical EU legislative act.

PART IV Competence to provide for the EU dimension in Education for Democratic Citizenship

Introduction: Actors

278 Actors designing and implementing the EU dimension in EDC curricula

In Part three, a reading of EDC standards jointly with EU law led to the identification of substantial content for the EU dimension of EDC. Given the importance of this dimension for the empowerment of EU citizens, the question for Part four is: who has the competence to incorporate the EU dimension into the national EDC curriculum?

A curriculum is 'a plan for learning in the form of the description of learning outcomes, of learning content and of learning processes for a specified period of study'.[2073] Actors at four levels can be distinguished: competent authorities prescribe the curriculum by laying down what must be learned at different stages of education (system level); teachers and pedagogical leaders develop the prescribed curriculum, adapting it to the school context and education needs (institutional level); teachers, and sometimes learners, develop, interpret and apply the prescribed and the institutional curriculum in teaching plans and instruction materials (subject or classroom level); learners experience the curriculum planned by teachers and develop (educational) competences (learner level).[2074] In Member States with centralised decision-making, public authorities responsible for education, or the bodies appointed by them, decide on the curriculum. In decentralised systems, educational institutions and teachers decide on the content and aims of the curriculum (e.g. school-based curriculum).[2075]

In addition to the actors at these four levels, other stakeholders may influence the curriculum: textbook authors and publishers, experts and scholars, quality assurance bodies, organisations assessing citizenship edu-

---

2073 CoE Reference Framework of Competences for Democratic Culture, Vol 3: Guidance for implementation (2018), p 13. Analogue: Commission/EACEA/Eurydice, Citizenship Education in Europe (2012), p 17 (curriculum: 'any official steering document (national or central-level) containing programmes of study, or learning content, learning objectives, attainment targets, guidelines on pupil assessment or syllabuses').

2074 Levels in CoE Reference Framework of Competences for Democratic Culture, Vol 3: Guidance for implementation (2018), p 14.

2075 Ibid, p 14.

cation, churches, etc.[2076] Taking formal, non-formal, and informal education together, other actors should also be mentioned, such as parents, youth organisations, NGOs, networks, media, and grassroots actors in civil society.[2077]

Part four will focus on the competence of public authorities as actors to formulate curricula. In Part three, 'competence' was an educational concept, a combination of knowledge, skills and attitudes.[2078] In Part four, 'competence' is used in the legal sense: who is authorised to regulate the EU dimension of EDC and on what legal basis?

279 Structure

This Part consists of two chapters. Chapter nine examines the conferral of competence on the EU. It starts by setting out the principles: the Member States enjoy the original competence in the field of education; the EU has a supporting competence based on Articles 165–166 TFEU, yet within limits. The requirement that the EU must fully respect Member States' responsibility for the content of teaching seems like an insurmountable obstacle,

---

2076 See e.g. Council Recommendation of 22 May 2018 on promoting common values, inclusive education, and the European dimension of teaching [2018] OJ C195/1, Explanatory memorandum: 'promoting awareness of EU citizenship and the values attached to it ... requires a joint effort of all actors concerned at all levels—the Member States, including their local and regional authorities, EU institutions and civil society'; Council Recommendation of 22 May 2017 on the European Qualifications Framework for lifelong learning and repealing the recommendation of the European Parliament and of the Council of 23 April 2008 on the establishment of the European Qualifications Framework for lifelong learning [2017] OJ C189/15, recital 7 and para 7. For the role of textbook authors, see e.g. F Piedade and others, 'Learning About the European Union in Times of Crisis: Portuguese Textbooks' Normative Visions of European Citizenship' (2018) 17 Journal of Social Science Education 31: the 'generalized resistance by textbook authors regarding the inclusion of pedagogical contents that transcend the national level' is identified as one of the main shortcomings in education in Portugal. See the role of experts and scholars in CoE work on EDC in § 31 ff. On the influence of churches in Spain, see Motos, 'The Controversy over Civic Education in Spain', 270–71: 'on claims of the Catholic Church and other conservative actors that moral education was exclusively reserved for families, not for schools and government via EDC' (n 462).

2077 On actors and stakeholders, see i.a. Charter paras 5(b), (d), (i), 6, and 8. Networks, i.a. NECE, DARE, EUROCLIO; see further <lllplatform.eu/who-we-are/members-and-partners/>.

2078 Council Recommendation of 22 May 2018 on key competences for lifelong learning, definition in Annex. Also text to n 849.

precluding any EU initiatives to formulate content for the EU dimension of EDC in mainstream education. Therefore, in order to understand to what extent the EU is competent to support the EU dimension of EDC in the Member States, three aspects of the legal basis for EU competence are examined in more detail. The Treaty expression 'quality education' (Article 165(1) TFEU) is linked to the third anchor point of the study, the right to education. The 'European dimension in education' in the legal basis (Article 165(2) first indent) is clarified and new elements are explored relating to the 'participation of young people in democratic life in Europe' (Article 165(2) fifth indent). The human rights-based approach to education (promoted by the UN and UNESCO) enriches the significance of the wording of Article 165 TFEU.

Chapter ten explores the exercise of education competences by the EU and the Member States. The EU has to respect the principles of subsidiarity and proportionality. Possible EU measures for the inclusion of an EU dimension in EDC are examined, with suggestions for the way ahead. The last section examines Member State competence in education and draws attention to certain limits to national educational autonomy.

CHAPTER 9 Conferral of competence to the EU

A *The principles*

280 *Conferral, subsidiarity and proportionality*

EU competences are governed by the principle of conferral: 'the Union shall act only within the limits of the competences conferred upon it by the Member States in the Treaties to attain the objectives set out therein'; competences not conferred upon the Union in the Treaties remain with the Member States (Articles 4 and 5(2) TEU). When the Union uses competences which are shared with the Member States or supporting competences (thus non-exclusive competences), it must respect the principle of subsidiarity: the Union can only act if and in so far as the objectives of the proposed action cannot be sufficiently achieved by the Member States, but can rather, by reason of the scale or effects of the proposed action, be better achieved at Union level (Article 5(3) TEU). In addition, the principle of proportionality requires that the content and form of all Union action shall not exceed what is necessary to achieve the objectives of the Treaties (Article 5(4) TEU).[2079]

Applied to citizenship education, three main questions arise. Does the EU *have* the competence to act in the field of EDC and its EU dimension? (the conferral question). Does the EU need to *use* that competence? (the subsidiarity question). Does the EU need to use its competence in a *specific* way, or could it be used in a *less intrusive* way? (the proportionality question).[2080]

In education, subsidiarity is a recurrent theme. Its multiple meanings must be differentiated.

2079 See also Protocol (No 2) and Art 352(2) TFEU.

2080 D Edward, 'Subsidiarity as a Legal Concept' in P Cardonnel, A Rosas and N Wahl (eds), *Constitutionalising the EU Judicial System: Essays in Honour of Pernilla Lindh* (Hart 2012) 99–100; Presidency Conclusions of the Edinburgh European Council of 11–12 December 1992, Overall approach to the application by the Council of the subsidiarity principle and article 3b of the Treaty on European Union (Annex 1 to Part A), SN 456/1/92 REV, 13: Should the EU act? What should be the intensity or nature of EU action?

281 *Subsidiarity as a meta-constitutional concept*

In the balance of powers between the EU and the Member States, subsidiarity relates to the fundamental issue of determining 'who does best what?'. The objective is, while creating an ever-closer union among the peoples of Europe, to take decisions as closely as possible to the citizen (Article 1 TEU). Subsidiarity thus operates at several levels. Firstly, at a meta-constitutional level, subsidiarity is the rationale underpinning the attribution of powers in the legal bases: are particular competences *conferred on the EU or not* by the Treaties? The Union can only act within the limits of conferred competences to attain the objectives set out in the Treaties. Secondly, at a legislative level, subsidiarity must be respected in the exercise of the conferred competences. The principle of subsidiarity laid down in the Treaties (Article 5(2) TEU) regulates the *use or not* of EU competences (subsidiarity in the strict sense). It is a political principle, the basis of sound multi-level governance, which is also reflected in the choice of legal instruments (no regulations where directives suffice, no directives where recommendations suffice).[2081] Compliance with the legal principle of subsidiarity is subject to review by the ECJ. The Treaties thus reflect the principle of subsidiarity in several ways. The principles of conferral, subsidiarity and proportionality are interrelated.

The understanding of subsidiarity as a meta-constitutional concept, the logic underpinning the conferral of competences on the Union, is highly relevant to the discussion of supporting competences, which have been spelled out in great detail in the Treaties.[2082] Education is a good illustration of this: within the conferral of competences, essential limits have been set, reflecting the subsidiarity concerns.[2083]

In the pre-Maastricht period, with no express Treaty powers for education, Community education policy developed (without being called such) as a result of the exercise of powers conferred on the Community in other

---

2081 Edward, ibid, 94, 96 (subsidiarity reflects a weighty principle of public morality, not to assign to a greater and higher association what lesser and subordinate organisations can do (Pope Pius XI); it is a principle of good governance); K Lenaerts and P Van Ypersele, 'Le principe et subsidiarité et son contexte: étude de l'article 3B du Traité CE' [1994] Cahiers de droit européen 3, 8–10. For the principle of proportionality and instruments, see § 314 .

2082 R Schütze, 'Cooperative federalism constitutionalised: the emergence of complementary competences in the EC legal order' (2006) 31 ELRev 167, 183: complementary competences associated with the principle of subsidiarity.

2083 For the example of health, see Schütze, ibid.

fields: a spill-over of the internal market,[2084] a surprising link, at the time, with the principle of non-discrimination[2085] and a far-reaching effect of vocational training.[2086] Some authors criticised the active role of the ECJ in case law such as *Gravier* (leading to 'competence creep').[2087] The ECJ paved the way for education competences in the Treaty, and maybe especially for the need to place constitutional limits on these competences in the Treaties.[2088]

2084 See early: Case 9/74 *Casagrande* ECLI:EU:C:1975:11: removal of educational obstacles to cross-border activities (implied powers). Interesting is Council Directive 77/486 of 25 July 1977 on the education of the children of migrant workers [1977] OJ L199/32: the objective of establishing an internal market persuaded Member States to adopt EU legislation which made inroads into their educational autonomy, including the learning content for children of workers in compulsory education (note, not higher education), residing with the worker in the host State. The Directive obliged the Member States to take appropriate measures to ensure teaching of the official language(s) of the host State and the mother tongue and culture of the country of origin (Art 2). Positive action had to be taken, four years were allowed for compliance and regular reporting required (Arts 4–5). The result was not satisfactory (Commission Report on the Education of Migrants' Children in the European Union COM(94) 423).

2085 Broad interpretation of 'vocational training' in Art 128 EEC brought situations within the scope of Art 7 EEC: Case 293/83 *Gravier* ECLI:EU:C:1985:69, paras 19–31; Case 24/86 *Blaizot* ECLI:EU:C:1988:43, paras 15–21; Case 263/86 *Humbel* ECLI:EU:C:1988:451.

2086 Case 242/87 *Commission v Council (Erasmus)* ECLI:EU:C:1989:217 (para 29: 'the perfectly legitimate aim that the development of a common policy should be in keeping with the general objectives of the Community, such as the achievement of a people's Europe, cannot lead to a change in the proper legal basis of measures which fall objectively under the common policy in question'); Case 56/88 *UK v CL (Petra)* ECLI:EU:C:1989:81; Joined Cases C-51/89, C-90/89 and C-94/89 *UK, France and Germany v Council* ECLI:EU:C:1991:241.

2087 For *Gravier*, see text to n 1377. Comments i.a. in J Field, *European Dimensions, Education, Training and the European Union* (Jessica Kingsley 1998) 56. See also J Lonbay, 'Education and the law: the Community context (European Community)' (1989) 14 ELRev 363; M Murphy, 'Covert action? Education, social policy and law in the European Union' (2003) 18 Journal of Education Policy 551; J-E Charlier and S Croché, 'How European Integration is Eroding National Control over Education Planning and Policy' (2005-2006) 37 European Education 7. Analysis also in A van den Brink, 'De begrenzing van de bevoegdheden van de Europese Unie als een gedeelde constitutionele opdracht' (2014) 62 SEW - Tijdschrift voor Europees en economisch Recht 266; and S Garben, 'Competence Creep Revisited' (2017) 55 JCMS 1.

2088 Shaw, 'Education and the Law in the European Community', 437; K Lenaerts, 'Education in European Community Law after "Maastricht"' (1994) 31 CML-

The 1992 Maastricht Treaty consolidated the *acquis communautaire* by introducing a legal basis for Community action in education.[2089] An important innovation was that the EU acquired competence for all types of education, including general education in primary and secondary schools.[2090] The 2009 Lisbon Treaty confirmed this: the EU 'shall have competence to carry out actions to support, coordinate or supplement the actions of the Member States' in the area of education, vocational training, and youth (Article 6 TFEU), with a legal basis in Articles 165 (education) and 166 (vocational training) TFEU. The Treaty uses careful language to authorise EU action and at the same time limit its scope, so as to preserve the paradigm of national educational autonomy.[2091] The length of the provision conferring competences in education is striking. There are 321 words in Article 165 TFEU (compare, e.g., with 131 words in Article 19 TFEU).

282 The legal basis in Articles 165 and 166 TFEU

Article 165(1) TFEU states that:

> The Union shall contribute to the development of quality education by encouraging cooperation between Member States and, if necessary, by supporting and supplementing their action, while fully respecting the responsibility of the Member States for the content of teaching and the organisation of education systems and their cultural and linguistic diversity.

The general objective of 'contributing to the development of quality education' may include EU action to promote the EU dimension in EDC in schools. It will be argued that quality education requires EDC with an EU dimension.[2092] Moreover, some specific objectives listed in paragraph 2 of Article 165 TFEU add to the potential of the legal basis for the EU to contribute to the development of the EU dimension of EDC: Union action

---

Rev 7, 9–10. See also B de Witte (ed) *European Community Law of Education* (Schriftenreihe Europäisches Recht 133, Nomos 1989).

2089 Art 126 EC, Art 149 EC through the Amsterdam Treaty, now Art 165 TFEU.

2090 Pépin, *The history of European cooperation in education and training. Europe in the making - an example*, 147.

2091 R Lane, 'New Community competences under the Maastricht Treaty' (1993) 30 CMLRev 939: 'clearly a softly-softly approach'.

2092 See also C Ferrari-Breeur, 'L'éducation et la formation professionnelle comme instruments de la citoyenneté européenne' in C Philip and P Soldatos (eds), *La citoyenneté européenne* (Collection études européennes, Chaire Jean Monnet 2000) 177.

shall be aimed at 'developing the European dimension in education, particularly through the teaching and dissemination of the languages of the Member States' (first indent) and at 'encouraging the participation of young people in democratic life in Europe' (fifth indent). Other specific objectives may be relevant as well.[2093] For vocational training, a legal basis for EU action supporting and supplementing the action of the Member States is provided in Article 166(1) TFEU.[2094] Here EU action to promote the EU dimension in EDC also dovetails with several of the specific aims mentioned in paragraph two of Article 166, i.a. the first, second, fourth and fifth aims.[2095]

Thus, in the EU legal order, providing for the EU dimension of EDC in the curriculum is first and foremost a task for the Member States. The EU only comes in to support, coordinate, or supplement.

In the period after 1992, tensions between the EU and Member State levels persisted.[2096] The Convention on the Future of Europe recalled that supporting measures 'apply to policy areas where the Member States have not transferred legislative competence to the Union, unless exceptionally and clearly specified in the relevant Treaty Article'; they allow the Union

2093 Such as 'promoting cooperation between educational establishments' and 'developing exchanges of information and experience on issues common to the education systems of the Member States' (Arts 165(2) third indent and fourth indent).

2094 Art 166 TFEU: 'The Union shall implement a vocational training policy which shall support and supplement the action of the Member States, while fully respecting the responsibility of the Member States for the content and organisation of vocational training.'.

2095 To 'facilitate adaptation to industrial changes', to 'improve initial and continuing vocational training in order to facilitate vocational integration and reintegration into the labour market', to 'develop exchanges of information and experience on issues common to the training systems of the Member States'. See also Regulation (EU) 2019/128 of the European Parliament and of the Council of 16 January 2019 establishing a European Centre for the Development of Vocational Training (Cedefop) and repealing Council Regulation (EEC) No 337/75 [2019] OJ L 30/90 (recital 4 refers to the needs of citizens and society). On the demarcation of Art 165 and 166 TFEU, see Ruffert, 'AEUV Art 165', Rn 11–12.

2096 In its White Paper, the Commission had highlighted the need to develop the European dimension in education (Commission White Paper of 29 November 1995 on education and training, Teaching and learning - towards the learning society COM(95) 590 final), but the Council expressed 'doubts and reservations', even about proposals concerning language learning. See Council Conclusions of 6 May 1996 on the White Paper "Teaching and learning: towards the learning society' [1996] OJ C195/1, e.g. para D.

to assist and supplement national policies 'where this is in the common interest of the Union and the Member States'.[2097] The Convention named the educational system among the 'basic public policy choices and social values of a Member State',[2098] an essential element of national identity. The Lisbon Treaty requires the EU to respect the national identities of Member States, inherent in their fundamental structures, political and constitutional (Article 4(2) TEU). In federal Member States, education policy is mostly reserved to the federated entities as part of their identity.[2099]

Member State competence in education corresponds to State responsibility for education in accordance with international agreements, such as the ICESCR and CRC, and underlined by the ECtHR.[2100] National educational autonomy is furthermore expressed in the paragraph-4 principle of the Charter on EDC/HRE.[2101]

283 The no-content limit

The EU has to respect several limits to its competence in the field of education. Firstly, Article 165(1) TFEU establishes some 'no go' areas: the EU can only act 'while fully respecting the responsibility of the Member States for the content of teaching and the organisation of education systems and their cultural and linguistic diversity'. Secondly, Article 165(4) TFEU prohibits the adoption of incentive measures which lead to the harmonisation of the laws or regulations of the Member States (in line with Article 2(5) TFEU). Since the Treaty excludes harmonisation in education, Article 352 TFEU cannot be used as a legal basis for harmonised EU citizenship education either.[2102]

For EU action aiming to develop the EU dimension in national school curricula, the requirement of full respect of Member States' responsibility for the content of teaching (the no-content limit) seems quite a significant

---

2097 European Convention, Working Group V 'Complementary Competencies, Final Report' (4 November 2002) CONV 375/1/02 REV 1, 5.

2098 Ibid, 10–11.

2099 See also *BVerfG, 2 BvE 2/08 (Lissabon)* 30 June 2009, Absatz-Nr (1-421), para 260. In his Opinion to Case 9/74 *Casagrande* ECLI:EU:C:1975:11, AG Warner described educational policy 'as almost the last in which the *Länder* retained any independence—so that any encroachment on them by Community law was regarded with some sensitivity'.

2100 *Valsamis v Greece* no 21787/93 (ECtHR 18 December 1996), para 28; *Folgerø and Others v Norway* no 15472/02 (ECtHR 29 June 2007), para 84 (g); text to n 687.

2101 See above § 29 .

2102 Comparable in Art 166 TFEU.

hurdle to have to overcome. After 1992, there was 'a marked decline in the Commission's eagerness to pursue its earlier curriculum-related ambitions'.[2103] On the basis of Article 165(2) second indent TFEU, the Union has been successful in promoting mobility in education (Erasmus[2104]), which is very valuable indeed for fostering EU citizenship and mutual understanding, and strengthens the EU dimension in EDC in various ways (especially at the level of higher education).[2105] However, the large majority of pupils (and students in higher education) remain at home. In Part three, substantive *content* was identified which is relevant for the EU dimension of EDC in mainstream education, especially for static citizens (criterion (iv), affecting the large majority of EU citizens).[2106] The obvious question therefore is whether Article 165 TFEU—requiring the EU to 'fully respect[ing] the responsibility of the Member States for the *content* of teaching'—precludes any EU initiatives to support the development of the substantive content of the EU dimension of EDC identified in Part three. Or, to put it differently, what action can the EU undertake—beyond mobility—to promote active, informed, and responsible EU citizenship in mainstream education for those who remain at home?[2107]

2103 T Theiler, 'The European union and the "European dimension" in schools: Theory and evidence' (1999) 21 Journal of European Integration 307, 331 (see also n 2242).

2104 I.a. Erasmus+ Regulation 1288/2013.

2105 See § 196 (the 'locals' also live in an area without internal frontiers) and 193 (conclusion). See i.a. Recommendation of the European Parliament and of the Council of 18 December 2006 on transnational mobility within the Community for education and training purposes: European Quality Charter for Mobility [2006] OJ L394/5. The *Erasmus* success story continues: Commission Proposal for a Regulation of the European Parliament and of the Council establishing 'Erasmus': the Union programme for education, training, youth and sport and repealing Regulation (EU) No 1288/2013, COM(2018) 367 final, reinforcing and extending mobility opportunities (see i.a. recital 20). See also Regulation (EU) 2019/499 of the European Parliament and of the Council of 25 March 2019 laying down provisions for the continuation of ongoing learning mobility activities under the Erasmus+ programme established by Regulation (EU) No 1288/2013, in the context of the withdrawal of the United Kingdom from the Union [2019] OJ L 85I/32.

2106 § 152 ff, § 276 .

2107 A thought-provoking, extreme hypothesis described in a fictious, provocative story by a French novelist: M Houellebecq, *Submission: A Novel* (Flammarion 2015). Through the accidental concurrence of factors after elections, the Muslim Brotherhood becomes part of the government in France in 2022. The party is not interested in Ministries like Finance and the Interior, but absolutely insists on occupying the Ministry of Education: 'What they care about is birth

An initial confirmation of competence is, as mentioned above, the fact that the Commission registered the European citizens' initiative 'More than education—Shaping active and responsible citizens'.[2108] This ECI aimed at incentive measures based on Article 165 TFEU. It reveals that the Commission considers that EU incentives to promote citizenship education do not manifestly fall outside its powers to propose legislation. In order to explore the issue of competence in greater depth, the key concepts of the conferral in Article 165 TFEU relevant to the EU dimension of EDC will now be analysed: quality education, the European dimension in education, and the participation of young people in democratic life in Europe. This analysis in sections B, C, and D will put the no-content limit in perspective.

B *Quality education*

284 *What is quality education?*

Pursuant to Article 165(1) TFEU, the Union 'shall contribute to the development of quality education'. To understand what 'quality education' means in the EU legal order, normative instruments at UN level (section 1), Council of Europe level (section 2) and EU level (section 3) must be looked at, in keeping with the terms of Article 220(1) TFEU in general and Article 165(3) TFEU in particular. There is no indication that when the competence for quality education was inserted into the Treaties, the Member States (as 'Masters of the Treaties') wanted to deviate from international standards on quality education.

What does an interpretation in the light of the international agreements by which the Member States were bound when they drafted Article 165 TFEU, signify for the concept of quality education inserted into that provision? This requires a short analysis of the international right to education,

---

rate and education. To them it's simple—whichever segment of the population has the highest birth rate, and does the best job of transmitting its values, wins. If you control the children, you control the future.' (Wednesday 18 May 2022). The curriculum itself would have to reflect the teachings of the Koran. They want France to withdraw from the EU. They impose school textbooks in mainstream education which are exclusively nation-state oriented and include *anti-EU* citizenship education. This hypothetical scenario may test the legal approach. To what extent is national educational autonomy framed by rights and obligations?

2108 See § 211 .

understood as a right to education directed to the aims listed in (binding) international agreements. This right relates to quality education, including human rights education and education for democracy. Quality education is relevant for all pupils, including the static ones, and it is undoubtedly linked to 'content of teaching'. A further section will thus have to address the question as to how the EU can contribute to the development of quality education (conferred competence) 'while fully respecting the responsibility of the Member States for the content of teaching' (limit to the competence conferred).

1. Quality education at UN level

285 The human rights-based approach to education

The analysis of possible content for the components of EDC based on EU law in Part three has demonstrated the need for an EU dimension in education to empower citizens. The UN and the UNESCO abandoned the needs-based approach to education and instead adopted a human rights-based approach (HRBA) some 15 years ago.[2109] Focusing on needs to achieve the intended educational goals had proved inadequate, whereas focusing on rights could help break through mere rhetoric.[2110] The human rights-based approach to education defines rights and obligations, and works towards 'strengthening the capacities of rights-holders to make their claims, and of duty-bearers to meet their obligations.'[2111] Taking a human rights-based approach inverts the top-down approach of traditional models of schooling, in which the education agenda is mostly defined from the perspective of the government, emphasising training, human capital investment, containment, and socialisation.[2112] The human rights-based

2109 UNGA 2005 World Summit Outcome (24 October 2005 UNGA Res 60/1) UN Doc A/RES/60/1, para 126; UNESCO-UNICEF, A Human Rights-Based Approach to Education for All: A framework for the realization of children's right to education and rights within education (2007), 3, 9; UNESCO The Right to Education: Law and Policy Review Guidelines (2014). See A Frankovits, *The Human Rights based approach and the United Nations system* (2006).

2110 UNESCO-UNICEF, A Human Rights-Based Approach to Education for All: A framework for the realization of children's right to education and rights within education (2007), 2.

2111 Ibid, 116.

2112 Ibid, 20.

approach starts from the individual and his or her human rights. He or she is to be empowered in a bottom-up model to participate in a free society. If education is not a privilege granted from above by governments, but a right that can be claimed from below, what does that imply for the EU citizen? Looking at education from this human rights-based perspective remains topical. In 2015, the 193 countries of the UN General Assembly adopted the 2030 Agenda for Sustainable Development, including a Global Goal on education, and recommitted to respecting rights and obligations under international law.[2113] The UN Human Rights Council urges States to take measures for '[e]nsuring that education is consistent with human rights standards and principles, including those laid down in the Universal Declaration of Human Rights and in international human rights treaties'.[2114]

286 Reception of UN standards in the EU legal order

For *the effects of* UN standards *in the EU legal order, I refer to the schema of modes of reception of exogenic norms in Part two.*[2115] In their education policy, EU institutions repeatedly refer to UN instruments by title (mode 3).[2116] In particular, the *Convention on the Rights of the Child was received in the EU legal order in this mode 3: many EU legal instruments, including legislation, refer to the CRC by title.*[2117] Article 24 CFR is based on the CRC (mode 4)

2113 UNGA Res 70/1 'Transforming our world: The 2030 Agenda for Sustainable Development' (25 September 2015) A/RES/70/1, paras 10, 18.

2114 UNHRC Res 29/7 'The right to education' (2 July 2015) UN Doc A/HRC/RES/29/7, 2(c). See also UNGA in § 294 .

2115 See i.a. §83 § 85 (i.a. n 642), §88 §100 (i.a. text to n 831), §140 §141 § 324 (i.a. n 2410).

2116 E.g. Council Recommendation of 22 May 2018 on key competences for lifelong learning, recital 13 (UN Sustainable Development Goals).

2117 E.g. Directive 2004/38, Art 28 (best interests of the child in cases of expulsion); Directive (EU) 2016/800 of the European Parliament and of the Council of 11 May 2016 on procedural safeguards for children who are suspects or accused persons in criminal proceedings [2016] OJ L132/1, Art 23 (non-regression). See also European Parliament Resolution of 16 January 2008: Towards an EU strategy on the rights of the child [2009] OJ C41E/24; Commission Communication 'An EU Agenda for the Rights of the Child' (15 February 2011) COM(2011) 60 final: 'The standards and principles of the UNCRC must continue to guide EU policies and actions that have an impact on the rights of the child'; European Parliament Resolution of 27 November 2014 on the 25th anniversary of the UN Convention on the Rights of the Child [2016] OJ C289/57, para 1: 'Considers that children's rights are at the heart of EU policies and that the 25th anniversary of the UN Convention on the Rights of the

and requires public authorities and private institutions to uphold the child's best interests as the primary consideration in all actions relating to children.[2118] Art 3(3) TEU states that the Union shall promote the protection of the rights of the child. Compliance with the rights of the child is a condition for accession to the EU.[2119] The ECJ takes UN and international standards into account in the interpretation of EU law (mode 6), e.g. the ICESCR in *Bressol* and the CRC in *Dynamic Medien*.[2120] Furthermore, no rights in the CFR shall be interpreted as restricting or adversely affecting human rights as recognised by international law and by international agreements to which the Union or all the Member States are parties (Article 53 CFR).

287 The international right to education: an umbrella right

The international right to education is defined by the international human rights framework, which is an evolving body of interrelated international instruments, some binding (covenants, conventions, treaties), others non-binding (declarations, recommendations, resolutions, conclusions, principles, guidelines, ...).[2121] *As is well known, the 1948 Universal Declaration of Human rights*

Child is an opportunity to ensure its full implementation in policy and in practice and to take additional measures to ensure respect for the rights of every child'; the Parliament proposes accession of the EU to the CRC.

2118 See the Explanations to the CFR. They refer in particular to Arts 3, 9, 12 and 13. Art 13 CFR gives the child the right to freedom of expression, which includes 'freedom to seek, receive and impart information and ideas of all kinds, regardless of frontiers'.

2119 Presidency Conclusions of the Copenhagen European Council of 21-22 June 1993, Bull EC 6-1993. See R Lamont, 'Article 24: The Rights of the Child' in S Peers and others (eds), *The EU Charter of Fundamental Rights: a Commentary* (Hart 2014) 670.

2120 Case C-73/08 *Bressol, Chaverot and Others* ECLI:EU:C:2010:181, paras 83–8: in this case the ECJ was asked to explain the effects of Member States' obligations under Art 13(2)(c) ICESCR (access to higher education); this provision was seen as compatible with Arts 18 and 21 TFEU as it does not require nor authorise a State Party to ensure wide access to quality higher education only for its own nationals. For the CRC, see i.a. Case C-244/06 *Dynamic Medien* ECLI:EU:C:2008:85, paras 39–40.

2121 Apart from CADE, ICESCR, and CRC (n 628), other binding international human rights instruments which include provisions on education are: *UN* Conventions such as the Convention relating to the Status of Refugees (1951); International Convention on the Elimination of All Forms of Racial Discrimination (1965); International Covenant on Civil and Political Rights (1966); Convention on the Elimination of All Forms of Discrimination against Women (1979); International Convention on the Protection of the Rights of

(UDHR, with high moral authority) was developed further in two 1966 Covenants (binding, ratified by all Member States, not by the EU), i.e. the International Covenant on Civil and Political Rights and the International Covenant on Economic, Social and Cultural Rights (ICESCR)*.*[2122] *The 1989 Convention on the Rights of the Child (CRC, binding, ratified by all Member States, not by the EU) sets out the full range of human rights from the perspective of the child.*[2123] *Treaty bodies adopt General Comments, which are authoritative interpretations of Treaty provisions.*[2124] *Documents of the Office of the UN High Commissioner for Human Rights (OHCHR) and of the* Special Rapporteur on the right to education are also authoritative. *International conferences of States on education summoned by the UNESCO General Confer-*

All Migrant Workers and Members of their Families (1990); Convention on the Rights of Persons with Disabilities (2006). Further *UNESCO* Convention on Technical and Vocational Education (1989); and *ILO* Conventions such as the Convention on the minimum age for employment (1973); Convention concerning Paid Educational Leave (1974); Worst Forms of Child Labour Convention (1999); Indigenous and Tribal Peoples Convention (1989); Convention concerning the Prohibition and Immediate Action for the Elimination of the Worst Forms of Child Labour (1999); Convention concerning Decent Work for Domestic Workers (2011). The 1924 Declaration of Geneva already adverted implicitly to a right to education with a number of 'musts'. For an understanding of the historic developement of the right to education, see D Hodson, *The Human Right to Education* (Ashgate/Dartmouth 1998); and M Nowak, 'The right to education' in A Eide, C Krause and A Rosas (eds), *Economic, social and cultural rights: a textbook* (2nd revised edn, Nijhoff 2001). See list of international standard-setting instruments in UNESCO The Right to Education: Law and Policy Review Guidelines (2014), p 49–50.

2122 Universal Declaration of Human Rights (adopted 10 December 1948) UNGA Res 217 A(III) (UDHR); International Covenant on Civil and Political Rights (adopted 16 December 1966, entered into force 23 March 1976) 999 UNTS 171 (ICCPR); International Covenant on Economic, Social and Cultural Rights (adopted 16 December 1966 A/RES/2200 (XXI), entered into force 3 January 1976) 993 UNTS3.

2123 Convention on the Rights of the Child (adopted 20 November 1989 UNGA Res 44/25, entered into force 2 September 1990) 15777 UNTS 3. See Art 1: 'a child means every human being below the age of eighteen years unless under the law applicable to the child, majority is attained earlier'.

2124 Implementation of the ICESCR is monitored by the Committee on Economic, Social and Cultural Rights (a body of independent experts); implementation of the ICCPR by the Human Rights Committee; and of the CRC by the Committee on the Rights of the Child (Treaty-based bodies). The UN Human Rights Council is a Charter based UN Human rights body. Overview of human rights bodies in <www.ohchr.org>.

ence adopt declarations and plans of action.[2125] *In short, a dégradé normatif appears (as at Council of Europe level*[2126]*): non-binding instruments complement and specify binding norms, expressing the political commitments of States.*[2127]

As Nowak writes, 'the right to education is one of the most complex human rights under present international law' as reflected in the abundancy of sources.[2128] *It encompasses several rights to which several types of obligations correspond. Scholars generally distinguish the social dimension of the right to education, including a* right of equal access to education and a right to quality education, and the freedom dimension, including the right of parents to choose schools, the freedom to establish education institutions, and academic freedom.[2129] The right to education cannot be ranked in a single category as a civil, a political, an economic, a social, or a cultural right: 'It embodies them all.'[2130] The right to education 'epitomizes the indivisibil-

2125 Art IV(3) UNESCO Constitution.

2126 See § 51 .

2127 See further O De Schutter, *International Human Rights Law* (2nd edn, Cambridge University Press 2014) 61 ff (human rights law as part of international law). Also *<en.unesco.org/themes/education/education-standards-norms>*. One of the main constitutional functions of UNESCO is standard-setting to realise the goals for which it was created.

2128 Nowak, 'The right to education', 268: the right is 'based on a variety of, sometimes antagonistic, philosophical foundations'; scholars and human rights bodies have only begun to provide answers to the most fundamental questions on the right to education.

2129 Social dimension: i.a. Art 13(2) ICESCR; Freedom dimension: i.a. Art 13(3) and (4) ICESCR, Art 18(4) ICCPR. See KD Beiter, *The Protection of the Right to Education by International Law* (Including a Systematic Analysis of Article 13 of the International Covenant on Economic, Social and Cultural Rights; International Studies in Human Rights vol 82, Nijhoff 2006) 459. Other ways of categorising the substance of the right to education: see CL Glenn and J De Groof, *Balancing Freedom, Autonomy and Accountability in Education*, vol 1 (Wolf Legal Publishers 2005) 53 (diversity of contents of the right to education in various countries); M Verheyde, 'Article 28: The Right to Education' in A Alen and others (eds), *A Commentary on the United Nations Convention on the Rights of the Child* (Martinus Nijhoff 2006) 1; Y Rabin, 'The Many Faces of the Right to Education' in D Barak-Erez and AM Gross (eds), *Exploring Social Rights: Between Theory and Practice* (Hart 2007) 266 (distinguishing between 3 different rights: the right to receive education, to choose (a stream of) education, and the right to equal education).

2130 Tomaševski, *Human rights obligations: making education available, accessible, acceptable and adaptable* 9. In the same sense: Nowak, 'The right to education', 268; Glenn and De Groof, *Balancing Freedom, Autonomy and Accountability in Education*; Verheyde, 'Article 28: The Right to Education', 1.

ity and interdependence of all human rights' and its different aspects must be considered in a holistic way.[2131]

288 Aims of education in binding instruments and corresponding obligations

In this interconnected set of rights, I will now focus on the right to quality education, especially in its relationship with the aims of education listed in international agreements (binding). These aims relate to the internal aspects of the right to education (by contrast with the external aspects, such as the right of equal access).[2132] *The importance of educational objectives is apparent throughout the development of human rights instruments.* The ICESCR and the CRC will get particular attention. *The aims of education are linked to quality education, including education for democratic citizenship. When applied in the EU, they require an EU dimension to EDC.*

A good understanding must start from the 1945 UNESCO Constitution, which connects education and peace: 'since wars begin in the minds of men, it is in the minds of men that the defences of peace must be constructed' (preamble). The 'purpose of the Organization is to contribute to peace and security by promoting collaboration among the nations through education (...) in order to further universal respect for justice, for the rule of law and for the human rights and fundamental freedoms (Article 1).[2133] *The 1948 UDHR proclaims in Article 26 that everyone has the right to education and immediately specifies four aims to which education 'shall be directed', inter alia strengthening of respect for human rights and fundamental freedoms.*[2134] *The aims, considered to be pivotal, reflect the UN 'Purposes and Principles' cited in the 1945 UN Charter.*[2135] *During the drafting of the UDHR, the importance of setting out the aims of education was repeatedly discussed and emphasised.*[2136] *A representative of UNESCO cited 'the example of Germany, where, under the Hitler regime, education had been*

2131 UN ComESCR 'General Comment No 11: Plans of action for primary education (article 14 ICESCR)' (1999), para 2.

2132 Beiter, *The Protection of the Right to Education by International Law* 463.

2133 Preamble and Art 1, para 1.

2134 Art 26: 'Education shall be directed to the full development of the human personality and to the strengthening of respect for human rights and fundamental freedoms. It shall promote understanding, tolerance and friendship among all nations, racial or religious groups, and shall further the activities of the United Nations for the maintenance of peace'.

2135 UN Charter Arts 1 and 2.

2136 See reports of work of the Commission on Human Rights in the Drafting of the Universal Declaration of Human Rights, e.g. SR 67en 68 (record of the 67th and 68th meeting).

admirably organised but had, nevertheless, produced disastrous results.'[2137] *Other fascist countries had also respected the right to education for everyone, yet 'the doctrines on which that education had been founded had led to two world wars. If the [UDHR] failed to define the spirit in which future generations were to be educated, it would lose its value as a guide for humanity.'*[2138] *Outlining the objectives of education was necessary to prevent some governments pursuing anti-social aims.*[2139]

The aims of education set out in the UDHR were confirmed in subsequent international agreements, giving them a binding character. A strong affirmation of the right to education is contained in the 1960 UNESCO Convention Against Discrimination in Education (CADE).[2140] *It stipulates that the term 'education' includes 'access to education, the standard and quality of education, and the conditions under which it is given'*[2141] *and repeats in Article 5(1) the aims listed in the UDHR to which education 'shall be directed'. The CADE leads to international obligations for Member States: '(t)he States Parties to this Convention undertake to take all necessary measures to ensure the application of the principles enunciated in paragraph 1 of this Article'.*[2142]

289 The ICESCR right to education and corresponding obligations

The 1966 ICESCR (binding) restates in Article 13(1) on the right to education the four educational aims of the UDHR[2143] *and adds a new aim: 'education shall enable all persons to participate effectively in a free society'.*[2144] The *travaux préparatoires* show how in the drafting of the Covenant, *'[s]ome doubt was expressed as to the desirability of including the definition of the aims of education (…) It was felt,* however, that, in the light of the widely differ-

2137 Commission on Human Rights, meeting of 10 June 1948, UN Economic and Social Council, UN Docs. E/CN.4/SR.67, p 12.

2138 Ibid, p 13.

2139 Ibid, p 14; also UN Docs. E/CN.4/SR.68, p 12; UN Docs E/CN.4/SR.288, p 7.

2140 Convention Against Discrimination in Education (adopted 14 December 1960, entered into force 22 May 1962) (CADE). For ratification, acceptance, or notification of succession by EU Member States, see <treaties.un.org>.

2141 Art 2(2).

2142 Art 5(2) CADE. Disputes may be referred to the International Court of Justice (Art 8).

2143 UN ComESCR 'General Comment No 13: The Right to Education (Art. 13)' UN Doc E/C.12/1999/10, para 4: also the ICESCR educational aims reflect the purposes and principles of the UN Charter Arts 1–2.

2144 Also, 'and the sense of its dignity' is added to the aim of ensuring the full development of the human personality and 'ethnic' groups added to the aim of promoting understanding, tolerance and friendship.

ing ends to which education could be used, it was important to state what those ends ought to be.'[2145] Not the 'higher interests of the State', but the full development of the human personality was the most fundamental aim.[2146]

The corollary of the right to education (as of all human rights) is an obligation to respect, to protect and to fulfil. To fulfil implies an obligation to facilitate and an obligation to provide.[2147] In its General Comment on Article 13, the *Committee on Economic, Social and Cultural Rights* cites among the specific legal obligations that 'States parties are required to ensure that curricula, for all levels of the educational system, are directed to the objectives identified in Article 13 (1)'.[2148] They must establish a transparent and effective system to monitor this. With regard to Article 13 (2), relating i.a. to primary, secondary and higher education, 'States have obligations to respect, protect and fulfil each of the "essential features" (availability, accessibility, acceptability, adaptability [the four A scheme]) of the right to education.'[2149] While the four 'A's are interrelated, for the EU dimension of EDC, 'acceptability' and 'adaptability' have specific relevance. The Committee emphasises that the form and *substance* of education, including *curricula* and teaching methods, must be 'acceptable (e.g. *relevant*, culturally appropriate and of *good quality*)', 'this is subject to the

2145 Annotations on the text of the draft International Covenants on Human Rights, UN Doc A/2929 (1 June 1955), p 112–113, para 37.

2146 UN ComESCR 'General Comment No 13: The Right to Education (Art. 13)' UN Doc E/C.12/1999/10, para 4; Beiter, *The Protection of the Right to Education by International Law* 464, 470.

2147 UN ComESCR 'General Comment No 13: The Right to Education (Art. 13)' UN Doc E/C.12/1999/10, paras 46–47. See also UN ComESCR 'General comment No 3: The nature of States parties' obligations (art. 2, para. 1, of the Covenant)' (1991), 3; The Maastricht Guidelines on Violations of Economic, Social and Cultural Rights (1997), UN Doc E/C.12/2000/13UN, paras 6–7. Typology of obligations in De Schutter, *International Human Rights Law* 279; on limited justiciability p 285. See illustration in Willems and Vernimmen, 'The fundamental human right to education for refugees: Some legal remarks': the question as to how to invoke the right to education against States remains delicate. On the justiciability of the right to an education adequate for citizenship under the US constitution, see class action law suit *Cook v Raimondo* (District Court of Rhode Island): MA Rebell, 'Major Federal Right to Education Lawsuit Filed in the U.S. (OxHRH Blog, 12 December 2018)' (2018). Also Friedman (n 2150).

2148 UN ComESCR 'General Comment No 13: The Right to Education (Art. 13)' UN Doc E/C.12/1999/10, para 49.

2149 Ibid, para 50 (see also fn 2 on adequacy).

educational objectives required by Article 13 (1) and such minimum educational standards as may be approved by the State'. Education must furthermore be 'adaptable', i.e. 'flexible so it can adapt to the needs of changing societies and communities and respond to the needs of students within their diverse social and cultural settings'.[2150] In assessing acceptability and adaptability, *the best interests of the child are a primary consideration.*[2151] The *Committee on Economic, Social and Cultural Rights* adds that States must 'fulfil (facilitate) the acceptability of education by taking positive measures' and 'fulfil (provide) the adaptability of education by designing and providing resources for curricula which reflect the contemporary needs of students in a changing world'.[2152] Every State party has a minimum core obligation to ensure the satisfaction of minimum essential levels of each of the ICESCR rights.[2153] For education, the Committee on Economic, Social and Cultural Rights holds that 'this core includes an obligation ... to ensure that education conforms to the objectives set out in Article 13(1)'.[2154] On the basis of a systematic interpretation, the normative con-

2150 Ibid, para 6 (emphasis added). On relevance, see UNESCO The Right to Education: Law and Policy Review Guidelines (2014) p 5, 12: 'In their effort to meet their commitments to making education for all a reality, countries are increasingly concerned with the delivery, quality and relevance of their education systems.' Also UNESCO The Dakar Framework for Action (Education for All) - Education for All: Meeting our Collective Commitments, adopted at the World Education Forum (Dakar, 26-28 April 2000), i.a. paras 44, 59 ('Providing quality education relevant to learners' needs and to the requirements of the changing society'), also p 28, 39. Further Tomaševski, *Human rights obligations: making education available, accessible, acceptable and adaptable*; Verheyde, 'Article 28: The Right to Education' 15; and application in *Three Country Audit of the lower secondary citizenship and human rights education curriculum: Reflection of the principles of the Charter on Education for Democratic Citizenship and Human Rights Education in the curricula of France, Finland and Ireland* (2013) 83 (what does education respecting the 4 'A's require; relationship with international agreements). See 'adequacy' in B Friedman and S Solow, 'The Federal Right to an Adequate Education' (2013) 81 George Washington Law Review 92 (authors argue the existence of a US federal constitutional right to a minimally adequate education, based on the text of the constitution, intentions, practice, and case law).

2151 UN ComESCR 'General Comment No 13: The Right to Education (Art. 13)' UN Doc E/C.12/1999/10, para 7.

2152 Ibid, para 50.

2153 UN ComESCR 'General comment No 3: The nature of States parties' obligations (art. 2, para. 1, of the Covenant)' (1991), para 10.

2154 UN ComESCR 'General Comment No 13: The Right to Education (Art. 13)' UN Doc E/C.12/1999/10, para 57. See also UN ComESCR 'General comment

tent of Article 13(1), including its aims, must be applied to the obligations based on Article 13(2), including the 4As.[2155] The *Committee* considers the use of curricula inconsistent with the educational aims of Article 13(1) to be a violation of Article 13. It includes acts of commission and of omission.[2156]

While Article 13(2) is drafted 'with a view of achieving the full realization of this right',[2157] States have an immediate obligation 'to take steps', i.a. to apply Article 13(2)(b), that is, to make secondary education generally available and accessible.[2158] Reading paragraphs 1 and 2 of Article 13 ICESCR in conjunction with one another, immediate steps must also be taken towards achieving acceptable and adaptable education.[2159] Those steps must be concrete and targeted,[2160] assured by all appropriate means, e.g. legislation, monitoring, international cooperation, domestic judicial effective remedies, administrative, financial, educational and social measures.[2161] 'Taking steps' is an obligation as to result. No deliberately retrogressive measures can be adopted.[2162]

The impact of Article 13 ICESCR on the content of teaching is clear. Rights and obligations must be respected, limiting the educational auton-

---

No 3: The nature of States parties' obligations (art. 2, para. 1, of the Covenant)' (1991), para 10.

2155 UN ComESCR 'General Comment No 13: The Right to Education (Art. 13)' UN Doc E/C.12/1999/10, para 58.

2156 Ibid, paras 58–59. See also The Maastricht Guidelines on Violations of Economic, Social and Cultural Rights (1997), UN Doc E/C.12/2000/13UN, para 11, paras 14–15: example of an act of commission is the 'adoption of any deliberately retrogressive measure that reduces the extent to which any such right is guaranteed' (an answer to the hypothesis of the novel *Submission*, n 2107). Acts of omission are the 'failure to monitor the realization of economic, social and cultural rights' (compare text to nn 2399 and 2400 on Eurydice and Chapter 11), the 'failure of a State to take into account its international legal obligations in the field of economic, social and cultural rights when entering into bilateral or multilateral agreements with other States, international organizations or multinational corporations'.

2157 In line with Art 2, calling for steps to be taken by all appropriate means to achieve the progressive full realisation of the rights.

2158 UN ComESCR 'General Comment No 13: The Right to Education (Art. 13)' UN Doc E/C.12/1999/10, para 52.

2159 In the same sense a combined reading of Arts 28 and 29 CFR, in Verheyde, 'Article 28: The Right to Education' 12.

2160 UN ComESCR 'General comment No 3: The nature of States parties' obligations (art. 2, para. 1, of the Covenant)' (1991), para 2.

2161 Ibid, paras 5 and 7.

2162 Ibid, para 9.

omy of Member States.[2163] Comparable rights and obligations flow from the CRC.

290 The CRC right to education

The 1989 CRC contains a separate provision on the aims of education, i.e. Article 29. It develops the ICESCR further, agreeing that education shall be directed to (inter alia) the 'preparation of the child for responsible life in a free society'. *The international consensus on the aims of education in the CRC is broad, as the CRC is the most widely ratified human rights treaty.*[2164] *Significantly, the first General Comment drafted by the Committee on the Rights of the Child was devoted to Article 29.*[2165] *The Committee immediately underlines 'its far-reaching importance'.*[2166] *The aims of education are directly linked to the realisation of the child's human dignity, the core value of the CRC. Article 29(1) stresses the need to empower children.* Education is an empowerment right.[2167] *The* 'child's right to education is not only a matter of access (art. 28) but also of *content*', content firmly rooted in the values of Article 29(1). The *right to quality education* appears: 'Article 29(1) underlines the individual and subjective right to a specific quality of education.' [2168] The Committee mentions in this context that 'the curriculum must be of direct *relevance* to the child's social, cultural, environmental and economic context and to his or her present and future needs'. As the *aims or values in Article 29(1) are formulated in fairly general terms, the Committee 'calls upon all States parties to take the necessary steps to formally incorporate these principles into their education policies and legislation at all levels' and states that '[t]he effective promotion of Article 29(1) requires the fundamental reworking of curricula to include the various aims of education and the systematic revision of*

2163 Cp the killer phrase (n 83).

2164 Convention on the Rights of the Child (adopted 20 November 1989 UNGA Res 44/25, entered into force 2 September 1990) 15777 UNTS 3. for the 196 'states parties', see <indicators.ohchr.org/>.

2165 UN ComRC 'General Comment No 1 (2001)- Article 29(1): The Aims of Education' Doc CRC/GC/2001/1. See also UN ComESCR 'General Comment No 13: The Right to Education (Art. 13)' UN Doc E/C.12/1999/10, paras 1, 4–5.

2166 UN ComRC 'General Comment No 1 (2001)- Article 29(1): The Aims of Education' Doc CRC/GC/2001/1, para 1.

2167 Ibid, paras 1- 2. See also UN ComESCR 'General Comment No 13: The Right to Education (Art. 13)' UN Doc E/C.12/1999/10, para 1; Tomaševski, *Human rights obligations: making education available, accessible, acceptable and adaptable*, p 10.

2168 UN ComRC 'General Comment No 1 (2001)- Article 29(1): The Aims of Education' Doc CRC/GC/2001/1, para 9, also para 22.

textbooks and other teaching materials and technologies, as well as school policies'.[2169]

As in the ICESCR, rig*hts of access and the right to quality education must be interlinked, in a systematic interpretation of Articles 28(1) and 29(1) CRC.*[2170]

291 Intermediate conclusion and significance for EU citizens

Education directed to the aims of education listed in international agreements is an essential part of the international right to education. The binding character of the provisions on aims follows from a textual interpretation: the UDHR, CADE, ICESCR and CRC all state that education 'shall be directed to', not 'should'. Other arguments in favour of their binding character, applying the rules on interpretation in the Vienna Convention on the law of Treaties, are, firstly, that the aims in Articles 5(1) CADE, 13(1) ICESCR and 29 CRC are laid down in the provisions of the body of the agreements (not in the preamble), secondly, that the *travaux préparatoires* show that including the aims was a deliberate decision, and, thirdly, that the practice of the Committee on Economic, Social and Cultural Rights and of the Committee on the Rights of the Child indicates that they perceive the aims as legally binding.[2171] *In short, the right to education includes a right to quality education. Quality education requires education to be directed to the aims listed, which has a real impact on the content of teaching. Obligations flow from this right*, as is confirmed by various UN bodies and scholars.[2172]

2169 Paras 17–18. 'Every child has the right to receive an education of good quality which in turn requires a focus on the quality of the learning environment, of teaching and learning processes and materials, and of learning outputs.' As to implemention, see CRC Art 4: 'States Parties shall undertake all appropriate legislative, administrative, and other measures for the implementation of the rights recognized in the present Convention'. Also Art 43 (the Committee calls upon States parties to develop a comprehensive national plan of action to promote and monitor realization of the objectives listed in Art 29(1)). Further UNHRC Res 26/17 'The right to education: follow-up to Human Rights Council resolution 8/4' (11 July 2014) UN Doc A/HRC/RES/26/17, on the role of communications procedures to promote the justiciability of the right to education, and the entry into force of the Optional Protocol to the Convention on the Rights of the Child on a communications procedure (14 April 2014).

2170 Verheyde, 'Article 28: The Right to Education' 12.

2171 Beiter uses these arguments with regard to the ICESCR (Beiter, *The Protection of the Right to Education by International Law* 469); they apply to the CRC as well.

2172 I.a. UN ComESCR 'General Comment No 13: The Right to Education (Art. 13)' UN Doc E/C.12/1999/10, 49; UNHRC Res 29/7 'The right to education' (2 July 2015) UN Doc A/HRC/RES/29/7 para 2, (c).

What do the international right to education and the compulsory aims of education mean for EU citizens and for the Member States (which all ratified the agreements cited)? To the extent that EDC (interconnected with HRE) prepares citizens for effective participation and responsible life in a free society, and to respect human rights (aims in Article 13(1) ICESCR and Article 29 CRC), and to the extent that for EU Member States EDC needs to include an EU dimension, as argued in Part three, the international right to education of citizens in Member States arguably includes a right to an EU dimension of EDC.[2173] Member States have obligations based on international law to provide acceptable and adaptable education, taking into account the best interests of the child.[2174] In the light of *the analysis in Part three, education in Member States which lacks an EU dimension cannot be considered to be acceptable (relevant and of good quality) or adapted to the needs of a changing society. The EU dimension is increasingly relevant in society. Relevant education should keep pace. Based on international law,* Member States have the obligation to work towards the progressive realisation of the EU dimension of EDC and to take immediate steps. Moreover, international cooperation for the realisation of economic, social and cultural rights is an obligation on all States, in line with the UN Charter. States parties to the ICESCR and CRC have 'an obligation to ensure that their actions as members of international organizations take due account of the right to education'.[2175] To fulfil their obligation of international cooperation to realise the right to education, I suggest that Member States should

---

2173 In the same vein, also Walkenhorst, 'Problems of Political Education in a Multi-level Polity: explaining Non-teaching of European Union Issues in German Secondary Schooling', 366: 'Since democratic participation requires political education, the EU should be expected to be a compulsory topic in school. Since the introduction of EU citizenship rights in 1993 the absence of EU secondary education is arguably a denial of a basic democratic right.'.

2174 Arts 28–29 CRC read in conjunction with Art 3 CRC.

2175 On the obligation to engage in international cooperation to realise the right to education, see Art 2(1) ICESCR; UN ComESCR 'General Comment No 13: The Right to Education (Art. 13)' UN Doc E/C.12/1999/10, paras 56, 59. See also Art 4 CRC: 'With regard to economic, social and cultural rights, States Parties shall undertake such measures to the maximum extent of their available resources and, where needed, *within the framework of international co-operation*' (emphasis added). Further UN ComESCR 'General comment No 3: The nature of States parties' obligations (art. 2, para. 1, of the Covenant)' (1991), para 11 and para 14: 'The Committee wishes to emphasize that in accordance with Articles 55 and 56 of the Charter of the United Nations, with well-established principles of international law, and with the provisions of the Covenant itself, international cooperation for development and thus for the realization

cooperate loyally with the Union when it uses its supporting competence to promote quality education (Article 165 TFEU).

292 Contemporary interpretations of the aims of education

The aims of education to which State parties have agreed in binding international agreements are abstract and do not define learning content precisely.[2176] Norm-setting and clarification comes from a range of bodies, which also adapt the aims to evolving situations.[2177] *The 1990 World Declaration on Education for All (Jomtien, Thailand) and the 1995 Plan of Action for the United Nations Decade for Human Rights Education* further developed the aims. In 1999, *the Committee on Economic, Social and Cultural Rights noted that these instruments reflect a 'contemporary interpretation' of the aims ('implicit' in the listed aims), given their worldwide endorsement, and accordingly took the view that State parties are required to ensure that their education conforms to the aims of Article 13 ICESCR as interpreted in the light of the recent instruments.*[2178]

Since 1999, many other international human rights instruments have been widely endorsed as well. Continuing the reasoning of the Committee on Economic, Social and Cultural Rights, they too give contemporary interpretations of the aims of the binding international agreements.[2179] *Declarations of international conferences give guidance as to the proper interpretation of the terms of the CADE, ICESCR and CRC in the current context.*[2180] General and specific, universal and regional human rights instruments recommit to the aims,

---

of economic, social and cultural rights is an obligation of all States'; UNGA Res 71/8 'Education for democracy' (17 November 2016) UN Doc A/RES/71/8, para 10; UN Doc A/RES/71/8.

2176 Tomaševski, *Human rights obligations: making education available, accessible, acceptable and adaptable*, p 11: written during the Cold War, deliberately vague and written to preclude litigation. See also Willems and Vernimmen, 'The fundamental human right to education for refugees: Some legal remarks', 228–9: non-committal provisions open to interpretation, leaving a large margin of appreciation for States.

2177 See also Vienna Convention on the Law of Treaties Arts 31–32.

2178 UN ComESCR 'General Comment No 13: The Right to Education (Art. 13)' UN Doc E/C.12/1999/10 para 5.

2179 The aims of ICESCR are somewhat outdated: Beiter, *The Protection of the Right to Education by International Law* 467.

2180 Example in UN ComESCR 'General Comment No 13: The Right to Education (Art. 13)' UN Doc E/C.12/1999/10, para 9: the Committee on Economic, Social and Cultural Rights used the 1990 'World Declaration on Education for All' to obtain guidance to intepret the term 'primary education' of the ICESCR.

update and adapt them.[2181] *If the aims of education in binding agreements are read in the light of widely accepted international human rights instruments, the right to quality education is confirmed, and the right to human rights education and education for democracy emerge.*

293 The right to quality education confirmed

The right to quality education—not mentioned as such in the ICESCR or the CRC—was emphasised by the Committee on the Rights of the Child[2182] *and is frequently restated in the later human rights framework.*[2183] *While in the Council of Europe the right to education of the ECHR focuses on equal access to the existing educational facilities,*[2184] *at UN level, it is frequently reiterated that the right to education is more than just the right to enter the school gates:*

> *getting children into schools is not enough; it is no guarantee of an education that enables individuals to achieve their economic and social objectives and to acquire the skills, knowledge, values and attitudes that bring about responsible and active citizenship.*[2185]

2181 For an overview of aims of education in regional and specific human rights instruments, see D Hodgson, 'The international human right to education and education concerning human rights' (1996) 4 The International Journal of Children's Rights 237, 251.

2182 Text to n 2168.

2183 E.g. UNESCO The Dakar Framework for Action (Education for All) - Education for All: Meeting our Collective Commitments, adopted at the World Education Forum (Dakar, 26-28 April 2000), para 32: 'All children must have the opportunity to fulfil *their right to quality education* in schools or alternative programmes at whatever level of education is considered "basic"'; UNESCO EFA Global Monitoring Report 2015. Education for All 2000-2015: Achievements and Challenges, p 185, reaffirming 'the *rights of all children to a good quality education*, one which provides the foundations for the rest of their lives' (i.a. with equality and without gender steroptypes). Emphasis added. See also various documents of UN Special Rapporteurs on the right to education, i.a. Tomaševski, *Human rights obligations: making education available, accessible, acceptable and adaptable*; and foreword of Vernor Muñoz to UNESCO-UNICEF, A Human Rights-Based Approach to Education for All: A framework for the realization of children's right to education and rights within education (2007); K Singh, *Report of the Special Rapporteur on the right to education: Normative action for quality education* (2012).

2184 See text to n 685.

2185 UNESCO-UNICEF, A Human Rights-Based Approach to Education for All: A framework for the realization of children's right to education and rights within education (2007), p 27.

Education without quality control can have nefarious consequences.[2186]

In the *2000 Dakar Framework for Action on Education for All (World Education Forum), the right to quality education was of central importance.*[2187] The Framework laid the basis for a *concept of quality education going beyond reading, writing and arithmetic, and saw 'competences for democratic citizenship and attitudes promoting solidarity as important outcomes.'*[2188] *In successive human rights instruments, descriptions of 'quality education' gradually include more objectives related to citizenship and citizenship education. UNESCO characterizes the right to quality education, as implying, inter alia, a broad, relevant and inclusive curriculum. Quality is defined by reference to learners' cognitive development, but also to education's role in promoting values and attitudes of responsible citizenship.*[2189] Quality education requires respect for the right *to* education, rights *in* and *through* education.[2190] *In 2015, the World Education Forum adopted the Incheon Declaration 'Education 2030: Towards inclusive*

2186 See K Tomaševski, *Removing Obstacles in the Way of the Right to Education* (Right to education Primer No 1, 2001), p 33: 'getting all children to school is still mistaken for their right to education, although they can be brainwashed, indoctrinated, abused, harmed for life'. The Special Rapporteur recounts how many schools in Rwanda taught pupils about 'scientific' ethnic differences between Hutus and Tutsis. This 'education' reinforcing mutual prejudices was a major factor in the 1994 genocide. See also Beiter, *The Protection of the Right to Education by International Law* 21, 493: the right to education is more than a right of access; it is a right to be educated.

2187 It underlays the six goals. See UNESCO The Dakar Framework for Action (Education for All) - Education for All: Meeting our Collective Commitments, adopted at the World Education Forum (Dakar, 26-28 April 2000), paras 7, 32, 42–44: 'Quality is at the heart of education (…) A quality education is one that satisfies basic learning needs'; it requires i.a. adequate facilities and learning materials, and a relevant curriculum; see especially the sixth goal: 'improving every aspect of the quality of education, and ensuring their excellence so that recognized and measurable learning outcomes are achieved by all'. See also UNESCO World Declaration on Education For All (Jomtien, Thailand, 1990): quality of basic education appears as a primary objective throughout the Declaration.

2188 UNHRC Res 15/28 'World Plan of Action for the second phase (2010-2014) of the World Programme for Human Rights Education' (27 July 2010) UN Doc A/HRC/15/28, para 19.

2189 UNESCO EFA Global Monitoring Report 2005, Education for All: The Quality Imperative, 31; UNESCO-UNICEF, A Human Rights-Based Approach to Education for All: A framework for the realization of children's right to education and rights within education (2007), 32.

2190 See i.a. UNESCO-UNICEF, A Human Rights-Based Approach to Education for All: A framework for the realization of children's right to education and rights within education (2007), 35. Also J De Groof, G Lauwers and K Singh,

and equitable quality education and lifelong learning for all',[2191] *in line with* UN Sustainable Development Goal 4 ('inclusive and equitable quality education').[2192]

294 The right to human rights education and education for democracy

Binding and non-binding instruments at UN and UNESCO level confirm the importance of human rights education. Based on the provisions in binding international agreements that education must strengthen respect for human rights and fundamental freedoms,[2193] several instruments mention 'a right to human rights education'. The right to human rights education is promoted by the Office of the High Commissioner for Human Rights[2194] and widely supported, *inter alia in* UN General Assembly Decla-

---

The right to education and rights in education (Wolf Legal Publishers 2006); and n 1261.

2191 UNESCO World Education Forum 2015, Incheon Declaration - Education 2030: Towards inclusive and equitable quality education and lifelong learning for all.

2192 UNGA Res 70/1 'Transforming our world: The 2030 Agenda for Sustainable Development' (25 September 2015) A/RES/70/1. The SDGs replaced the 2000 MDGs, Millenium Development Goals (Goal 2: to achieve universal primary education); United Nations Millennium Declaration UNGA Res 55/2, para 19. See in particular SDG target 4.7 on sustainable development and global citizenship ('By 2030, ensure that all learners acquire the knowledge and skills needed to promote sustainable development, including, among others, through education for sustainable development and sustainable lifestyles, human rights, gender equality, promotion of a culture of peace and non-violence, global citizenship and appreciation of cultural diversity and of culture's contribution to sustainable development').

2193 Art 5(1)(a) CADE, Art 13(1) ICESCR, and Art 29(1)(b) CRC; see also Art 55 UN Charter.

2194 'The Right to Human Rights Education', the title of a publication and website of the OHCHR, is widely supported as witnessed by the flag and icons of i.a. UNESCO, CoE, EU and EU Agency for Fundamental Rights: <www.ohchr.org/EN/Issues/Education/Training/Compilation/Pages/Listofcontents.aspx>. As normative basis for this right, the OHCHR refers to a 'compilation of provisions of international and regional instruments dealing with human rights education' (they include 'treaties, covenants, conventions and protocols; charters; declarations; recommendations; decisions; resolutions; principles; guidelines; rules; final documents; commitments; and conclusions or joint communiqués of intergovernmental meetings, congresses and conferences'): 'Despite their different legal status, and the different fora in which they were adopted which bear responsibility for their content, taken together these texts outline the human rights education commitments made by States in the context of international and regional intergovernmental forums, and

rations and Human Rights Council resolutions.[2195] *The Human Rights Council sees human rights education as an aspect of the right to quality education*[2196] *and asks States to respect the 2011 Declaration on Human Rights Education 'as a means to give full effect to the right to education'.*[2197] *UN bodies, the Special Rapporteur on the right to education, World conferences on education, all emphasise the importance of human rights education.*[2198] *Academic writers,*

---

provide the basis for the right to human rights education.' See also UN OHCHR 'Guidelines for National Plans of Action for Human Rights Education' (1997) UN Doc A/52/469/Add.1, A/52/469/Add.1/Corr.1 (20 October 1997 and 27 March 1998) para 16: 'Education in and for human rights is a fundamental human right'.

2195 I.a. UNGA Res 66/137 'United Nations Declaration on Human Rights Education and Training' (19 December 2011), Art 1 ('Everyone has the right to know, seek and receive information about all human rights and fundamental freedoms and should have access to human rights education and training'). See repeated resolutions of the HRC, e.g. UNHRC Res 8/4 'The right to education' (18 June 2008) UN Doc A/HRC/RES/8/4, para 7(f) (i); UNHRC Res 23/4 'The right to education: follow-up to Human Rights Council resolution 8/4' (19 June 2013) UN Doc A/HRC/23/2 (2013), para 4(f). See earlier UNGA 'Declaration on the Promotion among Youth of the Ideals of Peace, Mutual Respect and Understanding between Peoples' UNGA res 2037 (XX) (7 December 1965) UN Doc A/RES/20/2037, Principle III; and UNESCO Recommendation concerning Education for International Understanding, Co-operation and Peace and Education relating to Human Rights and Fundamental Freedoms (adopted 19 November 1974), Principles 7 and 18(c).

2196 UNHRC Res 8/4 'The right to education' (18 June 2008) UN Doc A/HRC/RES/8/4, para 7 (f) and (i).

2197 UNHRC Res 23/4 'The right to education: follow-up to Human Rights Council resolution 8/4' (19 June 2013) UN Doc A/HRC/23/2 (2013), para 5.

2198 UNESCO Recommendation concerning Education for International Understanding, Co-operation and Peace and Education relating to Human Rights and Fundamental Freedoms (adopted 19 November 1974); UNESCO World Plan of Action on Education for Human Rights and Democracy, adopted by the International Congress on Education for Human Rights and Democracy convened by the UNESCO (Montreal, 8-11 March 1993) Doc A/CONF.157/PC/42/Add.6; World Conference on Human Rights, Vienna Declaration and Programme of Action (25 June 1993) A/CONF.157/23, paras 33–34 and 78–82. The first phase of the UNGA 'World Programme for Human Rights Education' Res 59/113A (10 December 2004) A/RES/59/113 (2005–2009), focused on primary and secondary school systems. The second phase (2010–2014) focused on human rights education in higher education and i.a. in training for teachers and educators. Further: UNHRC Res 24/15 'Plan of Action for the third phase (2015–2019) of the World Programme for Human Rights Education' (8 October 2013) UN Doc A/HRC/27/28.

e.g. Nowak and Osler, refer to 'the right to human rights education', based on the UDHR and international treaties.[2199]

Human rights education overlaps with education for democracy. Since the implosion of the communist regimes and the end of the Cold War,[2200] *international human rights instruments have called for 'education for democracy'.* An International Congress convened by UNESCO adopted the *1993 World Plan of Action on Education for Human Rights and Democracy* (Montreal Declaration).[2201] *Human rights are construed in their broadest sense 'to include inter alia learning about tolerance and acceptance of others, solidarity, participatory citizenship and the importance of building mutual respect and understanding.' It declares that 'education for human rights and democracy is itself a human right and a prerequisite for the realization of human rights, democracy and social justice'.*[2202] *The Human Rights Council and UN General Assembly have adopted several resolutions on 'education for democracy'.*[2203] The Council of Europe Charter on EDC/HRE (Part one) is an example of the continua-

---

2199 M Nowak, 'Prioritising human rights education and training' [2004] European Human Rights Law Review 235; Osler, 'Human Rights Education: The Foundation of Education for Democratic Citizenship in our Global Age'.

2200 See also historic context in Arthur, Davies and Hahn, 'Introduction', 4–5.

2201 UNESCO World Plan of Action on Education for Human Rights and Democracy, adopted by the International Congress on Education for Human Rights and Democracy convened by the UNESCO (Montreal, 8-11 March 1993) Doc A/CONF.157/PC/42/Add.6. See earlier, pioneering citizenship education: UNESCO Recommendation concerning Education for International Understanding, Co-operation and Peace and Education relating to Human Rights and Fundamental Freedoms (adopted 19 November 1974), i.a. para 13: Member States should promote at every stage of education 'an active civic training (and learning) which will enable every person to gain a knowledge of the method of operation and the work of public institutions, whether local, national or inter-national, to become acquainted with the procedures for solving fundamental problems; and to participate in the cultural life of the community and in *public affairs*.' (emphasis added). See also before: UNGA 'Declaration on the Promotion among Youth of the Ideals of Peace, Mutual Respect and Understanding between Peoples' UNGA res 2037 (XX) (7 December 1965) UN Doc A/RES/20/2037.

2202 UNESCO World Plan of Action on Education for Human Rights and Democracy, adopted by the International Congress on Education for Human Rights and Democracy convened by the UNESCO (Montreal, 8-11 March 1993) Doc A/CONF.157/PC/42/Add.6.

2203 I.a. UNGA Res 67/18 'Education for democracy' (28 November 2012) UN Doc A/RES/67/18; UNHRC Res 19/36 'Human rights, democracy and the rule of law' (23 March 2012) UN Doc /HRC/RES/19/36; UNGA Res 69/268 'Education for democracy' (5 March 2015) UN Doc A/RES/69/268; UNHRC Res

tion of this work at regional level, transposing the aims of quality education—including human rights education and education for democracy—to the European context.[2204]

Interestingly, the concept of human rights education used at UN level includes components which the Council of Europe ranks under the concept of EDC (not under HRE), e.g. '[e]nabling all persons to participate effectively in a free and democratic society governed by the rule of law'.[2205] Human rights education clearly includes learning about political rights.[2206] *This shows that EDC and HRE are interlinked.*[2207]

28/14 'Human rights, democracy and the rule of law ' (26 March 2015) UN Doc HRC/RES/28/14; UNGA Res 71/8 'Education for democracy' (17 November 2016) UN Doc A/RES/71/8; UNGA Res 73/134 'Education for democracy' (13 December 2018) UN Doc A/RES/73/134; and work continues, i.a. reported in Secretary-General, Literacy for life: shaping future agendas and education for democracy (Note, A/71/177). On the status of resolutions in the EU legal order, see i.a. text to n 831.

2204 See § 57 (a strength of the Charter on EDC/HRE).

2205 See i.a. UNHRC Res 24/15 'Plan of Action for the third phase (2015-2019) of the World Programme for Human Rights Education' (8 October 2013) UN Doc A/HRC/27/28, para 4.

2206 See UNHRC Res 19/36 'Human rights, democracy and the rule of law' (23 March 2012) UN Doc /HRC/RES/19/36, paras 1, 4 and 5. Other human rights which relate to democracy are i.a. freedom of expression, of information, of thought, of assembly and association. See e.g. *All Human Beings: A Manual for Human Rights Education* (ed K Savolainen, The Teacher's Library series, UNESCO 1998) 8–11, explained in simple words, for educators and pupils.

2207 Interlinked, see UNHRC Res 19/36 'Human rights, democracy and the rule of law' (23 March 2012) UN Doc /HRC/RES/19/36, para 14; repeated in UNHRC Res 28/14 'Human rights, democracy and the rule of law ' (26 March 2015) UN Doc HRC/RES/28/14; also UN 'Guidance Note of the Secretary-General on Democracy' (2009): 'At the World Summit in 2005, as in the Millennium declaration in 2000, Member States of the United Nations (UN) recommitted themselves to protecting and promoting human rights, the rule of law and democracy, recognizing that they are interlinked and mutually reinforcing and that they belong to the universal and indivisible core values and principles of the United Nations.' These UN instruments show that CoE action is consistent with UN norms on education for human rights and for democracy. While the CoE usually refers to 'education for democratic citizenship', in one CoE document the expression 'education for democracy' indicates the link with action at UN level: CoE Standing Conference of European Ministers of Education, Resolution on education for democracy, human rights and tolerance (No 1) (Madrid, 23-24 March 1994).

The UN instruments on education for democracy confirm that education for democratic citizenship is not essentially linked to states,[2208] *but rather to 'society', or to 'policymaking at all levels'. Article 25 ICCPR proclaims that every citizen shall have the right and the opportunity to take part in 'the conduct of public affairs'. The 2009 UN Secretary General Guidance Note on Democracy refers to 'democratic values and principles in a society'.*[2209] *According to the UN General Assembly, education for democracy aims at the promotion of democratic values and democratic governance and human rights, and at facilitating* 'the empowerment of citizens and their participation in *political life and policymaking at all levels'.*[2210] *UN instruments frequently restate that democracy cannot be described on the basis of a single model.*[2211] *This should lead to openness to the EU model of democracy (as work in progress).*[2212] *The aim of education to 'enable all persons to participate effectively in a free society' (Article 13(1) ICESCR)* and to ensure the 'preparation of the child for responsible life in a free society' (Article 29 CRC) implicitly in*cludes the aim of education for democracy. Democracy is by definition a form of government based on the participation of all persons, based on the presumption of effective participation and a free society.*[2213]

This overview has highlighted aspects of the international right to education which are essential for quality education. The international right to education encompasses a right to education directed to the aims listed in binding agreements. This certainly has an impact on the curriculum. The requirement that education be acceptable and adaptable also relates to content of teaching. There is clearly a right to quality education comprising

---

2208 See §§ 150 -151 .

2209 UN 'Guidance Note of the Secretary-General on Democracy' (2009), in heading 3: '"Education for democracy" is a broad concept which can help to inculcate democratic values and principles in a society, encouraging citizens to be informed of their rights and the existing laws and policies designed to protect them, as well as training individuals to become democratic leaders in their societies.'. My emphasis.

2210 UNGA Res 71/8 'Education for democracy' (17 November 2016) UN Doc A/RES/71/8, para 6; idem in UNGA Res 67/18 'Education for democracy' (28 November 2012) UN Doc A/RES/67/18, para 4; UNGA Res 69/268 'Education for democracy' (5 March 2015) UN Doc A/RES/69/268, para 4. My emphasis.

2211 I.a. UN 'Guidance Note of the Secretary-General on Democracy' (2009), p 2; UNGA Res 69/268 'Education for democracy' (5 March 2015) UN Doc A/RES/69/268, p 2 ('Recognizing that, while democracies share common features, there is no single model of democracy and that democracy does not belong to any country or region').

2212 See i.a. § 225 and 228 .

2213 See also, *All Human Beings: A Manual for Human Rights Education* 8.

human rights education and education for democracy. Rights and obligations thus frame the educational autonomy of States. The interpretation 'quality education' in Article 165 TFEU in the light of international agreements is relevant for all learners, including the static ones.

2. Quality education at Council of Europe level

295 Democratic citizenship and human rights

The right to education in the ECHR (Art 2 Protocol 1) makes no reference to quality education.[2214] Indications are to be found in ECtHR case law. The ECtHR considers the State to be responsible for quality education and requires that the State, in fulfilling its educational functions, takes care to convey the information or knowledge included in the curriculum in an objective, critical and pluralistic manner, with no aim of indoctrination.[2215]

Quality education is defined in the 2012 Recommendation of the Committee of Ministers on ensuring quality education. The definition is consistent with the UN approach to quality education, including the aims of education for human rights and for democracy. Quality education, inter alia, 'promotes democracy, respect for human rights and social justice' and 'enables pupils and students to develop appropriate competences, self-confidence and critical thinking to help them become responsible citizens'.[2216]

2214 Art 2 Protocol 1 ECHR: 'No person shall be denied the right to education. In the exercise of any functions which it assumes in relation to education and to teaching, the State shall respect the right of parents to ensure such education and teaching in conformity with their own religious and philosophical convictions.' Yet, see Art 53 ECHR (no limitation or derogation of 'human rights and fundamental freedoms which may be ensured under the laws of any High Contracting Party or under any other agreement to which it is a part'). Arts 13(1) ICESCR and 29 CRC are thus indirectly relevant.

2215 See text to nn 693 and 696; and i.a. *Folgerø and Others v Norway* no 15472/02 (ECtHR 29 June 2007), para 84 (g), (h).

2216 CoE Recommendation CM/Rec(2012)13 of the Committee of Ministers to member States on ensuring quality education (12 December 2012), para 6: 'For the purposes of this recommendation, "quality education" is understood as education which: (a) gives access to learning to all pupils and students, particularly those in vulnerable or disadvantaged groups, adapted to their needs as appropriate; (b) provides a secure and non-violent learning environment in which the rights of all are respected; (c) develops each pupil's and student's personality, talents and mental and physical abilities to their fullest potential

The 2012 Recommendation refers to the 2010 Charter on EDC/HRE.[2217] Later instruments confirm this concept of quality education. In 2016, the Standing Conference of the Ministers of Education agreed on the strategic objective:

> To make the preparation for lifelong active democratic citizenship of all learners in education and training a hallmark of the quality of European education systems and an essential part of our response to the challenges Europe is facing.[2218]

Reinforced cooperation with EU institutions is sought, in particular to promote education for democratic citizenship and fundamental values,

---

and encourages them to complete the educational programmes in which they enrol; (d) promotes democracy, respect for human rights and social justice in a learning environment which recognises everyone's learning and social needs; (e) enables pupils and students to develop appropriate competences, self-confidence and critical thinking to help them become responsible citizens and improve their employability; (f) passes on universal and local cultural values to pupils and students while equipping them also to make their own decisions; (g) certifies outcomes of formal and non-formal learning in a transparent way based on fair assessment enabling acquired knowledge and competences to be recognised for further study, employment and other purposes; (h) relies on qualified teachers who are committed to continuous professional development; (i) is free of corruption.' See also preambular paras 25–6. Earlier: CoE Standing Conference of European Ministers of Education, Building a more humane and inclusive Europe: role of education policies, Resolution on the 2008-2010 programme of activities (Istanbul, 4-5 May 2007), paras 7–8 (asking, i.a., to reinforce work on indicators (with the European Commission) on quality assurance in the field of EDC/HRE); CoE Standing Conference of European Ministers of Education, Final Declaration on 'Education for Sustainable Democratic Societies: the Role of Teachers' (Ljubljana, 4-5 June 2010); and the 'Wroclaw Declaration on 50 Years of Cultural Cooperation', text to n 241.

2217 Recital 14 (having regard to).

2218 CoE Standing Conference of Ministers of Education, Securing Democracy through Education: The development of a Reference Framework of Competences for Democratic Culture (Brussels, 11-12 April 2016), para 13; also paras 20 and 31. See before: CoE Standing Conference of Ministers of Education, Governance and Quality Education (Helsinki, 26 -27 April 2013), paras 6, 15, 18 (1)-(2), 21(4).

fostering social and civic competences and intercultural understanding.[2219] The RFCDC is a means of responding to the call for quality education.[2220]

3. Quality education at EU level

296 *Quality education directed to key competences, including citizenship competence*

EU law provides several indications as to how to understand 'quality education' in Article 165 TFEU.

Firstly, pursuant to Article 9 TFEU, when defining and implementing its policies and activities, the Union shall take into account requirements linked to the promotion of 'a high level of education'. In the preamble to the TFEU, Member States declare their determination to promote the development of the highest possible level of knowledge for their peoples through wide access to education and through 'its continuous updating'. Interpreting quality education as 'a high level of education' and in the light of a commitment to 'its continuous updating', EU action should be able to support the EU dimension of EDC in the Member States.

Secondly, the right to education in the CFR (Article 14) must be interpreted in the light of the international agreements (ICESCR, CRC).[2221] Just like the right to education in the ECHR, the right to education in Article 14 CFR is silent about the aims of education (not present in the social dimension in paras 1 and 2).[2222] However, Article 53 CFR provides that no rights in the CFR 'shall be interpreted as restricting or adversely affecting human rights and fundamental freedoms as recognised…by international law and by international agreements to which the Union or

2219 CoE Standing Conference of Ministers of Education, Securing Democracy through Education: The development of a Reference Framework of Competences for Democratic Culture (Brussels, 11-12 April 2016), para 37.

2220 CoE Reference Framework of Competences for Democratic Culture, Vol 1: Context, concepts and model (2018), p 16.

2221 See n 2115. This right is based on the common constitutional traditions of Member States and on Art 2 Protocol ECHR (according to the Explanations).

2222 Some guidance in Art 17 European Social Charter (revised) ETS No 163 (Strasbourg, opening 3 May 1996, entry into force 1 July 1999): 'ensuring the effective exercise of the right of children and young persons to grow up in an environment which encourages the full development of their personality and of their physical and mental capacities'; see also the adjectives 'sufficient and adequate' in para 1(a).

all the Member States are party'. Education in the EU should therefore be understood in the sense of Article 13 ICESCR and 29 CRC, i.e. directed to the listed compulsory aims of education, part of the core of quality education. A contextual argument for an interpretation of the EU right to education in the light of the UN compulsory aims of education is moreover to be found in Article 24 of the UN Convention on the Rights of Persons with Disabilities, a Convention to which the EU has acceded and which is therefore part of EU law.[2223] It suggests that the EU right to education cannot be narrowly interpreted as relating to educational rights in crossborder situations only. The material scope of the EU right to education interpreted in the light of international agreements and staying within the field of application of EU law, is relevant for static citizens as well.[2224] The action undertaken by the EU with regard to the education of Roma and the reference made in this context to the right to education illustrates this point.[2225] Moreover, educational action must respect Article 24 CFR and take the child's best interests as a primary consideration.

This reading of the EU fundamental right to education is consistent with the approach of the 2017 European Pillar of Social Rights, jointly proclaimed by the European Parliament, the Council and the Commission. The very first provision of the European Pillar of Social Rights establishes the right to quality education:

2223 See arguments in Part two, first mode of reception (§ 83); Convention on the Rights of Persons with Disabilities (adopted 13 December 2006 A/RES/61/106, entry into force 3 May 2008); Council Decision of 26 November 2009 concerning the conclusion, by the European Community, of the United Nations Convention on the Rights of Persons with Disabilities [2010] OJ L23/35.

2224 Cp Gori, 'Article 14: Right to Education', 419, on the material scope of the current EU right to education (in short: right of equal access to education and training in another Member State; right of residence during the period of study; ancillary social rights; also crossborder educational services and establishment of private schools).

2225 See i.a. Commission Staff working document on the Application of the EU Charter of Fundamental Rights in 2016 Accompanying the document Communication from the Commission on 2016 Report on the Application of the EU Charter of Fundamental Rights SWD(2017) 162 final: in the European Semester, the Commission made specific reference to the inclusion of the Roma in mainstream education for three Member States (CZ, HU, SK). Also Council Recommendation of 9 December 2013 on effective Roma integration measures in the Member States [2013] OJ C378/1; M Roth and F Moisa, 'The right to education of Roma children in Romania: European policies and Romanian practices' 19 The International Journal of Children's Rights 501.

> Everyone has the right to quality and inclusive education, training and life-long learning in order to maintain and acquire skills that enable them to participate fully in society and manage successfully transitions in the labour market.[2226]

The reference to participating fully in society echoes the educational aim in the ICESCR of 'effective participation in a free society'. In focusing on quality and inclusiveness, the right to education in the European Pillar of Social Rights goes further than the right to education in Article 14 CFR.[2227]

Thirdly, several legal acts—based on Article 165 TFEU—develop the concept of quality education further, such as the 2006 and the 2018 Recommendations on key competences for lifelong learning.[2228] In the 2018 Recommendation, the Council states that the Member States should 'sup-

---

2226 The European Pillar of Social Rights, solemnly proclaimed by the European Parliament, the Council and the Commission on 17 November 2017: 'Education, training and life-long learning'.

2227 Commission Staff working document Accompanying the document Communication from the Commission Monitoring the implementation of the European Pillar of Social Rights SWD(2018) 67 final, 8.

2228 Recommendation of the European Parliament and of the Council of 18 December 2006 on key competences for lifelong learning [2006] OJ L394/10 (Annex: Key Competencies for Lifelong Learning- A European Reference Framework); Council Recommendation of 22 May 2018 on key competences for lifelong learning [2018] OJ C189/1. On quality education, see also Council Conclusions of 19 November 2010 on education for sustainable development [2010] OJ C327/11, paras 2–4; Commission staff working document 'Key European action supporting the 2030 Agenda and the Sustainable Development Goals Accompanying Commission Communication Next steps for a sustainable European future: European Union action for sustainability' SWD(2016) 390 final, heading 2.4, 'Ensure inclusive and equitable quality education and promote life-long learning opportunities for all' (Quality education is linked to an economic rationale: 'The most important Commission priorities contributing to this sustainable development goal are: jobs, growth and investment; a digital single market; a deeper and fairer economic and monetary union, a deeper and fairer internal market; a stronger global actor'. But '[s]ince end 2015 reinforced attention is also given to inclusive education, equality, equity, non-discrimination and the promotion of civic competences'); Conclusions of the Council and of the Representatives of the Governments of the Member States, meeting within the Council, on Inclusion in Diversity to achieve a High Quality Education For All - Council Conclusions (17 February 2017); Council Conclusions on moving towards a vision of a European Education Area [2018] OJ C195/7, para 12.2 (the Council ... underlines the 'the need to ensure high quality and inclusive education to support the development of

port the right to quality and inclusive education, training and lifelong learning' and use the European Reference Framework on key competences to do so. High quality education provides opportunities to develop the eight key competences. One of them is citizenship competence.[2229] That being so, adopting a measure to support the EU dimension in citizenship competence should be possible as a means to achieve quality education. Action to promote the EU dimension of EDC based on Article 165 TFEU would be consistent with present EU education policy.[2230]

297 Conclusion

Instruments at UN level indicate that quality education essentially includes education directed to the aims listed in binding international agreements (ICESCR and CRC), including enabling effective participation and responsible life in a free society and strengthening respect for human rights and fundamental freedoms. This requires education for human rights and democracy. In Council of Europe terminology, quality education includes EDC and HRE.[2231] This understanding of quality education is confirmed

---

all learners, including by focussing on the priorities set out in the November 2017 Council conclusions on school development and excellent teaching'). See also ECJ case law on quality education invoked in the justification of restrictions to fundamental freedoms e.g. *Bressol*, *Lyyski*, *Dirextra* (text to n 2424).

2229 Council Recommendation of 22 May 2018 on key competences for lifelong learning, para 1; see also Annex p 12 'Supporting the development of key competences'.

2230 Council Recommendation of 22 May 2018 on promoting common values, inclusive education, and the European dimension of teaching [2018] OJ C195/1; Council Recommendation of 22 May 2019 on a comprehensive approach to the teaching and learning of languages [2019] OJ C189/15 (and recital 6). See also Commission Communication 'Strengthening European Identity through Education and Culture' COM(2017) 673 final; Council Recommendation of 22 May 2017 on the European Qualifications Framework for lifelong learning and repealing the recommendation of the European Parliament and of the Council of 23 April 2008 on the establishment of the European Qualifications Framework for lifelong learning [2017] OJ C189/15; Council Conclusions on moving towards a vision of a European Education Area [2018] OJ C195/7. See also Council Conclusions on school development and excellent teaching (20 November 2017); Council Conclusions on moving towards a vision of a European Education Area [2018] OJ C195/7; Commission Communication 'Building a stronger Europe: the role of youth, education and culture policies' COM(2018) 268 final. Further Commission Erasmus Proposal COM(2018) 367 final.

2231 Academic writers also link quality education and EDC, see i.a.: Nussbaum, 'Education and Democratic Citizenship: Capabilities and Quality Education';

at EU level. The concept of quality education is relevant for all learners, including the static ones. In a human rights-based approach to education, all children have a right to quality education and states have corresponding obligations. In the light of the analysis in Part three, I conclude that EU action to support the EU dimension of EDC can be based on Article 165(1) TFEU and the concept of 'quality education'.

The interpretation of the concept of quality education in the light of international agreements puts the no-content limit in perspective. Admittedly, it remains intriguing that Article 165 TFEU, on the one hand, confers competence on the EU to contribute to the development of quality education—which undoubtedly also relates to content of teaching—and on the other hand, in the same provision, requires the EU to fully respect the responsibility of Member States for the content of teaching.[2232] Another concept in the legal basis will provide further indications in this regard: the European dimension in education.

C Developing the European dimension in education

298 The European dimension in education sensu stricto: a European dimension in school curricula

The European dimension in education *sensu stricto* is the first of the specific objectives of Union action for achieving quality education which appear in Article 165(2) TFEU: Union action shall be aimed at 'developing the European dimension in education, particularly through the teaching

D Wilson, *A Human Rights contribution to defining quality education* (Background paper prepared for the Education for All Global Monitoring Report 2005 The Quality Imperative, 2004). Further K Grimonprez, 'EU-burgerschap en vorming voor democratie: ijkpunten voor kwaliteitsvol onderwijs' (2019-20) Tijdschrift voor Onderwijsrecht en Onderwijsbeleid 5.

2232 See Snell, 'European Union and National Referendums: Need for Change after the Brexit Vote?': involving schools to educate citizens to become EU citizens is proposed as a solution, yet the competence question remains a stumbling block. On uncertainties with regard to supplementary competences in general, see i.a. Schütze, 'Cooperative federalism constitutionalised: the emergence of complementary competences in the EC legal order' (in the field of health and environment); S Garben, 'Confronting the Competence Conundrum: Democratising the European Union through an Expansion of its Legislative Powers' (2015) 35 Oxford Journal of Legal Studies 55, 59, 65. See further L Azoulai (ed) *The Question of Competence in the European Union* (Oxford University Press 2014).

and dissemination of the languages of the Member States' (first indent). The expression 'European dimension in education' is often used *sensu lato*, referring to the overarching aim of the whole of Article 165 TFEU: contributing to the development of quality education (paragraph 1), with the list of specific objectives (paragraph 2) as the further elaboration of this aim and thus including action to promote mobility.[2233] As an educational principle, the 'European dimension in education' has led to endless debates.[2234] As a Treaty expression, it merits a legal approach based on traditional interpretation methods. They all point in the same direction: the European dimension in education *sensu stricto* aims primarily at the insertion of 'European content' into national school curricula.[2235] That dimension (first indent) is not dependent on mobility (second indent).[2236] 'European content' includes languages and various themes for learning about

---

2233 H Ertl, 'European Union policies in education and training: the Lisbon agenda as a turning point?' (2006) 42 Comparative education 5, 8; Ruffert, 'AEUV Art 165', Rn 4 (on a citizens' right to transnational education, linked with Art 14 CFR, and the political integration-potential of EU education policy), Rn 13–14.

2234 Lane, 'New Community competences under the Maastricht Treaty', 951 ('Orwellian Newspeak'). See DG Mulcahy, 'In Search of the European Dimension in Education' (1991) 14 European Journal of Teacher Education 213; R Ryba, 'Unity in diversity: The enigma of the European dimension in education' (1995) 21 Oxford Review of Education 25; D Barthélemy, 'Analysis of the Concept of European Dimension' (1999) 31 European Education 64; Keating, Ortloff and Philippou, 'Citizenship Education Curricula: The Changes and Challenges Presented by Global and European Integration', 151.

2235 See K Grimonprez, 'The European dimension in citizenship education: unused potential of article 165 TFEU' (2014) 39 ELRev 3, 6. Also, the European dimension 'as such': expression used in Commission Report on the implementation of the Socrates programme 1995-1999, COM(2001) 75 final.

2236 Ruffert, 'AEUV Art 165', Rn 15: the first indent 'European dimension in education' impacts on the content of education. See, indeed, recommendation in Germany, Beschluss der Kultusministerkonferenz vom 08.06.1978 i. d. F. vom 05.05.2008, Empfehlung der Ständigen Konferenz der Kultusminister der Länder in der Bundesrepublik Deutschland 'Europabildung in der Schule', p 7: 'Zur Erschließung der europäischen Dimension in Unterricht und Erziehung sollen grundsätzlich alle Fächer und Lernbereiche der Schule einen Beitrag leisten. Die Lehrpläne und Bildungspläne der Länder enthalten dazu in differenzierter Weise konkrete Ziele und Themen sowie Hinweise auf geeignete Lerninhalte, zweckmäßige Arbeitsformen und wünschenswerte Einstellungen' (tr In order to develop the European dimension in instruction and education, all subjects and learning areas at school must in principle make a contribution. To achieve this the various curricula and educational plans of the *Länder* contain specific objectives and themes in a differentiated manner, as well as indi-

Europe.[2237] Developing the European dimension in education *sensu stricto* (first indent) is directly relevant for static citizens, pupils in classrooms in their own towns or villages, who do not cross borders.

299 Textual interpretation

The use of the words 'languages' and 'particularly' in a separate indent (preceding the mobility indent) is the first strong indication of a curricular concept for the European dimension in education.[2238] From the word 'particularly' it can be inferred that other curricular action is possible as well, for instance, courses on European history,[2239] or—indeed—the EU dimension of EDC.

300 Contextual and teleological interpretation

The maxim of consistent interpretation requires a reading of every provision of EU law in a way that does not contradict its normative context and is in keeping with the objectives pursued.[2240]

Firstly, in light of the increasing importance of the *travaux préparatoires* in ECJ case law, the objectives and actions envisaged in pre-Maastricht policy documents must be examined. These (public) documents show how the original 'European dimension in education' concept focused on the curriculum. The 1973 Janne Report launched the European dimension in

---

cations as to suitable learning content, appropriate working methods and desirable attitudes).

2237 K Lenaerts, 'Subsidiarity and Community competence in the field of education' [1995] Columbia Journal of European Law 1, 27: 'Under the [Arts 165–166] competence, the Community and the Member States may steer their political processes in the direction of giving education a truly European dimension. They may do so not only by promoting study of the various aspects of the European "polity" (such as history, geography, culture, economy, society, and politics), but also through such means as language training taught by native speakers or exchanges of teachers and students of the different Member States. Community competence in the field of education thus clearly contributes to the achievement of one of the basic objectives of the TEU, which under Article A, paragraph 2, was to "creat[e] an ever closer union among the peoples of Europe, in which decisions are taken as closely as possible to the citizen".'.

2238 See Council Recommendation of 22 May 2019 on a comprehensive approach to the teaching and learning of languages [2019] OJ C189/15.

2239 Example given by C Frazier, *L'éducation et la Communauté européenne* (CNRS 1995) 259, 261. See also Pépin, *The history of European cooperation in education and training. Europe in the making - an example* 148.

2240 Lenaerts and Gutiérrez-Fons, 'To Say What the Law of the EU Is: Methods of Interpretation and the European Court of Justice'.

education. All proposed actions concerned the curriculum: learning about Europe; learning about other Member States in history and geography; language learning; and 'Prudent and gradual teaching of European "civics" to be based mainly on Community practices and institutions, on pluralism and on democracy'.[2241] The 1985 Adonnino Report *A People's Europe*, seeking to give new impetus to the European dimension in education, proposed, inter alia, appropriate school books and teaching material, under the heading 'The European Image in Education'.[2242] The Adonnino report, clarifying the objective of what is now Article 165(2) TFEU, has the same value as the Delors report on which the ECJ based its interpretation of Article 125 TFEU in *Pringle*.[2243] After 1992, the objective of a curricular European dimension in education (apart from languages) moved silently from centre to backstage.[2244] Mobility became the focus of the European dimension in education *sensu lato*, as reflected in successful programmes such as Erasmus. Yet, this cannot allow us to forget the meaning and potential *sensu stricto* of the first indent Treaty concept.

2241 H Janne, *For a Community policy on education* (Report for the European Commission, Bull EC Supp 10-73, 1973) 52. The four first objectives of Art 165(2) TFEU can be traced back to this report.

2242 P Adonnino, *Adonnino Committee, A People's Europe, Reports from the ad hoc Committee* (Bull EC 7-1985, 1985), e.g. p 24. See also Keating, Ortloff and Philippou, 'Citizenship Education Curricula: The Changes and Challenges Presented by Global and European Integration'; R Ryba, 'Toward a European Dimension in Education: Intention and Reality in European Community Policy and Practice' (1992) 36 Comparative Education Review 10, 24. For later action, see Commission Staff working paper, First progress report of 23 September 1991 on action untertaken by the Member Sates and by the European Community with a view to strengthening the European dimension in education, SEC (91) 1753 final; Conclusions of the Council and of the Ministers of Education meeting within the Council of 27 November 1992 on measures for developing the European dimension in higher education [1992] OJ C336/4 (see Annex, point 3 about European content); Lonbay, 'Education and the law: the Community context (European Community)'; Theiler, 'The European union and the "European dimension" in schools: Theory and evidence', 323; *Pépin, The history of European cooperation in education and training. Europe in the making - an example*, 293.

2243 Case C-370/12 *Pringle* ECLI:EU:C:2012:756, paras 135–6; Case C-583/11 P *Inuit Tapiriit Kanatami and Others v Parliament and Council* ECLI:EU:C:2013:625, paras 59, 66, 70.

2244 Some EU instruments continued to refer to the European dimension in education, see i.a. Recommendation 2006 on key competences, recital 2: 'overall need to enhance the European dimension in Education'.

Secondly, the European dimension in education is linked to EU citizenship. The first objective of the European dimension in education in the 1993 Green Paper was contributing to European citizenship, based on shared values of interdependence, democracy, equal opportunity and mutual respect.[2245] European citizenship must be explained through education. It is a striking and significant coincidence that the European dimension in education was inserted into the Treaties at the same moment as EU citizenship (1992). It builds on Council of Europe action to develop the European dimension in education, interlinked with EDC.[2246]

Thirdly, a curricular European dimension in education harmonises with the wider context of the internal market. In its 1985 White Paper 'Completing the Internal Market',[2247] the Commission proposed to increase support for programmes 'helping young people, in whose hands the future of the Community's economy lies, to think in European terms'. Many initiatives for a European dimension in education aimed to raise European awareness through the curriculum (particularly in languages and geography). But after 1992, as reported by Field, because the impact of the internal market turned out to be less dramatic than anticipated, short-term enthusiasm was often followed by a loss of interest.[2248] However, free movement rules continue to presume a minimal understanding of, and confidence in, the system on the part of citizens.[2249]

Fourthly, some foundational principles of EU law are relevant for an interpretation of the European dimension in education *sensu stricto*. The normative context for systemic interpretation includes the principles of

2245 Commission Green Paper of 29 September 1993 on the European Dimension of Education COM(93) 457 final, para 13.

2246 See i.a. CoE Parlementary Assembly Recommendation 1111(1989) 'European dimension of education'; CoE Standing Conference of Ministers of Education, Resolution on 'the European dimension of education: teaming and curriculum content' (Vienna, 16-17 October 1991); CoE Recommendation R(99)2 of the Committee of Ministers to member states on secondary education (19 January 1999) . The relationship between the European dimension in education and EDC appears clearly in CoE Recommendation Rec(2002)12 of the Committee of Ministers to member states on education for democratic citizenship (16 October 2002), appendix, para 1 (text to n 236).

2247 Commission White Paper of 16 June 1986 'Completing the Internal Market' COM(85) 310 final, p.26.

2248 Field, *European Dimensions, Education, Training and the European Union*, 103–4.

2249 A Verhoeven, 'Redactionele Signalen' (2012) 60 SEW - Tijdschrift voor Europees en economisch Recht 269. For many citizens and (small) companies, the internal market is in practice still far from being a reality, not because rules are lacking, but because they are insufficiently known or trusted.

democracy, transparency and openness, access to documents and freedom of information.[2250] To be fully effective, these principles presuppose a minimal level of EDC for the whole population, not just for the mobile minority, as argued above.

301 The EU dimension of EDC as part of the European dimension in education

If the 'European dimension in education' in Article 165(2) first indent TFEU is read in harmony with the overall logic of the system, it implies a European dimension in education *sensu stricto* (a concept independent of learner mobility) referring essentially to European themes in the school curriculum. In its 2006 Resolution on initiatives to complement school curricula providing appropriate support measures to include the European dimension, the European Parliament recognised two different aspects of the European dimension: firstly, access to information about the EU (institutions, methods, practices, initiatives) and, secondly, knowledge of Europe's shared history and cultural heritage, linguistic skills, and an understanding of European current events, 'all of which may supplement national curricula'.[2251] The EU dimension of EDC falls mainly under the first heading, but also contributes to an understanding of European cultures and identities (second aspect). The European dimension in education thus includes the EU dimension of EDC. Compared to the European dimension in education, the EU dimension of EDC is a much more focused concept. As explained in Part three, it especially brings in additional elements with regard to the three empowerment aims (c-1–3), consistent with EU law. In the 2018 'Recommendation on promoting common values, inclusive education, and the European dimension of teaching', the Council states that Member States should promote 'the European dimension of teaching'.[2252] The *ratio legis* is to 'help learners experience European identity in all its diversity and strengthen a European

2250 TEU Arts 1, 10(1) and 11(2); TFEU Arts 1 and 15; CFR Art 42. See i.a. §§ 134 137 .

2251 European Parliament Resolution of 26 September 2006 on initiatives to complement school curricula providing appropriate support measures to include the European dimension [2006] OJ C306E/100, point 4. See also Commission Communication 'Investing efficiently in education and training: an imperative for Europe' COM(2002) 779 final, p 21–2, for a curricular European dimension in education.

2252 Council Recommendation of 22 May 2018 on promoting common values, inclusive education, and the European dimension of teaching [2018] OJ C195/1. See in the same spirit, European Parliament resolution of 12 June

positive and inclusive sense of belonging', in addition to promoting a better understanding of the Union and its Member States.[2253] The EU dimension of EDC is visible in many aspects of the European dimension of teaching (such as values, unity and diversity, and the functioning of the Union).[2254] This Recommendation is thus an important step. Yet, more specific action can be taken to support the development of the EU dimension of EDC.

302 Exception to the no-content limit

There seems to be a contradiction within Article 165 TFEU between the first and the second paragraphs. How can a blanket ban on content be reconciled with the EU competence to promote 'particularly' the teaching of languages? Languages are typically part of teaching content. As explained, the Treaty article was drafted at a time when the European dimension in education primarily had a curricular meaning. A reasonable solution to this apparent contradiction is to differentiate between the *lex generalis* and the *lex specialis*. An interpretation that gives full effect to the provisions within their context is that competence for the European dimension *sensu stricto* (second paragraph of Article 165 TFEU) is the *lex specialis* as compared with the *lex generalis* which requires full respect for Member States' responsibility for teaching content (first paragraph). This fits in well with the underlying philosophy and ratio of the 'no go' area. Member States wish to preserve their own identity through their (sub)national education system. Respect for the diversity of educational systems is guaranteed (*lex generalis*), while at the same time, teaching about the EU—of which Member States are part—is encouraged or coordinated (*lex specialis*). Unity in diversity. The one does not exclude the other.

2018 on modernisation of education in the EU (2017/2224(INI)), i.a. paras 36 and 134.

2253 Recital 18.

2254 Para 6: Promotion of a European dimension of teaching: 'encouraging: (a) an understanding of the European context and common heritage and values and an awareness of the unity and diversity, social, cultural and historical, of the Union and the Member States of the Union; (b) an understanding of the origins, values and functioning of the Union; (c) the participation of pupils and teachers in the e-Twinning network, in cross-border mobility, and transnational projects, especially for schools; (d) grass-roots projects to raise awareness of and improve understanding of the European Union in learning settings, notably through direct interaction with young people, such as an annual celebration, on a voluntary basis, of a "Day of the European Union" in learning settings'.

303 Illustration in the Jean Monnet programme

In a number of legal acts adopted on the basis of Article 165 TFEU, the Jean Monnet programme of the EU illustrates the *lex specialis* competence, of relevance for static citizens. Under the 2013 Erasmus+ Regulation, Jean Monnet activities aim to 'promote teaching and research on European integration'.[2255] The earlier 2006 Lifelong Learning Decision did so, too: the 'issues relating to European integration' which formed the core of the Jean Monnet programme are all expressions of the European dimension in education *sensu stricto*.[2256] In response to a request from the European Parliament,[2257] the Commission developed the 'Learning EU@school' initiative on the legal basis of the Jean Monnet programme (key activity 1) of the 2006 Lifelong Learning Decision,[2258] inter alia 'to develop content for EU teachers' or 'pedagogical content' and didactic material for the teaching of European integration in schools.[2259] This successful but limited initiative deserves broader EU support.[2260] Education initiatives which influence national curricula in order to promote the European dimension within the meaning of Article 165(2) *are* permitted.[2261]

From the Jean Monnet programme, albeit primarily aimed at higher education,[2262] I conclude that Article 165(2) first indent TFEU can reasonably be seen as a legal basis for action to encourage the EU dimension of

---

2255 Erasmus+ Regulation 1288/2013, Art 10.

2256 Decision 1720/2006 of the European Parliament and of the Council of 15 November 2006 establishing an action programme in the field of lifelong learning [2006] OJ L327/45; amended by Decision 1357/2008 [2008] OJ L350/56, Art 35(1)a, recital 31. See also Art 35(2) and Art 34(f). The programme aimed 'to stimulate teaching, research and reflection activities in the field of European integration studies'. See 'issues relating to European integration' in Arts 34–37; they can be linked to aspects of the EU dimension of EDC (knowledge, skills, attitudes, ...).

2257 See Draft General Budget 2011—Statement of revenue and expenditure COM(2010) 750 final, 397.

2258 Call for Proposals—EACEA/18/11 Jean Monnet programme: Key activity 1, Information and research activities for 'Learning EU@school' [2011] OJ C174/06, p.8.

2259 Learning EU@school, Call for Proposals [2011] OJ C174/06, Point 4.

2260 Jean Monnet Programme—"Learning EU@School", Report of Project Coordinators' Meeting, Best Practice and Cooperation, organized by EACEA (2012). New angles are explored in Innovation projects, including on Learning EU @school, in Jean-Monnet projects, Erasmus+ programme guide (2019), p 225.

2261 Yet, ibid: 'bearing in mind' p 5.

2262 Decision 1720/2006 of the European Parliament and of the Council of 15 November 2006 establishing an action programme in the field of lifelong

EDC. If the EU has the competence to promote teaching and research on European integration among specialist academics, including at home in their Member State, there is no reason to invoke the no-content limit to oppose—as a matter of principle—the EU competence to promote learning about European integration in schools.

In the Proposal for a new Erasmus programme, similarly based on Articles 165–166 TFEU, Jean Monnet activities 'will be partially refocused to target for example pupils in schools'.[2263] Jean Monnet actions will support 'teaching, learning, research and debates on European integration matters' in the field of higher education and 'in other fields of education and training'.[2264]

The Proposal is cautious as to the European dimension in static situations ('national activities with a strong European dimension').[2265] Yet, strengthening European identity is one of the general objectives (Article 3).[2266]

304 No harmonisation

Quality education presupposes a European dimension in education which includes the EU dimension of EDC. What is important is the term 'dimension'. The EU or European dimension does not interfere with the no harmonisation-limit.[2267] Part three argues for an EU *dimension* to national EDC from an adaptation perspective. The intention is not to impose a har-

---

learning [2006] OJ L327/45; amended by Decision 1357/2008 [2008] OJ L350/56, Art 34(a); Erasmus+ Regulation 1288/2013, Art 10.

2263 Commission Erasmus Proposal COM(2018) 367 final, explanatory memorandum 11.

2264 Commission Proposal for a Regulation of the European Parliament and of the Council establishing 'Erasmus': the Union programme for education, training, youth and sport and repealing Regulation (EU) No 1288/2013, COM(2018) 367 final, Art 7.

2265 Ibid, explanatory memorandum p 12: 'While Member States remain responsible for the content and organisation of their policies in the fields concerned, this Programme aims to boost transnational and international mobility and cooperation projects, and to support policy developments with a European dimension'; p 13: 'This action will also support flexible formats (generally transnational and, in exceptional cases, national activities with a strong European dimension) allowing organisations to reach out to people with fewer opportunities.'.

2266 Ibid, recital 31.

2267 The prohibition of harmonisation is in my view not problematic in the context of the EU *dimension* in EDC, integrated in the variety of national forms of citizenship education. Admittedly, much is unclear about the harmonisation

monised body of knowledge as EU citizenship education, to be learned by every EU citizen. The intention is to encourage the inclusion of an EU dimension of EDC—including critical thinking—in the very diverse forms and content of national citizenship education. The analysis has demonstrated that EU law impacts in such a decisive way on the substance of the EDC components, that EDC without an EU dimension can hardly be seen as 'quality education'. To be consistent with EU law, citizenship competences (and other key competences) as recommended by the Council in the 2018 Recommendation on key competences, should therefore include a genuine EU 'dimension'.[2268]

D Encouraging the participation of young people in democratic life in Europe

305 Political rights shed light on this part of the legal basis

In addition to 'quality education' and 'the European dimension in education', there is a third concept in the legal basis in Article 165 TFEU which is relevant to the promotion of the EU dimension in EDC: Union action shall be aimed at 'encouraging the participation of young people in democratic life in Europe' (para 2, fifth indent). Part three has already explained the significance of participation in democratic life in Europe, based on EU law on citizenship and democracy. Here, the human rights-based approach

---

restriction in the education field in general. See i.a. Garben, *EU Higher education law. The Bologna Process and harmonization by stealth*; S Garben, 'The Case to Correct Some of Maastricht's Mistakes: A Critical Assessment of Article 165 TFEU on Education and Suggestions for Reform' in M De Visser and AP van der Mei (eds), *The Treaty on European Union 1993-2013: Reflections from Maastricht* (Intersentia 2013); Garben, 'Confronting the Competence Conundrum: Democratising the European Union through an Expansion of its Legislative Powers'; M Dawson, 'Integration through Soft Law: No Competence Needed? Juridical and Bio-Power in the Realm of Soft Law' in S Garben and I Govaere (eds), *The Division of Competences between the EU and the Member States: Reflections on the Past, the Present and the Future* (Hart 2017); Garben S, 'Restating the Problem of Competence Creep, Tackling Harmonisation by Stealth and Reinstating the Legislator', in *The Division of Competences*, ibid, (2017).

2268 Council Recommendation of 22 May 2018 on key competences for lifelong learning: 'Citizenship competence is the ability to act as responsible citizens and to fully participate in civic and social life, based on understanding of social, economic, legal and political concepts and structures, as well as global developments and sustainability.' In the same vein see civic competences in Recommendation of the European Parliament and of the Council of 18 December 2006 on key competences for lifelong learning.

sheds extra light on this indent. The importance of the human rights-based approach to education was underlined in the context of quality education.[2269] As EDC is situated at the intersection of the right to education and political participation rights, the case law of the ECtHR on voting in elections and its relevance in the EU legal order is being recalled.[2270] A human rights-based approach requires action for effective political democracy in the EU. The political participation rights of EU citizens guaranteed by the CFR, too, give substance to the aim of 'the participation of young people in democratic life in Europe' in the fifth indent of Article 165(2) TFEU and underscore the importance for the EU of using this legal basis.[2271]

306 The fundamental right to vote in elections

Article 3 of Protocol 1 to the ECHR states that the member states 'undertake to hold free elections at reasonable intervals by secret ballot, under conditions which will ensure the free expression of the opinion of the people in the choice of the legislature'. Article 39(2) CFR provides that 'Members of the European Parliament shall be elected by direct universal suffrage in a free and secret ballot'.[2272] Remarkably, the ECHR and the CFR both formulate this in terms of an obligation, and the ECtHR as well as the ECJ have interpreted the respective provisions as establishing a right.[2273]

2269 See § 285 .

2270 Many more fundamental rights are relevant in EDC, i.a. the right to freedom of expression and the rights of the child. See i.a. Arts 19, 24 and 25 ICCPR. For fundamental rights *to*, *in* and *through* citizenship education, see UN ComRC 'General Comment No 1 (2001)- Article 29(1): The Aims of Education' Doc CRC/GC/2001/1; also UNESCO-UNICEF, A Human Rights-Based Approach to Education for All: A framework for the realization of children's right to education and rights within education (2007), 35; Tomaševski, *Human rights obligations: making education available, accessible, acceptable and adaptable*, 43; Verheyde, 'Article 28: The Right to Education' 2, 7.

2271 Including Arts 43–44 CFR (Ombudsman, petition).

2272 On correspondance in general, see Peers and Prechal, 'Article 52: Scope and Interpretation of Rights and Principles' 1491 ff.

2273 The ECtHR recognizes in Article 3 of Protocol No 1 a solemn commitment with a primary obligation to adopt positive measures to 'hold' democratic elections, and deduces a subjective right. See i.a. *Mathieu-Mohin and Clerfayt v Belgium* no 9267/81 (ECtHR 2 March 1987), paras 47–8, 50–53; also *Sitaropoulos and Giakoumopoulos v Greece* no 42202/07 (ECtHR 15 March 2012), para 67. Electoral rights in the UDHR (Art 21) and ICCPR (Art 25) are directly formulated as rights.

In *Matthews v UK*, the ECtHR decided that elections to the European Parliament fall within the scope of Article 3 Protocol 1 ECHR. The UK had not included Gibraltar in the franchise for the European Parliament elections. Ms Matthews, residing in Gibraltar, was denied any opportunity whatsoever of expressing her opinion on the choice of the members of the European Parliament.[2274] Firstly, the ECtHR rejected the argument of the UK that Article 3 was not applicable to elections for the European Parliament. Even though the European Parliament did not exist when Protocol 1 was drafted, the ECHR is a living instrument to be interpreted in the light of present-day conditions. In the obligation contained in Article 3, the word 'legislature' does not necessarily mean the national parliament.[2275] The ECtHR recalled that Article 3 enshrines a characteristic feature of an 'effective political democracy'[2276] and that elections for the European Parliament cannot be excluded from its scope on the ground that it is a supranational, rather than a purely domestic, representative organ.[2277] Subsequently, the ECtHR assessed whether the European Parliament has the characteristics of the 'legislature' in Gibraltar. The UK had argued that the European Parliament lacked the most fundamental attributes of a legislature, i.e. the power to initiate legislation and the power to adopt it. The Court referred to the 'the *sui generis* nature of the European Community, which does not follow in every respect the pattern common in many States of a more or less strict division of powers between the executive and the legislature'. Because the Court must ensure that effective political democracy is properly served in the territories to which the Convention applies, it had regard to the strictly legislative powers of the European Parliament *and* to its role in the overall legislative process (involving the participation of the European Parliament, the Council and the Commission).[2278] The Court found that

> the European Parliament represents the principal form of democratic, political accountability in the Community system. The Court considers that *whatever its limitations*, the European Parliament, which derives democratic legitimation from the direct elections by universal

2274 *Matthews v UK* no 24833/94 (ECtHR 18 February 1999), para 64.

2275 Paras 39–40.

2276 Para 42. Settled case law, see i.a. *Mathieu-Mohin and Clerfayt v Belgium* no 9267/81 (ECtHR 2 March 1987), para 47; *Sitaropoulos and Giakoumopoulos v Greece* no 42202/07 (ECtHR 15 March 2012), para 63.

2277 Para 44.

2278 Paras 48–9.

> suffrage, must be seen as that part of the European Community structure which best reflects concerns as to 'effective political democracy'.[2279]

The European Parliament constitutes a part of the legislature of Gibraltar for the purposes of Article 3 of Protocol 1. The UK had denied the very essence of Ms Matthews' right to vote and to elect the legislature.[2280]

This reasoning of the ECtHR in *Matthews* provides an argument with regard to other participation rights of EU citizens as well. *Whatever their limitations*, the rights to participate in the democratic life of the Union form part of the EU structure reflecting concerns as to 'effective political democracy'.[2281] The specific (non-statal) characteristics of these political rights in the EU do not deprive them of their relevance for democracy in the EU.[2282] In respect of other participation rights, too, it is necessary to bear in mind (in the words of the ECtHR) 'the *sui generis* nature of the European Community, which does not follow in every respect the pattern common in many States'.[2283] In this light, all reasonable measures must be taken to ensure the effectiveness of existing democratic participation rights. One such reasonable measure is to read them in the light of EDC standards. They help to guarantee effective political democracy, which constitutes 'one of the cornerstones of the Convention system'.[2284] The preamble to the ECHR affirms that fundamental human rights and freedoms are best maintained by an effective political democracy. As early as the 1987 *Mathieu-Mohin and Clerfayt* case, and ever since, the ECtHR has referred to this concept and objective.[2285] The ECtHR frequently reiterates that democracy is the only political model compatible with the ECHR.[2286] In order to establish and maintain the foundations of effective and mean-

---

2279 Para 52 (emphasis added).

2280 Paras 54 and 64–5.

2281 This applies *mutatis mutandis* to participatory opportunities based on Art 11 TEU, whatever their limitations.

2282 See § 213 . See also *BVerfG, 2 BvE 2/08 (Lissabon)* 30 June 2009, Absatz-Nr (1-421), para 280 'measured against requirements in a constitutional state...'.

2283 *Matthews*, para 48.

2284 *Karácsony and Others v Hungary* no 42461/13 et al (ECtHR 17 May 2016), para 138.

2285 *Mathieu-Mohin and Clerfayt v Belgium* no 9267/81 (ECtHR 2 March 1987), para 47; *Matthews*, para 42.

2286 *United Communist Party of Turkey and Others v Turkey* no 19392/92 (ECtHR 30 January 1998), para 45; *Hirst v UK* no 74025/01 (ECtHR 6 October 2005), para 58.

ingful democracy governed by the rule of law, the rights guaranteed under Article 3 of Protocol 1 are of prime importance: the ECHR 'establishes a close nexus between an effective political democracy and the effective operation of Parliament'.[2287] While the rights to vote and to stand for election are not absolute and member states have a wide margin of appreciation, they cannot hold elections in conditions that 'curtail the rights in question to such an extent as to impair their very essence and deprive them of their effectiveness'.[2288] National conditions 'must not thwart "the free expression of the opinion of the people in the choice of the legislature"'.[2289] Such 'free expression' implies freedom of expression in society.[2290] Free formation of the voter's opinion presupposes a minimal understanding of the system to which the vote relates. As analysed in Chapter two, the ECtHR has interpreted the ECHR rights in the light of recommendations of the Committee of Ministers.[2291] It can be assumed that the ECtHR would pay particular attention to the Recommendation on the Charter on EDC/HRE of the Committee of Ministers when interpreting Article 3 of Protocol 1 to the ECHR.[2292] Effective political democracy is closely related to EDC standards, as appears from the normative framework of the Council of Europe.[2293]

It is tempting to take the last step in the reasoning, i.e. to apply Article 52(3) CFR and to bring Article 3 of Protocol 1, thus interpreted in the light of EDC standards, into the EU legal order via an interpretation of Article 39(2) CFR, which corresponds to it.[2294] The mechanism is that recommendations of the Committee of Ministers of the Council of Europe

---

2287 *Karácsony and Others v Hungary* no 42461/13 et al (ECtHR 17 May 2016), para 141. Also *Scoppola v Italy (No 3)* no 126/05 (22 May 2012), paras 81–3.

2288 *Mathieu-Mohin and Clerfayt v Belgium* no 9267/81 (ECtHR 2 March 1987), paras 51–2; *Matthews v UK* no 24833/94 (ECtHR 18 February 1999), para 63; *Hirst v UK* no 74025/01 (ECtHR 6 October 2005), para 56.

2289 *Mathieu-Mohin* and *Clerfayt*, para 52; *Matthews*, para 63.

2290 I.a. *United Communist Party of Turkey and Others v Turkey* no 19392/92 (ECtHR 30 January 1998), para 45. See further van Dijk and others, *Theory and practice of the European Convention on human rights* 918; Grabenwarter, *European Convention on Human Rights: Commentary* 403: free formation of the voter's opinion, protection against indoctrination.

2291 *Demir and Baykara v Turkey* no 34503/97 (ECtHR 12 November 2008 ibid, para 76; with regard to the right to education, i.a. *Horváth and Kiss v Hungary* no 11146/11 (ECtHR 29 January 2013). See §§ 42 44 , and text to n 355.

2292 Text to n 370.

2293 §§ 30 -40 .

2294 In *Delvigne*, the ECJ implicitly included the ECtHR protection of the electoral right for prisoners: see analysis of Gundel, 'Der Verlust der bürgerlichen

can have legal effects in the interpretation of ECHR rights and that these rights thus interpreted have legal effects in the EU legal order via Article 52(3) CFR. However, the missing link here must be acknowledged: the Explanations to the CFR do not say that Article 39 CFR corresponds to any provision of the ECHR.[2295] The only authority is the application by the ECtHR of Article 3 Protocol 1 ECHR to the European Parliament in *Matthews*. The argument based on the requirement of effective political democracy in the ECHR legal order can thus not be transposed as such via Article 52(3) ECHR in conjunction with Article 39(2) CFR. However, the substance of the ECHR reasoning remains inspiring, particularly in the light of the Memorandum of Understanding.[2296] A reading of the right to vote for the European Parliament in the light of EDC standards—aiming at an effective political democracy—militates in favour of the incorporation of an EU dimension in national EDC. Moreover, the Explanations state that Article 39(2) CFR 'takes over the basic principles of the electoral system in a democratic State'. These principles include respect for the ECHR.[2297]

307 *Interpretation of the right to vote in harmony with constitutional traditions*

Another interpretation rule for the right to vote in the CFR is laid down in Article 52(4) CFR. In so far as Article 39(2) CFR recognises a right resulting from the constitutional traditions common to the Member States, it must be interpreted in harmony with them. Voting rights are explicitly set out in many Member State constitutions. As analysed in Part two, EDC

Ehrenrechte als Eingriff in die Grundrechtecharta—Neues zur Reichweite des EU-Grundrechtsschutzes gegenüber den Mitgliedstaaten und zur lex-mitior-Garantie', 181; van Eijken and van Rossem, 'Prisoner disenfranchisement and the right to vote in elections to the European Parliament: Universal suffrage key to unlocking political citizenship?', 128 (Charter-centrism).

2295 For other rights, the Explanations refer to corresponding rights, e.g. Art 48 on the presumption of innocence and right of defence. It is only 'in so far as'(Art 52(3) CFR) there is correspondance of rights, that the meaning and scope are the same as in the ECHR (as interpreted by the ECtHR).

2296 See § 22 .

2297 Cp J Shaw, 'Prisoner voting: now a matter of EU law' 2015 <eulawanalysis.blogspot.com/2015/10/prisoner-voting-now-matter-of-eu-law.html>: The adoption in Art 39(2) of the basic principles of the electoral system in a democratic state (Explanations) is presumably a reference to ECHR case law on Art 3 Protocol 1.

can—to a certain extent—be seen as part of the common constitutional traditions (or constitutional practices) linked with voting rights.[2298]

As no uniform procedure has yet been laid down, the election of the Members of the European Parliament must take place in accordance with the 'principles common to all Member States' (Article 223 TFEU).[2299] The Explanations to Article 39(2) CFR provide that it 'takes over the basic principles of the electoral system in a democratic State'. Can, on a wide interpretation, EDC standards be seen as part of these principles? All Member States are committed to the EDC principles in the Recommendation on the Charter on EDC/HRE. To prepare young voters for national elections, schools provide learning about national institutions. In the same way, schools should add an EU dimension to prepare for European Parliament elections. The elections for the European Parliament illustrate the intertwining of national and EU law (the Electoral Act states that the electoral procedure shall be governed in each Member State by its national provisions[2300]). This interlinking could be reflected by adding an EU dimension to national EDC on the topic of elections. It would be in line with the aim of future EU electoral law to enhance the effectiveness of the system and 'to bring Members of the European Parliament closer to their voters, in particular the youngest amongst them'.[2301]

308 Conclusion: a sound legal basis

The answer to the question as to whether the EU *has* the competence to act in the field of EDC and promote the EU dimension (the conferral question) is positive: Article 165 TFEU is a sound legal basis for EU action to support the EU dimension of EDC, including for static citizens, based on the general notion of quality education in paragraph 1 and on the specific objectives in paragraph 2, i.e. the European dimension in education (first indent) and the participation of young people in democratic life in Europe (fifth indent).

The next two questions are: Does the EU need to *use* that competence? (the subsidiarity question in the strict sense) and, if so, *to what extent* does it need to do so (proportionality)?

2298 See § 89 , nuanced § 94 .

2299 European Parliament Resolution of 11 November 2015 on the reform of the electoral law of the European Union [2017] OJ C366/7, recital J.

2300 Art 7 Act concerning the election of the representatives of the Assembly by direct universal suffrage [1976] OJ L278/5 (Electoral Act), as amended.

2301 European Parliament Resolution of 11 November 2015 on the reform of the electoral law of the European Union [2017] OJ C366/7, recital B.

CHAPTER 10 Subsidiarity, proportionality and Member State action

A Subsidiarity and proportionality of EU action

309 Subsidiarity as a principle regarding the use of competences

The effects of subsidiarity as a meta-constitutional concept, impacting on the *conferral* of competences, are so strong in the field of education that subsidiarity as a principle affecting the *use* of conferred competences, tends to occupy less space.[2302] Subsidiarity has already been taken into account in the very definition of the EU's competences in the legal basis: competences are conferred, but there are no-go areas and harmonisation is precluded. Articles 165 and 166 TFEU thus 'breathe the air of subsidiarity', especially in the limits set on the conferral of competences to the Union.[2303] Moreover, for supporting competences the subsidiarity question is less pressing, because there is no preemption of national competence in the policy fields concerned. When the EU exercises its supporting competence in education, the Member States retain their competences. By contrast, when the EU exercises shared competences, Member States are vigilant about guarding subsidiarity, because by using these shared competences, the EU preempts the field and Member States can no longer act (Article 2(2) TFEU).[2304]

However, subsidiarity must be respected. Pursuant to the general provision in Article 5 TEU, the use of Union competences is governed by the principles of subsidiarity and proportionality. The third paragraph only excludes those areas from the scope of subsidiarity which are a matter of exclusive EU competence—and education is not one of them.

2302 Lenaerts, 'Subsidiarity and Community competence in the field of education', 28.

2303 Ibid: 'fully breathe the air of subsidiarity'. Cp Schütze, 'Cooperative federalism constitutionalised: the emergence of complementary competences in the EC legal order', 183: not 'fully'; the limits in education such as the prohibition of harmonisation, may preclude EU action even if the objectives can be achieved better at Union level.

2304 See Commission, Better regulation toolbox, Tool 5, p 27 on subsidiarity: 'The point of departure is shared competence' (<ec.europa.eu/info/better-regulation-toolbox_en>).

310 Substantive and procedural conditions

What does compliance with the principle of subsidiarity require when conferred competences are used?

The substantive conditions are twofold: the objectives cannot be sufficiently achieved by the Member States at central, regional or local level (negative criterion) and can be better achieved at EU level (positive criterion).[2305] The institutions have developed guidelines for examining whether these conditions are fulfilled. In the 1992 Edinburgh conclusions, the European Council proposed that 'the issue under consideration has transnational aspects which cannot be satisfactorily regulated by action by Member States' and/or that action at Community level would produce clear benefits by reason of its scale or effects compared with action at the level of the Member States.[2306] The 1997 Amsterdam Protocol on the application of the principles of subsidiarity and proportionality continued the attempt to make subsidiarity operational.[2307] At present, Protocol 2 on the application of the principles of subsidiarity and proportionality, annexed to the Lisbon Treaty, sets out guidelines for determining whether the conditions are met.[2308]

Procedural conditions, too, must be respected. A statement of reasons (Article 296(2) TFEU), qualitative and (as far as possible) quantitative indicators, and impact assessments make it possible to check compliance with the principles of subsidiarity and proportionality.[2309] At a political level,

2305 See analysis in Calliess, 'EU-Vertrag (Lissabon) Art 5', Rn 33–41; K Granat, 'The Subsidiarity Principle in the EU Treaties' in *The Principle of Subsidiarity and its Enforcement in the EU Legal Order: The Role of National Parliaments in the Early Warning System* (Hart 2018) 20. Much literature on subsidiarity (extensive list in Calliess, EU-Vertrag (Lissabon) Art 5); see i.a. A Estella, *The EU principle of subsidiarity and its critique* (2005 edn, Oxford University Press 2002); T Blanke, 'The Principle of Subsidiarity in the Lisbon Treaty' in N Bruun and others (eds), *The Lisbon Treaty and Social Europe* (Hart 2012); Edward, 'Subsidiarity as a Legal Concept'; J Öberg, 'Subsidiarity as a Limit to the Exercise of EU Competences' (2017) 36 Yearbook of European Law 391.

2306 Edinburgh Presidency Conclusions (n 2080) 19.

2307 Protocol (No 30) on the application of the principles of subsidiarity and proportionality (Amsterdam, 2 October 1997); Case C-58/08 *Vodafone* ECLI:EU:C:2010:321, para 72.

2308 Case C-508/13 *Estonia v Parliament and Council* EU:C:2015:403, para 44; Case C 358/14 *Poland v Parliament and Council* ECLI:EU:C:2016:323, paras 111–113.

2309 Protocol (No 2) Art 5; Protocol (No 30) on the application of the principles of subsidiarity and proportionality (Amsterdam, 2 October 1997), para 4. See also Commission Staff Working Document 'Better Regulation Guidelines' SWD(2015) 111, and accompanying toolbox; Interinstitutional Agreement

national Parliaments review compliance in the pre-legislative phase (early warning system).[2310] At judicial level, in the case of litigation, the ECJ verifies whether the substantive conditions and the procedural safeguards have been met.[2311] While case law has been criticised for leaving wide discretion to the legislature and failing to examine issues of subsidiarity seriously, the EU legislature cannot merely assert, using a standard formula, that the principle of subsidiarity has been respected. The Court determines whether the EU legislature was entitled to consider, on the basis of a detailed statement of reasons, that the objective could be better achieved at EU level. In recent case law, the Court refers to specific evidence, to data and impact assessments, when reviewing compliance with the principles of subsidiarity and proportionality.[2312] In *Poland v Parliament and Council*, the impact assessment included 'sufficient information showing clearly and unequivocally the advantages of taking action at EU level rather than at Member State level'.[2313]

311 A dynamic concept

Can the objective of quality education, in particular in respect of the European dimension in education and the encouragement of the participation by young people in democratic life in Europe, not be sufficiently achieved by the Member States (negative criterion) and can it be better achieved at EU level (positive criterion)? For Lenaerts in 1994, Member States' responsibility for teaching content, the organisation of education systems, and their cultural and linguistic diversity, acknowledged in the Treaty provision conferring competence on the EU, 'boils down to the introduction of

---

between the European Parliament, the Council of the European Union and the European Commission on Better Law-Making [2016] OJ L123/1; Commission Annual report 2018 on the application of the principles of subsidiarity and proportionality and on relations with national parliaments COM(2019) 333 final.

2310 Granat, 'The Subsidiarity Principle in the EU Treaties'. See also Commission Communication 'The principles of subsidiarity and proportionality: Strengthening their role in the EU's policymaking' COM(2018) 703 final.

2311 Protocol (No 2) Art 8. See Case C-58/08 *Vodafone* ECLI:EU:C:2010:321; Case C-176/09 *Luxembourg v Parliament and Council* ECLI:EU:C:2011:290; Case C 358/14 *Poland v Parliament and Council* ECLI:EU:C:2016:323; *Poland v Parliament and Council* Case C-128/17 ECLI:EU:C:2019:194; and early cases as Case C-84/94 *UK v Council* ECLI:EU:C:1996:431.

2312 E.g. Case C-547/14 *Philip Morris Brands and Others v UK* ECLI:EU:C:2016:325, paras 214–227.

2313 Case C 358/14 *Poland v Parliament and Council* ECLI:EU:C:2016:323, para 123 (on the Tobacco Products Directive).

an irrebuttable presumption that they are better placed to deal with these policy matters'. He saw Community educational action as being confined to aspects 'which are manifestly cross-border and for which it would be difficult for each Member State to act efficiently on an individual basis'.[2314] I think that subsidiarity and proportionality should remain dynamic concepts, allowing EU cooperation to develop as new needs and expectations as to solidarity might arise.[2315] The 1992 Edinburgh conclusions already emphasised that subsidiarity is a dynamic concept to be applied in the light of the Treaty objectives: 'It allows Community action to be expanded where circumstances so require, and conversely, to be restricted or discontinued where it is no longer justified.'[2316] In a Europe facing economic, financial and migration crises and a civic deficit, the best level for achieving objectives must be sought objectively without a priori presumptions.

EU action supporting the EU dimension of EDC can satisfy both the negative and positive criteria[2317] and would be consistent with existing legal instruments on education and the reasons they state for compliance with subsidiarity. In 2018, five national parliaments submitted opinions on

---

2314 Lenaerts, 'Education in European Community Law after "Maastricht"', 41; also Lenaerts, 'Subsidiarity and Community competence in the field of education'. In the same vein: A Hingel, Education Policies and European Governance, Contribution to the Interservice Groups on European Governance (Commission, DG EAC, 2001), p 4: education is 'an ideal-type of a policy area for subsidiarity to play its full role', the most optimal level of decision-making being the (sub)national one 'where initiatives can be taken that are fully integrated while the nationally specific institutional set-ups as well as the historical and cultural heritage are respected'. Further H Ertl and D Phillips, 'Standardization in EU education and training policy: findings from a European research network' (2006) 42 Comparative Education 77, 78, observing that especially in the field of education, support for the principle of subsidiarity 'indicates that national and regional actors have been increasingly cautious in surrendering power to supranational bodies'.

2315 See C Calliess, *Subsidiaritäts-und Solidaritätsprinzip in der Europäischen Union* (Nomos 1996). See also Lenaerts and Van Nuffel, *European Union Law* (2011) 135; Pépin, *The History of European Cooperation in Education and Training* (2006) 146; O'Leary, *The Evolving Concept of Community Citizenship: From the Free Movement of Persons to Union Citizenship* 186: 'which level of authority is more suitable to deal with a specific problem may ultimately depend on a political decision'.

2316 Edinburgh Presidency Conclusions (n 2080) 16; also Protocol (No 30) on the application of the principles of subsidiarity and proportionality (Amsterdam, 2 October 1997), para 3.

2317 Text to n 2305.

proposals of the Commission in the education field, i.e. on key competences for lifelong learning, digital skills and common values. Some parliaments insisted that the EU should not go further than adopting legally non-binding recommendations. They asked to carefully examine the European added value and the administrative burden which the proposals generated. The Commission reassured the national parliaments that the proposals were drafted with subsidiarity in mind, fully respected the Member States' powers in education, and that future materials for support would be developed in close cooperation with the Member States, as voluntary tools for learning.[2318]

312 Objectives insufficiently achieved by Member States

Reports, academic research and case studies demonstrate in qualitative and quantitative terms that, in practice, the Treaty objectives of quality education, of the European dimension in education (*sensu stricto*, in particular with regard to the EU dimension of EDC), and of preparing young people for participation in democratic life in Europe, are not sufficiently achieved by Member States acting alone. Beyond rhetoric on citizenship education, figures and concrete examples reveal the specific shortcomings of Member States' action in the field. Fragmented EU learning in many Member States —or none at all—is reported by Eurydice and the International Civic and Citizenship Education Study, as mentioned in the Introduction to this work.[2319] The bEUcitizen project on barriers to EU citizenship concludes a

2318 Commission Annual report 2018 on the application of the principles of subsidiarity and proportionality and on relations with national parliaments COM(2019) 333 final, Opinions of CZ, DE, PT, and RO on the Education Package (see fn 79).

2319 See text and reports above in § 3 ; Losito B and others, Young People's Perceptions of Europe in a Time of Change: IEA International Civic and Citizenship Education Study- 2016 European Report (2017) 13 14; Commission/EACEA/ Eurydice, Citizenship Education in Europe (2012), 17 ff, 30, 32, 97 (in Germany, themes related to the European dimension were no longer included in the upper secondary level curriculum); Commission/EACEA/Eurydice, Citizenship Education at School in Europe (2017) 67. Also Commission, Learning Europe at School (DG for Education, Youth, Sport and Culture, ICF GHK, 2013); European Parliament Resolution of 12 April 2016 on Learning EU at school [2018] OJ C58/57; and Opinion of the European Economic and Social Committee on 'Education about the European Union' SOC/612 (21 March 2019), para 2.5. Further K Grimonprez, 'Beyond Rhetoric: Education for Democratic Citizenship in the European Union' in S Garben, I Govaere and P Nemitz (eds), *Critical Reflections on Constitutional Democracy in the European Union* (Hart 2019).

study of 7 Member States by stating that all countries share a very similar approach with regard to the European dimension of citizenship: 'it is a highly neglected area within the national curriculum'.[2320] While some schools and teachers do excellent work, in general the quality of the EU dimension in citizenship education seems largely unsatisfactory.[2321] It is worth recalling that Member States do not even sufficiently achieve the EDC objectives of the Council of Europe in terms of national EDC, that is, quite apart from the EU dimension. The second review cycle of the Charter on EDC/HRE gives evidence of implementation gaps, and even of commitment gaps.[2322] Work at Council of Europe level is important, but does not suffice.

The Commission guidelines on 'the necessity/relevance test' ask, as a key part for the negative criterion, to qualify the 'Union relevance' of the ini-

---

2320 WE Bakker and others, *The quest for a European civic culture: The EU and EU Citizenship in policies and practices of citizenship education in seven EU member states* (Utrecht University Repository 2017) 3, on the Netherlands, Croatia, France, Germany, Ireland, Spain and Hungary: 'The focus is dominantly on the factual and theoretical knowledge on the EU and especially its institutions rather than the promotion of values and the training of skills needed to exercise EU citizenship rights and needed for development of active, participating EU citizens. Hence, European citizenship education within the member states seems to be in its infancy'.

2321 See also P Ferreira, C Albanesi and I Menezes, 'European Identity and Citizenship in Textbooks/Educational Media' (2018) 17 Journal of Social Science Education 2; and 5 country reports in this special issue, uncovering gaps and differences, i.a. Piedade and others, 'Learning About the European Union in Times of Crisis: Portuguese Textbooks' Normative Visions of European Citizenship'; Missira V, 'Strengthening European citizenship education' (2019) 18 Journal of Social Science Education (3: European Citizenship Education: Business as Usual or Time for Change?) 55. Earlier, in the same vein: Theiler, 'The European union and the "European dimension" in schools: Theory and evidence', 332 ('Especially if contrasted against the fervour with which all the Member States continue to design their "civics", history, and geography curricula as vehicles to advance their specifically national socialization agendas, the "European dimension" is still a negligible entity in the school curricula throughout the Union'); Walkenhorst, 'Problems of Political Education in a Multi-level Polity: explaining Non-teaching of European Union Issues in German Secondary Schooling'; Keating, 'Educating Europe's citizens: moving from national to post-national models of educating for European citizenship', 147; A Keating, *Education for Citizenship in Europe: European Policies, National Adaptations and Young People's Attitudes* (Palgrave Macmillan 2014).

2322 See § 66 . Moreover, Member States cannot escape the negative criterion by referring to international cooperation. See Calliess, 'EU-Vertrag (Lissabon) Art 5', Rn 38.

tiative. The greater this relevance, the more likely it is that Member State action alone will be insufficient.[2323] Based on the analysis of the preceding chapters, the EU dimension of EDC can be said to have high Union relevance, as it concerns the very foundations of the EU, democracy and citizenship. The fact that some Member States are better at providing EU learning than others, does not detract from the legitimacy of the EU's use of its competence if the problem is widespread across the EU and not limited to a few Member States.[2324] In *Poland v European Parliament and Council*, the Court points out that the subsidiarity principle is not intended to limit the EU's competence on the basis of the situation of any particular Member State taken individually. It only requires that the proposed action can, by reason of its scale or effects, be better achieved at EU level in view of the EU objectives set out in Article 3 TEU, and provisions specific to various areas.[2325] The Proposal for a new Erasmus Regulation refers to an Erasmus+ mid-term evaluation which demonstrated that 'single initiatives of education institutions or Member States, though deemed efficient and beneficial at national level, have insufficient scale and volume, and do not reach a European-wide effect'.[2326]

313 Objectives better achieved by the EU

EU action to support the EU dimension in EDC has clear benefits. Its added value is apparent when compared with the fragmented action of the Member States. Transnational aspects (the *European* dimension of education) and an efficiency comparison, including economies of scale, may indicate that the EU is better placed to act than local, regional or national actors.[2327] As an argument for added value, the Council refers in its 'Recommendation on promoting common values, inclusive education, and the European dimension of teaching' inter alia to a common understanding of the importance of common values and to facilitating the sharing of knowl-

2323 Commission, Better regulation toolbox, Tool 5, p 27.

2324 Ibid. On this problem, Edward, 'Subsidiarity as a Legal Concept', 100; Granat, 'The Subsidiarity Principle in the EU Treaties', 21.

2325 Case C 358/14 *Poland v Parliament and Council* ECLI:EU:C:2016:323, para 119; earlier Case C-508/13 *Estonia v Parliament and Council* EU:C:2015:403, para 53.

2326 Commission Erasmus Proposal COM(2018) 367 final, explanatory memorandum 6–7; see also recital 57.

2327 See Calliess, 'EU-Vertrag (Lissabon) Art 5', Rn 41, on a comparison between the added value for integration and the loss of competence of Member States.

edge, expertise and good practice.[2328] These reasons would also be valid for EU action to promote EDC and its EU dimension. A common understanding of the EU dimension of EDC and the education of citizens in the values on which the EU is founded ('Werteverbund') are all the more important in a Union essentially based on mutual trust and are better supported at EU level.[2329] Even in the Council of Europe, the added value of action on EDC was justified by the advantages of using the same terminology and focusing on the same objectives.[2330] That argument holds true a fortiori in the EU. Given the interdependence of Member States' democracies, an EDC framework at EU level with common terminology and common objectives adds value to the disparate actions at national, regional, local and school level. That action for the EU dimension adds value to action for EDC at Member State and at Council of Europe level is clear from the preceding chapters. Part three identified specific additional and significant content for an EU dimension to national EDC and advanced concrete arguments for the added value of EU action to promote this dimension in mainstream education. EU measures have clear benefits for quality education and for empowering EU citizens in particular where they support specific learning outcomes for the EU dimension. At present, Member State norms on citizenship education and EU learning are often limited to general declarations and statements of intention.[2331] The Erasmus Regulation refers to gains in quality, improved knowledge and understanding of the

2328 Council Recommendation of 22 May 2018 on promoting common values, inclusive education, and the European dimension of teaching [2018] OJ C195/1, see preamble and Proposal, explanatory memorandum 6. See further Commission Staff working document Accompanying the document proposal for a Council Recommendation on common values, inclusive education and the European dimension of teaching (2018), p 23 ff.

2329 See i.a. §§ 173 247 , and text to n 1477.

2330 See i.a. in CoE Reference Framework of Competences for Democratic Culture, Vol 1: Context, concepts and model (2018), p 16, 21.

2331 Commission/EACEA/Eurydice, Citizenship Education at School in Europe (2017), and Annexes. See for *France*, 'Loi n° 2013–595 du 8 juillet 2013 d'orientation et de programmation pour la refondation de l'école de la République', Annexe 'La programmation des moyens et les orientations de la refondation de l'école de la République': 'Promouvoir une plus grande ouverture sur l'Europe et le monde. L'ecole doit favoriser l'intégration des futurs citoyens français dans l'espace politique de l'Union européenne et rendre possible la mobilité professionnelle dans l'espace économique européen. C'est pourquoi la France promouvra les initiatives visant à développer un esprit européen et un sentiment d'appartenance partagé à la communauté politique que constitue l'Union européenne. (...) L'apprentissage des langues vivantes constitue un

EU, to positive attitudes towards the EU, and the development of a European identity.[2332]

If the EU legislature has the political will to support the EU dimension of EDC, it should have no difficulties in establishing that the conditions applying to the principle of subsidiarity are satisfied.

314 EU supporting measures respecting proportionality

Pursuant to the principle of proportionality, the content and form of Union action must not exceed what is necessary to achieve the objectives of the Treaties. There is no sharp distinction between the principles of subsidiarity and proportionality, particularly in cases where the former principle permits *some* Union action and requires the 'to what extent' question to be addressed.[2333] The 1992 Edinburgh guidelines stated that, other things being equal, directives should be preferred to regulations and framework directives to detailed measures; where appropriate, non-binding measures such as recommendations should be preferred, and cooperation should be encouraged between Member States if this is sufficient to achieve the objectives.[2334] EU measures should leave as much scope as pos-

---

moyen privilégié de cette ouverture.' (To encourage greater openness to Europe and the World. School must promote the integration of future French citizens in the political space of the European Union and make professional mobility a reality in the European economic area. That is why France will promote initiatives to encourage a shared sense of being European and belonging to the political community of the European Union (...) Learning modern languages is an excellent way of achieving this openness.) Mobility is encouraged too. School, together with the family, must provide moral and civic teaching which includes learning about the values and symbols of the Republic and the European Union, their institutions, the national anthem and its origins, and prepare students for their role as citizens. For *Germany*, see i.a. Beschluss der Kultusministerkonferenz vom 08.06.1978 i. d. F. vom 05.05.2008, Empfehlung der Ständigen Konferenz der Kultusminister der Länder in der Bundesrepublik Deutschland 'Europabildung in der Schule'.

2332 Commission Erasmus Proposal COM(2018) 367 final, 6–7, see also recital 57. On added value, see further Grimonprez, 'The European dimension in citizenship education: unused potential of article 165 TFEU', 18–21.

2333 Lenaerts, 'Subsidiarity and Community competence in the field of education', 3, 25; Granat, 'The Subsidiarity Principle in the EU Treaties', 23, 29 (sharp distinction in Edinburgh conclusions, while confusion in Protocol 2).

2334 Edinburgh Presidency Conclusions (n 2080) 21; Protocol (No 30) on the application of the principles of subsidiarity and proportionality (Amsterdam, 2 October 1997), para 6.

sible for national decision consistent with achieving the aim of the measure.[2335]

Which type of instruments do the Treaties envisage in the field of education? The EU can exercise its supporting competence in education in two ways. Firstly, incentive measures may be adopted by the European Parliament and the Council acting in accordance with the ordinary legislative procedure, after consulting the Economic and Social Committee and the Committee of the Regions (Article 165(4) first indent TFEU). Educational incentive measures are thus legislative acts (Article 289 TFEU). Secondly, recommendations can be adopted by the Council (Article165(4) second indent TFEU).

Other options for promoting the EU dimension in EDC are measures adopted in a mixed form (combining an EU and an intergovernmental approach) and the creation of an EU Agency for Education for Democratic Citizenship. Finally, better reporting on EDC and its EU dimension in the Member States will help to identify gaps and prepare for future supporting action.

These options will now be explored.

315 Binding incentive measures

Binding incentive measures are the strongest form of action to support the EU dimension of EDC. The legal basis in Article 165(4) first indent TFEU has been used at regular intervals to adopt binding legislation to support quality education. It could equally be used to promote an EU dimension in EDC.

Contrary to common perception, EU education policy measures based on Articles 165–166 TFEU are not all just a matter of soft law.[2336]

2335 Edinburgh Conclusions (ibid) 20; Commission, Better regulation toolbox, Tool 5, p 30.

2336 The Convention Working Group considered that supporting measures authorise the Union to adopt 'recommendations, resolutions, guidelines, programmes, and other legally non-binding acts as well as legally binding decisions, to the extent specified' in the Treaty. See European Convention, Working Group V 'Complementary Competencies, Final Report' (4 November 2002) CONV 375/1/02 REV 1, p.1. See also L Martin, *L'Union européenne et l'économie de l'éducation: émergence d'un système éducatif européen* (Larcier 2011) 169: proliferation of EU documents on education, no hierarchy, unclear, unarticulated; European Parliament Resolution of 4 September 2007 on institutional and legal implications of the use of 'soft law' instruments [2008] OJ C187E/75: 'soft law' (an "ambiguous and pernicious" notion that should not be used) does not provide full judicial protection' (recitals A, D). The EU can

Although the word 'incentive measures' may give the opposite impression,[2337] incentive measures are binding when issued in the form of a regulation or decision (Article 288 TFEU). When they take the form of a recommendation they are not binding and their potential for the EU dimension in education is weaker (although recommendations are not without any legal effect[2338]). In EU education policy, incentive measures have mostly taken the form of decisions[2339] of the European Parliament and the Council establishing action programmes in education. Decision 819/95 established the Community action programme Socrates for the period 1995–1999, extended by Decision 253/2000 for the period 2000–2006.[2340] Decision 1720/2006 established an action programme in the field of lifelong learning for the period 2007–2013.[2341] The programme for the period 2014–2020 was adopted in the form of a regulation, the 2013 Erasmus+ Regulation.[2342]

---

take legally binding measures in education policy, see further Ruffert, 'AEUV Art 165', Rn 23.

2337 Compare Theiler, 'The European Union and the "European Dimension" in Schools' (1999) 21 Journal of European Integration 307, 323.

2338 The principle of sincere cooperation requires national administrations and courts to interpret national and Union provisions 'in a way which best corresponds to the aim of a recommendation': Lenaerts and Van Nuffel, *European Union Law* 919. See Joined Cases C-317-320/08 *Alassini* ECLI:EU:C:2010:146, para 40, referring, i.a., to Case C-322/88 *Grimaldi* ECLI:EU:C:1989:646, paras 7, 16, and 18.

2339 Before the Lisbon Treaty, decisions as defined in Art 249 EC needed specific addressees. Decisions *sui generis* were adopted, with no addressee. The Lisbon Treaty allows for addressed or non-addressed decisions (Art 288 TFEU).

2340 Decision 819/95 of the European Parliament and of the Council of 14 March 1995 establishing the Community action programme 'Socrates' [1995] OJ L87/10; Decision 253/2000 of the European Parliament and of the Council of 24 January 2000 establishing the second phase of the Community action programme in the field of education 'Socrates' [2000] OJ L28/1.

2341 Decision 1720/2006 of the European Parliament and of the Council of 15 November 2006 establishing an action programme in the field of lifelong learning [2006] OJ L327/45; amended by Decision 1357/2008 [2008] OJ L350/56.

2342 Erasmus+ Regulation 288/2013. The Erasmus+ programme covers 'education and training at all levels, in a lifelong learning perspective, including school education (Comenius), higher education (Erasmus), international higher education (Erasmus Mundus), vocational education and training (Leonardo da Vinci) and adult learning (Grundtvig)' (Art 1(3)(a)). See also Commission Erasmus Proposal COM(2018) 367 final.

What is the effect of educational incentive measures adopted by the EU? Member States retain their basic competence in education, but they have to exercise it in compliance with EU law including incentive measures. Incentive measures increasingly include obligations for Member States, i.e. obligations to cooperate and even take action, where that is necessary to achieve the objectives (proportionality).[2343] The incentive measure mechanism provides for an EU incentive if certain conditions are satisfied. The key question is: who benefits from the incentive? If Member States are the beneficiaries of the incentive, they have no obligation. If EU incentives, such as funding or quality labels, are intended to benefit schools or learners directly, Member States may be obliged, firstly, to adapt their legislation so that beneficiaries can satisfy the conditions applying and, secondly, to take all other necessary implementing measures. An example is the 2013 Erasmus+ Regulation.[2344] This lays down obligations for the Member States in unambiguous 'shall' and 'must' terms. They shall take all appropriate measures to remove legal and administrative obstacles to the proper functioning of the Programme; they shall appoint national authorities to act on their behalf, who in turn shall designate national agencies. All have obligations.[2345]

Incentive measures in the form of a regulation or decision have an important legal impact as they are binding on all the bodies of the Member State.[2346] Pursuant to the principle of primacy of Union law, national courts must refrain from applying any national provision which would be

2343 Lenaerts, 'Education in European Community Law after "Maastricht"', 31, 37–38; Field, *European Dimensions, Education, Training and the European Union*, 185. Cp before 1992: Shaw, 'Education and the Law in the European Community'.

2344 Erasmus+ Regulation 1288/2013. In the same sense, Decision 1720/2006 of the European Parliament and of the Council of 15 November 2006 establishing an action programme in the field of lifelong learning [2006] OJ L327/45; amended by Decision 1357/2008 [2008] OJ L350/56, Art 6(2); also obligations in Decision 253/2000 of the European Parliament and of the Council of 24 January 2000 establishing the second phase of the Community action programme in the field of education 'Socrates' [2000] OJ L28/1, Art 5. See further analysis in Grimonprez, 'The European dimension in citizenship education: unused potential of article 165 TFEU', 12.

2345 Arts 27 and 28. See further obligations in Erasmus+ Regulation 1288/2013, Arts 21–23, 31 and 37.

2346 If Member States do not implement them correctly in the period prescribed, individual actors can have the right to invoke them in court, to give the provisions 'effet utile'.

likely to hinder their implementation.[2347] If the Commission considers that a Member State has failed to fulfil an obligation imposed by an incentive measure, it can bring the matter before the ECJ (Article 258 TFEU).[2348]

A closer look at the incentive measures adopted puts the 'no content' and 'no harmonisation' limits in Article 165 TFEU in perspective, as EU education policy increasingly affects curricula and has converging effects.[2349] The 1995 Socrates Decision included the Comenius programme for schools.[2350] To 'develop the European dimension in education at all levels so as to strengthen the spirit of European citizenship' and to

---

2347 Case 249/85 *Albako* ECLI:EU:C:1987:245, para 17. Vertical, not horizontal direct effect: 80/06 *Carp* ECLI:EU:C:2007:327, para 22.

2348 Thus, although the educational autonomy of Member States is respected, this form of EU action potentially has far-reaching effects (in addition to the huge practical impact of financial incentives). See Lenaerts, 'Education in European Community Law after "Maastricht"', 15, 38; J Lonbay, 'Reflections on education and culture in EC law' in R Craufurd Smith (ed), *Culture and European Union law* (Oxford University Press 2004) 243, 250.

2349 It must be noted that a mere practice of EU institutions cannot derogate from the rules laid down in the Treaty and create precedents with regard to legal bases and competences conferred on the EU: see Case 68/86 *UK v Council* ECLI:EU:C:1988:85, para 24. A broader perspective relates to the context where EU measures taken on other legal bases may also impact on national educational content. A prime example is mutual recognition of diplomas (Art 53 TFEU), e.g. for medical and paramedical diplomas, coupled with the coordination of study curricula, and later Directive 2005/36 of the European Parliament and of the Council of 7 September 2005 on the recognition of professional qualifications [2005] OJ L255/22, with minimum harmonisation: see Lenaerts and Van Nuffel, *European Union Law* 260–265. Measures in other areas, such as culture, health, consumer protection, research and technological development or environment (Arts 167–169, 179 and 191 TFEU) can also influence school curricula and even have harmonising effects in accordance with case law (Case C-376/98 *Germany v Parliament and Council ('Tobacco Advertising')* ECLI:EU:C:2000:544, paras 77–78). Outside the EU, the intergovernmental Bologna process produced 'harmonisation by stealth': Garben, *EU Higher education law. The Bologna Process and harmonization by stealth*.

2350 Decision 819/95 of the European Parliament and of the Council of 14 March 1995 establishing the Community action programme 'Socrates' [1995] OJ L87/10. It included also the controversial *Lingua* programme. The 1989 Lingua Decision (Council Decision 89/489/EEC of 28 July 1989 establishing an action programme to promote foreign language competence in the European Community (Lingua) [1989] OJ L239/24) had been strongly opposed by the UK, who claimed that language teaching in secondary schools was outside the scope of the powers of the Community and confined *Lingua* to post-compul-

improve the knowledge of languages, the Parliament and the Council encouraged school partnerships developing 'subjects of European interest'.[2351] The 2000 Socrates Decision supported action to advance 'knowledge, skills and competences likely to foster active citizenship and employability', also awarding financial assistance for 'the development of curricula, courses, modules or teaching material in the context of reinforcing the European dimension of school education'.[2352] In the 2006 Lifelong Learning Decision, the Erasmus programme—encouraging mobility[2353]—inevitably brought changes in study curricula and the organisation of higher education, 'causing "convergence", if not "harmonisation"'.[2354] Within the overall objectives of the Decision and specifically of the Comenius programme, reference was made to developing a sense of European citizenship, skills for active citizenship, knowledge, and understanding of the diversity of European cultures, and of values such as human rights, democracy, and tolerance (undoubtedly aspects of the EU dimension of EDC), confirming the potential of the legal basis.[2355] Key activities in the transversal programme supported 'developing new language learning materials' and courses and 'innovative ICT-based content'.[2356] The 2013

---

sory education. After the 1992 Maastricht Treaty provided a new legal basis in Art 126 EC, the European Parliament and the Council incorporated the programme into the 1995 Socrates Decision.

2351 Decision 819/95 of the European Parliament and of the Council of 14 March 1995 establishing the Community action programme 'Socrates' [1995] OJ L87/10, Annex, Chapter II, Action 1; see also Art 3(a).

2352 Decision 253/2000 of the European Parliament and of the Council of 24 January 2000 establishing the second phase of the Community action programme in the field of education 'Socrates' [2000] OJ L28/1, Art 1, Action 1, 2(d).

2353 Decision 1720/2006 of the European Parliament and of the Council of 15 November 2006 establishing an action programme in the field of lifelong learning [2006] OJ L327/45; amended by Decision 1357/2008 [2008] OJ L350/56, Art 22.

2354 Shaw, 'From the Margins to the Centre: Education and Training Law and Policy', 555. See also J Pertek, 'Le processus de Bologne et l'action de la Communauté en matière d'éducation' [2005] Law & European affairs 51; LS Terry, 'The Bologna Process and Its Impact in Europe: It's So Much More than Degree Changes' (2008) 41 Vanderbilt Journal of Transnational Law 107.

2355 Decision 1720/2006 of the European Parliament and of the Council of 15 November 2006 establishing an action programme in the field of lifelong learning [2006] OJ L327/45; amended by Decision 1357/2008 [2008] OJ L350/56, Art 1(a)(d)(i); Art 17(1). Yet, insufficiently operationalised.

2356 Ibid, See i.a. Arts 33(2) and 33(3). For earlier action with curriculum implications, see e.g. Decision 2318/2003 of the European Parliament and of the

Erasmus+ Regulation supports curriculum development, e.g. in partnerships in the form of knowledge and skills alliances.[2357]

Applied to the EU dimension in EDC, the potential of Article 165 TFEU emerges clearly. Article 165 TFEU provides a legal basis for the EU to issue binding legislation to promote an EU dimension in EDC.[2358] Regulations or decisions can establish incentives for schools or learners, e.g. quality labels or funding, and oblige Member States to adapt their legislation to allow implementation. They should go no further than necessary and leave as much scope as possible to the Member States' national systems of citizenship education. In the Recommendation on promoting common values, inclusive education, and the European dimension of teaching, the Council declares that its content 'is without prejudice to existing national initiatives in these fields, notably in national civic education'.[2359]

316 Recommendations

Incentive measures can also take the form of recommendations. Recommendations of the Parliament and the Council containing incentives (based on Article 165(4) first indent TFEU) are to be distinguished from recommendations of the Council (based on Article 165(4) second indent), where neither the European Parliament nor the Economic and Social Committee or the Committee of the Regions are involved. [2360] Several

---

Council of 5 December 2003 adopting a multiannual programme (2004 to 2006) for the effective integration of information and communication technologies (ICT) in education and training systems in Europe (eLearning Programme) [2003] OJ L345/9.

2357 Erasmus+ Regulation 1288/2013, Art 8(1)b.

2358 I thus disagree with Theiler, 'The European union and the "European dimension" in schools: Theory and evidence', 323 and 325, for whom the Maastricht Treaty did 'not strengthen the Commission's and the EP's ability promote the "European dimension" in national school curricula in a significant way', arguing that it 'does not figure among the areas which the Treaty lists as subject to potential Union involvement', and even if this list were only illustrative, Community action 'could at the most be of a "soft" and non-binding type'. Neither do I agree with Lonbay, 'Reflections on education and culture in EC law' 273: 'the EC itself not being allowed to take … action'.

2359 Council Recommendation of 22 May 2018 on promoting common values, inclusive education, and the European dimension of teaching [2018] OJ C195/1, recital 19. Each Member State can decide on its approach in the implementing measures.

2360 E.g. Council Recommendation of 28 June 2011 on policies to reduce early school leaving [2011] OJ C191/1; Council Recommendation of 28 June 2011 'Youth on the move' — promoting the learning mobility of young people

recently adopted measures take the latter form.[2361] Remarkably, the Recommendation on key competences for lifelong learning adopted in 2006 by the European Parliament and the Council (ordinary legislative procedure) was replaced in 2018 by a Recommendation on key competences adopted solely by the Council.[2362]

Recommendations are appropriate instruments for supporting the EU dimension of EDC. Preferably adopted by the European Parliament and the Council (for increased legitimacy), or else by the Council alone, a recommendation promoting EDC and its EU dimension in Member States, would contribute to empowering EU citizens to exercise their democratic rights and responsibilities, to value diversity and to effectively participate in democratic life in Europe.

317 Respect of the no-content limit: learning outcomes

On the basis of Article 165 TFEU, the EU can use its 'competence' to support quality education, while fully respecting the 'responsibility' of Member States for the content of teaching.[2363]

If the curriculum is defined as 'a plan for learning in the form of the description of *learning outcomes*, of *learning content* and of *learning processes* for a specified period of study',[2364] the EU can recommend EDC and its EU dimension in the *learning outcomes*, yet leave the learning content to Member States, respecting the responsibility of Member States for the content of teaching. The paradigm in the field of education has shifted from inputs based on a static conception of curricular content to dynamically achieved

---

[2011] C199/1; Council Recommendation on the validation of non-formal and informal learning [2012] OJ C398/1.

2361 Council Recommendation of 19 December 2016 on Upskilling Pathways: New Opportunities for Adults [2016] OJ C484/1; Council Recommendation of 20 November 2017 on tracking graduates [2017] OJ C423/1; Council Recommendation of 22 May 2017 on the European Qualifications Framework for lifelong learning and repealing the recommendation of the European Parliament and of the Council of 23 April 2008 on the establishment of the European Qualifications Framework for lifelong learning [2017] OJ C189/15; Council Recommendation of 22 May 2018 on key competences for lifelong learning [2018] OJ C189/1; Council Recommendation of 22 May 2018 on promoting common values, inclusive education, and the European dimension of teaching [2018] OJ C195/1.

2362 Council Recommendation of 22 May 2018 on key competences for lifelong learning [2018] OJ C189/1.

2363 Competence and responsibility are not necessarily synonyms. For reflection, compare their use in Art 165(1) and Art 88(3) or Art 207(4)(b) TFEU.

2364 Text to n 2073.

learning outcomes and (educational) competences, defined as 'a combination of knowledge, skills and attitudes appropriate to the context'.[2365] The approach based on educational competences can be seen to be compatible with the 'no content' and 'no harmonisation' limits of the Treaty. In the 2018 Recommendation on key competences for lifelong learning the Council defines eight key competences but leaves the means of achieving them to the Member States (a wide variety of learning approaches and environments can be used to support their development[2366]). In order to overcome difficulties in the implementation, the Commission observed that 'translating key competences into learning outcomes is a major step', which 'can be done at different levels, by policy makers, but also teachers and learners within their individual education systems, institutions and programmes of learning'.[2367]

Admittedly, EU education policy recommendations have the capacity to influence the content of teaching.[2368] Although the words 'curriculum' and 'content' were not mentioned in the 2006 Recommendation on key

---

2365 Recommendation of the European Parliament and of the Council of 18 December 2006 on key competences for lifelong learning [2006] OJ L394/10 (Annex: Key Competencies for Lifelong Learning- A European Reference Framework). See also Erasmus+ Regulation 1288/2013, Art 2(19); Commission staff working document, Assessment of Key Competences in initial education and training: Policy Guidance Accompanying the document Communication from the Commission Rethinking Education: Investing in skills for better socio-economic outcomes SWD(2012) 371 final.

2366 Council Recommendation of 22 May 2018 on key competences for lifelong learning [2018] OJ C189/1, p 12.

2367 Commission Staff working document Accompanying the document Proposal for a Council Recommendation on Key Competences for LifeLong Learning SWD(2018) 14 final, 64 ('Policy makers can ensure that these learning outcomes are consistently specified across curricula, syllabi, specifications, standards or similar framework documents').

2368 In several recommendations 'learning plans' and elements of the European dimension in education (e.g. intercultural awareness) appear as preparation for learning mobility and it is suggested that they should be included in the curriculum, e.g. Recommendation of the European Parliament and of the Council of 18 December 2006 on transnational mobility within the Community for education and training purposes: European Quality Charter for Mobility [2006] OJ L394/5, recitals 1 and 2, and Annex on learning plans; Council Recommendation of 28 June 2011 'Youth on the move' — promoting the learning mobility of young people [2011] C199/1, point 3 and 4; Recommendation of the European Parliament and of the Council of 10 July 2001 on mobility within the Community for students, persons undergoing training, volunteers, teachers and trainers [2001] OJ L215/30, at I1(b).

competences, in practice the competences approach had a significant impact on curricula and content.[2369] Key competences are expressed in terms of indicators and benchmarks, where the pressure of publicity and the comparison of Member States' performances may have convergent effects.[2370] But I agree with Lonbay that creating 'convergence through commonly accepted outcomes is not at all the same as creating a rigid, Europe-wide curriculum'.[2371] Recommended learning outcomes should not be equated with forbidden content of teaching, nor as harmonisation, insofar as their implementation and the ways of achieving them are left to the educational freedom of the Member States. Learning outcomes leave room for differences in the precise content of teaching as Member States absorb them into the richness of national educational systems and cultures. The Member States also retain freedom as to learning processes, educational activities, choice of textbooks and methods, grouping of pupils, curricular or cross-curricular courses, distribution of annual taught time between subjects, methods of assessment, etc.

318 *An EU Reference Framework on Education for Democratic Citizenship and the EU Dimension*

On the legal basis of Article 165 TFEU and respecting the principles of subsidiarity and proportionality, a recommendation could be adopted on EDC and its EU dimension in order to elaborate on the components of the citizenship competence (key competence for lifelong learning) and to formulate learning outcomes for school education in a Reference Framework on Education for Democratic Citizenship and the EU Dimension. Inspiration could be drawn, for instance, from the Reference Framework for Lan-

2369 G Halász and A Michel, 'Key Competences in Europe: interpretation, policy formulation and implementation' (2011) 46 European Journal of Education 289; A Kleibrink, 'The EU as a Norm Entrepreneur: the case of lifelong learning' (2011) 46 European Journal of Education 70. See also Commission staff working document, Assessment of Key Competences in initial education and training: Policy Guidance Accompanying the document Communication from the Commission Rethinking Education: Investing in skills for better socio-economic outcomes SWD(2012) 371 final, p 6; Commission/EACEA/Eurydice, Citizenship Education in Europe (2012), p 17.

2370 See Council Conclusions on increasing the level of basic skills in the context of European cooperation on schools for the 21st century [2010] C323/04.

2371 Lonbay, 'Reflections on education and culture in EC law' 256.

guages[2372] or the Reference Framework for Competences for Democratic Culture[2373] of the Council of Europe. Learning outcomes could relate to the EDC components and their EU dimension as analysed in Part three, including the understanding of EU foundational values, objectives and principles, EU rights and obligations, and critical thinking.[2374] Member States would be encouraged to link their learning outcomes to the Reference Framework when determining content of teaching in national curricula. The Framework could be developed independently in cooperation with by (higher) education institutions (to avoid suspicion of Europropaganda by EU institutions).[2375] The projects supported in various actions, such as the 'Learning EU@school' projects under the Jean Monnet programme, and the outcomes they deliver, could be coordinated in harmony with this proposed Framework.[2376] At present, outcomes for EU learning at school and didactic materials are fragmented, scattered across many different websites, and teachers and pupils have no common database with which they can work throughout the learning process. Ideally, the Reference Framework would refer to a school-friendly version of selected provisions of the Treaties and CFR.[2377]

2372 The Common European Framework of Reference for Languages (see § 103), see i.a. appendix 1, B(4), 'a reference tool for the development and implementation of coherent and transparent language education policies', inviting member states to 'ensure that language instruction is fully integrated within the core of the educational aims'; 'The CEFR is intended to provide a shared basis for reflection and communication among the different partners in the field, including those involved in teacher education and in the elaboration of language syllabuses, curriculum guidelines, textbooks, examinations, etc., across the member states of the Council of Europe'.

2373 See § 38 .

2374 See also proposal to define a set of learning outcomes: Opinion of the European Economic and Social Committee on 'Education about the European Union' SOC/612 (21 March 2019), para 1.5.

2375 A common Reference Framework could be the answer to Commissioner Figel's emphasis on the importance of clear views on how to integrate the European dimension in school curricula and how to provide schools with both the material and the opportunities to learn about Europe in practice ([2006] OJ C306E/100). See also Opinion of the European Economic and Social Committee, Reconciling the national and European dimensions of communicating Europe [2009] OJ C27/152, point 3.4.

2376 See text to n 2259. Deserving much wider support.

2377 As proposed in § 175 . See further renewed action in Opinion of the European Economic and Social Committee on 'Teaching Europe — developing a toolkit for schools' [2019] OJ C 353/52.

Binding incentive measures could complement an EU recommendation on EDC and its EU dimension in order to encourage the inclusion of a high-quality EU dimension in key competences with financial and non-financial incentives (EU labels of excellence).[2378]

Upstream, Article 165(2) first indent TFEU is a basis for the sound development of the European dimension in teacher training (a prerequisite for the EU dimension in school education). 'EU schoolteachers' could be trained at Jean Monnet higher education institutions (teacher training with an EU label of excellency).[2379]

Existing programmes, such as the European Parliament Ambassador School Programme (EPAS), could be developed further and more widely implemented. EPAS is intended to promote the European dimension in school education and leads to the award of the 'Ambassador School' certificate.[2380]

A recommendation and incentive measures on EDC and its EU dimension would be consistent with other EU instruments in education policy and a major contribution to the realisation of the European Education Area (EEA).[2381]

319 Mixed instruments

As an *ad hoc* solution for action to promote the EU dimension of EDC, mixed instruments must be mentioned. Examples are 'conclusions of the Council and of the representatives of the Governments of the Member

---

2378 Mechanism set out in § 315 . Analogy to Erasmus+ Regulation 1288/2013, Art 10. See the support for EU learning@school projects.

2379 More recommendations in A. Dunne, D. Ulicna and S. Oberheidt, *Learning Europe at School* (DG EAC, Final report, submitted by ICF GHK, 2013); and B. Hoskins and D. Kerr, *Final Study Summary and Policy Recommendations: Participatory Citizenship in the European Union* (Report 4) (Institute of Education, University of London, commissioned by the European Commission, Europe for Citizens Programme, 2012).

2380 Launched in 2016, aiming to increase the turnout of young voters in the 2019 European Parliament elections.

2381 Consistent i.a. with Council Recommendation of 22 May 2018 on promoting common values, inclusive education, and the European dimension of teaching [2018] OJ C195/1. See further Council Conclusions on moving towards a vision of a European Education Area [2018] OJ C195/7. See also European Parliament Resolution of 12 December 2017 on the EU Citizenship Report 2017: Strengthening Citizens' Rights in a Union of Democratic Change (2017/2069(INI)), para 32.

States, meeting within the Council'[2382] or the Paris Declaration of the Education Ministers and the Commissioner for Education, Culture, Youth and Sport.[2383] Here EU action is combined with an intergovernmental

2382 Before competences were conferred in education, see i.a. Resolution of the Council and of the Ministers of Education, meeting within the Council, of 9 February 1976 comprising an action programme in the field of Education [1976] OJ C38/1; Conclusions of the Council and the Ministers for Education meeting within the Council of 3 June 1985 on improving the treatment of the European dimension in education; Resolution of the Council and of the Ministers for Education, meeting within the Council, of 3 June 1985 containing an action programme on equal opportunities for girls and boys in education [1985] OJ C166/1; Resolution of the Council and of the Ministers of Education meeting within the Council of 23 November 1988 concerning health education in schools. Even after the Treaty conferred competences in education: Conclusions of the Council and of the Ministers for Education meeting within the Council of 11 June 1993 on furthering an open European space for cooperation within higher education [1993] OJ C186/1; Resolution of the Council and the Representatives of the Governments of the Member States, meeting within the Council, on implementing the common objectives for participation by and information for young people in view of promoting their active European citizenship [2006] OJ C297/6; Conclusions of the Council and of the Representatives of the Governments of the Member States, meeting within the Council of 15 November 2007, on improving the quality of teacher education [2007] OJ C300/7; Conclusions of the Council and of the Representatives of the Governments of the Member States, meeting within the Council of 21 November 2008 on preparing young people for the 21st century: an agenda for European cooperation on schools [2008] OJ C319/20; Conclusions of the Council and of the Representatives of the Governments of the Member States, meeting within the Council, of 26 November 2009 on developing the role of education in a fully-functioning knowledge triangle [2009] OJ C302/3; Resolution of the Council and of the Representatives of the Governments of the Member States, meeting within the Council, of 24 February 2016 on promoting socio-economic development and inclusiveness in the EU through education: the contribution of education and training to the European Semester 2016 [2016] OJ C105/1; Conclusions of the Council and of the Representatives of the Governments of the Member States, meeting within the Council, on the role of the youth sector in an integrated and cross-sectoral approach to preventing and combating violent radicalisation of young people [2016] OJ C213/1; Conclusions of the Council and of the Representatives of the Governments of the Member States, meeting within the Council, on Inclusion in Diversity to achieve a High Quality Education For All - Council Conclusions (17 February 2017).

2383 EU Education Ministers and the Commissioner for Education, Culture, Youth and Sport, Paris Declaration on Promoting citizenship and the common values of freedom, tolerance and non-discrimination through education (17 March 2015).

approach. These instruments (partly) fall outside the scope of Article 165 TFEU.[2384]

Adopting a mixed instrument on the EU dimension of EDC would certainly respect Member State competences in education. However, there may be hesitation—and rightly so—in the light of the warning of the European Parliament that 'soft law cannot be a substitute for legal acts and instruments, which are available to ensure the continuity of the legislative process, especially in the field of culture and education'.[2385]

An alternative way of respecting Member State competences in education therefore deserves special attention: the creation of an EU Agency.

320 An EU Agency for Education for Democratic Citizenship

Inspiration for EU action—while respecting Member State competences in education and the principle of subsidiarity—might be drawn from Germany, where measures are adopted at federal level, while still respecting the education competences of the *Länder*. The *Bundeszentrale für politische Bildung* (Federal Agency for Civic Education) supports citizenship education in the *Länder* in cooperation with independent *Landeszentralen*. It is 'a federal public authority providing citizenship education and information on political issues to all people in Germany'.[2386] Originally, the Federal Centre for Homeland Service (1952) had the task of consolidating and spreading the democratic and European ideas among the German people[2387] (to erase the effects of Nazi-education). At present, the *Bundeszentrale für politische Bildung* has the task of promoting understanding of political issues through measures of political education, of strengthening demo-

---

2384 Resolution of the Council and the Representatives of the Governments of the Member States meeting within the Council on a framework for European cooperation in the youth field: The European Union Youth Strategy 2019–2027 [2018] OJ C 456/1. This instrument fosters youth participation in democratic life 'in line with' Article 165 TFEU and aims to 'Introduce and increase education about Europe and the EU in formal and non-formal settings' (Annex 3 European Youth Goals).

2385 European Parliament Resolution of 4 September 2007 on institutional and legal implications of the use of 'soft law' instruments [2008] OJ C187E/75, para 2, see also recital X.

2386 See n 497. On 26 May 1997 the Directors of the Federal and Regional Agencies for Civic Education submitted a public declaration entitled 'Demokratie braucht politische Bildung' (Democracy calls for political education), the Munich Manifesto.

2387 Erlaß über die Errichtung der Bundeszentrale für Heimatdienst, 25. November 1952, § 2.

cratic awareness, and of strengthening the readiness to political cooperation.[2388] A Board of trustees (22 members of the German *Bundestag*) monitors the politically balanced attitude and political effectiveness of the work of the *Bundeszentrale*. The *Bundeszentrale* has to maintain close links with the highest *Länder* authorities in all matters affecting their competences.[2389] The key activities of the *Bundeszentrale* include: the development of a wide variety of materials and instruments to support professionals in the field of citizenship education; providing them with training sessions and materials on teaching methods; providing teaching materials on complex issues adapted to different age groups and different learning environments (explained in simple terms and not contaminated by party politics); supporting social media activities; and providing funding for citizenship education to partners, with the task of making 'sure that citizenship education is provided on a local level in every region throughout the country'.[2390] The key activities of this German Federal Agency are inspired by respect of the German *Grundgesetz*.[2391]

In like vein, an EU agency could engage in comparable activities in respect of EU primary law in conjunction with national constitutions. It could provide information and develop educational materials for EDC and its EU dimension, while respecting EU and Member State competences. The Council of Europe has produced valuable materials (mainly in English or French) for implementing EDC in 47 member states (inter alia, in Turkey, Russia, or Azerbaijan). These materials are not sufficient for the EU Member States. An EU Agency could adapt materials to the specific EU

2388 Erlass über die Bundeszentrale für politische Bildung (BpB), 24. Januar 2001, § 2. See also T Krüger, 'Brauchen wir eine "Europäische Zentrale für politische Bildung"? Ich meine ja!' (2014) 144 Kulturpolitische Mitteilungen Kulturpolitik & Planung.

2389 Ibid, § 6 'Die politisch ausgewogene Haltung und die politische Wirksamkeit der Arbeit der Bundeszentrale werden von einem aus 22 Mitgliedern des Deutschen Bundestages bestehenden Kuratorium kontrolliert'; § 7 'Die Bundeszentrale hält in allen Angelegenheiten, welche die Zuständigkeit der Länder berühren, enge Verbindungen zu den obersten Landesbehörden.'.

2390 <www.bpb.de/die-bpb/138867/key-activities>.

2391 See n 506. Also T Krüger, *Politische Bildung—notwendiger denn je (27.5.2019) Jahresgespräch Politische Bildung* (2019), <www.bpb.de/presse/291890/politische-bildung-notwendiger-denn-je> ('die politische Bildung selbst—innerhalb eines inklusiven Gemeinwesens ...arbeitet an und auf Basis von einem "common ground": dem Grundgesetz').

context and make them available in all 24 EU languages.[2392] The Agency could offer training to citizenship education professionals from the Member States and provide funding for the development of the EU dimension of EDC to its partners, with the task of ensuring that that is provided in every Member State and region throughout the EU (including to static citizens). The European Parliament could monitor the activities of the Agency as to political correctness and effectiveness. The EU Agency would maintain close links with the highest educational authorities of the Member States, fully respecting their competences in education. The work of the Agency would be consistent with and support the decisions of the Ministers of Education of the EU, just as the activities of the *Bundeszentrale* respect the guidance given by the German Standing Conference of the Ministers of Education and Cultural Affairs. This Standing Conference has adopted resolutions recommending education for democracy and human rights education, as well as recommending the European dimension in education.[2393]

321 Reporting on the EU dimension of EDC

Finally, EU measures could at least provide for better reporting on EDC and its EU dimension in Member States, even if assessment is difficult.[2394]

2392 The existing Education, Audiovisual and Culture Executive Agency (EACEA) is an executive agency entrusted with the implementation of programmes as Erasmus+, Creative Europe, etc. It mainly manages funding. See Commission Implementing Decision of 18 December 2013 establishing the 'Education, Audiovisual and Culture Executive Agency' and repealing Decision 2009/336 [2013] OJ L343/46. Cp the idea of a centralised platform with learning and teaching materials in Opinion of the European Economic and Social Committee on 'Education about the European Union' SOC/612 (21 March 2019), paras 1.13, 4.4; Opinion of the European Economic and Social Committee on 'Teaching Europe — developing a toolkit for schools' [2019] OJ C 353/52, para 5.1.

2393 See text to n 504 ff. The 1978 Recommendation 'Europe in the classroom' (*Europa im Unterricht*) was amended in 1990 and updated in 2008 (*Europabildung in der Schule);* it recommends 'upholding the test criterion "European dimension in classroom teaching" when approving teaching and learning materials' (see <eacea.ec.europa.eu/national-policies/eurydice/content/other-dimensions-internationalisation-early-childhood-and-school-education-25_en>.

2394 The review cycles of the Charter on EDC/HRE concern EDC in general (no EU dimension). See §§ 62 66 and text to n 478. On the necessity of up-to-date studies mapping teaching about the EU, see Opinion of the European Economic and Social Committee on 'Education about the European Union' SOC/612 (21 March 2019), para 1.11.

Citizenship education continues to be an area characterised by gaps between policy and practice, between the curriculum as designed and the curriculum as implemented.[2395] In the face of the economic crisis, EU objectives in education have been pursued with targeted action, comprehensive strategies, due dates, and periodic reporting on progress.[2396] EU institutions have called for the modernisation of curricula to achieve the headline targets in education, aiming at an advanced knowledge-based economy, as a key to growth.[2397] These tools and endeavours could be envisaged with regard to the EU civic gap as well. Unfortunately, where reporting on the European dimension in education is concerned, there has been a step back.[2398] For years, the Member States were asked to report on their implementation of the European dimension in education in chapter 11 of the Eurydice Database, facilitating a comparative study.[2399] On the present Eurydice website, this chapter has been replaced by chapter 13 'Mobility and Internationalisation'.[2400] While some Member States (such as Germany) continue to report on the European dimension in education,

---

2395 Losito B and others, Young People's Perceptions of Europe in a Time of Change: IEA International Civic and Citizenship Education Study- 2016 European Report (2017), 13–14.

2396 See, e.g., Council Recommendation of 28 June 2011 on policies to reduce early school leaving [2011] OJ C191/1; or the EU benchmark for language teaching (Commission staff working document, Language competences for employability, mobility and growth Accompanying the document Communication From the Commission Rethinking Education: Investing in skills for better socio eco nomic outcomes SWD(2010) 372 final).

2397 I.e. reducing the proportion of early school leavers to less than 10% and increasing the proportion of 30–34 year olds having completed tertiary or equivalent education to at least 40%: Council Conclusions on the role of education and training in the implementation of the 'Europe 2020' strategy [2011] C70/1 ("Stresses", II at paras 6–7; "Considers" at para.4). See also European Parliament Resolution of 2 April 2009 on Better Schools: an agenda for European cooperation [2010] OJ C137E/43; Council Conclusions on increasing the level of basic skills in the context of European cooperation on schools for the 21st century [2010] C323/04; and especially Commission Communication 'Rethinking Education: Investing in skills for better socio-economic outcomes' COM(2012) 669 final, e.g. p 6, 11.

2398 Cp the international obligation of States (ICESCR) not to adopt deliberately retrogressive measures (n 2162).

2399 European Parliament, *The European Dimension in Secondary Education in Europe* (EDUC 11–2003), p 4, especially since 2002. Asking to report specifically on teaching about the European Union underscored its importance.

2400 <eacea.ec.europa.eu/national-policies/eurydice/national-description_en> (i.a. taking together 'the European, global and intercultural dimension in curricu-

others do not or scarcely do (such as Flanders, Belgium). The 'European, global and intercultural dimension in the curriculum' have been combined in one subject. Furthermore, a 'mobility score board' on the Eurydice website reveals the focus.

In the 1992 Maastricht Treaty, EU citizenship and the 'European dimension in education' were introduced together.[2401] As shown in Part three, the impact of EU citizenship has been consolidated in the case law of the ECJ. But the European dimension in education (*sensu stricto*) seems to be lagging far behind. While 'the European dimension in education'—Treaty concept—appeared in EU legislation containing action programmes in education for many years,[2402] the 2013 Erasmus+ Regulation aims to enhance 'the international dimension of education' (and only refers to a 'European dimension in sport').[2403] It is needless to explain that the European and the international dimension are very different concepts. In its Opinion, the Committee of the Regions rightly stressed the major challenge that 'the programme should strengthen EU citizenship by emphasising the European dimension'.[2404]

---

lum development'). See also Commission/EACEA/Eurydice E, Structural Indicators for Monitoring Education and Training Systems in Europe—2018. Eurydice Background Report (measuring of early childhood education, basic skills, early school leaving, higher education, employability, and mobility; no measuring of citizenship education).

2401 Now Arts 20 and 165 TFEU.

2402 The expression 'the European dimension in education' was central in the Decision 253/2000 of the European Parliament and of the Council of 24 January 2000 establishing the second phase of the Community action programme in the field of education 'Socrates' [2000] OJ L28/1, Arts 1(3) and 2(a), recital 1, and Annex: 'Comenius seeks to enhance the quality and reinforce the European dimension of school education, in particular by encouraging transnational cooperation between schools and contributing to improved professional development of staff directly involved in the school education sector, and to promote the learning of languages and intercultural awareness'. See also Decision 1720/2006 of the European Parliament and of the Council of 15 November 2006 establishing an action programme in the field of lifelong learning [2006] OJ L327/45; amended by Decision 1357/2008 [2008] OJ L350/56, recital 1.

2403 Erasmus+ Regulation 1288/2013, Art 5 1(d), and recital 8. Only a 'European dimension' in sport: Art 4(e). The 2018 Proposal for the Erasmus programme does not mention the European dimension in education either.

2404 Opinion of the Committee of the Regions of 3 and 4 May 2012 on 'Erasmus for All' [2012] OJ C225/200, p.3, para.13.

322 Unused potential

Article 165 TFEU provides an adequate legal basis for the EU to promote the EU dimension of EDC, especially with regard to achieving the Treaty objectives of quality education, the European dimension in education, and the participation of young people in democratic life in Europe (respect for the principle of conferral and seen in the light of subsidiarity as a meta-constitutional concept). The EU can exercise that competence and do so without going further than needed (respect for the principles of subsidiarity in the strict sense and proportionality). At present, the potential of Article 165 TFEU is not being fully used.[2405] If the Commission wants to make good use of the unexhausted potential of the Lisbon Treaty (sixth scenario for the future of Europe[2406]), then education is one of the areas available for action to build a more democratic and value-based Union close to its citizens. In addition to binding incentive measures and recommendations on the legal basis of Article 165 TFEU, action could take the form of mixed instruments, the creation of an EU Agency for Education for Democratic Citizenship, and better reporting on the state of play in the Member States.

B Member State action

323 National competence, but exercised in compliance with EU law

While the EU has a supporting competence in education, the main competence and responsibility for providing an EU dimension in EDC lies with the Member States. The so-called killer phrase in European citizenship education networks, 'Your work is incredibly important, but education is subject to national policies',[2407] is a correct reading of Article 4(1) TEU in conjunction with Article 165 TFEU. Competences not transferred to the Union do indeed remain with the Member States. However, when Member States use their competences in particular fields (such as personal names, taxes, nationality, and also education), they must still respect EU law. The ECJ recalls that 'whilst European Union law does not detract from the power of the Member States as regards the organisation of their

---

2405 Grimonprez, 'The European dimension in citizenship education: unused potential of article 165 TFEU'.

2406 Calliess, 'Bausteine einer erneuerten Europäischen Union- Auf der Suche nach dem europäischen Weg: Überlegungen im Lichte des Weißbuchs der Europäischen Kommission zur Zukunft Europas', 5.

2407 Text to n 83.

education systems and of vocational training—pursuant to Articles 165(1) and 166(1) TFEU—the fact remains that, when exercising that power, Member States must comply with European Union law'.[2408] Respect for EU law limits the discretion of Member States in the use of their education competences. This will be illustrated by EU educational rights in crossborder situations. Moreover, in a human rights-based approach to education, fundamental rights must be respected.

324 EU educational rights in crossborder situations

Because of the need to comply with EU law, a whole range of educational rights have developed in crossborder situations, which fall within the scope of the Treaties. Some of them were first addressed in ECJ case law and were later incorporated and specified in secondary legislation.

When exercising their competences in education, Member States must comply with the principle of free movement of workers (Article 45 TFEU). Articles 165 and 166 TFEU have no impact on the EU's express and implied powers concerning the internal market.[2409] Free movement of workers has to be guaranteed in compliance with the principles of liberty and dignity and respect for the right to family life. Seeking to ensure the best possible conditions for the integration of the migrant worker's family in the society of the host Member State, the ECJ has recognised several educational rights (rights to education and rights linked with education). [2410] The right of freedom of establishment (Article 49 TFEU) and the right

---

2408 I.a. Case C-73/08 *Bressol, Chaverot and Others* ECLI:EU:C:2010:181, para 28–29; Case C-281/06 *Jundt* ECLI:EU:C:2007:816, para 84–87; Case C-76/05 *Schwarz* ECLI:EU:C:2007:492, para 70. See also Ruffert, 'AEUV Art 165', Rn 2: (tr) The heart of the problem is that education policy affects too many other policy areas and, above all, fundamental freedoms, so that in its own right the Title on Education can only address partial aspects and thus cannot comprehensively limit the influence of EU law.

2409 Lenaerts, 'Education in European Community Law after "Maastricht"', 40, referring to Art 6(2) and art 49 EC; the *acquis communautaire* continues to exist in full in this area. On the *Casagrande* heritage, see Shaw, 'From the Margins to the Centre: Education and Training Law and Policy' 573. See also S Garben, 'The Bologna Process: From a European Law Perspective' (2010) 16 ELJ 186, arguing that there would have been legal competence to enact the content of the Bologna Declaration as a Community measure related to the internal market.

2410 Educational rights for workers flow from Art 45 TFEU and secondary legislation such as Council Regulation (EEC) No 1612/68 of 15 October 1968 on freedom of movement for workers within the Community [1968] OJ L257/2, and Regulation 492/2011 of the European Parliament and of the Council of 5

to provide services (Article 56 TFEU), too, have limited Member States' educational autonomy,[2411] as has (beyond the internal market) free movement of citizens[2412] and the principle of non-discrimination on the grounds of nationality[2413].

April 2011 on freedom of movement for workers within the Union [2011] OJ L141/1, construed generously by the ECJ on the basis of a teleological interpretation; see objectives in preambles. Human dignity and the right to family life imply that the worker cannot be separated from his family. See i.a. Case C-308/89 *di Leo* ECLI:EU:C:1990:400, para 13; Case C-413/99 *Baumbast* ECLI:EU:C:2002:493, para 50; Case C-337/07 *Ibrahim* ECLI:EU:C:2008:744, para 59; Case C-480/08 *Teixeira* ECLI:EU:C:2010:83, paras 61, 70; Case C-45/12 *Hadj* ECLI:EU:C:2013:390, para 44. For educational rights such as rights of equal access to education in the host Member State, or under conditions not restricting free movement; for derived residence rights for child and primary carer, etc., see Case 197/86 *Brown* ECLI:EU:C:1988:323; Case C-379/87 *Groener* ECLI:EU:C:1989:599; Case C-7/94 *Gaal* ECLI:EU:C:1995:11; Case C-281/98 *Angonese* ECLI:EU:C:2000:296; Case C-109/04 *Kranemann* ECLI:EU:C:2005:187; Case C-258/04 *Ioannidis* ECLI:EU:C:2005:559; Case C-529/11 *Alarape* ECLI:EU:C:2013:290; Case C-542/09 *Commission v the Netherlands* ECLI:EU:C:2012:346; Case C-317/14 *Commission v Belgium* ECLI:EU:C:2015:63.

2411 Both in requiring no discrimation and no hindrance. See Case C-337/97 *Meeusen* ECLI:EU:C:1999:284, paras 27–30; Case C-523/12 *Dirextra Alta Formazione* ECLI:EU:C:2013:831, paras 21–3, 26–9; Case C-76/05 *Schwarz* ECLI:EU:C:2007:492, paras 66–7. The situation of pupils, teachers and schools falls within the scope of the Treaties via the freedom of services provisions when education is seen as a 'service' within the meaning of the Treaty (private financing of a school and the intention to make an economic profit) and occurs crossborder. See Case C-109/92 *Wirth* ECLI:EU:C:1993:916, para 17; Case C-76/05 *Schwarz* ECLI:EU:C:2007:492, para 47. The distinction between publicly or privatly funded education can be criticised; see Garben, *EU Higher education law. The Bologna Process and harmonization by stealth*, 106; also Dougan, 'Fees, grants, loans and dole cheques: Who covers the costs of migrant education within the EU?'.

2412 Case C-359/13 *Martens* ECLI:EU:C:2015:118, para 23: 'although the Member States are competent, under Article 165(1) TFEU, as regards the content of teaching and the organisation of their respective education systems, they must exercise that competence in compliance with EU law and, in particular, in compliance with the Treaty provisions on the freedom to move and reside within the territory of the Member States, as conferred by Article 21(1) TFEU on every citizen of the Union'; repeated in Case C-679/16 *A* ECLI:EU:C:2018:601, para 58. See also Joined Cases C-11/06 and C-12/06 *Morgan and Bucher* ECLI:EU:C:2007:626, para 24; Case C-275/12 *Elrick* ECLI:EU:C:2013:684, para 21; Joined Cases C-523/11 and C-585/11 *Prinz* ECLI:EU:C:2013:524, para 26.

I am returning here briefly to the case law on free movement and educational rights in crossborder situations, not to downplay the relevance—argued above—of the EU dimension for static citizens, but to make two observations concerning the exercise of Member State competence in education.

The first observation is that in applying free movement rules to education contexts, the ECJ refused to apply the exception relating to the public service or the exercise of official authority. The *Commission v Greece* case is of interest in the context of citizenship education.[2414]

> According to the Commission, Greek legislation makes it impossible for nationals of other Member States to set up certain educational establisments and to give private lessons at home, and thus infringes free movement rules. The Greek Government invokes the exception to freedom of establishment for activities connected with the exercise of official authority in the State: 'it is for each Member State to define which activities in the State are connected with the exercise of official authority. That is the case as regards teaching activities in Greece, in view of the fact that, under the Greek Constitution, the provision of instruction is a fundamental duty of the State designed to ensure in particular the moral and spiritual education of its citizens and the development of their national consciousness, and that private individuals who carry on such activities do so in their capacity as repositories of official authority'.[2415] The ECJ emphasises that as a derogation from a fundamental freedom, the exception based on the exercise of official authority 'must be interpreted in a manner which limits its scope to what is strictly necessary in order to safeguard the interests which it allows the Member States to protect', to be appraised separately in respect of each Member State.[2416] The ECJ wants to prevent the effectiveness of the Treaty provisions on freedom of establishment being undermined by unilateral measures adopted by the Member States:

2413 Linking Arts 18 and 21 TFEU, D'Hoop (n 1393); also *Gravier* and other case law (§ 193).

2414 Case 147/86 *Commission v Greece* ECLI:EU:C:1988:150.

2415 Para 6. See actual Greek constitution on aims of citizenship education in Art 16(2): 'Education constitutes a basic mission for the State and shall aim at the moral, intellectual, professional and physical training of Greeks, the development of national and religious consciousness and at their formation as free and responsible citizens'.

2416 Paras 7–8.

'Although it is for each Member State to determine the role of, and the responsibilities attaching to, official authority with regard to instruction, it cannot be accepted that the mere fact that a private individual sets up a school such as a 'frontistirion' or a vocational training school, or gives private lessons at home, is connected with the exercise of official authority within the meaning of Article 55 of the Treaty.' Supervision by official authorities suffices to guarantee the protection of the interests entrusted to the State.[2417] The ECJ concludes that Greece has failed to fulfil its obligations under (now) Articles 49 and 56 TFEU.[2418]

In other cases, too, Member States have not been able to justify failure to comply with EU law in the education field by arguing that education concerns 'the general interest of the State'.[2419]

A second observation is the importance of the proportionality principle in case law for reconciling Member State prerogatives in education with EU rights and objectives. In *Bressol*, as explained in Part three, the ECJ found that the right of equal access to higher education cannot be limited by a requirement of local residence unless justified with specific evidence.[2420] The ECJ applied the proportionality principle in order to respect sensitive concerns of the Member States, yet at the same time to uphold the relevant EU principles.[2421] Shortly before the Lisbon Treaty was signed, Austria insisted on appending to the Treaty a special protocol allowing for a limitation on the number of non-national students who can be admitted to its universities. The Commission finally 'raised the white flag' and suspended its action against Austria for five years.[2422] Garben observes that Member States put mobility in education high on the European agenda yet face numerous problems in practice and are not very eager to implement

2417 Paras 8–10.

2418 Para 18.

2419 For workers, Case 66/85 *Lawrie-Blum* ECLI:EU:C:1986:284, paras 24–7 (because of her British nationality, Lawrie-Blum was refused access to a German education which prepared future teachers). In the same sense: Case C-290/94 *Commission v Greece* ECLI:EU:C:1996:265, para 37. For services, see Case C-281/06 *Jundt* ECLI:EU:C:2007:816, para 37.

2420 *Bressol*, see text to n 1385.

2421 Garben, 'Case C-73/08, Nicolas Bressol and Others, Céline Chaverot and Others v. Gouvernement de la Communaute française, Judgment of the Court (Grand Chamber) of 13 April 2010', 1510: in *Bressol*, 'the Court was stuck between a rock and a hard place'; 'The Court chose the middle way, exploiting the proportionality test to the fullest'.

2422 Analysis of this education saga in ibid, 1497–1498: the aftermath of the 2004 and 2005 *Commission v Belgium* and *Commission v Austria* cases.

it. Their 'political high-talk' on mobility in education sometimes 'feels like empty rhetoric'; 'Member States all too often want to have their cake and eat it too'.[2423] Garben discerns a lack of solidarity between Member States and a lack of commitment to their own policy objectives, but recognises the dangers of (excessive) Court driven integration.

If even mobility, which figures in the text of Article 165 TFEU (para 2, second indent) leads to tensions, the EU dimension of EDC, which is not specifically mentioned in the text of that provision, will a fortiori require caution.

The proportionality test has been decisive in other cases too. The ECJ accepts 'quality education' as an objective justifying restrictive measures, but only if the measure is suitable and does not go beyond what is necessary to achieve the objective. Quality education is not defined by the ECJ; concrete answers in this respect have to come from the referring court.[2424]

325 The right to vote and possible limitations

Voting rights for the European Parliament have effects on the relationship of static citizens with their own Member State. When determining who was entitled to vote in the elections for the European Parliament, France had to respect the conditions of Article 52(1) CFR (*Delvigne*). It seems natural to expect that, when organising education, Member States will include an EU dimension in national EDC to ensure effective participation in the electoral processes at EU level. The question arises as to whether Member State law on national EDC which fails to include an EU dimension, or—an extreme hypothesis to sharpen the reasoning—with a hostile,

2423 Ibid, 1494, 1509.

2424 In *Neri*, *Lyyski*, and *Bressol*, the ECJ left the application of the proportionality test to the referring court (Case C-153/02 *Neri* ECLI:EU:C:2003:614; Case C-40/05 *Lyyski* ECLI:EU:C:2007:10; *Bressol* (n 1385)). In *Dirextra*, however, the ECJ found that the freedom to provide services was restricted by Italian legislation and accepted the justification based on quality education as proportional (see paras 21–3, 26–9). In *Neri* the ECJ held that an Italian administrative practice constituted a restriction on the freedom of establishment as it was likely to deter students from attending these courses organised in Italy at a secondary establishment (certain degrees awarded by an UK university were not recognised when part of the studies had been completed in Italy at a secondary establishment of the UK university). Italy tried to justify this restriction by 'the need to ensure high standards of university education' and its attachment to a view of university education as 'a matter of "public interest", expressing as it does the cultural and historical values of the State'. The ECJ accepted quality education as an objective justifying a restrictive measure but the measure had to be proportional.

anti-EU dimension, can be considered to be a limitation of the right to vote for the European Parliament. If it is a limitation, it has to satisfy the conditions in Article 52(1) CFR, i.a. it must respect the essence of the right to vote. From a formal perspective, the absence of an EU dimension or even the inclusion of an anti-EU dimension in EDC does not prevent citizens from voting for the European Parliament. They can still be informed through the media or by EU information campaigns as part of the process of lifelong learning. Yet, from a substantive perspective, the right to vote may in certain circumstances be deprived of its core content where education fails. Will citizens exercise their right to vote for the European Parliament if teachers have told them previously at school (as happened to my youngest daughter) that the EU is not democratic 'at all' and that the European Parliament 'has no say'?[2425] And if they do, will they grasp the institutional significance of the electoral process they are participating in? Institutional efforts to engage with citizens in public debates on EU issues may be in vain if EDC at school is flawed and as a result citizens lack motivation. At the same time, EDC needs to include critical thinking. The role of the European Parliament is indeed limited to a certain extent, e.g. vis-à-vis the Troika or with regard to measures to tackle economic and financial crises. There may be a thin line between absorbing EU knowledge, exercising critical thinking, and listening to the unnuanced opinions of teachers. To what extent are teachers entitled to exercise their right to freedom of expression in the classroom?[2426]

326 Freedom rights and EDC

A human rights-based approach to EDC, which is situated at the intersection of the right to education and political participation rights, may be the right incentive for both the Member States and the EU to make use of their competences to establish and support the EU dimension of EDC. It

2425 Class of 18-year old pupils (teacher: 'Les membres du Parlement européen sont des guignoles qui sont payés pour ne rien faire': The Members of the European Parliament are puppets who are paid to do nothing.).

2426 See *Seurot v France* no 57383/00 (ECtHR Decision 18 May 2004) (n 323). See A Gardner, 'Preparing students for democratic participation: why teacher curricular speech should sometimes be protected by the First Amendment' (2008) 73 Missouri Law Review 213, 240 ('The court should employ a balancing test that is well grounded in the democratic purpose of education. While the government may articulate a legitimate interest which may limit teacher curricular speech, this interest should be weighed mightily against the interest of serving the fundamental purpose of our educational system'); Veny, *Onderwijsrecht 1: Dragende beginselen van het onderwijsbestel*, § 377 ff.

reflects the social dimension of the right to education and strengthens the effectiveness of participation rights.[2427] Yet, at the same time, the human rights-based approach constrains the use of these competences. When designing curricula and formulating learning outcomes, public authorities must respect fundamental rights. Equality rights, for instance, preclude the reinforcement of prejudices against ethnic groups at school.[2428] Freedom rights too, such as the right to freedom of thought, conscience and religion (Article 9 ECHR) or the right to freedom of expression (Article 10 ECHR), may limit the setting of compulsory school curricula.[2429] Importantly, the right to education itself has—in addition to a social dimension, including a right of equal access and to quality education—a freedom dimension, reflected in parents' right to educate their children in conformity with their religious and philosophical convictions, and in the freedom to found educational establishments (Article 2 Protocol 1 ECHR, Article 14(3) CRC).[2430] The ECtHR has upheld the obligation on States and state schools to provide education in an objective, critical and pluralistic way, with no aims of indoctrination. Non-state schools (identity driven or religious schools) have a larger degree of autonomy.[2431]

To what extent can schools, teachers, parents, or pupils rely on their freedom rights to oppose a compulsory curriculum on EDC and its EU dimension? Admittedly, the exercise of legal competences by public authorities (at EU or Member State level) in order to impose an EU dimension restricts freedom rights of actors in the education field. However,

---

2427 See n 2129.

2428 Extreme example above, n 2186 (reinforcing Hutu-Tutsi prejudices).

2429 *Siebenhaar v Germany* no 18136/02 (ECtHR 3 February 2011), para 36: freedom of religion includes in principle the right to try to convince others, for example by means of education. See also UN ComESCR 'General Comment No 13: The Right to Education (Art. 13)' UN Doc E/C.12/1999/10, para 28: teaching should be respectful of the freedoms of opinion, conscience and expression; *Handyside v UK* no 5493/72 (ECtHR 7 Dec 1976). For safe spaces, see n 1263. See also CoE Steering Committee for Human Rights (CDDH), Guide to good and promising practices on the way of reconciling freedom of expression with other rights and freedoms, in particular in culturally diverse societies (17 September 2019) CM(2019)148.

2430 Text to n 2129. See also Art 13(3)(4) ICESCR, Art 29(2) CRC, and several national constitutions (text to n 661).

2431 See i.a. *Kjeldsen, Busk Madsen and Pedersen v Denmark* no 5095/71 (ECtHR 7 December 1976), paras 50–53; *Hasan and Eylem Zengin v Turkey* no 1448/04 (ECtHR 9 October 2007), paras 52, 56, 57, 64; *Tarantino and Others v Italy* no 25851/09 et al (ECtHR 2 April 2013), Partly dissenting opinion of Judge Pinto de Albuquerque.

firstly, the provisions on the right to education circumscribe educational freedom: freedom is to be exercised 'with due respect for democratic principles' and 'in accordance with the national laws governing the exercise of such freedom and right' (Article 14 CFR); education in freely established institutions 'shall conform to such minimum standards as may be laid down by the State' (Article 13(4) ICESCR) and is subject always to the observance of the principle set forth in Article 29(1) CRC, i.e. the aims to which 'education shall be directed to' (Article 29(2) CRC).[2432] Moreover, while freedom rights limit to the action of public authorities, freedom rights themselves are not unlimited either. The constitutional core—for example, minority rights or equality rights—must be respected. Religious schools or individual teachers cannot invoke freedom of education to propagate views of *inequality* of men and women or of ethnic groups. In *Seurot*, the ECtHR decided that the limitation on the right to freedom of expression of a teacher (his dismissal) was legitimate: the indisputably racist content of the teacher's article in a school journal was incompatible with the teachers' special duties and responsibilities, i.e. their role as actors in EDC and their responsibility in the fight against racism and xenophobia.[2433] This echoes Popper's statement: in the name of tolerance, there should be no tolerance of intolerance.[2434] Limitations to fundamental

2432 In the same sense, text to n 2159.

2433 *Seurot v France* no 57383/00 (ECtHR Decision 18 May 2004) (above § 42). See also *Jersild v Denmark* no 15890/89 (ECtHR 23 September 1994), para 30: 'the vital importance of combating racial discrimination in all its forms and manifestations'.

2434 The paradox of tolerance: unlimited tolerance leads to the disappearance of tolerance. See also NM Stolzenberg, '"He drew a circle that shut me out": assimilation, indoctrination, and the paradox of a liberal education' (1993) 106 Harvard Law Review 581 ('indoctrination in tolerance'). Thought-provoking also is the Böckenförde dilemma: E-W Böckenförde, *Staat, Gesellschaft, Freiheit: Studien zur Staatstheorie und zum Verfassungsrecht* (Suhrkamp 1976), 60 ('Der freiheitliche, säkularisierte Staat lebt von Voraussetzungen, die er selbst nicht garantieren kann (...) Anderseits kann er diese inneren Regulierungskräfte nicht von sich aus, das heißt mit den Mitteln des Rechtszwanges und autoritativen Gebots zu garantieren suchen, ohne seine Freiheitlichkeit aufzugeben und—auf säkularisierter Ebene—in jenen Totalitätsanspruch zurückzufallen, aus dem er in den konfessionellen Bürgerkriegen herausgeführt hat'; (tr) The liberal secularised State is based on prerequisites which it cannot itself fulfil (...) On the other hand it cannot seek to preserve these inner regulatory forces itself, that is to say by enforcing the law and the prescriptions of public authority, without jettisoning its liberal ethos and—at the secular level—reverting to just that demand for totality from which it freed us after the wars of religion.).

rights and freedoms can in general be justified under the conditions of Article 52(1) CFR (that is, where they are necessary and genuinely meet objectives of general interest recognised by the Union or the need to protect the rights and freedoms of others) or—in the case of the freedom rights in Articles 9 and 10 ECHR—when they are 'necessary in a democratic society' and pursue the legitimate aims laid down in the second paragraphs. Applying these conditions, the ECtHR has ruled that limitations on freedom rights by a compulsory school curriculum were justified. In *Osmanoglu*, the ECtHR held that compulsory swimming lessons were a justified restriction on the freedom of religion of the (Muslim) parents, since the measures sought to achieve successful social integration and pursued the legitimate aim of protecting the public order or the rights and freedoms of others (set forth in Article 9 (2) ECHR).[2435] Contrary to the freedom in Articles 9 and 10 ECHR, the freedom of education in Article 2 of Protocol 1 ECHR does not bind the ECtHR with an exhaustive list of 'legitimate aims' justifying restrictions.[2436] The ECtHR held in *Kjeldsen* that the Danish legislation on compulsory integrated sex education did not offend the religious and philosophical convictions of parents to the extent forbidden by the second sentence of Article 2 of Protocol 1 (parents' rights), interpreted in the light of its first sentence and of the whole of the Convention.[2437] It is settled case law that Article 2 constitutes a whole that is dominated by its first sentence.[2438] In *Valsamis,* where pupils were obliged to participate in a school parade on the Greek National Day, the ECtHR weighed the general interests of the community against the right of parents and found no breach of Article 2 Protocol 1 ECHR.[2439]

Balancing compulsory citizenship education against freedom rights is a matter of debate in Europe and worldwide.[2440] Can the state impose its own versions of history and 'correct' diverging views in school textbooks

2435 *Osmanoglu and Kocabas v Switzerland* no 29086/12 (ECtHR 10 January 2017), paras 85, 96, 105.

2436 *Tarantino and Others v Italy* no 25851/09 et al (ECtHR 2 April 2013), para 45.

2437 *Kjeldsen, Busk Madsen and Pedersen v Denmark* no 5095/71 (ECtHR 7 December 1976), para 54.

2438 *Kjeldsen*, para 52; *Campbell and Cosans v UK* no 7511/76 et al (ECtHR 23 March 1983), para 40.

2439 Explained in text to n 699.

2440 See i.a. *Folgerø and Others v Norway* no 15472/02 (ECtHR 29 June 2007); *Hasan and Eylem Zengin v Turkey* no 1448/04 (ECtHR 9 October 2007); *Lautsi and Others v Italy* no 30814/06 (ECtHR 18 March 2011), and n 462. See also *Fernández Martínez v Spain* no 56030/07 (ECtHR 12 June 2014), para 123 (what is 'necessary in a democratic society'). Further E Janssen, *Faith in Public Debate:*

on citizenship education?[2441] Can public schools enforce compulsory readings on different religious and philosophical convictions if parents claim that 'there is but one acceptable view, the Biblical view'?[2442] Can public schools oblige pupils to salute the American flag and recite the Pledge of Allegiance? In *Barnette*, the US Supreme Court held that this obligation was contrary to free speech under the First Amendment.[2443] Case law of the ECtHR gives states a rather wide margin of appreciation when balancing the right to education in its social dimension with freedom rights. Yet, limitations must be proportional to the legitimate aims pursued.[2444]

As far as the question of the EU dimension in EDC is concerned, I submit that Member State measures which require quality education to include minimal, acceptable EDC and its EU dimension, satisfy the condi-

---

On Freedom of Expression, Hate Speech and Religion in France & the Netherlands (Intersentia 2015); Willems and Vernimmen, 'The fundamental human right to education for refugees: Some legal remarks', 229–230; K Willems, 'Balancing neutrality and religion in public schools: on educational curricula and religious signs' in P Meix Cereceda and J de Groof (eds), *Religious and Ideological Rights in Education* (Wolf Legal Publishers 2017); J Lievens, *De vrijheid van onderwijs* (Intersentia 2019).

2441 Supreme Court of Japan, *Ienaga v Japan*, No 1428 of 1986, Judgment of 16 March 1993, No 1119 of 1994, Judgment of 29 August 1997. Professor Ienaga lost the case against the Japanse government which had removed descriptions of atrocities committed by Japanese military during WWII from school textbooks. The government was deemed competent to decide on the content of education for children to the extent that is necessary and reasonable. See further Tomaševski, *Human rights in education as prerequisite for human rights education*, p 16, 19: changes of government and victories in political or armed conflicts often lead to re-writing of textbooks for history (see also n 2186); Beiter, *The Protection of the Right to Education by International Law* 495. Another example of State intervention in education is the required learning of creationism (no teaching of Darwin's evolution theory).

2442 No violation of the free exercise clause of the First Amendment: line of case law based on *Mozert v Hawkins County Board of Education*, 827 F. 2d 1058 (1987). The role of education is to prepare all pupils for pluralism in a democratic society.

2443 'I pledge allegiance to the Flag of the United States of America and to the Republic for which it stands; one Nation indivisible, with liberty and justice for al'. See *West Virginia State Board of Education v. Barnette*, 319 US 624 (1943), Justice Jackson: 'If there is any fixed star in our constitutional constellation, it is that no official, high or petty, can prescribe what shall be orthodox in politics, nationalism, religion, or other matters of opinion or force citizens to confess by word or act their faith therein'.

2444 *Tarantino and Others v Italy* no 25851/09 et al (ECtHR 2 April 2013), para 45; *Leyla Şahin v Turkey* no 44774/98 (ECtHR 10 November 2005), para 154.

tions justifying restrictions on freedom rights. It has been demonstrated in the preceding Parts that the EU dimension is necessary in a democratic society. Such measures are in the general interest of society and necessary for the protection of the rights and freedoms of others (EU rights). If a balance is to be struck between, on the one hand, the interests of educational actors invoking freedom rights and, on the other hand, the interests of citizens who wish to receive an adequate education to empower them as EU citizens and the needs of the community at large, then—in the light of the international consensus on EDC and the constitutional tenets of the system in which EU citizens live—requiring an EU dimension in EDC is a justified restriction of freedom rights. The state can impose minimum norms in education and in doing so fulfils its obligations corresponding to the right to education.[2445] Legislation requiring an EU dimension in the school curriculum pursues a legitimate aim and is proportional, in particular when based on EU primary law in conjunction with Member State constitutions, and thus clarifying the DNA of the system in which citizens live.[2446] It can be assumed that all actors, in state and non-state schools, in public and private teaching, aim to empower their learners. This requires minimal ('thin') EDC, learning about the foundational values, objectives and principles of the system, in keeping with the constitutional compound of EU law and Member State constitutions.[2447] How 'thick' they wish EDC to be, and how they colour the EU dimension, is a matter for schools and teachers to decide, in exercise of their freedom rights. Freedom rights in education aim to safeguard pluralism, which is essential for the preservation of a democratic society.[2448] Pluralism is protected if the compulsory curriculum starts from EU dimension based on EU primary law while remaining open to content input from the educational actors. The specific (philosophy and) identity of an individual school will still come to the fore in the way EU rights and obligations are appraised, and in the emphasis placed on certain values, objectives and principles. Case teaching and discussion of controversial issues (e.g. on valuing diversity) create opportunities for identity driven schools to highlight the school's own perspectives. The essence of the freedom rights is respected.

2445 The four A scheme includes the obligation to provide acceptable education. See State parties' obligations under the ICESCR and the CRC (§ 289).

2446 Text to n 1051.

2447 Third caveat, § 73 .

2448 *Kjeldsen*, para 50.

Admittedly, in many cases where education for democracy and the freedom of expression of teachers have to be weighed in the balance, it is hard to assess the appropriateness and the proportionality of teachers' actions to achieve the aims of learning and critical thinking. Lessons are not—and should not be—recorded. It must also be remembered that teachers are usually in a position of power with a captive audience of pupils in the classroom. In *Vogt,* the ECtHR considered the risk that teachers might possibly 'take advantage of [their] position to indoctrinate or exert improper influence in another way on pupils during lessons', a possibility at odds with the special duties and responsibilities incumbent on teachers.[2449] It is therefore important to establish curricular or learning outcomes *linked with* EU primary law (objectivity)[2450] and to provide clear guidelines for teaching controversial topics.[2451] EU primary law interconnected with national constitutions may provide guidance in conflicts. Some national constitutions stipulate that freedom in education does not release any person from the duty of allegiance to the constitution.[2452] In seeking to establish a balance with freedom rights, a safe path can be taken by including an EU dimension in mainstream education in accordance with the Treaties and CFR, while allowing critical thinking.

Recognising that in the European constitutional space, a constitutional core must be respected,[2453] is an application of Callan's normative view on citizenship education. He suggests differentiating between a minimal core of adequate citizenship education, where the role for individual autonomy is modest, and a wider sphere of respectable contention, where views can diverge.[2454] This confirms that an EU dimension of EDC based on EU primary law—including the fundamental rights laid down in the CFR— and on case teaching, is a good learning method, with no aim of indoctrination. The alternative would be to hold back and to lower ambitions for the EU dimension of EDC. That would definitely exclude the risk of indoctrinating pupils. Yet, avoiding this risk means one thing is certain: there will be a vacuum in the minds of young citizens, a lack of knowledge and understanding about the EU. This vacuum could be filled by populist indoctrination and one-liners unhindered by learning outcomes or founda-

---

2449 *Vogt v Germany* no 17851/91 (ECtHR 2 Sept 1996), para 60.
2450 § 164 ff.
2451 § 179 .
2452 Germany Art 5(3) Basic law, Greece Art 16(1), Cyprus Art 20(1). See n 672 and text.
2453 See i.a. §§ 167 and text to n 1159, also § 251 .
2454 Callan, *Creating Citizens: Political Education and Liberal Democracy* .

tional values and principles.[2455] This end-result could be worse than taking a risk (the 'beautiful risk of education'[2456]).

To conclude these reflections on the human rights-based approach, in the exercise of competences in education, national educational autonomy is limited, on the one hand, by the obligations corresponding to the social dimension of the right to education (the state must take action to achieve the compulsory aims in international agreements and provide quality education, upholding the link with constitutional texts) and, on the other hand, by freedom rights, such as the right to freedom of education and the right to freedom of expression.[2457]

Conclusion to Part four

327 Proposal for recitals

Based on Part four, these recitals are proposed for inclusion in the preamble of a hypothetical EU legislative act:

> *Whereas competence has been conferred on the EU to support and supplement Member State action in order to contribute to the development of quality education, to the European dimension in education and to encouraging young people to participate in democratic life in Europe, and to do so by providing incentives and making recommendations (Article 165 TFEU).*
> *Whereas quality education comprises education directed to the preparation of the learner for effective participation and responsible life in a free society, and to strengthening respect for human rights and fundamental freedoms, as stated in the International Covenant on Economic, Social and Cultural Rights and the Convention on the Rights of the Child, and therefore includes education for democratic citizenship and human rights.*
> *Whereas the Member States are invited to take more action to provide such education, including its EU dimension.*
> *Whereas quantitative and qualitative indictors reveal that Member States do not sufficiently achieve the objective of quality education including an EU*

2455 E.g. 'Hungarian PM to EU: "We won't be a Colony"' in <euobserver.com/843/115613>: '"We will not be a colony. Hungarians won't live according to the commands of foreign powers, they won't give up their independence or their freedom," Orban told over 100,000 people in Budapest.'.

2456 Biesta, *The Beautiful Risk of Education*. I do not agree with all the opinions expressed in this article, but space does not allow me to develop this here.

2457 Further nuancing the so-called killer phrase (n 83).

> *dimension in education for democratic citizenship; whereas EU action to support the EU dimension has added value compared to the fragmented action at national, regional, local or school level (respect for the principles of subsidiarity and proportionality).*
> *Whereas defining learning outcomes for the EU dimension in EDC does not disproportionately interfere with freedom rights in education to the extent that they are necessary in a democratic society and genuinely meet objectives of general interest recognised by the Union and the need to protect the rights and freedoms of others.*

Jean Monnet is alleged to have said: 'If I were to start again, I would start with education.'[2458] Today, Articles 165 and 166 TFEU would give him a sound legal basis for action to empower EU citizens for active, informed, critical and responsible EU citizenship.

2458 'He probably never did, but it is an aphorism which makes sense, where ever it comes from': Corbett, *Universities and the Europe of Knowledge: Ideas, Institutions and Policy Entrepreneurship in European Union Higher Education Policy* xi. See also Shaw, 'From the Margins to the Centre: Education and Training Law and Policy' 555, 586.

Summary and general conclusion

This study approached the democratic and civic deficit, which is often ascribed to the EU, from the educational perspective. That involved a double challenge, relating, on the one hand, to the concept of 'citizenship education' and, on the other, to that of 'EU citizenship'.[2459] Both concepts are to varying degrees, the subject of controversy in scholarship, yet need to be defined in order to address the issue of 'EU citizenship education'. From the outset, taking democracy seriously, I advocated not waiting until all the uncertainties about the two concepts have been resolved, but rather setting out immediately to examine the possible significance of adding an EU dimension to national citizenship education programmes, seen from the legal perspective.

To start with, firm anchor points had to be identified, founded on a sufficiently wide consensus among EU Member States, at either EU level itself or at the international level (the Council of Europe or the UN). Three anchor points were used: first, the concept of Education for Democratic Citizenship (EDC), interlinked with Human Rights Education (HRE), as defined in the Council of Europe Charter on EDC/HRE; second, EU citizenship as expressed in the EU Treaties; and third, the right to education in the International Covenant on Economic, Social and Cultural Rights (ICESCR) and the Convention on the Rights of the Child (CRC).[2460] As can readily be seen, the first and the third anchor points relate to norms which are exogenic to EU law. The Council of Europe Charter on EDC/HRE was chosen as the prism through which to look at the EU dimension to be added to national citizenship education, mainly because it establishes neutral standards for citizenship education accepted by all the EU Member States in their capacity as member states of the Council of Europe.[2461] This Charter provides guidance for discovering the additional content needed in national citizenship education programmes for nation states which are EU Member States. The use of exogenic norms for the first and the third anchor points made it necessary to carry out an in-depth analysis of the legal status of such norms in the EU legal order. This analytical

2459 §§ 5 6 .
2460 § 9.
2461 § 129 .

framework underpinned the research question of this study: what are the implications for citizenship education of EU citizens of a combined reading—as to form and substance—of the provisions on Education for Democratic Citizenship in the Council of Europe Charter on EDC/HRE, on EU citizenship in the EU Treaties, and on the right to education in the ICESCR and CRC?[2462]

The answer can now be articulated in four steps.

The *first step* is taken in Part one of the study, which draws on the Council of Europe legal order. Here it is concluded that the EDC concept and principles of the Charter on EDC/HRE form a reliable and neutral anchor point. The Charter contains a commonly accepted general concept of citizenship education. It can fulfil an interpretative function as a common European standard of great weight since it rests on a wide European consensus (including all EU Member States). Therefore throughout the study 'EDC standards' refer to the Charter's definition of EDC, interlinked with HRE, and its objectives and principles.[2463] The EDC components which specify the objectives of empowerment are essential: EDC aims to empower learners (c-1) to exercise and defend their democratic rights and responsibilities in society, (c-2) to value diversity, and (c-3) to play an active part in democratic life.[2464]

The *second step* is taken in Part two (Parts two, three, and four concern the EU legal order), in essence to meet the possible objection that the Charter on EDC/HRE has no binding force within the Council of Europe legal order, thus diminishing its legal significance within the EU legal order. That necessitated a close analysis of the different modes of reception of a wide variety of exogenic norms in the EU legal order. The spectrum ranged from—strongest mode as to legal effects—EU accession to conventions (mode 1), through reception via general principles of EU law (mode 2), reference to the title of exogenic instruments (mode 3), incorporation of the substance of exogenic instruments (mode 4), to—the weakest mode of normative reception—sharing inspiration and *de facto* cooperation (mode 5). Judicial interpretation complements these modes of reception (mode 6). At all times, reception must respect the autonomy of the EU legal order (red line).[2465] EDC standards are mostly received in modes 4 and 5. Occasionally, the title of Council of Europe instruments on EDC is

2462 § 10 .
2463 § 74 .
2464 § 27 .
2465 I.a. §§ 81 97 121 130 .

referred to (mode 3). The EU thus acknowledges EDC standards, which are a shared priority according to the Memorandum of Understanding between the Council of Europe and the EU. When taken into account in the interpretation of EU law (mode 6), EDC standards harmoniously fit with EU primary law, as they are linked to the EU's foundational values of democracy, respect for fundamental rights and the rule of law enshrined in Article 2 TEU.[2466]

The *third step* is taken in Part three, which constitutes the major part of the study. A substantive analysis is carried out of the meeting points between EDC standards and EU law. The rights and obligations of EU citizens are mapped and screened for their relevance for the EU dimension of EDC in mainstream education according to four criteria: (i) do they provide additional content to national EDC, (ii) is this content significant, i.e. relating to foundational (EU primary law) values, objectives and principles, (iii) do they invite critical thinking, and (iv) do they affect the large majority of EU citizens, including static citizens?[2467] The effects of a combined reading of EDC standards and EU law are considerable. EU law impacts in such a decisive and specific way on the EDC components that without an EU dimension, EDC in Member States is no longer adequate.

As to the first criterion (i), rights of EU citizens provide *additional* content to national EDC. Educational substance is added to the EDC components of knowledge, skills and understanding, attitudes and behaviour (b), and to the three empowerment aims (c-1–3). All the rights and obligations flowing from the TEU, TFEU and CFR add to EDC component (c-1) on exercising and defending democratic rights and responsibilities in society. The EU dimension of EDC should empower learners to exercise and respect these rights and responsibilities. Viewed through the lenses of EDC standards, EU citizens' rights are not limited to the classic citizenship rights listed in Articles 20–24 TFEU (conferred in the Maastricht Treaty) and the non-discrimination rights linked to free movement (Article 18 TFEU).[2468] EU citizens' rights are widened to include the political participation rights based on Title II TEU (conferred in the Lisbon Treaty, Articles 9–11; also 14(3) TEU).[2469] EU citizens are, moreover, holders of rights and bearers of obligations generated by EU law in various policy areas.[2470]

2466 I.a. §§ 22 115 116 118 124 125 145 .
2467 §§ 151 157 .
2468 §§ 186 215 .
2469 §§ 216 236 .
2470 § 238 .

Through the principle of direct effect, a whole series of Treaty provisions directly confer rights to citizens, independently from national law. Most EU rights, however, are contained in EU legal instruments not enjoying direct effect, but invokable as a standard for consistent interpretation of national law based on the primacy of EU law. Learning about EU rights and obligations in an area without internal frontiers inevitably adds content to EDC component (c-2) to empower citizens to value diversity, including respect for the fundamental rights of every individual. A number of EU rights directly concern EDC component (c-3) empowering citizens to play an active part in democratic life. The—often forgotten—EU citizenship right to participate in the democratic life of the Union (Article 10(3) TEU) relates to representative and participatory democracy and is expressed in specific rights, such as the right to vote for the European Parliament, to submit an ECI, to petition the European Parliament, or to apply to the Ombudsman.

As to the second criterion for relevance for mainstream education (ii), EU rights and obligations add *significant content* to national EDC to the extent that they relate to foundational values, objectives and principles laid down in EU primary law, the DNA of the system. The principle of conferral is frequently shown to be central to the EU dimension at school.[2471]

The third criterion, *inviting critical thinking* (iii), was not hard to fulfil. The case teaching method is particularly appropriate in this respect. The proposed learning method, based on the two pillars of EU primary law and case teaching, helps to convey the EU dimension of EDC in an objective, critical and pluralistic manner, with no aim of indoctrination, as required by the ECtHR.[2472] Several stories are used to illustrate how active citizens have defended their EU rights or been required to respect their EU obligations, providing food for debate. Case teaching can, furthermore, be seen as good practice for educating citizens to respect the values in Article 2 TEU and the CFR, values to be fostered as part of 'citizenship competence' within the meaning of the 2018 Council Recommendation on key competences for lifelong learning and the basis for a growing EU identity.

Finally, much of the proposed content for the EU dimension *affects the large majority of EU citizens, including static citizens* (fourth criterion, iv). The mobile /static citizens dichotomy does not correspond to reality. Free movement rights are relevant for the majority of EU citizens in multiple ways: all EU citizens enjoy these rights and can exercise them in various

2471 I.a. §§ 172 209 .
2472 § 163 .

forms and degrees of intensity. Living in an area without internal frontiers, citizens should moreover be aware of the implications of the mobility rules.[2473] EU law impacts on the daily life of EU citizens, including those who stay within the boundaries of their own Member State. To sum up, rights which static citizens derive from EU law include the right to vote for the European Parliament; the right to petition the European Parliament, to apply to the European Ombudsman, and to communicate in a Treaty language; the rights in participatory democracy, such as the ECI; all rights based on the direct effect and/or primacy of EU law (consistent interpretation of national law), combined with the right to effective judicial protection; fundamental rights when situations fall within the scope of EU law (even at home); rights related to the free movement of goods and services in the internal market (at home); rights based on the implementation of EU directives in national law (interpretation of national law in accordance with directives; autonomous EU concepts); rights in the area of freedom, security and justice; rights resulting from EU harmonisation (e.g. with regard to health, safety, food control, etc.); equality rights (non-discrimination on various grounds); working-time rights; privacy rights; consumer rights, such as protection against unfair terms in consumer contracts and rights with regard to the sale of consumer goods; rights in the digital single market; environmental rights, etc.[2474] A range of EU obligations correspond to these rights. In addition to the rights of static citizens, the increasingly important EU dimension of democratic life within the Member States was emphasised. In order to meaningfully exercise their national political participation rights—and to strengthen democratic legitimacy static citizens need an awareness of the EU dimension of national politics and its effect on their daily lives. To the extent that Member States are actors in EU governance and that the EU exercises public power, the quality of democracy at EU level is contingent on the quality of democracy at national level, which is in turn contingent on EDC and its EU dimension. The EU is 'work in progress' for all EU citizens, including the static ones. The EU dimension of EDC starts from the state of play in EU law and prepares the way for the next logical step by enabling citizens to participate in the best possible way. Bringing EU citizens on board in practice, beyond the rhetoric of democracy, calls for the education of Member State nationals in their capacity as EU citizens, empowering them for action at various levels.

2473 § 196 .
2474 I.a. §§ 254 255 258 260 262 .

To conclude, on the basis of EU law the third step identified substantial content for the EU dimension of EDC in mainstream education satisfying the four criteria (i)-(iv). The rights which citizens (in various capacities) derive from EU law are not thin, pale, or uncertain.[2475] They are broader and more significant than is often perceived in political or social science. The perception indeed persists that EU citizenship is in essence something of relevance only for mobile citizens, relating to the equality of treatment of citizens who move to another Member State.[2476] However, when one looks at EU law as a whole, the full significance of EU citizenship for nationals of Member States emerges. The question as to whether EU citizenship is sufficiently mature to justify the adaptation of citizenship education can be turned around: how mature is national citizenship education without an EU dimension, given the present state of EU law and its impact? EU law has become an essential part of the national legal orders and has led to additional rights and obligations for EU citizens. EDC must keep pace with EU law. In EU Member States quality education is no longer conceivable without an EU dimension.

Content for the EU dimension in education should, of course, not be limited to rights and obligations. Yet they may form the core of the EU dimension to EDC, as EU rights and obligations impact on all three empowerment aims of EDC and require additional knowledge, skills and attitudes. Moreover, rights and obligations provide a secure starting point from which the perspective can be widened and deepened to reflect on foundational values, objectives and principles of the EU reaching into cognitive and affective-behavioural domains.

The *fourth and final step*, in Part four, answers the question as to who has the competence to provide for the EU dimension to be added to national citizenship education. The EU enjoys conferred competence to support and supplement Member State action providing an EU dimension in national citizenship education programmes.[2477] This conclusion is reached through an analysis of the main terms used in the legal basis in Article 165 TFEU, i.e. quality education, the European dimension in education, and the participation of young people in democratic life in Europe. The central competence-conferring notion of quality education is properly understood by reference to the international right to education in the ICESCR and CRC (the third anchor point). Quality education comprises education

---

2475 Text to n 1017.
2476 Text to n 1809.
2477 § 282 .

directed to the preparation of learners for effective participation and responsible life in a free society and to strengthening respect for human rights, and must thus include education for human rights and democracy.[2478] This corresponds to EDC/HRE standards in the Charter on EDC/HRE. Furthermore, the EU dimension of EDC is included in the specific competence-conferring indent 'developing the European dimension in education' and finds further support in the indent 'encouraging the participation of young people in democratic life in Europe'.[2479]

The EU however only has supporting competence allowing it to adopt incentive measures, which have legislative status, or Council recommendations.[2480] There cannot be any preemption of Member State competence. The Member States remain the principal bearers of competence in education and the EU must fully respect the responsibility of Member States for content of teaching. The analysis combines a reading of the competence conferred on the Union with the autonomy of the Member States by concluding that the EU can promote key competences and learning outcomes for school curricula, and encourage Member States to adopt them, while the Member States remain free to take their own decisions on learning content and learning processes.[2481] This combined reading gives full effect to both the competence conferred on the EU and the constitutional protection of the Member States for their educational autonomy. The study has thus nuanced the widespread idea that the EU lacks relevant competence in citizenship education.[2482]

It has furthermore been argued that EU action to support the EU dimension of EDC respects the conditions of subsidiarity and proportionality: Member States are not sufficiently achieving the objectives of the EU dimension in EDC (evidence of absent or fragmented EU learning in reports) and EU action has clear benefits. Yet, in the exercise of its competence, the EU should not go further than necessary. Specific suggestions made are the establishment of a Reference Framework on Education for Democratic Citizenship and its EU Dimension, and the creation of an EU Agency for Education for Democratic Citizenship, clearly respecting the Member States' competence in education.

2478 §§ 288 291 294 .
2479 § 298 .
2480 § 314 .
2481 § 317 .
2482 Text to n 83.

For their part, Member States must respect general EU law when they exercise their competence in education. That applies in particular where Member States are obliged to respect binding EU legislative acts containing incentives for educational actors other than themselves, such as funding or quality labels to be awarded to schools or learners.[2483] Member States must also have regard to obligations corresponding to the international right to education in binding agreements and to commitments made on EDC standards in the Council of Europe, all of which constrain their margin of appreciation.

Based on the conclusions reached in the four steps of this study, I propose this preamble to an EU legislative act on EDC and its EU dimension as a comprehensive answer to the research question:

Having regard to the Treaty on the Functioning of the European Union, and in particular Articles 165 and 166 TFEU thereof,

(...)

(1) *Whereas a European consensus exists on the need, the concept and principles of education for democratic citizenship and human rights, as expressed in the Council of Europe Charter on Education for Democratic Citizenship (EDC) and Human Rights Education (HRE).*

(2) *Whereas EDC standards of the Council of Europe are not EU law and—as to their form—only have indirect effects in the EU legal order via partial normative reception and via an interpretation of EU law taking EDC standards into account while respecting the autonomy of the EU.*

(3) *Whereas EU law provides relevant content for the EU dimension to be incorporated into national EDC in mainstream education (hereafter 'the EU dimension of EDC').*

(4) *Whereas the content of the EU dimension of EDC is additional to national EDC; is significant, i.e. relating to foundational values, objectives and principles of the EU (based on EU primary law); invites critical thinking; and affects the large majority of EU citizens, including 'static' citizens.*

(5) *Whereas the EU dimension of EDC empowers EU citizens to exercise and respect the rights and obligations provided for under the Treaties and the Charter of Fundamental Rights of the EU, empowers to value diversity and to play an active part in democratic life at EU and at Member State level.*

(6) *Whereas competence has been conferred on the EU to support and supplement Member State action in order to contribute to the development of quality education, to the European dimension in education and to encour-*

2483 § 315.

aging young people to participate in democratic life in Europe, and to do so by providing incentives and making recommendations (Article 165 TFEU).

(7) *Whereas quality education comprises education directed to the preparation of the learner for effective participation and responsible life in a free society, and to strengthening respect for human rights and fundamental freedoms, as stated in the International Covenant on Economic, Social and Cultural Rights and the Convention on the Rights of the Child, and therefore includes education for democratic citizenship and human rights.*

(8) *Whereas the Member States are invited to take more action to provide such education, including its EU dimension.*

(9) *Whereas quantitative and qualitative indictors reveal that Member States do not sufficiently achieve the objective of quality education including an EU dimension in education for democratic citizenship; whereas EU action to support the EU dimension has added value compared to the fragmented action at national, regional, local or school level (respect for the principles of subsidiarity and proportionality).*

(10) *Whereas defining learning outcomes for the EU dimension in EDC does not disproportionately interfere with freedom rights in education to the extent that they are necessary in a democratic society and genuinely meet objectives of general interest recognised by the Union and the need to protect the rights and freedoms of others.*

EU citizenship is evolving.[2484] The 1992 Maastricht Treaty inserted EU citizenship into the Treaty and connected it to a limited list of citizenship rights. The 2009 Lisbon Treaty connected EU citizenship to the provisions on democratic principles in Title II TEU. Ten years later, the time has come to connect EU citizenship and democratic principles with EDC standards in mainstream education. Incorporating an EU dimension in EDC empowers citizens in their double role as national citizens and EU citizens and contributes to the dual democratic legitimacy of the Union, thus enhancing its social legitimacy. With a view to consolidating a Union based on the values of Article 2 TEU, going beyond a merely economic rationale, the European public sphere needs an educational substratum.[2485]

2484 S O'Leary, *The Evolving Concept of Community Citizenship: From the Free Movement of Persons to Union Citizenship* (European Monographs 13, Kluwer 1996).

2485 Central question 'Wie entstehen Öffentlichkeiten in der transnationalen Konstellation?' in C Calliess and M Hartmann, *Zur Demokratie in Europa: Unionsbürgerschaft und europäische Öffentlichkeit* (Mohr Siebeck 2014) 150. See n 117.

Annexes

1. The Charter on Education for Democratic Citizenship and Human Rights Education

Appendix to Recommendation CM/Rec(2010)7 of the Committee of Ministers to the member states of the Council of Europe, adopted on 11 May 2010.

Section I – General provisions

1. Scope

   The present Charter is concerned with education for democratic citizenship and human rights education as defined in paragraph 2. It does not deal explicitly with related areas such as intercultural education, equality education, education for sustainable development and peace education, except where they overlap and interact with education for democratic citizenship and human rights education.

2. Definitions

   For the purposes of the present Charter:

   a. "Education for democratic citizenship" means education, training, awareness-raising, information, practices and activities which aim, by equipping learners with knowledge, skills and understanding and developing their attitudes and behaviour, to empower them to exercise and defend their democratic rights and responsibilities in society, to value diversity and to play an active part in democratic life, with a view to the promotion and protection of democracy and the rule of law.

   b. "Human rights education" means education, training, awareness raising, information, practices and activities which aim, by equipping learners with knowledge, skills and understanding and developing their attitudes and behaviour, to empower learners to contribute to the building and defence of a universal culture of human rights in society, with a view to the promotion and protection of human rights and fundamental freedoms.

   c. "Formal education" means the structured education and training system that runs from pre-primary and primary through secondary school and on to university. It takes place, as a rule, at general or vocational educational institutions and leads to certification.

d. "Non-formal education" means any planned programme of education designed to improve a range of skills and competences, outside the formal educational setting.

e. "Informal education" means the lifelong process whereby every individual acquires attitudes, values, skills and knowledge from the educational influences and resources in his or her own environment and from daily experience (family, peer group, neighbours, encounters, library, mass media, work, play, etc).

3. Relationship between education for democratic citizenship and human rights education

Education for democratic citizenship and human rights education are closely inter-related and mutually supportive. They differ in focus and scope rather than in goals and practices. Education for democratic citizenship focuses primarily on democratic rights and responsibilities and active participation, in relation to the civic, political, social, economic, legal and cultural spheres of society, while human rights education is concerned with the broader spectrum of human rights and fundamental freedoms in every aspect of people's lives.

4. Constitutional structures and member state priorities

The objectives, principles and policies set out below are to be applied:

a. with due respect for the constitutional structures of each member state, using means appropriate to those structures.

b. having regard to the priorities and needs of each member state.

Section II – Objectives and principles

5. Objectives and principles

The following objectives and principles should guide member states in the framing of their policies, legislation and practice.

a. The aim of providing every person within their territory with the opportunity of education for democratic citizenship and human rights education.

b. Learning in education for democratic citizenship and human rights education is a lifelong process. Effective learning in this area involves a wide range of stakeholders including policy makers, educational professionals, learners, parents, educational institutions, educational authorities, civil servants, non-governmental organisations, youth organisations, media and the general public.

c. All means of education and training, whether formal, non-formal or informal, have a part to play in this learning process and are valuable in promoting its principles and achieving its objectives.

d. Non-governmental organisations and youth organisations have a valuable contribution to make to education for democratic citizenship and human rights education, particularly through non-formal and informal education, and accordingly need opportunities and support in order to make this contribution.

e. Teaching and learning practices and activities should follow and promote democratic and human rights values and principles; in particular, the governance of educational institutions, including schools, should reflect and promote human rights values and foster the empowerment and active participation of learners, educational staff and stakeholders, including parents.

f. An essential element of all education for democratic citizenship and human rights education is the promotion of social cohesion and intercultural dialogue and the valuing of diversity and equality, including gender equality; to this end, it is essential to develop knowledge, personal and social skills and understanding that reduce conflict, increase appreciation and understanding of the differences between faith and ethnic groups, build mutual respect for human dignity and shared values, encourage dialogue and promote non-violence in the resolution of problems and disputes.

g. One of the fundamental goals of all education for democratic citizenship and human rights education is not just equipping learners with knowledge, understanding and skills, but also empowering them with the readiness to take action in society in the defence and promotion of human rights, democracy and the rule of law.

h. Ongoing training and development for education professionals and youth leaders, as well as for trainers themselves, in the principles and practices of education for democratic citizenship and human rights education are a vital part of the delivery and sustainability of effective education in this area and should accordingly be adequately planned and resourced.

i. Partnership and collaboration should be encouraged among the wide range of stakeholders involved in education for democratic citizenship and human rights education at state, regional and local level so as to make the most of their contributions, including among policy makers, educational professionals, learners, parents, educational institutions, non-governmental organisations, youth organisations, media and the general public.

j. Given the international nature of human rights values and obligations and the common principles underpinning democracy and the rule of law, it is important for member states to pursue and encourage international and regional co-operation in the activities covered by the present Charter and the identification and exchange of good practice.

Section III – Policies

6. Formal general and vocational education

Member states should include education for democratic citizenship and human rights education in the curricula for formal education at pre-primary, primary and secondary school level as well as in general and vocational education and training. Member states should also continue to support, review and update education for democratic citizenship and human rights education in these curricula in order to ensure their relevance and encourage the sustainability of this area.

7. Higher education

Member states should promote, with due respect for the principle of academic freedom, the inclusion of education for democratic citizenship and human rights education in higher education institutions, in particular for future education professionals.

8. Democratic governance

Member states should promote democratic governance in all educational institutions both as a desirable and beneficial method of governance in its own right and as a practical means of learning and experiencing democracy and respect for human rights. They should encourage and facilitate, by appropriate means, the active participation of learners, educational staff and stakeholders, including parents, in the governance of educational institutions.

9. Training

Member states should provide teachers, other educational staff, youth leaders and trainers with the necessary initial and ongoing training and development in education for democratic citizenship and human rights education. This should ensure that they have a thorough knowledge and understanding of the discipline's objectives and principles and of appropriate teaching and learning methods, as well as other key skills appropriate to their area of education.

10. Role of non-governmental organisations, youth organisations and other stakeholders
    Member states should foster the role of non-governmental organisations and youth organisations in education for democratic citizenship and human rights education, especially in non-formal education. They should recognize these organisations and their activities as a valued part of the educational system, provide them where possible with the support they need and make full use of the expertise they can contribute to all forms of education. Member states should also promote and publicise education for democratic citizenship and human rights education to other stakeholders, notably the media and general public, in order to maximise the contribution that they can make to this area.
11. Criteria for evaluation
    Member states should develop criteria for the evaluation of the effectiveness of programmes on education for democratic citizenship and human rights education. Feedback from learners should form an integral part of all such evaluations.
12. Research
    Member states should initiate and promote research on education for democratic citizenship and human rights education to take stock of the current situation in the area and to provide stakeholders including policy makers, educational institutions, school leaders, teachers, learners, non-governmental organisations and youth organisations with comparative information to help them measure and increase their effectiveness and efficiency and improve their practices. This research could include, *inter alia*, research on curricula, innovative practices, teaching methods and development of evaluation systems, including evaluation criteria and indicators. Member states should share the results of their research with other member states and stakeholders where appropriate.
13. Skills for promoting social cohesion, valuing diversity and handling differences and conflict
    In all areas of education, member states should promote educational approaches and teaching methods which aim at learning to live

together in a democratic and multicultural society and at enabling learners to acquire the knowledge and skills to promote social cohesion, value diversity and equality, appreciate differences – particularly between different faith and ethnic groups – and settle disagreements and conflicts in a non-violent manner with respect for each others' rights, as well as to combat all forms of discrimination and violence, especially bullying and harassment.

Section IV – Evaluation and co-operation

14. Evaluation and review

Member states should regularly evaluate the strategies and policies they have undertaken with respect to the present Charter and adapt these strategies and policies as appropriate. They may do so in co-operation with other member states, for example on a regional basis. Any member state may also request assistance from the Council of Europe.

15. Co-operation in follow-up activities

Member states should, where appropriate, co-operate with each other and through the Council of Europe in pursuing the aims and principles of the present Charter by:

a. pursuing the topics of common interest and priorities identified;
b. fostering multilateral and transfrontier activities, including the existing network of co-ordinators on education for democratic citizenship and human rights education;
c. exchanging, developing, codifying and assuring the dissemination of good practices;
d. informing all stakeholders, including the public, about the aims and implementation of the Charter;
e. supporting European networks of non-governmental organisations, youth organisations and education professionals and co-operation among them.

16. International co-operation

Member states should share the results of their work on education for democratic citizenship and human rights education in the framework of the Council of Europe with other international organisations.

2. *Relationship between democracy, human rights and the rule of law*

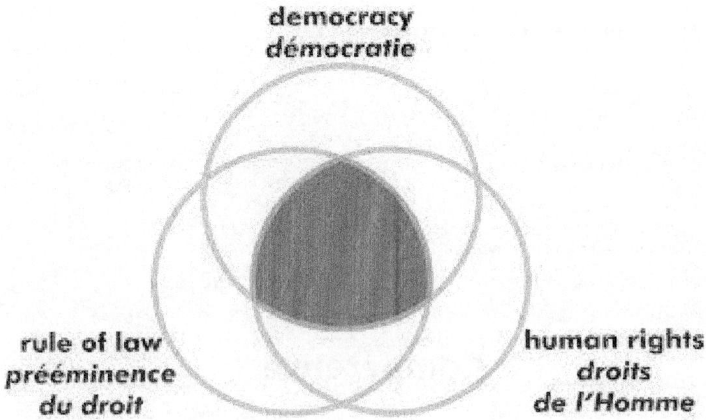

EDC and HRE have a comparable relationship.[2486]

2486 Figure in CoE Committee of Ministers, The Council of Europe and the Rule of Law, CM(2008)170, para 25. Above text to n 180.

3. *The Reference Framework of Competences for Democratic Culture*

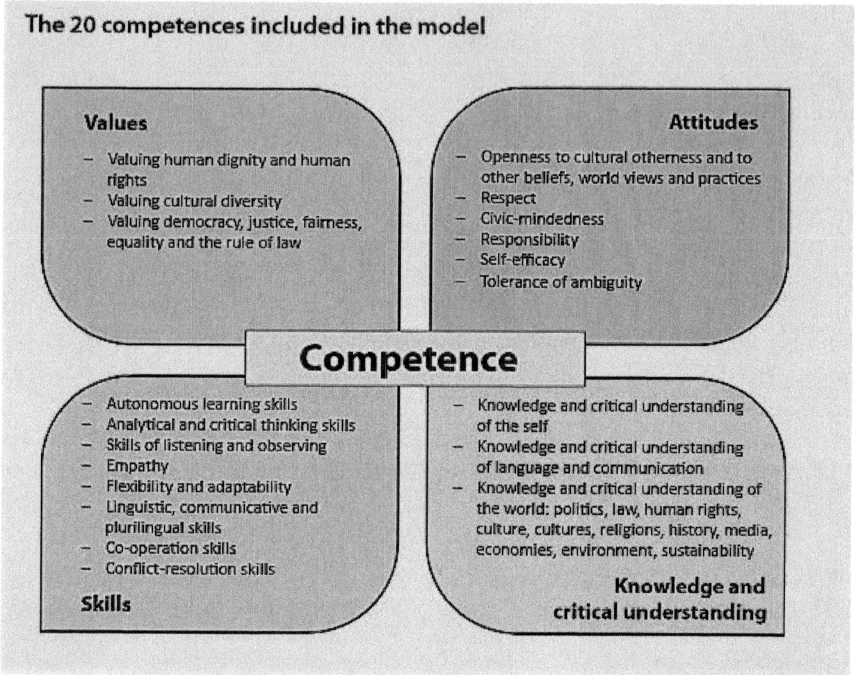

Council of Europe, 2018.[2487]

4. *EU Recommendation on key competences for lifelong learning*

Citizenship competence (sixth key competence)

Citizenship competence is the ability to act as responsible citizens and to fully participate in civic and social life, based on understanding of social, economic, legal and political concepts and structures, as well as global developments and sustainability.

2487 CoE Reference Framework of Competences for Democratic Culture, Vol 1: Context, concepts and model (2018) 38. Above § 38 .

Essential knowledge, skills and attitudes related to this competence

Citizenship competence is based on knowledge of basic concepts and phenomena relating to individuals, groups, work organisations, society, economy and culture. This involves an understanding of the European common values, as expressed in Article 2 of the Treaty on European Union and the Charter of Fundamental Rights of the European Union. It includes knowledge of contemporary events, as well as a critical understanding of the main developments in national, European and world history. In addition, it includes an awareness of the aims, values and policies of social and political movements, as well as of sustainable systems, in particular climate and demographic change at the global level and their underlying causes. Knowledge of European integration as well as an awareness of diversity and cultural identities in Europe and the world is essential. This includes an understanding of the multi-cultural and socioeconomic dimensions of European societies, and how national cultural identity contributes to the European identity.

Skills for citizenship competence relate to the ability to engage effectively with others in common or public interest, including the sustainable development of society. This involves critical thinking and integrated problem solving skills, as well as skills to develop arguments and constructive participation in community activities, as well as in decision-making at all levels, from local and national to the European and international level. This also involves the ability to access, have a critical understanding of, and interact with both traditional and new forms of media and understand the role and functions of media in democratic societies.

Respect for human rights as a basis for democracy lays the foundations for a responsible and constructive attitude. Constructive participation involves willingness to participate in democratic decision-making at all levels and civic activities. It includes support for social and cultural diversity, gender equality and social cohesion, sustainable lifestyles, promotion of culture of peace and non-violence, a readiness to respect the privacy of others, and to take responsibility for the environment. Interest in political and socioeconomic developments, humanities and intercultural communication is needed to be prepared both to overcome prejudices and to compromise where necessary and to ensure social justice and fairness.[2488]

2488 Council Recommendation of 22 May 2018 on key competences for lifelong learning [2018] OJ C189/1, Annex: Key competences for lifelong learning—A European reference framework.

5. Forms of citizenship education

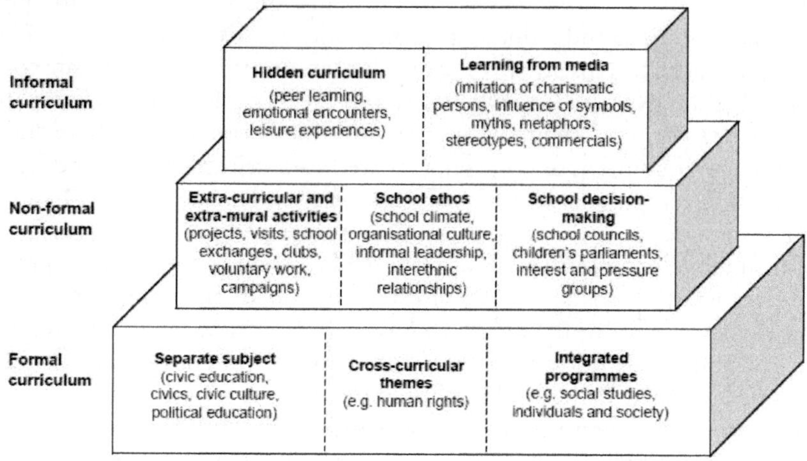

Citizenship Education in the School Context

Source[2489]

2489 Bîrzéa C, 'EDC policies in Europe – a synthesis' in *All-European Study on Education for Democratic Citizenship Policies* (CoE 2005) 38.

Bibliography

Sources are in principle ordered per year.

1. EU

EU primary law

Treaty on European Union, signed at Maastricht on 7 February 1992 [1992] OJ C191/1

Treaty of Lisbon amending the Treaty on European Union and the Treaty establishing the European Community, signed at Lisbon on 13 December 2007 [2007] OJ C306

Treaty of Accession of Croatia [2012] OJ L112

Protocol (No 1) On the role of the National Parliaments in the European Union [2012] OJ C326/1

Protocol (No 2) On the application of the principles of subsidiarity and proportionality [2012] OJ C326/1

Protocol (No 8) relating to Article 6(2) of the Treaty on European Union on the accession of the Union to the European Convention on the Protection of Human Rights and Fundamental Freedoms [2012] OJ C326/273

Consolidated versions of the Treaty on European Union and the Treaty on the Functioning of the European Union [2016] OJ C202/1

Charter of Fundamental Rights of the European Union [2016] OJ C202/389 (proclaimed at Strasbourg on 12 December 2007 by the European Parliament, the Council and the Commission [2007] OJ C303/1)

European Council/ Presidencies

Presidency Conclusions of the Birmingham European Council of 16 October 1992, Birmingham Declaration 'A Community close to its citizens', Bull EC 10–1992

Presidency Conclusions of the Edinburgh European Council of 11–12 December 1992, SN 456/1/92 REV 1

Presidency Conclusions of the Copenhagen European Council of 21–22 June 1993, Bull EC 6–1993

Presidency Conclusions of the Cologne European Council of 3–4 June 1999, 150/99 REV 1

Presidency Conclusions of the Lisbon European Council of 23 and 24 March 2000

Presidency Conclusions of the Brussels European Council of 21–22 June 2007, Annex I: IGC Mandate

European Council, The Stockholm Programme—An open and secure Europe serving and protecting citizens [2010] OJ C115/1

European Council Decision (EU) 2018/937 of 28 June 2018 establishing the composition of the European Parliament [2018] OJ L165I/1

European Council Decision (EU) 2019/584 taken in agreement with the United Kingdom of 11 April 2019 extending the period under Article 50(3) TEU [2019] OJ L 101/1

Other

Act concerning the election of the representatives of the Assembly by direct universal suffrage [1976] OJ L278/5 (Electoral Act), as amended

Community Charter of the Fundamental Social Rights of Workers (adopted by eleven of the Heads of State and Government at the European Council of Strasbourg on 8 and 9 December 1989)

Convention on the Future of Europe (2003) <european-convention.europa.eu/>

Praesidium European Convention, The democratic life of the Union (2 April 2003) CONV 650/03

European Convention, Working Group V 'Complementary Competencies, Final Report' (4 November 2002) CONV 375/1/02 REV 1

European Convention, Final report of Working Group IX on Simplification (29 November 2002) CONV 424/02

Treaty establishing a Constitution for Europe [2004] OJ C310 (signed in Rome on 29 October 2004, ratified by 15 of 25 Member States, no entry into force)

Final Act (2007/C306/02), Conference of the Representatives of the governments of the Member States [2007] OJ C306/231

Treaty establishing the European Stability Mechanism (ESM) (Brussels, 2 February 2012)

European Parliament and Council

Decision 819/95 of the European Parliament and of the Council of 14 March 1995 establishing the Community action programme 'Socrates' [1995] OJ L87/10

Directive 95/46/EC of the European Parliament and of the Council of 24 October 1995 on the protection of individuals with regard to the processing of personal data and on the free movement of such data [1995] OJ L281/31 (as amended)

Directive 97/7/EC of the European Parliament and of the Council of 20 May 1997 on the protection of consumers in respect of distance contracts [1997] OJ L144/19

Directive 1999/44/EC of the European Parliament and of the Council of 25 May 1999 on certain aspects of the sale of consumer goods and associated guarantees [1999] OJ L171/12

Decision 253/2000 of the European Parliament and of the Council of 24 January 2000 establishing the second phase of the Community action programme in the field of education 'Socrates' [2000] OJ L28/1

Decision 1934/2000 of the European Parliament and of the Council of 17 July 2000 on the European Year of Languages 2001 [2000] OJ L232/1

Regulation 1049/2001 of the European Parliament and of the Council of 30 May 2001 regarding public access to European Parliament, Council and Commission documents [2001] OJ L145/43

Recommendation of the European Parliament and of the Council of 10 July 2001 on mobility within the Community for students, persons undergoing training, volunteers, teachers and trainers [2001] OJ L215/30

Directive 2002/98/EC of the European Parliament and of the Council of 27 January 2003 setting standards of quality and safety for the collection, testing, processing, storage and distribution of human blood and blood components and amending Directive 2001/83/EC [2003] OJ L33/30

Directive 2003/87/EC of the European Parliament and of the Council of 13 October 2003 establishing a scheme for greenhouse gas emission allowance trading within the Community and amending Council Directive 96/61/EC [2003] OJ L275/32

Directive 2003/88/EC of the European Parliament and of the Council of 4 November 2003 concerning certain aspects of the organisation of working time [2003] OJ L299/9 (The Working Time Directive)

Decision 2318/2003 of the European Parliament and of the Council of 5 December 2003 adopting a multiannual programme (2004 to 2006) for the effective integration of information and communication technologies (ICT) in education and training systems in Europe (eLearning Programme) [2003] OJ L345/9

Regulation (EC) No 261/2004 of the European Parliament and of the Council of 11 February 2004 establishing common rules on compensation and assistance to passengers in the event of denied boarding and of cancellation or long delay of flights, and repealing Regulation (EEC) No 295/91 [2004] OJ L46/1

Directive 2004/35/CE of the European Parliament and of the Council of 21 April 2004 on environmental liability with regard to the prevention and remedying of environmental damage [2004] OJ L143/56, as amended (Environmental Liability Directive)

Regulation (EC) No 883/2004 of the European Parliament and of the Council of 29 April 2004 on the coordination of social security systems [2004] OJ L166/1, as amended

Directive 2004/38 of the European Parliament and of the Council of 29 April 2004 on the right of citizens of the Union and their family members to move and reside freely within the territory of the Member States [2004] OJ L158/77

Decision 2241/2004 of the European Parliament and of the Council of 15 December 2004 on a single Community framework for the transparency of qualifications and competences (Europass) [2004] OJ L390/6

Directive 2005/35/EC of the European Parliament and of the Council of 7 September 2005 on ship-source pollution and on the introduction of penalties for infringements [2005] OJ L255/11

Directive 2005/36 of the European Parliament and of the Council of 7 September 2005 on the recognition of professional qualifications [2005] OJ L255/22, as amended

Decision 771/2006/EC of the European Parliament and of the Council of 17 May 2006 establishing the European Year of Equal Opportunities for All (2007)—towards a just society [2006] OJ L146/1

Directive 2006/54/EC of the European Parliament and of the Council of 5 July 2006 on the implementation of the principle of equal opportunities and equal treatment of men and women in matters of employment and occupation [2006] OJ L204/23

Decision 1720/2006 of the European Parliament and of the Council of 15 November 2006 establishing an action programme in the field of lifelong learning [2006] OJ L327/45; amended by Decision 1357/2008 [2008] OJ L350/56

Decision 1904/2006 of the European Parliament and of the Council of 12 December 2006 establishing for the period 2007 to 2013 the programme 'Europe for Citizens' to promote active European citizenship [2006] OJ L378/32, amended by Decision 1358/2008 [2008] L350/58

Directive 2006/123 of the European Parliament and of the Council of 12 December 2006 on services in the internal market [2006] OJ L376/36

Recommendation of the European Parliament and of the Council of 18 December 2006 on key competences for lifelong learning [2006] OJ L394/10 (Annex: Key Competencies for Lifelong Learning- A European Reference Framework)

Recommendation of the European Parliament and of the Council of 18 December 2006 on transnational mobility within the Community for education and training purposes: European Quality Charter for Mobility [2006] OJ L394/5

Regulation (EC) No 1905/2006 of the European Parliament and of the Council of 18 December 2006 establishing a financing instrument for development cooperation [2006] OJ L378/41

Regulation (EC) No 862/2007 of the European Parliament and of the Council of 11 July 2007 on Community statistics on migration and international protection and repealing Council Regulation (EEC) No 311/76 on the compilation of statistics on foreign workers [2007] OJ L199/23

Directive 2008/50/EC of the European Parliament and of the Council of 21 May 2008 on ambient air quality and cleaner air for Europe [2008] OJ L152/1

Directive 2008/101/EC of the European Parliament and of the Council of 19 November 2008 amending Directive 2003/87/EC so as to include aviation activities in the scheme for greenhouse gas emission allowance trading within the Community [2009] OJ L8/3

Directive 2008/115/EC of the European Parliament and of the Council of 16 December 2008 on common standards and procedures in Member States for returning illegally staying third-country nationals [2008] OJ L348/98

Regulation (EC) No 1333/2008 of the European Parliament and of the Council of 16 December 2008 on food additives [2008] OJ L354/16

Directive 2009/48/EC of the European Parliament and of the Council of 18 June 2009 on the safety of toys [2009] OJ L170/1

Directive 2010/41/EU of the European Parliament and of the Council of 7 July 2010 on the application of the principle of equal treatment between men and women engaged in an activity in a self-employed capacity and repealing Council Directive 86/613/EEC [2010] OJ L 180/1

Regulation (EU) No 181/2011 of the European Parliament and of the Council of 16 February 2011 concerning the rights of passengers in bus and coach transport and amending Regulation (EC) No 2006/2004 [2011] OJ L55/1

Regulation (EU) No 211/2011 of the European Parliament and of the Council of 16 February 2011 on the citizens' initiative [2011] OJ L 65/1

Directive 2011/24/EU of the European Parliament and of the Council of 9 March 2011 on the application of patients' rights in cross-border healthcare [2011] OJ L88/45 (Patients' Mobility Directive)

Regulation 492/2011 of the European Parliament and of the Council of 5 April 2011 on freedom of movement for workers within the Union [2011] OJ L141/1

Directive 2011/36/EU of the European Parliament and of the Council of 5 April 2011 on preventing and combating trafficking in human beings and protecting its victims, and replacing Council Framework Decision 2002/629/JHA [2011] OJ L101/1 (Anti-Trafficking Directive)

Directive 2011/83/EU of the European Parliament and of the Council of 25 October 2011 on consumer rights, amending Council Directive 93/13/EEC and Directive 1999/44/EC of the European Parliament and of the Council and repealing Council Directive 85/577/EEC and Directive 97/7/EC of the European Parliament and of the Council [2011] OJ L304/64

Regulation (EU) No 1214/2011 of the European Parliament and of the Council of 16 November 2011 on the professional cross-border transport of euro cash by road between euro-area Member States [2011] OJ L316/1

Directive 2011/92/EU of the European Parliament and of the Council of 13 December 2011 on the assessment of the effects of certain public and private projects on the environment [2012] OJ L26/1 (amended by Directive 2014/52/EU)

Directive 2011/95/EU of the European Parliament and of the Council of 13 December 2011 on standards for the qualification of third-country nationals or stateless persons as beneficiaries of international protection, for a uniform status for refugees or for persons eligible for subsidiary protection, and for the content of the protection granted [2011] OJ L337/9

Directive 2012/29/EU of the European Parliament and of the Council of 25 October 2012 establishing minimum standards on the rights, support and protection of victims of crime, and replacing Council Framework Decision 2001/220/JHA [2012] L315/57 (Victims' Rights Directive)

Decision 1093/2012/EU of the European Parliament and of the Council of 21 November 2012 on the European Year of Citizens (2013) [2012] OJ L325/1

Directive 2013/33/EU of the European Parliament and of the Council of 26 June 2013 laying down standards for the reception of applicants for international protection [2013] OJ L180/96

Decision No 1386/2013/EU of the European Parliament and of the Council of 20 November 2013 on a General Union Environment Action Programme to 2020 'Living well, within the limits of our planet' [2013] OJ L354/171

Regulation 1288/2013 of the European Parliament and of the Council of 11 December 2013 establishing 'Erasmus+': the Union programme for education, training, youth and sport and repealing Decisions 1719/2006, 1720/2006 and 1298/2008 [2013] OJ L347/50

Regulation (EU) No 1293/2013 of the European Parliament and of the Council of 11 December 2013 on the establishment of a Programme for the Environment and Climate Action (LIFE) and repealing Regulation (EC) No 614/2007 [2013] OJ L347/185

Regulation 1381/2013 of the European Parliament and of the Council of 17 December 2013 establishing a Rights, Equality and Citizenship Programme for the period 2014 to 2020 [2013] OJ L354/62

Regulation (EU) No 235/2014 of the European Parliament and of the Council of 11 March 2014 establishing a financing instrument for democracy and human rights worldwide [2014] OJ L77/85

Directive (EU) 2015/2302 of the European Parliament and of the Council of 25 November 2015 on package travel and linked travel arrangements, amending Regulation (EC) No 2006/2004 and Directive 2011/83/EU of the European Parliament and of the Council and repealing Council Directive 90/314/EEC [2015] OJ L326/1

Regulation (EU) 2016/399 of the European Parliament and of the Council of 9 March 2016 on a Union Code on the rules governing the movement of persons across borders (Schengen Borders Code) [2016] OJ L77/1

Regulation (EU) 2016/679 of the European Parliament and of the Council of 27 April 2016 on the protection of natural persons with regard to the processing of personal data and on the free movement of such data, and repealing Directive 95/46/EC [2016] OJ L119/1 (General Data Protection Regulation)

Regulation (EU) 2016/794 of the European Parliament and of the Council of 11 May 2016 on the European Union Agency for Law Enforcement Cooperation (Europol) and replacing and repealing Council Decisions 2009/371/JHA, 2009/934/JHA, 2009/935/JHA, 2009/936/JHA and 2009/968/JHA [2016] OJ L135/53

Directive (EU) 2016/800 of the European Parliament and of the Council of 11 May 2016 on procedural safeguards for children who are suspects or accused persons in criminal proceedings [2016] OJ L132/1

Regulation (EU) 2017/826 of the European Parliament and of the Council of 17 May 2017 on establishing a Union programme to support specific activities enhancing the involvement of consumers and other financial services end-users in Union policy-making in the area of financial services for the period of 2017–2020 [2017] OJ L129/17

Regulation (EU) 2017/2394 of the European Parliament and of the Council of 12 December 2017 on cooperation between national authorities responsible for the enforcement of consumer protection laws and repealing Regulation (EC) No 2006/2004 [2017] OJ L 345/1

Decision (EU) 2018/646 of the European Parliament and of the Council of 18 April 2018 on a common framework for the provision of better services for skills and qualifications (Europass) and repealing Decision No 2241/2004/EC [2018] OJ L112/42

Regulation (EU) 2018/1475 of the European Parliament and of the Council of 2 October 2018 laying down the legal framework of the European Solidarity Corps and amending Regulation (EU) No 1288/2013, Regulation (EU) No 1293/2013 and Decision No 1313/2013/EU [2018] OJ L 250/1

Regulation (EU) 2018/1999 of the European Parliament and of the Council of 11 December 2018 on the Governance of the Energy Union and Climate Action, amending Regulations (EC) No 663/2009 and (EC) No 715/2009 of the European Parliament and of the Council, Directives 94/22/EC, 98/70/EC, 2009/31/EC, 2009/73/EC, 2010/31/EU, 2012/27/EU and 2013/30/EU of the European Parliament and of the Council, Council Directives 2009/119/EC and (EU) 2015/652 and repealing Regulation (EU) No 525/2013 of the European Parliament and of the Council [2018] L 328/1

Regulation (EU) 2019/128 of the European Parliament and of the Council of 16 January 2019 establishing a European Centre for the Development of Vocational Training (Cedefop) and repealing Council Regulation (EEC) No 337/75 [2019] OJ L 30/90

Regulation (EU) 2019/515 of the European Parliament and of the Council of 19 March 2019 on the mutual recognition of goods lawfully marketed in another Member State and repealing Regulation (EC) No 764/2008 [2019] OJ L 91/1

Regulation (EU) 2019/499 of the European Parliament and of the Council of 25 March 2019 laying down provisions for the continuation of ongoing learning mobility activities under the Erasmus+ programme established by Regulation (EU) No 1288/2013, in the context of the withdrawal of the United Kingdom from the Union [2019] OJ L 85I/32

Regulation (EU) 2019/631 of the European Parliament and of the Council of 17 April 2019 setting CO2 emission performance standards for new passenger cars and for new light commercial vehicles, and repealing Regulations (EC) No 443/2009 and (EU) No 510/2011 [2019] OJ L 111/13

Regulation (EU) 2019/788 of the European Parliament and of the Council of 17 April 2019 on the European citizens' initiative [2019] OJ L130/55

Directive (EU) 2019/771 of the European Parliament and of the Council of 20 May 2019 on certain aspects concerning contracts for the sale of goods, amending Regulation (EU) 2017/2394 and Directive 2009/22/EC, and repealing Directive 1999/44/EC [2019] OJ L 136/28

Directive (EU) 2019/1152 of the European Parliament and of the Council of 20 June 2019 on transparent and predictable working conditions in the European Union [2019] OJ L 186/105

Regulation (EU) 2019/1157 of the European Parliament and of the Council of 20 June 2019 on strengthening the security of identity cards of Union citizens and of residence documents issued to Union citizens and their family members exercising their right of free movement [2019] OJ L 188/67

Directive (EU) 2019/1158 of the European Parliament and of the Council of 20 June 2019 on work-life balance for parents and carers and repealing Council Directive 2010/18/EU [2019] OJ L 188/79

European Parliament

European Parliament Resolution of 12 April 1989 adopting the Declaration of fundamental rights and freedoms [1989] OJ C120/51

Decision of the European Parliament on the Regulations and General Conditions governing the performance of the Ombudsman's duties [1994] OJ L113/15, amended by Decisions of 14 March 2002 and 18 June 2008

European Parliament Resolution of 26 September 2006 on initiatives to complement school curricula providing appropriate support measures to include the European dimension [2006] OJ C306E/100

European Parliament Resolution of 4 September 2007 on institutional and legal implications of the use of 'soft law' instruments [2008] OJ C187E/75

European Parliament Resolution of 13 December 2007 on combating the rise of extremism in Europe [2008] OJ C323E/494

European Parliament Committee on Constitutional Affairs, Report on the Treaty of Lisbon (29 January 2008), Explanatory Statement to European Parliament resolution of 20 February 2008 on the Treaty of Lisbon

European Parliament Resolution of 16 January 2008: Towards an EU strategy on the rights of the child [2009] OJ C41E/24

European Parliament Resolution of 20 February 2008 on the Treaty of Lisbon [2009] OJ C184E/25

European Parliament Resolution of 24 March 2009 on Multilingualism: an asset for Europe and a shared commitment [2010] OJ C117E/59

European Parliament Resolution of 2 April 2009 on Better Schools: an agenda for European cooperation [2010] OJ C137E/43

European Parliament Resolution of 2 April 2009 on the application of Directive 2004/38/EC on the right of citizens of the Union and their family members to move and reside freely within the territory of the Member States [2010] OJ C137E/6

European Parliament Resolution of 18 May 2010 on 'An EU Strategy for Youth – Investing and Empowering' [2011] OJ C161E/21

European Parliament Resolution of 7 September 2010 on journalism and new media – creating a public sphere in Europe [2011] OJ C308E/55

European Parliament Resolution of 18 April 2012 on the Annual Report on Human Rights in the World and the European Union's policy on the matter, including implications for the EU's strategic human rights policy [2013] OJ C258E/8

European Parliament Resolution of 16 January 2014 on respect for the fundamental right of free movement in the EU [2016] OJ C482/114

European Parliament Decision of 15 April 2014 on the modification of the interinstitutional agreement on the Transparency Register [2017] OJ C443/228

European Parliament Resolution of 27 November 2014 on the 25th anniversary of the UN Convention on the Rights of the Child [2016] OJ C289/57

Written questions by Members of the European Parliament and their answers given by a European Union institution [2014] OJ C208/1

European Parliament Resolution of 15 January 2015 on the annual report on the activities of the European Ombudsman 2013 [2016] OJ C300/14

European Parliament Resolution of 28 October 2015 on the European Citizens' Initiative [2017] OJ C355/17

European Parliament Resolution of 11 November 2015 on the reform of the electoral law of the European Union [2017] OJ C366/7

European Parliament Resolution on Follow-up of the strategic framework for European cooperation in education and training (ET2020) [2018] OJ C91/6

European Parliament Resolution of 12 April 2016 on Learning EU at school [2018] OJ C58/57

European Parliament Resolution of 26 May 2016 on the Single Market Strategy [2018] OJ C76/112

European Parliament Resolution of 13 December 2016 on the situation of fundamental rights in the European Union in 2015 (2018/C 238/01)

European Parliament Resolution of 15 December 2016 on the activities of the Committee on Petitions 2015 [2018] OJ C238/132

Rules of Procedure of the European Parliament: 8th parliamentary term (January 2017)

European Parliament Resolution of 6 April 2017 on the adequacy of the protection afforded by the EU-US Privacy Shield

European Parliament Resolution of 15 November 2017 on the situation of the rule of law and democracy in Poland [2018] OJ C 356/44

European Parliament Resolution of 16 November 2017 on the annual report on the activities of the European Ombudsman in 2016 (2017/2126(INI))

European Parliament Resolution of 12 December 2017 on the EU Citizenship Report 2017: Strengthening Citizens' Rights in a Union of Democratic Change (2017/2069(INI))

Council

Council Regulation (EEC) No 1612/68 of 15 October 1968 on freedom of movement for workers within the Community [1968] OJ L257/2

Council Regulation (EEC) No 1408/71 of 14 June 1971 on the application of social security schemes to employed persons, to self-employed persons and to members of their families moving within the Community, as amended and updated by Council Regulation (EEC) No 2001/83 of 2 June 1983 [1983] OJ L230/6

Council Directive 77/486 of 25 July 1977 on the education of the children of migrant workers [1977] OJ L199/32

Council Directive 85/577/EEC of 20 December 1985 to protect the consumer in respect of contracts negotiated away from business premises [1985] OJ L372/31

Council Decision 89/489/EEC of 28 July 1989 establishing an action programme to promote foreign language competence in the European Community (Lingua) [1989] OJ L239/24

Council Directive 89/552/EEC of 3 October 1989 on the coordination of certain provisions laid down by law, regulation or administrative action in Member States concerning the pursuit of television broadcasting activities [1989] OJ L298/23, as amended by Directive 97/36/EC of the European Parliament and of the Council of 30 June 1997 [1997] OJ L202/60

Council Directive 93/13/EEC of 5 April 1993 on unfair terms in consumer contracts [1993] OJ L95/29

Council Directive 93/109/EC of 6 December 1993 laying down detailed arrangements for the exercise of the right to vote and stand as a candidate in elections to the European Parliament for citizens of the Union residing in a Member State of which they are not nationals [1993] OJ L329/34, amended by Council Directive 2013/1/EU of 20 December 2012

Council Directive 94/80/EC of 19 December 1994 laying down detailed arrangements for the exercise of the right to vote and to stand as a candidate in municipal elections by citizens of the Union residing in a Member State of which they are not nationals [1994] OJ L368/38, amended by Council Directive 96/30/EC of 13 May 1996

Council Resolution of 31 March 1995 on cooperation in the field of youth information and studies concerning youth [1995] OJ C207/5

Council Conclusions of 6 May 1996 on the White Paper 'Teaching and learning: towards the learning society' [1996] OJ C195/1

Council Directive 2000/43/EC of 29 June 2000 implementing the principle of equal treatment between persons irrespective of racial or ethnic origin [2000] OJ L180/22 (Racial Equality Directive)

Council Directive 2000/78/EC of 27 November 2000 establishing a general framework for equal treatment in employment and occupation [2000] OJ L303/16

Council Directive 2001/23/EC of 12 March 2001 on the approximation of the laws of the Member States relating to the safeguarding of employees' rights in the event of transfers of undertakings, businesses or parts of undertakings or businesses [2001] OJ L82/16

Council Decision of 25 June 2002 and 23 September 2002 amending the Act concerning the election of the representatives of the European Parliament by direct universal suffrage, annexed to Decision 76/787/ECSC, EEC, Euratom [2002] OJ L283/1

Council Framework Decision of 13 June 2002 on the European arrest warrant and the surrender procedures between Member States – Statements made by certain Member States on the adoption of the Framework Decision 2002/584/JHA [2002] OJ L190/1

Council Resolution of 19 December 2002 on the promotion of enhanced European cooperation in vocational education and training [2003] OJ C13/2

Council Directive 2003/86/EC of 22 September 2003 on the right to family reunification [2003] OJ L251/12

Council Directive 2004/113/EC of 13 December 2004 implementing the principle of equal treatment between men and women in the access to and supply of goods and services [2004] OJ L373/37 (Directive on Gender Equality)

Council Regulation (EC) No 2252/2004 of 13 December 2004 on standards for security features and biometrics in passports and travel documents issued by Member States [2004] OJ L385/1, as amended by Regulation (EC) No 444/2009 of the European Parliament and of the Council of 6 May 2009 [2009] OJ L142/1

Council Decision of 28 February 2008 relating to the conclusion of an Agreement between the European Community and the Council of Europe on cooperation between the European Union Agency for Fundamental Rights and the Council of Europe [2008] OJ L186/6

Council Conclusions of 12 May 2009 on a strategic framework for European cooperation in education and training (ET 2020) [2009] OJ C119/2

Council Conclusions of 19 November 2010 on education for sustainable development [2010] OJ C327/11

Council Resolution of 21 November 2008 on a European strategy for multilingualism [2008] OJ C320/1

Council Framework Decision 2008/909/JHA of 27 November 2008 on the application of the principle of mutual recognition to judgments in criminal matters imposing custodial sentences or measures involving deprivation of liberty for the purpose of their enforcement in the European Union [2008] OJ L327/27, as amended by Council Framework Decision 2009/299/JHA of 26 February 2009 [2009] OJ L81/24

Council Conclusions on increasing the level of basic skills in the context of European cooperation on schools for the 21st century [2010] C323/04

Council Decision of 26 November 2009 concerning the conclusion, by the European Community, of the United Nations Convention on the Rights of Persons with Disabilities [2010] OJ L23/35

Council Directive 2010/18/EU of 8 March 2010 implementing the revised Framework Agreement on parental leave concluded by BUSINESSEUROPE, UEAPME, CEEP and ETUC and repealing Directive 96/34/EC [2010] OJ L68/13

Council Resolution of 3 June 2010 concerning an updated handbook with recommendations for international police cooperation and measures to prevent and control violence and disturbances in connection with football matches with an international dimension, in which at least one Member State is involved [2010] OJ C165/1

Council Conclusions on the role of education and training in the implementation of the 'Europe 2020' strategy [2011] C70/1

Council Recommendation of 28 June 2011 'Youth on the move' — promoting the learning mobility of young people [2011] C199/1

Council Recommendation of 28 June 2011 on policies to reduce early school leaving [2011] OJ C191/1

Council Recommendation on the validation of non-formal and informal learning [2012] OJ C398/1

Council, EU Strategic Framework and Action Plan on Human Rights and Democracy (Luxembourg, 25 June 2012) 11855/12

Council Recommendation of 9 December 2013 on effective Roma integration measures in the Member States [2013] OJ C378/1

Council Regulation (EU) No 390/2014 of 14 April 2014 establishing the 'Europe for Citizens' programme for the period 2014–2020 [2014] OJ L115/3

Council Conclusions of 20 May 2014 on multilingualism and the development of language competences [2014] OJ C183/26

Council Directive (EU) 2015/637 of 20 April 2015 on the coordination and cooperation measures to facilitate consular protection for unrepresented citizens of the Union in third countries and repealing Decision 95/553/EC [2015] OJ L106/1

Council Conclusions on the Action Plan on Human Rights and Democracy 2015–2019 (20 July 2015)

Council Decision (EU) 2015/1601 of 22 September 2015 establishing provisional measures in the area of international protection for the benefit of Italy and Greece [2015] OJ L248/80

Council Resolution on encouraging political participation of young people in democratic life in Europe [2015] OJ C417/10

Conclusions of the Council and of the Representatives of the Governments of the Member States, meeting within the Council, on the prevention of radicalisation leading to violent extremism [2016] OJ C467/3

Council Conclusions of 30 May 2016 on developing media literacy and critical thinking through education and training [2016] OJ C212/5

Council Recommendation of 19 December 2016 on Upskilling Pathways: New Opportunities for Adults [2016] OJ C484/1

Conclusions of the Council and of the Representatives of the Governments of the Member States, meeting within the Council, on the role of the youth sector in an integrated and cross-sectoral approach to preventing and combating violent radicalisation of young people [2016] OJ C213/1

Council Recommendation of 22 May 2017 on the European Qualifications Framework for lifelong learning and repealing the recommendation of the European Parliament and of the Council of 23 April 2008 on the establishment of the European Qualifications Framework for lifelong learning [2017] OJ C189/15

Council Conclusions on school development and excellent teaching (20 November 2017)

Council Conclusions on the role of youth work in supporting young people's development of essential life skills that facilitate their successful transition to adulthood, active citizenship and working life [2017] OJ C189/30

Council Recommendation of 20 November 2017 on tracking graduates [2017] OJ C423/1

Council Resolution on the Structured Dialogue and the future development of the dialogue with young people in the context of policies for European cooperation in the youth field, post 2018 [2017] OJ C189/1

Council Conclusions on moving towards a vision of a European Education Area [2018] OJ C195/7

Council Conclusions on the role of young people in building a secure, cohesive and harmonious society in Europe [2018] OJ C195/13

Council Recommendation of 22 May 2018 on key competences for lifelong learning [2018] OJ C189/1

Council Recommendation of 22 May 2018 on promoting common values, inclusive education, and the European dimension of teaching [2018] OJ C195/1

Council Recommendation of 22 May 2019 on a comprehensive approach to the teaching and learning of languages [2019] OJ C189/15

Commission

Commission White Paper of 16 June 1986 'Completing the Internal Market' COM(85) 310 final

Commission Staff working paper, First progress report of 23 September 1991 on action untertaken by the Member Sates and by the European Community with a view to strengthening the European dimension in education, SEC (91) 1753 final

Commission, Europe and the challenge of enlargement (24 June 1992) Bull EC Suppl 3–92

Commission Green Paper of 29 September 1993 on the European Dimension of Education COM(93) 457 final

Commission Report on the Citizenship of the Union COM(93) 702 final

Commission Report on the Education of Migrants' Children in the European Union COM(94) 423

Commission White Paper of 29 November 1995 on education and training, Teaching and learning – towards the learning society COM(95) 590 final

Commission Second Report on Citizenship of the Union COM(97) 230 final

Commission Decision 2000/520/EC of 26 July 2000 pursuant to Directive 95/46 on the adequacy of the protection provided by the safe harbour privacy principles and related frequently asked questions issued by the US Department of Commerce [2000] OJ 2000 L215/7

Commission Report on the implementation of the Socrates programme 1995–1999, COM(2001) 75 final

Commission Third Report on Citizenship of the Union COM(2001) 506

Commission White Paper of 25 July 2001 on European Governance COM(2001) 428 final

Commission Communication 'Investing efficiently in education and training: an imperative for Europe' COM(2002) 779 final

Commission Communication 'Education & Training 2010': The success of the Lisbon Strategy hinges on urgent reforms (Draft joint interim report on the implementation of the detailed work programme on the follow-up of the objectives of education and training systems in Europe) COM(2003) 0685 final

Commission Communication on Article 7 of the Treaty on European Union: Respect for and promotion of values on which the Union is based COM(2003) 606 final

Commission Report Implementation of the 'Education & Training 2010' programme – Supporting document for the draft joint interim report on the implementation of the detailed work programme on the follow-up of the objectives of education and training systems in Europe SEC(2003) 1250 final

Commission Fourth Report on Citizenship of the Union (1 May 2001–30 April 2004) COM(2004) 695 final

Commission Communication 'The Commission's contribution to the period of reflection and beyond – Plan-D for Democracy, Dialogue and Debate' COM(2005) 494

Commission Communication 'The European Indicator of Language Competence' COM(2005) 356 final

Commission Communication 'A Common Agenda for Integration – Framework for the Integration of Third-Country Nationals in the European Union' COM(2005) 389 final

Commission White Paper of 1 February 2006 on a European Communication Policy COM(2006) 35

Commission Communication Follow-up to the Green Paper 'European Transparency Initiative' COM(2007) 127 final

Commission Fifth Report on citizenship of the Union (1 May 2004–30 June 2007) COM(2008) 85 final

Commission Proposal for a Council Directive on implementing the principle of equal treatment between persons irrespective of religion or belief, disability, age or sexual orientation COM(2008) 426 final (Horizontal Anti-Discrimination Directive)

Commission Report under Article 25 TFEU 'Progress towards effective EU Citizenship 2007–2010' COM(2010) 602 final

Commission EU Citizenship Report 2010 'Dismantling the obstacles to EU citizens' rights COM(2010) 603 final

Commission Communication 'An EU Agenda for the Rights of the Child' (15 February 2011) COM(2011) 60 final

Commission Implementing Reg (EU) No 1179/2011 of 17 November 2011 laying down technical specifications for online collection systems pursuant to Regulation (EU) No 211/2011 of the European Parliament and of the Council on the citizens' initiative [2018] OJ L301/3

Commission Staff working document 'Progress towards the common European objectives in education and training- Indicators and benchmarks 2010/2011'

Commission Staff working paper 'Consumer Empowerment in the EU' SEC(2011) 469 final

Commission Communication 'Rethinking Education: Investing in skills for better socio-economic outcomes' COM(2012) 669 final

Commission Decision to withdraw the Proposal for a Council Regulation on the exercise of the right to take collective action within the context of the freedom of establishment and the freedom to provide services COM(2012) 130

Commission staff working document, Assessment of Key Competences in initial education and training: Policy Guidance Accompanying the document Communication from the Commission Rethinking Education: Investing in skills for better socio-economic outcomes SWD(2012) 371 final

Commission staff working document, Language competences for employability, mobility and growth Accompanying the document Communication From the Commission Rethinking Education: Investing in skills for better socio-economic outcomes SWD(2010) 372 final

Jean Monnet Programme – "Learning EU@School", Report of Project Coordinators' Meeting, Best Practice and Cooperation, organised by EACEA (2012)

Commission Recommendation of 12 March 2013 on enhancing the democratic and efficient conduct of the elections to the European Parliament [2013] OJ L79/29

Commission Delegated Regulation (EU) No 887/2013 of 11 July 2013 replacing Annexes II and III to Regulation (EU) No 211/2011 of the European Parliament and of the Council on the citizens' initiative [2013] OJ L247/11

Commission Recommendation of 17 September 2013 on the principles governing SOLVIT [2013] OJ L249/10

Commission Implementing Decision of 18 December 2013 establishing the 'Education, Audiovisual and Culture Executive Agency' and repealing Decision 2009/336 [2013] OJ L343/46

Commission Report under Article 25 TFEU 'On progress towards effective EU Citizenship 2011–2013' COM(2013) 270 final

Co-creating European Union Citizenship: A Policy review (European Commission, 2013)

Commission Communication 'Empowering businesses and citizens in Europe's single market: An Action Plan for boosting Your Europe in cooperation with the Member States' COM(2013) 636 final

Commission EU Citizenship Report 2013: EU citizens: your rights, your future COM(2013) 269

Commission, *Learning Europe at School* (DG for Education, Youth, Sport and Culture, ICF GHK, 2013)

Commission Communication 'A new EU Framework to strengthen the Rule of Law' COM(2014) 0158 final

Commission Recommendation of 29 January 2014 addressing the consequences of disenfranchisement of Union citizens exercising their rights to free movement [2014] OJ L32/34

Commission Recommendation of 7 March 2014 on strengthening the principle of equal pay between men and women through transparency [2014] OJ L 69/112

Commission Report: Joint Report on the application of Council Directive 2000/43/EC of 29 June 2000 implementing the principle of equal treatment between persons irrespective of racial or ethnic origin ('Racial Equality Directive') and of Council Directive 2000/78/EC of 27 November 2000 establishing a general framework for equal treatment in employment and occupation ('Employment Equality Directive') COM(2014) 2 final

Did you know? 10 EU rights at a glance (European Commission Publications Office 2014)

Commission Communication 'A Digital Single Market Strategy for Europe' COM(2015) 0192 final

Commission Communication on the Transfer of Personal Data from the EU to the United States of America under Directive 95/46/EC following the Judgment by the Court of Justice in Case C-362/14 (Schrems) COM(2015) 566 final

Commission Delegated Regulation (EU) 2015/1070 of 31 March 2015 amending Annexes III, V and VII of Regulation (EC) No 211/2011 of the European Parliament and of the Council on the citizens' initiative [2015] OJ L178/1

Commission Report on the application of Regulation (EU) No 211/2011 on the citizens' initiative COM(2015) 145 final

Commission Staff Working Document 'Better Regulation Guidelines' SWD(2015) 111

Your Europe, your rights: A practical guide for citizens and businesses on their rights and opportunities in the EU's single market (European Commission, 2015)

Commission Communication 'Action Plan on the integration of third country nationals' COM(2016) 377 final

Commission Communication 'Action plan to strengthen the European response to travel document fraud' COM(2016) 790 final

Commission Communication 'Improving and modernising education' COM(2016) 941 final

Commission Communication supporting the prevention of radicalisation leading to violent extremism COM(2016) 379 final

Commission Directive (EU) 2016/882 of 1 June 2016 amending Directive 2007/59/EC of the European Parliament and of the Council as regards language requirements C/2016/3213 [2016] OJ L146/22

Commission Implementing Decision (EU) 2016/1250 of 12 July 2016 pursuant to Directive 95/46/EC of the European Parliament and of the Council on the adequacy of the protection provided by the EU-U.S. Privacy Shield [2016] OJ L 207/1

Commission Recommendation (EU) 2016/1374 of 27 July 2016 regarding the rule of law in Poland [2016] OJ L217/53

Commission Implementing Regulation (EU) 2016/2286 of 15 December 2016 laying down detailed rules on the application of fair use policy and on the methodology for assessing the sustainability of the abolition of retail roaming surcharges and on the application to be submitted by a roaming provider for the purposes of that assessment [2016] L344/46

Commission Proposal for a Interinstitutional Agreement on a mandatory Transparency Register COM(2016) 0627 final

Commission Recommendation (EU) 2017/146 of 21 December 2016 regarding the rule of law in Poland complementary to Recommendation (EU) 2016/1374 [2017] OJ L22/65

Commission staff working document 'Key European action supporting the 2030 Agenda and the Sustainable Development Goals Accompanying Commission Communication Next steps for a sustainable European future: European Union action for sustainability' SWD(2016) 390 final

Commission Citizenship Report 'Strengthening Citizens' Rights in a Union of Democratic Change EU Citizenship Report 2017' COM(2017) 030 final/2

Commission Communication 'Commission Work Programme 2017: Delivering a Europe that protects, empowers and defends' COM(2016) 710 final

Commission Communication 'Commission Work Programme 2018 An Agenda for a more united, stronger and more democratic Europe' COM(2017) 650 final/2

Commission Communication 'Completing the Better Regulation Agenda: Better solutions for better results' COM(2017) 651 final

Commission Communication 'Compliance Package- Action plan on the Reinforcement of SOLVIT: Bringing the benefits of the Single Market to citizens and businesses' COM(2017) 255 final

Commission Communication 'Eight progress report towards an effective and genuine Security Union' COM(2017) 0354 final

Commission Communication 'Establishing a European Pillar of Social Rights' COM(2017) 250 final

Commission Communication 'Exchanging and Protecting Personal Data in a Globalised World' COM(2017) 07 final

Commission Communication on 'Strengthening European Identity through Education and Culture' COM(2017) 673 final

Commission Communication on the Mid-Term Review on the implementation of the Digital Single Market Strategy A Connected Digital Single Market for All COM(2017) 228 final

Commission Communication 'School development and excellent teaching for a great start in life' COM(2017) 248 final

Commission Decision (EU) 2017/599 of 22 March 2017 on the proposed citizens' initiative entitled 'EU Citizenship for Europeans: United in Diversity in Spite of jus soli and jus sanguinis' [2017] OJ L81/18

Commission Recommendation (EU) 2017/761 of 26 April 2017 on the European Pillar of Social Rights [2017] OJ L113/56

Commission Decision of 27 July 2017 setting-up the High-Level Commission Expert Group on radicalisation [2017] OJ C252/3

Commission Proposal for a Council Decision on the determination of a clear risk of a serious breach by the Republic of Poland of the rule of law COM(2017) 835 final

Commission Recommendation (EU) 2017/1520 of 26 July 2017 regarding the rule of law in Poland complementary to Recommendations (EU) 2016/1374 and (EU) 2017/146 [2017] OJ L228/19

Commission Recommendation of 20 December 2017 regarding the rule of law in Poland complementary to Commission Recommendations (EU) 2016/1374, (EU) 2017/146 and (EU) 2017/1520 [2018] OJ L17/50

Commission Report on the application of Directive 2011/83/EU of the European Parliament and of the Council of 25 October 2011 on consumer rights COM(2017) 259 final

Commission Report on the first annual review of the functioning of the EU–US Privacy Shield COM(2017) 611 final

Commission Report on the implementation by Member States of Directive 2003/88/EC concerning certain aspects of the organisation of working time COM(2017) 254 final

Commission Report under Article 25 TFEU 'On progress towards effective EU citizenship 2013–2016' COM(2017) 32 final

Commission Staff working document Accompanying Commission Communication 'Establishing a European Pillar of Social Rights' SWD(2017) 201 final

Commission Staff working document Accompanying the document Proposal for a Regulation of the European Parliament and of the Council on the European citizens' initiative SWD(2017) 294 final

Commission Staff working document Evaluation of the Consumer Rights Directive Accompanying the document Report from the Commission to the European Parliament and the Council on the application of Directive 2011/83/EU of the European Parliament and of the Council of 25 October 2011 on consumer rights SWD(2017) 169 final

Commission Staff working document on the Application of the EU Charter of Fundamental Rights in 2016 Accompanying the document Communication from the Commission on 2016 Report on the Application of the EU Charter of Fundamental Rights SWD(2017) 162 final

Commission Staff working document Report of the public consultation Accompanying the document Commission Communication Establishing a European Pillar of Social Rights SWD(2017) 206 final

Commission White paper of 1 March 2017 on the future of Europe COM(2017) 2025 final

Commission, 12 Ideas for The Future of Europe: New narrative for Europe Communications campaign (2017)

Support of the stakeholder consultation in the context of the Key Competences Review: Report on the results of the stakeholder consultation EAC/2017/0150

Commission, Preparing teachers for diversity: the role of initial teacher education, Publications Office of the European Union (2017)

Commission Report on the Application of the EU Charter of Fundamental Rights COM(2017) 239 final

Commission Communication on the Digital Education Action Plan COM(2018) 22 final

Commission Communication 'A Europe that delivers: Institutional options for making the European Union's work more efficient' The European Commission's contribution to the Informal Leaders' meeting of 23 February 2018, COM(2018) 095 final

Commission Communication 'A Modern Budget for a Union that Protects, Empowers and Defends- The Multiannual Financial Framework for 2021–2027' COM(2018) 321 final

Commission Communication 'Building a stronger Europe: the role of youth, education and culture policies' COM(2018) 268 final

Commission Decision of 18 July 2018 on the proposed citizens' initiative entitled 'Permanent European Union Citizenship' [2018] OJ C264/4

Commission Proposal for a Regulation of the European Parliament and of the Council establishing 'Erasmus': the Union programme for education, training, youth and sport and repealing Regulation (EU) No 1288/2013, COM(2018) 367 final

Commission Recommendation (EU) 2018/234 of 14 February 2018 on enhancing the European nature and efficient conduct of the 2019 elections to the European Parliament [2018] OJ L45/40

Commission Report on the application of Regulation (EU) No 211/2011 on the citizens' initiative COM(2018) 157 final

Commission Communication 'The principles of subsidiarity and proportionality: Strengthening their role in the EU's policymaking' COM(2018) 703 final

Commission Staff working document Accompanying the document Communication from the Commission Monitoring the implementation of the European Pillar of Social Rights SWD(2018) 67 final

Commission Staff working document Accompanying the document proposal for a Council Recommendation on common values, inclusive education and the European dimension of teaching (2018)

Commission Staff working document Accompanying the document Proposal for a Council Recommendation on Key Competences for LifeLong Learning SWD(2018) 14 final

Commission Annual report 2018 on the application of the principles of subsidiarity and proportionality and on relations with national parliaments COM(2019) 333 final

Commission Communication 'Strengthening the rule of law within the Union: A blueprint for action' COM(2019) 343 final

Commission Report on the application in 2018 of Regulation (EC) No 1049/2001 regarding public access to European Parliament, Council and Commission documents COM(2019) 356 final

Commission Decision (EU) 2019/434 of 27 February 2019 on the proposed citizens' initiative entitled 'Europe CARES — Inclusive Quality Education for Children with Disabilities' [2019] OJ L 75/103

Commission Decision (EU) 2019/1182 of 3 July 2019 on the proposed citizens' initiative entitled 'EU law, minority rights and democratisation of Spanish institutions' [2019] OJ L 185/46

Commission Decision (EU) 2019/1564 of 4 September 2019 on the proposed citizens' initiative entitled 'Stop corruption in Europe at its root, by cutting off funds to countries with inefficient judiciary after deadline' [2019] OJ L 241/6

Commission Decision (EU) 2019/1565 of 4 September 2019 on the proposed citizens' initiative entitled 'Actions on Climate Emergency' [2019] OJ L 241/8

Interinstitutional

Joint Communication by the European Commission and the High Representative of the European Union for Foreign Affairs and Security Policy, Action Plan on Human Rights and Democracy (2015–2019) Keeping human rights at the heart of the EU agenda JOIN(2015) 16 final

Interinstitutional Agreement between the European Parliament, the Council of the European Union and the European Commission on Better Law-Making [2016] OJ L123/1

The European Pillar of Social Rights, solemnly proclaimed by the European Parliament, the Council and the Commission on 17 November 2017

Commission Joint Report on the application of Council Directive 2000/43/EC of 29 June 2000 implementing the principle of equal treatment between persons irrespective of racial or ethnic origin ('Racial Equality Directive') and of Council Directive 2000/78/EC of 27 November 2000 establishing a general framework for equal treatment in employment and occupation ('Employment Equality Directive') COM(2014) 2 final

Joint Report of the Council and the Commission on the implementation of the strategic framework for European cooperation in education and training (ET 2020) — New priorities for European cooperation in education and training [2015] OJ C 417/25

Eurydice

Commission/EACEA/Eurydice, Citizenship Education at School in Europe (2005)

Commission/EACEA/Eurydice, Citizenship Education in Europe (2012)

Commission/EACEA/Eurydice, Developing Key Competences at School in Europe: Challenges and Opportunities for Policy (2012)

Commission/EACEA/Eurydice, Promoting citizenship and the common values of freedom, tolerance and non-discrimination through education: Overview of education policy developments in Europe following the Paris Declaration of 17 March 2015 (2016)

Commission/EACEA/Eurydice, Citizenship Education at School in Europe (2017)

Commission/EACEA/Eurydice, Citizenship Education at School in Europe – Annexes: National Information and Websites (2017)

Commission/EACEA/Eurydice E, Structural Indicators for Monitoring Education and Training Systems in Europe – 2018. Eurydice Background Report

Commission/EACEA/Eurydice, Compulsory Education in Europe 2019/20 – Facts and Figures

Commission/EACEA/Eurydice, The teaching of regional and minority languages in schools in Europe (2019)

Eurobarometers

Flash Eurobarometer 319b, Youth on the Move: Education and training, mobility, employment and entrepreneurship (May 2011)

Special Eurobarometer 346, New Europeans (April 2011)

Flash Eurobarometer 430, European Union citizenship (March 2016)

Flash Eurobarometer 431, Electoral Rights (March 2016)

Flash Eurobarometer 443, e-Privacy (July 2016)

Special Eurobarometer 451, Future of Europe (December 2016)

Special Eurobarometer 471, Fairness, inequality and inter-generational mobility (December 2017)

Flash Eurobarometer 455, European Youth (January 2018)

Flash Eurobarometer 464, Fake News and Disinformation Online (March 2018)

Flash Eurobarometer 466, The European Education Area (May 2018)

Special Eurobarometer 469, Integration of immigrants in the European Union (April 2018)

Standard Eurobarometer 89, Public Opinion in the European Union (June 2018)

Standard Eurobarometer 91, 'European citizenship' (August 2019)

Eurobarometer Survey 91.5 of the European Parliament, The 2019 post-electoral survey: Have European elections entered a new dimension? (September 2019)

Special Eurobarometer 493, 'Discrimination in the EU (including LGBTI)' (October 2019)

Mixed instruments

Resolution of the Council and of the Ministers of Education, meeting within the Council, of 9 February 1976 comprising an action programme in the field of Education [1976] OJ C38/1

Conclusions of the Council and the Ministers for Education meeting within the Council of 3 June 1985 on improving the treatment of the European dimension in education

Resolution of the Council and of the Ministers for Education, meeting within the Council, of 3 June 1985 containing an action programme on equal opportunities for girls and boys in education [1985] OJ C166/1

Resolution of the Council and of the Ministers of Education meeting within the Council of 23 November 1988 concerning health education in schools

Resolution of the Council and the Representatives of the Governments of the Member States, meeting within the Council of 29 May 1990 on the fight against racism and xenophobia [1990] OJ C157/1

Conclusions of the Council and of the Ministers of Education meeting within the Council of 27 November 1992 on measures for developing the European dimension in higher education [1992] OJ C336/4

Conclusions of the Council and of the Ministers for Education meeting within the Council of 11 June 1993 on furthering an open European space for cooperation within higher education [1993] OJ C186/1

Conclusions of the Council and the Ministers for Youth meeting within the Council of 30 November 1994 on the promotion of voluntary service periods for young people [1994] OJ C348/2

Resolution of the Council and the Representatives of Member States' Governments meeting within the Council of 23 October 1995 on the response of educational systems to the problems of racism and xenophobia [1995] OJ C312/1

Resolution of the Council and of the Representatives of the Governments of the Member States, meeting within the Council, on the recognition of the value of non-formal and informal learning within the European youth field [2006] OJ C168/1

Resolution of the Council and the Representatives of the Governments of the Member States, meeting within the Council, on implementing the common objectives for participation by and information for young people in view of promoting their active European citizenship [2006] OJ C297/6

Conclusions of the Council and of the Representatives of the Governments of the Member States, meeting within the Council of 15 November 2007, on improving the quality of teacher education [2007] OJ C300/7

Conclusions of the Council and of the Representatives of the Governments of the Member States, meeting within the Council of 21 November 2008 on preparing young people for the 21st century: an agenda for European cooperation on schools [2008] OJ C319/20

Conclusions of the Council and of the Representatives of the Governments of the Member States, meeting within the Council, of 26 November 2009 on developing the role of education in a fully-functioning knowledge triangle [2009] OJ C302/3

EU Education Ministers and the Commissioner for Education, Culture, Youth and Sport, Paris Declaration on Promoting citizenship and the common values of freedom, tolerance and non-discrimination through education (17 March 2015)

Resolution of the Council and of the Representatives of the Governments of the Member States, meeting within the Council, of 24 February 2016 on promoting socio-economic development and inclusiveness in the EU through education: the contribution of education and training to the European Semester 2016 [2016] OJ C105/1

Conclusions of the Council and of the Representatives of the Governments of the Member States, meeting within the Council, on Inclusion in Diversity to achieve a High Quality Education For All – Council Conclusions (17 February 2017)

Resolution of the Council and the Representatives of the Governments of the Member States meeting within the Council on a framework for European cooperation in the youth field: The European Union Youth Strategy 2019–2027 [2018] OJ C 456/1

CoR and EESC

Opinion of the Committee of the Regions on the 'EU Citizenship Report 2010' [2011] OJ C166/3

Opinion of the Committee of the Regions of 3 and 4 May 2012 on 'Erasmus for All' [2012] OJ C225/200

Opinion of the Committee of the Regions on 'Strengthening EU citizenship: promotion of EU citizens' electoral rights' [2013] OJ C62/26

European Economic and Social Committee, European Passport to Active Citizenship (2015)

Opinion of the European Economic and Social Committee on The European Citizens' Initiative (review) [2016] OJ C389/35

Opinion of the European Economic and Social Committee on 'The transition towards a more sustainable European future—a strategy for 2050' [2018] OJ C81/44

Opinion of the Committee of the Regions 'Strengthening European Identity through Education and Culture' [2018] OJ C 361/19

Opinion of the European Economic and Social Committee on 'Education about the European Union' [2019] OJ C 228/68

Ombudsman

Decision of the European Ombudsman closing her own-initiative inquiry OI/9/2013/TN concerning the European Commission (4 March 2015)

Decision of the European Ombudsman adopting Implementing Provisions [2016] OJ C321/1

Ombudsman Emily O'Reilly, Annual report 2016 (16 May 2017)

Ombudsman Emily O'Reilly, Annual report 2018 (14 May 2019)

ECJ case law (alphabetical)

A Case C-679/16 ECLI:EU:C:2018:601

Accept Case C-81/12 ECLI:EU:C:2013:275

Achbita and Bougnaoui Cases C-157/15 and C-188/15 188 ECLI:EU:C:2017:203

Addou Case C-180/99 ECLI:EU:C:2001:532

Air Transport Association of America and Others Case C-366/10 ECLI:EU:C:2011:864

Åkerberg Fransson Case C-617/10 ECLI:EU:C:2013:280

Akzo Nobel Chemicals Case C-550/07 P ECLI:EU:C:2010:512

Alarape Case C-529/11 ECLI:EU:C:2013:290

Alassini Joined Cases C-317–320/08 ECLI:EU:C:2010:146

Albako Case 249/85 ECLI:EU:C:1987:245

Alimanovic Case C-67/14 ECLI:EU:C:2015:597

Alo and Osso Joined Cases C-443/14 and C-444/14 ECLI:EU:C:2016:127

Alokpa Case C-86/12 ECLI:EU:C:2013:645

Altun Case C-337/07 ECLI:EU:C:2018:63

Anagnostakis Case C-589/15 P ECLI:EU:C:2017:663

Angonese Case C-281/98 ECLI:EU:C:2000:296

Aranyosi and Căldăraru Joined Cases C-404/15 and C-659/15 PPU ECLI:EU:C:2016:198

Asbeek Brusse and de Man Garabito Case C-488/11 ECLI:EU:C:2013:341

Association de médiation sociale Case C-176/12 ECLI:EU:C:2014:2

Audiolux Case C-101/08 ECLI:EU:C:2009:626

Austria v Germany Case C-591/17 ECLI:EU:C:2019:504

Bauer Joined Cases C-569/16 and C-570/16 ECLI:EU:C:2018:871

Baumbast Case C-413/99 ECLI:EU:C:2002:493
Belgium v Commission Case C-323/97 ECLI:EU:C:1998:347
Bickel and Franz Case C-274/96 ECLI:EU:C:1998:563
Bidar Case C-209/03 ECLI:EU:C:2005:169
Blaizot Case 24/86 ECLI:EU:C:1988:43
Bogendorff von Wolffersdorff Case C-438/14 ECLI:EU:C:2016:401
Bosman Case C-415/93 ECLI:EU:C:1995:463
Bressol, Chaverot and Others Case C-73/08 ECLI:EU:C:2010:181
Brown Case 197/86 ECLI:EU:C:1988:323
Buivids Case C-345/17 ECLI:EU:C:2019:122
Bürgerausschuss für die Bürgerinitiative Minority SafePack — one million signatures for diversity in Europe Case T-646/13 ECLI:EU:T:2017:59
Câmpean Case C-200/14 ECLI:EU:C:2016:494
Carbonati Apuani Case C-72/03 ECLI:EU:C:2004:506
Carp 80/06 ECLI:EU:C:2007:327
Casagrande Case 9/74 ECLI:EU:C:1975:11
CCOO v Deutsche Bank Case C-55/18 ECLI:EU:C:2019:402
Centro Europa 7 Case C-380/05 ECLI:EU:C:2008:59
Chakroun Case C 578/08 ECLI:EU:C:2010:117
Chartry Case C-457/09 ECLI:EU:C:2011:101
CHEZ (Nikolova) Case C-83/14 ECLI:EU:C:2015:480
Cilfit Case 283/81 ECLI:EU:C:1982:335
ClientEarth Case C-404/13 ECLI:EU:C:2014:2382
ClientEarth Case C-57/16 P ECLI:EU:C:2018:660
Collins Case C 138/02 ECLI:EU:C:2004:172
Coman Case C-673/16 ECLI:EU:C:2018:385
Commission v Austria Case C-147/03 ECLI:EU:C:2005:427
Commission v Austria Case C-75/11 ECLI:EU:C:2012:605
Commission v Bavarian Lager Case C-28/08 P ECLI:EU:C:2010:378
Commission v Belgium Case 42/87 ECLI:EU:C:1988:454
Commission v Belgium Case C-11/95 ECLI:EU:C:1996:316
Commission v Belgium Case C-65/03 ECLI:EU:C:2004:402
Commission v Belgium Case C-533/11 ECLI:EU:C:2013:659
Commission v Belgium Case C-317/14 ECLI:EU:C:2015:63
Commission v Council (Erasmus) Case 242/87 ECLI:EU:C:1989:217
Commission v Council (Titanium dioxide) Case C 300/89 ECLI:EU:C:1991:244
Commission v European Investment Bank Case C-15/00 ECLI:EU:C:2003:396
Commission v Parliament and Council Case C-411/06 ECLI:EU:C:2009:518
Commission v France Case C-304/02 ECLI:EU:C:2005:444

Commission v Germany Case 29/84 ECLI:EU:C:1985:229
Commission v Germany Case C-433/03 ECLI:EU:C:2005:462
Commission v Germany Case C-518/07 ECLI:EU:C:2010:125
Commission v Greece Case 147/86 ECLI:EU:C:1988:150
Commission v Greece Case C-290/94 ECLI:EU:C:1996:265
Commission v Italy Case C-388/01 ECLI:EU:C:2003:30
Commission v Italy Case C-110/05 ECLI:EU:C:2009:66
Commission v Italy Case C-601/14 ECLI:EU:C:2016:759
Commission v Luxembourg Case C-111/91 ECLI:EU:C:1993:92
Commission v Poland, Order of the Court Case C-441/17 R ECLI:EU:C:2017:877
Commission v Poland Case C-441/17 ECLI:EU:C:2018:255
Commission v Poland Case C-619/18 ECLI:EU:C:2019:531
Commission v Poland Case C-192/18 pending
Commission v the Netherlands Case C-50/06 EU:C:2007:325
Commission v the Netherlands Case C-542/09 ECLI:EU:C:2012:346
Commission v the Netherlands Case C-233/14 ECLI:EU:C:2016:50
Commission v UK Case C-222/94 ECLI:EU:C:1996:314
Commission v UK Case C-308/14 ECLI:EU:C:2016:436
Commission v Kadi Joined Cases C-584/10 P, C-593/10 P and C-595/10 P ECLI:EU:C:2013:518
Compassion in World Farming Case C-1/96 ECLI:EU:C:1998:113
Confédération générale du travail and Others Case C-385/05 ECLI:EU:C:2007:37
Connolly Case C-274/99 P ECLI:EU:C:2001:127
Content Services Ltd Case C-49/11 ECLI:EU:C:2012:419
Costa v ENEL Case 6/64 ECLI:EU:C:1964:66
Costantini and Others Case T-44/14 ECLI:EU:T:2016:223
Council v Access Info Europe Case C-280/11 P ECLI:EU:C:2013:671
Council v Commission Case C-409/13 ECLI:EU:C:2015:217
Council v Front populaire pour la libération de la saguia-el-hamra et du rio de oro (Front Polisario) Case C-104/16 P ECLI:EU:C:2016:973
Cowan Case 186/87 ECLI:EU:C:1989:47
Craeynest and Others Case C-723/17 ECLI:EU:C:2019:533
Cresco Case C-193/17 ECLI:EU:C:2019:43
Cruciano Siragusa Case C-206/13 ECLI:EU:C:2014:126
CS Case C-304/14 ECLI:EU:C:2016:674
Dano Case C-333/13 ECLI:EU:C:2014:2358
De Capitani Case T-540/15 ECLI:EU:T:2018:167
Deckmyn and Vrijheidsfonds v Vandersteen and Others Case C-201/13 ECLI:EU:C:2014:2132

Defrenne II Case 43/75 ECLI:EU:C:1976:56
Defrenne III Case 149/77 ECLI:EU:C:1978:130
Delvigne Case C-650/13 ECLI:EU:C:2015:648
Demirel Case 12/86 ECLI:EU:C:1987:400
Dereci Case C-256/11 ECLI:EU:C:2011:734
Deutsche Grammophon Case 78/70 ECLI:EU:C:1971:59
Deutsche Schell Case C-188/91 ECLI:EU:C:1993:24
D'Hoop Case C-224/98 ECLI:EU:C:2002:432
di Leo Case C-308/89 ECLI:EU:C:1990:400
Dieter Kraus Case C-19/92 ECLI:EU:C:1993:125
Digital Rights Ireland Joined Cases C-293/12 and C-594/12 ECLI:EU:C:2014:238
Dirextra Alta Formazione Case C-523/12 ECLI:EU:C:2013:831
Dominguez Case C-282/10 ECLI:EU:C:2012:33
Duarte Hueros v Autociba SA and Automóviles Citroën España SA Case C-32/12 ECLI:EU:C:2013:637
Dynamic Medien Case C-244/06 ECLI:EU:C:2008:85
ebookers.com Deutschland Case C-112/11 ECLI:EU:C:2012:487
Efler Case T-754/14 ECLI:EU:T:2017:323
Egenberger Case C-414/16 ECLI:EU:C:2018:257
El Dridi Case C-61/11 PPU ECLI:EU:C:2011:268
Elrick Case C-275/12 ECLI:EU:C:2013:684
Eman and Sevinger Case C-300/04 ECLI:EU:C:2006:545
Erich Stauder v City of Ulm – Sozialamt Case 29–69 ECLI:EU:C:1969:57
ERT Case C-260/89 ECLI:EU:C:1991:254
Estonia v Parliament and Council Case C-508/13 EU:C:2015:403
European Ombudsman v Lamberts Case C-234/02 P ECLI:EU:C:2004:174
European Ombudsman v Staelen ECLI:EU:C:2017:256
Faccini Dori Case C-91/92 ECLI:EU:C:1994:292
Facebook Ireland and Schrems Case C-311/18 pending
Factortame I Case C 213/89 ECLI:EU:C:1990:257
Feryn Case C-54/07 ECLI:EU:C:2008:397
FOA (Fag og Arbejde) Case C-354/13 ECLI:EU:C:2014:2463
Folk Case C-529/15 ECLI:EU:C:2017:419
Forcheri Case 152/82 ECLI:EU:C:1983:205
Förster Case C-158/07 ECLI:EU:C:2008:630
Francovich and Bonifaci Joined Cases C-6/90 and C-9/90 ECLI:EU:C:1991:428
Fuß Case C-243/09 ECLI:EU:C:2010:609
Gaal Case C-7/94 ECLI:EU:C:1995:11
Garcia Avello Case C-148/02 ECLI:EU:C:2003:539

Germany v Council Case C-280/93 ECLI:EU:C:1994:367

Germany v Parliament and Council ('Tobacco Advertising') Case C-376/98 ECLI:EU:C:2000:544

Google Spain Case C-131/12 ECLI:EU:C:2014:317

Gottwald Case C-103/08 ECLI:EU:C:2009:597

Grad (Leberpfennig) Case 9/70 ECLI:EU:C:1970:78

Gravier Case 293/83 ECLI:EU:C:1985:69

Grimaldi Case C-322/88 ECLI:EU:C:1989:646

Groener Case C-379/87 ECLI:EU:C:1989:599

Grunkin and Paul Case C-353/06 EU:C:2008:559

Grzelczyk Case C-184/99 ECLI:EU:C:2001:458

Gutiérrez Naranjo and Others Joined Cases C-154/15 and C-307/15 ECLI:EU:C:2016:980

Hadj Case C-45/12 ECLI:EU:C:2013:390

Haegeman Case 181–73 ECLI:EU:C:1974:41

Haralambidis Case C-270/13 ECLI:EU:C:2014:2185

Hautala Case C-353/99 P ECLI:EU:C:2001:661

Huber Case C-524/06 ECLI:EU:C:2008:724

Humanplasma Case C-421/09 ECLI:EU:C:2010:760

Humbel Case 263/86 ECLI:EU:C:1988:451

Hungary v Slovakia Case C-364/10 EU:C:2012:630

Ibrahim Case C-337/07 ECLI:EU:C:2008:744

Iida Case C-40/11 ECLI:EU:C:2012:691

International Fruit Company Joined Cases 21 to 24–72 ECLI:EU:C:1972:115

Internationale Handelsgesellschaft Case 11–70 ECLI:EU:C:1970:114

Interporc Case C-41/00 P ECLI:EU:C:2003:125

Intertanko Case C-308/06 ECLI:EU:C:2008:312

Inuit Tapiriit Kanatami and Others v Commission Case C-398/13 P ECLI:EU:C:2015:535

Inuit Tapiriit Kanatami and Others v Parliament and Council Case C-583/11 P ECLI:EU:C:2013:625

Ioannidis Case C-258/04 ECLI:EU:C:2005:559

Izsák and Dabis Case C-420/16 P ECLI:EU:C:2019:177

Jippes Case C-189/01 ECLI:EU:C:2001:420

Juízes Portugueses Case C-64/16 ECLI:EU:C:2018:117

Jundt Case C-281/06 ECLI:EU:C:2007:816

K Case C-18/16 ECLI:EU:C:2017:680

Kadi Joined Cases C-402/05 P and C-415/05 P EU:C:2008:461

Kamberaj Case C-571/10 ECLI:EU:C:2012:233
Khalil and others Joined Cases C-95/99 to C-98/99 and C-180/99 ECLI:EU:C:2001:532
Kohll and Kohll-Schlesser Case C-300/15 ECLI:EU:C:2016:361
Konstantinidis Case C-168/91 ECLI:EU:C:1993:115
Kozłowski Case C-66/08 ECLI:EU:C:2008:437
Kranemann Case C-109/04 ECLI:EU:C:2005:187
Križan Case C-416/10 ECLI:EU:C:2013:8
Kücükdeveci Case C-555/07 ECLI:EU:C:2010:21
Las Case C-202/11 ECLI:EU:C:2013:239
Laval Case C-341/05 ECLI:EU:C:2007:809
Lawrie-Blum Case 66/85 ECLI:EU:C:1986:284
Ledra Joined Cases C-8/15 P to C-10/15 P ECLI:EU:C:2016:701
Liga Portuguesa de Futebol Profissional Case C-42/07 ECLI:EU:C:2009:519
Lindqvist Case C-101/01 ECLI:EU:C:2003:596
Liselotte Hauer Case 44/79 ECLI:EU:C:1979:290
LM Case C-216/18 PPU ECLI:EU:C:2018:586
Luxembourg v Parliament and Council Case C-176/09 ECLI:EU:C:2011:290
Lyyski Case C-40/05 ECLI:EU:C:2007:10
M and Others Case C-340/08 ECLI:EU:C:2010:232
Maizena v Council Case 139/79 ECLI:EU:C:1980:250
Mangold Case C-144/04 ECLI:EU:C:2005:709
Marshall Case 152/84 ECLI:EU:C:1986:84
Martens Case C-359/13 ECLI:EU:C:2015:118
Martínez Sala Case C-85/96 ECLI:EU:C:1998:217
MB Case C-451/16 ECLI:EU:C:2018:492
McCarthy Case C-434/09 ECLI:EU:C:2011:277
Meeusen Case C-337/97 ECLI:EU:C:1999:284
Melloni Case C-399/11 ECLI:EU:C:2013:107
Meneses Case C-220/12 ECLI:EU:C:2013:683
Metock Case C-127/08 ECLI:EU:C:2008:449
Microsoft Case T-167/08 ECLI:EU:T:2012:323
Monsanto Agricoltura Italia Case C-236/01 ECLI:EU:C:2003:43
Morgan and Bucher Joined Cases C-11/06 and C-12/06 ECLI:EU:C:2007:626
N Case C-601/15 PPU ECLI:EU:C:2016:85
NA Case C-115/15 ECLI:EU:C:2016:487
Nelson and TUI Travel Joined Cases C-581/10 and C-629/10 ECLI:EU:C:2012:657
Neri Case C-153/02 ECLI:EU:C:2003:614
The Netherlands v Parliament and Council Case C-377/98 ECLI:EU:C:2001:523

Nisttahuz Poclava v Ariza Toledano Case C-117/14 ECLI:EU:C:2015:60
Nold Case 4–73 ECLI:EU:C:1974:51
Novartis Pharmaceuticals Case C-106/01 ECLI:EU:C:2004:245
NS Joined Cases C-411/10 and C-493/10 ECLI:EU:C:2011:865
O, S & L Joined Cases C-356 and 357/11 ECLI:EU:C:2012:776
Ognyanov Case C-554/14 ECLI:EU:C:2016:835
Omega Spielhallen Case C-36/02 ECLI:EU:C:2004:614
One of Us and Others Case T-561/14 ECLI:EU:T:2018:210
Opinion 1/09 ECLI:EU:C:2011:123
Opinion 2/13 EU Accession to the ECHR ECLI:EU:C:2014:2454
Opinion 2/94 ECLI:EU:C:1996:140
Ordre des barreaux francophones et germanophone et autres Case C-305/05 ECLI:EU:C:2007:383
Orfanopoulos and Oliveri Joined Cases C-482/01 and C-493/01 ECLI:EU:C:2004:262
Orizzonte Salute Case C-61/14 ECLI:EU:C:2015:655
Oulane Case C-215/03 ECLI:EU:C:2005:95
P and S Case C-579/13 ECLI:EU:C:2015:369
Palacios de la Villa Case C-411/05 ECLI:EU:C:2007:604
Parliament v Council Case C-540/03 ECLI:EU:C:2006:429
Parliament v Council Case C-155/07 ECLI:EU:C:2008:605
Parti écologiste 'Les Verts' v Parliament Case 294/83 ECLI:EU:C:1986:166
Pešková and Peška Case C-315/15 ECLI:EU:C:2017:342
Petersen Case C-228/07 ECLI:EU:C:2008:494
Pfleger Case C-390/12 ECLI:EU:C:2014:281
Philip Morris Brands and Others v UK Case C-547/14 ECLI:EU:C:2016:325
Pignataro Case C-535/08 ECLI:EU:C:2009:20
Poland v Parliament and Council Case C 358/14 ECLI:EU:C:2016:323
Poland v Parliament and Council Case C-128/17 ECLI:EU:C:2019:194
Popławski II Case C-573/17 ECLI:EU:C:2019:530
PPK and KNK Case C-229/05 P ECLI:EU:C:2007:32
Pringle Case C-370/12 ECLI:EU:C:2012:756
Prinz Joined Cases C-523/11 and C-585/11 ECLI:EU:C:2013:524
Puppinck and Others v Commission Case C-418/18 P pending
Pusa Case C-224/02 ECLI:EU:C:2004:273
Rendón Marín Case C-165/14 ECLI:EU:C:2016:675
Rewe-Zentral (Cassis de Dijon) Case 120/78 ECLI:EU:C:1979:42
Roquette Frères Case 138/79 ECLI:EU:C:1980:249
Roquette Frères Case C-94/00 ECLI:EU:C:2002:603

Rottmann Case C-135/08 ECLI:EU:C:2010:104
RTI and Others Joined Cases C-320/94, C-328/94, C-329/94, C-337/94, C-338/94 and C-339/94 ECLI:EU:C:1996:486
Ruckdeschel Joined Cases 117/76 and 16/77 ECLI:EU:C:1977:160
Rüffer v Pokorná Case C-322/13 ECLI:EU:C:2014:189
Ruiz Zambrano Case C-34/09 ECLI:EU:C:2011:124
Runevič-Vardyn and Wardyn Case C-391/09 ECLI:EU:C:2011:291
Salahadin Abdulla and Others Joined Cases C-175/08, C-176/08, C-178/08 and C-179/08 ECLI:EU:C:2010:105
Satakunnan Markkinapörssi Oy and Satamedia Case C-73/07 ECLI:EU:C:2008:727
Sayn-Wittgenstein Case C-208/09 ECLI:EU:C:2010:806
Schecke and Eifert Joined Cases C-92/09 and C-93/09 ECLI:EU:C:2010:662
Schmidberger Case C-112/00 ECLI:EU:C:2003:333
Schönberger Case C-261/13 P ECLI:EU:C:2014:2423
Schrems Case C-362/14 ECLI:EU:C:2015:650
Schrems Case C-498/16 ECLI:EU:C:2018:37
Schwarz Case C-76/05 ECLI:EU:C:2007:492
Schwarz Case C-291/12 ECLI:EU:C:2013:670
Simma Federspiel Case C-419/16 ECLI:EU:C:2017:997
Simmenthal II Case 106/77 ECLI:EU:C:1978:49
Slovakia and Hungary v Council Joined Cases C-643/15 and C-647/15 ECLI:EU:C:2017:631
Slovenia v Croatia Case C-457/18 pending
Spain v Parliament Case C-377/16 ECLI:EU:C:2019:249
Spain v UK Case C-145/04 ECLI:EU:C:2006:543
Sturgeon Joined Cases C-402/07 and C-432/07 ECLI:EU:C:2009:716
Sweden and Turco Joined Cases C-39/05 P and C-52/05 P ECLI:EU:C:2008:374
Sweden v MyTravel and Commission Case C-506/08 P ECLI:EU:C:2011:496
T & L Sugars Case C-456/13 P ECLI:EU:C:2015:284
Teixeira Case C-480/08 ECLI:EU:C:2010:83
Tele2 Sverige and Watson and others Joined Cases C-203/15 and C-698/15 ECLI:EU:C:2016:970
Test-Achats Case C-236/09 ECLI:EU:C:2011:100
Tjebbes and Others Case C-221/17 ECLI:EU:C:2019:189
TNT Express Nederland Case C-533/08 ECLI:EU:C:2010:243
TopFit and Biffi Case C-22/18 ECLI:EU:C:2019:497
Transocean Marine Paint Association Case 17/74 ECLI:EU:C:1974:106
Trojani Case C-456/02 ECLI:EU:C:2004:488
UEAPME v Council Case T-135/96 ECLI:EU:T:1998:128

UK v CL (Petra) Case 56/88 ECLI:EU:C:1989:81

UK v Council Case 68/86 ECLI:EU:C:1988:85

UK v Council Case C-84/94 ECLI:EU:C:1996:431

UK, France and Germany v Council Joined Cases C-51/89, C-90/89 and C-94/89 ECLI:EU:C:1991:241

Unibet Case C-432/05 ECLI:EU:C:2007:163

Unión de Pequeños Agricultores v Council Case C-50/00 P ECLI:EU:C:2002:462

van Duyn Case 41/74 ECLI:EU:C:1974:133

Van Gend & Loos Case 26–62 ECLI:EU:C:1963:1

Viking Case C-438/05 ECLI:EU:C:2007:772

Vodafone Case C-58/08 ECLI:EU:C:2010:321

Walrave and Koch Case 36/74 ECLI:EU:C:1974:140

Wathelet Case C-149/15 ECLI:EU:C:2016:840

Weber and Others Joined Cases C-65/09 and C-87/09 ECLI:EU:C:2011:396

Wightman and Others Case C-621/18 ECLI:EU:C:2018:999

Winner Wetten Case C-409/06 ECLI:EU:C:2010:503

Wirth Case C-109/92 ECLI:EU:C:1993:916

Yanukovych Case T-348/14 ECLI:EU:T:2016:508

Ymeraga Case C-87/12 ECLI:EU:C:2013:291

Z Case C-363/12 ECLI:EU:C:2014:159

Zhu and Chen Case C-200/02 ECLI:EU:C:2004:639

2. *UN human rights instruments*

Universal Declaration of Human Rights (adopted 10 December 1948) UNGA Res 217 A(III) (UDHR)

International agreements

Convention Relating to the Status of Refugees (Geneva, signed 28 July 1951, UNGA resolution 429 (V) of 14 December 1950, entered into force 22 April 1954) UNTS, Vol 189, p 150, No 2545 (1954); Protocol Relating to the Status of Refugees (New York, 31 January 1967, entered into force 4 October 1967) (Geneva Convention)

Convention Against Discrimination in Education (adopted 14 December 1960, entered into force 22 May 1962) (CADE)

International Covenant on Civil and Political Rights (adopted 16 December 1966, entered into force 23 March 1976) 999 UNTS 171 (ICCPR)

International Covenant on Economic, Social and Cultural Rights (adopted 16 December 1966 A/RES/2200 (XXI), entered into force 3 January 1976) 993 UNTS3 (ICESCR)

Vienna Convention on the Law of Treaties (adopted 23 May 1969, entered into force 27 January 1980) 1155 UNTS 331

International Convention for the Prevention of Pollution from Ships (London, signed 2 November 1973); Protocol (17 February 1978) (Marpol 73/78)

Convention on the Elimination of All Forms of Discrimination against Women (adopted 18 December 1979 UNGA Res 34/180, entered into force 3 September 1981)

Convention against Torture and Other Cruel, Inhuman or Degrading Treatment or Punishment (adopted 10 December 1984 UNGA Res 39/46, entered into force 26 June 1987)

Convention on the Rights of the Child (adopted 20 November 1989 UNGA Res 44/25, entered into force 2 September 1990) 15777 UNTS 3 (CRC)

International Convention on the Protection of the Rights of All Migrant Workers and Members of Their Families (adopted 18 December 1990 UNGA Res 45/158)

Convention on the Rights of Persons with Disabilities (adopted 13 December 2006 A/RES/61/106, entry into force 3 May 2008)

General comments

UN ComESCR 'General comment No 3: The nature of States parties' obligations (art. 2, para. 1, of the Covenant)' (1991)

UN ComESCR 'General Comment No 11: Plans of action for primary education (article 14 ICESCR)' (1999)

UN ComESCR 'General Comment No 13: The Right to Education (Art. 13)' UN Doc E/C.12/1999/10

UN ComRC 'General Comment No 5 (2003): General measures of implementation of the Convention on the Rights of the Child (arts. 4, 42 and 44, para. 6)' UN Doc CRC/GC/2003/5

UN ComRC 'General Comment No 1 (2001)- Article 29(1): The Aims of Education' Doc CRC/GC/2001/1

Other

Annotations on the text of the draft International Covenants on Human Rights, UN Doc A/2929 (1 June 1955)

UNGA 'Declaration on the Promotion among Youth of the Ideals of Peace, Mutual Respect and Understanding between Peoples' UNGA res 2037 (XX) (7 December 1965)UN Doc A/RES/20/2037

UNESCO Recommendation concerning Education for International Understanding, Co-operation and Peace and Education relating to Human Rights and Fundamental Freedoms (adopted 19 November 1974)

UNESCO World Declaration on Education For All (Jomtien, Thailand, 1990)

World Conference on Human Rights, Vienna Declaration and Programme of Action (25 June 1993) A/CONF.157/23

UNESCO World Plan of Action on Education for Human Rights and Democracy, adopted by the International Congress on Education for Human Rights and Democracy convened by the UNESCO (Montreal, 8–11 March 1993) Doc A/CONF.157/PC/42/Add.6

UNGA 'United Nations Decade for Human Rights Education' Res 49/184 (23 December 1994) A/RES/49/184

The Maastricht Guidelines on Violations of Economic, Social and Cultural Rights (1997), UN Doc E/C.12/2000/13UN

UN OHCHR 'Guidelines for National Plans of Action for Human Rights Education' (1997) UN Doc A/52/469/Add.1, A/52/469/Add.1/Corr.1 (20 October 1997 and 27 March 1998)

UNGA Res 55/2 United Nations Millennium Declaration

UNESCO The Dakar Framework for Action (Education for All) – Education for All: Meeting our Collective Commitments, adopted at the World Education Forum (Dakar, 26–28 April 2000)

UNGA 'World Programme for Human Rights Education' Res 59/113A (10 December 2004) A/RES/59/113

UNESCO EFA Global Monitoring Report 2005, Education for All: The Quality Imperative

UNGA 2005 World Summit Outcome (24 October 2005 UNGA Res 60/1) UN Doc A/RES/60/1

UNGA 'International Year of Human Rights Learning (2007)' Res 62/171 (18 December 2007) UN Doc A/RES/62/171

UNHRC 'World Programme for Human Rights Education (Sept 2007): extending period first phase: 08–09' Res 6/24 (28 September 2007) UN Doc A/HRC/RES/6/24

UNESCO-UNICEF, A Human Rights-Based Approach to Education for All: A framework for the realization of children's right to education and rights within education (2007)

UNHRC Res 8/4 'The right to education' (18 June 2008) UN Doc A/HRC/RES/8/4

UN 'Guidance Note of the Secretary-General on Democracy' (2009)

UNHRC Res 15/28 'World Plan of Action for the second phase (2010–2014) of the World Programme for Human Rights Education' (27 July 2010) UN Doc A/HRC/15/28

UNGA Res 66/137 'United Nations Declaration on Human Rights Education and Training' (19 December 2011)

UN Secretary-General Global Education First Initiative, UN, NY, 2012

UNGA Res 67/18 'Education for democracy' (28 November 2012) UN Doc A/RES/67/18

UNHRC Res 20/7 'The right to education: follow-up to Human Rights Council resolution 8/4' (5 July 2012) UN Doc A/HRC/RES/20/7

UNHRC Res 19/36 'Human rights, democracy and the rule of law' (23 March 2012) UN Doc /HRC/RES/19/36

Singh K, *Report of the Special Rapporteur on the right to education: Normative action for quality education* (2012)

UNHRC Res 23/4 'The right to education: follow-up to Human Rights Council resolution 8/4' (19 June 2013) UN Doc A/HRC/23/2 (2013)

UNHRC Res 24/15 'Plan of Action for the third phase (2015–2019) of the World Programme for Human Rights Education' (8 October 2013) UN Doc A/HRC/27/28

UNESCO Global Citizenship Education: Preparing learners for the challenges of the 21st century (2014)

UNESCO The Right to Education: Law and Policy Review Guidelines (2014)

UNHRC Res 26/17 'The right to education: follow-up to Human Rights Council resolution 8/4' (11 July 2014) UN Doc A/HRC/RES/26/17

UNESCO World Education Forum 2015, Incheon Declaration – Education 2030: Towards inclusive and equitable quality education and lifelong learning for all

UNESCO Global Citizenship Education: Topics and Learning Objectives (2015)

UNESCO EFA Global Monitoring Report 2015. Education for All 2000–2015: Achievements and Challenges

UNGA Res 69/268 'Education for democracy' (5 March 2015) UN Doc A/RES/69/268

UNGA Res 70/1 'Transforming our world: The 2030 Agenda for Sustainable Development' (25 September 2015) A/RES/70/1

UNHRC Res 29/7 'The right to education' (2 July 2015) UN Doc A/HRC/RES/29/7

UNHRC Res 28/14 'Human rights, democracy and the rule of law ' (26 March 2015) UN Doc HRC/RES/28/14

Secretary-General, Literacy for life: shaping future agendas and education for democracy (Note, A/71/177)

UNGA Res 71/8 'Education for democracy' (17 November 2016) UN Doc A/RES/71/8

UNGA Res 73/134 'Education for democracy' (13 December 2018) UN Doc A/RES/73/134

3. *Council of Europe*

European Conventions

Statute of the Council of Europe (signed in London, 5 May 1949; entered into force 3 August 1949), ETS No 001

European Cultural Convention (Paris, 19 December 1954) ETS No 18

European Social Charter ETS No 35 (Turin, opened 18 October 1961, entered into force 26 February 1965)

European Agreement on the Instruction and Education of Nurses ETS No 59 (Strasbourg, opened 25 October 1967, entered into force 7 August 1969)

Convention on the Transfer of Sentenced Persons ETS No 112 (Strasbourg, opened 21 March 1983, entered into force 1 July 1985); Additional Protocol ETS 167 (Strasbourg, opened 18 December 1997, entered info force 1 June 2000)

European Convention on Transfrontier Television (5 May 1989)

Convention for the Protection of Individuals with regard to Automatic Processing of Personal Data ETS No 108 (Strasbourg, opened 28 January 1981, entered into force 1 October 1985)

European Convention on the Exercise of Children's Rights ETS No 160 (Strasbourg, opened 25 January 1996, entred into force 1 July 2000)

European Social Charter (revised) ETS No 163 (Strasbourg, opened 3 May 1996, entred into force 1 July 1999)

Convention on the Recognition of Qualifications concerning Higher Education in the European Region ETS No 165 (Lisbon, opened 11 April 1997, entred into force 1 February 1999)

Additional Protocol to the Convention for the Protection of Individuals with regard to Automatic Processing of Personal Data, regarding supervisory authorities and transborder data flows No 181 (Strasbourg, opened 8 November 2001, entered into force 1 July 2004)

CoE Convention on the Prevention of Terrorism CETS No 196 (Warsaw, opened 16 May 2005, entered into force 1 June 2007)

Convention on the Manipulation of Sports Competitions CETS No 215 (Magglingen, 18 September 2014)

CoE Summits

CoE First Summit of Heads of State and Government, Vienna Declaration (Vienna, 9 October 1993)

CoE Second Summit of Heads of State and Government, Final Declaration and Action Plan (Strasbourg, 10–11 October 1997)

CoE Third Summit of Heads of State and Government, The Declaration and the Action Plan (Warsaw, 16–17 May 2005)

CoE Committee of Ministers

CoE Committee of Ministers Resolution 77 (31) On the Protection of the Individuals in Relation to the Acts of Administrative Authorities (28 September 1977)

CoE Committee of Ministers Resolution (78)41 on the teaching of human rights (25 October 1978)

CoE Recommendation R(83)13 of the Committee of Ministers to member states on the role of the secondary school in preparing young people for life (23 September 1983)

CoE Recommendation R(85)7 of the Committee of Ministers to member states on teaching and learning about human rights in schools (14 May 1985)

CoE Recommendation No R(87)15 of the Committee of Ministers to the member States 'on regulating the use of personal data in the police sector' (17 September 1987)

CoE Recommendation R(87)3 of the Committee of Ministers to member states on the European Prison Rules (12 February 1987)

CoE Recommendation R(89)12 of the Committee of Ministers to member states on education in prison (13 October 1989)

CoE Committee of Ministers Statutory Resolution (93)27 on majorities required for decisions of the Committee of Ministers (14 May 1993)

CoE Committee of Ministers Declaration on compliance with commitments accepted by member states of the Council of Europe (10 November 1994)

CoE Committee of Ministers, Procedure for implementing the Declaration of 10 November 1994 on compliance with commitments accepted by member states of the Council of Europe (20 April 1995)

CoE Recommendation No R (95) 14 of the Committee of Ministers to the Member States of the Council of Europe on the protection of health of donors and recipients in the area of blood transfusion (12 October 1995)

CoE Recommendation R(98)3 of the Committee of Ministers to member states on access to higher education (17 March 1998)

CoE Recommendation R(98)6 of the Committee of Ministers to member states concerning modern languages (17 March 1998)

CoE Committee of Ministers Declaration and programme on education for democratic citizenship, based on the rights and responsibilities of citizens (Budapest, 7 May 1999)

CoE Recommendation R(99)2 of the Committee of Ministers to member states on secondary education (19 January 1999)

CoE Recommendation R(99)4 of the Committee of Ministers to member states on principles concerning the legal protection of incapable adults (23 February 1999)

CoE Recommendation R(2000)4 of the Committee of Ministers to member States on the education of Roma/Gypsy children in Europe (3 February 2000)

CoE Recommendation Rec(2000)12 of the Committee of Ministers to member states on the social sciences and the challenge of transition (13 July 2000)

CoE Recommendation Rec(2000)24 of the Committee of Ministers to member states on the Development of European Studies for Democratic Citizenship (20 December 2000)

CoE Recommendation Rec(2001)15 of the Committee of Ministers to member states on history teaching in twenty-first-century Europe (31 October 2001)

CoE Committee of Ministers Resolution Res(2002)8 on the statute of the European Commission against Racism and Intolerance (13 June 2002)

CoE Committee of Ministers Resolution(2002)3, Revised Statute of the European Commission for Democracy through Law (Venice Commission) (21 February 2002)

CoE Recommendation Rec(2002)12 of the Committee of Ministers to member states on education for democratic citizenship (16 October 2002)

CoE Recommendation Rec(2003)3 of the Committee of Ministers to member states on balanced participation of women and men in political and public decision making (12 March 2003)

CoE Recommendation Rec(2003)8 of the Committee of Ministers to member states on the promotion and recognition of non-formal education/learning of young people (30 April 2003)

CoE Recommendation Rec(2004)4 of the Committee of Ministers to member states on the European Convention on Human Rights in university education and professional training (12 May 2004)

CoE Recommendation Rec(2004)13 of the Committee of Ministers to member states on the participation of young people in local and regional life (17 November 2004), with in appendix the Revised European Charter on the Participation of Young People in Local and Regional Life

CoE Recommendation Rec(2004)15 of the Committee of Ministers to member states on electronic governance ('e-governance') (15 December 2004)

CoE Rules of Procedure of the Committee of Ministers (5th revised edn 2005)

CoE Committee of Ministers, Rules of Procedure for the meetings of the Ministers' Deputies (4th revised edn 2005)

CoE Recommendation Rec(2006)2 of the Committee of Ministers to member states on the European Prison Rules (1 January 2006)

CoE Recommendation Rec(2006)12 of the Committee of Ministers to member states on empowering children in the new information and communications environment (27 September 2006)

CoE Recommendation Rec(2006)14 of the Committee of Ministers to member states on citizenship and participation of young people in public life (25 October 2006)

CoE Committee of Ministers, Terms of reference of the Ad hoc Advisory Group on Education for Democratic Citizenship and Human Rights (ED-EDCHR) (5 February 2007) CM/Del/Dec(2007)985/7.2

CoE Recommendation CM/Rec(2007)6 of the Committee of Ministers to member states on the public responsibility for higher education and research (16 May 2007)

CoE Recommendation CM/Rec(2007)11 of the Committee of Ministers to member states on promoting freedom of expression and information in the new information and communications environment (26 September 2007)

CoE Recommendation CM/Rec(2007)13 of the Committee of Ministers to member states on gender mainstreaming in education (10 October 2007)

CoE Recommendation CM/Rec(2007)16 of the Committee of Ministers to member states on measures to promote the public service value of the Internet (7 November 2007)

Recommendation CM/Rec(2007)7 of the Committee of Ministers to member states on good administration (20 June 2007)

CoE Committee of Ministers, The Council of Europe and the Rule of Law, CM(2008)170

CoE Committee of Ministers, White Paper on Intercultural Dialogue: Living together as equals in dignity (2 May 2008)

CoE Recommendation CM/Rec(2008)4 of the Committee of Ministers to member states on strengthening the integration of children of migrants and of immigrant background (20 February 2008)

CoE Recommendation CM/Rec(2008)7 of the Committee of Ministers to member states on the use of the Council of Europe's Common European Framework of Reference for Languages (CEFR) and the promotion of plurilingualism (2 July 2008)

CoE Recommendation CM/Rec(2008)12 of the Committee of Ministers to member states on the dimension of religions and non-religious convictions within intercultural education (10 December 2008)

CoE Committee of Ministers Declaration on the Code of Good Practice for Civil Participation in the Decision-Making Process (21 October 2009)

CoE Recommendation CM/Rec(2009)4 of the Committee of Ministers to member States on the education of Roma and Travellers in Europe (17 June 2009)

CoE Recommendation CM/Rec(2010)7 of the Committee of Ministers to member states on the Council of Europe Charter on Education for Democratic Citizenship and Human Rights Education (11 May 2010)

CoE Recommendation CM/Rec(2010)12 of the Committee of Ministers of the Council of Europe on judges: independence, efficiency and responsibilities (17 November 2010)

CoE Recommendation CM/Rec(2011)4 of the Committee of Ministers to member states on education for global interdependence and solidarity (5 May 2011)

CoE Recommendation CM/Rec(2011)6 of the Committee of Ministers to member states on intercultural dialogue and the image of the other in history teaching (6 July 2011)

CoE Committee of Ministers, Council of Europe Strategy for the Rights of the Child (2012–2015) (15 February 2012) CM(2011)171final

CoE Committee of Ministers, Thematic debate: 'Living together implies having a level of common competences as regards intercultural and democratic dialogue, as well as a system of attitudes, behaviour and common values. Can these be taught?' – Follow-up (4 and 6 July 2012)

CoE Recommendation CM/Rec(2012)2 of the Committee of Ministers to member States on the participation of children and young people under the age of 18 (28 March 2012)

CoE Recommendation CM/Rec(2012)7 of the Committee of Ministers to member States on the responsibility of public authorities for academic freedom and institutional autonomy (20 June 2012)

CoE Recommendation CM/Rec(2012)13 of the Committee of Ministers to member States on ensuring quality education (12 December 2012)

CoE Recommendation CM/Rec(2014)5 of the Committee of Ministers to member States on the importance of competences in the language(s) of schooling for equity and quality in education and for educational success (2 April 2014)

CoE Committee of Ministers Declaration 'United around our principles against violent extremism and radicalisation leading to terrorism' (19 May 2015) CM(2015)74-final

CoE Committee of Ministers, The fight against violent extremism and radicalisation leading to terrorism – Action Plan (19 May 2015) CM(2015)74 add final

CoE Recommendation CM/Rec(2015)3 of the Committee of Ministers to member States on the access of young people from disadvantaged neighbourhoods to social rights (21 January 2015)

CoE Committee of Ministers Action Plan on Building Inclusive Societies (2016–2019) (15–16 March 2016) CM(2016)25

CoE Committee of Ministers, Council of Europe Strategy for the Rights of the Child (2016–2021): Children's human rights (3 March 2016) CM(2015)175final

CoE Exchange on the religious dimension of intercultural dialogue: the role of education in the prevention of radicalisation leading to terrorism and violent extremism (Strasbourg, 9–10 November 2016)

CoE Committee of Ministers, Terms of reference for the Steering Committee for education policy and practice (CDPPE), 1 January 2018 until 31 December 2019, CM(2017)131-addfinal (Education for Democracy)

Priorities of the Czech Chairmanship of the Committee of Ministers of the Council of Europe (May – November 2017) CM/Inf(2017)12

Priorities of the Finnish Presidency of the Committee of Ministers of the Council of Europe (21 November 2018–17 May 2019) CM/Inf(2018)30

CoE Recommendation CM/Rec(2018)7 of the Committee of Ministers to member States on Guidelines to respect, protect and fulfil the rights of the child in the digital environment (4 July 2018)

CoE Committee of Ministers, Summary Report on co-operation between the Council of Europe and the European Union Helsinki (16–17 May 2019) CM(2019)67-fina

CoE Recommendation CM/Rec(2019)5 of the Committee of Ministers to member States on the system of the European Convention Human Rights in university education and professional training (16 October 2019)

CoE Parlementary Assembly

CoE Parlementary Assembly Recommendation 1111(1989) 'European dimension of education'

CoE Parliamentary Assembly Recommendation 1346(1997) 'Human rights education'

CoE Parliamentary Assembly Recommendation 1353(1998) on the access of minorities to higher education

CoE Parliamentary Assembly Recommendation 1396(1999) 'Religion and democracy'

CoE Parliamentary Assembly Recommendation 1401(1999) 'Education in the responsibilities of the individual'

CoE Parliamentary Assembly Recommendation 1426(1999) 'European Democracies facing up to terrorism'

CoE Parliamentary Assembly Recommendation 1438(2000) 'Threat posed to democracy by extremist parties and movements in Europe'

CoE Parliamentary Assembly Recommendation 1682(2004) 'Education for Europe'

CoE Parliamentary Assembly Recommendation 1791(2007) 'State of human rights and democracy in Europe'

CoE Parliamentary Assembly Recommendation 1849(2008) 'For the promotion of a culture of democracy and human rights through teacher education'

CoE Parliamentary Assembly, Motion for a resolution tabled by Mr Luca Volontè and other members of the Assembly, 'Respect for human rights in education for democratic citizenship in Spain' (3 June 2010)

CoE Parliamentary Assembly Recommendation 2060(2015) 'The implementation of the Memorandum of Understanding between the Council of Europe and the European Union'

CoE Parliamentary Assembly Recommendation 2084(2016) 'Foreign fighters in Syria and Iraq'

CoE Parliamentary Assembly Recommendation 2088(2016) 'Towards a framework of competences for democratic citizenship'

CoE Parliamentary Assembly Resolution 2188(2017) 'New threats to the rule of law in Council of Europe member States: selected examples' (11 October 2017)

CoE Parliamentary Assembly Recommendation 2151 (2019) 'Establishment of a European Union mechanism on democracy, the rule of law and fundamental rights'

CoE Parliamentary Assembly Recommendation 2157 (2019) 'Towards an ambitious Council of Europe agenda for gender equality'

CoE Standing Conference of European Ministers of Education

CoE Standing Conference of European Ministers of Education, Resolution on the activities of international organisations in the fields of education and science (No 3) and Resolution on future meetings of the Ministers of Education (No 4) (The Hague, 12–13 November 1959)

CoE Standing Conference of Ministers of Education, Resolution on 'the European dimension of education: teaming and curriculum content' (Vienna, 16–17 October 1991)

CoE Standing Conference of European Ministers of Education, Resolution on education for democracy, human rights and tolerance (No 1) (Madrid, 23-24 March 1994)

CoE Standing Conference of European Ministers of Education, Resolution No 1 on trends and common issues in education in Europe, Resolution No 2 on fundamental values, aims and the future role of educational co-operation in the Council of Europe (Kristiansand, Norway, 22–24 June 1997)

CoE Standing Conference of European Ministers of Education, Resolution on results and conclusions of the completed projects on the 1997–2000 Medium-term programme: Educational policies for democratic citizenship and social cohesion: challenges and strategies for Europe (Cracow, 15–17 October 2000)

CoE Standing Conference of European Ministers of Education, Building a more humane and inclusive Europe: role of education policies, Resolution on the 2008–2010 programme of activities (Istanbul, 4–5 May 2007)

CoE Standing Conference of European Ministers of Education, Final Declaration on 'Education for Sustainable Democratic Societies: the Role of Teachers' (Ljubljana, 4–5 June 2010)

CoE Standing Conference of Ministers of Education, Governance and Quality Education (Helsinki, 26 -27 April 2013)

CoE Standing Conference of Ministers of Education, Securing Democracy through Education: The development of a Reference Framework of Competences for Democratic Culture (Brussels, 11–12 April 2016)

CoE other

CoE Congress of Local and Regional Authorities of Europe Recommendation 128(2003) on the revised European Charter on the Participation of Young People in Local and Regional Life (21 May 2003)

CoE Congress of Local and Regional Authorities of the Council of Europe Resolution 332(2011) 'Education for democratic citizenship: tools for cities'

CoE European Commission for Democracy through Law (Venice Commission), Rule of law checklist (11–12 March 2016)

CoE ECRI General Policy Recommendation No 10 on combating racism and racial discrimination in and through school education (15 December 2006)

CoE Secretary General, State of democracy, human rights and the rule of law in Europe. Report 2014

—, State of democracy, human rights and the rule of law: A shared responsibility for democratic security in Europe. Report 2015

—, State of democracy, human rights and the rule of law – a security imperative for Europe. Report 2016

—, The fight against violent extremism and radicalisation leading to terrorism – Implementing the Action Plan. Report (18 May 2016)

—, Opinion on the European Union initiative to establish a European Pillar of Social Rights (Strasbourg, 2 December 2016)

—, State of democracy, human rights and the rule of law: Populism – How strong are Europe's checks and balances? Report 2017

——, State of democracy, human rights and the rule of law: Role of institutions – Threats to institutions Report 2018

CoE, *Learning to live together: Council of Europe Report on the state of citizenship and human rights education in Europe* (in accordance with the objectives and principles of the Council of Europe Charter on Education for Democratic Citizenship and Human Rights, 2017)

CoE Ministers' Deputies, Effects of enlargement of the Council of Europe, Report (4 November 1994) CM/Del/Dec(94)519bis/2.2 (1994)

Council of Europe (2001) Common European framework of reference for languages: learning, teaching, assessment (CEFR)

CoE Europe-wide Global Education Congress, European Strategy Framework For Improving and Increasing Global Education In Europe to the Year 2015 (Maastricht Global Education Declaration) (Maastricht, 15–17 November 2002)

CoE, 50 years of the European Cultural Convention (2004)

Ministers responsible for culture, education, youth and sport from the States Parties to the European Cultural Convention, Wroclaw Declaration on 50 Years of Cultural Cooperation (9–10 December 2004) ETS No 18

CoE Conference of European Ministers responsible for Youth, Human dignity and social cohesion: youth policy responses to violence. Final Declaration (Budapest, 23–24 September 2005)

CoE Ad Hoc Committee of Experts for the European Year of Citizenship through Education (CAHCIT), Education for Democratic Citizenship and Human Rights: Programme of Activities (2006–2009), Learning and living democracy for all, DGIV/EDU/CAHCIT(2006)5

CoE Evaluation Conference of the 2005 European Year of Citizenship through Education: Conclusions (Sinaia, 27–28 April 2006)

CoE, Dialogue between Judges, European Court of Human Rights (2008)

CoE Committee of Ministers, Declaration and Action Plan, High Level Conference on the Future of the European Court of Human Rights (Interlaken, 19 February 2010)

CoE Report of the Group of Eminent Persons of the Council of Europe, *Living together: combining diversity and freedom in 21st century Europe* (2011)

CoE Conference of International Non-Governmental Organisations (INGOs), Declaration on genuine democracy (24 January 2013)

CoE Proceedings of the Conference on 'Human Rights and Democracy in Action – Looking Ahead: The Impact of the Council of Europe Charter on Education for Democratic Citizenship and Human Rights Education' (Strasbourg, 29–30 November 2012)

CoE European Committee of Social Rights, The relationship between European Union law and the European Social Charter (Working Document, 2014)

CoE, Pilot project, Teaching controversial issues: developing effective training for teachers and school leaders (2014)

CoE iGuide, Committee of Ministers: Procedures and working methods (24 September 2018)

CoE Secretariat, Compendium of the most relevant Council of Europe texts in the area of democracy CDDG(2016)Compendium

CoE, Government Replies to the Questionnaire, in 2016 Report on the State of citizenship and Human Rights Education in Europe

Competences for democratic culture: Living together as equals in culturally diverse democratic societies (CoE 2016)

CoE, Council of Europe Strategy for the Rights of the Child (2012–2015): Implementation report (2016)

World Forum for Democracy 2016, Democracy & equality: does education matter? (Strasbourg, 7–9 November 2016)

CoE Conference, Learning to Live Together: a Shared Commitment to Democracy: Conference on the Future of Citizenship and Human Rights Education in Europe (Strasbourg, 20–22 June 2017)

CoE Conference, Securing Democracy through Education (Nicosia, 22–23 March 2017)

CoE Reference Framework of Competences for Democratic Culture, Vol 1: Context, concepts and model (2018)

CoE Reference Framework of Competences for Democratic Culture, Vol 2: Descriptors of competences for democratic culture (2018)

CoE Reference Framework of Competences for Democratic Culture, Vol 3: Guidance for implementation (2018)

CoE Steering Committee for Human Rights (CDDH), Guide to good and promising practices on the way of reconciling freedom of expression with other rights and freedoms, in particular in culturally diverse societies (17 September 2019) CM(2019)148

CoE materials

All Human Beings: A Manual for Human Rights Education (ed K Savolainen, The Teacher's Library series, UNESCO 1998)

O'Shea K, 'EDC policies and regulatory frameworks' (Strasbourg, 6–7 December 2001)

O'Shea K, 'A Glossary of terms for Education for Democratic Citizenship: Education for Democratic Citizenship 2001–2004, Developing a Shared Understanding' CoE DGIV/EDU/CIT (2003)29

All-European Study on Education for Democratic Citizenship Policies (CoE 2005)

Human Rights Education in the School Systems of Europe, Central Asia and North America: A Compendium of Good Practice (CoE, OSCE/ODIHR, UNESCO, OHCHR, 2009)

Global Education Guidelines: a Handbook for Educators to Understand and Implement Global Education (Global Education Week Network, CoE, 2012)

Compass – Manual on human rights education with young people (CoE, 2012)

Three Country Audit of the lower secondary citizenship and human rights education curriculum: Reflection of the principles of the Charter on Education for Democratic Citizenship and Human Rights Education in the curricula of France, Finland and Ireland (2013)

Freedom(s) – Learning activities for secondary schools on the case law of the European Court of Human Rights (edited by P Kirschschlaeger, G Peter, B Dumont and D Hayward, Council of Europe 2015)

Curriculum Development and Review for Democratic Citizenship and Human Rights Education (prepared by Felisa Tibbits for UNESCO/CoE/Office for Democratic Institutions and Human Rights/Organization of American States, 2016)

ECtHR case law (alphabetical)

Al-Adsani v UK no 35763/97 (ECtHR 21 November 2001)

Alekseyev v Russia no 4916/07 et al (ECtHR 21 October 2010)

Altınay v Turkey no 37222/04 (ECtHR 9 July 2013)

Baka v Hungary no 20261/12 (ECtHR 23 June 2016)

Belgian Linguistic Cases no 1474/62 et al (ECtHR 23 July 1968)

Çam v Turkey no 51500/08 (ECtHR 23 February 2016)

Campbell and Cosans v UK no 7511/76 et al (ECtHR 23 March 1983)

Catan and Others v Moldova and Russia no 43370/04 et al (ECtHR 19 October 2012)

Cölgeçen and Others v Turkey no 50124/07 et al (ECtHR 12 December 2017)

Demir and Baykara v Turkey no 34503/97 (ECtHR 12 November 2008)

DH and Others v Czech Republic no 57325/00 (ECtHR 13 November 2007)

Enea v Italy no 74912/01 (ECtHR 17 September 2009)

Evans v UK no 6339/05 (ECtHR 10 April 2004)

Fernández Martínez v Spain no 56030/07 (ECtHR 12 June 2014)

Folgerø and Others v Norway no 15472/02 (ECtHR 29 June 2007)

Fretté v France no 36515/97 (ECtHR 26 February 2002)

Gäfgen v Germany no 22978/05 (ECtHR 1 June 2010)

Golder v UK no 4451/70 (ECtHR 21 February 1975)

Grori v Albania no 25336/04 (ECtHR 7 July 2009)

Guja v Moldova no 14277/04 (ECtHR 12 February 2008)

Gülay Çetin v Turkey no 44084/10 (ECtHR 5 March 2013)

Handyside v UK no 5493/72 (ECtHR 7 Dec 1976)

Hasan and Eylem Zengin v Turkey no 1448/04 (ECtHR 9 October 2007)

Hassan v UK no 29750/09 (ECtHR 16 September 2014)

Hirst v UK no 74025/01 (ECtHR 6 October 2005)

Horváth and Kiss v Hungary no 11146/11 (ECtHR 29 January 2013)

Jersild v Denmark no 15890/89 (ECtHR 23 September 1994)

Karácsony and Others v Hungary no 42461/13 et al (ECtHR 17 May 2016)
Kjeldsen, Busk Madsen and Pedersen v Denmark no 5095/71 (ECtHR 7 December 1976)
Lautsi and Others v Italy no 30814/06 (ECtHR 18 March 2011)
Leyla Şahin v Turkey no 44774/98 (ECtHR 10 November 2005)
Lindon and Others v France no 21279/02 et al (ECtHR 22 October 2007)
Mansur Yalçin and Others v Turkey no 21163/11 (ECtHR 16 September 2014)
Marckx v Belgium no 6833/74 (ECtHR 13 June 1979)
Mathieu-Mohin and Clerfayt v Belgium no 9267/81 (ECtHR 2 March 1987)
Matthews v UK no 24833/94 (ECtHR 18 February 1999)
MC v Bulgaria no 39272/98 (ECtHR 4 December 2003)
Mehmet Reşit Arslan and Orhan Bingöl v Turkey no 47121/06 et al (ECtHR 18 June 2019)
Mihalache v Romania no 54012/10 (ECtHR 8 July 2019)
Mosley v UK no 48009/08 (ECtHR 10 May 2011)
Murray v the Netherlands no 10511/10 (ECtHR 26 April 2016)
Muršić v Croatia no 7334/13 (ECtHR 20 October 2016)
National Union of Rail, Maritime and Transport Workers v UK no 31045/10 (ECtHR 8 April 2014)
Navalnyy v Russia no 29580/12 et al (ECtHR 15 November 2018)
Opuz v Turkey no 33401/02 (ECtHR 9 June 2009)
Oršuš and Others v Croatia no 15766/03 (ECtHR 16 March 2010)
Osmanoglu and Kocabas v Switzerland no 29086/12 (ECtHR 10 January 2017)
Perez v France no 47287/99 (ECtHR 12 February 2004)
Ponomaryovi v Bulgaria no 5335/05 (ECtHR 21 June 2011)
Rivière v France no 33834/03 (ECtHR 11 July 2006)
RMT v UK no 31045/10 (ECtHR, 8 April 2014)
Ruiz Rivera v Switzerland no 8300/06 (ECtHR 18 February 2014)
S v Switzerland no 12629/87 (ECtHR 28 November 1991)
Saadi v UK no 13229/03 (ECtHR 29 January 2008)
Salduz v Turkey no 36391/0227 (ECtHR November 2008)
Scoppola v Italy (No 3) no 126/05 (22 May 2012)
Selahattin Demirtaş v Turkey no 14305/17 (ECtHR 20 November 2018)
Seurot v France no 57383/00 (ECtHR Decision 18 May 2004)
SH and Others v Austria no 57813/00 (ECtHR 3 November 2011)
Shtukaturov v Russia no 44009/05 (ECtHR 27 March 2008)
Siebenhaar v Germany no 18136/02 (ECtHR 3 February 2011)
Siliadin v France no 73316/01 (ECtHR 26 July 2005)
Sindicatul "Păstorul cel Bun" v Romania no 2330/09 (ECtHR 9 July 2013)

Sitaropoulos and Giakoumopoulos v Greece no 42202/07 (ECtHR 15 March 2012)
Socialist Party and Others v Turkey no 20/1997/804/1007 (ECtHR 25 May 1998)
Soltysyak v Russia no 4663/05 (ECtHR 10 February 2011)
Tănase v Moldova no 7/08 (ECtHR 24 April 2010)
Tarantino and Others v Italy no 25851/09 et al (ECtHR 2 April 2013)
Telegraaf Media Nederland Landelijke Media v the Netherlands no 39315/06 (ECtHR 22 November 2012)
Üner v the Netherlands no 12629/87 (ECtHR 18 October 2006)
United Communist Party of Turkey and Others v Turkey no 19392/92 (ECtHR 30 January 1998)
V v UK no 24888/94 (ECtHR 16 December 1999)
Valsamis v Greece no 21787/93 (ECtHR 18 December 1996)
Velyo Velev v Bulgaria no 16032/07 (ECtHR 27 May 2014)
Vinter and Others v UK no 66069/09 et al (ECtHR 9 July 2013)
Vogt v Germany no 17851/91 (ECtHR 2 Sept 1996)
Von Hannover v Germany no 40660/08 et al (ECtHR 7 February 2012)
Pinto de Albuquerque, Partly dissenting opinion in *Muršić v Croatia* no 7334/13 (ECtHR 20 Oct 2016)

4. *EU/CoE*

Joint Declaration on co-operation and partnership between the Council of Europe and the European Commission (2001)
CoE Compendium of Texts governing the relations between the Council of Europe and the European Union (2001)
Memorandum of Understanding between the Council of Europe and the European Union (2007) (MOU)
Juncker J-C, *Council of Europe – European Union: 'A sole ambition for the European continent', Report to the attention of the Heads of State or Governments of the Member States of the Council of Europe* (2006)
CoE/EU Joint Programme- Human Rights and Democracy in Action- Pilot Projects Scheme

5. *Some comparative law sources*

Member State Constitutions

BE

Décret relatif à l'organisation d'un cours et d'une éducation à la philosophie et à la citoyenneté (D 22–10–2015, MB 09–12–2015)

Decreet 26 januari 2018 houdende wijziging van het decreet basisonderwijs van 25 februari 1997 en de Codex Secundair Onderwijs, wat de onderwijsdoelen betreft (opschrift gewijzigd door de commissie: ... tot wijziging van het decreet basisonderwijs van 25 februari 1997 en de Codex Secundair Onderwijs, wat onderwijsdoelen betreft, en tot wijziging van de decreten Rechtspositie onderwijspersoneel) BS 9 maart 2018, 2018030576

DE

Beschluss der Kultusministerkonferenz vom 04.12.1980 i.d.F. vom 14.12.2000, Empfehlung der Kultusministerkonferenz zur Förderung der Menschenrechtserziehung in der Schule

Beschluss der Kultusministerkonferenz vom 04.12.1980 i.d.F. vom 11.10.2018, 'Menschenrechtsbildung in der Schule'

Beschluss der Kultusministerkonferenz vom 08.06.1978 i. d. F. vom 05.05.2008, Empfehlung der Ständigen Konferenz der Kultusminister der Länder in der Bundesrepublik Deutschland 'Europabildung in der Schule'

Beschluss der Kultusministerkonferenz vom 06.03.2009, 'Stärkung der Demokratieerziehung'

Beschluss der Kultusministerkonferenz vom 06.03.2009 i. d. F. vom 11.10.2018, 'Demokratie als Ziel, Gegenstand und Praxis – historisch-politischer Bildung und Erziehung in der Schule'

Erlaß über die Errichtung der Bundeszentrale für Heimatdienst, 25. November 1952

Erlaß zur Änderung des Erlasses über die Errichtung der Bundeszentrale für Heimatdienst, 18. Mai 1963

BVerfG, 2 BvE 2/08 (Lissabon) 30 June 2009

FR

Code de l'éducation, Art L121–4–1 (crée par la Loi d'orientation et de programmation pour la refondation de l'École de la République n°2013–595 du 8 juillet 2013).

Décret relatif au Socle commun de connaissances, de compétences et de culture: Bulletin Officiel n°17 du 23–4–2015

Circulaire n° 2016–092 du 20–6–2016 relative au parcours citoyen de l'élève

Circulaire relative aux orientations générales pour les comités d'éducation à la santé et à la citoyenneté

Arrêté fixant le programme d'enseignement moral et civique à l'école élémentaire et au collège; Arrêté fixant les programmes d'enseignement moral et civique en classes de seconde générale et technologique, de première et terminale des séries générales (Arrêtés du 12–6–2015, Journal officiel du 21–6–2015): Bulletin officiel spécial n° 6 du 25 juin 2015

Condorcet, *Cinq mémoires sur l'instruction publique* (digital JM Tremblay edn, 1791)

—, *Rapport et project de décret relatifs à l'organisation générale de l'instruction publique, Présentation à l'Assemblée législative (20 et 21 avril 1792)* (1792)

Lepelletier M, *Plan d'Éducation Nationale, présenté à la Convention par Maximilien Robespierre au nom de la Commission d'Instruction publique, le 29 juillet 1793* (1793)

Talleyrand-Périgord, *Rapport sur l'Instruction Publique, fait au nom du Comité de Constitution à l'Assemblée Nationale, les 10, 11 et 19 Septembre 1791*

NL

Dutch Ministry of Education Culture and Science, *Citizenship – made in Europe: living together starts at school* (2004)

UK

Advisory Group on Citizenship, *Education for citizenship and the teaching of democracy in schools: the Crick Report* (Qualifications and Curriculum Authority, 1998)

Education (Independent School Standards) (England) (Amendment) Regulations 2014 (come into force on 29th September 2014)

UK Department of Education, Promoting fundamental British values as part of SMSC [spiritual, moral, social and cultural development] in schools: Departmental advice for maintained schools (November 2014)

UK, Department of Education, Improving the spiritual, moral, social and cultural (SMSC) development of pupils: supplementary information: Departmental advice for independent schools, academies and free schools (November 2014)

Other

Supreme Court of Japan, *Ienaga v Japan*, No 1428 of 1986, Judgment of 16 March 1993, No 1119 of 1994, Judgment of 29 August 1997

US Department of Education, Office of the Under Secretary and Office of Postsecondary Education, Advancing Civic Learning and Engagement in Democracy: A Road Map and Call to Action, Washington DC, 2012

Mozert v Hawkins County Board of Education, 827 F. 2d 1058 (1987)

West Virginia State Board of Education v. Barnette, 319 US 624 (1943)

<https://www.icivics.org/>

6. Authors

Abs HJ (ed), *Introducing Quality Assurance of Education for Democratic Citizenship in Schools: A comparative Study on Ten Countries* (CoE 2009)

Ach N, 'La citoyenneté européenne au service d'une Europe sociale' [2006] Journal des Tribunaux- Droit européen 129

Ackerman B, 'Revolution on a Human Scale (Moments of Change: Transformation in American Constitutionalism)' (1999) 108 Yale Law Journal 2279

Ackerman BA, *We the People*, vol 2: Transformations (Harvard University Press 1998)

Adam S and Van Elsuwege P, 'Citizenship rights and the federal balance between the European Union and its member states: comment on Dereci' (2012) 37 ELRev 176

—–, 'EU Citizenship and the European Federal Challenge through the Prism of Family Reunification' in Kochenov D (ed), *EU Citizenship and Federalism: The Role of Rights* (Cambridge University Press 2017)

Adonnino P, *Adonnino Committee, A People's Europe, Reports from the ad hoc Committee* (Bull EC 7–1985, 1985)

Ainley J, Schulz W and Friedman T (eds), *ICCS 2009 Encyclopedia: Approaches to civic and citizenship education around the world* (International Association for the Evaluation of Educational Achievement IEA 2013)

Alemanno A, 'Unpacking the Principle of Openness in EU Law: Transparency, Participation and Democracy' (2014) 1 ELRev 72

Alexy R, 'On the Structure of Legal Principles' (2000) 13 Ratio Juris 294

—–, 'The Construction of Constitutional Rights' (2010) 4 Law and Ethics of Human Rights 21

Amtenbrink F, 'The multidimensional constitutional legal order of the European Union – A successful case of cosmopolitan constitution building?' (2008) 39 Netherlands Yearbook of International Law 3

Amtenbrink F, 'Europe in Times of Economic Crisis: Bringing Europe's Citizens Closer to One Another?' in Dougan M, Nic Schuibhne N and Spaventa E (eds), *Empowerment and Disempowerment of the European Citizen* (Hart 2012)

Anderson BRO, *Imagined Communities: Reflections on the Origin and Spread of Nationalism* (revised edn, Verso 2006)

Anderson GW, 'Beyond "Constitutionalism Beyond the State"' (2012) 39 Journal of Law and Society 359

Arbués E, 'Civic Education in Europe: Pedagogic Challenge versus Social Reality' (2014) 4 Sociology Mind 226

Arnull A and others (eds), *A Constitutional Order of States: Essays in EU Law in Honour of Alan Dashwood* (Hart 2011)

Arthur J, Davies I and Hahn C (eds), *The SAGE Handbook of Education for Citizenship and Democracy* (Sage 2008)

Arthur J, Davies I and Hahn C, 'Introduction' in Arthur J, Davies I and Hahn C (eds), *The SAGE Handbook of Education for Citizenship and Democracy* (Sage 2008)

Arthur J and Lovat T, *The Routledge international handbook of education, religion and values* (Routledge 2013)

Arthur J and Wright D, *Teaching Citizenship in the Secondary School* (David Fulton 2001)

Audigier F, *Basic concepts and core competencies for education for democratic citizenship* (CoE 2000)

—, 'L'éducation civique dans l'école française' (2002) 1 Journal of Social Science Education 1

Avbelj M and Komárek J, *Constitutional Pluralism in the European Union and Beyond* (Hart 2012)

Aziz M, 'Implementation as the Test Case of European Citizenship' (2009) 15 Columbia Journal of European Law 281

Azoulai L, 'Constitution économique et citoyenneté de l'Union européenne' (2011) 25 Revue internationale de droit économique 543

Azoulai L (ed) *The Question of Competence in the European Union* (Oxford University Press 2014)

Azoulai L, 'Transfiguring European Citizenship: From Member State Territory to Union Territory' in Kochenov D (ed), *EU Citizenship and Federalism: The Role of Rights* (Cambridge University Press 2017)

Azoulai L and Jaeger E, 'Review: The Passage to Europe (van Middelaar)' (2014) 51 CMLRev 311

Baczko B, *Une éducation pour la démocratie: textes et projets de l'époque révolutionnaire* (2nd edn, Droz 2000)

Bakker WE and others, *The quest for a European civic culture: The EU and EU Citizenship in policies and practices of citizenship education in seven EU member states* (Utrecht University Repository 2017)

Balthasar A and Prosser A, '"Every citizen shall have the right to participate in the democratic life of the union": serious commitment or vain promise in an "ever closer union"?' (International Conference on electronic governance and open society, St Petersburg, 22 November 2016)

Bańkowski Z and Christodoulidis E, 'The European Union as an Essentially Contested Project' (1998) 4 ELJ 341

Banks JA, 'Diversity, Group Identity, and Citizenship Education in a Global Age' (2008) 37 Educational Researcher 129

—, 'Educating citizens in diverse societies' (2011) 22 Intercultural Education 243

Banks JA and others, *Democracy and diversity: principles and concepts for educating citizens in a global age* (University of Washington 2005)

Barents R, 'The Precedence of EU Law from the Perspective of Constitutional Pluralism' (2009) 5 European Constitutional Law Review 421

Barnard C, 'EU "Social" Policy: from Employment Law to Labour Market Reform' in Craig P and de Búrca G (eds), *The evolution of EU law* (Oxford University Press 2011)

Barnard C, 'EU employment law and the European social model: the past, the present, and the future' (2014) 67 Current Legal Problems 199

Barthélemy D, 'Analysis of the Concept of European Dimension' (1999) 31 European Education 64

Bartsch H-J, 'The Acceptance of Recommendations and Conventions within the Council of Europe' in *Le rôle de la volonté dans les actes juridiques: Etudes à la mémoire du Professeur Alfred Rieg* (Bruylant 2000)

Bauböck R, 'The three levels of citizenship within the European Union' (2014) 15 German Law Journal 751

Bauböck R, 'Still United in Diversity? The State of the Union Address' (Florence, 5 May 2017)

Bauer H and Calliess C (eds), *Constitutional principles in Europe* (Bruylant 2008)

Beaumont E, 'Education and the Constitution: Defining the Contours of Governance, Rights, and Citizenship' in Tushnet M, Graber MA and Levinson S (eds), *The Oxford Handbook of the US Constitution* (2015)

Becker H, 'Politische Bildung in Europa' Bundeszentrale für politische Bildung (2012) <www.bpb.de/apuz/148214/politische-bildung-in-europa?p=all>

Becker MA, 'Managing diversity in the European Union: inclusive European citizenship and third-country nationals' (2004) 7 Yale Human Rights and Development Law Journal 132

Beiter KD, *The Protection of the Right to Education by International Law* (Including a Systematic Analysis of Article 13 of the International Covenant on Economic, Social and Cultural Rights; International Studies in Human Rights vol 82, Nijhoff 2006)

Belanger P, *Education for Democratic Citizenship: Methods, Practices and Strategies* (CoE 2001)

Bellamy R, 'The European Constitution is Dead, Long Live European Constitutionalism' (2006) 13 Constellations 181

—, '"An Ever Closer Union Among the Peoples of Europe": Republican Intergovernmentalism and Demoicratic Representation within the EU' (2013) 35 Journal of European Integration 499

—, 'A Duty-Free Europe? What's Wrong with Kochenov's Account of EU Citizenship Rights' (2015) 21 ELJ 558

Bellamy R and Castiglione D, 'Three models of democracy, political community and representation in the EU' (2013) 20 Journal of European Public Policy 206

Benoît-Rohmer F, 'Valeurs et droits fondamentaux dans la Constitution' [2005] Revue trimestrielle de droit européen 261

Benoît-Rohmer F and Klebes H, *Le droit du Conseil de l'Europe – Vers un espace juridique paneuropéen* (CoE 2005)

—–, *Council of Europe Law – Towards a pan-European legal area* (CoE 2005)

Bergan S, Gallagher T and Harkavy I (eds), *Higher education for democratic innovation* (CoE Higher Education Series No 21, 2016)

Berthelet P, 'Les fondements théoriques du droit européen à l'épreuve de la constitutionnalisation de l'ordre juridique de l'Union: Entre permanence et changement' [2015] Revue du droit de l'Union européenne 529

Besselink LFM, *A Composite European Constitution* (Europa Law 2007)

Besselink LFM, 'The notion and nature of the European constitution after the Lisbon Treaty' in Wouters J, Verhey L and Kiiver P (eds), *European Constitutionalism beyond Lisbon* (Intersentia 2009)

Besselink LFM, 'Case C-208/09 Ilonka Sayn-Wittgenstein v Landeshauptmann von Wien: respecting constitutional identity in the EU' (2012) 49 CMLRev 671

Besselink LFM and others (eds), *Constitutional Law of the EU Member States* (Kluwer 2014)

Besson S, Cheneval F and Levrat N, *Des valeurs pour l'Europe? Values for Europe?* (Bruylant Academia 2008)

Besson S and Pichonnaz P (eds), *Les principes en droit européen/ Principles in European Law* (Schultess 2011)

Besson S and Utzinger A, 'Introduction: Future Challenges of European Citizenship – Facing a Wide-Open Pandora's Box' (2007) 13 ELJ 573

Besson S and Utzinger A, 'Towards European Citizenship' (2008) 39 Journal of Social Philosophy 196

Beukers TWB, van Harten HJ and Prechal S (eds), *Het recht van de Europese Unie in 50 klassieke arresten* (Juridische Uitgevers 2010)

Beutler Z and Lange D (eds), *Schlüsselkompetenzen für aktive BürgerInnenschaft. Handbuch für die Sekundarstufe* (Voice Agora Politische Bildung 2010)

Biesta G, *Learning Democracy in School and Society: Education, Lifelong Learning, and the Politics of Citizenship* (Sense 2011)

—–, *The Beautiful Risk of Education* (Paradigm 2014)

Biesta G and Lawy R, 'From teaching citizenship to learning democracy: Overcoming individualism in research, policy and practice' (2006) 36 Cambridge Journal of Education 63

Bîrzéa C, *Education for Democratic Citizenship: A LifeLong Learning Perspective* (CoE 2000)

Bîrzéa C, 'EDC policies in Europe – a synthesis' in *All-European Study on Education for Democratic Citizenship Policies* (CoE 2005)

Bîrzea C and others, *Tool for Quality Assurance of Education for Democratic Citizenship in Schools* (UNESCO, CoE, CEPS 2005)

Bîrzea C, Losito B and Veldhuis R, 'Editorial' (2005) 4 Journal of Social Science Education

Blanke T, 'The Principle of Subsidiarity in the Lisbon Treaty' in Bruun N and others (eds), *The Lisbon Treaty and Social Europe* (Hart 2012)

Blessing B, Grammes T and Schluss H, 'Civics Courses in the German Democratic Republic: A Case Study in the History of Curriculum and Educational Research' (2012) 11 Journal of Social Science Education 85

Blum L, 'Three educational values for a multicultural society: Difference recognition, national cohesion and equality' (2014) 43 Journal of Moral Education 332

Blumann C, 'Citoyenneté européenne et déficit démocratique' in Philip C and Soldatos P (eds), *La citoyenneté européenne* (Collection études européennes, Chaire Jean Monnet, 2000)

Böckenförde E-W, *Staat, Gesellschaft, Freiheit: Studien zur Staatstheorie und zum Verfassungsrecht* (Suhrkamp 1976)

—–, *Staat, Verfassung, Demokratie: Studien zur Verfassungstheorie und zum Verfassungsrecht* (Suhrkamp 1991)

Bolleyer N and Reh C, 'EU legitimacy revisited: the normative foundations of a multilevel polity' (2012) 19 Journal of European Public Policy 472

Borgmann-Prebil Y, 'The Rule of Reason in European Citizenship' (2008) 14 ELJ 328

Borgonovi F, 'The relationship between education and levels of trust and tolerance in Europe' (2012) 63 British Journal of Sociology 146

Borrás S and Conzelmann T, 'Democracy, Legitimacy and Soft Modes of Governance in the EU: The Empirical Turn' (2007) 29 Journal of European Integration 531

Boulouis J and Chevallier R-M, *Grands arrêts de la Cour de justice des Communautés européennes* (6 edn, Dalloz 1994)

Bouza García L, 'How Could the New Article 11 TEU Contribute to Reduce the EU's Democratic Malaise?' in Dougan M, Nic Shuibhne N and Spaventa E (eds), *Empowerment and Disempowerment of the European Citizen* (Hart 2012)

Bovens M and Yesilkagit K, 'The EU as lawmaker: the impact of EU directives on national regulation in the Netherlands' (2010) 88 Public Adminstration 57

Bredt S, 'Prospects and Limits of Democratic Governance in the EU' (2011) 17 ELJ 35

Brett P, Mompoint-Gaillard P and Salema MH, *How all teachers can support citizenship and human rights education: a framework for the development of competences* (CoE 2009)

Breyer S, *The Court and the World: American Law and the New Global Realities* (Vintage Books 2016)

Bribosia E and Ganty S, 'Arrêt *Dogan*: quelle légalité pour les tests d'intégration civique?' (2014) 22 Journal de droit européen 378

Brine J, 'Educational and Vocational Policy and Construction of the European Union' (1995) 5 International Studies in Sociology of Education 145

Brooks RM and Holford JAK, 'Citizenship, learning and education: themes and issues' (2009) 13 Citizenship Studies 85

Brubaker R, *Citizenship and nationhood in France and Germany* (3rd edn, Harvard University Press 1996)

Bruen J, 'From Dictatorship to Democracy? The Impact of the Collapse of the German Democratic Republic (GDR) on Political Education in its Schools' (2014) 10 Journal of Political Science Education 315

Buisson F, *Dictionnaire de pédagogie et d'instruction primaire* (1911 edn, 1882–1887)

Burgorgue-Larsen L, Levade A and Picod F (eds), *Traité établissant une Constitution pour l'Europe, Partie II La Charte des droits fondamentaux de l'Union: Commentaire article par article* (Bruylant 2005)

Callan E, 'Beyond sentimental civic education' (1994) 102 American Journal of Education 190

Callan E, *Creating Citizens: Political Education and Liberal Democracy* (Oxford University Press 1997)

—, 'The Great Sphere: Education against Servility' (1997) 31 Journal of Philosophy of Education 221

—, 'A Note on Patriotism and Utopianism: Response to Schrag' (1999) 18 Studies in philosophy and education 197

—, 'Liberal Legitimacy, Justice, and Civic Education' (2001) 111 Ethics: an international journal of social, political, and legal philosophy 141

—, 'Citizenship and Education' (2004) 7 Annual Review of Political Science 71

Calliess C, Subsidiaritäts-und Solidaritätsprinzip in der Europäischen Union (Nomos 1996)

—, 'Europa als Wertegemeinschaft — Integration und Identität durch europäisches Verfassungsrecht?' (2004) 59 JuristenZeitung 1033

—, 'Der Unionsbürger: Status, Dogmatik und Dynamik' (2007) 42 EuropaRecht 7

—, 'Europe as Transnational Law: The Transnationalization of Values by European Law' (2009) 10 German Law Journal 1367

—, 'EU-Vertrag (Lissabon) Art 2' in Calliess C, Ruffert M and Blanke H-J (eds), *EUV/AEUV: das Verfassungsrecht der Europäischen Union mit Europäischer Grundrechtecharta : Kommentar* (Beck 2016)

—, 'EU-Vertrag (Lissabon) Art 1' in Calliess C and Ruffert M (eds), *EUV/AEUV: das Verfassungsrecht der Europäischen Union mit Europäischer Grundrechtecharta : Kommentar* (5th edn, Beck 2016)

—, 'EU-Vertrag (Lissabon) Art 5' in Calliess C and Ruffert M (eds), *EUV/AEUV: das Verfassungsrecht der Europäischen Union mit Europäischer Grundrechtecharta : Kommentar* (5th edn, Beck 2016)

—, 'Bausteine einer erneuerten Europäischen Union- Auf der Suche nach dem europäischen Weg: Überlegungen im Lichte des Weißbuchs der Europäischen Kommission zur Zukunft Europas' (2018) 20 Neue Zeitschrift für Verwaltungsrecht 1

Calliess C and Hartmann M, *Zur Demokratie in Europa: Unionsbürgerschaft und europäische Öffentlichkeit* (Mohr Siebeck 2014)

Cambien N, 'Citizenship of the Union as a cornerstone of European integration: a study of its impact on policies and competences of the Member States' (KU Leuven 2011)

—, 'When does someone become a citizen? Dormant and active citizenship in recent case law of the European Court of Justice' (Politicologenetmaal, Maastricht, 12–13 June 2014)

Cardonnel P, Rosas A and Wahl N, *Constitutionalising the EU judicial systems: essays in honour of Pernilla Lindh* (Hart 2012)

Carey L and Forrester K, *Sites of Citizenship: Empowerment, Participation and Partnerships* (CoE 2000)

Castro AJ, 'What Makes a Citizen? Critical and Multicultural Citizenship and Preservice Teachers' Understanding of Citizenship Skills' (2013) 41 Theory & Research in Social Education 219

Chalmers D, Arnull A and Hillion C, *Accession and Withdrawal in the Law of the European Union* (Oxford University Press 2015)

Chalmers D, Davies G and Monti G, *European Union Law: cases and materials* (2 edn, Cambridge University Press 2011)

Chanet JF, *L'école républicaine et les petites patries* (Aubier 1996)

Chanet JF, 'Instruction publique, éducation nationale et liberté d'enseignement en Europe occidentale au XIXe siècle' (2005) 41 Paedagogica Historica 9

Charlier J-E and Croché S, 'How European Integration is Eroding National Control over Education Planning and Policy' (2005–2006) 37 European Education 7

Cheneval F, Lavenex S and Schimmelfennig F, 'Demoi-cracy in the European Union: principles, institutions, policies' (2015) 22 Journal of European Public Policy 1

Cheneval F and Schimmelfennig F, 'The Case for Demoicracy in the European Union' (2013) 51 JCMS 334

Chou M and others, *Young people, citizenship and political participation: combatting civic deficit* (Rowman & Littlefield 2017)

Christensen CR and Hansen AJ, *Teaching and the Case Method* (Harvard Business School 1987)

Christiansen T and Reh C, *Constitutionalizing the European Union* (Palgrave MacMillan 2009)

Claassen RL and Monson JQ, 'Does Civic Education Matter? The Power of Long-Term Observation and the Experimental Method' (2015) 11 Journal of Political Science Education 404

Claes E, 'Schools and Citizenship Education. A Comparative Investigation of Socialization Effects of Citizenship Education on Adolescents' (PhD in Social Science KULeuven, Faculteit Sociale Wetenschappen 2010)

Claes E and Hooghe M, 'The Effect of Political Science Education on Political Trust and Interest: Results from a 5-year Panel Study' (2017) 13 Journal of Political Science Education 33

Clausen KW, 'Alternative education versus the common will' (2010) 45 Journal of Thought 95

Clemitshaw G, 'Citizenship without history? Knowledge, skills and values in citizenship education' (2008) 3 Ethics and Education 135

Cloots E, *National Identity in EU Law* (Oxford University Press 2015)

Closa C, 'The concept of citizenship in the Treaty on European Union' (1992) 29 CMLRev 1137

Coles R, *The Call of Stories: Teaching and the Moral Imagination* (1990)

Colonna L, 'Schrems vs. Commissioner: A Precedent for the CJEU to Intervene in the National Intelligence Surveillance Activities of Member States?' (2016) 2 Europarättslig tidskrift 208

Compayré G, *Histoire critique des doctrines de l'éducation en France depuis le seizième siècle* (4th edn, Hachette 1883)

Conrad M, 'The ECI's Contribution to the Emergence of a European Public Sphere' in Conrad M, Knaut A and Böttger K (eds), *Bridging the Gap? Opportunities and Constraints of the European Citizens' Initiative* (Nomos 2016)

Conrad M and Steingrímsdóttir F, 'A Tool for European Citizens? A Typology of ECI Organizers 2012–2015' in Conrad M, Knaut A and Böttger K (eds), *Bridging the Gap?: Opportunities and Constraints of the European Citizens' Initiative* (Nomos 2016)

Corbett A, *Universities and the Europe of Knowledge: Ideas, Institutions and Policy Entrepreneurship in European Union Higher Education Policy* (Palgrave Macmillan 2005)

Cornu E, 'The impact of Council of Europe Standards on the European Union' in Wessel RA and Blockmans S (eds), *Between Autonomy and Dependence: The EU Legal Order Under the Influence of International Organisations* (Asser Press 2013)

Costello PJM, 'Education, citizenship and critical thinking' (1995) 107 Early Child Development and Care 105

Coutts S, 'Delvigne: A Multi-Levelled Political Citizenship' (2017) 42 ELRev 867

Craig P, 'Constitutions, Constitutionalism, and the European Union' (2001) 7 ELJ 125

—, 'Integration, Democracy and Legitimacy' in Craig P and de Búrca G (eds), *The evolution of EU law* (Oxford University Press 2011)

—, 'The Financial Crisis, the European Union Institutional Order, and Constitutional Responsibility' (2015) 22 Indiana Journal of Global Legal Studies 243

Craig P and de Búrca G, *EU Law: Text, Cases, and Materials* (6th edn, Oxford University Press 2015)

Cresson E, *Learning for active citizenship: a significant challenge in building a Europe of knowledge. Foreword* (1998)

Crick B, 'The Presuppositions of Citizenship Education' (1999) 33 Journal of Philosophy of Education 337

—, 'Education for Citizenship: the Citizenship Order' (2002) 55 Parliamentary Affairs 488

—, 'Citizenship: the political and the democratic' (2007) 55 British Journal of Educational Studies 235

Curren R, 'A neo-Aristotelian account of education, justice, and the human good' (2013) 11 Theory and Research in Education 231

Curtice J, 'Why Leave Won the UK's EU Referendum' (2017) 55 JCMS 19

Curtin D, *Executive Power of the European Union. Law, Practices, and the Living Constitution* (Oxford University Press 2009)

Curtin D, Mair P and Papadopoulos Y (eds), *Accountability and European Governance* (West European politics Series, Routledge 2010)

Curtin D and Meijer AJ, 'Does transparency strengthen legitimacy?' (2006) 11 Information Polity 109

Curtin D and Mendes J, 'Transparence et participation: des principes démocratiques pour l'administration de l'Union Européenne' (2011) 137 Revue Française d'Administration Publique 101

Cuypers SE and Haji I, 'Education for Critical Thinking: Can it be non-indoctrinative?' (2006) 38 Educational Philosophy and Theory 723

da Cruz Vilaça JL and others (eds), *The internal market and the digital economy*, vol 1 (XXVIII FIDE Congress Lisbon/Estoril (23–26 May 2018), Almedina 2018)

Dacheux É, 'La communication publique de l'Union européenne ne rapproche pas l'Europe des citoyens' (2017) 77 Hermès, La Revue 45

Dahl RA, *Democracy and its critics* (Yale University Press 1989)

—–, 'Justifying democracy' (1998) 35 Society 386

—–, *On democracy* (first edn 1998, Yale University 2000)

Dalessio TO, *Socializing Europe – Solidifying EU Citizenship* (Wolf Legal Publishers 2013)

Damay L and Mercenier H, 'Free movement and EU citizenship: a virtuous circle?' (2016) 23 Journal of European Public Policy 1139

Davies G, *Nationality discrimination in the European internal market* (European Monographs 44, Kluwer Law International 2003)

—–, 'The humiliation of the state as a constitutional tactic' in Amtenbrink F and van den Berg PAJ (eds), *The Constitutional Integrity of the European Union* (Asser Press 2010)

—–, 'The entirely conventional supremacy of Union citizenship and rights' in Shaw J (ed), *Has the European Court of Justice Challenged the Member State Sovereignty in Nationality Law?* (EUI Robert Schuman Centre for Advanced Studies Paper 62, 2011)

—–, 'Social Legitimacy and Purposive Power: The End, the Means and the Consent of the People' in Kochenov D, de Búrca G and A Williams (eds), *Europe's Justice Deficit?* (Hart 2015)

Davies I, 'Political Literacy' in Arthur J, Davies I and Hahn C (eds), *The SAGE Handbook of Education for Citizenship and Democracy* (Sage 2008)

Davies I and others, 'Young People's Community Engagement: What Does Research-Based and Other Literature Tell us About Young People's Perspectives and the Impact of Schools' Contributions?' (2013) 61 British Journal of Educational Studies 1

Davies M and Barnett R (eds), *The Palgrave handbook of critical thinking in higher education* (Palgrave Macmillan 2015)

Davis RW, 'Citizenship of the Union...rights for all?' (2002) 27 ELRev 121

Dawson M, 'Integration through Soft Law: No Competence Needed? Juridical and Bio-Power in the Realm of Soft Law' in Garben S and Govaere I (eds), *The Division of Competences between the EU and the Member States: Reflections on the Past, the Present and the Future* (Hart 2017

de Boer N, 'Addressing rights divergences under the Charter: Melloni' (2013) 50 CMLRev 1083

de Búrca G, 'The Drafting of the EU Charter of Fundamental Rights' (2001) 26 ELRev 126

—–, 'Developing Democracy beyond the State' (2007–2008) 46 Columbia Journal of Transnational Law 221

De Groof J, Gracienne L and Singh K, *The right to education and rights in education* (Wolf Legal Publishers 2006)

De Groof S and others, *Burgerschap bij 14-jarigen. Vlaanderen in internationaal perspectief. Vlaams eindrapport van de International civic and citizenship education study* (Vlaams Ministerie van Onderwijs en Vorming, 2010)

de Lange R, 'Paradoxes of European Citizenship' in Fitzpatrick P (ed), *Nationalism, racism and the rule of law* (Aldershot 1995)

De Schutter O, 'Europe in Search of its Civil Society' (2002) 8 ELJ 198

—–, 'The two Europes of human rights: the emerging division of tasks between the Council of Europe and the European Union in promoting human rights in Europe' (2008) 14 Columbia Journal of European Law 509

—–, *International Human Rights Law* (2nd edn, Cambridge University Press 2014)

De Vel G, *The Committee of Ministers of the Council of Europe* (CoE 1995)

De Vel G and Markert T, 'Importance and Weaknesses of the Council of Europe Conventions and of the Recommendations addressed by the Committee of Ministers to Member States' in Haller B, Krüger HC and Petzold H (eds), *Law in Greater Europe: Towards a Common Legal Area* (Kluwer Law International 2000)

de Vries S, 'Grondrechten binnen de Europese interne markt: een tragikomisch conflict tussen waarden in de "Domus Europaea"' (2016) 64 SEW – Tijdschrift voor Europees en economisch Recht 99

de Witte B (ed) *European Community Law of Education* (Schriftenreihe Europäisches Recht 133, Nomos 1989)

—–, 'Community Law and National Constitutional Values' (1991) 18 Legal Issues of Economic Integration 1

—–, 'Institutional Principles: A Special Category of General Principles of EC Law' in Bernitz U and Nergelius J (eds), *General Principles of European Community Law* (Kluwer Law International 2000)

—–, 'Non-market values in Internal Market Legislation' in Nic Schuibhne N (ed), *Regulating the Internal Market* (Edward Elgar 2006)

—–, 'The Continuous Significance of *Van Gend en Loos*' in Poiares Maduro M and Azoulai L (eds), *The Past and Future of EU Law: The Classics of EU Law Revisited on the 50th Anniversary of the Rome Treaty* (Hart 2010)

—–, 'Direct Effect, Supremacy, and the Nature of the Legal Order' in De Búrca G and Craig P (eds), *The Evolution of EU Law* (Oxford University Press 2011)

—–, 'Democratic Adjudication in Europe: How Can the European Court of Justice Be Responsive to the Citizens?' in Dougan M, Shuibhne NN and Spaventa E (eds), *Empowerment and Disempowerment of the European Citizen* (Hart 2012)

de Witte F, 'Union Citizenship and Constrained Democracy' in De Visser M and van der Mei AP (eds), *The Treaty on European Union 1993–2013: Reflections from Maastricht* (Intersentia 2013)

—–, *Justice in the EU: The Emergence of Transnational Solidarity* (Oxford Studies in European Law, 2015)

de Witte F, Bauböck R and Shaw J (eds), *Freedom of movement under attack: Is it worth defending as the core of EU citizenship?* (EUI Working Paper RSCAS 2016/69, 2016)

Dehousse F, *The European Citizens' Initiative: Next Big Thing of New False Good Idea?* (Egmont Paper 59, Academia Press 2013)

Delanty G, 'Citizenship as a learning process: disciplinary citizenship versus cultural citizenship' (2003) 22 International Journal of Lifelong Education 597

Delmas-Marty M, *Ordering Pluralism. A Conceptual Framework for Understanding the Transnational Legal World* (Hart 2009)

Delors J, 'Education: The Necessary Utopia' in *Learning: the Treasure Within, Report to Unesco of the International Commission on Education for the Twenty-first Century* (Unesco 1996)

Desomer M, *Reform of the Legal Instruments of the European Union* (Proefschrift, KUL 2008)

Dewey J, *Democracy and education: an introduction to the philosophy of education* (Macmillan 1916)

Diamandouros PN (ed) *The European Ombudsman: Origins, Establishment, Evolution* (Office for Official Publications of the European Communities 2005)

Domurath I, 'The Three Dimensions of Solidarity in the EU Legal Order: Limits of the Judicial and Legal Approach' (2012) 35 Journal of European Integration 459

Dougan M, 'Fees, grants, loans and dole cheques: Who covers the costs of migrant education within the EU?' (2005) 42 CMLRev 943

—–, 'The Constitutional Dimension to the Case Law on Union Citizenship' (2006) 31 ELRev 613

—–, 'Cross-border educational mobility and the exportation of student financial assistance' (2008) 33 ELRev 1

—–, 'What are we to make of the citizens' initiative?' (2011) 48 CMLRev 1807

Dougan M, Nic Shuibhne N and Spaventa E (eds), *Empowerment and disempowerment of the European citizen* (Hart 2012)

Dougan M and Spaventa E, '"Wish you weren't here..." New Models of Social Solidarity in the European Union' in Dougan M and Spaventa E (eds), *Social welfare and EU law* (Hart 2005)

Duda D, 'Case Teaching in der politikwissenschaftlichen Lehre' (2017) 27 Journal of Political Science 259

Dufeu S, *Valeurs et constitutions européennes. Une identité politique entre deux mythes: universalité et frontière* (Questions contemporaines, L'Harmattan 2005)

Dunn K, 'Left-Right identification and education in Europe: A contingent relationship' (2011) 9 Comparative European Politics 292

Dupré C, 'Article 1: Human Dignity' in Peers S and others (eds), *The EU Charter of Fundamental Rights: a Commentary* (Hart 2014)

—–, 'Re-Thinking European Constitutionalism: Dignity, Humanism, Democracy' in *The Age of Dignity: Human Rights and Constitutionalism in Europe* (Hart 2015)

Durner W, 'Streitbare Demokratie' (2003) 128 Archiv des oeffentlichen Rechts 340

Durr K, Spajic-Vrkaš V and Ferreira Martins I, *Strategies of Learning Democratic Citizenship* (CoE 2000)

Dusi P, Steinbach M and Messetti G, 'Citizenship Education in Multicultural Society: Teachers' Practices' (2012) 69 Procedia – Social and Behavioral Sciences 1410

Dworkin R, 'Hard Cases' (1975) 88 Harvard Law Review 1057

—–, *Law's Empire* (Harvard University Press 1987)

—–, *A matter of principle* (repr. edn, Clarendon 1992)

Dziuban CD and others, 'Developing the European Citizen: Investing in Europe's Democratic Future' (2007) 21 International Journal of Social Education 177

Edelstein W, 'Education for Democracy: reasons and strategies' (2011) 46 European Journal of Education 127

Editorial [JS], 'Is Opinion 2/13 Obsolescent?' (2017) 42 ELRev 449

Editorial Comments, 'Safeguarding EU values in the Member States – Is something finally happening?' (2015) 52 CMLRev 619

Editorial Comments, 'EU law as a way of life' (2017) 61 CMLRev 357

Edward D and Lane R, *Edward and Lane on European Union Law* (Edward Elgar 2013)

Eeckhout P, 'Human Rights and the Autonomy of EU Law: Pluralism or Integration?' (2013) 66 Current Legal Problems 169

Eeckhout P and Frantziou E, 'Brexit and Article 50: a constitutionalist reading' (2017) 54 CMLRev 695

Eichner D, 'Fallanalysen im Sachunterricht als Möglichkeit des Demokratie-Lernens' in Richter D (ed), *Politische Bildung von Anfang an: Demokratie-Lernen in der Grundschule* (Schriftenreihe Band 570, Bundeszentrale für politische Bildung 2007)

Eis A, 'Concepts and Perceptions of Democracy and Governance beyond the Nation State: Qualitative Research in Education for European Citizenship' (2010) 9 Journal of Social Science Education 35

Eleftheriadis P, 'Begging the Constitutional Question' (1998) 36 JCMS 255

——, 'The Content of European Citizenship' (2014) 15 German Law Journal 777

Ellis E and Watson P, *EU Anti-Discrimination Law* (2 edn, Oxford University Press 2012)

Emler N and Frazer E, 'Politics: the education effect' (1999) 25 Oxford Review Of Education 251

Ertl H, 'European Union policies in education and training: the Lisbon agenda as a turning point?' (2006) 42 Comparative education 5

Ertl H and Phillips D, 'Standardization in EU education and training policy: findings from a European research network' (2006) 42 Comparative Education 77

Estella A, *The EU principle of subsidiarity and its critique* (2005 edn, Oxford University Press 2002)

Evans D, Grassler H and Pouwels J (eds), *Human Rights and Values Education in Europe: Research in educational law, curricula and textbooks* (Fillibach Verlag 1997)

Evers H-U, *Die Befugnis des Staates zur Festlegung von Erziehungszielen in der pluralistischen Gesellschaft* (Duncker und Humblot 1979)

Feith D (ed) *Teaching America: the Case for Civic Education* (Rowman & Littlefield Education 2011)

Féron E, 'Citizenship Education in France' in Georgi VB (ed), *The Making of Citizens in Europe: New Perspectives on Citizenship Education* (Schriftenreihe Band 666, Bundeszentrale für politische Bildung 2008)

Ferrari A, 'The problem of civic cohesion and the role of the state school in France and Italy: historical, religious and secular comparisons' (2006) 35 Journal of Moral Education 533

Ferrari-Breeur C, 'L'éducation et la formation professionnelle comme instruments de la citoyenneté européenne' in Philip C and Soldatos P (eds), *La citoyenneté européenne* (Collection études européennes, Chaire Jean Monnet 2000)

Ferreira da Cunha P, *Political Ethics and European Constitution* (Springer 2015)

Ferreira P, Albanesi C and Menezes I, 'European Identity and Citizenship in Textbooks/Educational Media' (2018) 17 Journal of Social Science Education 2

Ferrera M and Bauböck R (eds), *Should EU Citizenship Be Duty-Free?* (EUI Working Paper RSCAS 2017/60, 2017)

Field J, *European Dimensions, Education, Training and the European Union* (Jessica Kingsley 1998)

Finkel SE, 'Can democracy be taught?' (2003) 14 Journal of Democracy 137

Fischman GE and Haas E, 'Beyond Idealized Citizenship Education: Embodied Cognition, Metaphors, and Democracy' (2012) 36 Review Of Research In Education 169

Follesdal A and Hix S, 'Why there is a democratic deficit in the EU: A response to Majone and Moravcsik' (2006) 44 JCMS 533

Forrester K, 'Leaving the academic towers: the Council of Europe and the Education for Democratic Citizenship Project' (2003) 22 International Journal of Lifelong Education 221

Frankovits A, *The Human Rights based approach and the United Nations system* (2006)

Frazier C, *L'éducation et la Communauté européenne* (CNRS 1995)

Freire S and others, 'Identity Construction through Schooling: listening to students' voices' (2009) 8 EERJ 80

Frevert U, 'How to become a Good European Citizen: Present Challenges and Past Experiences' in Georgi VB (ed), *The Making of Citizens in Europe: New Perspectives on Citizenship Education* (Schriftenreihe Band 666, Bundeszentrale für politische Bildung 2008)

Freyberg-Inan A, 'Equity as the missing link: the values of the European Union' (2010) 10 Romanian Journal of European Affairs 5

Friedman B and Solow S, 'The Federal Right to an Adequate Education' (2013) 81 George Washington Law Review 92

Füssel H-P, 'Cooperative Federalism in Education: About the Work of the Conference Education Ministers and the Joint Federal and Länder Commission on Education Planning and Research Promotion' in De Groof J and others (eds), *Power Sharing in Education: Dilemmas and Implications for Schools* (Acco 1998)

Galichet F, 'La citoyenneté comme pédagogie: réflexions sur l'éducation à la citoyenneté' (2002) 28 Revue des sciences de l'éducation 105

Garben S, 'The Bologna Process: From a European Law Perspective' (2010) 16 ELJ 186

—, 'Case C-73/08, Nicolas Bressol and Others, Céline Chaverot and Others v. Gouvernement de la Communaute française, Judgment of the Court (Grand Chamber) of 13 April 2010' (2010) 47 CMLRev 1493

—, *EU Higher education law. The Bologna Process and harmonization by stealth* (European Monographs 76, Kluwer Law 2011)

—, 'The Case to Correct Some of Maastricht's Mistakes: A Critical Assessment of Article 165 TFEU on Education and Suggestions for Reform' in De Visser M and van der Mei AP (eds), *The Treaty on European Union 1993–2013: Reflections from Maastricht* (Intersentia 2013)

—, 'Confronting the Competence Conundrum: Democratising the European Union through an Expansion of its Legislative Powers' (2015) 35 Oxford Journal of Legal Studies 55

—, 'Competence Creep Revisited' (2017) 55 JCMS 1

—, 'Restating the Problem of Competence Creep, Tackling Harmonisation by Stealth and Reinstating the Legislator' in S Garben and I Govaere (eds), *The Division of Competences between the EU and the Member States : Reflections on the Past, the Present and the Future* (Hart 2017)

Gardner A, 'Preparing students for democratic participation: why teacher curricular speech should sometimes be protected by the First Amendment' (2008) 73 Missouri Law Review 213

Gentner D and Smith LA, 'Analogical Learning and Reasoning' in Reisberg D (ed), *The Oxford Handbook of Cognitive Psychology* (Oxford Handbooks Online, Oxford University Press 2013)

Gerkrath J, *L'émergence d'un droit constitutionnel pour l'Europe* (Ed de l'Université de Bruxelles 1997)

Gilliams HM, 'Van "Gravier" tot "Erasmus": over de bijdrage van het Hof van Justitie tot de uitbouw van een Europees onderwijsbeleid' [1989–90] Rechtskundig weekblad 494

Glas LR, 'The European Court of Human Rights' use of non-binding and standard-setting Council of Europe documents' (2017) 17 Human Rights Law Review 97

Glenn CL and De Groof J, *Balancing Freedom, Autonomy and Accountability in Education*, vol 1 (Wolf Legal Publishers 2005)

Goleman D, *Emotional intelligence* (Bantam Books 1997)

Golich VL, 'The ABCs of Case Teaching' (2000) 1 International Studies Perspectives 11

Gollob R and Krapf P, *Exploring Children's Rights: Nine short projects for primary level* (EDC/HRE vol V, CoE 2007)

Gollob R and Krapf P (eds), *Living in democracy: EDC/HRE lesson plans for lower secondary level* (EDC/HRE vol III, CoE 2008)

—, *Teaching Democracy: A collection of models for democratic citizenship and human rights education* (EDC/HRE vol VI, CoE 2009)

Gollob R, Krapf P and Weidinger W (eds), *Taking Part in Democracy: Lesson plans for upper secondary level on democratic citizenship and human rights education* (EDC/HRE vol IV, CoE 2010)

Gollob R, Krapf P and Weidinger W (eds), *Educating for democracy: Background materials on democratic citizenship and human rights education for teachers* (EDC/HRE vol I, CoE 2011)

Gontard M, *L'oeuvre scolaire de la Troisième République : l'enseignement primaire en France de 1876 à 1914* (2nd edn, CRDP 1976)

Gordon RM, 'Freedom of expression and values inculcation in the public school curriculum' (1984) 13 The Journal of Law and Education 523

Gori G, *Towards an EU Right to Education* (European Monographs 28, Kluwer Law International 2001)

—, 'Article 14: Right to Education' in Peers S and others (eds), *The EU Charter of Fundamental Rights: a Commentary* (Hart 2014)

Gormley L, 'Brexit – Never Mind the Whys and Wherefores? Fog in the Channel, Continent Cut Off!' (2017) 40 Fordham International Law Journal 1175

—, 'Keeping EU Citizens out is wrong' (2013) 21 Journal de droit européen 316

Goudappel F, *The Effects of EU Citizenship* (TMC Asser Press 2010)

Grabenwarter C, 'National Constitutional Law Relating to the European Union' in von Bogdandy A and Bast J (eds), *Principles of European Constitutional Law* (2nd edn, Hart Beck Nomos 2010)

—, *European Convention on Human Rights: Commentary* (Beck Hart Nomos 2014)

Grammes T, 'Kontroversität' in Sander W (ed), *Handbuch politische Bildung* (Reihe Politik und Bildung 32, Bundeszentrale für politische Bildung 2005)

—, 'Exemplarisches Lernen' in Sander W (ed), *Handbuch politische Bildung* (Reihe Politik und Bildung 32, Bundeszentrale für politische Bildung 2005)

—, 'Different Cultures in Education for Democracy and Citizenship' (2012) 11 Journal of Social Science Education 3

Granat K, 'The Subsidiarity Principle in the EU Treaties' in *The Principle of Subsidiarity and its Enforcement in the EU Legal Order: The Role of National Parliaments in the Early Warning System* (Hart 2018)

Greer SL and Sokol T, 'Rules for Rights: European Law, Health Care and Social Citizenship' (2014) 20 ELJ 66

Grevet R, 'La réforme des études en France au siècle des Lumières' (1997) 297 Revue Historique 85

—, *L'avènement de l'école contemporaine en France (1789–1835): laïcisation et confessionnalisation de la culture scolaire* (Presses universitaires du Septentrion 2001)

Grimm D, 'Does Europe Need a Constitution?' (1995) 1 ELJ 282

—, 'Integration by constitution' (2005) 3 International Journal of Constitutional Law 193

—, 'The Democratic Costs of Constitutionalisation: The European Case' (2015) 21 ELJ 460

—, 'The Power of Restraint in the European Union' in Van Middelaar L and Van Parijs P (eds), *After the Storm: How to Save Democracy in Europe* (Lannoo 2015)

—, *The Constitution of European Democracy* (Oxford University Press 2017)

Grimonprez K, 'The European dimension in citizenship education: unused potential of article 165 TFEU' (2014) 39 ELRev 3

—, 'Conflicting ideas of Europe: the role of values in citizenship education' (European Conference NECE, Networking European Citizenship Education, '1914–2014: Lessons from History? Citizenship Education and Conflict Management', Vienna, 16–18 October 2014)

—, 'Beyond Rhetoric: Education for Democratic Citizenship in the European Union' in Garben S, Govaere I and Nemitz P (eds), *Critical Reflections on Constitutional Democracy in the European Union* (Hart 2019)

—, 'EU-burgerschap en vorming voor democratie: ijkpunten voor kwaliteitsvol onderwijs' (2019–2020) 1-2 Tijdschrift voor Onderwijsrecht en Onderwijsbeleid 5

Guidetti B, 'Intercultural education for citizenship in complex societies. Summary of the International Conference on Intercultural Education for citizenship' (2009) 4 Ricerche di Pedagogia e Didattica 1

Guild E and Peers S, *The EU Citizenship Directive: A Commentary* (Oxford University Press 2014)

Guiraudon V, 'Equality in the making: implementing European non-discrimination law' (2009) 13 Citizenship Studies 527

Guliyeva G, 'Education, Languages and Linguistic Minorities in the EU: Challenges and Perspectives' (2013) 19 ELJ 219

Gundel J, 'Der Verlust der bürgerlichen Ehrenrechte als Eingriff in die Grundrechtecharta – Neues zur Reichweite des EU-Grundrechtsschutzes gegenüber den Mitgliedstaaten und zur lex-mitior-Garantie' (2016) 51 Europarecht 176

Haav K, 'Civic Education in Estonia: Democratic or Authoritarian' (2008) 7 Journal of Social Science Education 121

Häberle P, *Verfassungslehre als Kulturwissenschaft* (2nd edn, Duncker und Humblot 1998)

Habermas J, 'Why Europe needs a constitution' (2001) New Left Review 5

—, *Zur Verfassung Europas. Ein Essay* (Suhrkamp 2011)

—, 'The Crisis of the European Union in the Light of a Constitutionalization of International Law' (2012) 23 European Journal Of International Law 335

—, 'Democracy, Solidarity and the European Crisis' (KU Leuven, 26 April 2013)

Hahn CL, 'Citizenship Education: an empirical study of policy, practices and outcomes' (1999) 25 Oxford Review Of Education 231

—, 'Teachers' perceptions of education for democratic citizenship in schools with transnational youth: A comparative study in the UK and Denmark' (2015) 10 Research in Comparative and International Education 95

Hailbronner K, 'Union Citizenship and Access to Social Benefits' (2015) 42 CMLRev 1245

Hailbronner K and Thym D, 'Gerardo Ruiz Zambrano v. Office national de l'emploi (Onem)' (2011) 48 CMLRev 1253

Halász G and Michel A, 'Key Competences in Europe: interpretation, policy formulation and implementation' (2011) 46 European Journal of Education 289

Halberstam D, 'The bride of Messina: constitutionalism and democracy in Europe' (2005) 30 ELRev 775

Haller B, Krüger H and Petzold H (eds), *Law in Greater Europe: Towards a Common Legal Area* (Kluwer Law International 2000)

Haller M, *European Integration as an Elite Project: the Failure of a Dream?* (Routledge 2008)

Hallinan MT (ed) *Handbook of the sociology of education* (Springer 2006)

Halstead JM and Pike MA, *Citizenship and Moral Education: Values in Action* (Routledge 2006)

Harden I, 'When Europeans Complain: The Work of the European Ombudsman' (2000) 3 Cambridge Yearbook of European Legal Studies 199

—, 'Article 43: European Ombudsman' in Peers S and others (eds), *The EU Charter of Fundamental Rights: a Commentary* (Hart 2014)

Hardy RJ, Rackaway C and Sonnier LE, 'In the Supreme Court Justices Shoes: Critical Thinking Through the Use of Hypothetical Case Law Analyses and Interactive Simulations' (2005) 38 Political Science and Politics 411

Harlow C and Rawlings R, 'Promoting Accountability in Multilevel Governance: A Network Approach' (2007) 13 ELJ 542

Hart H, *The Concept of Law* (2nd edn, Oxford University Press 1994)

Hartley M and Huddleston T, *School-community-university partnerships for a sustainable democracy: Education for Democratic Citizenship in Europe and the United States of America* (CoE 2010)

Haubenreich J, 'Education and the Constitution' (2012) 87 Peabody Journal of Education 436

Havel V, *Summer Meditations* (Wilson P tr, Vintage Books 1992)

Heater D, 'The history of citizenship education: a comparative outline' (2002) 55 Parliamentary Affairs (UK) 457

—, *Citizenship: the Civic Ideal in World History, Politics and Education* (3rd edn, Manchester University Press 2004)

—, *A Brief History of Citizenship* (New York University Press 2004)

—, *A history of education for citizenship* (Routledge Falmer 2004)

Hedtke R and Zimenkova T (eds), *Education for Civic and Political Participation: A Critical Approach* (Routledge 2013)

Hedtke R, Zimenkova T and Hippe T, 'A Trinity of Transformation, Europeanisation, and Democratisation? Current Research on Citizenship Education in Europe' (2007) 6 Journal of Social Science Education 5

Heijltjes A, van Gog T and Paas F, 'Improving students' critical thinking: Empirical support for explicit instructions combined with practice' (2014) 28 Applied Cognitive Psychology 518

Helskog GH, *Democracy and diversity in education. Report of the International conference at Buskerud University College (Norway 12–13 March 2013)*

Hendricks JS and Howerton DM, 'Teaching values, teaching stereotypes: sex education and indoctrination in public schools' (2011) 13 University of Pennsylvania Journal of Constitutional Law 587

Herdegen M, 'General Principles of EU Law: The Methodological Challenge' in Bernitz U and Nergelius J (eds), *General Principles of European Community Law* (European Monographs 25, Kluwer 2000)

Herlin-Karnell E, 'Is the Citizen Driving the EU's Criminal Law Agenda?' in Dougan M, Shuibhne NN and Spaventa E (eds), *Empowerment and Disempowerment of the European Citizen* (Hart 2012)

Hess D and Avery PG, 'Discussion of Controversial Issues as a Form and Goal of Democratic Education' in Arthur J, Davies I and Hahn C (eds), *The SAGE Handbook of Education for Citizenship and Democracy* (Sage 2008)

Hess DE, *Controversy in the Classroom: The Democratic Power of Discussion* (Routledge 2009)

—, 'Discussions that drive democracy' (2011) 69 Educational Leadership 69

—, *Courting Democracy: Teaching about Constitutions, Cases, and Courts* (Routledge 2016)

Hesselberger D, *Das Grundgesetz: Kommentar für die politische Bildung* (13 edn, Bundeszentrale für politische Bildung 2003)

Heuschling L, 'Wissenschaft vom Verfassungsrecht: Frankreich' in von Bogdandy A, Cruz Villalón P and Huber PM (eds), *Handbuch Ius Publicum Europaeum*, vol II Offene Staatlichkeit- Wissenschaft vom Verfassungsrecht (CF Müller Verlag 2007)

Heuschling L and Hummel J, 'Le libéralisme du Vormärz : la figure du « professeur politique »' (2006) 24 Revue Française d'Histoire des Idées Politiques 227

Heydt JM, *Education for Democratic Citizenship: Words and Actions* (CoE 2001)

Hilson C, 'Rights and principles in EU law: a distinction without foundation?' (2008) 15 Maastricht journal of European and comparative law 193

Hobsbawm E and Ranger T (eds), *The Invention of Tradition* (first published 1983, Cambridge University Press 1992)

Hochbaum I, 'The Federal Structure of Member States as a Limit to Common Educational Policy: The Case of Germany' in De Witte B (ed), *European Community Law of Education* (Nomos 1989)

Hodgson D, 'The international human right to education and education concerning human rights' (1996) 4 The International Journal of Children's Rights 237

Hodgson N, 'Educational research, governmentality and the construction of the cosmopolitan citizen' (2009) 4 Ethics and Education 177

Hodson D, *The Human Right to Education* (Ashgate/Dartmouth 1998)

Hoeksma J, *From Common Market to Common Democracy: A Theory of Democratic Integration* (Wolf Legal Publishers 2016)

Hoffmann-Riem W, 'The Venice Commission of the Council of Europe – Standards and Impact' (2014) 25 European Journal of International Law 579

Hofmann HCH and Mihaescu BC, 'The Relation between the Charter's Fundamental Rights and the Unwritten General Principles of EU Law: Good Administration as the Test Case' (2013) 9 European Constitutional Law Review 73

Hofmann HCH, Rowe GC and Türk AH, *Administrative law and policy of the European Union* (Oxford University Press 2011)

Hoogenboom A, 'In Search of a Rationale for the EU Citizenship Jurisprudence' (2015) 35 Oxford Journal of Legal Studies 301

Hooghe M and others, *Jongeren, politiek en burgerschap: politieke socialisatie bij Belgische jongeren* (Acco 2012)

Hoskins B, 'Brexit and its implications for Citizenship Education across Europe' 2 August 2016 <ec.europa.eu/epale/en/blog/brexit-and-its-implications-citizenship-education-across-europe>

Hoskins B and others, *Contextual Analysis Report: Participatory Citizenship in the European Union (Report 1)* (2012)

Hoskins B and Deakin Crick R, *Learning to Learn and Civic Competences: different currencies or two sides of the same coin?* (European Commission, JRC, CRELL, 2008)

Hoskins B, D'Hombres B and Campbell J, 'Does Formal Education Have an Impact on Active Citizenship Behaviour?' (2008) 7 EERJ 386

Hoskins B and others, *Measuring active citizenship in Europe* (CRELL Research Paper 4, European Communities 2006)

Hoskins B and Kerr D, *Final Study Summary and Policy Recommendations: Participatory Citizenship in the European Union (Report 4)* (2012)

Hoskins B and others, *Analytic Report: Participatory Citizenship in the European Union (Report 2)* (2012)

Hoskins B and Mascherini M, 'Measuring Active Citizenship through the Development of a Composite Indicator' (2009) 90 Social Indicators Research 459

Hoskins B, Saisana M and Harrison Villalba C, *The 2011 Civic Competence Composite Indicator (CCCI-2): Measuring Young People's Civic Competence across Europe based on the IEA International Citizenship and Civic Education study* (Publications Office of the European Union, 2012)

Houellebecq M, *Submission: A Novel* (Flammarion 2015)

Huddleston T, *Teaching about controversial issues: guidance for schools* (Citizenship Foundation 2003)

—— (ed) *Tool on Teacher Training for Education for Democratic Citizenship and Human rights Education* (revised, CoE 2007)

Huddleston T and Kerr D, *Managing controversy: developing a strategy for handling controversy and teaching controversial issues in schools* (CoE 2017)

Hufer K-P and Richter D (eds), *Politische Bildung als Profession: Verständnisse und Forschungen* (Schriftenreihe Band 1355, Bundeszentrale für politische Bildung 2013)

Hüfner K, 'The Human Rights Approach to Education in International Organisations' (2011) 46 European Journal of Education 117

Hüller T, 'Out of time? The democratic limits of EU demoicracy' (2015) 22 Journal of European Public Policy 1

Huntsinger JR and Schnall S, 'Emotion–Cognition Interactions' in Reisberg D (ed), *The Oxford Handbook of Cognitive Psychology* (Oxford Handbooks Online, Oxford University Press 2013)

Huyghe S, 'Construire une citoyenneté européenne' in Boniface P (ed), *Quelles valeurs pour l'Union européenne?* (Puf 2004)

Huyse L, *De democratie voorbij* (Van Halewijck 2014)

Ichilov O (ed), *Citizenship and Citizenship Education in a Changing World* (Woburn Press 1998)

Iliopoulou-Penot A, 'The Transnational Character of Union Citizenship' in Dougan M, Shuibhne NN and Spaventa E (eds), *Empowerment and Disempowerment of the European Citizen* (Hart 2012)

——, 'Citoyenneté de l'Union, mobilité et intégration dans l'espace européen' (2014) 134 Revue de l'OFCE 29

Isin EF, 'Citizens without Nations' 30 Environment and Planning D: Society and Space 450

Isin EF and Turner BS, *Handbook of Citizenship Studies* (Sage 2002)

Jääskinen N, 'Europeanisation of National Law: A Legal-theoretical Analysis' (2015) 40 ELRev 667

Jackson L, '"The Best Education Ever": Trumpism, Brexit, and new social learning' (2018) 50 Educational Philosophy and Theory 441

Jackson VC, 'Paradigms of public law: transnational constitutional values and democratic challenges' (2011) 8 International journal of constitutional law 517

Janne H, *For a Community policy on education* (Report for the European Commission, Bull EC Supp 10–73, 1973)

Janssen E, *Faith in Public Debate: On Freedom of Expression, Hate Speech and Religion in France & the Netherlands* (Intersentia 2015)

Jarass HD and Pieroth B, *Grundgesetz für die Bundesrepublik Deutschland: Kommentar* (11th edn, Beck 2011)

Jeliazkova M and Zimenkova T, 'Beyond description: Civic and political education in Europe – dialogue and comparison' (2017) 16 Journal of Social Science Education 2

Jessurun d'Oliveira HU, 'Union Citizenship: Pie in the Sky?' in Rosas A and Antola E (eds), *A citizens' Europe? In search of a new order* (Sage 1995)

Johnson L and Morris P, 'Critical citizenship education in England and France: a comparative analysis' (2012) 48 Comparative Education 283

Joris T and Vandenberghe J, 'The Council of Europe and the European Union: Natural Partners or Uneasy Bedfellows' (2008–2009) 15 Columbia Journal of European Law 1

Jung H, 'Die Empfehlungen des Ministerskomitees des Europarates: zugleich ein Beitrag zur europäischen Rechtsquellenlehre' in Bröhmer JR and Gerhard GR (eds), *Internationale Gemeinschaft und Menschenrechte: Festschrift für Georg Ress* (Carl Heymanns Verlag 2005)

Kamens DH, 'Education and Democracy: A Comparative Institutional Analysis' (1988) 61 Sociology of Education 114

Karatzia A, 'The European Citizens' Initiative in Practice: Legal Admissibility Concerns' (2015) 40 ELRev 509

Karatzia A, 'The European Citizens' Initiative and the EU institutional balance: On realism and the possibilities of affecting EU lawmaking' (2017) 54 CMLRev 177

Karpenschif MQM and Nourissat CQC, *Les grands arrêts de la jurisprudence de l'Union européenne* (PUF 2016)

Kavadias D and Dehertogh B, *Scholen en Burgerschapseducatie : de totstandkoming van de vraag tot ondersteuning binnen scholen* (Koning Boudewijnstichting 2010)

Keating A, 'Developing a European dimension to the sociology of education' (2006) 27 British Journal of Sociology of Education 269

—, 'Educating Europe's citizens: moving from national to post-national models of educating for European citizenship' (2009) 13 Citizenship Studies 135

—, *Education for Citizenship in Europe: European Policies, National Adaptations and Young People's Attitudes* (Palgrave Macmillan 2014)

—, 'Are cosmopolitan dispositions learned at home, at school, or through contact with others? Evidence from young people in Europe' (2016) 19 Journal of Youth Studies 338

Keating A, Benton T and Kerr D, 'Evaluating the impact of citizenship education in schools: What Works and What are we Measuring?' in Print M and Lange D (eds), *Schools, Curriculum and Civic Education for Building Democratic Citizens* (Series Civic and Political Education 2, Sense 2012)

Keating A, Ortloff DH and Philippou S, 'Citizenship Education Curricula: The Changes and Challenges Presented by Global and European Integration' (2009) 41 Journal of Curriculum Studies 145

Kelsen H, *Pure Theory of Law* (Knight tr, 2nd edn, University of California Press 1967)

Kennedy KJ, 'Global Trends in Civic and Citizenship Education: What are the Lessons for Nation States?' (2012) 2 Education Sciences 121

Kenney S, 'Using the master's tools to dismantle the master's house: can we harness the virtues of case teaching?' (2001) 20 Journal of policy analysis and management 346

Kerr D, 'Western Europe Regional Synthesis' in *All-European Study on Education for Democratic Citizenship Policies* (CoE 2004)

——, *Implementation of the Council of Europe Charter on Education for Democratic Citizenship and Human Rights Education: Final Report* (CoE Steering Committee for Educational Policy and Practice, 2012)

Kerr D and Keating A, 'Intercultural, citizenship and human rights education: the challenges of implementation for policy, practice and research' (2011) 53 Educational Research 119

Kerr D and Lopes J, *Implementation and outcomes of the 2005 European Year of Citizenship through Education: Learning and Living Democracy, Report DGIV/EDU/CAHCIT (2006)11*

Kerr D and others, *Vision versus Pragmatism: Citizenship in the Secondary School Curriculum in England. Citizenship Education Longitudinal Study* (5th Annual Report, National Foundation for Educational Research, 2007)

Kerr D and Losito B, *Tool on Key Issues for EDC Policies* (CoE 2004)

Kerr D and others, *Strategic support for decision makers: Policy tool for education for democratic citizenship and human rights* (CoE 2010)

Kerr D, McCarthy S and Smith A, 'Citizenship Education in England, Ireland and Northern Ireland' (2002) 37 European Journal of Education 179

Kerr D and others, *ICCS 2009 European Report: Civic knowledge, attitudes and engagement among lower-secondary students in 24 European countries* (International Association for the Evaluation of Educational Achievement IEA, 2010)

Khadar L and Shaw J, 'Article 39: Right to Vote and to Stand as a Candidate at Elections to the European Parliament' in Peers S and others (eds), *The EU Charter of Fundamental Rights: a Commentary* (Hart 2014)

Kiernan AK, 'Citizenship—the real democratic deficit of the European union? 1' (1997) 1 Citizenship Studies 323

Kiiver P, 'European Treaty reform and the national parliaments: towards a new assessment of Parliament-friendly Treaty provisions' in Wouters J, Verhey L and Kiiver P (eds), *European Constitutionalism beyond Lisbon* (Intersentia 2009)

—, 'Analysis and reflections: The early-warning system for the principle of subsidiarity: The national parliament as a Conseil d'Etat for Europe' (2011) 36 ELRev 98

Kilpatrick C, 'On the Rule of Law and Economic Emergency: The Degradation of Basic Legal Values in Europe's Bailouts" (2015) 35 Oxford Journal of Legal Studies 325' (2015) 35 Oxford Journal of Legal Studies 325

Kirchhof P, 'The European Union of States' in von Bogdandy A and Bast J (eds), *Principles of European Constitutional Law*, vol 8 (2nd edn, Hart Beck Nomos 2010)

Klabbers J, 'Straddling the Fence: The EU and International Law' in Chalmers D and Arnull A (eds), *The Oxford Handbook of European Union Law* (Oxford University Press 2015)

Kleibrink A, 'The EU as a Norm Entrepreneur: the case of lifelong learning' (2011) 46 European Journal of Education 70

Kluth W, 'AEUV Art 20' in Calliess C and Ruffert M (eds), *EUV/AEUV: das Verfassungsrecht der Europäischen Union mit Europäischer Grundrechtecharta : Kommentar* (5th edn, Beck 2016)

Kochenov D, 'Free movement and participation in the parliamentary elections in the member state of nationality: an ignored link?' (2009) 16 Maastricht Journal of European and Comparative Law 197

—, 'Ius tractum of many faces: European citizenship and the difficult relationship between status and rights' (2009) 15 Columbia Journal of European Law 169

—, 'Citizenship without Respect: The EU's Troubled Equality Ideal' (2010) 8 Jean Monnet Working Paper No 08/10

—, 'A Real European Citizenship: A New Jurisdiction Test; A Novel Chapter in the Development of the Union in Europe' (2011) 18 Columbia Journal of European Law 56

—, 'Two Sovereign States vs. a Human Being: CJEU as a Guardian of Arbitrariness in Citizenship Matters' in Shaw J (ed), *Has the European Court of Justice Challenged the Member State Sovereignty in Nationality Law?* (EUI Robert Schuman Centre for Advanced Studies Paper 62, 2011)

—, 'The essence of EU citizenship emerging from the last ten years of academic debate: beyond the cherry blossoms and the moon?' (2013) 62 International and Comparative Law Quarterly 97

—, 'The Citizenship Paradigm' (2013) 15 Cambridge Yearbook of European Legal Studies 197

—, 'The Right to Have What Rights? EU Citizenship in Need of Clarification' (2013) 19 ELJ 502

—, 'EU Citizenship without Duties' (2014) 20 ELJ 482

— (ed) *EU Citizenship and Federalism: The Role of Rights* (Cambridge University Press 2017)

—, 'On Tiles and Pillars: EU Citizenship as a Federal Denominator' in Kochenov D (ed), *EU Citizenship and Federalism: The Role of Rights* (Cambridge University Press 2017)

Kochenov D, de Búrca G and Williams A (eds), *Europe's Justice Deficit?* (Hart 2015)

Kochenov D and Plender R, 'EU Citizenship: From an Incipient Form to an Incipient Substance? The Discovery of the Treaty Text' (2012) 37 ELRev 369

Kohler-Koch B, 'Does participatory governance hold its promises?' in Kohler-Koch B and Larat F (eds), *Efficient and democratic governance in the European Union* (CONNEX Report Series No 9, Mannheim 2008)

Kohler-Koch B and Finke B, 'The Institutional Shaping of EU–Society Relations: A Contribution to Democracy via Participation?' (2007) 3 Journal of Civil Society 205

Kohler-Koch B and Rittberger B, 'The "Governance Turn" in EU studies' (2005) 44 JCMS 27

Kolb DA, *Experiential Learning: Experience as the Source of Learning and Development* (Prentice-Hall 1984)

Kolb M, *The European Union and the Council of Europe* (Palgrave Macmillan 2013)

Korostelina K, 'History Education and Social Identity' (2008) 8 Identity 25

Korostelina KV and Lässig S (eds), *History education and post-conflict reconciliation: reconsidering joint textbook projects* (Routledge 2013)

Kostadinova P, 'Improving the Transparency and Accountability of EU Institutions: The Impact of the Office of the European Ombudsman' (2015) 53 JCMS 1077

Kostakopoulou D, 'Ideas, Norms and European Citizenship: Explaining Institutional Change' (2005) 68 The Modern Law Review 233

—, 'European Union Citizenship: Writing the Future' (2007) 13 ELJ 623

—, 'When EU Citizens become Foreigners' (2014) 20 ELJ 447

—, 'Scala Civium: Citizenship Templates Post-Brexit and the European Union's Duty to Protect EU Citizens' (2018) 56 JCMS 1

Krastev I, 'Democracy of Rejection' in Van Middelaar L and Van Parijs P (eds), *After the Storm: How to Save Democracy in Europe* (Lannoo 2015)

Krek J and others, *Good Practices Report: Participatory Citizenship in the European Union (Report 3)* (2012)

Krek J and Sebart MK, 'Citizenship Education in Slovenia after the Formation of the Independent State' (2008) 9 Journal of Social Science Education 66

Kruger S, 'Learning Human Rights through Landmark Decisions of the European Court of Human Rights' (CoE Education Department, 2010)

Kuisma M, 'Rights or privileges? The challenge of globalization to the values of citizenship' (2008) 12 Citizenship Studies 613

Kunkler M and Stein T (eds), *Ernst-Wolfgang Böckenförde. Constitutional and political theory: selected writings* (Oxford University Press 2017)

La Chabeaussière AEX, *Catéchisme français, ou Principes de philosophie, de morale et de politique républicaine, à l'usage des écoles primaires* (L'An IV de la République, Chez Du Pont 1795)

Ladeur KH, '"We, the European People..."- Relâche?' (2008) 14 ELJ 147

Lamont R, 'Article 24: The Rights of the Child' in Peers S and others (eds), *The EU Charter of Fundamental Rights: a Commentary* (Hart 2014)

Lamy SL, 'Challenging Hegemonic Paradigms and Practices: Critical Thinking and Active Learning Strategies for International Relations' (2007) 40 APSC Political Science Politics 112

Lane R, 'New Community competences under the Maastricht Treaty' (1993) 30 CMLRev 939

Lange D, 'Citizenship Education in Germany' in Georgi VB (ed), *The Making of Citizens in Europe: New Perspectives on Citizenship Education* (Schriftenreihe Band 666, Bundeszentrale für politische Bildung 2008)

Lange D and Himmelmann G (eds), *Demokratiebewusstsein: Interdisziplinäre Annäherungen an ein zentrales Thema der Politischen Bildung* (VS Verlag für Sozialwissenschaften 2007)

Lansbergen A and Shaw J, 'National membership models in a multilevel Europe. Symposium: The Evolving Concept of Citizenship in Constitutional Law' (2010) 8 International Journal of Constitutional Law 50

Lantis JS, 'Ethics and Foreign Policy: Structured Debates for the International Studies Classroom' (2004) 5 International Studies Perspectives 17

Larik J, 'From specialty to a constitutional sense of purpose: on the changing role of the objectives of the European Union' (2014) 63 International and Comparative Law Quarterly 935

Lauglo J, 'Do more knowledgeable adolescents have more rationally based civic attitudes? Analysis of 38 countries' (2013) 33 Educational Psychology 262

Le Bon G, *The Crowd. A Study of the Popular Mind* (tr 'La psychologie des foules' 1895, Dover 2002)

Leino P and Petrov R, 'Between "Common Values" and Competing Universals—The Promotion of the EU's Common Values through the European Neighbourhood Policy' (2009) 15 ELJ 654

Lenaerts K, 'Constitutionalism and the Many Faces of Federalism' (1990) 38 The American Journal of Comparative Law 205

—, 'Education in European Community Law after "Maastricht"' (1994) 31 CMLRev 7

—, 'Subsidiarity and Community competence in the field of education' [1994–1995] Columbia Journal of European Law

—, 'De Europese Unie: doel of middel?' (1998) 21 Rechtskundig Weekblad 689

—, 'Interlocking Legal Orders in the European Union and Comparative Law' (2003) 52 International and Comparative Law Quarterly 873

—, '"In the Union we trust": trust-enhancing principles of Community law' (2004) 41 CMLRev 317

—, 'La constitutionnalisation de l'ordre juridique de l'Union européenne' in *Mélanges en l'honneur du Professeur Francis Delpérée: Itinéraires d'un constitutionnaliste* (Bruylant 2007)

—, 'A Community Based on a "Constitutional Charter": Community Law as a Complete and Coherent Constitutional System' in Maduro MP and Azoulai L (eds), *The Past and Future of EU Law: The Classics of EU Law Revisited on the 50th Anniversary of the Rome Treaty* (Hart 2010)

—, 'Federalism and the Rule of Law: Perspectives from the European Court of Justice' (2011) 33 Fordham International Law Journal 1338

—, '"Civis Europaeus Sum": From the Cross-border Link to the Status of Citizen of the Union' in Cardonnel P, Rosas A and Wahl N (eds), *Constitutionalising The EU Judicial System – Essays in Honour of Pernilla Lindh* (Hart 2012)

—, 'EU Federalism in 3-D' in Cloots E, De Baere G and Sottiaux S (eds), *Federalism in the European Union* (Hart 2012)

—, 'EU Citizenship and the Social Solidarity Link' in Foblets M-C, Hildebrandt M and Steenbergen J (eds), *Liber Amicorum René Foqué* (Larcier 2012)

—, 'In the Name of EU Citizenship' in Verbeke A and others (eds), *Confronting the Frontiers of Family and Succession Law – Liber Amicorum Walter Pintens* (Intersentia 2012)

—, 'The principle of democracy in the case law of the European Court of Justice' (2013) 62 International and Comparative Law Quarterly 271

—, 'The concept of EU citizenship in the case law of the European Court of Justice' (2013) 13 ERA Forum 569

—, 'EU Values and Constitutional Pluralism: The EU System of Fundamental Rights Protection' (2014) XXXIV Polish Yearbook of International Law 135

—, 'EU citizenship and the European Court of Justice's "stone-by-stone" approach' (2015) 1 International Comparative Jurisprudence 1

—, 'Some thoughts on the State of the European Union as a rights-based legal order' [2015] Il Diritto dell'Unione Europea 5

—, 'Linking EU Citizenship to Democracy' (2015) 11 Croatian Yearbook of European Law and Policy VII

—, 'Demoicracy, Constitutional Pluralism and the Court of Justice of the European Union' in Van Middelaar L and Van Parijs P (eds), *After the Storm: How to Save Democracy in Europe* (Lannoo 2015)

—, 'Cogito ergo civis europaeus sum: Discours à l'occasion de l'attribution du titre de docteur honoris causa de l'Université de Poitiers' (10 October 2016)

—, 'L'apport de la Cour de justice à la construction européenne' (2017) 25 Journal de droit européen 134

—, 'La vie après l'avis: Exploring the principle of mutual (yet not blind) trust' (2017) 54 CMLRev 805

—, 'Au droit citoyen: Discours à l'occasion de l'attribution du titre de docteur honoris causa de l'Université de Namur' (50 ans de la Faculté de Droit de Namur, 13 October 2017)

Lenaerts K and Desomer M, 'Bricks for a Constitutional Treaty of the European Union: Values, Objectives and Means' (2002) 27 ELRev 377

Lenaerts K and Gutiérrez-Fons, JA, 'The constitutional allocation of powers and general principles of EU law' (2010) 47 CMLRev 1629

—, 'The Role of General Principles of EU Law' in Arnull A and others (eds), *A Constitutional Order of States? Essays in EU Law in Honour of Alan Dashwood* (Hart 2011)

—, 'To Say What the Law of the EU Is: Methods of Interpretation and the European Court of Justice' (2014) 20 Columbia Journal of European Law 3

—, 'The Place of the Charter in the EU Constitutional Edifice' in Peers S and others (eds), *The EU Charter of Fundamental Rights: a Commentary* (Hart 2014)

—, 'Epilogue on EU Citizenship: Hopes and Fears' in Kochenov D (ed), *EU Citizenship and Federalism: The Role of Rights* (Cambridge University Press 2017)

Lenaerts K and Van Nuffel P, *European Union Law* (R Bray and N Cambien, eds 3rd edn, Sweet & Maxwell 2011)

—, *Europees Recht* (6 edn, Intersentia 2017)

Lenaerts K and Van Ypersele P, 'Le principe et subsidiarité et son contexte: étude de l'article 3B du Traité CE' [1994] Cahiers de droit européen 3

Lessig L, 'Against transparency. The perils of openness in government' (2009) 240 The New Republic 37

Levade A, 'Citoyenneté de l'Union européenne et identité constitutionnelle' [2011] 1 Law & European affairs 97

Liebert U, 'The European Citizenship Paradox: Renegotiating Equality and Diversity in the New Europe' (2007) 10 Critical Review of International Social and Political Philosophy 417

Lindfelt M, 'Article 44: Right to Petition' in Peers S and others (eds), *The EU Charter of Fundamental Rights: a Commentary* (Hart 2014)

Liu G, 'Education, Equality, and National Citizenship' (2006) 116 The Yale Law Journal 330

Lockyer A, Crick B and Annette J, *Education for Democratic Citizenship: Issues of Theory and Practice* (Ashgate 2003)

Lödén H, McCallion MS and Wall P, 'Teaching Citizenship: What if the EU Is Part of the Solution and Not the Problem?' (2014) 10 Journal of Political Science Education 386

Lohrenscheit C, 'Dialogue and Dignity – Linking Human Rights Education with Paulo Freire's "Education for Liberation"' (2006) 5 Journal of Social Science Education 126

Lonbay J, 'Education and the law: the Community context (European Community)' (1989) 14 ELRev 363

—, 'Reflections on education and culture in EC law' in Craufurd Smith R (ed), *Culture and European Union law* (Oxford University Press 2004)

Loobuyck P, *Meer LEF in het onderwijs: levensbeschouwing, ethiek en filosofie voor iedereen* (Paul Verbraeken Lezing, VUBPress 2014)

—, *Samenleven met gezond verstand* (Polis 2017)

Lorenz TM, 'Value Training: Education or Indoctrination? A Constitutional Analysis' (1992) 34 Arizona Law Review 593

Lösch B and Thimmel A (eds), *Kritische politische Bildung: Ein Handbuch* (Reihe Politik und Bildung, Band 54, Wochenschau Verlag 2011)

Losito B and others, *Young People's Perceptions of Europe in a Time of Change: IEA International Civic and Citizenship Education Study- 2016 European Report* (2017)

Louis J-V, 'Le droit de retrait de l'Union européene' (2006) 42 Cahiers de Droit européen 293

Lücke M and others (eds), *CHANGE – Handbook for History Learning and Human Rights Education* (Wochenschau Verlag 2016)

Luiz P, 'On the relationship between emotion and cognition' (2008) 9 Nature Reviews Neuroscience 148

Maas W, 'Unrespected, unequal, hollow? Contingent Citizenship and Reversible Rights in the European Union' (2008–2009) 15 Columbia Journal of European Law 265

—, 'The Origins, Evolution, and Political Objectives of EU Citizenship' (2014) 15 German Law Journal 797

Macedo S, 'Community, Diversity, and Civic Education: toward a Liberal Political Science of Group Life' [1996] Social Philosophy and Policy Foundation 240

—, 'School Choice, Civic Values and Problems of Policy Comparison,' in Wolf P and Macedo S (eds), *Educating Citizens: International Perspectives on Civic Values and School Choice* (Brookings Institution Press 2004)

Magnette P, 'European Governance and Civic Participation: Beyond Elitist Citizenship?' (2003) 51 Political Studies 144

—, 'How can one be European? Reflections on the Pillars of European Civic Identity' (2007) 13 ELJ 664

Maillard S, *L'émergence de la citoyenneté sociale européenne* (Presses Universitaires d'Aix-Marseille 2008)

Majone G, *Dilemmas of European integration: the ambiguities and pitfalls of integration by stealth* (Oxford University Press 2005)

Mancini GF, 'The making of a constitution for Europe' (1989) 26 CMLRev 595

—, 'Europe: The Case for Statehood' (1998) 4 ELJ 29

Marks S, 'The European Convention on Human Rights and its Democratic Society' (1996) 66 The British Year Book of International Law 209

Marshall TH, *Citizenship and Social Class* (Cambridge University Press 1950)

Martens AM and Gainous J, 'Civic Education and Democratic Capacity: How Do Teachers Teach and What Works?' (2013) 94 Social Science Quarterly 956

Martin D, 'L'arrêt Mangold: Vers une hiérarchie inversée du droit à l'égalité en droit communautaire?' [2006] Journal des tribunaux du travail 941

Martin L, *L'Union européenne et l'économie de l'éducation: émergence d'un système éducatif européen* (Larcier 2011)

Mascherini M, Manca AR and Hoskins B, *The characterization of Active Citizenship in Europe* (European Commission, JRC, CRELL, 2009)

Massing P, 'Institutionenkundliches Lernen' in Sander W (ed), *Handbuch politische Bildung* (Reihe Politik und Bildung 32, Bundeszentrale für politische Bildung 2005)

—–, 'Die Infrastruktur der politischen Bildung in der Bundesrepublik Deutschland – Fächer, Institutionen, Verbände, Träger' in Sander W (ed), *Handbuch politische Bildung* (Bundeszentrale für politische Bildung 2005)

—–, 'Politische Bildung in der Grundschule: Uberblick, Kritik, Perspektiven' in Richter D (ed), *Politische Bildung von Anfang an: Demokratie-Lernen in der Grundschule* (Schriftenreihe Band 570, Bundeszentrale für politische Bildung 2007)

Maurer HPD and Neuhold C, 'Problem-Based Learning in European Studies' in Baroncelli S and others (eds), *Teaching and Learning the European Union: Traditional and Innovative Methods* (Springer 2014)

Mazák J and Moser M, 'Adjudication by reference to general principles of EU law: a second look at the Mangold case law' in Adams M and others (eds), *Judging Europe's judges: The Legitimacy of the Case Law of the European Court of Justice* (Hart 2013)

McCormick JP, 'Habermas, Supranational Democracy and the European Constitution' (2006) 2 European Constitutional Law Review 398

McCowan T, 'Approaching the political in citizenship education: The perspectives of Paulo Freire and Bernard Crick' (2006) 6 Educate 57

McCowan T, *Rethinking Citizenship Education: a Curriculum for Participatory Democracy* (Continuum 2009)

McNabb L, 'Civic Outreach Programs: Common Models, Shared Challenges, and Strategic Recommendations' (2013) 90 Denver University Law Review 871

Meduna M, 'Institutional report' in Neergaard U, Jacqueson C and Holst-Christensen N (eds), *Union Citizenship: Development, Impact and Challenges – The XXVI FIDE Congress in Copenhagen, 2014 Congress Publications Vol* 2 (DJØF 2014)

Meeusen J, *Recht van de Europese Unie: basisjurisprudentie* (3 edn, Intersentia 2015)

Mendes J, 'Participation and the role of law after Lisbon: a legal view on Article 11 TEU' (2011) 48 CMLRev 1849

—–, *Participation in EU Rule-Making: A Rights-Based Approach* (Oxford University Press 2011)

—–, *Participation in a New Regulatory Paradigm: Collaboration and Constraint in TTIP's Regulatory Cooperation* (IILJ Working Paper 2016/5 2016)

Menéndez J, 'European Citizenship after Martínez Sala and Baumbast: Has European Law Become More Human but Less Social' in Maduro M and Azoulai L (eds), *The Past and Future of EU Law; The Classics of EU Law Revisited on the 50th Anniversary of the Rome Treaty* (Hart 2010)

—–, 'Which Citizenship? Whose Europe? – The Many Paradoxes of European Citizenship' (2014) 15 German Law Journal 928

Menkel-Meadow C, 'Telling Stories in School: Using Case Studies and Stories to Teach Legal Ethics' (2000–2001) 69 Fordham Law Review 787

Menthe J, 'Education for Democratic Citizenship: Values vs Process' in Print M and Lange D (eds), *Schools, Curriculum and Civic Education for Building Democratic Citizens* (Sense 2012)

Mertens de Wilmars J, 'Réflexions sur les méthodes d'interprétation de la Cour de justice des Communautés européennes' (1986) 22 Cahiers de Droit européen 5

Mihaescu Evans BC, *The right to good administration at the crossroads of the various sources of fundamental rights in the EU integrated administrative system* (Luxembourg Legal Studies 7, Nomos 2015)

Miklin E, 'Beyond subsidiarity: the indirect effect of the Early Warning System on national parliamentary scrutiny in European Union affairs' (2016) 23 Journal of European Public Policy 1

Minow M, 'What the rule of law should mean in civics education: from the "Following Orders" defence to the classroom' (2006) 35 Journal of Moral Education 137

Mintrop H, 'The Old and New Face of Civic Education: expert, teacher, and student views' (2003) 2 EERJ 446

Missira V, 'Strengthening European citizenship education' (2019) 18 Journal of Social Science Education (3: European Citizenship Education: Business as Usual or Time for Change?) 55

Möllers C, 'Pouvoir Constituant- Constitution-Constitutionalisation' in von Bogdandy A and Bast J (eds), *Principles of European Constitutional Law*, vol 8 (2 edn, Hart Beck Nomos 2010)

Montesquieu, *De l'esprit des lois* (digital JM Tremblay 2002 edn, Barillot 1748)

Morijn J, 'Balancing Fundamental Rights and Common Market Freedoms in Union Law: Schmidberger and Omega in the Light of the European Constitution' (2006) 12 ELJ 15

Moskowitz GB, *Social cognition: understanding self and others* (Guilford 2005)

Motos CR, 'The Controversy over Civic Education in Spain' (2010) 9 European Political Science 269

Muir E, *EU Equality Law: The First Fundamental Rights Policy of the EU* (Oxford Studies in European Law, OUP 2018)

Mulcahy DG, 'In Search of the European Dimension in Education' (1991) 14 European Journal of Teacher Education 213

Müller JW, 'A general theory of constitutional patriotism' (2007) 6 International Journal of Constitutional Law 72

——, 'A European Constitutional Patriotism? The Case Restated' (2008) 14 ELJ 542

Müller R, 'Politische Bildung (und Europa)' Bundeszentrale für politische Bildung (2016) <www.bpb.de/nachschlagen/lexika/177197/politische-bildung-und-europ a>

Muller WC and others, 'Legal Europeanization: comparative perspectives' (2010) 88 Public Administration 75

Mulnix JW, 'Thinking Critically about Critical Thinking' (2012) 44 Educational Philosophy and Theory 464

Murdoch J, *Protecting the right to freedom of thought, conscience and religion under the European Convention on Human Rights* (Council of Europe Human Rights Handbooks, 2012)

—, 'Using self- and peer assessment at honours level: bridging the gap between law school and the workplace' (2015) 49 The Law Teacher 73

Murphy M, 'Covert action? Education, social policy and law in the European Union' (2003) 18 Journal of Education Policy 551

Naval C, Print M and Veldhuis R, 'Education for Democratic Citizenship in the New Europe: context and reform' (2002) 37 European Journal of Education 107

Naylor, 'Educating for citizenship with law-related education' (1981) 20 Theory into Practice 194

Neergaard U, Jacqueson C and Holst-Christensen N (eds), *Union Citizenship: Development, Impact and Challenges – The XXVI FIDE Congress in Copenhagen, 2014 Congress Publications Vol 2* (DJØF 2014)

Neframi E, *Objectifs et compétences dans l'Union européenne* (Droit de l'Union européenne Colloques, Bruylant 2013)

—, 'Principe de coopération loyale et principe d'attribution dans le cadre de la mise en oeuvre du droit de l'Union' (2016) 52 Cahiers droit européen 221

Neuvonen PJ, *Equal Citizenship and its Limits in EU Law: We the Burden?* (Hart 2016)

Nic Shuibhne N, 'The Resilience of EU Market Citizenship' (2010) 47 CMLRev 1597

—, 'Three paradoxes of EU citizenship (Editorial)' (2010) ELRev 129

—, 'The Developing Legal Dimensions of Union Citizenship' in Chalmers D and Arnull A (eds), *The Oxford Handbook of European Union Law* (Oxford University Press 2015)

Nic Shuibhne N and Shaw J, 'General report' in Neergaard U, Jacqueson C and Holst-Christensen N (eds), *Union Citizenship, FIDE Congress 2014* (DJØF 2014)

Nicola F and Davies B (eds), *EU Law Stories: Contextual and Critical Histories of European Jurisprudence* (Cambridge University Press 2017)

Nicolaïdis K, 'The New Constitution as European "Demoi-cracy"?' (2004) 7 Critical Review of International Social and Political Philosophy 76

—, 'European Demoicracy and Its Crisis' (2013) 51 JCMS 351

Niemi RG and Hepburn MA, 'The Rebirth of Political Socialization' (1995) 24 Perspectives on Political Science 7

Niemi RG and Sanders M, 'Assessing Student Performance in Civics: The NAEP 1998 Civics Assessment' (2004) 32 Theory & Research in Social Education 326

Niens U, O'Connor U and Smith A, 'Citizenship education in divided societies: teachers' perspectives in Northern Ireland' (2013) 17 Citizenship Studies 128

Nora P, 'Ernest Lavisse: son rôle dans la formation du sentiment national' (1962) 228 Revue Historique 73

Norris P, *Democratic Deficit: Critical Citizens Revisited* (Cambridge University Press 2011)

Nowak M, 'The right to education' in Eide A, Krause C and Rosas A (eds), *Economic, social and cultural rights: a textbook* (2nd revised edn, Nijhoff 2001)

—, 'Prioritising human rights education and training' [2004] European Human Rights Law Review 235

Nussbaum M, 'Education for Citizenship in an Era of Global Connection' (2002) 21 Studies in Philosophy and Education 289

—, 'Cultivating Humanity in Legal Education' (2003) 70 University of Chicago Law Review 265

—, 'Political Soul-Making and the Imminent Demise of Liberal Education' (2006) 37 Journal of Social Philosophy 301

—, 'Education and Democratic Citizenship: Capabilities and Quality Education' (2006) 7 Journal of Human Development 385

—, 'Toward a globally sensitive patriotism' (2008) 137 Daedalus 78

—, 'Education for Profit, Education for Freedom' (2009) 95 Liberal Education 6

—, 'Teaching patriotism: love and critical freedom' (2012) 79 University of Chicago Law Review 213

—, *Political Emotions: Why Love Matters for Justice* (Harvard University Press 2015)

Nussbaum M and Cohen J, *For love of country: debating the limits of patriotism* (Beacon 1996)

O'Brien C, 'Real links, abstract rights and false alarms: the relationship between the ECJ's "real link" case law and national solidarity' (2008) 33 ELRev 643

O'Brien C, 'I trade, therefore I am: legal personhood in the European Union' (2013) 50 CMLRev 1643

O'Leary S, 'The relationship between Community citizenship and the protection of fundamental rights in Community law' (1995) 32 CMLRev 519

—, *The Evolving Concept of Community Citizenship: From the Free Movement of Persons to Union Citizenship* (European Monographs 13, Kluwer 1996)

—, 'The Past, Present and Future of the Purely Internal Rule in EU Law' in Dougan M, Nic Schuibhne N and Spaventa E (eds), *Empowerment and Disempowerment of the European Citizen* (Hart 2012)

—, 'The Charter and the Future Contours of EU Social and Employment Law' in Cardonnel P, Rosas A and Wahl N (eds), *Constitutionalising the EU judicial systems: essays in honour of Pernilla Lindh* (Hart 2012)

—, 'Europe and the Rule of Law' (Keynote speech, ESCB Annual Legal Conference, Frankfurt 6 September 2018)

Öberg J, 'Subsidiarity as a Limit to the Exercise of EU Competences' (2017) 36 Yearbook of European Law 391

Oberreuter H, 'Rechtserziehung' in Sander W (ed), *Handbuch politische Bildung* (Reihe Politik und Bildung 32, 3rd edn, Wochenschau 2005)

Oelkers J, 'The European Crisis and Education for Democracy' (2017) 22 The European Legacy 832

Olafsdottir O, 'Education for Democratic Citizenship and Human Rights: A Project by the Council of Europe' in Georgi VB (ed), *The Making of Citizens in Europe: New Perspectives on Citizenship Education* (Schriftenreihe Band 666, Bundeszentrale für politische Bildung 2008)

Olgers T, 'Escaping the Box of Pandora, in K O'Shea, EDC policies and regulatory frameworks' (Strasbourg, 6–7 December 2001)

Olsen EDH, 'European Citizenship: Mixing Nation State and Federal Features with a Cosmopolitan Twist' (2013) 14 Perspectives on European Politics and Society 1

Olsen TV, 'The political constitution of the EU citizen rights regime' (2011) 18 Journal of European Public Policy 35

Organ J, 'Decommissioning Direct Democracy? A Critical Analysis of Commission Decision-Making on the Legal Admissibility of European Citizens Initiative Proposals' (2014) 10 European Constitutional Law Review 422

Orlenius K, 'Tolerance of intolerance: values and virtues at stake in education' (2008) 37 Journal of Moral Education 467

Ortino M, 'A reading of the EU constitutional legal system through the meta-principle of effectiveness' [2016] Cahiers droit européen 91

Osler A, 'European Citizenship and Study Abroad: student teachers' experiences and identities' (1998) 28 Cambridge Journal of Education 77

––, 'Human Rights Education: The Foundation of Education for Democratic Citizenship in our Global Age' in Arthur J, Davies I and Hahn C (eds), *The SAGE Handbook of Education for Citizenship and Democracy* (Sage 2008)

––, 'Patriotism, multiculturalism and belonging: political discourse and the teaching of history' (2009) 61 Educational Review 85

––, 'Teacher interpretations of citizenship education: national identity, cosmopolitan ideals, and political realities' (2011) 43 Journal of Curriculum Studies 1

––, 'Bringing Human Rights Back Home: Learning from "Superman" and Addressing Political Issues at School' (2013) 104 The Social Studies 67

––, *General Rapporteur Conference report, in CoE Proceedings of the Conference on 'Human Rights and Democracy in Action – Looking Ahead: The Impact of the Council of Europe Charter on Education for Democratic Citizenship and Human Rights Education' (Strasbourg, 29–30 November 2012)* (2013)

Osler A and Leung YW, 'Human rights education, politics and power' (2011) 6 Education, Citizenship and Social Justice 199

Osler A and Starkey H, 'Fundamental Issues in Teacher Education for Human Rights: a European perspective' (1994) 23 Journal of Moral Education 349

––, 'Citizenship Education and National Identities in France and England: Inclusive or exclusive?' (2001) 27 Oxford Review of Education 287

––, 'Education for Citizenship: Mainstreaming the Fight against Racism?' (2002) 37 European Journal of Education 143

––, *Citizenship and Language Learning: international perspectives* (Trentham Books 2005)

—–, *Changing citizenship: democracy and inclusion in education* (Osler A and Starkey H eds, Open University Press and McGraw-Hill Education 2005)

—–, 'Education for democratic citizenship: a review of research, policy and practice 1995–2005' (2006) 21 Research Papers in Education 433

—–, 'Education for Cosmopolitan Citizenship' in Georgi VB (ed), *The Making of Citizens in Europe: New Perspectives on Citizenship Education* (Schriftenreihe Band 666, Bundeszentrale für politische Bildung 2008)

—–, *Teachers and Human Rights Education* (Trentham 2010)

Osler A and Zhu J, 'Narratives in teaching and research for justice and human rights' (2011) 6 Education, Citizenship and Social Justice 223

Ost F and van de Kerchove M, *De la pyramide au réseau? Pour une théorie dialectique du droit* (Facultés universitaires Saint-Louis 2002)

Otte R, 'The Council of Europe's work on "Education for Democratic Citizenship and Human Rights Education" and its links to the PIDOP project' in Barrett M and Zani B (eds), *Political and Civic Engagement: Multidisciplinary Perspectives* (Routledge 2014)

Palombella G, 'Whose Europe? After the constitution: A goal-based citizenship' (2005) 3 International Journal of Constitutional Law 357

Papastephanou M, 'Philosophical Presuppositions of Citizenship Education and Political Liberalism' in Arthur J, Davies I and Hahn C (eds), *The SAGE Handbook of Education for Citizenship and Democracy* (Sage 2008)

Parker W, 'Diversity, globalization and democratic education: Curriculum possibilities' in Banks JA (ed), *Diversity and citizenship education: Global perspectives* (2004)

Parker WC, Ninomiya A and Cogan J, 'Educating World Citizens: Toward Multinational Curriculum Development' (1999) 36 American Educational Research Journal 117

Pech L, 'A Union Founded on the Rule of Law': Meaning and Reality of the Rule of Law as a Constitutional Principle of EU Law' (2010) 6 European Constitutional Law Review 359

Peers S and Prechal S, 'Article 52: Scope and Interpretation of Rights and Principles' in Peers S and others (eds), *The EU Charter of Fundamental Rights: a Commentary* (Hart 2014)

Pépin L, *The history of European cooperation in education and training. Europe in the making – an example* (European Commission 2006)

Pérez-Díaz V, 'The European Civic Deficit' (2004) <www.essayandscience.com/article/24/the-european-civic-deficit/>

Pernice I, 'Bestandssicherung der Verfassungen: Verfassungsrechtliche Mechanismen zur Wahrung der Verfassungsordnung' in Bieber R and Widmer P (eds), *Der europäische Vefassungsraum* (Schulthess Juristische Medien 1995)

—–, 'Multilevel constitutionalism in the European Union' (2002) 27 ELRev 511

—–, 'Does Europe need a Constitution?' in *Arnull A and others (eds), A Constitutional Order of States: Essays in EU Law in Honour of Alan Dashwood* (Hart 2011)

—, 'Solidarität in Europa: Eine Ortsbestimmung im Verhältnis zwischen Bürger, Staat und Europäischer Union' in Calliess C (ed), *Uberlegungen im Kontext der Krise im Euroraum* (Mohr Siebeck 2013)

—, 'Editorial: Nationale Wahlen sind Europäische Wahlen' [2017] Europäische Zeitschrift für Wirtschaftsrecht 441

Pertek J, 'L'éducation et la Communauté: une relation mouvementée et incertaine' [2005] Law & European affairs 7

—, 'Le processus de Bologne et l'action de la Communauté en matière d'éducation' [2005] Law & European affairs 51

Peters A, 'European democracy after the 2003 Convention' (2004) 41 CMLRev 37

—, 'The European Ombudsman and the European constitution' (2005) 42 CMLRev 697

Petovka B, 'Data Privacy Rights and Citizenship: Notes on Federalism All the Way Up' in Kochenov D (ed), *EU Citizenship and Federalism: The Role of Rights* (Cambridge University Press 2017)

Petrik A (ed) *Formate fachdidaktischer Forschung in der politischen Bildung* (Gesellschaft für Politikdidaktik und politische Jugend- und Erwachsenenbildung, Band 14, Schwalbach/Ts 2015)

Philip C and Soldatos P (eds), *La citoyenneté européenne* (Collection études européennes, Chaire Jean Monnet, 2000)

Philippou S, 'Policy, curriculum and the struggle for change in Cyprus: the case of the European dimension in education' (2007) 17 International Studies in Sociology of Education 249

Philippou S, Keating A and Hinderliter Ortloff D, 'Citizenship education curricula: comparing the multiple meanings of supra-national citizenship in Europe and beyond' (2009) 42 Journal of curriculum studies 291

Piedade F and others, 'Learning About the European Union in Times of Crisis: Portuguese Textbooks' Normative Visions of European Citizenship' (2018) 17 Journal of Social Science Education 31

Pilcher J and Kaufmann B (eds), *The European Citizens Initiative: Into New Democratic Territory* (Intersentia 2010)

Pina FH, 'Constitution, Education and Research' (2013) 12 EERJ 34

Poiares Maduro M, 'The importance of being called a constitution: Constitutional authority and the authority of constitutionalism' (2005) 3 International Journal of Constitutional Law 332

Poiares Maduro M and Azoulai L (eds), *The Past and Future of EU Law: The Classics of EU Law Revisited on the 50th Anniversary of the Rome Treaty* (Hart 2010)

Ponzano P, 'L'initiative citoyenne européenne: la démocratie participative à l'épreuve' [2012] Revue du droit de l'Union européenne 615

Potvin-Solis L, 'La liaison entre le principe de non-discrimination et les libertés et droits fondamentaux des personnes dans les jurisprudences européennes' (2009) 20 Revue trimestrielle des droits de l'homme 967

— (ed) *Les valeurs communes dans l'Union européenne* (Bruylant 2014)

Prechal S, 'Defrenne: de Europese gelijkebeloningsaga met verstrekkende gevolgen' in Schutgens and others (eds), *Canon van het recht* (Ars Aequi Libri 2010)

—, 'Competence creep and general principles of law' (2010) 3 Review of European administrative law 1

Prechal S and de Leeuw ME, 'Transparency: A General Principle of EU Law?' in Bernitz U, Nergelius J and Cardner C (eds), *General Principles of EC Law in a Process of Development* (Kluwer 2008)

Print M and Lange D (eds), *Schools, Curriculum and Civic Education for Building Democratic Citizens* (Series Civic and Political Education 2, Sense 2012)

— (eds), *Civic Education and Competences for Engaging Citizens in Democracies* (Springer 2013)

Priollaud F-X and Siritzky D, *Le traité de Lisbonne: Commentaire, article par article, des nouveaux traités européens (TUE et TFUE)* (La documentation française 2008)

Prost A, *Histoire de l'enseignement en France 1800–1967* (2nd edn, Colin 1970)

Putnam RD, 'Bowling Alone: America's Declining Social Capital' (1995) 6 Journal of Democracy 65

Quinn G, 'The European Union and the Council of Europe on the Issue of Human Rights: Twins Separated at Birth?' (2001) 46 McGill Law Journal 849

Quintelier E, 'The effect of schools on political participation: A multilevel logistic analysis' (2008) 25 Research Papers in Education 137–154

Rabin Y, 'The Many Faces of the Right to Education' in Barak-Erez D and Gross AM (eds), *Exploring Social Rights: Between Theory and Practice* (Hart 2007)

Raines T, Goodwin M and Cutts D, *The Future of Europe: Comparing Public and Elite Attitudes* (Research Paper, Europe Programme, Chatham House, The Royal Institute of International Affairs, 2017)

Raskin JB, *We the Students: Supreme Court Cases for and about Students* (4th edn, Sage 2015)

Raskin JB, Ahranjani M and Ferguson AG, *Youth Justice in America* (2 edn, Sage 2015)

Rawls J, *Political Liberalism* (2005 edn, Columbia University Press 1993)

Raz J, 'On the Authority and Interpretations of Constitutions: Some Preliminaries' in Alexander L (ed), *Constitutionalism* (Cambridge University Press 2001)

Rebell MA, 'Major Federal Right to Education Lawsuit Filed in the U.S. (OxHRH Blog, 12 December 2018)'

Recchi E, 'Pathways to European identity formation: a tale of two models' (2014) 27 Innovation: The European Journal of Social Science Research 119

Recchi E and Favell A (eds), *Pioneers of European Integration. Citizenship and Mobility in the EU* (Edward Elgar 2009)

Recchi E and others, 'Cross-border mobilities in the European Union: An evidence-based typology' in *EUCROSS, Final report, 'The Europeanisation of Everyday Life: Cross-Border Practices and Transnational Identifications Among EU and Third-Country Citizens'* (2014)

Redish MH and Finnertyt K, 'What did you Learn in School Today? Free Speech, Values Inculcation, and the Democratic Educational Paradox' (2002–2003) 88 Cornell Law Review 62

Reh C, 'The Lisbon Treaty: De-Constitutionalizing the European Union?' (2009) 47 JCMS 625

Reilly E, 'Education and the Constitution: Shaping Each Other & the Next Century' (2000–2001) 34 Akron Law Review 1

Reimer F, 'Ziele und Zuständigkeiten: Die Funktionen der Unionszielbestimmungen' (2003) 38 Europarecht 992

Reinhardt S, 'The Case of (East-) Germany' (2008) 6 Journal of Social Science Education 67

—, *Teaching Civics: A Manual for Secondary Education Teachers* (Barbara Budrich 2015)

—, 'The Beutelsbach Consensus' (2016) 15 Journal of Social Science Education 11

Reynolds S, 'Union citizenship: Placing limitations on a human-centred approach?' in Ferreira N and Kostakopoulou D (eds), *The Human Face of the European Union: Are EU Law and Policy Humane Enough?* (Cambridge University Press 2016)

Richter D (ed) *Politische Bildung von Anfang an. Demokratie-Lernen in der Grundschule* (Schriftenreihe Band 570, Bundeszentrale für politische Bildung 2007)

Riesenberg P, *A History of Citizenship: Sparta to Washington* (Anvil Series, Krieger 2002)

Rosas A and Armati L, *EU Constitutional Law: An Introduction* (Hart 2018)

Ross A, 'Multiple Identities and Education for Active Citizenship' (2007) 55 British Journal of Educational Studies 286

—, 'Organizing a Curriculum for Active Citizenship Education' in Arthur J, Davies I and Hahn C (eds), *The SAGE Handbook of Education for Citizenship and Democracy* (Sage 2008)

—, *A European Education. Citizenship, identities and young people. European issues in Children's Identity and Citizenship* (Trentham Books, CiCe 2009)

—, 'Controversies and Generational Differences: Young People's Identities in Some European States' (2012) 2 Education Sciences 91

—, *Finding Political Identities: Young People in a Changing Europe* (Springer 2018)

Ross M, 'The Struggle for EU Citizenship: Why Solidarity Matters' in Arnull A and others (eds), *A Constitutional Order of States: Essays in EU Law in Honour of Alan Dashwood* (Hart 2011)

Rossi LS and Casolari F, *The Principle of Equality in EU Law* (Springer International 2017)

Roth M and Moisa F, 'The right to education of Roma children in Romania: European policies and Romanian practices' 19 The International Journal of Children's Rights 501

Rousseau J-J, *Emile ou de l'éducation* (1762, Flammarion ed 2009)

Rousseau J-J, *The government of Poland* (Kendall W tr, Bobbs-Merrill 1972)

Rowe D, 'Value pluralism, democracy and education for citizenship' in *Values, Culture & Education* (1999)

Ruffert M, 'EU-Vertrag (Lissabon) Art 10' in Calliess C and Ruffert M (eds), *EUV/AEUV: das Verfassungsrecht der Europäischen Union mit Europäischer Grundrechtecharta : Kommentar* (5th edn, Beck 2016)

—–, 'AEUV Art 165' in Calliess C and Ruffert M (eds), *EUV/AEUV: das Verfassungsrecht der Europäischen Union mit Europäischer Grundrechtecharta : Kommentar* (5th edn, Beck 2016)

Rummens S and Sottiaux S, 'Democratic Legitimacy in the Bund or 'Federation of States': the Cases of Belgium and the EU' (2014) 20 ELJ 568

Russo CJ and Thro WE, 'Reflections on the Law and Curricular Values in American Schools' (2012) 87 Peabody Journal of Education 402

Ryba R, 'Toward a European Dimension in Education: Intention and Reality in European Community Policy and Practice' (1992) 36 Comparative Education Review 10

—–, 'Unity in diversity: The enigma of the European dimension in education' (1995) 21 Oxford Review of Education 25

Safjan M and Düsterhaus D, 'A Union of Effective Judicial Protection: Addressing a Multi-level Challenge through the Lens of Article 47 CFREU' (2014) 33 Yearbook of European Law 3

Salamońska J and Recchi E, *Europe between mobility and sedentarism: Patterns of cross-border practices and their consequences for European identification* (EUI Working Paper RSCAS 2016/50, 2016)

Salema MH, 'Teacher and Trainer Training in Education for Democratic Citizenship Competencies' (2005) 4 Journal of Social Science Education 39

Salomone RC, 'Common Schools, Uncommon Values: Listening to the Voices of Dissent' (1996) 14 Yale Law & Policy Review 169

Sampermans D and others, *ICCS 2016 Rapport Vlaanderen, Een onderzoek naar burgerschapseducatie in Vlaanderen. Eindrapport november 2017* (KU Leuven, Centrum voor Politicologie, 2017)

Sander TH and Putnam RD, 'Still Bowling Alone? The Post-9/11 Split' (2010) 21 Journal of Democracy 9

Sander W (ed) *Handbuch politische Bildung* (Reihe Politik und Bildung 32, Bundeszentrale für politische Bildung 2005)

—–, 'Theorie der politischen Bildung: Geschichte – didaktische Konzeptionen – aktuelle Tendenzen und Probleme' in Sander W (ed), *Handbuch politische Bildung* (Reihe Politik und Bildung 32, Bundeszentrale für politische Bildung 2005)

Sander W and Scheunpflug A (eds), *Politische Bildung in der Weltgeschellschaft. Herausforderungen, Positionen, Kontroversen. Perspektiven politischer Bildung* (Schriftenreihe Band 1201, Bundeszentrale für politische Bildung 2011)

Sander W and Steinbach P (eds), *Politische Bildung in Deutschland* (Schriftenreihe Band 1449, Bundeszentrale für politische Bildung 2014)

Sandström Kjellin M and others, 'Pupils' voices about citizenship education: comparative case studies in Finland, Sweden and England' (2010) 33 European Journal of Teacher Education 201

Sangiovanni A, 'Solidarity in the European Union' (2013) 33 Oxford Journal of Legal Studies 1

Sarmiento D and Sharpston E, 'European Citizenship and Its New Union: Time to Move on?' in Kochenov D (ed), *EU Citizenship and Federalism: The Role of Rights* (Cambridge University Press 2017)

Sasse G, 'The Council of Europe as a Norm Entrepreneur: The Political Strengths of a Weak International Institution' in Walker N, Shaw J and Tierney S (eds), *Europe's Constitutional Mosaic* (Hart 2011)

Sayer J and Erler L (eds), *Schools for the Future Europe: Values and Change beyond Lisbon* (Continuum 2012)

Schaffar B, 'Changing the Definition of Education. On Kant's Educational Paradox Between Freedom and Restraint' (2014) 33 Studies in Philosophy and Education 5

Scharpf FW, 'After the Crash: A Multilevel European Democracy' in van Middelaar L and Van Parijs P (eds), *After the Storm: How to Save Democracy in Europe* (Lannoo 2015)

Schenberg S and Frick K, 'Finishing, Refining, Polishing: On the Use of Travaux Préparatoires as an Aid to the Interpretation of Community Legislation' (2003) 28 ELRev 149

Scherb A, *Der Bürger in der Streitbaren Demokratie: Über die normativen Grundlagen Politischer Bildung* (Springer Verlag 2008)

Schermers HG and Blokker NM, *International Institutional Law: Unity within Diversity* (5th edn, Martinus Nijhoff 2011)

Schlenker A, 'Supranational, Intergovernmental or Demoicratic Legitimacy? Citizens' Evaluations of the EU' (2015) 16 European Politics and Society 581

Schmahl S and Breuer M (eds), *The Council of Europe: Its Law and Policies* (Oxford University Press 2017)

Schmidt VA, *Democracy in Europe: the EU and national polities* (Oxford University Press 2006)

Schönberger C, 'European Citizenship as Federal Citizenship: Some Citizenship Lessons of Comparative Federalism' (2007) 19 European Review of Public Law 63

—, 'Foreword. European citizenship as federal citizenship: studying EU citizenship through the federal lens' in Kochenov D (ed), *EU Citizenship and Federalism: The Role of Rights* (Cambridge University Press 2017)

Schreiner P (ed) *'Education for Democratic Citizenship' in the Context of Europe* (CSC/CEC 2013)

Schuitema J and others, 'Guiding classroom discussions for democratic citizenship education' (2017) 44 Educational Studies 377

Schulz W and others, *ICCS 2009 International Report: Civic knowledge, attitudes, and engagement among lower-secondary school students in 38 countries* (International Association for the Evaluation of Educational Achievement IEA, 2010)

Schulz W and others, *IEA International Civic and Citizenship Education Study 2016: Assessment Framework* (2016)

Schütze R, 'Cooperative federalism constitutionalised: the emergence of complementary competences in the EC legal order' (2006) 31 ELRev 167

Schütze R, 'On "federal" Ground: The European Union as an (Inter)national Phenomenon' (2009) 46 CMLRev 1069

—, *European constitutional law* (2 edn, Cambridge University Press 2016)

Schwarze J, 'Die Abwägung von Zielen der europäischen Integration und mitgliedstaatlichen Interessen in der Rechtsprechung des EuGH' (2013) 48 Europarecht 253

Schweitzer M, Hummer W and Obwexer W, *Europarecht: das Recht der Europäischen Union* (Manz 2007)

Scott J, 'Can the EU Deliver on Citizen Expectations in the Fight against Climate Change?' in Dougan M, Shuibhne NN and Spaventa E (eds), *Empowerment and Disempowerment of the European Citizen* (Hart 2012)

Sebart K and Krek J, 'Citizenship education in educational research: description of knowledge, skills and values and their explanation in school evaluation' in Kovzuh B and others (eds), *New paradigms and methods in educational and social research* (University of California 2007)

Semmelmann C, 'General Principles in EU Law between a Compensatory Role and an Intrinsic Value' (2013) 19 ELJ 457

Senden L, *Soft Law in European Community Law* (Hart 2004)

Seubert S and others (eds), *Moving Beyond Barriers: Prospects for EU Citizenship* (Edward Elgar 2018)

Shapiro BP, *Hints for case teaching* (Harvard Business 2014)

Sharpston E, 'Citizenship and Fundamental Rights – Pandora's Box or a Natural Step Towards Maturity?' in Cardonnel P, Rosas A and Wahl N (eds), *Constitutionalising the EU Judicial System: Essays in Honour of Pernilla Lindh* (Hart 2012)

Shaw J, 'Education and the Law in the European Community' (1992) 21 Journal of Law & Education 415

—, 'The many pasts and futures of citizenship in the European Union' (1997) 22 ELRev 554

—, 'From the Margins to the Centre: Education and Training Law and Policy' in Craig P and de Búrca G (eds), *The evolution of EU law* (Oxford University Press 1999)

—, 'Mainstreaming Equality and Diversity in the European Union' (2005) 58 Current Legal Problems 255

—, *The Transformation of Citizenship in the European Union: Electoral Rights and the Restructuring of Political Space* (Cambridge University Press 2007)

—, 'E.U. Citizenship and Political Rights in an Evolving European Union' (2007) 75 Fordham Law Review 2549

—, 'One or Many Constitutions: The Constitutional Future of the European Union in the 2000s from a Legal Perspective' (2007) 52 Scandinavian Studies in Law 393

—, 'The Treaty of Lisbon and Citizenship' [2008] The Federal Trust for education & research (June)

—, 'Political Rights and Multilevel Citizenship in Europe' in Carrera S and Guild E (eds), *Illiberal Liberal States: Immigration, Citizenship and Integration in the EU* (Ashgate 2009)

—, 'The constitutional development of citizenship in the EU context: with or without the Treaty of Lisbon' in Pernice I, Tanchev, E (ed), *Ceci n'est pas une Constitution – Constitutionalisation without a Constitution?* (Nomos 2009)

—, 'Citizenship and Political Participation: The Role of Electoral Rights Under European Union Law' in Fanning B and Munck R (eds), *Immigration and the Irish Experience of European and Global Social Transformation* (Ashgate 2010/11)

— (ed) *Has the European Court of Justice Challenged the Member State Sovereignty in Nationality Law?* (EUI Robert Schuman Centre for Advanced Studies Paper 62, 2011)

—, 'Citizenship: Contrasting Dynamics at the Interface of Integration and Constitutionalism' in Craig P and de Búrca G (eds), *The evolution of EU law* (Oxford University Press 2011)

—, 'Prisoner voting: now a matter of EU law' 2015 <eulawanalysis.blogspot.com/2015/10/prisoner-voting-now-matter-of-eu-law.html>

—, 'The quintessentially democratic act? Democracy, political community and citizenship in and after the UK's EU referendum of June 2016' (2017) 39 Journal of European Integration 559

Shore C, '"European Governance" or Governmentality? The European Commission and the Future of Democratic Government' (2011) 17 ELJ 287

Smismans S, *Law, Legitimacy, and European Governance: Functional Participation in Social Regulation* (Oxford Studies in European Law, Oxford University Press 2004)

—, 'The constitutional labelling of "the democratic life of the EU": "representative" and "participatory" democracy' in Follesdal A and Dobson L (eds), *Political Theory and the European Constitution* (Routledge 2004)

—, 'New governance: the solution for active European citizenship, or the end of citizenship?' (2007) 13 Columbia Journal of European Law 595

—, 'New Modes of Governance and the Participatory Myth' (2008) 31 West European Politics 874

—, 'Should participatory democracy become the normative model for EU governance?' [2012] Re-Public

—, 'Regulating interest group participation in the European Union: changing paradigms between transparency and representation' (2014) 39 ELRev 470

Smith G, 'The European Citizens' Initiative: A New Institution for Empowering Europe's Citizens?' in Dougan M, Nic Shuibhne N and Spaventa E (eds), *Empowerment and Disempowerment of the European Citizen* (Hart 2012)

Snell J, 'European Union and National Referendums: Need for Change after the Brexit Vote?' (2017) 28 European Business Law Review 767

Snyder F (ed) *The Europeanisation of Law: The Legal Effects of European Integration* (Hart 2000)

Somek A, 'Solidarity decomposed: being and time in European citizenship' (2007) 32 ELRev 787

—, 'The Individualisation of Liberty: Europe's Move from Emancipation to Empowerment' (2013) 4 Transnational Legal Theory 258

—, 'Europe: Political, Not Cosmopolitan' (2014) 20 ELJ 142

Spaventa E, 'Seeing the wood despite the trees? On the scope of union citizenship and its constitutional effects' (2008) 45 CMLRev 13

—, 'Article 45: Freedom of Movement and of Residence' in Peers S and others (eds), *The EU Charter of Fundamental Rights: a Commentary* (Hart 2014)

Sprogøe J and Winther-Jensen T (eds), *Identity, education and citizenship – multiple interrelations* (Comparative studies series 13 Peter Lang 2006)

Sprungk C, 'A New Type of Representative Democracy? Reconsidering the Role of National Parliaments in the European Union' (2013) 35 Journal of European Integration 547

Starkey H, 'Back to Basic Values: Education for Justice and Peace in the World' (1992) 21 Journal of Moral Education 185

—, 'Diversity and citizenship in the curriculum' (2008) 6 London Review of Education 5

—, 'Human rights, cosmopolitanism and utopias: implications for citizenship education' (2012) 42 Cambridge Journal of Education 21

—, 'Fundamental British Values and citizenship education: tensions between national and global perspectives' (2018) 100 Geografiska Annaler: Series B, Human Geography 1

Starup P and Elsmore MJ, 'Taking a logical step forward? Comment on Ibrahim and Teixeira' (2010) 35 ELRev 571

Stein E, 'International integration and democracy: no love at first sight' (2001) 95 American Journal of International Law 489

Stolzenberg NM, '"He drew a circle that shut me out": assimilation, indoctrination, and the paradox of a liberal education' (1993) 106 Harvard Law Review 581

Storbeck J and Clore GL, 'On the interdependence of cognition and emotion' (2007) 21 Cognition & Emotion 1212

Streinz T, 'Fraternal twins: the European Union and the Council of Europe' in de Waele H and Kuipers J-J (eds), *The European Union's emerging international identity: Views from the Global Arena* (Martinus Nijhoff 2013)

Struthers AEC, 'Human Rights: A Topic Too Controversial for Mainstream Education?' (2016) 16 Human Rights Law Review 131

Stute D, 'Privacy Almighty? The CJEU's Judgment in Google Spain SL v AEPD' [2015] Michigan Journal of International Law 649

Subotic J, 'Europe is a State of Mind: Identity and Europeanization in the Balkans' (2011) 55 International Studies Quarterly 309

Sultana RG, 'A Uniting Europe, a Dividing Education? Euro-centrism and the Curriculum' (1995) 5 International Studies in Sociology of Education 115

Sundstrom M and Fernandez C, 'Citizenship education and diversity in liberal societies: Theory and policy in a comparative perspective' (2013) 8 Education, Citizenship and Social Justice 103

Sutor B, 'Politische Bildung im Streit um die "intellektuelle Gründung" der Bundesrepublik Deutschland. Die Kontroversen der siebziger und achtziger Jahre' (2002) 52 Aus Politik und Zeitgeschichte: APuZ 17

Tarozzi M, Rapanà F and Ghirotto L, 'Ambiguities of Citizenship. Reframing the Notion of Citizenship Education' (2013) 8 Ricerche di Pedagogia e Didattica – Journal of Theories and Research in Education 201

Telman DAJ, 'Langdellian limericks (case teaching method)' (2011) 61 Journal of Legal Education 110

Temple Lang J, 'The Development by the Court of Justice of the Duties of Cooperation of National Authorities and Community Institutions under Article 10 EC' (2007–2008) 31 Fordham International Law Journal 1483

Ten Dam G and Volman M, 'Critical thinking as a citizenship competence: Teaching strategies' (2004) 14 Learning and Instruction 359

Terry LS, 'The Bologna Process and Its Impact in Europe: It's So Much More than a Degree Changes' (2008) 41 Vanderbilt Journal of Transnational Law 107

Theiler T, 'The European union and the "European dimension" in schools: Theory and evidence' (1999) 21 Journal of European Integration 307

Thym D, 'The Elusive Limits of Solidarity: Residence Rights of and Social Benefits for Economically Inactive Union Citizens' (2015) 52 CMLRev 17

—, 'Ambiguities of Personhood, Citizenship, Migration and Fundamental Rights' in Azoulai L, Barbou des Places S and Pataut E (eds), *Constructing the Person in EU Law: Rights, Roles, Identities* (Hart 2016)

—, 'Citizens' and 'Foreigners' in EU Law: Migration Law and its Cosmopolitan Outlook' (2016) 22 ELJ 296

—, 'The Failure of Union citizenship beyond the Single Market' in De Witte B, Bauböck R and Shaw J (eds), *Freedom of movement under attack: Is it worth defending as the core of EU citizenship?* (EUI Working Paper RSCAS 2016/69, 2016)

—, 'Frontiers of EU Citizenship: Three Trajectories and Their Methodological Limitations' in Kochenov D (ed), *EU Citizenship and Federalism: The Role of Rights* (Cambridge University Press 2017)

Timmermans C, 'How to Define the European Union?' in Goudappel F and Hirsch Ballin E (eds), *Democracy and Rule of Law in the European Union: Essays in Honour of Jaap W de Zwaan* (Springer 2014)

Töller AE, 'Concepts of Causality in Quantitative Approaches to Europeanization' in Radaelli C and Exadactylos T (eds), *Establishing Causality in Europeanization Research* (Palgrave Macmillan 2012)

Tomaševski K, *Human rights obligations: making education available, accessible, acceptable and adaptable* (Right to education Primers No 3, 2001)

—, *Removing Obstacles in the Way of the Right to Education* (Right to education Primer No 1, 2001)

Tomaševski K, *Human rights in education as prerequisite for human rights education* (Right to Education Primers No 4, Novum Grafiska 2001)

Torney-Purta J, 'The School's Role in Developing Civic Engagement: A Study of Adolescents in Twenty-Eight Countries' (2002) 6 Applied Developmental Science 203

Torney-Purta J and Barber C, 'Democratic School Engagement and Civic Participation among European Adolescents: Analysis of Data from the IEA Civic Education Study' (2005) 4 Journal of Social Science Education 13

Torney-Purta J and others, *Citizenship and education in twenty-eight countries: Civic knowledge and engagement at age fourteen* (IEA 2001)

Treaty establishing a Constitution for Europe [2004] OJ C310/1

Tridimas T, *The General Principles of EU Law* (Oxford University Press 2006)

Tröhler D, 'La construction de la société et les conceptions sur l'éducation. Visions comparées en Allemagne, en France et aux États-Unis dans les années 1900' [2013] Education et sociétés 35

Trstenjak V, 'Civis Europeus Sum: Union Citizenship and the Influence of the Court of Justice of the European Union' (2015) 23 European Review 71

Tryfonidou A, *The impact of Union citizenship on the EU's market freedoms* (Hart 2016)

Tsadiras A, 'The European Ombudsman's remedial powers: an empirical analysis in context' (2013) 38 ELRev 52

—, 'Maladministration and life beyond legality: The European Ombudsman's paradigm' (2015) 3 International Review of Law 11

Tschentscher A, 'Comparing Constitutions and International Constitutional Law: A Primer' (10 February 2011)

Tulkens F, 'Freedom of Religion under the European Convention on Human Rights: A Precious Asset' [2014] Brigham Young University Law Review 509

Tulkens F, Van Drooghenbroeck S and Krenc F, 'Le soft law et la Cour européenne des droits de l'homme: questions de légitimité et de méthode' (2012) 23 Revue trimestrielle des droits de l'homme 433

Valcke P, 'General Report' in da Cruz Vilaça JL and others (eds), *The internal market and the digital economy*, vol 1 (XXVIII FIDE Congress Lisbon/Estoril (23–26 May 2018), Almedina 2018)

Van Bossuyt A, 'Is there an effective European legal framework for the protection of minority languages? The European Union and the Council of Europe screened' (2007) 32 ELRev 860

van den Brink A, 'De begrenzing van de bevoegdheden van de Europese Unie als een gedeelde constitutionele opdracht' (2014) 62 SEW – Tijdschrift voor Europees en economisch Recht 266

van den Brink M, 'The Court and the Legislators: who should define the scope of free movement in the EU?' in De Witte F, Bauböck R and Shaw J (eds), *Freedom of movement under attack: Is it worth defending as the core of EU citizenship?* (EUI Working Papers RSCAS 2016/69, 2016)

van den Brink T, 'National Parliaments and EU Economic Governance. In Search of New ways to Enhance Democratic Legitimacy' in Goudappel F and Hirsch Ballin E (eds), *Democracy and Rule of Law in the European Union: Essays in Honour of Jaap W de Zwaan* (Springer 2015)

van der Jeught S, 'Conflicting Language Policies in the European Union and its Member States' (Proefschrift, Vrije Universiteit Brussel 2015)

van der Mei AP, 'Movement of Students and the Protection of National Educational Interests: Reflections on Bressol and Chaverot' (2011) 13 European Journal of Migration and Law 123

van der Ploeg P and Guérin L, 'Questioning Participation and Solidarity as Goals of Citizenship Education' (2016) 28 Critical Review 248

van der Schyff G, 'The constitutional relationship between the European Union and its Member States: the role of national identity in article 4(2) TEU' (2012) 37 ELRev 563

Van Deth JW, 'In Search of the "Good European Citizen": WYSIWYG?' in Kohler-Koch B and Larat F (eds), *Efficient and democratic governance in the European Union* (CONNEX Report Series No 9, 2008)

van Dijk P and others (eds), *Theory and practice of the European Convention on human rights* (4 edn, Intersentia 2006)

van Eijken H, *European Citizenship and the Constitutionalisation of the European Union* (Europa Law 2015)

van Eijken H and de Vries SA, 'A New Route into the Promised Land? Being a European Citizen after Ruiz Zambrano' (2011) 36 ELRev 704

van Eijken H and Marguery TP, 'The Federal Entrenchment of Citizens in the European Union Member States' Criminal Laws: Or How EU Citizenship Is Shaping Criminal Law' in Kochenov D (ed), *EU Citizenship and Federalism: The Role of Rights* (Cambridge University Press 2017)

van Eijken H and van Rossem JW, 'Prisoner disenfranchisement and the right to vote in elections to the European Parliament: Universal suffrage key to unlocking political citizenship?' (2016) 12 European Constitutional Law Review 114

van Gerven W, 'Gemeenschapstrouw: goede trouw in E.G.-verband' [1989–90] Rechtskundig Weekblad 1158

—, *The European Union: A Polity of States and Peoples* (Hart 2005)

van Middelaar L, *De passage naar Europa. Geschiedenis van een begin* (Historische uitgeverij 2009)

—, *The passage to Europe: How a Continent became a Union* (Waters L tr, Yale University Press 2013)

Van Middelaar L and Van Parijs P (eds), *After the Storm: How to Save Democracy in Europe* (Lannoo 2015)

Van Parijs P, 'Justifying Europe' in van Middelaar L and Van Parijs P (eds), *After the Storm: How to Save Democracy in Europe* (Lannoo 2015)

Van Reybrouck D, 'Democratie is meer dan een bolletje kleuren' *De Standaard* (19 November 2016) <www.standaard.be/cnt/dmf20161118_02579747>

Van Rijckevorsel E, 'Initiative citoyenne et "dérapages démocratiques" dans l'Union européenne' (2016) 24 Journal de droit européen 52

Van Roosmalen M and others, *Fundamental rights and principles: liber amicorum Pieter van Dijk* (Intersentia 2012)

Vandenabeele J, Vanassche E and Wildemeersch D, 'Stories of/on citizenship education: a case of participatory planning' (2011) 30 International Journal of Lifelong Education 171

Vandenbroucke F, 'EU citizenship should speak to both the mobile and the non-mobile European' in Ferrera M and Bauböck R (eds), *Should EU citizenship be duty-free?* (EUI Working Papers RSCAS 2017/60, 2017)

Vargova M, 'Democratic Deficits of a Dualist Deliberative Constitutionalism: Bruce Ackerman and Jürgen Habermas' (2005) 18 Ratio Juris 365

Vaujany J, *L'école primaire en France sous la Troisième République : les lois fondamentales, l'école nouvelle, l'évolution de l'école* (Perrin 1912)

Veldhuis R, *Education for democratic citizenship: dimensions of citizenship, core competencies, variables and international activities* (CoE 1997)

Veny L, *Rechtsbescherming in het onderwijs* (Die Keure 1990)

—, *Onderwijsrecht 1: Dragende beginselen van het onderwijsbestel* (Die Keure 2010)

—, 'The right to education according to the case-law of the European court of human rights' in Fodor EM (ed), *Education and law: interferences* (Pro Universitaria 2016)

Verhaegen S, Hooghe M and Meeusen C, 'Opportunities to learn about Europe at school. A comparative analysis among European adolescents in 21 European member states' (2013) 45 Journal of Curriculum Studies 838

Verheyde M, 'Article 28: The Right to Education' in Alen A and others (eds), *A Commentary on the United Nations Convention on the Rights of the Child* (Martinus Nijhoff 2006)

Verhoeven A, *The European Union in Search of a Democratic and Constitutional Theory* (European Monographs 38, Kluwer Law International 2002)

—, 'Redactionele Signalen' (2012) 60 SEW – Tijdschrift voor Europees en economisch Recht 269

Vermeulen B, 'The right to education (Article 2 of Protocol No. 1)' in Van Dijk P and others (eds), *Theory and practice of the European Convention on human rights* (4th edn, Intersentia 2006)

Vincent M-B, '« La Constitution doit devenir un livre populaire »: Enseigner le patriotisme constitutionnel sous la République de Weimar' (2009) Histoire de l'éducation 71

Vogiatzis N, 'The linguistic policy of the EU institutions and political participation post-Lisbon' (2016) 41 ELRev 176

von Bogdandy A, 'The European Union as a Human Rights Organisation? Human Rights and the Core of the European Union' (2000) 37 CMLRev 1307

—, 'Founding Principles of EU Law: A Theoretical and Doctrinal Sketch' (2010) 16 ELJ 95

—, 'Founding Principles' in von Bogdandy A and Bast J (eds), *Principles of European Constitutional Law*, vol 8 (2nd edn, Hart Beck Nomos 2010)

—, 'The European lesson for international democracy: the significance of Articles 9 to 12 EU Treaty for International Organizations' (2012) 23 European Journal of International Law 315

von Bogdandy A, Arndt F and Bast J, 'Legal instruments in European Union law and their reform: A systematic approach on an empirical basis' (2004) 21 Yearbook of European Law 91

von Bogdandy A and Sonnevend P (eds), *Constitutional Crisis in the European Constitutional Area: Theory, Law and Politics in Hungary and Romania* (Hart Beck 2015)

Voßkuhle A, 'European Integration Through Law: The Contribution of the Federal Constitutional Court' (2017) 58 European Journal of Sociology 145

—, 'Multilevel cooperation of the European Constitutional Courts: Der Europäische Verfassungsgerichtsverbund' (2010) 6 European Constitutional Law Review 175

Walkenhorst H, 'Problems of Political Education in a Multi-level Polity: explaining Non-teaching of European Union Issues in German Secondary Schooling' (2006) 14 Journal of Contemporary European Studies 353

Walker N, 'The Idea of Constitutional Pluralism' (2002) 65 Modern Law Review 317

—, 'Postnational constitutionalism and the problem of translation' in Weiler JHH and Wind M (eds), *European Constitutionalism Beyond the State* (Cambridge University Press 2003)

—, 'The Legacy of Europe's Constitutional Moment' (2004) 11 Constellations 368

—, 'Europe's constitutional momentum and the search for polity legitimacy' (2005) 3 International Journal of Constitutional Law 211

—, 'European Constitutionalism in the State Constitutional Tradition' (2006) 59 Current Legal Problems 51

—, 'Not the European Constitution' (2008) 15 Maastricht journal of European and comparative law 135

––, 'Opening or Closure? The Constitutional Intimations of the ECJ' in Maduro MP and Azoulai L (eds), *The Past and Future of EU Law: The Classics of EU Law Revisited on the 50th Anniversary of the Rome Treaty* (Hart 2010)

––, 'The Philosophy of European Union Law' in Chalmers D and Arnull A (eds), *The Oxford Handbook of European Union Law* (Oxford Handbooks Online 2015)

Walker N, Shaw J and Tierney S, *Europe's Constitutional Mosaic* (Hart 2011)

Weber E, *Peasants Into Frenchmen: The Modernization of Rural France, 1880–1914* (Stanford UP 1976)

Wehling H-G, 'Der Beutelsbacher Konsens: Entstehung und Wirkung' Landeszentrale für politische Bildung Baden-Württemberg (1977) <www.lpb-bw.de/wiebeutelbacherkonsensentstand.html>

Weiler JHH, 'The European Union belongs to its citizens: three immodest proposals' 22 ELRev 150

––, 'To be a European Citizen -Eros and Civilization' (1997) 4 Journal of European Public Policy 495

––, 'A Constitution for Europe? Some hard choices' (2002) 40 JCMS 563

––, *The constitution of Europe: do the new clothes have an emperor? and other essays on European integration* (reprint edn, Cambridge University Press 2004)

––, 'On the Distinction between Values and Virtues in the Process of European Integration' (IILJ International Legal Theory Colloqium, The Turn to Governance: The Exercise of Power in the International Public Space, New York Law School, 3 March 2010, unpublished)

––, 'In the Face of Crisis: Input Legitimacy, Output Legitimacy and the Political Messianism of European Integration' (2012) 34 Journal of European Integration 825

––, 'Deciphering the Political and Legal DNA of European Integration' in Dickson X and Eleftheriadis P (eds), *Philosophical Foundations of European Union Law* (Oxford University Press 2012)

––, 'United in Fear: The Loss of Heimat and the Crises of Europe' in Papadopoulou L, Pernice I and Weiler JHH (eds), *Legitimacy issues of the European Union in the face of crisis: Dimitris Tsatsos in memoriam* (Nomos 2017)

Weißeno G, 'Standards für die politische Bildung' (2005) 55 Aus Politik und Zeitgeschichte: APuZ 32

Weißeno G (ed), *Politikkompetenz. Was Unterricht zu leisten hat* (Schriftenreihe Band 645, Bundeszentrale für politische Bildung 2008)

––, 'Dimensionen der Politikkompetenz' in Weiseno G and Buchstein H (eds), *Politisch Handeln Modelle, Möglichkeite, Kompetenzen* (Schriftenreihe Band 1191, Bundeszentrale für politische Bildung 2012)

Weißeno G and Buchstein H (eds), *Politisch Handeln. Modelle, Möglichkeiten, Kompetenzen* (Schriftenreihe Band 1191, Bundeszentrale für politische Bildung 2012)

Wessel RA and Blockmans S, *Between Autonomy and Dependence: The EU Legal Order Under the Influence of International Organisations* (Asser Press 2013)

Widmaier B and Overwien B (eds), *Was heisst heute Kritische Politische Bildung?* (Non-Formale Politische Bildung, Band 2, Wochenschau Verlag 2013)

Wiener A, 'Going Home? "European" Citizenship Practice Twenty Years After' in Kochenov D (ed), *EU Citizenship and Federalism: The Role of Rights* (Cambridge University Press 2017)

Wilkinson MA, 'Political Constitutionalism and the European Union' (2013) 76 The Modern Law Review 191

Willems K, 'Balancing neutrality and religion in public schools: on educational curricula and religious signs' in Meix Cereceda P and de Groof J (eds), *Religious and Ideological Rights in Education* (Wolf Legal Publishers 2017)

Willems K and Vernimmen J, 'The fundamental human right to education for refugees: Some legal remarks' (2017) 17 EERJ 219

Williams AT, 'Taking Values Seriously: Towards a Philosophy of EU Law' (2009) 29 Oxford Journal of Legal Studies 549

—, *The Ethos of Europe: Values, Law and Justice in the EU* (Cambridge University Press 2010)

Wilson D, *A Human Rights contribution to defining quality education* (Background paper prepared for the Education for All Global Monitoring Report 2005 The Quality Imperative, 2004)

Wimmel A, 'Theorizing the Democratic Legitimacy of European Governance: a Labyrinth with No Exit?' (2009) 31 Journal of European Integration 181

Wind M, 'Post-national citizenship in Europe: the EU as a "welfare rights generator"?' (2009) 15 Columbia Journal of European Law 239

Winther-Jensen T (ed) *Challenges to European Education: Cultural Values, National identities, and Global Responsibilities* (Comparative Studies Series 6, Peter Lang 1996)

Wolf PJ and Macedo S (eds), *Educating Citizens: International Perspectives on Civic Values and School Choice* (Brookings Institution Press 2004)

Wollenschläger F, 'A New Fundamental Freedom beyond Market Integration: Union Citizenship and its Dynamics for Shifting the Economic Paradigm of European Integration' (2011) 17 ELJ 1

Wouters J, Verhey L and Kiiver P (eds), *European Constitutionalism beyond Lisbon* (Intersentia 2009)

Zajda J, Daun H and L. Saha L (eds), *Nation-building, identity and citizenship education* (Springer 2009)

Ziemes JF, Hahn-Laudenberg K and Abs HJ, 'From Connectedness and Learning to European and National Identity: Results from Fourteen European Countries' (2019) 18 Journal of Social Science Education (3: European Citizenship Education: Business as Usual or Time for Change?) 5

Ziller J, 'European models of government: Towards a patchwork with missing pieces' (2001) 54 Parliamentary Affairs 102

Zimenkova T, 'Citizenship Through Faith and Feelings: Defining Citizenship in Citizenship Education. An Exemplary Textbook Analysis' (2008) 7 Journal of Social Science Education 81

Zimenkova T and Hedtke R, 'The Talk-and-Action Approach to Citizenship Education. An Outline of a Methodology of Critical Studies in Citizenship Education' (2008) 7 Journal of Social Science Education 5